Spanish
Dictionary
and Grammar

Spanish Dictionary and Grammar

Christine Lea
John Butt

Oxford   New York

OXFORD UNIVERSITY PRESS

Oxford University Press, Great Clarendon Street, Oxford OX2 6DP

Oxford New York
Athens Auckland Bangkok Bogota Bombay
Buenos Aires Calcutta Cape Town Dar es Salaam
Delhi Florence Hong Kong Istanbul Karachi
Kuala Lumpur Madras Madrid Melbourne
Mexico City Nairobi Paris Singapore
Taipei Tokyo Toronto Warsaw

and associated companies in
Berlin Ibadan

Oxford is a trade mark of Oxford University Press

Dictionary © Oxford University Press, 1993
Grammar © Oxford University Press, 1996

This combined edition first published 1997

British Library Cataloguing in Publication Data
Data available

Library of Congress Cataloging in Publication Data
Data available
ISBN 0-19-860079-8

10 9 8 7 6 5 4 3 2

Printed in Great Britain by
Mackays of Chatham

Preface

Part of the Oxford Paperback Dictionary and Grammar series, the present work combines an up-to-date and compact dictionary, offering comprehensive coverage of modern Spanish and English, with a practical and user-friendly guide to Spanish grammar. This unique feature makes it the perfect all-in-one reference tool for students, tourists and business people alike.

Acknowledgements

On behalf of Christine Lea and John Butt, the Publisher would like to thank Mary-Carmen Beaven for her constructive comments on the dictionary and Dr M. Janes and Mrs J. Andrews, whose French and Italian Mini-dictionaries have served as models for the compilation of the A–Z text, as well as Antonia Moreira Rodríguez, and the staff and students of King's College in London for their help and advice on the grammar text.

Contents

Dictionary

Christine Lea

Grammar

John Butt

Dictionary

Contents

Introduction
Pronunciation of Spanish
Abbreviations

Introduction

The swung dash (~) is used to replace a headword or that part of a headword preceding the vertical bar (|). In both English and Spanish only irregular plurals are given. Normally Spanish nouns and adjectives ending in an unstressed vowel form the plural by adding *s* (e.g. *libro*, *libros*). Nouns and adjectives ending in a stressed vowel or a consonant add *es* (e.g. *rubí*, *rubíes*; *pared*, *paredes*). An accent on the final syllable is not required when *es* is added (e.g. *nación*, *naciones*). Final *z* becomes *ces* (e.g. *vez*, *veces*). Spanish nouns and adjectives ending in *o* form the feminine by changing the final *o* to *a* (e.g. *hermano*, *hermana*). Most Spanish nouns and adjectives ending in anything other than final *o* do not have a separate feminine form with the exception of those denoting nationality etc; these add *a* to the masculine singular form (e.g. *español*, *española*). An accent on the final syllable is then not required (e.g. *inglés*, *inglesa*). Adjectives ending in *án*, *ón*, or *or* behave like those denoting nationality with the following exceptions: *inferior*, *mayor*, *mejor*, *menor*, *peor*, *superior* where the feminine has the same form as the masculine. Spanish verb tables will be found in the appendix.

The Spanish alphabet

In Spanish *ch*, *ll* and *ñ* are considered separate letters and in the Spanish–English section, therefore, they will be found after *cu*, *lu* and *ny* respectively.

Pronunciation of Spanish

Vowels:

a   is between pronunciation of *a* in English *cat* and *arm*
e   is like *e* in English *bed*
i   is like *ee* in English *see* but a little shorter
o   is like *o* in English *hot* but a little longer
u   is like *oo* in English *too*
y   when a vowel is as Spanish **i**

Consonants:

b   1) in initial position or after nasal consonant is like English *b*
    2) in other positions is between English *b* and English *v*
c   1) before **e** or **i** is like *th* in English *thin*
    2) in other positions is like *c* in English *cat*
ch is like *ch* in English *chip*
d   1) in initial position, after nasal consonants and after **l** is like English *d*
    2) in other positions is like *th* in English *this*
f   is like English *f*
g   1) before **e** or **i** is like *ch* in Scottish *loch*
    2) in initial position is like *g* in English *get*
    3) in other positions is like 2) but a little softer
h   is silent in Spanish but see also **ch**
j   is like *ch* in Scottish *loch*
k   is like English *k*
l   is like English *l* but see also **ll**
ll is like *lli* in English *million*
m   is like English *m*
n   is like English *n*
ñ   is like *ni* in English *opinion*
p   is like English *p*
q   is like English *k*
r   is rolled or trilled
s   is like *s* in English *sit*
t   is like English *t*
v   1) in initial position or after nasal consonant is like English *b*
    2) in other positions is between English *b* and English *v*
w   is like Spanish **b** or **v**
x   is like English *x*
y   is like English *y*
z   is like *th* in English *thin*

Abbreviations

adjective	*a*	adjetivo
abbreviation	*abbr/abrev*	abreviatura
administration	*admin*	administración
adverb	adv	adverbio
American	*Amer*	americano
anatomy	*anat*	anatomía
architecture	*archit/arquit*	arquitectura
definite article	*art def*	artículo definido
indefinite article	*art indef*	artículo indefinido
astrology	*astr*	astrología
motoring	*auto*	automóvil
auxiliary	*aux*	auxiliar
aviation	*aviat/aviac*	aviación
biology	*biol*	biología
botany	*bot*	botánica
commerce	*com*	comercio
conjunction	*conj*	conjunción
cookery	*culin*	cocina
electricity	*elec*	electricidad
school	*escol*	enseñanza
Spain	*Esp*	España
feminine	*f*	femenino
familiar	*fam*	familiar
figurative	*fig*	figurado
philosophy	*fil*	filosofía
photography	*foto*	fotografía
geography	*geog*	geografía
geology	*geol*	geología
grammar	*gram*	gramática
humorous	*hum*	humorístico
interjection	*int*	interjección
interrogative	*inter*	interrogativo
invariable	*invar*	invariable
legal, law	*jurid*	jurídico
Latin American	*LAm*	latinoamericano
language	*lang*	lengua(je)
masculine	*m*	masculino
mathematics	*mat(h)*	matemáticas
mechanics	*mec*	mecánica
medicine	*med*	medicina
military	*mil*	militar
music	*mus*	música
mythology	*myth*	mitología
noun	*n*	nombre
nautical	*naut*	náutica
oneself	*o.s.*	uno mismo, se
proprietary term	*P*	marca registrada
pejorative	*pej*	peyorativo
philosophy	*phil*	filosofía
photography	*photo*	fotografía

plural	*pl*	plural
politics	*pol*	política
possessive	*poss*	posesivo
past participle	*pp*	participio de pretérito
prefix	*pref*	prefijo
preposition	*prep*	preposición
present participle	*pres p*	participio de presente
pronoun	*pron*	pronombre
psychology	*psych*	psicología
past tense	*pt*	tiempo pasado
railway	*rail*	ferrocarril
relative	*rel*	relativo
religion	*relig*	religión
school	*schol*	enseñanza
singular	*sing*	singular
slang	*sl*	argot
someone	*s.o.*	alguien
something	*sth*	algo
technical	*tec*	técnico
television	*TV*	televisión
university	*univ*	universidad
auxiliary verb	*v aux*	verbo auxiliar
verb	*vb*	verbo
intransitive verb	*vi*	verbo intransitivo
pronominal verb	*vpr*	verbo pronominal
transitive verb	*vt*	verbo transitivo
transitive & intransitive verb	*vti*	verbo transitivo e intransitivo

Proprietary terms

This dictionary includes some words which are, or are asserted to be, proprietary names or trademarks. Their inclusion does not imply that they have acquired for legal purposes a non-proprietary or general significance, nor is any other judgement implied concerning their legal status. In cases where the editor has some evidence that a word is used as a proprietary name or trade mark this is indicated by the letter (P), but no judgement concerning the legal status of such words is made or implied thereby.

A

a *prep* in, at; (*dirección*) to; (*tiempo*) at; (*hasta*) to, until; (*fecha*) on; (*más tarde*) later; (*medio*) by; (*precio*) for, at. **~ 5 km** 5 km away. **¿~ cuántos estamos?** what's the date? **~l día siguiente** the next day. **~ la francesa** in the French fashion. **~ las 2** at 2 o'clock. **~ los 25 años** (*edad*) at the age of 25; (*después de*) after 25 years. **~ no ser por** but for. **~ que** I bet. **~ 28 de febrero** on the 28th of February

ábaco *m* abacus

abad *m* abbot

abadejo *m* (*pez*) cod

abad|esa *f* abbess. **~ía** *f* abbey

abajo *adv* (down) below; (*dirección*) down(wards); (*en casa*) downstairs. ● *int* down with. **calle ~** down the street. **el ~ firmante** the undersigned. **escaleras ~** downstairs. **la parte de ~** the bottom part. **los de ~** those at the bottom. **más ~** below.

abalanzarse [10] *vpr* rush towards

abalorio *m* glass bead

abanderado *m* standard-bearer

abandon|ado *adj* abandoned; (*descuidado*) neglected; ⟨*personas*⟩ untidy. **~ar** *vt* leave ⟨*un lugar*⟩; abandon ⟨*personas, cosas*⟩. ● *vi* give up. **~arse** *vpr* give in; (*descuidarse*) let o.s. go. **~o** *m* abandonment; (*estado*) abandon

abani|car [7] *vt* fan. **~co** *m* fan. **~queo** *m* fanning

abarata|miento *m* reduction in price. **~r** *vt* reduce. **~rse** *vpr* ⟨*precios*⟩ come down

abarca *f* sandal

abarcar [7] *vt* put one's arms around, embrace; (*comprender*) embrace; (*LAm, acaparar*) monopolize

abarquillar *vt* warp. **~se** *vpr* warp

abarrotar *vt* overfill, pack full

abarrotes *mpl* (*LAm*) groceries

abast|ecer [11] *vt* supply. **~ecimiento** *m* supply; (*acción*) supplying. **~o** *m* supply. **dar ~o** a supply

abati|do *a* depressed. **~miento** *m* depression. **~r** *vt* knock down, demolish; (*fig, humillar*) humiliate. **~rse** *vpr* swoop (**sobre** on); (*ponerse abatido*) get depressed

abdica|ción *f* abdication. **~r** [7] *vt* give up. ● *vi* abdicate

abdom|en *m* abdomen. **~inal** *a* abdominal

abec|é *m* (*fam*) alphabet, ABC. **~edario** *m* alphabet

abedul *m* birch (tree)

abej|a *f* bee. **~arrón** *m* bumble-bee. **~ón** *m* drone. **~orro** *m* bumble-bee; (*insecto coleóptero*) cockchafer

aberración *f* aberration

abertura *f* opening

abet|al *m* fir wood. **~o** *m* fir (tree)

abierto *pp véase* **abrir**. ● *a* open

abigarra|do *a* multi-coloured; (*fig, mezclado*) mixed. **~miento** *m* variegation

abigeato *m* (*Mex*) rustling

abism|al *a* abysmal; (*profundo*) deep. **~ar** *vt* throw into an abyss; (*fig, abatir*) humble. **~arse** *vpr* be absorbed (**en** in), be lost (**en** in). **~o** *m* abyss; (*fig, diferencia*) world of difference

abizcochado *a* spongy

abjura|ción *f* abjuration. **~r** *vt* forswear. ● *vi.* **~r de** forswear

ablanda|miento *m* softening. **~r** *vt* soften. **~rse** *vpr* soften

ablución *f* ablution

abnega|ción *f* self-sacrifice. **~do** *a* self-sacrificing

aboba|do *a* silly. **~miento** *m* silliness

aboca|do *a* ⟨*vino*⟩ medium. **~r** [7] *vt* pour out

abocetar *vt* sketch

abocinado *a* trumpet-shaped

abochornar vt suffocate; (fig, avergonzar) embarrass. ~se vpr feel embarrassed; ⟨plantas⟩ wilt

abofetear vt slap

aboga|cía f legal profession. ~do m lawyer; (notario) solicitor; (en el tribunal) barrister, attorney (Amer). ~r [12] vi plead

abolengo m ancestry

aboli|ción f abolition. ~cionismo m abolitionism. ~cionista m & f abolitionist. ~r [24] vt abolish

abolsado a baggy

abolla|dura f dent. ~r vt dent

abomba|do a convex; (Arg, borracho) drunk. ~r vt make convex. ~rse vpr (LAm, corromperse) start to rot, go bad

abomina|ble a abominable. ~ción f abomination. ~r vt detest. ● vi. ~r de detest

abona|ble a payable. ~do a paid. ● m subscriber

abonanzar vi ⟨tormenta⟩ abate; ⟨tiempo⟩ improve

abon|ar vt pay; (en agricultura) fertilize. ~aré m promissory note. ~arse vpr subscribe. ~o m payment; (estiércol) fertilizer; (a un periódico) subscription

aborda|ble a reasonable; ⟨persona⟩ approachable. ~je m boarding. ~r vt tackle ⟨un asunto⟩; approach ⟨una persona⟩; (naut) come alongside

aborigen a & m native

aborrascarse [7] vpr get stormy

aborrec|er [11] vt hate; (exasperar) annoy. ~ible a loathsome. ~ido a hated. ~imiento m hatred

aborregado a ⟨cielo⟩ mackerel

abort|ar vi have a miscarriage. ~ivo a abortive. ~o m miscarriage; (voluntario) abortion; (fig, monstruo) abortion. **hacerse** ~**ar** have an abortion

abotaga|miento m swelling. ~rse [12] vpr swell up

abotonar vt button (up)

aboveda|do a vaulted. ~r vt vault

abra f cove

abracadabra m abracadabra

abrasa|dor a burning. ~r vt burn; (fig, consumir) consume. ~rse vpr burn

abrasi|ón f abrasion; (geología) erosion. ~vo a abrasive

abraz|adera f bracket. ~ar vt [10] embrace; (encerrar) enclose. ~arse

vpr embrace. ~o m hug. **un fuerte** ~**o de** (en una carta) with best wishes from

abrecartas m paper-knife

ábrego m south wind

abrelatas m invar tin opener (Brit), can opener

abreva|dero m watering place. ~r vt water ⟨animales⟩. ~rse vpr ⟨animales⟩ drink

abrevia|ción f abbreviation; (texto abreviado) abridged text. ~do a brief; ⟨texto⟩ abridged. ~r vt abbreviate; abridge ⟨texto⟩; cut short ⟨viaje etc⟩. ● vi be brief. ~tura f abbreviation

abrig|ada f shelter. ~adero m shelter. ~ado a ⟨lugar⟩ sheltered; ⟨personas⟩ well wrapped up. ~ar [12] vt shelter; cherish ⟨esperanza⟩; harbour ⟨duda, sospecha⟩. ~arse vpr (take) shelter; (con ropa) wrap up. ~o m (over)coat; ⟨lugar⟩ shelter

abril m April. ~eño a April

abrillantar vt polish

abrir [pp abierto] vt/i open. ~se vpr open; (extenderse) open out; ⟨el tiempo⟩ clear

abrocha|dor m buttonhook. ~r vt do up; (con botones) button up

abrojo m thistle

abroncar [7] vt (fam) tell off; (abuchear) boo; (avergonzar) shame. ~se vpr be ashamed; (enfadarse) get annoyed

abroquelarse vpr shield o.s.

abruma|dor a overwhelming. ~r vt overwhelm

abrupto a steep; (áspero) harsh

abrutado a brutish

absceso m abscess

absentismo m absenteeism

ábside m apse

absintio m absinthe

absolución f (relig) absolution; (jurid) acquittal

absolut|amente adv absolutely, completely. ~ismo m absolutism. ~ista a & m & f absolutist. ~o a absolute. ~orio a of acquittal. **en** ~**o** (de manera absoluta) absolutely; (con sentido negativo) (not) at all

absolver [2, pp absuelto] vt (relig) absolve; (jurid) acquit

absor|bente a absorbent; (fig, interesante) absorbing. ~ber vt absorb. ~ción f absorption. ~to a absorbed

abstemio a teetotal. ● m teetotaller

absten|ción f abstention. **~erse** [40] vpr abstain, refrain (**de** from)

abstinen|cia f abstinence. **~te** a abstinent

abstra|cción f abstraction. **~cto** a abstract. **~er** [41] vt abstract. **~erse** vpr be lost in thought. **~ído** a absent-minded

abstruso a abstruse

absuelto a (relig) absolved; (jurid) acquitted

absurdo a absurd. ● m absurd thing

abuche|ar vt boo. **~o** m booing

abuel|a f grandmother. **~o** m grandfather. **~os** mpl grandparents

ab|ulia f lack of willpower. **~úlico** a weak-willed

abulta|do a bulky. **~miento** m bulkiness. **~r** vt enlarge; (hinchar) swell; (fig, exagerar) exaggerate. ● vi be bulky

abunda|ncia f abundance. **~nte** a abundant, plentiful. **~r** vi be plentiful. **nadar en la ~ncia** be rolling in money

aburguesa|miento m conversion to a middle-class way of life. **~rse** vpr become middle-class

aburri|do a (con estar) bored; (con ser) boring. **~miento** m boredom; (cosa pesada) bore. **~r** vt bore. **~rse** vpr be bored, get bored

abus|ar vi take advantage. **~ar de la bebida** drink too much. **~ivo** a excessive. **~o** m abuse. **~ón** a (fam) selfish

abyec|ción f wretchedness. **~to** a abject

acá adv here; (hasta ahora) until now. **~ y allá** here and there. **de ~ para allá** to and fro. **de ayer ~** since yesterday

acaba|do a finished; (perfecto) perfect; (agotado) worn out. ● m finish. **~miento** m finishing; (fin) end. **~r** vt/i finish. **~rse** vpr finish; (agotarse) run out; (morirse) die. **~r con** put an end to. **~r de** (+ infinitivo) have just (+ pp). **~ de llegar** he has just arrived. **~r por** (+ infinitivo) end up (+ gerundio). **¡se acabó!** that's it!

acabóse m. **ser el ~** be the end, be the limit

acacia f acacia

acad|emia f academy. **~émico** a academic

acaec|er [11] vi happen. **~imiento** m occurrence

acalora|damente adv heatedly. **~do** a heated. **~miento** m heat. **~r** vt warm up; (fig, excitar) excite. **~rse** vpr get hot; (fig, excitarse) get excited

acallar vt silence

acampanado a bell-shaped

acampar vi camp

acanala|do a grooved. **~dura** f groove. **~r** vt groove

acantilado a steep. ● m cliff

acanto m acanthus

acapara|r vt hoard; (monopolizar) monopolize. **~miento** m hoarding; (monopolio) monopolizing

acaracolado a spiral

acaricia|dor a caressing. **~r** vt caress; (rozar) brush; (proyectos etc) have in mind

ácaro m mite

acarre|ar vt transport; (desgracias etc) cause. **~o** m transport

acartona|do a (persona) wizened. **~rse** vpr (ponerse rígido) go stiff; (persona) become wizened

acaso adv maybe, perhaps. ● m chance. **~ llueva mañana** perhaps it will rain tomorrow. **al ~** at random. **por si ~** in case

acata|miento m respect (**a** for). **~r** vt respect

acatarrarse vpr catch a cold, get a cold

acaudalado a well off

acaudillar vt lead

acceder vi agree; (tener acceso) have access

acces|ibilidad f accessibility. **~ible** a accessible; (persona) approachable. **~o** m access, entry; (med, ataque) attack; (llegada) approach

accesorio a & m accessory

accidentado a (terreno) uneven; (agitado) troubled; (persona) injured

accident|al a accidental. **~arse** vpr have an accident. **~e** m accident

acci|ón f (incl jurid) action; (hecho) deed. **~onar** vt work. ● vi gesticulate. **~onista** m & f shareholder

acebo m holly (tree)

acebuche m wild olive tree

acecinar vt cure (carne). **~se** vpr become wizened

acech|ar vt spy on; (aguardar) lie in wait for. **~o** m spying. **al ~o** on the look-out

acedera f sorrel

acedía f (*pez*) plaice; (*acidez*) heartburn

aceit|ar vt oil; (*culin*) add oil to. **~e** m oil; (*de oliva*) olive oil. **~era** f oil bottle; (*para engrasar*) oilcan. **~ero** a oil. **~oso** a oily

aceitun|a f olive. **~ado** a olive. **~o** m olive tree

acelera|ción f acceleration. **~damente** adv quickly. **~dor** m accelerator. **~r** vt accelerate; (*fig*) speed up, quicken

acelga f chard

ac|émila f mule; (*como insulto*) ass (*fam*). **~emilero** m muleteer

acendra|do a pure. **~r** vt purify; refine (*metales*)

acensuar vt tax

acent|o m accent; (*énfasis*) stress. **~uación** f accentuation. **~uar** [21] vt stress; (*fig*) emphasize. **~uarse** vpr become noticeable

aceña f water-mill

acepción f meaning, sense

acepta|ble a acceptable. **~ción** f acceptance; (*aprobación*) approval. **~r** vt accept

acequia f irrigation channel

acera f pavement (*Brit*), sidewalk (*Amer*)

acerado a steel; (*fig, mordaz*) sharp

acerca de prep about

acerca|miento m approach; (*fig*) reconciliation. **~r** [7] vt bring near. **~rse** vpr approach

acería f steelworks

acerico m pincushion

acero m steel. **~ inoxidable** stainless steel

acérrimo a (*fig*) staunch

acert|ado a right, correct; (*apropiado*) appropriate. **~ar** [1] vt hit (*el blanco*); (*adivinar*) get right, guess. ● vi get right. **~ar a** happen to. **~ar con** hit on. **~ijo** m riddle

acervo m pile; (*bienes*) common property

acetato m acetate

acético a acetic

acetileno m acetylene

acetona f acetone

aciago a unlucky

aciano m cornflower

ac|íbar m aloes; (*planta*) aloe; (*fig, amargura*) bitterness. **~ibarar** vt add aloes to; (*fig, amargar*) embitter

acicala|do a dressed up, overdressed. **~r** vt dress up. **~rse** vpr get dressed up

acicate m spur

acid|ez f acidity. **~ificar** [7] vt acidify. **~ificarse** vpr acidify

ácido a sour. ● m acid

acierto m success; (*idea*) good idea; (*habilidad*) skill

aclama|ción f acclaim; (*aplausos*) applause. **~r** vt acclaim; (*aplaudir*) applaud

aclara|ción f explanation. **~r** vt lighten (*colores*); (*explicar*) clarify; (*enjuagar*) rinse. ● vi (*el tiempo*) brighten up. **~rse** vpr become clear. **~torio** a explanatory

aclimata|ción f acclimatization, acclimation (*Amer*). **~r** vt acclimatize, acclimate (*Amer*). **~rse** vpr become acclimatized, become acclimated (*Amer*)

acné m acne

acobardar vt intimidate. **~se** vpr get frightened

acocil m (*Mex*) freshwater shrimp

acod|ado a bent. **~ar** vt (*doblar*) bend; (*agricultura*) layer. **~arse** vpr lean on (**en** on). **~o** m layer

acog|edor a welcoming; (*ambiente*) friendly. **~er** [14] vt welcome; (*proteger*) shelter; (*recibir*) receive. **~erse** vpr take refuge. **~ida** f welcome; (*refugio*) refuge

acogollar vi bud. **~se** vpr bud

acolcha|do a quilted. **~r** vt quilt, pad

acólito m acolyte; (*monaguillo*) altar boy

acomet|edor a aggressive; (*emprendedor*) enterprising. **~er** vt attack; (*emprender*) undertake; (*llenar*) fill. **~ida** f attack. **~ividad** f aggression; (*iniciativa*) enterprise

acomod|able a adaptable. **~adizo** a accommodating. **~ado** a well off. **~ador** m usher. **~adora** f usherette. **~amiento** m suitability. **~ar** vt arrange; (*adaptar*) adjust. ● vi be suitable. **~arse** vpr settle down; (*adaptarse*) conform. **~aticio** a accommodating. **~o** m position

acompaña|do a accompanied; (*concurrido*) busy. **~miento** m accompaniment. **~nta** f companion. **~nte** m companion; (*mus*) accompanist. **~r** vt accompany; (*adjuntar*) enclose. **~rse** vpr (*mus*) accompany o.s.

acompasa|do *a* rhythmic. **~r** *vt* keep in time; (*fig, ajustar*) adjust

acondiciona|do *a* equipped. **~miento** *m* conditioning. **~r** *vt* fit out; (*preparar*) prepare

acongojar *vt* distress. **~se** *vpr* get upset

acónito *m* aconite

aconseja|ble *a* advisable. **~do** *a* advised. **~r** *vt* advise. **~rse vpr** take advice. **~rse con** consult

aconsonantar *vt/i* rhyme

acontec|er [11] *vi* happen. **~imiento** *m* event

acopi|ar *vt* collect. **~o** *m* store

acopla|do *a* coordinated. **~miento** *m* coupling; (*elec*) connection. **~r** *vt* fit; (*elec*) connect; (*rail*) couple

acoquina|miento *m* intimidation. **~r** *vt* intimidate. **~rse** *vpr* be intimidated

acoraza|do *a* armour-plated. ● *m* battleship. **~r** [10] *vt* armour

acorazonado *a* heart-shaped

acorcha|do *a* spongy. **~rse** *vpr* go spongy; (*parte del cuerpo*) go to sleep

acord|ado *a* agreed. **~ar** [2] *vt* agree (upon); (*decidir*) decide; (*recordar*) remind. **~e** *a* in agreement; (*mus*) harmonious. ● *m* chord

acorde|ón *m* accordion. **~onista** *m* & *f* accordionist

acordona|do *a* (*lugar*) cordoned off. **~miento** *m* cordoning off. **~r** *vt* tie, lace; (*rodear*) surround, cordon off

acorrala|miento *m* (*de animales*) rounding up; (*de personas*) cornering. **~r** *vt* round up (*animales*); corner (*personas*)

acorta|miento *m* shortening. **~r** *vt* shorten; (*fig*) cut down

acos|ar *vt* hound; (*fig*) pester. **~o** *m* pursuit; (*fig*) pestering

acostar [2] *vt* put to bed; (*naut*) bring alongside. ● *vi* (*naut*) reach land. **~se** *vpr* go to bed; (*echarse*) lie down; (*Mex, parir*) give birth

acostumbra|do *a* (*habitual*) usual. **~do a** used to, accustomed to. **~r** *vt* get used. **me ha acostumbrado a levantarme por la noche** he's got me used to getting up at night. ● *vi.* **~r (a)** be accustomed to. **acostumbro comer a la una** I usually have lunch at one o'clock. **~rse** *vpr* become accustomed, get used

acota|ción *f* (*nota*) marginal note; (*en el teatro*) stage direction; (*cota*) elevation mark. **~do** *a* enclosed. **~r** *vt* mark out (*terreno*); (*anotar*) annotate

ácrata *a* anarchistic. ● *m* & *f* anarchist

acre *m* acre. ● *a* (*olor*) pungent; (*sabor*) sharp, bitter

acrecenta|miento *m* increase. **~r** [1] *vt* increase. **~rse** *vpr* increase

acrec|er [11] *vt* increase. **~imiento** *m* increase

acredita|do *a* reputable; (*pol*) accredited. **~r** *vt* prove; accredit (*representante diplomático*); (*garantizar*) guarantee; (*autorizar*) authorize. **~rse** *vpr* make one's name

acreedor *a* worthy (a of). ● *m* creditor

acribillar *vt* (*a balazos*) riddle (a with); (*a picotazos*) cover (a with); (*fig, a preguntas etc*) pester (a with)

acrimonia *f* (*de sabor*) sharpness; (*de olor*) pungency; (*fig*) bitterness

acrisola|do *a* pure; (*fig*) proven. **~r** *vt* purify; (*confirmar*) prove

acritud *f* (*de sabor*) sharpness; (*de olor*) pungency; (*fig*) bitterness

acr|obacia *f* acrobatics. **~obacias aéreas** aerobatics. **~óbata** *m* & *f* acrobat. **~obático** *a* acrobatic. **~obatismo** *m* acrobatics

acrónimo *m* acronym

acróstico *a* & *m* acrostic

acta *f* minutes; (*certificado*) certificate

actinia *f* sea anemone

actitud *f* posture, position; (*fig*) attitude, position

activ|ación *f* speed-up. **~amente** *adv* actively. **~ar** *vt* activate; (*acelerar*) speed up. **~idad** *f* activity. **~o** *a* active. ● *m* assets

acto *m* act; (*ceremonia*) ceremony. **en el ~** immediately

act|or *m* actor. **~riz** *f* actress

actuación *f* action; (*conducta*) behaviour; (*theat*) performance

actual *a* present; (*asunto*) topical. **~idad** *f* present. **~idades** *fpl* current affairs. **~ización** *f* modernization. **~izar** [10] *vt* modernize. **~mente** *adv* now, at the present time. **en la ~idad** nowadays

actuar [21] *vt* work. ● *vi* act. **~ como**, **~ de** act as

actuario *m* clerk of the court. ～ **(de seguros)** actuary

acuarel|a *f* watercolour. ～**ista** *m & f* watercolourist

acuario *m* aquarium. **A～** Aquarius

acuartela|do *a* quartered. ～**miento** *m* quartering. ～**r** *vt* quarter, billet; *(mantener en cuartel)* confine to barracks

acuático *a* aquatic

acuci|ador pressing. ～**ar** *vt* urge on; *(dar prisa a)* hasten. ～**oso** *a* keen

acuclillarse *vpr* crouch down, squat down

acuchilla|do *a* slashed; *⟨persona⟩* stabbed. ～**r** *vt* slash; stab *⟨persona⟩*; *(alisar)* smooth

acudir *vi.* ～ **a** go to, attend; keep *⟨una cita⟩*; *(en auxilio)* go to help

acueducto *m* aqueduct

acuerdo *m* agreement. ● *vb véase* **acordar**. **¡de ～!** OK! **de ～ con** in accordance with. **estar de ～** agree. **ponerse de ～** agree

acuesto *vb véase* **acostar**

acuidad *f* acuity, sharpness

acumula|ción *f* accumulation. ～**dor** *a* accumulative. ● *m* accumulator. ～**r** *vt* accumulate. ～**rse** *vpr* accumulate

acunar *vt* rock

acuña|ción *f* minting, coining. ～**r** *vt* mint, coin

acuos|idad *f* wateriness. ～**o** *a* watery

acupuntura *f* acupuncture

acurrucarse [7] *vpr* curl up

acusa|ción *f* accusation. ～**do** *a* accused; *(destacado)* marked. ● *m* accused. ～**dor** *a* accusing. ● *m* accuser. ～**r** *vt* accuse; *(mostrar)* show; *(denunciar)* denounce. ～**rse** *vpr* confess; *(notarse)* become marked. ～**torio** *a* accusatory

acuse *m.* ～ **de recibo** acknowledgement of receipt

acus|ica *m & f (fam)* telltale. ～**ón** *a & m* telltale

acústic|a *f* acoustics. ～**o** *a* acoustic

achacar [7] *vt* attribute

achacoso *a* sickly

achaflanar *vt* bevel

achantar *vt (fam)* intimidate. ～**se** *vpr* hide; *(fig)* back down

achaparrado *a* stocky

achaque *m* ailment

achares *mpl (fam)*. **dar ～** make jealous

achata|miento *m* flattening. ～**r** *vt* flatten

achica|do *a* childish. ～**r** [7] *vt* make smaller; *(fig, empequeñecer, fam)* belittle; *(naut)* bale out. ～**rse** *vpr* become smaller; *(humillarse)* be humiliated

achicopalado *a (Mex)* depressed

achicoria *f* chicory

achicharra|dero *m* inferno. ～**nte** *a* sweltering. ～**r** *vt* burn; *(fig)* pester. ～**rse** *vpr* burn

achispa|do *a* tipsy. ～**rse** *vpr* get tipsy

achocolatado *a* (chocolate-)brown

achuch|ado *a (fam)* hard. ～**ar** *vt* jostle, push. ～**ón** *m* shove, push

achulado *a* cocky

adagio *m* adage, proverb; *(mus)* adagio

adalid *m* leader

adamascado *a* damask

adapta|ble *a* adaptable. ～**ción** *f* adaptation. ～**dor** *m* adapter. ～**r** *vt* adapt; *(ajustar)* fit. ～**rse** *vpr* adapt o.s.

adecentar *vt* clean up. ～**se** *vpr* tidy o.s. up

adecua|ción *f* suitability. ～**damente** *adv* suitably. ～**do** *a* suitable. ～**r** *vt* adapt, make suitable

adelant|ado *a* advanced; *⟨niño⟩* precocious; *⟨reloj⟩* fast. ～**amiento** *m* advance(ment); *(auto)* overtaking. ～**ar** *vt* advance, move forward; *(acelerar)* speed up; put forward *⟨reloj⟩*; *(auto)* overtake. ● *vi* advance, go forward; *⟨reloj⟩* gain, be fast. ～**arse** *vpr* advance, move forward; *⟨reloj⟩* gain; *(auto)* overtake. ～**e** *adv* forward. ● *int* come in!; *(¡siga!)* carry on! ～**o** *m* advance; *(progreso)* progress. **más ～e** *(lugar)* further on; *(tiempo)* later on. **pagar por ～ado** pay in advance.

adelfa *f* oleander

adelgaza|dor *a* slimming. ～**miento** *m* slimming. ～**r** [10] *vt* make thin. ● *vi* lose weight; *(adrede)* slim. ～**rse** *vpr* lose weight; *(adrede)* slim

ademán *m* gesture. **ademanes** *mpl (modales)* manners. **en ～ de** as if to

además *adv* besides; *(también)* also. ～ **de** besides

adentr|arse *vpr.* ～ **en** penetrate into; study thoroughly *⟨tema etc⟩*. ～**o** *adv* in(side). **mar ～o** out at sea. **tierra ～o** inland

adepto *m* supporter

aderez|ar [10] *vt* flavour ⟨*bebidas*⟩; (*condimentar*) season; dress ⟨*ensalada*⟩. ∼**o** *m* flavouring; (*con condimentos*) seasoning; (*para ensalada*) dressing

adeud|ar *vt* owe. ∼**o** *m* debit

adhe|rencia *f* adhesion; (*fig*) adherence. ∼**rente** *a* adherent. ∼**rir** [4] *vt* stick on. ● *vi* stick. ∼**rirse** *vpr* stick; (*fig*) follow. ∼**sión** *f* adhesion; (*fig*) support. ∼**sivo** *a* & *m* adhesive

adici|ón *f* addition. ∼**onal** *a* additional. ∼**onar** *vt* add

adicto *a* devoted. ● *m* follower

adiestra|do *a* trained. ∼**miento** *m* training. ∼**r** *vt* train. ∼**rse** *vpr* practise

adinerado *a* wealthy

adiós *int* goodbye!; (*al cruzarse con alguien*) hello!

adit|amento *m* addition; (*accesorio*) accessory. ∼**ivo** *m* additive

adivin|ación *f* divination; (*por conjeturas*) guessing. ∼**ador** *m* fortune-teller. ∼**anza** *f* riddle. ∼**ar** *vt* foretell; (*acertar*) guess. ∼**o** *m* fortune-teller

adjetivo *a* adjectival. ● *m* adjective

adjudica|ción *f* award. ∼**r** [7] *vt* award. ∼**rse** *vpr* appropriate. ∼**tario** *m* winner of an award

adjunt|ar *vt* enclose. ∼**o** *a* enclosed; (*auxiliar*) assistant. ● *m* assistant

adminículo *m* thing, gadget

administra|ción *f* administration; (*gestión*) management. ∼**dor** *m* administrator; (*gerente*) manager. ∼**dora** *f* administrator; manageress. ∼**r** *vt* administer. ∼**tivo** *a* administrative

admira|ble *a* admirable. ∼**ción** *f* admiration. ∼**dor** *m* admirer. ∼**r** *vt* admire; (*asombrar*) astonish. ∼**rse** *vpr* be astonished. ∼**tivo** *a* admiring

admi|sibilidad *f* admissibility. ∼**sible** *a* acceptable. ∼**sión** *f* admission; (*aceptación*) acceptance. ∼**tir** *vt* admit; (*aceptar*) accept

adobar *vt* (*culin*) pickle; (*fig*) twist

adobe *m* sun-dried brick. ∼**ra** *f* mould for making (sun-dried) bricks

adobo *m* pickle

adocena|do *a* common. ∼**rse** *vpr* become common

adoctrinamiento *m* indoctrination

adolecer [11] *vi* be ill. ∼ **de** suffer with

adolescen|cia *f* adolescent. ∼**te** *a* & *m* & *f* adolescent

adonde *conj* where

adónde *adv* where?

adop|ción *f* adoption. ∼**tar** *vt* adopt. ∼**tivo** *a* adoptive; ⟨*patria*⟩ of adoption

adoqu|ín *m* paving stone; (*imbécil*) idiot. ∼**inado** *m* paving. ∼**inar** *vt* pave

adora|ble *a* adorable. ∼**ción** *f* adoration. ∼**dor** *a* adoring. ● *n* worshipper. ∼**r** *vt* adore

adormec|edor *a* soporific; ⟨*droga*⟩ sedative. ∼**er** [11] *vt* send to sleep; (*fig, calmar*) calm, soothe. ∼**erse** *vpr* fall asleep; (*un miembro*) go to sleep. ∼**ido** *a* sleepy; ⟨*un miembro*⟩ numb. ∼**imiento** *m* sleepiness; (*de un miembro*) numbness

adormidera *f* opium poppy

adormilarse *vpr* doze

adorn|ar *vt* adorn (**con, de** with). ∼**o** *m* decoration

adosar *vt* lean (**a** against)

adqui|rido *a* acquired. ∼**rir** [4] *vt* acquire; (*comprar*) buy. ∼**sición** *f* acquisition; (*compra*) purchase. ∼**sitivo** *a* acquisitive. **poder** *m* ∼**sitivo** purchasing power

adrede *adv* on purpose

adrenalina *f* adrenalin

adscribir [*pp* adscrito] *vt* appoint

aduan|a *f* customs. ∼**ero** *a* customs. ● *m* customs officer

aducir [47] *vt* allege

adueñarse *vpr* take possession

adul|ación *f* flattery. ∼**ador** *a* flattering. ● *m* flatterer. ∼**ar** *vt* flatter

ad|ulteración *f* adulteration. ∼**ulterar** *vt* adulterate. ● *vi* commit adultery. ∼**ulterino** *a* adulterous. ∼**ulterio** *m* adultery. ∼**últera** *f* adulteress. ∼**último** *a* adulterous. ● *m* adulterer

adulto *a* & *m* adult, grown-up

adusto *a* severe, harsh

advenedizo *a* & *m* upstart

advenimiento *m* advent, arrival; (*subida al trono*) accession

adventicio *a* accidental

adverbi|al *a* adverbial. ∼**o** *m* adverb

advers|ario *m* adversary. ∼**idad** *f* adversity. ∼**o** *a* adverse, unfavourable

advert|encia *f* warning; (*prólogo*) foreword. ∼**ido** *a* informed. ∼**ir** [4] *vt* warn; (*notar*) notice

adviento *m* Advent
advocación *f* dedication
adyacente *a* adjacent
aéreo *a* air; (*photo*) aerial; ⟨*ferrocarril*⟩ overhead; (*fig*) flimsy
aeróbica *f* aerobics
aerodeslizador *m* hovercraft
aerodinámic|a *f* aerodynamics. **∼o** *a* aerodynamic
aeródromo *m* aerodrome, airdrome (*Amer*)
aero|espacial *a* aerospace. **∼faro** *m* beacon. **∼lito** *m* meteorite. **∼nauta** *m* & *f* aeronaut. **∼náutica** *f* aeronautics. **∼náutico** *a* aeronautical. **∼nave** *f* airship. **∼puerto** *m* airport. **∼sol** *m* aerosol
afab|ilidad *f* affability. **∼le** *a* affable
afamado *a* famous
af|án *m* hard work; (*deseo*) desire. **∼anar** *vt* (*fam*) pinch. **∼anarse** *vpr* strive (**en, por** to). **∼anoso** *a* laborious
afea|miento *m* disfigurement. **∼r** *vt* disfigure, make ugly; (*censurar*) censure
afección *f* disease
afecta|ción *f* affectation. **∼do** *a* affected. **∼r** *vt* affect
afect|ísimo *a* affectionate. **∼ísimo amigo** (*en cartas*) my dear friend. **∼ividad** *f* emotional nature. **∼ivo** *a* sensitive. **∼o** *m* (*cariño*) affection. ● *a*. **∼o a** attached to. **∼uosidad** *f* affection. **∼uoso** *a* affectionate. **con un ∼uoso saludo** (*en cartas*) with kind regards. **suyo ∼ísimo** (*en cartas*) yours sincerely
afeita|do *m* shave. **∼dora** *f* electric razor. **∼r** *vt* shave. **∼rse** *vpr* (have a) shave
afelpado *a* velvety
afemina|do *a* effeminate. ● *m* effeminate person. **∼miento** *m* effeminacy. **∼rse** *vpr* become effeminate
aferrar [1] *vt* grasp
afgano *a* & *m* Afghan
afianza|miento *m* (*reforzar*) strengthening; (*garantía*) guarantee. **∼rse** [10] *vpr* become established
afici|ón *f* liking; (*conjunto de aficionados*) fans. **∼onado** *a* keen (**a** on), fond (**a of**). ● *m* fan. **∼onar** *vt* make fond. **∼onarse** *vpr* take a liking to. **por ∼ón** as a hobby
afila|do *a* sharp. **∼dor** *m* knifegrinder. **∼dura** *f* sharpening. **∼r** *vt*

sharpen. **∼rse** *vpr* get sharp; (*ponerse flaco*) grow thin
afilia|ción *f* affiliation. **∼do** *a* affiliated. **∼rse** *vpr* become a member (**a** of)
afiligranado *a* filigreed; (*fig*) delicate
afín *a* similar; (*próximo*) adjacent; ⟨*personas*⟩ related
afina|ción *f* refining; (*auto, mus*) tuning. **∼do** *a* finished; (*mus*) in tune. **∼r** *vt* refine; (*afilar*) sharpen; (*acabar*) finish; (*auto, mus*) tune. ● *vi* be in tune. **∼rse** *vpr* become more refined
afincarse [7] *vpr* settle
afinidad *f* affinity; (*parentesco*) relationship
afirma|ción *f* affirmation. **∼r** *vt* make firm; (*asentir*) affirm. **∼rse** *vpr* steady o.s.; (*confirmar*) confirm. **∼tivo** *a* affirmative
aflic|ción *f* affliction. **∼tivo** *a* distressing
afligi|do *a* distressed. ● *m* afflicted. **∼r** [14] *vt* distress. **∼rse** *vpr* grieve
afloja|miento *m* loosening. **∼r** *vt* loosen; (*relajar*) ease. ● *vi* let up
aflora|miento *m* outcrop. **∼r** *vi* appear on the surface
aflu|encia *f* flow. **∼ente** *a* flowing. ● *m* tributary. **∼ir** [17] *vi* flow (**a** into)
af|onía *f* hoarseness. **∼ónico** *a* hoarse
aforismo *m* aphorism
aforo *m* capacity
afortunado *a* fortunate, lucky
afrancesado *a* francophile
afrent|a *f* insult; (*vergüenza*) disgrace. **∼ar** *vt* insult. **∼oso** *a* insulting
África *f* Africa. **∼ del Sur** South Africa
africano *a* & *m* African
afrodisíaco *a* & *m*, **afrodisiaco** *a* & *m* aphrodisiac
afrontar *vt* bring face to face; (*enfrentar*) face, confront
afuera *adv* out(side). **¡∼!** out of the way! **∼s** *fpl* outskirts
agachar *vt* lower. **∼se** *vpr* bend over
agalla *f* (*de los peces*) gill. **∼s** *fpl* (*fig*) guts
agarrada *f* row
agarrader|a *f* (*LAm*) handle. **∼o** *m* handle. **tener ∼as** (*LAm*), **tener ∼os** have influence

agarr|ado *a* (*fig, fam*) mean. **~ador** *a* (*Arg*) ⟨*bebida*⟩ strong. **~ar** *vt* grasp; (*esp LAm*) take, catch. ● *vi* ⟨*plantas*⟩ take root. **~arse** *vpr* hold on; (*reñirse, fam*) fight. **~ón** *m* tug; (*LAm, riña*) row

agarrota|miento *m* tightening; (*auto*) seizing up. **~r** *vt* tie tightly; ⟨*el frío*⟩ stiffen; garotte ⟨*un reo*⟩. **~rse** *vpr* go stiff; (*auto*) seize up

agasaj|ado *m* guest of honour. **~ar** *vt* look after well. **~o** *m* good treatment

ágata *f* agate

agavilla|dora *f* (*máquina*) binder. **~r** *vt* bind

agazaparse *vpr* hide

agencia *f* agency. **~ de viajes** travel agency. **~ inmobiliaria** estate agency (*Brit*), real estate agency (*Amer*). **~r** *vt* find. **~rse** *vpr* find (out) for o.s.

agenda *f* notebook

agente *m* agent; (*de policía*) policeman. **~ de aduanas** customs officer. **~ de bolsa** stockbroker

ágil *a* agile

agilidad *f* agility

agita|ción *f* waving; (*de un líquido*) stirring; (*intranquilidad*) agitation. **~do** *a* ⟨*el mar*⟩ rough; (*fig*) agitated. **~dor** *m* (*pol*) agitator

agitanado *a* gypsy-like

agitar *vt* wave; shake ⟨*botellas etc*⟩; stir ⟨*líquidos*⟩; (*fig*) stir up. **~se** *vpr* wave; ⟨*el mar*⟩ get rough; (*fig*) get excited

aglomera|ción *f* agglomeration; (*de tráfico*) traffic jam. **~r** *vt* amass. **~rse** *vpr* form a crowd

agn|osticismo *m* agnosticism. **~óstico** *a* & *m* agnostic

agobi|ador *a* ⟨*trabajo*⟩ exhausting; ⟨*calor*⟩ oppressive. **~ante** *a* ⟨*trabajo*⟩ exhausting; ⟨*calor*⟩ oppressive. **~ar** *vt* weigh down; (*fig, abrumar*) overwhelm. **~o** *m* weight; (*cansancio*) exhaustion; (*opresión*) oppression

agolpa|miento *m* (*de gente*) crowd; (*de cosas*) pile. **~rse** *vpr* crowd together

agon|ía *f* death throes; (*fig*) agony. **~izante** *a* dying; ⟨*luz*⟩ failing. **~izar** [10] *vi* be dying

agor|ar [16] *vt* prophesy. **~ero** *a* of ill omen. ● *m* soothsayer

agostar *vt* wither

agosto *m* August. **hacer su ~** feather one's nest

agota|do *a* exhausted; ⟨*libro*⟩ out of print. **~dor** *a* exhausting. **~miento** *m* exhaustion. **~r** *vt* exhaust. **~rse** *vpr* be exhausted; ⟨*libro*⟩ go out of print

agracia|do *a* attractive; (*que tiene suerte*) lucky. **~r** *vt* make attractive

agrada|ble *a* pleasant, nice. **~r** *vi* please. **esto me ~** I like this

agradec|er [11] *vt* thank ⟨*persona*⟩; be grateful for ⟨*cosa*⟩. **~ido** *a* grateful. **~imiento** *m* gratitude. **¡muy ~ido!** thanks a lot!

agrado *m* pleasure; (*amabilidad*) friendliness

agrandar *vt* enlarge; (*fig*) exaggerate. **~se** *vpr* get bigger

agrario *a* agrarian, land; ⟨*política*⟩ agricultural

agrava|miento *m* worsening. **~nte** *a* aggravating. ● *f* additional problem. **~r** *vt* aggravate; (*aumentar el peso*) make heavier. **~rse** *vpr* get worse

agravi|ar *vt* offend; (*perjudicar*) wrong. **~arse** *vpr* be offended. **~o** *m* offence

agraz *m*. **en ~** prematurely

agredir [24] *vt* attack. **~ de palabra** insult

agrega|do *m* aggregate; (*funcionario diplomático*) attaché. **~r** [12] *vt* add; (*unir*) join; appoint ⟨*persona*⟩

agremiar *vt* form into a union. **~se** *vpr* form a union

agres|ión *f* aggression; (*ataque*) attack. **~ividad** *f* aggressiveness. **~ivo** *a* aggressive. **~or** *m* aggressor

agreste *a* country

agria|do *a* (*fig*) embittered. **~r** [*regular, o raramente* 20] *vt* sour. **~rse** *vpr* turn sour; (*fig*) become embittered

agr|ícola *a* agricultural. **~icultor** *a* agricultural. ● *m* farmer. **~icultura** *f* agriculture, farming

agridulce *a* bitter-sweet; (*culin*) sweet-and-sour

agriera *f* (*LAm*) heartburn

agrietar *vt* crack. **~se** *vpr* crack; ⟨*piel*⟩ chap

agrimens|or *m* surveyor. **~ura** *f* surveying

agrio *a* sour; (*fig*) sharp. **~s** *mpl* citrus fruits

agronomía *f* agronomy

agropecuario *a* farming

agrupa|ción *f* group; (*acción*) grouping. **~r** *vt* group. **~rse** *vpr* form a group

agua *f* water; (*lluvia*) rain; (*marea*) tide; (*vertiente del tejado*) slope. **~ abajo** downstream. **~ arriba** upstream. **~ bendita** holy water. **~ caliente** hot water. **estar entre dos ~s** sit on the fence. **hacer ~** (*naut*) leak. **nadar entre dos ~s** sit on the fence

aguacate *m* avocado pear; (*árbol*) avocado pear tree

aguacero *m* downpour, heavy shower

agua f corriente running water

aguachinarse *vpr* (*Mex*) ⟨*cultivos*⟩ be flooded

aguada *f* watering place; (*naut*) drinking water; (*acuarela*) water-colour

agua f de colonia eau-de-Cologne

aguad|o *a* watery. **~ucho** *m* refreshment kiosk

agua: ~ dulce fresh water. **~fiestas** *m & f invar* spoil-sport, wet blanket. **~ fría** cold water. **~fuerte** *m* etching

aguaje *m* spring tide

agua: ~mala f, ~mar *m* jellyfish

aguamarina *f* aquamarine

agua: ~miel f mead. **~ mineral con gas** fizzy mineral water. **~ mineral sin gas** still mineral water. **~nieve f** sleet

aguanoso *a* watery; ⟨*tierra*⟩ waterlogged

aguant|able *a* bearable. **~aderas** *fpl* patience. **~ar** *vt* put up with, bear; (*sostener*) support. ● *vi* hold out. **~arse** *vpr* restrain o.s. **~e** *m* patience; (*resistencia*) endurance

agua: ~pié *m* watery wine. **~ potable** drinking water. **~r** [15] *vt* water down. **~ salada** salt water.

aguardar *vt* wait for. ● *vi* wait

agua: ~rdiente *m* (cheap) brandy. **~rrás** *m* turpentine, turps (*fam*). **~turma** *f* Jerusalem artichoke. **~zal** *m* puddle

agud|eza *f* sharpness; (*fig, perspicacia*) insight; (*fig, ingenio*) wit. **~izar** [10] *vt* sharpen. **~izarse** *vpr* ⟨*enfermedad*⟩ get worse. **~o** *a* sharp; ⟨*ángulo, enfermedad*⟩ acute; (*voz*) high-pitched

agüero *m* omen. **ser de buen ~** augur well

aguij|ada *f* goad. **~ar** *vt* (*incl fig*) goad. **~ón** *m* point of a goad. **~onazo** *m* prick. **~onear** *vt* goad

águila *f* eagle; (*persona perspicaz*) astute person

aguileña *f* columbine

aguil|eño *a* aquiline. **~ucho** *m* eaglet

aguinaldo *m* Christmas box

aguja *f* needle; (*del reloj*) hand; (*arquit*) steeple. **~s fpl** (*rail*) points

agujer|ear *vt* make holes in. **~o** *m* hole

agujetas *fpl* stiffness. **tener ~** be stiff

agujón *m* hairpin

agusanado *a* full of maggots

agutí *m* (*LAm*) guinea pig

aguza|do *a* sharp. **~miento** *m* sharpening. **~r** [10] *vt* sharpen

ah *int* ah!, oh!

aherrojar *vt* (*fig*) oppress

ahí *adv* there. **de ~ que** so that. **por ~** over there; (*aproximadamente*) thereabouts

ahija|da *f* god-daughter, godchild. **~do** *m* godson, godchild. **~r** *vt* adopt

ahínco *m* enthusiasm; (*empeño*) insistence

ahíto *a* full up

ahog|ado *a* (*en el agua*) drowned; (*asfixiado*) suffocated. **~ar** [12] *vt* (*en el agua*) drown; (*asfixiar*) suffocate; put out ⟨*fuego*⟩. **~arse** *vpr* (*en el agua*) drown; (*asfixiarse*) suffocate. **~o** *m* breathlessness; (*fig, angustia*) distress; (*apuro*) financial trouble

ahondar *vt* deepen. ● *vi* go deep. **~ en** (*fig*) examine in depth. **~se** *vpr* get deeper

ahora *adv* now; (*hace muy poco*) just now; (*dentro de poco*) very soon. **~ bien** but. **~ mismo** right now. **de ~ en adelante** from now on, in future. **por ~** for the time being

ahorca|dura *f* hanging. **~r** [7] *vt* hang. **~rse** *vpr* hang o.s.

ahorita *adv* (*fam*) now. **~ mismo** right now

ahorquillar *vt* shape like a fork

ahorr|ador *a* thrifty. **~ar** *vt* save. **~arse** *vpr* save o.s. **~o** *m* saving; (*cantidad ahorrada*) savings. **~os** *mpl* savings

ahuecar [7] *vt* hollow; fluff up ⟨*colchón*⟩; deepen ⟨*la voz*⟩; (*marcharse, fam*) clear off (*fam*)

ahuizote m (Mex) bore

ahulado m (LAm) oilskin

ahuma|do a (culin) smoked; (de colores) smoky. ~r vt (culin) smoke; (llenar de humo) fill with smoke. ● vi smoke. ~rse vpr become smoky; ‹comida› acquire a smoky taste; (emborracharse, fam) get drunk

ahusa|do a tapering. ~rse vpr taper

ahuyentar vt drive away; banish ‹pensamientos etc›

airado a annoyed

aire m air; (viento) breeze; (corriente) draught; (aspecto) appearance; (mus) tune, air. ~ación f ventilation. ~ acondicionado air-conditioned. ~ar vt air; (ventilar) ventilate; (fig, publicar) make public. ~arse vpr. salir para ~arse go out for some fresh air. al ~ libre in the open air. darse ~s give o.s. airs

airón m heron

airos|amente adv gracefully. ~o a draughty; (fig) elegant

aisla|do a isolated; (elec) insulated. ~dor a (elec) insulating. ● m (elec) insulator. ~miento m isolation; (elec) insulation. ~nte a insulating. ~r [23] vt isolate; (elec) insulate

ajajá int good! splendid!

ajar vt crumple; (estropear) spoil

ajedre|cista m & f chess-player. ~z m chess. ~zado a chequered, checked

ajenjo m absinthe

ajeno a (de otro) someone else's; (de otros) other people's; (extraño) alien

ajetre|arse vpr be busy. ~o m bustle

ají m (LAm) chilli; (salsa) chilli sauce

aj|iaceite m garlic sauce. ~ilimójili m piquant garlic sauce. ~illo m garlic. al ~illo cooked with garlic. ~o m garlic. ~o-a-rriero m cod in garlic sauce

ajorca f bracelet

ajuar m furnishings; (de novia) trousseau

ajuma|do a (fam) drunk. ~rse vpr (fam) get drunk

ajust|ado a right; ‹vestido› tight. ~ador m fitter. ~amiento m fitting; (adaptación) adjustment; (acuerdo) agreement; (de una cuenta) settlement. ~ar vt fit; (adaptar) adapt; (acordar) agree; settle ‹una cuenta›;

(apretar) tighten. ● vi fit. ~arse vpr fit; (adaptarse) adapt o.s.; (acordarse) come to an agreement. ~e m fitting; (adaptación) f adjustment; (acuerdo) agreement; (de una cuenta) settlement

ajusticiar vt execute

al = a ¦ el

ala f wing; (de sombrero) brim; (deportes) winger

alaba|ncioso a boastful. ~nza f praise. ~r vt praise. ~rse vpr boast

alabastro m alabaster

álabe m (paleta) paddle; (diente) cog

alabe|ar vt warp. ~arse vpr warp. ~o m warping

alacena f cupboard (Brit), closet (Amer)

alacrán m scorpion

alacridad f alacrity

alado a winged

alambi|cado a distilled; (fig) subtle. ~camiento m distillation; (fig) subtlety. ~car [7] vt distil. ~que m still

alambr|ada f wire fence; (de alambre de espinas) barbed wire fence. ~ar vt fence. ~e m wire. ~e de espinas barbed wire. ~era f fireguard

alameda f avenue; (plantío de álamos) poplar grove

álamo m poplar. ~ temblón aspen

alano m mastiff

alarde m show. ~ar vi boast

alarga|dera f extension. ~do a long. ~dor m extension. ~miento m lengthening. ~r [12] vt lengthen; stretch out ‹mano etc›; (dar) give, pass. ~rse vpr lengthen, get longer

alarido m shriek

alarm|a f alarm. ~ante a alarming. ~ar vt alarm, frighten. ~arse vpr be alarmed. ~ista m & f alarmist

alba f dawn

albacea m executor. ● f executrix

albacora (culin) tuna(-fish)

albahaca f basil

albanés a & m Albanian

Albania f Albania

albañal m sewer, drain

albañil m bricklayer. ~ería f (arte) bricklaying

albarán m delivery note

albarda f packsaddle; (Mex) saddle. ~r vt saddle

albaricoque m apricot. ~ro m apricot tree

albatros m albatross

albedrío m will. **libre** ~ free will

albéitar *m* veterinary surgeon (*Brit*), veterinarian (*Amer*), vet (*fam*)

alberca *f* tank, reservoir

alberg|ar [12] *vt* (*alojar*) put up; ⟨*viviendas*⟩ house; (*dar asilo*) shelter. ~**arse** *vpr* stay; (*refugiarse*) shelter. ~**ue** *m* accommodation; (*refugio*) shelter. ~**ue de juventud** youth hostel

albóndiga *f* meatball, rissole

albor *m* dawn. ~**ada** *f* dawn; (*mus*) dawn song. ~**ear** *vi* dawn

albornoz *m* (*de los moros*) burnous; (*para el baño*) bathrobe

alborot|adizo *a* excitable. ~**ado** *a* excited; (*aturdido*) hasty. ~**ador** *a* rowdy. ● *m* trouble-maker. ~**ar** *vt* disturb, upset. ● *vi* make a racket. ~**arse** *vpr* get excited; ⟨*el mar*⟩ get rough. ~**o** *m* row, uproar

alboroz|ado *a* overjoyed. ~**ar** [10] *vt* make laugh; (*regocijar*) make happy. ~**arse** *vpr* be overjoyed. ~**o** *m* joy

albufera *f* lagoon

álbum *m* (*pl* ~**es** *o* ~**s**) album

alcachofa *f* artichoke

alcald|e *m* mayor. ~**esa** *f* mayoress. ~**ía** *f* mayoralty; (*oficina*) mayor's office

álcali *m* alkali

alcalino *a* alkaline

alcance *m* reach; (*de arma, telescopio etc*) range; (*déficit*) deficit

alcancía *f* money-box

alcanzar [10] *vt* (*llegar a*) catch up; (*coger*) reach; catch ⟨*un autobús*⟩; ⟨*bala etc*⟩ strike, hit. ● *vi* reach; (*ser suficiente*) be enough. ~ **a** manage

alcaparra *f* caper

alcaucil *m* artichoke

alcayata *f* hook

alcazaba *f* fortress

alcázar *m* fortress

alcoba *f* bedroom

alcoh|ol *m* alcohol. ~**ol desnaturalizado** methylated spirits, meths (*fam*). ~**ólico** *a* & *m* alcoholic. ~**olímetro** *m* breathalyser (*Brit*). ~**olismo** *m* alcoholism. ~**olizarse** [10] *vpr* become an alcoholic

Alcorán *m* Koran

alcornoque *m* cork-oak; (*persona torpe*) idiot

alcuza *f* (olive) oil bottle

aldaba *f* door-knocker. ~**da** *f* knock at the door

alde|a *f* village. ~**ano** *a* village; (*campesino*) rustic, country. ~**huela** *f* hamlet

alea|ción *f* alloy. ~**r** *vt* alloy

aleatorio *a* uncertain

alecciona|dor *a* instructive. ~**miento** *m* instruction. ~**r** *vt* instruct

aledaños *mpl* outskirts

alega|ción *f* allegation; (*Arg, Mex, disputa*) argument. ~**r** [12] *vt* claim; (*jurid*) allege. ● *vi* (*LAm*) argue. ~**to** *m* plea

aleg|oría *f* allegory. ~**órico** *a* allegorical

alegr|ar *vt* make happy; (*avivar*) brighten up. ~**arse** *vpr* be happy; (*emborracharse*) get merry. ~**e** *a* happy; (*achispado*) merry, tight. ~**emente** *adv* happily. ~**ía** *f* happiness. ~**ón** *m* sudden joy, great happiness

aleja|do *a* distant. ~**miento** *m* removal; (*entre personas*) estrangement; (*distancia*) distance. ~**r** *vt* remove; (*ahuyentar*) get rid of; (*fig, apartar*) separate. ~**rse** *vpr* move away

alela|do *a* stupid. ~**r** *vt* stupefy. ~**rse** *vpr* be stupefied

aleluya *m* & *f* alleluia

alemán *a* & *m* German

Alemania *f* Germany. ~ **Occidental** (*historia*) West Germany. ~ **Oriental** (*historia*) East Germany

alenta|dor *a* encouraging. ~**r** [1] *vt* encourage. ● *vi* breathe

alerce *m* larch

al|ergia *f* allergy. ~**érgico** *a* allergic

alero *m* (*del tejado*) eaves

alerón *m* aileron

alerta *adv* alert, on the alert. ¡~! look out! ~**r** *vt* alert

aleta *f* wing; (*de pez*) fin

aletarga|do *a* lethargic. ~**miento** *m* lethargy. ~**r** [12] *vt* make lethargic. ~**rse** *vpr* become lethargic

alet|azo *m* (*de un ave*) flap of the wings; (*de un pez*) flick of the fin. ~**ear** *vi* flap its wings, flutter. ~**eo** *m* flapping (of the wings)

aleve *a* treacherous

alevín *m* young fish

alevos|ía *f* treachery. ~**o** *a* treacherous

alfab|ético *a* alphabetical. ~**etizar** [10] *vt* alphabetize; teach to read

and write ‹*a uno*›. ～**eto** *m* alphabet.
～**eto Morse** Morse code

alfalfa *f* lucerne (*Brit*), alfalfa
(*Amer*)

alfar *m* pottery. ～**ería** *f* pottery.
～**ero** *m* potter

alféizar *m* window-sill

alferecía *f* epilepsy

alférez *m* second lieutenant

alfil *m* (*en ajedrez*) bishop

alfile|r *m* pin. ～**razo** *m* pinprick.
～**tero** *m* pin-case

alfombr|a *f* (*grande*) carpet;
(*pequeña*) rug, mat. ～**ar** *vt* carpet.
～**illa** *f* rug, mat; (*med*) German
measles

alforja *f* saddle-bag

algas *fpl* seaweed

algarabía *f* (*fig, fam*) gibberish,
nonsense

algarada *f* uproar

algarrob|a *f* carob bean. ～**o** *m* carob
tree

algazara *f* uproar

álgebra *f* algebra

algebraico *a* algebraic

álgido *a* (*fig*) decisive

algo *pron* something; (*en frases
interrogativas*) anything. ● *adv*
rather. ¿～ **más?** is there anything
else? **¿quieres tomar algo?** (*de beber*)
would you like a drink?; (*de comer*)
would you like something to eat?

algodón *m* cotton. ～**ón de azúcar**
candy floss (*Brit*), cotton candy
(*Amer*). ～**onero** *a* cotton. ● *m* cotton plant. ～**ón hidrófilo** cotton
wool

alguacil *m* bailiff

alguien *pron* someone, somebody;
(*en frases interrogativas*) anyone,
anybody

alguno *a* (*delante de nombres mas-
culinos en singular* **algún**) some; (*en
frases interrogativas*) any; (*pospuesto al nombre en frases negativas*) at all. **no tiene idea alguna** he
hasn't any idea at all. ● *pron* one;
(*en plural*) some; (*alguien*)
someone. **alguna que otra vez** from
time to time. **algunas veces, alguna
vez** sometimes

alhaja *f* piece of jewellery; (*fig*) treasure. ～**r** *vt* deck with jewels; (*amueblar*) furnish

alharaca *f* fuss

alhelí *m* wallflower

alheña *f* privet

alhucema *f* lavender

alia|do *a* allied. ● *m* ally. ～**nza** *f* alli-
ance; (*anillo*) wedding ring. ～**r** [20]
vt combine. ～**rse** *vpr* be combined;
(*formar una alianza*) form an
alliance

alias *adv* & *m* alias

alicaído *a* (*fig, débil*) weak; (*fig, abatido*) depressed

alicates *mpl* pliers

aliciente *m* incentive; (*de un lugar*)
attraction

alien|ado *a* mentally ill. ～**ista** *m* & *f*
psychiatrist

aliento *m* breath; (*ánimo*) courage

aligera|miento *m* lightening; (*ali-
vio*) alleviation. ～**r** *vt* make lighter;
(*aliviar*) alleviate, ease; (*apresurar*)
quicken

alij|ar *vt* (*descargar*) unload;
smuggle ‹*contrabando*›. ～**o** *m*
unloading; (*contrabando*) contraband

alimaña *f* vicious animal

aliment|ación *f* food; (*acción*) feed-
ing. ～**ar** *vt* feed; (*nutrir*) nourish.
● *vi* be nourishing. ～**arse** *vpr* feed
(*con, de* on). ～**icio** *a* nourishing.
～**o** *m* food. ～**os** *mpl* (*jurid*)
alimony. **productos** *mpl* ～**icios**
foodstuffs

alimón. al ～ *adv* jointly

alinea|ción *f* alignment; (*en
deportes*) line-up. ～**r** *vt* align, line
up

aliñ|ar *vt* (*culin*) season. ～**o** *m*
seasoning

alioli *m* garlic sauce

alisar *vt* smooth

alisios *apl.* **vientos** *mpl* ～ trade
winds

aliso *m* alder (tree)

alista|miento *m* enrolment. ～**r** *vt*
put on a list; (*mil*) enlist. ～**rse** *vpr*
enrol; (*mil*) enlist

aliteración *f* alliteration

alivi|ador *a* comforting. ～**ar** *vt*
lighten; relieve ‹*dolor, etc*›; (*hurtar,
fam*) steal, pinch (*fam*). ～**arse** *vpr*
‹*dolor*› diminish; ‹*persona*› get
better. ～**o** *m* relief

aljibe *m* tank

alma *f* soul; (*habitante*) inhabitant

almac|én *m* warehouse; (*LAm,
tienda*) grocer's shop; (*de un arma*)
magazine. ～**enes** *mpl* department
store. ～**enaje** *m* storage; (*derechos*)
storage charges. ～**enamiento** *m*
storage; (*mercancías almacenadas*)
stock. ～**enar** *vt* store; stock up with

⟨provisiones⟩. **~enero** *m* (*Arg*) shopkeeper. **~enista** *m* & *f* shopkeeper

almádena *f* sledge-hammer

almanaque *m* almanac

almeja *f* clam

almendr|a *f* almond. **~ado** *a* almond-shaped. **~o** *m* almond tree

almiar *m* haystack

alm|íbar *m* syrup. **~ibarado** *a* syrupy. **~ibarar** *vt* cover in syrup

almid|ón *m* starch. **~onado** *a* starched; (*fig, estirado*) starchy

alminar *m* minaret

almirant|azgo *m* admiralty. **~e** *m* admiral

almirez *m* mortar

almizcle *m* musk

almohad|a *f* cushion; (*de la cama*) pillow; (*funda*) pillowcase. **~illa** *f* small cushion; (*acerico*) pincushion. **~ón** *m* large pillow, bolster. **consultar con la ~a** sleep on it

almorranas *fpl* haemorrhoids, piles

alm|orzar [2 & 10] *vt* (*a mediodía*) have for lunch; (*desayunar*) have for breakfast. ● *vi* (*a mediodía*) have lunch; (*desayunar*) have breakfast. **~uerzo** *m* (*a mediodía*) lunch; (*desayuno*) breakfast

alocado *a* scatter-brained

alocución *f* address, speech

aloja|do *m* (Mex) lodger, guest. **~miento** *m* accommodation. **~r** *vt* put up. **~rse** *vpr* stay

alondra *f* lark

alpaca *f* alpaca

alpargat|a *f* canvas shoe, espadrille. **~ería** *f* shoe shop

Alpes *mpl* Alps

alpin|ismo *m* mountaineering, climbing. **~ista** *m* & *f* mountaineer, climber. **~o** *a* Alpine

alpiste *m* birdseed

alquil|ar *vt* (*tomar en alquiler*) hire ⟨vehículo⟩, rent ⟨piso, casa⟩; (*dar en alquiler*) hire (out) ⟨vehículo⟩, rent (out) ⟨piso, casa⟩. **~arse** *vpr* ⟨casa⟩ be let; ⟨vehículo⟩ be on hire. **se alquila** to let (*Brit*), for rent (*Amer*). **~er** *m* (*acción de alquilar un piso etc*) renting; (*acción de alquilar un vehículo*) hiring; (*precio por el que se alquila un piso etc*) rent; (*precio por el que se alquila un vehículo*) hire charge. **de ~er** for hire

alquimi|a *f* alchemy. **~sta** *m* alchemist

alquitara *f* still. **~r** *vt* distil

alquitr|án *m* tar. **~anar** *vt* tar

alrededor *adv* around. **~ de** around; (*con números*) about. **~es** *mpl* surroundings; (*de una ciudad*) outskirts

alta *f* discharge

altamente *adv* highly

altaner|ía *f* (*orgullo*) pride. **~o** *a* proud, haughty

altar *m* altar

altavoz *m* loudspeaker

altera|bilidad *f* changeability. **~ble** *a* changeable. **~ción** *f* change, alteration. **~do** *a* changed, altered; (*perturbado*) disturbed. **~r** *vt* change, alter; (*perturbar*) disturb; (*enfadar*) anger, irritate. **~rse** *vpr* change, alter; (*agitarse*) get upset; (*enfadarse*) get angry; ⟨comida⟩ go off

alterca|do *m* argument. **~r** [7] *vi* argue

altern|ado *a* alternate. **~ador** *m* alternator. **~ante** *a* alternating. **~ar** *vt/i* alternate. **~arse** *vpr* take turns. **~ativa** *f* alternative. **~ativo** *a* alternating. **~o** *a* alternate

alteza *f* height. **A~** (*título*) Highness

altibajos *mpl* (*de terreno*) unevenness; (*fig*) ups and downs

altiplanicie *f* high plateau

altísimo *a* very high. ● *m*. **el A~** the Almighty

altisonante *a*, **altísono** *a* pompous

altitud *f* height; (*aviat, geog*) altitude

altiv|ez *f* arrogance. **~o** *a* arrogant

alto *a* high; ⟨persona⟩ tall; ⟨voz⟩ loud; (*fig, elevado*) lofty; (*mus*) ⟨nota⟩ high(-pitched); (*mus*) ⟨voz, instrumento⟩ alto; ⟨horas⟩ early. **tiene 3 metros de ~** it is 3 metres high. ● *adv* high; (*de sonidos*) loud(ly). ● *m* height; (*de un edificio*) high floor; (*viola*) viola; (*voz*) alto; (*parada*) stop. ● *int* halt!, stop! **en lo ~ de** on the top of

altoparlante *m* (*esp LAm*) loudspeaker

altruis|mo *m* altruism. **~ta** *a* altruistic. ● *m* & *f* altruist

altura *f* height; (*altitud*) altitude; (*de agua*) depth; (*fig, cielo*) sky. **a estas ~s** at this stage. **tiene 3 metros de ~** it is 3 metres high

alubia *f* French bean

alucinación *f* hallucination

alud *m* avalanche

aludi|do *a* in question. **darse por ~do** take it personally. **no darse por ~do** turn a deaf ear. **~r** *vi* mention

alumbra|do *a* lit; (*achispado, fam*) tipsy. ● *m* lighting. **~miento** *m* lighting; (*parto*) childbirth. **~r** *vt* light. ● *vi* give birth. **~rse** *vpr* (*emborracharse*) get tipsy

aluminio *m* aluminium (*Brit*), aluminum (*Amer*)

alumno *m* pupil; (*univ*) student

aluniza|je *m* landing on the moon. **~r** [10] *vi* land on the moon

alusi|ón *f* allusion. **~vo** *a* allusive

alverja *f* vetch; (*LAm, guisante*) pea

alza *f* rise. **~cuello** *m* clerical collar, dog-collar (*fam*). **~da** *f* (*de caballo*) height; (*jurid*) appeal. **~do** *a* raised; (*persona*) fraudulently bankrupt; (*Mex, soberbio*) vain; (*precio*) fixed. **~miento** *m* raising; (*aumento*) rise, increase; (*pol*) revolt. **~r** [10] *vt* raise, lift (up); raise (*precios*). **~rse** *vpr* rise; (*ponerse en pie*) stand up; (*pol*) revolt; (*quebrar*) go fraudulently bankrupt; (*apelar*) appeal

allá *adv* there. **¡~ él!** that's his business. **~ fuera** out there. **~ por el 1970** around about 1970. **el más ~** the beyond. **más ~** further on. **más ~ de** beyond. **por ~** over there

allana|miento *m* levelling; (*de obstáculos*) removal. **~miento de morada** burglary. **~r** *vt* level; remove (*obstáculos*); (*fig*) iron out (*dificultades etc*); burgle (*una casa*). **~rse** *vpr* level off; (*hundirse*) fall down; (*ceder*) submit (**a** to)

allega|do *a* close. ● *m* relation. **~r** [12] *vt* collect

allí *adv* there; (*tiempo*) then. **~ donde** wherever. **~ fuera** out there. **por ~** over there

ama *f* lady of the house. **~ de casa** housewife. **~ de cría** wet-nurse. **~ de llaves** housekeeper

amab|ilidad *f* kindness. **~le** *a* kind; (*simpático*) nice

amado *a* dear. **~r** *m* lover

amaestra|do *a* trained; (*en circo*) performing. **~miento** *m* training. **~r** *vt* train

amag|ar [12] *vt* (*amenazar*) threaten; (*mostrar intención de*) show signs of. ● *vi* threaten; (*algo bueno*) be in the offing. **~o** *m* threat; (*señal*) sign; (*med*) sympton

amalgama *f* amalgam. **~r** *vt* amalgamate

amamantar *vt* breast-feed

amancebarse *vpr* live together

amanecer *m* dawn. ● *vi* dawn; (*persona*) wake up. **al ~** at dawn, at daybreak

amanera|do *a* affected. **~miento** *m* affectation. **~rse** *vpr* become affected

amanezca *f* (*Mex*) dawn

amansa|dor *m* tamer. **~miento** *m* taming. **~r** *vt* tame; break in (*un caballo*); soothe (*dolor etc*). **~rse** *vpr* calm down

amante *a* fond. ● *m & f* lover

amañ|ar *vt* arrange. **~o** *m* scheme

amapola *f* poppy

amar *vt* love

amara|je *m* landing on the sea; (*de astronave*) splash-down. **~r** *vt* land on the sea; (*astronave*) splash down

amarg|ado *a* embittered. **~ar** [12] *vt* make bitter; embitter (*persona*). **~arse** *vpr* get bitter. **~o** *a* bitter. ● *m* bitterness. **~ura** *f* bitterness

amariconado *a* effeminate

amarill|ear *vi* go yellow. **~ento** *a* yellowish; (*tez*) sallow. **~ez** *f* yellow; (*de una persona*) paleness. **~o** *a & m* yellow

amarra *f* mooring rope. **~s** *fpl* (*fig, fam*) influence. **~do** *a* (*LAm*) mean. **~r** *vt* moor; (*atar*) tie. ● *vi* (*empollar, fam*) study hard, swot (*fam*)

amartillar *vt* cock (*arma de fuego*)

amas|ar *vt* knead; (*fig, tramar, fam*) concoct, cook up (*fam*). **~ijo** *m* dough; (*acción*) kneading; (*fig, mezcla, fam*) hotchpotch

amate *m* (*Mex*) fig tree

amateur *a & m & f* amateur

amatista *f* amethyst

amazona *f* Amazon; (*mujer varonil*) mannish woman; (*que monta a caballo*) horsewoman

Amazonas *m*. **el río ~** the Amazon

ambages *mpl* circumlocutions. **sin ~** in plain language

ámbar *m* amber

ambarino *a* amber

ambici|ón *f* ambition. **~onar** *vt* strive after. **~onar ser** have an ambition to be. **~oso** *a* ambitious. ● *m* ambitious person

ambidextro *a* ambidextrous. ● *m* ambidextrous person

ambient|ar *vt* give an atmosphere to. **~arse** *vpr* adapt o.s. **~e** *m* atmosphere; (*medio*) environment

ambig|uamente *adv* ambiguously. **~üedad** *f* ambiguity. **~uo** *a* ambiguous; (*fig, afeminado, fam*) effeminate

ámbito *m* ambit

ambos *a & pron* both. **~ a dos** both (of them)

ambulancia *f* ambulance; (*hospital móvil*) field hospital

ambulante *a* travelling

ambulatorio *m* out-patients' department

amedrentar *vt* frighten, scare. **~se** *vpr* be frightened

amén *m* amen. ● *int* amen! **en un decir ~** in an instant

amenaza *f* threat. **~dor** *a*, **~nte** *a* threatening. **~r** [10] *vt* threaten

amen|idad *f* pleasantness. **~izar** [10] *vt* brighten up. **~o** *a* pleasant

América *f* America. **~ Central** Central America. **~ del Norte** North America. **~ del Sur** South America. **~ Latina** Latin America

american|a *f* jacket. **~ismo** *m* Americanism. **~ista** *m & f* Americanist. **~o** *a* American

amerindio *a & m & f* Amerindian, American Indian

ameriza|je *m* landing on the sea; (*de astronave*) splash-down. **~r** [10] *vt* land on the sea; ⟨*astronave*⟩ splash down

ametralla|dora *f* machine-gun. **~r** *vt* machine-gun

amianto *m* asbestos

amig|a *f* friend; (*novia*) girl-friend; (*amante*) lover. **~able** *a* friendly. **~ablemente** *adv* amicably. **~rse** [12] *vpr* live together

am|ígdala *f* tonsil. **~igdalitis** *f* tonsillitis

amigo *a* friendly. ● *m* friend; (*novio*) boy-friend; (*amante*) lover. **ser ~ de** be fond of. **ser muy ~s** be good friends

amilanar *vt* frighten, scare. **~se** *vpr* be frightened

aminorar *vt* lessen; slow down ⟨*velocidad*⟩

amist|ad *f* friendship. **~ades** *mpl* friends. **~osamente** *adv* amicably. **~oso** *a* friendly

amnesia *f* amnesia

amnist|ía *f* amnesty. **~iar** [20] *vt* grant an amnesty to

amo *m* master; (*dueño*) owner; (*jefe*) boss; (*cabeza de familia*) head of the family

amodorra|miento *m* sleepiness. **~rse** *vpr* get sleepy

amojonar *vt* mark out

amola|dor *m* knife-grinder. **~r** [2] *vt* sharpen; (*molestar, fam*) annoy

amoldar *vt* mould; (*acomodar*) fit

amonedar *vt* coin, mint

amonesta|ción *f* rebuke, reprimand; (*de una boda*) banns. **~r** *vt* rebuke, reprimand; (*anunciar la boda*) publish the banns

amoníaco *m*, **amoniaco** *m* ammonia

amontillado *m* Amontillado, pale dry sherry

amontona|damente *adv* in a heap. **~miento** *m* piling up. **~r** *vt* pile up; (*fig, acumular*) accumulate. **~rse** *vpr* pile up; ⟨*gente*⟩ crowd together; (*amancebarse, fam*) live together

amor *m* love. **~es** *mpl* (*relaciones amorosas*) love affairs. **con mil ~es**, **de mil ~es** with (the greatest of) pleasure. **hacer el ~** make love. **por (el) ~ de Dios** for God's sake

amorata|do *a* purple; (*de frío*) blue. **~rse** *vpr* go black and blue

amorcillo *m* Cupid

amordazar [10] *vt* gag; (*fig*) silence

amorfo *a* amorphous, shapeless

amor: ~ío *m* affair. **~oso** *a* loving; ⟨*cartas*⟩ love

amortajar *vt* shroud

amortigua|dor *a* deadening. ● *m* (*auto*) shock absorber. **~miento** *m* deadening; (*de la luz*) dimming. **~r** [15] *vt* deaden ⟨*ruido*⟩; dim ⟨*luz*⟩; cushion ⟨*golpe*⟩; tone down ⟨*color*⟩

amortiza|ble *a* redeemable. **~ción** *f* (*de una deuda*) repayment; (*recuperación*) redemption. **~r** [10] *vt* repay ⟨*una deuda*⟩

amoscarse [7] *vpr* (*fam*) get cross, get irritated

amostazarse [10] *vpr* get cross

amotina|do *a & m* insurgent, rebellious. **~miento** *m* riot; (*mil*) mutiny. **~r** *vt* incite to riot. **~rse** *vpr* rebel; (*mil*) mutiny

ampar|ar *vt* help; (*proteger*) protect. **~arse** *vpr* seek protection; (*de la lluvia*) shelter. **~o** *m* protection; (*de la lluvia*) shelter. **al ~o de** under the protection of

amperio *m* ampere, amp (*fam*)

amplia|ción *f* extension; (*photo*) enlargement. **~r** [20] *vt* enlarge, extend; (*photo*) enlarge

amplifica|ción f amplification. ~**dor** m amplifier. ~**r** [7] amplify

ampli|o a wide; (*espacioso*) spacious; (*ropa*) loose-fitting. ~**tud** f extent; (*espaciosidad*) spaciousness; (*espacio*) space

ampolla f (*med*) blister; (*frasco*) flask; (*de medicamento*) ampoule, phial

ampuloso a pompous

amputa|ción f amputation; (*fig*) deletion. ~**r** vt amputate; (*fig*) delete

amueblar vt furnish

amuinar vt (*Mex*) annoy

amuralla|do a walled. ~**r** vt build a wall around

anacardo m (*fruto*) cashew nut

anaconda f anaconda

anacr|ónico a anachronistic. ~**onismo** m anachronism

ánade m & f duck

anagrama m anagram

anales mpl annals

analfabet|ismo m illiteracy. ~**o** a & m illiterate

analgésico a & m analgesic, pain-killer

an|álisis m invar analysis. ~**álisis de sangre** blood test. ~**alista** m & f analyst. ~**alítico** a analytical. ~**alizar** [10] vt analyze

an|alogía f analogy. ~**álogo** a analogous

ananás m pineapple

anaquel m shelf

anaranjado a orange

an|arquía f anarchy. ~**árquico** a anarchic. ~**arquismo** m anarchism. ~**arquista** a anarchistic. ● m & f anarchist

anatema m anathema

anat|omía f anatomy. ~**ómico** a anatomical

anca f haunch; (*parte superior*) rump; (*nalgas, fam*) bottom. ~**s** fpl **de rana** frogs' legs

ancestral a ancestral

anciano a elderly, old. ● m elderly man, old man; (*relig*) elder. **los** ~**s** old people

ancla f anchor. ~**dero** m anchorage. ~**r** vi anchor, drop anchor. **echar** ~**s** anchor. **levar** ~**s** weigh anchor

áncora f anchor; (*fig*) refuge

ancho a wide; (*ropa*) loose-fitting; (*fig*) relieved; (*demasiado grande*) too big; (*ufano*) smug. ● m width; (*rail*) gauge. **a mis anchas, a sus**

anchas etc comfortable, relaxed. **quedarse tan ancho** behave as if nothing has happened. **tiene 3 metros de** ~ it is 3 metres wide

anchoa f anchovy

anchura f width; (*medida*) measurement

andaderas fpl baby-walker

andad|or a good at walking. ● m baby-walker. ~**ura** f walking; (*manera de andar*) walk

Andalucía f Andalusia

andaluz a & m Andalusian

andamio m platform. ~**s** mpl scaffolding

andar [25] vt (*recorrer*) cover, go. ● vi walk; (*máquina*) go, work; (*estar*) be; (*moverse*) move. ● m walk. **¡anda!** go on! come on! ~**iego** a fond of walking; (*itinerante*) wandering. ~ **por** be about. ~**se** vpr (*marcharse*) go away

andén m platform; (*de un muelle*) quayside; (*LAm, acera*) pavement (*Brit*), sidewalk (*Amer*)

Andes mpl Andes

andino a Andean

Andorra f Andorra

andrajo m rag. ~**so** a ragged

andurriales mpl (*fam*) out-of-the-way place

anduve vb véase **andar**

anécdota f anecdote

anega|dizo a subject to flooding. ~**r** [12] vt flood. ~**rse** vpr be flooded, flood

anejo a attached. ● m annexe; (*de libro etc*) appendix

an|emia f anaemia. ~**émico** a anaemic

anest|esia f anaesthesia. ~**ésico** a & m anaesthetic. ~**esista** m & f anaesthetist

anex|ión f annexation. ~**ionar** vt annex. ~**o** a attached. ● m annexe

anfibio a amphibious. ● m amphibian

anfiteatro m amphitheatre; (*en un teatro*) upper circle

anfitri|ón m host. ~**ona** f hostess

ángel m angel; (*encanto*) charm

angelical a, **angélico** a angelic

angina f. ~ **de pecho** angina (pectoris). **tener** ~**s** have tonsillitis

anglicano a & m Anglican

anglicismo m Anglicism

anglófilo a & m Anglophile

anglo|hispánico a Anglo-Spanish. ~**sajón** a & m Anglo-Saxon

angosto *a* narrow

anguila *f* eel

angula *f* elver, baby eel

angular *a* angular

ángulo *m* angle; (*rincón, esquina*) corner; (*curva*) bend

anguloso *a* angular

angusti|a *f* anguish. **~ar** *vt* distress; (*inquietar*) worry. **~arse** *vpr* get distressed; (*inquietarse*) get worried. **~oso** *a* anguished; (*que causa angustia*) distressing

anhel|ante *a* panting; (*deseoso*) longing. **~ar** *vt* (+ *nombre*) long for; (+ *verbo*) long to. ● *vi* pant. **~o** *m* (*fig*) yearning. **~oso** *a* panting; (*fig*) eager

anidar *vi* nest

anill|a *f* ring. **~o** *m* ring. **~o de boda** wedding ring

ánima *f* soul

anima|ción *f* (*de personas*) life; (*de cosas*) liveliness; (*bullicio*) bustle; (*en el cine*) animation. **~do** *a* lively; ⟨*sitio etc*⟩ busy. **~dor** *m* compère, host

animadversión *f* ill will

animal *a* animal; (*fig, torpe, fam*) stupid. ● *m* animal; (*fig, idiota, fam*) idiot; (*fig, bruto, fam*) brute

animar *vt* give life to; (*dar ánimo*) encourage; (*dar vivacidad*) liven up. **~se** *vpr* (*decidirse*) decide; (*ponerse alegre*) cheer up. **¿te animas a venir al cine?** do you fancy coming to the cinema?

ánimo *m* soul; (*mente*) mind; (*valor*) courage; (*intención*) intention. **¡~!** come on!, cheer up! **dar ~s** encourage

animosidad *f* animosity

animoso *a* brave; (*resuelto*) determined

aniquila|ción *f* annihilation. **~miento** *m* annihilation. **~r** *vt* annihilate; (*acabar con*) ruin. **~rse** *vpr* deteriorate

anís *m* aniseed; (*licor*) anisette

aniversario *m* anniversary

ano *m* anus

anoche *adv* last night, yesterday evening

anochecer [11] *vi* get dark; ⟨*persona*⟩ be at dusk. **anochecí en Madrid** I was in Madrid at dusk. ● *m* nightfall, dusk. **al ~** at nightfall

anodino *a* indifferent

an|omalía *f* anomaly. **~ómalo** *a* anomalous

an|onimato *m* anonymity. **~ónimo** *a* anonymous; (*sociedad*) limited. ● *m* anonymity; (*carta*) anonymous letter

anormal *a* abnormal; (*fam*) stupid, silly. **~idad** *f* abnormality

anota|ción *f* noting; (*acción de poner notas*) annotation; (*nota*) note. **~r** *vt* (*poner nota*) annotate; (*apuntar*) make a note of

anquilosa|miento *m* paralysis. **~r** *vt* paralyze. **~rse** *vpr* become paralyzed

ansi|a *f* anxiety, worry; (*anhelo*) yearning. **~ar** [20 *o regular*] *vt* long for. **~edad** *f* anxiety. **~oso** *a* anxious; (*deseoso*) eager

antag|ónico *a* antagonistic. **~onismo** *m* antagonism. **~onista** *m & f* antagonist

antaño *adv* in days gone by

antártico *a & m* Antarctic

ante *prep* in front of, before; (*en comparación con*) compared with; (*frente a peligro, enemigo*) in the face of; (*en vista de*) in view of. ● *m* (*piel*) suede. **~anoche** *adv* the night before last. **~ayer** *adv* the day before yesterday. **~brazo** *m* forearm

ante... *pref* ante...

antece|dente *a* previous. ● *m* antecedent. **~dentes** *mpl* history, background. **~dentes penales** criminal record. **~der** *vt* precede. **~sor** *m* predecessor; (*antepasado*) ancestor

antedicho *a* aforesaid

antelación *f* advance. **con ~** in advance

antemano *adv.* **de ~** beforehand

antena *f* antenna; (*radio, TV*) aerial

anteojeras *fpl* blinkers

anteojo *m* telescope. **~s** *mpl* (*gemelos*) opera glasses; (*prismáticos*) binoculars; (*LAm, gafas*) glasses, spectacles

ante: ~pasados *mpl* forebears, ancestors. **~pecho** *m* rail; (*de ventana*) sill. **~poner** [34] *vt* put in front (**a** of); (*fig*) put before, prefer. **~proyecto** *m* preliminary sketch; (*fig*) blueprint. **~puesto** *a* put before

anterior *a* previous; (*delantero*) front, fore. **~idad** *f.* **con ~idad** previously. **~mente** *adv* previously

antes *adv* before; (*antiguamente*) in days gone by; (*mejor*) rather; (*primero*) first. **~ de** before. **~ de ayer**

the day before yesterday. ∼ **de que** + *subj* before. ∼ **de que llegue** before he arrives. **cuanto** ∼**, lo** ∼ **posible** as soon as possible

antesala *f* anteroom; (*sala de espera*) waiting-room. **hacer** ∼ wait (to be received)

anti... *pref* anti...

anti: ∼**aéreo** *a* anti-aircraft. ∼**biótico** *a & m* antibiotic. ∼**ciclón** *m* anticyclone

anticip|**ación** *f* anticipation. **con** ∼**ación** in advance. **con media hora de** ∼**ación** half an hour early. ∼**adamente** *adv* in advance. ∼**ado** *a*. **por** ∼**ado** in advance. ∼**ar** *vt* bring forward; advance ⟨*dinero*⟩. ∼**arse** *vpr* be early. ∼**o** *m* (*dinero*) advance; (*fig*) foretaste

anti: ∼**concepcional** *a & m* contraceptive. ∼**conceptivo** *a & m* contraceptive. ∼**congelante** *m* antifreeze

anticua|**do** *a* old-fashioned. ∼**rio** *m* antique dealer. ∼**rse** *vpr* go out of date

anticuerpo *m* antibody

antídoto *m* antidote

anti: ∼**estético** *a* ugly. ∼**faz** *m* mask. ∼**gás** *a invar*. **careta** ∼**gás** gas mask

antig|**ualla** *f* old relic. ∼**uamente** *adv* formerly; (*hace mucho tiempo*) long ago. ∼**üedad** *f* antiquity; (*objeto*) antique; (*en un empleo*) length of service. ∼**uo** *a* old, ancient. **chapado a la** ∼**ua** old-fashioned

antílope *m* antelope

Antillas *fpl* West Indies

antinatural *a* unnatural

antip|**atía** *f* dislike; (*cualidad de antipático*) unpleasantness. ∼**ático** *a* unpleasant, unfriendly

anti: ∼**semita** *m & f* anti-Semite. ∼**semítico** *a* anti-Semitic. ∼**semitismo** *m* anti-Semitism. ∼**séptico** *a & m* antiseptic. ∼**social** *a* antisocial

antítesis *f invar* antithesis

antoj|**adizo** *a* capricious. ∼**arse** *vpr* fancy. **se le** ∼**a un caramelo** he fancies a sweet. ∼**o** *m* whim; (*de embarazada*) craving

antología *f* anthology

antorcha *f* torch

antro *m* cavern; (*fig*) dump, hole. ∼ **de perversión** den of iniquity

antropófago *m* cannibal

antrop|**ología** *f* anthropology. ∼**ólogo** *m & f* anthropologist

anua|**l** *a* annual. ∼**lidad** *f* annuity. ∼**lmente** *adv* yearly. ∼**rio** *m* yearbook

anudar *vt* tie, knot; (*fig, iniciar*) begin; (*fig, continuar*) resume. ∼**se** *vpr* get into knots. ∼**se la voz** get a lump in one's throat

anula|**ción** *f* annulment, cancellation. ∼**r** *vt* annul, cancel. ● *a* ⟨*dedo*⟩ ring. ● *m* ring finger

Anunciación *f* Annunciation

anunci|**ante** *m & f* advertiser. ∼**ar** *vt* announce; advertise ⟨*producto comercial*⟩; (*presagiar*) be a sign of. ∼**arse** *vpr* promise to be. ∼**o** *m* announcement; (*para vender algo*) advertisement, advert (*fam*); (*cartel*) poster

anzuelo *m* (fish)hook; (*fig*) bait. **tragar el** ∼ be taken in, fall for it

añadi|**do** *a* added. ∼**dura** *f* addition. ∼**r** *vt* add. **por** ∼**dura** besides

añejo *a* ⟨*vino*⟩ mature; ⟨*jamón etc*⟩ cured

añicos *mpl* bits. **hacer** ∼ (*romper*) smash (to pieces); (*dejar cansado*) wear out

añil *m* indigo

año *m* year. ∼ **bisiesto** leap year. ∼ **nuevo** new year. **al** ∼ per year, a year. **¿cuántos** ∼**s tiene? tiene 5** ∼**s** how old is he? he's 5 (years old). **el** ∼ **pasado** last year. **el** ∼ **que viene** next year. **entrado en** ∼**s** elderly. **los** ∼**s 60** the sixties

añora|**nza** *f* nostalgia. ∼**r** *vt* miss. ● *vi* pine

apabullar *vt* crush; (*fig*) intimidate

apacentar [1] *vt* graze. ∼**se** *vpr* graze

apacib|**ilidad** *f* gentleness; (*calma*) peacefulness. ∼**le** *a* gentle; ⟨*tiempo*⟩ mild

apacigua|**dor** *a* pacifying. ∼**miento** *m* appeasement. ∼**r** [15] *vt* pacify; (*calmar*) calm; relieve ⟨*dolor etc*⟩. ∼**rse** *vpr* calm down

apadrina|**miento** *m* sponsorship. ∼**r** *vt* sponsor; be godfather to ⟨*a un niño*⟩; (*en una boda*) be best man for

apaga|**dizo** *a* slow to burn. ∼**do** *a* extinguished; ⟨*color*⟩ dull; ⟨*aparato eléctrico*⟩ off; ⟨*persona*⟩ lifeless; ⟨*sonido*⟩ muffled. ∼**r** [12] *vt* put out ⟨*fuego, incendio*⟩; turn off, switch off ⟨*aparato eléctrico*⟩; quench ⟨*sed*⟩; muffle ⟨*sonido*⟩. ∼**rse** *vpr* ⟨*fuego*⟩ go out; ‹*luz*› go out; ‹*sonido*› die away; (*fig*) pass away

apagón *m* blackout

apalabrar *vt* make a verbal agreement; (*contratar*) engage. ~**se** *vpr* come to a verbal agreement

apalanca|miento *m* leverage. ~**r** [7] *vt* (*levantar*) lever up; (*abrir*) lever open

apalea|miento *m* (*de grano*) winnowing; (*de alfombras, frutos, personas*) beating. ~**r** *vt* winnow ‹*grano*›; beat ‹*alfombras, frutos, personas*›; (*fig*) be rolling in ‹*dinero*›

apantallado *a* (*Mex*) stupid

apañ|ado *a* handy. ~**ar** *vt* (*arreglar*) fix; (*remendar*) mend; (*agarrar*) grasp, take hold of. ~**arse** *vpr* get along, manage. ¡estoy ~ado! that's all I need!

aparador *m* sideboard

aparato *m* apparatus; (*máquina*) machine; (*teléfono*) telephone; (*rad, TV*) set; (*ostentación*) show, pomp. ~**samente** *adv* ostentatiously; (*impresionante*) spectacularly. ~**si-dad** *f* ostentation. ~**so** *a* showy, ostentatious; ‹*caída*› spectacular

aparca|miento *m* car park (*Brit*), parking lot (*Amer*). ~**r** [7] *vt/i* park

aparea|miento *m* pairing off. ~**r** *vt* pair off; mate ‹*animales*›. ~**rse** *vpr* match; ‹*animales*› mate

aparecer [11] *vi* appear. ~**se** *vpr* appear

aparej|ado *a* ready; (*adecuado*) fitting. **llevar** ~**ado, traer** ~**ado** mean, entail. ~**o** *m* preparation; (*avíos*) equipment

aparent|ar *vt* (*afectar*) feign; (*parecer*) look. ● *vi* show off. ~**a 20 años** she looks like she's 20. ~**e** *a* apparent; (*adecuado, fam*) suitable

apari|ción *f* appearance; (*visión*) apparition. ~**encia** *f* appearance; (*fig*) show. **cubrir las** ~**encias** keep up appearances

apartad|ero *m* lay-by; (*rail*) siding. ~**o** *a* separated; (*aislado*) isolated. ● *m* (*de un texto*) section. ~**o** (**de correos**) post-office box, PO box

apartamento *m* flat (*Brit*), apartment

apart|amiento *m* separation; (*LAm, piso*) flat (*Brit*), apartment; (*aislamiento*) seclusion. ~**ar** *vt* separate; (*quitar*) remove. ~**arse** *vpr* leave; abandon ‹*creencia*›; (*quitarse*

de en medio) get out of the way; (*aislarse*) cut o.s. off. ~**e** *adv* apart; (*por separado*) separately; (*además*) besides. ● *m* aside; (*párrafo*) new paragraph. ~**e de** apart from. **dejar** ~**e** leave aside. **eso** ~**e** apart from that

apasiona|do *a* passionate; (*entusiasta*) enthusiastic; (*falto de objetividad*) biassed. ● *m* lover (**de** of). ~**miento** *m* passion. ~**r** *vt* excite. ~**rse** *vpr* get excited (**de, por** about), be mad (**de, por** about); (*ser parcial*) become biassed

ap|atía *f* apathy. ~**ático** *a* apathetic

apea|dero *m* (*rail*) halt. ~**r** *vt* fell ‹*árbol*›; (*disuadir*) dissuade; overcome ‹*dificultad*›; sort out ‹*problema*›. ~**rse** *vpr* (*de un vehículo*) get off

apechugar [12] *vi* push (with one's chest). ~ **con** put up with

apedrear *vt* stone

apeg|ado *a* attached. ~**o** *m* (*fam*) affection. **tener** ~**o a** be fond of

apela|ción *f* appeal. ~**r** *vi* appeal; (*recurrir*) resort (**a** to)

apelmazar [10] *vt* compress

apellid|ar *vt* call. ~**arse** *vpr* be called. **¿cómo te apellidas?** what's your surname? ~**o** *m* surname

apenar *vt* pain. ~**se** *vpr* grieve

apenas *adv* hardly, scarcely; (*enseguida que*) as soon as. ~ **si** (*fam*) hardly

ap|éndice *m* (*med*) appendix; (*fig*) appendage; (*de un libro*) appendix. ~**endicitis** *f* appendicitis

apercibi|miento *m* warning. ~**r** *vt* warn (**de** of, about); (*amenazar*) threaten. ~**rse** *vpr* prepare; (*percatarse*) provide o.s. (**de** with)

apergaminado *a* ‹*piel*› wrinkled

aperitivo *m* (*bebida*) aperitif; (*comida*) appetizer

aperos *mpl* agricultural equipment

apertura *f* opening

apesadumbrar *vt* upset. ~**se** *vpr* be upset

apestar *vt* stink out; (*fastidiar*) pester. ● *vi* stink (**a** of)

apet|ecer [11] *vt* long for; (*interesar*) appeal to. **¿te** ~**ece una copa?** do you fancy a drink? do you feel like a drink? ● *vi* be welcome. ~**ecible** *a* attractive. ~**ito** *m* appetite; (*fig*) desire. ~**itoso** *a* tempting

apiadarse *vpr* feel sorry (**de** for)

ápice *m* (*nada, en frases negativas*) anything. **no ceder un ~** not give an inch

apicult|or *m* bee-keeper. **~ura** *f* bee-keeping

apilar *vt* pile up

apiñar *vt* pack in. **~se** *vpr* ⟨*personas*⟩ crowd together; ⟨*cosas*⟩ be packed tight

apio *m* celery

apisonadora *f* steamroller

aplacar [7] *vt* placate; relieve ⟨*dolor*⟩

aplanar *vt* smooth. **~se** *vpr* become smooth; ⟨*persona*⟩ lose heart

aplasta|nte *a* overwhelming. **~r** *vt* crush. **~rse** *vpr* flatten o.s.

aplatanarse *vpr* become lethargic

aplau|dir *vt* clap, applaud; (*fig*) applaud. **~so** *m* applause; (*fig*) praise

aplaza|miento *m* postponement. **~r** [10] *vt* postpone; defer ⟨*pago*⟩

aplebeyarse *vpr* lower o.s.

aplica|ble *a* applicable. **~ción** *f* application. **~do** *a* ⟨*persona*⟩ diligent. **~r** [7] *vt* apply; (*fijar*) attach. **~rse** *vpr* apply o.s.

aplom|ado *a* self-confident; (*vertical*) vertical. **~o** *m* (self-) confidence, aplomb; (*verticalidad*) verticality

apocado *a* timid

Apocalipsis *f* Apocalypse

apocalíptico *a* apocalyptic

apoca|miento *m* diffidence. **~r** [7] *vt* belittle ⟨*persona*⟩. **~rse** *vpr* feel small

apodar *vt* nickname

apodera|do *m* representative. **~r** *vt* authorize. **~rse** *vpr* seize

apodo *m* nickname

apogeo *m* (*fig*) height

apolilla|do *a* moth-eaten. **~rse** *vpr* get moth-eaten

apolítico *a* non-political

apología *f* defence

apoltronarse *vpr* get lazy

apoplejía *f* stroke

apoquinar *vt/i* (*fam*) fork out

aporrear *vt* hit, thump; beat up ⟨*persona*⟩

aporta|ción *f* contribution. **~r** *vt* contribute

aposent|ar *vt* put up, lodge. **~o** *m* room, lodgings

apósito *m* dressing

aposta *adv* on purpose

apostar[1] [2] *vt/i* bet

apostar[2] *vt* station. **~se** *vpr* station o.s.

apostilla *f* note. **~r** *vt* add notes to

apóstol *m* apostle

apóstrofo *m* apostrophe

apoy|ar *vt* lean (**en** against); (*descansar*) rest; (*asentar*) base; (*reforzar*) support. **~arse** *vpr* lean, rest. **~o** *m* support

apreci|able *a* appreciable; (*digno de estima*) worthy. **~ación** *f* appreciation; (*valoración*) appraisal. **~ar** *vt* value; (*estimar*) appreciate. **~ativo** *a* appreciative. **~o** *m* appraisal; (*fig*) esteem

aprehensión *f* capture

apremi|ante *a* urgent, pressing. **~ar** *vt* urge; (*obligar*) compel; (*dar prisa a*) hurry up. ● *vi* be urgent. **~o** *m* urgency; (*obligación*) obligation

aprender *vt/i* learn. **~se** *vpr* learn (by heart)

aprendiz *m* apprentice. **~aje** *m* apprenticeship

aprensi|ón *f* apprehension; (*miedo*) fear. **~vo** *a* apprehensive, fearful

apresa|dor *m* captor. **~miento** *m* capture. **~r** *vt* seize; (*prender*) capture

aprestar *vt* prepare. **~se** *vpr* prepare

apresura|damente *adv* hurriedly, in a hurry. **~do** *a* in a hurry; (*hecho con prisa*) hurried. **~miento** *m* hurry. **~r** *vt* hurry. **~rse** *vpr* hurry

apret|ado *a* tight; (*difícil*) difficult; (*tacaño*) stingy, mean. **~ar** [1] *vt* tighten; press ⟨*botón*⟩; squeeze ⟨*persona*⟩; (*comprimir*) press down. ● *vi* be too tight. **~arse** *vpr* crowd together. **~ón** *m* squeeze. **~ón de manos** handshake

aprieto *m* difficulty. **verse en un ~** be in a tight spot

aprisa *adv* quickly

aprisionar *vt* imprison

aproba|ción *f* approval. **~r** [2] *vt* approve (of); pass ⟨*examen*⟩. ● *vi* pass

apropia|do *a* appropriate. **~rse** *vpr*. **~rse de** appropriate, take

aprovecha|ble *a* usable. **~do** *a* (*aplicado*) diligent; (*ingenioso*) resourceful; (*egoísta*) selfish; (*económico*) thrifty. **~miento** *m* advantage; (*uso*) use. **~r** *vt* take advantage of; (*utilizar*) make use of. ● *vi* be useful. **~rse** *vpr* make the most of it. **~rse de** take advantage of. **¡que aproveche!** enjoy your meal!

aprovisionar *vt* supply (**con, de** with)

aproxima|ción *f* approximation; (*proximidad*) closeness; (*en la lotería*) consolation prize. **~damente** *adv* roughly, approximately. **~do** *a* approximate, rough. **~r** *vt* bring near; (*fig*) bring together ⟨*personas*⟩. **~rse** *vpr* come closer, approach

apt|itud *f* suitability; (*capacidad*) ability. **~o** *a* (*capaz*) capable; (*adecuado*) suitable

apuesta *f* bet

apuesto *m* smart. ● *vb véase* **apostar**

apunta|ción *f* note. **~do** *a* sharp. **~dor** *m* prompter

apuntalar *vt* shore up

apunt|amiento *m* aiming; (*nota*) note. **~ar** *vt* aim ⟨*arma*⟩; (*señalar*) point at; (*anotar*) make a note of, note down; (*sacar punta*) sharpen; (*en el teatro*) prompt. **~arse** *vpr* put one's name down; score ⟨*triunfo, tanto etc*⟩. **~e** *m* note; (*bosquejo*) sketch. **tomar ~s** take notes

apuñalar *vt* stab

apur|adamente *adv* with difficulty. **~ado** *a* difficult; (*sin dinero*) hard up; (*agotado*) exhausted; (*exacto*) precise, carefully done. **~ar** *vt* exhaust; (*acabar*) finish; drain ⟨*vaso etc*⟩; (*fastidiar*) annoy; (*causar vergüenza*) embarrass. **~arse** *vpr* worry; (*esp LAm, apresurarse*) hurry up. **~o** *m* tight spot, difficult situation; (*vergüenza*) embarrassment; (*estrechez*) hardship, want; (*esp LAm, prisa*) hurry

aquejar *vt* trouble

aquel *a* (*f* **aquella,** *mpl* **aquellos,** *fpl* **aquellas**) that; (*en plural*) those; (*primero de dos*) former

aquél *pron* (*f* **aquélla,** *mpl* **aquéllos,** *fpl* **aquéllas**) that one; (*en plural*) those; (*primero de dos*) the former

aquello *pron* that; (*asunto*) that business

aquí *adv* here. **de ~** from here. **de ~ a 15 días** in a fortnight's time. **de ~ para allí** to and fro. **de ~ que** so that. **hasta ~** until now. **por ~** around here

aquiescencia *f* acquiescence

aquietar *vt* calm (down)

aquí: ~ fuera out here. **~ mismo** right here

árabe *a* & *m* & *f* Arab; (*lengua*) Arabic

Arabia *f* Arabia. **~ saudita, ~ saudí** Saudi Arabia

arábigo *a* Arabic

arado *m* plough. **~r** *m* ploughman

Aragón *m* Aragon

aragonés *a* & *m* Aragonese

arancel *m* tariff. **~ario** *a* tariff

arandela *f* washer

araña *f* spider; (*lámpara*) chandelier

arañar *vt* scratch

arar *vt* plough

arbitra|je *m* arbitration; (*en deportes*) refereeing. **~r** *vt/i* arbitrate; (*en fútbol etc*) referee; (*en tenis etc*) umpire

arbitr|ariedad *f* arbitrariness. **~ario** *a* arbitrary. **~io** *m* (*free*) will; (*jurid*) decision, judgement

árbitro *m* arbitrator; (*en fútbol etc*) referee; (*en tenis etc*) umpire

árbol *m* tree; (*eje*) axle; (*palo*) mast

arbol|ado *m* trees. **~adura** *f* rigging. **~eda** *f* wood

árbol: ~ genealógico family tree. **~ de navidad** Christmas tree

arbusto *m* bush

arca *f* (*caja*) chest. **~ de Noé** Noah's ark

arcada *f* arcade; (*de un puente*) arches; (*náuseas*) retching

arca|ico *a* archaic. **~ísmo** *m* archaism

arcángel *m* archangel

arcano *m* mystery. ● *a* mysterious, secret

arce *m* maple (tree)

arcén *m* (*de autopista*) hard shoulder; (*de carretera*) verge

arcilla *f* clay

arco *m* arch; (*de curva*) arc; (*arma, mus*) bow. **~ iris** *m* rainbow

archipiélago *m* archipelago

archiv|ador *m* filing cabinet. **~ar** *vt* file (away). **~o** *m* file; (*de documentos históricos*) archives

arder *vt/i* burn; (*fig, de ira*) seethe. **~se** *vpr* burn (up). **estar que arde** be very tense. **y va que arde** and that's enough

ardid *m* trick, scheme

ardiente *a* burning. **~mente** *adv* passionately

ardilla *f* squirrel

ardor *m* heat; *(fig)* ardour. ~ **del estómago** *m* heartburn. ~**oso** *a* burning

arduo *a* arduous

área *f* area

arena *f* sand; *(en deportes)* arena; *(en los toros)* (bull)ring. ~**l** *m* sandy area

arenga *f* harangue. ~**r** [12] *vt* harangue

aren|isca *f* sandstone. ~**isco** *a*, ~**oso** *a* sandy

arenque *m* herring. ~ **ahumado** kipper

argamasa *f* mortar

Argel *m* Algiers. ~**ia** *f* Algeria

argelino *a* & *m* Algerian

argentado *a* silver-plated

Argentina *f*. **la** ~ Argentina

argentin|ismo *m* Argentinism. ~**o** *a* silvery; *(de la Argentina)* Argentinian, Argentine. ● *m* Argentinian

argolla *f* ring

argot *m* slang

argucia *f* sophism

argüir [19] *vt* *(deducir)* deduce; *(probar)* prove, show; *(argumentar)* argue; *(echar en cara)* reproach. ● *vi* argue

argument|ación *f* argument. ~**ador** *a* argumentative. ~**ar** *vt/i* argue. ~**o** *m* argument; *(de libro, película etc)* story, plot; *(resumen)* synopsis

aria *f* aria

aridez *f* aridity, dryness

árido *a* arid, dry. ● *m*. ~**s** *mpl* dry goods

Aries *m* Aries

arisco *a* ⟨persona⟩ unsociable; ⟨animal⟩ vicious

arist|ocracia *f* aristocracy. ~**ócrata** *m* & *f* aristocrat. ~**ocrático** *a* aristocratic

aritmética *f* arithmetic

arma *f* arm, weapon; *(sección)* section. ~**da** *f* navy; *(flota)* fleet. ~ **de fuego** firearm. ~**do** *a* armed *(de* with). ~**dura** *f* armour; *(de gafas etc)* frame; *(tec)* framework. ~**mento** *m* arms, armaments; *(acción de armar)* armament. ~**r** *vt* arm *(de* with); *(montar)* put together. ~**r un lío** kick up a fuss. **La A~da Invencible** the Armada

armario *m* cupboard; *(para ropa)* wardrobe. ~ **ropero** wardrobe

armatoste *m* monstrosity, hulk *(fam)*

armazón *m* & *f* frame(work)

armer|ía *f* gunsmith's shop; *(museo)* war museum. ~**o** *m* gunsmith

armiño *m* ermine

armisticio *m* armistice

armonía *f* harmony

armónica *f* harmonica, mouth organ

armoni|oso harmonious. ~**zación** *f* harmonizing. ~**zar** [10] *vt* harmonize. ● *vi* harmonize; ⟨personas⟩ get on well *(con* with); ⟨colores⟩ go well *(con* with)

arnés *m* armour. **arneses** *mpl* harness

aro *m* ring, hoop; *(Arg, pendiente)* ear-ring

arom|a *m* aroma; *(de vino)* bouquet. ~**ático** *a* aromatic. ~**atizar** [10] *vt* perfume; *(culin)* flavour

arpa *f* harp

arpado *a* serrated

arpía *f* harpy; *(fig)* hag

arpillera *f* sackcloth, sacking

arpista *m* & *f* harpist

arp|ón *m* harpoon. ~**onar** *vt*, ~**onear** *vt* harpoon

arque|ar *vt* arch, bend. ~**arse** *vpr* arch, bend. ~**o** *m* arching, bending

arque|ología *f* archaeology. ~**ológico** *a* archaeological. ~**ólogo** *m* archaeologist

arquería *f* arcade

arquero *m* archer; *(com)* cashier

arqueta *f* chest

arquetipo *m* archetype; *(prototipo)* prototype

arquitect|o *m* architect. ~**ónico** *a* architectural. ~**ura** *f* architecture

arrabal *m* suburb; *(LAm, tugurio)* slum. ~**es** *mpl* outskirts. ~**ero** *a* suburban; *(de modales groseros)* common

arracima|do *a* in a bunch; *(apiñado)* bunched together. ~**rse** *vpr* bunch together

arraiga|damente *adv* firmly. ~**r** [12] *vi* take root. ~**rse** *vpr* take root; *(fig)* settle

arran|cada *f* sudden start. ~**car** [7] *vt* pull up ⟨planta⟩; extract ⟨diente⟩; *(arrebatar)* snatch; *(auto)* start. ● *vi* start. ~**carse** *vpr* start. ~**que** *m* sudden start; *(auto)* start; *(de emoción)* outburst

arras *fpl* security

arrasa|dor *a* overwhelming, devastating. ~**r** *vt* level, smooth; raze to the ground ⟨edificio etc⟩; *(llenar)* fill to the brim. ● *vi* ⟨el cielo⟩ clear.

~**rse** *vpr* ‹*el cielo*› clear; ‹*los ojos*› fill with tears; (*triunfar*) triumph

arrastr|ado *a* (*penoso*) wretched. ~**ar** *vt* pull; (*rozar contra el suelo*) drag (along); give rise to ‹*consecuencias*›. ● *vi* trail on the ground. ~**arse** *vpr* crawl; (*humillarse*) grovel. ~**e** *m* dragging; (*transporte*) haulage. **estar para el** ~**e** (*fam*) have had it, be worn out. **ir** ~**ado** be hard up

arrayán *m* myrtle

arre *int* gee up! ~**ar** *vt* urge on; give ‹*golpe*›

arrebañar *vt* scrape together; scrape clean ‹*plato etc*›

arrebat|ado *a* enraged; (*irreflexivo*) impetuous; ‹*cara*› flushed. ~**ar** *vt* snatch (away); ‹*el viento*› blow away; (*fig*) win (over); captivate ‹*corazón etc*›. ~**arse** *vpr* get carried away. ~**o** *m* (*de cólera etc*) fit; (*éxtasis*) extasy

arrebol *m* red glow

arreciar *vi* get worse, increase

arrecife *m* reef

arregl|ado *a* neat; (*bien vestido*) well-dressed; (*moderado*) moderate. ~**ar** *vt* arrange; (*poner en orden*) tidy up; sort out ‹*asunto, problema etc*›; (*reparar*) mend. ~**arse** *vpr* (*ponerse bien*) improve; (*prepararse*) get ready; (*apañarse*) manage, make do; (*ponerse de acuerdo*) come to an agreement. ~**árselas** manage, get by. ~**o** *m* (*incl mus*) arrangement; (*acción de reparar*) repair; (*acuerdo*) agreement; (*orden*) order. **con** ~**o a** according to

arrellanarse *vpr* lounge, sit back

arremangar [12] *vt* roll up ‹*mangas*›; tuck up ‹*falda*›. ~**se** *vpr* roll up one's sleeves

arremet|er *vt/i* attack. ~**ida** *f* attack

arremolinarse *vpr* mill about

arrenda|dor *m* (*que da en alquiler*) landlord; (*que toma en alquiler*) tenant. ~**miento** *m* renting; (*contrato*) lease; (*precio*) rent. ~**r** [1] *vt* (*dar casa en alquiler*) let; (*dar cosa en alquiler*) hire out; (*tomar en alquiler*) rent. ~**tario** *m* tenant

arreos *mpl* harness

arrepenti|miento *m* repentance, regret. ~**rse** [4] *vpr*. ~**rse de** sorry, regret; repent ‹*pecados*›

arrest|ar *vt* arrest, detain; (*encarcelar*) imprison. ~**o** *m* arrest; (*encarcelamiento*) imprisonment

arriar [20] *vt* lower ‹*bandera, vela*›; (*aflojar*) loosen; (*inundar*) flood. ~**se** *vpr* be flooded

arriba *adv* (up) above; (*dirección*) up(wards); (*en casa*) upstairs. ● *int* up with; (*¡levántate!*) up you get!; (*¡ánimo!*) come on! ¡~ **España!** long live Spain! ~ **mencionado** aforementioned. **calle** ~ up the street. **de** ~ **abajo** from top to bottom. **de 100 pesetas para** ~ more than 100 pesetas. **escaleras** ~ upstairs. **la parte de** ~ the top part. **los de** ~ those at the top. **más** ~ above

arribar *vi* ‹*barco*› reach port; (*esp LAm, llegar*) arrive

arribista *m & f* self-seeking person, arriviste

arribo *m* (*esp LAm*) arrival

arriero *m* muleteer

arriesga|do *a* risky. ~**r** [12] *vt* risk; (*aventurar*) venture. ~**rse** *vpr* take a risk

arrim|ar *vt* bring close(r); (*apartar*) move out of the way ‹*cosa*›; (*apartar*) push aside ‹*persona*›. ~**arse** *vpr* come closer, approach; (*apoyarse*) lean (a on). ~**o** *m* support. **al** ~**o de** with the support of

arrincona|do *a* forgotten. ~**rse** *vt* put in a corner; (*perseguir*) corner; (*arrumbar*) put aside; (*apartar a uno*) leave out, ignore. ~**rse** *vpr* become a recluse

arriscado *a* ‹*terreno*› uneven

arrobar *vt* entrance. ~**se** *vpr* be enraptured

arrocero *a* rice

arrodillarse *vpr* kneel (down)

arrogan|cia *f* arrogance; (*orgullo*) pride. ~**te** *a* arrogant; (*orgulloso*) proud

arrogarse [12] *vpr* assume

arroj|ado *a* brave. ~**ar** *vt* throw; (*dejar caer*) drop; (*emitir*) give off, throw out; (*producir*) produce. ● *vi* (*esp LAm, vomitar*) be sick. ~**arse** *vpr* throw o.s. ~**o** *m* courage

arrolla|dor *a* overwhelming. ~**r** *vt* roll (up); (*atropellar*) run over; ‹*ejército*› crush; ‹*agua*› sweep away; (*tratar sin respeto*) have no respect for

arropar *vt* wrap up; (*en la cama*) tuck up; (*fig, amparar*) protect. ~**se** *vpr* wrap (o.s.) up

arroy|o *m* stream; (*de una calle*) gutter; (*fig, de lágrimas*) flood; (*fig, de sangre*) pool. **poner en el ~o** throw into the street. **~uelo** *m* small stream

arroz *m* rice. **~al** *m* rice field. **~ con leche** rice pudding

arruga *f* (*en la piel*) wrinkle, line; (*en tela*) crease. **~r** [12] *vt* wrinkle; crumple (*papel*); crease (*tela*). **~rse** *vpr* (*la piel*) wrinkle, get wrinkled; (*tela*) crease, get creased

arruinar *vt* ruin; (*destruir*) destroy. **~se** *vpr* (*persona*) be ruined; (*edificio*) fall into ruins

arrullar *vt* lull to sleep. ● *vi* (*palomas*) coo. **~se** *vpr* bill and coo

arrumaco *m* caress; (*zalamería*) flattery

arrumbar *vt* put aside

arsenal *m* (*astillero*) shipyard; (*de armas*) arsenal; (*fig*) store

arsénico *m* arsenic

arte *m en singular*, *f en plural* art; (*habilidad*) skill; (*astucia*) cunning. **bellas ~s** fine arts. **con ~** skilfully. **malas ~s** trickery. **por amor al ~** for nothing, for love

artefacto *m* device

arter|amente *adv* artfully. **~ía** *f* cunning

arteria *f* artery; (*fig, calle*) main road

artero *a* cunning

artesan|al *a* craft. **~ía** *f* handicrafts. **~o** *m* artisan, craftsman. **objeto** *m* **de ~ía** hand-made article

ártico *a & m* Arctic

articula|ción *f* joint; (*pronunciación*) articulation. **~damente** *adv* articulately. **~do** *a* articulated; (*lenguaje*) articulate. **~r** *vt* articulate

articulista *m & f* columnist

artículo *m* article. **~s** *mpl* (*géneros*) goods. **~ de exportación** export commodity. **~ de fondo** editorial, leader

artificial *a* artificial

artificiero *m* bomb-disposal expert

artificio *m* (*habilidad*) skill; (*dispositivo*) device; (*engaño*) trick. **~so** *a* clever; (*astuto*) artful

artilugio *m* gadget

artiller|ía *f* artillery. **~o** *m* artilleryman, gunner

artimaña *f* trap

art|ista *m & f* artist; (*en espectáculos*) artiste. **~ísticamente** *adv* artistically. **~ístico** *a* artistic

artr|ítico *a* arthritic. **~itis** *f* arthritis

arveja *f* vetch; (*LAm, guisante*) pea

arzobispo *m* archbishop

as *m* ace

asa *f* handle

asad|o *a* roast(ed). ● *m* roast (meat), joint. **~o a la parrilla** grilled. **~o al horno** (*sin grasa*) baked; (*con grasa*) roast. **~or** *m* spit. **~ura** *f* offal

asalariado *a* salaried. ● *m* employee

asalt|ante *m* attacker; (*de un banco*) robber. **~ar** *vt* storm (*fortaleza*); attack (*persona*); raid (*banco etc*); (*fig*) (*duda*) assail; (*fig*) (*idea etc*) cross one's mind. **~o** *m* attack; (*en boxeo*) round

asamble|a *f* assembly; (*reunión*) meeting; (*congreso*) conference. **~ísta** *m & f* member of an assembly

asapán *m* (*Mex*) flying squirrel

asar *vt* roast; (*fig, acosar*) pester (**a** with). **~se** *vpr* be very hot. **~ a la parrilla** grill. **~ al horno** (*sin grasa*) bake; (*con grasa*) roast

asbesto *m* asbestos

ascendencia *f* descent

ascend|ente *a* ascending. **~er** [1] *vt* promote. ● *vi* go up, ascend; (*cuenta etc*) come to, amount to; (*ser ascendido*) be promoted. **~iente** *m & f* ancestor; (*influencia*) influence

ascens|ión *f* ascent; (*de grado*) promotion. **~ional** *a* upward. **~o** *m* ascent; (*de grado*) promotion. **día** *m* **de la A~ión** Ascension Day

ascensor *m* lift (*Brit*), elevator (*Amer*). **~ista** *m & f* lift attendant (*Brit*), elevator operator (*Amer*)

asc|eta *m & f* ascetic. **~ético** *a* ascetic

asco *m* disgust. **dar ~** be disgusting; (*fig, causar enfado*) be infuriating. **estar hecho un ~** be disgusting. **hacer ~s de algo** turn up one's nose at sth. **me da ~ el ajo** I can't stand garlic. **¡qué ~!** how disgusting! **ser un ~** be a disgrace

ascua *f* ember. **estar en ~s** be on tenterhooks

asea|damente *adv* cleanly. **~do** *a* clean; (*arreglado*) neat. **~r** *vt* (*lavar*) wash; (*limpiar*) clean; (*arreglar*) tidy up

asedi|ar *vt* besiege; (*fig*) pester. **~o** *m* siege

asegura|do *a & m* insured. **~dor** *m* insurer. **~r** *vt* secure, make safe; (*decir*) assure; (*concertar un seguro*) insure; (*preservar*) safeguard. ~**rse** *vpr* make sure

asemejarse *vpr* be alike

asenta|da *f*. **de una ~da** at a sitting. ~**do** *a* situated; (*arraigado*) established. ~**r** [1] *vt* place; (*asegurar*) settle; (*anotar*) note down. ● *vi* be suitable. ~**rse** *vpr* settle; (*estar situado*) be situated

asenti|miento *m* consent. ~**r** [4] *vi* agree (a to). ~**r con la cabeza** nod

aseo *m* cleanliness. ~**s** *mpl* toilets

asequible *a* obtainable; (*precio*) reasonable; (*persona*) approachable

asesin|ar *vt* murder; (*pol*) assassinate. ~**ato** *m* murder; (*pol*) assassination. ~**o** *m* murderer; (*pol*) assassin

asesor *m* adviser, consultant. ~**amiento** *m* advice. ~**ar** *vt* advise. ~**arse** *vpr*. ~**arse con/de** consult. ~**ía** *f* consultancy; (*oficina*) consultant's office

asestar *vt* aim (*arma*); strike (*golpe etc*); (*disparar*) fire

asevera|ción *f* assertion. ~**r** *vt* assert

asfalt|ado *a* asphalt. ~**ar** *vt* asphalt. ~**o** *m* asphalt

asfixia *f* suffocation. ~**nte** *a* suffocating. ~**r** *vt* suffocate. ~**rse** *vpr* suffocate

así *adv* so; (*de esta manera*) like this, like that. ● *a* such. ~ ~, ~ **asá**, ~ **asado** so-so. ~ **como** just as. ~**...** **como** both... and. ~ **pues** so. ~ **que** so; (*enseguida*) as soon as. ~ **sea** so be it. ~ **y todo** even so. **aun** ~ even so. **¿no es** ~? isn't that right? **y** ~ **(sucesivamente)** and so on

Asia *f* Asia

asiático *a* & *m* Asian

asidero *m* handle; (*fig, pretexto*) excuse

asidu|amente *adv* regularly. ~**idad** *f* regularity. ~**o** *a* & *m* regular

asiento *m* seat; (*situación*) site. ~ **delantero** front seat. ~ **trasero** back seat. **tome Vd** ~ please take a seat

asigna|ción *f* assignment; (*sueldo*) salary. ~**r** *vt* assign; allot (*porción, tiempo etc*)

asignatura *f* subject. ~ **pendiente** (*escol*) failed subject; (*fig*) matter still to be resolved

asil|ado *m* inmate. ~**ado político** refugee. ~**o** *m* asylum; (*fig*) shelter;

(*de ancianos etc*) home. ~**o de huérfanos** orphanage. **pedir** ~**o político** ask for political asylum

asimétrico *a* asymmetrical

asimila|ción *f* assimilation. ~**r** *vt* assimilate. ~**rse** *vpr* be assimilated. ~**rse a** resemble

asimismo *adv* in the same way, likewise

asir [45] *vt* grasp. ~**se** *vpr* grab hold (a, de of)

asist|encia *f* attendance; (*gente*) people (present); (*en un teatro etc*) audience; (*ayuda*) assistance. ~**encia médica** medical care. ~**enta** *f* assistant; (*mujer de la limpieza*) charwoman. ~**ente** *m* assistant. ~**ente social** social worker. ~**ido** *a* assisted. ~**ir** *vt* assist, help; (*un médico*) treat. ● *vi*. ~**ir a** attend, be present at

asm|a *f* asthma. ~**ático** *a* & *m* asthmatic

asn|ada *f* (*fig*) silly thing. ~**o** *m* donkey; (*fig*) ass

asocia|ción *f* association; (*com*) partnership. ~**do** *a* associated; (*miembro etc*) associate. ● *m* associate. ~**r** *vt* associate; (*com*) take into partnership. ~**rse** *vpr* associate; (*com*) become a partner

asolador *a* destructive

asolar[1] [1] *vt* destroy. ~**se** *vpr* be destroyed

asolar[2] *vt* dry up (*plantas*)

asoma|da *f* brief appearance. ~**r** *vt* show. ● *vi* appear, show. ~**rse** *vpr* (*persona*) lean out (a, por of); (*cosa*) appear

asombr|adizo *a* easily frightened. ~**ar** *vt* (*pasmar*) amaze; (*sorprender*) surprise. ~**arse** *vpr* (*sorprenderse*) be amazed; surprised. ~**o** *m* amazement, surprise. ~**osamente** *adv* amazingly. ~**oso** *a* amazing, astonishing

asomo *m* sign. **ni por** ~ by no means

asonada *f* mob; (*motín*) riot

aspa *f* cross, X-shape; (*de molino*) (windmill) sail. ~**do** *a* X-shaped

aspaviento *m* show, fuss. ~**s** *mpl* gestures. **hacer** ~**s** make a big fuss

aspecto *m* look, appearance; (*fig*) aspect

aspereza *f* roughness; (*de sabor etc*) sourness

áspero *a* rough; (*sabor etc*) bitter

aspersión *f* sprinkling

aspiración *f* breath; (*deseo*) ambition

aspirador *a* suction. ~**a** *f* vacuum cleaner

aspira|nte *m* candidate. ~**r** *vt* breathe in; ‹*máquina*› suck up. ● *vi* breathe in; ‹*máquina*› suck. ~**r a** aspire to

aspirina *f* aspirin

asquear *vt* sicken. ● *vi* be sickening. ~**se** *vpr* be disgusted

asqueros|amente *adv* disgustingly. ~**idad** *f* filthiness. ~**o** *a* disgusting

asta *f* spear; (*de la bandera*) flagpole; (*mango*) handle; (*cuerno*) horn. **a media** ~ at half-mast. ~**do** *a* horned

asterisco *m* asterisk

astilla *f* splinter. ~**s** *fpl* firewood. ~**r** *vt* splinter. **hacer** ~**s** smash. **hacerse** ~**s** shatter

astillero *m* shipyard

astringente *a* & *m* astringent

astro *m* star

astr|ología *f* astrology. ~**ólogo** *m* astrologer

astrona|uta *m* & *f* astronaut. ~**ve** *f* spaceship

astr|onomía *f* astronomy. ~**onómico** *a* astronomical. ~**ónomo** *m* astronomer

astu|cia *f* cleverness; (*ardid*) cunning. ~**to** *a* astute; (*taimado*) cunning

asturiano *a* & *m* Asturian

Asturias *fpl* Asturias

asueto *m* time off, holiday

asumir *vt* assume

asunción *f* assumption. **A**~ Assumption

asunto *m* subject; (*cuestión*) matter; (*de una novela*) plot; (*negocio*) business. ~**s** *mpl* **exteriores** foreign affairs. **el** ~ **es que** the fact is that

asusta|dizo *a* easily frightened. ~**r** *vt* frighten. ~**rse** *vpr* be frightened

ataca|nte *m* & *f* attacker. ~**r** [7] *vt* attack

atad|ero *m* rope; (*cierre*) fastening; (*gancho*) hook. ~**ijo** *m* bundle. ~**o** *a* tied; (*fig*) timid. ● *m* bundle. ~**ura** *f* tying; (*cuerda*) string

ataj|ar *vi* take a short cut. ~**o** *m* short cut; (*grupo*) bunch. **echar por el** ~**o** take the easy way out

atalaya *f* watch-tower; (*fig*) vantage point

atañer [22] *vt* concern

ataque *m* attack; (*med*) fit, attack. ~ **al corazón** heart attack. ~ **de nervios** hysterics

atar *vt* tie (up). ~**se** *vpr* get tied up

atardecer [11] *vi* get dark. ● *m* dusk. **al** ~ at dusk

atarea|do *a* busy. ~**rse** *vpr* work hard

atasc|adero *m* (*fig*) stumbling block. ~**ar** [7] *vt* block; (*fig*) hinder. ~**arse** *vpr* get stuck; ‹*tubo etc*› block. ~**o** *m* obstruction; (*auto*) traffic jam

ataúd *m* coffin

atav|iar [20] *vt* dress up. ~**iarse** *vpr* dress up, get dressed up. ~**ío** *m* dress, attire

atemorizar [10] *vt* frighten. ~**se** *vpr* be frightened

Atenas *fpl* Athens

atenazar [10] *vt* (*fig*) torture; ‹*duda, miedo*› grip

atención *f* attention; (*cortesía*) courtesy, kindness; (*interés*) interest. ¡~! look out! ~ **a** beware of. **llamar la** ~ attract attention, catch the eye. **prestar** ~ pay attention

atender [1] *vt* attend to; heed ‹*consejo etc*›; (*cuidar*) look after. ● *vi* pay attention

atenerse [40] *vpr* abide (**a** by)

atentado *m* offence; (*ataque*) attack. ~ **contra la vida de uno** attempt on s.o.'s life

atentamente *adv* attentively; (*con cortesía*) politely; (*con amabilidad*) kindly. **le saluda** ~ (*en cartas*) yours faithfully

atentar *vi* commit an offence. ~ **contra la vida de uno** make an attempt on s.o.'s life

atento *a* attentive; (*cortés*) polite; (*amable*) kind

atenua|nte *a* extenuating. ● *f* extenuating circumstance. ~**r** [21] *vt* attenuate; (*hacer menor*) diminish, lessen. ~**rse** *vpr* weaken

ateo *a* atheistic. ● *m* atheist

aterciopelado *a* velvety

aterido *a* frozen (stiff), numb (with cold)

aterra|dor *a* terrifying. ~**r** *vt* terrify. ~**rse** *vpr* be terrified

aterriza|je *m* landing. ~**je forzoso** emergency landing. ~**r** [10] *vt* land

aterrorizar [10] *vt* terrify

atesorar *vt* hoard

atesta|do *a* packed, full up. ● *m* sworn statement. ~**r** *vt* fill up, pack; (*jurid*) testify

atestiguar [15] *vt* testify to; *(fig)* prove

atiborrar *vt* fill, stuff. **~se** *vpr* stuff o.s.

ático *m* attic

atilda|do *a* elegant, neat. **~r** *vt* put a tilde over; *(arreglar)* tidy up. **~rse** *vpr* smarten o.s. up

atina|damente *adv* rightly. **~do** *a* right; *(juicioso)* wise, sensible. **~r** *vt/i* hit upon; *(acertar)* guess right

atípico *a* exceptional

atiplado *a* high-pitched

atirantar *vt* tighten

atisb|ar *vt* spy on; *(vislumbrar)* make out. **~o** *m* spying; *(indicio)* hint, sign

atizar [10] *vt* poke; give *⟨golpe⟩*; *(fig)* stir up; arouse, excite *⟨pasión etc⟩*

atlántico *a* Atlantic. **el (océano) A~** the Atlantic (Ocean)

atlas *m* atlas

atl|eta *m & f* athlete. **~ético** *a* athletic. **~etismo** *m* athletics

atm|ósfera *f* atmosphere. **~osférico** *a* atmospheric

atolondra|do *a* scatter-brained; *(aturdido)* bewildered. **~miento** *m* bewilderment; *(irreflexión)* thoughtlessness. **~r** *vt* bewilder; *(pasmar)* stun. **~rse** *vpr* be bewildered

atolladero *m* bog; *(fig)* tight corner

at|ómico *a* atomic. **~omizador** *m* atomizer. **~omizar** [10] *vt* atomize

átomo *m* atom

atónito *m* amazed

atonta|do *a* bewildered; *(tonto)* stupid. **~r** *vt* stun. **~rse** *vpr* get confused

atormenta|dor *a* tormenting. • *m* tormentor. **~r** *vt* torture. **~rse** *vpr* worry, torment o.s.

atornillar *vt* screw on

atosigar [12] *vt* pester

atracadero *m* quay

atracador *m* bandit

atracar [7] *vt* *(amarrar)* tie up; *(arrimar)* bring alongside; rob *⟨banco, persona⟩*. • *vi ⟨barco⟩* tie up; *⟨astronave⟩* dock. **~se** *vpr* stuff o.s. (de with)

atracci|ón *f* attraction. **~ones** *fpl* entertainment, amusements

atrac|o *m* hold-up, robbery. **~ón** *m*. **darse un ~ón** stuff o.s.

atractivo *a* attractive. • *m* attraction; *(encanto)* charm

atraer [41] *vt* attract

atragantarse *vpr* choke (**con** on). **la historia se me atraganta** I can't stand history

atranc|ar [7] *vt* bolt *⟨puerta⟩*; block up *⟨tubo etc⟩*. **~arse** *vpr* get stuck; *⟨tubo⟩* get blocked. **~o** *m* difficulty

atrapar *vt* trap; *(fig)* land *⟨empleo etc⟩*; catch *⟨resfriado⟩*

atrás *adv* behind; *(dirección)* back(wards); *(tiempo)* previously, before. • *int* back! **dar un paso ~** step backwards. **hacia ~, para ~** backwards

atras|ado *a* behind; *⟨reloj⟩* slow; *(con deudas)* in arrears; *⟨país⟩* backward. **llegar ~ado** arrive late. **~ar** *vt* slow down; *(retrasar)* put back; *(demorar)* delay, postpone. • *vi ⟨reloj⟩* be slow. **~arse** *vpr* be late; *⟨reloj⟩* be slow; *(quedarse atrás)* be behind. **~o** *m* delay; *(de un reloj)* slowness; *(de un país)* backwardness. **~os** *mpl* arrears

atravesa|do *a* lying across; *(bizco)* cross-eyed; *(fig, malo)* wicked. **~r** [1] *vt* cross; *(traspasar)* go through; *(poner transversalmente)* lay across. **~rse** *vpr* lie across; *(en la garganta)* get stuck, stick; *(entrometerse)* interfere

atrayente *a* attractive

atrev|erse *vpr* dare. **~erse con** tackle. **~ido** *a* daring, bold; *(insolente)* insolent. **~imiento** *m* daring, boldness; *(descaro)* insolence

atribuci|ón *f* attribution. **atribuciones** *fpl* authority

atribuir [17] *vt* attribute; confer *⟨función⟩*. **~se** *vpr* take the credit for

atribular *vt* afflict. **~se** *vpr* be distressed

atribut|ivo *a* attributive. **~o** *m* attribute; *(símbolo)* symbol

atril *m* lectern; *(mus)* music stand

atrincherar *vt* fortify with trenches. **~se** *vpr* entrench (o.s.)

atrocidad *f* atrocity. **decir ~es** make silly remarks. **¡qué ~!** how terrible!

atrochar *vi* take a short cut

atrojarse *vpr* (*Mex*) be cornered

atrona|dor *a* deafening. **~r** [2] *vt* deafen

atropell|adamente *adv* hurriedly. **~ado** *a* hasty. **~ar** *vt* knock down, run over; *(empujar)* push aside; *(maltratar)* bully; *(fig)* outrage, insult. **~arse** *vpr* rush. **~o** *m* *(auto)* accident; *(fig)* outrage

atroz *a* atrocious; (*fam*) huge. **∼mente** *adv* atrociously, awfully

atuendo *m* dress, attire

atufar *vt* choke; (*fig*) irritate. **∼se** *vpr* be overcome; (*enfadarse*) get cross

atún *m* tuna (fish)

aturdi|do *a* bewildered; (*irreflexivo*) thoughtless. **∼r** *vt* bewilder, stun; ⟨*ruido*⟩ deafen. **∼rse** *vpr* be stunned; (*intentar olvidar*) try to forget

atur(r)ullar *vt* bewilder

atusar *vt* smooth; trim ⟨*pelo*⟩

auda|cia *f* boldness, audacity. **∼z** *a* bold

audib|ilidad *f* audibility. **∼le** *a* audible

audición *f* hearing; (*concierto*) concert

audiencia *f* audience; (*tribunal*) court

auditor *m* judge-advocate; (*de cuentas*) auditor

auditorio *m* audience; (*sala*) auditorium

auge *m* peak; (*com*) boom

augur|ar *vt* predict; ⟨*cosas*⟩ augur. **∼io** *m* omen. **∼ios** *mpl*. **con nuestros ∼ios para** with our best wishes for

augusto *a* august

aula *f* class-room; (*univ*) lecture room

aulaga *f* gorse

aull|ar [23] *vi* howl. **∼ido** *m* howl

aument|ar *vt* increase; put up ⟨*precios*⟩; magnify ⟨*imagen*⟩; step up ⟨*producción, voltaje*⟩. ● *vi* increase. **∼arse** *vpr* increase. **∼ativo** *a* & *m* augmentative. **∼o** *m* increase; (*de sueldo*) rise

aun *adv* even. **∼ así** even so. **∼ cuando** although. **más ∼** even more. **ni ∼** not even

aún *adv* still, yet. **∼ no ha llegado** it still hasn't arrived, it hasn't arrived yet

aunar [23] *vt* join. **∼se** *vpr* join together

aunque *conj* although, (even) though

aúpa *int* up! **de ∼** wonderful

aureola *f* halo

auricular *m* (*de teléfono*) receiver. **∼es** *mpl* headphones

aurora *f* dawn

ausen|cia *f* absence. **∼tarse** *vpr* leave. **∼te** *a* absent. ● *m* & *f* absentee; (*jurid*) missing person. **en ∼ de** in the absence of

auspicio *m* omen. **bajo los ∼s de** sponsored by

auster|idad *f* austerity. **∼o** *a* austere

austral *a* southern. ● *m* (*unidad monetaria argentina*) austral

Australia *m* Australia

australiano *a* & *m* Australian

Austria *f* Austria

austriaco, austríaco *a* & *m* Austrian

aut|enticar [7] authenticate. **∼enticidad** *f* authenticity. **∼éntico** *a* authentic

auto *m* sentence; (*auto, fam*) car. **∼s** *mpl* proceedings

auto... *pref* auto...

auto|ayuda *f* self-help. **∼biografía** *f* autobiography. **∼biográfico** *a* autobiographical. **∼bombo** *m* self-glorification

autobús *m* bus. **en ∼** by bus

autocar *m* coach (*Brit*), (long-distance) bus (*Amer*)

aut|ocracia *f* autocracy. **∼ócrata** *m* & *f* autocrat. **∼ocrático** *a* autocratic

autóctono *a* autochthonous

auto: ∼determinación *f* self-determination. **∼defensa** *f* self-defence. **∼didacto** *a* self-taught. ● *m* autodidact. **∼escuela** *f* driving school. **∼giro** *m* autogiro

autógrafo *m* autograph

automación *f* automation

autómata *m* robot

autom|ático *a* automatic. ● *m* press-stud. **∼atización** *f* automation. **∼atizar** [10] *vt* automate

automotor *a* (*f* **automotriz**) self-propelled. ● *m* diesel train

autom|óvil *a* self-propelled. ● *m* car. **∼ovilismo** *m* motoring. **∼ovilista** *m* & *f* driver, motorist

aut|onomía *f* autonomy. **∼onómico** *a*, **∼ónomo** *a* autonomous

autopista *f* motorway (*Brit*), freeway (*Amer*)

autopsia *f* autopsy

autor *m* author. **∼a** *f* author(ess)

autori|dad *f* authority. **∼tario** *a* authoritarian. **∼tarismo** *m* authoritarianism

autoriza|ción *f* authorization. **∼damente** *adv* officially. **∼do** *a* authorized, official; ⟨*opinión etc*⟩ authoritative. **∼r** [10] *vt* authorize

auto: ~**rretrato** *m* self-portrait. ~**servicio** *m* self-service restaurant. ~**stop** *m* hitch-hiking. **hacer** ~**stop** hitch-hike

autosuficien|cia *f* self-sufficiency. ~**te** *a* self-sufficient

autovía *f* dual carriageway

auxili|ar *a* assistant; ⟨*servicios*⟩ auxiliary. ● *m* assistant. ● *vt* help. ~**o** *m* help. ¡~**o**! help! ~**os espirituales** last rites. **en** ~**o de** in aid of. **pedir** ~**o** shout for help. **primeros** ~**os** first aid

Av. *abrev* (*Avenida*) Ave, Avenue

aval *m* guarantee

avalancha *f* avalanche

avalar *vt* guarantee

avalorar *vt* enhance; (*fig*) encourage

avance *m* advance; (*en el cine*) trailer; (*balance*) balance; (*de noticias*) early news bulletin. ~ **informativo** publicity hand-out

avante *adv* (*esp LAm*) forward

avanza|do *a* advanced. ~**r** [10] *vt* move forward. ● *vi* advance

avar|icia *f* avarice. ~**icioso** *a*, ~**iento** *a* greedy; (*tacaño*) miserly. ~**o** *a* miserly. ● *m* miser

avasalla|dor *a* overwhelming. ~**r** *vt* dominate

Avda. *abrev* (*Avenida*) Ave, Avenue

ave *f* bird. ~ **de paso** (*incl fig*) bird of passage. ~ **de presa**, ~ **de rapiña** bird of prey

avecinarse *vpr* approach

avecindarse *vpr* settle

avejentarse *vpr* age

avellan|a *f* hazel-nut. ~**o** *m* hazel (tree)

avemaría *f* Hail Mary. **al** ~ at dusk

avena *f* oats

avenar *vt* drain

avenida *f* (*calle*) avenue; (*de río*) flood

avenir [53] *vt* reconcile. ~**se** *vpr* come to an agreement

aventaja|do *a* outstanding. ~**r** *vt* surpass

aventar [1] *vt* fan; winnow ⟨*grano etc*⟩; ⟨*viento*⟩ blow away

aventur|a *f* adventure; (*riesgo*) risk. ~**a amorosa** love affair. ~**ado** *a* risky. ~**ar** *vt* risk. ~**arse** *vpr* dare. ~**a sentimental** love affair. ~**ero** *a* adventurous. ● *m* adventurer

avergonza|do *a* ashamed; (*embarazado*) embarrassed. ~**r** [10 & 16] *vt* shame; (*embarazar*) embar-

rass. ~**rse** *vpr* be ashamed; (*embarazarse*) be embarrassed

aver|ía *f* (*auto*) breakdown; (*daño*) damage. ~**iado** *a* broken down; ⟨*fruta*⟩ damaged, spoilt. ~**iar** [20] *vt* damage. ~**iarse** *vpr* get damaged; ⟨*coche*⟩ break down

averigua|ble *a* verifiable. ~**ción** *f* verification; (*investigación*) investigation; (*Mex, disputa*) argument. ~**dor** *m* investigator. ~**r** [15] *vt* verify; (*enterarse de*) find out; (*investigar*) investigate. ● *vi* (*Mex*) quarrel

aversión *f* aversion (**a, hacia, por** for)

avestruz *m* ostrich

aviación *f* aviation; (*mil*) air force

aviado *a* (*Arg*) well off. **estar** ~ be in a mess

aviador *m* (*aviat*) member of the crew; (*piloto*) pilot; (*Arg, prestamista*) money-lender; (*Arg, de minas*) mining speculator

aviar [20] *vt* get ready, prepare; (*arreglar*) tidy; (*reparar*) repair; (*LAm, prestar dinero*) lend money; (*dar prisa*) hurry up. ~**se** *vpr* get ready. ¡**aviate!** hurry up!

av|ícula *a* poultry. ~**icultor** *m* poultry farmer. ~**icultura** *f* poultry farming

avidez *f* eagerness, greed

ávido *a* eager, greedy

avieso *a* (*maligno*) wicked

avinagra|do *a* sour. ~**r** *vt* sour; (*fig*) embitter. ~**rse** *vpr* go sour; (*fig*) become embittered

avío *m* preparation. ~**s** *mpl* provisions; (*utensilios*) equipment

avi|ón *m* aeroplane (*Brit*), airplane (*Amer*). ~**oneta** *f* light aircraft

avis|ado *a* wise. ~**ar** *vt* warn; (*informar*) notify, inform; call ⟨*médico etc*⟩. ~**o** *m* warning; (*anuncio*) notice. **estar sobre** ~**o** be on the alert. **mal** ~**ado** ill-advised. **sin previo** ~**o** without notice

avisp|a *f* wasp. ~**ado** *a* sharp. ~**ero** *m* wasps' nest; (*fig*) mess. ~**ón** *m* hornet

avistar *vt* catch sight of

avitualla|miento *m* supplying. ~**r** *vt* provision

avivar *vt* stoke up ⟨*fuego*⟩; brighten up ⟨*color*⟩; arouse ⟨*interés, pasión*⟩; intensify ⟨*dolor*⟩. ~**se** *vpr* revive; (*animarse*) cheer up

axila *f* axilla, armpit

axiom|a *m* axiom. **∼ático** *a* axiomatic
ay *int* (*de dolor*) ouch!; (*de susto*) oh!; (*de pena*) oh dear! ∼ **de** poor. **¡∼ de ti!** poor you!
aya *f* governess, child's nurse
ayer *adv* yesterday. ● *m* past. **antes de ∼** the day before yesterday. ∼ **por la mañana** yesterday morning. ∼ **(por la) noche** last night
ayo *m* tutor
ayote *m* (*Mex*) pumpkin
ayuda *f* help, aid. ∼ **de cámara** valet. **∼nta** *f*, **∼nte** *m* assistant; (*mil*) adjutant. **∼nte técnico sanitario (ATS)** nurse. **∼r** *vt* help
ayun|ar *vi* fast. **∼as** *fpl*. **estar en ∼as** have had no breakfast; (*fig, fam*) be in the dark. **∼o** *m* fasting
ayuntamiento *m* town council, city council; (*edificio*) town hall
azabache *m* jet
azad|a *f* hoe. **∼ón** *m* (large) hoe
azafata *f* air hostess
azafrán *m* saffron
azahar *m* orange blossom
azar *m* chance; (*desgracia*) misfortune. **al ∼** at random. **por ∼** by chance
azararse *vpr* go wrong; (*fig*) get flustered
azaros|amente *adv* hazardously. **∼o** *a* hazardous, risky; (*persona*) unlucky
azoga|do *a* restless. **∼rse** [12] *vpr* be restless
azolve *m* (*Mex*) obstruction
azora|do *a* flustered, excited, alarmed. **∼miento** *m* confusion, embarrassment. **∼r** *vt* embarrass; (*aturdir*) alarm. **∼rse** *vpr* get flustered, be alarmed
Azores *fpl* Azores
azot|aina *f* beating. **∼ar** *vt* whip, beat. **∼e** *m* whip; (*golpe*) smack; (*fig, calamidad*) calamity
azotea *f* flat roof. **estar mal de la ∼** be mad
azteca *a* & *m* & *f* Aztec
az|úcar *m* & *f* sugar. **∼ucarado** *a* sweet. **∼ucarar** *vt* sweeten. **∼ucarero** *m* sugar bowl
azucena *f* (white) lily
azufre *m* sulphur
azul *a* & *m* blue. **∼ado** *a* bluish. **∼ de lavar** (washing) blue. **∼ marino** navy blue
azulejo *m* tile
azuzar *vt* urge on, incite

B

bab|a *f* spittle. **∼ear** *vi* drool, slobber; (*niño*) dribble. **caerse la ∼a** be delighted
babel *f* bedlam
babe|o *m* drooling; (*de un niño*) dribbling. **∼ro** *m* bib
Babia *f*. **estar en ∼** have one's head in the clouds
babieca *a* stupid. ● *m* & *f* simpleton
babor *m* port. **a ∼** to port, on the port side
babosa *f* slug
babosada *f* (*Mex*) silly remark
babos|ear *vt* slobber over; (*niño*) dribble over. **∼eo** *m* drooling; (*de niño*) dribbling. **∼o** *a* slimy; (*LAm, tonto*) silly
babucha *f* slipper
babuino *m* baboon
baca *f* luggage rack
bacaladilla *f* small cod
bacalao *m* cod
bacon *m* bacon
bacteria *f* bacterium
bache *m* hole; (*fig*) bad patch
bachillerato *m* school-leaving examination
badaj|azo *m* stroke (of a bell). **∼o** *m* clapper; (*persona*) chatterbox
bagaje *m* baggage; (*animal*) beast of burden; (*fig*) knowledge
bagatela *f* trifle
Bahamas *fpl* Bahamas
bahía *f* bay
bail|able *a* dance. **∼ador** *a* dancing. ● *m* dancer. **∼aor** *m* Flamenco dancer. **∼ar** *vt/i* dance. **∼arín** dancer. **∼arina** *f* dancer; (*de baile clásico*) ballerina. **∼e** *m* dance. **∼e de etiqueta** ball. **ir a ∼ar** go dancing
baja *f* drop, fall; (*mil*) casualty. **∼ por maternidad** maternity leave. **∼da** *f* slope; (*acto de bajar*) descent. **∼mar** *m* low tide. **∼r** *vt* lower; (*llevar abajo*) get down; bow (*la cabeza*). **∼r la escalera** go downstairs. ● *vi* go down; (*temperatura, precio*) fall. **∼rse** *vpr* bend down. **∼r(se) de** get out of (*coche*); get off (*autobús, caballo, tren, bicicleta*). **dar(se) de ∼** take sick leave
bajeza *f* vile deed
bajío *m* sandbank

bajo *a* low; (*de estatura*) short, small; ‹*cabeza, ojos*› lowered; (*humilde*) humble, low; (*vil*) vile, low; ‹*color*› pale; ‹*voz*› low; (*mus*) deep. ● *m* lowland; (*bajío*) sandbank; (*mus*) bass. ● *adv* quietly; ‹*volar*› low. ● *prep* under; (*temperatura*) below. ~ **la lluvia** in the rain. **los ~s fondos** the low district. **por lo ~** under one's breath; (*fig*) in secret

bajón *m* drop; (*de salud*) decline; (*com*) slump

bala *f* bullet; (*de algodón etc*) bale. ~ **perdida** stray bullet. **como una ~** like a shot

balada *f* ballad

baladí *a* trivial

baladrón *a* boastful

baladron|ada *f* boast. ~**ear** *vi* boast

balan|ce *m* swinging; (*de una cuenta*) balance; (*documento*) balance sheet. ~**cear** *vt* balance. ● *vi* hesitate. ~**cearse** *vpr* swing; (*vacilar*) hesitate. ~**ceo** *m* swinging. ~**za** *f* scales; (*com*) balance

balar *vi* bleat

balaustrada *f* balustrade, railing(s); (*de escalera*) banisters

balay *m* (*LAm*) wicker basket

balazo *m* (*disparo*) shot; (*herida*) bullet wound

balboa *f* (*unidad monetaria panameña*) balboa

balbuc|ear *vt/i* stammer; ‹*niño*› babble. ~**eo** *m* stammering; (*de niño*) babbling. ~**iente** *a* stammering; ‹*niño*› babbling. ~**ir** [24] *vt/i* stammer; ‹*niño*› babble

balc|ón *m* balcony. ~**onada** *f* row of balconies. ~**onaje** *m* row of balconies

balda *f* shelf

baldado *a* disabled, crippled; (*rendido*) shattered. ● *m* disabled person, cripple

baldaquín *m*, **baldaquino** *m* canopy

baldar *vt* cripple

balde *m* bucket. **de ~** free (of charge). **en ~** in vain. ~**ar** *vt* wash down

baldío *a* ‹*terreno*› waste; (*fig*) useless

baldosa *f* (*floor*) tile; (*losa*) flagstone

balduque *m* (*incl fig*) red tape

balear *a* Balearic. ● *m* native of the Balearic Islands. **las Islas** *fpl* **B~es** the Balearics, the Balearic Islands

baleo *m* (*LAm, tiroteo*) shooting; (*Mex, abanico*) fan

balido *m* bleat; (*varios sonidos*) bleating

bal|ín *m* small bullet. ~**ines** *mpl* shot

balística *f* ballistics

baliza *f* (*naut*) buoy; (*aviat*) beacon

balneario *m* spa; (*con playa*) seaside resort. ● *a.* **estación** *f* **balnearia** spa; (*con playa*) seaside resort

balompié *m* football (*Brit*), soccer

bal|ón *m* ball, football. ~**oncesto** *m* basketball. ~**onmano** *m* handball. ~**volea** *m* volleyball

balotaje *m* (*LAm*) voting

balsa *f* (*de agua*) pool; (*plataforma flotante*) raft

bálsamo *m* balsam; (*fig*) balm

balsón *m* (*Mex*) stagnant water

baluarte *m* (*incl fig*) bastion

balumba *f* mass, mountain

ballena *f* whale

ballesta *f* crossbow

ballet /ba'le/ (*pl* **ballets** uba'le/) *m* ballet

bambole|ar *vi* sway; ‹*mesa etc*› wobble. ~**arse** *vpr* sway; ‹*mesa etc*› wobble. ~**o** *m* swaying; (*de mesa etc*) wobbling

bambú *m* (*pl* **bambúes**) bamboo

banal *a* banal. ~**idad** *f* banality

banan|a *f* (*esp LAm*) banana. ~**o** *m* (*LAm*) banana tree

banast|a *f* large basket. ~**o** *m* large round basket

banc|a *f* banking; (*en juegos*) bank; (*LAm, asiento*) bench. ~**ario** *a* bank, banking. ~**arrota** *f* bankruptcy. ~**o** *m* (*asiento*) bench; (*com*) bank; (*bajío*) sandbank. **hacer ~arrota, ir a la ~arrota** go bankrupt

banda *f* (*incl mus, radio*) band; (*grupo*) gang, group; (*lado*) side. ~**da** *f* (*de aves*) flock; (*de peces*) shoal. ~ **de sonido,** ~ **sonora** sound-track

bandeja *f* tray; (*LAm, plato*) serving dish. **servir algo en ~ a uno** hand sth to s.o. on a plate

bandera *f* flag; (*estandarte*) banner, standard

banderill|a *f* banderilla. ~**ear** *vt* stick the banderillas in. ~**ero** *m* banderillero

banderín *m* pennant, small flag; banner

bandido *m* bandit

bando m edict, proclamation; (partido) faction. ~s mpl banns. **pasarse al otro** ~ go over to the other side

bandolero m bandit

bandolina f mandolin

bandoneón m large accordion

banjo m banjo

banquero m banker

banqueta f stool; (LAm, acera) pavement (Brit), sidewalk (Amer)

banquete m banquet; (de boda) wedding reception. ~ar vt/i banquet

banquillo m bench; (jurid) dock; (taburete) footstool

bañ|ado m (LAm) swamp. ~ador m (de mujer) swimming costume; (de hombre) swimming trunks. ~ar vt bathe, immerse; bath ⟨niño⟩; (culin, recubrir) coat. ~arse vpr go swimming, have a swim; (en casa) have a bath. ~era f bath, bath-tub. ~ero m life-guard. ~ista m & f bather. ~o m bath; (en piscina, mar etc) swim; (bañera) bath, bath-tub; (capa) coat(ing)

baptisterio m baptistery; (pila) font

baquet|a f (de fusil) ramrod; (de tambor) drumstick. ~ear vt bother. ~eo m nuisance, bore

bar m bar

barahúnda f uproar

baraja f pack of cards. ~r vt shuffle; juggle, massage ⟨cifras etc⟩. ● vi argue (con with); (enemistarse) fall out (con with). ~s fpl argument. **jugar a la** ~ play cards. **jugar a dos** ~s, **jugar con dos** ~s be deceitful, indulge in double-dealing

baranda f, **barandal** m, **barandilla** f handrail; (de escalera) banisters

barat|a f (Mex) sale. ~ija f trinket. ~illo m junk shop; (géneros) cheap goods. ~o a cheap. ● m sale. ● adv cheap(ly). ~ura f cheapness

baraúnda f uproar

barba f chin; (pelo) beard. ~do a bearded

barbacoa f barbecue; (Mex, carne) barbecued meat

bárbaramente adv savagely; (fig) tremendously

barbari|dad f barbarity; (fig) outrage; (mucho, fam) awful lot (fam). **¡qué ~dad!** how awful! ~e f barbarity; (fig) ignorance. ~smo m barbarism

bárbaro a barbaric, cruel; (bruto) uncouth; (estupendo, fam) terrific (fam). ● m barbarian. **¡qué ~!** how marvellous!

barbear vt (afeitar) shave; (Mex, lisonjear) fawn on

barbecho m fallow

barber|ía f barber's (shop). ~o m barber; (Mex, adulador) flatterer

barbi|lampiño a beardless; (fig) inexperienced, green. ~lindo m dandy

barbilla f chin

barbitúrico m barbiturate

barbo m barbel. ~ **de mar** red mullet

barbot|ar vt/i mumble. ~ear vt/i mumble. ~eo m mumbling

barbudo a bearded

barbullar vi jabber

barca f (small) boat. ~ **de pasaje** ferry. ~je m fare. ~za f barge

Barcelona f Barcelona

barcelonés a of Barcelona, from Barcelona. ● m native of Barcelona

barco m boat; (navío) ship. ~ **cisterna** tanker. ~ **de vapor** steamer. ~ **de vela** sailing boat. **ir en** ~ go by boat

bario m barium

barítono m baritone

barman m (pl barmans) barman

barniz m varnish; (para loza etc) glaze; (fig) veneer. ~ar [10] vt varnish; glaze ⟨loza etc⟩

bar|ométrico a barometric. ~ómetro m barometer

bar|ón m baron. ~onesa f baroness

barquero m boatman

barra f bar; (pan) French bread; (de oro o plata) ingot; (palanca) lever. ~ **de labios** lipstick. **no pararse en** ~s stop at nothing

barrabasada f mischief, prank

barraca f hut; (vivienda pobre) shack, shanty

barranco m ravine, gully; (despeñadero) cliff, precipice

barre|dera f road-sweeper. ~dura f rubbish. ~minas m invar mine-sweeper

barren|a f drill, bit. ~ar vt drill. ~o m large (mechanical) drill. **entrar en** ~a ⟨avión⟩ go into a spin

barrer vt sweep; (quitar) sweep aside

barrera f barrier. ~ **del sonido** sound barrier

barriada f district

barrica f barrel
barricada f barricade
barrido m sweeping
barrig|a f (pot-)belly. **~ón** a, **~udo** a pot-bellied
barril m barrel. **~ete** m keg, small barrel
barrio m district, area. **~bajero** a vulgar, common. **~s bajos** poor quarter, poor area. **el otro ~** (fig, fam) the other world
barro m mud; (arcilla) clay; (arcilla cocida) earthenware
barroco a Baroque. ● m Baroque style
barrote m heavy bar
barrunt|ar vt sense, have a feeling. **~e** m, **~o** m sign; (presentimiento) feeling
bartola f. **tenderse a la ~, tumbarse a la ~** take it easy
bártulos mpl things. **liar los ~** pack one's bags
barullo m uproar; (confusión) confusion. **a ~** galore
basa f, **basamento** m base; (fig) basis
basar vt base. **~se** vpr. **~se en** be based on
basc|a f crowd. **~as** fpl nausea. **~osidad** f filth. **la ~a** the gang
báscula f scales
bascular vi tilt
base f base; (fig) basis, foundation. **a ~ de** thanks to; (mediante) by means of; (en una receta) as the basic ingredient(s). **a ~ de bien** very well. **partiendo de la ~ de, tomando como ~** on the basis of
básico a basic
basílica f basilica
basilisco m basilisk. **hecho un ~** furious
basta f tack, tacking stitch
bastante a enough; (varios) quite a few, quite a lot of. ● adv rather, fairly; (mucho tiempo) long enough; (suficiente) enough; (Mex, muy) very
bastar vi be enough. **¡basta!** that's enough! **basta decir que** suffice it to say that. **basta y sobra** that's more than enough
bastardilla f italics. **poner en ~** italicize
bastardo m bastard; (fig, vil) mean, base
bastidor m frame; (auto) chassis. **~es** mpl (en el teatro) wings. **entre ~es** behind the scenes

bastión f (incl fig) bastion
basto a coarse. **~s** mpl (naipes) clubs
bast|ón m walking stick. **empuñar el ~ón** take command. **~onazo** m blow with a stick
basur|a f rubbish, garbage (Amer); (en la calle) litter. **~ero** m dustman (Brit), garbage collector (Amer); (sitio) rubbish dump; (recipiente) dustbin (Brit), garbage can (Amer). **cubo** m **de la ~a** dustbin (Brit), garbage can (Amer)
bata f dressing-gown; (de médico etc) white coat. **~ de cola** Flamenco dress
batall|a f battle. **~a campal** pitched battle. **~ador** a fighting. ● m fighter. **~ar** vi battle, fight. **~ón** m battalion. ● a. **cuestión** f **batallona** vexed question. **de ~a** everyday
batata f sweet potato
bate m bat. **~ador** m batter; (cricket) batsman
batería f battery; (mus) percussion. **~ de cocina** kitchen utensils, pots and pans
batido a beaten; ⟨nata⟩ whipped. ● m batter; (bebida) milk shake. **~ra** f beater. **~ra eléctrica** mixer
batín m dressing-gown
batir vt beat; (martillar) hammer; mint ⟨monedas⟩; whip ⟨nata⟩; (derribar) knock down. **~ el récord** break the record. **de ~ palmas** clap. **~se** vpr fight
batuta f baton. **llevar la ~** be in command, be the boss
baúl m trunk; (LAm, auto) boot (Brit), trunk (Amer)
bauti|smal a baptismal. **~smo** m baptism, christening. **~sta** a & m & f Baptist. **~zar** [10] vt baptize, christen
baya f berry
bayeta f (floor-)cloth
bayoneta f bayonet. **~zo** m (golpe) bayonet thrust; (herida) bayonet wound
baza f (naipes) trick; (fig) advantage. **meter ~** interfere
bazar m bazaar
bazofia f leftovers; (basura) rubbish
beat|itud f (fig) bliss. **~o** a blessed; (de religiosidad afectada) sanctimonious
bebé m baby
beb|edero m drinking trough; (sitio) watering place. **~edizo** a

drinkable. ● *m* potion; (*veneno*) poison. ∼edor *a* drinking. ● *m* heavy drinker. ∼er *vt/i* drink. **dar de ∼er a uno** give s.o. a drink. ∼ida *f* drink. ∼ido *a* tipsy, drunk

beca *f* grant, scholarship. ∼rio *m* scholarship holder, scholar

becerro *m* calf

befa *f* jeer, taunt. ∼r *vt* scoff at. ∼rse *vpr*. ∼rse de scoff at. **hacer ∼ de** scoff at

beige /beis, bes/ *a & m* beige

béisbol *m* baseball

beldad *f* beauty

belén *m* crib, nativity scene; (*barullo*) confusion

belga *a & m & f* Belgian

Bélgica *f* Belgium

bélico *a*, **belicoso** *a* warlike

beligerante *a* belligerent

bella|co *a* wicked. ● *m* rogue. ∼quear *vi* cheat. ∼quería *f* dirty trick

bell|eza *f* beauty. ∼o *a* beautiful. ∼as artes *fpl* fine arts

bellota *f* acorn

bemol *m* flat. **tener (muchos) ∼es** be difficult

bencina *f* (*Arg, gasolina*) petrol (*Brit*), gasoline (*Amer*)

bend|ecir [46 *pero imperativo* **bendice**, *futuro, condicional y pp regulares*] *vt* bless. ∼ición *f* blessing. ∼ito *a* blessed, holy; (*que tiene suerte*) lucky; (*feliz*) happy

benefactor *m* benefactor. ∼a *f* benefactress

benefic|encia *f* (*organización pública*) charity. ∼iar *vt* benefit. ∼iarse *vpr* benefit. ∼iario *m* beneficiary; (*de un cheque etc*) payee. ∼io *m* benefit; (*ventaja*) advantage; (*ganancia*) profit, gain. ∼ioso *a* beneficial, advantageous

benéfico *a* beneficial; (*de beneficencia*) charitable

benemérito *a* worthy

beneplácito *m* approval

ben|evolencia *f* benevolence. ∼évolo *a* benevolent

bengala *f* flare. **luz** *f* **de B∼** flare

benign|idad *f* kindness; (*falta de gravedad*) mildness. ∼o *a* kind; (*moderado*) gentle, mild; (*tumor*) benign

beodo *a* drunk

berberecho *m* cockle

berenjena *f* aubergine (*Brit*), eggplant. ∼l *m* (*fig*) mess

bermejo *a* red

berr|ear *vi* (*animales*) low, bellow; (*niño*) howl; (*cantar mal*) screech. ∼ido *m* bellow; (*de niño*) howl; (*de cantante*) screech

berrinche *m* temper; (*de un niño*) tantrum

berro *m* watercress

berza *f* cabbage

besamel(a) *f* white sauce

bes|ar *vt* kiss; (*rozar*) brush against. ∼arse *vpr* kiss (each other); (*tocarse*) touch each other. ∼o *m* kiss

bestia *f* beast; (*bruto*) brute; (*idiota*) idiot. ∼ **de carga** beast of burden. ∼l *a* bestial, animal; (*fig, fam*) terrific. ∼lidad *f* bestiality; (*acción brutal*) horrid thing

besugo *m* sea-bream. **ser un ∼** be stupid

besuquear *vt* cover with kisses

betún *m* bitumen; (*para el calzado*) shoe polish

biberón *m* feeding-bottle

Biblia *f* Bible

bíblico *a* biblical

bibliografía *f* bibliography

biblioteca *f* library; (*librería*) bookcase. ∼ **de consulta** reference library. ∼ **de préstamo** lending library. ∼rio *m* librarian

bicarbonato *m* bicarbonate. ∼ **sódico** bicarbonate of soda

bici *f* (*fam*) bicycle, bike (*fam*). ∼cleta *f* bicycle. **ir en ∼cleta** go by bicycle, cycle. **montar en ∼cleta** ride a bicycle

bicolor *a* two-colour

bicultural *a* bicultural

bicho *m* (*animal*) small animal, creature; (*insecto*) insect. ∼ **raro** odd sort. **cualquier ∼ viviente, todo ∼ viviente** everyone

bidé *m*, **bidet** *m* bidet

bidón *m* drum, can

bien *adv* (*mejor*) well; (*muy*) very, quite; (*correctamente*) right; (*de buena gana*) willingly. ● *m* good; (*efectos*) property; (*provecho*) advantage, benefit. **¡∼!** fine!, OK!, good! **∼... (o) ∼** either... or. **∼ que** although. **¡está ∼!** fine! alright! **más ∼** rather. **¡muy ∼!** good! **no ∼** as soon as. **¡qué ∼!** marvellous!, great! (*fam*). **si ∼** although

bienal *a* biennial

bien: ∼aventurado *a* fortunate. ∼estar *m* well-being. ∼hablado *a* well-spoken. ∼hechor *m* benefactor.

~**hechora** f benefactress. ~**intencionado** a well-meaning

bienio m two years, two year-period

bien: ~**quistar** vt reconcile. ~**quistarse** vpr become reconciled. ~**quisto** a well-liked

bienvenid|a f welcome. ~**o** a welcome. ¡~**o!** welcome! **dar la** ~**a a uno** welcome s.o.

bife m (Arg), **biftek** m steak

bifurca|ción f fork, junction. ~**rse** [7] vpr fork

b|igamia f bigamy. ~**ígamo** a bigamous. ● m & f bigamist

bigot|e m moustache. ~**udo** a with a big moustache

bikini m bikini; (culin) toasted cheese and ham sandwich

bilingüe a bilingual

billar m billiards

billete m ticket; (de banco) note (Brit), bill (Amer). ~ **de banco** banknote. ~ **de ida y vuelta** return ticket (Brit), round-trip ticket (Amer). ~ **sencillo** single ticket (Brit), one-way ticket (Amer). ~**ro** m, ~**ra** f wallet, billfold (Amer)

billón m billion (Brit), trillion (Amer)

bimbalete m (Mex) swing

bi|mensual a fortnightly, twice-monthly. ~**mestral** a two-monthly. ~**motor** a twin-engined. ● m twin-engined plane

binocular a binocular. ~**es** mpl binoculars

biodegradable a biodegradable

bi|ografía f biography. ~**ográfico** a biographical. ~**ógrafo** m biographer

bi|ología f biology. ~**ológico** a biological. ~**ólogo** m biologist

biombo m folding screen

biopsia f biopsy

bioquímic|a f biochemistry; (persona) biochemist. ~**o** m biochemist

bípedo m biped

biplano m biplane

biquini m bikini

birlar vt (fam) steal, pinch (fam)

birlibirloque m. **por arte de** ~ (as if) by magic

Birmania f Burma

birmano a & m Burmese

biromen m (Arg) ball-point pen

bis m encore. ● adv twice. ¡~**!** encore! **vivo en el 3** ~ I live at 3A

bisabuel|a f great-grandmother. ~**o** m great-grandfather. ~**os** mpl great-grandparents

bisagra f hinge

bisar vt encore

bisbise|ar vt whisper. ~**o** m whisper(ing)

bisemanal a twice-weekly

bisiesto a leap. **año** m ~ leap year

bisniet|a f great-granddaughter. ~**o** m great-grandson. ~**os** mpl great-grandchildren

bisonte m bison

bisté m, **bistec** m steak

bisturí m scalpel

bisutería f imitation jewellery, costume jewellery

bizco a cross-eyed. **quedarse** ~ be dumbfounded

bizcocho m sponge (cake); (Mex, galleta) biscuit

bizquear vi squint

blanc|a f white woman; (mus) minim. ~**o** a white; (tez) fair. ● m white; (persona) white man; (intervalo) interval; (espacio) blank; (objetivo) target. ~**o de huevo** white of egg, egg-white. **dar en el** ~**o** hit the mark. **dejar en** ~**o** leave blank. **pasar la noche en** ~**o** have a sleepless night. ~**o y negro** black and white. ~**ura** f whiteness. ~**uzco** a whitish

blandir [24] vt brandish

bland|o a soft; ⟨carácter⟩ weak; (cobarde) cowardly; ⟨palabras⟩ gentle, tender. ~**ura** f softness. ~**uzco** a softish

blanque|ar vt whiten; white-wash ⟨paredes⟩; bleach ⟨tela⟩. ● vi turn white; (presentarse blanco) look white. ~**cino** a whitish. ~**o** m whitening

blasfem|ador a blasphemous. ● m blasphemer. ~**ar** vi blaspheme. ~**ia** f blasphemy. ~**o** a blasphemous. ● m blasphemer

blas|ón m coat of arms; (fig,) honour, glory. ~**onar** vt emblazon. ● vi boast (**de** of, about)

bledo m nothing. **me importa un** ~, **no se me da un** ~ I couldn't care less

blinda|je m armour. ~**r** vt armour

bloc m (pl blocs) pad

bloque m block; (pol) bloc. ~**ar** vt block; (mil) blockade; (com) freeze. ~**o** m blockade; (com) freezing. **en** ~ en bloc

blusa f blouse

boato m show, ostentation

bob|ada f silly thing. **~alicón** a stupid. **~ería** f silly thing. **decir ~adas** talk nonsense

bobina f bobbin, reel; (foto) spool; (elec) coil

bobo a silly, stupid. ● m idiot, fool

boca f mouth; (fig, entrada) entrance; (de cañón) muzzle; (agujero) hole. **~ abajo** face down. **~ arriba** face up. **a ~ de jarro** point-blank. **con la ~ abierta** dumbfounded

bocacalle f junction. **la primera ~ a la derecha** the first turning on the right

bocad|illo m sandwich; (comida ligera, fam) snack. **~o** m mouthful; (mordisco) bite; (de caballo) bit

boca: ~jarro. a ~jarro point-blank. **~manga** f cuff

bocanada f puff; (de vino etc) mouthful

bocaza f invar, **bocazas** f invar big-mouth

boceto m outline, sketch

bocina f horn. **~zo** m toot, blast. **tocar la ~** sound one's horn

bock m beer mug

bocha f bowl. **~s** fpl bowls

bochinche m uproar

bochorno m sultry weather; (fig, vergüenza) embarrassment. **~so** a oppressive; (fig) embarrassing. **¡qué ~!** how embarrassing!

boda f marriage; (ceremonia) wedding

bodeg|a f cellar; (de vino) wine cellar; (almacén) warehouse; (de un barco) hold. **~ón** m cheap restaurant; (pintura) still life

bodoque m pellet; (tonto, fam) thickhead

bofes mpl lights. **echar los ~** slog away

bofet|ada f slap; (fig) blow. **dar una ~ada a uno** slap s.o. in the face. **darse de ~adas** clash. **~ón** m punch

boga m & f rower; (hombre) oarsman; (mujer) oarswoman; (moda) fashion. **estar en ~** be in fashion, be in vogue. **~da** f stroke (of the oar). **~dor** rower, oarsman. **~r** [12] vt row. **~vante** m (crustáceo) lobster

Bogotá f Bogotá

bogotano a from Bogotá. ● m native of Bogotá

bohemio a & m Bohemian

bohío m (LAm) hut

boicot m (pl **boicots**) boycott. **~ear** vt boycott. **~eo** m boycott. **hacer el ~** boycott

boina f beret

boîte /bwat/ m night-club

bola f ball; (canica) marble; (naipes) slam; (betún) shoe polish; (mentira) fib; (Mex, reunión desordenada) rowdy party. **~ del mundo** (fam) globe. **contar ~s** tell fibs. **dejar que ruede la ~** let things take their course. **meter ~s** tell fibs

bolas fpl (LAm) bolas

boleada f (Mex) polishing of shoes

boleadoras (LAm) fpl bolas

bolera f bowling alley

bolero m (baile, chaquetilla) bolero; (fig, mentiroso, fam) liar; (Mex, limpiabotas) bootblack

boletín m bulletin; (publicación periódica) journal; (escolar) report. **~ de noticias** news bulletin. **~ de precios** price list. **~ informativo** news bulletin. **~ meteorológico** weather forecast

boleto m (esp LAm) ticket

boli m (fam) Biro (P), ball-point pen

boliche m (juego) bowls; (bolera) bowling alley

bolígrafo m Biro (P), ball-point pen

bolillo m bobbin; (Mex, panecillo) (bread) roll

bolívar m (unidad monetaria venezolana) bolívar

Bolivia f Bolivia

boliviano a Bolivian. ● m Bolivian; (unidad monetaria de Bolivia) boliviano

bolo m skittle

bolsa f bag; (monedero) purse; (LAm, bolsillo) pocket; (com) stock exchange; (cavidad) cavity. **~ de agua caliente** hot-water bottle

bolsillo m pocket; (monedero) purse. **de ~** pocket

bolsista m & f stockbroker

bolso m (de mujer) handbag

boll|ería f baker's shop. **~ero** m baker. **~o** m roll; (con azúcar) bun; (abolladura) dent; (chichón) lump; (fig, jaleo, fam) fuss

bomba f bomb; (máquina) pump; (noticia) bombshell. **~ de aceite** (auto) oil pump. **~ de agua** (auto) water pump. **~ de incendios** fire-engine. **pasarlo ~** have a marvellous time

bombach|as fpl (LAm) knickers, pants. **~o** m (esp Mex) baggy trousers, baggy pants (Amer)

bombarde|ar vt bombard; (mil) bomb. ∼o m bombardment; (mil) bombing. ∼ro m (avión) bomber

bombazo m explosion

bombear vt pump; (mil) bomb

bombero m fireman. **cuerpo** m **de** ∼s fire brigade (Brit), fire department (Amer)

bombilla f (light) bulb; (LAm, para maté) pipe for drinking maté; (Mex, cucharón) ladle

bombín m pump; (sombrero, fam) bowler (hat) (Brit), derby (Amer)

bombo m (tambor) bass drum. **a** ∼ **y platillos** with a lot of fuss

bomb|ón m chocolate. **ser un** ∼**ón** be a peach. ∼**ona** f container. ∼**onera** f chocolate box

bonachón a easygoing; (bueno) good-natured

bonaerense a from Buenos Aires. ● m native of Buenos Aires

bonanza f (naut) fair weather; (prosperidad) prosperity. **ir en** ∼ (naut) have fair weather; (fig) go well

bondad f goodness; (amabilidad) kindness. **tenga la** ∼ **de** would you be kind enough to. ∼**osamente** adv kindly. ∼**oso** a kind

bongo m (LAm) canoe

boniato m sweet potato

bonito a nice; (mono) pretty. ¡**muy** ∼!, ¡**qué** ∼! that's nice!, very nice!. ● m bonito

bono m voucher; (título) bond. ∼ **del Tesoro** government bond

boñiga f dung

boqueada f gasp. **dar las** ∼s be dying

boquerón m anchovy

boquete m hole; (brecha) breach

boquiabierto a open-mouthed; (fig) amazed, dumbfounded. **quedarse** ∼ be amazed

boquilla f mouthpiece; (para cigarillos) cigarette-holder; (filtro de cigarillo) tip

borboll|ar vi bubble. ∼**ón** m bubble. **hablar a** ∼**ones** gabble. **salir a** ∼**ones** gush out

borbot|ar vt bubble. ∼**ón** m bubble. **hablar a** ∼**ones** gabble. **salir a** ∼**ones** gush out

bordado a embroidered. ● m embroidery. **quedar** ∼, **salir** ∼ come out very well

bordante m (Mex) lodger

bordar vt embroider; (fig, fam) do very well

bord|e m edge; (de carretera) side; (de plato etc) rim; (de un vestido) hem. ∼**ear** vt go round the edge of; (fig) border on. ∼**illo** m kerb. **al** ∼**e de** on the edge of; (fig) on the brink of

bordo m board. **a** ∼ on board

borinqueño a & m Puerto Rican

borla f tassel

borra f flock; (pelusa) fluff; (sedimento) sediment

borrach|era f drunkenness. ∼**ín** m drunkard. ∼**o** a drunk. ● m drunkard; (temporalmente) drunk. **estar** ∼**o** be drunk. **ni** ∼**o** never in a million years. **ser** ∼**o** be a drunkard

borrador m rough copy; (libro) rough notebook

borradura f crossing-out

borrajear vt/i scribble

borrar vt rub out; (tachar) cross out

borrasc|a f storm. ∼**oso** a stormy

borreg|o m year-old lamb; (fig) simpleton; (Mex, noticia falsa) hoax. ∼**uil** a meek

borric|ada f silly thing. ∼**o** m donkey; (fig, fam) ass

borrón m smudge; (fig, imperfección) blemish; (de una pintura) sketch. ∼ **y cuenta nueva** let's forget about it!

borroso a blurred; (fig) vague

bos|caje m thicket. ∼**coso** a wooded. ∼**que** m wood, forest. ∼**quecillo** m copse

bosquej|ar vt sketch. ∼**o** m sketch

bosta f dung

bostez|ar [10] vi yawn. ∼**o** m yawn

bota f boot; (recipiente) leather wine bottle

botadero m (Mex) ford

botánic|a f botany. ∼**o** a botanical. ● m botanist

botar vt launch. ● vi bounce. **estar que bota** be hopping mad

botarat|ada f silly thing. ∼**e** m idiot

bote m bounce; (golpe) blow; (salto) jump; (sacudida) jolt; (lata) tin, can; (vasija) jar; (en un bar) jar for tips; (barca) boat. ∼ **salvavidas** lifeboat. **de** ∼ **en** ∼ packed

botell|a f bottle. ∼**ita** f small bottle

botica f chemist's (shop) (Brit), drugstore (Amer). ∼**rio** m chemist (Brit), druggist (Amer)

botija f, **botijo** m earthenware jug

botín m half boot; (despojos) booty; (LAm, calcetín) sock

botiquín m medicine chest; (de primeros auxilios) first aid kit

bot|ón m button; (yema) bud. ∼onadura f buttons. ∼ón de oro buttercup. ∼ones m invar bellboy (Brit), bellhop (Amer)

botulismo m botulism

boutique /bu'tik/ m boutique

bóveda f vault

boxe|ador m boxer. ∼ar vi box. ∼o m boxing

boya f buoy; (corcho) float. ∼nte a buoyant

bozal m (de perro etc) muzzle; (de caballo) halter

bracear vi wave one's arms; (nadar) swim, crawl

bracero m labourer. de ∼ (fam) arm in arm

braga f underpants, knickers; (cuerda) rope. ∼dura f crotch. ∼s fpl knickers, pants. ∼zas m invar (fam) henpecked man

bragueta f flies

braille /breil/ m Braille

bram|ar vi roar; (vaca) moo; (viento) howl. ∼ido m roar

branquia f gill

bras|a f hot coal. a la ∼a grilled. ∼ero m brazier; (LAm, hogar) hearth

Brasil m. el ∼ Brazil

brasile|ño a & m Brazilian. ∼ro a & m (LAm) Brazilian

bravata f boast

bravío a wild; (persona) coarse, uncouth

brav|o a brave; (animales) wild; (mar) rough. ¡∼! int well done! bravo! ∼ura f ferocity; (valor) courage

braz|a f fathom. nadar a ∼a do the breast-stroke. ∼ada f waving of the arms; (en natación) stroke; (cantidad) armful. ∼ado m armful. ∼al m arm-band. ∼alete m bracelet; (brazal) arm-band. ∼o m arm; (de animales) foreleg; (rama) branch. ∼o derecho right-hand man. a ∼o by hand. del ∼o arm in arm

brea f tar, pitch

brear vt ill-treat

brécol m broccoli

brecha f gap; (mil) breach; (med) gash. estar en la ∼ be in the thick of it

brega f struggle. ∼r [12] vi struggle; (trabajar mucho) work hard, slog away. andar a la ∼ work hard

breña f, **breñal** m scrub

Bretaña f Brittany. **Gran** ∼ Great Britain

breve a short. ∼dad f shortness. en ∼ soon, shortly. en ∼s momentos soon

brez|al m moor. ∼o m heather

brib|ón m rogue, rascal. ∼onada f, ∼onería f dirty trick

brida f bridle. a toda ∼ at full speed

bridge /britʃ/ m bridge

brigada f squad; (mil) brigade. **general de** ∼ brigadier (Brit), brigadier-general (Amer)

brill|ante a brilliant. ● m diamond. ∼antez f brilliance. ∼ar vi shine; (centellear) sparkle. ∼o m shine; (brillantez) brilliance; (centelleo) sparkle. dar ∼o, sacar ∼o polish

brinc|ar [7] vi jump up and down. ∼o m jump. dar un ∼o jump. estar que brinca be hopping mad. pegar un ∼o jump

brind|ar vt offer. ● vi. ∼ar por toast, drink a toast to. ∼is m toast

br|ío m energy; (decisión) determination. ∼ioso a spirited; (garboso) elegant

brisa f breeze

británico a British. ● m Briton, British person

brocado m brocade

bróculi m broccoli

brocha f paintbrush; (para afeitarse) shaving-brush

broche m clasp, fastener; (joya) brooch; (Arg, sujetapapeles) paperclip

brocheta f skewer

brom|a f joke. ∼a pesada practical joke. ∼ear vi joke. ∼ista a fun-loving. ● m & f joker. de ∼a, en ∼a in fun. ni de ∼a never in a million years

bronca f row; (reprensión) telling-off

bronce m bronze. ∼ado a bronze; (por el sol) tanned, sunburnt. ∼ar vt tan (piel). ∼arse vpr get a suntan

bronco a rough

bronquitis f bronchitis

broqueta f skewer

brot|ar vi (plantas) bud, sprout; (med) break out; (líquido) gush forth; (lágrimas) well up. ∼e m bud, shoot; (med) outbreak; (de líquido) gushing; (de lágrimas) welling-up

bruces mpl. de ∼ face down(wards). caer de ∼ fall flat on one's face

bruj|a _f_ witch. ● _a_ (_Mex_) penniless. **~ear** _vi_ practise witchcraft. **~ería** _f_ witchcraft. **~o** _m_ wizard, magician; (_LAm_) medicine man

brújula _f_ compass

brum|a _f_ mist; (_fig_) confusion. **~oso** _a_ misty, foggy

bruñi|do _m_ polish. **~r** [22] _vt_ polish

brusco _a_ (_repentino_) sudden; ‹persona› brusque

Bruselas _fpl_ Brussels

brusquedad _f_ abruptness

brut|al _a_ brutal. **~alidad** _f_ brutality; (_estupidez_) stupidity. **~o** _a_ (_estúpido_) stupid; (_tosco_) rough, uncouth; ‹peso, sueldo› gross

bucal _a_ oral

buce|ar _vi_ dive; (_fig_) explore. **~o** _m_ diving

bucle _m_ curl

budín _m_ pudding

budis|mo _m_ Buddhism. **~ta** _m & f_ Buddhist

buen _véase_ **bueno**

buenamente _adv_ easily; (_voluntariamente_) willingly

buenaventura _f_ good luck; (_adivinación_) fortune. **decir la ~ a uno, echar la ~ a uno** tell s.o.'s fortune

bueno _a_ (_delante de nombre masculino en singular_ **buen**) good; (_apropiado_) fit; (_amable_) kind; ‹tiempo› fine. ● _int_ well!; (_de acuerdo_) OK!, very well! **¡buena la has hecho!** you've gone and done it now! **¡buenas noches!** good night! **¡buenas tardes!** (_antes del atardecer_) good afternoon!; (_después del atardecer_) good evening! **¡~s días!** good morning! **estar de buenas** be in a good mood. **por las buenas** willingly

Buenos Aires _m_ Buenos Aires

buey _m_ ox

búfalo _m_ buffalo

bufanda _f_ scarf

bufar _vi_ snort. **estar que bufa** be hopping mad

bufete _m_ (_mesa_) writing-desk; (_despacho_) lawyer's office

bufido _m_ snort; (_de ira_) outburst

buf|o _a_ comic. **~ón** _a_ comical. ● _m_ buffoon. **~onada** _f_ joke

bugle _m_ bugle

buharda _f_, **buhardilla** _f_ attic; (_ventana_) dormer window

búho _m_ owl

buhoner|ía _f_ pedlar's wares. **~o** _m_ pedlar

buitre _m_ vulture

bujía _f_ candle; (_auto_) spark(ing)-plug

bula _f_ bull

bulbo _m_ bulb

bulevar _m_ avenue, boulevard

Bulgaria _f_ Bulgaria

búlgaro _a & m_ Bulgarian

bulo _m_ hoax

bulto _m_ (_volumen_) volume; (_tamaño_) size; (_forma_) shape; (_paquete_) package; (_protuberancia_) lump. **a ~** roughly

bulla _f_ uproar; (_muchedumbre_) crowd

bullicio _m_ hubbub; (_movimiento_) bustle. **~so** _a_ bustling; (_ruidoso_) noisy

bullir [22] _vt_ stir, move. ● _vi_ boil; (_burbujear_) bubble; (_fig_) bustle

buñuelo _m_ doughnut; (_fig_) mess

BUP _abrev_ (_Bachillerato Unificado Polivalente_) secondary school education

buque _m_ ship, boat

burbuj|a _f_ bubble. **~ear** _vi_ bubble; ‹vino› sparkle. **~eo** _m_ bubbling

burdel _m_ brothel

burdo _a_ rough, coarse; ‹excusa› clumsy

burgu|és _a_ middle-class, bourgeois. ● _m_ middle-class person. **~esía** _f_ middle class, bourgeoisie

burla _f_ taunt; (_broma_) joke; (_engaño_) trick. **~dor** _a_ mocking. ● _m_ seducer. **~r** _vt_ trick, deceive; (_seducir_) seduce. **~rse** _vpr._ **~rse de** mock, make fun of

burlesco _a_ funny

burlón _a_ mocking

bur|ocracia _f_ civil service. **~ócrata** _m & f_ civil servant. **~ocrático** _a_ bureaucratic

burro _m_ donkey; (_fig_) ass

bursátil _a_ stock-exchange

bus _m_ (_fam_) bus

busca _f_ search. **a la ~ de** in search of. **en ~ de** in search of

busca: ~pié _m_ feeler. **~pleitos** _m_ _invar_ (_LAm_) trouble-maker

buscar [7] _vt_ look for. ● _vi_ look. **buscársela** ask for it. **ir a ~ a uno** fetch s.o.

buscarruidos _m_ _invar_ trouble-maker

buscona _f_ prostitute

busilis _m_ snag

búsqueda _f_ search

busto _m_ bust

butaca *f* armchair; *(en el teatro etc)* seat

butano *m* butane

buzo *m* diver

buzón *m* postbox *(Brit)*, mailbox *(Amer)*

C

Cu *abrev (Calle)* St, Street, Rd, Road

cabal *a* exact; *(completo)* complete. **no estar en sus ~es** not be in one's right mind

cabalga|dura *f* mount, horse. **~r** [12] *vt* ride. ● *vi* ride, go riding. **~ta** *f* ride; *(desfile)* procession

cabalmente *adv* completely; *(exactamente)* exactly

caballa *f* mackerel

caballada *f (LAm)* stupid thing

caballeresco *a* gentlemanly. **literatura f caballeresca** books of chivalry

caballer|ía *f* mount, horse. **~iza** *f* stable. **~izo** *m* groom

caballero *m* gentleman; *(de orden de caballería)* knight; *(tratamiento)* sir. **~samente** *adv* like a gentleman. **~so** *a* gentlemanly

caballete *m (del tejado)* ridge; *(de la nariz)* bridge; *(de pintor)* easel

caballito *m* pony. **~ del diablo** dragonfly. **~ de mar** sea-horse. **los ~s** *(tiovivo)* merry-go-round

caballo *m* horse; *(del ajedrez)* knight; *(de la baraja española)* queen. **~ de vapor** horsepower. **a ~** on horseback

cabaña *f* hut

cabaret /kabaˈre/ *m (pl* **cabarets** /kabaˈre/) night-club

cabece|ar *vi* nod; *(para negar)* shake one's head. **~o** *m* nodding, nod; *(acción de negar)* shake of the head

cabecera *f (de la cama, de la mesa)* head; *(en un impreso)* heading

cabecilla *m* leader

cabell|o *m* hair. **~os** *mpl* hair. **~udo** *a* hairy

caber [28] *vi* fit **(en** into). **los libros no caben en la caja** the books won't fit into the box. **no cabe duda** there's no doubt

cabestr|illo *m* sling. **~o** *m* halter

cabeza *f* head; *(fig, inteligencia)* intelligence. **~da** *f* butt; *(golpe recibido)* blow; *(saludo, al dormirse)* nod. **~zo** *m* butt; *(en fútbol)* header. **andar de ~** have a lot to do. **dar una ~da** nod off

cabida *f* capacity; *(extensión)* area. **dar ~ a** leave room for, leave space for

cabina *f (de avión)* cabin, cockpit; *(electoral)* booth; *(de camión)* cab. **~ telefónica** telephone box *(Brit)*, telephone booth *(Amer)*

cabizbajo *a* crestfallen

cable *m* cable

cabo *m* end; *(trozo)* bit; *(mil)* corporal; *(mango)* handle; *(geog)* cape; *(naut)* rope. **al ~** eventually. **al ~ de una hora** after an hour. **de ~ a rabo** from beginning to end. **llevar(se) a ~** carry out

cabr|a *f* goat. **~a montesa** *f* mountain goat. **~iola** *f* jump, skip. **~itilla** *f* kid. **~ito** *m* kid

cabrón *m* cuckold

cabuya *f (LAm)* pita, agave

cacahuate *m (Mex)*, **cacahuete** *m* peanut

cacao *m (planta y semillas)* cacao; *(polvo)* cocoa; *(fig)* confusion

cacare|ar *vt* boast about. ● *vi (gallo)* crow; *(gallina)* cluck. **~o** *m (incl fig)* crowing; *(de gallina)* clucking

cacería *f* hunt

cacerola *f* casserole, saucepan

caciqu|e *m* cacique, Indian chief; *(pol)* cacique, local political boss. **~il** *a* despotic. **~ismo** *m* caciquism, despotism

caco *m* pickpocket, thief

cacof|onía *f* cacophony. **~ónico** *a* cacophonous

cacto *m* cactus

cacumen *m* acumen

cacharro *m* earthenware pot; *(para flores)* vase; *(coche estropeado)* wreck; *(cosa inútil)* piece of junk; *(chisme)* thing. **~s** *mpl* pots and pans

cachear *vt* frisk

cachemir *m*, **cachemira** *f* cashmere

cacheo *m* frisking

cachetada *f (LAm)*, **cachete** *m* slap

cachimba *f* pipe

cachiporra *f* club, truncheon. **~zo** *m* blow with a club

cachivache *m* thing, piece of junk

cacho *m* bit, piece; *(LAm, cuerno)* horn; *(miga)* crumb

cachondeo *m (fam)* joking, joke

cachorro *m (perrito)* puppy; *(de otros animales)* young

cada *a invar* each, every. ~ **uno** each one, everyone. **uno de ~ cinco** one in five

cadalso *m* scaffold

cadáver *m* corpse. **ingresar ~** be dead on arrival

cadena *f* chain; *(TV)* channel. ~ **de fabricación** production line. ~ **de montañas** mountain range. ~ **perpetua** life imprisonment

cadencia *f* cadence, rhythm

cadera *f* hip

cadete *m* cadet

caduc|ar [7] *vi* expire. ~**idad** *f*. **fecha** *f* **de** ~**idad** sell-by date. ~**o** *a* decrepit

cae|dizo *a* unsteady. ~**r** [29] *vi* fall. ~**rse** *vpr* fall (over). **dejar** ~**r** drop. **estar al** ~**r** be about to happen. **este vestido no me** ~ **bien** this dress doesn't suit me. **hacer** ~**r** knock over. **Juan me** ~ **bien** I get on well with Juan. **su cumpleaños cayó en Martes** his birthday fell on a Tuesday

café *m* coffee; *(cafetería)* café. ● *a*. **color** ~ coffee-coloured. ~ **con leche** white coffee. ~ **cortado** coffee with a little milk. ~ **(solo)** black coffee

cafe|ína *f* caffeine. ~**tal** *m* coffee plantation. ~**tera** *f* coffee-pot. ~**tería** *f* café. ~**tero** *a* coffee

caíd|a *f* fall; *(disminución)* drop; *(pendiente)* slope. ~**o** *a* fallen; *(abatido)* dejected. ● *m* fallen

caigo *vb véase* **caer**

caimán *m* cayman, alligator

caj|a *f* box; *(grande)* case; *(de caudales)* safe; *(donde se efectúan los pagos)* cash desk; *(en supermercado)* check-out. ~**a de ahorros** savings bank. ~**a de caudales,** ~**a fuerte** safe. ~**a postal de ahorros** post office savings bank. ~**a registradora** till. ~**ero** *m* cashier. ~**etilla** *f* packet. ~**ita** *f* small box. ~**ón** *m* large box; *(de mueble)* drawer; *(puesto de mercado)* stall. **ser de** ~**ón** be a matter of course

cal *m* lime

cala *f* cove

calaba|cín *m* marrow; *(fig, idiota, fam)* idiot. ~**za** *f* pumpkin; *(fig, idiota, fam)* idiot

calabozo *m* prison; *(celda)* cell

calado *a* soaked. ● *m* *(naut)* draught. **estar ~ hasta los huesos** be soaked to the skin

calamar *m* squid

calambre *m* cramp

calami|dad *f* calamity, disaster. ~**toso** *a* calamitous, disastrous

calar *vt* soak; *(penetrar)* pierce; *(fig, penetrar)* see through; sample *(fruta)*. ~**se** *vpr* get soaked; *(zapatos)* leak; *(auto)* stall

calavera *f* skull

calcar [7] *vt* trace; *(fig)* copy

calceta *f*. **hacer** ~ knit

calcetín *m* sock

calcinar *vt* burn

calcio *m* calcium

calco *m* tracing. ~**manía** *f* transfer. **papel** *m* **de** ~ tracing-paper

calcula|dor *a* calculating. ~**dora** *f* calculator. ~**dora de bolsillo** pocket calculator. ~**r** *vt* calculate; *(suponer)* reckon, think

cálculo *m* calculation; *(fig)* reckoning

caldea|miento *m* heating. ~**r** *vt* heat, warm. ~**rse** *vpr* get hot

calder|a *f* boiler; *(Arg, para café)* coffee-pot; *(Arg, para té)* teapot. ~**eta** *f* small boiler

calderilla *f* small change, coppers

calder|o *m* small boiler. ~**ón** *m* large boiler

caldo *m* stock; *(sopa)* soup, broth. **poner a ~ a uno** give s.o. a dressing-down

calefacción *f* heating. ~ **central** central heating

caleidoscopio *m* kaleidoscope

calendario *m* calendar

caléndula *f* marigold

calenta|dor *m* heater. ~**miento** *m* heating; *(en deportes)* warm-up. ~**r** [1] *vt* heat, warm. ~**rse** *vpr* get hot, warm up

calentur|a *f* fever, (high) temperature. ~**iento** *a* feverish

calibr|ar *vt* calibrate; *(fig)* measure. ~**e** *m* calibre; *(diámetro)* diameter; *(fig)* importance

calidad *f* quality; *(función)* capacity. **en ~ de** as

cálido *a* warm

calidoscopio *m* kaleidoscope

caliente *a* hot, warm; *(fig, enfadado)* angry

califica|ción *f* qualification; *(evaluación)* assessment; *(nota)* mark. ~**r** [7] *vt* qualify; *(evaluar)* assess; mark *(examen etc)*. ~**r de** describe as, label. ~**tivo** *a* qualifying. ● *m* epithet

caliza f limestone. **~o** a lime
calm|a f calm. ¡**~a!** calm down!
~ante a & m sedative. **~ar** vt calm,
soothe. ● vi ⟨viento⟩ abate. **~arse**
vpr calm down; ⟨viento⟩ abate.
~oso a calm; ⟨flemático, fam⟩
phlegmatic. **en ~a** calm. **perder la
~a** lose one's composure
calor m heat, warmth. **hace ~** it's
hot. **tener ~** be hot
caloría f calorie
calorífero m heater
calumni|a f calumny; ⟨oral⟩ slander;
⟨escrita⟩ libel. **~ar** vt slander; ⟨por
escrito⟩ libel. **~oso** a slanderous;
⟨cosa escrita⟩ libellous
caluros|amente adv warmly. **~o** a
warm
calv|a f bald patch. **~ero** m clearing.
~icie f baldness. **~o** a bald; ⟨te-
rreno⟩ barren
calza f (fam) stocking; ⟨cuña⟩ wedge
calzada f road
calza|do a wearing shoes. ● m foot-
wear, shoe. **~dor** m shoehorn. **~r**
[10] vt put shoes on; ⟨llevar⟩ wear.
● vi wear shoes. ● vpr put on. **¿qué
número calza Vd?** what size shoe do
you take?
calz|ón m shorts; ⟨ropa interior⟩
knickers, pants. **~ones** mpl shorts.
~oncillos mpl underpants
calla|do a quiet. **~r** vt silence; keep
⟨secreto⟩; hush up ⟨asunto⟩. ● vi be
quiet, keep quiet, shut up (fam).
~rse vpr be quiet, keep quiet, shut
up (fam). ¡**cállate!** be quiet! shut up!
(fam)
calle f street, road; (en deportes, en
autopista) lane. **~ de dirección
única** one-way street. **~ mayor** high
street, main street. **abrir ~** make
way
callej|a f narrow street. **~ear** vi wan-
der about the streets. **~ero** a street.
● m street plan. **~ón** m alley. **~uela**
f back street, side street. **~ón sin
salida** cul-de-sac
call|ista m & f chiropodist. **~o** m
corn, callus. **~os** mpl tripe. **~oso** a
hard, rough
cama f bed. **~ de matrimonio** double
bed. **~ individual** single bed. **caer en
la ~** fall ill. **guardar ~** be confined
to bed
camada f litter; (fig, de ladrones)
gang
camafeo m cameo
camaleón m chameleon

cámara f room; (de reyes) royal
chamber; (fotográfica) camera; (de
armas, pol) chamber. **~ fotográfica**
camera. **a ~ lenta** in slow motion
camarada f colleague; (amigo)
companion
camarer|a f chambermaid; (de
restaurante etc) waitress; (en casa)
maid. **~o** m waiter
camarín m dressing-room; (naut)
cabin
camarón m shrimp
camarote m cabin
cambi|able a changeable; (com etc)
exchangeable. **~ante** a variable.
~ar vt change; (trocar) exchange.
● vi change. **~ar de idea** change
one's mind. **~arse** vpr change. **~o**
m change; (com) exchange rate;
(moneda menuda) (small) change.
~sta m & f money-changer. **en ~o**
on the other hand
camelia f camellia
camello m camel
camilla f stretcher; (sofá) couch
camina|nte m traveller. **~r** vt cover.
● vi travel; (andar) walk; ⟨río,
astros etc⟩ move. **~ta** f long walk
camino m road; (sendero) path,
track; (dirección, medio) way. **~ de**
towards, on the way to. **abrir ~**
make way. **a medio ~, a la mitad
del ~** half-way. **de ~** on the way.
ponerse en ~ set out
cami|ón m lorry; (Mex, autobús)
bus. **~onero** m lorry-driver.
~oneta f van
camis|a f shirt; (de un fruto) skin. **~a
de dormir** nightdress. **~a de fuerza**
strait-jacket. **~ería** f shirt shop.
~eta f T-shirt; (ropa interior) vest.
~ón m nightdress
camorra f (fam) row. **buscar ~** look
for trouble, pick a quarrel
camote m (LAm) sweet potato
campamento m camp
campan|a f bell. **~ada** f stroke of a
bell; (de reloj) striking. **~ario** m bell
tower, belfry. **~eo** m peal of bells.
~illa f bell. **~udo** a bell-shaped;
⟨estilo⟩ bombastic
campaña f countryside; (mil, pol)
campaign. **de ~** (mil) field
campe|ón a & m champion. **~onato**
m championship
campes|ino a country. ● m peasant.
~tre a country
camping /'kampin/ m (pl **campings**
/'kampin/) camping; (lugar)
campsite. **hacer ~** go camping

campiña *f* countryside

campo *m* country; (*agricultura, fig*) field; (*de tenis*) court; (*de fútbol*) pitch; (*de golf*) course. **~santo** *m* cemetery

camufla|do *a* camouflaged. **~je** *m* camouflage. **~r** *vt* camouflage

cana *f* grey hair, white hair. **echar una ~ al aire** have a fling. **peinar ~s** be getting old

Canadá *m*. **el ~** Canada

canadiense *a & m* Canadian

canal *m* (*incl TV*) channel; (*artificial*) canal; (*del tejado*) gutter. **~ de la Mancha** English Channel. **~ de Panamá** Panama Canal. **~ón** *m* (*horizontal*) gutter; (*vertical*) drain-pipe

canalla *f* rabble. ● *m* (*fig, fam*) swine. **~da** *f* dirty trick

canapé *m* sofa, couch; (*culin*) canapé

Canarias *fpl*. **(las islas) ~** the Canary Islands, the Canaries

canario *a* of the Canary Islands. ● *m* native of the Canary Islands; (*pájaro*) canary

canast|a *f* (large) basket. **~illa** *f* small basket; (*para un bebé*) layette. **~illo** *m* small basket. **~o** *m* (large) basket

cancela *f* gate

cancela|ción *f* cancellation . **~r** *vt* cancel; write off ‹*deuda*›; (*fig*) forget

cáncer *m* cancer. **C~** Cancer

canciller *m* chancellor; (*LAm, ministro de asuntos exteriores*) Minister of Foreign Affairs

canci|ón *f* song. **~ón de cuna** lullaby. **~onero** *m* song-book. **¡siempre la misma ~ón!** always the same old story!

cancha *f* (*de fútbol*) pitch, ground; (*de tenis*) court

candado *m* padlock

candel|a *f* candle. **~ero** *m* candlestick. **~illa** *f* candle

candente *a* (*rojo*) red-hot; (*blanco*) white-hot; (*fig*) burning

candidato *m* candidate

candidez *f* innocence; (*ingenuidad*) naïvety

cándido *a* naïve

candil *m* oil-lamp; (*Mex, araña*) chandelier. **~ejas** *fpl* footlights

candinga *m* (*Mex*) devil

candor *m* innocence; (*ingenuidad*) naïvety. **~oso** *a* innocent; (*ingenuo*) naïve

canela *f* cinnamon. **ser ~** be beautiful

cangrejo *m* crab. **~ de río** crayfish

canguro *m* kangaroo; (*persona*) baby-sitter

can|íbal *a & m* cannibal. **~ibalismo** *m* cannibalism

canica *f* marble

canijo *m* weak

canino *a* canine. ● *m* canine (tooth)

canje *m* exchange. **~ar** *vt* exchange

cano *a* grey-haired

canoa *f* canoe; (*con motor*) motor boat

canon *m* canon

can|ónigo *m* canon. **~onizar** [10] *vt* canonize

canoso *a* grey-haired

cansa|do *a* tired. **~ncio** *m* tiredness. **~r** *vt* tire; (*aburrir*) bore. ● *vi* be tiring; (*aburrir*) get boring. **~rse** *vpr* get tired

cantábrico *a* Cantabrian. **el mar ~** the Bay of Biscay

canta|nte *a* singing. ● *m* singer; (*en óperas*) opera singer. **~or** *m* Flamenco singer. **~r** *vt/i* sing. ● *m* singing; (*canción*) song; (*poema*) poem. **~rlas claras** speak frankly

cántar|a *f* pitcher. **~o** *m* pitcher. **llover a ~os** pour down

cante *m* folk song. **~ flamenco, ~ jondo** Flamenco singing

cantera *f* quarry

cantidad *f* quantity; (*número*) number; (*de dinero*) sum. **una ~ de** lots of

cantilena *f*, **cantinela** *f* song

cantimplora *f* water-bottle

cantina *f* canteen; (*rail*) buffet

canto *m* singing; (*canción*) song; (*borde*) edge; (*de un cuchillo*) blunt edge; (*esquina*) corner; (*piedra*) pebble. **~ rodado** boulder. **de ~** on edge

cantonés *a* Cantonese

cantor *a* singing. ● *m* singer

canturre|ar *vt/i* hum. **~o** *m* humming

canuto *m* tube

caña *f* stalk, stem; (*planta*) reed; (*vaso*) glass; (*de la pierna*) shin. **~ de azúcar** sugar-cane. **~ de pescar** fishing-rod

cañada *f* ravine; (*camino*) track

cáñamo *m* hemp. **~ índio** cannabis

cañ|ería *f* pipe; (*tubería*) piping. **~o** *m* pipe, tube; (*de fuente*) jet. **~ón** *m* pipe, tube; (*de órgano*) pipe; (*de* *chimenea)* flue; *(arma de fuego)* cannon; *(desfiladero)* canyon. **~onazo** *m* gunshot. **~onera** *f* gunboat

caoba *f* mahogany

ca|os *m* chaos. **~ótico** *a* chaotic

capa *f* cloak; *(de pintura)* coat; *(culin)* coating; *(geol)* stratum, layer

capacidad *f* capacity; *(fig)* ability

capacitar *vt* qualify, enable; *(instruir)* train

caparazón *m* shell

capataz *m* foreman

capaz *a* capable, able; *(espacioso)* roomy. **~ para** which holds, with a capacity of

capazo *m* large basket

capcioso *a* sly, insidious

capellán *m* chaplain

caperuza *f* hood; *(de pluma)* cap

capilla *f* chapel; *(mus)* choir

capita *f* small cloak, cape

capital *a* capital, very important. ● *m* *(dinero)* capital. ● *f* *(ciudad)* capital; *(LAm, letra)* capital (letter). **~ de provincia** county town

capitali|smo *m* capitalism. **~sta** *a & m & f* capitalist. **~zar** [10] *vt* capitalize

capit|án *m* captain. **~anear** *vt* lead, command; *(un equipo)* captain

capitel *m* *(arquit)* capital

capitulaci|ón *f* surrender; *(acuerdo)* agreement. **~ones** *fpl* marriage contract

capítulo *m* chapter. **~s matrimoniales** marriage contract

capó *m* bonnet *(Brit)*, hood *(Amer)*

capón *m* *(pollo)* capon

caporal *m* chief, leader

capota *f* *(de mujer)* bonnet; *(auto)* folding top, sliding roof

capote *m* cape

Capricornio *m* Capricorn

capricho *m* whim. **~so** *a* capricious, whimsical. **a ~** capriciously

cápsula *f* capsule

captar *vt* harness ‹agua›; grasp ‹sentido›; hold ‹atención›; win ‹confianza›; *(radio)* pick up

captura *f* capture. **~r** *vt* capture

capucha *f* hood

capullo *m* bud; *(de insecto)* cocoon

caqui *m* khaki

cara *f* face; *(de una moneda)* obverse; *(de un objeto)* side; *(aspecto)* look, appearance; *(descaro)* cheek. **~ a** towards; *(frente a)* facing. **~ a ~** face to face. **~ o cruz** heads or tails.

dar la ~ face up to. **hacer ~ a** face. **no volver la ~ atrás** not look back. **tener ~ de** look, seem to be. **tener ~ para** have the face to. **tener mala ~** look ill. **volver la ~** look the other way

carabela *f* caravel, small light ship

carabina *f* rifle; *(fig, señora, fam)* chaperone

Caracas *m* Caracas

caracol *m* snail; *(de pelo)* curl. **¡~es!** Good Heavens! **escalera** *f* **de ~** spiral staircase

carácter *m* *(pl* **caracteres)** character. **con ~ de, por su ~ de** as

característic|a *f* characteristic; *(LAm, teléfonos)* dialling code. **~o** *a* characteristic, typical

caracteriza|do *a* characterized; *(prestigioso)* distinguished. **~r** [10] *vt* characterize

cara: ~ dura cheek, nerve. **~dura** *m & f* cheeky person, rotter *(fam)*

caramba *int* good heavens!, goodness me!

carámbano *m* icicle

caramelo *m* sweet *(Brit)*, candy *(Amer)*; *(azúcar fundido)* caramel

carancho *m* *(Arg)* vulture

carapacho *m* shell

caraqueño *a* from Caracas. ● *m* native of Caracas

carátula *f* mask; *(fig, teatro)* theatre; *(Mex, esfera del reloj)* face

caravana *f* caravan; *(fig, grupo)* group; *(auto)* long line, traffic jam

caray *int* *(fam)* good heavens!, goodness me!

carb|ón *m* coal; *(papel)* carbon (paper); *(para dibujar)* charcoal. **~oncillo** *m* charcoal. **~onero** *a* coal. ● *m* coal-merchant. **~onizar** [10] *vt* *(fig)* burn (to a cinder). **~ono** *m* carbon

carburador *m* carburettor

carcajada *f* burst of laughter. **reírse a ~s** roar with laughter. **soltar una ~** burst out laughing

cárcel *m* prison, jail; *(en carpintería)* clamp

carcel|ario *a* prison. **~ero** *a* prison. ● *m* prison officer

carcom|a *f* woodworm. **~er** *vt* eat away; *(fig)* undermine. **~erse** *vpr* be eaten away; *(fig)* waste away

cardenal *m* cardinal; *(contusión)* bruise

cárdeno *a* purple

cardiaco, **cardíaco** *a* cardiac, heart. • *m* heart patient
cardinal *a* cardinal
cardiólogo *m* cardiologist, heart specialist
cardo *m* thistle
carear *vt* bring face to face ⟨*personas*⟩; compare ⟨*cosas*⟩
carecer [11] *vi*. ~ **de** lack. ~ **de sentido** not to make sense
caren|cia *f* lack. **~te** *a* lacking
carero *a* expensive
carestía *f* ⟨*precio elevado*⟩ high price; ⟨*escasez*⟩ shortage
careta *f* mask
carey *m* tortoiseshell
carga *f* load; ⟨*fig*⟩ burden; ⟨*acción*⟩ loading; ⟨*de barco*⟩ cargo; ⟨*obligación*⟩ obligation. **~do** *a* loaded; ⟨*fig*⟩ burdened; ⟨*tiempo*⟩ heavy; ⟨*hilo*⟩ live; ⟨*pila*⟩ charged. **~mento** *m* load; ⟨*acción*⟩ loading; ⟨*de un barco*⟩ cargo. **~nte** *a* demanding. **~r** [12] *vt* load; ⟨*fig*⟩ burden; ⟨*mil, elec*⟩ charge; fill ⟨*pluma etc*⟩; ⟨*fig, molestar, fam*⟩ annoy. • *vi* load. **~r con** pick up. **~rse** *vpr* ⟨*llenarse*⟩ fill; ⟨*cielo*⟩ become overcast; ⟨*enfadarse, fam*⟩ get cross. **llevar la ~ de algo** be responsible for sth
cargo *m* load; ⟨*fig*⟩ burden; ⟨*puesto*⟩ post; ⟨*acusación*⟩ accusation, charge; ⟨*responsabilidad*⟩ charge. **a ~ de** in the charge of. **hacerse ~ de** take responsibility for. **tener a su ~** be in charge of
carguero *m* ⟨*Arg*⟩ beast of burden; ⟨*naut*⟩ cargo ship
cari *m* ⟨*LAm*⟩ grey
cariacontecido *a* crestfallen
caria|do *a* decayed. **~rse** *vpr* decay
caribe *a* Caribbean. **el mar** *m* **C~** the Caribbean (Sea)
caricatura *f* caricature
caricia *f* caress
caridad *f* charity. ¡**por ~!** for goodness sake!
caries *f invar* ⟨*dental*⟩ decay
carilampiño *a* clean-shaven
cariño *m* affection; ⟨*caricia*⟩ caress. ~ **mío** my darling. **~samente** *adv* tenderly, lovingly; ⟨*en carta*⟩ with love from. **~so** *a* affectionate. **con mucho ~** ⟨*en carta*⟩ with love from. **tener ~ a** be fond of. **tomar ~ a** take a liking to. **un ~** ⟨*en carta*⟩ with love from
carism|a *m* charisma. **~ático** *a* charismatic

caritativo *a* charitable
cariz *m* look
carlinga *f* cockpit
carmesí *a* & *m* crimson
carmín *m* ⟨*de labios*⟩ lipstick; ⟨*color*⟩ red
carnal *a* carnal; ⟨*pariente*⟩ blood, full. **primo** ~ first cousin
carnaval *m* carnival. **~esco** *a* carnival. **martes** *m* **de** ~ Shrove Tuesday
carne *f* ⟨*incl de frutos*⟩ flesh; ⟨*para comer*⟩ meat. ~ **de cerdo** pork. ~ **de cordero** lamb. ~ **de gallina** gooseflesh. ~ **picada** mince. ~ **de ternera** veal. ~ **de vaca** beef. **me pone la** ~ **de gallina** it gives me the creeps. **ser de** ~ **y hueso** be only human
carné *m* card; ⟨*cuaderno*⟩ notebook. ~ **de conducir** driving licence ⟨*Brit*⟩, driver's license ⟨*Amer*⟩. ~ **de identidad** identity card.
carnero *m* sheep; ⟨*culin*⟩ lamb
carnet /kar'ne/ *m* card; ⟨*cuaderno*⟩ notebook. ~ **de conducir** driving licence ⟨*Brit*⟩, driver's license ⟨*Amer*⟩. ~ **de identidad** identity card
carnicer|ía *f* butcher's (shop); ⟨*fig*⟩ massacre. **~o** *a* carnivorous; ⟨*fig, cruel*⟩ cruel, savage. • *m* butcher; ⟨*animal*⟩ carnivore
carnívoro *a* carnivorous. • *m* carnivore
carnoso *a* fleshy
caro *a* dear. • *adv* dear, dearly. **costar ~ a uno** cost s.o. dear
carpa *f* carp; ⟨*tienda*⟩ tent
carpeta *f* file, folder. **~zo** *m*. **dar ~zo a** shelve, put on one side
carpinter|ía *f* carpentry. **~o** *m* carpinter, joiner
carraspe|ar *vi* clear one's throat. **~ra** *f*. **tener ~ra** have a frog in one's throat
carrera *f* run; ⟨*prisa*⟩ rush; ⟨*concurso*⟩ race; ⟨*recorrido, estudios*⟩ course; ⟨*profesión*⟩ profession, career
carreta *f* cart. **~da** *f* cart-load
carrete *m* reel; ⟨*película*⟩ 35mm film
carretera *f* road. ~ **de circunvalación** bypass, ring road. ~ **nacional** A road ⟨*Brit*⟩, highway ⟨*Amer*⟩. ~ **secundaria** B road ⟨*Brit*⟩, secondary road ⟨*Amer*⟩
carret|illa *f* trolley; ⟨*de una rueda*⟩ wheelbarrow; ⟨*de bebé*⟩ baby-walker. **~ón** *m* small cart

carril *m* rut; (*rail*) rail; (*de autopista etc*) lane
carrillo *m* cheek; (*polea*) pulley
carrizo *m* reed
carro *m* cart; (*LAm, coche*) car. ~ **de asalto**, ~ **de combate** tank
carrocería *f* (*auto*) bodywork; (*taller*) car repairer's
carroña *f* carrion
carroza *f* coach, carriage; (*en desfile de fiesta*) float
carruaje *m* carriage
carrusel *m* merry-go-round
carta *f* letter; (*documento*) document; (*lista de platos*) menu; (*lista de vinos*) list; (*geog*) map; (*naipe*) card. ~ **blanca** free hand. ~ **de crédito** credit card
cartearse *vpr* correspond
cartel *m* poster; (*de escuela etc*) wall-chart. ~**era** *f* hoarding; (*en periódico*) entertainments. ~**ito** *m* notice. **de** ~ celebrated. **tener** ~ be a hit, be successful
cartera *f* wallet; (*de colegial*) satchel; (*para documentos*) briefcase
cartería *f* sorting office
carterista *m & f* pickpocket
cartero *m* postman, mailman (*Amer*)
cartílago *m* cartilage
cartilla *f* first reading book. ~ **de ahorros** savings book. **leerle la** ~ **a uno** tell s.o. off
cartón *m* cardboard
cartucho *m* cartridge
cartulina *f* thin cardboard
casa *f* house; (*hogar*) home; (*empresa*) firm; (*edificio*) building. ~ **de correos** post office. ~ **de huéspedes** boarding-house. ~ **de socorro** first aid post. **amigo** *m* **de la** ~ family friend. **ir a** ~ go home. **salir de** ~ go out
casad|a *f* married woman. ~**o** *a* married. ● *m* married man. **los recién** ~**os** the newly-weds
casamentero *m* matchmaker
casa|miento *m* marriage; (*ceremonia*) wedding. ~**r** *vt* marry. ● *vi* get married. ~**rse** *vpr* get married
cascabel *m* small bell. ~**eo** *m* jingling
cascada *f* waterfall
cascado *a* broken; (*voz*) harsh
cascanueces *m invar* nutcrackers
cascar [7] *vt* break; crack (*frutos secos*); (*pegar*) beat. ● *vi* (*fig, fam*) chatter, natter (*fam*). ~**se** *vpr* crack

cáscara *f* (*de huevo, frutos secos*) shell; (*de naranja*) peel; (*de plátano*) skin
casco *m* helmet; (*de cerámica etc*) piece, fragment; (*cabeza*) head; (*de barco*) hull; (*envase*) empty bottle; (*de caballo*) hoof; (*de una ciudad*) part, area
cascote *m* rubble
caserío *m* country house; (*conjunto de casas*) hamlet
casero *a* home-made; (*doméstico*) domestic, household; (*amante del hogar*) home-loving; (*reunión*) family. ● *m* owner; (*vigilante*) caretaker
caseta *f* small house, cottage. ~ **de baño** bathing hut
caset(t)e *m & f* cassette
casi *adv* almost, nearly; (*en frases negativas*) hardly. ~ ~ very nearly. ~ **nada** hardly any. **¡**~ **nada!** is that all! ~ **nunca** hardly ever
casilla *f* small house; (*cabaña*) hut; (*de mercado*) stall; (*en ajedrez etc*) square; (*departamento de casillero*) pigeon-hole
casillero *m* pigeon-holes
casimir *m* cashmere
casino *m* casino; (*sociedad*) club
caso *m* case; (*atención*) notice. ~ **perdido** hopeless case. ~ **urgente** emergency. **darse el** ~ **(de) que** happen. **el** ~ **es que** the fact is that. **en** ~ **de** in the event of. **en cualquier** ~ in any case, whatever happens. **en ese** ~ in that case. **en todo** ~ in any case. **en último** ~ as a last resort. **hacer** ~ **de** take notice of. **poner por** ~ suppose
caspa *f* dandruff
cáspita *int* good heavens!, goodness me!
casquivano *a* scatter-brained
cassette *m & f* cassette
casta *f* (*de animal*) breed; (*de persona*) descent
castaña *f* chestnut
castañet|a *f* click of the fingers. ~**ear** *vi* (*dientes*) chatter
castaño *a* chestnut, brown. ● *m* chestnut (tree)
castañuela *f* castanet
castellano *a* Castilian. ● *m* (*persona*) Castilian; (*lengua*) Castilian, Spanish. ~**parlante** *a* Castilian-speaking, Spanish-speaking. **¿habla Vd** ~**?** do you speak Spanish?

castidad *f* chastity

castig|ar [12] *vt* punish; (*en deportes*) penalize. **~o** *m* punishment; (*en deportes*) penalty

Castilla *f* Castille. **~ la Nueva** New Castille. **~ la Vieja** Old Castille

castillo *m* castle

cast|izo *a* true; ‹*lengua*› pure. **~o** *a* pure

castor *m* beaver

castra|ción *f* castration. **~r** *vt* castrate

castrense *m* military

casual *a* chance, accidental. **~idad** *f* chance, coincidence. **~mente** *adv* by chance. **dar la ~idad** happen. **de ~idad, por ~idad** by chance. **¡qué ~idad!** what a coincidence!

cataclismo *m* cataclysm

catador *m* taster; (*fig*) connoisseur

catalán *a & m* Catalan

catalejo *m* telescope

catalizador *m* catalyst

cat|alogar [12] *vt* catalogue; (*fig*) classify. **~álogo** *m* catalogue

Cataluña *f* Catalonia

catamarán *m* catamaran

cataplúm *int* crash! bang!

catapulta *f* catapult

catar *vt* taste, try

catarata *f* waterfall, falls; (*med*) cataract

catarro *m* cold

cat|ástrofe *m* catastrophe. **~astrófico** *a* catastrophic

catecismo *m* catechism

catedral *f* cathedral

catedrático *m* professor; (*de instituto*) teacher, head of department

categ|oría *f* category; (*clase*) class. **~órico** *a* categorical. **de ~oría** important. **de primera ~oría** first-class

catinga *f* (*LAm*) bad smell

catita *f* (*Arg*) parrot

catoche *m* (*Mex*) bad mood

cat|olicismo *m* catholicism. **~ólico** *a* (Roman) Catholic. **●** *m* (Roman) Catholic

catorce *a & m* fourteen

cauce *m* river bed; (*fig, artificial*) channel

caución *f* caution; (*jurid*) guarantee

caucho *m* rubber

caudal *m* (*de río*) flow; (*riqueza*) wealth. **~oso** *a* ‹*río*› large

caudillo *m* leader, caudillo

causa *f* cause; (*motivo*) reason; (*jurid*) lawsuit. **~r** *vt* cause. **a ~ de, por ~ de** because of

cáustico *a* caustic

cautel|a *f* caution. **~arse** *vpr* guard against. **~osamente** *adv* warily, cautiously. **~oso** *a* cautious, wary

cauterizar [10] *vt* cauterize; (*fig*) apply drastic measures to

cautiv|ar *vt* capture; (*fig, fascinar*) captivate. **~erio** *m*, **~idad** *f* captivity. **~o** *a & m* captive

cauto *a* cautious

cavar *vt/i* dig

caverna *f* cave, cavern

caviar *m* caviare

cavidad *f* cavity

cavil|ar *vi* ponder, consider. **~oso** *a* worried

cayado *m* (*de pastor*) crook; (*de obispo*) crozier

caza *f* hunting; (*una expedición*) hunt; (*animales*) game. **●** *m* fighter. **~dor** *m* hunter. **~dora** *f* jacket. **~ mayor** big game hunting. **~ menor** small game hunting. **~r** [10] *vt* hunt; (*fig*) track down; (*obtener*) catch, get. **andar a (la) ~ de** be in search of. **dar ~** chase, go after

cazo *m* saucepan; (*cucharón*) ladle. **~leta** *f* (small) saucepan

cazuela *f* casserole

cebada *f* barley

ceb|ar *vt* fatten (up); (*con trampa*) bait; prime ‹*arma de fuego*›. **~o** *m* bait; (*de arma de fuego*) charge

ceboll|a *f* onion. **~ana** *f* chive. **~eta** *f* spring onion. **~ino** *m* chive

cebra *f* zebra

cece|ar *vi* lisp. **~o** *m* lisp

cedazo *m* sieve

ceder *vt* give up. **●** *vi* give in; (*disminuir*) ease off; (*fallar*) give way, collapse. **ceda el paso** give way

cedilla *f* cedilla

cedro *m* cedar

cédula *f* document; (*ficha*) index card

CE(E) *abrev* (*Comunidad (Económica) Europea*) E(E)C, European (Economic) Community

cefalea *f* severe headache

ceg|ador *a* blinding. **~ar** [1 & 12] *vt* blind; (*tapar*) block up. **~arse** *vpr* be blinded (**de** by). **~ato** *a* short-sighted. **~uera** *f* blindness

ceja *f* eyebrow

cejar *vi* move back; (*fig*) give way

celada *f* ambush; (*fig*) trap

cela|dor *m* (*de niños*) monitor; (*de cárcel*) prison warder; (*de museo etc*) attendant. **~r** *vt* watch

celda f cell
celebra|ción f celebration. **~r** vt celebrate; (alabar) praise. **~rse** vpr take place
célebre a famous; (fig, gracioso) funny
celebridad f fame; (persona) celebrity
celeridad f speed
celest|e a heavenly. **~ial** a heavenly. **azul ~e** sky-blue
celibato m celibacy
célibe a celibate
celo m zeal. **~s** mpl jealousy. **dar ~s** make jealous. **papel** m **~** adhesive tape, Sellotape (P). **tener ~s** be jealous
celofán m cellophane
celoso a enthusiastic; (que tiene celos) jealous
celta a Celtic. ● m & f Celt
céltico a Celtic
célula f cell
celular a cellular
celuloide m celluloid
celulosa f cellulose
cellisca f sleetstorm
cementerio m cemetery
cemento m cement; (hormigón) concrete; (LAm, cola) glue
cena f dinner; (comida ligera) supper. **~duría** f (Mex) restaurant
cenag|al m marsh, bog; (fig) tight spot. **~oso** a muddy
cenar vt have for dinner; (en cena ligera) have for supper. ● vi have dinner; (tomar cena ligera) have supper
cenicero m ashtray
cenit m zenith
ceniz|a f ash. **~o** a ashen. ● m jinx
censo m census. **~ electoral** electoral roll
censura f censure; (de prensa etc) censorship. **~r** vt censure; censor ⟨prensa etc⟩
centavo a & m hundredth; (moneda) centavo
centell|a f flash; (chispa) spark. **~ar** vi, **~ear** vi sparkle. **~eo** m sparkle, sparkling
centena f hundred. **~r** m hundred. **a ~res** by the hundred
centenario a centenary; ⟨persona⟩ centenarian. ● m centenary; (persona) centenarian
centeno m rye
centésim|a f hundredth. **~o** a hundredth; (moneda) centésimo

cent|ígrado a centigrade, Celsius. **~igramo** m centigram. **~ilitro** m centilitre. **~ímetro** m centimetre
céntimo a hundredth. ● m cent
centinela f sentry
centolla f, **centollo** m spider crab
central a central. ● f head office. **~ de correos** general post office. **~ eléctrica** power station. **~ nuclear** nuclear power station. **~ telefónica** telephone exchange. **~ismo** m centralism. **~ita** f switchboard
centraliza|ción f centralization. **~r** [10] vt centralize
centrar vt centre
céntrico a central
centrífugo a centrifugal
centro m centre. **~ comercial** shopping centre
Centroamérica f Central America
centroamericano a & m Central American
centuplicar [7] vt increase a hundredfold
ceñi|do a tight. **~r** [5 & 22] vt surround, encircle; ⟨vestido⟩ be a tight fit. **~rse** vpr limit o.s. (**a** to)
ceñ|o m frown. **~udo** a frowning. **fruncir el ~o** frown
cepill|ar vt brush; (en carpintería) plane. **~o** m brush; (en carpintería) plane. **~o de dientes** toothbrush
cera f wax
cerámic|a f ceramics; (materia) pottery; (objeto) piece of pottery. **~o** a ceramic
cerca f fence. ● adv near, close. **~s** mpl foreground. **~ de** prep near; (con números, con tiempo) nearly. **de ~** from close up, closely
cercado m enclosure
cercan|ía f nearness, proximity. **~ías** fpl outskirts. **tren** m **de ~ías** local train. **~o** a near, close. **C~o Oriente** m Near East
cercar [7] vt fence in, enclose; ⟨gente⟩ surround, crowd round; (asediar) besiege
cerciorar vt convince. **~se** vpr make sure, find out
cerco m (grupo) circle; (cercado) enclosure; (asedio) siege
Cerdeña f Sardinia
cerdo m pig; (carne) pork
cereal m cereal
cerebr|al a cerebral. **~o** m brain; (fig, inteligencia) intelligence, brains

ceremoni|a *f* ceremony. **~al** *a* ceremonial. **~oso** *a* ceremonious, stiff

céreo *a* wax

cerez|a *f* cherry. **~o** cherry tree

cerill|a *f* match. **~o** *m* (*Mex*) match

cern|er [1] *vt* sieve. **~erse** *vpr* hover; (*fig*, *amenazar*) hang over. **~idor** *m* sieve

cero *m* nought, zero; (*fútbol*) nil (*Brit*), zero (*Amer*); (*tenis*) love; (*persona*) nonentity. **partir de ~** start from scratch

cerquillo *m* (*LAm*, *flequillo*) fringe

cerquita *adv* very near

cerra|do *a* shut, closed; (*espacio*) shut in, enclosed; ⟨*cielo*⟩ overcast; ⟨*curva*⟩ sharp. **~dura** *f* lock; (*acción de cerrar*) shutting, closing. **~jero** *m* locksmith. **~r** [1] *vt* shut, close; (*con llave*) lock; (*con cerrojo*) bolt; (*cercar*) enclose; turn off ⟨*grifo*⟩; block up ⟨*agujero etc*⟩. ● *vi* shut, close. **~rse** *vpr* shut, close; ⟨*herida*⟩ heal. **~r con llave** lock

cerro *m* hill. **irse por los ~s de Úbeda** ramble on

cerrojo *m* bolt. **echar el ~** bolt

certamen *m* competition, contest

certero *a* accurate

certeza *f*, **certidumbre** *f* certainty

certifica|do *a* ⟨*carta etc*⟩ registered. ● *m* certificate; (*carta*) registered letter. **~r** [7] *vt* certify; register ⟨*carta etc*⟩

certitud *f* certainty

cervato *m* fawn

cerve|cería *f* beerhouse, bar; (*fábrica*) brewery. **~za** *f* beer. **~za de barril** draught beer. **~za de botella** bottled beer

cesa|ción *f* cessation, suspension. **~nte** *a* out of work. **~r** *vt* stop. ● *vi* stop, cease; (*dejar un empleo*) give up. **sin ~r** incessantly

cesáreo *a* Caesarian. **operación** *f* **cesárea** Caesarian section

cese *m* cessation; (*de un empleo*) dismissal

césped *m* grass, lawn

cest|a *f* basket. **~ada** *f* basketful. **~o** *m* basket. **~o de los papeles** wastepaper basket

cetro *m* sceptre; (*fig*) power

cianuro *m* cyanide

ciática *f* sciatica

cibernética *f* cibernetics

cicatriz *f* scar. **~ación** *f* healing. **~ar** [10] *vt/i* heal. **~arse** *vpr* heal

ciclamino *m* cyclamen

cíclico *a* cyclic(al)

ciclis|mo *m* cycling. **~ta** *m* & *f* cyclist

ciclo *m* cycle; (*LAm*, *curso*) course

ciclomotor *m* moped

ciclón *m* cyclone

ciclostilo *m* cyclostyle, duplicating machine

ciego *a* blind. ● *m* blind man, blind person. **a ciegas** in the dark

cielo *m* sky; (*relig*) heaven; (*persona*) darling. **¡~s!** good heavens!, goodness me!

ciempiés *m invar* centipede

cien *a* a hundred. **~ por ~** (*fam*) completely, one hundred per cent. **me pone a ~** it drives me mad

ciénaga *f* bog, swamp

ciencia *f* science; (*fig*) knowledge. **~s** *fpl* (*univ etc*) science. **~s empresariales** business studies. **saber a ~ cierta** know for a fact, know for certain

cieno *m* mud

científico *a* scientific. ● *m* scientist

ciento *a* & *m* (*delante de nombres, y numerales a los que multiplica* **cien**) a hundred, one hundred. **por ~** per cent

cierne *m* blossoming. **en ~** in blossom; (*fig*) in its infancy

cierre *m* fastener; (*acción de cerrar*) shutting, closing. **~ de cremallera** zip, zipper (*Amer*)

cierro *vb véase* **cerrar**

cierto *a* certain; (*verdad*) true. **estar en lo ~** be right. **lo ~ es que** the fact is that. **no es ~** that's not true. **¿no es ~?** right? **por ~** certainly, by the way. **si bien es ~ que** although

ciervo *m* deer

cifra *f* figure, number; (*cantidad*) sum. **~do** *a* coded. **~r** *vt* code; (*resumir*) summarize. **en ~** code, in code

cigala *f* (Norway) lobster

cigarra *f* cicada

cigarr|illo *m* cigarette. **~o** *m* (*cigarillo*) cigarette; (*puro*) cigar

cigüeña *f* stork

cil|índrico *a* cylindrical. **~indro** *m* cylinder; (*Mex*, *organillo*) barrel organ

cima *f* top; (*fig*) summit

címbalo *m* cymbal

cimbrear *vt* shake. **~se** *vpr* sway

cimentar [1] *vt* lay the foundations of; (*fig*, *reforzar*) strengthen

cimer|a *f* crest. **~o** *a* highest

cimiento *m* foundations; (*fig*) source. **desde los ~s** from the very beginning

cinc *m* zinc

cincel *m* chisel. **~ar** *vt* chisel

cinco *a & m* five

cincuent|a *a & m* fifty; (*quincuagésimo*) fiftieth. **~ón** *a* about fifty

cine *m* cinema. **~matografiar** [20] *vt* film

cinético *a* kinetic

cínico *a* cynical; (*desvergonzado*) shameless. ● *m* cynic

cinismo *m* cynicism; (*desvergüenza*) shamelessness

cinta *f* band; (*adorno de pelo etc*) ribbon; (*película*) film; (*magnética*) tape; (*de máquina de escribir etc*) ribbon. **~ aisladora**, **~ aislante** insulating tape. **~ magnetofónica** magnetic tape. **~ métrica** tape measure

cintur|a *f* waist. **~ón** *m* belt. **~ón de seguridad** safety belt. **~ón salvavidas** lifebelt

ciprés *m* cypress (tree)

circo *m* circus

circuito *m* circuit; (*viaje*) tour. **~ cerrado** closed circuit. **corto ~** short circuit

circula|ción *f* circulation; (*vehículos*) traffic. **~r** *a* circular. ● *vt* circulate. ● *vi* circulate; ⟨*líquidos*⟩ flow; (*conducir*) drive; ⟨*autobús etc*⟩ run

círculo *m* circle. **~ vicioso** vicious circle. **en ~** in a circle

circunci|dar *vt* circumcise. **~sión** *f* circumcision

circunda|nte *a* surrounding. **~r** *vt* surround

circunferencia *f* circumference

circunflejo *m* circumflex

circunscri|bir [*pp* **circunscrito**] *vt* confine. **~pción** *f* (*distrito*) district. **~pción electoral** constituency

circunspecto *a* wary, circumspect

circunstan|cia *f* circumstance. **~te** *a* surrounding. ● *m* bystander. **los ~tes** those present

circunvalación *f*. **carretera** *f* **de ~** bypass, ring road

cirio *m* candle

ciruela *f* plum. **~ claudia** greengage. **~ damascena** damson

ciru|gía *f* surgery. **~jano** *m* surgeon

cisne *m* swan

cisterna *f* tank, cistern

cita *f* appointment; (*entre chico y chica*) date; (*referencia*) quotation. **~ción** *f* quotation; (*jurid*) summons. **~do** *a* aforementioned. **~r** *vt* make an appointment with; (*mencionar*) quote; (*jurid*) summons. **~rse** *vpr* arrange to meet

cítara *f* zither

ciudad *f* town; (*grande*) city. **~anía** *f* citizenship; (*habitantes*) citizens. **~ano** *a* civic ● *m* citizen, inhabitant; (*habitante de ciudad*) city dweller

cívico *a* civic

civil *a* civil. ● *m* civil guard. **~idad** *f* politeness

civiliza|ción *f* civilization. **~r** [10] *vt* civilize. **~rse** *vpr* become civilized

civismo *m* community spirit

cizaña *f* (*fig*) discord

clam|ar *vi* cry out, clamour. **~or** *m* cry; (*griterío*) noise, clamour; (*protesta*) outcry. **~oroso** *a* noisy

clandestin|idad *f* secrecy. **~o** *a* clandestine, secret

clara *f* (*de huevo*) egg white

claraboya *f* skylight

clarear *vi* dawn; (*aclarar*) brighten up. **~se** *vpr* be transparent

clarete *m* rosé

claridad *f* clarity; (*luz*) light

clarifica|ción *f* clarification. **~r** [7] *vt* clarify

clarín *m* bugle

clarinet|e *m* clarinet; (*músico*) clarinettist. **~ista** *m & f* clarinettist

clarividen|cia *f* clairvoyance; (*fig*) far-sightedness. **~te** *a* clairvoyant; (*fig*) far-sighted

claro *a* (*con mucha luz*) bright; (*transparente*, *evidente*) clear; ⟨*colores*⟩ light; ⟨*líquido*⟩ thin. ● *m* (*en bosque etc*) clearing; (*espacio*) gap. ● *adv* clearly. ● *int* of course! **~ de luna** moonlight. **¡~ que sí!** yes of course! **¡~ que no!** of course not!

clase *f* class; (*aula*) classroom. **~ media** middle class. **~ obrera** working class. **~ social** social class. **dar ~s** teach. **toda ~ de** all sorts of

clásico *a* classical; (*fig*) classic. ● *m* classic

clasifica|ción *f* classification; (*deportes*) league. **~r** [7] *vt* classify; (*seleccionar*) sort

claudia *f* greengage

claudicar [7] (*ceder*) give in; (*cojear*) limp

claustro m cloister; (*univ*) staff
claustrof|obia f claustrophobia.
~**óbico** a claustrophobic
cláusula f clause
clausura f closure; (*ceremonia*) closing ceremony. ~**r** vt close
clava|do a fixed; (*con clavo*) nailed.
~**r** vt knock in <*clavo*>; (*introducir a mano*) stick; (*fijar*) fix; (*juntar*) nail together. **es** ~**do a su padre** he's the spitting image of his father
clave f key; (*mus*) clef; (*clavicémbalo*) harpsichord
clavel m carnation
clavicémbalo m harpsichord
clavícula f collar bone, clavicle
clavija f peg; (*elec*) plug
clavo m nail; (*culin*) clove
claxon m (*pl* **claxons** /ˈklakson/) horn
clemen|cia f clemency, mercy. ~**te** a clement, merciful
clementina f tangerine
cleptómano m kleptomaniac
cler|ecía f priesthood. ~**ical** a clerical
clérigo m priest
clero m clergy
cliché m cliché; (*foto*) negative
cliente m & f client, customer; (*de médico*) patient. ~**la** f clientele, customers; (*de médico*) patients, practice
clim|a m climate. ~**ático** a climatic. ~**atizado** a air-conditioned. ~**atológico** a climatological
clínic|a f clinic. ~**o** a clinical. ● m clinician
clip m (*pl* **clips**) clip
clo m cluck. **hacer** ~ ~ cluck
cloaca f drain, sewer
cloque|ar vi cluck. ~**o** m clucking
cloro m chlorine
club m (*pl* **clubs** o **clubes**) club
coacci|ón f coercion, compulsion.
~**onar** vt coerce, compel
coagular vt coagulate; clot <*sangre*>;
curdle <*leche*>. ~**se** vpr coagulate;
<*sangre*> clot; <*leche*> curdle
coalición f coalition
coartada f alibi
coartar vt hinder; restrict <*libertad etc*>
cobard|e a cowardly. ● m coward.
~**ía** f cowardice
cobaya f, **cobayo** m guinea pig
cobert|era f (*tapadera*) lid. ~**izo** m lean-to, shelter. ~**or** m bedspread; (*manta*) blanket. ~**ura** f covering

cobij|a f (*LAm, ropa de cama*) bedclothes; (*Mex, manta*) blanket. ~**ar** vt shelter. ~**arse** vpr shelter, take shelter. ~**o** m shelter
cobra f cobra
cobra|dor m conductor. ~**dora** f conductress. ~**r** vt collect; (*ganar*) earn; charge <*precio*>; cash <*cheque*>; (*recuperar*) recover. ● vi be paid. ~**rse** vpr recover
cobre m copper; (*mus*) brass (instruments)
cobro m collection; (*de cheque*) cashing; (*pago*) payment. **ponerse en** ~ go into hiding. **presentar al** ~ cash
cocada f (*LAm*) sweet coconut
cocaína f cocaine
cocci|ón f cooking; (*tec*) baking, firing
cocear vt/i kick
coc|er [2 & 9] vt/i cook; (*hervir*) boil; (*en horno*) bake. ~**ido** a cooked. ● m stew
cociente m quotient. ~ **intelectual** intelligence quotient, IQ
cocin|a f kitchen; (*arte de cocinar*) cookery, cuisine; (*aparato*) cooker.
~**a de gas** gas cooker. ~**a eléctrica** electric cooker. ~**ar** vt/i cook. ~**ero** m cook
coco m coconut; (*árbol*) coconut palm; (*cabeza*) head; (*duende*) bogeyman. **comerse el** ~ think hard
cocodrilo m crocodile
cocotero m coconut palm
cóctel m (*pl* **cócteles** o **cócteles**) cocktail; (*reunión*) cocktail party
coche m car (*Brit*), motor car (*Brit*), automobile (*Amer*); (*de tren*) coach, carriage. ~**cama** sleeper. ~ **fúnebre** hearse. ~**ra** f garage; (*de autobuses*) depot. ~ **restaurante** dining-car. ~**s de choque** dodgems
cochin|ada f dirty thing. ~**o** a dirty, filthy. ● m pig
cod|azo m nudge (with one's elbow); (*Mex, aviso secreto*) tip-off. ~**ear** vt/i elbow, nudge
codici|a f greed. ~**ado** a coveted, sought after. ~**ar** vt covet. ~**oso** a greedy (**de** for)
código m code. ~ **de la circulación** Highway Code
codo m elbow; (*dobladura*) bend.
hablar por los ~**s** talk too much.
hasta los ~**s** up to one's neck
codorniz m quail
coeducación f coeducation

coerción f coercion
coetáneo a & m contemporary
coexist|encia f coexistence. ~**ir** vi coexist
cofradía f brotherhood
cofre m chest
coger [14] vt (España) take; catch ⟨tren, autobús, pelota, catarro⟩; (agarrar) take hold of; (del suelo) pick up; pick ⟨frutos etc⟩. ● vi (caber) fit. ~**se** vpr trap, catch
cogollo m (de lechuga etc) heart; (fig, lo mejor) cream; (fig, núcleo) centre
cogote m back of the neck
cohech|ar vt bribe. ~**o** m bribery
coherente a coherent
cohesión f cohesion
cohete m rocket; (Mex, pistola) pistol
cohibi|ción f inhibition. ~**r** vt restrict; inhibit ⟨persona⟩. ~**rse** vpr feel inhibited; (contenerse) restrain o.s.
coincid|encia f coincidence. ~**ente** a coincidental. ~**ir** vt coincide. **dar la ~encia** happen
coje|ar vi limp; ⟨mueble⟩ wobble. ~**ra** f lameness
coj|ín m cushion. ~**inete** m small cushion. ~**inete de bolas** ball bearing
cojo a lame; ⟨mueble⟩ wobbly. ● m lame person
col f cabbage. ~**es de Bruselas** Brussel sprouts
cola f tail; (fila) queue; (para pegar) glue. **a la ~** at the end. **hacer ~** queue (up). **tener ~, traer ~** have serious consequences
colabora|ción f collaboration. ~**dor** m collaborator. ~**r** vi collaborate
colada f washing. **hacer la ~** do the washing
colador m strainer
colapso m collapse; (fig) stoppage
colar [2] vt strain ⟨líquidos⟩; (lavar) wash; pass ⟨moneda falsa etc⟩. ● vi ⟨líquido⟩ seep through; (fig) be believed, wash (fam). ~**se** vpr slip; (no hacer caso de la cola) jump the queue; (en fiesta) gatecrash; (meter la pata) put one's foot in it
colch|a f bedspread. ~**ón** m mattress. ~**oneta** f mattress
colear vi wag its tail; ⟨asunto⟩ not be resolved. **vivito y coleando** alive and kicking
colecci|ón f collection; (fig, gran número de) a lot of. ~**onar** vt collect. ~**onista** m & f collector

colecta f collection
colectiv|idad f community. ~**o** a collective. ● m (Arg) minibus
colector m (en las alcantarillas) main sewer
colega m & f colleague
colegi|al m schoolboy. ~**ala** f schoolgirl. ~**o** m private school; (de ciertas profesiones) college. ~**o mayor** hall of residence
colegir [5 & 14] vt gather
cólera f cholera; (ira) anger, fury. **descargar su ~** vent one's anger. **montar en ~** fly into a rage
colérico a furious, irate
colesterol m cholesterol
coleta f pigtail
colga|nte a hanging. ● m pendant. ~**r** [2 & 12] vt hang; hang out ⟨colada⟩; hang up ⟨abrigo etc⟩. ● vi hang; (teléfono) hang up, ring off. ~**rse** vpr hang o.s. **dejar a uno ~do** let s.o. down
cólico m colic
coliflor m cauliflower
colilla f cigarette end
colina f hill
colinda|nte a adjacent. ~**r** vt border (con on)
colisión f collision, crash; (fig) clash
colmar vt fill to overflowing; (fig) fulfill. ~ **a uno de amabilidad** overwhelm s.o. with kindness
colmena f beehive, hive
colmillo m eye tooth, canine (tooth); (de elefante) tusk; (de otros animales) fang
colmo m height. **ser el ~** be the limit, be the last straw
coloca|ción f positioning; (empleo) job, position. ~**r** [7] vt put, place; (buscar empleo) find work for. ~**rse** vpr find a job
Colombia f Colombia
colombiano a & m Colombian
colon m colon
colón m (unidad monetaria de Costa Rica y El Salvador) colón
Colonia f Cologne
coloni|a f colony; (agua de colonia) eau-de-Cologne; (LAm, barrio) suburb. ~**a de verano** holiday camp. ~**al** a colonial. ~**ales** mpl imported foodstuffs; (comestibles en general) groceries. ~**alista** m & f colonialist. ~**zación** f colonization. ~**zar** [10] colonize
coloqui|al a colloquial. ~**o** m conversation; (congreso) conference

color *m* colour. **~ado** *a* (*rojo*) red. **~ante** *m* colouring. **~ar** *vt* colour. **~ear** *vt/i* colour. **~ete** *m* rouge. **~ido** *m* colour. **de ~** colour. **en ~** (*fotos, película*) colour

colosal *a* colossal; (*fig, magnífico, fam*) terrific

columna *f* column; (*fig, apoyo*) support

columpi|ar *vt* swing. **~arse** *vpr* swing. **~o** *m* swing

collar *m* necklace; (*de perro etc*) collar

coma *f* comma. ● *m* (*med*) coma

comadre *f* midwife; (*madrina*) godmother; (*vecina*) neighbour. **~ar** *vi* gossip

comadreja *f* weasel

comadrona *f* midwife

comand|ancia *f* command. **~ante** *m* commander. **~o** *m* command; (*soldado*) commando

comarca *f* area, region

comba *f* bend; (*juguete*) skipping-rope. **~r** *vt* bend. **~rse** *vpr* bend. **saltar a la ~** skip

combat|e *m* fight; (*fig*) struggle. **~iente** *m* fighter. **~ir** *vt/i* fight

combina|ción *f* combination; (*bebida*) cocktail; (*arreglo*) plan, scheme; (*prenda*) slip. **~r** *vt* combine; (*arreglar*) arrange; (*armonizar*) match, go well with. **~rse** *vpr* combine; (*ponerse de acuerdo*) agree (**para** to)

combustible *m* fuel

comedia *f* comedy; (*cualquier obra de teatro*) play. **hacer la ~** pretend

comedi|do *a* reserved. **~rse** [5] *vpr* be restrained

comedor *m* dining-room; (*restaurante*) restaurant; (*persona*) glutton. **ser buen ~** have a good appetite

comensal *m* companion at table, fellow diner

comentar *vt* comment on; (*anotar*) annotate. **~io** *m* commentary; (*observación*) comment; (*fam*) gossip. **~ista** *m & f* commentator

comenzar [1 & 10] *vt/i* begin, start

comer *vt* eat; (*a mediodía*) have for lunch; (*corroer*) eat away; (*en ajedrez*) take. ● *vi* eat; (*a mediodía*) have lunch. **~se** *vpr* eat (up). **dar de ~ a** feed

comerci|al *a* commercial. **~ante** *m* trader; (*de tienda*) shopkeeper. **~ar**

vt trade (**con, en** in); (*con otra persona*) do business. **~o** *m* commerce; (*actividad*) trade; (*tienda*) shop; (*negocio*) business

comestible *a* edible. **~s** *mpl* food. **tienda de ~s** grocer's (shop) (*Brit*), grocery (*Amer*)

cometa *m* comet. ● *f* kite

comet|er *vt* commit; make ⟨*falta*⟩. **~ido** *m* task

comezón *m* itch

comicastro *m* poor actor, ham (*fam*)

comicios *mpl* elections

cómico *a* comic(al). ● *m* comic actor; (*cualquier actor*) actor

comida *f* food; (*a mediodía*) lunch. **hacer la ~** prepare the meals

comidilla *f* topic of conversation. **ser la ~ del pueblo** be the talk of the town

comienzo *m* beginning, start. **a ~s de** at the beginning of

comil|ón *a* greedy. **~ona** *f* feast

comillas *fpl* inverted commas

comino *m* cumin. **(no) me importa un ~** I couldn't care less

comisar|ía *f* police station. **~io** *m* commissioner; (*deportes*) steward. **~io de policía** police superintendent

comisión *f* assignment; (*comité*) commission, committee; (*com*) commission

comisura *f* corner. **~ de los labios** corner of the mouth

comité *m* committee

como *adv* like, as. ● *conj* as; (*en cuanto*) as soon as. **~ quieras** as you like. **~ sabes** as you know. **~ si** as if

cómo *a* how? ¿**~**? I beg your pardon? ¿**~ está Vd?** how are you? ¡**~ no!** (*esp LAm*) of course! ¿**~ son?** what are they like? ¿**~ te llamas?** what's your name? ¡**y ~!** and how!

cómoda *f* chest of drawers

comodidad *f* comfort. **a su ~** at your convenience

cómodo *a* comfortable; (*útil*) handy

comoquiera *conj*. **~ que** since. **~ que sea** however it may be

compacto *a* compact; (*denso*) dense; ⟨*líneas etc*⟩ close

compadecer [11] *vt* feel sorry for. **~se** *vpr*. **~se de** feel sorry for

compadre *m* godfather; (*amigo*) friend

compañ|ero *m* companion; (*de trabajo*) colleague; (*amigo*) friend. **~ía** *f* company. **en ~ía de** with

compara|ble *a* comparable. ~ción *f* comparison. ~r *vt* compare. ~tivo *a & m* comparative. en ~ción con in comparison with, compared with

comparecer [11] *vi* appear

comparsa *f* group; (*en el teatro*) extra

compartimiento *m* compartment

compartir *vt* share

compás *m* (*instrumento*) (pair of) compasses; (*ritmo*) rhythm; (*división*) bar (*Brit*), measure (*Amer*); (*naut*) compass. a ~ in time

compasi|ón *f* compassion, pity. tener ~ón de feel sorry for. ~vo *a* compassionate

compatib|ilidad *f* compatibility. ~le *a* compatible

compatriota *m & f* compatriot

compeler *vt* compel, force

compendi|ar *vt* summarize. ~o *m* summary

compenetración *f* mutual understanding

compensa|ción *f* compensation. ~ción por despido redundancy payment. ~r *vt* compensate

competen|cia *f* competition; (*capacidad*) competence; (*terreno*) field, scope. ~te *a* competent; (*apropiado*) appropriate, suitable

competi|ción *f* competition. ~dor *m* competitor. ~r [5] *vi* compete

compilar *vt* compile

compinche *m* accomplice; (*amigo*, *fam*) friend, mate (*fam*)

complac|encia *f* pleasure; (*indulgencia*) indulgence. ~er [32] *vt* please; (*prestar servicio*) help. ~erse *vpr* have pleasure, be pleased. ~iente *a* helpful; (*marido*) complaisant

complej|idad *f* complexity. ~o *a & m* complex

complement|ario *a* complementary. ~o *m* complement; (*gram*) object, complement

complet|ar *vt* complete. ~o *a* complete; (*lleno*) full; (*perfecto*) perfect

complexión *f* disposition; (*constitución*) constitution

complica|ción *f* complication. ~r [7] *vt* complicate; involve (*persona*). ~rse *vpr* become complicated

cómplice *m* accomplice

complot *m* (*pl* complots) plot

compon|ente *m* a component. ● *m* component; (*culin*) ingredient; (*miembro*) member. ~er [34] *vt* make up; (*mus, literatura etc*) write, compose; (*reparar*) mend; (*culin*) prepare; (*arreglar*) restore; settle (*estómago*); reconcile (*diferencias*). ~erse *vpr* be made up; (*arreglarse*) get ready. ~érselas manage

comporta|miento *m* behaviour. ~r *vt* involve. ~rse *vpr* behave. ~rse como es debido behave properly. ~rse mal misbehave

composi|ción *f* composition. ~tor *m* composer

compostelano *a* from Santiago de Compostela. ● *m* native of Santiago de Compostela

compostura *f* composition; (*arreglo*) repair; (*culin*) condiment; (*comedimiento*) composure

compota *f* stewed fruit

compra *f* purchase. ~ a plazos hire purchase. ~dor *m* buyer; (*en una tienda*) customer. ~r *vt* buy. ~venta *f* dealing. hacer la ~, ir a la ~, ir de ~s do the shopping, go shopping. negocio *m* de ~venta second-hand shop

compren|der *vt* understand; (*incluir*) include. ~sible *a* understandable. ~sión *f* understanding. ~sivo *a* understanding; (*que incluye*) comprehensive

compresa *f* compress; (*de mujer*) sanitary towel

compr|esión *f* compression. ~imido *a* compressed. ● *m* pill, tablet. ~imir *vt* compress; keep back (*lágrimas*); (*fig*) restrain

comproba|nte *m* (*recibo*) receipt. ~r *vt* check; (*confirmar*) confirm

comprometer *vt* compromise; (*arriesgar*) endanger. ~erse *vpr* compromise o.s.; (*obligarse*) agree to. ~ido *a* (*situación*) awkward, embarrassing

compromiso *m* obligation; (*apuro*) predicament; (*cita*) appointment; (*acuerdo*) agreement. sin ~ without obligation

compuesto *a* compound; (*persona*) smart. ● *m* compound

compungido *a* sad, sorry

computador *m*, computadora *f* computer

computar *vt* calculate

cómputo *m* calculation

comulgar [12] *vi* take Communion

común *a* common. ● *m* community. en ~ in common. por lo ~ generally

comunal *a* municipal, communal

comunica|ción *f* communication. **~do** *m* communiqué. **~do a la prensa** press release. **~r** [7] *vt/i* communicate; pass on ⟨*enfermedad*, *información*⟩. **~rse** *vpr* communicate; ⟨*enfermedad*⟩ spread. **~tivo** *a* communicative. **está ~ndo** (*al teléfono*) it's engaged, the line's engaged

comunidad *f* community. **~ de vecinos** residents' association. **C~ (Económica) Europea** European (Economic) Community. **en ~** together

comunión *f* communion; (*relig*) (Holy) Communion

comunis|mo *m* communism. **~ta** *a* & *m* & *f* communist

comúnmente *adv* generally, usually

con *prep* with; (*a pesar de*) in spite of; (+ *infinitivo*) by. **~ decir la verdad** by telling the truth. **~ que** so. **~ tal que** as long as

conato *m* attempt

concatenación *f* chain, linking

cóncavo *a* concave

concebir [5] *vt/i* conceive

conceder *vt* concede, grant; award ⟨*premio*⟩; (*admitir*) admit

concej|al *m* councillor. **~o** *m* town council

concentra|ción *f* concentration. **~do** *m* concentrated. **~r** *vt* concentrate. **~rse** *vpr* concentrate

concep|ción *f* conception. **~to** *m* concept; (*opinión*) opinion. **bajo ningún ~to** in no way. **en mi ~to** in my view. **por ningún ~to** in no way

concerniente *a* concerning. **en lo ~ a** with regard to

concertar [1] *vt* (*mus*) harmonize; (*coordinar*) coordinate; (*poner de acuerdo*) agree. ● *vi* be in tune; (*fig*) agree. **~se** *vpr* agree

concertina *f* concertina

concesión *f* concession

conciencia *f* conscience; (*conocimiento*) consciousness. **~ción** *f* awareness. **~ limpia** clear conscience. **~ sucia** guilty conscience. **a ~ de que** fully aware that. **en ~** honestly. **tener ~ de** be aware of. **tomar ~ de** become aware of

concienzudo *a* conscientious

concierto *m* concert; (*acuerdo*) agreement; (*mus*, *composición*) concerto

concilia|ble *a* reconcilable. **~ción** *f* reconciliation. **~r** *vt* reconcile. **~r el sueño** get to sleep. **~rse** *vpr* gain

concilio *m* council

conciso *a* concise

conciudadano *m* fellow citizen

conclu|ir [17] *vt* finish; (*deducir*) conclude. ● *vi* finish, end. **~irse** *vpr* finish, end. **~sión** *f* conclusion. **~yente** *a* conclusive

concord|ancia *f* agreement. **~ar** [2] *vt* reconcile. **~e** *a* in agreement. **~ia** *f* harmony

concret|amente *adv* specifically, to be exact. **~ar** *vt* make specific. **~arse** *vpr* become definite; (*limitarse*) confine o.s. **~o** *a* concrete; (*determinado*) specific, particular. ● *m* (*LAm*, *hormigón*) concrete. **en ~o** definite; (*concretamente*) to be exact; (*en resumen*) in short

concurr|encia *f* coincidence; (*reunión*) crowd, audience. **~ido** *a* crowded, busy. **~ir** *vi* meet; (*asistir*) attend; (*coincidir*) coincide; (*contribuir*) contribute; (*en concurso*) compete

concurs|ante *m* & *f* competitor, contestant. **~ar** *vi* compete, take part. **~o** *m* competition; (*concurrencia*) crowd; (*ayuda*) help

concha *f* shell; (*carey*) tortoiseshell

condado *m* county

conde *m* earl, count

condena *f* sentence. **~ción** *f* condemnation. **~do** *m* convict. **~r** *vt* condemn; (*jurid*) convict

condensa|ción *f* condensation. **~r** *vt* condense. **~rse** *vpr* condense

condesa *f* countess

condescende|ncia *f* condescension; (*tolerancia*) indulgence. **~r** [1] *vi* agree; (*dignarse*) condescend

condici|ón *f* condition; (*naturaleza*) nature. **~onado** *a*, **~onal** *a* conditional. **~onar** *vt* condition. **a ~ón de (que)** on the condition that

condiment|ar *vt* season. **~o** *m* condiment

condolencia *f* condolence

condominio *m* joint ownership

condón *m* condom

condonar *vt* (*perdonar*) reprieve; cancel ⟨*deuda*⟩

conducir [47] *vt* drive ⟨*vehículo*⟩; carry ⟨*electricidad*, *gas*, *agua etc*⟩. ● *vi* drive; (*fig*, *llevar*) lead. **~se** *vpr* behave. **¿a qué conduce?** what's the point?

conducta *f* behaviour

conducto *m* pipe, tube; *(anat)* duct. **por ~ de** through

conductor *m* driver; *(jefe)* leader; *(elec)* conductor

conduzco *vb véase* **conducir**

conectar *vt/i* connect; *(enchufar)* plug in

conejo *m* rabbit

conexión *f* connection

confabularse *vpr* plot

confecci|ón *f* making; *(prenda)* ready-made garment. **~ones** *fpl* clothing, clothes. **~onado** *a* ready-made. **~onar** *vt* make

confederación *f* confederation

conferencia *f* conference; *(al teléfono)* long-distance call; *(univ etc)* lecture. **~ cumbre, ~ en la cima, ~ en la cumbre** summit conference. **~nte** *m & f* lecturer

conferir [4] *vt* confer; award *(premio)*

confes|ar [1] *vt/i* confess. **~arse** *vpr* confess. **~ión** *f* confession. **~ional** *a* confessional. **~ionario** *m* confessional. **~or** *m* confessor

confeti *m* confetti

confia|do *a* trusting; *(seguro de sí mismo)* confident. **~nza** *f* trust; *(en sí mismo)* confidence; *(intimidad)* familiarity. **~r** [20] *vt* entrust. ● *vi* trust. **~rse** *vpr* put one's trust in

confiden|cia *f* confidence, secret. **~cial** *a* confidential. **~te** *m & f* close friend; *(de policía)* informer

configuración *f* configuration, shape

conf|ín *m* border. **~inar** *vt* confine; *(desterrar)* banish. ● *vi* border **(con** on). **~ines** *mpl* outermost parts

confirma|ción *f* confirmation. **~r** *vt* confirm

confiscar [7] *vt* confiscate

confit|ería *f* sweet-shop *(Brit)*, candy store *(Amer)*. **~ura** *f* jam

conflagración *f* conflagration

conflicto *m* conflict

confluencia *f* confluence

conforma|ción *f* conformation, shape. **~r** *vt (acomodar)* adjust. ● *vi* agree. **~rse** *vpr* conform

conform|e *a* in agreement; *(contento)* happy, satisfied; *(según)* according **(con** to). ● *conj* as. ● *int* OK! **~e a** in accordance with, according to. **~idad** *f* agreement; *(tolerancia)* resignation. **~ista** *m & f* conformist

conforta|ble *a* comfortable. **~nte** *a* comforting. **~r** *vt* comfort

confronta|ción *f* confrontation; *(comparación)* comparison. **~r** *vt* confront; *(comparar)* compare

confu|ndir *vt* blur; *(equivocar)* mistake, confuse; *(perder)* lose; *(mezclar)* mix up, confuse. **~ndirse** *vpr* become confused; *(equivocarse)* make a mistake. **~sión** *f* confusion; *(vergüenza)* embarrassment. **~so** *a* confused; *(avergonzado)* embarrassed

congela|do *a* frozen. **~dor** *m* freezer. **~r** *vt* freeze

congeniar *vi* get on

congesti|ón *f* congestion. **~onado** *a* congested. **~onar** *vt* congest. **~onarse** *vpr* become congested

congoja *f* distress

congraciar *vt* win over. **~se** *vpr* ingratiate o.s.

congratular *vt* congratulate

congrega|ción *f* gathering; *(relig)* congregation. **~rse** [12] *vpr* gather, assemble

congres|ista *m & f* delegate, member of a congress. **~o** *m* congress, conference. **C~o de los Diputados** House of Commons

cónico *a* conical

conífer|a *f* conifer. **~o** *a* coniferous

conjetura *f* conjecture, guess. **~r** *vt* conjecture, guess

conjuga|ción *f* conjugation. **~r** [12] *vt* conjugate

conjunción *f* conjunction

conjunto *a* joint. ● *m* collection; *(mus)* band; *(ropa)* suit, outfit. **en ~** altogether

conjura *f*, **conjuración** *f* conspiracy

conjurar *vt* plot, conspire

conmemora|ción *f* commemoration. **~r** *vt* commemorate. **~tivo** *a* commemorative

conmigo *pron* with me

conminar *vt* threaten; *(avisar)* warn

conmiseración *f* commiseration

conmo|ción *f* shock; *(tumulto)* upheaval; *(terremoto)* earthquake. **~cionar** *vt* shock. **~ cerebral** concussion. **~ver** [2] *vt* shake; *(emocionar)* move

conmuta|dor *m* switch. **~r** *vt* exchange

connivencia *f* connivance

connota|ción *f* connotation. **~r** *vt* connote

cono *m* cone

conoc|edor *a & m* expert. **~er** [11] *vt* know; (*por primera vez*) meet; (*reconocer*) recognize, know. **~erse** *vpr* know o.s.; ⟨*dos personas*⟩ know each other; (*notarse*) be obvious. **dar a ~er** make known. **darse a ~er** make o.s. known. **~ido** *a* well-known. ● *m* acquaintance. **~imiento** *m* knowledge; (*sentido*) consciousness; (*conocido*) acquaintance. **perder el ~imiento** faint. **se ~e que** apparently. **tener ~imiento de** know about

conozco *vb véase* **conocer**

conque *conj* so

conquense *a* from Cuenca. ● *m* native of Cuenca

conquista *f* conquest. **~dor** *a* conquering. ● *m* conqueror; (*de América*) conquistador; (*fig*) lady-killer. **~r** *vt* conquer, win

consabido *a* well-known

consagra|ción *f* consecration. **~r** *vt* consecrate; (*fig*) devote. **~rse** *vpr* devote o.s.

consanguíneo *m* blood relation

consciente *a* conscious

consecución *f* acquisition; (*de un deseo*) realization

consecuen|cia *f* consequence; (*firmeza*) consistency. **~te** *a* consistent. **a ~cia de** as a result of. **en ~cia, por ~cia** consequently

consecutivo *a* consecutive

conseguir [5 & 13] *vt* get, obtain; (*lograr*) manage; achieve ⟨*objetivo*⟩

conseja *f* story, fable

consej|ero *m* adviser; (*miembro de consejo*) member. **~o** *m* advice; (*pol*) council. **~o de ministros** cabinet

consenso *m* assent, consent

consenti|do *a* ⟨*niño*⟩ spoilt. **~miento** *m* consent. **~r** [4] *vt* allow. ● *vi* consent. **~rse** *vpr* break

conserje *m* porter, caretaker. **~ría** *f* porter's office

conserva *f* preserves; (*mermelada*) jam, preserve; (*en lata*) tinned food. **~ción** *f* conservation; (*de alimentos*) preservation; (*de edificio*) maintenance. **en ~** preserved

conservador *a & m* (*pol*) conservative

conservar *vt* keep; preserve ⟨*alimentos*⟩. **~se** *vpr* keep; ⟨*costumbre etc*⟩ survive

conservatorio *m* conservatory

considera|ble *a* considerable. **~ción** *f* consideration; (*respeto*) respect. **~do** *a* considered; (*amable*) considerate; (*respetado*) respected. **~r** *vt* consider; (*respetar*) respect. **de ~ción** considerable. **de su ~ción** (*en cartas*) yours faithfully. **tomar en ~ción** take into consideration

consigna *f* order; (*rail*) left luggage office (*Brit*), baggage room (*Amer*); (*eslogan*) slogan

consigo *pron* (*él*) with him; (*ella*) with her; (*Ud, Uds*) with you; (*uno mismo*) with o.s.

consiguiente *a* consequent. **por ~** consequently

consist|encia *f* consistency. **~ente** *a* consisting (**en** of); (*firme*) solid. **~ir** *vi* consist (**en** of); (*deberse*) be due (**en** to)

consola|ción *f* consolation. **~r** [2] *vt* console, comfort

consolidar *vt* consolidate. **~se** *vpr* consolidate

consomé *m* clear soup, consommé

consonan|cia *f* consonance. **~te** *a* consonant. ● *f* consonant

consorcio *m* consortium

consorte *m & f* consort

conspicuo *a* eminent; (*visible*) visible

conspira|ción *f* conspiracy. **~dor** *m* conspirator. **~r** *vi* conspire

constan|cia *f* constancy. **~te** *a* constant

constar *vi* be clear; (*figurar*) appear, figure; (*componerse*) consist. **hacer ~** point out. **me consta que** I'm sure that. **que conste que** believe me

constatar *vt* check; (*confirmar*) confirm

constelación *f* constellation

consternación *f* consternation

constipa|do *m* cold. ● *a.* **estar ~do** have a cold. **~rse** *vpr* catch a cold

constitu|ción *f* constitution; (*establecimiento*) setting up. **~cional** *a* constitutional. **~ir** [17] *vt* constitute; (*formar*) form; (*crear*) set up, establish. **~irse** *vpr* set o.s. up (**en** as); (*presentarse*) appear. **~tivo** *a*, **~yente** *a* constituent

constreñir [5 & 22] *vt* force, oblige; (*restringir*) restrain

constricción *f* constriction

constru|cción *f* construction. **~ctor** *m* builder. **~ir** [17] *vt* construct; build ⟨*edificio*⟩

consuelo *m* consolation, comfort
consuetudinario *a* customary
cónsul *m* consul
consula|do *m* consulate. **~r** *a* consular
consult|a *f* consultation. **~ar** *vt* consult. **~orio** *m* surgery. **~orio sentimental** problem page. **horas** *fpl* de **~a** surgery hours. **obra** *f* de **~a** reference book
consumar *vt* complete; commit ⟨*crimen*⟩; consummate ⟨*matrimonio*⟩
consum|ición *f* consumption; (*bebida*) drink; (*comida*) food. **~ido** *a* ⟨*persona*⟩ skinny, wasted; ⟨*frutas*⟩ shrivelled. **~idor** *m* consumer. **~ir** *vt* consume. **~irse** *vpr* ⟨*persona*⟩ waste away; ⟨*cosa*⟩ wear out; (*quedarse seco*) dry up. **~ismo** *m* consumerism. **~o** *m* consumption
contab|ilidad *f* book-keeping; (*profesión*) accountancy. **~le** *m* & *f* accountant
contacto *m* contact. **ponerse en ~ con** get in touch with
contado *a* counted. **~s** *apl* few. **~r** *m* meter; (*LAm*, *contable*) accountant. **al ~** cash
contagi|ar *vt* infect ⟨*persona*⟩; pass on ⟨*enfermedd*⟩; (*fig*) contaminate. **~o** *m* infection. **~oso** *a* infectious
contamina|ción *f* contamination, pollution. **~r** *vt* contaminate, pollute
contante *a*. **dinero** *m* **~** cash
contar [2] *vt* count; tell ⟨*relato*⟩. ● *vi* count. **~ con** rely on, count on. **~se** *vpr* be included (**entre** among); (*decirse*) be said
contempla|ción *f* contemplation. **~r** *vt* look at; (*fig*) contemplate. **sin ~ciones** unceremoniously
contemporáneo *a* & *m* contemporary
contend|er [1] *vi* compete. **~iente** *m* & *f* competitor
conten|er [40] *vt* contain; (*restringir*) restrain. **~erse** *vpr* restrain o.s. **~ido** *a* contained. ● *m* contents
content|ar *vt* please. **~arse** *vpr*. **~arse de** be satisfied with, be pleased with. **~o** *a* (*alegre*) happy; (*satisfecho*) pleased
contesta|ción *f* answer. **~dor** *m*. **~ automático** answering machine. **~r** *vt/i* answer; (*replicar*) answer back
contexto *m* context

contienda *f* struggle
contigo *pron* with you
contiguo *a* adjacent
continen|cia *f* continence. **~tal** *a* continental. **~te** *m* continent
contingen|cia *f* contingency. **~te** *a* contingent. ● *m* contingent; (*cuota*) quota
continu|ación *f* continuation. **~ar** [21] *vt* continue, resume. ● *vi* continue. **~ará** (*en revista*, *TV etc*) to be continued. **~idad** *f* continuity. **~o** *a* continuous; (*muy frecuente*) continual. **a ~ación** immediately after.
corriente *f* **~a** direct current
contorno *m* outline; (*geog*) contour. **~s** *mpl* surrounding area
contorsión *f* contortion
contra *adv* & *prep* against. ● *m* cons. **en ~** against
contraalmirante *m* rear-admiral
contraata|car [7] *vt/i* counterattack. **~que** *m* counter-attack
contrabajo *m* double-bass; (*persona*) double-bass player
contrabalancear *vt* counterbalance
contraband|ista *m* & *f* smuggler. **~o** *m* contraband
contracción *f* contraction
contrachapado *m* plywood
contrad|ecir [46] *vt* contradict. **~icción** *f* contradiction. **~ictorio** *a* contradictory
contraer [41] *vt* contract. **~ matrimonio** marry. **~se** *vpr* contract; (*limitarse*) limit o.s.
contrafuerte *m* buttress
contragolpe *m* backlash
contrahecho *a* fake; ⟨*moneda*⟩ counterfeit; ⟨*persona*⟩ hunchbacked
contraindicación *f* contraindication
contralto *m* alto. ● *f* contralto
contramano. a ~ in the wrong direction
contrapartida *f* compensation
contrapelo. a ~ the wrong way
contrapes|ar *vt* counterbalance. **~o** *m* counterbalance
contraponer [34] oppose; (*comparar*) compare
contraproducente *a* counterproductive
contrari|ar [20] *vt* oppose; (*molestar*) annoy. **~edad** *f* obstacle; (*disgusto*) annoyance. **~o** *a* contrary; ⟨*dirección*⟩ opposite; ⟨*persona*⟩ opposed. **al ~o** on the contrary. **al**

~o de contrary to. de lo ~o otherwise. en ~o against. llevar la ~a contradict. por el ~o on the contrary

contrarrestar *vt* counteract

contrasentido *m* contradiction

contraseña *f* secret mark; (*palabra*) password

contrast|ar *vt* check, verify. • *vi* contrast. ~e *m* contrast; (*en oro, plata etc*) hallmark

contratar *vt* sign a contract for; engage (*empleados*)

contratiempo *m* setback; (*accidente*) accident

contrat|ista *m & f* contractor. ~o *m* contract

contraven|ción *f* contravention. ~ir [53] *vi.* ~ir a contravene

contraventana *f* shutter

contribu|ción *f* contribution; (*tributo*) tax. ~ir [17] *vt/i* contribute. ~yente *m & f* contributor; (*que paga impuestos*) taxpayer

contrincante *m* rival, opponent

contrito *a* contrite

control *m* control; (*inspección*) check. ~ar *vt* control; (*examinar*) check

controversia *f* controversy

contundente *a* (*arma*) blunt; (*argumento etc*) convincing

conturbar *vt* perturb

contusión *f* bruise

convalec|encia *f* convalescence. ~er [11] *vi* convalesce. ~iente *a & m & f* convalescent

convalidar *vt* confirm; recognize (*título*)

convenc|er [9] *vt* convince. ~imiento *m* conviction

convenci|ón *f* convention. ~onal *a* conventional

conveni|encia *f* convenience; (*aptitud*) suitability. ~encias (sociales) conventions. ~ente *a* suitable; (*aconsejable*) advisable; (*provechoso*) useful, advantageous. ~o *m* agreement. ~r [53] *vt* agree. • *vi* agree; (*ser conveniente*) be convenient for, suit; (*ser aconsejable*) be advisable

convento *m* (*de monjes*) monastery; (*de monjas*) convent

convergente *a* converging

converger [14] *vi*, **convergir** [14] *vi* converge

conversa|ción *f* conversation. ~r *vi* converse, talk

conver|sión *f* conversion. ~so *a* converted. • *m* convert. ~tible *a* convertible. ~tir [4] *vt* convert. ~tirse *vpr* be converted

convexo *a* convex

convic|ción *f* conviction. ~to *a* convicted

convida|do *m* guest. ~r *vt* invite. te convido a un helado I'll treat you to an ice-cream

convincente *a* convincing

convite *m* invitation; (*banquete*) banquet

conviv|encia *f* coexistence. ~ir *vi* live together

convocar [7] *vt* convene (*reunión*); summon (*personas*)

convoy *m* convoy; (*rail*) train; (*vinagrera*) cruet

convulsión *f* convulsion; (*fig*) upheaval

conyugal *a* conjugal; (*vida*) married

cónyuge *m* spouse. ~s *mpl* (married) couple

coñac *m* (*pl* coñacs) brandy

coopera|ción *f* co-operation. ~r *vi* co-operate. ~tiva *f* co-operative. ~tivo *a* co-operative

coord|enada *f* coordinate. ~inación *f* co-ordination. ~inar *vt* co-ordinate

copa *f* glass; (*deportes, fig*) cup. ~s *fpl* (*naipes*) hearts. tomar una ~ have a drink

copia *f* copy. ~ en limpio fair copy. ~r *vt* copy. sacar una ~ make a copy

copioso *a* copious; (*lluvia, nevada etc*) heavy

copla *f* verse; (*canción*) song

copo *m* flake. ~ de nieve snowflake. ~s de maíz cornflakes

coquet|a *f* flirt; (*mueble*) dressing-table. ~ear *vi* flirt. ~eo *m* flirtation. ~o *a* flirtatious

coraje *m* courage; (*rabia*) anger. dar ~ make mad, make furious

coral *a* choral. • *m* (*materia, animal*) coral

Corán *m* Koran

coraza *f* (*naut*) armour-plating; (*de tortuga*) shell

coraz|ón *m* heart; (*persona*) darling. ~onada *f* hunch; (*impulso*) impulse. sin ~ón heartless. tener buen ~ón be good-hearted

corbata *f* tie, necktie (*esp Amer*). ~ de lazo bow tie

corcova f hump. ~**do** a hunch-backed

corchea f quaver

corchete m fastener, hook and eye; (*gancho*) hook; (*paréntesis*) square bracket

corcho m cork

cordel m cord, thin rope

cordero m lamb

cordial a cordial, friendly. ● m tonic. ~**idad** f cordiality, warmth

cordillera f mountain range

córdoba m (*unidad monetaria de Nicaragua*) córdoba

Córdoba f Cordova

cordón m string; (*de zapatos*) lace; (*cable*) flex; (*fig*) cordon. ~ **umbilical** umbilical cord

corear vt chant

coreografía f choreography

corista m & f member of the chorus. ● f (*bailarina*) chorus girl

cornet|a f bugle. ~**in** m cornet

Cornualles m Cornwall

cornucopia f cornucopia

cornudo a horned. ● m cuckold

coro m chorus; (*relig*) choir

corona f crown; (*de flores*) wreath, garland. ~**ción** f coronation. ~**r** vt crown

coronel m colonel

coronilla f crown. **estar hasta la** ~ be fed up

corporación f corporation

corporal a corporal

corpulento a stout

corpúsculo m corpuscle

corral m pen. **aves** fpl **de** ~ poultry

correa f strap; (*de perro*) lead; (*cinturón*) belt

correc|ción f correction; (*reprensión*) rebuke; (*cortesía*) good manners. ~**to** a correct; (*cortés*) polite

corre|dizo a running. **nudo** ~**dizo** slip knot. **puerta** f ~**diza** sliding door. ~**dor** m runner; (*pasillo*) corridor; (*agente*) agent, broker. ~**dor automovilista** racing driver

corregir [5 & 14] vt correct; (*reprender*) rebuke

correlaci|ón f correlation. ~**onar** vt correlate

correo m courier; (*correos*) post, mail; (*tren*) mail train. ~**s** mpl post office. **echar al** ~ post

correr vt run; (*viajar*) travel; draw (*cortinas*). ● vi run; (*agua, electricidad etc*) flow; (*tiempo*) pass. ~**se** vpr (*apartarse*) move along;

(*pasarse*) go too far; (*colores*) run. ~**se una juerga** have a ball

correspond|encia f correspondence. ~**er** vi correspond; (*ser adecuado*) be fitting; (*contestar*) reply; (*pertenecer*) belong; (*incumbir*) fall to. ~**erse** vpr (*amarse*) love one another. ~**iente** a corresponding

corresponsal m correspondent

corrid|a f run. ~**a de toros** bullfight. ~**o** a (*peso*) good; (*continuo*) continuous; (*avergonzado*) embarrassed. **de** ~**a** from memory

corriente a (*agua*) running; (*monedas, publicación, cuenta, año etc*) current; (*ordinario*) ordinary. ● f current; (*de aire*) draught; (*fig*) tendency. ● m current month. **al** ~ (*al día*) up-to-date; (*enterado*) aware

corr|illo m small group, circle. ~**o** m circle

corroborar vt corroborate

corroer [24 & 37] vt corrode; (*geol*) erode; (*fig*) eat away. ~**se** vpr corrode

corromper vt rot (*madera*); turn bad (*alimentos*); (*fig*) corrupt. ● vi (*fam*) stink. ~**se** vpr (*madera*) rot; (*alimentos*) go bad; (*fig*) be corrupted

corrosi|ón f corrosion. ~**vo** a corrosive

corrupción f (*de madera etc*) rot; (*soborno*) bribery; (*fig*) corruption

corsé m corset

cortacésped m invar lawn-mower

cortad|o a cut; (*leche*) sour; (*avergonzado*) embarrassed; (*confuso*) confused. ● m coffee with a little milk. ~**ura** f cut

corta|nte a sharp; (*viento*) biting; (*frío*) bitter. ~**r** vt cut; (*recortar*) cut out; (*aislar, detener*) cut off; (*interrumpir*) cut in. ● vi cut. ~**rse** vpr cut o.s.; (*leche etc*) curdle; (*al teléfono*) be cut off; (*fig*) be embarrassed, become tongue-tied. ~**rse el pelo** have one's hair cut. ~**rse las uñas** cut one's nails

cortauñas m invar nail-clippers

corte m cutting; (*de instrumento cortante*) cutting edge; (*de corriente*) cut; (*de prendas de vestir*) cut; (*de tela*) length. ● f court. ~ **de luz** power cut. ~ **y confección** dressmaking. **hacer la** ~ court. **las C**~**s** the Spanish parliament

cortej|ar *vt* court. **~o** *m* (*de rey etc*) entourage. **~o fúnebre** cortège, funeral procession. **~o nupcial** wedding procession

cortés *a* polite

cortesan|a *f* courtesan. **~o** *m* courtier

cortesía *f* courtesy

corteza *f* bark; (*de naranja etc*) peel, rind; (*de pan*) crust

cortijo *m* farm; (*casa*) farmhouse

cortina *f* curtain

corto *a* short; (*escaso*) scanty; (*apocado*) shy. **~circuito** *m* short circuit. **~ de alcances** dim, thick. **~ de oído** hard of hearing. **~ de vista** short-sighted. **a la corta o a la larga** sooner or later. **quedarse ~** fall short; (*miscalcular*) under-estimate

Coruña *f*. **La ~** Corunna

corvo *a* bent

cosa *f* thing; (*asunto*) business; (*idea*) idea. **~ de** about. **como si tal ~** just like that; (*como si no hubiera pasado nada*) as if nothing had happened. **decirle a uno cuatro ~s** tell s.o. a thing or two. **lo que son las ~s** much to my surprise

cosaco *a* & *m* Cossack

cosech|a *f* harvest; (*de vino*) vintage. **~ar** *vt* harvest. **~ero** *m* harvester

coser *vt/i* sew. **~se** *vpr* stick to s.o. **eso es ~ y cantar** it's as easy as pie

cosmético *a* & *m* cosmetic

cósmico *a* cosmic

cosmonauta *m* & *f* cosmonaut

cosmopolita *a* & *m* & *f* cosmopolitan

cosmos *m* cosmos

cosquillas *fpl* ticklishness. **buscar a uno las ~** provoke s.o. **hacer ~** tickle. **tener ~** be ticklish

costa *f* coast. **a ~ de** at the expense of. **a toda ~** at any cost

costado *m* side

costal *m* sack

costar [2] *vt/i* cost. **~ caro** be expensive. **cueste lo que cueste** at any cost

Costa Rica *f* Costa Rica

costarricense *a* & *m*, **costarriqueño** *a* & *m* Costa Rican

coste *m* cost. **~ar** *vt* pay for; (*naut*) sail along the coast

costero *a* coastal

costilla *f* rib; (*chuleta*) chop

costo *m* cost. **~so** *a* expensive

costumbre *f* custom, habit. **de ~** *a* usual. ● *adv* usually

costur|a *f* sewing; (*línea*) seam; (*confección*) dressmaking. **~era** *f* dressmaker. **~ero** *m* sewing box

cotejar *vt* compare

cotidiano *a* daily

cotille|ar *vt* gossip. **~o** *m* gossip

cotiza|ción *f* quotation, price. **~r** [10] *vt* (*en la bolsa*) quote. ● *vi* pay one's subscription. **~rse** *vpr* fetch; (*en la bolsa*) stand at; (*fig*) be valued

coto *m* enclosure; (*de caza*) preserve. **~ de caza** game preserve

cotorr|a *f* parrot; (*urraca*) magpie; (*fig*) chatterbox. **~ear** *vi* chatter

coyuntura *f* joint; (*oportunidad*) opportunity; (*situación*) situation; (*circunstancia*) occasion, juncture

coz *f* kick

cráneo *m* skull

cráter *m* crater

crea|ción *f* creation. **~dor** *a* creative. ● *m* creator. **~r** *vt* create

crec|er [11] *vi* grow; (*aumentar*) increase. **~ida** *f* (*de río*) flood. **~ido** *a* (*persona*) grown-up; (*número*) large, considerable; (*plantas*) fully-grown. **~iente** *a* growing; (*luna*) crescent. **~imiento** *m* growth

credencial *a* credential. **~es** *fpl* credentials

credibilidad *f* credibility

crédito *m* credit. **digno de ~** reliable, trustworthy

credo *m* creed. **en un ~** in a flash

crédulo *a* credulous

cre|encia *f* belief. **~er** [18] believe; (*pensar*) think. **~o que no** I don't think so, I think not. **~o que sí** I think so. ● *vi* believe. **~erse** *vpr* consider o.s. **no me lo ~o** I don't believe it. **~íble** *a* credible. ¡**ya lo ~o!** I should think so!

crema *f* cream; (*culin*) custard. **~ bronceadora** sun-tan cream

cremación *f* cremation; (*de basura*) incineration

cremallera *f* zip, zipper (*Amer*)

crematorio *m* crematorium; (*de basura*) incinerator

crepitar *vi* crackle

crepúsculo *m* twilight

crescendo *m* crescendo

cresp|o *a* frizzy. **~ón** *m* crêpe

cresta *f* crest; (*tupé*) toupee; (*geog*) ridge

Creta *f* Crete

cretino *m* cretin

creyente *m* believer

cría f breeding; (animal) baby animal

cria|da f maid, servant. **~dero** nursery. **~do** a brought up. ● m servant. **~dor** m breeder. **~nza** f breeding. **~r** [20] vt suckle; grow ⟨plantas⟩; breed ⟨animales⟩; (educar) bring up. **~rse** vpr grow up

criatura f creature; (niño) baby

crim|en m crime. **~inal** a & m & f criminal

crin m mane; (relleno) horsehair

crinolina f crinoline

crío m child

criollo a & m Creole

cripta f crypt

crisantemo m chrysanthemum

crisis f crisis

crisol m melting-pot

crispar vt twitch; (irritar, fam) annoy. **~ los nervios a uno** get on s.o.'s nerves

cristal m crystal; (vidrio) glass; (de una ventana) pane of glass. **~ de aumento** magnifying glass. **~ino** a crystalline; (fig) crystal-clear. **~izar** [10] crystallize. **limpiar los ~es** clean the windows

cristian|amente adv in a Christian way. **~dad** f Christianity. **~ismo** m Christianity. **~o** a & m Christian

Cristo m Christ

cristo m crucifix

criterio m criterion; (opinión) opinion

cr|ítica f criticism; (reseña) review. **~iticar** [7] vt criticize. **~ítico** a critical. ● m critic

croar vi croak

crom|ado a chromium-plated. **~o** m chromium, chrome

cromosoma m chromosome

crónic|a f chronicle; (de periódico) news. **~o** a chronic

cronista m & f reporter

cronol|ogía f chronology. **~ógico** a chronological

cron|ometraje m timing. **~ometrar** vt time. **~ómetro** m chronometer; (en deportes) stop-watch

croquet /'kroket/ m croquet

croqueta f croquette

cruce m crossing; (de calles, de carreteras) crossroads; (de peatones) (pedestrian) crossing

crucial a crucial

crucifi|car [7] vt crucify. **~jo** m crucifix. **~xión** f crucifiction

crucigrama m crossword (puzzle)

crudo a raw; (fig) crude. **petróleo** m **~** crude oil

cruel a cruel. **~dad** f cruelty

cruji|do m (de seda, de hojas secas etc) rustle; (de muebles etc) creak. **~r** vi ⟨seda, hojas secas etc⟩ rustle; ⟨muebles etc⟩ creak

cruz f cross; (de moneda) tails. **~ gamada** swastika. **la C~ Roja** the Red Cross

cruzada f crusade

cruzar [10] vt cross; (poner de un lado a otro) lay across. **~se** vpr cross; (pasar en la calle) pass

cuaderno m exercise book; (para apuntes) notebook

cuadra f (caballeriza) stable; (LAm, manzana) block

cuadrado a & m square

cuadragésimo a fortieth

cuadr|ar vt square. ● vi suit; (estar de acuerdo) agree. **~arse** vpr (mil) stand to attention; (fig) dig one's heels in. **~ilátero** a quadrilateral. ● m quadrilateral; (boxeo) ring

cuadrilla f group; (pandilla) gang

cuadro m square; (pintura) painting; (de obra de teatro, escena) scene; (de jardín) bed; (de números) table; (de mando etc) panel; (conjunto del personal) staff. **~ de distribución** switchboard. **a ~s, de ~s** check. **en ~** in a square. **¡qué ~!, ¡vaya un ~!** what a sight!

cuadrúpedo m quadruped

cuádruple a & m quadruple

cuajar vt thicken; clot ⟨sangre⟩; curdle ⟨leche⟩; (llenar) fill up. ● vi ⟨nieve⟩ settle; (fig, fam) work out. **cuajado de** full of. **~se** vpr coagulate; ⟨sangre⟩ clot; ⟨leche⟩ curdle. **~ón** m clot

cual pron. **el ~, la ~ etc** ⟨animales y cosas⟩ that, which; ⟨personas, sujeto⟩ who, that; ⟨personas, objeto⟩ whom. ● adv as, like. ● a such as. **~ si** as if. **~... tal** like... like. **cada ~** everyone. **por lo ~** because of which

cuál pron which

cualidad f quality; (propiedad) property

cualquiera a (delante de nombres cualquier, pl cualesquiera) any. ● pron (pl cualesquiera) anyone, anybody; (cosas) whatever, whichever. **un ~** a nobody

cuando adv when. ● conj when; (aunque) even if. **~ más** at the most.

~ menos at the least. **~ no** if not. **aun ~** even if. **de ~ en ~** from time to time

cuándo *adv & conj* when. **¿de ~ acá?, ¿desde~?** since when?

cuant|ía *f* quantity; (*extensión*) extent. **~ioso** *a* abundant

cuanto *a* as much... as, as many... as. ● *pron* as much as, as many as. ● *adv* as much as. **~ más, mejor** the more the merrier. **en ~** as soon as. **en ~ a** as for. **por ~** since. **unos ~s** a few, some

cuánto *a* (*interrogativo*) how much?; (*interrogativo en plural*) how many?; (*exclamativo*) what a lot of! ● *pron* how much?; (*en plural*) how many? ● *adv* how much. **¡~ tiempo?** how long? **¡~ tiempo sin verte!** it's been a long time! **¿a ~?** how much? **¿a ~s estamos?** what's the date today? **un Sr. no sé ~s** Mr So-and-So

cuáquero *m* Quaker

cuarent|a *a & m* forty; (*cuadragésimo*) fortieth. **~ena** *f* (about) forty; (*med*) quarantine. **~ón** *a* about forty

cuaresma *f* Lent

cuarta *f* (*palmo*) span

cuartear *vt* quarter, divide into four; (*zigzaguear*) zigzag. **~se** *vpr* crack

cuartel *m* (*mil*) barracks. **~ general** headquarters. **no dar ~** show no mercy

cuarteto *m* quartet

cuarto *a* fourth. ● *m* quarter; (*habitación*) room. **~ de baño** bathroom. **~ de estar** living room. **~ de hora** quarter of an hour. **estar sin un ~** be broke. **menos ~** (a) quarter to. **y ~** (a) quarter past

cuarzo *m* quartz

cuatro *a & m* four. **~cientos** *a & m* four hundred

Cuba *f* Cuba

cuba: ~libre *m* rum and Coke (P). **~no** *a & m* Cuban

cúbico *a* cubic

cubículo *m* cubicle

cubiert|a *f* cover, covering; (*de la cama*) bedspread; (*techo*) roof; (*neumático*) tyre; (*naut*) deck. **~o** *a* covered; (*cielo*) overcast. ● *m* place setting, cutlery; (*comida*) meal. **a ~o de** safe from

cubis|mo *m* cubism. **~ta** *a & m & f* cubist

cubil *m* den, lair. **~ete** *m* bowl; (*molde*) mould; (*para echar los dados*) cup

cubo *m* bucket; (*en geometría y matemáticas*) cube

cubrecama *m* bedspread

cubrir *vt* [*pp* **cubierto**] cover; (*sonido*) drown; fill (*vacante*). **~se** *vpr* cover o.s.; (*ponerse el sombrero*) put on one's hat; (*el cielo*) cloud over, become overcast

cucaracha *f* cockroach

cuclillas. en ~ *adv* squatting

cuclillo *m* cuckoo

cuco *a* shrewd; (*mono*) pretty, nice. ● *m* cuckoo; (*insecto*) grub

cucurucho *m* cornet

cuchar|a *f* spoon. **~ada** *f* spoonful. **~adita** *f* teaspoonful. **~illa** *f*, **~ita** *f* teaspoon. **~ón** *m* ladle

cuchiche|ar *vi* whisper. **~o** *m* whispering

cuchill|a *f* large knife; (*de carnicero*) cleaver; (*hoja de afeitar*) razor blade. **~ada** *f* slash; (*herida*) knife wound. **~o** *m* knife

cuchitril *m* pigsty; (*fig*) hovel

cuello *m* neck; (*de camisa*) collar. **cortar el ~ a uno** cut s.o.'s throat

cuenc|a *f* hollow; (*del ojo*) (eye) socket; (*geog*) basin. **~o** *m* hollow; (*vasija*) bowl

cuenta *f* count; (*acción de contar*) counting; (*factura*) bill; (*en banco, relato*) account; (*asunto*) affair; (*de collar etc*) bead. **~ corriente** current account, checking account (*Amer*). **ajustar las ~s** settle accounts. **caer en la ~ de que** realize that. **darse ~ de** realize. **en resumidas ~s** in short. **por mi ~** for myself. **tener en ~, tomar en ~** bear in mind

cuentakilómetros *m* *invar* milometer

cuent|ista *m & f* story-writer; (*de mentiras*) fibber. **~o** *m* story; (*mentira*) fib, tall story. ● *vb véase* **contar**

cuerda *f* rope; (*más fina*) string; (*mus*) string. **~ floja** tightrope. **dar ~ a** wind up (*un reloj*)

cuerdo *a* (*persona*) sane; (*acción*) sensible

cuern|a *f* horns. **~o** *m* horn

cuero *m* leather; (*piel*) skin; (*del grifo*) washer. **~ cabelludo** scalp. **en ~s (vivos)** stark naked

cuerpo *m* body

cuervo *m* crow

cuesta f slope, hill. ~ **abajo** downhill. ~ **arriba** uphill. **a** ~**s** on one's back

cuesti|ón f matter; (altercado) quarrel; (dificultad) trouble. ~**onario** m questionnaire

cueva f cave; (sótano) cellar

cuida|do m care; (preocupación) worry; (asunto) affair. **¡~do!** (be) careful! ~**doso** a careful. ~**dosamente** adv carefully. ~**r** vt look after. ● vi. ~**r de** look after. ~**rse** vpr look after o.s. ~**rse de** be careful to. **tener** ~**do** be careful

culata f (de arma de fuego) butt; (auto) cylinder head. ~**zo** m recoil

culebra f snake

culebrón m (LAm) soap opera

culinario a culinary

culmina|ción f culmination. ~**r** vi culminate

culo m (fam) bottom. **ir de** ~ go downhill

culpa f fault; (jurid) guilt. ~**bilidad** f guilt. ~**ble** a guilty. ● m culprit. ~**r** vt blame (**de** for). **echar la** ~ blame. **por** ~ **de** because of. **tener la** ~ **de** be to blame for

cultiv|ar vt farm; grow (plantas); (fig) cultivate. ~**o** m farming; (de plantas) growing

cult|o a (tierra etc) cultivated; (persona) educated. ● m cult; (homenaje) worship. ~**ura** f culture. ~**ural** a cultural

culturismo m body-building

cumbre f summit; (fig) height

cumpleaños m invar birthday

cumplido a perfect; (grande) large; (cortés) polite. ● m compliment. ~**r** a reliable. **de** ~ courtesy. **por** ~ out of politeness

cumplim|entar vt carry out; (saludar) pay a courtesy call to; (felicitar) congratulate. ~**iento** m carrying out, execution

cumplir vt carry out; observe (ley); serve (condena); reach (años); keep (promesa). ● vi do one's duty. ~**se** vpr expire; (realizarse) be fulfilled. **hoy cumple 3 años** he's 3 (years old) today. **por** ~ as a mere formality

cumulativo a cumulative

cúmulo m pile, heap

cuna f cradle; (fig, nacimiento) birthplace

cundir vi spread; (rendir) go a long way

cuneta f gutter

cuña f wedge

cuñad|a f sister-in-law. ~**o** m brother-in-law

cuño m stamp. **de nuevo** ~ new

cuota f quota; (de sociedad etc) subscription, fees

cupe vb véase **caber**

cupé m coupé

Cupido m Cupid

cupo m cuota

cupón m coupon

cúpula f dome

cura f cure; (tratamiento) treatment. ● m priest. ~**ble** a curable. ~**ción** f healing. ~**ndero** m faith-healer. ~**r** vt (incl culin) cure; dress (herida); (tratar) treat; (fig) remedy; tan (pieles). ● vi (persona) get better; (herida) heal; (fig) be cured. ~**rse** vpr get better

curios|ear vi pry; (mirar) browse. ~**idad** f curiosity; (limpieza) cleanliness. ~**o** a curious; (raro) odd, unusual; (limpio) clean

curriculum vitae m curriculum vitae

cursar vt send; (estudiar) study

cursi a pretentious, showy. ● m affected person

cursillo m short course

cursiva f italics

curso m course; (univ etc) year. **en** ~ under way; (año etc) current

curtir vt tan; (fig) harden. ~**se** vpr become tanned; (fig) become hardened

curv|a f curve; (de carretera) bend. ~**o** a curved

cúspide f peak

custodi|a f care, safe-keeping. ~**ar** vt take care of. ~**o** a & m guardian

cutáneo a skin. **enfermedad** f **cutánea** skin disease

cutícula f cuticle

cutis m skin, complexion

cuyo pron (de persona) whose, of whom; (de cosa) whose, of which. **en** ~ **caso** in which case

CH

chabacano a common; (chiste etc) vulgar. ● m (Mex, albaricoque) apricot

chabola f shack. ~**s** fpl shanty town

chacal m jackal

chacota f fun. **echar a** ~ make fun of

chacra f (*LAm*) farm

cháchara f chatter

chacharear vt (*Mex*) sell. ● vi chatter

chafar vt crush. **quedar chafado** be nonplussed

chal m shawl

chalado a (*fam*) crazy

chalé m house (with a garden), villa

chaleco m waistcoat, vest (*Amer*). ~ **salvavidas** life-jacket

chalequear vt (*Arg, Mex*) trick

chalet m (*pl* **chalets**) house (with a garden), villa

chalón m (*LAm*) shawl

chalote m shallot

chalupa f boat

chamac|a f (*esp Mex*) girl. ~**o** m (*esp Mex*) boy

chamagoso a (*Mex*) filthy

chamarr|a f sheepskin jacket. ~**o** m (*LAm*) coarse blanket

chamba f (*fam*) fluke; (*Mex, empleo*) job. **por** ~ by fluke

champán m, **champaña** f champagne

champiñón m mushroom

champú m (*pl* **champúes** o **champús**) shampoo

chamuscar [7] vt scorch; (*Mex, vender*) sell cheaply

chance m (*esp LAm*) chance

chanclo m clog; (*de caucho*) rubber overshoe

chancho m (*LAm*) pig

chanchullo m swindle, fiddle (*fam*)

chandal m tracksuit

chanquete m whitebait

chantaj|e m blackmail. ~**ista** m & f blackmailer

chanza f joke

chapa f plate, sheet; (*de madera*) plywood; (*de botella*) metal top. ~**do a la antigua** old-fashioned. ~**do de oro** gold-plated

chaparrón m downpour. **llover a chaparrones** pour (down), rain cats and dogs

chapotear vi splash

chapuce|ar vt botch; (*Mex, engañar*) deceive. ~**ro** a (*persona*) careless; (*cosas*) shoddy. ● m careless worker

chapurrar vt, **chapurrear** vt speak badly, speak a little; mix (*licores*)

chapuza f botched job, mess; (*de poca importancia*) odd job

chaqueta f jacket. **cambiar la** ~ change sides

chaquetero m turncoat

charada f charade

charc|a f pond, pool. ~**o** m puddle, pool. **cruzar el** ~**o** cross the water; (*ir a América*) cross the Atlantic

charla f chat; (*conferencia*) talk. ~**dor** a talkative. ~**r** vi (*fam*) chat

charlatán a talkative. ● m chatterbox; (*curandero*) charlatan

charol m varnish; (*cuero*) patent leather

chárter a charter

chascar [7] vt crack ⟨látigo⟩; click ⟨lengua⟩; snap ⟨dedos⟩. ● vi ⟨látigo⟩ crack; (*con la lengua*) click one's tongue; ⟨los dedos⟩ snap

chascarrillo m joke, funny story

chasco m disappointment; (*broma*) joke; (*engaño*) trick

chasis m (*auto*) chassis

chasqu|ear vt crack ⟨látigo⟩; click ⟨lengua⟩; snap ⟨dedos⟩. ● vi ⟨látigo⟩ crack; (*con la lengua*) click one's tongue; ⟨los dedos⟩ snap. ~**ido** m crack; (*de la lengua*) click; (*de los dedos*) snap

chatarra f scrap iron; (*fig*) scrap

chato a ⟨nariz⟩ snub; ⟨persona⟩ snub-nosed; ⟨objetos⟩ flat. ● m wine glass; (*niño, mujer, fam*) dear, darling; (*hombre, fam*) mate (*fam*)

chaval m (*fam*) boy, lad. ~**a** f girl, lass

che int (*Arg*) listen!, hey!

checo a & m Czech. **la república** f **Checa** the Czech Republic

checoslovaco a & m (*history*) Czechoslovak

Checoslovaquia f (*history*) Czechoslovakia

chelín m shilling

chelo a (*Mex, rubio*) fair

cheque m cheque. ~ **de viaje** traveller's cheque. ~**ra** f cheque-book

chica f girl; (*criada*) maid, servant

chicano a & m Chicano, Mexican-American

chicle m chewing-gum

chico a (*fam*) small. ● m boy. ~**s** mpl children

chicoleo m compliment

chicoria f chicory

chicharra f cicada; (*fig*) chatterbox

chicharrón m (*de cerdo*) crackling; (*fig*) sunburnt person

chichón m bump, lump

chifla|do a (*fam*) crazy, daft. ~**r** vt (*fam*) drive crazy. ~**rse** vpr be mad (**por** about). **le chifla el chocolate**

he's mad about chocolate. **le tiene chiflado esa chica** he's crazy about that girl

Chile m Chile

chile m chilli

chileno a & m Chilean

chill|ar vi scream, shriek; ⟨gato⟩ howl; ⟨ratón⟩ squeak; ⟨cerdo⟩ squeal. **~ido** m scream, screech; ⟨de gato etc⟩ howl. **~ón** a noisy; ⟨colores⟩ loud; ⟨sonido⟩ shrill

chimenea f chimney; ⟨hogar⟩ fireplace

chimpancé m chimpanzee

China f China

chinch|ar vt ⟨fam⟩ annoy, pester. **~e** m drawing-pin ⟨Brit⟩, thumbtack ⟨Amer⟩; ⟨insecto⟩ bedbug; ⟨fig⟩ nuisance. **~eta** f drawing-pin ⟨Brit⟩, thumbtack ⟨Amer⟩

chinela f slipper

chino a & m Chinese

Chipre m Cyprus

chipriota a & m & f Cypriot

chiquillo a childish. ● m child, kid ⟨fam⟩

chiquito a small, tiny. ● m child, kid ⟨fam⟩

chiribita f spark. **estar que echa ~s** be furious

chirimoya f custard apple

chiripa f fluke. **por ~** by fluke

chirivía f parsnip

chirri|ar vi creak; ⟨pájaro⟩ chirp. **~do** m creaking; ⟨al freir⟩ sizzling; ⟨de pájaros⟩ chirping

chis int sh!, hush!; ⟨para llamar a uno, fam⟩ hey!, psst!

chism|e m gadget, thingumajig ⟨fam⟩; ⟨chismorreo⟩ piece of gossip. **~es** mpl things, bits and pieces. **~orreo** m gossip. **~oso** a gossipy. ● m gossip

chispa f spark; ⟨gota⟩ drop; ⟨gracia⟩ wit; ⟨fig⟩ sparkle. **estar que echa ~(s)** be furious

chispe|ante a sparkling. **~r** vi spark; ⟨lloviznar⟩ drizzle; ⟨fig⟩ sparkle

chisporrotear vt throw out sparks; ⟨fuego⟩ crackle; ⟨aceite⟩ sizzle

chistar vi speak. **sin ~** without saying a word

chiste m joke, funny story. **hacer ~ de** make fun of. **tener ~** be funny

chistera f ⟨fam⟩ top hat, topper ⟨fam⟩

chistoso a funny

chiva|r vi inform ⟨policía⟩; ⟨niño⟩ tell. **~tazo** m tip-off. **~to** m informer; ⟨niño⟩ telltale

chivo m kid, young goat

choca|nte a surprising; ⟨persona⟩ odd. **~r** [7] vt clink ⟨vasos⟩; shake ⟨la mano⟩. ● vi collide, hit. **~r con**, **~r contra** crash into. **lo ~nte es que** the surprising thing is that

chocolate m chocolate. **tableta** f **de ~** bar of chocolate

choch|ear vi be senile. **~o** a senile; ⟨fig⟩ soft

chófer m chauffeur; ⟨conductor⟩ driver

cholo a & m ⟨LAm⟩ half-breed

chopo m poplar

choque m collision; ⟨fig⟩ clash; ⟨eléctrico⟩ shock; ⟨auto, rail etc⟩ crash, accident; ⟨sacudida⟩ jolt

chorizo m salami

chorr|ear vi gush forth; ⟨fig⟩ be dripping. **~o** m jet, stream; ⟨caudal pequeño⟩ trickle; ⟨fig⟩ stream. **a ~os** ⟨fig⟩ in abundance. **hablar a ~os** jabber

chovinis|mo m chauvinism. **~ta** a chauvinistic. ● m & f chauvinist

choza f hut

chubas|co m squall, heavy shower; ⟨fig⟩ bad patch. **~quero** m raincoat, anorak

chuchería f trinket; ⟨culin⟩ sweet

chufa f tiger nut

chuleta f chop

chulo a insolent; ⟨vistoso⟩ showy. ● m ruffian; ⟨rufián⟩ pimp

chumbo m prickly pear; ⟨fam⟩ bump. **higo** m **~** prickly pear

chup|ada f suck; ⟨al cigarro etc⟩ puff. **~ado** a skinny; ⟨fácil, fam⟩ very easy. **~ar** vt suck, lick; puff at ⟨cigarro etc⟩; ⟨absorber⟩ absorb. **~arse** vpr lose weight. **~ete** m dummy ⟨Brit⟩, pacifier ⟨Amer⟩

churro m fritter; ⟨fam⟩ mess. **me salió un ~** I made a mess of it

chusco a funny

chusma f riff-raff

chutar vi shoot. **¡va que chuta!** it's going well!

D

dactilógrafo m typist

dado m dice. ● a given; ⟨hora⟩ gone. **~ que** since, given that

dalia f dahlia

daltoniano a colour-blind

dama *f* lady; *(en la corte)* lady-in-waiting. **~s** *fpl* draughts *(Brit)*, checkers *(Amer)*

damasco *m* damask

danés *a* Danish. ● *m* Dane; *(idioma)* Danish

danza *f* dance; *(acción)* dancing; *(enredo)* affair. **~r** [10] *vt/i* dance

dañ|ado *a* damaged. **~ar** *vt* damage; harm *(persona)*. **~ino** *a* harmful. **~o** *m* damage; *(a una persona)* harm. **~oso** *a* harmful. **~os y perjuicios** damages. **hacer ~o a** harm; hurt *(persona)*. **hacerse ~o** hurt o.s.

dar [26] *vt* give; *(producir)* yield; strike *(la hora)*. ● *vi* give. **da igual** it doesn't matter. **¡dale!** go on! **da lo mismo** it doesn't matter. **~ a** *(ventana)* look on to; *(edificio)* face. **~ a luz** give birth. **~ con** meet *(persona)*; find *(cosa)*; **~ de cabeza** fall flat on one's face. **~ por** assume; (*+ infinitivo*) decide. **~se** *vpr* give o.s. up; *(suceder)* happen. **dárselas de** make o.s. out to be. **~se por** consider o.s. **¿qué más da?** it doesn't matter!

dardo *m* dart

dársena *f* dock

datar *vt* date. ● *vi*. **~ de** date from

dátil *m* date

dato *m* fact. **~s** *mpl* data, information

de *prep* of; *(procedencia)* from; *(suposición)* if. **~ día** by day. **~ dos en dos** two by two. **~ haberlo sabido** if I (you, he etc) had known. **~ niño** as a child. **el libro ~ mi amigo** my friend's book. **las 2 ~ la madrugada** 2 (o'clock) in the morning. **un puente ~ hierro** an iron bridge. **soy ~ Loughborough** I'm from Loughborough

deambular *vi* stroll

debajo *adv* underneath. **~ de** underneath, under. **el de ~** the one underneath. **por ~** underneath. **por ~ de** below

debat|e *m* debate. **~ir** *vt* debate

deber *vt* owe. ● *vi* have to, must. ● *m* duty. **~es** *mpl* homework. **~se** *vpr*. **~se a** be due to. **debo marcharme** I must go, I have to go

debido *a* due; *(correcto)* proper. **~ a** due to. **como es ~** as is proper. **con el respeto ~** with due respect

débil *a* weak; *(ruido)* faint; *(luz)* dim

debili|dad *f* weakness. **~tar** *vt* weaken. **~tarse** *vpr* weaken, get weak

débito *m* debit; *(deuda)* debt

debutar *vi* make one's debut

década *f* decade

deca|dencia *f* decline. **~dente** *a* decadent. **~er** [29] *vi* decline; *(debilitarse)* weaken. **~ído** *a* depressed. **~imiento** *m* decline, weakening

decano *m* dean; *(miembro más antiguo)* senior member

decantar *vt* decant *(vino etc)*

decapitar *vt* behead

decena *f* ten; *(aproximadamente)* about ten

decencia *f* decency, honesty

decenio *m* decade

decente *a* *(persona)* respectable, honest; *(cosas)* modest; *(limpio)* clean, tidy

decepci|ón *f* disappointment. **~onar** *vt* disappoint

decibelio *m* decibel

decidi|do *a* decided; *(persona)* determined, resolute. **~r** *vt* decide; settle *(cuestión etc)*. ● *vi* decide. **~rse** *vpr* make up one's mind

decimal *a & m* decimal

décimo *a & m* tenth. ● *m* *(de lotería)* tenth part of a lottery ticket

decimo: ~ctavo *a & m* eighteenth. **~cuarto** *a & m* fourteenth. **~nono** *a & m*, **~noveno** *a & m* nineteenth. **~quinto** *a & m* fifteenth. **~séptimo** *a & m* seventeenth. **~sexto** *a & m* sixteenth. **~tercero** *a & m*, **~tercio** *a & m* thirteenth

decir [46] *vt* say; *(contar)* tell. ● *m* saying. **~se** *vpr* be said. **~ que no** say no. **~ que sí** say yes. **dicho de otro modo** in other words. **dicho y hecho** no sooner said than done. **¿dígame?** can I help you? **¡dígame!** *(al teléfono)* hello! **digamos** let's say. **es ~** that is to say. **mejor dicho** rather. **¡no me digas!** you don't say!, really! **por así ~, por ~lo así** so to speak, as it were. **querer ~** mean. **se dice que** it is said that, they say that

decisi|ón *f* decision. **~vo** *a* decisive

declamar *vt* declaim

declara|ción *f* statement. **~ción de renta** income tax return. **~r** *vt/i* declare. **~rse** *vpr* declare o.s.; *(epidemia etc)* break out

declina|ción *f* *(gram)* declension. **~r** *vt/i* decline; *(salud)* deteriorate

declive *m* slope; (*fig*) decline. **en ~** sloping

decolorar *vt* discolour, fade. **~se** *vpr* become discoloured, fade

decora|ción *f* decoration. **~do** *m* (*en el teatro*) set. **~dor** *m* decorator. **~r** *vt* decorate. **~tivo** *a* decorative

decoro *m* decorum; (*respeto*) respect. **~so** *a* proper; (*modesto*) modest; ⟨*profesión*⟩ honourable

decrecer [11] *vi* decrease, diminish; ⟨*aguas*⟩ subside

decrépito *a* decrepit

decret|ar *vt* decree. **~o** *m* decree

dedal *m* thimble

dedica|ción *f* dedication. **~r** [7] *vt* dedicate; devote ⟨*tiempo*⟩. **~toria** *f* dedication, inscription

ded|il *m* finger-stall. **~illo** *m*. **al ~illo** at one's fingertips. **~o** *m* finger; (*del pie*) toe. **~o anular** ring finger. **~ corazón** middle finger. **~o gordo** thumb. **~o índice** index finger. **~o meñique** little finger. **~o pulgar** thumb

deduc|ción *f* deduction. **~ir** [47] *vt* deduce; (*descontar*) deduct

defect|o *m* fault, defect. **~uoso** *a* defective

defen|der [1] *vt* defend. **~sa** *f* defence. **~sivo** *a* defensive. **~sor** *m* defender. **abogado** *m* **~sor** defence counsel

deferen|cia *f* deference. **~te** *a* deferential

deficien|cia *f* deficiency. **~cia mental** mental handicap. **~te** *a* deficient; (*imperfecto*) defective. **~te mental** mentally handicapped

déficit *m invar* deficit

defini|ción *f* definition. **~do** *a* defined. **~r** *vt* define; (*aclarar*) clarify. **~tivo** *a* definitive. **en ~tiva** (*en resumen*) in short

deflación *f* deflation

deform|ación *f* deformation; (*TV etc*) distortion. **~ar** *vt* deform; (*TV etc*) distort. **~arse** *vpr* go out of shape. **~e** *a* deformed; (*feo*) ugly

defraudar *vt* cheat; (*decepcionar*) disappoint; evade ⟨*impuestos etc*⟩

defunción *f* death

degenera|ción *f* degeneration; (*moral*) degeneracy. **~do** *a* degenerate. **~r** *vi* degenerate

deglutir *vt/i* swallow

degollar [16] *vt* cut s.o.'s throat; (*fig, arruinar*) ruin

degradar *vt* degrade. **~se** *vpr* lower o.s.

degusta|ción *f* tasting. **~r** *vt* taste

dehesa *f* pasture

dei|dad *f* deity. **~ficar** [7] *vt* deify

deja|ción *f* surrender. **~dez** *f* abandon; (*pereza*) laziness. **~do** *a* negligent. **~r** *vt* leave; (*abandonar*) abandon; (*prestar*) lend; (*permitir*) let. **~r aparte**, **~r a un lado** leave aside. **~r de** stop. **no ~r de** not fail to

dejo *m* aftertaste; (*tonillo*) accent

del = **de** ¦ **el**

delantal *m* apron

delante *adv* in front; (*enfrente*) opposite. **~ de** in front of. **de ~** front

delanter|a *f* front; (*de teatro etc*) front row; (*ventaja*) advantage. **coger la ~a** get ahead. **~o** *a* front. ● *m* forward. **llevar la ~a** be ahead

delat|ar *vt* denounce. **~or** *m* informer

delega|ción *f* delegation; (*sucursal*) branch. **~do** *m* delegate; (*com*) agent, representative. **~r** [12] *vt* delegate

deleit|ar *vt* delight. **~e** *m* delight

deletéreo *a* deleterious

deletre|ar *vt* spell (out). **~o** *m* spelling

deleznable *a* brittle, crumbly; ⟨*argumento etc*⟩ weak

delfín *m* dolphin

delgad|ez *f* thinness. **~o** *a* thin; (*esbelto*) slim. **~ucho** *a* skinny

delibera|ción *f* deliberation. **~r** *vt* discuss, decide. ● *vi* deliberate

delicad|eza *f* delicacy; (*fragilidad*) frailty; (*tacto*) tact. **~o** *a* delicate; (*sensible*) sensitive; (*discreto*) tactful, discreet. **falta de ~eza** tactlessness

delici|a *f* delight. **~oso** *a* delightful; ⟨*sabor etc*⟩ delicious; (*gracioso, fam*) funny

delimitar *vt* delimit

delincuen|cia *f* delinquency. **~te** *a* & *m* delinquent

delinea|nte *m* draughtsman. **~r** *vt* outline; (*dibujar*) draw

delinquir [8] *vi* commit an offence

delir|ante *a* delirious. **~ar** *vi* be delirious; (*fig*) talk nonsense. **~io** *m* delirium; (*fig*) frenzy

delito *m* crime, offence

delta *f* delta

demacrado *a* emaciated

demagogo *m* demagogue

demanda *f.* **en ~ de** asking for; (*en busca de*) in search of. **~nte** *m & f* (*jurid*) plaintiff. **~r** *vt* (*jurid*) bring an action against

demarca|ción *f* demarcation. **~r** [7] *vt* demarcate

demás *a* rest of the, other. ● *pron* rest, others. **lo ~** the rest. **por ~** useless; (*muy*) very. **por lo ~** otherwise

demasía *f* excess; (*abuso*) outrage; (*atrevimiento*) insolence. **en ~** too much

demasiado *a* too much; (*en plural*) too many. ● *adv* too much; (*con adjetivo*) too

demen|cia *f* madness. **~te** *a* demented, mad

dem|ocracia *f* democracy. **~ócrata** *m & f* democrat. **~ocrático** *a* democratic

demol|er [2] *vt* demolish. **~ición** *f* demolition

demonio *m* devil, demon. **¡~s!** hell! **¿cómo ~s?** how the hell? **¡qué ~s!** what the hell!

demora *f* delay. **~r** *vt* delay. ● *vi* stay on. **~rse** *vpr* be a long time

demostra|ción *f* demonstration, show. **~r** [2] *vt* demonstrate; (*mostrar*) show; (*probar*) prove. **~tivo** *a* demonstrative

denegar [1 & 12] *vt* refuse

deng|oso *a* affected, finicky. **~ue** *m* affectation

denigrar *vt* denigrate

denomina|ción *f* denomination. **~do** *a* called. **~dor** *m* denominator. **~r** *vt* name

denotar *vt* denote

dens|idad *f* density. **~o** *a* dense, thick

denta|dura *f* teeth. **~dura postiza** denture, false teeth. **~l** *a* dental

dentera *f.* **dar ~ a uno** set s.o.'s teeth on edge; (*dar envidia*) make s.o. green with envy

dentífrico *m* toothpaste

dentista *m & f* dentist

dentro *adv* inside; (*de un edificio*) indoors. **~ de** in. **~ de poco** soon. **por ~** inside

denuncia *f* report; (*acusación*) accusation. **~r** *vt* report (a crime); ⟨*periódico etc*⟩ denounce; (*indicar*) indicate

departamento *m* department; (*Arg, piso*) flat (*Brit*), apartment (*Amer*)

dependencia *f* dependence; (*sección*) section; (*sucursal*) branch

depender *vi* depend (**de** on)

dependient|a *f* shop assistant. **~e** *a* dependent (**de** on). ● *m* employee; (*de oficina*) clerk; (*de tienda*) shop assistant

depila|ción *f* depilation. **~r** *vt* depilate. **~torio** *a* depilatory

deplora|ble *a* deplorable. **~r** *vt* deplore, regret

deponer [34] *vt* remove from office. ● *vi* give evidence

deporta|ción *f* deportation. **~r** *vt* deport

deport|e *m* sport. **~ista** *m* sportsman. ● *f* sportswoman. **~ivo** *a* sports. ● *m* sports car. **hacer ~e** take part in sports

deposición *f* deposition; (*de un empleo*) removal from office

dep|ositador *m* depositor. **~ositante** *m & f* depositor. **~ositar** *vt* deposit; (*poner*) put, place. **~ósito** *m* deposit; (*conjunto de cosas*) store; (*almacén*) warehouse; (*mil*) depot; (*de líquidos*) tank

deprava|ción *f* depravity. **~do** *a* depraved. **~r** *vt* deprave. **~rse** *vpr* become depraved

deprecia|ción *f* depreciation. **~r** *vt* depreciate. **~rse** *vpr* depreciate

depresión *f* depression

deprim|ente *a* depressing. **~ido** *a* depressed. **~ir** *vt* depress. **~irse** *vpr* get depressed

depura|ción *f* purification; (*pol*) purging. **~r** *vt* purify; (*pol*) purge

derech|a *f* (*mano*) right hand; (*lado*) right. **~ista** *a* right-wing. ● *m & f* right-winger. **~o** *a* right; (*vertical*) upright; (*recto*) straight. ● *adv* straight. ● *m* right; (*ley*) law; (*lado*) right side. **~os** *mpl* dues. **~os de autor** royalties. **a la ~a** on the right; (*hacia el lado derecho*) to the right. **todo ~o** straight on

deriva *f* drift. **a la ~** drifting, adrift

deriva|ción *f* derivation; (*cambio*) diversion. **~do** *a* derived. ● *m* derivative, by-product. **~r** *vt* derive; (*cambiar la dirección de*) divert. ● *vi.* **~r de** derive from, be derived from. **~rse** *vpr* be derived

derram|amiento *m* spilling. **~amiento de sangre** bloodshed. **~ar** *vt* spill; (*verter*) pour; shed ⟨*lágrimas*⟩. **~arse** *vpr* spill. **~e** *m* spilling; (*pérdida*) leakage; (*cantidad perdida*) spillage; (*med*) discharge; (*med, de sangre*) haemorrhage

derretir [5] vt melt. ~**se** vpr melt; (*enamorarse*) fall in love (**por** with)

derriba|do a fallen down. ~**r** vt knock down; bring down, overthrow ⟨*gobierno etc*⟩. ~**rse** vpr fall down

derrocar [7] vt bring down, overthrow ⟨*gobierno etc*⟩

derroch|ar vt squander. ~**e** m waste

derrot|a f defeat; (*rumbo*) course. ~**ar** vt defeat. ~**ado** a defeated; ⟨*vestido*⟩ shabby. ~**ero** m course

derrumba|miento m collapse. ~**r** vt (*derribar*) knock down. ~**rse** vpr collapse

desaborido a tasteless; ⟨*persona*⟩ dull

desabotonar vt unbutton, undo. ● vi bloom. ~**se** vpr come undone

desabrido a tasteless; ⟨*tiempo*⟩ unpleasant; ⟨*persona*⟩ surly

desabrochar vt undo. ~**se** vpr come undone

desacat|ar vt have no respect for. ~**o** m disrespect

desac|ertado a ill-advised; (*erróneo*) wrong. ~**ertar** [1] vt be wrong. ~**ierto** m mistake

desaconseja|ble a inadvisable. ~**do** a unwise, ill-advised. ~**r** vt advise against, dissuade

desacorde a discordant

desacostumbra|do a unusual. ~**r** vt give up

desacreditar vt discredit

desactivar vt defuse

desacuerdo m disagreement

desafiar [20] vt challenge; (*afrontar*) defy

desafilado a blunt

desafina|do a out of tune. ~**r** vi be out of tune. ~**rse** vpr go out of tune

desafío m challenge; (*combate*) duel

desaforado a ⟨*comportamiento*⟩ outrageous; (*desmedido*) excessive; ⟨*sonido*⟩ loud; (*enorme*) huge

desafortunad|amente adv unfortunately. ~**o** a unfortunate

desagrada|ble a unpleasant. ~**r** vt displease. ● vi be unpleasant. **me ~ el sabor** I don't like the taste

desagradecido a ungrateful

desagrado m displeasure. **con ~** unwillingly

desagravi|ar vt make amends to. ~**o** m amends; (*expiación*) atonement

desagregar [12] vt break up. ~**se** vpr disintegrate

desagüe m drain; (*acción*) drainage. **tubo** m **de ~** drain-pipe

desaguisado a illegal. ● m offence; (*fam*) disaster

desahog|ado a roomy; (*adinerado*) well-off; (*fig, descarado, fam*) impudent. ~**ar** [12] vt relieve; vent (*ira*). ~**arse** vpr (*desfogarse*) let off steam. ~**o** m comfort; (*alivio*) relief

desahuci|ar vt deprive of hope; give up hope for ⟨*enfermo*⟩; evict ⟨*inquilino*⟩. ~**o** m eviction

desair|ado a humiliating; ⟨*persona*⟩ humiliated, spurned. ~**ar** vt snub ⟨*persona*⟩; disregard ⟨*cosa*⟩. ~**e** m rebuff

desajuste m maladjustment; (*avería*) breakdown

desal|entador a disheartening. ~**entar** [1] vt (*fig*) discourage. ~**iento** m discouragement

desaliño m untidiness, scruffiness

desalmado a wicked

desalojar vt eject ⟨*persona*⟩; evacuate ⟨*sitio*⟩. ● vi move (house)

desampar|ado a helpless; (*abandonado*) abandoned. ~**ar** vt abandon. ~**o** m helplessness; (*abandono*) abandonment

desangelado a insipid, dull

desangrar vt bleed. ~**se** vpr bleed

desanima|do a down-hearted. ~**r** vt discourage. ~**rse** vpr lose heart

desánimo m discouragement

desanudar vt untie

desapacible a unpleasant; ⟨*sonido*⟩ harsh

desapar|ecer [11] vi disappear; (*efecto*) wear off. ~**ecido** a disappeared. ● m missing person. ~**ecidos** mpl missing. ~**ición** f disappearance

desapasionado a dispassionate

desapego m indifference

desapercebido a unnoticed

desaplicado a lazy

desaprensi|ón f unscrupulousness. ~**vo** a unscrupulous

desaproba|ción f disapproval. ~**r** [2] vt disapprove of; (*rechazar*) reject.

desaprovecha|do a wasted; ⟨*alumno*⟩ lazy. ~**r** vt waste

desarm|ar vt disarm; (*desmontar*) take to pieces. ~**e** m disarmament

desarraig|ado a rootless. ~**ar** [12] vt uproot; (*fig, erradicar*) wipe out. ~**o** m uprooting; (*fig*) eradication

desarregl|ado *a* untidy; (*desordenado*) disorderly. **~ar** *vt* mess up; (*deshacer el orden*) make untidy. **~o** *m* disorder; (*de persona*) untidiness

desarroll|ado *a* (well-) developed. **~ar** *vt* develop; (*desenrollar*) unroll, unfold. **~arse** *vpr* (*incl foto*) develop; (*desenrollarse*) unroll; ‹*suceso*› take place. **~o** *m* development

desarrugar [12] *vt* smooth out

desarticular *vt* dislocate ‹*hueso*›; (*fig*) break up

desaseado *a* dirty; (*desordenado*) untidy

desasirse [45] *vpr* let go (**de** of)

desasos|egar [1 & 12] *vt* disturb. **~egarse** *vpr* get uneasy. **~iego** *m* anxiety; (*intranquilidad*) restlessness

desastr|ado *a* scruffy. **~e** *m* disaster. **~oso** *a* disastrous

desata|do *a* untied; (*fig*) wild. **~r** *vt* untie; (*fig, soltar*) unleash. **~rse** *vpr* come undone

desatascar [7] *vt* pull out of the mud; unblock ‹*tubo etc*›

desaten|ción *f* inattention; (*descortesía*) discourtesy. **~der** [1] *vt* not pay attention to; neglect ‹*deber etc*›. **~to** *a* inattentive; (*descortés*) discourteous

desatin|ado *a* silly. **~o** *m* silliness; (*error*) mistake

desatornillar *vt* unscrew

desatracar [7] *vt/i* cast off

desautorizar [10] *vt* declare unauthorized; (*desmentir*) deny

desavenencia *f* disagreement

desayun|ar *vt* have for breakfast. **●** *vi* have breakfast. **~o** *m* breakfast

desazón *m* (*fig*) anxiety

desbandarse *vpr* (*mil*) disband; (*dispersarse*) disperse

desbarajust|ar *vt* throw into confusion. **~e** *m* confusion

desbaratar *vt* spoil

desbloquear *vt* unfreeze

desbocado *a* ‹*vasija etc*› chipped; ‹*caballo*› runaway; ‹*persona*› foul-mouthed

desborda|nte *a* overflowing. **~r** *vt* go beyond; (*exceder*) exceed. **●** *vi* overflow. **~rse** *vpr* overflow

descabalgar [12] *vi* dismount

descabellado *a* crazy

descabezar [10] *vt* behead

descafeinado *a* decaffeinated. **●** *m* decaffeinated coffee

descalabr|ar *vt* injure in the head; (*fig*) damage. **~o** *m* disaster

descalificar [7] *vt* disqualify; (*desacreditar*) discredit

descalz|ar [10] *vt* take off ‹*zapato*›. **~o** *a* barefoot

descaminar *vt* misdirect; (*fig*) lead astray

descamisado *a* shirtless; (*fig*) shabby

descampado *a* open. **●** *m* open ground

descans|ado *a* rested; ‹*trabajo*› easy. **~apiés** *m* footrest. **~ar** *vt/i* rest. **~illo** *m* landing. **~o** *m* rest; (*descansillo*) landing; (*en deportes*) half-time; (*en el teatro etc*) interval

descapotable *a* convertible

descarado *a* insolent, cheeky; (*sin vergüenza*) shameless

descarg|a *f* unloading; (*mil, elec*) discharge. **~ar** [12] *vt* unload; (*mil, elec*) discharge, shock; deal ‹*golpe etc*›. **●** *vi* flow into. **~o** *m* unloading; (*recibo*) receipt; (*jurid*) evidence

descarnado *a* scrawny, lean; (*fig*) bare

descaro *m* insolence, cheek; (*cinismo*) nerve, effrontery

descarriar [20] *vt* misdirect; (*fig*) lead astray. **~se** *vpr* go the wrong way; ‹*res*› stray; (*fig*) go astray

descarrila|miento *m* derailment. **~r** *vi* be derailed. **~se** *vpr* be derailed

descartar *vt* discard; (*rechazar*) reject. **~se** *vpr* discard

descascarar *vt* shell

descen|dencia *f* descent; (*personas*) descendants. **~dente** *a* descending. **~der** [1] *vt* lower, get down; go down ‹*escalera etc*›. **●** *vi* go down; (*provenir*) be descended (**de** from). **~diente** *m* & *f* descendent. **~so** *m* descent; (*de temperatura, fiebre etc*) fall, drop

descentralizar [10] *vt* decentralize

descifrar *vt* decipher; decode ‹*clave*›

descolgar [2 & 12] *vt* take down; pick up ‹*el teléfono*›. **~se** *vpr* let o.s. down; (*fig, fam*) turn up

descolorar *vt* discolour, fade

descolori|do *a* discoloured, faded; ‹*persona*› pale. **~r** *vt* discolour, fade

descomedido *a* rude; (*excesivo*) excessive, extreme

descomp|ás *m* disproportion. **~as-ado** *a* disproportionate

descomp|oner [34] *vt* break down; decompose ‹*substancia*›; distort ‹*rasgos*›; (*estropear*) break; (*desarreglar*) disturb, spoil. **~onerse** *vpr* decompose; ‹*persona*› lose one's temper. **~osición** *f* decomposition; (*med*) diarrhoea. **~ostura** *f* breaking; (*de un motor*) breakdown; (*desorden*) disorder. **~uesto** *a* broken; (*podrido*) decomposed; (*encolerizado*) angry. **estar ~uesto** have diarrhoea

descomunal *a* (*fam*) enormous

desconc|ertante *a* disconcerting. **~ertar** [1] *vt* disconcert; (*dejar perplejo*) puzzle. **~ertarse** *vpr* be put out, be disconcerted; ‹*mecanismo*› break down. **~ierto** *m* confusion

desconectar *vt* disconnect

desconfia|do *a* distrustful. **~nza** *f* distrust, suspicion. **~r** [20] *vi*. **~r de** not trust; (*no creer*) doubt

descongelar *vt* defrost; (*com*) unfreeze

desconoc|er [11] *vt* not know, not recognize. **~ido** *a* unknown; (*cambiado*) unrecognizable. ● *m* stranger. **~imiento** *m* ignorance

desconsidera|ción *f* lack of consideration. **~do** *a* inconsiderate

descons|olado *a* distressed. **~olar** [2] *vt* distress. **~olarse** *vpr* despair. **~uelo** *m* distress; (*tristeza*) sadness

desconta|do *a*. **dar por ~do** take for granted. **por ~do** of course. **~r** [2] *vt* discount

descontent|adizo *a* hard to please. **~ar** *vt* displease. **~o** *a* unhappy (**de** about), discontented (**de** with). ● *m* discontent

descontrolado *a* uncontrolled

descorazonar *vt* discourage. **~se** *vpr* lose heart

descorchar *vt* uncork

descorrer *vt* draw ‹*cortina*›. **~ el cerrojo** unbolt the door

descort|és *a* rude, discourteous. **~esía** *f* rudeness

descos|er *vt* unpick. **~erse** *vpr* come undone. **~ido** *a* unstitched; (*fig*) disjointed. **como un ~ido** a lot

descoyuntar *vt* dislocate

descrédito *m* disrepute. **ir en ~ de** damage the reputation of

descreído *a* unbelieving

descremar *vt* skim

descri|bir [*pp* **descrito**] *vt* describe. **~pción** *f* description. **~ptivo** *a* descriptive

descuartizar [10] *vt* cut up

descubierto *a* discovered; (*no cubierto*) uncovered; (*expuesto*) exposed; ‹*cielo*› clear; (*sin sombrero*) bareheaded. ● *m* overdraft; (*déficit*) deficit. **poner al ~** expose

descubri|miento *m* discovery. **~r** [*pp* **descubierto**] *vt* discover; (*quitar lo que cubre*) uncover; (*revelar*) reveal; unveil ‹*estatua*›. **~rse** *vpr* be discovered; ‹*cielo*› clear; (*quitarse el sombrero*) take off one's hat

descuento *m* discount

descuid|ado *a* careless; ‹*aspecto etc*› untidy; (*desprevenido*) unprepared. **~ar** *vt* neglect. ● *vi* not worry. **~arse** *vpr* be careless; (*no preocuparse*) not worry. **¡~a!** don't worry! **~o** *m* carelessness; (*negligencia*) negligence. **al ~o** nonchalantly. **estar ~ado** not worry, rest assured

desde *prep* (*lugar etc*) from; (*tiempo*) since, from. **~ hace poco** for a short time. **~ hace un mes** for a month. **~ luego** of course. **~ Madrid hasta Barcelona** from Madrid to Barcelona. **~ niño** since childhood

desdecir [46, *pero imperativo* **desdice**, *futuro y condicional regulares*] *vi*. **~ de** be unworthy of; (*no armonizar*) not match. **~se** *vpr*. **~ de** take back ‹*palabras etc*›; go back on ‹*promesa*›

desd|én *m* scorn. **~eñable** *a* contemptible. **~eñar** *vt* scorn. **~eñoso** *a* scornful

desdicha *f* misfortune. **~do** *a* unfortunate. **por ~** unfortunately

desdoblar *vt* straighten; (*desplegar*) unfold

desea|ble *a* desirable. **~r** *vt* want; wish ‹*algo a uno*›. **de ~r** desirable. **le deseo un buen viaje** I hope you have a good journey. **¿qué desea Vd?** can I help you?

desecar [7] *vt* dry up

desech|ar *vt* throw out. **~o** *m* rubbish

desembalar *vt* unpack

desembarazar [10] *vt* clear. **~se** *vpr* free o.s.

desembarca|dero *m* landing stage. **~r** [7] *vt* unload. ● *vi* disembark

desemboca|dura *f* (*de río*) mouth; (*de calle*) opening. **~r** [7] *vi*. **~r en**

⟨*río*⟩ flow into; ⟨*calle*⟩ join; (*fig*) lead to, end in

desembols|ar *vt* pay. **~o** *m* payment

desembragar [12] *vi* declutch

desembrollar *vt* unravel

desembuchar *vi* tell, reveal a secret

desemejan|te *a* unlike, dissimilar. **~za** *f* dissimilarity

desempapelar *vt* unwrap

desempaquetar *vt* unpack, unwrap

desempat|ar *vi* break a tie. **~e** *m* tie-breaker

desempeñ|ar *vt* redeem; play ⟨*papel*⟩; hold ⟨*cargo*⟩; perform, carry out ⟨*deber etc*⟩. **~arse** *vpr* get out of debt. **~o** *m* redemption; (*de un papel, de un cargo*) performance

desemple|ado *a* unemployed. ● *m* unemployed person. **~o** *m* unemployment. **los ~ados** *mpl* the unemployed

desempolvar *vt* dust; (*fig*) unearth

desencadenar *vt* unchain; (*fig*) unleash. **~se** *vpr* break loose; ⟨*guerra etc*⟩ break out

desencajar *vt* dislocate; (*desconectar*) disconnect. **~se** *vpr* become distorted

desencant|ar *vt* disillusion. **~o** *m* disillusionment

desenchufar *vt* unplug

desenfad|ado *a* uninhibited. **~ar** *vt* calm down. **~arse** *vpr* calm down. **~o** *m* openness; (*desenvoltura*) assurance

desenfocado *a* out of focus

desenfren|ado *a* unrestrained. **~arse** *vpr* rage. **~o** *m* licentiousness

desenganchar *vt* unhook

desengañ|ar *vt* disillusion. **~arse** *vpr* be disillusioned; (*darse cuenta*) realize. **~o** *m* disillusionment, disappointment

desengrasar *vt* remove the grease from. ● *vi* lose weight

desenla|ce *m* outcome. **~zar** [10] *vt* undo; solve ⟨*problema*⟩

desenmarañar *vt* unravel

desenmascarar *vt* unmask

desenojar *vt* calm down. **~se** *vpr* calm down

desenred|ar *vt* unravel. **~arse** *vpr* extricate o.s. **~o** *m* denoument

desenrollar *vt* unroll, unwind

desenroscar [7] *vt* unscrew

desentenderse [1] *vpr* want nothing to do with; (*afectar ignorancia*) pretend not to know. **hacerse el desentendido** (*fingir no oir*) pretend not to hear

desenterrar [1] *vt* exhume; (*fig*) unearth

desenton|ar *vi* be out of tune; ⟨*colores*⟩ clash. **~o** *m* rudeness

desentrañar *vt* work out

desenvoltura *f* ease; (*falta de timidez*) confidence; (*descaro*) insolence

desenvolver [2, *pp* **desenvuelto**] *vt* unwrap; expound ⟨*idea etc*⟩. **~se** *vpr* act with confidence

deseo *m* wish, desire. **~so** *a* desirous. **ardér en ~s de** long for. **buen ~** good intentions. **estar ~so de** be eager to

desequilibr|ado *a* unbalanced. **~io** *m* imbalance

des|erción *f* desertion; (*pol*) defection. **~ertar** *vt* desert. **~értico** *a* desert-like. **~ertor** *m* deserter

desespera|ción *f* despair. **~do** *a* desperate. **~nte** *a* infuriating. **~r** *vt* drive to despair. ● *vi* despair (**de** of). **~rse** *vpr* despair

desestimar *vt* (*rechazar*) reject

desfachat|ado *a* brazen, impudent. **~ez** *f* impudence

desfalc|ar [7] *vt* embezzle. **~o** *m* embezzlement

desfallec|er [11] *vt* weaken. ● *vi* get weak; (*desmayarse*) faint. **~imiento** *m* weakness

desfas|ado *a* ⟨*persona*⟩ out of place, out of step; ⟨*máquina etc*⟩ out of phase. **~e** *m* jet-lag. **estar ~ado** have jet-lag

desfavor|able *a* unfavourable. **~ecer** [11] *vt* ⟨*ropa*⟩ not suit

desfigurar *vt* disfigure; (*desdibujar*) blur; (*fig*) distort

desfiladero *m* pass

desfil|ar *vi* march (past). **~e** *m* procession, parade. **~e de modelos** fashion show

desfogar [12] *vt* vent (**en, con** on). **~se** *vpr* let off steam

desgajar *vt* tear off; (*fig*) uproot ⟨*persona*⟩. **~se** *vpr* come off

desgana *f* (*falta de apetito*) lack of appetite; (*med*) weakness, faintness; (*fig*) unwillingness

desgarr|ador *a* heart-rending. **~ar** *vt* tear; (*fig*) break ⟨*corazón*⟩. **~o** *m* tear, rip; (*descaro*) insolence. **~ón** *m* tear

desgast|ar *vt* wear away; wear out ‹*ropa*›. **~arse** *vpr* wear away; ‹*ropa*› be worn out; ‹*persona*› wear o.s. out. **~e** *m* wear

desgracia *f* misfortune; (*accidente*) accident; (*mala suerte*) bad luck. **~damente** *adv* unfortunately. **~do** *a* unlucky; (*pobre*) poor; (*desagradable*) unpleasant. ● *m* unfortunate person, poor devil (*fam*). **~r** *vt* spoil. **caer en ~** fall from favour. **estar en ~** be unfortunate. **por ~** unfortunately. **¡qué ~!** what a shame!

desgranar *vt* shell ‹*guisantes etc*›

desgreñado *a* ruffled, dishevelled

desgua|ce *m* scrapyard. **~zar** [10] *vt* scrap

deshabitado *a* uninhabited

deshabituarse [21] *vpr* get out of the habit

deshacer [31] *vt* undo; strip ‹*cama*›; unpack ‹*maleta*›; (*desmontar*) take to pieces; break ‹*trato*›; (*derretir*) melt; (*en agua*) dissolve; (*destruir*) destroy; (*estropear*) spoil; (*derrotar*) defeat. **~se** *vpr* come undone; (*descomponerse*) fall to pieces; (*derretirse*) melt. **~se de algo** get rid of sth. **~se en lágrimas** burst into tears. **~se por hacer algo** go out of one's way to do sth

deshelar [1] *vt* thaw. **~se** *vpr* thaw

desheredar *vt* disinherit

deshidratar *vt* dehydrate. **~se** *vpr* become dehydrated

deshielo *m* thaw

deshilachado *a* frayed

deshincha|do *a* ‹*neumático*› flat. **~r** *vt* deflate. **~rse** *vpr* go down

deshollina|dor *m* (chimney-)sweep. **~r** *vt* sweep ‹*chimenea*›

deshon|esto *a* dishonest; (*obsceno*) indecent. **~or** *m*, **~ra** *f* disgrace. **~rar** *vt* dishonour

deshora *f*. **a ~** (*a hora desacostumbrada*) at an unusual time; (*a hora inoportuna*) at an inconvenient time; (*a hora avanzada*) very late

deshuesar *vt* bone ‹*carne*›; stone ‹*fruta*›

desidia *f* laziness

desierto *a* deserted. ● *m* desert

designa|ción *f* designation. **~r** *vt* designate; (*fijar*) fix

desigual *a* unequal; ‹*terreno*› uneven; (*distinto*) different. **~dad** *f* inequality

desilusi|ón *f* disappointment; (*pérdida de ilusiones*) disillusionment. **~onar** *vt* disappoint; (*quitar las ilusiones*) disillusion. **~onarse** *vpr* become disillusioned

desinfecta|nte *m* disinfectant. **~r** *vt* disinfect

desinfestar *vt* decontaminate

desinflar *vt* deflate. **~se** *vpr* go down

desinhibido *a* uninhibited

desintegra|ción *f* disintegration. **~r** *vt* disintegrate. **~rse** *vpr* disintegrate

desinter|és *m* impartiality; (*generosidad*) generosity. **~esado** *a* impartial; (*liberal*) generous

desistir *vi*. **~ de** give up

desleal *a* disloyal. **~tad** *f* disloyalty

desleír [51] *vt* thin down, dilute

deslenguado *a* foul-mouthed

desligar [12] *vt* untie; (*separar*) separate; (*fig*, *librar*) free. **~se** *vpr* break away; (*de un compromiso*) free o.s.

deslizar [10] *vt* slide, slip. **~se** *vpr* slide, slip; ‹*tiempo*› slide by, pass; (*fluir*) flow

deslucido *a* tarnished; (*gastado*) worn out; (*fig*) undistinguished

deslumbrar *vt* dazzle

deslustrar *vt* tarnish

desmadr|ado *a* unruly. **~arse** *vpr* get out of control. **~e** *m* excess

desmán *m* outrage

desmandarse *vpr* get out of control

desmantelar *vt* dismantle; (*despojar*) strip

desmañado *a* clumsy

desmaquillador *m* make-up remover

desmay|ado *a* unconscious. **~ar** *vi* lose heart. **~arse** *vpr* faint. **~o** *m* faint; (*estado*) unconsciousness; (*fig*) depression

desmedido *a* excessive

desmedrarse *vpr* waste away

desmejorarse *vpr* deteriorate

desmelenado *a* dishevelled

desmembrar *vt* (*fig*) divide up

desmemoriado *a* forgetful

desmentir [4] *vt* deny. **~se** *vpr* contradict o.s.; (*desdecirse*) go back on one's word

desmenuzar [10] *vt* crumble; chop ‹*carne etc*›

desmerecer [11] *vt* be unworthy of. ● *vi* deteriorate

desmesurado a excessive; (*enorme*) enormous

desmigajar vt, **desmigar** [12] vt crumble

desmonta|ble a collapsible. ~**r** vt (*quitar*) remove; (*desarmar*) take to pieces; (*derribar*) knock down; (*allanar*) level. ● vi dismount

desmoralizar [10] vt demoralize

desmoronar vt wear away; (*fig*) make inroads into. ~**se** vpr crumble

desmovilizar [10] vt/i demobilize

desnatar vt skim

desnivel m unevenness; (*fig*) difference, inequality

desnud|ar vt strip; undress, strip (*persona*). ~**arse** vpr get undressed; (*fig*) bare. ● m nude

desnutri|ción f malnutrition. ~**do** a undernourished

desobed|ecer [11] vt disobey. ~**iencia** f disobedience. ~**iente** a disobedient

desocupa|do a (*asiento etc*) vacant, free; (*sin trabajo*) unemployed; (*ocioso*) idle. ~**r** vt vacate

desodorante m deodorant

desoír [50] vt take no notice of

desola|ción f desolation; (*fig*) distress. ~**do** a desolate; (*persona*) sorry, sad. ~**r** vt ruin; (*desconsolar*) distress

desollar vt skin; (*fig, criticar*) criticize; (*fig, hacer pagar demasiado, fam*) fleece

desorbitante a excessive

desorden m disorder, untidiness; (*confusión*) confusion. ~**ado** a untidy. ~**ar** vt disarrange, make a mess of

desorganizar [10] vt disorganize; (*trastornar*) disturb

desorienta|do a confused. ~**r** vt disorientate. ~**rse** vpr lose one's bearings

desovar vi (*pez*) spawn; (*insecto*) lay eggs

despabila|do a wide awake; (*listo*) quick. ~**r** vt (*despertar*) wake up; (*avivar*) brighten up. ~**rse** vpr wake up; (*avivarse*) brighten up. ¡**despabílate**! get a move on!

despaci|o adv slowly. ● int easy does it! ~**to** adv slowly

despach|ar vt finish; (*tratar con*) deal with; (*vender*) sell; (*enviar*) send; (*despedir*) send away; issue

(*billete*). ● vi hurry up. ~**arse** vpr get rid; (*terminar*) finish. ~**o** m dispatch; (*oficina*) office; (*venta*) sale; (*del teatro*) box office

despampanante a stunning

desparejado a odd

desparpajo m confidence; (*descaro*) impudence

desparramar vt scatter; spill (*líquidos*); squander (*fortuna*)

despavorido a terrified

despectivo a disparaging; (*sentido etc*) pejorative

despecho m spite. **a** ~ **de** in spite of. **por** ~ out of spite

despedazar [10] vt tear to pieces

despedi|da f goodbye, farewell. ~**da de soltero** stag-party. ~**r** [5] vt say goodbye, see off; dismiss (*empleado*); evict (*inquilino*); (*arrojar*) throw; give off (*olor etc*). ~**rse** vpr. ~**rse de** say goodbye to

despeg|ado a cold, indifferent. ~**ar** [12] vt unstick. ● vi (*avión*) take off. ~**o** m indifference. ~**ue** m take-off

despeinar vt ruffle the hair of

despeja|do a clear; (*persona*) wide awake. ~**r** vt clear; (*aclarar*) clarify. ● vi clear. ~**rse** vpr (*aclararse*) become clear; (*cielo*) clear; (*tiempo*) clear up; (*persona*) liven up

despellejar vt skin

despensa f pantry, larder

despeñadero m cliff

desperdici|ar vt waste. ~**o** m waste. ~**os** mpl rubbish. **no tener** ~**o** be good all the way through

desperezarse [10] vpr stretch

desperfecto m flaw

desperta|dor m alarm clock. ~**r** [1] vt wake up; (*fig*) awaken. ~**rse** vpr wake up

despiadado a merciless

despido m dismissal

despierto a awake; (*listo*) bright

despilfarr|ar vt waste. ~**o** m squandering; (*gasto innecesario*) extravagance

despista|do a (*con estar*) confused; (*con ser*) absent-minded. ~**r** vt throw off the scent; (*fig*) mislead. ~**rse** vpr go wrong; (*fig*) get confused

despiste m swerve; (*error*) mistake; (*confusión*) muddle

desplaza|do a out of place. ~**miento** m displacement; (*de opinión etc*) swing, shift. ~**r** [10] vt displace. ~**rse** vpr travel

despl|egar [1 & 12] *vt* open out; spread ⟨*alas*⟩; (*fig*) show. **~iegue** *m* opening; (*fig*) show

desplomarse *vpr* lean; (*caerse*) collapse

desplumar *vt* pluck; (*fig, fam*) fleece

despobla|do *m* deserted area. **~r** [2] *vt* depopulate

despoj|ar *vt* deprive ⟨*persona*⟩; strip ⟨*cosa*⟩. **~o** *m* plundering; (*botín*) booty. **~os** *mpl* left-overs; (*de res*) offal; (*de ave*) giblets

desposado *a & m* newly-wed

déspota *m & f* despot

despreci|able *a* despicable; ⟨*cantidad*⟩ negligible. **~ar** *vt* despise; (*rechazar*) scorn. **~o** *m* contempt

desprend|er *vt* remove; give off ⟨*olor*⟩. **~erse** *vpr* fall off; (*fig*) part with; (*deducirse*) follow. **~imiento** *m* loosening; (*generosidad*) generosity

despreocupa|ción *f* carelessness. **~do** *a* unconcerned; (*descuidado*) careless. **~rse** *vpr* not worry

desprestigiar *vt* discredit

desprevenido *a* unprepared. **coger a uno ~** catch s.o. unawares

desproporci|ón *f* disproportion. **~onado** *a* disproportionate

despropósito *m* irrelevant remark

desprovisto *a*. **~ de** lacking, without

después *adv* after, afterwards; (*más tarde*) later; (*a continuación*) then. **~ de** after. **~ de comer** after eating. **~ de todo** after all. **~ que** after. **poco ~** soon after. **una semana ~** a week later

desquiciar *vt* (*fig*) disturb

desquit|ar *vt* compensate. **~arse** *vpr* make up for; (*vengarse*) take revenge. **~e** *m* compensation; (*venganza*) revenge

destaca|do *a* outstanding. **~r** [7] *vt* emphasize. ● *vi* stand out. **~rse** *vpr* stand out

destajo *m* piece-work. **hablar a ~** talk nineteen to the dozen

destap|ar *vt* uncover; open ⟨*botella*⟩. **~arse** *vpr* reveal one's true self. **~e** *m* (*fig*) permissiveness

destartalado *a* ⟨*habitación*⟩ untidy; ⟨*casa*⟩ rambling

destell|ar *vi* sparkle. **~o** *m* sparkle; (*de estrella*) twinkle; (*fig*) glimmer

destemplado *a* out of tune; (*agrio*) harsh; ⟨*tiempo*⟩ unsettled; ⟨*persona*⟩ out of sorts

desteñir [5 & 22] *vt* fade; (*manchar*) discolour. ● *vi* fade. **~se** *vpr* fade; ⟨*color*⟩ run

desterra|do *m* exile. **~r** [1] *vt* banish

destetar *vt* wean

destiempo *m*. **a ~** at the wrong moment

destierro *m* exile

destil|ación *f* distillation. **~ar** *vt* distil. **~ería** *f* distillery

destin|ar *vt* destine; (*nombrar*) appoint. **~atario** *m* addressee. **~o** *m* (*uso*) use, function; (*lugar*) destination; (*empleo*) position; (*suerte*) destiny. **con ~ a** going to, bound for. **dar ~ a** find a use for

destitu|ción *f* dismissal. **~ir** [17] *vt* dismiss

destornilla|dor *m* screwdriver. **~r** *vt* unscrew

destreza *f* skill

destripar *vt* rip open

destroz|ar [10] *vt* ruin; (*fig*) shatter. **~o** *m* destruction. **causar ~os**, **hacer ~os** ruin

destru|cción *f* destruction. **~ctivo** *a* destructive. **~ir** [17] *vt* destroy; demolish ⟨*edificio*⟩

desunir *vt* separate

desus|ado *a* old-fashioned; (*insólito*) unusual. **~o** *m* disuse. **caer en ~o** become obsolete

desvaído *a* pale; (*borroso*) blurred; ⟨*persona*⟩ dull

desvalido *a* needy, destitute

desvalijar *vt* rob; burgle ⟨*casa*⟩

desvalorizar [10] *vt* devalue

desván *m* loft

desvanec|er [11] *vt* make disappear; tone down ⟨*colores*⟩; (*borrar*) blur; (*fig*) dispel. **~erse** *vpr* disappear; (*desmayarse*) faint. **~imiento** *m* (*med*) fainting fit

desvariar [20] *vi* be delirious; (*fig*) talk nonsense

desvel|ar *vt* keep awake. **~arse** *vpr* stay awake, have a sleepless night. **~o** *m* insomnia, sleeplessness

desvencijar *vt* break; (*agotar*) exhaust

desventaja *f* disadvantage

desventura *f* misfortune. **~do** *a* unfortunate

desverg|onzado *a* impudent, cheeky. **~üenza** *f* impudence, cheek

desvestirse [5] *vpr* undress

desv|iación *f* deviation; (*auto*) diversion. **~iar** [20] *vt* deflect, turn aside.

~**iarse** *vpr* be deflected; (*del camino*) make a detour; (*del tema*) stray. ~**io** *m* diversion; (*frialdad*) *f* indifference

desvivirse *vpr* long (**por** for); (*afanarse*) strive, do one's utmost

detall|ar *vt* relate in detail. ~**e** *m* detail; (*fig*) gesture. ~**ista** *m* & *f* retailer. **al** ~**e** in detail; (*al por menor*) retail. **con todo** ~**e** in great detail. **en** ~**es** in detail. **¡qué** ~**e!** how thoughtful!

detect|ar *vt* detect. ~**ive** *m* detective

deten|ción *f* stopping; (*jurid*) arrest; (*en la cárcel*) detention. ~**er** [40] *vt* stop; (*jurid*) arrest; (*encarcelar*) detain; (*retrasar*) delay. ~**erse** *vpr* stop; (*entretenerse*) spend a lot of time. ~**idamente** *adv* carefully. ~**ido** *a* (*jurid*) under arrest; (*minucioso*) detailed. ● *m* prisoner

detergente *a* & *m* detergent

deterior|ar *vt* damage, spoil. ~**arse** *vpr* deteriorate. ~**o** *m* damage

determina|ción *f* determination; (*decisión*) decison. ~**nte** *a* decisive. ~**r** *vt* determine; (*decidir*) decide; (*fijar*) fix. **tomar una** ~**ción** make a decision

detestar *vt* detest

detonar *vi* explode

detrás *adv* behind; (*en la parte posterior*) on the back. ~ **de** behind. **por** ~ on the back; (*detrás de*) behind

detrimento *m* detriment. **en** ~ **de** to the detriment of

detrito *m* debris

deud|a *f* debt. ~**or** *m* debtor

devalua|ción *f* devaluation. ~**r** [21] *vt* devalue

devanar *vt* wind

devasta|dor *a* devastating. ~**r** *vt* devastate

devoción *f* devotion

devol|ución *f* return; (*com*) repayment, refund. ~**ver** [5] (*pp* **devuelto**) *vt* return; (*com*) repay, refund; restore ‹*edificio etc*›. ● *vi* be sick

devorar *vt* devour

devoto *a* devout; ‹*amigo etc*› devoted. ● *m* enthusiast

di *vb véase* **dar**

día *m* day. ~ **de fiesta** (public) holiday. ~ **del santo** saint's day. ~ **festivo** (public) holiday. ~ **hábil**, ~ **laborable** working day. **al** ~ up to

date. **al** ~ **siguiente** (on) the following day. **¡buenos** ~**s!** good morning! **dar los buenos** ~**s** say good morning. **de** ~ by day. **el** ~ **de hoy** today. **el** ~ **de mañana** tomorrow. **en pleno** ~ in broad daylight. **en su** ~ in due course. **todo el santo** ~ all day long. **un** ~ **de estos** one of these days. **un** ~ **sí y otro no** every other day. **vivir al** ~ live from hand to mouth

diab|etes *f* diabetes. ~**ético** *a* diabetic

diab|lo *m* devil. ~**lura** *f* mischief. ~**ólico** *a* diabolical

diácono *m* deacon

diadema *f* diadem

diáfano *a* diaphanous

diafragma *m* diaphragm

diagn|osis *f* diagnosis. ~**osticar** [7] *vt* diagnose. ~**óstico** *a* diagnostic

diagonal *a* & *f* diagonal

diagrama *m* diagram

dialecto *m* dialect

diálisis *f* dialysis

di|alogar [12] *vi* talk. ~**álogo** *m* dialogue

diamante *m* diamond

diámetro *m* diameter

diana *f* reveille; (*blanco*) bull's-eye

diapasón *m* (*para afinar*) tuning fork

diapositiva *f* slide, transparency

diari|amente *adv* every day. ~**o** *a* daily. ● *m* newspaper; (*libro*) diary. **a** ~**o** daily. ~**o** **hablado** (*en la radio*) news bulletin. **de** ~**o** everyday, ordinary

diarrea *f* diarrhoea

diatriba *f* diatribe

dibuj|ar *vt* draw. ~**o** *m* drawing. ~**os animados** cartoon (film)

diccionario *m* dictionary

diciembre *m* December

dictado *m* dictation

dictad|or *m* dictator. ~**ura** *f* dictatorship

dictamen *m* opinion; (*informe*) report

dictar *vt* dictate; pronounce ‹*sentencia etc*›

dich|a *f* happiness. ~**o** *a* said; (*susodicho*) aforementioned. ● *m* saying. ~**oso** *a* happy; (*afortunado*) fortunate. ~**o y hecho** no sooner said than done. **mejor** ~**o** rather. **por** ~**a** fortunately

didáctico *a* didactic

dieci|nueve *a & m* nineteen. **~ocho** *a & m* eighteen. **~séis** *a & m* sixteen. **~siete** *a & m* seventeen

diente *m* tooth; (*de tenedor*) prong; (*de ajo*) clove. **~ de león** dandelion. **hablar entre ~s** mumble

diesel /'disel/ *a* diesel

diestr|a *f* right hand. **~o** *a* (*derecho*) right; (*hábil*) skillful

dieta *f* diet

diez *a & m* ten

diezmar *vt* decimate

difama|ción *f* (*con palabras*) slander; (*por escrito*) libel. **~r** *vt* (*hablando*) slander; (*por escrito*) libel

diferen|cia *f* difference; (*desacuerdo*) disagreement. **~ciar** *vt* differentiate between. ● *vi* differ. **~ciarse** *vpr* differ. **~te** *a* different

difer|ido *a* (*TV etc*) recorded. **~ir** [4] *vt* postpone, defer. ● *vi* differ

dif|ícil *a* difficult. **~icultad** *f* difficulty; (*problema*) problem. **~icultar** *vt* make difficult

difteria *f* diphtheria

difundir *vt* spread; (*TV etc*) broadcast. **~se** *vpr* spread

difunto *a* late, deceased. ● *m* deceased

difusión *f* spreading

dige|rir [4] *vt* digest. **~stión** *f* digestion. **~stivo** *a* digestive

digital *a* digital; (*de los dedos*) finger

dignarse *vpr* deign. **dígnese Vd** be so kind as

dign|atario *m* dignitary. **~idad** *f* dignity; (*empleo*) office. **~o** *a* worthy; (*apropiado*) appropriate

digo *vb véase* **decir**

digresión *f* digression

dije *vb véase* **decir**

dila|ción *f* delay. **~tación** *f* dilation, expansion. **~tado** *a* extensive; (*tiempo*) long. **~tar** *vt* expand; (*med*) dilate; (*prolongar*) prolong. **~tarse** *vpr* expand; (*med*) dilate; (*extenderse*) extend. **sin ~ción** immediately

dilema *m* dilemma

diligen|cia *f* diligence; (*gestión*) job; (*historia*) stagecoach. **~te** *a* diligent

dilucidar *vt* explain; solve (*misterio*)

diluir [17] *vt* dilute

diluvio *m* flood

dimensión *f* dimension; (*tamaño*) size

diminut|ivo *a & m* diminutive. **~o** *a* minute

dimi|sión *f* resignation. **~tir** *vt/i* resign

Dinamarca *f* Denmark

dinamarqués *a* Danish. ● *m* Dane

din|ámica *f* dynamics. **~ámico** *a* dynamic. **~amismo** *m* dynamism

dinamita *f* dynamite

dínamo *m*, **dinamo** *m* dynamo

dinastía *f* dynasty

dineral *m* fortune

dinero *m* money. **~ efectivo** cash. **~ suelto** change

dinosaurio *m* dinosaur

diócesis *f* diocese

dios *m* god. **~a** *f* goddess. **¡D~ mío!** good heavens! **¡gracias a D~!** thank God! **¡válgame D~!** bless my soul!

diploma *m* diploma

diplomacia *f* diplomacy

diplomado *a* qualified

diplomático *a* diplomatic. ● *m* diplomat

diptongo *m* diphthong

diputa|ción *f* delegation. **~ción provincial** county council. **~do** *m* delegate; (*pol, en España*) member of the Cortes; (*pol, en Inglaterra*) Member of Parliament; (*pol, en Estados Unidos*) congressman

dique *m* dike

direc|ción *f* direction; (*señas*) address; (*los que dirigen*) management; (*pol*) leadership. **~ción prohibida** no entry. **~ción única** one-way. **~ta** *f* (*auto*) top gear. **~tiva** *f* directive, guideline. **~tivo** *m* executive. **~to** *a* direct; (*línea*) straight; (*tren*) through. **~tor** *m* director; (*mus*) conductor; (*de escuela etc*) headmaster; (*de periódico*) editor; (*gerente*) manager. **~tora** *f* (*de escuela etc*) headmistress. **en ~to** (*TV etc*) live. **llevar la ~ción de** direct

dirig|ente *a* ruling. ● *m & f* leader; (*de empresa*) manager. **~ible** *a & m* dirigible. **~ir** [14] *vt* direct; (*mus*) conduct; run (*empresa etc*); address (*carta etc*). **~irse** *vpr* make one's way; (*hablar*) address

discernir [1] *vt* distinguish

disciplina *f* discipline. **~r** *vt* discipline. **~rio** *a* disciplinary

discípulo *m* disciple; (*alumno*) pupil

disco *m* disc; (*mus*) record; (*deportes*) discus; (*de teléfono*) dial; (*auto*) lights; (*rail*) signal

disconforme *a* not in agreement

discontinuo *a* discontinuous

discord|ante *a* discordant. **~e** *a* discordant. **~ia** *f* discord

discoteca *f* discothèque, disco (*fam*); (*colección de discos*) record library

discreción *f* discretion

discrepa|ncia *f* discrepancy; (*desacuerdo*) disagreement. **~r** *vi* differ

discreto *a* discreet; (*moderado*) moderate; ⟨*color*⟩ subdued

discrimina|ción *f* discrimination. **~r** *vt* (*distinguir*) discriminate between; (*tratar injustamente*) discriminate against

disculpa *f* apology; (*excusa*) excuse. **~r** *vt* excuse, forgive. **~rse** *vpr* apologize. **dar ~s** make excuses. **pedir ~s** apologize

discurrir *vt* think up. ● *vi* think (*en* about); ⟨*tiempo*⟩ pass

discurs|ante *m* speaker. **~ar** *vi* speak (**sobre** about). **~o** *m* speech

discusión *f* discussion; (*riña*) argument. **eso no admite ~** there can be no argument about that

discuti|ble *a* debatable. **~r** *vt* discuss; (*argumentar*) argue about; (*contradecir*) contradict. ● *vi* discuss; (*argumentar*) argue

disec|ar [7] *vt* dissect; stuff ⟨*animal muerto*⟩. **~ción** *f* dissection

disemina|ción *f* dissemination. **~r** *vt* disseminate, spread

disentería *f* dysentery

disenti|miento *m* dissent, disagreement. **~r** [4] *vi* disagree (**de** with) (**en** on)

diseñ|ador *m* designer. **~ar** *vt* design. **~o** *m* design; (*fig*) sketch

disertación *f* dissertation

disfraz *m* disguise; (*vestido*) fancy dress. **~ar** [10] *vt* disguise. **~arse** *vpr*. **~arse de** disguise o.s. as

disfrutar *vt* enjoy. ● *vi* enjoy o.s. **~ de** enjoy

disgregar [12] *vt* disintegrate

disgust|ar *vt* displease; (*molestar*) annoy. **~arse** *vpr* get annoyed, get upset; ⟨*dos personas*⟩ fall out. **~o** *m* annoyance; (*problema*) trouble; (*repugnancia*) disgust; (*riña*) quarrel; (*dolor*) sorrow, grief

disiden|cia *f* disagreement, dissent. **~te** *a & m & f* dissident

disímil *a* (*LAm*) dissimilar

disimular *vt* conceal. ● *vi* pretend

disipa|ción *f* dissipation; (*de dinero*) squandering. **~r** *vt* dissipate; (*derrochar*) squander

diskette *m* floppy disk

dislocarse [7] *vpr* dislocate

disminu|ción *f* decrease. **~ir** [17] *vi* diminish

disociar *vt* dissociate

disolver [2, *pp* **disuelto**] *vt* dissolve. **~se** *vpr* dissolve

disonante *a* dissonant

dispar *a* different

disparar *vt* fire. ● *vi* shoot (**contra** at)

disparat|ado *a* absurd. **~ar** *vi* talk nonsense. **~e** *m* silly thing; (*error*) mistake. **decir ~es** talk nonsense. **¡qué ~e!** how ridiculous! **un ~e** (*mucho, fam*) a lot, an awful lot (*fam*)

disparidad *f* disparity

disparo *m* (*acción*) firing; (*tiro*) shot

dispensar *vt* distribute; (*disculpar*) excuse. **¡Vd dispense!** forgive me

dispers|ar *vt* scatter, disperse. **~arse** *vpr* scatter, disperse. **~ión** *f* dispersion. **~o** *a* scattered

dispon|er [34] *vt* arrange; (*preparar*) prepare. ● *vi*. **~er de** have; (*vender etc*) dispose of. **~erse** *vpr* get ready. **~ibilidad** *f* availability. **~ible** *a* available

disposición *f* arrangement; (*aptitud*) talent; (*disponibilidad*) disposal; (*jurid*) order, decree. **~ de ánimo** frame of mind. **a la ~ de** at the disposal of. **a su ~** at your service

dispositivo *m* device

dispuesto *a* ready; (*hábil*) clever; (*inclinado*) disposed; (*servicial*) helpful

disputa *f* dispute. **~r** *vt* dispute. ● *vi*. **~r por** argue about; (*competir para*) compete for. **sin ~** undoubtedly

distan|cia *f* distance. **~ciar** *vt* space out; (*en deportes*) outdistance. **~ciarse** *vpr* ⟨*dos personas*⟩ fall out. **~te** *a* distant. **a ~cia** from a distance. **guardar las ~cias** keep one's distance

distar *vi* be away; (*fig*) be far. **dista 5 kilómetros** it's 5 kilometres away

distin|ción *f* distinction. **~guido** *a* distinguished; (*en cartas*) Honoured. **~guir** [13] *vt/i* distinguish. **~guirse** *vpr* distinguish o.s.; (*diferenciarse*) differ; (*verse*) be visible. **~tivo** *a* distinctive. ● *m* badge. **~to** *a* different; (*claro*) distinct

distorsión *f* distortion; (*med*) sprain

distra|cción *f* amusement; (*descuido*) absent-mindedness, inattention. **~er** [41] *vt* distract; (*divertir*) amuse; embezzle ⟨*fondos*⟩. ● *vi* be entertaining. ~**erse** *vpr* amuse o.s.; (*descuidarse*) not pay attention. ~**ído** *a* amusing; (*desatento*) absent-minded

distribu|ción *f* distribution. ~**idor** *m* distributor, agent. ~**idor automático** vending machine. ~**ir** [17] *vt* distribute

distrito *m* district

disturbio *m* disturbance

disuadir *vt* dissuade

diurético *a & m* diuretic

diurno *a* daytime

divagar [12] *vi* (*al hablar*) digress

diván *m* settee, sofa

diverg|encia *f* divergence. ~**ente** *a* divergent. ~**ir** [14] *vi* diverge

diversidad *f* diversity

diversificar [7] *vt* diversify

diversión *f* amusement, entertainment; (*pasatiempo*) pastime

diverso *a* different

diverti|do *a* amusing; (*que tiene gracia*) funny; (*agradable*) enjoyable. ~**r** [4] *vt* amuse, entertain. ~**rse** *vpr* enjoy o.s.

dividir *vt* divide; (*repartir*) share out

divin|idad *f* divinity. ~**o** *a* divine

divisa *f* emblem. ~**s** *fpl* foreign exchange

divisar *vt* make out

divis|ión *f* division. ~**or** *m* divisor. ~**orio** *a* dividing

divorci|ado *a* divorced. ● *m* divorcee. ~**ar** *vt* divorce. ~**arse** *vpr* get divorced. ~**o** *m* divorce

divulgar [12] *vt* divulge; (*propagar*) spread. ~**se** *vpr* become known

do *m* C; (*solfa*) doh

dobl|adillo *m* hem; (*de pantalón*) turn-up (*Brit*), cuff (*Amer*). ~**ado** *a* double; (*plegado*) folded; ⟨*película*⟩ dubbed. ~**ar** *vt* double; (*plegar*) fold; (*torcer*) bend; turn ⟨*esquina*⟩; dub ⟨*película*⟩. ● *vi* turn; ⟨*campana*⟩ toll. ~**arse** *vpr* double; (*encorvarse*) bend; (*ceder*) give in. ~**e** *a* double. ● *m* double; (*pliegue*) fold. ~**egar** [12] *vt* (*fig*) force to give in. ~**egarse** *vpr* give in. **el** ~**e** twice as much

doce *a & m* twelve. ~**na** *f* dozen. ~**no** *a* twelfth

docente *a* teaching. ● *m & f* teacher

dócil *a* obedient

doct|o *a* learned. ~**or** *m* doctor. ~**orado** *m* doctorate. ~**rina** *f* doctrine

document|ación *f* documentation, papers. ~**al** *a & m* documentary.

~**ar** *vt* document. ~**arse** *vpr* gather information. ~**o** *m* document. **D~o Nacional de Identidad** national identity card

dogm|a *m* dogma. ~**ático** *a* dogmatic

dólar *m* dollar

dol|er [2] *vi* hurt, ache; (*fig*) grieve. **me duele la cabeza** my head hurts. **le duele el estómago** he has a pain in his stomach. ~**erse** *vpr* regret; (*quejarse*) complain. ~**or** *m* pain; (*sordo*) ache; (*fig*) sorrow. ~**oroso** *a* painful. ~**or de cabeza** headache. ~**or de muelas** toothache

domar *vt* tame; break in ⟨*caballo*⟩

dom|esticar [7] *vt* domesticate. ~**éstico** *a* domestic. ● *m* servant

domicilio *m* home. **a** ~ at home. **servicio a** ~ home delivery service

domina|ción *f* domination. ~**nte** *a* dominant; ⟨*persona*⟩ domineering. ~**r** *vt* dominate; (*contener*) control; (*conocer*) have a good knowledge of. ● *vi* dominate; (*destacarse*) stand out. ~**rse** *vpr* control o.s.

domin|go *m* Sunday. ~**guero** *a* Sunday. ~**ical** *a* Sunday

dominio *m* authority; (*territorio*) domain; (*fig*) good knowledge

dominó *m* (*juego*) dominoes

don *m* talent, gift; (*en un sobre*) Mr. ~ **Pedro** Pedro. **tener** ~ **de lenguas** have a gift for languages. **tener** ~ **de gentes** have a way with people

donación *f* donation

donaire *m* grace, charm

dona|nte *m* (*de sangre*) donor. ~**r** *vt* donate

doncella *f* (*criada*) maid

donde *adv* where

dónde *adv* where? **¿hasta** ~**?** how far? **¿por** ~**?** whereabouts? (*¿por qué camino?*) which way? **¿a** ~ **vas?** where are you going? **¿de** ~ **eres?** where are you from?

dondequiera *adv* anywhere; (*en todas partes*) everywhere. ~ **que** wherever. **por** ~ everywhere

doña *f* (*en un sobre*) Mrs. ~ **María** María

dora|do *a* golden; (*cubierto de oro*) gilt. ~**dura** *f* gilding. ~**r** *vt* gilt; (*culin*) brown

dormi|lón *m* sleepyhead. ● *a* lazy. ~**r** [6] *vt* send to sleep. ● *vi* sleep. ~**rse** *vpr* go to sleep. ~**tar** *vi* doze. ~**torio** *m* bedroom. ~**r la siesta**

have an afternoon nap, have a siesta. **echarse a dormir** go to bed
dors|al *a* back. ● *m* (*en deportes*) number. **~o** *m* back
dos *a* & *m* two. **~cientos** *a* & *m* two hundred. **cada ~ por tres** every five minutes. **de ~ en ~** in twos, in pairs. **en un ~ por tres** in no time. **los dos, las dos** both (of them)
dosi|ficar [7] *vt* dose; (*fig*) measure out. **~s** *f* dose
dot|ado *a* gifted. **~ar** *vt* give a dowry; (*proveer*) endow (**de** with). **~e** *m* dowry
doy *vb véase* **dar**
dragar [12] *vt* dredge
drago *m* dragon tree
dragón *m* dragon
dram|a *m* drama; (*obra de teatro*) play. **~ático** *a* dramatic. **~atizar** [10] *vt* dramatize. **~aturgo** *m* playwright
drástico *a* drastic
droga *f* drug. **~dicto** *m* drug addict. **~do** *a* drugged. ● *m* drug addict. **~r** [12] *vt* drug. **~rse** *vpr* take drugs. **~ta** *m* & *f* (*fam*) drug addict
droguería *f* hardware shop (*Brit*), hardware store (*Amer*)
dromedario *m* dromedary
ducha *f* shower. **~rse** *vpr* have a shower
dud|a *f* doubt. **~ar** *vt/i* doubt. **~oso** *a* doubtful; (*sospechoso*) dubious. **poner en ~a** a question. **sin ~a (alguna)** without a doubt
duelo *m* duel; (*luto*) mourning
duende *m* imp
dueñ|a *f* owner, proprietress; (*de una pensión*) landlady. **~o** *m* owner, proprietor; (*de una pensión*) landlord
duermo *vb véase* **dormir**
dul|ce *a* sweet; (*agua*) fresh; (*suave*) soft, gentle. ● *m* sweet. **~zura** *f* sweetness; (*fig*) gentleness
duna *f* dune
dúo *m* duet, duo
duodécimo *a* & *m* twelfth
duplica|do *a* in duplicate. ● *m* duplicate. **~r** [7] *vt* duplicate. **~rse** *vpr* double
duque *m* duke. **~sa** *f* duchess
dura|ción *f* duration, length. **~dero** *a* lasting
durante *prep* during, in; (*medida de tiempo*) for. **~ todo el año** all year round
durar *vi* last

durazno *m* (*LAm, fruta*) peach
dureza *f* hardness, toughness; (*med*) hard patch
durmiente *a* sleeping
duro *a* hard; (*culin*) tough; (*fig*) harsh. ● *adv* hard. ● *m* five-peseta coin. **ser ~ de oído** be hard of hearing

E

e *conj* and
ebanista *m* & *f* cabinet-maker
ébano *m* ebony
ebri|edad *f* drunkenness. **~o** *a* drunk
ebullición *f* boiling
eccema *m* eczema
eclesiástico *a* ecclesiastical. ● *m* clergyman
eclipse *m* eclipse
eco *m* echo. **hacer(se) ~** echo
ecolog|ía *f* ecology. **~ista** *m* & *f* ecologist
economato *m* cooperative store
econ|omía *f* economy; (*ciencia*) economics. **~ómicamente** *adv* economically. **~ómico** *a* economic(al); (*no caro*) inexpensive. **~omista** *m* & *f* economist. **~omizar** [10] *vt/i* economize
ecuación *f* equation
ecuador *m* equator. **el E~** Ecuador
ecuánime *a* level-headed; (*imparcial*) impartial
ecuanimidad *f* equanimity
ecuatoriano *a* & *m* Ecuadorian
ecuestre *a* equestrian
echar *vt* throw; post (*carta*); give off (*olor*); pour (*líquido*); sprout (*hojas etc*); (*despedir*) throw out; dismiss (*empleado*); (*poner*) put on; put out (*raíces*); show (*película*). **~se** *vpr* throw o.s.; (*tumbarse*) lie down. **~ a** start. **~ a perder** spoil. **~ de menos** miss. **~se atrás** (*fig*) back down. **echárselas de** feign
edad *f* age. **~ avanzada** old age. **E~ de Piedra** Stone Age. **E~ Media** Middle Ages. **¿qué ~ tiene?** how old is he?
edición *f* edition; (*publicación*) publication
edicto *m* edict
edific|ación *f* building. **~ante** *a* edifying. **~ar** [7] *vt* build; (*fig*) edify. **~io** *m* building; (*fig*) structure

Edimburgo *m* Edinburgh

edit|ar *vt* publish. **~or** *a* publishing. ● *m* publisher. **~orial** *a* editorial. ● *m* leading article. ● *f* publishing house

edredón *m* eiderdown

educa|ción *f* upbringing; *(modales)* (good) manners; *(enseñanza)* education. **~do** *a* polite. **~dor** *m* teacher. **~r** [7] *vt* bring up; *(enseñar)* educate. **~tivo** *a* educational. **bien ~do** polite. **falta de ~ción** rudeness, bad manners. **mal ~do** rude

edulcorante *m* sweetener

EE.UU. *abrev (Estados Unidos)* USA, United States (of America)

efect|ivamente *adv* really; *(por supuesto)* indeed. **~ivo** *a* effective; *(auténtico)* real; *(empleo)* permanent. ● *m* cash. **~o** *m* effect; *(impresión)* impression. **~os** *mpl* belongings; *(com)* goods. **~uar** [21] *vt* carry out, effect; make *(viaje, compras etc)*. **en ~o** in fact; *(por supuesto)* indeed

efervescente *a* effervescent; *(bebidas)* fizzy

efica|cia *f* effectiveness; *(de persona)* efficiency. **~z** *a* effective; *(persona)* efficient

eficien|cia *f* efficiency. **~te** *a* efficient

efigie *f* effigy

efímero *a* ephemeral

efluvio *m* outflow

efusi|ón *n* effusion. **~vo** *a* effusive; *(gracias)* warm

Egeo *m.* **mar ~** Aegean Sea

égida *f* aegis

egipcio *a & m* Egyptian

Egipto *m* Egypt

ego|céntrico *a* egocentric. ● *m* egocentric person. **~ísmo** *m* selfishness. **~ista** *a* selfish. ● *m* selfish person

egregio *a* eminent

egresar *vi (LAm)* leave; *(univ)* graduate

eje *m* axis; *(tec)* axle

ejecu|ción *f* execution; *(mus etc)* performance. **~tante** *m & f* executor; *(mus etc)* performer. **~tar** *vt* carry out; *(mus etc)* perform; *(matar)* execute

ejecutivo *m* director, manager

ejempl|ar *a* exemplary. ● *m* *(ejemplo)* example, specimen; *(libro)* copy; *(revista)* issue, number. **~ificar** [7] *vt* exemplify. **~o** *m* example.

dar ~o set an example. **por ~o** for example. **sin ~** unprecedented

ejerc|er [9] *vt* exercise; practise *(profesión)*; exert *(influencia)*. ● *vi* practise. **~icio** *m* exercise; *(de una profesión)* practice. **~itar** *vt* exercise. **~itarse** *vpr* exercise. **hacer ~icios** take exercise

ejército *m* army

el *art def m (pl* **los**) the. ● *pron (pl* **los**) the one. **~ de Antonio** Antonio's. **~ que** whoever, the one

él *pron (persona)* he; *(persona con prep)* him; *(cosa)* it. **el libro de ~** his book

elabora|ción *f* processing; *(fabricación)* manufacture. **~r** *vt* process; manufacture *(producto)*; *(producir)* produce

el|asticidad *f* elasticity. **~ástico** *a & m* elastic

elec|ción *f* choice; *(de político etc)* election. **~ciones** *fpl (pol)* election. **~tor** *m* voter. **~torado** *m* electorate. **~toral** *a* electoral

electri|cidad *f* electricity. **~sta** *m & f* electrician

eléctrico *a* electric; *(de la electricidad)* electrical

electrificar [7] *vt*, **electrizar** [10] *vt* electrify

electrocutar *vt* electrocute

electrodo *m* electrode

electrodoméstico *a* electrical household. **~s** *mpl* electrical household appliances

electrólisis *f* electrolysis

electrón *m* electron

electrónic|a *f* electronics. **~o** *a* electronic

elefante *m* elephant

elegan|cia *f* elegance. **~te** *a* elegant

elegía *f* elegy

elegi|ble *a* eligible. **~do** *a* chosen. **~r** [5 & 14] *vt* choose; *(por votación)* elect

element|al *a* elementary. **~o** *m* element; *(persona)* person, bloke *(fam)*. **~os** *mpl (nociones)* basic principles

elenco *m (en el teatro)* cast

eleva|ción *f* elevation; *(de precios)* rise, increase; *(acción)* raising. **~dor** *m (LAm)* lift. **~r** *vt* raise; *(promover)* promote

elimina|ción *f* elimination. **~r** *vt* eliminate. **~toria** *f* preliminary heat

el|ipse *f* ellipse. **~íptico** *a* elliptical

élite /e'lit, e'lite/ *f* elite

elixir *m* elixir

elocución *f* elocution

elocuen|cia *f* eloquence. **~te** *a* eloquent

elogi|ar *vt* praise. **~o** *m* praise

elote *m* (*Mex*) corn on the cob

eludir *vt* avoid, elude

ella *pron* (*persona*) she; (*persona con prep*) her; (*cosa*) it. **~s** *pron pl* they; (*con prep*) them. **el libro de ~** her book. **el libro de ~s** their book

ello *pron* it

ellos *pron pl* they; (*con prep*) them. **el libro de ~** their book

emaciado *a* emaciated

emana|ción *f* emanation. **~r** *vi* emanate (**de** from); (*originarse*) originate (**de** from, in)

emancipa|ción *f* emancipation. **~do** *a* emancipated. **~r** *vt* emancipate. **~rse** *vpr* become emancipated

embadurnar *vt* smear

embajad|a *f* embassy. **~or** *m* ambassador

embalar *vt* pack

embaldosar *vt* tile

embalsamar *vt* embalm

embalse *m* dam; (*pantano*) reservoir

embaraz|ada *a* pregnant. **•** *f* pregnant woman. **~ar** [10] *vt* hinder. **~o** *m* hindrance; (*de mujer*) pregnancy. **~oso** *a* awkward, embarrassing

embar|cación *f* boat. **~cadero** *m* jetty, pier. **~car** [7] *vt* embark (*personas*); ship (*mercancías*). **~carse** *vpr* embark. **~carse en** (*fig*) embark upon

embargo *m* embargo; (*jurid*) seizure. **sin ~** however

embarque *m* loading

embarullar *vt* muddle

embaucar [7] *vt* deceive

embeber *vt* absorb; (*empapar*) soak. **•** *vi* shrink. **~se** *vpr* be absorbed

embelesar *vt* delight. **~se** *vpr* be delighted

embellecer [11] *vt* embellish

embesti|da *f* attack. **~r** [5] *vt/i* attack

emblema *m* emblem

embobar *vt* amaze

embobecer [11] *vt* make silly. **~se** *vpr* get silly

embocadura *f* (*de un río*) mouth

emboquillado *a* tipped

embolsar *vt* pocket

emborrachar *vt* get drunk. **~se** *vpr* get drunk

emborrascarse [7] *vpr* get stormy

emborronar *vt* blot

embosca|da *f* ambush. **~rse** [7] *vpr* lie in wait

embotar *vt* blunt; (*fig*) dull

embotella|miento *m* (*de vehículos*) traffic jam. **~r** *vt* bottle

embrague *m* clutch

embriag|ar [12] *vt* get drunk; (*fig*) intoxicate; (*fig, enajenar*) enrapture. **~arse** *vpr* get drunk. **~uez** *f* drunkenness; (*fig*) intoxication

embrión *m* embryo

embroll|ar *vt* mix up; involve (*personas*). **~arse** *vpr* get into a muddle; *en un asunto*) get involved. **~o** *m* tangle; (*fig*) muddle. **~ón** *m* troublemaker

embromar *vt* make fun of; (*engañar*) fool

embruja|do *a* bewitched; (*casa etc*) haunted. **~r** *vt* bewitch

embrutecer [11] *vt* brutalize

embuchar *vt* wolf (*comida*)

embudo *m* funnel

embuste *m* lie. **~ro** *a* deceitful. **•** *m* liar

embuti|do *m* (*culin*) sausage. **~r** *vt* stuff

emergencia *f* emergency; (*acción de emerger*) emergence. **en caso de ~** in case of emergency

emerger [14] *vi* appear, emerge; (*submarino*) surface

emigra|ción *f* emigration. **~nte** *m* & *f* emigrant. **~r** *vi* emigrate

eminen|cia *f* eminence. **~te** *a* eminent

emisario *m* emissary

emis|ión *f* emission; (*de dinero*) issue; (*TV etc*) broadcast. **~or** *a* issuing; (*TV etc*) broadcasting. **~ora** *f* radio station

emitir *vt* emit; let out (*grito*); (*TV etc*) broadcast; (*expresar*) express; (*poner en circulación*) issue

emoci|ón *f* emotion; (*excitación*) excitement. **~onado** *a* moved. **~onante** *a* exciting; (*conmovedor*) moving. **~onar** *vt* excite; (*conmover*) move. **~onarse** *vpr* get excited; (*conmoverse*) be moved. **¡qué ~ón!** how exciting!

emotivo *a* emotional; (*conmovedor*) moving

empacar [7] *vt* (*LAm*) pack

empacho *m* indigestion; (*vergüenza*) embarrassment

empadronar *vt* register. **~se** *vpr* register

empalagoso *a* sickly; (*demasiado amable*) ingratiating; (*demasiado sentimental*) mawkish

empalizada *f* fence

empalm|ar *vt* connect, join. ● *vi* meet. **~e** *m* junction; (*de trenes*) connection

empanad|a *f* (savoury) pie. **~illa** *f* (small) pie. **~o** *a* fried in breadcrumbs

empanizado *a* (*Mex*) fried in breadcrumbs

empantanar *vt* flood. **~se** *vpr* become flooded; (*fig*) get bogged down

empañar *vt* mist; dull ⟨*metales etc*⟩; (*fig*) tarnish. **~se** *vpr* ⟨*cristales*⟩ steam up

empapar *vt* soak; (*absorber*) soak up. **~se** *vpr* be soaked

empapela|do *m* wallpaper. **~r** *vt* paper; (*envolver*) wrap (in paper)

empaquetar *vt* package; pack together ⟨*personas*⟩

emparedado *m* sandwich

emparejar *vt* match; (*nivelar*) make level. **~se** *vpr* pair off

empast|ar *vt* fill ⟨*muela*⟩. **~e** *m* filling

empat|ar *vi* draw. **~e** *m* draw

empedernido *a* inveterate; (*insensible*) hard

empedrar [1] *vt* pave

empeine *m* instep

empeñ|ado *a* in debt; (*decidido*) determined; (*acalorado*) heated. **~ar** *vt* pawn; pledge ⟨*palabras*⟩; (*principiar*) start. **~arse** *vpr* (*endeudarse*) get into debt; (*meterse*) get involved; (*estar decidido a*) insist (*en* on). **~o** *m* pledge; (*resolución*) determination. **casa de ~s** pawnshop

empeorar *vt* make worse. ● *vi* get worse. **~se** *vpr* get worse

empequeñecer [11] *vt* dwarf; (*fig*) belittle

empera|dor *m* emperor. **~triz** *f* empress

empezar [1 & 10] *vt/i* start, begin. **para ~** to begin with

empina|do *a* upright; ⟨*cuesta*⟩ steep. **~r** *vt* raise. **~rse** *vpr* ⟨*persona*⟩ stand on tiptoe; ⟨*animal*⟩ rear

empírico *a* empirical

emplasto *m* plaster

emplaza|miento *m* (*jurid*) summons; (*lugar*) site. **~r** [10] *vt* summon; (*situar*) site

emple|ado *m* employee. **~ar** *vt* use; employ ⟨*persona*⟩; spend ⟨*tiempo*⟩. **~arse** *vpr* be used; ⟨*persona*⟩ be employed. **~o** *m* use; (*trabajo*) employment; (*puesto*) job

empobrecer [11] *vt* impoverish. **~se** *vpr* become poor

empolvar *vt* powder

empoll|ar *vt* incubate ⟨*huevos*⟩; (*estudiar, fam*) swot up (*Brit*), grind away at (*Amer*). ● *vi* ⟨*ave*⟩ sit; ⟨*estudiante*⟩ swot (*Brit*), grind away (*Amer*). **~ón** *m* swot

emponzoñar *vt* poison

emporio *m* emporium; (*LAm, almacén*) department store

empotra|do *a* built-in, fitted. **~r** *vt* fit

emprendedor *a* enterprising

emprender *vt* undertake; set out on ⟨*viaje etc*⟩. **~la con uno** pick a fight with s.o.

empresa *f* undertaking; (*com*) company, firm. **~rio** *m* impresario; (*com*) contractor

empréstito *m* loan

empuj|ar *vt* push; press ⟨*botón*⟩. **~e** *m* push, shove; (*fig*) drive. **~ón** *m* push, shove

empuñar *vt* grasp; take up ⟨*pluma, espada*⟩

emular *vt* emulate

emulsión *f* emulsion

en *prep* in; (*sobre*) on; (*dentro*) inside, in; (*con dirección*) into; (*medio de transporte*) by. **~ casa** at home. **~ coche** by car. **~ 10 días** in 10 days. **de pueblo ~ pueblo** from town to town

enagua *f* petticoat

enajena|ción *f* alienation; (*éxtasis*) rapture. **~r** *vt* alienate; (*volver loco*) drive mad; (*fig, extasiar*) enrapture. **~ción mental** insanity

enamora|do *a* in love. ● *m* lover. **~r** *vt* win the love of. **~rse** *vpr* fall in love (*de* with)

enan|ito *m* dwarf. **~o** *a & m* dwarf

enardecer [11] *vt* inflame. **~se** *vpr* get excited (*por* about)

encabeza|miento *m* heading; (*de periódico*) headline. **~r** [10] *vt* introduce ⟨*escrito*⟩; (*poner título a*) entitle; head ⟨*una lista*⟩; lead ⟨*revolución etc*⟩; (*empadronar*) register

encadenar vt chain; (fig) tie down

encaj|ar vt fit; fit together ⟨varias piezas⟩. ● vi fit; (estar de acuerdo) tally. ~**arse** vpr squeeze into. ~**e** m lace; (acción de encajar) fitting

encajonar vt box; (en sitio estrecho) squeeze in

encalar vt whitewash

encallar vt run aground; (fig) get bogged down

encaminar vt direct. ~**se** vpr make one's way

encandilar vt (pasmar) bewilder; (estimular) stimulate

encanecer [11] vi go grey

encant|ado a enchanted; (hechizado) bewitched; ⟨casa etc⟩ haunted. ~**ador** a charming. ● m magician. ~**amiento** m magic. ~**ar** vt bewitch; (fig) charm, delight. ~**o** m magic; (fig) delight. ¡~**ado!** pleased to meet you! **me** ~**a la leche** I love milk

encapotado a ⟨cielo⟩ overcast

encapricharse vpr. ~ **con** take a fancy to

encarar vt face. ~**se** vpr. ~**se con** face

encarcelar vt imprison

encarecer [11] vt put up the price of; (alabar) praise. ● vi go up

encarg|ado a in charge. ● m manager, attendant, person in charge. ~**ar** [12] vt entrust; (pedir) order. ~**arse** vpr take charge (de of). ~**o** m job; (com) order; (recado) errand. **hecho de** ~**o** made to measure

encariñarse vpr. ~ **con** take to, become fond of

encarna|ción f incarnation. ~**do** a incarnate; (rojo) red. ● m red

encarnizado a bitter

encarpetar vt file; (LAm, dar carpetazo) shelve

encarrilar vt put back on the rails; (fig) direct, put on the right road

encasillar vt pigeonhole

encastillarse vpr. ~ **en** (fig) stick to

encauzar [10] vt channel

encend|edor m lighter. ~**er** [1] vt light; (pegar fuego a) set fire to; switch on, turn on ⟨aparato eléctrico⟩; (fig) arouse. ~**erse** vpr light; (prender fuego) catch fire; (excitarse) get excited; (ruborizarse) blush. ~**ido** a lit; ⟨aparato eléctrico⟩ on; (rojo) bright red. ● m (auto) ignition

encera|do a waxed. ● m (pizarra) blackboard. ~**r** vt wax

encerr|ar [1] vt shut in; (con llave) lock up; (fig, contener) contain. ~**ona** f trap

encía f gum

encíclica f encyclical

enciclop|edia f encyclopaedia. ~**édico** a encyclopaedic

encierro m confinement; (cárcel) prison

encima adv on top; (arriba) above. ~ **de** on, on top of; (sobre) over; (además de) besides, as well as. **por** ~ on top; (a la ligera) superficially. **por** ~ **de todo** above all

encina f holm oak

encinta a pregnant

enclave m enclave

enclenque a weak; (enfermizo) sickly

encog|er [14] vt shrink; (contraer) contract. ~**erse** vpr shrink. ~**erse de hombros** shrug one's shoulders. ~**ido** a shrunk; (fig, tímido) timid

encolar vt glue; (pegar) stick

encolerizar [10] vt make angry. ~**se** vpr get angry, lose one's temper

encomendar [1] vt entrust

encomi|ar vt praise. ~**o** m praise

encono m bitterness, ill will

encontra|do a contrary, conflicting. ~**r** [2] vt find; (tropezar con) meet. ~**rse** vpr meet; (hallarse) be. **no** ~**rse** feel uncomfortable

encorvar vt bend, curve. ~**se** vpr stoop

encrespado a ⟨pelo⟩ curly; ⟨mar⟩ rough

encrucijada f crossroads

encuaderna|ción f binding. ~**dor** m bookbinder. ~**r** vt bind

encuadrar vt frame

encub|ierto a hidden. ~**rir** [pp **encubierto**] vt hide, conceal; shelter ⟨delincuente⟩

encuentro m meeting; (colisión) crash; (en deportes) match; (mil) skirmish

encuesta f survey; (investigación) inquiry

encumbra|do a eminent. ~**r** vt (fig, elevar) exalt. ~**rse** vpr rise

encurtidos mpl pickles

encharcar [7] vt flood. ~**se** vpr be flooded

enchuf|ado a switched on. ~**ar** vt plug in; fit together ⟨tubos etc⟩. ~**e** m socket; (clavija) plug; (de tubos

etc) joint; (*fig, empleo, fam*) cushy job; (*influencia, fam*) influence. **tener ~e** have friends in the right places
endeble *a* weak
endemoniado *a* possessed; (*malo*) wicked
enderezar [10] *vt* straighten out; (*poner vertical*) put upright (again); (*fig, arreglar*) put right, sort out; (*dirigir*) direct. **~se** *vpr* straighten out
endeudarse *vpr* get into debt
endiablado *a* possessed; (*malo*) wicked
endomingarse [12] *vpr* dress up
endosar *vt* endorse ⟨*cheque etc*⟩; (*fig, fam*) lumber
endrogarse [12] *vpr* (*Mex*) get into debt
endulzar [10] *vt* sweeten; (*fig*) soften
endurecer [11] *vt* harden. **~se** *vpr* harden; (*fig*) become hardened
enema *m* enema
enemi|go *a* hostile. ● *m* enemy. **~stad** *f* enmity. **~star** *vt* make an enemy of. **~starse** *vpr* fall out (**con** with)
en|ergía *f* energy. **~érgico** *a* ⟨*persona*⟩ lively; ⟨*decisión*⟩ forceful
energúmeno *m* madman
enero *m* January
enervar *vt* enervate
enésimo *a* nth, umpteenth (*fam*)
enfad|adizo *a* irritable. **~ado** *a* cross, angry. **~ar** *vt* make cross, anger; (*molestar*) annoy. **~arse** *vpr* get cross. **~o** *m* anger; (*molestia*) annoyance
énfasis *m invar* emphasis, stress. **poner ~** stress, emphasize
enfático *a* emphatic
enferm|ar *vi* fall ill. **~edad** *f* illness. **~era** *f* nurse. **~ería** *f* sick bay. **~ero** *m* (male) nurse. **~izo** *a* sickly. **~o** *a* ill. ● *m* patient
enflaquecer [11] *vt* make thin. ● *vi* lose weight
enfo|car [7] *vt* shine on; focus ⟨*lente etc*⟩; (*fig*) consider. **~que** *m* focus; (*fig*) point of view
enfrascarse [7] *vpr* (*fig*) be absorbed
enfrentar *vt* face, confront; (*poner frente a frente*) bring face to face. **~se** *vpr*. **~se con** confront; (*en deportes*) meet
enfrente *adv* opposite. **~ de** opposite. **de ~** opposite

enfria|miento *m* cooling; (*catarro*) cold. **~r** [20] *vt* cool (down); (*fig*) cool down. **~rse** *vpr* go cold; (*fig*) cool off
enfurecer [11] *vt* infuriate. **~se** *vpr* lose one's temper; (*mar*) get rough
enfurruñarse *vpr* sulk
engalanar *vt* adorn. **~se** *vpr* dress up
enganchar *vt* hook; hang up ⟨*ropa*⟩. **~se** *vpr* get caught; (*mil*) enlist
engañ|ar *vt* deceive, trick; (*ser infiel*) be unfaithful. **~arse** *vpr* be wrong, be mistaken; (*no admitir la verdad*) deceive o.s. **~o** *m* deceit, trickery; (*error*) mistake. **~oso** *a* deceptive; ⟨*persona*⟩ deceitful
engarzar [10] *vt* string ⟨*cuentas*⟩; set ⟨*joyas*⟩; (*fig*) link
engatusar *vt* (*fam*) coax
engendr|ar *vt* breed; (*fig*) produce. **~o** *m* (*monstruo*) monster; (*fig*) brainchild
englobar *vt* include
engomar *vt* glue
engordar [2] *vt* fatten. ● *vi* get fatter, put on weight
engorro *m* nuisance
engranaje *m* (*auto*) gear
engrandecer [11] *vt* (*enaltecer*) exalt, raise
engrasar *vt* grease; (*con aceite*) oil; (*ensuciar*) make greasy
engreído *a* arrogant
engrosar [2] *vt* swell. ● *vi* ⟨*persona*⟩ get fatter; ⟨*río*⟩ swell
engullir [22] *vt* gulp down
enharinar *vt* sprinkle with flour
enhebrar *vt* thread
enhorabuena *f* congratulations. **dar la ~** congratulate
enigm|a *m* enigma. **~ático** *a* enigmatic
enjabonar *vt* soap; (*fig, fam*) butter up
enjalbegar [12] *vt* whitewash
enjambre *m* swarm
enjaular *vt* put in a cage
enjuag|ar [12] *vt* rinse (out). **~atorio** *m* mouthwash. **~ue** *m* rinsing; (*para la boca*) mouthwash
enjugar [12] *vt* dry; (*limpiar*) wipe; cancel ⟨*deuda*⟩
enjuiciar *vt* pass judgement on
enjuto *a* ⟨*persona*⟩ skinny
enlace *m* connection; (*matrimonial*) wedding
enlatar *vt* tin, can

enlazar [10] *vt* tie together; *(fig)* relate, connect

enlodar *vt*, **enlodazar** [10] *vt* cover in mud

enloquecer [11] *vt* drive mad. ● *vi* go mad. **~se** *vpr* go mad

enlosar *vt* *(con losas)* pave; *(con baldosas)* tile

enlucir [11] *vt* plaster

enluta|do *a* in mourning. **~r** *vt* dress in mourning; *(fig)* sadden

enmarañar *vt* tangle (up), entangle; *(confundir)* confuse. **~se** *vpr* get into a tangle; *(confundirse)* get confused

enmarcar [7] *vt* frame

enmascarar *vt* mask. **~se de** masquerade as

enm|endar *vt* correct. **~endarse** *vpr* mend one's way. **~ienda** *f* correction; *(de ley etc)* amendment

enmohecerse [11] *vpr* *(con óxido)* go rusty; *(con hongos)* go mouldy

enmudecer [11] *vi* be dumbstruck; *(callar)* say nothing

ennegrecer [11] *vt* blacken

ennoblecer [11] *vt* ennoble; *(fig)* add style to

enoj|adizo *a* irritable. **~ado** *a* angry, cross. **~ar** *vt* make cross, anger; *(molestar)* annoy. **~arse** *vpr* get cross. **~o** *m* anger; *(molestia)* annoyance. **~oso** *a* annoying

enorgullecerse [11] *vpr* be proud

enorm|e *a* enormous; *(malo)* wicked. **~emente** *adv* enormously. **~idad** *f* immensity; *(atrocidad)* enormity. **me gusta una ~idad** I like it enormously

enrabiar *vt* infuriate

enraizar [10 & 20] *vi* take root

enrarecido *a* rarefied

enrasar *vt* make level

enred|adera *f* creeper. **~adero** *a* climbing. **~ar** *vt* tangle (up), entangle; *(confundir)* confuse; *(comprometer a uno)* involve, implicate; *(sembrar la discordia)* cause trouble between. ● *vi* get up to mischief. **~ar con** fiddle with, play with. **~arse** *vpr* get into a tangle; *(confundirse)* get confused; *(persona)* get involved. **~o** *m* tangle; *(fig)* muddle, mess

enrejado *m* bars

enrevesado *a* complicated

enriquecer [11] *vt* make rich; *(fig)* enrich. **~se** *vpr* get rich

enrojecer [11] *vt* turn red, redden. **~se** *vpr* *(persona)* go red, blush

enrolar *vt* enlist

enrollar *vt* roll (up); wind *(hilo etc)*

enroscar [7] *vt* coil; *(atornillar)* screw in

ensalad|a *f* salad. **~era** *f* salad bowl. **~illa** *f* Russian salad. **armar una ~a** make a mess

ensalzar [10] *vt* praise; *(enaltecer)* exalt

ensambladura *f*, **ensamblaje** *m* *(acción)* assembling; *(efecto)* joint

ensamblar *vt* join

ensanch|ar *vt* widen; *(agrandar)* enlarge. **~arse** *vpr* get wider. **~e** *m* widening; *(de ciudad)* new district

ensangrentar [1] *vt* stain with blood

ensañarse *vpr*. **~ con** treat cruelly

ensartar *vt* string *(cuentas etc)*

ensay|ar *vt* test; rehearse *(obra de teatro etc)*. **~arse** *vpr* rehearse. **~o** *m* test, trial; *(composición literaria)* essay

ensenada *f* inlet, cove

enseña|nza *f* education; *(acción de enseñar)* teaching. **~nza media** secondary education. **~r** *vt* teach; *(mostrar)* show

enseñorearse *vpr* take over

enseres *mpl* equipment

ensillar *vt* saddle

ensimismarse *vpr* be lost in thought

ensoberbecerse [11] *vpr* become conceited

ensombrecer [11] *vt* darken

ensordecer [11] *vt* deafen. ● *vi* go deaf

ensortijar *vt* curl *(pelo etc)*

ensuciar *vt* dirty. **~se** *vpr* get dirty

ensueño *m* dream

entablar *vt* *(empezar)* start

entablillar *vt* put in a splint

entalegar [12] *vt* put into a bag; *(fig)* hoard

entallar *vt* fit *(un vestido)*. ● *vi* fit

entarimado *m* parquet

ente *m* entity, being; *(persona rara, fam)* odd person; *(com)* firm, company

entend|er [1] *vt* understand; *(opinar)* believe, think; *(querer decir)* mean. ● *vi* understand. **~erse** *vpr* make o.s. understood; *(comprenderse)* be understood. **~er de** know all about. **~erse con** get on with. **~ido** *a* understood; *(enterado)* well-informed. ● *interj* agreed!, OK! *(fam)*. **~imiento** *m* understanding.

a mi ~er in my opinion. **dar a ~er** hint. **no darse por ~ido** pretend not to understand, turn a deaf ear
entenebrecer [11] *vt* darken. **~se** *vpr* get dark
enterado *a* well-informed; (*que sabe*) aware. **no darse por ~** pretend not to understand, turn a deaf ear
enteramente *adv* entirely, completely
enterar *vt* inform. **~se** *vpr*. **~se de** find out about, hear of. **¡entérate!** listen! **¿te enteras?** do you understand?
entereza *f* (*carácter*) strength of character
enternecer [11] *vt* (*fig*) move, touch. **~se** *vpr* be moved, be touched
entero *a* entire, whole; (*firme*) firm. **por ~** entirely, completely
enterra|dor *m* gravedigger. **~r** [1] *vt* bury
entibiar *vt* cool. **~se** *vpr* cool down; (*fig*) cool off
entidad *f* entity; (*organización*) organization; (*com*) company
entierro *m* burial; (*ceremonia*) funeral
entona|ción *f* intonation; (*fig*) arrogance. **~r** *vt* intone. ● *vi* (*mus*) be in tune; (*colores*) match. **~rse** *vpr* (*fortalecerse*) tone o.s. up; (*engreírse*) be arrogant
entonces *adv* then. **en aquel ~, por aquel ~** at that time, then
entontecer [11] *vt* make silly. **~se** *vpr* get silly
entornar *vt* half close; leave ajar (*puerta*)
entorpecer [11] *vt* (*frío etc*) numb; (*dificultar*) hinder
entra|da *f* entrance; (*acceso*) admission, entry; (*billete*) ticket; (*de datos, tec*) input. **~do** *a*. **~do en años** elderly. **ya ~da la noche** late at night. **~nte** *a* next, coming. **dar ~da a** (*admitir*) admit. **de ~da** right away.
entraña *f* (*fig*) heart. **~s** *fpl* entrails; (*fig*) heart. **~ble** *a* (*cariño etc*) deep; (*amigo*) close. **~r** *vt* involve
entrar *vt* put; (*traer*) bring. ● *vi* go in, enter; (*venir*) come in, enter; (*empezar*) start, begin. **no ~ ni salir en** have nothing to do with
entre *prep* (*de dos personas o cosas*) between; (*más de dos*) among(st)

entreab|ierto *a* half-open. **~rir** [*pp* **entreabierto**] *vt* half open
entreacto *m* interval
entrecano *a* (*pelo*) greying; (*persona*) who is going grey
entrecejo *m* forehead. **arrugar el ~, fruncir el ~** frown
entrecerrar [1] *vt* (*Amer*) half close
entrecortado *a* (*voz*) faltering; (*respiración*) laboured
entrecruzar [10] *vt* intertwine
entrega *f* handing over; (*de mercancías etc*) delivery; (*de novela etc*) instalment; (*dedicación*) commitment. **~r** [12] *vt* hand over, deliver, give. **~rse** *vpr* surrender, give o.s. up; (*dedicarse*) devote o.s. (**a** to)
entrelazar [10] *vt* intertwine
entremés *m* hors-d'oeuvre; (*en el teatro*) short comedy
entremet|er *vt* insert. **~erse** *vpr* interfere. **~ido** *a* interfering
entremezclar *vt* mix
entrena|dor *m* trainer. **~miento** *m* training. **~r** *vt* train. **~rse** *vpr* train
entrepierna *f* crotch
entresacar [7] *vt* pick out
entresuelo *m* mezzanine
entretanto *adv* meanwhile
entretejer *vt* interweave
entreten|er [40] *vt* entertain, amuse; (*detener*) delay, keep; (*mantener*) keep alive, keep going. **~erse** *vpr* amuse o.s.; (*tardar*) delay, linger. **~ido** *a* entertaining. **~imiento** *m* entertainment; (*mantenimiento*) upkeep
entrever [43] *vt* make out, glimpse
entrevista *f* interview; (*reunión*) meeting. **~rse** *vpr* have an interview
entristecer [11] *vt* sadden, make sad. **~se** *vpr* be sad
entromet|erse *vpr* interfere. **~ido** *a* interfering
entroncar [7] *vi* be related
entruchada *f*, **entruchado** *m* (*fam*) plot
entumec|erse [11] *vpr* go numb. **~ido** *a* numb
enturbiar *vt* cloud
entusi|asmar *vt* fill with enthusiasm; (*gustar mucho*) delight. **~asmarse** *vpr*. **~asmarse con** get enthusiastic about; (*ser aficionado a*) be mad about, love. **~asmo** *m* enthusiasm. **~asta** *a* enthusiastic.

● *m* & *f* enthusiast. **~ástico** *a* enthusiastic
enumera|ción *f* count, reckoning. **~r** *vt* enumerate
enuncia|ción *f* enunciation. **~r** *vt* enunciate
envainar *vt* sheathe
envalentonar *vt* encourage. **~se** *vpr* be brave, pluck up courage
envanecer [11] *vt* make conceited. **~se** *vpr* be conceited
envas|ado *a* tinned. ● *m* packaging. **~ar** *vt* package; (*en latas*) tin, can; (*en botellas*) bottle. **~e** *m* packing; (*lata*) tin, can; (*botella*) bottle
envejec|er [11] *vt* make old. ● *vi* get old, grow old. **~erse** *vpr* get old, grow old. **~ido** *a* aged, old
envenenar *vt* poison
envergadura *f* (*alcance*) scope
envés *m* wrong side
envia|do *a* sent. ● *m* representative; (*de la prensa*) correspondent. **~r** *vt* send
enviciar *vt* corrupt
envidi|a *f* envy; (*celos*) jealousy. **~able** *a* enviable. **~ar** *vt* envy, be envious of. **~oso** *a* envious. **tener ~a** a envy
envilecer [11] *vt* degrade
envío *m* sending, dispatch; (*de mercancías*) consignment; (*de dinero*) remittance. **~ contra reembolso** cash on delivery. **gastos** *mpl* **de envío** postage and packing (costs)
enviudar *vi* 〈*mujer*〉 become a widow, be widowed; 〈*hombre*〉 become a widower, be widowed
env|oltura *f* wrapping. **~olver** [2, *pp* **envuelto**] *vt* wrap; (*cubrir*) cover; (*fig, acorralar*) corner; (*fig, enredar*) involve; (*mil*) surround. **~olvimiento** *m* involvement. **~uelto** *a* wrapped (up)
enyesar *vt* plaster; (*med*) put in plaster
enzima *f* enzyme
épica *f* epic
epicentro *m* epicentre
épico *a* epic
epid|emia *f* epidemic. **~émico** *a* epidemic
epil|epsia *f* epilepsy. **~éptico** *a* epileptic
epílogo *m* epilogue
episodio *m* episode
epístola *f* epistle
epitafio *m* epitaph
epíteto *m* epithet

epítome *m* epitome
época *f* age; (*período*) period. **hacer ~** make history, be epoch-making
equidad *f* equity
equilátero *a* equilateral
equilibr|ar *vt* balance. **~io** *m* balance; (*de balanza*) equilibrium. **~ista** *m* & *f* tightrope walker
equino *a* horse, equine
equinoccio *m* equinox
equipaje *m* luggage (*esp Brit*), baggage (*esp Amer*); (*de barco*) crew
equipar *vt* equip; (*de ropa*) fit out
equiparar *vt* make equal; (*comparar*) compare
equipo *m* equipment; (*en deportes*) team
equitación *f* riding
equivale|ncia *f* equivalence. **~nte** *a* equivalent. **~r** [42] *vi* be equivalent; (*significar*) mean
equivoca|ción *f* mistake, error. **~do** *a* wrong. **~r** [7] *vt* mistake. **~rse** *vpr* be mistaken, be wrong, make a mistake. **~rse de** be wrong about. **~rse de número** dial the wrong number. **si no me equivoco** if I'm not mistaken
equívoco *a* equivocal; (*sospechoso*) suspicious. ● *m* ambiguity; (*juego de palabras*) pun; (*doble sentido*) double meaning
era *f* era. ● *vb véase* **ser**
erario *m* treasury
erección *f* erection; (*fig*) establishment
eremita *m* hermit
eres *vb véase* **ser**
erguir [48] *vt* raise. **~ la cabeza** hold one's head high. **~se** *vpr* straighten up
erigir [14] *vt* erect. **~se** *vpr* set o.s. up (**en** as)
eriza|do *a* prickly. **~rse** [10] *vpr* stand on end
erizo *m* hedgehog; (*de mar*) sea urchin. **~ de mar**, **~ marino** sea urchin
ermita *f* hermitage. **~ño** *m* hermit
erosi|ón *f* erosion. **~onar** *vt* erode
er|ótico *a* erotic. **~otismo** *m* eroticism
errar [1, *la* **i** *inicial se escribe* **y**] *vt* miss. ● *vi* wander; (*equivocarse*) make a mistake, be wrong
errata *f* misprint
erróneo *a* erroneous, wrong
error *m* error, mistake. **estar en un ~** be wrong, be mistaken

eructar vi belch

erudi|ción f learning, erudition. **~to** a learned

erupción f eruption; (med) rash

es vb véase **ser**

esa a véase **ese**

ésa pron véase **ése**

esbelto a slender, slim

esboz|ar [10] vt sketch, outline. **~o** m sketch, outline

escabeche m pickle. **en ~** pickled

escabroso a ⟨terreno⟩ rough; ⟨asunto⟩ difficult; ⟨atrevido⟩ crude

escabullirse [22] vpr slip away

escafandra f, **escafandro** m diving-suit

escala f scale; (escalera de mano) ladder; (de avión) stopover. **~da** f climbing; (pol) escalation. **~r** vt scale; break into ⟨una casa⟩. ● vi (pol) escalate. **hacer ~ en** stop at. **vuelo sin ~s** non-stop flight

escaldar vt scald

escalera f staircase, stairs; (de mano) ladder. **~ de caracol** spiral staircase. **~ de incendios** fire escape. **~ mecánica** escalator. **~ plegable** step-ladder

escalfa|do a poached. **~r** vt poach

escalinata f flight of steps

escalofrío m shiver

escal|ón m step; (de escalera interior) stair; (de escala) rung. **~onar** vt spread out

escalope m escalope

escam|a f scale; (de jabón) flake; (fig) suspicion. **~oso** a scaly

escamotear vt make disappear; (robar) steal, pinch (fam); disregard ⟨dificultad⟩

escampar vi stop raining

esc|andalizar [10] vt scandalize, shock. **~andalizarse** vpr be shocked. **~ándalo** m scandal; (alboroto) uproar. **~andaloso** a scandalous; (alborotador) noisy

Escandinavia f Scandinavia

escandinavo a & m Scandinavian

escaño m bench; (pol) seat

escapa|da f escape; (visita) flying visit. **~do** a in a hurry. **~r** vi escape. **~rse** vpr escape; ⟨líquido, gas⟩ leak. **dejar ~r** let out

escaparate m (shop) window. **ir de ~s** go window-shopping

escapatoria f (fig, fam) way out

escape m (de gas, de líquido) leak; (fuga) escape; (auto) exhaust

escarabajo m beetle

escaramuza f skirmish

escarbar vt scratch; pick ⟨dientes, herida etc⟩; (fig, escudriñar) delve (en into)

escarcha f frost. **~do** a ⟨fruta⟩ crystallized

escarlat|a a invar scarlet. **~ina** f scarlet fever

escarm|entar [1] vt punish severely. ● vi learn one's lesson. **~iento** m punishment; (lección) lesson

escarn|ecer [11] vt mock. **~io** m ridicule

escarola f endive

escarpa f slope. **~do** a steep

escas|ear vi be scarce. **~ez** f scarcity, shortage; (pobreza) poverty. **~o** a scarce; (poco) little; (insuficiente) short; (muy justo) barely

escatimar vt be sparing with

escayola f plaster. **~r** vt put in plaster

escena f scene; (escenario) stage. **~rio** m stage; (en el cine) scenario; (fig) scene

escénico a scenic

escenografía f scenery

esc|epticismo m scepticism. **~éptico** a sceptical. ● m sceptic

esclarecer [11] vt (fig) throw light on, clarify

esclavina f cape

esclav|itud f slavery. **~izar** [10] vt enslave. **~o** m slave

esclerosis f sclerosis

esclusa f lock

escoba f broom

escocer [2 & 9] vt hurt. ● vi sting

escocés a Scottish. ● m Scotsman

Escocia f Scotland

escog|er [14] vt choose, select. **~ido** a chosen; (de buena calidad) choice

escolar a school. ● m schoolboy. ● f schoolgirl. **~idad** f schooling

escolta f escort

escombros mpl rubble

escond|er vt hide. **~erse** vpr hide. **~idas. a ~idas** secretly. **~ite** m hiding place; (juego) hide-and-seek. **~rijo** m hiding place

escopeta f shotgun. **~zo** m shot

escoplo m chisel

escoria f slag; (fig) dregs

Escorpión m Scorpio

escorpión m scorpion

escot|ado a low-cut. **~adura** f low neckline. **~ar** vt cut out. ● vi pay

one's share. **~e** *m* low neckline. **ir a ~e, pagar a ~e** share the expenses
escozor *m* pain
escri|bano *m* clerk. **~biente** *m* clerk. **~bir** [*pp* **escrito**] *vt/i* write. **~bir a máquina** type. **~birse** *vpr* write to each other; (*deletrearse*) be spelt. **~to** *a* written. ● *m* writing; (*documento*) document. **~tor** *m* writer. **~torio** *m* desk; (*oficina*) office. **~tura** *f* (hand)writing; (*documento*) document; (*jurid*) deed. **¿cómo se escribe...?** how do you spell...? **poner por ~to** put into writing
escr|úpulo *m* scruple; (*escrupulosidad*) care, scrupulousness. **~uloso** *a* scrupulous
escrut|ar *vt* scrutinize; count (*votos*). **~inio** *m* count. **hacer el ~inio** count the votes
escuadr|a *f* (*instrumento*) square; (*mil*) squad; (*naut*) fleet. **~ón** *m* squadron
escuálido *a* skinny; (*sucio*) squalid
escuchar *vt* listen to. ● *vi* listen
escudilla *f* bowl
escudo *m* shield. **~ de armas** coat of arms
escudriñar *vt* examine
escuela *f* school. **~ normal** teachers' training college
escueto *a* simple
escuincle *m* (*Mex*, *perro*) stray dog; (*Mex*, *muchacho*, *fam*) child, kid (*fam*)
escul|pir *vt* sculpture. **~tor** *m* sculptor. **~tora** *f* sculptress. **~tura** *f* sculpture; (*en madera*) carving
escupir *vt/i* spit
escurr|eplatos *m invar* plate-rack. **~idizo** *a* slippery. **~ir** *vt* drain; wring out (*ropa*). ● *vi* drip; (*ser resbaladizo*) be slippery. **~irse** *vpr* slip
ese *a* (*f* **esa**, *mpl* **esos**, *fpl* **esas**) that; (*en plural*) those
ése *pron* (*f* **ésa**, *mpl* **ésos**, *fpl* **ésas**) that one; (*en plural*) those; (*primero de dos*) the former. **ni por ésas** on no account
esencia *f* essence. **~l** *a* essential. **lo ~l** the main thing
esf|era *f* sphere; (*de reloj*) face. **~érico** *a* spherical
esfinge *f* sphinx
esf|orzarse [2 & 10] *vpr* make an effort. **~uerzo** *m* effort

esfumarse *vpr* fade away; (*persona*) vanish
esgrim|a *f* fencing. **~ir** *vt* brandish; (*fig*) use
esguince *m* swerve; (*med*) sprain
eslab|ón *m* link. **~onar** *vt* link (together)
eslavo *a* Slav, Slavonic
eslogan *m* slogan
esmalt|ar *vt* enamel; varnish (*uñas*); (*fig*) adorn. **~e** *m* enamel. **~ de uñas**, **~e para las uñas** nail varnish (*Brit*), nail polish (*Amer*)
esmerado *a* careful
esmeralda *f* emerald
esmerarse *vpr* take care (**en** over)
esmeril *m* emery
esmero *m* care
esmoquin *m* dinner jacket, tuxedo (*Amer*)
esnob *a invar* snobbish. ● *m* & *f* (*pl* **esnobs**) snob. **~ismo** *m* snobbery
esnórkel *m* snorkel
eso *pron* that. **¡~ es!** that's it! **~ mismo** exactly. **¡~ no!** certainly not! **¡~ sí!** of course. **a ~ de** about. **en ~** at that moment. **¿no es ~?** isn't that right? **por ~** therefore. **y ~ que** although
esos *a pl véase* **ese**
ésos *pron pl véase* **ése**
espabila|do *a* bright. **~r** *vt* snuff (*vela*); (*avivar*) brighten up; (*despertar*) wake up. **~rse** *vpr* wake up; (*apresurarse*) hurry up
espaci|al *a* space. **~ar** *vt* space out. **~o** *m* space. **~oso** *a* spacious
espada *f* sword. **~s** *fpl* (*en naipes*) spades
espagueti *m* spaghetti
espald|a *f* back. **~illa** *f* shoulder-blade. **a ~as de uno** behind s.o.'s back. **a las ~as** on one's back. **tener las ~as anchas** be broad-shouldered. **volver la ~a a uno**, **volver las ~as a uno** give s.o. the cold shoulder
espant|ada *f* stampede. **~adizo** *a* timid, timorous. **~ajo** *m*, **~apájaros** *m inv* scarecrow. **~ar** *vt* frighten; (*ahuyentar*) frighten away. **~arse** *vpr* be frightened; (*ahuyentarse*) be frightened away. **~o** *m* terror; (*horror*) horror. **~oso** *a* frightening; (*muy grande*) terrible. **¡qué ~ajo!** what a sight!
España *f* Spain
español *a* Spanish. ● *m* (*persona*) Spaniard; (*lengua*) Spanish. **los**

~es the Spanish. **~izado** a Hispanicized

esparadrapo m sticking-plaster, plaster (*Brit*)

esparci|do a scattered; (*fig*) widespread. **~r** [9] vt scatter; (*difundir*) spread. **~rse** vpr be scattered; (*difundirse*) spread; (*divertirse*) enjoy o.s.

espárrago m asparagus

esparto m esparto (grass)

espasm|o m spasm. **~ódico** a spasmodic

espátula f spatula; (*en pintura*) palette knife

especia f spice

especial a special. **~idad** f speciality (*Brit*), specialty (*Amer*). **~ista** a & m & f specialist. **~ización** f specialization. **~izar** [10] vt specialize. **~izarse** vpr specialize. **~mente** adv especially. **en ~** especially

especie f kind, sort; (*en biología*) species; (*noticia*) piece of news. **en ~** in kind

especifica|ción f specification. **~r** [7] vt specify

específico a specific

espect|áculo m sight; (*diversión*) entertainment, show. **~ador** m & f spectator. **~acular** a spectacular

espectro m spectre; (*en física*) spectrum

especula|ción f speculation. **~dor** m speculator. **~r** vi speculate. **~tivo** a speculative

espej|ismo m mirage. **~o** m mirror. **~o retrovisor** (*auto*) rear-view mirror

espeleólogo m potholer

espeluznante a horrifying

espera f wait. **sala f de ~** waiting room

espera|nza f hope. **~r** vt hope; (*aguardar*) wait for; (*creer*) expect. ● vi hope; (*aguardar*) wait. **~r en uno** trust in s.o. **en ~ de** awaiting. **espero que no** I hope not. **espero que sí** I hope so

esperma f sperm

esperpento m fright; (*disparate*) nonsense

espes|ar vt thicken. **~arse** vpr thicken. **~o** a thick; (*pasta etc*) stiff. **~or** m, **~ura** f thickness; (*bot*) thicket

espetón m spit

esp|ía f spy. **~iar** [20] vt spy on. ● vi spy

espiga f (*de trigo etc*) ear

espina f thorn; (*de pez*) bone; (*dorsal*) spine; (*astilla*) splinter; (*fig, dificultad*) difficulty. **~ dorsal** spine

espinaca f spinach

espinazo m spine

espinilla f shin; (*med*) blackhead

espino m hawthorn. **~ artificial** barbed wire. **~so** a thorny; (*pez*) bony; (*fig*) difficult

espionaje m espionage

espiral a & f spiral

espirar vt/i breathe out

esp|iritismo m spiritualism. **~iritoso** a spirited. **~iritista** m & f spiritualist. **~íritu** m spirit; (*mente*) mind; (*inteligencia*) intelligence. **~iritual** a spiritual. **~iritualismo** m spiritualism

espita f tap, faucet (*Amer*)

espl|éndido a splendid; (*persona*) generous. **~endor** m splendour

espliego m lavender

espolear vt (*fig*) spur on

espoleta f fuse

espolvorear vt sprinkle

esponj|a f sponge; (*tejido*) towelling. **~oso** a spongy. **pasar la ~a** forget about it

espont|aneidad f spontaneity. **~áneo** a spontaneous

esporádico a sporadic

espos|a f wife. **~as** fpl handcuffs. **~ar** vt handcuff. **~o** m husband. **los ~os** the couple

espuela f spur; (*fig*) incentive. **dar de ~s** spur on

espum|a f foam; (*en bebidas*) froth; (*de jabón*) lather. **~ar** vt skim. ● vi foam; (*bebidas*) froth; (*jabón*) lather. **~oso** a (*vino*) sparkling. **echar ~a** foam, froth

esqueleto m skeleton

esquem|a m outline. **~ático** a sketchy

esqu|í m (pl **esquís**) ski; (*el deporte*) skiing. **~iador** m skier. **~iar** [20] vi ski

esquilar vt shear

esquimal a & m Eskimo

esquina f corner

esquirol m blackleg

esquiv|ar vt avoid. **~o** a aloof

esquizofrénico a & m schizophrenic

esta a véase **este**

ésta pron véase **éste**

estab|ilidad f stability. **~ilizador** m stabilizer. **~ilizar** [10] vt stabilize. **~le** a stable

establec|er [11] *vt* establish. **~erse** *vpr* settle; (*com*) start a business. **~imiento** *m* establishment

establo *m* cowshed

estaca *f* stake; (*para apalear*) stick. **~da** *f* (*cerca*) fence

estación *f* station; (*del año*) season; (*de vacaciones*) resort. **~ de servicio** service station

estaciona|miento *m* parking. **~r** *vt* station; (*auto*) park. **~rio** *a* stationary

estadio *m* stadium; (*fase*) stage

estadista *m* statesman. **●f** stateswoman

estadístic|a *f* statistics. **~o** *a* statistical

estado *m* state. **~ civil** marital status. **~ de ánimo** frame of mind. **~ de cuenta** bank statement. **~ mayor** (*mil*) staff. **en buen ~** in good condition. **en ~ (interesante)** pregnant

Estados Unidos *mpl* United States

estadounidense *a* American, United States. **●** *m & f* American

estafa *f* swindle. **~r** *vt* swindle

estafeta *f* (*oficina de correos*) (sub-)post office

estala|ctita *f* stalactite. **~gmita** *f* stalagmite

estall|ar *vi* explode; ‹*olas*› break; ‹*guerra, epidemia etc*› break out; (*fig*) burst. **~ar en llanto** burst into tears. **~ar de risa** burst out laughing. **~ido** *m* explosion; (*de guerra, epidemia etc*) outbreak; (*de risa etc*) outburst

estamp|a *f* print; (*aspecto*) appearance. **~ado** *a* printed. **●** *m* printing; (*tela*) cotton print. **~ar** *vt* stamp; (*imprimir*) print. **dar a la ~a** (*imprimir*) print; (*publicar*) publish. **la viva ~a** the image

estampía. de ~ía suddenly

estampido *m* explosion

estampilla *f* stamp; (*Mex*) (postage) stamp

estanca|do *a* stagnant. **~miento** *m* stagnation. **~r** [7] *vt* stem; (*com*) turn into a monopoly

estanci|a *f* stay; (*Arg, finca*) ranch, farm; (*cuarto*) room. **~ero** *m* (*Arg*) farmer

estanco *a* watertight. **●** *m* tobacconist's (shop)

estandarte *m* standard, banner

estanque *m* lake; (*depósito de agua*) reservoir

estanquero *m* tobacconist

estante *m* shelf. **~ría** *f* shelves; (*para libros*) bookcase

estañ|o *m* tin. **~adura** *f* tin-plating

estar [27] *vi* be; (*quedarse*) stay; (*estar en casa*) be in. **¿estamos?** alright? **estamos a 29 de noviembre** it's the 29th of November. **~ para** be about to. **~ por** remain to be; (*con ganas de*) be tempted to; (*ser partidario de*) be in favour of. **~se** *vpr* stay. **¿cómo está Vd?, ¿cómo estás?** how are you?

estarcir [9] *vt* stencil

estatal *a* state

estático *a* static; (*pasmado*) dumb-founded

estatua *f* statue

estatura *f* height

estatut|ario *a* statutory. **~o** *m* statute

este *m* east; (*viento*) east wind. **●** *a* (*f* **esta,** *mpl* **estos,** *fpl* **estas**) this; (*en plural*) these. **●** *int* (*LAm*) well, er

éste *pron* (*f* **ésta,** *mpl* **éstos,** *fpl* **éstas**) this one, (*en plural*) these; (*segundo de dos*) the latter

estela *f* wake; (*arquit*) carved stone

estera *f* mat; (*tejido*) matting

est|éreo *a* stereo. **~ereofónico** *a* stereo, stereophonic

esterilla *f* mat

estereotip|ado *a* stereotyped. **~o** *m* stereotype

est|éril *a* sterile; ‹*mujer*› infertile; ‹*terreno*› barren. **~erilidad** *f* sterility; (*de mujer*) infertility; (*de terreno*) barrenness

esterlina *a* sterling. **libra** *f* **~** pound sterling

estético *a* aesthetic

estevado *a* bow-legged

estiércol *m* dung; (*abono*) manure

estigma *m* stigma. **~s** *mpl* (*relig*) stigmata

estilarse *vpr* be used

estil|ista *m & f* stylist. **~izar** [10] *vt* stylize. **~o** *m* style. **por el ~o** of that sort

estilográfica *f* fountain pen

estima *f* esteem. **~do** *a* esteemed. **~do señor** (*en cartas*) Dear Sir. **~r** *vt* esteem; have great respect for ‹*persona*›; (*valorar*) value; (*juzgar*) think

est|imulante *a* stimulating. **●** *m* stimulant. **~imular** *vt* stimulate; (*incitar*) incite. **~ímulo** *m* stimulus

estipular *vt* stipulate

estir|ado a stretched; ⟨persona⟩ haughty. **~ar** vt stretch; (fig) stretch out. **~ón** m pull, tug; ⟨crecimiento⟩ sudden growth

estirpe m stock

estival a summer

esto pron neutro this; ⟨este asunto⟩ this business. **en ~** at this point. **en ~ de** in this business of. **por ~** therefore

estofa f class. **de baja ~** ⟨gente⟩ low-class

estofa|do a stewed. ● m stew. **~r** vt stew

estoic|ismo m stoicism. **~o** a stoical. ● m stoic

estómago m stomach. **dolor** m **de ~** stomach-ache

estorb|ar vt hinder, obstruct; ⟨molestar⟩ bother, annoy. ● vi be in the way. **~o** m hindrance; ⟨molestia⟩ nuisance

estornino m starling

estornud|ar vi sneeze. **~o** m sneeze

estos a mpl véase **este**

éstos pron mpl véase **éste**

estoy vb véase **estar**

estrabismo m squint

estrado m stage; (mus) bandstand

estrafalario a outlandish

estrag|ar [12] vt devastate. **~o** m devastation. **hacer ~os** devastate

estragón m tarragon

estrambótico a outlandish

estrangula|ción f strangulation. **~dor** m strangler; (auto) choke. **~miento** m blockage; (auto) bottleneck. **~r** vt strangle

estraperlo m black market. **comprar algo de ~** buy sth on the black market

estratagema f stratagem

estrateg|a m & f strategist. **~ia** f strategy

estratégic|amente adv strategically. **~o** a strategic

estrato m stratum

estratosfera f stratosphere

estrech|ar vt make narrower; take in ⟨vestido⟩; ⟨apretar⟩ squeeze; hug ⟨persona⟩. **~ar la mano a uno** shake hands with s.o. **~arse** vpr become narrower; ⟨apretarse⟩ squeeze up. **~ez** f narrowness; ⟨apuro⟩ tight spot; ⟨falta de dinero⟩ want. **~o** a narrow; ⟨vestido etc⟩ tight; (fig, íntimo) close. ● m straits. **~o de miras, de miras ~as** narrow-minded

estregar [1 & 12] vt rub

estrella f star. **~ de mar, ~mar** m starfish

estrellar vt smash; fry ⟨huevos⟩. **~se** vpr smash; ⟨fracasar⟩ fail. **~se contra** crash into

estremec|er [11] vt shake. **~erse** vpr tremble (**de** with). **~imiento** m shaking

estren|ar vt use for the first time; wear for the first time ⟨vestido etc⟩; show for the first time ⟨película⟩. **~arse** vpr make one's début; ⟨película⟩ have its première; ⟨obra de teatro⟩ open. **~o** m first use; ⟨de película⟩ première; ⟨de obra de teatro⟩ first night

estreñi|do a constipated. **~miento** m constipation

estr|épito m din. **~epitoso** a noisy; (fig) resounding

estreptomicina f streptomycin

estrés m stress

estría f groove

estribar vt rest (**en** on); ⟨consistir⟩ lie (**en** in)

estribillo m refrain; ⟨muletilla⟩ catchphrase

estribo m stirrup; ⟨de vehículo⟩ step; ⟨contrafuerte⟩ buttress. **perder los ~s** lose one's temper

estribor m starboard

estricto a strict

estridente a strident, raucous

estrofa f strophe

estropajo m scourer. **~so** a ⟨carne etc⟩ tough; ⟨persona⟩ slovenly

estropear vt spoil; ⟨romper⟩ break. **~se** vpr be damaged; ⟨fruta etc⟩ go bad; ⟨fracasar⟩ fail

estructura f structure. **~l** a structural

estruendo m din; ⟨de mucha gente⟩ uproar. **~so** a deafening

estrujar vt squeeze; (fig) drain

estuario m estuary

estuco m stucco

estuche m case

estudi|ante m & f student. **~antil** a student. **~ar** vt study. **~o** m study; ⟨de artista⟩ studio. **~oso** a studious

estufa f heater; (LAm) cooker

estupefac|ción f astonishment. **~iente** a astonishing. ● m narcotic. **~to** a astonished

estupendo a marvellous; ⟨hermoso⟩ beautiful

est|upidez f stupidity; ⟨acto⟩ stupid thing. **~úpido** a stupid

estupor *m* amazement

esturión *m* sturgeon

estuve *vb véase* **estar**

etapa *f* stage. **hacer ~ en** break the journey at. **por ~s** in stages

etc *abrev* (*etcétera*) etc

etcétera *adv* et cetera

éter *m* ether

etéreo *a* ethereal

etern|amente *adv* eternally. **~idad** *f* eternity. **~izar** [10] *vt* drag out. **~izarse** *vpr* be interminable. **~o** *a* eternal

étic|a *f* ethics. **~o** *a* ethical

etimología *f* etymology

etiqueta *f* ticket, tag; (*ceremonial*) etiquette. **de ~** formal

étnico *a* ethnic

eucalipto *m* eucalyptus

eufemismo *m* euphemism

euforia *f* euphoria

Europa *f* Europe

europe|o *a* & *m* European. **~izar** [10] *vt* Europeanize

eutanasia *f* euthanasia

evacua|ción *f* evacuation. **~r** [21 *o regular*] *vt* evacuate

evadir *vt* avoid. **~se** *vpr* escape

evaluar [21] *vt* evaluate

evang|élico *a* evangelical. **~elio** *m* gospel. **~elista** *m* & *f* evangelist

evapora|ción *f* evaporation. **~r** *vi* evaporate. **~rse** *vpr* evaporate; (*fig*) disappear

evasi|ón *f* evasion; (*fuga*) escape. **~vo** *a* evasive

evento *m* event. **a todo ~** at all events

eventual *a* possible. **~idad** *f* eventuality

eviden|cia *f* evidence. **~ciar** *vt* show. **~ciarse** *vpr* be obvious. **~te** *a* obvious. **~temente** *adv* obviously. **poner en ~cia** show; (*fig*) make a fool of

evitar *vt* avoid; (*ahorrar*) spare

evocar [7] *vt* evoke

evoluci|ón *f* evolution. **~onado** *a* fully-developed. **~onar** *vi* evolve; (*mil*) manoeuvre

ex *pref* ex-, former

exacerbar *vt* exacerbate

exact|amente *adv* exactly. **~itud** *f* exactness. **~o** *a* exact; (*preciso*) accurate; (*puntual*) punctual. **¡~!** exactly!. **con ~itud** exactly

exagera|ción *f* exaggeration. **~do** *a* exaggerated. **~r** *vt/i* exaggerate

exalta|do *a* exalted; (*fanático*) fanatical. **~r** *vt* exalt. **~rse** *vpr* get excited

exam|en *m* examination; (*escol, univ*) exam(ination). **~inador** *m* examiner. **~inar** *vt* examine. **~inarse** *vpr* take an exam

exánime *a* lifeless

exaspera|ción *f* exasperation. **~r** *vt* exasperate. **~rse** *vpr* get exasperated

excava|ción *f* excavation. **~dora** *f* digger. **~r** *vt* excavate

excede|ncia *f* leave of absence. **~nte** *a* & *m* surplus. **~r** *vi* exceed. **~rse** *vpr* go too far. **~rse a sí mismo** excel o.s.

excelen|cia *f* excellence; (*tratamiento*) Excellency. **~te** *a* excellent

exc|entricidad *f* eccentricity. **~éntrico** *a* & *m* eccentric

excepci|ón *f* exception. **~onal** *a* exceptional. **a ~ón de, con ~ón de** except (for)

except|o *prep* except (for). **~uar** [21] *vt* except

exces|ivo *a* excessive. **~o** *m* excess. **~o de equipaje** excess luggage (*esp Brit*), excess baggage (*esp Amer*)

excita|ble *a* excitable. **~ción** *f* excitement. **~nte** *a* exciting. **● m** stimulant. **~r** *vt* excite; (*incitar*) incite. **~rse** *vpr* get excited

exclama|ción *f* exclamation. **~r** *vi* exclaim

exclu|ir [17] *vt* exclude. **~sión** *f* exclusion. **~siva** *f* sole right; (*en la prensa* exclusive (story). **~sive** *adv* exclusive; (*exclusivamente*) exclusively. **~sivo** *a* exclusive

excomu|lgar [12] *vt* excommunicate. **~nión** *f* excommunication

excremento *m* excrement

exculpar *vt* exonerate; (*jurid*) acquit

excursi|ón *f* excursion, trip. **~onista** *m* & *f* day-tripper. **ir de ~ón** go on an excursion

excusa *f* excuse; (*disculpa*) apology. **~r** *vt* excuse. **presentar sus ~s** apologize

execra|ble *a* loathsome. **~r** *vt* loathe

exento *a* exempt; (*libre*) free

exequias *fpl* funeral rites

exhala|ción *f* shooting star. **~r** *vt* exhale, breath out; give off (*olor etc*). **~rse** *vpr* hurry. **como una ~ción** at top speed

exhaust|ivo *a* exhaustive. **~o** *a* exhausted

exhibi|ción *f* exhibition. **~cionista** *m* & *f* exhibitionist. **~r** *vt* exhibit

exhortar *vt* exhort (**a** to)

exhumar *vt* exhume; (*fig*) dig up

exig|encia *f* demand. **~ente** *a* demanding. **~ir** [14] *vt* demand. **tener muchas ~encias** be very demanding

exiguo *a* meagre

exil|(i)ado *a* exiled. ● *m* exile. **~(i)arse** *vpr* go into exile. **~io** *m* exile

eximio *a* distinguished

eximir *vt* exempt; (*liberar*) free

existencia *f* existence. **~s** *fpl* stock

existencial *a* existential. **~ismo** *m* existentialism

exist|ente *a* existing. **~ir** *vi* exist

éxito *m* success. **no tener ~** fail. **tener ~** be successful

exitoso *a* successful

éxodo *m* exodus

exonerar *vt* (*de un empleo*) dismiss; (*de un honor etc*) strip

exorbitante *a* exorbitant

exorci|smo *m* exorcism. **~zar** [10] *vt* exorcise

exótico *a* exotic

expan|dir *vt* expand; (*fig*) spread. **~dirse** *vpr* expand. **~sión** *f* expansion. **~sivo** *a* expansive

expatria|do *a* & *m* expatriate. **~r** *vt* banish. **~rse** *vpr* emigrate; (*exiliarse*) go into exile

expectativa *f*. **estar a la ~** be on the lookout

expedición *f* dispatch; (*cosa expedida*) shipment; (*mil, científico etc*) expedition

expediente *m* expedient; (*jurid*) proceedings; (*documentos*) record, file

expedi|r [5] *vt* dispatch, send; issue ⟨*documento*⟩. **~to** *a* clear

expeler *vt* expel

expende|dor *m* dealer. **~dor automático** vending machine. **~duría** *f* shop; (*de billetes*) ticket office. **~r** *vt* sell

expensas *fpl*. **a ~ de** at the expense of. **a mis ~** at my expense

experiencia *f* experience

experiment|al *a* experimental. **~ar** *vt* test, experiment with; (*sentir*) experience. **~o** *m* experiment

experto *a* & *m* expert

expiar [20] *vt* atone for

expirar *vi* expire; (*morir*) die

explana|da *f* levelled area; (*paseo*) esplanade. **~r** *vt* level

explayar *vt* extend. **~se** *vpr* spread out, extend; (*hablar*) be long-winded; (*confiarse*) confide (**a** in)

expletivo *m* expletive

explica|ción *f* explanation. **~r** [7] *vt* explain. **~rse** *vpr* understand; (*hacerse comprender*) explain o.s. **no me lo explico** I can't understand it

explícito *a* explicit

explora|ción *f* exploration. **~dor** *m* explorer; (*muchacho*) boy scout. **~r** *vt* explore. **~torio** *a* exploratory

explosi|ón *f* explosion; (*fig*) outburst. **~onar** *vt* blow up. **~vo** *a* & *m* explosive

explota|ción *f* working; (*abuso*) exploitation. **~r** *vt* work ⟨*mina*⟩; farm ⟨*tierra*⟩; (*abusar*) exploit. ● *vi* explode

expone|nte *m* exponent. **~r** [34] *vt* expose; display ⟨*mercancías*⟩; (*explicar*) expound; exhibit ⟨*cuadros etc*⟩; (*arriesgar*) risk. ● *vi* hold an exhibition. **~rse** *vpr* run the risk (**a** of)

exporta|ción *f* export. **~dor** *m* exporter. **~r** *vt* export

exposición *f* exposure; (*de cuadros etc*) exhibition; (*en escaparate etc*) display; (*explicación*) exposition, explanation

expresamente *adv* specifically

expres|ar *vt* express. **~arse** *vpr* express o.s. **~ión** *f* expression. **~ivo** *a* expressive; (*cariñoso*) affectionate

expreso *a* express. ● *m* express messenger; (*tren*) express

exprimi|dor *m* squeezer. **~r** *vt* squeeze; (*explotar*) exploit

expropiar *vt* expropriate

expuesto *a* on display; ⟨*lugar etc*⟩ exposed; (*peligroso*) dangerous. **estar ~ a** be liable to

expuls|ar *vt* expel; throw out ⟨*persona*⟩; send off ⟨*jugador*⟩. **~ión** *f* expulsion

expurgar [12] *vt* expurgate

exquisit|o *a* exquisite. **~amente** *adv* exquisitely

extasiar [20] *vt* enrapture

éxtasis *m invar* ecstasy

extático *a* ecstatic

extend|er [1] *vt* spread (out); draw up ⟨*documento*⟩. **~erse** *vpr* spread;

⟨*paisaje etc*⟩ extend, stretch; ⟨*tenderse*⟩ stretch out. **~ido** *a* spread out; ⟨*generalizado*⟩ widespread; ⟨*brazos*⟩ outstretched

extens|amente *adv* widely; ⟨*detalladamente*⟩ in full. **~ión** *f* extension; ⟨*amplitud*⟩ expanse; ⟨*mus*⟩ range. **~o** *a* extensive

extenuar [21] *vt* exhaust

exterior *a* external, exterior; ⟨*del extranjero*⟩ foreign; ⟨*aspecto etc*⟩ outward. ● *m* exterior; ⟨*países extranjeros*⟩ abroad. **~izar** [10] *vt* show

extermin|ación *f* extermination. **~ar** *vt* exterminate. **~io** *m* extermination

externo *a* external; ⟨*signo etc*⟩ outward. ● *m* day pupil

extin|ción *f* extinction. **~guir** [13] *vt* extinguish. **~guirse** *vpr* die out; ⟨*fuego*⟩ go out. **~to** *a* extinguished; ⟨*raza etc*⟩ extinct. **~tor** *m* fire extinguisher

extirpa|r *vt* uproot; extract ⟨*muela etc*⟩; remove ⟨*tumor*⟩. **~ción** *f* (*fig*) eradication

extorsi|ón *f* (*fig*) inconvenience. **~onar** *vt* inconvenience

extra *a invar* extra; ⟨*de buena calidad*⟩ good-quality; ⟨*huevos*⟩ large. **paga** *f* **~** bonus

extrac|ción *f* extraction; ⟨*de lotería*⟩ draw. **~to** *m* extract

extradición *f* extradition

extraer [41] *vt* extract

extranjero *a* foreign. ● *m* foreigner; ⟨*países*⟩ foreign countries. **del ~** from abroad. **en el ~, por el ~** abroad

extrañ|ar *vt* surprise; ⟨*encontrar extraño*⟩ find strange; (*LAm, echar de menos*) miss; ⟨*desterrar*⟩ banish. **~arse** *vpr* be surprised (**de** at); ⟨*2 personas*⟩ grow apart. **~eza** *f* strangeness; ⟨*asombro*⟩ surprise. **~o** *a* strange. ● *m* stranger

extraoficial *a* unofficial

extraordinario *a* extraordinary. ● *m* ⟨*correo*⟩ special delivery; ⟨*plato*⟩ extra dish; ⟨*de periódico etc*⟩ special edition. **horas** *fpl* **extraordinarias** overtime

extrarradio *m* suburbs

extrasensible *a* extra-sensory

extraterrestre *a* extraterrestrial. ● *m* alien

extravagan|cia *f* oddness, eccentricity. **~te** *a* odd, eccentric

extravertido *a & m* extrovert

extrav|iado *a* lost; ⟨*lugar*⟩ isolated. **~iar** [20] *vt* lose. **~iarse** *vpr* get lost; ⟨*objetos*⟩ be missing. **~ío** *m* loss

extremar *vt* overdo. **~se** *vpr* make every effort

extremeño *a* from Extremadura. ● *m* person from Extremadura

extrem|idad *f* extremity. **~idades** *fpl* extremities. **~ista** *a & m & f* extremist. **~o** *a* extreme. ● *m* end; ⟨*colmo*⟩ extreme. **en ~o** extremely. **en último ~o** as a last resort

extrovertido *a & m* extrovert

exuberan|cia *f* exuberance. **~te** *a* exuberant

exulta|ción *f* exultation. **~r** *vi* exult

eyacular *vt/i* ejaculate

F

fa *m* F; (*solfa*) fah

fabada *f* Asturian stew

fábrica *f* factory. **marca** *f* **de ~** trade mark

fabrica|ción *f* manufacture. **~ción en serie** mass production. **~nte** *m & f* manufacturer. **~r** [7] *vt* manufacture; ⟨*inventar*⟩ fabricate

fábula *f* fable; ⟨*mentira*⟩ story, lie; ⟨*chisme*⟩ gossip

fabuloso *a* fabulous

facci|ón *f* faction. **~ones** *fpl* ⟨*de la cara*⟩ features

faceta *f* facet

fácil *a* easy; ⟨*probable*⟩ likely; ⟨*persona*⟩ easygoing

facili|dad *f* ease; ⟨*disposición*⟩ aptitude. **~dades** *fpl* facilities. **~tar** *vt* facilitate; ⟨*proporcionar*⟩ provide

fácilmente *adv* easily

facistol *m* lectern

facón *m* (*Arg*) gaucho knife

facsímil(e) *m* facsimile

factible *a* feasible

factor *m* factor

factoría *f* agency; (*esp LAm, fábrica*) factory

factura *f* bill, invoice; ⟨*hechura*⟩ manufacture. **~r** *vt* (*hacer la factura*) invoice; ⟨*cobrar*⟩ charge; ⟨*en ferrocarril*⟩ register (*Brit*), check (*Amer*)

faculta|d *f* faculty; ⟨*capacidad*⟩ ability; ⟨*poder*⟩ power. **~tivo** *a* optional

facha *f* ⟨*aspecto, fam*⟩ look

fachada f façade; (fig, apariencia) show

faena f job. ~s **domésticas** housework

fagot m bassoon; (músico) bassoonist

faisán m pheasant

faja f (de tierra) strip; (corsé) corset; (mil etc) sash

fajo m bundle; (de billetes) wad

falang|e f (política española) Falange. ~**ista** m & f Falangist

falda f skirt; (de montaña) side

fálico a phallic

fals|ear vt falsify, distort. ~**edad** f falseness; (mentira) lie, falsehood. ~**ificación** f forgery. ~**ificador** m forger. ~**ificar** [7] vt forge. ~**o** a false; (equivocado) wrong; (falsificado) fake

falt|a f lack; (ausencia) absence; (escasez) shortage; (defecto) fault, defect; (culpa) fault; (error) mistake; (en fútbol etc) foul; (en tenis) fault. ~**ar** vi be lacking; (estar ausente) be absent. ~**o** a lacking (**de** in). **a** ~**a de** for lack of. **echar en** ~**a** miss. **hacer** ~**a** be necessary. **me hace** ~**a** I need. **¡no** ~**aba más!** don't mention it! (naturalmente) of course! **sacar** ~**as** find fault

falla f (incl geol) fault. ~**r** vi fail; (romperse) break, give way; ‹motor, tiro etc› miss. **sin** ~**r** without fail

fallec|er [11] vi die. ~**ido** a late. • m deceased

fallido a vain; (fracasado) unsuccessful

fallo m failure; (defecto) fault; (jurid) sentence

fama f fame; (reputación) reputation. **de mala** ~ of ill repute. **tener** ~ **de** have the reputation of

famélico a starving

famili|a f family. ~ **numerosa** large family. ~**r** a familiar; (de la familia) family; (sin ceremonia) informal. ~**ridad** f familiarity. ~**rizarse** [10] vpr become familiar (**con** with)

famoso a famous

fanático a fanatical. • m fanatic

fanfarr|ón a boastful. • m braggart. ~**onada** f boasting; (dicho) boast. ~**onear** vi show off

fango m mud. ~**so** a muddy

fantas|ear vi daydream; (imaginar) fantasize. ~**ía** f fantasy. **de** ~ fancy

fantasma m ghost

fantástico a fantastic

fantoche m puppet

faringe f pharynx

fardo m bundle

farfullar vi jabber, gabble

farmac|éutico a pharmaceutical. • m chemist (Brit), pharmacist, druggist (Amer). ~**ia** f (ciencia) pharmacy; (tienda) chemist's (shop) (Brit), pharmacy, drugstore (Amer)

faro m lighthouse; (aviac) beacon; (auto) headlight

farol m lantern; (de la calle) street lamp. ~**a** f street lamp. ~**ita** f small street lamp

farsa f farce

fas adv. **por** ~ **o por nefas** rightly or wrongly

fascículo m instalment

fascina|ción f fascination. ~**r** vt fascinate

fascis|mo m fascism. ~**ta** a & m & f fascist

fase f phase

fastidi|ar vt annoy; (estropear) spoil. ~**arse** vpr (aguantarse) put up with it; (hacerse daño) hurt o.s. ~**o** m nuisance; (aburrimiento) boredom. ~**oso** a annoying. **¡para que te** ~**es!** so there! **¡qué** ~**o!** what a nuisance!

fatal a fateful; (mortal) fatal; (pésimo, fam) terrible. ~**idad** f fate; (desgracia) misfortune. ~**ista** m & f fatalist

fatig|a f fatigue. ~**as** fpl troubles. ~**ar** [12] vt tire. ~**arse** vpr get tired. ~**oso** a tiring

fatuo a fatuous

fauna f fauna

fausto a lucky

favor m favour. ~**able** a favourable. **a** ~ **de, en** ~ **de** in favour of. **haga el** ~ **de** would you be so kind as to, please. **por** ~ please

favorec|edor a flattering. ~**er** [11] vt favour; ‹vestido, peinado etc› suit. ~**ido** a favoured

favorit|ismo m favouritism. ~**o** a & m favourite

faz f face

fe f faith. **dar** ~ certify. **de buena** ~ in good faith

fealdad f ugliness

febrero m February

febril a feverish

fecund|ación f fertilization. ~**ación artificial** artificial insemination. ~**ar** vt fertilize. ~**o** a fertile; (fig) prolific

fecha *f* date. **~r** *vt* date. **a estas ~s** now; (*todavía*) still. **hasta la ~** so far. **poner la ~** date
fechoría *f* misdeed
federa|ción *f* federation. **~l** *a* federal
feísimo *a* hideous
felici|dad *f* happiness. **~dades** *fpl* best wishes; (*congratulaciones*) congratulations. **~tación** *f* congratulation. **~tar** *vt* congratulate. **~tarse** *vpr* be glad
feligr|és *m* parishioner. **~esía** *f* parish
felino *a* & *m* feline
feliz *a* happy; (*afortunado*) lucky. **¡Felices Pascuas!** Happy Christmas! **¡F~ Año Nuevo!** Happy New Year!
felpudo *a* plush. ● *m* doormat
femeni|l *a* feminine. **~no** *a* feminine; (*biol, bot*) female. ● *m* feminine. **~nidad** *f* femininity. **~sta** *a* & *m* & *f* feminist
fen|omenal *a* phenomenal. **~ómeno** *m* phenomenon; (*monstruo*) freak
feo *a* ugly; (*desagradable*) nasty; (*malo*) bad
féretro *m* coffin
feria *f* fair; (*verbena*) carnival; (*descanso*) holiday; (*Mex, cambio*) change. **~do** *a*. **día ~do** holiday
ferment|ación *f* fermentation. **~ar** *vt/i* ferment. **~o** *m* ferment
fero|cidad *f* ferocity. **~z** *a* fierce; (*persona*) savage
férreo *a* iron. **vía férrea** railway (*Brit*), railroad (*Amer*)
ferreter|ía *f* ironmonger's (shop) (*Brit*), hardware store (*Amer*). **~o** *m* ironmonger (*Brit*), hardware dealer (*Amer*)
ferro|bús *m* local train. **~carril** *m* railway (*Brit*), railroad (*Amer*). **~viario** *a* rail. ● *m* railwayman (*Brit*), railroad worker (*Amer*)
fértil *a* fertile
fertili|dad *f* fertility. **~zante** *m* fertilizer. **~zar** [10] *vt* fertilize
férvido *a* fervent
ferv|iente *a* fervent. **~or** *m* fervour
festej|ar *vt* celebrate; entertain (*persona*); court (*novia etc*); (*Mex, golpear*) beat. **~o** *m* entertainment; (*celebración*) celebration
festiv|al *m* festival. **~idad** *f* festivity. **~o** *a* festive; (*humorístico*) humorous. **día ~o** feast day, holiday

festonear *vt* festoon
fétido *a* stinking
feto *m* foetus
feudal *a* feudal
fiado *m*. **al ~** on credit. **~r** *m* fastener; (*jurid*) guarantor
fiambre *m* cold meat
fianza *f* (*dinero*) deposit; (*objeto*) surety. **bajo ~** on bail. **dar ~** pay a deposit
fiar [20] *vt* guarantee; (*vender*) sell on credit; (*confiar*) confide. ● *vi* trust. **~se** *vpr*. **~se de** trust
fiasco *m* fiasco
fibra *f* fibre; (*fig*) energy. **~ de vidrio** fibreglass
fic|ción *f* fiction. **~ticio** *a* fictitious; (*falso*) false
fich|a *f* token; (*tarjeta*) index card; (*en los juegos*) counter. **~ar** *vt* file. **~ero** *m* card index. **estar ~ado** have a (police) record
fidedigno *a* reliable
fidelidad *f* faithfulness. **alta ~** hi-fi (*fam*), high fidelity
fideos *mpl* noodles
fiebre *f* fever. **~ del heno** hay fever. **tener ~** have a temperature
fiel *a* faithful; (*memoria, relato etc*) reliable. ● *m* believer; (*de balanza*) needle. **los ~es** the faithful
fieltro *m* felt
fier|a *f* wild animal; (*persona*) brute. **~o** *a* fierce; (*cruel*) cruel. **estar hecho una ~a** be furious
fierro *m* (*LAm*) iron
fiesta *f* party; (*día festivo*) holiday. **~s** *fpl* celebrations. **~ nacional** bank holiday (*Brit*), national holiday
figura *f* figure; (*forma*) shape; (*en obra de teatro*) character; (*en naipes*) court-card. **~r** *vt* feign; (*representar*) represent. ● *vi* figure; (*ser importante*) be important. **~rse** *vpr* imagine. **¡figúrate!** just imagine! **~tivo** *a* figurative
fij|ación *f* fixing. **~ar** *vt* fix; stick (*sello*); post (*cartel*). **~arse** *vpr* settle; (*fig, poner atención*) notice. **¡fíjate!** just imagine! **~o** *a* fixed; (*firme*) stable; (*persona*) settled. **de ~o** certainly
fila *f* line; (*de soldados etc*) file; (*en el teatro, cine etc*) row; (*cola*) queue. **ponerse en ~** line up
filamento *m* filament
fil|antropía *f* philanthropy. **~antrópico** *a* philanthropic. **~ántropo** *m* philanthropist

filarmónico *a* philharmonic

filat|elia *f* stamp collecting, philately. ~**élico** *a* philatelic. ● *m* stamp collector, philatelist

filete *m* fillet

filfa *f* (*fam*) hoax

filial *a* filial. ● *f* subsidiary

filigrana *f* filigree (work); (*en papel*) watermark

Filipinas *fpl.* **las (islas)** ~ the Philippines

filipino *a* Philippine, Filipino

filmar *vt* film

filo *m* edge; (*de hoja*) cutting edge; (*Mex, hambre*) hunger. **al** ~ **de las doce** at exactly twelve o'clock. **dar** ~ **a, sacar** ~ **a** sharpen

filología *f* philology

filón *m* vein; (*fig*) gold-mine

fil|osofía *f* philosophy. ~**osófico** *a* philosophical. ~**ósofo** *m* philosopher

filtr|ar *vt* filter. ~**arse** *vpr* filter; (*dinero*) disappear. ~**o** *m* filter; (*bebida*) philtre

fin *m* end; (*objetivo*) aim. ~ **de semana** weekend. **a** ~ **de** in order to. ~ **de cuentas** all things considered. **a** ~ **de que** in order that. **a** ~**es de** at the end of. **al** ~ finally. **al** ~ **y al cabo** after all. **dar** ~ **a** end. **en** ~ in short. **poner** ~ **a** end. **por** ~ finally. **sin** ~ endless

final *a* final, last. ● *m* end. ● *f* final. ~**idad** *f* aim. ~**ista** *m & f* finalist. ~**izar** [10] *vt/i* end. ~**mente** *adv* finally

financi|ar *vt* finance. ~**ero** *a* financial. ● *m* financier

finca *f* property; (*tierras*) estate; (*LAm, granja*) farm

finés *a* Finnish. ● *m* Finn; (*lengua*) Finnish

fingi|do *a* false. ~**r** [14] *vt* feign; (*simular*) simulate. ● *vi* pretend. ~**rse** *vpr* pretend to be

finito *a* finite

finlandés *a* Finnish. ● *m* (*persona*) Finn; (*lengua*) Finnish

Finlandia *f* Finland

fin|o *a* fine; (*delgado*) slender; (*astuto*) shrewd; (*sentido*) keen; (*cortés*) polite; (*jerez*) dry. ~**ura** *f* fineness; (*astucia*) shrewdness; (*de sentido*) keenness; (*cortesía*) politeness

fiordo *m* fiord

firma *f* signature; (*empresa*) firm

firmamento *m* firmament

firmar *vt* sign

firme *a* firm; (*estable*) stable, steady; (*persona*) steadfast. ● *m* (*pavimento*) (road) surface. ● *adv* hard. ~**za** *f* firmness. **de** ~ hard. **en** ~ firm, definite

fisc|al *a* fiscal. ● *m & f* public prosecutor. ~**o** *m* treasury

fisg|ar [12] *vt* pry into (*asunto*); spy on (*persona*). ● *vi* pry. ~**ón** *a* prying. ● *m* busybody

físic|a *f* physics. ~**o** *a* physical. ● *m* physique; (*persona*) physicist

fisi|ología *f* physiology. ~**ológico** *a* physiological. ~**ólogo** *m* physiologist

fisioterap|euta *m & f* physiotherapist. ~**ia** *f* physiotherapy. ~**ista** *m & f* (*fam*) physiotherapist

fisonom|ía *f* physiognomy, face. ~**ista** *m & f.* **ser buen** ~**ista** be good at remembering faces

fisura *f* (*Med*) fracture

fláccido *a* flabby

flaco *a* thin, skinny; (*débil*) weak

flagelo *m* scourge

flagrante *a* flagrant. **en** ~ redhanded

flamante *a* splendid; (*nuevo*) brand-new

flamenco *a* flamenco; (*de Flandes*) Flemish. ● *m* (*música etc*) flamenco

flan *m* crème caramel

flaqueza *f* thinness; (*debilidad*) weakness

flash *m* flash

flato *m*, **flatulencia** *f* flatulence

flaut|a *f* flute. ● *m & f* (*músico*) flautist, flutist (*Amer*). ~**ín** *m* piccolo. ~**ista** *m & f* flautist, flutist (*Amer*)

fleco *m* fringe

flecha *f* arrow

flem|a *f* phlegm. ~**ático** *a* phlegmatic

flequillo *m* fringe

fletar *vt* charter

flexib|ilidad *f* flexibility. ~**le** *a* flexible. ● *m* flex, cable

flirte|ar *vi* flirt. ~**o** *m* flirting

floj|ear *vi* ease up. ~**o** *a* loose; (*poco fuerte*) weak; (*viento*) light; (*perezoso*) lazy

flor *f* flower; (*fig*) cream. ~**a** *f* flora. ~**al** *a* floral. ~**ecer** [11] *vi* flower, bloom; (*fig*) flourish. ~**eciente** *a* (*fig*) flourishing. ~**ero** *m* flower vase. ~**ido** *a* flowery; (*selecto*) select; (*lenguaje*) florid. ~**ista** *m & f* florist

flota f fleet

flot|ador m float. **~ar** vi float. **~e** m. **a ~e** afloat

flotilla f flotilla

fluctua|ción f fluctuation. **~r** [21] vi fluctuate

flu|idez f fluidity; (*fig*) fluency. **~ido** a fluid; (*fig*) fluent. ● m fluid. **~ir** [17] vi flow. **~jo** m flow. **~o y reflujo** ebb and flow

fluorescente a fluorescent

fluoruro m fluoride

fluvial a river

fobia f phobia

foca f seal

foc|al a focal. **~o** m focus; (*lámpara*) floodlight; (*LAm*, *bombilla*) light bulb

fogón m (*cocina*) cooker

fogoso a spirited

folio m leaf

folk|lore m folklore. **~órico** a folk

follaje m foliage

follet|ín m newspaper serial. **~o** m pamphlet

follón m (*lío*) mess; (*alboroto*) row

fomentar vt foment, stir up

fonda f (*pensión*) boarding-house

fondo m bottom; (*parte más lejana*) bottom, end; (*de escenario, pintura etc*) background; (*profundidad*) depth. **~s** mpl funds, money. **a ~** thoroughly. **en el ~** deep down

fonétic|a f phonetics. **~o** a phonetic

fono m (*LAm, del teléfono*) earpiece

fontaner|ía plumbing. **~o** m plumber

footing /'futin/ m jogging

forastero a alien. ● m stranger

forceje|ar vi struggle. **~o** m struggle

fórceps m invar forceps

forense a forensic

forjar vt forge

forma f form, shape; (*horma*) mould; (*modo*) way; (*de zapatero*) last. **~s** fpl conventions. **~ción** f formation; (*educación*) training. **dar ~ a** shape; (*expresar*) formulate. **de ~ que** so (that). **de todas ~s** anyway. **estar en ~** be in good form. **guardar ~s** keep up appearances

formal a formal; (*de fiar*) reliable; (*serio*) serious. **~idad** f formality; (*fiabilidad*) reliability; (*seriedad*) seriousness

formar vt form; (*hacer*) make; (*enseñar*) train. **~se** vpr form; (*desarrollarse*) develop

formato m format

formidable a formidable; (*muy grande*) enormous; (*muy bueno, fam*) marvellous

fórmula f formula; (*receta*) recipe

formular vt formulate; make ‹*queja etc*›; (*expresar*) express

fornido a well-built

forraje m fodder. **~ar** vt/i forage

forr|ar vt (*en el interior*) line; (*en el exterior*) cover. **~o** m lining; (*cubierta*) cover. **~o del freno** brake lining

fortale|cer [11] vt strengthen. **~za** f strength; (*mil*) fortress; (*fuerza moral*) fortitude

fortificar [7] vt fortify

fortuito a fortuitous. **encuentro** m **~** chance meeting

fortuna f fortune; (*suerte*) luck. **por ~** fortunately

forz|ado a hard. **~ar** [2 & 10] vt force. **~osamente** adv necessarily. **~oso** a inevitable; (*necesario*) necessary

fosa f grave

fosfato m phosphate

fósforo m phosphorus; (*cerilla*) match

fósil a & m fossil

fosilizarse [10] vpr fossilize

foso m ditch

foto f photo, photograph. **sacar ~s** take photographs .

fotocopia f photocopy. **~dora** f photocopier. **~r** vt photocopy

fotogénico a photogenic

fot|ografía f photography; (*foto*) photograph. **~ografiar** [20] vt photograph. **~ográfico** a photographic. **~ógrafo** m photographer. **sacar ~ografías** take photographs

foyer m foyer

frac m (*pl* **fraques** o **fracs**) tails

fracas|ar vi fail. **~o** m failure

fracción f fraction; (*pol*) faction

fractura f fracture. **~r** vt fracture, break. **~rse** vpr fracture, break

fragan|cia f fragrance. **~te** a fragrant

fragata f frigate

fr|ágil a fragile; (*débil*) weak. **~agilidad** f fragility; (*debilidad*) weakness

fragment|ario a fragmentary. **~o** m fragment

fragor m din

fragoso a rough

fragua f forge. ~r [15] vt forge; (fig) concoct. ● vi harden

fraile m friar; (monje) monk

frambuesa f raspberry

francés a French. ● m (persona) Frenchman; (lengua) French

Francia f France

franco a frank; (com) free. ● m (moneda) franc

francotirador m sniper

franela f flannel

franja f border; (fleco) fringe

franque|ar vt clear; stamp ⟨carta⟩; overcome ⟨obstáculo⟩. ~o m stamping; (cantidad) postage

franqueza f frankness; (familiaridad) familiarity

franquis|mo m General Franco's regime; (política) Franco's policy. ~ta a pro-Franco

frasco m small bottle

frase f phrase; (oración) sentence. ~ hecha set phrase

fratern|al a fraternal. ~idad f fraternity

fraud|e m fraud. ~ulento a fraudulent

fray m brother, friar

frecuen|cia f frequency. ~tar vt frequent. ~te a frequent. con ~cia frequently

frega|dero m sink. ~r [1 & 12] vt scrub; wash up ⟨los platos⟩; mop ⟨el suelo⟩; (LAm, fig, molestar, fam) annoy

freír [51, pp frito] vt fry; (fig, molestar, fam) annoy. ~se vpr fry; ⟨persona⟩ be very hot, be boiling (fam)

frenar vt brake; (fig) check

fren|esí m frenzy. ~ético a frenzied

freno m (de caballería) bit; (auto) brake; (fig) check

frente m front. ● f forehead. ~ a opposite; (en contra de) opposed to. ~ por ~ opposite; (en un choque) head-on. al ~ at the head; (hacia delante) forward. arrugar la ~ frown. de ~ forward. hacer ~ a face ⟨cosa⟩; stand up to ⟨persona⟩

fresa f strawberry

fresc|a f fresh air. ~o a (frío) cool; (nuevo) fresh; (descarado) cheeky. ● m fresh air; (frescor) coolness; (mural) fresco; (persona) impudent person. ~or m coolness. ~ura f freshness; (frío) coolness; (descaro) cheek. al ~o in the open air. hacer

~o be cool. **tomar el** ~o get some fresh air

fresno m ash (tree)

friable a friable

frialdad f coldness; (fig) indifference

fricci|ón f rubbing; (fig, tec) friction; (masaje) massage. ~onar vt rub

frigidez f coldness; (fig) frigidity

frígido a frigid

frigorífico m refrigerator, fridge (fam)

frijol m bean. ~es refritos (Mex) purée of black beans

frío a & m cold. **coger** ~ catch cold. **hacer** ~ be cold

frisar vi. ~ en be getting on for, be about

frito a fried; (exasperado) exasperated. **me tiene** ~ I'm sick of him

fr|ivolidad f frivolity. ~ívolo a frivolous

fronda f foliage

fronter|a f frontier; (fig) limit. ~izo a frontier. ~o a opposite

frontón m pelota court

frotar vt rub; strike ⟨cerilla⟩

fructífero a fruitful

frugal a frugal

fruncir [9] vt gather ⟨tela⟩; wrinkle ⟨piel⟩

fruslería f trifle

frustra|ción f frustration. ~r vt frustrate. ~rse vpr (fracasar) fail. **quedar** ~do be disappointed

frut|a f fruit. ~ería f fruit shop. ~ero a fruit. ● m fruiterer; (recipiente) fruit bowl. ~icultura f fruit-growing. ~illa f (LAm) strawberry. ~o m fruit

fucsia f fuchsia

fuego m fire. ~s artificiales fireworks. **a** ~ lento on a low heat. **tener** ~ have a light

fuente f fountain; (manantial) spring; (plato) serving dish; (fig) source

fuera adv out; (al exterior) outside; (en otra parte) away; (en el extranjero) abroad. ● vb véase ir y ser. ~ de outside; (excepto) except for, besides. **por** ~ on the outside

fuerte a strong; ⟨color⟩ bright; ⟨sonido⟩ loud; ⟨dolor⟩ severe; (duro) hard; (grande) large; ⟨lluvia, nevada⟩ heavy. ● m fort; (fig) strong point. ● adv hard; (con hablar etc) loudly; (mucho) a lot

fuerza f strength; (poder) power; (en física) force; (mil) forces. ~ de

voluntad will-power. **a ~ de** by dint of, by means of. **a la ~** by necessity. **por ~** by force; (*por necesidad*) by necessity. **tener ~s para** have the strength to

fuese *vb véase* **ir** *y* **ser**

fug|a *f* flight, escape; (*de gas etc*) leak; (*mus*) fugue. **~arse** [12] *vpr* flee, escape. **~az** *a* fleeting. **~itivo** *a & m* fugitive. **ponerse en ~a** take to flight

fui *vb véase* **ir** *y* **ser**

fulano *m* so-and-so. **~, mengano y zutano** Tom, Dick and Harry

fulgor *m* brilliance; (*fig*) splendour

fulminar *vt* strike by lightning; (*fig, mirar*) look daggers at

fuma|dor *a* smoking. ● *m* smoker. **~r** *vt/i* smoke. **~rse** *vpr* smoke; (*fig, gastar*) squander. **~rada** *f* puff of smoke. **~r en pipa** smoke a pipe. **prohibido ~r** no smoking

funámbulo *m* tightrope walker

funci|ón *f* function; (*de un cargo etc*) duties; (*de teatro*) show, performance. **~onal** *a* functional. **~onar** *vi* work, function. **~onario** *m* civil servant. **no ~ona** out of order

funda *f* cover. ● **~ de almohada** pillowcase

funda|ción *f* foundation. **~mental** *a* fundamental. **~mentar** *vt* lay the foundations of; (*fig*) base. **~mento** *m* foundation. **~r** *vt* found; (*fig*) base. **~rse** *vpr* be based

fundi|ción *f* melting; (*de metales*) smelting; (*taller*) foundry. **~r** *vt* melt; smelt ⟨*metales*⟩; cast ⟨*objeto*⟩; blend ⟨*colores*⟩; (*fusionar*) merge. **~rse** *vpr* melt; (*unirse*) merge

fúnebre *a* funeral; (*sombrío*) gloomy

funeral *a* funeral. ● *m* funeral. **~es** *mpl* funeral

funicular *a & m* funicular

furg|ón *m* van. **~oneta** *f* van

fur|ia *f* fury; (*violencia*) violence. **~ibundo** *a* furious. **~ioso** *a* furious. **~or** *m* fury

furtivo *a* furtive

furúnculo *m* boil

fuselaje *m* fuselage

fusible *m* fuse

fusil *m* gun. **~ar** *vt* shoot

fusión *f* melting; (*unión*) fusion; (*com*) merger

fútbol *m* football

futbolista *m* footballer

fútil *a* futile

futur|ista *a* futuristic. ● *m & f* futurist. **~o** *a & m* future

G

gabán *m* overcoat

garbardina *f* raincoat; (*tela*) gabardine

gabinete *m* (*pol*) cabinet; (*en museo etc*) room; (*de dentista, médico etc*) consulting room

gacela *f* gazelle

gaceta *f* gazette

gachas *fpl* porridge

gacho *a* drooping

gaélico *a* Gaelic

gafa *f* hook. **~s** *fpl* glasses, spectacles. **~s de sol** sun-glasses

gaf|ar *vt* hook; (*fam*) bring bad luck to. **~e** *m* jinx

gaita *f* bagpipes

gajo *m* (*de naranja, nuez etc*) segment

gala|s *fpl* finery, best clothes. **estar de ~** be dressed up. **hacer ~ de** show off

galán *m* (*en el teatro*) male lead; (*enamorado*) lover

galante *a* gallant. **~ar** *vt* court. **~ría** *f* gallantry

galápago *m* turtle

galardón *m* reward

galaxia *f* galaxy

galeón *m* galleon

galera *f* galley

galería *f* gallery

Gales *m* Wales. **país de ~** Wales

gal|és *a* Welsh. ● *m* Welshman; (*lengua*) Welsh. **~esa** *f* Welshwoman

galgo *m* greyhound

Galicia *f* Galicia

galimatías *m invar* (*fam*) gibberish

galón *m* gallon; (*cinta*) braid; (*mil*) stripe

galop|ar *vi* gallop. **~e** *m* gallop

galvanizar [10] *vt* galvanize

gallard|ía *f* elegance. **~o** *a* elegant

gallego *a & m* Galician

galleta *f* biscuit (*Brit*), cookie (*Amer*)

gall|ina *f* hen, chicken; (*fig, fam*) coward. **~o** *m* cock

gama *f* scale; (*fig*) range

gamba *f* prawn (*Brit*), shrimp (*Amer*)

gamberro *m* hooligan

gamuza *f* (*piel*) chamois leather

gana *f* wish, desire; (*apetito*) appetite. **de buena ~** willingly. **de mala ~** reluctantly. **no me da la ~** I don't feel like it. **tener ~s de** (+ *infinitivo*) feel like (+ *gerundio*)

ganad|ería *f* cattle raising; (*ganado*) livestock. **~o** *m* livestock. **~o de cerda** pigs. **~o lanar** sheep. **~o vacuno** cattle

ganar *vt* earn; (*en concurso, juego etc*) win; (*alcanzar*) reach; (*aventajar*) beat. ● *vi* (*vencer*) win; (*mejorar*) improve. **~se la vida** earn a living. **salir ganando** come out better off

ganch|illo *m* crochet. **~o** *m* hook. **~oso** *a*, **~udo** *a* hooked. **echar el ~o a** hook. **hacer ~illo** crochet. **tener ~o** be very attractive

gandul *a & m & f* good-for-nothing

ganga *f* bargain; (*buena situación*) easy job, cushy job (*fam*)

gangrena *f* gangrene

gans|ada *f* silly thing. **~o** *m* goose

gañi|do *m* yelping. **~r** [22] *vi* yelp

garabat|ear *vt/i* (*garrapatear*) scribble. **~o** *m* (*garrapato*) scribble

garaj|e *m* garage. **~ista** *m & f* garage attendant

garant|e *m & f* guarantor. **~ía** *f* guarantee. **~ir** [24] *vt* (*esp LAm*), **~izar** [10] *vt* guarantee

garapiñado *a*. **almendras** *fpl* **garapiñadas** sugared almonds

garbanzo *m* chick-pea

garbo *m* poise; (*de escrito*) style. **~so** *a* elegant

garfio *m* hook

garganta *f* throat; (*desfiladero*) gorge; (*de botella*) neck

gárgaras *fpl*. **hacer ~** gargle

gargarismo *m* gargle

gárgola *f* gargoyle

garita *f* hut; (*de centinela*) sentry box

garito *m* gambling den

garra *f* (*de animal*) claw; (*de ave*) talon

garrafa *f* carafe

garrapata *f* tick

garrapat|ear *vi* scribble. **~o** *m* scribble

garrote *m* club, cudgel; (*tormento*) garrotte

gárrulo *a* garrulous

garúa *f* (*LAm*) drizzle

garza *f* heron

gas *m* gas. **con ~** fizzy. **sin ~** still

gasa *f* gauze

gaseosa *f* lemonade

gasfitero *m* (*Arg*) plumber

gas|óleo *m* diesel. **~olina** *f* petrol (*Brit*), gasoline (*Amer*), gas (*Amer*). **~olinera** *f* petrol station (*Brit*), gas station (*Amer*); (*lancha*) motor boat. **~ómetro** *m* gasometer

gast|ado *a* spent; (*vestido etc*) worn out. **~ador** *m* spendthrift. **~ar** *vt* spend; (*consumir*) use; (*malgastar*) waste; wear (*vestido etc*); crack (*broma*). ● *vi* spend. **~arse** *vpr* wear out. **~o** *m* expense; (*acción de gastar*) spending

gástrico *a* gastric

gastronomía *f* gastronomy

gat|a *f* cat. **a ~as** on all fours. **~ear** *vi* crawl

gatillo *m* trigger; (*de dentista*) (dental) forceps

gat|ito *m* kitten. **~o** *m* cat. **dar ~o por liebre** take s.o. in

gaucho *a & m* Gaucho

gaveta *f* drawer

gavilla *f* sheaf; (*de personas*) band, gang

gaviota *f* seagull

gazpacho *m* gazpacho, cold soup

géiser *m* geyser

gelatina *f* gelatine; (*jalea*) jelly

gelignita *f* gelignite

gema *f* gem

gemelo *m* twin. **~s** *mpl* (*anteojos*) binoculars; (*de camisa*) cuff-links. **G~s** Gemini

gemido *m* groan

Géminis *mpl* Gemini

gemir [5] *vi* groan; (*animal*) whine, howl

gen *m*, **gene** *m* gene

geneal|ogía *f* genealogy. **~ógico** *a* genealogical. **árbol** *m* **~ógico** family tree

generación *f* generation

general *a* general; (*corriente*) common. ● *m* general. **~ísimo** *m* generalissimo, supreme commander. **~ización** *f* generalization. **~izar** [10] *vt/i* generalize. **~mente** *adv* generally. **en ~** in general. **por lo ~** generally

generar *vt* generate

género *m* type, sort; (*biol*) genus; (*gram*) gender; (*producto*) product. **~s de punto** knitwear. **~ humano** mankind

generos|idad *f* generosity. **~o** *a* generous; (*vino*) full-bodied

génesis *m* genesis

genétic|a *f* genetics. **~o** *a* genetic

genial *a* brilliant; *(agradable)* pleasant

genio *m* temper; *(carácter)* nature; *(talento, persona)* genius

genital *a* genital. **~es** *mpl* genitals

gente *f* people; *(nación)* nation; *(familia, fam)* family; *(Mex, persona)* person

gentil *a* charming; *(pagano)* pagan. **~eza** *f* elegance; *(encanto)* charm; *(amabilidad)* kindness

gentío *m* crowd

genuflexión *f* genuflection

genuino *a* genuine

ge|ografía *f* geography. **~ográfico** *a* geographical. **~ógrafo** *m* geographer

ge|ología *f* geology. **~ólogo** *m* geologist

geom|etría *f* geometry. **~étrico** *a* geometrical

geranio *m* geranium

geren|cia *f* management. **~te** *m* manager

geriatría *f* geriatrics

germánico *a* & *m* Germanic

germen *m* germ

germicida *f* germicide

germinar *vi* germinate

gestación *f* gestation

gesticula|ción *f* gesticulation. **~r** *vi* gesticulate; *(hacer muecas)* grimace

gesti|ón *f* step; *(administración)* management. **~onar** *vt* take steps to arrange; *(dirigir)* manage

gesto *m* expression; *(ademán)* gesture; *(mueca)* grimace

Gibraltar *m* Gibraltar

gibraltareño *a* & *m* Gibraltarian

gigante *a* gigantic. ● *m* giant. **~sco** *a* gigantic

gimn|asia *f* gymnastics. **~asio** *m* gymnasium, gym *(fam)*. **~asta** *m* & *f* gymnast. **~ástica** *f* gymnastics

gimotear *vi* whine

ginebra *f* gin

Ginebra *f* Geneva

ginec|ología *f* gynaecology. **~ólogo** *m* gynaecologist

gira *f* excursion; *(a varios sitios)* tour

girar *vt* spin; *(por giro postal)* transfer. ● *vi* rotate, go round; *‹camino etc›* turn

girasol *m* sunflower

gir|atorio *a* revolving. **~o** *m* turn; *(com)* draft; *(locución)* expression. **~o postal** postal order

giroscopio *m* gyroscope

gis *m* chalk

gitano *a* & *m* gypsy

glacia|l *a* icy. **~r** *m* glacier

gladiador *m* gladiator

glándula *f* gland

glasear *vt* glaze; *(culin)* ice

glicerina *f* glycerine

glicina *f* wisteria

glob|al *a* global; *(fig)* overall. **~o** *m* globe; *(aeróstato, juguete)* balloon

glóbulo *m* globule; *(med)* corpuscle

gloria *f* glory. **~rse** *vpr* boast (**de** about)

glorieta *f* bower; *(auto)* roundabout *(Brit)*, (traffic) circle *(Amer)*

glorificar [7] *vt* glorify

glorioso *a* glorious

glosario *m* glossary

glot|ón *a* gluttonous. ● *m* glutton. **~onería** *f* gluttony

glucosa *f* glucose

gnomo /'nomo/ *m* gnome

gob|ernación *f* government. **~ernador** *a* governing. ● *m* governor. **~ernante** *a* governing. **~ernar** [1] *vt* govern; *(dirigir)* manage, direct. **~ierno** *m* government; *(dirección)* management, direction. **~ierno de la casa** housekeeping. **Ministerio** *m* **de la G~ernación** Home Office *(Brit)*, Department of the Interior *(Amer)*

goce *m* enjoyment

gol *m* goal

golf *m* golf

golfo *m* gulf; *(niño)* urchin; *(holgazán)* layabout

golondrina *f* swallow

golos|ina *f* titbit; *(dulce)* sweet. **~o** *a* fond of sweets

golpe *m* blow; *(puñetazo)* punch; *(choque)* bump; *(de emoción)* shock; *(acceso)* fit; *(en fútbol)* shot; *(en tenis, de remo)* stroke. **~ar** *vt* hit; *(dar varios golpes)* beat; *(con mucho ruido)* bang; *(con el puño)* punch. ● *vi* knock. **~ de estado** coup d'etat. **~ de fortuna** stroke of luck. **~ de mano** raid. **~ de vista** glance. **~ militar** military coup. **de ~** suddenly. **de un ~** at one go

gom|a *f* rubber; *(para pegar)* glue; *(anillo)* rubber band; *(elástico)* elastic. **~a de borrar** rubber. **~a de pegar** glue. **~a espuma** foam rubber. **~ita** *f* rubber band

gongo *m* gong

gord|a *f* *(Mex)* thick tortilla. **~iflón** *m* *(fam)*, **~inflón** *m* *(fam)* fatty. **~o** *a* *‹persona›* fat; *‹carne›* fatty;

(*grande*) large, big. ● *m* first prize. ~**ura** *f* fatness; (*grasa*) fat
gorila *f* gorilla
gorje|ar *vi* chirp. ~**o** *m* chirping
gorra *f* cap
gorrión *m* sparrow
gorro *m* cap; (*de niño*) bonnet
got|a *f* drop; (*med*) gout. ~**ear** *vi* drip. ~**eo** *m* dripping. ~**era** *f* leak. **ni** ~**a** nothing
gótico *a* Gothic
gozar [10] *vt* enjoy. ● *vi*. ~ **de** enjoy. ~**se** *vpr* enjoy
gozne *m* hinge
gozo *m* pleasure; (*alegría*) joy. ~**so** *a* delighted
graba|ción *f* recording. ~**do** *m* engraving, print; (*en libro*) illustration. ~**r** *vt* engrave; record (*discos etc*)
gracejo *m* wit
graci|a *f* grace; (*favor*) favour; (*humor*) wit. ~**as** *fpl* thanks. ¡~**as!** thank you!, thanks! ~**oso** *a* funny. ● *m* fool, comic character. **dar las** ~**as** thank. **hacer** ~**a** amuse; (*gustar*) please. ¡**muchas** ~**as!** thank you very much! **tener** ~**a** be funny
grad|a *f* step; (*línea*) row; (*de anfiteatro*) tier. ~**ación** *f* gradation. ~**o** *m* degree; (*escol*) year (*Brit*), grade (*Amer*); (*voluntad*) willingness
gradua|ción *f* graduation; (*de alcohol*) proof. ~**do** *m* graduate. ~**l** *a* gradual. ~**r** [21] *vt* graduate; (*medir*) measure; (*univ*) confer a degree on. ~**rse** *vpr* graduate
gráfic|a *f* graph. ~**o** *a* graphic. ● *m* graph
grajo *m* rook
gram|ática *f* grammar. ~**atical** *a* grammatical
gramo *m* gram, gramme (*Brit*)
gramófono *m* record-player, gramophone (*Brit*), phonograph (*Amer*)
gran *a véase* **grande**
grana *f* (*color*) scarlet
granada *f* pomegranate; (*mil*) grenade
granate *m* garnet
Gran Bretaña *f* Great Britain
grande *a* (*delante de nombre en singular* **gran**) big, large; (*alto*) tall; (*fig*) great. ● *m* grandee. ~**za** *f* greatness
grandioso *a* magnificent
granel *m*. **a** ~ in bulk; (*suelto*) loose; (*fig*) in abundance

granero *m* barn
granito *m* granite; (*grano*) small grain
graniz|ado *m* iced drink. ~**ar** [10] *vi* hail. ~**o** *m* hail
granj|a *f* farm. ~**ero** *m* farmer
grano *m* grain; (*semilla*) seed; (*de café*) bean; (*med*) spot. ~**s** *mpl* cereals
granuja *m & f* rogue
gránulo *m* granule
grapa *f* staple
gras|a *f* grease; (*culin*) fat. ~**iento** *a* greasy
gratifica|ción *f* (*propina*) tip; (*de sueldo*) bonus. ~**r** [7] *vt* (*dar propina*) tip
gratis *adv* free
gratitud *f* gratitude
grato *a* pleasant; (*bienvenido*) welcome
gratuito *a* free; (*fig*) uncalled for
grava *f* gravel
grava|men *m* obligation. ~**r** *vt* tax; (*cargar*) burden
grave *a* serious; (*pesado*) heavy; (*sonido*) low; (*acento*) grave. ~**dad** *f* gravity
gravilla *f* gravel
gravita|ción *f* gravitation. ~**r** *vi* gravitate; (*apoyarse*) rest (**sobre** on); (*fig, pesar*) weigh (**sobre** on)
gravoso *a* onerous; (*costoso*) expensive
graznar *vi* (*cuervo*) caw; (*pato*) quack
Grecia *f* Greece
gregario *a* gregarious
greguería *f* uproar
gremio *m* union
greñ|a *f* mop of hair. ~**udo** *a* unkempt
gresca *f* uproar; (*riña*) quarrel
griego *a & m* Greek
grieta *f* crack
grifo *m* tap, faucet (*Amer*); (*animal fantástico*) griffin
grilletes *mpl* shackles
grillo *m* cricket; (*bot*) shoot. ~**s** *mpl* shackles
grima *f*. **dar** ~ annoy
gringo *m* (*LAm*) Yankee (*fam*), American
gripe *f* flu (*fam*), influenza
gris *a* grey. ● *m* grey; (*policía, fam*) policeman
grit|ar *vt* shout (for); (*como protesta*) boo. ● *vi* shout. ~**ería** *f*, ~**erío** *m*

uproar. **~o** m shout; (de dolor, sorpresa) cry; (chillido) scream. **dar ~s** shout

grosella f redcurrant. **~ negra** blackcurrant

groser|ía f coarseness; (palabras etc) coarse remark. **~o** a coarse; (descortés) rude

grosor m thickness

grotesco a grotesque

grúa f crane

grues|a f gross. **~o** a thick; (persona) fat, stout. ● m thickness; (fig) main body

grulla f crane

grumo m clot; (de leche) curd

gruñi|do m grunt; (fig) grumble. **~r** [22] vi grunt; (perro) growl; (refunfuñar) grumble

grupa f hindquarters

grupo m group

gruta f grotto

guacamole m (Mex) avocado purée

guadaña f scythe

guagua f trifle; (esp LAm, autobús, fam) bus

guante m glove

guapo a good-looking; (chica) pretty; (elegante) smart

guarapo m (LAm) sugar cane liquor

guarda m & f guard; (de parque etc) keeper. ● f protection. **~barros** invar mudguard. **~bosque** m gamekeeper. **~costas** m invar coastguard vessel. **~dor** a careful. ● m keeper. **~espaldas** m invar bodyguard. **~meta** m invar goalkeeper. **~r** vt keep; (vigilar) guard; (proteger) protect; (reservar) save, keep. **~rse** vpr be on one's guard. **~rse de** (+ infinitivo) avoid (+ gerundio). **~rropa** m wardrobe; (en local público) cloakroom. **~vallas** m invar (LAm) goalkeeper

guardería f nursery

guardia f guard; (custodia) care. ● f guard. **G~ Civil** Civil Guard. **~ municipal** policeman. **~ de tráfico** traffic policeman. **estar de ~** be on duty. **estar en ~** be on one's guard. **montar la ~** mount guard

guardián m guardian; (de parque etc) keeper; (de edificio) caretaker

guardilla f attic

guar|ecer [11] (albergar) give shelter to. **~ecerse** vpr take shelter. **~ida** f den, lair; (de personas) hideout

guarn|ecer [11] vt provide; (adornar) decorate; (culin) garnish. **~ición** m decoration; (de caballo) harness; (culin) garnish; (mil) garrison; (de piedra preciosa) setting

guarro m pig

guasa f joke; (ironía) irony

guaso a (Arg) coarse

guasón a humorous. ● m joker

Guatemala f Guatemala

guatemalteco a from Guatemala. ● m person from Guatemala

guateque m party

guayaba f guava; (dulce) guava jelly

guayabera f (Mex) shirt

gubernamental a, **gubernativo** a governmental

güero a (Mex) fair

guerr|a f war; (método) warfare. **~a civil** civil war. **~ear** vi wage war. **~ero** a war; (belicoso) fighting. ● m warrior. **~illa** f band of guerillas. **~illero** m guerilla. **dar ~a** annoy

guía m & f guide. ● f guidebook; (de teléfonos) directory; (de ferrocarriles) timetable

guiar [20] vt guide; (llevar) lead; (auto) drive. **~se** vpr be guided (**por** by)

guij|arro m pebble. **~o** m gravel

guillotina f guillotine

guind|a f morello cherry. **~illa** f chilli

guiñapo m rag; (fig, persona) reprobate

guiñ|ar vt/i wink. **~o** m wink. **hacer ~os** wink

gui|ón m hyphen, dash; (de película etc) script. **~onista** m & f scriptwriter

guirnalda f garland

güiro m (LAm) gourd

guisa f manner, way. **a ~ de** as. **de tal ~** in such a way

guisado m stew

guisante m pea. **~ de olor** sweet pea

guis|ar vt/i cook. **~o** m dish

güisqui m whisky

guitarr|a f guitar. **~ista** m & f guitarist

gula f gluttony

gusano m worm; (larva de mosca) maggot

gustar vt taste. ● vi please. **¿te gusta?** do you like it? **me gusta el vino** I like wine

gusto m taste; (placer) pleasure. **~so** a tasty; (agradable) pleasant. **a ~** comfortable. **a mi ~** to my liking.

buen ~ (good) taste. **con mucho** ~ with pleasure. **dar** ~ please. **mucho** ~ pleased to meet you

gutural *a* guttural

H

ha *vb véase* **haber**

haba *f* broad bean; (*de café etc*) bean

Habana *f*. **la** ~ Havana

haban|era *f* habanera, Cuban dance. ~**ero** *a* from Havana. ● *m* person from Havana. ~**o** *m* (*puro*) Havana

haber *v aux* [30] have. ● *v imper-sonal* (*presente s & pl* **hay**, *imper-fecto s & pl* **había**, *pretérito s & pl* **hubo**) be. **hay 5 bancos en la plaza** there are 5 banks in the square. **hay que hacerlo** it must be done, you have to do it. **he aquí** here is, here are. **no hay de qué** don't mention it, not at all. ¿**qué hay?** (¿*qué pasa?*) what's the matter?; (¿*qué tal?*) how are you?

habichuela *f* bean

hábil *a* skilful; (*listo*) clever; (*adec-uado*) suitable

habilidad *f* skill; (*astucia*) clever-ness

habilita|ción *f* qualification. ~**r** *vt* qualify

habita|ble *a* habitable. ~**ción** *f* room; (*casa etc*) dwelling; (*cuarto de dormir*) bedroom; (*en biología*) hab-itat. ~**ción de matrimonio**, ~**ción doble** double room. ~**ción indi-vidual** , ~**ción sencilla** single room. ~**do** *a* inhabited. ~**nte** *m* inhabit-ant. ~**r** *vt* live in. ● *vi* live

hábito *m* habit

habitual *a* usual, habitual; ‹*cliente*› regular. ~**mente** *adv* usually

habituar [21] *vt* accustom. ~**se** *vpr*. ~**se a** get used to

habla *f* speech; (*idioma*) language; (*dialecto*) dialect. **al** ~ (*al teléfono*) speaking. **ponerse al** ~ **con** get in touch with. ~**dor** *a* talkative. ● *m* chatterbox. ~**duría** *f* rumour. ~**durías** *fpl* gossip. ~**nte** *a* speak-ing. ● *m & f* speaker. ~**r** *vt* speak. ● *vi* speak, talk (**con** to). ~**rse** *vpr* speak. ¡**ni** ~**r!** out of the question! **se** ~ **español** Spanish spoken

hacedor *m* creator, maker

hacendado *m* landowner; (*LAm*) farmer

hacendoso *a* hard-working

hacer [31] *vt* do; (*fabricar, producir etc*) make; (*en matemáticas*) make, be. ● *v impersonal* (*con expresiones meteorológicas*) be; (*con deter-minado periodo de tiempo*) ago. ~**se** *vpr* become; (*acostumbrarse*) get used (**a** to); (*estar hecho*) be made. ~ **de** act as. ~**se a la mar** put to sea. ~**se el sordo** pretend to be deaf. **hace buen tiempo** it's fine weather. **hace calor** it's hot. **hace frío** it's cold. **hace poco** recently. **hace 7 años** 7 years ago. **hace sol** it's sunny. **hace viento** it's windy. ¿**qué le vamos a** ~? what are we going to do?

hacia *prep* towards; (*cerca de*) near; (*con tiempo*) at about. ~ **abajo** down(wards). ~ **arriba** up(wards). ~ **las dos** at about two o'clock

hacienda *f* country estate; (*en LAm*) ranch; (*LAm, ganado*) livestock; (*pública*) treasury. **Ministerio** *m* **de H**~ Ministry of Finance; (*en Gran Bretaña*) Exchequer; (*en Estados Unidos*) Treasury. **ministro** *m* **de H**~ Minister of Finance; (*en Gran Bretaña*) Chancellor of the Exchequer; (*en Estados Unidos*) Secretary of the Treasury

hacinar *vt* stack

hacha *f* axe; (*antorcha*) torch

hachís *m* hashish

hada *f* fairy. **cuento** *m* **de** ~**s** fairy tale

hado *m* fate

hago *vb véase* **hacer**

Haití *m* Haiti

halag|ar [12] *vt* flatter. ~**üeño** *a* flattering

halcón *m* falcon

hálito *m* breath

halo *m* halo

hall /xol/ *m* hall

halla|r *vt* find; (*descubrir*) discover. ~**rse** *vpr* be. ~**zgo** *m* discovery

hamaca *f* hammock; (*asiento*) deck-chair

hambr|e *f* hunger; (*de muchos*) famine. ~**iento** *a* starving. **tener** ~**e** be hungry

Hamburgo *m* Hamburg

hamburguesa *f* hamburger

hamp|a *f* underworld. ~**ón** *m* thug

handicap /'xandikap/ *m* handicap

hangar *m* hangar

haragán a lazy, idle. ● m layabout
harap|iento a in rags. ∼o m rag
harina f flour
harpa f harp
hart|ar vt satisfy; (fastidiar) annoy. ∼arse vpr (comer) eat one's fill; (cansarse) get fed up (de with). ∼azgo m surfeit. ∼o a full; (cansado) tired; (fastidiado) fed up (de with). ● adv enough; (muy) very. ∼ura f surfeit; (abundancia) plenty; (de deseo) satisfaction
hasta prep as far as; (con tiempo) until, till; (Mex) not until. ● adv even. ¡∼ **la vista!** goodbye!, see you! (fam). ¡∼ **luego!** see you later! ¡∼ **mañana!** see you tomorrow! ¡∼ **pronto!** see you soon!
hast|iar [20] vt annoy; (cansar) weary, tire; (aburrir) bore. ∼iarse vpr get fed up (de with). ∼ío m weariness; (aburrimiento) boredom; (asco) disgust
hat|illo m bundle (of belongings); (ganado) small flock. ∼o m belongings; (ganado) flock, herd
haya f beech (tree). ● vb véase **haber**
Haya f. **la** ∼ the Hague
haz m bundle; (de trigo) sheaf; (de rayos) beam
hazaña f exploit
hazmerreír m laughing-stock
he vb véase **haber**
hebdomadario a weekly
hebilla f buckle
hebra f thread; (fibra) fibre
hebreo a Hebrew; (actualmente) Jewish. ● m Hebrew; (actualmente) Jew; (lengua) Hebrew
hecatombe m (fig) disaster
hechi|cera f witch. ∼cería f witchcraft. ∼cero a magic. ● m wizard. ∼zar [10] vt cast a spell on; (fig) fascinate. ∼zo m witchcraft; (un acto de brujería) spell; (fig) fascination
hech|o pp de **hacer**. ● a mature; (terminado) finished; (vestidos etc) ready-made; (culin) done. ● m fact; (acto) deed; (cuestión) matter; (suceso) event. ∼ura f making; (forma) form; (del cuerpo) build; (calidad de fabricación) workmanship. **de** ∼o in fact
hed|er [1] vi stink. ∼iondez f stench. ∼iondo a stinking, smelly. ∼or m stench
hela|da f freeze; (escarcha) frost. ∼dera f (LAm) refrigerator, fridge (Brit, fam). ∼dería f ice-cream

shop. ∼do a frozen; (muy frío) very cold. ● m ice-cream. ∼dora f freezer. ∼r [1] vt freeze. ∼rse vpr freeze
helecho m fern
hélice f spiral; (propulsor) propeller
heli|cóptero m helicopter. ∼puerto m heliport
hembra f female; (mujer) woman
hemisferio m hemisphere
hemorragia f haemorrhage
hemorroides fpl haemorrhoids, piles
henchir [5] vt fill. ∼se vpr stuff o.s.
hend|er [1] vt split. ∼idura f crack, split; (geol) fissure
heno m hay
heráldica f heraldry
herb|áceo a herbaceous. ∼olario m herbalist. ∼oso a grassy
hered|ad f country estate. ∼ar vt/i inherit. ∼era f heiress. ∼ero m heir. ∼itario a hereditary
herej|e m heretic. ∼ía f heresy
herencia f inheritance; (fig) heritage
heri|da f injury. ∼do a injured, wounded. ● m injured person. ∼r [4] vt injure, wound; (fig) hurt. ∼rse vpr hurt o.s. **los** ∼dos the injured; (cantidad) the number of injured
herman|a f sister. ∼a **política** sister-in-law. ∼astra f stepsister. ∼astro m stepbrother. ∼dad f brotherhood. ∼o m brother. ∼o **político** brother-in-law. ∼os **gemelos** twins
hermético a hermetic; (fig) watertight
hermos|o a beautiful; (espléndido) splendid; (hombre) handsome. ∼ura f beauty
hernia f hernia
héroe m hero
hero|ico a heroic. ∼ína f heroine; (droga) heroin. ∼ísmo m heroism
herr|adura f horseshoe. ∼amienta f tool. ∼ería f smithy. ∼ero m blacksmith. ∼umbre f rust
herv|idero m (manantial) spring; (fig) hotbed; (multitud) throng. ∼ir [4] vt/i boil. ∼or m boiling; (fig) ardour
heterogéneo a heterogeneous
heterosexual a & m & f heterosexual
hex|agonal a hexagonal. ∼ágono m hexagon
hiato m hiatus

hiberna|ción f hibernation. **~r** vi hibernate

hibisco m hibiscus

híbrido a & m hybrid

hice vb véase **hacer**

hidalgo m nobleman

hidrata|nte a moisturizing. **~r** vt hydrate; (crema etc) moisturize. **crema** f **~nte** moisturizing cream

hidráulico a hydraulic

hidroavión m seaplane

hidroeléctrico a hydroelectric

hidrófilo a absorbent

hidr|ofobia f rabies. **~ófobo** a rabid

hidrógeno m hydrogen

hidroplano m seaplane

hiedra f ivy

hiel f (fig) bitterness

hielo m ice; (escarcha) frost; (fig) coldness

hiena f hyena; (fig) brute

hierba f grass; (culin, med) herb. **~buena** f mint. **mala ~** weed; (gente) bad people, evil people

hierro m iron

hígado m liver

higi|ene f hygiene. **~énico** a hygienic

hig|o m fig. **~uera** f fig tree

hij|a f daughter. **~a política** daughter-in-law. **~astra** f stepdaughter. **~astro** m stepson. **~o** m son. **~o político** son-in-law. **~s** mpl sons; (chicos y chicas) children

hilar vt spin. **~ delgado** split hairs

hilaridad f laughter, hilarity

hilera f row; (mil) file

hilo m thread; (elec) wire; (de líquido) trickle; (lino) linen

hilv|án m tacking. **~anar** vt tack; (fig, bosquejar) outline

himno m hymn. **~ nacional** anthem

hincapié m. **hacer ~ en** stress, insist on

hincar [7] vt drive in. **~se** vpr sink into. **~se de rodillas** kneel down

hincha f (fam) grudge; (aficionado, fam) fan

hincha|do a inflated; (med) swollen; (persona) arrogant. **~r** vt inflate, blow up. **~rse** vpr swell up; (fig, comer mucho, fam) gorge o.s. **~zón** f swelling; (fig) arrogance

hindi m Hindi

hindú a Hindu

hiniesta f (bot) broom

hinojo m fennel

hiper... pref hyper...

hiper|mercado m hypermarket. **~sensible** a hypersensitive. **~tensión** f high blood pressure

hípico a horse

hipn|osis f hypnosis. **~ótico** a hypnotic. **~otismo** m hypnotism. **~otizador** m hypnotist. **~otizar** [10] vt hypnotize

hipo m hiccup. **tener ~** have hiccups

hipocondríaco a & m hypochondriac

hip|ocresía f hypocrisy. **~ócrita** a hypocritical. ● m & f hypocrite

hipodérmico a hypodermic

hipódromo m racecourse

hipopótamo m hippopotamus

hipoteca f mortgage. **~r** [7] vt mortgage

hip|ótesis f invar hypothesis. **~otético** a hypothetical

hiriente a offensive, wounding

hirsuto a shaggy

hirviente a boiling

hispánico a Hispanic

hispano... pref Spanish

Hispanoamérica f Spanish America

hispano|americano a Spanish American. **~hablante** a, **~parlante** a Spanish-speaking

hist|eria f hysteria. **~érico** a hysterical. **~erismo** m hysteria

hist|oria f history; (cuento) story. **~oriador** m historian. **~órico** a historical. **~orieta** f tale; (con dibujos) strip cartoon. **pasar a la ~oria** go down in history

hito m milestone

hizo vb véase **hacer**

hocico m snout; (fig, de enfado) grimace

hockey m hockey. **~ sobre hielo** ice hockey

hogar m hearth; (fig) home. **~eño** a home; (persona) home-loving

hogaza f large loaf

hoguera f bonfire

hoja f leaf; (de papel, metal etc) sheet; (de cuchillo, espada etc) blade. **~ de afeitar** razor blade. **~lata** f tin. **~latería** f tinware. **~latero** m tinsmith

hojaldre m puff pastry, flaky pastry

hojear vt leaf through; (leer superficialmente) glance through

hola int hello!

Holanda f Holland

holand|és a Dutch. ● m Dutchman; (lengua) Dutch. **~esa** f Dutchwoman

holg|ado *a* loose; (*fig*) comfortable. **~ar** [2 & 12] *vt* (*no trabajar*) not work, have a day off; (*sobrar*) be unnecessary. **~azán** *a* lazy. ● *m* idler. **~ura** *f* looseness; (*fig*) comfort; (*en mecánica*) play. **huelga decir que** needless to say

holocausto *m* holocaust

hollín *m* soot

hombre *m* man; (*especie humana*) man(kind). ● *int* Good Heavens!; (*de duda*) well. **~ de estado** statesman. **~ de negocios** businessman. **~ rana** frogman. **el ~ de la calle** the man in the street

hombr|era *f* epaulette; (*almohadilla*) shoulder pad. **~o** *m* shoulder

hombruno *a* masculine

homenaje *m* homage; (*fig*) tribute. **rendir ~** a pay tribute to

home|ópata *m* homoeopath. **~opatía** *f* homoeopathy. **~opático** *a* homoeopathic

homicid|a *a* murderous. ● *m & f* murderer. **~io** *m* murder

homogéneo *a* homogeneous

homosexual *a & m & f* homosexual. **~idad** *f* homosexuality

hond|o *a* deep. **~onada** *f* hollow. **~ura** *f* depth

Honduras *fpl* Honduras

hondureño *a & m* Honduran

honest|idad *f* decency. **~o** *a* proper

hongo *m* fungus; (*culin*) mushroom; (*venenoso*) toadstool

hon|or *m* honour. **~orable** *a* honourable. **~orario** *a* honorary. **~orarios** *mpl* fees. **~ra** *f* honour; (*buena fama*) good name. **~radez** *f* honesty. **~rado** *a* honest. **~rar** *vt* honour. **~rarse** *vpr* be honoured

hora *f* hour; (*momento determinado, momento oportuno*) time. **~ avanzada** late hour. **~ punta** rush hour. **~s** *fpl* **de trabajo** working hours. **~s** *fpl* **extraordinarias** overtime. **a estas ~s** now. **¿a qué ~?** at what time? when? **de ~ en ~** hourly. **de última ~** last-minute. **en buena ~** at the right time. **media ~** half an hour. **¿qué ~ es?** what time is it? **¿tiene Vd ~?** can you tell me the time?

horario *a* time; (*cada hora*) hourly. ● *m* timetable. **a ~** (*LAm*) on time

horca *f* gallows

horcajadas. a ~ astride

horchata *f* tiger-nut milk

horda *f* horde

horizont|al *a & f* horizontal. **~e** *m* horizon

horma *f* mould; (*para fabricar calzado*) last; (*para conservar forma del calzado*) shoe-tree

hormiga *f* ant

hormigón *m* concrete

hormigue|ar *vt* tingle; (*bullir*) swarm. **me ~a la mano** I've got pins and needles in my hand. **~o** *m* tingling; (*fig*) anxiety

hormiguero *m* anthill; (*de gente*) swarm

hormona *f* hormone

horn|ada *f* batch. **~ero** *m* baker. **~illo** *m* cooker. **~o** *m* oven; (*para ladrillos, cerámica etc*) kiln; (*tec*) furnace

horóscopo *m* horoscope

horquilla *f* pitchfork; (*para el pelo*) hairpin

horr|endo *a* awful. **~ible** *a* horrible. **~ipilante** *a* terrifying. **~or** *m* horror; (*atrocidad*) atrocity. **~orizar** [10] *vt* horrify. **~orizarse** *vpr* be horrified. **~oroso** *a* horrifying. **¡qué ~or!** how awful!

hort|aliza *f* vegetable. **~elano** *m* market gardener. **~icultura** *f* horticulture

hosco *a* surly; ⟨*lugar*⟩ gloomy

hospeda|je *m* lodging. **~r** *vt* put up. **~rse** *vpr* lodge

hospital *m* hospital

hospital|ario *a* hospitable. **~idad** *f* hospitality

hostal *m* boarding-house

hostería *f* inn

hostia *f* (*relig*) host; (*golpe, fam*) punch

hostigar [12] *vt* whip; (*fig, excitar*) urge; (*fig, molestar*) pester

hostil *a* hostile. **~idad** *f* hostility

hotel *m* hotel. **~ero** *a* hotel. ● *m* hotelier

hoy *adv* today. **~ (en) día** nowadays. **~ mismo** this very day. **~ por ~** for the time being. **de ~ en adelante** from now on

hoy|a *f* hole; (*sepultura*) grave. **~o** *m* hole; (*sepultura*) grave. **~uelo** *m* dimple

hoz *f* sickle; (*desfiladero*) pass

hube *vb* *véase* **haber**

hucha *f* money box

hueco *a* hollow; (*vacío*) empty; (*esponjoso*) spongy; (*resonante*) resonant. ● *m* hollow

huelg|a *f* strike. **~a de brazos caídos** sit-down strike. **~a de celo** work-to-rule. **~a de hambre** hunger strike. **~uista** *m* & *f* striker. **declarar la ~a, declararse en ~a** come out on strike

huelo *vb véase* **oler**

huella *f* footprint; (*de animal, vehículo etc*) track. **~ dactilar, ~ digital** fingerprint

huérfano *a* orphaned. ● *m* orphan. **~ de** without

huero *a* empty

huert|a *f* market garden (*Brit*), truck farm (*Amer*); (*terreno de regadío*) irrigated plain. **~o** *m* vegetable garden; (*de árboles frutales*) orchard

huesa *f* grave

hueso *m* bone; (*de fruta*) stone. **~so** *a* bony

huésped *m* guest; (*que paga*) lodger; (*animal*) host

huesudo *a* bony

huev|a *f* roe. **~era** *f* eggcup. **~o** *m* egg. **~o duro** hard-boiled egg. **~o escalfado** poached egg. **~o estrellado, ~o frito** fried egg. **~o pasado por agua** boiled egg. **~os revueltos** scrambled eggs

hui|da *f* flight, escape. **~dizo** *a* (*tímido*) shy; (*fugaz*) fleeting. **~r** [17] *vt/i* flee, run away; (*evitar*) avoid

huipil *m* (*Mex*) embroidered smock

huitlacoche *m* (*Mex*) edible black fungus

hule *m* oilcloth, oilskin

human|idad *f* mankind; (*fig*) humanity. **~idades** *fpl* humanities. **~ismo** *m* humanism. **~ista** *m* & *f* humanist. **~itario** *a* humanitarian. **~o** *a* human; (*benévolo*) humane. ● *m* human (being)

hum|areda *f* cloud of smoke. **~ear** *vi* smoke; (*echar vapor*) steam

humed|ad *f* dampness (*en meteorología*) humidity. **~ecer** [11] *vt* moisten. **~ecerse** *vpr* become moist

húmedo *a* damp; (*clima*) humid; (*mojado*) wet

humi|ldad *f* humility. **~lde** *a* humble. **~llación** *f* humiliation. **~llar** *vt* humiliate. **~llarse** *vpr* humble o.s.

humo *m* smoke; (*vapor*) steam; (*gas nocivo*) fumes. **~s** *mpl* conceit

humor *m* mood, temper; (*gracia*) humour. **~ismo** *m* humour. **~ista**

m & *f* humorist. **~ístico** *a* humorous. **estar de mal ~** be in a bad mood

hundi|do *a* sunken. **~miento** *m* sinking. **~r** *vt* sink; destroy (*edificio*). **~rse** *vpr* sink; (*edificio*) collapse

húngaro *a* & *m* Hungarian

Hungría *f* Hungary

huracán *m* hurricane

huraño *a* unsociable

hurg|ar [12] *vt* poke; (*fig*) stir up. **~ón** *m* poker

hurón *m* ferret. ● *a* unsociable

hurra *int* hurray!

hurraca *f* magpie

hurtadillas. a ~ stealthily

hurt|ar *vt* steal. **~o** *m* theft; (*cosa robada*) stolen object

husmear *vt* sniff out; (*fig*) pry into

huyo *vb véase* **huir**

I

Iberia *f* Iberia

ibérico *a* Iberian

ibero *a* & *m* Iberian

íbice *m* ibex, mountain goat

Ibiza *f* Ibiza

iceberg /iθ'ber/ *m* iceberg

icono *m* icon

ictericia *f* jaundice

ida *f* outward journey; (*salida*) departure. **de ~ y vuelta** return (*Brit*), round-trip (*Amer*)

idea *f* idea; (*opinión*) opinion. **cambiar de ~** change one's mind. **no tener la más remota ~, no tener la menor ~** not have the slightest idea, not have a clue (*fam*)

ideal *a* ideal; (*imaginario*) imaginary. ● *m* ideal. **~ista** *m* & *f* idealist. **~izar** [10] *vt* idealize

idear *vt* think up, conceive; (*inventar*) invent

ídem *pron* & *adv* the same

idéntico *a* identical

identi|dad *f* identity. **~ficación** *f* identification. **~ficar** [7] *vt* identify. **~ficarse** *vpr*. **~ficarse con** identify with

ideol|ogía *f* ideology. **~ógico** *a* ideological

idílico *a* idyllic

idilio *m* idyll

idiom|a *m* language. **~ático** *a* idiomatic

idiosincrasia *f* idiosyncrasy
idiot|a *a* idiotic. ● *m* & *f* idiot. ∼**ez** *f* idiocy
idiotismo *m* idiom
idolatrar *vt* worship; (*fig*) idolize
ídolo *m* idol
idóneo *a* suitable (**para** for)
iglesia *f* church
iglú *m* igloo
ignición *f* ignition
ignomini|a *f* ignominy, disgrace. ∼**oso** *a* ignominious
ignora|ncia *f* ignorance. ∼**nte** *a* ignorant. ● *m* ignoramus. ∼**r** *vt* not know, be unaware of
igual *a* equal; (*mismo*) the same; (*similar*) like; (*llano*) even; (*liso*) smooth. ● *adv* easily. ● *m* equal. ∼ **que** (the same) as. **al** ∼ **que** the same as. **da** ∼, **es** ∼ it doesn't matter
igual|ar *vt* make equal; (*ser igual*) equal; (*allanar*) level. ∼**arse** *vpr* be equal. ∼**dad** *f* equality. ∼**mente** *adv* equally; (*también*) also, likewise; (*respuesta de cortesía*) the same to you
ijada *f* flank
ilegal *a* illegal
ilegible *a* illegible
ilegítimo *a* illegitimate
ileso *a* unhurt
ilícito *a* illicit
ilimitado *a* unlimited
ilógico *a* illogical
ilumina|ción *f* illumination; (*alumbrado*) lighting; (*fig*) enlightenment. ∼**r** *vt* light (up); (*fig*) enlighten. ∼**rse** *vpr* light up
ilusi|ón *f* illusion; (*sueño*) dream; (*alegría*) joy. ∼**onado** *a* excited. ∼**onar** *vt* give false hope. ∼**onarse** *vpr* have false hopes. **hacerse** ∼**ones** build up one's hopes. **me hace** ∼**ón** I'm thrilled; I'm looking forward to ⟨*algo en el futuro*⟩
ilusionis|mo *m* conjuring. ∼**ta** *m* & *f* conjurer
iluso *a* easily deceived. ● *m* dreamer. ∼**rio** *a* illusory
ilustra|ción *f* learning; (*dibujo*) illustration. ∼**do** *a* learned; (*con dibujos*) illustrated. ∼**r** *vt* explain; (*instruir*) instruct; (*añadir dibujos etc*) illustrate. ∼**rse** *vpr* acquire knowledge. ∼**tivo** *a* illustrative
ilustre *a* illustrious
imagen *f* image; (*TV etc*) picture

imagina|ble *a* imaginable. ∼**ción** *f* imagination. ∼**r** *vt* imagine. ∼**rse** *vpr* imagine. ∼**rio** *m* imaginary. ∼**tivo** *a* imaginative
imán *m* magnet
imantar *vt* magnetize
imbécil *a* stupid. ● *m* & *f* imbecile, idiot
imborrable *a* indelible; ⟨*recuerdo etc*⟩ unforgettable
imbuir [17] *vt* imbue (**de** with)
imita|ción *f* imitation. ∼**r** *vt* imitate
impacien|cia *f* impatience. ∼**tarse** *vpr* lose one's patience. ∼**te** *a* impatient; (*intranquilo*) anxious
impacto *m* impact
impar *a* odd
imparcial *a* impartial. ∼**idad** *f* impartiality
impartir *vt* impart
impasible *a* impassive
impávido *a* fearless; (*impasible*) impassive
impecable *a* impeccable
impedi|do *a* disabled. ∼**menta** *f* (*esp mil*) baggage. ∼**mento** *m* hindrance. ∼**r** [5] *vt* prevent; (*obstruir*) hinder
impeler *vt* drive
impenetrable *a* impenetrable
impenitente *a* unrepentant
impensa|ble *a* unthinkable. ∼**do** *a* unexpected
imperar *vi* reign
imperativo *a* imperative; ⟨*persona*⟩ imperious
imperceptible *a* imperceptible
imperdible *m* safety pin
imperdonable *a* unforgivable
imperfec|ción *f* imperfection. ∼**to** *a* imperfect
imperial *a* imperial. ● *f* upper deck. ∼**ismo** *m* imperialism
imperio *m* empire; (*poder*) rule; (*fig*) pride. ∼**so** *a* imperious
impermeable *a* waterproof. ● *m* raincoat
impersonal *a* impersonal
impertérrito *a* undaunted
impertinen|cia *f* impertinence. ∼**te** *a* impertinent
imperturbable *a* imperturbable
ímpetu *m* impetus; (*impulso*) impulse; (*impetuosidad*) impetuosity
impetuos|idad *f* impetuosity; (*violencia*) violence. ∼**o** *a* impetuous; (*violento*) violent

impío *a* ungodly; ⟨*acción*⟩ irreverent

implacable *a* implacable

implantar *vt* introduce

implica|ción *f* implication. **~r** [7] *vt* implicate; (*significar*) imply

implícito *a* implicit

implora|ción *f* entreaty. **~r** *vt* implore

imponderable *a* imponderable; (*inapreciable*) invaluable

impon|ente *a* imposing; (*fam*) terrific. **~er** [34] *vt* impose; (*requerir*) demand; deposit ⟨*dinero*⟩. **~erse** *vpr* be imposed; (*hacerse obedecer*) assert o.s.; (*hacerse respetar*) command respect. **~ible** *a* taxable

impopular *a* unpopular. **~idad** *f* unpopularity

importa|ción *f* import; (*artículo*) import. **~dor** *a* importing. ● *m* importer

importa|ncia *f* importance; (*tamaño*) size. **~nte** *a* important; (*en cantidad*) considerable. **~r** *vt* import; (*valer*) cost. ● *vi* be important, matter. ¡**le importa...?** would you mind...? **no ~** it doesn't matter

importe *m* price; (*total*) amount

importun|ar *vt* bother. **~o** *a* troublesome; (*inoportuno*) inopportune

imposib|ilidad *f* impossibility. **~le** *a* impossible. **hacer lo ~le** do all one can

imposición *f* imposition; (*impuesto*) tax

impostor *m* & *f* impostor

impotable *a* undrinkable

impoten|cia *f* impotence. **~te** *a* powerless, impotent

impracticable *a* impracticable; (*intransitable*) unpassable

impreca|ción *f* curse. **~r** [7] *vt* curse

imprecis|ión *f* vagueness. **~o** *a* imprecise

impregnar *vt* impregnate; (*empapar*) soak; (*fig*) cover

imprenta *f* printing; (*taller*) printing house, printer's

imprescindible *a* indispensable, essential

impresi|ón *f* impression; (*acción de imprimir*) printing; (*tirada*) edition; (*huella*) imprint. **~onable** *a* impressionable. **~onante** *a* impressive; (*espantoso*) frightening. **~onar** *vt* impress; (*conmover*) move; (*foto*) expose. **~onarse**

vpr be impressed; (*conmover*) be moved

impresionis|mo *m* impressionism. **~ta** *a* & *m* & *f* impressionist

impreso *a* printed. ● *m* printed paper, printed matter. **~ra** *f* printer

imprevis|ible *a* unforeseeable. **~to** *a* unforeseen

imprimir [*pp* impreso] *vt* impress; print ⟨*libro etc*⟩

improbab|ilidad *f* improbability. **~le** *a* unlikely, improbable

improcedente *a* unsuitable

improductivo *a* unproductive

improperio *m* insult. **~s** *mpl* abuse

impropio *a* improper

improvis|ación *f* improvisation. **~adamente** *adv* suddenly. **~ado** *a* improvised. **~ar** *vt* improvise. **~o** *a*. **de ~o** suddenly

impruden|cia *f* imprudence. **~te** *a* imprudent

impuden|cia *f* impudence. **~te** *a* impudent

imp|údico *a* immodest; (*desvergonzado*) shameless. **~udor** *m* immodesty; (*desvergüenza*) shamelessness

impuesto *a* imposed. ● *m* tax. **~ sobre el valor añadido** VAT, value added tax

impugnar *vt* contest; (*refutar*) refute

impulsar *vt* impel

impuls|ividad *f* impulsiveness. **~ivo** *a* impulsive. **~o** *m* impulse

impun|e *a* unpunished. **~idad** *f* impunity

impur|eza *f* impurity. **~o** *a* impure

imputa|ción *f* charge. **~r** *vt* attribute; (*acusar*) charge

inacabable *a* interminable

inaccesible *a* inaccessible

inaceptable *a* unacceptable

inacostumbrado *a* unaccustomed

inactiv|idad *f* inactivity. **~o** *a* inactive

inadaptado *a* maladjusted

inadecuado *a* inadequate; (*inapropiado*) unsuitable

inadmisible *a* inadmissible; (*intolerable*) intolerable

inadvert|ido *a* unnoticed. **~encia** *f* inadvertence

inagotable *a* inexhaustible

inaguantable *a* unbearable; ⟨*persona*⟩ insufferable

inaltera|ble *a* unchangeable; ⟨*color*⟩ fast; ⟨*carácter*⟩ calm. **~do** *a* unchanged

inanimado *a* inanimate
inaplicable *a* inapplicable
inapreciable *a* imperceptible
inapropiado *a* inappropriate
inarticulado *a* inarticulate
inasequible *a* out of reach
inaudito *a* unheard-of
inaugura|ción *f* inauguration. **~l** *a* inaugural. **~r** *vt* inaugurate
inca *a* Incan. ● *m & f* Inca. **~ico** *a* Incan
incalculable *a* incalculable
incandescen|cia *f* incandescence. **~te** *a* incandescent
incansable *a* tireless
incapa|cidad *f* incapacity. **~citar** *vt* incapacitate. **~z** *a* incapable
incauto *a* unwary; (*fácil de engañar*) gullible
incendi|ar *vt* set fire to. **~arse** *vpr* catch fire. **~ario** *a* incendiary. ● *m* arsonist. **~o** *m* fire
incentivo *m* incentive
incertidumbre *f* uncertainty
incesante *a* incessant
incest|o *m* incest. **~uoso** *a* incestuous
inciden|cia *f* incidence; (*incidente*) incident. **~tal** *a* incidental. **~te** *m* incident
incidir *vi* fall; (*influir*) influence
incienso *m* incense
incierto *a* uncertain
incinera|ción *f* incineration; (*de cadáveres*) cremation. **~dor** *m* incinerator. **~r** *vt* incinerate; cremate ⟨*cadáver*⟩
incipiente *a* incipient
incisión *f* incision
incisivo *a* incisive. ● *m* incisor
incitar *vt* incite
incivil *a* rude
inclemen|cia *f* harshness. **~te** *a* harsh
inclina|ción *f* slope; (*de la cabeza*) nod; (*fig*) inclination. **~r** *vt* incline. **~rse** *vpr* lean; (*encorvarse*) stoop; (*en un saludo*) bow; (*fig*) be inclined. **~rse a** (*parecerse*) resemble
inclu|ido *a* included; ⟨*precio*⟩ inclusive; (*en cartas*) enclosed. **~ir** [17] *vt* include; (*en cartas*) enclose. **~sión** *f* inclusion. **~sive** *adv* inclusive. **hasta el lunes ~sive** up to and including Monday. **~so** *a* included; (*en cartas*) enclosed. ● *adv* including; (*hasta*) even
incógnito *a* unknown. **de ~** incognito

incoheren|cia *f* incoherence. **~te** *a* incoherent
incoloro *a* colourless
incólume *a* unharmed
incomestible *a*, **incomible** *a* uneatable, inedible
incomodar *vt* inconvenience; (*molestar*) bother. **~se** *vpr* trouble o.s.; (*enfadarse*) get angry
incómodo *a* uncomfortable; (*inoportuno*) inconvenient
incomparable *a* imcomparable
incompatib|ilidad *f* incompatibility. **~le** *a* incompatible
incompeten|cia *f* incompetence. **~te** *a* incompetent
incompleto *a* incomplete
incompren|dido *a* misunderstood. **~sible** *a* incomprehensible. **~sión** *f* incomprehension
incomunicado *a* isolated; ⟨*preso*⟩ in solitary confinement
inconcebible *a* inconceivable
inconciliable *a* irreconcilable
inconcluso *a* unfinished
incondicional *a* unconditional
inconfundible *a* unmistakable
incongruente *a* incongruous
inconmensurable *a* (*fam*) enormous
inconscien|cia *f* unconsciousness; (*irreflexión*) recklessness. **~te** *a* unconscious; (*irreflexivo*) reckless
inconsecuente *a* inconsistent
inconsiderado *a* inconsiderate
inconsistente *a* insubstantial
inconsolable *a* unconsolable
inconstan|cia *f* inconstancy. **~te** *a* changeable; ⟨*persona*⟩ fickle
incontable *a* countless
incontaminado *a* uncontaminated
incontenible *a* irrepressible
incontestable *a* indisputable
incontinen|cia *f* incontinence. **~te** *a* incontinent
inconvenien|cia *f* disadvantage. **~te** *a* inconvenient; (*inapropiado*) inappropriate; (*incorrecto*) improper. ● *m* difficulty; (*desventaja*) drawback
incorpora|ción *f* incorporation. **~r** *vt* incorporate; (*culin*) mix. **~rse** *vpr* sit up; join ⟨*sociedad, regimiento etc*⟩
incorrecto *a* incorrect; ⟨*acción*⟩ improper; (*descortés*) discourteous
incorregible *a* incorrigible
incorruptible *a* incorruptible
incrédulo *a* incredulous

increíble *a* incredible

increment|ar *vt* increase. **~o** *m* increase

incriminar *vt* incriminate

incrustar *vt* encrust

incuba|ción *f* incubation. **~dora** *f* incubator. **~r** *vt* incubate; *(fig)* hatch

incuestionable *a* unquestionable

inculcar [7] *vt* inculcate

inculpar *vt* accuse; *(culpar)* blame

inculto *a* uncultivated; ⟨*persona*⟩ uneducated

incumplimiento *m* non-fulfilment; *(de un contrato)* breach

incurable *a* incurable

incurrir *vi*. **~ en** incur; fall into ⟨*error*⟩; commit ⟨*crimen*⟩

incursión *f* raid

indaga|ción *f* investigation. **~r** [12] *vt* investigate

indebido *a* undue

indecen|cia *f* indecency. **~te** *a* indecent

indecible *a* inexpressible

indecis|ión *f* indecision. **~o** *a* undecided

indefenso *a* defenceless

indefini|ble *a* indefinable. **~do** *a* indefinite

indeleble *a* indelible

indelicad|eza *f* indelicacy. **~o** *a* indelicate; *(falto de escrúpulo)* unscrupulous

indemn|e *a* undamaged; ⟨*persona*⟩ unhurt. **~idad** *f* indemnity. **~izar** [10] *vt* indemnify, compensate

independ|encia *f* independence. **~iente** *a* independent

independizarse [10] *vpr* become independent

indescifrable *a* indecipherable, incomprehensible

indescriptible *a* indescribable

indeseable *a* undesirable

indestructible *a* indestructible

indetermina|ble *a* indeterminable. **~do** *a* indeterminate

India *f*. **la ~** India. **las ~s** *fpl* the Indies

indica|ción *f* indication; *(sugerencia)* suggestion. **~ciones** *fpl* directions. **~dor** *m* indicator; *(tec)* gauge. **~r** [7] *vt* show, indicate; *(apuntar)* point at; *(hacer saber)* point out; *(aconsejar)* advise. **~tivo** *a* indicative. ● *m* indicative; *(al teléfono)* dialling code

índice *m* indication; *(dedo)* index finger; *(de libro)* index; *(catálogo)* catalogue; *(aguja)* pointer

indicio *m* indication, sign; *(vestigio)* trace

indiferen|cia *f* indifference. **~te** *a* indifferent. **me es ~te** it's all the same to me

indígena *a* indigenous. ● *m & f* native

indigen|cia *f* poverty. **~te** *a* needy

indigest|ión *f* indigestion. **~o** *a* undigested; *(difícil de digerir)* indigestible

indign|ación *f* indignation. **~ado** *a* indignant. **~ar** *vt* make indignant. **~arse** *vpr* be indignant. **~o** *a* unworthy; *(despreciable)* contemptible

indio *a & m* Indian

indirect|a *f* hint. **~o** *a* indirect

indisciplina *f* lack of discipline. **~do** *a* undisciplined

indiscre|ción *f* indiscretion. **~to** *a* indiscreet

indiscutible *a* unquestionable

indisoluble *a* indissoluble

indispensable *a* indispensable

indisp|oner [34] *vt* ⟨*enemistar*⟩ set against. **~onerse** *vpr* fall out; *(ponerse enfermo)* fall ill. **~osición** *f* indisposition. **~uesto** *a* indisposed

indistinto *a* indistinct

individu|al *a* individual; ⟨*cama*⟩ single. **~alidad** *f* individuality. **~alista** *m & f* individualist. **~alizar** [10] *vt* individualize. **~o** *a & m* individual

índole *f* nature; *(clase)* type

indolen|cia *f* indolence. **~te** *a* indolent

indoloro *a* painless

indomable *a* untameable

indómito *a* indomitable

Indonesia *f* Indonesia

inducir [47] *vt* induce; *(deducir)* infer

indudable *a* undoubted. **~mente** *adv* undoubtedly

indulgen|cia *f* indulgence. **~te** *a* indulgent

indult|ar *vt* pardon; exempt *(de un pago etc)*. **~o** *m* pardon

industria *f* industry. **~l** *a* industrial. ● *m* industrialist. **~lización** *f* industrialization. **~lizar** [10] *vt* industrialize

industriarse *vpr* do one's best

industrioso *a* industrious

inédito *a* unpublished; (*fig*) unknown

ineducado *a* impolite

inefable *a* inexpressible

ineficaz *a* ineffective

ineficiente *a* inefficient

inelegible *a* ineligible

ineludible *a* inescapable, unavoidable

inept|itud *f* ineptitude. ~o *a* inept

inequívoco *a* unequivocal

iner|cia *f* inertia

inerme *a* unarmed; (*fig*) defenceless

inerte *a* inert

inesperado *a* unexpected

inestable *a* unstable

inestimable *a* inestimable

inevitable *a* inevitable

inexacto *a* inaccurate; (*incorrecto*) incorrect; (*falso*) untrue

inexistente *a* non-existent

inexorable *a* inexorable

inexper|iencia *f* inexperience. ~to *a* inexperienced

inexplicable *a* inexplicable

infalible *a* infallible

infam|ar *vt* defame. ~atorio *a* defamatory. ~e *a* infamous; (*fig, muy malo, fam*) awful. ~ia *f* infamy

infancia *f* infancy

infant|a *f* infanta, princess. ~e *m* infante, prince; (*mil*) infantryman. ~ería *f* infantry. ~il *a* (*de niño*) child's; (*como un niño*) infantile

infarto *m* coronary (thrombosis)

infatigable *a* untiring

infatua|ción *f* conceit. ~rse *vpr* get conceited

infausto *a* unlucky

infec|ción *f* infection. ~cioso *a* infectious. ~tar *vt* infect. ~tarse *vpr* become infected. ~to *a* infected; (*fam*) disgusting

infecundo *a* infertile

infeli|cidad *f* unhappiness. ~z *a* unhappy

inferior *a* inferior. ● *m & f* inferior. ~idad *f* lower; (*calidad*) inferiority

inferir [4] *vt* infer; (*causar*) cause

infernal *a* infernal, hellish

infestar *vt* infest; (*fig*) inundate

infi|delidad *f* unfaithfulness. ~el *a* unfaithful

infierno *m* hell

infiltra|ción *f* infiltration. ~rse *vpr* infiltrate

ínfimo *a* lowest

infini|dad *f* infinity. ~tivo *m* infinitive. ~to *a* infinite. ● *m* infinite;

(*en matemáticas*) infinity. **una ~dad de** countless

inflación *f* inflation; (*fig*) conceit

inflama|ble *a* (in)flammable. ~ción *f* inflammation. ~r *vt* set on fire; (*fig, med*) inflame. ~rse *vpr* catch fire; (*med*) become inflamed

inflar *vt* inflate; (*fig, exagerar*) exaggerate

inflexi|ble *a* inflexible. ~ón *f* inflexion

infligir [14] *vt* inflict

influ|encia *f* influence. ~enza *f* flu (*fam*), influenza. ~ir [17] *vt/i* influence. ~jo *m* influence. ~yente *a* influential

informa|ción *f* information. ~ciones *fpl* (*noticias*) news; (*de teléfonos*) directory enquiries. ~dor *m* informant

informal *a* informal; (*incorrecto*) incorrect

inform|ante *m & f* informant. ~ar *vt/i* inform. ~arse *vpr* find out. ~ática *f* information technology. ~ativo *a* informative

informe *a* shapeless. ● *m* report; (*información*) information

infortun|ado *a* unfortunate. ~io *m* misfortune

infracción *f* infringement

infraestructura *f* infrastructure

infranqueable *a* impassable; (*fig*) insuperable

infrarrojo *a* infrared

infrecuente *a* infrequent

infringir [14] *vt* infringe

infructuoso *a* fruitless

infundado *a* unfounded

infu|ndir *vt* instil. ~sión *f* infusion

ingeniar *vt* invent

ingenier|ía *f* engineering. ~o *m* engineer

ingenio *m* ingenuity; (*agudeza*) wit; (*LAm, de azúcar*) refinery. ~so *a* ingenious

ingenu|idad *f* ingenuousness. ~o *a* ingenuous

ingerir [4] *vt* swallow

Inglaterra *f* England

ingle *f* groin

ingl|és *a* English. ● *m* Englishman; (*lengua*) English. ~esa *f* Englishwoman

ingrat|itud *f* ingratitude. ~o *a* ungrateful; (*desagradable*) thankless

ingrediente *m* ingredient

ingres|ar vt deposit. ● vi. ~**ar en** come in, enter; join ⟨sociedad⟩. ~**o** m entry; (en sociedad, hospital etc) admission. ~**os** mpl income

inh|ábil a unskillful; (no apto) unfit. ~**abilidad** f unskillfulness

inhabitable a uninhabitable

inhala|ción f inhalation. ~**dor** m inhaler. ~**r** vt inhale

inherente a inherent

inhibi|ción f inhibition. ~**r** vt inhibit

inhospitalario a, **inhóspito** a inhospitable

inhumano a inhuman

inicia|ción f beginning. ~**l** a & f initial. ~**r** vt initiate; (comenzar) begin, start. ~**tiva** f initiative

inicio m beginning

inicuo a iniquitous

inigualado a unequalled

ininterrumpido a continuous

injer|encia f interference. ~**ir** [4] vt insert. ~**irse** vpr interfere

injert|ar vt graft. ~**to** m graft

injuri|a f insult; (ofensa) offence. ~**ar** vt insult. ~**oso** a offensive

injust|icia f injustice. ~**o** a unjust

inmaculado a immaculate

inmaduro a unripe; ⟨persona⟩ immature

inmediaciones fpl neighbourhood

inmediat|amente adv immediately. ~**o** a immediate; (contiguo) next

inmejorable a excellent

inmemorable a immemorial

inmens|idad f immensity. ~**o** a immense

inmerecido a undeserved

inmersión f immersion

inmigra|ción f immigration. ~**nte** a & m immigrant. ~**r** vt immigrate

inminen|cia f imminence. ~**te** a imminent

inmiscuirse [17] vpr interfere

inmobiliario a property

inmoderado a immoderate

inmodesto a immodest

inmolar vt sacrifice

inmoral a immoral. ~**idad** f immorality

inmortal a immortal. ~**izar** [10] vt immortalize

inmóvil a immobile

inmueble a. **bienes** ~**s** property

inmund|icia f filth. ~**icias** fpl rubbish. ~**o** a filthy

inmun|e a immune. ~**idad** f immunity. ~**ización** f immunization. ~**izar** [10] vt immunize

inmuta|ble a unchangeable. ~**rse** vpr turn pale

innato a innate

innecesario a unnecessary

innegable a undeniable

innoble a ignoble

innova|ción f innovation. ~**r** vt/i innovate

innumerable a innumerable

inocen|cia f innocence. ~**tada** f practical joke. ~**te** a innocent. ~**tón** a naïve

inocuo a innocuous

inodoro a odourless. ● m toilet

inofensivo a inoffensive

inolvidable a unforgettable

inoperable a inoperable

inopinado a unexpected

inoportuno a untimely; (incómodo) inconvenient

inorgánico a inorganic

inoxidable a stainless

inquebrantable a unbreakable

inquiet|ar vt worry. ~**arse** vpr get worried. ~**o** a worried; (agitado) restless. ~**ud** f anxiety

inquilino m tenant

inquirir [4] vt enquire into, investigate

insaciable a insatiable

insalubre a unhealthy

insanable a incurable

insatisfecho a unsatisfied; (descontento) dissatisfied

inscri|bir [pp **inscrito**] vt inscribe; (en registro etc) enrol, register. ~**birse** vpr register. ~**pción** f inscription; (registro) registration

insect|icida m insecticide. ~**o** m insect

insegur|idad f insecurity. ~**o** a insecure; (dudoso) uncertain

insemina|ción f insemination. ~**r** vt inseminate

insensato a senseless

insensible a insensitive; (med) insensible; (imperceptible) imperceptible

inseparable a inseparable

insertar vt insert

insidi|a f trap. ~**oso** a insidious

insigne a famous

insignia f badge; (bandera) flag

insignificante a insignificant

insincero a insincere

insinua|ción f insinuation. ~**nte** a insinuating. ~**r** [21] vt insinuate. ~**rse** vpr ingratiate o.s. ~**rse en** creep into

insípido *a* insipid

insist|encia *f* insistence. **~ente** *a* insistent. **~ir** *vi* insist; (*hacer hincapié*) stress

insolación *f* sunstroke

insolen|cia *f* rudeness, insolence. **~te** *a* rude, insolent

insólito *a* unusual

insoluble *a* insoluble

insolven|cia *f* insolvency. **~te** *a* & *m* & *f* insolvent

insomn|e *a* sleepless. **~io** *m* insomnia

insondable *a* unfathomable

insoportable *a* unbearable

insospechado *a* unexpected

insostenible *a* untenable

inspec|ción *f* inspection. **~cionar** *vt* inspect. **~tor** *m* inspector

inspira|ción *f* inspiration. **~r** *vt* inspire. **~rse** *vpr* be inspired

instala|ción *f* installation. **~r** *vt* install. **~rse** *vpr* settle

instancia *f* request

instant|ánea *f* snapshot. **~áneo** *a* instantaneous; (*café etc*) instant. **~e** *m* instant. **a cada ~e** constantly. **al ~e** immediately

instar *vt* urge

instaura|ción *f* establishment. **~r** *vt* establish

instiga|ción *f* instigation. **~dor** *m* instigator. **~r** [12] *vt* instigate; (*incitar*) incite

instint|ivo *a* instinctive. **~o** *m* instinct

institu|ción *f* institution. **~cional** *a* institutional. **~ir** [17] *vt* establish. **~to** *m* institute; (*escol*) (secondary) school. **~triz** *f* governess

instru|cción *f* instruction. **~ctivo** *a* instructive. **~ctor** *m* instructor. **~ir** [17] *vt* instruct; (*enseñar*) teach

instrument|ación *f* instrumentation. **~al** *a* instrumental. **~o** *m* instrument; (*herramienta*) tool

insubordina|ción *f* insubordination. **~r** *vt* stir up. **~rse** *vpr* rebel

insuficien|cia *f* insufficiency; (*inadecuación*) inadequacy. **~te** *a* insufficient

insufrible *a* insufferable

insular *a* insular

insulina *f* insulin

insulso *a* tasteless; (*fig*) insipid

insult|ar *vt* insult. **~o** *m* insult

insuperable *a* insuperable; (*excelente*) excellent

insurgente *a* insurgent

insurrec|ción *f* insurrection. **~to** *a* insurgent

intacto *a* intact

intachable *a* irreproachable

intangible *a* intangible

integra|ción *f* integration. **~l** *a* integral; (*completo*) complete; ⟨*pan*⟩ wholemeal (*Brit*), wholewheat (*Amer*). **~r** *vt* make up

integridad *f* integrity; (*entereza*) wholeness

íntegro *a* complete; (*fig*) upright

intelect|o *m* intellect. **~ual** *a* & *m* & *f* intellectual

inteligen|cia *f* intelligence. **~te** *a* intelligent

inteligible *a* intelligible

intemperancia *f* intemperance

intemperie *f* bad weather. **a la ~** in the open

intempestivo *a* untimely

intenci|ón *f* intention. **~onado** *a* deliberate. **~onal** *a* intentional. **bien ~onado** well-meaning. **mal ~onado** malicious. **segunda ~ón** duplicity

intens|idad *f* intensity. **~ificar** [7] *vt* intensify. **~ivo** *a* intensive. **~o** *a* intense

intent|ar *vt* try. **~o** *m* intent; (*tentativa*) attempt. **de ~o** intentionally

intercalar *vt* insert

intercambio *m* exchange

interceder *vt* intercede

interceptar *vt* intercept

intercesión *f* intercession

interdicto *m* ban

inter|és *m* interest; (*egoísmo*) self-interest. **~esado** *a* interested; (*parcial*) biassed; (*egoísta*) selfish. **~esante** *a* interesting. **~esar** *vt* interest; (*afectar*) concern. ● *vi* be of interest. **~esarse** *vpr* take an interest (**por** in)

interfer|encia *f* interference. **~ir** [4] *vi* interfere

interino *a* temporary; ⟨*persona*⟩ acting. ● *m* stand-in; (*médico*) locum

interior *a* interior. ● *m* inside. **Ministerio** *m* **del l~** Home Office (*Brit*), Department of the Interior (*Amer*)

interjección *f* interjection

interlocutor *m* speaker

interludio *m* interlude

intermediario *a* & *m* intermediary

intermedio *a* intermediate. ● *m* interval

interminable *a* interminable
intermitente *a* intermittent. ● *m* indicator
internacional *a* international
intern|ado *m* (*escol*) boarding-school. ~**ar** *vt* intern; (*en manicomio*) commit. ~**arse** *vpr* penetrate. ~**o** *a* internal; (*escol*) boarding. ● *m* (*escol*) boarder
interpelar *vt* appeal
interponer [34] *vt* interpose. ~**se** *vpr* intervene
int|erpretación *f* interpretation. ~**erpretar** *vt* interpret. ~**érprete** *m* interpreter; (*mus*) performer
interroga|ción *f* question; (*acción*) interrogation; (*signo*) question mark. ~**r** [12] *vt* question. ~**tivo** *a* interrogative
interru|mpir *vt* interrupt; (*suspender*) stop. ~**pción** *f* interruption. ~**ptor** *m* switch
intersección *f* intersection
interurbano *a* inter-city; 〈*conferencia*〉 long-distance
intervalo *m* interval; (*espacio*) space. **a** ~**s** at intervals
interven|ir [53] *vt* control; (*med*) operate on. ● *vi* intervene; (*participar*) take part. ~**tor** *m* inspector; (*com*) auditor
intestino *m* intestine
intim|ar *vi* become friendly. ~**idad** *f* intimacy
intimidar *vt* intimidate
íntimo *a* intimate. ● *m* close friend
intitular *vt* entitle
intolera|ble *a* intolerable. ~**nte** *a* intolerant
intoxicar [7] *vt* poison
intranquil|izar [10] *vt* worry. ~**o** *a* worried
intransigente *a* intransigent
intransitable *a* impassable
intransitivo *a* intransitive
intratable *a* intractable
intrépido *a* intrepid
intriga *f* intrigue. ~**nte** *a* intriguing. ~**r** [12] *vt/i* intrigue
intrincado *a* intricate
intrínseco *a* intrinsic
introduc|ción *f* introduction. ~**ir** [47] *vt* introduce; (*meter*) insert. ~**irse** *vpr* get into; (*entrometerse*) interfere
intromisión *f* interference
introvertido *a* & *m* introvert
intrus|ión *f* intrusion. ~**o** *a* intrusive. ● *m* intruder

intui|ción *f* intuition. ~**r** [17] *vt* sense. ~**tivo** *a* intuitive
inunda|ción *f* flooding. ~**r** *vt* flood
inusitado *a* unusual
in|útil *a* useless; (*vano*) futile. ~**utilidad** *f* uselessness
invadir *vt* invade
inv|alidez *f* invalidity; (*med*) disability. ~**álido** *a* & *m* invalid
invaria|ble *a* invariable. ~**do** *a* unchanged
invas|ión *f* invasion. ~**or** *a* invading. ● *m* invader
invectiva *f* invective
invencible *a* invincible
inven|ción *f* invention. ~**tar** *vt* invent
inventario *m* inventory
invent|iva *f* inventiveness. ~**ivo** *a* inventive. ~**or** *m* inventor
invernadero *m* greenhouse
invernal *a* winter
inverosímil *a* improbable
inversión *f* inversion; (*com*) investment
inverso *a* inverse; (*contrario*) opposite. **a la inversa** the other way round
invertebrado *a* & *m* invertebrate
inverti|do *a* inverted; (*homosexual*) homosexual. ● *m* homosexual. ~**r** [4] *vt* reverse; (*volcar*) turn upside down; (*com*) invest; spend 〈*tiempo*〉
investidura *f* investiture
investiga|ción *f* investigation; (*univ*) research. ~**dor** *m* investigator. ~**r** [12] *vt* investigate
investir [5] *vt* invest
inveterado *a* inveterate
invicto *a* unbeaten
invierno *m* winter
inviolable *a* inviolate
invisib|ilidad *f* invisibility. ~**le** *a* invisible
invita|ción *f* invitation. ~**do** *m* guest. ~**r** *vt* invite. **te invito a una copa** I'll buy you a drink
invoca|ción *f* invocation. ~**r** [7] *vt* invoke
involuntario *a* involuntary
invulnerable *a* invulnerable
inyec|ción *f* injection. ~**tar** *vt* inject
ion *m* ion
ir [49] *vi* go; 〈*ropa*〉 (*convenir*) suit. ● *m* going. ~**se** *vpr* go away. ~ **a hacer** be going to do. ~ **a pie** walk. ~ **de paseo** go for a walk. ~ **en coche** go by car. **no me va ni me viene** it's all the same to me. **no**

vaya a ser que in case. ¡qué va! nonsense! va mejorando it's gradually getting better. ¡vamos!, ¡vámonos! come on! let's go! ¡vaya! fancy that! ¡vete a saber! who knows? ¡ya voy! I'm coming!

ira f anger. ~cundo a irascible

Irak m Iraq

Irán m Iran

iraní a & m & f Iranian

iraquí a & m & f Iraqi

iris m (anat) iris; (arco iris) rainbow

Irlanda f Ireland

irland|és a Irish. ● m Irishman; (lengua) Irish. ~esa f Irishwoman

ir|onía f irony. ~ónico a ironic

irracional a irrational

irradiar vt/i radiate

irrazonable a unreasonable

irreal a unreal. ~idad f unreality

irrealizable a unattainable

irreconciliable a irreconcilable

irreconocible a unrecognizable

irrecuperable a irretrievable

irreducible a irreducible

irreflexión f impetuosity

irrefutable a irrefutable

irregular a irregular. ~idad f irregularity

irreparable a irreparable

irreprimible a irrepressible

irreprochable a irreproachable

irresistible a irresistible

irresoluto a irresolute

irrespetuoso a disrespectful

irresponsable a irresponsible

irrevocable a irrevocable

irriga|ción f irrigation. ~r [12] vt irrigate

irrisorio a derisive; (insignificante) ridiculous

irrita|ble a irritable. ~ción f irritation. ~r vt irritate. ~rse vpr get annoyed

irrumpir vi burst (en in)

irrupción f irruption

isla f island. las I~s Británicas the British Isles

Islam m Islam

islámico a Islamic

islandés a Icelandic. ● m Icelander; (lengua) Icelandic

Islandia f Iceland

isleño a island. ● m islander

Israel m Israel

israelí a & m Israeli

istmo /'ismo/ m isthmus

Italia f Italy

italiano a & m Italian

itinerario a itinerary

IVA abrev (impuesto sobre el valor añadido) VAT, value added tax

izar [10] vt hoist

izquierd|a f left(-hand); (pol) left (-wing). ~ista m & f leftist. ~o a left. a la ~a on the left; (con movimiento) to the left

J

ja int ha!

jabalí m wild boar

jabalina f javelin

jab|ón m soap. ~onar vt soap. ~onoso a soapy

jaca f pony

jacinto m hyacinth

jacta|ncia f boastfulness; (acción) boasting. ~rse vpr boast

jadea|nte a panting. ~r vi pant

jaez m harness

jaguar m jaguar

jalea f jelly

jaleo m row, uproar. armar un ~ kick up a fuss

jalón m (LAm, tirón) pull; (Mex, trago) drink

Jamaica f Jamaica

jamás adv never; (en frases afirmativas) ever

jamelgo m nag

jamón m ham. ~ de York boiled ham. ~ serrano cured ham

Japón m. el ~ Japan

japonés a & m Japanese

jaque m check. ~ mate checkmate

jaqueca f migraine. dar ~ bother

jarabe m syrup

jardín m garden. ~ de la infancia kindergarten, nursery school

jardiner|ía f gardening. ~o m gardener

jarocho a (Mex) from Veracruz

jarr|a f jug. ~o m jug. echar un ~o de agua fría a throw cold water on. en ~as with hands on hips

jaula f cage

jauría f pack of hounds

jazmín m jasmine

jef|a f boss. ~atura f leadership; (sede) headquarters. ~e m boss; (pol etc) leader. ~e de camareros head waiter. ~e de estación stationmaster. ~e de ventas sales manager

jengibre m ginger

jeque *m* sheikh
jer|arquía *f* hierarchy. **~árquico** *a* hierarchical
jerez *m* sherry. **al ~** with sherry
jerga *f* coarse cloth; (*argot*) jargon
jerigonza *f* jargon; (*galimatías*) gibberish
jeringa *f* syringe; (*LAm, molestia*) nuisance. **~r** [12] *vt* (*fig, molestar, fam*) annoy
jeroglífico *m* hieroglyph(ic)
jersey *m* (*pl* jerseys) jersey
Jerusalén *m* Jerusalem
Jesucristo *m* Jesus Christ. **antes de ~** BC, before Christ
jesuita *a & m & f* Jesuit
Jesús *m* Jesus. ● *int* good heavens!; (*al estornudar*) bless you!
jícara *f* small cup
jilguero *m* goldfinch
jinete *m* rider, horseman
jipijapa *f* straw hat
jirafa *f* giraffe
jirón *m* shred, tatter
jitomate *m* (*Mex*) tomato
jocoso *a* funny, humorous
jorna|da *f* working day; (*viaje*) journey; (*etapa*) stage. **~l** *m* day's wage; (*trabajo*) day's work. **~lero** *m* day labourer
joroba *f* hump. **~do** *a* hunchbacked. ● *m* hunchback. **~r** *vt* annoy
jota *f* letter J; (*danza*) jota, popular dance; (*fig*) iota. **ni ~** nothing
joven (*pl* jóvenes) *a* young. ● *m* young man, youth. ● *f* young woman, girl
jovial *a* jovial
joy|a *f* jewel. **~as** *fpl* jewellery. **~ería** *f* jeweller's (shop). **~ero** *m* jeweller; (*estuche*) jewellery box
juanete *m* bunion
jubil|ación *f* retirement. **~ado** *a* retired. **~ar** *vt* pension off. **~arse** *vpr* retire. **~eo** *m* jubilee
júbilo *m* joy
jubiloso *a* jubilant
judaísmo *m* Judaism
judía *f* Jewish woman; (*alubia*) bean. **~ blanca** haricot bean. **~ escarlata** runner bean. **~ verde** French bean
judicial *a* judicial
judío *a* Jewish. ● *m* Jewish man
judo *m* judo

juego *m* game; (*de niños, tec*) play; (*de azar*) gambling; (*conjunto*) set. ● *vb véase* jugar. **estar en ~** be at stake. **estar fuera de ~** be offside. **hacer ~** match
juerga *f* spree
jueves *m* Thursday
juez *m* judge. **~ de instrucción** examining magistrate. **~ de línea** linesman
juga|dor *m* player; (*en juegos de azar*) gambler. **~r** [3] *vt* play. ● *vi* play; (*a juegos de azar*) gamble; (*apostar*) bet. **~rse** *vpr* risk. **~r al fútbol** play football
juglar *m* minstrel
jugo *m* juice; (*de carne*) gravy; (*fig*) substance. **~so** *a* juicy; (*fig*) substantial
juguet|e *m* toy. **~ear** *vi* play. **~ón** *a* playful
juicio *m* judgement; (*opinión*) opinion; (*razón*) reason. **~so** *a* wise. **a mi ~** in my opinion
juliana *f* vegetable soup
julio *m* July
junco *m* rush, reed
jungla *f* jungle
junio *m* June
junt|a *f* meeting; (*consejo*) board, committee; (*pol*) junta; (*tec*) joint. **~ar** *vt* join; (*reunir*) collect. **~arse** *vpr* join; (*gente*) meet. **~o** *a* joined; (*en plural*) together. **~o a** next to. **~ura** *f* joint. **por ~o** all together
jura|do *a* sworn. ● *m* jury; (*miembro de jurado*) juror. **~mento** *m* oath. **~r** *vt/i* swear. **~r en falso** commit perjury. **jurárselas a uno** have it in for s.o. **prestar ~mento** take the oath
jurel *m* (type of) mackerel
jurídico *a* legal
juris|dicción *f* jurisdiction. **~prudencia** *f* jurisprudence
justamente *a* exactly; (*con justicia*) fairly
justicia *f* justice
justifica|ción *f* justification. **~r** [7] *vt* justify
justo *a* fair, just; (*exacto*) exact; (*ropa*) tight. ● *adv* just. **~ a tiempo** just in time
juven|il *a* youthful. **~tud** *f* youth; (*gente joven*) young people
juzga|do *m* (*tribunal*) court. **~r** [12] *vt* judge. **a ~r por** judging by

K

kilo *m*, **kilogramo** *m* kilo, kilogram
kil|ometraje *m* distance in kilometres, mileage. ~**ométrico** *a* (*fam*) endless. ~**ómetro** *m* kilometre. ~**ómetro cuadrado** square kilometre
kilovatio *m* kilowatt
kiosco *m* kiosk

L

la *m* A; (*solfa*) lah. ● *art def f* the. ● *pron* (*ella*) her; (*Vd*) you; (*ello*) it. ~ **de** the one. ~ **de Vd** your one, yours. ~ **que** whoever, the one
laberinto *m* labyrinth, maze
labia *f* glibness
labio *m* lip
labor *f* work; (*tarea*) job. ~**able** *a* working. ~**ar** *vi* work. ~**es** *fpl* **de aguja** needlework. ~**es** *fpl* **de ganchillo** crochet. ~**es** *fpl* **de punto** knitting. ~**es** *fpl* **domésticas** housework
laboratorio *m* laboratory
laborioso *a* laborious
laborista *a* Labour. ● *m & f* member of the Labour Party
labra|do *a* worked; ⟨*madera*⟩ carved; ⟨*metal*⟩ wrought; ⟨*tierra*⟩ ploughed. ~**dor** *m* farmer; (*obrero*) labourer. ~**nza** *f* farming. ~**r** *vt* work; carve ⟨*madera*⟩; cut ⟨*piedra*⟩; till ⟨*la tierra*⟩; (*fig, causar*) cause
labriego *m* peasant
laca *f* lacquer
lacayo *m* lackey
lacerar *vt* lacerate
lacero *m* lassoer; (*cazador*) poacher
lacio *a* straight; (*flojo*) limp
lacón *m* shoulder of pork
lacónico *a* laconic
lacra *f* scar
lacr|ar *vt* seal. ~**e** *m* sealing wax
lactante *a* breast-fed
lácteo *a* milky. **productos** *mpl* ~**s** dairy products
ladear *vt/i* tilt. ~**se** *vpr* lean
ladera *f* slope
ladino *a* astute
lado *m* side. **al** ~ near. **al** ~ **de** at the side of, beside. **los de al** ~ the next

door neighbours. **por otro** ~ on the other hand. **por todos** ~**s** on all sides. **por un** ~ on the one hand
ladr|ar *vi* bark. ~**ido** *m* bark
ladrillo *m* brick; (*de chocolate*) block
ladrón *a* thieving. ● *m* thief
lagart|ija *f* (small) lizard. ~**o** *m* lizard
lago *m* lake
lágrima *f* tear
lagrimoso *a* tearful
laguna *f* small lake; (*fig, omisión*) gap
laico *a* lay
lamé *m* lamé
lamedura *f* lick
lament|able *a* lamentable, pitiful. ~**ar** *vt* be sorry about. ~**arse** *vpr* lament; (*quejarse*) complain. ~**o** *m* moan
lamer *vt* lick; ⟨*olas etc*⟩ lap
lámina *f* sheet; (*foto*) plate; (*dibujo*) picture
lamina|do *a* laminated. ~**r** *vt* laminate
lámpara *f* lamp; (*bombilla*) bulb; (*lamparón*) grease stain. ~ **de pie** standard lamp
lamparón *m* grease stain
lampiño *a* clean-shaven, beardless
lana *f* wool. ~**r** *a*. **ganado** *m* ~**r** sheep. **de** ~ wool(len)
lanceta *f* lancet
lancha *f* boat. ~ **motora** *f* motor boat. ~ **salvavidas** lifeboat
lanero *a* wool(len)
langost|a *f* (*crustáceo marino*) lobster; (*insecto*) locust. ~**ino** *m* prawn
languide|cer [11] *vi* languish. ~**z** *f* languor
lánguido *a* languid; (*decaído*) listless
lanilla *f* nap; (*tela fina*) flannel
lanudo *a* woolly
lanza *f* lance, spear
lanza|llamas *m* invar flamethrower. ~**miento** *m* throw; (*acción de lanzar*) throwing; (*de proyectil, de producto*) launch. ~**r** [10] *vt* throw; (*de un avión*) drop; launch ⟨*proyectil, producto*⟩. ~**rse** *vpr* fling o.s.
lapicero *m* (propelling) pencil
lápida *f* memorial tablet. ~ **sepulcral** tombstone
lapidar *vt* stone
lápiz *m* pencil; (*grafito*) lead. ~ **de labios** lipstick
Laponia *f* Lapland

lapso m lapse

larg|a f. **a la ~a** in the long run. **dar ~as** put off. **~ar** [12] vt slacken; (dar, fam) give; (fam) deal ⟨bofetada etc⟩. **~arse** vpr (fam) go away, clear off (fam). **~o** a long; (demasiado) too long. ● m length. **¡~o!** go away! **~ueza** f generosity. **a lo ~o** lengthwise. **a lo ~o de** along. **tener 100 metros de ~o** be 100 metres long

laring|e f larynx. **~itis** f laryngitis

larva f larva

las art def fpl the. ● pron them. **~ de** those, the ones. **~ de Vd** your ones, yours. **~ que** whoever, the ones

lascivo a lascivious

láser m laser

lástima f pity; (queja) complaint. **dar ~** be pitiful. **ella me da ~** I feel sorry for her. **¡qué ~!** what a pity!

lastim|ado a hurt. **~ar** vt hurt. **~arse** vpr hurt o.s. **~ero** a doleful. **~oso** a pitiful

lastre m ballast

lata f tinplate; (envase) tin (esp Brit), can; (molestia, fam) nuisance. **dar la ~** be a nuisance. **¡qué ~!** what a nuisance!

latente a latent

lateral a side, lateral

latido m beating; (cada golpe) beat

latifundio m large estate

latigazo m (golpe) lash; (chasquido) crack

látigo m whip

latín m Latin. **saber ~** (fam) not be stupid

latino a Latin. **L~américa** f Latin America. **~americano** a & m Latin American

latir vi beat; ⟨herida⟩ throb

latitud f latitude

latón m brass

latoso a annoying; (pesado) boring

laucha f (Arg) mouse

laúd m lute

laudable a laudable

laureado a honoured; (premiado) prize-winning

laurel m laurel; (culin) bay

lava f lava

lava|ble a washable. **~bo** m washbasin; (retrete) toilet. **~dero** m sink, wash-basin. **~do** m washing. **~do de cerebro** brainwashing. **~do en seco** dry-cleaning. **~dora** f washing machine. **~ndería** f laundry. **~ndería automática** launderette, laundromat (esp Amer). **~parabrisas** m invar windscreen washer (Brit), windshield washer (Amer). **~platos** m & f invar dishwasher; (Mex, fregadero) sink. **~r** vt wash. **~r en seco** dry-clean. **~rse** vpr have a wash. **~rse las manos** (incl fig) wash one's hands. **~tiva** f enema. **~vajillas** m & f inv dishwasher

lax|ante a & m laxative. **~o** a loose

laz|ada f bow. **~o** m knot; (lazada) bow; (fig, vínculo) tie; (cuerda con nudo corredizo) lasso; (trampa) trap

le pron (acusativo, él) him; (acusativo, Vd) you; (dativo, él) (to) him; (dativo, ella) (to) her; (dativo, ello) (to) it; (dativo, Vd) (to) you

leal a loyal; (fiel) faithful. **~tad** f loyalty; (fidelidad) faithfulness

lebrel m greyhound

lección f lesson; (univ) lecture

lect|or m reader; (univ) language assistant. **~ura** f reading

leche f milk; (golpe) bash. **~ condensada** condensed milk. **~ desnatada** skimmed milk. **~ en polvo** powdered milk. **~ra** f (vasija) milk jug. **~ría** f dairy. **~ro** a milk, dairy. ● m milkman. **~ sin desnatar** whole milk. **tener mala ~** be spiteful

lecho m bed

lechoso a milky

lechuga f lettuce

lechuza f owl

leer [18] vt/i read

legación f legation

legado m legacy; (enviado) legate

legajo m bundle, file

legal a legal. **~idad** f legality. **~izar** [10] vt legalize; (certificar) authenticate. **~mente** adv legally

legar [12] vt bequeath

legendario a legendary

legible a legible

legi|ón f legion. **~onario** m legionary

legisla|ción f legislation. **~dor** m legislator. **~r** vi legislate. **~tura** f legislature

leg|itimidad f legitimacy. **~ítimo** a legitimate; (verdadero) real

lego a lay; (ignorante) ignorant. ● m layman

legua f league

legumbre f vegetable

lejan|ía f distance. **~o** a distant

lejía f bleach

lejos adv far. **~ de** far from. **a lo ~** in the distance. **desde ~** from a distance, from afar

lelo a stupid
lema m motto
lencería f linen; (de mujer) lingerie
lengua f tongue; (idioma) language.
  irse de la ~ talk too much. **mor-**
  derse la ~ hold one's tongue. **tener**
  mala ~ have a vicious tongue
lenguado m sole
lenguaje m language
lengüeta f (de zapato) tongue
lengüetada f, **lengüetazo** m lick
lente f lens. **~s** mpl glasses. **~s de**
  contacto contact lenses
lentej|a f lentil. **~uela** f sequin
lentilla f contact lens
lent|itud f slowness. **~o** a slow
leñ|a f firewood. **~ador** m wood-
  cutter. **~o** m log
Leo m Leo
le|ón m lion. **León** Leo. **~ona** f
  lioness
leopardo m leopard
leotardo m thick tights
lepr|a f leprosy. **~oso** m leper
lerdo a dim; (torpe) clumsy
les pron (acusativo) them; (acusativo, Vds) you; (dativo) (to) them;
  (dativo, Vds) (to) you
lesbia(na) f lesbian
lesbiano a, **lesbio** a lesbian
lesi|ón f wound. **~onado** a injured.
  ~onar vt injure; (dañar) damage
letal a lethal
letanía f litany
let|árgico a lethargic. **~argo** m
  lethargy
letr|a f letter; (escritura) hand-
  writing; (de una canción) words,
  lyrics. **~a de cambio** bill of
  exchange. **~a de imprenta** print.
  ~ado a learned. **~ero** m notice;
  (cartel) poster
letrina f latrine
leucemia f leukaemia
levadizo a. **puente** m **~** drawbridge
levadura f yeast. **~ en polvo** baking
  powder
levanta|miento m lifting; (sub-
  levación) uprising. **~r** vt raise, lift;
  (construir) build; (recoger) pick up;
  (separar) take off. **~rse** vpr get up;
  (ponerse de pie) stand up; (erguirse,
  sublevarse) rise up
levante m east; (viento) east wind.
  L~ Levant
levar vt weigh ⟨ancla⟩. ● vi set sail
leve a light; ⟨enfermedad etc⟩ slight;
  (de poca importancia) trivial. **~dad**
  f lightness; (fig) slightness

léxico m vocabulary
lexicografía f lexicography
ley f law; (parlamentaria) act. **plata** f
  de ~ sterling silver
leyenda f legend
liar [20] vt tie; (envolver) wrap up;
  roll ⟨cigarillo⟩; (fig, confundir) confuse; (fig, enredar) involve. **~se** vpr
  get involved
libanés a & m Lebanese
Líbano m. **el ~** Lebanon
libel|ista m & f satirist. **~o** m satire
libélula f dragonfly
libera|ción f liberation. **~dor** a lib-
  erating. ● m liberator
liberal a & m & f liberal. **~idad** f lib-
  erality. **~mente** adv liberally
liber|ar vt free. **~tad** f freedom.
  ~tad de cultos freedom of worship.
  ~tad de imprenta freedom of the
  press. **~tad provisional** bail. **~tar**
  vt free. **en ~tad** free
libertino m libertine
Libia f Libya
libido m libido
libio a & m Libyan
libra f pound. **~ esterlina** pound
  sterling
Libra f Libra
libra|dor m (com) drawer. **~r** vt free;
  (de un peligro) rescue. **~rse** vpr free
  o.s. **~rse de** get rid of
libre a free; ⟨aire⟩ open; (en natación) freestyle. **~ de impuestos**
  tax-free. ● m (Mex) taxi
librea f livery
libr|ería f bookshop (Brit), book-
  store (Amer); (mueble) bookcase.
  ~ero m bookseller. **~eta** f
  notebook. **~o** m book. **~o de a**
  bordo logbook. **~o de bolsillo**
  paperback. **~o de ejercicios** exercise book. **~o de reclamaciones**
  complaints book
licencia f permission; (documento)
  licence. **~do** m graduate. **~ para**
  manejar (LAm) driving licence. **~r**
  vt (mil) discharge; (echar) dismiss.
  ~tura f degree
licencioso a licentious
liceo m (esp LAm) (secondary)
  school
licita|dor m bidder. **~r** vt bid for
lícito a legal; (permisible) permissible
licor m liquid; (alcohólico) liqueur
licua|dora f liquidizer. **~r** [21]
  liquefy
lid f fight. **en buena ~** by fair means

líder *m* leader

liderato *m*, **liderazgo** *m* leadership

lidia *f* bullfighting; (*lucha*) fight; (*LAm, molestia*) nuisance. **~r** *vt/i* fight

liebre *f* hare

lienzo *m* linen; (*del pintor*) canvas; (*muro, pared*) wall

liga *f* garter; (*alianza*) league; (*mezcla*) mixture. **~dura** *f* bond; (*mus*) slur; (*med*) ligature. **~mento** *m* ligament. **~r** [12] *vt* tie; (*fig*) join; (*mus*) slur. ● *vi* mix. **~r con** (*fig*) pick up. **~rse** *vpr* (*fig*) commit o.s.

liger|eza *f* lightness; (*agilidad*) agility; (*rapidez*) swiftness; (*de carácter*) fickleness. **~o** *a* light; (*rápido*) quick; (*ágil*) agile; (*superficial*) superficial; (*de poca importancia*) slight. ● *adv* quickly. **a la ~a** lightly, superficially

liguero *m* suspender belt

lija *f* dogfish; (*papel de lija*) sandpaper. **~r** *vt* sand

lila *f* lilac

Lima *f* Lima

lima *f* file; (*fruta*) lime. **~duras** *fpl* filings. **~r** *vt* file (down)

limbo *m* limbo

limita|ción *f* limitation. **~do** *a* limited. **~r** *vt* limit. **~r con** border on. **~tivo** *a* limiting

límite *m* limit. **~ de velocidad** speed limit

limítrofe *a* bordering

limo *m* mud

lim|ón *m* lemon. **~onada** *f* lemonade

limosn|a *f* alms. **~ear** *vi* beg. **pedir ~a** beg

limpia *f* cleaning. **~botas** *m invar* bootblack. **~parabrisas** *m inv* windscreen wiper (*Brit*), windshield wiper (*Amer*). **~pipas** *m invar* pipe-cleaner. **~r** *vt* clean; (*enjugar*) wipe

limpi|eza *f* cleanliness; (*acción de limpiar*) cleaning. **~eza en seco** dry-cleaning. **~o** *a* clean; (*cielo*) clear; (*fig, honrado*) honest. ● *adv* fairly. **en ~o** (*com*) net. **jugar ~o** play fair

linaje *m* lineage; (*fig, clase*) kind

lince *m* lynx

linchar *vt* lynch

lind|ante *a* bordering (**con** on). **~ar** *vi* border (**con** on). **~e** *f* boundary. **~ero** *m* border

lindo *a* pretty, lovely. **de lo ~** (*fam*) a lot

línea *f* line. **en ~s generales** in broad outline. **guardar la ~** watch one's figure

lingote *m* ingot

lingü|ista *m & f* linguist. **~ística** *f* linguistics. **~ístico** *a* linguistic

lino *m* flax; (*tela*) linen

linóleo *m*, **linóeum** *m* lino, linoleum

linterna *f* lantern; (*de bolsillo*) torch, flashlight (*Amer*)

lío *m* bundle; (*jaleo*) fuss; (*embrollo*) muddle; (*amorío*) affair

liquen *m* lichen

liquida|ción *f* liquidation; (*venta especial*) (clearance) sale. **~r** *vt* liquify; (*com*) liquidate; settle ⟨*cuenta*⟩

líquido *a* liquid; (*com*) net. ● *m* liquid

lira *f* lyre; (*moneda italiana*) lira

líric|a *f* lyric poetry. **~o** *a* lyric(al)

lirio *m* iris. **~ de los valles** lily of the valley

lirón *m* dormouse; (*fig*) sleepyhead. **dormir como un ~** sleep like a log

Lisboa *f* Lisbon

lisia|do *a* disabled. **~r** *vt* disable; (*herir*) injure

liso *a* smooth; ⟨*pelo*⟩ straight; ⟨*tierra*⟩ flat; (*sencillo*) plain

lisonj|a *f* flattery. **~eador** *a* flattering. ● *m* flatterer. **~ear** *vt* flatter. **~ero** *a* flattering

lista *f* stripe; (*enumeración*) list; (*de platos*) menu. **~ de correos** poste restante. **~do** *a* striped. **a ~s** striped

listo *a* clever; (*preparado*) ready

listón *m* ribbon; (*de madera*) strip

lisura *f* smoothness

litera *f* (*en barco*) berth; (*en tren*) sleeper; (*en habitación*) bunk bed

literal *a* literal

litera|rio *a* literary. **~tura** *f* literature

litig|ar [12] *vi* dispute; (*jurid*) litigate. **~io** *m* dispute; (*jurid*) litigation

litografía *f* (*arte*) lithography; (*cuadro*) lithograph

litoral *a* coastal. ● *m* coast

litro *m* litre

lituano *a & m* Lithuanian

liturgia *f* liturgy

liviano *a* fickle, inconstant

lívido *a* livid

lizo *m* warp thread

lo *art def neutro.* ~ **importante** what is important, the important thing. ● *pron* (*él*) him; (*ello*) it. ~ **que** what(ever), that which

loa *f* praise. ~**ble** *a* praiseworthy. ~**r** *vt* praise

lobo *m* wolf

lóbrego *a* gloomy

lóbulo *m* lobe

local *a* local. ● *m* premises; (*lugar*) place. ~**idad** *f* locality; (*de un espectáculo*) seat; (*entrada*) ticket. ~**izar** [10] *vt* localize; (*encontrar*) find, locate

loción *f* lotion

loco *a* mad; (*fig*) foolish. ● *m* lunatic. ~ **de alegría** mad with joy. **estar ~ por** be crazy about. **volverse ~** go mad

locomo|ción *f* locomotion. ~**tora** *f* locomotive

locuaz *a* talkative

locución *f* expression

locura *f* madness; (*acto*) crazy thing. **con ~** madly

locutor *m* announcer

locutorio *m* (*de teléfono*) telephone booth

lod|azal *m* quagmire. ~**o** *m* mud

logaritmo *m* logarithm, log

lógic|a *f* logic. ~**o** *a* logical

logística *f* logistics

logr|ar *vt* get; win (*premio*). ~ **hacer** manage to do. ~**o** *m* achievement; (*de premio*) winning; (*éxito*) success

loma *f* small hill

lombriz *f* worm

lomo *m* back; (*de libro*) spine; (*doblez*) fold. ~ **de cerdo** loin of pork

lona *f* canvas

loncha *f* slice; (*de tocino*) rasher

londinense *a* from London. ● *m* Londoner

Londres *m* London

loneta *f* thin canvas

longánimo *a* magnanimous

longaniza *f* sausage

longev|idad *f* longevity. ~**o** *a* long-lived

longitud *f* length; (*geog*) longitude

lonja *f* slice; (*de tocino*) rasher; (*com*) market

lord *m* (*pl* **lores**) lord

loro *m* parrot

los *art def mpl* the. ● *pron* them. ~ **de Antonio** Antonio's. ~ **que** whoever, the ones

losa *f* slab; (*baldosa*) flagstone. ~ **sepulcral** tombstone

lote *m* share

lotería *f* lottery

loto *m* lotus

loza *f* crockery

lozano *a* fresh; (*vegetación*) lush; (*persona*) lively

lubri(fi)ca|nte *a* lubricating. ● *m* lubricant. ~**r** [7] *vt* lubricate

lucero *m* (*estrella*) bright star; (*planeta*) Venus

lucid|ez *f* lucidity. ~**o** *a* splendid

lúcido *a* lucid

luciérnaga *f* glow-worm

lucimiento *m* brilliance

lucir [11] *vt* (*fig*) show off. ● *vi* shine; (*lámpara*) give off light; (*joya*) sparkle. ~**se** *vpr* (*fig*) shine, excel

lucr|ativo *a* lucrative. ~**o** *m* gain

lucha *f* fight. ~**dor** *m* fighter. ~**r** *vi* fight

luego *adv* then; (*más tarde*) later. ● *conj* therefore. ~ **que** as soon as. **desde ~** of course

lugar *m* place. ~ **común** cliché. ~**eño** *a* village. **dar ~ a** give rise to. **en ~ de** instead of. **en primer ~** in the first place. **hacer ~** make room. **tener ~** take place

lugarteniente *m* deputy

lúgubre *a* gloomy

lujo *m* luxury. ~**so** *a* luxurious. **de ~** de luxe

lujuria *f* lust

lumbago *m* lumbago

lumbre *f* fire; (*luz*) light. ¿**tienes ~?** have you got a light?

luminoso *a* luminous; (*fig*) brilliant

luna *f* moon; (*de escaparate*) window; (*espejo*) mirror. ~ **de miel** honeymoon. ~**r** *a* lunar. ● *m* mole. **claro de ~** moonlight. **estar en la ~** be miles away

lunes *m* Monday. **cada ~ y cada martes** day in, day out

lupa *f* magnifying glass

lúpulo *m* hop

lustr|abotas *m inv* (*LAm*) bootblack. ~**ar** *vt* shine, polish. ~**e** *m* shine; (*fig*, *esplendor*) splendour. ~**oso** *a* shining. **dar ~e a**, **sacar ~e a** polish

luto *m* mourning. **estar de ~** be in mourning

luxación *f* dislocation

Luxemburgo *m* Luxemburg

luz *f* light; (*electricidad*) electricity. **luces** *fpl* intelligence. ~ **antiniebla**

(*auto*) fog light. **a la ~ de** in the light of. **a todas luces** obviously. **dar a ~** give birth. **hacer la ~ sobre** shed light on. **sacar a la ~** bring to light

LL

llaga *f* wound; (*úlcera*) ulcer

llama *f* flame; (*animal*) llama

llamada *f* call; (*golpe*) knock; (*señal*) sign

llama|do *a* known as. **~miento** *m* call. **~r** *vt* call; (*por teléfono*) ring (up). ● *vi* call; (*golpear en la puerta*) knock; (*tocar el timbre*) ring. **~rse** *vpr* be called. **~r por teléfono** ring (up), telephone. **¿cómo te ~s?** what's your name?

llamarada *f* blaze; (*fig*) blush; (*fig, de pasión etc*) outburst

llamativo *a* loud, gaudy

llamear *vi* blaze

llan|eza *f* simplicity. **~o** *a* flat, level; (*persona*) natural; (*sencillo*) plain. ● *m* plain

llanta *f* (*auto*) (wheel) rim; (*LAm, neumático*) tyre

llanto *m* weeping

llanura *f* plain

llave *f* key; (*para tuercas*) spanner; (*grifo*) tap (*Brit*), faucet (*Amer*); (*elec*) switch. **~ inglesa** monkey wrench. **~ro** *m* key-ring. **cerrar con ~** lock. **echar la ~** lock up

llega|da *f* arrival. **~r** [12] *vi* arrive, come; (*alcanzar*) reach; (*bastar*) be enough. **~rse** *vpr* come near; (*ir*) go (round). **~r a** (*conseguir*) manage to. **~r a saber** find out. **~r a ser** become

llen|ar *vt* fill (up); (*rellenar*) fill in. **~o** *a* full. ● *m* (*en el teatro etc*) full house. **de ~** completely

lleva|dero *a* tolerable. **~r** *vt* carry; (*inducir, conducir*) lead; (*acompañar*) take; wear (*ropa*); (*traer*) bring. **~rse** *vpr* run off with (*cosa*). **~rse bien** get on well together. **¿cuánto tiempo ~s aquí?** how long have you been here? **llevo 3 años estudiando inglés** I've been studying English for 3 years

llor|ar *vi* cry; (*ojos*) water. **~iquear** *vi* whine. **~iqueo** *m* whining. **~o** *m* crying. **~ón** *a* whining. ● *m* crybaby. **~oso** *a* tearful

llov|er [2] *vi* rain. **~izna** *f* drizzle. **~iznar** *vi* drizzle

llueve *vb véase* **llover**

lluvi|a *f* rain; (*fig*) shower. **~oso** *a* rainy; (*clima*) wet

M

maca *f* defect; (*en fruta*) bruise

macabro *a* macabre

macaco *a* (*LAm*) ugly. ● *m* macaque (monkey)

macadam *m*, **macadán** *m* Tarmac (*P*)

macanudo *a* (*fam*) great

macarrón *m* macaroon. **~es** *mpl* macaroni

macerar *vt* macerate

maceta *f* mallet; (*tiesto*) flowerpot

macilento *a* wan

macizo *a* solid. ● *m* mass; (*de plantas*) bed

macrobiótico *a* macrobiotic

mácula *f* stain

macuto *m* knapsack

mach /mak/ *m*. **(número de) ~** Mach (number)

machac|ar [7] *vt* crush. ● *vi* go on (**en** about). **~ón** *a* boring. ● *m* bore

machamartillo. a ~ *adv* firmly

machaqueo *m* crushing

machet|azo *m* blow with a machete; (*herida*) wound from a machete. **~e** *m* machete

mach|ista *m* male chauvinist. **~o** *a* male; (*varonil*) macho

machón *m* buttress

machucar [7] *vt* crush; (*estropear*) damage

madera *m* (*vino*) Madeira. ● *f* wood; (*naturaleza*) nature. **~ble** *a* yielding timber. **~je** *m*, **~men** *m* woodwork

madero *m* log; (*de construcción*) timber

madona *f* Madonna

madr|astra *f* stepmother. **~e** *f* mother. **~eperla** *f* mother-of-pearl. **~eselva** *f* honeysuckle

madrigal *m* madrigal

madriguera *f* den; (*de liebre*) burrow

madrileño *a* of Madrid. ● *m* person from Madrid

madrina *f* godmother; (*en una boda*) chief bridesmaid

madroño *m* strawberry-tree

madrug|ada f dawn. **~ador** a who gets up early. ● m early riser. **~ar** [12] vi get up early. **~ón** m. **darse un ~ón** get up very early

madur|ación f maturing; (de fruta) ripening. **~ar** vt/i mature; (fruta) ripen. **~ez** f maturity; (de fruta) ripeness. **~o** a mature; (fruta) ripe

maestr|a f teacher. **~ía** f skill. **~o** m master. **~a**, **~o** (de escuela) schoolteacher

mafia f Mafia

magdalena f madeleine, small sponge cake

magia f magic

mágico a magic; (maravilloso) magical

magín m (fam) imagination

magisterio m teaching (profession); (conjunto de maestros) teachers

magistrado m magistrate; (juez) judge

magistral a teaching; (bien hecho) masterly; (lenguaje) pedantic

magistratura f magistracy

magn|animidad f magnanimity. **~ánimo** a magnanimous

magnate m magnate

magnesia f magnesia. **~ efervescente** milk of magnesia

magnético a magnetic

magneti|smo m magnetism. **~zar** [10] vt magnetize

magnetofón m, **magnetófono** m tape recorder

magnificencia f magnificence

magnífico a magnificent

magnitud f magnitude

magnolia f magnolia

mago m magician. **los (tres) reyes ~s** the Magi

magr|a f slice of ham. **~o** a lean; (tierra) poor; (persona) thin

magulla|dura f bruise. **~r** vt bruise

mahometano a & m Muhammadan

maíz m maize, corn (Amer)

majada f sheepfold; (estiércol) manure; (LAm) flock of sheep

majader|ía f silly thing. **~o** m idiot; (mano del mortero) pestle. ● a stupid

majador m crusher

majagranzas m idiot

majar vt crush; (molestar) bother

majest|ad f majesty. **~uoso** a majestic

majo a nice

mal adv badly; (poco) poorly; (difícilmente) hardly; (equivocadamente) wrongly. ● a see

malo. ● m evil; (daño) harm; (enfermedad) illness. **~ que bien** somehow (or other). **de ~ en peor** worse and worse. **hacer ~ en** be wrong to. **¡menos ~!** thank goodness!

malabar a. **juegos ~es** juggling. **~ismo** m juggling. **~ista** m & f juggler

malaconsejado a ill-advised

malacostumbrado a with bad habits

malagueño a of Málaga. ● m person from Málaga

malamente adv badly; (fam) hardly enough

malandanza f misfortune

malapata m & f nuisance

malaria f malaria

Malasia f Malaysia

malasombra m & f clumsy person

malavenido a incompatible

malaventura f misfortune. **~do** a unfortunate

malayo a Malay(an)

malbaratar vt sell off cheap; (malgastar) squander

malcarado a ugly

malcasado a unhappily married; (infiel) unfaithful

malcomer vi eat poorly

malcriad|eza f (LAm) bad manners. **~o** a (niño) spoilt

maldad f evil; (acción) wicked thing

maldecir [46 pero imperativo **maldice**, futuro y condicional regulares, pp **maldecido** o **maldito**] vt curse. ● vi speak ill (**de** of); (quejarse) complain (**de** about)

maldici|ente a backbiting; (que blasfema) foul-mouthed. **~ón** f curse

maldit|a f tongue. **¡~a sea!** damn it! **~o** a damned. ● m (en el teatro) extra

maleab|ilidad f malleability. **~le** a malleable

malea|nte a wicked. ● m vagrant. **~r** vt damage; (pervertir) corrupt. **~rse** vpr be spoilt; (pervertirse) be corrupted

malecón m breakwater; (rail) embankment; (para atracar) jetty

maledicencia f slander

maleficio m curse

maléfico a evil

malestar m indisposition; (fig) uneasiness

malet|a f (suit)case; (auto) boot, trunk (Amer); (LAm, lío de ropa) bundle; (*LAm, de bicicleta*) saddle-bag. **hacer la ~a** pack one's bags. ● *m* & *f* (*fam*) bungler. **~ero** *m* porter; (*auto*) boot, trunk (*Amer*). **~ín** *m* small case

malevolencia *f* malevolence

malévolo *a* malevolent

maleza *f* weeds; (*matorral*) undergrowth

malgasta|dor *a* wasteful. ● *m* spendthrift. **~r** *vt* waste

malgeniado *a* (*LAm*) bad-tempered

malhablado *a* foul-mouthed

malhadado *a* unfortunate

malhechor *m* criminal

malhumorado *a* bad-tempered

malici|a *f* malice. **~arse** *vpr* suspect. **~as** *fpl* (*fam*) suspicions. **~oso** *a* malicious

malign|idad *f* malice; (*med*) malignancy. **~o** *a* malignant; ⟨*persona*⟩ malicious

malintencionado *a* malicious

malmandado *a* disobedient

malmirado *a* (*con estar*) disliked; (*con ser*) inconsiderate

malo *a* (*delante de nombre masculino en singular* **mal**) bad; (*enfermo*) ill. **~ de** difficult. **estar de malas** be out of luck; (*malhumorado*) be in a bad mood. **lo ~ es que** the trouble is that. **ponerse a malas con uno** fall out with s.o. **por las malas** by force

malogr|ar *vt* waste; (*estropear*) spoil. **~arse** *vpr* fall through. **~o** *m* failure

maloliente *a* smelly

malparto *m* miscarriage

malpensado *a* nasty, malicious

malquerencia *f* dislike

malquist|ar *vt* set against. **~arse** *vpr* fall out. **~o** *a* disliked

malsano *a* unhealthy; (*enfermizo*) sickly

malsonante *a* ill-sounding; (*grosero*) offensive

malta *f* malt; (*cerveza*) beer

maltés *a* & *m* Maltese

maltratar *vt* ill-treat

maltrecho *a* battered

malucho *a* (*fam*) poorly

malva *f* mallow. **(color de) ~** *a invar* mauve

malvado *a* wicked

malvavisco *m* marshmallow

malvender *vt* sell off cheap

malversa|ción *f* embezzlement. **~dor** *a* embezzling. ● *m* embezzler. **~r** *vt* embezzle

Malvinas *fpl.* **las islas ~** the Falkland Islands

malla *f* mesh. **cota de ~** coat of mail

mallo *m* mallet

Mallor|ca *f* Majorca. **~quín** *a* & *m* Majorcan

mama *f* teat; (*de mujer*) breast

mamá *f* mum(my)

mama|da *f* sucking. **~r** *vt* suck; (*fig*) grow up with; (*engullir*) gobble

mamario *a* mammary

mamarrach|adas *fpl* nonsense. **~o** *m* clown; (*cosa ridícula*) (ridiculous) sight

mameluco *a* Brazilian half-breed; (*necio*) idiot

mamífero *a* mammalian. ● *m* mammal

mamola *f.* **hacer la ~** chuck (under the chin); (*fig*) make fun of

mamotreto *m* notebook; (*libro voluminoso*) big book

mampara *f* screen

mamporro *m* blow

mampostería *f* masonry

mamut *m* mammoth

maná *f* manna

manada *f* herd; (*de lobos*) pack. **en ~** in crowds

manager /'manaʒer/ *m* manager

mana|ntial *m* spring; (*fig*) source. **~r** *vi* flow; (*fig*) abound. ● *vt* run with

manaza *f* big hand; (*sucia*) dirty hand. **ser un ~s** be clumsy

manceb|a *f* concubine. **~ía** *f* brothel. **~o** *m* youth; (*soltero*) bachelor

mancera *f* plough handle

mancilla *f* stain. **~r** *vt* stain

manco *a* (*de una mano*) one-handed; (*de las dos manos*) handless; (*de un brazo*) one-armed; (*de los dos brazos*) armless

mancomún *adv.* **de ~** jointly

mancomun|adamente *adv* jointly. **~ar** *vt* unite; (*jurid*) make jointly liable. **~arse** *vpr* unite. **~idad** *f* union

mancha *f* stain

Mancha *f.* **la ~** la Mancha (region of Spain). **el canal de la ~** the English Channel

mancha|do *a* dirty; ⟨*animal*⟩ spotted. **~r** *vt* stain. **~rse** *vpr* get dirty

manchego *a* of la Mancha. ● *m* person from la Mancha

manchón *m* large stain

manda f legacy
manda|dero m messenger. **~miento** m order; (*relig*) commandment. **~r** vt order; (*enviar*) send; (*gobernar*) rule. ● vi be in command. **¿mande?** (*esp LAm*) pardon?
mandarín m mandarin
mandarin|a f (*naranja*) mandarin; (*lengua*) Mandarin. **~o** m mandarin tree
mandat|ario m attorney. **~o** m order; (*jurid*) power of attorney
mandíbula f jaw
mandil m apron
mandioca f cassava
mando m command; (*pol*) term of office. **~ a distancia** remote control. **los ~s** the leaders
mandolina f mandolin
mandón a bossy
manducar [7] vt (*fam*) stuff oneself with
manecilla f needle; (*de reloj*) hand
manej|able a manageable. **~ar** vt handle; (*fig*) manage; (*LAm, conducir*) drive. **~arse** vpr behave. **~o** m handling; (*intriga*) intrigue
manera f way. **~s** fpl manners. **de ~ que** so (that). **de ninguna ~** not at all. **de otra ~** otherwise. **de todas ~s** anyway
manga f sleeve; (*tubo de goma*) hose-(pipe); (*red*) net; (*para colar*) filter
mangante m beggar; (*fam*) scrounger
mangle m mangrove
mango m handle; (*fruta*) mango
mangonear vt boss about. ● vi (*entrometerse*) interfere
manguera f hose(pipe)
manguito m muff
manía f mania; (*antipatía*) dislike
maniaco a, **maníaco** a maniac(al). ● m maniac
maniatar vt tie s.o.'s hands
maniático a maniac(al); (*fig*) crazy
manicomio m lunatic asylum
manicura f manicure; (*mujer*) manicurist
manido a stale; (*carne*) high
manifesta|ción f manifestation; (*pol*) demonstration. **~nte** m demonstrator. **~r** [1] vi manifest; (*pol*) state. **~rse** vpr show; (*pol*) demonstrate
manifiesto a clear; (*error*) obvious; (*verdad*) manifest. ● m manifesto
manilargo a light-fingered

manilla f bracelet; (*de hierro*) handcuffs
manillar m handlebar(s)
maniobra f manoeuvring; (*rail*) shunting; (*fig*) manoeuvre. **~r** vt operate; (*rail*) shunt. ● vi manoeuvre. **~s** fpl (*mil*) manoeuvres
manipula|ción f manipulation. **~r** vt manipulate
maniquí m dummy. ● f model
manirroto a extravagant. ● m spendthrift
manita f little hand
manivela f crank
manjar m (*special*) dish
mano f hand; (*de animales*) front foot; (*de perros, gatos*) front paw. **~ de obra** work force. **¡~s arriba!** hands up! **a ~** by hand; (*próximo*) handy. **de segunda ~** second hand. **echar una ~** lend a hand. **tener buena ~ para** be good at
manojo m bunch
manose|ar vt handle; (*fig*) overwork. **~o** m handling
manotada f, **manotazo** m slap
manote|ar vi gesticulate. **~o** m gesticulation
mansalva. a ~ adv without risk
mansarda f attic
mansedumbre f gentleness; (*de animal*) tameness
mansión f stately home
manso a gentle; (*animal*) tame
manta f blanket. **~ eléctrica** electric blanket. **a ~ (de Dios)** a lot
mantec|a f fat; (*LAm*) butter. **~ado** m bun; (*helado*) ice-cream. **~oso** a greasy
mantel m tablecloth; (*del altar*) altar cloth. **~ería** f table linen
manten|er [40] vt support; (*conservar*) keep; (*sostener*) maintain. **~erse** vpr remain. **~ de/con** live off. **~imiento** m maintenance
mantequ|era f butter churn. **~ería** f dairy. **~illa** f butter
mantilla f mantilla
manto m cloak
mantón m shawl
manual a & m manual
manubrio m crank
manufactura f manufacture; (*fábrica*) factory
manuscrito a handwritten. ● m manuscript
manutención f maintenance

manzana f apple. ~r m (apple) orchard

manzanilla f camomile tea; (vino) manzanilla, pale dry sherry

manzano m apple tree

maña f skill. ~s fpl cunning

mañan|a f morning; (el día siguiente) tomorrow. ● m future. ● adv tomorrow. ~ero a who gets up early. ● m early riser. ~a por la ~a tomorrow morning. **pasado** ~a the day after tomorrow. **por la** ~a in the morning

mañoso a clever; (astuto) crafty

mapa m map. ~**mundi** m map of the world

mapache m racoon

mapurite m skunk

maqueta f scale model

maquiavélico a machiavellian

maquilla|je m make-up. ~r vt make up. ~**rse** vpr make up

máquina f machine; (rail) engine. ~ **de escribir** typewriter. ~ **fotográfica** camera

maquin|ación f machination. ~**al** a mechanical. ~**aria** f machinery. ~**ista** m & f operator; (rail) engine driver

mar m & f sea. **alta** ~ high seas. **la** ~ **de** (fam) lots of

maraña f thicket; (enredo) tangle; (embrollo) muddle

maravedí m (pl **maravedís, maravedises**) maravedi, old Spanish coin

maravill|a f wonder. ~**ar** vt astonish. ~**arse** vpr be astonished (con at). ~**oso** a marvellous, wonderful. **a** ~**a, a las mil** ~**as** marvellously. **contar/decir** ~**as de** speak wonderfully of. **hacer** ~**as** work wonders

marbete m label

marca f mark; (de fábrica) trademark; (deportes) record. ~**do** a marked. ~**dor** m marker; (deportes) scoreboard. ~r [7] vt mark; (señalar) show; (anotar) note down; score ‹un gol›; dial ‹número de teléfono›. ● vi score. **de** ~ brand name; (fig) excellent. **de** ~ **mayor** (fam) first-class

marcial a martial

marciano a & m Martian

marco m frame; (moneda alemana) mark; (deportes) goal-posts

marcha f (incl mus) march; (auto) gear; (curso) course. **a toda** ~ at full speed. **dar/hacer** ~ **atrás** put into reverse. **poner en** ~ start; (fig) set in motion

marchante m (f **marchanta**) dealer; (LAm, parroquiano) client

marchar vi go; (funcionar) work, go. ~**se** vpr go away, leave

marchit|ar vt wither. ~**arse** vpr wither. ~**o** a withered

marea f tide. ~**do** a sick; (en el mar) seasick; (aturdido) dizzy; (borracho) drunk. ~r vt sail, navigate; (baquetear) annoy. ~**rse** vpr feel sick; (en un barco) be seasick; (estar aturdido) feel dizzy; (irse la cabeza) feel faint; (emborracharse) get slightly drunk

marejada f swell; (fig) wave

maremagno m (de cosas) sea; (de gente) (noisy) crowd

mareo m sickness; (en el mar) seasickness; (aturdimiento) dizziness; (fig, molestia) nuisance

marfil m ivory. ~**eño** a ivory. **torre** f **de** ~ ivory tower

margarina f margarine

margarita f pearl; (bot) daisy

marg|en m margin; (borde) edge, border; (de un río) bank; (de un camino) side; (nota marginal) marginal note. ~**inado** a on the edge. ● m outcast. ~**inal** a marginal. ~**inar** vt (excluir) exclude; (dejar márgenes) leave margins; (poner notas) write notes in the margin. **al** ~**en** (fig) outside

mariachi (Mex) m (música popular de Jalisco) Mariachi; (conjunto popular) Mariachi band

mariano a Marian

marica f (hombre afeminado) sissy; (urraca) magpie

maricón m homosexual, queer (sl)

marid|aje m married life; (fig) harmony. ~**o** m husband

mariguana f, **marihuana** f marijuana

marimacho m mannish woman

marimandona f bossy woman

marimba f (type of) drum; (LAm, especie de xilofón) marimba

marimorena f (fam) row

marin|a f coast; (cuadro) seascape; (conjunto de barcos) navy; (arte de navegar) seamanship. ~**era** f seamanship; (conjunto de marineros) crew. ~**ero** a marine; (barco) seaworthy. ● m sailor. ~**o** a marine. ~**a de guerra** navy. ~**a mercante** merchant navy. **a la** ~**era** in tomato

and garlic sauce. **azul** ~o navy blue
marioneta *f* puppet. ~s *fpl* puppet
show
maripos|a *f* butterfly. ~**ear** *vi* be
fickle; (*galantear*) flirt. ~**n** *m* flirt.
~**a nocturna** moth
mariquita *f* ladybird, ladybug
(*Amer*)
marisabidilla *f* know-all
mariscador *m* shell-fisher
mariscal *m* marshal
maris|co *m* seafood, shellfish.
~**quero** *m* (*persona que pesca mariscos*) seafood fisherman; (*persona
que vende mariscos*) seafood seller
marital *a* marital
marítimo *a* maritime; ‹*ciudad etc*›
coastal, seaside
maritornes *f* uncouth servant
marmit|a *f* pot. ~**ón** *m* kitchen boy
mármol *m* marble
marmol|era *f* marblework, marbles.
~**ista** *m & f* marble worker
marmóreo *a* marble
marmota *f* marmot
maroma *f* rope; (*LAm, función de
volatines*) tightrope walking
marqu|és *m* marquess. ~**esa** *f* mar-
chioness. ~**esina** *f* glass canopy
marquetería *f* marquetry
marrajo *a* ‹*toro*› vicious; ‹*persona*›
cunning. ● *m* shark
marran|a *f* sow. ~**ada** *f* filthy thing;
(*cochinada*) dirty trick. ~**o** *a* filthy.
● *m* hog
marrar *vt* (*errar*) miss; (*fallar*) fail
marrón *a & m* brown
marroquí *a & m & f* Moroccan. ● *m*
(*tafilete*) morocco
marrubio *m* (*bot*) horehound
Marruecos *m* Morocco
marruller|ía *f* cajolery. ~**o** *a* cajol-
ing. ● *m* cajoler
marsopa *f* porpoise
marsupial *a & m* marsupial
marta *f* marten
martajar *vt* (*Mex*) grind ‹*maíz*›
Marte *m* Mars
martes *m* Tuesday
martill|ada *f* blow with a hammer.
~**ar** *vt* hammer. ~**azo** *m* blow with
a hammer. ~**ear** *vt* hammer. ~**eo**
m hammering. ~**o** *m* hammer
martín *m* **pescador** kingfisher
martinete *m* (*macillo del piano*)
hammer; (*mazo*) drop hammer
martingala *f* (*ardid*) trick
mártir *m & f* martyr

martir|io *m* martyrdom. ~**izar** [10]
vt martyr; (*fig*) torment, torture.
~**ologio** *m* martyrology
marxis|mo *m* Marxism. ~**ta** *a & m*
& f Marxist
marzo *m* March
más *adv & a* (*comparativo*) more;
(*superlativo*) most. ~ **caro** dearer.
~ **curioso** more curious. **el** ~ **caro**
the dearest; (*de dos*) the dearer. **el** ~
curioso the most curious; (*de dos*)
the more curious. ● *conj* and, plus.
● *m* plus (sign). ~ **bien** rather. ~
de (*cantidad indeterminada*) more
than. ~ **o menos** more or less. ~
que more than. ~ **y** ~ more and
more. **a lo** ~ at (the) most. **de** ~ too
many. **es** ~ moreover. **no** ~ no
more
masa *f* dough; (*cantidad*) mass; (*física*) mass. **en** ~ en masse
masacre *f* massacre
masaj|e *m* massage. ~**ista** *m*
masseur. ● *f* masseuse
masca|da *f* (*LAm*) plug of tobacco.
~**dura** *f* chewing. ~**r** [7] *vt* chew
máscara *f* mask; (*persona*) masked
figure/person
mascar|ada *f* masquerade. ~**illa** *f*
mask. ~**ón** *m* (large) mask
mascota *f* mascot
masculin|idad *f* masculinity. ~**o** *a*
masculine; ‹*sexo*› male. ● *m* masculine
mascullar [3] *vt* mumble
masilla *f* putty
masivo *a* massive, large-scale
mas|ón *m* (free)mason. ~**onería** *f*
(free)masonry. ~**ónico** *a* masonic
masoquis|mo *m* masochism. ~**ta** *a*
masochistic. ● *m & f* masochist
mastate *m* (*Mex*) loincloth
mastelero *m* topmast
mastica|ción *f* chewing. ~**r** [7] *vt*
chew; (*fig*) chew over
mástil *m* mast; (*palo*) pole; (*en
instrumentos de cuerda*) neck
mastín *m* mastiff
mastitis *f* mastitis
mastodonte *m* mastodon
mastoides *a & f* mastoid
mastuerzo *m* cress
masturba|ción *f* masturbation.
~**rse** *vpr* masturbate
mata *f* grove; (*arbusto*) bush
matad|ero *m* slaughterhouse. ~**or**
a killing. ● *m* killer; (*torero*)
matador
matadura *f* sore

matamoscas *m invar* fly swatter

mata|nza *f* killing. **~r** *vt* kill ⟨*personas*⟩; slaughter ⟨*reses*⟩. **~rife** *m* butcher. **~rse** *vpr* commit suicide; (*en un acidente*) be killed. **estar a ~r con uno** be deadly enemies with s.o.

matarratas *m invar* cheap liquor

matasanos *m invar* quack

matasellos *m invar* postmark

match *m* match

mate *a* matt, dull; ⟨*sonido*⟩ dull. ● *m* (*ajedrez*) (check)mate; (*LAm, bebida*) maté

matemátic|as *fpl* mathematics, maths (*fam*), math (*Amer, fam*). **~o** *a* mathematical. ● *m* mathematician

materia *f* matter; (*material*) material. **~ prima** raw material. **en ~ de** on the question of

material *a* & *m* material. **~idad** *f* material nature. **~ismo** *m* materialism. **~ista** *a* materialistic. ● *m* & *f* materialist. **~izar** [10] *vt* materialize. **~izarse** *vpr* materialize. **~mente** *adv* materially; (*absolutamente*) absolutely

matern|al *a* maternal; (*como de madre*) motherly. **~idad** *f* motherhood; (*casa de maternidad*) maternity home. **~o** *a* motherly; ⟨*lengua*⟩ mother

matin|al *a* morning. **~ée** *m* matinée

matiz *m* shade. **~ación** *f* combination of colours. **~ar** [10] *vt* blend ⟨*colores*⟩; (*introducir variedad*) vary; (*teñir*) tinge (**de** with)

matojo *m* bush

mat|ón *m* bully. **~onismo** *m* bullying

matorral *m* scrub; (*conjunto de matas*) thicket

matra|ca *f* rattle. **~quear** *vt* rattle; (*dar matraca*) pester. **dar ~ca** pester. **ser un(a) ~ca** be a nuisance

matraz *m* flask

matriarca|do *m* matriarchy. **~l** *a* matriarchal

matr|ícula *f* (*lista*) register, list; (*acto de matricularse*) registration; (*auto*) registration number. **~icular** *vt* register. **~icularse** *vpr* enrol, register

matrimoni|al *a* matrimonial. **~o** *m* marriage; (*pareja*) married couple

matritense *a* from Madrid

matriz *f* matrix; (*anat*) womb, uterus

matrona *f* matron; (*partera*) midwife

Matusalén *m* Methuselah. **más viejo que ~** as old as Methuselah

matute *m* smuggling. **~ro** *m* smuggler

matutino *a* morning

maula *f* piece of junk

maull|ar *vi* miaow. **~ido** *m* miaow

mauritano *a* & *m* Mauritanian

mausoleo *m* mausoleum

maxilar *a* maxillary. **hueso ~** jaw(bone)

máxima *f* maxim

máxime *adv* especially

máximo *a* maximum; (*más alto*) highest. ● *m* maximum

maya *f* daisy; (*persona*) Maya Indian

mayestático *a* majestic

mayo *m* May; (*palo*) maypole

mayólica *f* majolica

mayonesa *f* mayonnaise

mayor *a* (*más grande, comparativo*) bigger; (*más grande, superlativo*) biggest; (*de edad, comparativo*) older; (*de edad, superlativo*) oldest; (*adulto*) grown-up; (*principal*) main, major; (*mus*) major. ● *m* & *f* boss; (*adulto*) adult. **~al** *m* foreman; (*pastor*) head shepherd. **~azgo** *m* entailed estate. **al por ~** wholesale

mayordomo *m* butler

mayor|ía *f* majority. **~ista** *m* & *f* wholesaler. **~mente** *adv* especially

mayúscul|a *f* capital (letter). **~o** *a* capital; (*fig, grande*) big

maza *f* mace

mazacote *m* hard mass

mazapán *m* marzipan

mazmorra *f* dungeon

mazo *m* mallet; (*manojo*) bunch

mazorca *f*. **~ de maíz** corn on the cob

me *pron* (*acusativo*) me; (*dativo*) (to) me; (*reflexivo*) (to) myself

meandro *m* meander

mecánic|a *f* mechanics. **~o** *a* mechanical. ● *m* mechanic

mecani|smo *m* mechanism. **~zación** *f* mechanization. **~zar** [10] *vt* mechanize

mecanograf|ía *f* typing. **~iado** *a* typed, typewritten. **~iar** [20] *vt* type

mecanógrafo *m* typist

mecate *m* (*LAm*) (*pita*) rope

mecedora *f* rocking chair

mecenazgo *m* patronage

mecer [9] *vt* rock; swing ‹*columpio*›. **~se** *vpr* rock; (*en un columpio*) swing

mecha *f* (*de vela*) wick; (*de mina*) fuse

mechar *vt* stuff, lard

mechero *m* (cigarette) lighter

mechón *m* (*de pelo*) lock

medall|a *f* medal. **~ón** *m* medallion; (*relicario*) locket

media *f* stocking; (*promedio*) average

mediación *f* mediation

mediado *a* half full; ‹*trabajo etc*› halfway through. **a ~s de marzo** in the middle of March

mediador *m* mediator

medialuna *f* croissant

median|amente *adv* fairly. **~era** *f* party wall. **~ero** *a* ‹*muro*› party. **~a** *f* average circumstances. **~o** *a* average, medium; (*mediocre*) mediocre

medianoche *f* midnight; (*culin*) small sandwich

mediante *prep* through, by means of

mediar *vi* mediate; (*llegar a la mitad*) be halfway (**en** through)

mediatizar [10] *vt* annex

medic|ación *f* medication. **~amento** *m* medicine. **~ina** *f* medicine. **~inal** *a* medicinal. **~inar** *vt* administer medicine

medición *f* measurement

médico *a* medical. ● *m* doctor. **~ de cabecera** GP, general practitioner

medid|a *f* measurement; (*unidad*) measure; (*disposición*) measure, step; (*prudencia*) moderation. **~or** *m* (*LAm*) meter. **a la ~a** made to measure. **a ~a que** as. **en cierta ~a** to a certain point

mediero *m* share-cropper

medieval *a* medieval. **~ista** *m & f* medievalist

medio *a* half (a); (*mediano*) average. **~ litro** half a litre. ● *m* middle; (*manera*) means; (*en deportes*) half(-back). **en ~** in the middle (**de** of). **por ~ de** through

mediocr|e *a* (*mediano*) average; (*de escaso mérito*) mediocre. **~idad** *f* mediocrity

mediodía *m* midday, noon; (*sur*) south

medioevo *m* Middle Ages

Medio Oriente *m* Middle East

medir [5] *vt* medir; weigh up ‹*palabras etc*›. ● *vi* measure, be. **~se** *vpr* (*moderarse*) be moderate

medita|bundo *a* thoughtful. **~ción** *f* meditation. **~r** *vt* think about. ● *vi* meditate

Mediterráneo *m* Mediterranean

mediterráneo *a* Mediterranean

médium *m & f* medium

medrar *vi* thrive

medroso *a* (*con estar*) frightened; (*con ser*) fearful

médula *f* marrow

medusa *f* jellyfish

mefítico *a* noxious

mega... *pref* mega...

megáfono *m* megaphone

megal|ítico *a* megalithic. **~ito** *m* megalith

megal|omanía *f* megalomania. **~ómano** *m* megalomaniac

mejicano *a & m* Mexican

Méjico *m* Mexico

mejido *a* ‹*huevo*› beaten

mejilla *f* cheek

mejillón *m* mussel

mejor *a & adv* (*comparativo*) better; (*superlativo*) best. **~a** *f* improvement. **~able** *a* improvable. **~amiento** *m* improvement. **~ dicho** rather. **a lo ~** perhaps. **tanto ~** so much the better

mejorana *f* marjoram

mejorar *vt* improve, better. ● *vi* get better

mejunje *m* mixture

melanc|olía *f* melancholy. **~ólico** *a* melancholic

melaza *f* molasses, treacle (*Amer*)

melen|a *f* long hair; (*de león*) mane. **~udo** *a* long-haired

melifluo *a* mellifluous

melillense *a* of/from Melilla. ● *m* person from Melilla

melindr|e *m* (*mazapán*) sugared marzipan cake; (*masa frita con miel*) honey fritter. **~oso** *a* affected

melocot|ón *m* peach. **~onero** *m* peach tree

mel|odía *f* melody. **~ódico** *a* melodic. **~odioso** *a* melodious

melodram|a *m* melodrama. **~áticamente** *adv* melodramatically. **~ático** *a* melodramatic

melómano *m* music lover

mel|ón *m* melon; (*bobo*) fool. **~onada** *f* something stupid

meloncillo *m* (*animal*) mongoose

melos|idad *f* sweetness. **~o** *a* sweet

mella *f* notch. **~do** *a* jagged. **~r** *vt* notch

mellizo *a & m* twin

membran|a *f* membrane. **~oso** *a* membranous

membrete *m* letterhead

membrill|ero *m* quince tree. **~o** *m* quince

membrudo *a* burly

memez *f* something silly

memo *a* stupid. ● *m* idiot

memorable *a* memorable

memorando *m*, **memorándum** *m* notebook; (*nota*) memorandum

memoria *f* memory; (*informe*) report; (*tesis*) thesis. **~s** *fpl* (*recuerdos personales*) memoirs. **de ~** from memory

memorial *m* memorial. **~ista** *m* amanuensis

memor|ión *m* good memory. **~ista** *a* having a good memory. **~ístico** *a* memory

mena *f* ore

menaje *m* furnishings

menci|ón *f* mention. **~onado** *a* aforementioned. **~onar** *vt* mention

menda|cidad *f* mendacity. **~z** *a* lying

mendi|cante *a & m* mendicant. **~cidad** *f* begging. **~gar** [12] *vt* beg (for). ● *vi* beg. **~go** *m* beggar

mendrugo *m* (*pan*) hard crust; (*zoquete*) blockhead

mene|ar *vt* move, shake. **~arse** *vpr* move, shake. **~o** *m* movement, shake

menester *m* need. **~oso** *a* needy. **ser ~** be necessary

menestra *f* stew

menestral *m* artesan

mengano *m* so-and-so

mengua *f* decrease; (*falta*) lack; (*descrédito*) discredit. **~do** *a* miserable; (*falto de carácter*) spineless. **~nte** *a* decreasing; ‹*luna*› waning; ‹*marea*› ebb. ● *f* (*del mar*) ebb tide; (*de un río*) low water. **~r** [15] *vt/i* decrease, diminish

meningitis *f* meningitis

menisco *m* meniscus

menjurje *m* mixture

menopausia *f* menopause

menor *a* ‹*más pequeño, comparativo*› smaller; (*más pequeño, superlativo*) smallest; (*más joven, comparativo*) younger; (*más joven*) youngest; (*mus*) minor. ● *m & f*

(*menor de edad*) minor. **al por ~** retail

Menorca *f* Minorca

menorquín *a & m* Minorcan

menos *a* (*comparativo*) less; (*comparativo, con plural*) fewer; (*superlativo*) least; (*superlativo, con plural*) fewest. ● *adv* (*comparativo*) less; (*superlativo*) least. ● *prep* except. **~cabar** *vt* lessen; (*fig, estropear*) damage. **~cabo** *m* lessening. **~preciable** *a* contemptible. **~preciar** *vt* despise. **~precio** *m* contempt. **a ~ que** unless. **al ~** at least. **ni mucho ~** far from it. **por lo ~ at least**

mensaje *m* message. **~ro** *m* messenger

menso *a* (*Mex*) stupid

menstru|ación *f* menstruation. **~al** *a* menstrual. **~ar** [21] *vi* menstruate. **~o** *m* menstruation

mensual *a* monthly. **~idad** *f* monthly pay

ménsula *f* bracket

mensurable *a* measurable

menta *f* mint

mental *a* mental. **~idad** *f* mentality. **~mente** *adv* mentally

mentar [1] *vt* mention, name

mente *f* mind

mentecato *a* stupid. ● *m* idiot

mentir [4] *vi* lie. **~a** *f* lie. **~oso** *a* lying. ● *m* liar. **de ~ijillas** for a joke

mentís *m invar* denial

mentol *m* menthol

mentor *m* mentor

menú *m* menu

menudear *vi* happen frequently

menudencia *f* trifle

menudeo *m* retail trade

menudillos *mpl* giblets

menudo *a* tiny; ‹*lluvia*› fine; (*insignificante*) insignificant. **~s** *mpl* giblets. **a ~** often

meñique *a* ‹*dedo*› little. ● *m* little finger

meollo *m* brain; (*médula*) marrow; (*parte blanda*) soft part; (*fig, inteligencia*) brains

meramente *adv* merely

mercachifle *m* hawker; (*fig*) profiteer

mercader *m* (*LAm*) merchant

mercado *m* market. **M~ Común** Common Market. **~ negro** black market

mercan|cía *f* article. **~cías** *fpl* goods, merchandise. **~te** *a & m* merchant. ∼**til** *a* mercantile, commercial. ∼**tilismo** *m* mercantilism

mercar [7] *vt* buy

merced *f* favour. **su/vuestra** ∼ your honour

mercenario *a & m* mercenary

mercer|ía *f* haberdashery, notions (*Amer*). ∼**o** *m* haberdasher

mercurial *a* mercurial

Mercurio *m* Mercury

mercurio *m* mercury

merec|edor *a* deserving. ∼**er** [11] *vt* deserve. ● *vi* be deserving. ∼**idamente** *adv* deservedly. ∼**ido** *a* well deserved. ∼**imiento** *m* (*mérito*) merit

merend|ar [1] *vt* have as an afternoon snack. ● *vi* have an afternoon snack. ∼**ero** *m* snack bar; (*lugar*) picnic area

merengue *m* meringue

meretriz *f* prostitute

mergo *m* cormorant

meridian|a *f* (*diván*) couch. ∼**o** *a* midday; (*fig*) dazzling. ● *m* meridian

meridional *a* southern. ● *m* southerner

merienda *f* afternoon snack

merino *a* merino

mérito *m* merit; (*valor*) worth

meritorio *a* meritorious. ● *m* unpaid trainee

merlo *m* black wrasse

merluza *f* hake

merma *f* decrease. ∼**r** *vt/i* decrease, reduce

mermelada *f* jam

mero *a* mere; (*Mex, verdadero*) real. ● *adv* (*Mex, precisamente*) exactly; (*Mex, verdaderamente*) really. ● *m* grouper

merode|ador *a* marauding. ● *m* marauder. ∼**ar** *vi* maraud. ∼**o** *m* marauding

merovingio *a & m* Merovingian

mes *m* month; (*mensualidad*) monthly pay

mesa *f* table; (*para escribir o estudiar*) desk. **poner la** ∼ lay the table

mesana *f* (*palo*) mizen-mast

mesarse *vpr* tear at one's hair

mesenterio *m* mesentery

meseta *f* plateau; (*descansillo*) landing

mesiánico *a* Messianic

Mesías *m* Messiah

mesilla *f* small table. ∼ **de noche** bedside table

mesón *m* inn

mesoner|a *f* landlady. ∼**o** *m* landlord

mestiz|aje *m* crossbreeding. ∼**o** *a* (*persona*) half-caste; (*animal*) cross-bred. ● *m* (*persona*) half-caste; (*animal*) cross-breed

mesura *f* moderation. ∼**do** *a* moderate

meta *f* goal; (*de una carrera*) finish

metabolismo *m* metabolism

metacarpiano *m* metacarpal

metafísic|a *f* metaphysics. ∼**o** *a* metaphysical

met|áfora *f* metaphor. ∼**afórico** *a* metaphorical

met|al *m* metal; (*instrumentos de latón*) brass; (*de la voz*) timbre. ∼**álico** *a* (*objeto*) metal; (*sonido*) metallic. ∼**alizarse** [10] *vpr* (*fig*) become mercenary

metal|urgia *f* metallurgy. ∼**úrgico** *a* metallurgical

metam|órfico *a* metamorphic. ∼**orfosear** *vt* transform. ∼**orfosis** *f* metamorphosis

metano *m* methane

metatarsiano *m* metatarsal

metátesis *f* invar metathesis

metedura *f*. ∼ **de pata** blunder

mete|órico *a* meteoric. ∼**orito** *m* meteorite. ∼**oro** *m* meteor. ∼**orología** *f* meteorology. ∼**orológico** *m* meteorological. ∼**orólogo** *m* meteorologist

meter *vt* put, place; (*ingresar*) deposit; score (*un gol*); (*enredar*) involve; (*causar*) make. ∼**se** *vpr* get; (*entrometerse*) meddle. ∼**se con uno** pick a quarrel with s.o.

meticulos|idad *f* meticulousness. ∼**o** *a* meticulous

metido *m* reprimand. ● *a*. ∼ **en años** getting on. **estar muy** ∼ **con uno** be well in with s.o.

metilo *m* methyl

metódico *a* methodical

metodis|mo *m* Methodism. ∼**ta** *a & m & f* Methodist

método *m* method

metodología *f* methodology

metomentodo *m* busybody

metraje *m* length. **de largo** ∼ (*película*) feature

metrall|a *f* shrapnel. ∼**eta** *f* submachine gun

métric|a *f* metrics. ∼**o** *a* metric; (*verso*) metrical

metro *m* metre; (*tren*) underground, subway (*Amer*). ~ **cuadrado** cubic metre

metrónomo *m* metronome

metr|ópoli *f* metropolis. ~**opolitano** *a* metropolitan. ● *m* metropolitan; (*tren*) underground, subway (*Amer*)

mexicano *a* & *m* (*LAm*) Mexican

México *m* (*LAm*) Mexico. ~ **D. F.** Mexico City

mezcal *m* (*Mex*) (type of) brandy

mezc|la *f* (*acción*) mixing; (*substancia*) mixture; (*argamasa*) mortar. ~**lador** *m* mixer. ~**lar** *vt* mix; shuffle ‹*los naipes*›. ~**larse** *vpr* mix; (*intervenir*) interfere. ~**olanza** *f* mixture

mezquin|dad *f* meanness. ~**o** *a* mean; (*escaso*) meagre. ● *m* mean person

mezquita *f* mosque

mi *a* my. ● *m* (*mus*) E; (*solfa*) mi

mí *pron* me

miaja *f* crumb

miasma *m* miasma

miau *m* miaow

mica *f* (*silicato*) mica; (*Mex, embriaguez*) drunkenness

mico *m* (long-tailed) monkey

micro... *pref* micro...

microbio *m* microbe

micro: ~**biología** *f* microbiology. ~**cosmo** *m* microcosm. ~**film(e)** *m* microfilm

micrófono *m* microphone

micrómetro *m* micrometer

microonda *f* microwave. **horno** *m* **de** ~**s** microwave oven

microordenador *m* microcomputer

microsc|ópico *a* microscopic. ~**opio** *m* microscope

micro: ~**surco** *m* long-playing record. ~**taxi** *m* minicab

miedo *m* fear. ~**so** *a* fearful. **dar** ~ frighten. **morirse de** ~ be scared to death. **tener** ~ be frightened

miel *f* honey

mielga *f* lucerne, alfalfa (*Amer*)

miembro *m* limb; (*persona*) member

mientras *conj* while. ● *adv* meanwhile. ~ **que** whereas. ~ **tanto** in the meantime

miércoles *m* Wednesday. ~ **de ceniza** Ash Wednesday

mierda *f* (*vulgar*) shit

mies *f* corn, grain (*Amer*)

miga *f* crumb; (*fig, meollo*) essence. ~**jas** *fpl* crumbs. ~**r** [12] *vt* crumble

migra|ción *f* migration. ~**torio** *a* migratory

mijo *m* millet

mil *a* & *m* a/one thousand. ~**es de** thousands of. ~ **novecientos noventa y dos** nineteen ninety-two. ~ **pesetas** a thousand pesetas

milagro *m* miracle. ~**so** *a* miraculous

milano *m* kite

mildeu *m*, **mildiu** *m* mildew

milen|ario *a* millenial. ~**io** *m* millennium

milenrama *f* milfoil

milésimo *a* & *m* thousandth

mili *f* (*fam*) military service

milicia *f* soldiering; (*gente armada*) militia

mili|gramo *m* milligram. ~**litro** *m* millilitre

milímetro *m* millimetre

militante *a* militant

militar *a* military. ● *m* soldier. ~**ismo** *m* militarism. ~**ista** *a* militaristic. ● *m* & *f* militarist. ~**izar** [10] *vt* militarize

milonga *f* (*Arg, canción*) popular song; (*Arg, baile*) popular dance

milord *m*. **vivir como un** ~ live like a lord

milpies *m invar* woodlouse

milla *f* mile

millar *m* thousand. **a** ~**es** by the thousand

mill|ón *m* million. ~**onada** *f* fortune. ~**onario** *m* millionaire. ~**onésimo** *a* & *m* millionth. **un** ~**n de libros** a million books

mimar *vt* spoil

mimbre *m* & *f* wicker. ~**arse** *vpr* sway. ~**ra** *f* osier. ~**ral** *m* osier-bed

mimetismo *m* mimicry

mímic|a *f* mime. ~**o** *a* mimic

mimo *m* mime; (*a un niño*) spoiling; (*caricia*) caress

mimosa *f* mimosa

mina *f* mine. ~**r** *vt* mine; (*fig*) undermine

minarete *m* minaret

mineral *m* mineral; (*mena*) ore. ~**ogía** *f* mineralogy. ~**ogista** *m* & *f* mineralogist

miner|ía *f* mining. ~**o** *a* mining. ● *m* miner

mini... *pref* mini...

miniar *vt* paint in miniature

miniatura *f* miniature

minifundio *m* smallholding

minimizar [10] *vt* minimize

mínim|o *a & m* minimum. **~um** *m* minimum

minino *m* (*fam*) cat, puss (*fam*)

minio *m* red lead

minist|erial *a* ministerial. **~erio** *m* ministry. **~ro** *m* minister

minor|ación *f* diminution. **~a** *f* minority. **~idad** *f* minority. **~ista** *m & f* retailer

minuci|a *f* trifle. **~osidad** *f* thoroughness. **~oso** *a* thorough; (*con muchos detalles*) detailed

minué *m* minuet

minúscul|a *f* small letter, lower case letter. **~o** *a* tiny

minuta *f* draft; (*menú*) menu

minut|ero *m* minute hand. **~o** *m* minute

mío *a & pron* mine. **un amigo ~** a friend of mine

miop|e *a* short-sighted. ● *m & f* short-sighted person. **~ía** *f* short-sightedness

mira *f* sight; (*fig, intención*) aim. **~da** *f* look. **~do** *a* thought of; (*comedido*) considerate; (*cirunspecto*) circumspect. **~dor** *m* windowed balcony; (*lugar*) viewpoint. **~miento** *m* consideration. **~r** *vt* look at; (*observar*) watch; (*considerar*) consider. **~r fijamente a** stare at. ● *vi* look; (*edificio etc*) face. **~rse** *vpr* (*personas*) look at each other. **a la ~** on the lookout. **con ~s a** with a view to. **echar una ~da a** glance at

mirilla *f* peephole

miriñaque *m* crinoline

mirlo *m* blackbird

mirón *a* nosey. ● *m* nosey-parker; (*espectador*) onlooker

mirra *f* myrrh

mirto *m* myrtle

misa *f* mass

misal *m* missal

mis|antropía *f* misanthropy. **~antrópico** *a* misanthropic. **~ántropo** *m* misanthropist

miscelánea *f* miscellany; (*Mex, tienda*) corner shop

miser|able *a* very poor; (*lastimoso*) miserable; (*tacaño*) mean. **~ia** *f* extreme poverty; (*suciedad*) squalor

misericordi|a *f* pity; (*piedad*) mercy. **~oso** *a* merciful

mísero *a* very poor; (*lastimoso*) miserable; (*tacaño*) mean

misil *m* missile

misi|ón *f* mission. **~onal** *a* missionary. **~onero** *m* missionary

misiva *f* missive

mism|amente *adv* just. **~ísimo** *a* very same. **~o** *a* same; (*después de pronombre personal*) myself, yourself, himself, herself, itself, ourselves, yourselves, themselves; (*enfático*) very. ● *adv* right. **ahora ~** right now. **aquí ~** right here

mis|oginia *f* misogyny. **~ógino** *m* misogynist

misterio *m* mystery. **~so** *a* mysterious

místic|a *f* mysticism. **~o** *a* mystical

mistifica|ción *f* falsification; (*engaño*) trick. **~r** [7] *vt* falsify; (*engañar*) deceive

mitad *f* half; (*centro*) middle

mítico *a* mythical

mitiga|ción *f* mitigation. **~r** [12] *vt* mitigate; quench ‹*sed*›; relieve ‹*dolor etc*›

mitin *m* meeting

mito *m* myth. **~logía** *f* mythology. **~lógico** *a* mythological

mitón *m* mitten

mitote *m* (*LAm*) Indian dance

mitra *f* mitre. **~do** *m* prelate

mixteca *f* (*Mex*) southern Mexico

mixt|o *a* mixed. ● *m* passenger and goods train; (*cerilla*) match. **~ura** *f* mixture

mnemotécnic|a *f* mnemonics. **~o** *a* mnemonic

moaré *m* moiré

mobiliario *m* furniture

moblaje *m* furniture

moca *m* mocha

moce|dad *f* youth. **~ro** *m* young people. **~tón** *m* strapping lad

moción *f* motion

moco *m* mucus

mochales *a invar.* **estar ~** be round the bend

mochila *f* rucksack

mocho *a* blunt. ● *m* butt end

mochuelo *m* little owl

moda *f* fashion. **~l** *a* modal. **~les** *mpl* manners. **~lidad** *f* kind. **de ~** in fashion

model|ado *m* modelling. **~ador** *m* modeller. **~ar** *vt* model; (*fig, configurar*) form. **~o** *m* model

modera|ción *f* moderation. **~do** *a* moderate. **~r** *vt* moderate; reduce ‹*velocidad*›. **~rse** *vpr* control oneself

modern|amente *adv* recently. **~idad** *f* modernity. **~ismo** *m* modernism. **~ista** *m & f* modernist. **~izar** [10] *vt* modernize. **~o** *a* modern

modest|ia *f* modesty. **~o** *a* modest

modicidad *f* reasonableness

módico *a* moderate

modifica|ción *f* modification. **~r** [7] *vt* modify

modismo *m* idiom

modist|a *f* dressmaker. **~o** *m & f* designer

modo *m* manner, way; (*gram*) mood; (*mus*) mode. **~ de ser** character. **de ~ que** so that. **de ningún ~** certainly not. **de todos ~s** anyhow

modorr|a *f* drowsiness. **~o** *a* drowsy

modoso *a* well-behaved

modula|ción *f* modulation. **~dor** *m* modulator. **~r** *vt* modulate

módulo *m* module

mofa *f* mockery. **~rse** *vpr*. **~rse de** make fun of

mofeta *f* skunk

moflet|e *m* chubby cheek. **~udo** *a* with chubby cheeks

mogol *m* Mongol. **el Gran M~** the Great Mogul

moh|ín *m* grimace. **~ino** *a* sulky. **hacer un ~ín** pull a face

moho *m* mould; (*óxido*) rust. **~so** *a* mouldy; ⟨*metales*⟩ rusty

moisés *m* Moses basket

mojado *a* damp, wet

mojama *f* salted tuna

mojar *vt* wet; (*empapar*) soak; (*humedecer*) moisten, dampen. ● *vi*. **~ en** get involved in

mojicón *m* blow in the face; (*bizcocho*) sponge cake

mojiganga *f* masked ball; (*en el teatro*) farce

mojigat|ería *f* hypocrisy. **~o** *m* hypocrite

mojón *m* boundary post; (*señal*) signpost

molar *m* molar

mold|e *m* mould; (*aguja*) knitting needle. **~ear** *vt* mould, shape; (*fig*) form. **~ura** *f* moulding

mole *f* mass, bulk. ● *m* (*Mex, guisado*) (Mexican) stew with chili sauce

mol|écula *f* molecule. **~ecular** *a* molecular

mole|dor *a* grinding. ● *m* grinder; (*persona*) bore. **~r** [2] grind; (*hacer polvo*) pulverize

molest|ar *vt* annoy; (*incomodar*) bother. **¿le ~a que fume?** do you mind if I smoke? **no ~ar** do not disturb. ● *vi* be a nuisance. **~arse** *vpr* bother; (*ofenderse*) take offence. **~ia** *f* bother, nuisance; (*inconveniente*) inconvenience; (*incomodidad*) discomfort. **~o** *a* annoying; (*inconveniente*) inconvenient; (*ofendido*) offended

molicie *f* softness; (*excesiva comodidad*) easy life

molido *a* ground; (*fig, muy cansado*) worn out

molienda *f* grinding

molin|ero *m* miller. **~ete** *m* toy windmill. **~illo** *m* mill; (*juguete*) toy windmill. **~o** *m* (water) mill. **~o de viento** windmill

molusco *m* mollusc

mollar *a* soft

molleja *f* gizzard

mollera *f* (*de la cabeza*) crown; (*fig, sesera*) brains

moment|áneamente *adv* momentarily; (*por el momento*) right now. **~áneo** *a* momentary. **~o** *m* moment; (*mecánica*) momentum

momi|a *f* mummy. **~ficación** *f* mummification. **~ficar** [7] *vt* mummify. **~ficarse** *vpr* become mummified

momio *a* lean. ● *m* bargain; (*trabajo*) cushy job

monaca|l *a* monastic. **~to** *m* monasticism

monada *f* beautiful thing; (*de un niño*) charming way; (*acción tonta*) silliness

monaguillo *m* altar boy

mon|arca *m & f* monarch. **~arquía** *f* monarchy. **~árquico** *a* monarchic(al). **~arquismo** *m* monarchism

mon|asterio *m* monastery. **~ástico** *a* monastic

monda *f* pruning; (*peladura*) peel

mond|adientes *m invar* toothpick. **~adura** *f* pruning; (*peladura*) peel. **~ar** *vt* peel ⟨*fruta etc*⟩; dredge ⟨*un río*⟩. **~o** *a* (*sin pelo*) bald; (*sin dinero*) broke; (*sencillo*) plain

mondongo *m* innards

moned|a *f* coin; (*de un país*) currency. **~ero** *m* minter; (*portamonedas*) purse

monetario a monetary

mongol a & m Mongolian

mongolismo m Down's syndrome

monigote m weak character; (muñeca) rag doll; (dibujo) doodle

monises mpl money, dough (fam)

monitor m monitor

monj|a f nun. ~e m monk. ~il a nun's; (como de monja) like a nun

mono m monkey; (sobretodo) overalls. ● a pretty

mono... pref mono...

monocromo a & m monochrome

monóculo m monocle

mon|ogamia f monogamy. ~ógamo a monogamous

monografía f monograph

monograma m monogram

monol|ítico a monolithic. ~ito m monolith

mon|ologar [12] vi soliloquize. ~ólogo m monologue

monoman|ía f monomania. ~iaco m monomaniac

monoplano m monoplane

monopoli|o m monopoly. ~zar [10] vt monopolize

monos|ilábico a monosyllabic. ~ílabo m monosyllable

monoteís|mo m monotheism. ~ta a monotheistic. ● m & f monotheist

mon|otonía f monotony. ~ótono m monotonous

monseñor m monsignor

monserga f boring talk

monstruo m monster. ~sidad f monstrosity. ~so a monstrous

monta f mounting; (valor) value

montacargas m invar service lift

monta|do a mounted. ~dor m fitter. ~je m assembly; (cine) montage; (teatro) staging, production

montañ|a f mountain. ~ero a mountaineer. ~és a mountain. ● m highlander. ~ismo m mountaineering. ~oso a mountainous. ~a rusa big dipper

montaplatos m invar service lift

montar vt ride; (subirse) get on; (ensamblar) assemble; cock ‹arma›; set up ‹una casa, un negocio›. ● vi ride; (subirse a) mount. ~ a caballo ride a horse

montaraz a ‹animales› wild; ‹personas› mountain

monte m (montaña) mountain; (terreno inculto) scrub; (bosque) forest. ~ de piedad pawn-shop. **ingeniero m de ~s** forestry expert

montepío m charitable fund for dependents

monter|a f cloth cap. ~o m hunter

montés a wild

Montevideo m Montevideo

montevideano a & m Montevidean

montículo m hillock

montón m heap, pile. **a montones** in abundance, lots of

montuoso a hilly

montura f mount; (silla) saddle

monument|al a monumental; (fig, muy grande) enormous. ~o m monument

monzón m & f monsoon

moñ|a f hair ribbon. ~o m bun

moque|o m runny nose. ~ro m handkerchief

moqueta f fitted carpet

moquillo m distemper

mora f mulberry; (zarzamora) blackberry

morada f dwelling

morado a purple

morador m inhabitant

moral m mulberry tree. ● f morals. ● a moral. ~eja f moral. ~idad f morality. ~ista m & f moralist. ~izador a moralizing. ● m moralist. ~izar [10] vt moralize

morapio m (fam) cheap red wine

morar vi live

moratoria f moratorium

morbidez f softness

mórbido a soft; (malsano) morbid

morbo m illness. ~sidad f morbidity. ~so a unhealthy

morcilla f black pudding

morda|cidad f bite. ~z a biting

mordaza f gag

mordazmente adv bitingly

morde|dura f bite. ~r [2] vt bite; (fig, quitar porciones a) eat into; (denigrar) gossip about. ● vi bite

mordis|car [7] vt nibble (at). ● vi nibble. ~co m bite. ~quear vt nibble (at)

morelense a (Mex) from Morelos. ● m & f person from Morelos

morena f (geol) moraine

moreno a dark; (de pelo obscuro) dark-haired; (de raza negra) negro

morera f mulberry tree

morería f Moorish lands; (barrio) Moorish quarter

moretón m bruise

morfema m morpheme

morfin|a f morphine. ~ómano a morphine. ● m morphine addict

morfol|ogía f morphology. ~**ógico** a morphological

moribundo a moribund

morillo m andiron

morir [6] (pp **muerto**) vi die; (fig, extinguirse) die away; (fig, terminar) end. ~**se** vpr die. ~**se de hambre** starve to death; (fig) be starving. **se muere por una flauta** she's dying to have a flute

moris|co a Moorish. ● m Moor. ~**ma** f Moors

morm|ón m & f Mormon. ~**ónico** a Mormon. ~**onismo** m Mormonism

moro a Moorish. ● m Moor

moros|idad f dilatoriness. ~**o** a dilatory

morrada f butt; (puñetazo) punch

morral m (mochila) rucksack; (del cazador) gamebag; (para caballos) nosebag

morralla f rubbish

morrillo m nape of the neck

morriña f homesickness

morro m snout

morrocotudo a (esp Mex) (fam) terrific (fam)

morsa f walrus

mortaja f shroud

mortal a & m & f mortal. ~**idad** f mortality. ~**mente** adv mortally

mortandad f death toll

mortecino a failing; (color) faded

mortero m mortar

mortífero a deadly

mortifica|ción f mortification. ~**r** [7] vt (med) damage; (atormentar) plague; (humillar) humiliate. ~**rse** vpr (Mex) feel embarassed

mortuorio a death

morueco m ram

moruno a Moorish

mosaico a of Moses, Mosaic. ● m mosaic

mosca f fly. ~**rda** f blowfly. ~**rdón** m botfly; (mosca de cuerpo azul) bluebottle

moscatel a muscatel

moscón m botfly; (mosca de cuerpo azul) bluebottle

moscovita a & m & f Muscovite

Moscú m Moscow

mosque|arse vpr get cross. ~**o** m resentment

mosquete m musket. ~**ro** m musketeer

mosquit|ero m mosquito net. ~**o** m mosquito; (mosca pequeña) fly, gnat

mostacho m moustache

mostachón m macaroon

mostaza f mustard

mosto m must

mostrador m counter

mostrar [2] vt show. ~**se** vpr (show oneself to) be. **se mostró muy amable** he was very kind

mostrenco a ownerless; (animal) stray; (torpe) thick; (gordo) fat

mota f spot, speck

mote m nickname; (lema) motto

motea|do a speckled. ~**r** vt speckle

motejar vt call

motel m motel

motete m motet

motín m riot; (rebelión) uprising; (de tropas) mutiny

motiv|ación f motivation. ~**ar** vt motivate; (explicar) explain. ~**o** m reason. **con** ~**o de** because of

motocicl|eta f motor cycle, motor bike (fam). ~**ista** m & f motorcyclist

motón m pulley

motonave f motor boat

motor a motor. ● m motor, engine. ~**a** f motor boat. ~ **de arranque** starter motor

motoris|mo m motorcycling. ~**ta** m & f motorist; (de una moto) motorcyclist

motorizar [10] vt motorize

motriz af motive, driving

move|dizo a movable; (poco firme) unstable; (persona) fickle. ~**r** [2] vt move; shake (la cabeza); (provocar) cause. ~**rse** vpr move; (darse prisa) hurry up. **arenas** fpl ~**dizas** quicksand

movi|ble a movable. ~**do** a moved; (foto) blurred; (inquieto) fidgety

móvil a movable. ● m motive

movili|dad f mobility. ~**zación** f mobilization. ~**zar** [10] vt mobilize

movimiento m movement, motion; (agitación) bustle

moza f girl; (sirvienta) servant, maid. ~**lbete** m young lad

mozárabe a Mozarabic. ● m & f Mozarab

moz|o m boy, lad. ~**uela** f young girl. ~**uelo** m young boy/lad

muaré m moiré

mucam|a f (Arg) servant. ~**o** m (Arg) servant

mucos|idad f mucus. ~**o** a mucous

muchach|a f girl; (sirvienta) servant, maid. ~**o** m boy, lad; (criado) servant

muchedumbre *f* crowd

muchísimo *a* very much. ● *adv* a lot

mucho *a* much (*pl* **many**), a lot of. ● *pron* a lot; (*personas*) many (people). ● *adv* a lot, very much; (*de tiempo*) long, a long time. **ni ∼ menos** by no means. **por ∼ que** however much

muda *f* change of clothing; (*de animales*) moult. **∼ble** *a* changeable; ⟨*personas*⟩ fickle. **∼nza** *f* change; (*de casa*) removal. **∼r** *vt/i* change. **∼rse** (*de ropa*) change one's clothes; (*de casa*) move (house)

mudéjar *a* & *m* & *f* Mudéjar

mud|ez *f* dumbness. **∼o** *a* dumb; (*callado*) silent

mueble *a* movable. ● *m* piece of furniture

mueca *f* grimace, face. **hacer una ∼** pull a face

muela *f* (*diente*) tooth; (*diente molar*) molar; (*piedra de afilar*) grindstone; (*piedra de molino*) millstone

muelle *a* soft. ● *m* spring; (*naut*) wharf; (*malecón*) jetty

muérdago *m* mistletoe

muero *vb véase* **morir**

muert|e *f* death; (*homicidio*) murder. **∼o** *a* dead; (*matado, fam*) killed; ⟨*colores*⟩ pale. ● *m* dead person; (*cadáver*) body, corpse

muesca *f* nick; (*ranura*) slot

muestra *f* sample; (*prueba*) proof; (*modelo*) model; (*seal*) sign. **∼rio** *m* collection of samples

muestro *vb véase* **mostrar**

muevo *vb véase* **mover**

mugi|do *m* moo. **∼r** [14] *vi* moo; (*fig*) roar

mugr|e *m* dirt. **∼iento** *a* dirty, filthy

mugrón *m* sucker

muguete *m* lily of the valley

mujer *f* woman; (*esposa*) wife. ● *int* my dear! **∼iego** *a* ⟨*hombre*⟩ fond of the women. **∼il** *a* womanly. **∼ío** *m* (crowd of) women. **∼zuela** *f* prostitute

mújol *m* mullet

mula *f* mule; (*Mex*) unsaleable goods. **∼da** *f* drove of mules

mulato *a* & *m* mulatto

mulero *m* muleteer

mulet|a *f* crutch; (*fig*) support; (*toreo*) stick with a red flag

mulo *m* mule

multa *f* fine. **∼r** *vt* fine

multi... *pref* multi...

multicolor *a* multicolour(ed)

multicopista *m* copying machine

multiforme *a* multiform

multilateral *a* multilateral

multilingüe *a* multilingual

multimillonario *m* multimillionaire

múltiple *a* multiple

multiplic|ación *f* multiplication. **∼ar** [7] *vt* multiply. **∼arse** *vpr* multiply; (*fig*) go out of one's way. **∼idad** *f* multiplicity

múltiplo *a* & *m* multiple

multitud *f* multitude, crowd. **∼inario** *a* multitudinous

mulli|do *a* soft. ● *m* stuffing. **∼r** [22] *vt* soften

mund|ano *a* wordly; (*de la sociedad elegante*) society. **∼ial** *a* world-wide. **la segunda guerra ∼ial** the Second World War. **∼illo** *m* world, circles. **∼o** *m* world. **∼ología** *f* worldly wisdom. **todo el ∼o** everybody

munición *f* ammunition; (*provisiones*) supplies

municip|al *a* municipal. **∼alidad** *f* municipality. **∼io** *m* municipality; (*ayuntamiento*) town council

mun|ificencia *f* munificence. **∼ífico** *a* munificent

muñe|ca *f* (*anat*) wrist; (*juguete*) doll; (*maniquí*) dummy. **∼co** *m* boy doll. **∼quera** *f* wristband

muñón *m* stump

mura|l *a* mural, wall. ● *m* mural. **∼lla** *f* (city) wall. **∼r** *vt* wall

murciélago *m* bat

murga *f* street band; (*lata*) bore, nuisance. **dar la ∼** bother, be a pain (*fam*)

murmullo *m* (*de personas*) whisper(ing), murmur(ing); (*del agua*) rippling; (*del viento*) sighing, rustle

murmura|ción *f* gossip. **∼dor** *a* gossiping. ● *m* gossip. **∼r** *vi* murmur; (*hablar en voz baja*) whisper; (*quejarse en voz baja*) mutter; (*criticar*) gossip

muro *m* wall

murri|a *f* depression. **∼o** *a* depressed

mus *m* card game

musa *f* muse

musaraña *f* shrew

muscula|r *a* muscular. **∼tura** *f* muscles

músculo *m* muscle

musculoso *a* muscular

muselina *f* muslin

museo *m* museum. ~ **de arte** art gallery

musgaño *m* shrew

musgo *m* moss. ~**so** *a* mossy

música *f* music

musical *a & m* musical

músico *a* musical. ● *m* musician

music|ología *f* musicology. ~**ólogo** *m* musicologist

musitar *vt/i* mumble

muslímico *a* Muslim

muslo *m* thigh

mustela *a* weasel

musti|arse *vpr* wither, wilt. ~**o** *a* ⟨*plantas*⟩ withered; ⟨*cosas*⟩ faded; ⟨*personas*⟩ gloomy; (*Mex, hipócrita*) hypocritical

musulmán *a & m* Muslim

muta|bilidad *f* mutability. ~**ción** *f* change; (*en biología*) mutation

mutila|ción *f* mutilation. ~**do** *a* cripple. ● *m* cripple. ~**r** *vt* mutilate; cripple, maim ⟨*persona*⟩

mutis *m* (*en el teatro*) exit. ~**mo** *m* silence

mutu|alidad *f* mutuality; (*asociación*) friendly society. ~**amente** *adv* mutually. ~**o** *a* mutual

muy *adv* very; (*demasiado*) too

N

nab|a *f* swede. ~**o** *m* turnip

nácar *m* mother-of-pearl

nac|er [11] *vi* be born; ⟨*huevo*⟩ hatch; ⟨*planta*⟩ sprout. ~**ido** *a* born. ~**iente** *a* ⟨*sol*⟩ rising. ~**imiento** *m* birth; (*de río*) source; (*belén*) crib. **dar** ~**imiento a** give rise to. **lugar** *m* **de** ~**imiento** place of birth. **recien** ~**ido** newborn. **volver a** ~**er** have a narrow escape

naci|ón *f* nation. ~**onal** *a* national. ~**onalidad** *f* nationality. ~**onalismo** *m* nationalism. ~**onalista** *m & f* nationalist. ~**onalizar** [10] *vt* nationalize. ~**onalizarse** *vpr* become naturalized

nada *pron* nothing, not anything. ● *adv* not at all. **¡~ de eso!** nothing of the sort! **antes de** ~ first of all. **¡de** ~**!** (*después de 'gracias'*) don't mention it! **para** ~ (not) at all. **por** ~ **del mundo** not for anything in the world

nada|dor *m* swimmer. ~**r** *vi* swim

nadería *f* trifle

nadie *pron* no one, nobody

nado *adv.* **a** ~ swimming

nafta *f* (*LAm, gasolina*) petrol, (*Brit*), gas (*Amer*)

nailon *m* nylon

naipe *m* (playing) card. **juegos** *mpl* **de** ~**s** card games

nalga *f* buttock. ~**s** *fpl* bottom

nana *f* lullaby

Nápoles *m* Naples

naranj|a *f* orange. ~**ada** *f* orange-ade. ~**al** *m* orange grove. ~**o** *m* orange tree

narcótico *a & m* narcotic

nariz *f* nose; (*orificio de la nariz*) nostril. **¡narices!** rubbish!

narra|ción *f* narration. ~**dor** *m* narrator. ~**r** *vt* tell. ~**tivo** *a* narrative

nasal *a* nasal

nata *f* cream

natación *f* swimming

natal *a* birth; ⟨*pueblo etc*⟩ home. ~**idad** *f* birth rate

natillas *fpl* custard

natividad *f* nativity

nativo *a & m* native

nato *a* born

natural *a* natural. ● *m* native. ~**eza** *f* nature; (*nacionalidad*) nationality; (*ciudadanía*) naturalization. ~**eza muerta** still life. ~**idad** *f* naturalness. ~**ista** *m & f* naturalist. ~**izar** [10] *vt* naturalize. ~**izarse** *vpr* become naturalized. ~**mente** *adv* naturally. ● *int* of course!

naufrag|ar [12] *vi* ⟨*barco*⟩ sink; ⟨*persona*⟩ be shipwrecked; (*fig*) fail. ~**io** *m* shipwreck

náufrago *a* shipwrecked. ● *m* shipwrecked person

náusea *f* nausea. **dar** ~**s a uno** make s.o. feel sick. **sentir** ~**s** feel sick

nauseabundo *a* sickening

náutico *a* nautical

navaja *f* penknife; (*de afeitar*) razor. ~**zo** *m* slash

naval *a* naval

Navarra *f* Navarre

nave *f* ship; (*de iglesia*) nave. ~ **espacial** spaceship. **quemar las** ~**s** burn one's boats

navega|ble *a* navigable; ⟨*barco*⟩ seaworthy. ~**ción** *f* navigation. ~**nte** *m & f* navigator. ~**r** [12] *vi* sail; (*avión*) fly

Navid|ad *f* Christmas. ~**eño** *a* Christmas. **en** ~**ades** at Christmas. **¡feliz** ~**ad!** Happy Christmas! **por** ~**ad** at Christmas

navío *m* ship
nazi *a & m & f* Nazi
neblina *f* mist
nebuloso *a* misty; (*fig*) vague
necedad *f* foolishness. **decir ~es**
talk nonsense. **hacer una ~** do sth
stupid
necesari|amente *adv* necessarily.
~o *a* necessary
necesi|dad *f* necessity; (*pobreza*)
poverty. **~dades** *fpl* hardships. **por**
~dad (out) of necessity. **~tado** *a* in
need (**de** of); (*pobre*) needy. **~tar** *vt*
need. ● *vi.* **~tar de** need
necio *a* silly. ● *m* idiot
necrología *f* obituary column
néctar *m* nectar
nectarina *f* nectarine
nefasto *a* unfortunate, ominous
nega|ción *f* negation; (*desmen-*
timiento) denial; (*gram*) negative.
~do *a* incompetent. **~r** [1 & 12] *vt*
deny; (*rehusar*) refuse. **~rse** *vpr.*
~rse a refuse. **~tiva** *f* negative;
(*acción*) denial; (*acción de rehusar*)
refusal. **~tivo** *a & m* negative
negligen|cia *f* negligence. **~te** *a*
negligent
negoci|able *a* negotiable. **~ación** *f*
negotiation. **~ante** *m & f* dealer.
~ar *vt/i* negotiate. **~ar en** trade in.
~o *m* business; (*com, trato*) deal.
~os *mpl* business. **hombre** *m* **de**
~os businessman
negr|a *f* Negress; (*mus*) crotchet. **~o**
a black; (*persona*) Negro. ● *m*
(*color*) black; (*persona*) Negro.
~ura *f* blackness. **~uzco** *a* blackish
nene *m & f* baby, child
nenúfar *m* water lily
neo... *pref* neo...
neocelandés *a* from New Zealand.
● *m* New Zealander
neolítico *a* Neolithic
neón *m* neon
nepotismo *m* nepotism
nervio *m* nerve; (*tendón*) sinew;
(*bot*) vein. **~sidad** *f*, **~sismo** *m*
nervousness; (*impaciencia*) impatience. **~so** *a* nervous; (*de tem-*
peramento) highly-strung. **crispar**
los ~s a uno (*fam*) get on s.o.'s
nerves. **ponerse ~so** get excited
neto *a* clear; (*verdad*) simple; (*com*)
net
neumático *a* pneumatic. ● *m* tyre
neumonía *f* pneumonia
neuralgia *f* neuralgia

neur|ología *f* neurolgy. **~ólogo** *m*
neurologist
neur|osis *f* neurosis. **~ótico** *a*
neurotic
neutr|al *a* neutral. **~alidad** *f* neut-
rality. **~alizar** [10] *vt* neutralize. **~o**
a neutral; (*gram*) neuter
neutrón *m* neutron
neva|da *f* snowfall. **~r** [1] *vi* snow.
~sca *f* blizzard
nevera *f* fridge (*Brit, fam*), refrigerator
nevisca *f* light snowfall. **~r** [7] *vi*
snow lightly
nexo *m* link
ni *conj* nor, neither; (*ni siquiera*) not
even. **~...** ~ neither... nor. **~ que** as
if. **~ siquiera** not even
Nicaragua *f* Nicaragua
nicaragüense *a & m & f* Nicaraguan
nicotina *f* nicotine
nicho *m* niche
nido *m* nest; (*de ladrones*) den;
(*escondrijo*) hiding-place
niebla *f* fog; (*neblina*) mist. **hay ~**
it's foggy
niet|a *f* granddaughter. **~o** *m*
grandson. **~os** *mpl* grandchildren
nieve *f* snow; (*LAm, helado*) ice-
cream
Nigeria *f* Nigeria. **~no** *a* Nigerian
niki *m* T-shirt
nilón *m* nylon
nimbo *m* halo
nimi|edad *f* triviality. **~o** *a* in-
significant
ninfa *f* nymph
ninfea *f* water lily
ningún *véase* **ninguno**
ninguno *a* (*delante de nombre mas-*
culino en singular **ningún**) no, not
any. ● *pron* none; (*persona*) no-one,
nobody; (*de dos*) neither. **de nin-**
guna manera, de ningún modo by
no means. **en ninguna parte**
nowhere
niñ|a *f* (little) girl. **~ada** *f* childish
thing. **~era** *f* nanny. **~ería** *f* childish thing. **~ez** *f* childhood. **~o** *a*
childish. ● *m* (little) boy. **de ~o** as a
child. **desde ~o** from childhood
níquel *m* nickel
níspero *m* medlar
nitidez *f* clearness
nítido *a* clear; (*foto*) sharp
nitrato *m* nitrate
nítrico *a* nitric
nitrógeno *m* nitrogen

nivel *m* level; (*fig*) standard. **~ar** *vt* level. **~arse** *vpr* become level. **~ de vida** standard of living

no *adv* not; (*como respuesta*) no. **¿~?** isn't it? **~ más** only. **¡a que ~!** I bet you don't! **¡cómo ~!** of course! **Felipe ~ tiene hijos** Felipe has no children. **¡que ~!** certainly not!

nob|iliario *a* noble. **~le** *a & m & f* noble. **~leza** *f* nobility

noción *f* notion. **nociones** *fpl* rudiments

nocivo *a* harmful

nocturno *a* nocturnal; (*clase*) evening; (*tren etc*) night. ● *m* nocturne

noche *f* night. **~ vieja** New Year's Eve. **de ~** at night. **hacer ~** spend the night. **media ~** midnight. **por la ~** at night

Nochebuena *f* Christmas Eve

nodo *m* (*Esp, película*) newsreel

nodriza *f* nanny

nódulo *m* nodule

nogal *m* walnut(-tree)

nómada *a* nomadic. ● *m & f* nomad

nombr|adía *f* fame. **~ado** *a* famous; (*susodicho*) aforementioned. **~amiento** *m* appointment. **~ar** *vt* appoint; (*citar*) mention. **~e** *m* name; (*gram*) noun; (*fama*) renown. **~e de pila** Christian name. **en ~e de** in the name of. **no tener ~e** be unspeakable. **poner de ~e** call

nomeolvides *m invar* forget-me-not

nómina *f* payroll

nomina|l *a* nominal. **~tivo** *a & m* nominative. **~tivo** *a* (*cheque etc*) made out to

non *a* odd. ● *m* odd number

nonada *f* trifle

nono *a* ninth

nordeste *a* (*región*) north-eastern; (*viento*) north-easterly. ● *m* north-east

nórdico *a* northern. ● *m* northerner

noria *f* water-wheel; (*en una feria*) ferris wheel

norma *f* rule

normal *a* normal. ● *f* teachers' training college. **~idad** normality (*Brit*), normalcy (*Amer*). **~izar** [10] *vt* normalize. **~mente** *adv* normally, usually

Normandía *f* Normandy

noroeste *a* (*región*) north-western; (*viento*) north-westerly. ● *m* north-west

norte *m* north; (*viento*) north wind; (*fig, meta*) aim

Norteamérica *f* (North) America

norteamericano *a & m* (North) American

norteño *a* northern. ● *m* northerner

Noruega *f* Norway

noruego *a & m* Norwegian

nos *pron* (*acusativo*) us; (*dativo*) (to) us; (*reflexivo*) (to) ourselves; (*recíproco*) (to) each other

nosotros *pron* we; (*con prep*) us

nost|algia *f* nostalgia; (*de casa, de patria*) homesickness. **~álgico** *a* nostalgic

nota *f* note; (*de examen etc*) mark. **~ble** *a* notable. **~ción** *f* notation. **~r** *vt* notice; (*apuntar*) note down. **de mala ~** notorious. **de ~** famous. **digno de ~** notable. **es de ~r** it should be noted. **hacerse ~r** stand out

notario *m* notary

notici|a *f* (piece of) news. **~as** *fpl* news. **~ario** *m* news. **~ero** *a* news. **atrasado de ~as** behind the times. **tener ~as de** hear from

notifica|ción *f* notification. **~r** [7] *vt* notify

notori|edad *f* notoriety. **~o** *a* well-known; (*evidente*) obvious

novato *m* novice

novecientos *a & m* nine hundred

noved|ad *f* newness; (*noticia*) news; (*cambio*) change; (*moda*) latest fashion. **~oso** *a* (*LAm*) novel. **sin ~ad** no news

novel|a *f* novel. **~ista** *m & f* novelist

noveno *a* ninth

novent|a *a & m* ninety; (*nonagésimo*) ninetieth. **~ón** *a & m* ninety-year-old

novia *f* girlfriend; (*prometida*) fiancée; (*en boda*) bride. **~zgo** *m* engagement

novicio *m* novice

noviembre *m* November

novilunio *m* new moon

novill|a *f* heifer. **~o** *m* bullock. **hacer ~os** play truant

novio *m* boyfriend; (*prometido*) fiancé; (*en boda*) bridegroom. **los ~s** the bride and groom

novísimo *a* very new

nub|arrón *m* large dark cloud. **~e** *f* cloud; (*de insectos etc*) swarm. **~lado** *a* cloudy, overcast. ● *m* cloud. ~**lar** vt cloud. ~**larse** vpr become cloudy. ~**loso** a cloudy

nuca f back of the neck

nuclear a nuclear

núcleo m nucleus

nudillo m knuckle

nudis|mo m nudism. ~**ta** m & f nudist

nudo m knot; (de asunto etc) crux. ~**so** a knotty. **tener un ~ en la garganta** have a lump in one's throat

nuera f daughter-in-law

nuestro a our; (pospuesto al sustantivo) of ours. ● pron ours. ~ **coche** our car. **un coche** ~ a car of ours

nueva f (piece of) news. ~**s** fpl news. ~**mente** adv newly; (de nuevo) again

Nueva York f New York

Nueva Zelanda f, **Nueva Zelandia** f (LAm) New Zealand

nueve a & m nine

nuevo a new. **de ~** again

nuez f nut; (del nogal) walnut; (anat) Adam's apple. ~ **de Adán** Adam's apple. ~ **moscada** nutmeg

nul|idad f incompetence; (persona, fam) nonentity. ~**o** a useless; (jurid) null and void

num|eración f numbering. ~**eral** a & m numeral. ~**erar** vt number. ~**érico** a numerical

número m number; (arábigo, romano) numeral; (de zapatos etc) size. **sin ~** countless

numeroso a numerous

nunca adv never, not ever. ~ (ja)**más** never again. **casi ~** hardly ever. **más que ~** more than ever

nupcia|l a nuptial. ~**s** fpl wedding. **banquete ~l** wedding breakfast

nutria f otter

nutri|ción f nutrition. ~**do** a nourished, fed; (fig) large; ⟨aplausos⟩ loud; ⟨fuego⟩ heavy. ~**r** vt nourish, feed; (fig) feed. ~**tivo** a nutritious. **valor** m ~**tivo** nutritional value

nylon m nylon

Ñ

ña f (LAm, fam) Mrs

ñacanina f (Arg) poisonous snake

ñame m yam

ñapindá m (Arg) mimosa

ñato (LAm) snub-nosed

ño m (LAm, fam) Mr

ñoñ|ería f, ~**ez** f insipidity. ~**o** a insipid; (tímido) bashful; (quisquilloso) prudish

ñu m gnu

O

o conj or. ~ **bien** rather. ~... ~ either... or. ~ **sea** in other words

oasis m invar oasis

obcecar [7] vt blind

obed|ecer [11] vt/i obey. ~**iencia** f obedience. ~**iente** a obedient

obelisco m obelisk

obertura f overture

obes|idad f obesity. ~**o** a obese

obispo m bishop

obje|ción f objection. ~**tar** vt/i object

objetiv|idad f objectivity. ~**o** a objective. ● m objective; (foto etc) lens

objeto m object

objetor m objector. ~ **de conciencia** conscientious objector

oblicuo a oblique; ⟨mirada⟩ sidelong

obliga|ción f obligation; (com) bond. ~**do** a obliged; (forzoso) obligatory; ~**r** [12] vt force, oblige. ~**rse** vpr. ~**rse a** undertake to. ~**torio** a obligatory

oboe m oboe; (músico) oboist

obra f work; (de teatro) play; (construcción) building. ~ **maestra** masterpiece. **en ~s** under construction. **por ~s** de thanks to. ~**r** vt do; (construir) build

obrero a labour; ⟨clase⟩ working. ● m workman; (en fábrica) worker

obscen|idad f obscenity. ~**o** a obscene

obscu... véase oscu...

obsequi|ar vt lavish attention on. ~**ar con** give, present with. ~**o** m gift, present; (agasajo) attention. ~**oso** a obliging. **en ~o de** in honour of

observa|ción f observation; (objeción) objection. ~**dor** m observer. ~**ncia** f observance. ~**nte** a observant. ~**r** vt observe; (notar) notice. ~**rse** vpr be noted. ~**torio** m observatory. **hacer una ~ción** make a remark

obsesión 149 ojete

obses|ión *f* obsession. **∼ionar** *vt* obsess. **∼ivo** *a* obsessive. **∼o** *a* obsessed

obst|aculizar [10] *vt* hinder. **∼áculo** *m* obstacle

obstante. no ∼ *adv* however, nevertheless. ● *prep* in spite of

obstar *vi*. **∼ para** prevent

obstétrico *a* obstetric

obstina|ción *f* obstinacy. **∼do** *a* obstinate. **∼rse** *vpr* be obstinate. **∼rse en** (+ *infinitivo*) persist in (+ *gerundio*)

obstru|cción *f* obstruction. **∼ir** [17] *vt* obstruct

obtener [40] *vt* get, obtain

obtura|dor *m* (*foto*) shutter. **∼r** *vt* plug; fill ⟨*muela etc*⟩

obtuso *a* obtuse

obviar *vt* remove

obvio *a* obvious

oca *f* goose

ocasi|ón *f* occasion; (*oportunidad*) opportunity; (*motivo*) cause. **∼onal** *a* chance. **∼onar** *vt* cause. **aprovechar la ∼ón** take the opportunity. **con ∼ón de** on the occasion of. **de ∼ón** bargain; (*usado*) second-hand. **en ∼ones** sometimes. **perder una ∼ón** miss a chance

ocaso *m* sunset; (*fig*) decline

occident|al *a* western. ● *m & f* westerner. **∼e** *m* west

océano *m* ocean

ocio *m* idleness; (*tiempo libre*) leisure time. **∼sidad** *f* idleness. **∼so** *a* idle; (*inútil*) pointless

oclusión *f* occlusion

octano *m* octane. **índice** *m* **de ∼** octane number, octane rating

octav|a *f* octave. **∼o** *a & m* eighth

octogenario *a & m* octogenarian, eighty-year-old

oct|ogonal *a* octagonal. **∼ógono** *m* octagon

octubre *m* October

oculista *m & f* oculist, optician

ocular *a* eye

ocult|ar *vt* hide. **∼arse** *vpr* hide. **∼o** *a* hidden; (*secreto*) secret

ocupa|ción *f* occupation. **∼do** *a* occupied; ⟨*persona*⟩ busy. **∼nte** *m* occupant. **∼r** *vt* occupy. **∼rse** *vpr* look after

ocurr|encia *f* occurrence, event; (*idea*) idea; (*que tiene gracia*) witty remark. **∼ir** *vi* happen. **∼irse** *vpr* occur. **¿qué ∼e?** what's the matter? **se me ∼e que** it occurs to me that

ochent|a *a & m* eighty. **∼ón** *a & m* eighty-year-old

ocho *a & m* eight. **∼cientos** *a & m* eight hundred

oda *f* ode

odi|ar *vt* hate. **∼o** *m* hatred. **∼oso** *a* hateful

odisea *f* odyssey

oeste *m* west; (*viento*) west wind

ofen|der *vt* offend; (*insultar*) insult. **∼derse** *vpr* take offence. **∼sa** *f* offence. **∼siva** *f* offensive. **∼sivo** *a* offensive

oferta *f* offer; (*en subasta*) bid; (*regalo*) gift. **∼s de empleo** situations vacant. **en ∼** on (special) offer

oficial *a* official. ● *m* skilled worker; (*funcionario*) civil servant; (*mil*) officer. **∼a** *f* skilled (woman) worker

oficin|a *f* office. **∼a de colocación** employment office. **∼a de Estado** government office. **∼a de turismo** tourist office. **∼ista** *m & f* office worker. **horas** *fpl* **de ∼a** business hours

oficio *m* job; (*profesión*) profession; (*puesto*) post. **∼so** *a* (*no oficial*) unofficial

ofrec|er [11] *vt* offer; give ⟨*fiesta, banquete etc*⟩; (*prometer*) promise. **∼erse** *vpr* ⟨*persona*⟩ volunteer; ⟨*cosa*⟩ occur. **∼imiento** *m* offer

ofrenda *f* offering. **∼r** *vt* offer

ofusca|ción *f* blindness; (*confusión*) confusion. **∼r** [7] *vt* blind; (*confundir*) confuse. **∼rse** *vpr* be dazzled

ogro *m* ogre

oí|ble *a* audible. **∼da** *f* hearing. **∼do** *m* hearing; (*anat*) ear. **al ∼do** in one's ear. **de ∼das** by hearsay. **de ∼do** by ear. **duro de ∼do** hard of hearing

oigo *vb véase* **oír**

oír [50] *vt* hear. **∼ misa** go to mass. **¡oiga!** listen!; (*al teléfono*) hello!

ojal *m* buttonhole

ojalá *int* I hope so! ● *conj* if only

ojea|da *f* glance. **∼r** *vt* eye; (*para inspeccionar*) see; (*ahuyentar*) scare away. **dar una ∼da a, echar una ∼da a** glance at

ojeras *fpl* (*del ojo*) bags

ojeriza *f* ill will. **tener ∼ a** have a grudge against

ojete *m* eyelet

ojo *m* eye; (*de cerradura*) keyhole; (*de un puente*) span. ¡~! careful!

ola *f* wave

olé *int* bravo!

olea|da *f* wave. ~**je** *m* swell

óleo *m* oil; (*cuadro*) oil painting

oleoducto *m* oil pipeline

oler [2, *las formas que empezarían por* **ue** *se escriben* **hue**] *vt* smell; (*curiosear*) pry into; (*descubrir*) discover. ● *vi* smell (**a** of)

olfat|ear *vt* smell, sniff; (*fig*) sniff out. ~**o** *m* (sense of) smell; (*fig*) intuition

olimpiada *f*, **olimpíada** *f* Olympic games, Olympics

olímpico *a* ⟨*juegos*⟩ Olympic

oliv|a *f* olive; (*olivo*) olive tree. ~**ar** *m* olive grove. ~**o** *m* olive tree

olmo *m* elm (tree)

olor *m* smell. ~**oso** *a* sweet-smelling

olvid|adizo *a* forgetful. ~**ar** *vt* forget. ~**arse** *vpr* forget; (*estar olvidado*) be forgotten. ~**o** *m* oblivion; (*acción de olvidar*) forgetfulness. **se me** ~**ó** I forgot

olla *f* pot, casserole; (*guisado*) stew. ~ **a/de presión**, ~ **exprés** pressure cooker. ~ **podrida** Spanish stew

ombligo *m* navel

ominoso *a* awful, abominable

omi|sión *f* omission; (*olvido*) forgetfulness. ~**tir** *vt* omit

ómnibus *a* omnibus

omnipotente *a* omnipotent

omóplato *m*, **omoplato** *m* shoulder blade

once *a & m* eleven

ond|a *f* wave. ~**a corta** short wave. ~**a larga** long wave. ~**ear** *vi* wave; ⟨*agua*⟩ ripple. ~**ulación** *f* undulation; (*del pelo*) wave. ~**ular** *vi* wave. **longitud** *f* **de** ~**a** wavelength

oneroso *a* onerous

ónice *m* onyx

onomástico *a*. **día** ~, **fiesta onomástica** name-day

ONU *abrev* (*Organización de las Naciones Unidas*) UN, United Nations

onza *f* ounce

opa *a* (*LAm*) stupid

opaco *a* opaque; (*fig*) dull

ópalo *m* opal

opción *f* option

ópera *f* opera

opera|ción *f* operation; (*com*) transaction. ~**dor** *m* operator; (*cirujano*) surgeon; (*TV*) cameraman. ~**r** *vt* operate on; work ⟨*milagro etc*⟩. ● *vi* operate; (*com*) deal. ~**rse** *vpr* occur; (*med*) have an operation. ~**torio** *a* operative

opereta *f* operetta

opin|ar *vi* think. ~**ión** *f* opinion. **la** ~**ión pública** public opinion

opio *m* opium

opone|nte *a* opposing. ● *m & f* opponent. ~**r** *vt* oppose; offer ⟨*resistencia*⟩; raise ⟨*objeción*⟩. ~**rse** *vpr* be opposed; ⟨*dos personas*⟩ oppose each other

oporto *m* port (wine)

oportun|idad *f* opportunity; (*cualidad de oportuno*) timeliness. ~**ista** *m & f* opportunist. ~**o** *a* opportune; (*apropiado*) suitable

oposi|ción *f* opposition. ~**ciones** *fpl* competition, public examination. ~**tor** *m* candidate

opres|ión *f* oppression; (*ahogo*) difficulty in breathing. ~**ivo** *a* oppressive. ~**o** *a* oppressed. ~**or** *m* oppressor

oprimir *vt* squeeze; press ⟨*botón etc*⟩; ⟨*ropa*⟩ be too tight for; (*fig*) oppress

oprobio *m* disgrace

optar *vi* choose. ~ **por** opt for

óptic|a *f* optics; (*tienda*) optician's (shop). ~**o** *a* optic(al). ● *m* optician

optimis|mo *m* optimism. ~**ta** *a* optimistic. ● *m & f* optimist

opuesto *a* opposite; (*enemigo*) opposed

opulen|cia *f* opulence. ~**to** *a* opulent

oración *f* prayer; (*discurso*) speech; (*gram*) sentence

oráculo *m* oracle

orador *m* speaker

oral *a* oral

orar *vi* pray

oratori|a *f* oratory. ~**o** *a* oratorical. ● *m* (*mus*) oratorio

orbe *m* orb

órbita *f* orbit

orden *m & f* order; (*Mex, porción*) portion. ~**ado** *a* tidy. ~ **del día** agenda. **órdenes** *fpl* **sagradas** Holy Orders. **a sus órdenes** (*esp Mex*) can I help you? **en** ~ in order. **por** ~ in turn

ordenador *m* computer

ordena|nza *f* order. ● *m* (*mil*) orderly. ~**r** *vt* put in order; (*mandar*) order; (*relig*) ordain

ordeñar *vt* milk

ordinal *a & m* ordinal

ordinario *a* ordinary; (*grosero*) common

orear *vt* air

orégano *m* oregano

oreja *f* ear

orfanato *m* orphanage

orfebre *m* goldsmith, silversmith

orfeón *m* choral society

orgánico *a* organic

organigrama *m* flow chart

organillo *m* barrel-organ

organismo *m* organism

organista *m & f* organist

organiza|ción *f* organization. **∼dor** *m* organizer. **∼r** [10] *vt* organize. **∼rse** *vpr* get organized

órgano *m* organ

orgasmo *m* orgasm

orgía *f* orgy

orgullo *m* pride. **∼so** *a* proud

orientación *f* direction

oriental *a & m & f* oriental

orientar *vt* position. **∼se** *vpr* point; (*persona*) find one's bearings

oriente *m* east. **O∼ Medio** Middle East

orificio *m* hole

orig|en *m* origin. **∼inal** *a* original; (*excéntrico*) odd. **∼inalidad** *f* originality. **∼inar** *vt* give rise to. **∼inario** *a* original; (*nativo*) native. **dar ∼en a** give rise to. **ser ∼inario de** come from

orilla *f* (*del mar*) shore; (*de río*) bank; (*borde*) edge

orín *m* rust

orina *f* urine. **∼l** *m* chamber-pot. **∼r** *vi* urinate

oriundo *a*. **∼ de** (*persona*) (originating) from; (*animal etc*) native to

orla *f* border

ornamental *a* ornamental

ornitología *f* ornithology

oro *m* gold. **∼s** *mpl* Spanish card suit. **∼ de ley** 9 carat gold. **hacerse de ∼** make a fortune. **prometer el ∼ y el moro** promise the moon

oropel *m* tinsel

orquesta *f* orchestra. **∼l** *a* orchestral. **∼r** *vt* orchestrate

orquídea *f* orchid

ortiga *f* nettle

ortodox|ia *f* orthodoxy. **∼o** *a* orthodox

ortografía *f* spelling

ortop|edia *f* orthopaedics. **∼édico** *a* orthopaedic

oruga *f* caterpillar

orzuelo *m* sty

os *pron* (*acusativo*) you; (*dativo*) (to) you; (*reflexivo*) (to) yourselves; (*recíproco*) (to) each other

osad|ía *f* boldness. **∼o** *a* bold

oscila|ción *f* swinging; (*de precios*) fluctuation; (*tec*) oscillation. **∼r** *vi* swing; (*precio*) fluctuate; (*tec*) oscillate; (*fig, vacilar*) hesitate

oscur|ecer [11] *vi* darken; (*fig*) obscure. **∼ecerse** *vpr* grow dark; (*nublarse*) cloud over. **∼idad** *f* darkness; (*fig*) obscurity. **∼o** *a* dark; (*fig*) obscure. **a ∼as** in the dark

óseo *a* bony

oso *m* bear. **∼ de felpa, ∼ de peluche** teddy bear

ostensible *a* obvious

ostent|ación *f* ostentation. **∼ar** *vt* show off; (*mostrar*) show. **∼oso** *a* ostentatious

osteoartritis *f* osteoarthritis

oste|ópata *m & f* osteopath. **∼opatía** *f* osteopathy

ostión *m* (*esp Mex*) oyster

ostra *f* oyster

ostracismo *m* ostracism

Otan *abrev* (*Organización del Tratado del Atlántico Norte*) NATO, North Atlantic Treaty Organization

otear *vt* observe; (*escudriñar*) scan, survey

otitis *f* inflammation of the ear

otoño *m* autumn (*Brit*), fall (*Amer*)

otorga|miento *m* granting; (*documento*) authorization. **∼r** [12] *vt* give; (*jurid*) draw up

otorrinolaringólogo *m* ear, nose and throat specialist

otro *a* other; (*uno más*) another. ● *pron* another (one); (*en plural*) others; (*otra persona*) someone else. **el ∼** the other. **el uno al ∼** one another, each other

ovación *f* ovation

oval *a* oval

óvalo *m* oval

ovario *m* ovary

oveja *f* sheep; (*hembra*) ewe

overol *m* (*LAm*) overalls

ovino *a* sheep

ovillo *m* ball. **hacerse un ∼** curl up

OVNI *abrev* (*objeto volante no identificado*) UFO, unidentified flying object

ovulación *f* ovulation

oxida|ción f rusting. ~**r** vi rust. ~**rse** vpr go rusty
óxido m oxide
oxígeno m oxygen
oye vb véase **oír**
oyente a listening. ● m & f listener
ozono m ozone

P

pabellón m bell tent; (edificio) building; (de instrumento) bell; (bandera) flag
pabilo m wick
paceño a from La Paz. ● m person from La Paz
pacer [11] vi graze
pacien|cia f patience. ~**te** a & m & f patient
pacificar [7] vt pacify; reconcile ‹dos personas›. ~**se** vpr calm down
pacífico a peaceful. **el (Océano** m **) P~** the Pacific (Ocean)
pacifis|mo m pacifism. ~**ta** a & m & f pacifist
pact|ar vi agree, make a pact. ~**o** m pact, agreement
pachucho a ‹fruta› overripe; ‹persona› poorly
padec|er [11] vt/i suffer (**de** from); (soportar) bear. ~**imiento** m suffering; (enfermedad) ailment
padrastro m stepfather
padre a (fam) great. ● m father. ~**s** mpl parents
padrino m godfather; (en boda) best man
padrón m census
paella f paella
paga f pay, wages. ~**ble** a, ~**dero** a payable
pagano a & m pagan
pagar [12] vt pay; pay for ‹compras›. ● vi pay. ~**é** m IOU
página f page
pago m payment
pagoda f pagoda
país m country; (región) region. ~ **natal** native land. **el P~ Vasco** the Basque Country. **los P~es Bajos** the Low Countries
paisa|je m countryside. ~**no** a of the same country. ● m compatriot
paja f straw; (fig) nonsense
pajarera f aviary
pájaro m bird. ~ **carpintero** woodpecker

paje m page
Pakistán m. **el** ~ Pakistan
pala f shovel; (laya) spade; (en deportes) bat; (de tenis) racquet
palabr|a f word; (habla) speech. ~**ota** f swear-word. **decir** ~**otas** swear. **pedir la** ~**a** ask to speak. **soltar** ~**otas** swear. **tomar la** ~**a** (begin to) speak
palacio m palace; (casa grande) mansion
paladar m palate
paladino a clear; (público) public
palanca f lever; (fig) influence. ~ **de cambio (de velocidades)** gear lever (Brit), gear shift (Amer)
palangana f wash-basin
palco m (en el teatro) box
Palestina f Palestine
palestino a & m Palestinian
palestra f (fig) arena
paleta f (de pintor) palette; (de albañil) trowel
paleto m yokel
paliativo a & m palliative
palide|cer [11] vi turn pale. ~**z** f paleness
pálido a pale
palillo m small stick; (de dientes) toothpick
palique m. **estar de** ~ be chatting
paliza f beating
palizada f fence; (recinto) enclosure
palma f (de la mano) palm; (árbol) palm (tree); (de dátiles) date palm. ~**s** fpl applause. ~**da** f slap. ~**das** fpl applause. **dar** ~**(da)s** clap. **tocar las** ~**s** clap
palmera f date palm
palmo m span; (fig, pequeña cantidad) small amount. ~ **a** ~ inch by inch
palmote|ar vi clap, applaud. ~**o** m clapping, applause
palo m stick; (del teléfono etc) pole; (mango) handle; (de golf) club; (golpe) blow; (de naipes) suit; (mástil) mast
paloma f pigeon, dove
palomitas fpl popcorn
palpa|ble a palpable. ~**r** vt feel
palpita|ción f palpitation. ~**nte** a throbbing. ~**r** vi throb; (latir) beat
palta f (LAm) avocado pear
pal|údico a marshy; (de paludismo) malarial. ~**udismo** m malaria
pamp|a f pampas. ~**ear** vi (LAm) travel across the pampas. ~**ero** a of the pampas

pan *m* bread; (*barra*) loaf. **~ integral** wholemeal bread (*Brit*), wholewheat bread (*Amer*). **~ tostado** toast. **~ rallado** breadcrumbs. **ganarse el ~** earn one's living

pana *f* corduroy

panacea *f* panacea

panader|ía *f* bakery; (*tienda*) baker's (shop). **~o** *m* baker

panal *m* honeycomb

Panamá *f* Panama

panameño *a & m* Panamanian

pancarta *f* placard

panda *m* panda; (*pandilla*) gang

pander|eta *f* (small) tambourine. **~o** *m* tambourine

pandilla *f* gang

panecillo *m* (bread) roll

panel *m* panel

panfleto *m* pamphlet

pánico *m* panic

panor|ama *m* panorama. **~ámico** *a* panoramic

panqué *m* (*LAm*) pancake

pantaletas *fpl* (*LAm*) underpants, knickers

pantal|ón *m* trousers. **~ones** *mpl* trousers. **~ón corto** shorts. **~ón tejano, ~ón vaquero** jeans

pantalla *f* screen; (*de lámpara*) (lamp)shade

pantano *m* marsh; (*embalse*) reservoir. **~so** *a* boggy

pantera *f* panther

pantomima *f* pantomime

pantorrilla *f* calf

pantufla *f* slipper

panucho *m* (*Mex*) stuffed tortilla

panz|a *f* belly. **~ada** *f* (*hartazgo, fam*) bellyful; (*golpe, fam*) blow in the belly. **~udo** *a* fat, pot-bellied

pañal *m* nappy (*Brit*), diaper (*Amer*)

pañ|ería *f* draper's (shop). **~o** *m* material; (*de lana*) woollen cloth; (*trapo*) cloth. **~o de cocina** dishcloth; (*para secar*) tea towel. **~o higiénico** sanitary towel. **en ~os menores** in one's underclothes

pañuelo *m* handkerchief; (*de cabeza*) scarf

papa *m* pope. **●** *f* (*esp LAm*) potato. **~s francesas** (*LAm*) chips

papá *m* dad(dy). **~s** *mpl* parents. **P~ Noel** Father Christmas

papada *f* (*de persona*) double chin

papado *m* papacy

papagayo *m* parrot

papal *a* papal

papanatas *m inv* simpleton

paparrucha *f* (*tontería*) silly thing

papaya *f* pawpaw

papel *m* paper; (*en el teatro etc*) role. **~ carbón** carbon paper. **~ celofán** celophane paper. **~ de calcar** carbon paper. **~ de embalar, ~ de envolver** wrapping paper. **~ de plata** silver paper. **~ de seda** tissue paper. **~era** *f* waste-paper basket. **~ería** *f* stationer's (shop). **~eta** *f* ticket; (*para votar*) paper. **~ higiénico** toilet paper. **~ pintado** wallpaper. **~ secante** blotting paper. **blanco como el ~** as white as a sheet. **desempeñar un ~, hacer un ~** play a role

paperas *fpl* mumps

paquebote *m* packet (boat)

paquete *m* packet; (*paquebote*) packet (boat); (*Mex, asunto difícil*) difficult job. **~ postal** parcel

paquistaní *a & m* Pakistani

par *a* equal; (*número*) even. **●** *m* couple; (*dos cosas iguales*) pair; (*igual*) equal; (*título*) peer. **a la ~** at the same time; (*monedas*) at par. **al ~ que** at the same time. **a ~es** two by two. **de ~ en ~** wide open. **sin ~** without equal

para *prep* for; (*hacia*) towards; (*antes del infinitivo*) (in order) to. **~ con** to(wards). **¿~ qué?** why? **~ que** so that

parabienes *mpl* congratulations

parábola *f* (*narración*) parable

parabrisas *m inv* windscreen (*Brit*), windshield (*Amer*)

paraca *f* (*LAm*) strong wind (from the Pacific)

paraca|ídas *m inv* parachute. **~idista** *m & f* parachutist; (*mil*) paratrooper

parachoques *m inv* bumper (*Brit*), fender (*Amer*); (*rail*) buffer

parad|a *f* (*acción*) stopping; (*sitio*) stop; (*de taxis*) rank; (*mil*) parade. **~ero** *m* whereabouts; (*alojamiento*) lodging. **~o** *a* stationary; (*obrero*) unemployed; (*lento*) slow. **dejar ~o** confuse. **tener mal ~ero** come to a sticky end

paradoja *f* paradox

parador *m* state-owned hotel

parafina *f* paraffin

par|afrasear *vt* paraphrase. **~áfrasis** *f inv* paraphrase

paraguas *m inv* umbrella

Paraguay *m* Paraguay

paraguayo *a & m* Paraguayan

paraíso *m* paradise; (*en el teatro*) gallery

paralel|a *f* parallel (line). **~as** *fpl* parallel bars. **~o** *a* & *m* parallel

par|álisis *f inv* paralysis. **~alítico** *a* paralytic. **~alizar** [10] *vt* paralyse

paramilitar *a* paramilitary

páramo *m* barren plain

parang|ón *m* comparison. **~onar** *vt* compare

paraninfo *m* hall

paranoi|a *f* paranoia. **~co** *a* paranoiac

parapeto *m* parapet; (*fig*) barricade

parapléjico *a* & *m* paraplegic

parar *vt/i* stop. **~se** *vpr* stop. **sin ~** continuously

pararrayos *m inv* lightning conductor

parásito *a* parasitic. ● *m* parasite

parasol *m* parasol

parcela *f* plot. **~r** *vt* divide into plots

parcial *a* partial. **~idad** *f* prejudice; (*pol*) faction. **a tiempo ~** part-time

parco *a* sparing, frugal

parche *m* patch

pardo *a* brown

parear *vt* pair off

parec|er *m* opinion; (*aspecto*) appearance. ● *vi* [11] seem; (*asemejarse*) look like; (*aparecer*) appear. **~erse** *vpr* resemble, look like. **~ido** *a* similar. ● *m* similarity. **al ~er** apparently. **a mi ~er** in my opinion. **bien ~ido** good-looking. **me ~e** I think. **¿qué te parece?** what do you think? **según ~e** apparently

pared *f* wall. **~ón** *m* thick wall; (*de ruinas*) standing wall. **~ por medio** next door. **llevar al ~ón** shoot

parej|a *f* pair; (*hombre y mujer*) couple; (*la otra persona*) partner. **~o** *a* alike, the same; (*liso*) smooth

parente|la *f* relations. **~sco** *m* relationship

paréntesis *m inv* parenthesis; (*signo ortográfico*) bracket. **entre ~** (*fig*) by the way

paria *m* & *f* outcast

paridad *f* equality

pariente *m* & *f* relation, relative

parihuela *f*, **parihuelas** *fpl* stretcher

parir *vt* give birth to. ● *vi* have a baby, give birth

París *m* Paris

parisiense *a* & *m* & *f*, **parisino** *a* & *m* Parisian

parking /'parkin/ *m* car park (*Brit*), parking lot (*Amer*)

parlament|ar *vi* discuss. **~ario** *a* parliamentary. ● *m* member of parliament (*Brit*), congressman (*Amer*). **~o** *m* parliament

parlanchín *a* talkative. ● *m* chatterbox

parmesano *a* Parmesan

paro *m* stoppage; (*desempleo*) unemployment; (*pájaro*) tit

parodia *f* parody. **~r** *vt* parody

parpadear *vi* blink; (*luz*) flicker; (*estrella*) twinkle

párpado *m* eyelid

parque *m* park. **~ de atracciones** funfair. **~ infantil** children's playground. **~ zoológico** zoo, zoological gardens

parqué *m* parquet

parquedad *f* frugality; (*moderación*) moderation

parra *f* grapevine

párrafo *m* paragraph

parrilla *f* grill; (*LAm*, *auto*) radiator grill. **~da** *f* grill. **a la ~** grilled

párroco *m* parish priest

parroquia *f* parish; (*iglesia*) parish church. **~no** *m* parishioner; (*cliente*) customer

parsimoni|a *f* thrift. **~oso** *a* thrifty

parte *m* message; (*informe*) report. ● *f* part; (*porción*) share; (*lado*) side; (*jurid*) party. **dar ~** report. **de mi ~** for me. **de ~ de** from. **¿de ~ de quién?** (*al teléfono*) who's speaking? **en cualquier ~** anywhere. **en gran ~** largely. **en ~** partly. **en todas ~s** everywhere. **la mayor ~** the majority. **ninguna ~** nowhere. **por otra ~** on the other hand. **por todas ~s** everywhere

partera *f* midwife

partición *f* sharing out

participa|ción *f* participation; (*noticia*) notice; (*de lotería*) lottery ticket. **~nte** *a* participating. ● *m* & *f* participant. **~r** *vt* notify. ● *vi* take part

participio *m* participle

partícula *f* particle

particular *a* particular; (*clase*) private. ● *m* matter. **~idad** *f* peculiarity. **~izar** [10] *vt* distinguish; (*detallar*) give details about. **en ~** in particular. **nada de ~** nothing special

partida *f* departure; (*en registro*) entry; (*documento*) certificate; (*juego*) game; (*de gente*) group. **mala ~** dirty trick

partidario *a & m* partisan. ~ **de** keen on

parti|do *a* divided. ● *m* (*pol*) party; (*encuentro*) match, game; (*equipo*) team. ~**r** *vt* divide; (*romper*) break; (*repartir*) share; crack ⟨*nueces*⟩. ● *vi* leave; (*empezar*) start. ~**rse** *vpr* (*romperse*) break; (*dividirse*) split. **a** ~**r de** (starting) from

partitura *f* (*mus*) score

parto *m* birth; (*fig*) creation. **estar de** ~ be in labour

párvulo *m*. **colegio de** ~**s** nursery school

pasa *f* raisin. ~ **de Corinto** currant. ~ **de Esmirna** sultana

pasa|ble *a* passable. ~**da** *f* passing; (*de puntos*) row. ~**dero** *a* passable. ~**dizo** *m* passage. ~**do** *a* past; ⟨*día, mes etc*⟩ last; (*anticuado*) old-fashioned; ⟨*comida*⟩ bad, off. ~**do mañana** the day after tomorrow. ~**dor** *m* bolt; (*de pelo*) hair-slide; (*culin*) strainer. **de** ~**da** in passing. **el lunes** ~**do** last Monday

pasaje *m* passage; (*naut*) crossing; (*viajeros*) passengers. ~**ro** *a* passing. ● *m* passenger

pasamano(s) *m* handrail; (*barandilla de escalera*) banister(s)

pasamontañas *m inv* Balaclava (helmet)

pasaporte *m* passport

pasar *vt* pass; (*poner*) put; (*filtrar*) strain; spend ⟨*tiempo*⟩; (*tragar*) swallow; show ⟨*película*⟩; (*tolerar*) tolerate, overlook; give ⟨*mensaje, enfermedad*⟩. ● *vi* pass; (*suceder*) happen; (*ir*) go; (*venir*) come; ⟨*tiempo*⟩ go by. ~ **de** have no interest in. ~**se** *vpr* pass; (*terminarse*) be over; ⟨*flores*⟩ wither; ⟨*comida*⟩ go bad; spend ⟨*tiempo*⟩ (*excederse*) go too far. ~**lo bien** have a good time. ~ **por alto** leave out. **como si no hubiese pasado nada** as if nothing had happened. **lo que pasa es que** the fact is that. **pase lo que pase** whatever happens. **¡pase Vd!** come in!, go in! **¡que lo pases bien!** have a good time! **¿qué pasa?** what's the matter?, what's happening?

pasarela *f* footbridge; (*naut*) gangway

pasatiempo *m* hobby, pastime

pascua *f* (*fiesta de los hebreos*) Passover; (*de Resurrección*) Easter; (*Navidad*) Christmas. ~**s** *fpl* Christmas. **hacer la** ~ **a uno** mess things up for s.o. **¡y santas** ~**s!** and that's that!

pase *m* pass

pase|ante *m & f* passer-by. ~**ar** *vt* take for a walk; (*exhibir*) show off. ● *vi* go for a walk; (*en coche etc*) go for a ride. ~**arse** *vpr* go for a walk; (*en coche etc*) go for a ride. ~**o** *m* walk; (*en coche etc*) ride; (*calle*) avenue. ~**o marítimo** promenade. **dar un** ~**o** go for a walk. **¡vete a** ~**o!** (*fam*) go away!, get lost! (*fam*)

pasillo *m* passage

pasión *f* passion

pasiv|idad *f* passiveness. ~**o** *a* passive

pasm|ar *vt* astonish. ~**arse** *vpr* be astonished. ~**o** *m* astonishment. ~**oso** *a* astonishing

paso *a* ⟨*fruta*⟩ dried ● *m* step; (*acción de pasar*) passing; (*huella*) footprint; (*manera de andar*) walk; (*camino*) way through; (*entre montañas*) pass; (*estrecho*) strait(s). ~ **a nivel** level crossing (*Brit*), grade crossing (*Amer*). ~ **de cebra** Zebra crossing. ~ **de peatones** pedestrian crossing. ~ **elevado** flyover. **a cada** ~ at every turn. **a dos** ~**s** very near. **al** ~ **que** at the same time as. **a** ~ **lento** slowly. **ceda el** ~ give way. **de** ~ in passing. **de** ~ **por** on the way through. **prohibido el** ~ no entry

pasodoble *m* (*baile*) pasodoble

pasota *m & f* drop-out

pasta *f* paste; (*masa*) dough; (*dinero, fam*) money. ~**s** *fpl* pasta; (*pasteles*) pastries. ~ **de dientes**, ~ **dentífrica** toothpaste

pastar *vt/i* graze

pastel *m* cake; (*empanada*) pie; (*lápiz*) pastel. ~**ería** *f* cakes; (*tienda*) cake shop, confectioner's

paste(u)rizar [10] *vt* pasteurize

pastiche *m* pastiche

pastilla *f* pastille; (*de jabón*) bar; (*de chocolate*) piece

pastinaca *f* parsnip

pasto *m* pasture; (*hierba*) grass; (*Mex, césped*) lawn. ~**r** *m* shepherd; (*relig*) minister. ~**ral** *a* pastoral

pata *f* leg; (*pie*) paw, foot. ~**s arriba** upside down. **a cuatro** ~**s** on all fours. **meter la** ~ put one's foot in it. **tener mala** ~ have bad luck

pataca *f* Jerusalem artichoke

pata|da *f* kick. ~**lear** *vt* stamp; ⟨*niño pequeño*⟩ kick

pataplum *int* crash!

patata *f* potato. **~s fritas** chips (*Brit*), French fries (*Amer*). **~s fritas (a la inglesa)** (*potato*) crisps (*Brit*), potato chips (*Amer*)

patent|ar *vt* patent. **~e** *a* obvious. ● *f* licence. **~e de invención** patent

patern|al *a* paternal; ⟨*cariño etc*⟩ fatherly. **~idad** *f* paternity. **~o** *a* paternal; ⟨*cariño etc*⟩ fatherly

patético *a* moving

patillas *fpl* sideburns

patín *m* skate; (*juguete*) scooter

pátina *f* patina

patina|dero *m* skating rink. **~dor** *m* skater. **~je** *m* skating. **~r** *vi* skate; (*deslizarse*) slide. **~zo** *m* skid; (*fig*, *fam*) blunder

patio *m* patio. **~ de butacas** stalls (*Brit*), orchestra (*Amer*)

pato *m* duck

patol|ogía *f* pathology. **~ógico** *a* pathological

patoso *a* clumsy

patraña *f* hoax

patria *f* native land

patriarca *m* patriarch

patrimonio *m* inheritance; (*fig*) heritage

patri|ota *a* patriotic. ● *m & f* patriot. **~ótico** *a* patriotic. **~otismo** *m* patriotism

patrocin|ar *vt* sponsor. **~io** *m* sponsorship

patr|ón *m* patron; (*jefe*) boss; (*de pensión etc*) landlord; (*modelo*) pattern. **~onato** *m* patronage; (*fundación*) trust, foundation

patrulla *f* patrol; (*fig*, *cuadrilla*) group. **~r** *vt/i* patrol

paulatinamente *adv* slowly

pausa *f* pause. **~do** *a* slow

pauta *f* guideline

paviment|ar *vt* pave. **~o** *m* pavement

pavo *m* turkey. **~ real** peacock

pavor *m* terror. **~oso** *a* terrifying

payas|ada *f* buffoonery. **~o** *m* clown

paz *f* peace. **La P~** La Paz

peaje *m* toll

peatón *m* pedestrian

pebet|a *f* (*LAm*) little girl. **~e** *m* little boy

peca *f* freckle

peca|do *m* sin; (*defecto*) fault. **~dor** *m* sinner. **~minoso** *a* sinful. **~r** [7] *vi* sin

pecoso *a* freckled

pectoral *a* pectoral; (*para la tos*) cough

peculiar *a* peculiar, particular. **~idad** *f* peculiarity

pech|era *f* front. **~ero** *m* bib. **~o** *m* chest; (*de mujer*) breast; (*fig*, *corazón*) heart. **~uga** *f* breast. **dar el ~o** breast-feed ⟨*a un niño*⟩; (*afrontar*) confront. **tomar a ~o** take to heart

pedagogo *m* teacher

pedal *m* pedal. **~ear** *vi* pedal

pedante *a* pedantic

pedazo *m* piece, bit. **a ~s** in pieces. **hacer ~s** break to pieces. **hacerse ~s** fall to pieces

pedernal *m* flint

pedestal *m* pedestal

pedestre *a* pedestrian

pediatra *m & f* paediatrician

pedicuro *m* chiropodist

pedi|do *m* order. **~r** [5] *vt* ask (for); (*com, en restaurante*) order. ● *vi* ask. **~r prestado** borrow

pegadizo *a* sticky; (*mus*) catchy

pegajoso *a* sticky

pega|r [12] *vt* stick (on); (*coser*) sew on; give ⟨*enfermedad etc*⟩; (*juntar*) join; (*golpear*) hit; (*dar*) give. ● *vi* stick. **~rse** *vpr* stick; (*pelearse*) hit each other. **~r fuego a** set fire to. **~tina** *f* sticker

pein|ado *m* hairstyle. **~ar** *vt* comb. **~arse** *vpr* comb one's hair. **~e** *m* comb. **~eta** *f* ornamental comb

p.ej. *abrev* (*por ejemplo*) e.g., for example

pela|do *a* ⟨*fruta*⟩ peeled; ⟨*cabeza*⟩ bald; ⟨*número*⟩ exactly; ⟨*terreno*⟩ barren. ● *m* bare patch. **~dura** *f* (*acción*) peeling; (*mondadura*) peelings

pela|je *m* (*de animal*) fur; (*fig*, *aspecto*) appearance. **~mbre** *m* (*de animal*) fur; (*de persona*) thick hair

pelar *vt* cut the hair; (*mondar*) peel; (*quitar el pellejo*) skin

peldaño *m* step; (*de escalera de mano*) rung

pelea *f* fight; (*discusión*) quarrel. **~r** *vi* fight. **~rse** *vpr* fight

peletería *f* fur shop

peliagudo *a* difficult, tricky

pelícano *m*, **pelicano** *m* pelican

película *f* film (*esp Brit*), movie (*Amer*). **~ de dibujos (animados)** cartoon (film). **~ en colores** colour film

peligro *m* danger; (*riesgo*) risk. **~so** *a* dangerous. **poner en ~** endanger

pelirrojo *a* red-haired

pelma *m & f*, **pelmazo** *m* bore, nuisance

pel|o *m* hair; (*de barba o bigote*) whisker. **~ón** *a* bald; (*rapado*) with very short hair. **no tener ~os en la lengua** be outspoken. **tomar el ~o a uno** pull s.o.'s leg

pelota *f* ball; (*juego vasco*) pelota. **~ vasca** pelota. **en ~(s)** naked

pelotera *f* squabble

pelotilla *f*. **hacer la ~ a** ingratiate o.s. with

peluca *f* wig

peludo *a* hairy

peluquer|ía *f* (*de mujer*) hairdresser's; (*de hombre*) barber's. **~o** *m* (*de mujer*) hairdresser; (*de hombre*) barber

pelusa *f* down; (*celos, fam*) jealousy

pelvis *f* pelvis

pella *f* lump

pelleja *f*, **pellejo** *m* skin

pellizc|ar [7] *vt* pinch. **~o** *m* pinch

pena *f* sadness; (*dificultad*) difficulty. **~ de muerte** death penalty. **a duras ~s** with difficulty. **da ~ que** it's a pity that. **me da ~ que** I'm sorry that. **merecer la ~** be worthwhile. **¡qué ~!** what a pity! **valer la ~** be worthwhile

penacho *m* tuft; (*fig*) plume

penal *a* penal; (*criminal*) criminal. ● *m* prison. **~idad** *f* suffering; (*jurid*) penalty. **~izar** [10] *vt* penalize

penalty *m* penalty

penar *vt* punish. ● *vi* suffer. **~ por** long for

pend|er *vi* hang. **~iente** *a* hanging; ⟨*terreno*⟩ sloping; ⟨*cuenta*⟩ outstanding; (*fig*) ⟨*asunto etc*⟩ pending. ● *m* earring. ● *f* slope

pendón *m* banner

péndulo *a* hanging. ● *m* pendulum

pene *m* penis

penetra|nte *a* penetrating; ⟨*sonido*⟩ piercing; ⟨*herida*⟩ deep. **~r** *vt* penetrate; (*fig*) pierce; (*entender*) understand. ● *vi* penetrate; (*entrar*) go into

penicilina *f* penicillin

pen|ínsula *f* peninsula. **península Ibérica** Iberian Peninsula. **~insular** *a* peninsular

penique *m* penny

peniten|cia *f* penitence; (*castigo*) penance. **~te** *a & m & f* penitent

penoso *a* painful; (*difícil*) difficult

pensa|do *a* thought. **~dor** *m* thinker. **~miento** *m* thought. **~r** [1] *vt* think; (*considerar*) consider. ● *vi* think. **~r en** think about. **~tivo** *a* thoughtful. **bien ~do** all things considered. **cuando menos se piensa** when least expected. **menos ~do** least expected. **¡ni ~rlo!** certainly not! **pienso que sí** I think so

pensi|ón *f* pension; (*casa de huéspedes*) guest-house. **~ón completa** full board. **~onista** *m & f* pensioner; (*huésped*) lodger; (*escol*) boarder

pentágono *m* pentagon

pentagrama *m* stave

Pentecostés *m* Whitsun; (*fiesta judía*) Pentecost

penúltimo *a & m* penultimate, last but one

penumbra *f* half-light

penuria *f* shortage

peñ|a *f* rock; (*de amigos*) group; (*club*) club. **~ón** *m* rock. **el peñón de Gibraltar** The Rock (of Gibraltar)

peón *m* labourer; (*en ajedrez*) pawn; (*en damas*) piece; (*juguete*) (spinning) top

peonía *f* peony

peonza *f* (spinning) top

peor *a* (*comparativo*) worse; (*superlativo*) worst. ● *adv* worse. **~ que ~** worse and worse. **lo ~** the worst thing. **tanto ~** so much the worse

pepin|illo *m* gherkin. **~o** *m* cucumber. **(no) me importa un ~o** I couldn't care less

pepita *f* pip

pepitoria *f* fricassee

pequeñ|ez *f* smallness; (*minucia*) trifle. **~ito** *a* very small, tiny. **~o** *a* small, little. **de ~o** as a child. **en ~o** in miniature

pequinés *m* (*perro*) Pekingese

pera *f* (*fruta*) pear. **~l** *m* pear (tree)

percance *m* setback

percatarse *vpr*. **~ de** notice

perc|epción *f* perception. **~eptible** *a* perceptible. **~eptivo** *a* perceptive. **~ibir** *vt* perceive; earn ⟨*dinero*⟩

percusión *f* percussion

percutir *vt* tap

percha *f* hanger; (*de aves*) perch. **de ~** off the peg

perde|dor *a* losing. ● *m* loser. **~r** [1] *vt* lose; (*malgastar*) waste; miss ⟨*tren etc*⟩. ● *vi* lose; ⟨*tela*⟩ fade. **~rse** *vpr* get lost; (*desaparecer*) disappear;

(*desperdiciarse*) be wasted; (*estropearse*) be spoilt. **echar(se) a ∼r** spoil
pérdida *f* loss; (*de líquido*) leak; (*de tiempo*) waste
perdido *a* lost
perdiz *f* partridge
perd|ón *m* pardon, forgiveness. ● *int* sorry! **∼onar** *vt* excuse, forgive; (*jurid*) pardon. ¡**∼one (Vd)!** sorry! **pedir ∼ón** apologize
perdura|ble *a* lasting. **∼r** *vi* last
perece|dero *a* perishable. **∼r** [11] *vi* perish
peregrin|ación *f* pilgrimage. **∼ar** *vi* go on a pilgrimage; (*fig, fam*) travel. **∼o** *a* strange. ● *m* pilgrim
perejil *m* parsley
perengano *m* so-and-so
perenne *a* everlasting; (*bot*) perennial
perentorio *a* peremptory
perez|a *f* laziness. **∼oso** *a* lazy
perfec|ción *f* perfection. **∼cionamiento** *m* perfection; (*mejora*) improvement. **∼cionar** *vt* perfect; (*mejorar*) improve. **∼cionista** *m & f* perfectionist. **∼tamente** *adv* perfectly. ● *int* of course! **∼to** *a* perfect; (*completo*) complete. **a la ∼ción** perfectly, to perfection
perfidia *f* treachery
pérfido *a* treacherous
perfil *m* profile; (*contorno*) outline; **∼es** *mpl* (*fig, rasgos*) features. **∼ado** *a* (*bien terminado*) well-finished. **∼ar** *vt* draw in profile; (*fig*) put the finishing touches to
perfora|ción *f* perforation. **∼do** *m* perforation. **∼dora** *f* punch. **∼r** *vt* pierce, perforate; punch ⟨*papel, tarjeta etc*⟩
perfum|ar *vt* perfume. **∼arse** *vpr* put perfume on. **∼e** *m* perfume, scent. **∼ería** *f* perfumery
pergamino *m* parchment
pericia *f* expertise
pericón *m* popular Argentinian dance
perif|eria *f* (*de población*) outskirts. **∼érico** *a* peripheral
perilla *f* (*barba*) goatee
perímetro *m* perimeter
periódico *a* periodic(al). ● *m* newspaper
periodis|mo *m* journalism. **∼ta** *m & f* journalist
período *m*, **periodo** *m* period
periquito *m* budgerigar

periscopio *m* periscope
perito *a & m* expert
perju|dicar [7] *vt* harm; (*desfavorecer*) not suit. **∼dicial** *a* harmful. **∼icio** *m* harm. **en ∼icio de** to the detriment of
perjur|ar *vi* perjure o.s. **∼io** *m* perjury
perla *f* pearl. **de ∼s** *adv* very well. ● *a* excellent
permane|cer [11] *vi* remain. **∼ncia** *f* permanence; (*estancia*) stay. **∼nte** *a* permanent. ● *f* perm
permeable *a* permeable
permi|sible *a* permissible. **∼sivo** *a* permissive. **∼so** *m* permission; (*documento*) licence; (*mil etc*) leave. **∼so de conducción, ∼so de conducir** driving licence (*Brit*), driver's license (*Amer*). **∼tir** *vt* allow, permit. **∼tirse** *vpr* be allowed. **con ∼so** excuse me. ¿**me ∼te?** may I?
permutación *f* exchange; (*math*) permutation
pernicioso *a* pernicious; ⟨*persona*⟩ wicked
pernio *m* hinge
perno *m* bolt
pero *conj* but. ● *m* fault; (*objeción*) objection
perogrullada *f* platitude
perol *m* pan
peronista *m & f* follower of Juan Perón
perorar *vi* make a speech
perpendicular *a & f* perpendicular
perpetrar *vt* perpetrate
perpetu|ar [21] *vt* perpetuate. **∼o** *a* perpetual
perplej|idad *f* perplexity. **∼o** *a* perplexed
perr|a *f* (*animal*) bitch; (*moneda*) coin, penny (*Brit*), cent (*Amer*); (*rabieta*) tantrum. **∼era** *f* kennel. **∼ería** *f* (*mala jugada*) dirty trick; (*palabra*) harsh word. **∼o** *a* awful. ● *m* dog. **∼o corredor** hound. **∼o de aguas** spaniel. **∼o del hortelano** dog in the manger. **∼o galgo** greyhound. **de ∼os** awful. **estar sin una ∼a** be broke
persa *a & m & f* Persian
perse|cución *f* pursuit; (*tormento*) persecution. **∼guir** [5 & 13] *vt* pursue; (*atormentar*) persecute
persevera|ncia *f* perseverance. **∼nte** *a* persevering. **∼r** *vi* persevere
persiana *f* (Venetian) blind

persist|encia f persistence. **~ente** a persistent. **~ir** vi persist

person|a f person. **~as** fpl people. **~aje** m (*persona importante*) important person; (*de obra literaria*) character. **~al** a personal; (*para una persona*) single. ● m staff. **~alidad** f personality. **~arse** vpr appear in person. **~ificar** [7] vt personify. **~ificación** f personification

perspectiva f perspective

perspica|cia f shrewdness; (*de vista*) keen eye-sight. **~z** a shrewd; (*vista*) keen

persua|dir vt persuade. **~sión** f persuasion. **~sivo** a persuasive

pertenecer [11] vi belong

pertinaz a persistent

pertinente a relevant

perturba|ción f disturbance. **~r** vt perturb

Perú m. **el ~** Peru

peruano a & m Peruvian

perver|sión f perversion. **~so** a perverse. ● m pervert. **~tir** [4] vt pervert

pervivir vi live on

pesa f weight. **~dez** f weight; (*de cabeza etc*) heaviness; (*lentitud*) sluggishness; (*cualidad de fastidioso*) tediousness; (*cosa fastidiosa*) bore, nuisance

pesadilla f nightmare

pesad|o a heavy; (*lento*) slow; (*duro*) hard; (*aburrido*) boring, tedious. **~umbre** f (*pena*) sorrow

pésame m sympathy, condolences

pesar vt/i weigh. ● m sorrow; (*remordimiento*) regret. **a ~ de (que)** in spite of. **me pesa que** I'm sorry that. **pese a (que)** in spite of

pesario m pessary

pesca f fishing; (*peces*) fish; (*pescado*) catch. **~da** f hake. **~dería** f fish shop. **~dilla** f whiting. **~do** m fish. **~dor** a fishing. ● m fisherman. **~r** [7] vt catch. ● vi fish. **ir de ~** go fishing

pescuezo m neck

pesebre m manger

pesero m (*Mex*) minibus taxi

peseta f peseta; (*Mex*) twenty-five centavos

pesimis|mo m pessimism. **~ta** a pessimistic. ● m & f pessimist

pésimo a very bad, awful

peso m weight; (*moneda*) peso. **~ bruto** gross weight. **~ neto** net

weight. **a ~** by weight. **de ~** influential

pesquero a fishing

pesquisa f inquiry

pestañ|a f eyelash. **~ear** vi blink. **sin ~ear** without batting an eyelid

pest|e f plague; (*hedor*) stench. **~icida** m pesticide. **~ilencia** f pestilence; (*hedor*) stench

pestillo m bolt

pestiño m pancake with honey

petaca f tobacco case; (*LAm, maleta*) suitcase

pétalo m petal

petardo m firework

petición f request; (*escrito*) petition. **a ~ de** at the request of

petirrojo m robin

petrificar [7] vt petrify

petr|óleo m oil. **~olero** a oil. ● m oil tanker. **~olífero** a oil-bearing

petulante a arrogant

peyorativo a pejorative

pez f fish; (*substancia negruzca*) pitch. **~ espada** swordfish

pezón m nipple; (*bot*) stalk

pezuña f hoof

piada f chirp

piadoso a compassionate; (*devoto*) devout

pian|ista m & f pianist. **~o** m piano. **~o de cola** grand piano

piar [20] vi chirp

pib|a f (*LAm*) little girl. **~e** m (*LAm*) little boy

picad|illo m mince; (*guiso*) stew. **~o** a perforated; (*carne*) minced; (*ofendido*) offended; (*mar*) choppy; (*diente*) bad. **~ura** f bite, sting; (*de polilla*) moth hole

picante a hot; (*palabras etc*) cutting

picaporte m door-handle; (*aldaba*) knocker

picar [7] vt prick, pierce; (*ave*) peck; (*insecto, pez*) bite; (*avispa*) sting; (*comer poco*) pick at; mince (*carne*). ● vi prick; (*ave*) peck; (*insecto, pez*) bite; (*sol*) scorch; (*sabor fuerte*) be hot. **~ alto** aim high

picard|ear vt corrupt. **~ía** f wickedness; (*travesura*) naughty thing

picaresco a roguish; (*literatura*) picaresque

pícaro a villainous; (*niño*) mischievous. ● m rogue

picatoste m toast; (*frito*) fried bread

picazón f itch

pico m beak; (*punta*) corner; (*herramienta*) pickaxe; (*cima*) peak.

∼**tear** vt peck; (comer, fam) pick at.
y ∼ (con tiempo) a little after; (con
cantidad) a little more than
picudo a pointed
pich|ona f (fig) darling; ∼**ón** m
pigeon
pido vb véase **pedir**
pie m foot; (bot, de vaso) stem. ∼ **cuadrado** square foot. **a cuatro** ∼**s** on
all fours. **al** ∼ **de la letra** literally. **a**
∼ on foot. **a** ∼**(s) juntillas** (fig)
firmly. **buscarle tres** ∼**s al gato** split
hairs. **de** ∼ standing (up). **de** ∼**s a
cabeza** from head to foot. **en** ∼
standing (up). **ponerse de/en** ∼
stand up
piedad f pity; (relig) piety
piedra f stone; (de mechero) flint;
(granizo) hailstone
piel f skin; (cuero) leather. **artículos
de** ∼ leather goods
pienso vb véase **pensar**
pierdo vb véase **perder**
pierna f leg. **estirar las** ∼**s** stretch
one's legs
pieza f piece; (parte) part; (obra
teatral) play; (moneda) coin; (habitación) room. ∼ **de recambio** spare
part
pífano m fife
pigment|ación f pigmentation. ∼**o**
m pigment
pigmeo a & m pygmy
pijama m pyjamas
pila f (montón) pile; (recipiente)
basin; (eléctrica) battery. ∼ **bautismal** font
píldora f pill
pilot|ar vt pilot. ∼**o** m pilot
pilla|je m pillage. ∼**r** vt pillage;
(alcanzar, agarrar) catch; (atropellar) run over
pillo a wicked. ● m rogue
pim|entero m (vasija) pepper-pot.
∼**entón** m paprika, cayenne
pepper. ∼**ienta** f pepper. ∼**iento** m
pepper. **grano** m **de** ∼**ienta**
peppercorn
pináculo m pinnacle
pinar m pine forest
pincel m paintbrush. ∼**ada** f brush-
stroke. **la última** ∼**ada** (fig) the finishing touch
pinch|ar vt pierce, prick; puncture
⟨neumático⟩; (fig, incitar) push;
(med, fam) give an injection to.
∼**azo** m prick; (en neumático) puncture. ∼**itos** mpl kebab(s); (tapas)
savoury snacks. ∼**o** m point

ping|ajo m rag. ∼**o** m rag
ping-pong m table tennis, ping-
pong
pingüino m penguin
pino m pine (tree)
pint|a f spot; (fig, aspecto) appear-
ance. ∼**ada** f graffiti. ∼**ar** vt paint.
∼**arse** vpr put ón make-up. ∼**or** m
painter. ∼**or de brocha gorda**
painter and decorator. ∼**oresco** a
picturesque. ∼**ura** f painting. **no**
∼**a nada** (fig) it doesn't count. **tener**
∼**a de** look like
pinza f (clothes-)peg (Brit), (clothes-)
pin (Amer); (de cangrejo etc) claw.
∼**s** fpl tweezers
pinzón m chaffinch
piñ|a f pine cone; (ananás) pine-
apple; (fig, grupo) group. ∼**ón** m
(semilla) pine nut
pío a pious; ⟨caballo⟩ piebald. ● m
chirp. **no decir (ni)** ∼ not say a word
piocha f pickaxe
piojo m louse
pionero m pioneer
pipa f pipe; (semilla) seed; (de girasol) sunflower seed
pipián m (LAm) stew
pique m resentment; (rivalidad)
rivalry. **irse a** ∼ sink
piqueta f pickaxe
piquete m picket
piragua f canoe
pirámide f pyramid
pirata a & f pirate
Pirineos mpl Pyrenees
piropo m (fam) compliment
piruet|a f pirouette. ∼**ear** vi
pirouette
pirulí m lollipop
pisa|da f footstep; (huella) footprint.
∼**papeles** m invar paperweight. ∼**r**
vt tread on; (apretar) press; (fig)
walk over. ● vi tread. **no** ∼**r el
césped** keep off the grass
piscina f swimming pool; (para
peces) fish-pond
Piscis m Pisces
piso m floor; (vivienda) flat (Brit),
apartment (Amer); (de zapato) sole
pisotear vt trample (on)
pista f track; (fig, indicio) clue. ∼ **de
aterrizaje** runway. ∼ **de baile** dance
floor. ∼ **de hielo** skating-rink. ∼ **de
tenis** tennis court
pistacho m pistachio (nut)
pisto m fried vegetables
pistol|a f pistol. ∼**era** f holster. ∼**ero**
m gunman

pistón *m* piston

pit|ar *vt* whistle at. ● *vi* blow a whistle; (*auto*) sound one's horn. **~ido** *m* whistle

pitill|era *f* cigarette case. **~o** *m* cigarette

pito *m* whistle; (*auto*) horn

pitón *m* python

pitorre|arse *vpr.* **~arse de** make fun of. **~o** *m* teasing

pitorro *m* spout

pivote *m* pivot

pizarr|a *f* slate; (*encerrado*) blackboard. **~ón** *m* (*LAm*) blackboard

pizca *f* (*fam*) tiny piece; (*de sal*) pinch. **ni ~** not at all

pizz|a *f* pizza. **~ería** *f* pizzeria

placa *f* plate; (*conmemorativa*) plaque; (*distintivo*) badge

pláceme *m* congratulations

place|ntero *a* pleasant. **~r** [32] *vt* please. **me ~** I like. ● *m* pleasure

plácido *a* placid

plaga *f* plague; (*fig, calamidad*) disaster; (*fig, abundancia*) glut. **~r** [12] *vt* fill

plagi|ar *vt* plagiarize. **~o** *m* plagiarism

plan *m* plan; (*med*) course of treatment. **a todo ~** on a grand scale. **en ~ de** as

plana *f* (*llanura*) plain; (*página*) page. **en primera ~** on the front page

plancha *f* iron; (*lámina*) sheet. **~do** *m* ironing. **~r** *vt/i* iron. **a la ~** grilled. **tirarse una ~** put one's foot in it

planeador *m* glider

planear *vt* plan. ● *vi* glide

planeta *m* planet. **~rio** *a* planetary. ● *m* planetarium

planicie *f* plain

planifica|ción *f* planning. **~r** [7] *vt* plan

planilla *f* (*LAm*) list

plano *a* flat. ● *m* plane; (*de ciudad*) plan. **primer ~** foreground; (*foto*) close-up

planta *f* (*anat*) sole; (*bot, fábrica*) plant; (*plano*) ground plan; (*piso*) floor. **~ baja** ground floor (*Brit*), first floor (*Amer*)

planta|ción *f* plantation. **~do** *a* planted. **~r** *vt* plant; deal ‹*golpe*›. **~r en la calle** throw out. **~rse** *vpr* stand; (*fig*) stand firm. **bien ~do** good-looking

plantear *vt* (*exponer*) expound; (*causar*) create; raise ‹*cuestión*›

plantilla *f* insole; (*modelo*) pattern; (*personal*) personnel

plaqué *m* plate

plasma *m* plasma

plástico *a & m* plastic

plata *f* silver; (*fig, dinero, fam*) money. **~ de ley** sterling silver. **~ alemana** nickel silver

plataforma *f* platform

plátano *m* plane (tree); (*fruta*) banana; (*platanero*) banana tree

platea *f* stalls (*Brit*), orchestra (*Amer*)

plateado *a* silver-plated; (*color de plata*) silver

pl|ática *f* chat, talk. **~aticar** [7] *vi* chat, talk

platija *f* plaice

platillo *m* saucer; (*mus*) cymbal. **~ volante** flying saucer

platino *m* platinum. **~s** *mpl* (*auto*) points

plato *m* plate; (*comida*) dish; (*parte de una comida*) course

platónico *a* platonic

plausible *a* plausible; (*loable*) praiseworthy

playa *f* beach; (*fig*) seaside

plaza *f* square; (*mercado*) market; (*sitio*) place; (*empleo*) job. **~ de toros** bullring

plazco *vb véase* **placer**

plazo *m* period; (*pago*) instalment; (*fecha*) date. **comprar a ~s** buy on hire purchase (*Brit*), buy on the installment plan (*Amer*)

plazuela *f* little square

pleamar *f* high tide

plebe *f* common people. **~yo** *a & m* plebeian

plebiscito *m* plebiscite

plectro *m* plectrum

plega|ble *a* pliable; ‹*silla etc*› folding. **~r** [1 & 12] *vt* fold. **~rse** *vpr* bend; (*fig*) give way

pleito *m* (*court*) case; (*fig*) dispute

plenilunio *m* full moon

plen|itud *f* fullness; (*fig*) height. **~o** *a* full. **en ~o día** in broad daylight. **en ~o verano** at the height of the summer

pleuresía *f* pleuresy

plieg|o *m* sheet. **~ue** *m* fold; (*en ropa*) pleat

plinto *m* plinth

plisar *vt* pleat

plom|ero *m* (*esp LAm*) plumber. **~o** *m* lead; (*elec*) fuse. **de ~o** lead

pluma *f* feather; (*para escribir*) pen. **~ estilográfica** fountain pen. **~je** *m* plumage

plúmbeo *a* leaden

plum|ero *m* feather duster; (*para plumas, lapices etc*) pencil-case. **~ón** *m* down

plural *a* & *m* plural. **~idad** *f* plurality; (*mayoría*) majority. **en ~** in the plural

pluriempleo *m* having more than one job

plus *m* bonus

pluscuamperfecto *m* pluperfect

plusvalía *f* appreciation

plut|ocracia *f* plutocracy. **~ócrata** *m* & *f* plutocrat. **~ocrático** *a* plutocratic

plutonio *m* plutonium

pluvial *a* rain

pobla|ción *f* population; (*ciudad*) city, town; (*pueblo*) village. **~do** *a* populated. ● *m* village. **~r** [2] *vt* populate; (*habitar*) inhabit. **~rse** *vpr* get crowded

pobre *a* poor. ● *m* & *f* poor person; (*fig*) poor thing. ¡**~cito!** poor (little) thing! ¡**~ de mí!** poor (old) me! **~za** *f* poverty

pocilga *f* pigsty

poción *f* potion

poco *a* not much, little; (*en plural*) few; (*unos*) a few. ● *m* (a) little. ● *adv* little, not much; (*con adjetivo*) not very; (*poco tiempo*) not long. **a ~** little by little, gradually. **a ~ de** soon after. **dentro de ~** soon. **hace ~** not long ago. **poca cosa** nothing much. **por ~** (*fam*) nearly

podar *vt* prune

poder [33] *vi* be able. **no pudo venir** he couldn't come. ¿**puedo hacer algo?** can I do anything? ¿**puedo pasar?** may I come in? ● *m* power. **~es** *mpl* **públicos** authorities. **~oso** *a* powerful. **en el ~** in power. **no ~ con** not be able to cope with; (*no aguantar*) not be able to stand. **no ~ más** be exhausted; (*estar harto de algo*) not be able to manage any more. **no ~ menos que** not be able to help. **puede que** it is possible that. **puede ser** it is possible. ¿**se puede ...?** may I ...?

podrido *a* rotten

po|ema *m* poem. **~esía** *f* poetry; (*poema*) poem. **~eta** *m* poet. **~ético** *a* poetic

polaco *a* Polish. ● *m* Pole; (*lengua*) Polish

polar *a* polar. **estrella ~** polestar

polarizar [10] *vt* polarize

polca *f* polka

polea *f* pulley

pol|émica *f* controversy. **~émico** *a* polemic(al). **~emizar** [10] *vi* argue

polen *m* pollen

policía *f* police (force); (*persona*) policewoman. ● *m* policeman. **~co** *a* police; (*novela etc*) detective

policlínica *f* clinic, hospital

policromo, polícromo *a* polychrome

polideportivo *m* sports centre

poliéster *m* polyester

poliestireno *m* polystyrene

polietileno *m* polythene

pol|igamia *f* polygamy. **~ígamo** *a* polygamous

políglota *m* & *f* polyglot

polígono *m* polygon

polilla *f* moth

polio(mielitis) *f* polio(myelitis)

pólipo *m* polyp

politécnic|a *f* polytechnic. **~o** *a* polytechnic

polític|a *f* politics. **~o** *a* political; (*pariente*) -in-law. ● *m* politician. **padre m ~o** father-in-law

póliza *f* document; (*de seguros*) policy

polo *m* pole; (*helado*) ice lolly (*Brit*); (*juego*) polo. **~ helado** ice lolly (*Brit*). **~ norte** North Pole

Polonia *f* Poland

poltrona *f* armchair

polución *f* (*contaminación*) pollution

polv|areda *f* cloud of dust; (*fig, escándalo*) scandal. **~era** *f* compact. **~o** *m* powder; (*suciedad*) dust. **~os** *mpl* powder. **en ~o** powdered. **estar hecho ~o** be exhausted. **quitar el ~o** dust

pólvora *f* gunpowder; (*fuegos artificiales*) fireworks

polvor|iento *a* dusty. **~ón** *m* Spanish Christmas shortcake

poll|ada *f* brood. **~era** *f* (*para niños*) baby-walker; (*LAm, falda*) skirt. **~ería** *f* poultry shop. **~o** *m* chicken; (*gallo joven*) chick

pomada *f* ointment

pomelo *m* grapefruit

pómez *a*. **piedra f ~** pumice stone

pomp|a *f* bubble; (*esplendor*) pomp. **~as fúnebres** funeral. **~oso** *a* pompous; (*espléndido*) splendid

pómulo *m* cheek; (*hueso*) cheekbone
poncha|do *a* (*Mex*) punctured, flat. **~r** *vt* (*Mex*) puncture
ponche *m* punch
poncho *m* poncho
ponderar *vt* (*alabar*) speak highly of
poner [34] *vt* put; put on ⟨*ropa, obra de teatro, TV etc*⟩; (*suponer*) suppose; lay ⟨*la mesa, un huevo*⟩; (*hacer*) make; (*contribuir*) contribute; give ⟨*nombre*⟩; show ⟨*película, interés*⟩; open ⟨*una tienda*⟩; equip ⟨*una casa*⟩. ● *vi* lay. **~se** *vpr* put o.s.; (*volverse*) get; put on ⟨*ropa*⟩; (*sol*) set. **~ con** (*al teléfono*) put through to. **~ en claro** clarify. **~ por escrito** put into writing. **~ una multa** fine. **~se a** start to. **~se a mal con uno** fall out with s.o. **pongamos** let's suppose
pongo *vb véase* **poner**
poniente *m* west; (*viento*) west wind
pont|ificado *m* pontificate. **~ifical** *a* pontifical. **~ificar** [7] *vi* pontificate. **~ífice** *m* pontiff
pontón *m* pontoon
popa *f* stern
popelín *m* poplin
popul|acho *m* masses. **~ar** *a* popular; ⟨*lenguaje*⟩ colloquial. **~aridad** *f* popularity. **~arizar** [10] *vt* popularize. **~oso** *a* populous
póquer *m* poker
poquito *m* a little bit. ● *adv* a little
por *prep* for; (*para*) (in order) to; (*a través de*) through; (*a causa de*) because of; (*como agente*) by; (*en matemática*) times; (*como función*) as; (*en lugar de*) instead of. **~ la calle** along the street. **~ mí** as for me, for my part. **~ si** in case. **~ todo el país** throughout the country. **50 kilómetros ~ hora** 50 kilometres per hour
porcelana *f* china
porcentaje *m* percentage
porcino *a* pig. ● *m* small pig
porción *f* portion; (*de chocolate*) piece
pordiosero *m* beggar
porf|ía *f* persistence; (*disputa*) dispute. **~iado** *a* persistent. **~iar** [20] *vi* insist. **a ~ía** in competition
pormenor *m* detail
pornogr|afía *f* pornography. **~áfico** *a* pornographic
poro *m* pore. **~so** *a* porous
poroto *m* (*LAm, judía*) bean

porque *conj* because; (*para que*) so that
porqué *m* reason
porquería *f* filth; (*basura*) rubbish; (*grosería*) dirty trick
porra *f* club; (*culin*) fritter
porrón *m* wine jug (with a long spout)
portaaviones *m invar* aircraft-carrier
portada *f* façade; (*de libro*) title page
portador *m* bearer
porta|equipaje(s) *m invar* boot (*Brit*), trunk (*Amer*); (*encima del coche*) roof-rack. **~estandarte** *m* standard-bearer
portal *m* hall; (*puerta principal*) main entrance; (*soportal*) porch
porta|lámparas *m invar* socket. **~ligas** *m invar* suspender belt. **~monedas** *m invar* purse
portarse *vpr* behave
portátil *a* portable
portavoz *m* megaphone; (*fig, persona*) spokesman
portazgo *m* toll
portazo *m* bang. **dar un ~** slam the door
porte *m* transport; (*precio*) carriage. **~ador** *m* carrier
portento *m* marvel
porteño *a* (*de Buenos Aires*) from Buenos Aires. ● *m* person from Buenos Aires
porter|ía *f* caretaker's lodge, porter's lodge; (*en deportes*) goal. **~o** *m* caretaker, porter; (*en deportes*) goalkeeper. **~o automático** intercom (*fam*)
portezuela *f* small door; (*auto*) door
pórtico *m* portico
portill|a *f* gate; (*en barco*) porthole. **~o** *m* opening
portorriqueño *a* Puerto Rican
Portugal *m* Portugal
portugués *a* & *m* Portuguese
porvenir *m* future
posada *f* guest house; (*mesón*) inn
posaderas *fpl* (*fam*) bottom
posar *vt* put. ● *vi* ⟨*pájaro*⟩ perch; ⟨*modelo*⟩ sit. **~se** *vpr* settle
posdata *f* postscript
pose|edor *m* owner. **~er** [18] *vt* have, own; (*saber*) know well. **~ído** *a* possessed. **~sión** *f* possession. **~sionar** *vt*. **~sionar de** hand over. **~sionarse** *vpr*. **~sionarse de** take possession of. **~sivo** *a* possessive
posfechar *vt* postdate

posguerra f post-war years
posib|ilidad f possibility. ~le a possible. **de ser** ~le if possible. **en lo** ~le as far as possible. **hacer todo lo** ~le **para** do everything possible to. **si es** ~le if possible
posición f position
positivo a positive
poso m sediment
posponer [34] vt put after; (diferir) postpone
posta f. **a** ~ on purpose
postal a postal. ● f postcard
poste m pole
postergar [12] vt pass over; (diferir) postpone
posteri|dad f posterity. ~**or** a back; (ulterior) later. ~**ormente** adv later
postigo m door; (contraventana) shutter
postizo a false, artificial. ● m hairpiece
postra|do a prostrate. ~**r** vt prostrate. ~**rse** vpr prostrate o.s.
postre m dessert, sweet (Brit). **de** ~ for dessert
postular vt postulate; collect ⟨dinero⟩
póstumo a posthumous
postura f position, stance
potable a drinkable; ⟨agua⟩ drinking
potaje m vegetable stew
potasio m potassium
pote m jar
poten|cia f power. ~**cial** a & m potential. ~**te** a powerful. **en** ~**cia** potential
potingue m (fam) concoction
potr|a f filly. ~**o** m colt; (en gimnasia) horse. **tener** ~**a** be lucky
pozo m well; (hoyo seco) pit; (de mina) shaft
pozole m (Mex) stew
práctica f practice; (destreza) skill. **en la** ~ in practice. **poner en** ~ put into practice
practica|ble a practicable. ~**nte** a & f nurse. ~**r** [7] vt practise; play ⟨deportes⟩; (ejecutar) carry out
práctico a practical; (diestro) skilled. ● m practitioner
prad|era f meadow; (terreno grande) prairie. ~**o** m meadow
pragmático a pragmatic
preámbulo m preamble
precario a precarious
precaución f precaution; (cautela) caution. **con** ~ cautiously

precaver vt guard against
precede|ncia f precedence; (prioridad) priority. ~**nte** a preceding. ● m precedent. ~**r** vt/i precede
precepto m precept. ~**r** m tutor
precia|do a valuable; (estimado) esteemed. ~**rse** vpr boast
precinto m seal
precio m price. ~ **de venta al público** retail price. **al** ~ **de** at the cost of. **no tener** ~ be priceless. ¿**qué** ~ **tiene?** how much is it?
precios|idad f value; (cosa preciosa) beautiful thing. ~**o** a precious; (bonito) beautiful. **¡es una** ~**idad!** it's beautiful!
precipicio m precipice
precipita|ción f precipitation. ~**damente** adv hastily. ~**do** a hasty. ~**r** vt hurl; (acelerar) accelerate; (apresurar) hasten. ~**rse** vpr throw o.s.; (correr) rush; (actuar sin reflexionar) act rashly
precis|amente a exactly. ~**ar** vt require; (determinar) determine. ~**ión** f precision; (necesidad) need. ~**o** a precise; (necesario) necessary
preconcebido a preconceived
precoz a early; ⟨niño⟩ precocious
precursor m forerunner
predecesor m predecessor
predecir [46]; o [46, pero imperativo **predice**, futuro y condicional regulares] vt foretell
predestina|ción f predestination. ~**r** vt predestine
prédica f sermon
predicamento m influence
predicar [7] vt/i preach
predicción f prediction; (del tiempo) forecast
predilec|ción f predilection. ~**to** a favourite
predisponer [34] vt predispose
predomin|ante a predominant. ~**ar** vt dominate. ● vi predominate. ~**io** m predominance
preeminente a pre-eminent
prefabricado a prefabricated
prefacio m preface
prefect|o m prefect. ~**ura** f prefecture
prefer|encia f preference. ~**ente** a preferential. ~**ible** a preferable. ~**ido** a favourite. ~**ir** [4] vt prefer. **de** ~**encia** preferably
prefigurar vt foreshadow
prefij|ar vt fix beforehand; (gram) prefix. ~**o** m prefix; (telefónico) dialling code

preg|ón *m* announcement. **~onar** *vt* announce
pregunta *f* question. **~r** *vt/i* ask. **~rse** *vpr* wonder. **hacer ~s** ask questions
prehistórico *a* prehistoric
preju|icio *m* prejudice. **~zgar** [12] *vt* prejudge
prelado *m* prelate
preliminar *a & m* preliminary
preludio *m* prelude
premarital *a*, **prematrimonial** *a* premarital
prematuro *a* premature
premedita|ción *f* premeditation. **~r** *vt* premeditate
premi|ar *vt* give a prize to; (*recompensar*) reward. **~o** *m* prize; (*recompensa*) reward; (*com*) premium. **~o gordo** first prize
premonición *f* premonition
premura *f* urgency; (*falta*) lack
prenatal *a* antenatal
prenda *f* pledge; (*de vestir*) article of clothing, garment; (*de cama etc*) linen. **~s** *fpl* (*cualidades*) talents; (*juego*) forfeits. **~r** *vt* captivate. **~rse** *vpr* be captivated (**de** by); (*enamorarse*) fall in love (**de** with)
prender *vt* capture; (*sujetar*) fasten. ● *vi* catch; (*arraigar*) take root. **~se** *vpr* (*encenderse*) catch fire
prensa *f* press. **~r** *vt* press
preñado *a* pregnant; (*fig*) full
preocupa|ción *f* worry. **~do** *a* worried. **~r** *vt* worry. **~rse** *vpr* worry. **~rse de** look after. **¡no te preocupes!** don't worry!
prepara|ción *f* preparation. **~do** *a* prepared. ● *m* preparation. **~r** *vt* prepare. **~rse** *vpr* get ready. **~tivo** *a* preparatory. ● *m* preparation. **~torio** *a* preparatory
preponderancia *f* preponderance
preposición *f* preposition
prepotente *a* powerful; (*fig*) presumptuous
prerrogativa *f* prerogative
presa *f* (*acción*) capture; (*cosa*) catch; (*embalse*) dam
presagi|ar *vt* presage. **~o** *m* omen; (*premonición*) premonition
présbita *a* long-sighted
presb|iteriano *a & m* Presbyterian. **~iterio** *m* presbytery. **~ítero** *m* priest
prescindir *vi.* **~ de** do without; (*deshacerse de*) dispense with

prescri|bir (*pp* **prescrito**) *vt* prescribe. **~pción** *f* prescription
presencia *f* presence; (*aspecto*) appearance. **~r** *vt* be present at; (*ver*) witness. **en ~ de** in the presence of
presenta|ble *a* presentable. **~ción** *f* presentation; (*aspecto*) appearance; (*de una persona a otra*) introduction. **~dor** *m* presenter. **~r** *vt* present; (*ofrecer*) offer; (*hacer conocer*) introduce; show (*película*). **~rse** *vpr* present o.s.; (*hacerse conocer*) introduce o.s.; (*aparecer*) turn up
presente *a* present; (*este*) this. ● *m* present. **los ~s** those present. **tener ~** remember
presenti|miento *m* presentiment; (*de algo malo*) foreboding. **~r** [4] *vt* have a presentiment of
preserva|ción *f* preservation. **~r** *vt* preserve. **~tivo** *m* condom
presiden|cia *f* presidency; (*de asamblea*) chairmanship. **~cial** *a* presidential. **~ta** *f* (*woman*) president. **~te** *m* president; (*de asamblea*) chairman. **~te del gobierno** leader of the government, prime minister
presidi|ario *m* convict. **~o** *m* prison
presidir *vt* preside over
presilla *f* fastener
presi|ón *f* pressure. **~onar** *vt* press; (*fig*) put pressure on. **a ~ón** under pressure. **hacer ~ón** press
preso *a* under arrest; (*fig*) stricken. ● *m* prisoner
presta|do *a* (*a uno*) lent; (*de uno*) borrowed. **~mista** *m & f* moneylender. **pedir ~do** borrow
préstamo *m* loan; (*acción de pedir prestado*) borrowing
prestar *vt* lend; give ⟨*ayuda etc*⟩; pay ⟨*atención*⟩. ● *vi* lend
prestidigita|ción *f* conjuring. **~dor** *m* magician
prestigio *m* prestige. **~so** *a* prestigious
presu|mido *a* presumptuous. **~mir** *vt* presume. ● *vi* be conceited. **~nción** *f* presumption. **~nto** *a* presumed. **~ntuoso** *a* presumptuous
presup|oner [34] *vt* presuppose. **~uesto** *m* budget
presuroso *a* quick
preten|cioso *a* pretentious. **~der** *vt* try to; (*afirmar*) claim; (*solicitar*) apply for; (*cortejar*) court. **~dido** *a* so-called. **~diente** *m* pretender; (*a*

una mujer) suitor. **~sión** *f* pretension; (*aspiración*) aspiration

pretérito *m* preterite, past

pretexto *m* pretext. **a ~ de** on the pretext of

prevalec|er [11] *vi* prevail. **~iente** *a* prevalent

prevalerse [42] *vpr* take advantage

preven|ción *f* prevention; (*prejuicio*) prejudice. **~ido** *a* (*precavido*) cautious. **~ir** [53] *vt* prepare; (*proveer*) provide; (*precaver*) prevent; (*advertir*) warn. **~tivo** *a* preventive

prever [43] *vt* foresee; (*prepararse*) plan

previo *a* previous

previs|ible *a* predictable. **~ión** *f* forecast; (*prudencia*) prudence. **~ión de tiempo** weather forecast. **~to** *a* foreseen

prima *f* (*pariente*) cousin; (*cantidad*) bonus

primario *a* primary

primate *m* primate; (*fig, persona*) important person

primavera *f* spring. **~l** *a* spring

primer *a véase* **primero**

primer|a *f* (*auto*) first (gear); (*en tren etc*) first class. **~o** *a* (*delante de nombre masculino en singular* **primer**) first; (*principal*) main; (*anterior*) former; (*mejor*) best. ● *n* (the) first. ● *adv* first. **~a enseñanza** primary education. **a ~os de** at the beginning of. **de ~a** first-class

primitivo *a* primitive

primo *m* cousin; (*fam*) fool. **hacer el ~** be taken for a ride

primogénito *a & m* first-born, eldest

primor *m* delicacy; (*cosa*) beautiful thing

primordial *a* basic

princesa *f* princess

principado *m* principality

principal *a* principal. ● *m* (*jefe*) head, boss (*fam*)

príncipe *m* prince

principi|ante *m & f* beginner. **~ar** *vt/i* begin, start. **~o** *m* beginning; (*moral, idea*) principle; (*origen*) origin. **al ~o** at first. **a ~o(s) de** at the beginning of. **dar ~o a** a start. **desde el ~o** from the outset. **en ~o** in principle. **~os** *mpl* (*nociones*) rudiments

pring|oso *a* greasy. **~ue** *m* dripping; (*mancha*) grease mark

prior *m* prior. **~ato** *m* priory

prioridad *f* priority

prisa *f* hurry, haste. **a ~** quickly. **a toda ~** (*fam*) as quickly as possible. **correr ~** be urgent. **darse ~** hurry (up). **de ~** quickly. **tener ~** be in a hurry

prisi|ón *f* prison; (*encarcelamiento*) imprisonment. **~onero** *m* prisoner

prism|a *m* prism. **~áticos** *mpl* binoculars

priva|ción *f* deprivation. **~do** *a* (*particular*) private. **~r** *vt* deprive (**de** of); (*prohibir*) prevent (**de** from). ● *vi* be popular. **~tivo** *a* exclusive (**de** to)

privilegi|ado *a* privileged; (*muy bueno*) exceptional. **~o** *m* privilege

pro *prep* for. ● *m* advantage. ● *pref* pro-. **el ~ y el contra** the pros and cons. **en ~ de** on behalf of. **los ~s y los contras** the pros and cons

proa *f* bows

probab|ilidad *f* probability. **~le** *a* probable, likely. **~lemente** *adv* probably

proba|dor *m* fitting-room. **~r** [2] *vt* try; try on (*ropa*); (*demostrar*) prove. ● *vi* try. **~rse** *vpr* try on

probeta *f* test-tube

problem|a *m* problem. **~ático** *a* problematic

procaz *a* insolent

proced|encia *f* origin. **~ente** *a* (*razonable*) reasonable. **~ente de** (coming) from. **~er** *m* conduct. ● *vi* proceed. **~er contra** start legal proceedings against. **~er de** come from. **~imiento** *m* procedure; (*sistema*) process; (*jurid*) proceedings

procesador *m*. **~ de textos** word processor

procesal *a*. **costas ~es** legal costs

procesamiento *m* processing. **~ de textos** word-processing

procesar *vt* prosecute

procesión *f* procession

proceso *m* process; (*jurid*) trial; (*transcurso*) course

proclama *f* proclamation. **~ción** *f* proclamation. **~r** *vt* proclaim

procrea|ción *f* procreation. **~r** *vt* procreate

procura|dor *m* attorney, solicitor. **~r** *vt* try; (*obtener*) get; (*dar*) give

prodigar [12] *vt* lavish. **~se** *vpr* do one's best

prodigio *m* prodigy; (*milagro*) miracle. ~**ioso** *a* prodigious

pródigo *a* prodigal

produc|ción *f* production. ~**ir** [47] *vt* produce; (*causar*) cause. ~**irse** *vpr* (*aparecer*) appear; (*suceder*) happen. ~**tivo** *a* productive. ~**to** *m* product. ~**tor** *m* producer. ~**to derivado** by-product. ~**tos agrícolas** farm produce. ~**tos de belleza** cosmetics. ~**tos de consumo** consumer goods

proeza *f* exploit

profan|ación *f* desecration. ~**ar** *vt* desecrate. ~**o** *a* profane

profecía *f* prophecy

proferir [4] *vt* utter; hurl (*insultos etc*)

profes|ar *vt* profess; practise (*profesión*). ~**ión** *f* profession. ~**ional** *a* professional. ~**or** *m* teacher; (*en universidad etc*) lecturer. ~**orado** *m* teaching profession; (*conjunto de profesores*) staff

prof|eta *m* prophet. ~**ético** *a* prophetic. ~**etizar** [10] *vt/i* prophesize

prófugo *a* & *m* fugitive

profund|idad *f* depth. ~**o** *a* deep; (*fig*) profound

profus|ión *f* profusion. ~**o** *a* profuse. **con** ~**ión** profusely

progenie *f* progeny

programa *m* programme; (*de ordenador*) program; (*de estudios*) curriculum. ~**ción** *f* programming; (*TV etc*) programmes; (*en periódico*) TV guide. ~**r** *vt* programme; program (*ordenador*). ~**dor** *m* computer programmer

progres|ar *vi* (make) progress. ~**ión** *f* progression. ~**ista** *a* progressive. ~**ivo** *a* progressive. ~**o** *m* progress. **hacer** ~**os** make progress

prohibi|ción *f* prohibition. ~**do** *a* forbidden. ~**r** *vt* forbid. ~**tivo** *a* prohibitive

prójimo *m* fellow man

prole *f* offspring

proletari|ado *m* proletariat. ~**o** *a* & *m* proletarian

prol|iferación *f* proliferation. ~**iferar** *vi* proliferate. ~**ífico** *a* prolific

prolijo *a* long-winded, extensive

prólogo *m* prologue

prolongar [12] *vt* prolong; (*alargar*) lengthen. ~**se** *vpr* go on

promedio *m* average

prome|sa *f* promise. ~**ter** *vt/i* promise. ~**terse** *vpr* (*novios*) get engaged. ~**térselas muy felices** have high hopes. ~**tida** *f* fiancée. ~**tido** *a* promised; (*novios*) engaged. ● *m* fiancé

prominen|cia *f* prominence. ~**te** *a* prominent

promiscu|idad *f* promiscuity. ~**o** *a* promiscuous

promoción *f* promotion

promontorio *m* promontory

promo|tor *m* promoter. ~**ver** [2] *vt* promote; (*causar*) cause

promulgar [12] *vt* promulgate

pronombre *m* pronoun

pron|osticar [7] *vt* predict. ~**óstico** *m* prediction; (*del tiempo*) forecast; (*med*) prognosis

pront|itud *f* quickness. ~**o** *a* quick; (*preparado*) ready. ● *adv* quickly; (*dentro de poco*) soon; (*temprano*) early. ● *m* urge. **al** ~**o** at first. **de** ~**o** suddenly. **por lo** ~**o** for the time being; (*al menos*) anyway. **tan** ~**o como** as soon as

pronuncia|ción *f* pronunciation. ~**miento** *m* revolt. ~**r** *vt* pronounce; deliver (*discurso*). ~**rse** *vpr* be pronounced; (*declarase*) declare o.s.; (*sublevarse*) rise up

propagación *f* propagation

propaganda *f* propaganda; (*anuncios*) advertising

propagar [12] *vt/i* propagate. ~**se** *vpr* spread

propano *m* propane

propasarse *vpr* go too far

propens|ión *f* inclination. ~**o** *a* inclined

propiamente *adv* exactly

propici|ar *vt* (*provocar*) cause, bring about. ~**o** *a* favourable

propie|dad *f* property; (*posesión*) possession. ~**tario** *m* owner

propina *f* tip

propio *a* own; (*característico*) typical; (*natural*) natural; (*apropiado*) proper. **de** ~ on purpose. **el médico** ~ the doctor himself

proponer [34] *vt* propose. ~**se** *vpr* propose

proporci|ón *f* proportion. ~**onado** *a* proportioned. ~**onal** *a* proportional. ~**onar** *vt* proportion; (*facilitar*) provide

proposición *f* proposition

propósito *m* intention. **a** ~ (*adrede*) on purpose; (*de paso*) incidentally.

a ～ de with regard to. **de ～** on purpose

propuesta *f* proposal

propuls|ar *vt* propel; (*fig*) promote. **～ión** *f* propulsion. **～ión a chorro** jet propulsion

prórroga *f* extension

prorrogar [12] *vt* extend

prorrumpir *vi* burst out

prosa *f* prose. **～ico** *a* prosaic

proscri|bir (*pp* **proscrito**) *vt* banish; (*prohibido*) ban. **～to** *a* banned. ● *m* exile; (*persona*) outlaw

prosecución *f* continuation

proseguir [5 & 13] *vt/i* continue

prospección *f* prospecting

prospecto *m* prospectus

prosper|ar *vi* prosper. **～idad** *f* prosperity; (*éxito*) success

próspero *a* prosperous. **¡P～ Año Nuevo!** Happy New Year!

prostit|ución *f* prostitution. **～uta** *f* prostitute

protagonista *m & f* protagonist

prote|cción *f* protection. **～ctor** *a* protective. ● *m* protector; (*patrocinador*) patron. **～ger** [14] *vt* protect. **～gida** *f* protegée. **～gido** *a* protected. ● *m* protegé

proteína *f* protein

protesta *f* protest; (*declaración*) protestation

protestante *a & m & f* (*relig*) Protestant

protestar *vt/i* protest

protocolo *m* protocol

protuberan|cia *f* protuberance. **～te** *a* protuberant

provecho *m* benefit. **¡buen ～!** enjoy your meal! **de ～** useful. **en ～ de** to the benefit of. **sacar ～ de** benefit from

proveer [18] (*pp* **proveído** *y* **provisto**) *vt* supply, provide

provenir [53] *vi* come (**de** from)

proverbi|al *a* proverbial. **～o** *m* proverb

providencia *f* providence. **～l** *a* providential

provincia *f* province. **～l** *a*, **～no** *a* provincial

provisi|ón *f* provision; (*medida*) measure. **～onal** *a* provisional

provisto *a* provided (**de** with)

provoca|ción *f* provocation. **～r** [7] *vt* provoke; (*causar*) cause. **～tivo** *a* provocative

próximamente *adv* soon

proximidad *f* proximity

próximo *a* next; (*cerca*) near

proyec|ción *f* projection. **～tar** *vt* hurl; cast ‹*luz*›; show ‹*película*›. **～til** *m* missile. **～to** *m* plan. **～to de ley** bill. **～tor** *m* projector. **en ～to** planned

pruden|cia *f* prudence. **～nte** *a* prudent, sensible

prueba *f* proof; (*examen*) test; (*de ropa*) fitting. **a ～** on trial. **a ～ de** proof against. **a ～ de agua** waterproof. **en ～ de** in proof of. **poner a ～** test

pruebo *vb véase* **probar**

psicoan|álisis *f* psychoanalysis. **～alista** *m & f* psychoanalyst. **～alizar** [10] *vt* psychoanalyse

psicodélico *a* psychedelic

psic|ología *f* psychology. **～ológico** *a* psychological. **～ólogo** *m* psychologist

psicópata *m & f* psychopath

psicosis *f* psychosis

psique *f* psyche

psiqui|atra *m & f* psychiatrist. **～atría** *f* psychiatry. **～átrico** *a* psychiatric

psíquico *a* psychic

ptas, pts *abrev* (*pesetas*) pesetas

púa *f* sharp point; (*bot*) thorn; (*de erizo*) quill; (*de peine*) tooth; (*mus*) plectrum

pubertad *f* puberty

publica|ción *f* publication. **～r** [7] *vt* publish; (*anunciar*) announce

publici|dad *f* publicity; (*com*) advertising. **～tario** *a* advertising

público *a* public. ● *m* public; (*de espectáculo etc*) audience. **dar al ～** publish

puchero *m* cooking pot; (*guisado*) stew. **hacer ～s** (*fig, fam*) pout

pude *vb véase* **poder**

púdico *a* modest

pudiente *a* rich

pudín *m* pudding

pudor *m* modesty. **～oso** *a* modest

pudrir (*pp* **podrido**) *vt* rot; (*fig, molestar*) annoy. **～se** *vpr* rot

puebl|ecito *m* small village. **～o** *m* town; (*aldea*) village; (*nación*) nation, people

puedo *vb véase* **poder**

puente *m* bridge; (*fig, fam*) long weekend. **～ colgante** suspension bridge. **～ levadizo** drawbridge. **hacer ～** (*fam*) have a long weekend

puerco *a* filthy; (*grosero*) coarse. ● *m* pig. **～ espín** porcupine

pueril *a* childish

puerro *m* leek

puerta *f* door; (*en deportes*) goal; (*de ciudad*) gate. ~ **principal** main entrance. **a** ~ **cerrada** behind closed doors

puerto *m* port; (*fig, refugio*) refuge; (*entre montañas*) pass. ~ **franco** free port

Puerto Rico *m* Puerto Rico

puertorriqueño *a* & *m* Puerto Rican

pues *adv* (*entonces*) then; (*bueno*) well. ● *conj* since

puest|a *f* setting; (*en juegos*) bet. ~**a de sol** sunset. ~**a en escena** staging. ~**a en marcha** starting. ~**o** *a* put; (*vestido*) dressed. ● *m* place; (*empleo*) position, job; (*en mercado etc*) stall. ● *conj.* ~**o que** since. ~**o de socorro** first aid post

pugna *f* fight. ~**r** *vt* fight

puja *f* effort; (*en subasta*) bid. ~**r** *vt* struggle; (*en subasta*) bid

pulcro *a* neat

pulga *f* flea; (*de juego*) tiddly-wink. **tener malas** ~**s** be bad-tempered

pulga|da *f* inch. ~**r** *m* thumb; (*del pie*) big toe

puli|do *a* neat. ~**mentar** *vt* polish. ~**mento** *m* polishing; (*substancia*) polish. ~**r** *vt* polish; (*suavizar*) smooth

pulm|ón *m* lung. ~**onar** *a* pulmonary. ~**onía** *f* pneumonia

pulpa *f* pulp

pulpería *f* (*LAm*) grocer's shop (*Brit*), grocery store (*Amer*)

púlpito *m* pulpit

pulpo *m* octopus

pulque *m* (*Mex*) pulque, alcoholic Mexican drink

pulsa|ción *f* pulsation. ~**dor** *a* pulsating. ● *m* button. ~**r** *vt* (*mus*) play

pulsera *f* bracelet; (*de reloj*) strap

pulso *m* pulse; (*muñeca*) wrist; (*firmeza*) steady hand; (*fuerza*) strength; (*fig, tacto*) tact. **tomar el** ~ **a uno** take s.o.'s pulse

pulular *vi* teem with

pulveriza|dor *m* (*de perfume*) atomizer. ~**r** [10] *vt* pulverize; atomize ‹*líquido*›

pulla *f* cutting remark

pum *int* bang!

puma *m* puma

puna *f* puna, high plateau

punitivo *a* punitive

punta *f* point; (*extremo*) tip; (*clavo*) (small) nail. **estar de** ~ be in a bad mood. **estar de** ~ **con uno** be at odds with s.o. **ponerse de** ~ **con uno** fall out with s.o.. **sacar** ~ **a** sharpen; (*fig*) find fault with

puntada *f* stitch

puntal *m* prop, support

puntapié *m* kick

puntear *vt* mark; (*mus*) pluck

puntera *f* toe

puntería *f* aim; (*destreza*) markmanship

puntiagudo *a* sharp, pointed

puntilla *f* (*encaje*) lace. **de** ~**s** on tiptoe

punto *m* point; (*señal*) dot; (*de examen*) mark; (*lugar*) spot, place; (*de taxis*) stand; (*momento*) moment; (*punto final*) full stop (*Brit*), period (*Amer*); (*puntada*) stitch; (*de tela*) mesh. ~ **de admiración** exclamation mark. ~ **de arranque** starting point. ~ **de exclamación** exclamation mark. ~ **de interrogación** question mark. ~ **de vista** point of view. ~ **final** full stop. ~ **muerto** (*auto*) neutral (gear). ~ **y aparte** full stop, new paragraph (*Brit*), period, new paragraph (*Amer*). ~ **y coma** semicolon. **a** ~ on time; (*listo*) ready. **a** ~ **de** on the point of. **de** ~ knitted. **dos** ~**s** colon. **en** ~ exactly. **hacer** ~ knit. **hasta cierto** ~ to a certain extent

puntuación *f* punctuation; (*en deportes, acción*) scoring; (*en deportes, número de puntos*) score

puntual *a* punctual; (*exacto*) accurate. ~**idad** *f* punctuality; (*exactitud*) accuracy

puntuar [21] *vt* punctuate. ● *vi* score

punza|da *f* prick; (*dolor*) pain; (*fig*) pang. ~**nte** *a* sharp. ~**r** [10] *vt* prick

puñado *m* handful. **a** ~**s** by the handful

puñal *m* dagger. ~**ada** *f* stab

puñ|etazo *m* punch. ~**o** *m* fist; (*de ropa*) cuff; (*mango*) handle. **de su** ~**o (y letra)** in his own handwriting

pupa *f* spot; (*en los labios*) cold sore. **hacer** ~ hurt. **hacerse** ~ hurt o.s.

pupila *f* pupil

pupitre *m* desk

puquio *m* (*Arg*) spring

puré *m* purée; (*sopa*) thick soup. ~ **de patatas** mashed potato

pureza *f* purity

purga *f* purge. ~**r** [12] *vt* purge. ~**torio** *m* purgatory

purifica|ción *f* purification. **~r** [7] *vt* purify

purista *m & f* purist

puritano *a* puritanical. ● *m* puritan

puro *a* pure; *(cielo)* clear; *(fig)* simple. ● *m* cigar. **de ~** so. **de pura casualidad** by sheer chance

púrpura *f* purple

purpúreo *a* purple

pus *m* pus

puse *vb véase* **poner**

pusilánime *a* cowardly

pústula *f* spot

puta *f* whore

putrefacción *f* putrefaction

pútrido *a* rotten, putrid

Q

que *pron rel (personas, sujeto)* who; *(personas, complemento) (cosas)* which, that. ● *conj* that. **¡~ tengan Vds buen viaje!** have a good journey! **¡que venga!** let him come! **~ venga o no venga** whether he comes or not. **a que** I bet. **creo que tiene razón** I think (that) he is right. **de ~** from which. **yo ~ tú** if I were you

qué *a (con sustantivo)* what; *(con a o adv)* how. ● *pron* what. **¡~ bonito!** how nice. **¿en ~ piensas?** what are you thinking about?

quebra|da *f* gorge; *(paso)* pass. **~dizo** *a* fragile. **~do** *a* broken; *(com)* bankrupt. ● *m (math)* fraction. **~dura** *f* fracture; *(hondonada)* gorge. **~ntar** *vt* break; *(debilitar)* weaken. **~nto** *m (pérdida)* loss; *(daño)* damage. **~r** [1] *vt* break. ● *vi* break; *(com)* go bankrupt. **~rse** *vpr* break

quechua *a & m & f* Quechuan

queda *f* curfew

quedar *vi* stay, remain; *(estar)* be; *(faltar, sobrar)* be left. **~ bien** come off well. **~se** *vpr* stay. **~ con** arrange to meet. **~ en** agree to. **~ en nada** come to nothing. **~ por** (+ *infinitivo*) remain to be (+ *pp*)

quehacer *m* job. **~es domésticos** household chores

quej|a *f* complaint; *(de dolor)* moan. **~arse** *vpr* complain (**de** about); *(gemir)* moan. **~ido** *m* moan. **~oso** *a* complaining

quema|do *a* burnt; *(fig, fam)* bitter. **~dor** *m* burner. **~dura** *f* burn. **~r** *vt* burn; *(prender fuego a)* set fire to. ● *vi* burn. **~rse** *vpr* burn o.s.; *(consumirse)* burn up; *(con el sol)* get sunburnt. **~rropa** *adv.* **a ~rropa** point-blank

quena *f* Indian flute

quepo *vb véase* **caber**

queque *m (Mex)* cake

querella *f (riña)* quarrel, dispute; *(jurid)* charge

quer|er [35] *vt* want; *(amar)* love; *(necesitar)* need. **~er decir** mean. **~ido** *a* dear; *(amado)* loved. ● *m* darling; *(amante)* lover. **como quiera que** since; *(de cualquier modo)* however. **cuando quiera que** whenever. **donde quiera** wherever. **¿quieres darme ese libro?** would you pass me that book? **quiere llover** it's trying to rain. **¿quieres un helado?** would you like an ice-cream? **quisiera ir a la playa** I'd like to go to the beach. **sin ~er** without meaning to

queroseno *m* kerosene

querubín *m* cherub

ques|adilla *f* cheesecake; *(Mex, empanadilla)* pie. **~o** *m* cheese. **~o de bola** Edam cheese

quiá *int* never!, surely not!

quicio *m* frame. **sacar de ~ a uno** infuriate s.o.

quiebra *f* break; *(fig)* collapse; *(com)* bankruptcy

quiebro *m* dodge

quien *pron rel (sujeto)* who; *(complemento)* whom

quién *pron interrogativo (sujeto)* who; *(tras preposición)* whom. **¿de ~?** whose. **¿de ~ son estos libros?** whose are these books?

quienquiera *pron* whoever

quiero *vb véase* **querer**

quiet|o *a* still; *(inmóvil)* motionless; *(carácter etc)* calm. **~ud** *f* stillness

quijada *f* jaw

quilate *m* carat

quilla *f* keel

quimera *f (fig)* illusion

químic|a *f* chemistry. **~o** *a* chemical. ● *m* chemist

quincalla *f* hardware; *(de adorno)* trinket

quince *a & m* fifteen. **~ días** a fortnight. **~na** *f* fortnight. **~nal** *a* fortnightly

quincuagésimo *a* fiftieth

quiniela f pools coupon. **~s** fpl (football) pools

quinientos a & m five hundred

quinino m quinine

quinqué m oil-lamp; (fig, fam) shrewdness

quinquenio m (period of) five years

quinta f (casa) villa

quintaesencia f quintessence

quintal m a hundred kilograms

quinteto m quintet

quinto a & m fifth

quiosco m kiosk; (en jardín) summerhouse; (en parque etc) bandstand

quirúrgico a surgical

quise vb véase **querer**

quisque pron. **cada ~** (fam) (absolutely) everybody

quisquill|a f trifle; (camarón) shrimp. **~oso** a irritable; (chinchorrero) fussy

quita|manchas m invar stain remover. **~nieves** m invar snow plough. **~r** vt remove, take away; take off ⟨ropa⟩; (robar) steal. **~ndo** (a excepción de, fam) apart from. **~rse** vpr be removed; take off ⟨ropa⟩. **~rse de** (no hacerlo más) stop. **~rse de en medio** get out of the way. **~sol** m invar sunshade

Quito m Quito

quizá(s) adv perhaps

quórum m quorum

R

rábano m radish. **~ picante** horseradish. **me importa un ~** I couldn't care less

rabi|a f rabies; (fig) rage. **~ar** vi (de dolor) be in great pain; (estar enfadado) be furious; (fig, tener ganas, fam) long. **~ar por algo** long for sth. **~ar por hacer algo** long to do sth. **~eta** f tantrum. **dar ~a** infuriate

rabino m Rabbi

rabioso a rabid; (furioso) furious; ⟨dolor etc⟩ violent

rabo m tail

racial a racial

racimo m bunch

raciocinio m reason; (razonamiento) reasoning

ración f share, ration; (de comida) portion

racional a rational. **~izar** [10] vt rationalize

racionar vt (limitar) ration; (repartir) ration out

racis|mo m racism. **~ta** a racist

racha f gust of wind; (fig) spate

radar m radar

radiación f radiation

radiactiv|idad f radioactivity. **~o** a radioactive

radiador m radiator

radial a radial

radiante a radiant

radical a & m & f radical

radicar [7] vi (estar) be. **~ en** (fig) lie in

radio m radius; (de rueda) spoke; (elemento metálico) radium. **●** f radio

radioactiv|idad f radioactivity. **~o** a radioactive

radio|difusión f broadcasting. **~emisora** f radio station. **~escucha** m & f listener

radiografía f radiography

radi|ología f radiology. **~ólogo** m radiologist

radioterapia f radiotherapy

radioyente m & f listener

raer [36] vt scrape off

ráfaga f (de viento) gust; (de luz) flash; (de ametralladora) burst

rafia f raffia

raído a threadbare

raigambre f roots; (fig) tradition

raíz f root. **a ~ de** immediately after. **echar raíces** (fig) settle

raja f split; (culin) slice. **~r** vt split. **~rse** vpr split; (fig) back out

rajatabla. a ~ vigorously

ralea f sort

ralo a sparse

ralla|dor m grater. **~r** vt grate

rama f branch. **~je** m branches. **~l** m branch. **en ~** raw

rambla f gully; (avenida) avenue

ramera f prostitute

ramifica|ción f ramification. **~rse** [7] vpr branch out

ramilla f twig

ramillete m bunch

ramo m branch; (de flores) bouquet

rampa f ramp, slope

ramplón a vulgar

rana f frog. **ancas** fpl **de ~** frogs' legs. **no ser ~** not be stupid

rancio a rancid; ⟨vino⟩ old; (fig) ancient

ranch|ero *m* cook; (*LAm, jefe de rancho*) farmer. **~o** *m* (*LAm*) ranch, farm

rango *m* rank

ranúnculo *m* buttercup

ranura *f* groove; (*para moneda*) slot

rapar *vt* shave; crop (*pelo*)

rapaz *a* rapacious; (*ave*) of prey. ● *m* bird of prey

rapidez *f* speed

rápido *a* fast, quick. ● *adv* quickly. ● *m* (*tren*) express. **~s** *mpl* rapids

rapiña *f* robbery. **ave** *f* **de ~** bird of prey

rapsodia *f* rhapsody

rapt|ar *vt* kidnap. **~o** *m* kidnapping; (*de ira etc*) fit; (*éxtasis*) ecstasy

raqueta *f* racquet

raramente *adv* seldom, rarely

rarefacción *f* rarefaction

rar|eza *f* rarity; (*cosa rara*) oddity. **~o** *a* rare; (*extraño*) odd. **es ~o que** it is strange that. **¡qué ~o!** how strange!

ras *m.* **a ~ de** level with

rasar *vt* level; (*rozar*) graze

rasca|cielos *m invar* skyscraper. **~dura** *f* scratch. **~r** [7] *vt* scratch; (*raspar*) scrape

rasgar [12] *vt* tear

rasgo *m* stroke. **~s** *mpl* (*facciones*) features

rasguear *vt* strum; (*fig, escribir*) write

rasguñ|ar *vt* scratch. **~o** *m* scratch

raso *a* (*llano*) flat; (*liso*) smooth; (*cielo*) clear; (*cucharada etc*) level; (*vuelo etc*) low. ● *m* satin. **al ~** in the open air. **soldado** *m* **~** private

raspa *f* (*de pescado*) backbone

raspa|dura *f* scratch; (*acción*) scratching. **~r** *vt* scratch; (*rozar*) scrape

rastr|a *f* rake. **a ~as** dragging. **~ear** *vt* track. **~eo** *m* dragging. **~ero** *a* creeping; (*vuelo*) low. **~illar** *vt* rake. **~illo** *m* rake. **~o** *m* rake; (*huella*) track; (*señal*) sign. **el R~o** the flea market in Madrid. **ni ~o** not a trace

rata *f* rat

rate|ar *vt* steal. **~ría** *f* pilfering. **~ro** *m* petty thief

ratifica|ción *f* ratification. **~r** [7] *vt* ratify

rato *m* moment, short time. **~s libres** spare time. **a ~s** at times. **hace un ~** a moment ago. **¡hasta otro ~!** (*fam*) see you soon! **pasar mal ~** have a rough time

rat|ón *m* mouse. **~onera** *f* mousetrap; (*madriguera*) mouse hole

raud|al *m* torrent; (*fig*) floods. **~o** *a* swift

raya *f* line; (*lista*) stripe; (*de pelo*) parting. **~r** *vt* rule. ● *vi* border (**con** on). **a ~s** striped. **pasar de la ~** go too far

rayo *m* ray; (*descarga eléctrica*) lightning. **~s X** X-rays

raza *f* race; (*de animal*) breed. **de ~** (*caballo*) thoroughbred; (*perro*) pedigree

raz|ón *f* reason. **a ~ón de** at the rate of. **perder la ~ón** go out of one's mind. **tener ~ón** be right. **~onable** *a* reasonable. **~onamiento** *m* reasoning. **~onar** *vt* reason out. ● *vi* reason

re *m* D; (*solfa*) re

reac|ción *f* reaction. **~cionario** *a* & *m* reactionary. **~ción en cadena** chain reaction. **~tor** *m* reactor; (*avión*) jet

real *a* real; (*de rey etc*) royal. ● *m* real, old Spanish coin

realce *m* relief; (*fig*) splendour

realidad *f* reality; (*verdad*) truth. **en ~** in fact

realis|mo *m* realism. **~ta** *a* realistic. ● *m* & *f* realist; (*monárquico*) royalist

realiza|ción *f* fulfilment. **~r** [10] *vt* carry out; make (*viaje*); achieve (*meta*); (*vender*) sell. **~rse** *vpr* (*plan etc*) be carried out; (*sueño, predicción etc*) come true; (*persona*) fulfil o.s.

realzar [10] *vt* (*fig*) enhance

reanima|ción *f* revival. **~r** *vt* revive. **~rse** *vpr* revive

reanudar *vt* resume; renew (*amistad*)

reaparecer [11] *vi* reappear

rearm|ar *vt* rearm. **~e** *m* rearmament

reavivar *vt* revive

rebaja *f* reduction. **~do** *a* (*precio*) reduced. **~r** *vt* lower. **en ~s** in the sale

rebanada *f* slice

rebaño *m* herd; (*de ovejas*) flock

rebasar *vt* exceed; (*dejar atrás*) leave behind

rebatir *vt* refute

rebel|arse *vpr* rebel. **~de** *a* rebellious. ● *m* rebel. **~día** *f* rebelliousness. **~ión** *f* rebellion

reblandecer [11] *vt* soften

rebosa|nte *a* overflowing. **~r** *vi* overflow; (*abundar*) abound

rebot|ar *vt* bounce; (*rechazar*) repel. • *vi* bounce; ‹*bala*› ricochet. **~e** *m* bounce, rebound. **de ~e** on the rebound

rebozar [10] *vt* wrap up; (*culin*) coat in batter

rebullir [22] *vi* stir

rebusca|do *a* affected. **~r** [7] *vt* search thoroughly

rebuznar *vi* bray

recabar *vt* claim

recado *m* errand; (*mensaje*) message. **dejar ~** leave a message

reca|er [29] *vi* fall back; (*med*) relapse; (*fig*) fall. **~ída** *f* relapse

recalcar [7] *vt* squeeze; (*fig*) stress

recalcitrante *a* recalcitrant

recalentar [1] *vt* (*de nuevo*) reheat; (*demasiado*) overheat

recamar *vt* embroider

recámara *f* small room; (*de arma de fuego*) chamber; (*LAm, dormitorio*) bedroom

recambio *m* change; (*de pluma etc*) refill. **~s** *mpl* spare parts. **de ~** spare

recapitula|ción *f* summing up. **~r** *vt* sum up

recarg|ar [12] *vt* overload; (*aumentar*) increase; recharge ‹*batería*›. **~o** *m* increase

recat|ado *a* modest. **~ar** *vt* hide. **~arse** *vpr* hide o.s. away; (*actuar discretamente*) act discreetly. **~o** *m* prudence; (*modestia*) modesty. **sin ~arse, sin ~o** openly

recauda|ción *f* (*cantidad*) takings. **~dor** *m* tax collector. **~r** *vt* collect

recel|ar *vt/i* suspect. **~o** *m* distrust; (*temor*) fear. **~oso** *a* suspicious

recepci|ón *f* reception. **~onista** *m & f* receptionist

receptáculo *m* receptacle

recept|ivo *a* receptive. **~or** *m* receiver

recesión *f* recession

receta *f* recipe; (*med*) prescription

recib|imiento *m* (*acogida*) welcome. **~ir** *vt* receive; (*acoger*) welcome. • *vi* entertain. **~irse** *vpr* graduate. **~o** *m* receipt. **acusar ~o** acknowledge receipt

reci|én *adv* recently; ‹*casado, nacido etc*› newly. **~ente** *a* recent; (*culin*) fresh

recinto *m* enclosure

recio *a* strong; ‹*voz*› loud. • *adv* hard; (*en voz alta*) loudly

recipiente *m* (*persona*) recipient; (*cosa*) receptacle

recíproco *a* reciprocal. **a la recíproca** vice versa

recita|l *m* recital; (*de poesías*) reading. **~r** *vt* recite

reclama|ción *f* claim; (*queja*) complaint. **~r** *vt* claim. • *vi* appeal

reclinar *vi* lean. **~se** *vpr* lean

reclu|ir [17] *vt* shut away. **~sión** *f* seclusion; (*cárcel*) prison. **~so** *m* prisoner

recluta *m* recruit. • *f* recruitment. **~miento** *m* recruitment; (*conjunto de reclutas*) recruits. **~r** *vt* recruit

recobrar *vt* recover. **~se** *vpr* recover

recodo *m* bend

recog|er [14] *vt* collect; pick up ‹*cosa caída*›; (*cosechar*) harvest; (*dar asilo*) shelter. **~erse** *vpr* withdraw; (*ir a casa*) go home; (*acostarse*) go to bed. **~ida** *f* collection; (*cosecha*) harvest. **~ido** *a* withdrawn; (*pequeño*) small

recolección *f* harvest

recomenda|ción *f* recommendation. **~r** [1] *vt* recommend; (*encomendar*) entrust

recomenzar [1 & 10] *vt/i* start again

recompensa *f* reward. **~r** *vt* reward

recomponer [34] *vt* mend

reconcilia|ción *f* reconciliation. **~r** *vt* reconcile. **~rse** *vpr* be reconciled

recóndito *a* hidden

reconoc|er [11] *vt* recognize; (*admitir*) acknowledge; (*examinar*) examine. **~imiento** *m* recognition; (*admisión*) acknowledgement; (*agradecimiento*) gratitude; (*examen*) examination

reconozco *vb véase* **reconocer**

reconquista *f* reconquest. **~r** *vt* reconquer; (*fig*) win back

reconsiderar *vt* reconsider

reconstitu|ir [17] *vt* reconstitute. **~yente** *m* tonic

reconstru|cción *f* reconstruction. **~ir** [17] *vt* reconstruct

récord /'rekor/ *m* record. **batir un ~** break a record

recordar [2] *vt* remember; (*hacer acordar*) remind; (*Lam, despertar*) wake up. • *vi* remember. **que yo recuerde** as far as I remember. **si mal no recuerdo** if I remember rightly

recorr|er *vt* tour ‹*país*›; (*pasar por*) travel through; cover ‹*distancia*›; (*registrar*) look over. **~ido** *m* journey; (*itinerario*) route

recort|ado *a* jagged. **~ar** *vt* cut (out). **~e** *m* cutting (out); (*de periódico etc*) cutting

recoser *vt* mend

recostar [2] *vt* lean. **~se** *vpr* lie back

recoveco *m* bend; (*rincón*) nook

recre|ación *f* recreation. **~ar** *vt* recreate; (*divertir*) entertain. **~arse** *vpr* amuse o.s. **~ativo** *a* recreational. **~o** *m* recreation; (*escol*) break

recrimina|ción *f* recrimination. **~r** *vt* reproach

recrudecer [11] *vi* increase, worsen, get worse

recta *f* straight line

rect|angular *a* rectangular; ‹*triángulo*› right-angled. **~ángulo** *a* rectangular; ‹*triángulo*› right-angled. ● *m* rectangle

rectifica|ción *f* rectification. **~r** [7] *vt* rectify

rect|itud *f* straightness; (*fig*) honesty. **~o** *a* straight; (*fig, justo*) fair; (*fig, honrado*) honest. ● *m* rectum. **todo ~o** straight on

rector *a* governing. ● *m* rector

recuadro *m* (*en periódico*) box

recubrir [*pp* **recubierto**] *vt* cover

recuerdo *m* memory; (*regalo*) souvenir. ● *vb véase* **recordar**. **~s** *mpl* (*saludos*) regards

recupera|ción *f* recovery. **~r** *vt* recover. **~rse** *vpr* recover. **~r el tiempo perdido** make up for lost time

recur|rir *vi*. **~rir a** resort to ‹*cosa*›; turn to ‹*persona*›. **~so** *m* resort; (*medio*) resource; (*jurid*) appeal. **~sos** *mpl* resources

recusar *vt* refuse

rechaz|ar [10] *vt* repel; reflect ‹*luz*›; (*no aceptar*) refuse; (*negar*) deny. **~o** *m*. **de ~o** on the rebound; (*fig*) consequently

rechifla *f* booing; (*burla*) derision

rechinar *vi* squeak; ‹*madera etc*› creak; ‹*dientes*› grind

rechistar *vt* murmur. **sin ~** without saying a word

rechoncho *a* stout

red *f* network; (*malla*) net; (*para equipaje*) luggage rack; (*fig, engaño*) trap

redac|ción *f* editing; (*conjunto de redactores*) editorial staff; (*oficina*) editorial office; (*escol, univ*) essay. **~tar** *vt* write. **~tor** *m* writer; (*de periódico*) editor

redada *f* casting; (*de policía*) raid

redecilla *f* small net; (*para el pelo*) hairnet

rededor *m*. **al ~**, **en ~** around

reden|ción *f* redemption. **~tor** *a* redeeming

redil *f* sheepfold

redimir *vt* redeem

rédito *m* interest

redoblar *vt* redouble; (*doblar*) bend back

redoma *f* flask

redomado *a* sly

redond|a *f* (*de imprenta*) roman (type); (*mus*) semibreve (*Brit*), whole note (*Amer*). **~amente** *adv* (*categóricamente*) flatly. **~ear** *vt* round off. **~el** *m* circle; (*de plaza de toros*) arena. **~o** *a* round; (*completo*) complete. ● *m* circle. **a la ~a** around. **en ~o** round; (*categóricamente*) flatly

reduc|ción *f* reduction. **~ido** *a* reduced; (*limitado*) limited; (*pequeño*) small; ‹*precio*› low. **~ir** [47] *vt* reduce. **~irse** *vpr* be reduced; (*fig*) amount

reduje *vb véase* **reducir**

redundan|cia *f* redundancy. **~te** *a* redundant

reduplicar [7] *vt* (*aumentar*) redouble

reduzco *vb véase* **reducir**

reedificar [7] *vt* reconstruct

reembols|ar *vt* reimburse. **~o** *m* repayment. **contra ~o** cash on delivery

reemplaz|ar [10] *vt* replace. **~o** *m* replacement

reemprender *vt* start again

reenviar [20] *vt*, **reexpedir** [5] *vt* forward

referencia *f* reference; (*información*) report. **con ~** a with reference to. **hacer ~ a** refer to

referéndum *m* (*pl* **referéndums**) referendum

referir [4] *vt* tell; (*remitir*) refer. **~se** *vpr* refer. **por lo que se refiere a** as regards

refiero *vb véase* **referir**

refilón. de ~ obliquely

refin|amiento *m* refinement. **~ar** *vt* refine. **~ería** *f* refinery

reflector *m* reflector; (*proyector*) searchlight

reflej|ar *vt* reflect. **~o** *a* reflected; (*med*) reflex. • *m* reflection; (*med*) reflex; (*en el pelo*) highlights

reflexi|ón *f* reflection. **~onar** *vi* reflect. **~vo** *a* ⟨*persona*⟩ thoughtful; (*gram*) reflexive. **con ~ón** on reflection. **sin ~ón** without thinking

reflujo *m* ebb

reforma *f* reform. **~s** *fpl* (*reparaciones*) repairs. **~r** *vt* reform. **~rse** *vpr* reform

reforzar [2 & 10] *vt* reinforce

refrac|ción *f* refraction. **~tar** *vt* refract. **~tario** *a* heat-resistant

refrán *m* saying

refregar [1 & 12] *vt* rub

refrenar *vt* rein in ⟨*caballo*⟩; (*fig*) restrain

refrendar *vt* endorse

refresc|ar [7] *vt* refresh; (*enfriar*) cool. • *vi* get cooler. **~arse** *vpr* refresh o.s.; (*salir*) go out for a walk. **~o** *m* cold drink. **~os** *mpl* refreshments

refrigera|ción *f* refrigeration; (*aire acondicionado*) air-conditioning. **~r** *vt* refrigerate. **~dor** *m*, **~dora** *f* refrigerator

refuerzo *m* reinforcement

refugi|ado *m* refugee. **~arse** *vpr* take refuge. **~o** *m* refuge, shelter

refulgir [14] *vi* shine

refundir *vt* (*fig*) revise, rehash

refunfuñar *vi* grumble

refutar *vt* refute

regadera *f* watering-can; (*Mex, ducha*) shower

regala|damente *adv* very well. **~do** *a* as a present, free; (*cómodo*) comfortable. **~r** *vt* give; (*agasajar*) treat very well. **~rse** *vpr* indulge o.s.

regaliz *m* liquorice

regalo *m* present, gift; (*placer*) joy; (*comodidad*) comfort

regañ|adientes. a ~adientes reluctantly. **~ar** *vt* scold. • *vi* moan; (*dos personas*) quarrel. **~o** *m* (*reprensión*) scolding

regar [1 & 12] *vt* water

regata *f* regatta

regate *m* dodge; (*en deportes*) dribbling. **~ar** *vt* haggle over; (*economizar*) economize on. • *vi* haggle; (*en deportes*) dribble. **~o** *m* haggling; (*en deportes*) dribbling

regazo *m* lap

regencia *f* regency

regenerar *vt* regenerate

regente *m & f* regent; (*director*) manager

régimen *m* (*pl* **regímenes**) rule; (*pol*) regime; (*med*) diet. **~ alimenticio** diet

regimiento *m* regiment

regio *a* royal

regi|ón *f* region. **~onal** *a* regional

regir [5 & 14] *vt* rule; govern ⟨*país*⟩; run ⟨*colegio, empresa*⟩. • *vi* apply, be in force

registr|ado *a* registered. **~ador** *m* recorder; (*persona*) registrar. **~ar** *vt* register; (*grabar*) record; (*examinar*) search. **~arse** *vpr* register; (*darse*) be reported. **~o** *m* (*acción de registrar*) registration; (*libro*) register; (*cosa anotada*) entry; (*inspección*) search. **~o civil** (*oficina*) register office

regla *f* ruler; (*norma*) rule; (*menstruación*) period, menstruation. **~mentación** *f* regulation. **~mentar** *vt* regulate. **~mentario** *a* obligatory. **~mento** *m* regulations. **en ~** in order. **por o ~ general** as a rule

regocij|ar *vt* delight. **~arse** *vpr* be delighted. **~o** *m* delight. **~os** *mpl* festivities

regodearse *vpr* be delighted. **~o** *m* delight

regordete *a* chubby

regres|ar *vi* return. **~ión** *f* regression. **~ivo** *a* backward. **~o** *m* return

reguer|a *f* irrigation ditch. **~o** *m* irrigation ditch; (*señal*) trail

regula|dor *m* control. **~r** *a* regular; (*mediano*) average; (*no bueno*) so-so. • *vt* regulate; (*controlar*) control. **~ridad** *f* regularity. **con ~ridad** regularly. **por lo ~r** as a rule

rehabilita|ción *f* rehabilitation; (*en un empleo etc*) reinstatement. **~r** *vt* rehabilitate; (*al empleo etc*) reinstate

rehacer [31] *vt* redo; (*repetir*) repeat; (*reparar*) repair. **~se** *vpr* recover

rehén *m* hostage

rehogar [12] *vt* sauté

rehuir [17] *vt* avoid

rehusar *vt/i* refuse

reimpr|esión *f* reprinting. **~imir** (*pp* **reimpreso**) *vt* reprint

reina *f* queen. **~do** *m* reign. **~nte** *a* ruling; (*fig*) prevailing. **~r** *vi* reign; (*fig*) prevail

reincidir *vi* relapse, repeat an offence

reino *m* kingdom. **R~ Unido** United Kingdom

reinstaurar *vt* restore

reintegr|ar *vt* reinstate ⟨persona⟩; refund ⟨cantidad⟩. **~arse** *vpr* return. **~o** *m* refund

reír [51] *vi* laugh. **~se** *vpr* laugh. **~se de** laugh at. **echarse a ~** burst out laughing

reivindica|ción *f* claim. **~r** [7] *vt* claim; (restaurar) restore

rej|a *f* grille, grating. **~illa** *f* grille, grating; (red) luggage rack; (de mimbre) wickerwork. **entre ~as** behind bars

rejuvenecer [11] *vt/i* rejuvenate. **~se** *vpr* be rejuvenated

relaci|ón *f* relation(ship); (relato) tale; (lista) list. **~onado** *a* concerning. **~onar** *vt* relate (con to). **~onarse** *vpr* be connected. **bien ~onado** well-connected. **con ~ón a, en ~ón a** in relation to. **hacer ~ón a** refer to

relaja|ción *f* relaxation; (aflojamiento) slackening. **~do** *a* loose. **~r** *vt* relax; (aflojar) slacken. **~rse** *vpr* relax

relamerse *vpr* lick one's lips

relamido *a* overdressed

rel|ámpago *m* (flash of) lightning. **~ampaguear** *vi* thunder; (fig) sparkle

relatar *vt* tell, relate

relativ|idad *f* relativity. **~o** *a* relative. **en lo ~o a** in relation to

relato *m* tale; (informe) report

relegar [12] *vt* relegate. **~ al olvido** forget about

relev|ante *a* outstanding. **~ar** *vt* relieve; (substituir) replace. **~o** *m* relief. **carrera** *f* **de ~os** relay race

relieve *m* relief; (fig) importance. **de ~** important. **poner de ~** emphasize

religi|ón *f* religion. **~osa** *f* nun. **~oso** *a* religious. ● *m* monk

relinch|ar *vi* neigh. **~o** *m* neigh

reliquia *f* relic

reloj *m* clock; (de bolsillo o pulsera) watch. **~ de caja** grandfather clock. **~ de pulsera** wrist-watch. **~ de sol** sundial. **~ despertador** alarm clock. **~ería** *f* watchmaker's (shop). **~ero** *m* watchmaker

reluci|ente *a* shining. **~r** [11] *vi* shine; (destellar) sparkle

relumbrar *vi* shine

rellano *m* landing

rellen|ar *vt* refill; (culin) stuff; fill in ⟨formulario⟩. **~o** *a* full up; (culin) stuffed. ● *m* filling; (culin) stuffing

remach|ar *vt* rivet; (fig) drive home. **~e** *m* rivet

remangar [12] *vt* roll up

remanso *m* pool; (fig) haven

remar *vi* row

remat|ado *a* (total) complete; ⟨niño⟩ very naughty. **~ar** *vt* finish off; (agotar) use up; (com) sell off cheap. **~e** *m* end; (fig) finishing touch. **de ~e** completely

remedar *vt* imitate

remedi|ar *vt* remedy; (ayudar) help; (poner fin a) put a stop to; (fig, resolver) solve. **~o** *m* remedy; (fig) solution. **como último ~o** as a last resort. **no hay más ~o** there's no other way. **no tener más ~o** have no choice

remedo *m* imitation

rem|endar [1] *vt* repair. **~iendo** *m* patch; (fig, mejora) improvement

remilg|ado *a* fussy; (afectado) affected. **~o** *m* fussiness; (afectación) affectation

reminiscencia *f* reminiscence

remirar *vt* look again at

remisión *f* sending; (referencia) reference; (perdón) forgiveness

remiso *a* remiss

remit|e *m* sender's name and address. **~ente** *m* sender. **~ir** *vt* send; (referir) refer. ● *vi* diminish

remo *m* oar

remoj|ar *vt* soak; (fig, fam) celebrate. **~o** *m* soaking. **poner a ~o** soak

remolacha *f* beetroot. **~ azucarera** sugar beet

remolcar [7] *vt* tow

remolino *m* swirl; (de aire etc) whirl; (de gente) throng

remolque *m* towing; (cabo) towrope; (vehículo) trailer. **a ~** on tow. **dar ~ a** tow

remontar *vt* mend. **~se** *vpr* soar; (con tiempo) go back to

rémora *f* (fig) hindrance

remord|er [2] (fig) worry. **~imiento** *m* remorse. **tener ~imientos** feel remorse

remoto *a* remote

remover [2] *vt* move; stir ⟨líquido⟩; turn over ⟨tierra⟩; (quitar) remove; (fig, activar) revive

remozar [10] *vt* rejuvenate ⟨*persona*⟩; renovate ⟨*edificio etc*⟩

remunera|ción *f* remuneration. **~r** *vt* remunerate

renac|er [11] *vi* be reborn; (*fig*) revive. **~imiento** *m* rebirth. **R~** Renaissance

renacuajo *m* tadpole; (*fig*) tiddler

rencilla *f* quarrel

rencor *m* bitterness. **~oso** *a* (*estar*) resentful; (*ser*) spiteful. **guardar ~ a** have a grudge against

rendi|ción *f* surrender. **~do** *a* submissive; (*agotado*) exhausted

rendija *f* crack

rendi|miento *m* efficiency; (*com*) yield. **~r** [5] *vt* yield; (*vencer*) defeat; (*agotar*) exhaust; pay ⟨*homenaje*⟩. ● *vi* pay; (*producir*) produce. **~rse** *vpr* surrender

renega|do *a & m* renegade. **~r** [1 & 12] *vt* deny. ● *vi* grumble. **~r de** renounce ⟨*fe etc*⟩; disown ⟨*personas*⟩

RENFE *abrev* (*Red Nacional de los Ferrocarriles Españoles*) Spanish National Railways

renglón *m* line; (*com*) item. **a ~ seguido** straight away

reno *m* reindeer

renombr|ado *a* renowned. **~e** *m* renown

renova|ción *f* renewal; (*de edificio*) renovation; (*de cuarto*) decorating. **~r** *vt* renew; renovate ⟨*edificio*⟩; decorate ⟨*cuarto*⟩

rent|a *f* income; (*alquiler*) rent; (*deuda*) national debt. **~able** *a* profitable. **~ar** *vt* produce, yield; (*LAm, alquilar*) rent, hire. **~a vitalicia** (life) annuity. **~ista** *m & f* person of independent means

renuncia *f* renunciation. **~r** *vi*. **~r a** renounce, give up

reñi|do *a* hard-fought. **~r** [5 & 22] *vt* tell off. ● *vi* quarrel. **estar ~do con** be incompatible with ⟨*cosas*⟩; be on bad terms with ⟨*personas*⟩

reo *m & f* culprit; (*jurid*) accused. **~ de Estado** person accused of treason. **~ de muerte** prisoner sentenced to death

reojo. mirar de ~ look out of the corner of one's eye at; (*fig*) look askance at

reorganizar [10] *vt* reorganize

repanchigarse [12] *vpr*, **repantigarse** [12] *vpr* sprawl out

repar|ación *f* repair; (*acción*) repairing; (*fig, compensación*) reparation.

~ar *vt* repair; (*fig*) make amends for; (*notar*) notice. ● *vi*. **~ar en** notice; (*hacer caso de*) pay attention to. **~o** *m* fault; (*objeción*) objection. **poner ~os** raise objections

repart|ición *f* division. **~idor** *m* delivery man. **~imiento** *m* distribution. **~ir** *vt* distribute, share out; deliver ⟨*cartas, leche etc*⟩; hand out ⟨*folleto, premio*⟩. **~o** *m* distribution; (*de cartas, leche etc*) delivery; (*actores*) cast

repas|ar *vt* go over; check ⟨*cuenta*⟩; revise ⟨*texto*⟩; (*leer a la ligera*) glance through; (*coser*) mend. ● *vi* go back. **~o** *m* revision; (*de ropa*) mending. **dar un ~o** look through

repatria|ción *f* repatriation. **~r** *vt* repatriate

repecho *m* steep slope

repele|nte *a* repulsive. **~r** *vt* repel

repensar [1] *vt* reconsider

repent|e. de ~ suddenly. **~ino** *a* sudden

repercu|sión *f* repercussion. **~tir** *vi* reverberate; (*fig*) have repercussions (**en** on)

repertorio *m* repertoire; (*lista*) index

repeti|ción *f* repetition; (*mus*) repeat. **~damente** *adv* repeatedly. **~r** [5] *vt* repeat; (*imitar*) copy; ● *vi*. **~r de** have a second helping of. **¡que se repita!** encore!

repi|car [7] *vt* ring ⟨*campanas*⟩. **~que** *m* peal

repisa *f* shelf. **~ de chimenea** mantlepiece

repito *vb véase* **repetir**

replegarse [1 & 12] *vpr* withdraw

repleto *a* full up

réplica *a* answer; (*copia*) replica

replicar [7] *vi* answer

repliegue *m* crease; (*mil*) withdrawal

repollo *m* cabbage

reponer [34] *vt* replace; revive ⟨*obra de teatro*⟩; (*contestar*) reply. **~se** *vpr* recover

report|aje *m* report. **~ero** *m* reporter

repos|ado *a* quiet; (*sin prisa*) unhurried. **~ar** *vi* rest. **~arse** *vpr* settle. **~o** *m* rest

repost|ar *vt* replenish; refuel ⟨*avión*⟩; fill up ⟨*coche etc*⟩. **~ería** *f* cake shop

repren|der *vt* reprimand. **~sible** *a* reprehensible

represalia *f* reprisal. **tomar ∼s** retaliate

representa|ción *f* representation; *(en el teatro)* performance. **en ∼ción de** representing. **∼nte** *m* representative; *(actor)* actor. ● *f* representative; *(actriz)* actress. **∼r** *vt* represent; perform ⟨*obra de teatro*⟩; play ⟨*papel*⟩; *(aparentar)* look. **∼rse** *vpr* imagine. **∼tivo** *a* representative

represi|ón *f* repression. **∼vo** *a* repressive

reprimenda *f* reprimand

reprimir *vt* supress. **∼se** *vpr* stop o.s.

reprobar [2] *vt* condemn; reproach ⟨*persona*⟩

réprobo *a & m* reprobate

reproch|ar *vt* reproach. **∼e** *m* reproach

reproduc|ción *f* reproduction. **∼ir** [47] *vt* reproduce. **∼tor** *a* reproductive

reptil *m* reptile

rep|ública *f* republic. **∼ublicano** *a & m* republican

repudiar *vt* repudiate

repuesto *m* store; *(auto)* spare (part). **de ∼** in reserve

repugna|ncia *f* disgust. **∼nte** *a* repugnant. **∼r** *vt* disgust

repujar *vt* emboss

repuls|a *f* rebuff. **∼ión** *f* repulsion. **∼ivo** *a* repulsive

reputa|ción *f* reputation. **∼do** *a* reputable. **∼r** *vt* consider

requebrar [1] *vt* flatter

requemar *vt* scorch; *(culin)* burn; tan ⟨*piel*⟩

requeri|miento *m* request; *(jurid)* summons. **∼r** [4] *vt* need; *(pedir)* ask

requesón *m* cottage cheese

requete... *pref* extremely

requiebro *m* compliment

réquiem *m* (*pl* **réquiems**) *m* requiem

requis|a *f* inspection; *(mil)* requisition. **∼ar** *vt* requisition. **∼ito** *m* requirement

res *f* animal. **∼ lanar** sheep. **∼ vacuna** ⟨*vaca*⟩ cow; ⟨*toro*⟩ bull; ⟨*buey*⟩ ox. **carne de ∼** *(Mex)* beef

resabido *a* well-known; ⟨*persona*⟩ pedantic

resabio *m* (unpleasant) after-taste; *(vicio)* bad habit

resaca *f* undercurrent; *(después de beber alcohol)* hangover

resaltar *vi* stand out. **hacer ∼** emphasize

resarcir [9] *vt* repay; *(compensar)* compensate. **∼se** *vpr* make up for

resbal|adizo *a* slippery. **∼ar** *vi* slip; *(auto)* skid; ⟨*líquido*⟩ trickle. **∼arse** *vpr* slip; *(auto)* skid; ⟨*líquido*⟩ trickle. **∼ón** *m* slip; *(de vehículo)* skid

rescat|ar *vt* ransom; *(recuperar)* recapture; *(fig)* recover. **∼e** *m* ransom; *(recuperación)* recapture; *(salvamento)* rescue

rescindir *vt* cancel

rescoldo *m* embers

resecar [7] *vt* dry up; *(med)* remove. **∼se** *vpr* dry up

resenti|do *a* resentful. **∼miento** *m* resentment. **∼rse** *vpr* feel the effects; *(debilitarse)* be weakened; *(ofenderse)* take offence **(de** at)

reseña *f* account; *(en periódico)* report, review. **∼r** *vt* describe; *(en periódico)* report on, review

resero *m* *(Arg)* herdsman

reserva *f* reservation; *(provisión)* reserve(s). **∼ción** *f* reservation. **∼do** *a* reserved. **∼r** *vt* reserve; *(guardar)* keep, save. **∼rse** *vpr* save o.s. **a ∼ de** except for. **a ∼ de que** unless. **de ∼** in reserve

resfria|do *m* cold; *(enfriamiento)* chill. **∼r** *vt*. **∼r a uno** give s.o. a cold. **∼rse** *vpr* catch a cold; *(fig)* cool off

resguard|ar *vt* protect. **∼arse** *vpr* protect o.s.; *(fig)* take care. **∼o** *m* protection; *(garantía)* guarantee; *(recibo)* receipt

resid|encia *f* residence; *(univ)* hall of residence, dormitory *(Amer)*; *(de ancianos etc)* home. **∼encial** *a* residential. **∼ente** *a & m & f* resident. **∼ir** *vi* reside; *(fig)* lie

residu|al *a* residual. **∼o** *m* remainder. **∼os** *mpl* waste

resigna|ción *f* resignation. **∼damente** *adv* with resignation. **∼r** *vt* resign. **∼rse** *vpr* resign o.s. **(a, con** to)

resina *f* resin

resist|encia *f* resistence. **∼ente** *a* resistent. **∼ir** *vt* resist; *(soportar)* bear. ● *vi* resist. **oponer ∼encia** *a* resist

resma *f* ream

resobado *a* trite

resol|ución *f* resolution; *(solución)* solution; *(decisión)* decision. **∼ver**

[2] (*pp* **resuelto**) resolve; solve ‹*problema etc*›. **~verse** *vpr* be solved; (*resultar bien*) work out; (*decidirse*) make up one's mind

resollar [2] *vi* breathe heavily. **sin ~** without saying a word

resona|ncia *f* resonance. **~nte** *a* resonant; (*fig*) resounding. **~r** [2] *vi* resound. **tener ~ncia** cause a stir

resopl|ar *vi* puff; (*por enfado*) snort; (*por cansancio*) pant. **~ido** *m* heavy breathing; (*de enfado*) snort; (*de cansancio*) panting

resorte *m* spring. **tocar (todos los) ~s** (*fig*) pull strings

respald|ar *vt* back; (*escribir*) endorse. **~arse** *vpr* lean back. **~o** *m* back

respect|ar *vi* concern. **~ivo** *a* respective. **~o** *m* respect. **al ~o** on the matter. **(con) ~o a** as regards. **en/por lo que ~a** as regards

respet|able *a* respectable. ● *m* audience. **~ar** *vt* respect. **~o** *m* respect. **~uoso** *a* respectful. **de ~o** best. **faltar al ~o a** be disrespectful to. **hacerse ~ar** command respect

respingo *m* start

respir|ación *f* breathing; (*med*) respiration; (*ventilación*) ventilation. **~ador** *a* respiratory. **~ar** *vi* breathe; (*fig*) breathe a sigh of relief. **no ~ar** (*no hablar*) not say a word. **~o** *m* breathing; (*fig*) rest

respland|ecer [11] *vi* shine. **~eciente** *a* shining. **~or** *m* brilliance; (*de llamas*) glow

responder *vi* answer; (*replicar*) answer back; (*fig*) reply, respond. **~ de** answer for

responsab|ilidad *f* responsibility. **~le** *a* responsible. **hacerse ~le de** assume responsibilty for

respuesta *f* reply, answer

resquebra|dura *f* crack. **~jar** *vt* crack. **~jarse** *vpr* crack

resquemor *m* (*fig*) uneasiness

resquicio *m* crack; (*fig*) possibility

resta *f* subtraction

restablecer [11] *vt* restore. **~se** *vpr* recover

restallar *vi* crack

restante *a* remaining. **lo ~** the rest

restar *vt* take away; (*substraer*) subtract. ● *vi* be left

restaura|ción *f* restoration. **~nte** *m* restaurant. **~r** *vt* restore

restitu|ción *f* restitution. **~ir** [17] *vt* return; (*restaurar*) restore

resto *m* rest, remainder; (*en matemática*) remainder. **~s** *mpl* remains; (*de comida*) leftovers

restorán *m* restaurant

restregar [1 & 12] *vt* rub

restri|cción *f* restriction. **~ngir** [14] *vt* restrict, limit

resucitar *vt* resuscitate; (*fig*) revive. ● *vi* return to life

resuelto *a* resolute

resuello *m* breath; (*respiración*) breathing

resulta|do *m* result. **~r** *vi* result; (*salir*) turn out; (*ser*) be; (*ocurrir*) happen; (*costar*) come to

resum|en *m* summary. **~ir** *vt* summarize; (*recapitular*) sum up; (*abreviar*) abridge. **en ~en** in short

resur|gir [14] *vi* reappear; (*fig*) revive. **~gimiento** *m* resurgence. **~rección** *f* resurrection

retaguardia *f* (*mil*) rearguard

retahíla *f* string

retal *m* remnant

retama *f*, **retamo** *m* (*LAm*) broom

retar *vt* challenge

retardar *vt* slow down; (*demorar*) delay

retazo *m* remnant; (*fig*) piece, bit

retemblar [1] *vi* shake

rete... *pref* extremely

reten|ción *f* retention. **~er** [40] *vt* keep; (*en la memoria*) retain; (*no dar*) withhold

reticencia *f* insinuation; (*reserva*) reticence, reluctance

retina *f* retina

retintín *m* ringing. **con ~** (*fig*) sarcastically

retir|ada *f* withdrawal. **~ado** *a* secluded; (*jubilado*) retired. **~ar** *vt* move away; (*quitar*) remove; withdraw ‹*dinero*›; (*jubilar*) pension off. **~arse** *vpr* draw back; (*mil*) withdraw; (*jubilarse*) retire; (*acostarse*) go to bed. **~o** *m* retirement; (*pensión*) pension; (*lugar apartado*) retreat

reto *m* challenge

retocar [7] *vt* retouch

retoño *m* shoot

retoque *m* (*acción*) retouching; (*efecto*) finishing touch

retorc|er [2 & 9] *vt* twist; wring ‹*ropa*›. **~erse** *vpr* get twisted up; (*de dolor*) writhe. **~imiento** *m* twisting; (*de ropa*) wringing

retóric|a *f* rhetoric; (*grandilocuencia*) grandiloquence. **~o** *m* rhetorical

retorn|ar *vt/i* return. **~o** *m* return
retortijón *m* twist; (*de tripas*) stomach cramp
retoz|ar [10] *vi* romp, frolic. **~ón** *a* playful
retractar *vt* retract. **~se** *vpr* retract
retra|er [41] *vt* retract. **~erse** *vpr* withdraw. **~ído** *a* retiring
retransmitir *vt* relay
retras|ado *a* behind; (*reloj*) slow; (*poco desarrollado*) backward; (*anticuado*) old-fashioned; (*med*) mentally retarded. **~ar** *vt* delay; put back (*reloj*); (*retardar*) slow down. ● *vi* fall behind; (*reloj*) be slow. **~arse** *vpr* be behind; (*reloj*) be slow. **~o** *m* delay; (*poco desarrollo*) backwardness; (*de reloj*) slowness. **~os** *mpl* arrears. **con 5 minutos de ~o** 5 minutes late. **traer ~o** be late
retrat|ar *vt* paint a portrait of; (*foto*) photograph; (*fig*) protray. **~ista** *m & f* portrait painter. **~o** *m* portrait; (*fig, descripción*) description. **ser el vivo ~o de** be the living image of
retreparse *vpr* lean back
retreta *f* retreat
retrete *m* toilet
retribu|ción *f* payment. **~ir** [17] *vt* pay
retroce|der *vi* move back; (*fig*) back down. **~so** *m* backward movement; (*de arma de fuego*) recoil; (*med*) relapse
retrógrado *a & m* (*pol*) reactionary
retropropulsión *f* jet propulsion
retrospectivo *a* retrospective
retrovisor *m* rear-view mirror
retumbar *vt* echo; (*trueno etc*) boom
reuma *m*, **reúma** *m* rheumatism
reum|ático *a* rheumatic. **~atismo** *m* rheumatism
reuni|ón *f* meeting; (*entre amigos*) reunion. **~r** [23] *vt* join together; (*recoger*) gather (together). **~rse** *vpr* join together; (*personas*) meet
rev|álida *f* final exam. **~alidar** *vt* confirm; (*escol*) take an exam in
revancha *f* revenge. **tomar la ~** get one's own back
revela|ción *f* revelation. **~do** *m* developing. **~dor** *a* revealing. **~r** *vt* reveal; (*foto*) develop
revent|ar [1] *vi* burst; (*tener ganas*) be dying to. **~arse** *vpr* burst. **~ón** *m* burst; (*auto*) puncture
reverbera|ción *f* (*de luz*) reflection; (*de sonido*) reverberation. **~r** *vi*

(*luz*) be reflected; (*sonido*) reverberate
reveren|cia *f* reverence; (*muestra de respeto*) bow; (*muestra de respeto de mujer*) curtsy. **~ciar** *vt* revere. **~do** *a* respected; (*relig*) reverend. **~te** *a* reverent
revers|ible *a* reversible. **~o** *m* reverse
revertir [4] *vi* revert
revés *m* wrong side; (*desgracia*) misfortune; (*en deportes*) backhand. **al ~** the other way round; (*con lo de arriba abajo*) upside down; (*con lo de dentro fuera*) inside out
revesti|miento *m* coating. **~r** [5] *vt* cover; put on (*ropa*); (*fig*) take on
revis|ar *vt* check; overhaul (*mecanismo*); service (*coche etc*). **~ión** *f* check(ing); (*inspección*) inspection; (*de coche etc*) service. **~or** *m* inspector
revist|a *f* magazine; (*inspección*) inspection; (*artículo*) review; (*espectáculo*) revue. **~ero** *m* critic; (*mueble*) magazine rack. **pasar ~a a** inspect
revivir *vi* come to life again
revocar [7] *vt* revoke; whitewash (*pared*)
revolcar [2 & 7] *vt* knock over. **~se** *vpr* roll
revolotear *vi* flutter
revoltijo *m*, **revoltillo** *m* mess. **~ de huevos** scrambled eggs
revoltoso *a* rebellious; (*niño*) naughty
revoluci|ón *f* revolution. **~onar** *vt* revolutionize. **~onario** *a & m* revolutionary
revolver [2, *pp* **revuelto**] *vt* mix; stir (*líquido*); (*desordenar*) mess up; (*pol*) stir up. **~se** *vpr* turn round. **~se contra** turn on
revólver *m* revolver
revoque *m* (*con cal*) whitewashing
revuelo *m* fluttering; (*fig*) stir
revuelt|a *f* turn; (*de calle etc*) bend; (*motín*) revolt; (*conmoción*) disturbance. **~o** *a* mixed up; (*líquido*) cloudy; (*mar*) rough; (*tiempo*) unsettled; (*huevos*) scrambled
rey *m* king. **~es** *mpl* king and queen
reyerta *f* quarrel
rezagarse [12] *vpr* fall behind
rez|ar [10] *vt* say. ● *vi* pray; (*decir*) say. **~o** *m* praying; (*oración*) prayer
rezongar [12] *vi* grumble

rezumar *vt/i* ooze
ría *f* estuary
riachuelo *m* stream
riada *f* flood
ribera *f* bank
ribete *m* border; (*fig*) embellishment
ricino *m*. **aceite de ~** castor oil
rico *a* rich; (*culin, fam*) delicious. ● *m* rich person
rid|ículo *a* ridiculous. **~iculizar** [10] *vt* ridicule
riego *m* watering; (*irrigación*) irrigation
riel *m* rail
rienda *f* rein
riesgo *m* risk. **a ~ de** at the risk of. **correr (el) ~ de** run the risk of
rifa *f* raffle. **~r** *vt* raffle. **~rse** *vpr* (*fam*) quarrel over
rifle *m* rifle
rigidez *f* rigidity; (*fig*) inflexibility
rígido *a* rigid; (*fig*) inflexible
rig|or *m* strictness; (*exactitud*) exactness; (*de clima*) severity. **~uroso** *a* rigorous. **de ~or** compulsory. **en ~or** strictly speaking
rima *f* rhyme. **~r** *vt/i* rhyme
rimbombante *a* resounding; ⟨*lenguaje*⟩ pompous; (*fig, ostentoso*) showy
rimel *m* mascara
rincón *m* corner
rinoceronte *m* rhinoceros
riña *f* quarrel; (*pelea*) fight
riñ|ón *m* kidney. **~onada** *f* loin; (*guiso*) kidney stew
río *m* river; (*fig*) stream. ● *vb véase* **reír. ~ abajo** downstream. **~ arriba** upstream
rioja *m* Rioja wine
riqueza *f* wealth; (*fig*) richness. **~s** *fpl* riches
riquísimo *a* delicious
risa *f* laugh. **desternillarse de ~** split one's sides laughing. **la ~** laughter
risco *m* cliff
ris|ible *a* laughable. **~otada** *f* guffaw
ristra *f* string
risueño *a* smiling; (*fig*) happy
rítmico *a* rhythmic(al)
ritmo *m* rhythm; (*fig*) rate
rit|o *m* rite; (*fig*) ritual. **~ual** *a & m* ritual. **de ~ual** customary
rival *a & m & f* rival. **~idad** *f* rivalry. **~izar** [10] *vi* rival
riz|ado *a* curly. **~ar** [10] *vt* curl; ripple ⟨*agua*⟩. **~o** *m* curl; (*en agua*) ripple. **~oso** *a* curly

róbalo *m* bass
robar *vt* steal ⟨*cosa*⟩; rob ⟨*persona*⟩; (*raptar*) kidnap
roble *m* oak (tree)
roblón *m* rivet
robo *m* theft; (*fig, estafa*) robbery
robot (*pl* **robots**) *m* robot
robust|ez *f* strength. **~o** *a* strong
roca *f* rock
roce *m* rubbing; (*toque ligero*) touch; (*señal*) mark; (*fig, entre personas*) contact
rociar [20] *vt* spray
rocín *m* nag
rocío *m* dew
rodaballo *m* turbot
rodado *m* (*Arg, vehículo*) vehicle
rodaja *f* disc; (*culin*) slice
roda|je *m* (*de película*) shooting; (*de coche*) running in. **~r** [2] *vt* shoot ⟨*película*⟩; run in ⟨*coche*⟩; (*recorrer*) travel. ● *vi* roll; ⟨*coche*⟩ run; (*hacer una película*) shoot
rode|ar *vt* surround. **~arse** *vpr* surround o.s. (**de** with). **~o** *m* long way round; (*de ganado*) round-up. **andar con ~os** beat about the bush. **sin ~os** plainly
rodill|a *f* knee. **~era** *f* knee-pad. **de ~as** kneeling
rodillo *m* roller; (*culin*) rolling-pin
rododendro *m* rhododendron
rodrigón *m* stake
roe|dor *m* rodent. **~r** [37] *vt* gnaw
rogar [2 & 12] *vt/i* ask; (*relig*) pray. **se ruega a los Sres pasajeros...** passengers are requested.... **se ruega no fumar** please do not smoke
roj|ete *m* rouge. **~ez** *f* redness. **~izo** *a* reddish. **~o** *a & m* red. **ponerse ~o** blush
roll|izo *a* round; ⟨*persona*⟩ plump. **~o** *m* roll; (*de cuerda*) coil; (*culin, rodillo*) rolling-pin; (*fig, pesadez, fam*) bore
romance *a* Romance. ● *m* Romance language; (*poema*) romance. **hablar en ~** speak plainly
rom|ánico *a* Romanesque; ⟨*lengua*⟩ Romance. **~ano** *a & m* Roman. **a la ~ana** (*culin*) (deep-)fried in batter
rom|anticismo *m* romanticism. **~ántico** *a* romantic
romería *f* pilgrimage
romero *m* rosemary
romo *a* blunt; ⟨*nariz*⟩ snub; (*fig, torpe*) dull
rompe|cabezas *m invar* puzzle; (*con tacos de madera*) jigsaw (puzzle).

~**nueces** *m invar* nutcrackers. ~**olas** *m invar* breakwater

romp|er (*pp* **roto**) *vt* break; break off ⟨*relaciones etc*⟩. ● *vi* break; ⟨*sol*⟩ break through. ~**erse** *vpr* break. ~**er** a burst out. ~**imiento** *m* (*de relaciones etc*) breaking off

ron *m* rum

ronc|ar [7] *vi* snore. ~**o** *a* hoarse

roncha *f* lump; (*culin*) slice

ronda *f* round; (*patrulla*) patrol; (*carretera*) ring road. ~**lla** *f* group of serenaders; (*invención*) story. ~**r** *vt/i* patrol

rondón. de ~ unannounced

ronquedad *f*, **ronquera** *f* hoarseness

ronquido *m* snore

ronronear *vi* purr

ronzal *m* halter

roñ|a *f* (*suciedad*) grime. ~**oso** *a* dirty; (*oxidado*) rusty; (*tacaño*) mean

rop|a *f* clothes, clothing. ~**a blanca** linen; (*ropa interior*) underwear. ~**a de cama** bedclothes. ~**a hecha** ready-made clothes. ~**a interior** underwear. ~**aje** *m* robes; (*excesivo*) heavy clothing. ~**ero** *m* wardrobe

ros|a *a invar* pink. ● *f* rose; (*color*) pink. ~**áceo** *a* pink. ~**ado** *a* rosy. ● *m* (*vino*) rosé. ~**al** *m* rose-bush

rosario *m* rosary; (*fig*) series

rosbif *m* roast beef

rosc|a *f* coil; (*de tornillo*) thread; (*de pan*) roll. ~**o** *m* roll

rosetón *m* rosette

rosquilla *f* doughnut; (*oruga*) grub

rostro *m* face

rota|ción *f* rotation. ~**tivo** *a* rotary

roto *a* broken

rótula *f* kneecap

rotulador *m* felt-tip pen

rótulo *m* sign; (*etiqueta*) label

rotundo *a* emphatic

rotura *f* break

roturar *vt* plough

roza *f* groove. ~**dura** *f* scratch

rozagante *a* showy

rozar [10] *vt* rub against; (*ligeramente*) brush against; (*ensuciar*) dirty; (*fig*) touch on. ~**se** *vpr* rub; (*con otras personas*) mix

Rte. *abrev* (*Remite*(*nte*)) sender

rúa *f* (small) street

rubéola *f* German measles

rubí *m* ruby

rubicundo *a* ruddy

rubio *a* ⟨*pelo*⟩ fair; ⟨*persona*⟩ fair-haired; ⟨*tabaco*⟩ Virginian

rubor *m* blush; (*fig*) shame. ~**izado** *a* blushing; (*fig*) ashamed. ~**izar** [10] *vt* make blush. ~**izarse** *vpr* blush

rúbrica *f* red mark; (*de firma*) flourish; (*título*) heading

rudeza *f* roughness

rudiment|al *a* rudimentary. ~**os** *mpl* rudiments

rudo *a* rough; (*sencillo*) simple

rueda *f* wheel; (*de mueble*) castor; (*de personas*) ring; (*culin*) slice. ~ **de prensa** press conference

ruedo *m* edge; (*redondel*) arena

ruego *m* request; (*súplica*) entreaty. ● *vb véase* **rogar**

rufi|án *m* pimp; (*granuja*) villain. ~**anesco** *a* roguish

rugby *m* Rugby

rugi|do *m* roar. ~**r** [14] *vi* roar

ruibarbo *m* rhubarb

ruido *m* noise; (*alboroto*) din; (*escándalo*) commotion. ~**so** *a* noisy; (*fig*) sensational

ruin *a* despicable; (*tacaño*) mean

ruina *f* ruin; (*colapso*) collapse

ruindad *f* meanness

ruinoso *a* ruinous

ruiseñor *m* nightingale

ruleta *f* roulette

rulo *m* (*culin*) rolling-pin; (*del pelo*) curler

Rumania *f* Romania

rumano *a & m* Romanian

rumba *f* rumba

rumbo *m* direction; (*fig*) course; (*fig, generosidad*) lavishness. ~**so** *a* lavish. **con** ~ **a** in the direction of. **hacer** ~ **a** head for

rumia|nte *a & m* ruminant. ~**r** *vt* chew; (*fig*) chew over. ● *vi* ruminate

rumor *m* rumour; (*ruido*) murmur. ~**earse** *vpr* be rumoured. ~**oso** *a* murmuring

runr|ún *m* rumour; (*ruido*) murmur. ~**unearse** *vpr* be rumoured

ruptura *f* break; (*de relaciones etc*) breaking off

rural *a* rural

Rusia *f* Russia

ruso *a & m* Russian

rústico *a* rural; (*de carácter*) coarse. **en rústica** paperback

ruta *f* route; (*camino*) road; (*fig*) course

rutina *f* routine. ~**rio** *a* routine

S

S.A. *abrev* (*Sociedad Anónima*) Ltd, Limited, plc, Public Limited Company

sábado *m* Saturday

sabana *f* (*esp LAm*) savannah

sábana *f* sheet

sabandija *f* bug

sabañón *m* chilblain

sabático *a* sabbatical

sab|elotodo *m & f invar* know-all (*fam*). **~er** [38] *vt* know; (*ser capaz de*) be able to, know how to; (*enterarse de*) learn. ● *vi*. **~er a** taste of. **~er** *m* knowledge. **~ido** *a* well-known. **~iduría** *f* wisdom; (*conocimientos*) knowledge. **a ~er si** I wonder if. **¡haberlo ~ido!** if only I'd known! **hacer ~er** let know. **no sé cuántos** what's-his-name. **para que lo sepas** let me tell you. **¡qué sé yo!** how should I know? **que yo sepa** as far as I know. **¿~es nadar?** can you swim? **un no sé qué** a certain sth. **¡yo qué sé!** how should I know?

sabiendas. a ~ knowingly; (*a propósito*) on purpose

sabio *a* learned; (*prudente*) wise

sabor *m* taste, flavour; (*fig*) flavour. **~ear** *vt* taste; (*fig*) savour

sabot|aje *m* sabotage. **~eador** *m* saboteur. **~ear** *vt* sabotage

sabroso *a* tasty; (*fig, substancioso*) meaty

sabueso *m* (*perro*) bloodhound; (*fig, detective*) detective

saca|corchos *m invar* corkscrew. **~puntas** *m invar* pencil-sharpener

sacar [7] *vt* take out; put out (*parte del cuerpo*); (*quitar*) remove; take (*foto*); win (*premio*); get (*billete, entrada etc*); withdraw (*dinero*); reach (*solución*); draw (*conclusión*); make (*copia*). **~ adelante** bring up (*niño*); carry on (*negocio*)

sacarina *f* saccharin

sacerdo|cio *m* priesthood. **~tal** *a* priestly. **~te** *m* priest

saciar *vt* satisfy

saco *m* bag; (*anat*) sac; (*LAm, chaqueta*) jacket; (*de mentiras*) pack. **~ de dormir** sleeping-bag

sacramento *m* sacrament

sacrific|ar [7] *vt* sacrifice. **~arse** *vpr* sacrifice o.s. **~io** *m* sacrifice

sacr|ilegio *m* sacrilege. **~ílego** *a* sacrilegious

sacro *a* sacred, holy. **~santo** *a* sacrosanct

sacudi|da *f* shake; (*movimiento brusco*) jolt, jerk; (*fig*) shock. **~da eléctrica** electric shock. **~r** *vt* shake; (*golpear*) beat; (*ahuyentar*) chase away. **~rse** *vpr* shake off; (*fig*) get rid of

sádico *a* sadistic. ● *m* sadist

sadismo *m* sadism

saeta *f* arrow; (*de reloj*) hand

safari *m* safari

sagaz *a* shrewd

Sagitario *m* Sagittarius

sagrado *a* sacred, holy. ● *m* sanctuary

Sahara *m*, **Sáhara** /'saxara/ *m* Sahara

sainete *m* short comedy

sal *f* salt

sala *f* room; (*en teatro*) house. **~ de espectáculos** concert hall, auditorium. **~ de espera** waiting-room. **~ de estar** living-room. **~ de fiestas** nightclub

sala|do *a* salty; (*agua del mar*) salt; (*vivo*) lively; (*encantador*) cute; (*fig*) witty. **~r** *vt* salt

salario *m* wages

salazón *f* (*carne*) salted meat; (*pescado*) salted fish

salchich|a *f* (*pork*) sausage. **~ón** *m* salami

sald|ar *vt* pay (*cuenta*); (*vender*) sell off; (*fig*) settle. **~o** *m* balance; (*venta*) sale; (*lo que queda*) remnant

salero *m* salt-cellar

salgo *vb véase* **salir**

sali|da *f* departure; (*puerta*) exit, way out; (*de gas, de líquido*) leak; (*de astro*) rising; (*com, posibilidad de venta*) opening; (*chiste*) witty remark; (*fig*) way out. **~da de emergencia** emergency exit. **~ente** *a* projecting; (*fig*) outstanding. **~r** [52] *vi* leave; (*de casa etc*) go out; (*revista etc*) be published; (*resultar*) turn out; (*astro*) rise; (*aparecer*) appear. **~rse** *vpr* leave; (*recipiente, líquido etc*) leak. **~r adelante** get by. **~rse con la suya** get one's own way

saliva *f* saliva

salmo *m* psalm

salm|ón *m* salmon. **~onete** *m* red mullet

salmuera *f* brine

salón *m* lounge, sitting-room. **~ de actos** assembly hall. **~ de fiestas** dancehall

salpica|dero m (auto) dashboard. **~dura** f splash; (acción) splashing. **~r** [7] vt splash; (fig) sprinkle

sals|a f sauce; (para carne asada) gravy; (fig) spice. **~a verde** parsley sauce. **~era** f sauce-boat

salt|amontes m invar grasshopper. **~ar** vt jump (over); (fig) miss out. ● vi jump; (romperse) break; ⟨líquido⟩ spurt out; (desprenderse) come off; ⟨pelota⟩ bounce; (estallar) explode. **~eador** m highwayman. **~ear** vt rob; (culin) sauté. ● vi skip through

saltimbanqui m acrobat

salt|o m jump; (al agua) dive. **~o de agua** waterfall. **~ón** a ⟨ojos⟩ bulging. ● m grasshopper. a **~os** by jumping; (fig) by leaps and bounds. **de un ~o** with one jump

salud f health; (fig) welfare. ● int cheers! **~able** a healthy

salud|ar vt greet, say hello to; (mil) salute. **~o** m greeting; (mil) salute. **~os** mpl best wishes. **le ~a atentamente** (en cartas) yours faithfully

salva f salvo; (de aplausos) thunders

salvación f salvation

salvado m bran

Salvador m. **El ~** El Salvador

salvaguardia f safeguard

salvaje a ⟨planta, animal⟩ wild; (primitivo) savage. ● m & f savage

salvamanteles m invar table-mat

salva|mento m rescue. **~r** vt save, rescue; (atravesar) cross; (recorrer) travel; (fig) overcome. **~rse** vpr save o.s. **~vidas** m invar lifebelt. **chaleco ~vidas** life-jacket

salvia f sage

salvo a safe. ● adv & prep except (for). **~ que** unless. **~conducto** m safe-conduct. **a ~** out of danger. **poner a ~** put in a safe place

samba f samba

San a Saint, St. **~ Miguel** St Michael

sana|r vt cure. ● vi recover. **~torio** m sanatorium

sanci|ón f sanction. **~onar** vt sanction

sancocho m (LAm) stew

sandalia f sandal

sándalo m sandalwood

sandía f water melon

sandwich /'sambitʃ/ m (pl **sandwichs, sandwiches**) sandwich

sanear vt drain

sangr|ante a bleeding; (fig) flagrant. **~ar** vt/i bleed. **~e** f blood. **a ~e fría** in cold blood

sangría f (bebida) sangria

sangriento a bloody

sangu|ijuela f leech. **~íneo** a blood

san|idad f health. **~itario** a sanitary. **~o** a healthy; (seguro) sound. **~o y salvo** safe and sound. **cortar por lo ~o** settle things once and for all

santiamén m. **en un ~** in an instant

sant|idad f sanctity. **~ificar** [7] vt sanctify. **~iguar** [15] vt make the sign of the cross over. **~iguarse** vpr cross o.s. **~o** a holy; (delante de nombre) Saint, St. ● m saint; (día) saint's day, name day. **~uario** m sanctuary. **~urrón** a sanctimonious, hypocritical

sañ|a f fury; (crueldad) cruelty. **~oso** a, **~udo** a furious

sapo m toad; (bicho, fam) small animal, creature

saque m (en tenis) service; (en fútbol) throw-in; (inicial en fútbol) kick-off

saque|ar vt loot. **~o** m looting

sarampión m measles

sarape m (Mex) blanket

sarc|asmo m sarcasm. **~ástico** a sarcastic

sardana f Catalonian dance

sardina f sardine

sardo a & m Sardinian

sardónico a sardonic

sargento m sergeant

sarmiento m vine shoot

sarpullido m rash

sarta f string

sartén f frying-pan (Brit), fry-pan (Amer)

sastre m tailor. **~ría** f tailoring; (tienda) tailor's (shop)

Satanás m Satan

satánico a satanic

satélite m satellite

satinado a shiny

sátira f satire

satírico a satirical. ● m satirist

satisf|acción f satisfaction. **~acer** [31] vt satisfy; (pagar) pay; (gustar) please; meet ⟨gastos, requisitos⟩. **~acerse** vpr satisfy o.s.; (vengarse) take revenge. **~actorio** a satisfactory. **~echo** a satisfied. **~echo de sí mismo** smug

satura|ción f saturation. **~r** vt saturate

Saturno m Saturn

sauce m willow. **~ llorón** weeping willow

saúco *m* elder

savia *f* sap

sauna *f* sauna

saxofón *m*, **saxófono** *m* saxophone

saz|ón *f* ripeness; *(culin)* seasoning. **~onado** *a* ripe; *(culin)* seasoned. **~onar** *vt* ripen; *(culin)* season. **en ~ón** in season

se *pron* *(él)* him; *(ella)* her; *(Vd)* you; *(reflexivo, él)* himself; *(reflexivo, ella)* herself; *(reflexivo, ello)* itself; *(reflexivo, uno)* oneself; *(reflexivo, Vd)* yourself; *(reflexivo, ellos, ellas)* themselves; *(reflexivo, Vds)* yourselves; *(recíproco)* (to) each other. **~ dice** people say, they say, it is said *(que* that). **~ habla español** Spanish spoken

sé *vb véase* **saber** *y* **ser**

sea *vb véase* **ser**

sebo *m* tallow; *(culin)* suet

seca|dor *m* drier; *(de pelo)* hairdrier. **~nte** *a* drying. ● *m* blotting-paper. **~r** [7] *vt* dry. **~rse** *vpr* dry; ‹río etc› dry up; ‹persona› dry o.s.

sección *f* section

seco *a* dry; *(frutos, flores)* dried; *(flaco)* thin; *(respuesta)* curt; *(escueto)* plain. **a secas** just. **en ~** *(bruscamente)* suddenly. **lavar en ~** dry-clean

secre|ción *f* secretion. **~tar** *vt* secrete

secretar|ía *f* secretariat. **~io** *m* secretary

secreto *a & m* secret

secta *f* sect. **~rio** *a* sectarian

sector *m* sector

secuela *f* consequence

secuencia *f* sequence

secuestr|ar *vt* confiscate; kidnap ‹persona›; hijack ‹avión›. **~o** *m* seizure; *(de persona)* kidnapping; *(de avión)* hijack(ing)

secular *a* secular

secundar *vt* second, help. **~io** *a* secondary

sed *f* thirst. ● *vb véase* **ser**. **tener ~** be thirsty. **tener ~ de** *(fig)* be hungry for

seda *f* silk

sedante *a & m*, **sedativo** *a & m* sedative

sede *f* seat; *(relig)* see

sedentario *a* sedentary

sedici|ón *f* sedition. **~oso** *a* seditious

sediento *a* thirsty

sediment|ar *vi* deposit. **~arse** *vpr* settle. **~o** *m* sediment

seduc|ción *f* seduction. **~ir** [47] *vt* seduce; *(atraer)* attract. **~tor** *a* seductive. ● *m* seducer

sega|dor *m* harvester. **~dora** *f* harvester, mower. **~r** [1 & 12] *vt* reap

seglar *a* secular. ● *m* layman

segmento *m* segment

segoviano *m* person from Segovia

segrega|ción *f* segregation. **~r** [12] *vt* segregate

segui|da *f*. **en ~da** immediately. **~do** *a* continuous; *(en plural)* consecutive. ● *adv* straight; *(después)* after. **todo ~do** straight ahead. **~dor** *a* following. ● *m* follower. **~r** [5 & 13] *vt* follow *(continuar)* continue

según *prep* according to. ● *adv* it depends; *(a medida que)* as

segundo *a* a second. ● *m* second; *(culin)* second course

segur|amente *adv* certainly; *(muy probablemente)* surely. **~idad** *f* safety; *(certeza)* certainty; *(aplomo)* confidence. **~idad en sí mismo** self-confidence. **~idad social** social security. **~o** *a* safe; *(cierto)* certain, sure; *(firme)* secure; *(de fiar)* reliable. ● *adv* for certain. ● *m* insurance; *(dispositivo de seguridad)* safety device. **~o de sí mismo** self-confident. **~o de terceros** third-party insurance

seis *a & m* six. **~cientos** *a & m* six hundred

seísmo *m* earthquake

selec|ción *f* selection. **~cionar** *vt* select, choose. **~tivo** *a* selective. **~to** *a* selected; *(fig)* choice

selva *f* forest; *(jungla)* jungle

sell|ar *vt* stamp; *(cerrar)* seal. **~o** *m* stamp; *(en documento oficial)* seal; *(fig, distintivo)* hallmark

semáforo *m* semaphore; *(auto)* traffic lights; *(rail)* signal

semana *f* week. **~l** *a* weekly. **~rio** *a & m* weekly. **S~ Santa** Holy Week

semántic|a *f* semantics. **~o** *a* semantic

semblante *m* face; *(fig)* look

sembrar [1] *vt* sow; *(fig)* scatter

semeja|nte *a* similar; *(tal)* such. ● *m* fellow man; *(cosa)* equal. **~nza** *f* similarity. **~r** *vi* seem. **~rse** *vpr* look alike. **a ~nza de** like. **tener ~nza con** resemble

semen *m* semen. ~**tal** *a* stud. ● *m* stud animal

semestr|al *a* half-yearly. ~**e** *m* six months

semibreve *m* semibreve (*Brit*), whole note (*Amer*)

semic|ircular *a* semicircular. ~**írculo** *m* semicircle

semicorchea *f* semiquaver (*Brit*), sixteenth note (*Amer*)

semifinal *f* semifinal

semill|a *f* seed. ~**ero** *m* nursery; (*fig*) hotbed

seminario *m* (*univ*) seminar; (*relig*) seminary

sem|ita *a* Semitic. ● *m* Semite. ~**ítico** *a* Semitic

sémola *f* semolina

senado *m* senate; (*fig*) assembly. ~**r** *m* senator

sencill|ez *f* simplicity. ~**o** *a* simple; (*uno solo*) single

senda *f*, **sendero** *m* path

sendos *apl* each

seno *m* bosom. ~ **materno** womb

sensaci|ón *f* sensation. ~**onal** *a* sensational

sensat|ez *f* good sense. ~**o** *a* sensible

sensi|bilidad *f* sensibility. ~**ble** *a* sensitive; (*notable*) notable; (*lamentable*) lamentable. ~**tivo** *a* (*órgano*) sense

sensual *a* sensual. ~**idad** *f* sensuality

senta|do *a* sitting (down). **dar algo por** ~**do** take something for granted. ~**r** [1] *vt* place; (*establecer*) establish. ● *vi* suit; (*de medidas*) fit; (*comida*) agree with. ~**rse** *vpr* sit (down); (*sedimento*) settle

sentencia *f* saying; (*jurid*) sentence. ~**r** *vt* sentence

sentido *a* deeply felt; (*sincero*) sincere; (*sensible*) sensitive. ● *m* sense; (*dirección*) direction. ~ **común** common sense. ~ **del humor** sense of humour. ~ **único** one-way. **doble** ~ double meaning. **no tener** ~ not make sense. **perder el** ~ faint. **sin** ~ unconscious; (*cosa*) senseless

sentim|ental *a* sentimental. ~**iento** *m* feeling; (*sentido*) sense; (*pesar*) regret

sentir [4] *vt* feel; (*oír*) hear; (*lamentar*) be sorry for. ● *vi* feel; (*lamentarse*) be sorry. ● *m* (*opinión*) opinion. ~**se** *vpr* feel. **lo siento** I'm sorry

seña *f* sign. ~**s** *fpl* (*dirección*) address; (*descripción*) description

señal *f* sign; (*rail etc*) signal; (*telefónico*) tone; (*com*) deposit. ~**ado** *a* notable. ~**ar** *vt* signal; (*poner señales en*) mark; (*apuntar*) point out; (*manecilla, aguja*) point to; (*determinar*) fix. ~**arse** *vpr* stand out. **dar** ~**es de** show signs of. **en** ~ **de** as a token of

señero *a* alone; (*sin par*) unique

señor *m* man; (*caballero*) gentleman; (*delante de nombre propio*) Mr; (*tratamiento directo*) sir. ~**a** *f* lady, woman; (*delante de nombre propio*) Mrs; (*esposa*) wife; (*tratamiento directo*) madam. ~**ial** *a* (*casa*) stately. ~**ita** *f* young lady; (*delante de nombre propio*) Miss; (*tratamiento directo*) miss. ~**ito** *m* young gentleman. **el** ~ **alcalde** the mayor. **el** ~ **Mr. muy** ~ **mío** Dear Sir. **¡no** ~**!** certainly not! **ser** ~ **de** be master of, control

señuelo *m* lure

sepa *vb véase* **saber**

separa|ción *f* separation. ~**do** *a* separate. ~**r** *vt* separate; (*apartar*) move away; (*de empleo*) dismiss. ~**rse** *vpr* separate; (*amigos*) part. ~**tista** *a* & *m* & *f* separatist. **por** ~**do** separately

septentrional *a* north(ern)

séptico *a* septic

septiembre *m* September

séptimo *a* seventh

sepulcro *m* sepulchre

sepult|ar *vt* bury. ~**ura** *f* burial; (*tumba*) grave. ~**urero** *m* gravedigger

sequ|edad *f* dryness. ~**ía** *f* drought

séquito *m* entourage; (*fig*) aftermath

ser [39] *vi* be. ● *m* being. ~ **de** be made of; (*provenir de*) come from; (*pertenecer a*) belong to. ~ **humano** human being. **a no** ~ **que** unless. **¡así sea!** so be it! **es más** what is more. **lo que sea** anything. **no sea que, no vaya a** ~ **que** in case. **o sea** in other words. **sea lo que fuere** be that as it may. **sea... sea** either... or. **siendo así que** since. **soy yo** it's me

seren|ar *vt* calm down. ~**arse** *vpr* calm down; (*tiempo*) clear up. ~**ata** *f* serenade. ~**idad** *f* serenity. ~**o** *a* (*cielo*) clear; (*tiempo*) fine; (*fig*) calm. ● *m* night watchman. **al** ~**o** in the open

seri|al *m* serial. **∼e** *f* series. **fuera de ∼e** (*fig, extraordinario*) special. **producción f en ∼** mass production

seri|edad *f* seriousness. **∼o** *a* serious; (*confiable*) reliable. **en ∼o** seriously. **poco ∼o** frivolous

sermón *m* sermon

serp|enteante *a* winding. **∼entear** *vi* wind. **∼iente** *f* snake. **∼iente de cascabel** rattlesnake

serrano *a* mountain; ⟨*jamón*⟩ cured

serr|ar [1] *vt* saw. **∼ín** *m* sawdust. **∼ucho** *m* (hand)saw

servi|cial *a* helpful. **∼cio** *m* service; (*conjunto*) set; (*aseo*) toilet. **∼cio a domicilio** delivery service. **∼dor** *m* servant. **∼dumbre** *f* servitude; (*criados*) servants, staff. **∼l** *a* servile. **su (seguro) ∼dor** (*en cartas*) yours faithfully

servilleta *f* serviette, (table) napkin

servir [5] *vt* serve; (*ayudar*) help; (*en restaurante*) wait on. ● *vi* serve; (*ser útil*) be of use. **∼se** *vpr* help o.s. **∼se de** use. **no ∼ de nada** be useless. **para ∼le** at your service. **sírvase sentarse** please sit down

sesear *vi* pronounce the Spanish *c* as an *s*

sesent|a *a & m* sixty. **∼ón** *a & m* sixty-year-old

seseo *m* pronunciation of the Spanish *c* as an *s*

sesg|ado *a* slanting. **∼o** *m* slant; (*fig, rumbo*) turn

sesión *f* session; (*en el cine*) showing; (*en el teatro*) performance

ses|o *m* brain; (*fig*) brains. **∼udo** *a* inteligent; (*sensato*) sensible

seta *f* mushroom

sete|cientos *a & m* seven hundred. **∼nta** *a & m* seventy. **∼ntón** *a & m* seventy-year-old

setiembre *m* September

seto *m* fence; (*de plantas*) hedge. **∼ vivo** hedge

seudo... *pref* pseudo...

seudónimo *m* pseudonym

sever|idad *f* severity. **∼o** *a* severe; ⟨*disciplina, profesor etc*⟩ strict

Sevilla *f* Seville

sevillan|as *fpl* popular dance from Seville. **∼o** *m* person from Seville

sexo *m* sex

sext|eto *m* sextet. **∼o** *a* sixth

sexual *a* sexual. **∼idad** *f* sexuality

si *m* (*mus*) B; (*solfa*) te. ● *conj* if; (*dubitativo*) whether. **∼ no** or else. **por ∼ (acaso)** in case

sí *pron reflexivo* (*él*) himself; (*ella*) herself; (*ello*) itself; (*uno*) oneself; (*Vd*) yourself; (*ellos, ellas*) themselves; (*Vds*) yourselves; (*recíproco*) each other

sí *adv* yes. ● *m* consent

Siamés *a & m* Siamese

Sicilia *f* Sicily

sida *m* Aids

siderurgia *f* iron and steel industry

sidra *f* cider

siega *f* harvesting; (*época*) harvest time

siembra *f* sowing; (*época*) sowing time

siempre *adv* always. **∼ que** if. **como ∼** as usual. **de ∼** (*acostumbrado*) usual. **lo de ∼** the same old story. **para ∼** for ever

sien *f* temple

siento *vb véase* **sentar** *y* **sentir**

sierra *f* saw; (*cordillera*) mountain range

siervo *m* slave

siesta *f* siesta

siete *a & m* seven

sífilis *f* syphilis

sifón *m* U-bend; (*de soda*) syphon

sigilo *m* secrecy

sigla *f* initials, abbreviation

siglo *m* century; (*época*) time, age; (*fig, mucho tiempo, fam*) ages; (*fig, mundo*) world

significa|ción *f* meaning; (*importancia*) significance. **∼do** *a* (*conocido*) well-known. ● *m* meaning. **∼r** [7] *vt* mean; (*expresar*) express. **∼rse** *vpr* stand out. **∼tivo** *a* significant

signo *m* sign. **∼ de admiración** exclamation mark. **∼ de interrogación** question mark

sigo *vb véase* **seguir**

siguiente *a* following, next. **lo ∼** the following

sílaba *f* syllable

silb|ar *vt/i* whistle. **∼ato** *m*, **∼ido** *m* whistle

silenci|ador *m* silencer. **∼ar** *vt* hush up. **∼o** *m* silence. **∼oso** *a* silent

sílfide *f* sylph

silicio *m* silicon

silo *m* silo

silueta *f* silhouette; (*dibujo*) outline

silvestre *a* wild

sill|a *f* chair; (*de montar*) saddle; (*relig*) see. **∼a de ruedas** wheelchair. **∼ín** *m* saddle. **∼ón** *m* armchair

simb|ólico *a* symbolic(al). **~olismo** *m* symbolism. **~olizar** [10] *vt* symbolize

símbolo *m* symbol

sim|etría *f* symmetry. **~étrico** *a* symmetric(al)

simiente *f* seed

similar *a* similar

simp|atía *f* liking; (*cariño*) affection; (*fig, amigo*) friend. **~ático** *a* nice, likeable; (*amable*) kind. **~atizante** *m* & *f* sympathizer. **~atizar** [10] *vi* get on (well together). **me es ~ático** I like

simpl|e *a* simple; (*mero*) mere. **~eza** *f* simplicity; (*tontería*) stupid thing; (*insignificancia*) trifle. **~icidad** *f* simplicity. **~ificar** [7] *vt* simplify. **~ón** *m* simpleton

simposio *m* symposium

simula|ción *f* simulation. **~r** *vt* feign

simultáneo *a* simultaneous

sin *prep* without. **~ que** without

sinagoga *f* synagogue

sincer|idad *f* sincerity. **~o** *a* sincere

síncopa *f* (*mus*) syncopation

sincopar *vt* syncopate

sincronizar [10] *vt* synchronize

sindica|l *a* (trade-)union. **~lista** *m* & *f* trade-unionist. **~to** *m* trade union

síndrome *m* syndrome

sinfín *m* endless number

sinf|onía *f* symphony. **~ónico** *a* symphonic

singular *a* singular; (*excepcional*) exceptional. **~izar** [10] *vt* single out. **~izarse** *vpr* stand out

siniestro *a* sinister; (*desgraciado*) unlucky. ● *m* disaster

sinnúmero *m* endless number

sino *m* fate. ● *conj* but; (*salvo*) except

sínodo *m* synod

sinónimo *a* synonymous. ● *m* synonym

sinrazón *f* wrong

sintaxis *f* syntax

síntesis *f invar* synthesis

sint|ético *a* synthetic. **~etizar** [10] *vt* synthesize; (*resumir*) summarize

síntoma *f* sympton

sintomático *a* symptomatic

sinton|ía *f* (*en la radio*) signature tune. **~izar** [10] *vt* (*con la radio*) tune (in)

sinuoso *a* winding

sinvergüenza *m* & *f* scoundrel

sionis|mo *m* Zionism. **~ta** *m* & *f* Zionist

siquiera *conj* even if. ● *adv* at least. **ni ~** not even

sirena *f* siren

Siria *f* Syria

sirio *a* & *m* Syrian

siroco *m* sirocco

sirvienta *f*, **sirviente** *m* servant

sirvo *vb* *véase* **servir**

sise|ar *vt/i* hiss. **~o** *m* hissing

sísmico *a* seismic

sismo *m* earthquake

sistem|a *m* system. **~ático** *a* systematic. **por ~a** as a rule

sitiar *vt* besiege; (*fig*) surround

sitio *m* place; (*espacio*) space; (*mil*) siege. **en cualquier ~** anywhere

situa|ción *f* position. **~r** [21] *vt* situate; (*poner*) put; (*depositar*) deposit. **~rse** *vpr* be successful, establish o.s.

slip /es'lip/ *m* (*pl* **slips** /es'lip/) underpants, briefs

slogan /es'logan/ *m* (*pl* **slogans** /es'logan/) slogan

smoking /es'mokin/ *m* (*pl* **smokings** /es'mokin/) dinner jacket (*Brit*), tuxedo (*Amer*)

sobaco *m* armpit

sobar *vt* handle; knead ⟨*masa*⟩

soberan|ía *f* sovereignty. **~o** *a* sovereign; (*fig*) supreme. ● *m* sovereign

soberbi|a *f* pride; (*altanería*) arrogance. **~o** *a* proud; (*altivo*) arrogant

soborn|ar *vt* bribe. **~o** *m* bribe

sobra *f* surplus. **~s** *fpl* leftovers. **~do** *a* more than enough. **~nte** *a* surplus. **~r** *vi* be left over; (*estorbar*) be in the way. **de ~** more than enough

sobrasada *f* Majorcan sausage

sobre *prep* on; (*encima de*) on top of; (*más o menos*) about; (*por encima de*) above; (*sin tocar*) over; (*además de*) on top of. ● *m* envelope. **~cargar** [12] *vt* overload. **~coger** [14] *vt* startle. **~cogerse** *vpr* be startled. **~cubierta** *f* dust cover. **~dicho** *a* aforementioned. **~entender** [1] *vt* understand, infer. **~entendido** *a* implicit. **~humano** *a* superhuman. **~llevar** *vt* bear. **~mesa** *f*. **de ~mesa** after-dinner. **~natural** *a* supernatural. **~nombre** *m* nickname. **~pasar** *vt* exceed. **~poner** [34] *vt* superimpose; (*fig, anteponer*) put before. **~ponerse** *vpr* overcome. **~pujar** *vt* surpass. **~saliente** *a* (*fig*) outstanding. ● *m* excellent mark. **~salir** [52] *vi* stick out;

(fig) stand out. **~saltar** *vt* startle. **~salto** *m* fright. **~sueldo** *m* bonus. **~todo** *m* overall; *(abrigo)* overcoat. **~ todo** above all, especially. **~venir** [53] *vi* happen. **~viviente** *a* surviving. ● *m* & *f* survivor. **~vivir** *vi* survive. **~volar** *vt* fly over

sobriedad *f* restraint

sobrin|a *f* niece. **~o** *m* nephew

sobrio *a* moderate, sober

socarr|ón *a* sarcastic; *(taimado)* sly. **~onería** *f* sarcasm

socavar *vt* undermine

soci|able *a* sociable. **~al** *a* social. **~aldemocracia** *f* social democracy. **~aldemócrata** *m* & *f* social democrat. **~alismo** *m* socialsim. **~alista** *a* & *m* & *f* socialist. **~alizar** [10] *vt* nationalize. **~edad** *f* society; *(com)* company. **~edad anónima** limited company. **~o** *m* member; *(com)* partner. **~ología** *f* sociology. **~ólogo** *m* sociologist

socorr|er *vt* help. **~o** *m* help

soda *f* *(bebida)* soda (water)

sodio *m* sodium

sofá *m* sofa, settee

sofistica|ción *f* sophistication. **~do** *a* sophisticated. **~r** [7] *vt* adulterate

sofoca|ción *f* suffocation. **~nte** *a* *(fig)* stifling. **~r** [7] *vt* suffocate; *(fig)* stifle. **~rse** *vpr* suffocate; *(ruborizarse)* blush

soga *f* rope

soja *f* soya (bean)

sojuzgar [12] *vt* subdue

sol *m* sun; *(luz solar)* sunlight; *(mus)* G; *(solfa)* soh. **al ~** in the sun. **día** *m* **de ~** sunny day. **hace ~, hay ~** it is sunny. **tomar el ~** sunbathe

solamente *adv* only

solapa *f* lapel; *(de bolsillo etc)* flap. **~do** *a* sly. **~r** *vt/i* overlap

solar *a* solar. ● *m* plot

solariego *a* *(casa)* ancestral

solaz *m* relaxation

soldado *m* soldier. **~ raso** private

solda|dor *m* welder; *(utensilio)* soldering iron. **~r** [2] *vt* weld, solder

solea|do *a* sunny. **~r** *vt* put in the sun

soledad *f* solitude; *(aislamiento)* loneliness

solemn|e *a* solemn. **~idad** *f* solemnity; *(ceremonia)* ceremony

soler [2] *vi* be in the habit of. **suele despertarse a las 6** he usually wakes up at 6 o'clock

sol|icitar *vt* request; apply for *(empleo)*; attract *(atención)*. **~ícito** *a* solicitous. **~icitud** *f* *(atención)* concern; *(petición)* request; *(para un puesto)* application

solidaridad *f* solidarity

solid|ez *f* solidity; *(de color)* fastness. **~ificar** [7] *vt* solidify. **~ificarse** *vpr* solidify

sólido *a* solid; *(color)* fast; *(robusto)* strong. ● *m* solid

soliloquio *m* soliloquy

solista *m* & *f* soloist

solitario *a* solitary; *(aislado)* lonely. ● *m* recluse; *(juego, diamante)* solitaire

solo *a* *(sin compañía)* alone; *(aislado)* lonely; *(único)* only; *(mus)* solo; *(café)* black. ● *m* solo; *(juego)* solitaire. **a solas** alone

sólo *adv* only. **~ que** only. **aunque ~ sea** even if it is only. **con ~ que** if; *(con tal que)* as long as. **no ~... sino también** not only... but also... **tan ~** only

solomillo *m* sirloin

solsticio *m* solstice

soltar [2] *vt* let go of; *(dejar caer)* drop; *(dejar salir, decir)* let out; give *(golpe etc)*. **~se** *vpr* come undone; *(librarse)* break loose

solter|a *f* single woman. **~o** *a* single. ● *m* bachelor. **apellido** *m* **de ~a** maiden name

soltura *f* looseness; *(agilidad)* agility; *(en hablar)* ease, fluency

solu|ble *a* soluble. **~ción** *f* solution. **~cionar** *vt* solve; settle *(huelga, asunto)*

solvent|ar *vt* resolve; settle *(deuda)*. **~e** *a* & *m* solvent

sollo *m* sturgeon

solloz|ar [10] *vi* sob. **~o** *m* sob

sombr|a *f* shade; *(imagen oscura)* shadow. **~eado** *a* shady. **a la ~a** in the shade

sombrero *m* hat. **~ hongo** bowler hat

sombrío *a* sombre

somero *a* shallow

someter *vt* subdue; subject *(persona)*; *(presentar)* submit. **~se** *vpr* give in

somn|oliento *a* sleepy. **~ífero** *m* sleeping-pill

somos *vb véase* **ser**

son *m* sound. ● *vb véase* **ser**

sonámbulo *m* sleepwalker

sonar [2] *vt* blow; ring ‹*timbre*›. ● *vi* sound; ‹*timbre, teléfono etc*› ring; ‹*reloj*› strike; (*pronunciarse*) be pronounced; (*mus*) play; (*fig, ser conocido*) be familiar. ~**se** *vpr* blow one's nose. ~**a** sound like

sonata *f* sonata

sonde|ar *vt* sound; (*fig*) sound out. ~**o** *m* sounding; (*fig*) poll

soneto *m* sonnet

sónico *a* sonic

sonido *m* sound

sonoro *a* sonorous; (*ruidoso*) loud

sonr|eír [51] *vi* smile. ~**eírse** *vpr* smile. ~**iente** *a* smiling. ~**isa** *f* smile

sonroj|ar *vt* make blush. ~**arse** *vpr* blush. ~**o** *m* blush

sonrosado *a* rosy, pink

sonsacar [7] *vt* wheedle out

soñ|ado *a* dream. ~**ador** *m* dreamer. ~**ar** [2] *vi* dream (con of). ¡**ni** ~**arlo!** not likely! (**que**) **ni** ~**ado** marvellous

sopa *f* soup

sopesar *vt* (*fig*) weigh up

sopl|ar *vt* blow; blow out ‹*vela*›; blow off (*polvo*); (*inflar*) blow up. ● *vi* blow. ~**ete** *m* blowlamp. ~**o** *m* puff; (*fig, momento*) moment

soporífero *a* soporific. ● *m* sleeping-pill

soport|al *m* porch. ~**ales** *mpl* arcade. ~**ar** *vt* support; (*fig*) bear. ~**e** *m* support

soprano *f* soprano

sor *f* sister

sorb|er *vt* suck; sip ‹*bebida*›; (*absorber*) absorb. ~**ete** *m* sorbet, water-ice. ~**o** *m* swallow; (*pequeña cantidad*) sip

sord|amente *adv* silently, dully. ~**era** *f* deafness

sórdido *a* squalid; (*tacaño*) mean

sordo *a* deaf; (*silencioso*) quiet. ● *m* deaf person. ~**mudo** *a* deaf and dumb. **a la sorda, a sordas** on the quiet. **hacerse el** ~ turn a deaf ear

sorna *f* sarcasm. **con** ~ sarcastically

soroche *m* (*LAm*) mountain sickness

sorpre|ndente *a* surprising. ~**nder** *vt* surprise; (*coger desprevenido*) catch. ~**sa** *f* surprise

sorte|ar *vt* draw lots for; (*rifar*) raffle; (*fig*) avoid. ● *vi* draw lots; (*con moneda*) toss up. ~**o** *m* draw; (*rifa*) raffle; (*fig*) avoidance

sortija *f* ring; (*de pelo*) ringlet

sortilegio *m* witchcraft; (*fig*) spell

sos|egado *a* calm. ~**egar** [1 & 12] *vt* calm. ● *vi* rest. ~**iego** *m* calmness. **con** ~**iego** calmly

soslayo. al ~, **de** ~ sideways

soso *a* tasteless; (*fig*) dull

sospech|a *f* suspicion. ~**ar** *vt/i* suspect. ~**oso** *a* suspicious. ● *m* suspect

sost|én *m* support; (*prenda femenina*) bra (*fam*), brassière. ~**ener** [40] *vt* support; (*sujetar*) hold; (*mantener*) maintain; (*alimentar*) sustain. ~**enerse** *vpr* support o.s.; (*continuar*) remain. ~**enido** *a* sustained; (*mus*) sharp. ● *m* (*mus*) sharp

sota *f* (*de naipes*) jack

sótano *m* basement

sotavento *m* lee

soto *m* grove; (*matorral*) thicket

soviético *a* (*historia*) Soviet

soy *vb véase* **ser**

Sr *abrev* (*Señor*) Mr. ~**a** *abrev* (*Señora*) Mrs. ~**ta** *abrev* (*Señorita*) Miss

su *a* (*de él*) his; (*de ella*) her; (*de ello*) its; (*de uno*) one's; (*de Vd*) your; (*de ellos, de ellas*) their; (*de Vds*) your

suav|e *a* smooth; (*fig*) gentle; ‹*color, sonido*› soft. ~**idad** *f* smoothness, softness. ~**izar** [10] *vt* smooth, soften

subalimentado *a* underfed

subalterno *a* secondary; ‹*persona*› auxiliary

subarrendar [1] *vt* sublet

subasta *f* auction; (*oferta*) tender. ~**r** *vt* auction

sub|campeón *m* runner-up. ~**consciencia** *f* subconscious. ~**consciente** *a & m* subconscious. ~**continente** *m* subcontinent. ~**desarrollado** *a* under-developed. ~**director** *m* assistant manager

súbdito *m* subject

sub|dividir *vt* subdivide. ~**estimar** *vt* underestimate. ~**gerente** *m & f* assistant manager

subi|da *f* ascent; (*aumento*) rise; (*pendiente*) slope. ~**do** *a* ‹*precio*› high; ‹*color*› bright; ‹*olor*› strong. ~**r** *vt* go up; (*poner*) put; (*llevar*) take up; (*aumentar*) increase. ● *vi* go up. ~**r a** get into ‹*coche*›; get on ‹*autobús, avión, barco, tren*›; (*aumentar*) increase. ~**rse** *vpr* climb up. ~**rse a** get on ‹*tren etc*›

súbito *a* sudden. ● *adv* suddenly. **de** ~ suddenly

subjetivo *a* subjective

subjuntivo *a & m* subjunctive

subleva|ción *f* uprising. **~r** *vt* incite to rebellion. **~rse** *vpr* rebel

sublim|ar *vt* sublimate. **~e** *a* sublime

submarino *a* underwater. ● *m* submarine

subordinado *a & m* subordinate

subrayar *vt* underline

subrepticio *a* surreptitious

subsanar *vt* remedy; overcome ⟨dificultad⟩

subscri|bir *vt* (*pp* **subscrito**) sign. **~birse** *vpr* subscribe. **~pción** *f* subscription

subsidi|ario *a* subsidiary. **~o** *m* subsidy. **~o de paro** unemployment benefit

subsiguiente *a* subsequent

subsist|encia *f* subsistence. **~ir** *vi* subsist; (*perdurar*) survive

substanci|a *f* substance. **~al** *a* important. **~oso** *a* substantial

substantivo *m* noun

substitu|ción *f* substitution. **~ir** [17] *vt/i* substitute. **~to** *a & m* substitute

substraer [41] *vt* take away

subterfugio *m* subterfuge

subterráneo *a* underground. ● *m* (*bodega*) cellar; (*conducto*) underground passage

subtítulo *m* subtitle

suburb|ano *a* suburban. ● *m* suburban train. **~io** *m* suburb; (*en barrio pobre*) slum

subvenci|ón *f* grant. **~onar** *vt* subsidize

subver|sión *f* subversion. **~sivo** *a* subversive. **~tir** [4] *vt* subvert

subyugar [12] *vt* subjugate; (*fig*) subdue

succión *f* suction

suce|der *vi* happen; (*seguir*) follow; (*substituir*) succeed. **~dido** *m* event. **lo ~dido** what happened. **~sión** *f* succession. **~sivo** *a* successive; (*consecutivo*) consecutive. **~so** *m* event; (*incidente*) incident. **~sor** *m* successor. **en lo ~sivo** in future. **lo que ~de es que** the trouble is that. **¿qué ~de?** what's the matter?

suciedad *f* dirt; (*estado*) dirtiness

sucinto *a* concise; ⟨prenda⟩ scanty

sucio *a* dirty; (*vil*) mean; ⟨conciencia⟩ guilty. **en ~** in rough

sucre *m* (*unidad monetaria del Ecuador*) sucre

suculento *a* succulent

sucumbir *vi* succumb

sucursal *f* branch (office)

Sudáfrica *m & f* South Africa

sudafricano *a & m* South African

Sudamérica *f* South America

sudamericano *a & m* South American

sudar *vt* work hard for. ● *vi* sweat

sud|este *m* south-east; (*viento*) south-east wind. **~oeste** *m* southwest; (*viento*) south-west wind

sudor *m* sweat

Suecia *f* Sweden

sueco *a* Swedish. ● *m* (*persona*) Swede; (*lengua*) Swedish. **hacerse el ~** pretend not to hear

suegr|a *f* mother-in-law. **~o** *m* father-in-law. **mis ~os** my in-laws

suela *f* sole

sueldo *m* salary

suelo *m* ground; (*dentro de edificio*) floor; (*tierra*) land. *véase* **soler**

suelto *a* loose; (*libre*) free; (*sin pareja*) odd; ⟨lenguaje⟩ fluent. ● *m* (*en periódico*) item; (*dinero*) change

sueño *m* sleep; (*ilusión*) dream. **tener ~** be sleepy

suero *m* serum; (*de leche*) whey

suerte *f* luck; (*destino*) fate; (*azar*) chance. **de otra ~** otherwise. **de ~ que** so. **echar ~s** draw lots. **por ~** fortunately. **tener ~** be lucky

suéter *m* jersey

suficien|cia *f* sufficiency; (*presunción*) smugness; (*aptitud*) suitability. **~te** *a* sufficient; (*presumido*) smug. **~temente** *adv* enough

sufijo *m* suffix

sufragio *m* (*voto*) vote

sufri|do *a* ⟨persona⟩ long-suffering; ⟨tela⟩ hard-wearing. **~miento** *m* suffering. **~r** *vt* suffer; (*experimentar*) undergo; (*soportar*) bear. ● *vi* suffer

suge|rencia *f* suggestion. **~rir** [4] *vt* suggest. **~stión** *f* suggestion. **~stionable** *a* impressionable. **~stionar** *vt* influence. **~stivo** *a* (*estimulante*) stimulating; (*atractivo*) attractive

suicid|a *a* suicidal. ● *m & f* suicide; (*fig*) maniac. **~arse** *vpr* commit suicide. **~io** *m* suicide

Suiza *f* Switzerland

suizo *a* Swiss. ● *m* Swiss; (*bollo*) bun

suje|ción f subjection. **∼tador** m
fastener; (de pelo, papeles etc) clip;
(prenda femenina) bra (fam), brassière. **∼tapapeles** m invar paperclip. **∼tar** vt fasten; (agarrar) hold;
(fig) restrain. **∼tarse** vr subject o.s.;
(ajustarse) conform. **∼to** a
fastened; (susceptible) subject. ● m
individual
sulfamida f sulpha (drug)
sulfúrico a sulphuric
sult|án m sultan. **∼ana** f sultana
suma f sum; (total) total. **en ∼** in
short. **∼mente** adv extremely. **∼r**
vt add (up); (fig) gather. ● vi add up.
∼rse vpr. **∼rse a** join in
sumario a brief. ● m summary;
(jurid) indictment
sumergi|ble a submarine. ● a sub-
mersible. **∼r** [14] vt submerge
sumidero m drain
suministr|ar vt supply. **∼o** m sup-
ply; (acción) supplying
sumir vt sink; (fig) plunge
sumis|ión f submission. **∼o** a
submissive
sumo a greatest; (supremo)
supreme. **a lo ∼** at the most
suntuoso a sumptuous
supe vb véase **saber**
superar vt surpass; (vencer) overcome; (dejar atrás) get past. **∼se**
vpr excel o.s.
superchería f swindle
superestructura f superstructure
superfici|al a superficial. **∼e** f sur-
face; (extensión) area. **de ∼e**
surface
superfluo a superfluous
superhombre m superman
superintendente m superintendent
superior a superior; (más alto)
higher; (mejor) better; (piso) upper.
● m superior. **∼idad** f superiority
superlativo a & m superlative
supermercado m supermarket
supersónico a supersonic
supersticí|ón f superstition. **∼oso** a
superstitious
supervis|ión f supervision. **∼or** m
supervisor
superviviente a surviving. ● m & f
survivor
suplantar vt supplant
suplement|ario a supplementary.
∼o m supplement
suplente a & m & f substitute
súplica f entreaty; (petición) request
suplicar [7] vt beg

suplicio m torture
suplir vt make up for; (reemplazar)
replace
supo|ner [34] vt suppose; (significar)
mean; (costar) cost. **∼sición** f
supposition
supositorio m suppository
suprem|acía f supremacy. **∼o** a
supreme; (momento etc) critical
supr|esión f suppression. **∼imir** vt
suppress; (omitir) omit
supuesto a supposed. ● m assumption. **∼ que** if. **¡por ∼!** of course!
sur m south; (viento) south wind
surc|ar [7] vt plough. **∼o** m furrow;
(de rueda) rut; (en la piel) wrinkle
surgir [14] vi spring up; (elevarse)
loom up; (aparecer) appear; (dificultad, oportunidad) arise, crop
up
surrealis|mo m surrealism. **∼ta** a &
m & f surrealist
surti|do a well-stocked; (variado)
assorted. ● m assortment, selection. **∼dor** m (de gasolina) petrol
pump (Brit), gas pump (Amer). **∼r**
vt supply; have (efecto). **∼rse** vpr
provide o.s. (de with)
susceptib|ilidad f susceptibility;
(sensibilidad) sensitivity. **∼le** a susceptible; (sensible) sensitive
suscitar vt provoke; arouse (curiosidad, interés, sospechas)
suscr... véase **subscr...**
susodicho a aforementioned
suspen|der vt hang (up); (inte-
rrumpir) suspend; (univ etc) fail.
∼derse vpr stop. **∼sión** f suspension. **∼so** a hanging; (pasmado)
amazed; (univ etc) failed. ● m fail.
en ∼so pending
suspicaz a suspicious
suspir|ar vi sigh. **∼o** m sigh
sust... véase **subst...**
sustent|ación f support. **∼ar** vt sup-
port; (alimentar) sustain; (mantener) maintain. **∼o** m support;
(alimento) sustenance
susto m fright. **caerse del ∼** be
frightened to death
susurr|ar vi (persona) whisper;
(agua) murmur; (hojas) rustle. **∼o**
m (de persona) whisper; (de agua)
murmur; (de hojas) rustle
sutil a fine; (fig) subtle. **∼eza** f fine-
ness; (fig) subtlety
suyo a & pron (de él) his; (de ella)
hers; (de ello) its; (de uno) one's; (de
Vd) yours; (de ellos, de ellas) theirs;

(*de Vds*) yours. **un amigo** ∼ a friend of his, a friend of theirs, etc

T

taba *f* (*anat*) ankle-bone; (*juego*) jacks

tabac|alera *f* (state) tobacconist. ∼**alero** *a* tobacco. ∼**o** *m* tobacco; (*cigarillos*) cigarettes; (*rapé*) snuff

tabalear *vi* drum (with one's fingers)

Tabasco *m* Tabasco (**P**)

tabern|a *f* bar. ∼**ero** *m* barman; (*dueño*) landlord

tabernáculo *m* tabernacle

tabique *m* (thin) wall

tabl|a *f* plank; (*de piedra etc*) slab; (*estante*) shelf; (*de vestido*) pleat; (*lista*) list; (*índice*) index; (*en matemática etc*) table. ∼**ado** *m* platform; (*en el teatro*) stage. ∼**ao** *m* place where flamenco shows are held. ∼**as reales** backgammon. ∼**ero** *m* board. ∼**ero de mandos** dashboard. **hacer** ∼**a rasa de** disregard

tableta *f* tablet; (*de chocolate*) bar

tabl|illa *f* small board. ∼**ón** *m* plank. ∼**ón de anuncios** notice board (*esp Brit*), bulletin board (*Amer*)

tabú *m* taboo

tabular *vt* tabulate

taburete *m* stool

tacaño *a* mean

tacita *f* small cup

tácito *a* tacit

taciturno *a* taciturn; (*triste*) miserable

taco *m* plug; (*LAm, tacón*) heel; (*de billar*) cue; (*de billetes*) book; (*fig, lío, fam*) mess; (*Mex, culin*) filled tortilla

tacógrafo *m* tachograph

tacón *m* heel

táctic|a *f* tactics. ∼**o** *a* tactical

táctil *a* tactile

tacto *m* touch; (*fig*) tact

tacuara *f* (*Arg*) bamboo

tacurú *m* (small) ant

tacha *f* fault; (*clavo*) tack. **poner** ∼**s a** find fault with. **sin** ∼ flawless

tachar *vt* (*borrar*) rub out; (*con raya*) cross out. ∼ **de** accuse of

tafia *f* (*LAm*) rum

tafilete *m* morocco

tahúr *m* card-sharp

Tailandia *f* Thailand

tailandés *a & m* Thai

taimado *a* sly

taj|ada *f* slice. ∼**ante** *a* sharp. ∼**o** *m* slash; (*fig, trabajo, fam*) job; (*culin*) chopping block. **sacar** ∼**ada** profit

Tajo *m* Tagus

tal *a* such; (*ante sustantivo en singular*) such a. ● *pron* (*persona*) someone; (*cosa*) such a thing. ● *adv* so; (*de tal manera*) in such a way. ∼ **como** the way. ∼ **cual** (*tal como*) the way; (*regular*) fair. ∼ **para cual** (*fam*) two of a kind. **con** ∼ **que** as long as. **¿qué** ∼**?** how are you? **un** ∼ a certain

taladr|ar *vt* drill. ∼**o** *m* drill; (*agujero*) drill hole

talante *m* mood. **de buen** ∼ willingly

talar *vt* fell; (*fig*) destroy

talco *m* talcum powder

talcualillo *a* (*fam*) so so

talega *f*, **talego** *m* sack

talento *m* talent

TALGO *m* high-speed train

talismán *m* talisman

tal|ón *m* heel; (*recibo*) counterfoil; (*cheque*) cheque. ∼**onario** *m* receipt book; (*de cheques*) cheque book

talla *f* carving; (*grabado*) engraving; (*de piedra preciosa*) cutting; (*estatura*) height; (*medida*) size; (*palo*) measuring stick; (*Arg, charla*) gossip. ∼**do** *a* carved. ● *m* carving. ∼**dor** *m* engraver

tallarín *m* noodle

talle *m* waist; (*figura*) figure; (*medida*) size

taller *m* workshop; (*de pintor etc*) studio

tallo *m* stem, stalk

tamal *m* (*LAm*) tamale

tamaño *a* (*tan grande*) so big a; (*tan pequeño*) so small a. ● *m* size. **de** ∼ **natural** life-size

tambalearse *vpr* ⟨*persona*⟩ stagger; ⟨*cosa*⟩ wobble

también *adv* also, too

tambor *m* drum. ∼ **del freno** brake drum. ∼**ilear** *vi* drum

Támesis *m* Thames

tamiz *m* sieve. ∼**ar** [10] *vt* sieve

tampoco *adv* nor, neither, not either

tampón *m* tampon; (*para entintar*) ink-pad

tan *adv* so. **tan... ∼** as... as

tanda *f* group; (*capa*) layer; (*de obreros*) shift

tangente *a* & *f* tangent

Tánger *m* Tangier

tangible *a* tangible

tango *m* tango

tanque *m* tank; (*camión, barco*) tanker

tante|ar *vt* estimate; (*ensayar*) test; (*fig*) weigh up. ● *vi* score. **~o** *m* estimate; (*prueba*) test; (*en deportes*) score

tanto *a* (*en singular*) so much; (*en plural*) so many; (*comparación en singular*) as much; (*comparación en plural*) as many. ● *pron* so much; (*en plural*) so many. ● *adv* so much; (*tiempo*) so long. ● *m* certain amount; (*punto*) point; (*gol*) goal. **~ como** as well as; (*cantidad*) as much as. **~ más... cuanto que** all the more... because. **~ si... como si** whether... or. **a ~s de** sometime in. **en ~, entre ~** meanwhile. **en ~ que** while. **entre ~** meanwhile. **estar al ~ de** be up to date with. **hasta ~ que** until. **no es para ~** it's not as bad as all that. **otro ~** the same; (*el doble*) as much again. **por (lo) ~** so. **un ~** *adv* somewhat

tañer [22] *vt* play

tapa *f* lid; (*de botella*) top; (*de libro*) cover. **~s** *fpl* savoury snacks

tapacubos *m invar* hub-cap

tapa|dera *f* cover, lid; (*fig*) cover. **~r** *vt* cover; (*abrigar*) wrap up; (*obturar*) plug; put the top on ‹*botella*›

taparrabo(s) *m invar* loincloth; (*bañador*) swimming-trunks

tapete *m* (*de mesa*) table cover; (*alfombra*) rug

tapia *f* wall. **~r** *vt* enclose

tapicería *f* tapestry; (*de muebles*) upholstery

tapioca *f* tapioca

tapiz *m* tapestry. **~ar** [10] *vt* hang with tapestries; upholster ‹*muebles*›

tap|ón *m* stopper; (*corcho*) cork; (*med*) tampon; (*tec*) plug. **~onazo** *m* pop

taqu|igrafía *f* shorthand. **~ígrafo** *m* shorthand writer

taquill|a *f* ticket office; (*archivador*) filing cabinet; (*fig, dinero*) takings. **~ero** *m* clerk, ticket seller. ● *a* box-office

tara *f* (*peso*) tare; (*defecto*) defect

taracea *f* marquetry

tarántula *f* tarantula

tararear *vt/i* hum

tarda|nza *f* delay. **~r** *vi* take; (*mucho tiempo*) take a long time. **a más ~r** at the latest. **sin ~r** without delay

tard|e *adv* late. ● *f* (*antes del atardecer*) afternoon; (*después del atardecer*) evening. **~e o temprano** sooner or later. **~ío** *a* late. **de ~e en ~e** from time to time. **por la ~e** in the afternoon

tardo *a* (*torpe*) slow

tarea *f* task, job

tarifa *f* rate, tariff

tarima *f* platform

tarjeta *f* card. **~ de crédito** credit card. **~ postal** postcard

tarro *m* jar

tarta *f* cake; (*torta*) tart. **~ helada** ice-cream gateau

tartamud|ear *vi* stammer. **~o** *a* stammering. ● *m* stammerer. **es ~o** he stammers

tártaro *m* tartar

tarugo *m* chunk

tasa *f* valuation; (*precio*) fixed price; (*índice*) rate. **~r** *vt* fix a price for; (*limitar*) ration; (*evaluar*) value

tasca *f* bar

tatarabuel|a *f* great-great-grandmother. **~o** *m* great-great-grandfather

tatua|je *m* (*acción*) tattooing; (*dibujo*) tattoo. **~r** [21] *vt* tattoo

taurino *a* bullfighting

Tauro *m* Taurus

tauromaquia *f* bullfighting

tax|i *m* taxi. **~ímetro** *m* taxi meter. **~ista** *m* & *f* taxi-driver

tayuyá *m* (*Arg*) water melon

taz|a *f* cup. **~ón** *m* bowl

te *pron* (*acusativo*) you; (*dativo*) (to) you; (*reflexivo*) (to) yourself

té *m* tea. **dar el ~** bore

tea *f* torch

teatr|al *a* theatre; (*exagerado*) theatrical. **~alizar** [10] *vt* dramatize. **~o** *m* theatre; (*literatura*) drama. **obra** *f* **~al** play

tebeo *m* comic

teca *f* teak

tecla *f* key. **~do** *m* keyboard. **tocar la ~, tocar una ~** pull strings

técnica *f* technique

tecn|icismo *m* technicality

técnico *a* technical. ● *m* technician

tecnol|ogía *f* technology. **~ógico** *a* technological

tecolote m (Mex) owl

tecomate m (Mex) earthenware cup

tech|ado m roof. **~ar** vt roof. **~o** m (interior) ceiling; (exterior) roof. **~umbre** f roofing. **bajo ~ado** indoors

teja f tile. **~do** m roof. **a toca ~** cash

teje|dor m weaver. **~r** vt weave; (hacer punto) knit

tejemaneje m (fam) fuss; (intriga) scheming

tejido m material; (anat, fig) tissue. **~s** mpl textiles

tejón m badger

tela f material; (de araña) web; (en líquido) skin

telar m loom. **~es** mpl textile mill

telaraña f spider's web, cobweb

tele f (fam) television

tele|comunicación f telecommunication. **~diario** m television news. **~dirigido** a remote-controlled. **~férico** m cable-car; (tren) cable-railway

tel|efonear vt/i telephone. **~efónico** a telephone. **~efonista** m & f telephonist. **~éfono** m telephone. **al ~éfono** on the phone

tel|egrafía f telegraphy. **~egrafiar** [20] vt telegraph. **~egráfico** a telegraphic. **~égrafo** m telegraph

telegrama m telegram

telenovela f television soap opera

teleobjetivo m telephoto lens

telep|atía f telepathy. **~ático** a telepathic

telesc|ópico a telescopic. **~opio** m telescope

telesilla m ski-lift, chair-lift

telespectador m viewer

telesquí m ski-lift

televi|dente m & f viewer. **~sar** vt televise. **~sión** f television. **~sor** m television (set)

télex m telex

telón m curtain. **~ de acero** (historia) Iron Curtain

tema m subject; (mus) theme

tembl|ar [1] vi shake; (de miedo) tremble; (de frío) shiver; (fig) shudder. **~or** m shaking; (de miedo) trembling; (de frío) shivering. **~or de tierra** earthquake. **~oroso** a trembling

temer vt be afraid (of). • vi be afraid. **~se** vpr be afraid

temerario a reckless

tem|eroso a frightened. **~ible** a fearsome. **~or** m fear

témpano m floe

temperamento m temperament

temperatura f temperature

temperie f weather

tempest|ad f storm. **~uoso** a stormy. **levantar ~ades** (fig) cause a storm

templ|ado a moderate; (tibio) warm; ‹clima, tiempo› mild; (valiente) courageous; (listo) bright. **~anza** f moderation; (de clima o tiempo) mildness. **~ar** vt temper; (calentar) warm; (mus) tune. **~e** m tempering; (temperatura) temperature; (humor) mood

templ|ete m niche; (pabellón) pavilion. **~o** m temple

tempora|da f time; (época) season. **~l** a temporary. • m (tempestad) storm; (período de lluvia) rainy spell

tempran|ero a ‹frutos› early. **~o** a & adv early. **ser ~ero** be an early riser

tena|cidad f tenacity

tenacillas fpl tongs

tenaz a tenacious

tenaza f, **tenazas** fpl pliers; (para arrancar clavos) pincers; (para el fuego, culin) tongs

tende|ncia f tendency. **~nte** a. **~nte a** aimed at. **~r** [1] vt spread (out); hang out ‹ropa a secar›; (colocar) lay. • vi have a tendency (a to). **~rse** vpr stretch out

tender|ete m stall. **~o** m shopkeeper

tendido a spread out; ‹ropa› hung out; ‹persona› stretched out. • m (en plaza de toros) front rows. **~s** mpl (ropa lavada) washing

tendón m tendon

tenebroso a gloomy; (turbio) shady

tenedor m fork; (poseedor) holder

tener [40] vt have (got); (agarrar) hold; be ‹años, calor, celos, cuidado, frío, ganas, hambre, miedo, razón, sed etc›. **¡ten cuidado!** be careful! **tengo calor** I'm hot. **tiene 3 años** he's 3 (years old). **~se** vpr stand up; (considerarse) consider o.s., think o.s. **~ al corriente, ~ al día** keep up to date. **~ 2 cm de largo** be 2 cms long. **~ a uno por** consider s.o. **~ que** have (got) to. **tenemos que comprar pan** we've got to buy some bread. **¡ahí tienes!** there you are! **no ~ nada que ver con** have nothing to do with. **¿qué tienes?** what's the matter (with you)? ¡**tenga!** here you are!

tengo vb véase **tener**

teniente m lieutenant. ~ **de alcalde** deputy mayor

tenis m tennis. ~**ta** m & f tennis player

tenor m sense; (mus) tenor. **a este** ~ in this fashion

tens|ión f tension; (presión) pressure; (arterial) blood pressure; (elec) voltage; (de persona) tenseness. ~**o** a tense

tentación f temptation

tentáculo m tentacle

tenta|dor a tempting. ~**r** [1] vt feel; (seducir) tempt

tentativa f attempt

tenue a thin; ⟨luz, voz⟩ faint

teñi|do m dye. ~**r** [5 & 22] vt dye; (fig) tinge (**de** with). ~**rse** vpr dye one's hair

te|ología f theology. ~**ológico** a theological. ~**ólogo** m theologian

teorema m theorem

te|oría f theory. ~**órico** a theoretical

tepache m (Mex) (alcoholic) drink

tequila f tequila

TER m high-speed train

terap|éutico a therapeutic. ~**ia** f therapy

tercer a véase **tercero**. ~**a** f (auto) third (gear). ~**o** a (delante de nombre masculino en singular **tercer**) third. ● m third party

terceto m trio

terciar vi mediate. ~ **en** join in. ~**se** vpr occur

tercio m third

terciopelo m velvet

terco a obstinate

tergiversar vt distort

terma|l a thermal. ~**s** fpl thermal baths

termes m invar termite

térmico a thermal

termina|ción f ending; (conclusión) conclusion. ~**l** a & m terminal. ~**nte** a categorical. ~**r** vt finish, end. ~**rse** vpr come to an end. ~**r por** end up

término m end; (palabra) term; (plazo) period. ~ **medio** average. ~ **municipal** municipal district. **dar** ~ **a** finish off. **en último** ~ as a last resort. **estar en buenos** ~**s con** be on good terms with. **llevar a** ~ carry

out. **poner** ~ **a** put an end to. **primer** ~ foreground

terminología f terminology

termita f termite

termo m Thermos flask (P), flask

termómetro m thermometer

termo|nuclear a thermonuclear. ~**sifón** m boiler. ~**stato** m thermostat

tern|a f (carne) veal. ~**o** m calf

ternura f tenderness

terquedad f stubbornness

terracota f terracotta

terrado m flat roof

terraplén m embankment

terrateniente m & f landowner

terraza f terrace; (terrado) flat roof

terremoto m earthquake

terre|no a earthly. ● m land; (solar) plot; (fig) field. ~**stre** a earthly; (mil) ground

terr|ible a terrible. ~**iblemente** adv awfully. ~**ífico** a terrifying

territori|al a territorial. ~**o** m territory

terrón m (de tierra) clod; (culin) lump

terror m terror. ~**ífico** a terrifying. ~**ismo** m terrorism. ~**ista** m & f terrorist

terr|oso a earthy; (color) brown. ~**uño** m land; (patria) native land

terso a polished; ⟨piel⟩ smooth

tertulia f social gathering, get-together (fam). ~**r** vi (LAm) get together. **estar de** ~ chat. **hacer** ~ get together

tesi|na f dissertation. ~**s** f invar thesis; (opinión) theory

tesón m perseverance

tesor|ería f treasury. ~**ero** m treasurer. ~**o** m treasure; (tesorería) treasury; (libro) thesaurus

testa f (fam) head. ~**ferro** m figurehead

testa|mento m will. **T~mento** (relig) Testament. ~**r** vi make a will

testarudo a stubborn

testículo m testicle

testi|ficar [7] vt/i testify. ~**go** m witness. ~**go de vista**, ~**go ocular**, ~**go presencial** eyewitness. ~**monio** m testimony

teta f nipple; (de biberón) teat

tétanos m tetanus

tetera f (para el té) teapot; (Mex, biberón) feeding-bottle

tetilla f nipple; (de biberón) teat

tétrico a gloomy

textil *a & m* textile

text|o *m* text. **~ual** *a* textual

textura *f* texture

teyú *m* (*Arg*) iguana

tez *f* complexion

ti *pron* you

tía *f* aunt; (*fam*) woman

tiara *f* tiara

tibio *a* lukewarm. **ponerle ~ a uno** insult s.o.

tiburón *m* shark

tic *m* tic

tiempo *m* time; (*atmosférico*) weather; (*mus*) tempo; (*gram*) tense; (*en deportes*) half. **a su ~** in due course. **a ~** in time. **¿cuánto ~?** how long? **hace buen ~** the weather is fine. **hace ~** some time ago. **mucho ~** a long time. **perder el ~** waste time. **¿qué ~ hace?** what is the weather like?

tienda *f* shop; (*de campaña*) tent. **~ de comestibles**, **~ de ultramarinos** grocer's (shop) (*Brit*), grocery store (*Amer*)

tiene *vb véase* **tener**

tienta. a ~s gropingly. **andar a ~s** grope one's way

tiento *m* touch; (*de ciego*) blind person's stick; (*fig*) tact

tierno *a* tender; (*joven*) young

tierra *f* land; (*planeta, elec*) earth; (*suelo*) ground; (*geol*) soil, earth. **caer por ~** (*fig*) crumble. **por ~** overland, by land

tieso *a* stiff; (*firme*) firm; (*engreído*) conceited; (*orgulloso*) proud

tiesto *m* flowerpot

tifoideo *a* typhoid

tifón *m* typhoon

tifus *m* typhus; (*fiebre tifoidea*) typhoid (fever); (*en el teatro*) people with complimentary tickets

tigre *m* tiger

tijera *f*, **tijeras** *fpl* scissors; (*de jardín*) shears

tijeret|a *f* (*insecto*) earwig; (*bot*) tendril. **~ear** *vt* snip

tila *f* lime(-tree); (*infusión*) lime tea

tild|ar *vt*. **~ar de** (*fig*) call. **~e** *m* tilde

tilín *m* tinkle. **hacer ~** appeal

tilingo *a* (*Arg, Mex*) silly

tilma *f* (*Mex*) poncho

tilo *m* lime(-tree)

timar *vt* swindle

timbal *m* drum; (*culin*) timbale, meat pie

timbiriche *m* (*Mex*) (alcoholic) drink

timbr|ar *vt* stamp. **~e** *m* (*sello*) stamp; (*elec*) bell; (*sonido*) timbre. **tocar el ~e** ring the bell

timidez *f* shyness

tímido *a* shy

timo *m* swindle

timón *m* rudder; (*fig*) helm

tímpano *m* kettledrum; (*anat*) eardrum. **~s** *mpl* (*mus*) timpani

tina *f* tub. **~ja** *f* large earthenware jar

tinglado *m* (*fig*) intrigue

tinieblas *fpl* darkness; (*fig*) confusion

tino *f* (*habilidad*) skill; (*moderación*) moderation; (*tacto*) tact

tint|a *f* ink. **~e** *m* dyeing; (*color*) dye; (*fig*) tinge. **~ero** *m* ink-well. **de buena ~a** on good authority

tint|ín *m* tinkle; (*de vasos*) chink, clink. **~inear** *vi* tinkle; ⟨*vasos*⟩ chink, clink

tinto *a* ⟨*vino*⟩ red

tintorería *f* dyeing; (*tienda*) dry cleaner's

tintura *f* dyeing; (*color*) dye; (*noción superficial*) smattering

tío *m* uncle; (*fam*) man. **~s** *mpl* uncle and aunt

tiovivo *m* merry-go-round

típico *a* typical

tipo *m* type; (*persona, fam*) person; (*figura de mujer*) figure; (*figura de hombre*) build; (*com*) rate

tip|ografía *f* typography. **~ográfico** *a* typographic(al). **~ógrafo** *m* printer

típula *f* crane-fly, daddy-long-legs

tique *m*, **tíquet** *m* ticket

tiquete *m* (*LAm*) ticket

tira *f* strip. **la ~ de** lots of

tirabuzón *m* corkscrew; (*de pelo*) ringlet

tirad|a *f* distance; (*serie*) series; (*de libros etc*) edition. **~o** *a* (*barato*) very cheap; (*fácil, fam*) very easy. **~or** *m* (*asa*) handle; (*juguete*) catapult (*Brit*), slingshot (*Amer*). **de una ~a** at one go

tiran|ía *f* tyranny. **~izar** [10] *vt* tyrannize. **~o** *a* tyrannical. ● *m* tyrant

tirante *a* tight; (*fig*) tense; ⟨*relaciones*⟩ strained. ● *m* shoulder strap. **~s** *mpl* braces (*esp Brit*), suspenders (*Amer*)

tirar *vt* throw; (*desechar*) throw away; (*derribar*) knock over; give ⟨*golpe, coz etc*⟩; (*imprimir*) print. ● *vi* (*disparar*) shoot. **~se** *vpr*

throw o.s.; (*tumbarse*) lie down. ∼ **a**
tend to (be); (*parecerse a*) resemble.
∼ **de** pull; (*atraer*) attract. **a todo** ∼
at the most. **ir tirando** get by
tirita *f* sticking-plaster, plaster
(*Brit*)
tirit|ar *vi* shiver. ∼**ón** *m* shiver
tiro *m* throw; (*disparo*) shot; (*alcance*) range. ∼ **a gol** shot at goal.
a ∼ within range. **errar el** ∼ miss.
pegarse un ∼ shoot o.s.
tiroides *m* thyroid (gland)
tirón *m* tug. **de un** ∼ in one go
tirote|ar *vt* shoot at. ∼**o** *m* shooting
tisana *f* herb tea
tisis *f* tuberculosis
tisú *m* (*pl* **tisus**) tissue
títere *m* puppet. ∼ **de guante** glove
puppet. ∼**s** *mpl* puppet show
titilar *vi* quiver; ⟨*estrella*⟩ twinkle
titiritero *m* puppeteer; (*acróbata*)
acrobat; (*malabarista*) juggler
titube|ante *a* shaky; (*fig*) hesistant.
∼**ar** *vi* stagger; ⟨*cosa*⟩ be unstable;
(*fig*) hesitate. ∼**o** *m* hesitation
titula|do *a* ⟨*libro*⟩ entitled; ⟨*per-
sona*⟩ qualified. ∼**r** *m* headline;
(*persona*) holder. ● *vt* call. ∼**rse** *vpr*
be called
título *m* title; (*persona*) titled person; (*académico*) qualification;
(*univ*) degree; (*de periódico etc*)
headline; (*derecho*) right. **a** ∼ **de** as,
by way of
tiza *f* chalk
tiz|nar *vt* dirty. ∼**ne** *m* soot. ∼**ón** *m*
half-burnt stick; (*fig*) stain
toall|a *f* towel. ∼**ero** *m* towel-rail
tobillo *m* ankle
tobogán *m* slide; (*para la nieve*)
toboggan
tocadiscos *m invar* record-player
toca|do *a* (*con sombrero*) wearing.
● *m* hat. ∼**dor** *m* dressing-table.
∼**dor de señoras** ladies' room.
∼**nte** *a* touching. ∼**r** [7] *vt* touch;
(*mus*) play; ring ⟨*timbre*⟩; (*mencionar*) touch on; ⟨*barco*⟩ stop at.
● *vi* knock; (*corresponder a uno*) be
one's turn. ∼**rse** *vpr* touch each
other; (*cubrir la cabeza*) cover one's
head. **en lo que** ∼ **a**, **en lo** ∼**nte a**
as for. **estar** ∼**do (de la cabeza)** be
mad. **te** ∼ **a ti** it's your turn
tocateja. a ∼ cash
tocayo *m* namesake
tocino *m* bacon
tocólogo *m* obstetrician
todavía *adv* still, yet. ∼ **no** not yet

todo *a* all; (*entero*) the whole; (*cada*)
every. ● *adv* completely, all. ● *m*
whole. ● *pron* everything, all; (*en
plural*) everyone. ∼ **el día** all day.
∼ **el mundo** everyone. ∼ **el que**
anyone who. ∼ **incluido** all in. ∼ **lo
contrario** quite the opposite. ∼ **lo
que** anything which. ∼**s los días**
every day. ∼**s los dos** both (of
them). ∼**s los tres** all three. **ante** ∼
above all. **a** ∼ **esto** meanwhile. **con**
∼ still, however. **del** ∼ completely.
en ∼ **el mundo** anywhere. **estar en**
∼ be on the ball. **es** ∼ **uno** it's all
the same. **nosotros** ∼**s** all of us.
sobre ∼ above all
toldo *m* sunshade
tolera|ncia *f* tolerance. ∼**nte** *a* tol-
erant. ∼**r** *vt* tolerate
tolondro *m* (*chichón*) lump
toma *f* taking; (*med*) dose; (*de agua*)
outlet; (*elec*) socket; (*elec, clavija*)
plug. ● *int* well!, fancy that! ∼ **de
corriente** power point. ∼**dura** *f*.
∼**dura de pelo** hoax. ∼**r** *vt* take;
catch ⟨*autobús, tren etc*⟩; (*beber*)
drink, have; (*comer*) eat, have. ● *vi*
take; (*dirigirse*) go. ∼**rse** *vpr* take;
(*beber*) drink, have; (*comer*) eat,
have. ∼**r a bien** take well. ∼**r a mal**
take badly. ∼**r en serio** take seriously. ∼**rla con uno** pick on s.o. ∼**r
nota** take note. ∼**r por** take for. ∼ **y
daca** give and take. **¿qué va a** ∼**r?**
what would you like?
tomate *m* tomato
tomavistas *m invar* cine-camera
tómbola *f* tombola
tomillo *m* thyme
tomo *m* volume
ton. sin ∼ **ni son** without rhyme or
reason
tonada *f*, **tonadilla** *f* tune
tonel *m* barrel. ∼**ada** *f* ton. ∼**aje** *m*
tonnage
tónic|a *f* tonic water; (*mus*) tonic.
∼**o** *a* tonic; ⟨*sílaba*⟩ stressed. ● *m*
tonic
tonificar [7] *vt* invigorate
tono *m* tone; (*mus, modo*) key;
(*color*) shade
tont|ería *f* silliness; (*cosa*) silly
thing; (*dicho*) silly remark. ∼**o** *a*
silly. ● *m* fool, idiot; (*payaso*) clown.
dejarse de ∼**erías** stop wasting
time. **hacer el** ∼**o** act the fool.
hacerse el ∼**o** feign ignorance
topacio *m* topaz

topar vt ⟨animal⟩ butt; ⟨persona⟩ bump into; (fig) run into. ● vi. ~ **con** run into

tope a maximum. ● m end; (de tren) buffer. **hasta los ~s** crammed full. **ir a ~** go flat out

tópico a topical. ● m cliché

topo m mole

topogr|afía f topography. **~áfico** a topographical

toque m touch; (sonido) sound; (de campana) peal; (de reloj) stroke; (fig) crux. **~ de queda** curfew. **~tear** vt keep fingering, fiddle with. **dar el último ~** put the finishing touches

toquilla f shawl

tórax m thorax

torbellino m whirlwind; (de polvo) cloud of dust; (fig) whirl

torcer [2 & 9] vt twist; (doblar) bend; wring out ⟨ropa⟩. ● vi turn. **~se** vpr twist; (fig, desviarse) go astray; (fig, frustrarse) go wrong

tordo a dapple grey. ● m thrush

tore|ar vt fight; (evitar) dodge; (entretener) put off. ● vi fight (bulls). **~o** m bullfighting. **~ro** m bullfighter

torment|a f storm. **~o** m torture. **~oso** a stormy

tornado m tornado

tornar vt return

tornasolado a irridescent

torneo m tournament

tornillo m screw

torniquete m (entrada) turnstile

torno m lathe; (de alfarero) wheel. **en ~ a** around

toro m bull. **~s** mpl bullfighting. **ir a los ~s** go to a bullfight

toronja f grapefruit

torpe a clumsy; (estúpido) stupid

torped|ero m torpedo-boat. **~o** m torpedo

torpeza f clumsiness; (de inteligencia) slowness

torpor m torpor

torrado m toasted chick-pea

torre f tower; (en ajedrez) castle, rook

torrefac|ción f roasting. **~to** a roasted

torren|cial a torrential. **~te** m torrent; (circulatorio) bloodstream; (fig) flood

tórrido a torrid

torrija f French toast

torsión f twisting

torso m torso

torta f tart; (bollo, fam) cake; (golpe) slap, punch; (Mex, bocadillo) sandwich. **~zo** m slap, punch. **no entender ni ~** not understand a word of it. **pegarse un ~zo** have a bad accident

tortícolis f stiff neck

tortilla f omelette; (Mex, de maíz) tortilla, maize cake. **~ francesa** plain omelette

tórtola f turtle-dove

tortuga f tortoise; (de mar) turtle

tortuoso a winding; (fig) devious

tortura f torture. **~r** vt torture

torvo a grim

tos f cough. **~ ferina** whooping cough

tosco a crude; ⟨persona⟩ coarse

toser vi cough

tósigo m poison

tosquedad f crudeness; (de persona) coarseness

tost|ada f toast. **~ado** a ⟨pan⟩ toasted; ⟨café⟩ roasted; ⟨persona⟩ tanned; (marrón) brown. **~ar** vt toast ⟨pan⟩; roast ⟨café⟩; tan ⟨piel⟩. **~ón** m (pan) crouton; (lata) bore

total a total. ● adv after all. ● m total; (totalidad) whole. **~idad** f whole. **~itario** a totalitarian. **~izar** [10] vt total. **~ que** so, to cut a long story short

tóxico a toxic

toxicómano m drug addict

toxina f toxin

tozudo a stubborn

traba f bond; (fig, obstáculo) obstacle. **poner ~s a** hinder

trabaj|ador a hard-working. ● m worker. **~ar** vt work (de as); knead ⟨masa⟩; (estudiar) work at; ⟨actor⟩ act. ● vi work. **~o** m work. **~os** mpl hardships. **~os forzados** hard labour. **~oso** a hard. **costar ~o** be difficult. ¿**en qué ~as?** what work do you do?

trabalenguas m invar tonguetwister

traba|r vt (sujetar) fasten; (unir) join; (empezar) start; (culin) thicken. **~rse** vpr get tangled up. **trabársele la lengua** get tonguetied. **~zón** f joining; (fig) connection

trabucar [7] vt mix up

trácala f (Mex) trick

tracción f traction

tractor m tractor

tradici|ón f tradition. **~onal** a traditional. **~onalista** m & f traditionalist

traduc|ción f translation. **~ir** [47] vt translate (**al** into). **~tor** m translator

traer [41] vt bring; (*llevar*) carry; (*atraer*) attract. **traérselas** be difficult

trafica|nte m & f dealer. **~r** [7] vi deal

tráfico m traffic; (*com*) trade

traga|deras fpl (*fam*) throat. **tener buenas ~deras** (*ser crédulo*) swallow anything; (*ser tolerante*) be easygoing. **~luz** m skylight. **~perras** f invar slot-machine. **~r** [12] vt swallow; (*comer mucho*) devour; (*absorber*) absorb; (*fig*) swallow up. **no (poder) ~r** not be able to stand. **~rse** vpr swallow; (*fig*) swallow up

tragedia f tragedy

trágico a tragic. ● m tragedian

trag|o m swallow, gulp; (*pequeña porción*) sip; (*fig, disgusto*) blow. **~ón** a greedy. ● m glutton. **echar(se) un ~o** have a drink

trai|ción f treachery; (*pol*) treason. **~cionar** vt betray. **~cionero** a treacherous. **~dor** a treacherous. ● m traitor

traigo vb véase **traer**

traje m dress; (*de hombre*) suit. ● vb véase **traer**. **~ de baño** swimming-costume. **~ de ceremonia**, **~ de etiqueta**, **~ de noche** evening dress

traj|ín m (*transporte*) haulage; (*jaleo, fam*) bustle. **~inar** vt transport. ● vi bustle about

trama m weft; (*fig*) link; (*fig, argumento*) plot. **~r** vt weave; (*fig*) plot

tramitar vt negotiate

trámite m step. **~s** mpl procedure. **en ~** in hand

tramo m (*parte*) section; (*de escalera*) flight

tramp|a f trap; (*puerta*) trapdoor; (*fig*) trick. **~illa** f trapdoor. **hacer ~a** cheat

trampolín m trampoline; (*fig, de piscina*) springboard

tramposo a cheating. ● m cheat

tranca f stick; (*de puerta*) bar

trance m moment; (*hipnótico etc*) trance. **a todo ~** at all costs

tranco m stride

tranquil|idad f (*peace and*) quiet; (*de espíritu*) peace of mind. **~izar** [10] vt reassure. **~o** a quiet; ‹*conciencia*›

clear; ‹*mar*› calm; (*despreocupado*) thoughtless. **estáte ~o** don't worry

trans... pref (véase también **tras...**) trans...

transacción f transaction; (*acuerdo*) compromise

transatlántico a transatlantic. ● m (ocean) liner

transbord|ador m ferry. **~ar** vt transfer. **~arse** vpr change. **~o** m transfer. **hacer ~o** change (**en** at)

transcri|bir (pp **transcrito**) vt transcribe. **~pción** f transcription

transcur|rir vi pass. **~so** m course

transeúnte a temporary. ● m & f passer-by

transfer|encia f transfer. **~ir** [4] vt transfer

transfigurar vt transfigure

transforma|ción f transformation. **~dor** m transformer. **~r** vt transform

transfusión f transfusion. **hacer una ~** give a blood transfusion

transgre|dir vt transgress. **~sión** f transgression

transición f transition

transido a overcome

transigir [14] vi give in, compromise

transistor m transistor; (*radio*) radio

transita|ble a passable. **~r** vi go

transitivo a transitive

tránsito m transit; (*tráfico*) traffic

transitorio a transitory

translúcido a translucent

transmi|sión f transmission; (*radio, TV*) broadcast. **~sor** m transmitter. **~sora** f broadcasting station. **~tir** vt transmit; (*radio, TV*) broadcast; (*fig*) pass on

transparen|cia f transparency. **~tar** vt show. **~te** a transparent

transpira|ción f perspiration. **~r** vi transpire; (*sudar*) sweat

transponer [34] vt move. ● vi disappear round ‹*esquina etc*›; disappear behind ‹*montaña etc*›. **~se** vpr disappear

transport|ar vt transport. **~e** m transport. **empresa** f **de ~es** removals company

transversal a transverse; ‹*calle*› side

tranvía m tram

trapacería f swindle

trapear vt (*LAm*) mop

trapecio m trapeze; (*math*) trapezium

trapiche m (para azúcar) mill; (para aceitunas) press

trapicheo m fiddle

trapisonda f (jaleo, fam) row; (enredo, fam) plot

trapo m rag; (para limpiar) cloth. ∼s mpl (fam) clothes. **a todo** ∼ out of control

tráquea f windpipe, trachea

traquete|ar vt bang, rattle. ∼o m banging, rattle

tras prep after; (detrás) behind; (encima de) as well as

tras... pref (véase también **trans...**) trans...

trascende|ncia f importance. ∼ntal a transcendental; (importante) important. ∼r [1] vi (oler) smell (a of); (saberse) become known; (extenderse) spread

trasegar [1 & 12] vt move around

trasero a back, rear. ● m (anat) bottom

trasgo m goblin

traslad|ar vt move; (aplazar) postpone; (traducir) translate; (copiar) copy. ∼o m transfer; (copia) copy; (mudanza) removal. **dar** ∼o send a copy

trasl|úcido a translucent. ∼ucirse [11] vpr be translucent; (dejarse ver) show through; (fig, revelarse) be revealed. ∼uz m. **al** ∼uz against the light

trasmano m. **a** ∼ out of reach; (fig) out of the way

trasnochar vt (acostarse tarde) go to bed late; (no acostarse) stay up all night; (no dormir) be unable to sleep; (pernoctar) spend the night

traspas|ar vt pierce; (transferir) transfer; (pasar el límite) go beyond. ∼o m transfer. **se** ∼**a** for sale

traspié m trip; (fig) slip. **dar un** ∼ stumble; (fig) slip up

trasplant|ar vt transplant. ∼e m transplanting; (med) transplant

trastada f stupid thing; (jugada) dirty trick, practical joke

traste m fret. **dar al** ∼ **con** ruin. **ir al** ∼ fall through

trastero m storeroom

trastienda f back room; (fig) shrewdness

trasto m piece of furniture; (cosa inútil) piece of junk; (persona) useless person, dead loss (fam)

trastorn|ado a mad. ∼ar vt upset; (volver loco) drive mad; (fig, gustar

mucho, fam) delight. ∼**arse** vpr get upset; (volverse loco) go mad. ∼o m (incl med) upset; (pol) disturbance; (fig) confusion

trastrocar [2 & 7] vt change round

trat|able a friendly. ∼**ado** m treatise; (acuerdo) treaty. ∼**amiento** m treatment; (título) title. ∼**ante** m & f dealer. ∼**ar** vt (incl med) treat; deal with ‹asunto etc›; (com) deal; (manejar) handle; (de tú, de Vd) address (de as); (llamar) call. ● vi treat (with). ∼**ar con** have to do with; know ‹persona›; (com) deal in. ∼**ar de** be about; (intentar) try. ∼o m treatment; (acuerdo) agreement; (título) title; (relación) relationship. **¡**∼**o hecho!** agreed! ∼os mpl dealings. **¿de qué se** ∼**a?** what's it about?

traum|a m trauma. ∼**ático** a traumatic

través m (inclinación) slant. **a** ∼ **de** through; (de un lado a otro) across. **de** ∼ across; (de lado) sideways. **mirar de** ∼ look askance at

travesaño m crosspiece

travesía f crossing; (calle) side-street

trav|esura f prank. ∼**ieso** a ‹niño› mischievous, naughty

trayecto m road; (tramo) stretch; (ruta) route; (viaje) journey. ∼**ria** f trajectory; (fig) course

traz|a f plan; (aspecto) look, appearance; (habilidad) skill. ∼**ado** a. **bien** ∼**ado** good-looking. **mal** ∼**ado** unattractive. ● m plan. ∼**ar** [10] vt draw; (bosquejar) sketch. ∼o m line

trébol m clover. ∼**es** mpl (en naipes) clubs

trece a & m thirteen

trecho m stretch; (distancia) distance; (tiempo) while. **a** ∼s in places. **de** ∼ **en** ∼ at intervals

tregua f truce; (fig) respite

treinta a & m thirty

tremendo a terrible; (extraordinario) terrific

trementina f turpentine

tren m train; (equipaje) luggage. ∼ **de aterrizaje** landing gear. ∼ **de vida** lifestyle

tren|cilla f braid. ∼**za** f braid; (de pelo) plait. ∼**zar** [10] vt plait

trepa|dor a climbing. ∼**r** vt/i climb

tres a & m three. ∼**cientos** a & m three hundred. ∼**illo** m three-piece suite; (mus) triplet

treta f trick

tri|angular *a* triangular. **~ángulo** *m* triangle

trib|al *a* tribal. **~u** *f* tribe

tribulación *f* tribulation

tribuna *f* platform; (*de espectadores*) stand

tribunal *m* court; (*de examen etc*) board; (*fig*) tribunal

tribut|ar *vt* pay. **~o** *m* tribute; (*impuesto*) tax

triciclo *m* tricycle

tricolor *a* three-coloured

tricornio *a* three-cornered. ● *m* three-cornered hat

tricotar *vt/i* knit

tridimensional *a* three-dimensional

tridente *m* trident

trigésimo *a* thirtieth

trig|al *m* wheat field. **~o** *m* wheat

trigonometría *f* trigonometry

trigueño *a* olive-skinned; ⟨*pelo*⟩ dark blonde

trilogía *f* trilogy

trilla|do *a* (*fig, manoseado*) trite; (*fig, conocido*) well-known. **~r** *vt* thresh

trimestr|al *a* quarterly. **~e** *m* quarter; (*escol, univ*) term

trin|ar *vi* warble. **estar que trina** be furious

trinchar *vt* carve

trinchera *f* ditch; (*mil*) trench; (*rail*) cutting; (*abrigo*) trench coat

trineo *m* sledge

trinidad *f* trinity

Trinidad *f* Trinidad

trino *m* warble

trío *m* trio

tripa *f* intestine; (*culin*) tripe; (*fig, vientre*) tummy, belly. **~s** *fpl* (*de máquina etc*) parts, workings. **me duele la ~** I've got tummy-ache. **revolver las ~s** turn one's stomach

tripicallos *mpl* tripe

tripl|e *a* triple. ● *m*. **el ~e (de)** three times as much (as). **~icado** *a*. **por ~icado** in triplicate. **~icar** [7] *vt* treble

trípode *m* tripod

tríptico *m* triptych

tripula|ción *f* crew. **~nte** *m & f* member of the crew. **~r** *vt* man

triquitraque *m* (*ruido*) clatter

tris *m* crack; (*de papel etc*) ripping noise. **estar en un ~** be on the point of

triste *a* sad; ⟨*paisaje, tiempo etc*⟩ gloomy; (*fig, insignificante*) miserable. **~za** *f* sadness

tritón *m* newt

triturar *vt* crush

triunf|al *a* triumphal. **~ante** *a* triumphant. **~ar** *vi* triumph (**de**, **sobre** over). **~o** *m* triumph

triunvirato *m* triumvirate

trivial *a* trivial

triza *f* piece. **hacer algo ~s** smash sth to pieces

trocar [2 & 7] *vt* (ex)change

trocear *vt* cut up, chop

trocito *m* small piece

trocha *f* narrow path; (*atajo*) short cut

trofeo *m* trophy

tromba *f* waterspout. **~ de agua** heavy downpour

trombón *m* trombone; (*músico*) trombonist

trombosis *f invar* thrombosis

trompa *f* horn; (*de orquesta*) French horn; (*de elefante*) trunk; (*hocico*) snout; (*juguete*) (spinning) top; (*anat*) tube. ● *m* horn player. **coger una ~** (*fam*) get drunk

trompada *f*, **trompazo** *m* bump

trompet|a *f* trumpet; (*músico*) trumpeter, trumpet player; (*clarín*) bugle. **~illa** *f* ear-trumpet

trompicar [7] *vi* trip

trompo *m* (*juguete*) (spinning) top

trona|da *f* thunder storm. **~r** *vt* (*Mex*) shoot. ● *vi* thunder

tronco *m* trunk. **dormir como un ~** sleep like a log

tronchar *vt* bring down; (*fig*) cut short. **~se de risa** laugh a lot

trono *m* throne

trop|a *f* troops. **~el** *m* mob. **ser de ~a** be in the army

tropero *m* (*Arg, vaquero*) cowboy

tropez|ar [1 & 10] *vi* trip; (*fig*) slip up. **~ar con** run into. **~ón** *m* stumble; (*fig*) slip

tropical *a* tropical

trópico *a* tropical. ● *m* tropic

tropiezo *m* slip; (*desgracia*) mishap

trot|ar *vi* trot. **~e** *m* trot; (*fig*) toing and froing. **al ~e** trotting; (*de prisa*) in a rush. **de mucho ~e** hard-wearing

trozo *m* piece, bit. **a ~s** in bits

truco *m* knack; (*ardid*) trick. **coger el ~** get the knack

trucha *f* trout

trueno *m* thunder; (*estampido*) bang

trueque *m* exchange. **aun a ~ de** even at the expense of

trufa *f* truffle. **~r** *vt* stuff with truffles

truhán *m* rogue; (*gracioso*) jester

truncar [7] *vt* truncate; (*fig*) cut short

tu *a* your

tú *pron* you

tuba *f* tuba

tubérculo *m* tuber

tuberculosis *f* tuberculosis

tub|ería *f* pipes; (*oleoducto etc*) pipeline. **~o** *m* tube. **~o de ensayo** test tube. **~o de escape** (*auto*) exhaust (pipe). **~ular** *a* tubular

tuerca *f* nut

tuerto *a* one-eyed, blind in one eye. ● *m* one-eyed person

tuétano *m* marrow; (*fig*) heart. **hasta los ~s** completely

tufo *m* fumes; (*olor*) bad smell

tugurio *m* hovel, slum

tul *m* tulle

tulipán *m* tulip

tulli|do *a* paralysed. **~r** [22] *vt* cripple

tumba *f* grave, tomb

tumb|ar *vt* knock down, knock over; (*fig, en examen, fam*) fail; (*pasmar, fam*) overwhelm. **~arse** *vpr* lie down. **~o** *m* jolt. **dar un ~o** tumble. **~ona** *f* settee; (*sillón*) armchair; (*de lona*) deckchair

tumefacción *f* swelling

tumido *a* swollen

tumor *m* tumour

tumulto *m* turmoil; (*pol*) riot

tuna *f* prickly pear; (*de estudiantes*) student band

tunante *m & f* rogue

túnel *m* tunnel

Túnez *m* (*ciudad*) Tunis; (*país*) Tunisia

túnica *f* tunic

Tunicia *f* Tunisia

tupé *m* toupee; (*fig*) nerve

tupido *a* thick

turba *f* peat; (*muchedumbre*) mob

turba|ción *f* disturbance, upset; (*confusión*) confusion. **~do** *a* upset

turbante *m* turban

turbar *vt* upset; (*molestar*) disturb. **~se** *vpr* be upset

turbina *f* turbine

turbi|o *a* cloudy; ⟨*vista*⟩ blurred; ⟨*asunto etc*⟩ unclear. **~ón** *m* squall

turbulen|cia *f* turbulence; (*disturbio*) disturbance. **~te** *a* turbulent; ⟨*persona*⟩ restless

turco *a* Turkish. ● *m* Turk; (*lengua*) Turkish

tur|ismo *m* tourism; (*coche*) car. **~ista** *m & f* tourist. **~ístico** *a* tourist. **oficina** *f* **de ~ismo** tourist office

turn|arse *vpr* take turns (**para** to). **~o** *m* turn; (*de trabajo*) shift. **por ~o** in turn

turquesa *f* turquoise

Turquía *f* Turkey

turrón *m* nougat

turulato *a* (*fam*) stunned

tutear *vt* address as *tú*. **~se** *vpr* be on familiar terms

tutela *f* (*jurid*) guardianship; (*fig*) protection

tuteo *m* use of the familiar *tú*

tutor *m* guardian; (*escol*) form master

tuve *vb véase* **tener**

tuyo *a & pron* yours. **un amigo ~** a friend of yours

U

u *conj* or

ubicuidad *f* ubiquity

ubre *f* udder

ucraniano *a & m* Ukranian

Ud *abrev* (*Usted*) you

uf *int* phew!; (*de repugnancia*) ugh!

ufan|arse *vpr* be proud (**con, de** of); (*jactarse*) boast (**con, de** about). **~o** *a* proud

ujier *m* usher

úlcera *f* ulcer

ulterior *a* later; ⟨*lugar*⟩ further. **~mente** *adv* later, subsequently

últimamente *adv* (*recientemente*) recently; (*al final*) finally; (*en último caso*) as a last resort

ultim|ar *vt* complete. **~átum** *m* ultimatum

último *a* last; (*más reciente*) latest; (*más lejano*) furthest; (*más alto*) top; (*más bajo*) bottom; (*fig, extremo*) extreme. **estar en las últimas** be on one's last legs; (*sin dinero*) be down to one's last penny. **por ~** finally. **ser lo ~** (*muy bueno*) be marvellous; (*muy malo*) be awful. **vestido a la última** dressed in the latest fashion

ultra *a* ultra, extreme

ultraj|ante *a* outrageous. **~e** *m* outrage

ultramar *m* overseas countries. **de ~, en ~** overseas

ultramarino a overseas. ~s mpl groceries. **tienda de** ~s grocer's (shop) (Brit), grocery store (Amer)

ultranza a ~ (con decisión) decisively; (extremo) extreme

ultra|sónico a ultrasonic. ~violeta a invar ultraviolet

ulular vi howl; ‹búho› hoot

umbilical a umbilical

umbral m threshold

umbrío a, **umbroso** a shady

un art indef m (pl unos) a. ● a one. ~os a pl some

una art indef f a. **la** ~ one o'clock

un|ánime a unanimous. ~animidad f unanimity

undécimo a eleventh

ung|ir [14] vt anoint. ~üento m ointment

únic|amente adv only. ~o a only; (fig, incomparable) unique

unicornio m unicorn

unid|ad f unit; (cualidad) unity. ~o a united

unifica|ción f unification. ~r [7] vt unite, unify

uniform|ar vt standardize; (poner uniforme a) put into uniform. ~e a & m uniform. ~idad f uniformity

uni|génito a only. ~lateral a unilateral

uni|ón f union; (cualidad) unity; (tec) joint. ~r vt join; mix ‹líquidos›. ~rse vpr join together

unísono m unison. **al** ~ in unison

unitario a unitary

universal a universal

universi|dad f university. **U~dad a Distancia** Open University. ~tario a university

universo m universe

uno a one; (en plural) some. ● pron one; (alguien) someone, somebody. ● m one. ~ **a otro** each other. ~ **y otro** both. **(los)** ~**s... (los) otros** some... others

untar vt grease; (med) rub; (fig, sobornar, fam) bribe

uña f nail; (de animal) claw; (casco) hoof

upa int up!

uranio m uranium

Urano m Uranus

urban|idad f politeness. ~ismo m town planning. ~ístico a urban. ~ización f development. ~izar [10] vt civilize; develop ‹terreno›. ~o a urban

urbe f big city

urdimbre f warp

urdir vt (fig) plot

urg|encia f urgency; (emergencia) emergency; (necesidad) urgent need. ~ente a urgent. ~ir [14] vi be urgent. **carta** f ~**ente** express letter

urinario m urinal

urna f urn; (pol) ballot box

urraca f magpie

URSS abrev (historia) (Unión de Repúblicas Socialistas Soviéticas) USSR, Union of Soviet Socialist Republics

Uruguay m. **el** ~ Uruguay

uruguayo a & m Uruguayan

us|ado a used; ‹ropa etc› worn. ~anza f usage, custom. ~ar vt use; (llevar) wear. ~o m use; (costumbre) usage, custom. **al** ~o (de moda) in fashion; (a la manera de) in the style of. **de** ~o **externo** for external use

usted pron you

usual a usual

usuario a user

usur|a f usury. ~ero m usurer

usurpar vt usurp

usuta f (Arg) sandal

utensilio m tool; (de cocina) utensil. ~s mpl equipment

útero m womb

útil a useful. ~es mpl implements

utili|dad f usefulness. ~tario a utilitarian; ‹coche› utility. ~zación f use, utilization. ~zar [10] vt use, utilize

uva f grape. ~ **pasa** raisin. **mala** ~ bad mood

V

vaca f cow; (carne) beef

vacaciones fpl holiday(s). **estar de** ~ be on holiday. **ir de** ~ go on holiday

vaca|nte a vacant. ● f vacancy. ~r [7] vi fall vacant

vaci|ar [20] vt empty; (ahuecar) hollow out; (en molde) cast; (afilar) sharpen. ~edad f emptiness; (tontería) silly thing, frivolity

vacila|ción f hesitation. ~nte a unsteady; (fig) hesitant. ~r vi sway; (dudar) hesitate; (fam) tease

vacío a empty; (vanidoso) vain. ● m empty space; (estado) emptiness; (en física) vacuum; (fig) void

vacuidad *f* emptiness; *(tontería)* silly thing, frivolity

vacuna *f* vaccine. **∼ción** *f* vaccination. **∼r** *vt* vaccinate

vacuno *a* bovine

vacuo *a* empty

vade *m* folder

vad|ear *vt* ford. **∼o** *m* ford

vaga|bundear *vi* wander. **∼bundo** *a* vagrant; ⟨perro⟩ stray. ● *m* tramp. **∼r** [12] *vi* wander (about)

vagina *f* vagina

vago *a* vague; *(holgazán)* idle; ⟨foto⟩ blurred. ● *m* idler

vag|ón *m* carriage; *(de mercancías)* truck, wagon. **∼ón restaurante** dining-car. **∼oneta** *f* truck

vahído *m* dizzy spell

vaho *m* breath; *(vapor)* steam. **∼s** *mpl* inhalation

vaina *f* sheath; *(bot)* pod

vainilla *f* vanilla

vaivén *m* swaying; *(de tráfico)* coming and going; *(fig, de suerte)* change. **vaivenes** *mpl (fig)* ups and downs

vajilla *f* dishes, crockery. **lavar la ∼** wash up

vale *m* voucher; *(pagaré)* IOU. **∼dero** *a* valid

valenciano *a* from Valencia

valent|ía *f* courage; *(acción)* brave deed. **∼ón** *m* braggart

valer [42] *vt* be worth; *(costar)* cost; *(fig, significar)* mean. ● *vi* be worth; *(costar)* cost; *(servir)* be of use; *(ser valedero)* be valid; *(estar permitido)* be allowed. ● *m* worth. **∼ la pena** be worthwhile, be worth it. **¿cuánto vale?** how much is it? **no ∼ para nada** be useless. **¡vale!** all right!, OK! *(fam).* **¿vale?** all right?, OK? *(fam)*

valeroso *a* courageous

valgo *vb véase* **valer**

valía *f* worth

validez *f* validity. **dar ∼ a** validate

válido *a* valid

valiente *a* brave; *(valentón)* boastful; *(en sentido irónico)* fine. ● *m* brave person; *(valentón)* braggart

valija *f* case; *(de correos)* mailbag. **∼ diplomática** diplomatic bag

val|ioso *a* valuable. **∼or** *m* value, worth; *(descaro, fam)* nerve. **∼ores** *mpl* securities. **∼oración** *f* valuation. **∼orar** *vt* value. **conceder ∼or a** attach importance to. **objetos**

∼ *mpl* **de ∼or** valuables. **sin ∼or** worthless

vals *m invar* waltz

válvula *f* valve

valla *f* fence; *(fig)* barrier

valle *m* valley

vampiro *m* vampire

vanagloriarse [20 *o regular*] *vpr* boast

vanamente *adv* uselessly, in vain

vandalismo *m* vandalism

vándalo *m* vandal

vanguardia *f* vanguard. **de ∼** *(en arte, música etc)* avant-garde

vanid|ad *f* vanity. **∼oso** *a* vain

vano *a* vain; *(inútil)* useless. **en ∼** in vain

vapor *m* steam; *(gas)* vapour; *(naut)* steamer. **∼izador** *m* spray. **∼izar** [10] vaporize. **al ∼** *(culin)* steamed

vaquer|ía *f* dairy. **∼o** *m* cow-herd, cowboy. **∼os** *mpl* jeans

vara *f* stick; *(de autoridad)* staff; *(medida)* yard

varar *vi* run aground

varia|ble *a* & *f* variable. **∼ción** *f* variation. **∼nte** *f* version. **∼ntes** *fpl* hors d'oeuvres. **∼r** [20] *vt* change; *(dar variedad a)* vary. ● *vi* vary; *(cambiar)* change

varice *f* varicose vein

varicela *f* chickenpox

varicoso *a* having varicose veins

variedad *f* variety

varilla *f* stick; *(de metal)* rod

vario *a* varied; *(en plural)* several

varita *f* wand

variz *f* varicose vein

var|ón *a* male. ● *m* man; *(niño)* boy. **∼onil** *a* manly

vasc|o *a* & *m* Basque. **∼ongado** *a* Basque. **∼uence** *a* & *m* Basque. **las V∼ongadas** the Basque provinces

vasectomía *f* vasectomy

vaselina *f* Vaseline (P), petroleum jelly

vasija *f* pot, container

vaso *m* glass; *(anat)* vessel

vástago *m* shoot; *(descendiente)* descendant; *(varilla)* rod

vasto *a* vast

Vaticano *m* Vatican

vaticin|ar *vt* prophesy. **∼io** *m* prophesy

vatio *m* watt

vaya *vb véase* **ir**

Vd *abrev* *(Usted)* you

vecin|dad *f* neighbourhood, vicinity; *(vecinos)* neighbours. **∼dario** *m*

inhabitants, neighbourhood. ∼o *a*
neighbouring; (*de al lado*) next-
door. ● *m* neighbour

veda|do *m* preserve. ∼**do de caza**
game preserve. ∼**r** *vt* prohibit

vega *f* fertile plain

vegeta|ción *f* vegetation. ∼**l** *a*
vegetable. ● *m* plant, vegetable. ∼**r**
vi grow; ⟨*persona*⟩ vegetate. ∼**riano**
a & m vegetarian

vehemente *a* vehement

vehículo *m* vehicle

veinte *a & m* twenty. ∼**na** *f* score

veinti|cinco *a & m* twenty-five. ∼**cu-
atro** *a & m* twenty-four. ∼**dós** *a &
m* twenty-two. ∼**nueve** *a & m*
twenty-nine; ∼**ocho** *a & m* twenty-
eight. ∼**séis** *a & m* twenty-six. ∼**siete** *a & m* twenty-seven. ∼**trés** *a &
m* twenty-three. ∼**ún** *a* twenty-one.
∼**uno** *a & m* (*delante de nombre
masculino* **veintún**) twenty-one

vejar *vt* humiliate; (*molestar*) vex

vejez *f* old age

vejiga *f* bladder; (*med*) blister

vela *f* (*naut*) sail; (*de cera*) candle;
(*falta de sueño*) sleeplessness;
(*vigilia*) vigil. **pasar la noche en** ∼
have a sleepless night

velada *f* evening party

vela|do *a* veiled; (*foto*) blurred. ∼**r**
vt watch over; (*encubrir*) veil; (*foto*)
blur. ● *vi* stay awake, not sleep. ∼**r
por** look after. ∼**rse** *vpr* (*foto*) blur

velero *m* sailing-ship

veleta *f* weather vane

velo *m* veil

veloc|idad *f* speed; (*auto etc*) gear.
∼**ímetro** *m* speedometer. ∼**ista** *m
& f* sprinter. **a toda** ∼**idad** at full
speed

velódromo *m* cycle-track

veloz *a* fast, quick

vell|o *m* down. ∼**ón** *m* fleece. ∼**udo**
a hairy

vena *f* vein; (*en madera*) grain. **estar
de/en** ∼ be in the mood

venado *m* deer; (*culin*) venison

vencedor *a* winning. ● *m* winner

vencejo *m* (*pájaro*) swift

venc|er [9] *vt* beat; (*superar*) over-
come. ● *vi* win; ⟨*plazo*⟩ expire.
∼**erse** *vpr* collapse; ⟨*persona*⟩ control o.s. ∼**ido** *a* beaten; (*com, atrasado*) in arrears. **darse por** ∼**ido**
give up. **los** ∼**idos** *mpl* (*en deportes
etc*) the losers

venda *f* bandage. ∼**je** *m* dressing.
∼**r** *vt* bandage

vendaval *m* gale

vende|dor *a* selling. ● *m* seller,
salesman. ∼**dor ambulante** pedlar.
∼**r** *vt* sell. ∼**rse** *vpr* sell. ∼**rse caro**
play hard to get. **se** ∼ for sale

vendimia *f* grape harvest; (*de vino*)
vintage, year

Venecia *f* Venice

veneciano *a* Venetian

veneno *m* poison; (*fig, malevolencia*) spite. ∼**so** *a* poisonous

venera *f* scallop shell

venera|ble *a* venerable. ∼**ción** *f* rev-
erence. ∼**r** *vt* revere

venéreo *a* venereal

venero *m* (*yacimiento*) seam; (*de
agua*) spring; (*fig*) source

venezolano *a & m* Venezuelan

Venezuela *f* Venezuela

venga|nza *f* revenge. ∼**r** [12] *vt*
avenge. ∼**rse** *vpr* take revenge (**de,
por** for) (**de, en** on). ∼**tivo** *a*
vindictive

vengo *vb véase* **venir**

venia *f* (*permiso*) permission

venial *a* venial

veni|da *f* arrival; (*vuelta*) return.
∼**dero** *a* coming. ∼**r** [53] *vi* come;
(*estar, ser*) be. ∼**r a para** come to. ∼**r
bien** suit. **la semana que viene** next
week. **¡venga!** come on!

venta *f* sale; (*posada*) inn. **en** ∼ for
sale

ventaj|a *f* advantage. ∼**oso** *a*
advantageous

ventan|a *f* window; (*de la nariz*) nos-
tril. ∼**illa** *f* window

ventarrón *m* (*fam*) strong wind

ventear *vt* (*olfatear*) sniff

ventero *m* innkeeper

ventila|ción *f* ventilation. ∼**dor** *m*
fan. ∼**r** *vt* air

vent|isca *f* blizzard. ∼**olera** *f* gust of
wind. ∼**osa** *f* sucker. ∼**osidad** *f*
wind, flatulence. ∼**oso** *a* windy

ventrílocuo *m* ventriloquist

ventrudo *a* pot-bellied

ventur|a *f* happiness; (*suerte*) luck.
∼**oso** *a* happy, lucky. **a la** ∼**a** at random. **echar la buena** ∼**a a uno** tell
s.o.'s fortune. **por** ∼**a** by chance;
(*afortunadamente*) fortunately

Venus *f* Venus

ver [43] *vt* see; watch ⟨*televisión*⟩.
● *vi* see. ∼**se** *vpr* see o.s.; (*encontrarse*) find o.s.; ⟨*dos personas*⟩
meet. **a mi** (*modo de*) ∼ in my view.
a ∼ let's see. **de buen** ∼ good-
looking. **dejarse** ∼ show. **¡habráse**

visto! did you ever! **no poder** ~ not be able to stand. **no tener nada que** ~ **con** have nothing to do with. **¡para que veas!** so there! **vamos a** ~ let's see. **ya lo veo** that's obvious. **ya** ~**ás** you'll see. **ya** ~**emos** we'll see

vera f edge; (de río) bank

veracruzano a from Veracruz

veran|eante m & f tourist, holiday-maker. ~**ear** vi spend one's holiday. ~**eo** m (summer) holiday. ~**iego** a summer. ~**o** m summer. **casa** f **de** ~**eo** summer-holiday home. **ir de** ~**eo** go on holiday. **lugar** m **de** ~**eo** holiday resort

veras fpl. **de** ~ really

veraz a truthful

verbal a verbal

verbena f (bot) verbena; (fiesta) fair; (baile) dance

verbo m verb. ~**so** a verbose

verdad f truth. **¿**~**?** isn't it?, aren't they?, won't it? etc. ~**eramente** adv really. ~**ero** a true; (fig) real. **a decir** ~ to tell the truth. **de** ~ really. **la pura** ~ the plain truth. **si bien es** ~ **que** although

verd|e a green; (fruta etc) unripe; (chiste etc) dirty, blue. ● m green; (hierba) grass. ~**or** m greenness

verdugo m executioner; (fig) tyrant

verdu|lería f greengrocer's (shop). ~**lero** m greengrocer. ~**ra** f (green) vegetable(s)

vereda f path; (LAm, acera) pavement (Brit), sidewalk (Amer)

veredicto m verdict

vergel m large garden; (huerto) orchard

verg|onzoso a shameful; (tímido) shy. ~**üenza** f shame; (timidez) shyness. **¡es una** ~**üenza!** it's a disgrace! **me da** ~**üenza** I'm ashamed; (tímido) I'm shy about. **tener** ~**üenza** be ashamed; (tímido) be shy

verídico a true

verifica|ción f verification. ~**r** [7] vt check. ~**rse** vpr take place; (resultar verdad) come true

verja f grating; (cerca) railings; (puerta) iron gate

vermú m, **vermut** m vermouth

vernáculo a vernacular

verosímil a likely; (relato etc) credible

verraco m boar

verruga f wart

versado a versed

versar vi turn. ~ **sobre** be about

versátil a versatile; (fig) fickle

versión f version; (traducción) translation

verso m verse; (línea) line

vértebra f vertebra

verte|dero m rubbish tip; (desaguadero) drain. ~**dor** m drain. ~**r** [1] vt pour; (derramar) spill. ● vi flow

vertical a & f vertical

vértice f vertex

vertiente f slope

vertiginoso a dizzy

vértigo m dizziness; (med) vertigo. **de** ~ (fam) amazing

vesania f rage; (med) insanity

vesícula f blister. ~ **biliar** gall-bladder

vespertino a evening

vestíbulo m hall; (de hotel, teatro etc) foyer

vestido m (de mujer) dress; (ropa) clothes

vestigio m trace. ~**s** mpl remains

vest|imenta f clothing. ~**ir** [5] vt (ponerse) put on; (llevar) wear; dress (niño etc). ● vi dress; (llevar) wear. ~**irse** vpr get dressed; (llevar) wear. ~**uario** m wardrobe; (cuarto) dressing-room

Vesuvio m Vesuvius

vetar vt veto

veterano a veteran

veterinari|a f veterinary science. ~**o** a veterinary. ● m vet (fam), veterinary surgeon (Brit), veterinarian (Amer)

veto m veto. **poner el** ~ **a** veto

vetusto a ancient

vez f time; (turno) turn. **a la** ~ at the same time; (de una vez) in one go. **alguna que otra** ~ from time to time. **alguna** ~ sometimes; (en preguntas) ever. **algunas veces** sometimes. **a su** ~ in (his) turn. **a veces** sometimes. **cada** ~ **más** more and more. **de una** ~ in one go. **de una** ~ **para siempre** once and for all. **de** ~ **en cuando** from time to time. **dos veces** twice. **2 veces 4** 2 times 4. **en** ~ **de** instead of. **érase una** ~, **había una** ~ once upon a time. **muchas veces** often. **otra** ~ again. **pocas veces**, **rara** ~ rarely. **repetidas veces** again and again. **tal** ~ perhaps. **una** ~ (**que**) once

vía f road; (rail) line; (anat) tract; (fig) way. ● prep via. ~ **aérea** by air.

~ de comunicación f means of communication. **~ férrea** railway (*Brit*), railroad (*Amer*). **~ rápida** fast lane. **estar en ~s de** be in the process of

viab|ilidad f viability. **~le** a viable

viaducto m viaduct

viaj|ante m & f commercial traveller. **~ar** vi travel. **~e** m journey; (*corto*) trip. **~e de novios** honeymoon. **~ero** m traveller; (*pasajero*) passenger. **¡buen ~e!** have a good journey!

víbora f viper

vibra|ción f vibration. **~nte** a vibrant. **~r** vt/i vibrate

vicario m vicar

vice... pref vice-...

viceversa adv vice versa

vici|ado a corrupt; (*aire*) stale. **~ar** vt corrupt; (*estropear*) spoil. **~o** m vice; (*mala costumbre*) bad habit. **~oso** a dissolute; (*círculo*) vicious

vicisitud f vicissitude

víctima f victim; (*de un accidente*) casualty

victori|a f victory. **~oso** a victorious

vid f vine

vida f life; (*duración*) lifetime. **¡~ mía!** my darling! **de por ~** for life. **en mi ~** never (in my life). **en ~ de** during the lifetime of. **estar en ~** be alive

vídeo m video recorder

video|cinta f videotape. **~juego** m video game

vidriar vt glaze

vidri|era f stained glass window; (*puerta*) glass door; (*LAm, escaparate*) shop window. **~ería** f glass works. **~ero** m glazier. **~o** m glass. **~oso** a glassy

vieira f scallop

viejo a old. ● m old person

Viena f Vienna

viene vb véase **venir**

viento m wind. **hacer ~** be windy

vientre f belly; (*matriz*) womb; (*intestino*) bowels. **llevar un niño en el ~** be pregnant

viernes m Friday. **V~ Santo** Good Friday

viga f beam; (*de metal*) girder

vigen|cia f validity. **~te** a valid; (*ley*) in force. **entrar en ~cia** come into force

vigésimo a twentieth

vigía f (*torre*) watch-tower; (*persona*) lookout

vigil|ancia f vigilance. **~ante** a vigilant. ● m watchman, supervisor. **~ar** vt keep an eye on. ● vi be vigilant; (*vigía etc*) keep watch. **~ia** f vigil; (*relig*) fasting

vigor m vigour; (*vigencia*) force. **~oso** a vigorous. **entrar en ~** come into force

vil a vile. **~eza** f vileness; (*acción*) vile deed

vilipendiar vt abuse

vilo. en ~ in the air

villa f town; (*casa*) villa. **la V~** Madrid

villancico m (Christmas) carol

villano a rustic; (*grosero*) coarse

vinagre m vinegar. **~ra** f vinegar bottle. **~ras** fpl cruet. **~ta** f vinaigrette (sauce)

vincular vt bind

vínculo m bond

vindicar [7] vt avenge; (*justificar*) vindicate

vine vb véase **venir**

vinicult|or m wine-grower. **~ura** f wine growing

vino m wine. **~ de Jerez** sherry. **~ de la casa** house wine. **~ de mesa** table wine

viña f, **viñedo** m vineyard

viola f viola; (*músico*) viola player

violación f violation; (*de una mujer*) rape

violado a & m violet

violar vt violate; break (*ley*); rape (*mujer*)

violen|cia f violence; (*fuerza*) force; (*embarazo*) embarrassment. **~tar** vt force; break into (*casa etc*). **~tarse** vpr force o.s. **~to** a violent; (*fig*) awkward. **hacer ~cia a** force

violeta a invar & f violet

viol|ín m violin; (*músico*) violinist. **~inista** m & f violinist. **~ón** m double bass; (*músico*) double-bass player. **~onc(h)elista** m & f cellist. **~onc(h)elo** m cello

vira|je m turn. **~r** vt turn. ● vi turn; (*fig*) change direction

virg|en a & f virgin. **~inal** a virginal. **~inidad** f virginity

Virgo m Virgo

viril a virile. **~idad** f virility

virtual a virtual

virtud f virtue; (*capacidad*) ability. **en ~ de** by virtue of

virtuoso a virtuous. ● m virtuoso

viruela *f* smallpox. **picado de ∼s** pock-marked

virulé. a la ∼ (*fam*) crooked; (*estropeado*) damaged

virulento *a* virulent

virus *m invar* virus

visa|do *m* visa. **∼r** *vt* endorse

vísceras *fpl* entrails

viscos|a *f* viscose. **∼o** *a* viscous

visera *f* visor; (*de gorra*) peak

visib|ilidad *f* visibility. **∼le** *a* visible

visig|odo *a* Visigothic. ● *m* Visigoth. **∼ótico** *a* Visigothic

visillo *m* (*cortina*) net curtain

visi|ón *f* vision; (*vista*) sight. **∼onario & m** visionary.

visita *f* visit; (*persona*) visitor. **∼ de cumplido** courtesy call. **∼nte** *m & f* visitor. **∼r** *vt* visit. **tener ∼** have visitors

vislumbr|ar *vt* glimpse. **∼e** *f* glimpse; (*resplandor, fig*) glimmer

viso *m* sheen; (*aspecto*) appearance

visón *m* mink

visor *m* viewfinder

víspera *f* day before, eve

vista *f* sight, vision; (*aspecto, mirada*) look; (*panorama*) view. **apartar la ∼** look away; (*fig*) turn a blind eye. **a primera ∼, a simple ∼** at first sight. **clavar la ∼ en** stare at. **con ∼s a** with a view to. **en ∼ de** in view of, considering. **estar a la ∼** be obvious. **hacer la ∼ gorda** turn a blind eye. **perder de ∼** lose sight of. **tener a la ∼** have in front of one. **volver la ∼ atrás** look back

vistazo *m* glance. **dar/echar un ∼ a** glance at

visto *a* seen; (*corriente*) common; (*considerado*) considered. ● *vb véase* **vestir**. **∼ bueno** passed. **∼ que** since. **bien ∼** acceptable. **está ∼ que** it's obvious that. **lo nunca ∼** an unheard-of thing. **mal ∼** unacceptable. **por lo ∼** apparently

vistoso *a* colourful, bright

visual *a* visual. ● *f* glance. **echar una ∼ a** have a look at

vital *a* vital. **∼icio** *a* life. ● *m* (life) annuity. **∼idad** *f* vitality

vitamina *f* vitamin

viticult|or *m* wine-grower. **∼ura** *f* wine growing

vitorear *vt* cheer

vítreo *a* vitreous

vitrina *f* showcase

vituper|ar *vt* censure. **∼io** *m* censure. **∼ios** *mpl* abuse

viud|a *f* widow. **∼ez** *f* widowhood. **∼o** *a* widowed. ● *m* widower

viva *m* cheer

vivacidad *f* liveliness

vivamente *adv* vividly; (*sinceramente*) sincerely

vivaz *a* (*bot*) perennial; (*vivo*) lively

víveres *mpl* supplies

vivero *m* nursery; (*fig*) hotbed

viveza *f* vividness; (*de inteligencia*) sharpness; (*de carácter*) liveliness

vívido *a* true

vívido *a* vivid

vivienda *f* housing; (*casa*) house; (*piso*) flat

viviente *a* living

vivificar [7] *vt* (*animar*) enliven

vivir *vt* live through. ● *vi* live. ● *m* life. **∼ de** live on. **de mal ∼** dissolute. **¡viva!** hurray! **¡viva el rey!** long live the king!

vivisección *f* vivisection

vivo *a* alive; (*viviente*) living; ⟨*color*⟩ bright; (*listo*) clever; (*fig*) lively. **a lo ∼, al ∼** vividly

Vizcaya *f* Biscay

vizconde *m* viscount. **∼sa** *f* viscountess

vocab|lo *m* word. **∼ulario** *m* vocabulary

vocación *f* vocation

vocal *a* vocal. ● *f* vowel. ● *m & f* member. **∼ista** *m & f* vocalist

voce|ar *vt* call ⟨*mercancías*⟩; (*fig*) proclaim. ● *vi* shout. **∼río** *m* shouting

vociferar *vi* shout

vodka *m & f* vodka

vola|da *f* flight. **∼dor** *a* flying. ● *m* rocket. **∼ndas. en ∼ndas** in the air; (*fig, rápidamente*) very quickly. **∼nte** *a* flying. ● *m* (*auto*) steering-wheel; (*nota*) note; (*rehilete*) shuttlecock; (*tec*) flywheel. **∼r** [2] *vt* blow up. ● *vi* fly; (*desaparecer, fam*) disappear

volátil *a* volatile

volcán *m* volcano. **∼ico** *a* volcanic

vol|car [2 & 7] *vt* knock over; (*adrede*) empty out. ● *vi* overturn. **∼carse** *vpr* fall over; ⟨*vehículo*⟩ overturn; (*fig*) do one's utmost. **∼carse en** throw o.s. into

vol(e)ibol *m* volleyball

volquete *m* tipper, dump truck

voltaje *m* voltage

volte|ar *vt* turn over; (*en el aire*) toss; ring ⟨*campanas*⟩. **∼reta** *f* somersault

voltio *m* volt

voluble *a* (*fig*) fickle

volum|en *m* volume; (*importancia*) importance. **~inoso** *a* voluminous

voluntad *f* will; (*fuerza de voluntad*) will-power; (*deseo*) wish; (*intención*) intention. **buena ~** goodwill. **mala ~** ill will

voluntario *a* voluntary. ● *m* volunteer. **~so** *a* willing; (*obstinado*) wilful

voluptuoso *a* voluptuous

volver [2, *pp* **vuelto**] *vt* turn; (*de arriba a abajo*) turn over; (*devolver*) restore. ● *vi* return; (*fig*) revert. **~se** *vpr* turn round; (*regresar*) return; (*hacerse*) become. **~ a hacer algo** do sth again. **~ en sí** come round

vomit|ar *vt* bring up. ● *vi* be sick, vomit. **~ivo** *m* emetic. ● *a* disgusting

vómito *m* vomit; (*acción*) vomiting

vorágine *f* maelstrom

voraz *a* voracious

vos *pron* (*LAm*) you

vosotros *pron* you; (*reflexivo*) yourselves. **el libro de ~** your book

vot|ación *f* voting; (*voto*) vote. **~ante** *m & f* voter. **~ar** *vt* vote for. ● *vi* vote. **~o** *m* vote; (*relig*) vow; (*maldición*) curse. **hacer ~os por** hope for

voy *vb véase* **ir**

voz *f* voice; (*grito*) shout; (*rumor*) rumour; (*palabra*) word. **~ pública** public opinion. **aclarar la ~** clear one's throat. **a media ~** softly. **a una ~** unanimously. **dar voces** shout. **en ~ alta** loudly

vuelco *m* upset. **el corazón me dio un ~** my heart missed a beat

vuelo *m* flight; (*acción*) flying; (*de ropa*) flare. **al ~** in flight; (*fig*) in passing

vuelta *f* turn; (*curva*) bend; (*paseo*) walk; (*revolución*) revolution; (*regreso*) return; (*dinero*) change. **a la ~** on one's return; (*de página*) over the page. **a la ~ de la esquina** round the corner. **dar la ~ al mundo** go round the world. **dar una ~** go for a walk. **estar de ~** be back. **¡hasta la ~!** see you soon!

vuelvo *vb véase* **volver**

vuestro *a* your. ● *pron* yours. **un amigo ~** a friend of yours

vulg|ar *a* vulgar; (*persona*) common. **~aridad** *f* ordinariness;

(*trivialidad*) triviality; (*grosería*) vulgarity. **~arizar** [10] *vt* popularize. **~o** *m* common people

vulnerab|ilidad *f* vulnerability. **~le** *a* vulnerable

W

wáter *m* toilet

whisky /ˈwiski/ *m* whisky

X

xenofobia *f* xenophobia

xilófono *m* xylophone

Y

y *conj* and

ya *adv* already; (*ahora*) now; (*luego*) later; (*en seguida*) immediately; (*pronto*) soon. ● *int* of course! **~ no** no longer. **~ que** since. **¡~!, ~!** oh yes!, all right!

yacaré *m* (*LAm*) alligator

yac|er [44] *vi* lie. **~imiento** *m* deposit; (*de petróleo*) oilfield

yanqui *m & f* American, Yank(ee)

yate *m* yacht

yegua *f* mare

yeísmo *m* pronunciation of the Spanish *ll* like the Spanish *y*

yelmo *m* helmet

yema *f* (*bot*) bud; (*de huevo*) yolk; (*golosina*) sweet. **~ del dedo** fingertip

yergo *vb véase* **erguir**

yermo *a* uninhabited; (*no cultivable*) barren. ● *m* wasteland

yerno *m* son-in-law

yerro *m* mistake. ● *vb véase* **errar**

yerto *a* stiff

yeso *m* gypsum; (*arquit*) plaster. **~ mate** plaster of Paris

yo *pron* I. ● *m* ego. **~ mismo** I myself. **soy ~** it's me

yodo *m* iodine

yoga *m* yoga

yogur *m* yog(h)urt

York. de ~ (*jamón*) cooked

yuca *f* yucca

Yucatán *m* Yucatán

yugo *m* yoke

Yugoslavia *f* Yugoslavia
yugoslavo *a & m* Yugoslav
yunque *m* anvil
yunta *f* yoke
yuxtaponer [34] *vt* juxtapose
yuyo *m* (*Arg*) weed

Z

zafarse *vpr* escape; get out of ⟨*obligación etc*⟩
zafarrancho *m* (*confusión*) mess; (*riña*) quarrel
zafio *a* coarse
zafiro *m* sapphire
zaga *f* rear. **no ir en ~** not be inferior
zaguán *m* hall
zaherir [4] *vt* hurt one's feelings
zahorí *m* clairvoyant; (*de agua*) water diviner
zaino *a* ⟨*caballo*⟩ chestnut; ⟨*vaca*⟩ black
zalamer|ía *f* flattery. **~o** *a* flattering. ● *m* flatterer
zamarra *f* (*piel*) sheepskin; (*prenda*) sheepskin jacket
zamarrear *vt* shake
zamba *f* (*esp LAm*) South American dance; (*samba*) samba
zambull|ida *f* dive. **~r** [22] *vt* plunge. **~rse** *vpr* dive
zamparse *vpr* fall; (*comer*) gobble up
zanahoria *f* carrot
zancad|a *f* stride. **~illa** *f* trip. **echar la ~illa a uno, poner la ~illa a uno** trip s.o. up
zanc|o *m* stilt. **~udo** *a* long-legged. ● *m* (*LAm*) mosquito
zanganear *vi* idle
zángano *m* drone; (*persona*) idler
zangolotear *vt* fiddle with. ● *vi* rattle; ⟨*persona*⟩ fidget
zanja *f* ditch. **~r** *vt* (*fig*) settle
zapapico *m* pickaxe

zapat|ear *vt/i* tap with one's feet. **~ería** *f* shoe shop; (*arte*) shoemaking. **~ero** *m* shoemaker; (*el que remienda zapatos*) cobbler. **~illa** *f* slipper. **~illas deportivas** trainers. **~o** *m* shoe
zaragata *f* turmoil
Zaragoza *f* Saragossa
zarand|a *f* sieve. **~ear** *vt* sieve; (*sacudir*) shake
zarcillo *m* earring
zarpa *f* claw, paw
zarpar *vi* weigh anchor
zarza *f* bramble. **~mora** *f* blackberry
zarzuela *f* musical, operetta
zascandil *m* scatterbrain
zenit *m* zenith
zigzag *m* zigzag. **~uear** *vi* zigzag
zinc *m* zinc
zipizape *m* (*fam*) row
zócalo *m* skirting-board; (*pedestal*) plinth
zodiaco *m*, **zodíaco** *m* zodiac
zona *f* zone; (*área*) area
zoo *m* zoo. **~logía** *f* zoology. **~lógico** *a* zoological
zoólogo *m* zoologist
zopenco *a* stupid. ● *m* idiot
zoquete *m* (*de madera*) block; (*persona*) blockhead
zorr|a *f* fox; (*hembra*) vixen. **~o** *m* fox
zozobra *f* (*fig*) anxiety. **~r** *vi* be shipwrecked; (*fig*) be ruined
zueco *m* clog
zulú *a & m* Zulu
zumb|ar *vt* (*fam*) give ⟨*golpe etc*⟩. ● *vi* buzz. **~ido** *m* buzzing
zumo *m* juice
zurci|do *m* darning. **~r** [9] *vt* darn
zurdo *a* left-handed; ⟨*mano*⟩ left
zurrar *vt* (*fig, dar golpes, fam*) beat up
zurriago *m* whip
zutano *m* so-and-so

ENGLISH-SPANISH
INGLÉS-ESPAÑOL

A

a /ə, eɪ/ *indef art* (*before vowel* **an**) un *m*; una *f*

aback /ə'bæk/ *adv.* **be taken ~** quedar desconcertado

abacus /'æbəkəs/ *n* ábaco *m*

abandon /ə'bændən/ *vt* abandonar. ● *n* abandono *m*, desenfado *m*. ~**ed** *a* abandonado; ‹*behaviour*› perdido. ~**ment** *n* abandono *m*

abase /ə'beɪs/ *vt* degradar. ~**ment** *n* degradación *f*

abashed /ə'bæʃt/ *a* confuso

abate /ə'beɪt/ *vt* disminuir. ● *vi* disminuir; ‹*storm etc*› calmarse. ~**ment** *n* disminución *f*

abattoir /'æbətwɑ:(r)/ *n* matadero *m*

abbess /'æbɪs/ *n* abadesa *f*

abbey /'æbɪ/ *n* abadía *f*

abbot /'æbət/ *n* abad *m*

abbreviat|e /ə'bri:vɪeɪt/ *vt* abreviar. ~**ion** /-'eɪʃn/ *n* abreviatura *f*; (*act*) abreviación *f*

ABC /'eɪbi:'si:/ *n* abecé *m*, abecedario *m*

abdicat|e /'æbdɪkeɪt/ *vt/i* abdicar. ~**ion** /-'eɪʃn/ *n* abdicación *f*

abdom|en /'æbdəmən/ *n* abdomen *m*. ~**inal** /-'dɒmɪnl/ *a* abdominal

abduct /æb'dʌkt/ *vt* secuestrar. ~**ion** /-ʃn/ *n* secuestro *m*. ~**or** *n* secuestrador *m*

aberration /æbə'reɪʃn/ *n* aberración *f*

abet /ə'bet/ *vt* (*pt* **abetted**) (*jurid*) ser cómplice de

abeyance /ə'beɪəns/ *n.* **in ~** en suspenso

abhor /əb'hɔ:(r)/ *vt* (*pt* **abhorred**) aborrecer. ~**rence** /-'hɒrəns/ *n* aborrecimiento *m*; (*thing*) abominación *f*. ~**rent** /-'hɒrənt/ *a* aborrecible

abide /ə'baɪd/ *vt* (*pt* **abided**) soportar. ● *vi* (*old use, pt* **abode**) morar. ~ **by** atenerse a; cumplir ‹*promise*›

abiding /ə'baɪdɪŋ/ *a* duradero, permanente

ability /ə'bɪlətɪ/ *n* capacidad *f*; (*cleverness*) habilidad *f*

abject /'æbdʒekt/ *a* (*wretched*) miserable; (*vile*) abyecto

ablaze /ə'bleɪz/ *a* en llamas

able /'eɪbl/ *a* (**-er, -est**) capaz. **be ~** poder; (*know how to*) saber

ablutions /ə'blu:ʃnz/ *npl* ablución *f*

ably /'eɪblɪ/ *adv* hábilmente

abnormal /æb'nɔ:ml/ *a* anormal. ~**ity** /-'mælətɪ/ *n* anormalidad *f*

aboard /ə'bɔ:d/ *adv* a bordo. ● *prep* a bordo de

abode /ə'bəʊd/ *see* **abide**. ● *n* (*old use*) domicilio *m*

abolish /ə'bɒlɪʃ/ *vt* suprimir, abolir

abolition /æbə'lɪʃn/ *n* supresión *f*, abolición *f*

abominable /ə'bɒmɪnəbl/ *a* abominable

abominat|e /ə'bɒmɪneɪt/ *vt* abominar. ~**ion** /-'neɪʃn/ *n* abominación *f*

aborigin|al /æbə'rɪdʒənl/ *a & n* aborigen (*m & f*), indígena (*m & f*). ~**es** /-i:z/ *npl* aborígenes *mpl*

abort /ə'bɔ:t/ *vt* hacer abortar. ● *vi* abortar. ~**ion** /-ʃn/ *n* aborto *m* provocado; (*fig*) aborto *m*. ~**ionist** *n* abortista *m & f*. ~**ive** *a* abortivo; (*fig*) fracasado

abound /ə'baʊnd/ *vi* abundar (**in** de, en)

about /ə'baʊt/ *adv* (*approximately*) alrededor de; (*here and there*) por todas partes; (*in existence*) por aquí. **~ here** por aquí. **be ~ to** estar a punto de. **be up and ~** estar levantado. ● *prep* sobre; (*around*) alrededor de; (*somewhere in*) en. **talk ~** hablar de. ~**-face** *n* (*fig*) cambio *m* rotundo. ~**-turn** *n* (*fig*) cambio *m* rotundo

above /ə'bʌv/ *adv* arriba. ● *prep* encima de; (*more than*) más de. **~ all** sobre todo. ~**-board** *a* honrado.

● *adv* abiertamente. **~mentioned** *a* susodicho

abrasi|on /ə'breɪʒn/ *n* abrasión *f*. **~ve** /ə'breɪsɪv/ *a & n* abrasivo (*m*); (*fig*) agresivo, brusco

abreast /ə'brest/ *adv* de frente. **keep ~ of** mantenerse al corriente de

abridge /ə'brɪdʒ/ *vt* abreviar. **~ment** *n* abreviación *f*; (*abstract*) resumen *m*

abroad /ə'brɔːd/ *adv* (*be*) en el extranjero; (*go*) al extranjero; (*far and wide*) por todas partes

abrupt /ə'brʌpt/ *a* brusco. **~ly** *adv* (*suddenly*) repentinamente; (*curtly*) bruscamente. **~ness** *n* brusquedad *f*

abscess /'æbsɪs/ *n* absceso *m*

abscond /əb'skɒnd/ *vi* fugarse

absen|ce /'æbsəns/ *n* ausencia *f*; (*lack*) falta *f*. **~t** /'æbsənt/ *a* ausente. /æb'sent/ *vr*. **~ o.s.** ausentarse. **~tly** *adv* distraídamente. **~t-minded** *a* distraído. **~t-mindedness** *n* distracción *f*, despiste *m*

absentee /æbsən'tiː/ *n* ausente *m & f*. **~ism** *n* absentismo *m*

absinthe /'æbsɪnθ/ *n* ajenjo *m*

absolute /'æbsəluːt/ *a* absoluto. **~ly** *adv* absolutamente

absolution /æbsə'luːʃn/ *n* absolución *f*

absolve /əb'zɒlv/ *vt* (*from sin*) absolver; (*from obligation*) liberar

absor|b /əb'zɔːb/ *vt* absorber. **~bent** *a* absorbente. **~ption** *n* absorción *f*

abstain /əb'steɪn/ *vi* abstenerse (*from* de)

abstemious /əb'stiːmɪəs/ *a* abstemio

abstention /əb'stenʃn/ *n* abstención *f*

abstinen|ce /'æbstɪnəns/ *n* abstinencia *f*. **~t** *a* abstinente

abstract /'æbstrækt/ *a* abstracto. ● *n* (*quality*) abstracto *m*; (*summary*) resumen *m*. /əb'strækt/ *vt* extraer; (*summarize*) resumir. **~ion** /-ʃn/ *n* abstracción *f*

abstruse /əb'struːs/ *a* abstruso

absurd /əb'sɜːd/ *a* absurdo. **~ity** *n* absurdo *m*, disparate *m*

abundan|ce /ə'bʌndəns/ *n* abundancia *f*. **~t** *a* abundante

abuse /ə'bjuːz/ *vt* (*misuse*) abusar de; (*ill-treat*) maltratar; (*insult*) insultar. /ə'bjuːs/ *n* abuso *m*; (*insults*) insultos *mpl*

abusive /ə'bjuːsɪv/ *a* injurioso

abut /ə'bʌt/ *vi* (*pt* abutted) confinar (**on** con)

abysmal /ə'bɪzməl/ *a* abismal; (*bad, fam*) pésimo; (*fig*) profundo

abyss /ə'bɪs/ *n* abismo *m*

acacia /ə'keɪʃə/ *n* acacia *f*

academic /ækə'demɪk/ *a* académico; (*pej*) teórico. ● *n* universitario *m*, catedrático *m*. **~ian** /-də'mɪʃn/ *n* académico *m*

academy /ə'kædəmɪ/ *n* academia *f*. **~ of music** conservatorio *m*

accede /ək'siːd/ *vi*. **~ to** acceder a (*request*); tomar posesión de (*office*). **~ to the throne** subir al trono

accelerat|e /ək'seləreɪt/ *vt* acelerar. **~ion** /-'reɪʃn/ *n* aceleración *f*. **~or** *n* acelerador *m*

accent /'æksənt/ *n* acento *m*. /æk'sent/ *vt* acentuar

accentuate /ək'sentʃʊeɪt/ *vt* acentuar

accept /ək'sept/ *vt* aceptar. **~able** *a* aceptable. **~ance** *n* aceptación *f*; (*approval*) aprobación *f*

access /'ækses/ *n* accceso *m*. **~ibility** /-ɪ'bɪlətɪ/ *n* accesibilidad *f*. **~ible** /ək'sesəbl/ *a* accesible; (*person*) tratable

accession /æk'seʃn/ *n* (*to power, throne etc*) ascenso *m*; (*thing added*) adquisición *f*

accessory /ək'sesərɪ/ *a* accesorio. ● *n* accesorio *m*, complemento *m*; (*jurid*) cómplice *m & f*

accident /'æksɪdənt/ *n* accidente *m*; (*chance*) casualidad *f*. **by ~** por accidente, por descuido, sin querer; (*by chance*) por casualidad. **~al** /-'dentl/ *a* accidental, fortuito. **~ally** /-'dentəlɪ/ *adv* por accidente, por descuido, sin querer; (*by chance*) por casualidad

acclaim /ə'kleɪm/ *vt* aclamar. ● *n* aclamación *f*

acclimatiz|ation /əklaɪmətaɪ'zeɪʃn/ *n* aclimatación *f*. **~e** /ə'klaɪmətaɪz/ *vt* aclimatar. ● *vi* aclimatarse

accolade /'ækəleɪd/ *n* (*of knight*) acolada *f*; (*praise*) encomio *m*

accommodat|e /ə'kɒmədeɪt/ *vt* (*give hospitality to*) alojar; (*adapt*) acomodar; (*supply*) proveer; (*oblige*) complacer. **~ing** *a* complaciente. **~ion** /-'deɪʃn/ *n* alojamiento *m*; (*rooms*) habitaciones *fpl*

accompan|iment /ə'kʌmpənɪmənt/ *n* acompañamiento *m*. **~ist** *n* acompañante *m & f*. **~y** /ə'kʌmpənɪ/ *vt* acompañar

accomplice /ə'kʌmplɪs/ *n* cómplice *m & f*

accomplish /ə'kʌmplɪʃ/ *vt* (*complete*) acabar; (*achieve*) realizar; (*carry out*) llevar a cabo. **~ed** *a* consumado. **~ment** *n* realización *f*; (*ability*) talento *m*; (*thing achieved*) triunfo *m*, logro *m*

accord /ə'kɔːd/ *vi* concordar. • *vt* conceder. • *n* acuerdo *m*; (*harmony*) armonía *f*. **of one's own ~** espontáneamente. **~ance** *n*. **in ~ance with** de acuerdo con

according /ə'kɔːdɪŋ/ *adv*. **~ to** según. **~ly** *adv* en conformidad; (*therefore*) por consiguiente

accordion /ə'kɔːdɪən/ *n* acordeón *m*

accost /ə'kɒst/ *vt* abordar

account /ə'kaʊnt/ *n* cuenta *f*; (*description*) relato *m*; (*importance*) importancia *f*. **on ~ of** a causa de. **on no ~** de ninguna manera. **on this ~** por eso. **take into ~** tener en cuenta. • *vt* considerar. **~ for** dar cuenta de, explicar

accountab|ility /əkaʊntə'bɪlətɪ/ *n* responsabilidad *f*. **~le** *a* responsable (**for** de)

accountan|cy /ə'kaʊntənsɪ/ *n* contabilidad *f*. **~t** *n* contable *m & f*

accoutrements /ə'kuːtrəmənts/ *npl* equipo *m*

accredited /ə'kredɪtɪd/ *a* acreditado; (*authorized*) autorizado

accrue /ə'kruː/ *vi* acumularse

accumulat|e /ə'kjuːmjʊleɪt/ *vt* acumular. • *vi* acumularse. **~ion** /-'leɪʃn/ *n* acumulación *f*. **~or** *n* (*elec*) acumulador *m*

accura|cy /'ækjərəsɪ/ *n* exactitud *f*, precisión *f*. **~te** *a* exacto, preciso

accus|ation /ækjuː'zeɪʃn/ *n* acusación *f*. **~e** *vt* acusar

accustom /ə'kʌstəm/ *vt* acostumbrar. **~ed** *a* acostumbrado. **get ~ed (to)** acostumbrarse (a)

ace /eɪs/ *n* as *m*

acetate /'æsɪteɪt/ *n* acetato *m*

ache /eɪk/ *n* dolor *m*. • *vi* doler. **my leg ~s** me duele la pierna

achieve /ə'tʃiːv/ *vt* realizar; lograr (*success*). **~ment** *n* realización *f*; (*feat*) éxito *m*; (*thing achieved*) proeza *f*, logro *m*

acid /'æsɪd/ *a & n* ácido (*m*). **~ity** /ə'sɪdətɪ/ *n* acidez *f*

acknowledge /ək'nɒlɪdʒ/ *vt* reconocer. **~ receipt of** acusar recibo de.

~ment *n* reconocimiento *m*; (*com*) acuse *m* de recibo

acme /'ækmɪ/ *n* cima *f*

acne /'æknɪ/ *n* acné *m*

acorn /'eɪkɔːn/ *n* bellota *f*

acoustic /ə'kuːstɪk/ *a* acústico. **~s** *npl* acústica *f*

acquaint /ə'kweɪnt/ *vt*. **~ s.o. with** poner a uno al corriente de. **be ~ed with** conocer (*person*); saber (*fact*). **~ance** *n* conocimiento *m*; (*person*) conocido *m*

acquiesce /ækwɪ'es/ *vi* consentir (**in** en). **~nce** *n* aquiescencia *f*, consentimiento *m*

acqui|re /ə'kwaɪə(r)/ *vt* adquirir; aprender (*language*). **~re a taste for** tomar gusto a. **~sition** /ækwɪ'zɪʃn/ *n* adquisición *f*. **~sitive** /-'kwɪzətɪv/ *a* codicioso

acquit /ə'kwɪt/ *vt* (*pt* **acquitted**) absolver; **~ o.s. well** defenderse bien, tener éxito. **~tal** *n* absolución *f*

acre /'eɪkə(r)/ *n* acre *m*. **~age** *n* superficie *f* (en acres)

acrid /'ækrɪd/ *a* acre

acrimon|ious /ækrɪ'məʊnɪəs/ *a* cáustico, mordaz. **~y** /'ækrɪmənɪ/ *n* acrimonia *f*, acritud *f*

acrobat /'ækrəbæt/ *n* acróbata *m & f*. **~ic** /-'bætɪk/ *a* acrobático. **~ics** /-'bætɪks/ *npl* acrobacia *f*

acronym /'ækrənɪm/ *n* acrónimo *m*, siglas *fpl*

across /ə'krɒs/ *adv & prep* (*side to side*) de un lado al otro; (*on other side*) del otro lado de; (*crosswise*) a través. **go** *or* **walk ~** atravesar

act /ækt/ *n* acto *m*; (*action*) acción *f*; (*in variety show*) número *m*; (*decree*) decreto *m*. • *vt* hacer (*part, role*). • *vi* actuar; (*pretend*) fingir; (*function*) funcionar. **~ as** actuar de. **~ for** representar. **~ing** *a* interino. • *n* (*of play*) representación *f*; (*by actor*) interpretación *f*; (*profession*) profesión *f* de actor

action /'ækʃn/ *n* acción *f*; (*jurid*) demanda *f*; (*plot*) argumento *m*. **out of ~** (*on sign*) no funciona. **put out of ~** inutilizar. **take ~** tomar medidas

activate /'æktɪveɪt/ *vt* activar

activ|e /'æktɪv/ *a* activo; (*energetic*) enérgico; (*volcano*) en actividad. **~ity** /-'tɪvətɪ/ *n* actividad *f*

act|or /'æktə(r)/ *n* actor *m*. **~ress** *n* actriz *f*

actual /'æktʃʊəl/ a verdadero. ~**ity** /-'ælətɪ/ n realidad f. ~**ly** adv en realidad, efectivamente; (even) incluso

actuary /'æktʃʊərɪ/ n actuario m

actuate /'æktʃʊeɪt/ vt accionar, impulsar

acumen /'ækjʊmen/ n perspicacia f

acupunctur|e /'ækjʊpʌŋktʃə(r)/ n acupuntura f. ~**ist** n acupunturista m & f

acute /ə'kjuːt/ a agudo. ~**ly** adv agudamente. ~**ness** n agudeza f

ad /æd/ n (fam) anuncio m

AD /eɪ'diː/ abbr (Anno Domini) d.J.C.

adamant /'ædəmənt/ a inflexible

Adam's apple /'ædəmz'æpl/ n nuez f (de Adán)

adapt /ə'dæpt/ vt adaptar. ● vi adaptarse

adaptab|ility /ədæptə'bɪlətɪ/ n adaptabilidad f. ~**le** /ə'dæptəbl/ a adaptable

adaptation /ædæp'teɪʃn/ n adaptación f; (of book etc) versión f

adaptor /ə'dæptə(r)/ n (elec) adaptador m

add /æd/ vt añadir. ● vi sumar. ~ **up** sumar; (fig) tener sentido. ~ **up to** equivaler a

adder /'ædə(r)/ n víbora f

addict /'ædɪkt/ n adicto m; (fig) entusiasta m & f. ~**ed** /ə'dɪktɪd/ a. ~**ed to** adicto a; (fig) fanático de. ~**ion** /-ʃn/ n (med) dependencia f; (fig) afición f. ~**ive** a que crea dependencia

adding machine /'ædɪŋməʃiːn/ n máquina f de sumar, sumadora f

addition /ə'dɪʃn/ n suma f. **in** ~ además. ~**al** /-ʃənl/ a suplementario

additive /'ædɪtɪv/ a & n aditivo (m)

address /ə'dres/ n señas fpl, dirección f; (speech) discurso m. ● vt poner la dirección; (speak to) dirigirse a. ~**ee** /ædre'siː/ n destinatario m

adenoids /'ædɪnɔɪdz/ npl vegetaciones fpl adenoideas

adept /'ædept/ a & n experto (m)

adequa|cy /'ædɪkwəsɪ/ n suficiencia f. ~**te** a suficiente, adecuado. ~**tely** adv suficientemente, adecuadamente

adhere /əd'hɪə(r)/ vi adherirse (**to** a); observar (rule). ~**nce** /-rəns/ n adhesión f; (to rules) observancia f

adhesion /əd'hiːʒn/ n adherencia f

adhesive /əd'hiːsɪv/ a & n adhesivo (m)

ad infinitum /ædɪnfɪ'naɪtəm/ adv hasta el infinito

adjacent /ə'dʒeɪsnt/ a contiguo

adjective /'ædʒɪktɪv/ n adjetivo m

adjoin /ə'dʒɔɪn/ vt lindar con. ~**ing** a contiguo

adjourn /ə'dʒɜːn/ vt aplazar; suspender (meeting etc). ● vi suspenderse. ~ **to** trasladarse a

adjudicate /ə'dʒuːdɪkeɪt/ vt juzgar. ● vi actuar como juez

adjust /ə'dʒʌst/ vt ajustar (machine); (arrange) arreglar. ● vi. ~ (**to**) adaptarse (a). ~**able** a ajustable. ~**ment** n adaptación f; (tec) ajuste m

ad lib /æd'lɪb/ a improvisado. ● vi (pt -**libbed**) (fam) improvisar

administer /əd'mɪnɪstə(r)/ vt administrar, dar, proporcionar

administrat|ion /ədmɪnɪ'streɪʃn/ n administración f. ~**or** n administrador m

admirable /'ædmərəbl/ a admirable

admiral /'ædmərəl/ n almirante m

admiration /ædmə'reɪʃn/ n admiración f

admire /əd'maɪə(r)/ vt admirar. ~**r** /-'maɪərə(r)/ n admirador m; (suitor) enamorado m

admissible /əd'mɪsəbl/ a admisible

admission /əd'mɪʃn/ n admisión f; (entry) entrada f

admit /əd'mɪt/ vt (pt **admitted**) dejar entrar; (acknowledge) admitir, reconocer. ~ **to** confesar. **be** ~**ted** (to hospital etc) ingresar. ~**tance** n entrada f. ~**tedly** adv es verdad que

admoni|sh /əd'mɒnɪʃ/ vt reprender; (advise) aconsejar. ~**tion** /-'nɪʃn/ n reprensión f

ado /ə'duː/ n alboroto m; (trouble) dificultad f. **without more** ~ en seguida, sin más

adolescen|ce /ædə'lesns/ n adolescencia f. ~**t** a & n adolescente (m & f)

adopt /ə'dɒpt/ vt adoptar. ~**ed** a (child) adoptivo. ~**ion** /-ʃn/ n adopción f. ~**ive** a adoptivo

ador|able /ə'dɔːrəbl/ a adorable. ~**ation** /ædə'reɪʃn/ n adoración f. ~**e** /ə'dɔː(r)/ vt adorar

adorn /ə'dɔːn/ vt adornar. ~**ment** n adorno m

adrenalin /ə'drenəlɪn/ n adrenalina f

adrift /ə'drɪft/ a & adv a la deriva

adroit /ə'drɔɪt/ a diestro

adulation /ædjʊ'leɪʃn/ n adulación f

adult /'ædʌlt/ a & n adulto (m)

adulterat|ion /ədʌltə'reɪʃn/ n adulteración f. ~e /ə'dʌltəreɪt/ vt adulterar

adulter|er /ə'dʌltərə(r)/ n adúltero m. ~ess n adúltera f. ~ous a adúltero. ~y n adulterio m

advance /əd'vɑːns/ vt adelantar. ● vi adelantarse. ● n adelanto m. in ~ con anticipación, por adelantado. ~d a avanzado; ⟨studies⟩ superior. ~ment n adelanto m; (in job) promoción f

advantage /əd'vɑːntɪdʒ/ n ventaja f. take ~ of aprovecharse de; abusar de ⟨person⟩. ~ous /ædvən'teɪdʒəs/ a ventajoso

advent /'ædvənt/ n venida f. A~ n adviento m

adventur|e /əd'ventʃə(r)/ n aventura f. ~er n aventurero m. ~ous a ⟨persona⟩ aventurero; ⟨cosa⟩ arriesgado; (fig, bold) llamativo

adverb /'ædvɜːb/ n adverbio m

adversary /'ædvəsərɪ/ n adversario m

advers|e /'ædvɜːs/ a adverso, contrario, desfavorable. ~ity /əd'vɜːsətɪ/ n infortunio m

advert /'ædvɜːt/ n (fam) anuncio m. ~ise /'ædvətaɪz/ vt anunciar. ● vi hacer publicidad; (seek, sell) poner un anuncio. ~isement /əd'vɜːtɪsmənt/ n anuncio m. ~iser /-ə(r)/ n anunciante m & f

advice /əd'vaɪs/ n consejo m; (report) informe m

advis|able /əd'vaɪzəbl/ a aconsejable. ~e vt aconsejar; (inform) avisar. ~e against aconsejar en contra de. ~er n consejero m; (consultant) asesor m. ~ory a consultivo

advocate /'ædvəkət/ n defensor m; (jurid) abogado m. /'ædvəkeɪt/ vt recomendar

aegis /'iːdʒɪs/ n égida f. under the ~ of bajo la tutela de, patrocinado por

aeon /'iːən/ n eternidad f

aerial /'eərɪəl/ a aéreo. ● n antena f

aerobatics /eərə'bætɪks/ npl acrobacia f aérea

aerobics /eə'rəʊbɪks/ npl aeróbica f

aerodrome /'eərədrəʊm/ n aeródromo m

aerodynamic /eərəʊdaɪ'næmɪk/ a aerodinámico

aeroplane /'eərəpleɪn/ n avión m

aerosol /'eərəsɒl/ n aerosol m

aesthetic /iːs'θetɪk/ a estético

afar /ə'fɑː(r)/ adv lejos

affable /'æfəbl/ a afable

affair /ə'feə(r)/ n asunto m. (love) ~ aventura f, amorío m. ~s npl (business) negocios mpl

affect /ə'fekt/ vt afectar; (pretend) fingir

affect|ation /æfek'teɪʃn/ n afectación f. ~ed a afectado, amanerado

affection /ə'fekʃn/ n cariño m; (disease) afección f. ~ate /-ʃənət/ a cariñoso

affiliat|e /ə'fɪlɪeɪt/ vt afiliar. ~ion /-'eɪʃn/ n afiliación f

affinity /ə'fɪnətɪ/ n afinidad f

affirm /ə'fɜːm/ vt afirmar. ~ation /æfə'meɪʃn/ n afirmación f

affirmative /ə'fɜːmətɪv/ a afirmativo. ● n respuesta f afirmativa

affix /ə'fɪks/ vt sujetar; añadir ⟨signature⟩; pegar ⟨stamp⟩

afflict /ə'flɪkt/ vt afligir. ~ion /-ʃn/ n aflicción f, pena f

affluen|ce /'æfluəns/ n riqueza f. ~t a rico. ● n (geog) afluente m

afford /ə'fɔːd/ vt permitirse; (provide) dar

affray /ə'freɪ/ n reyerta f

affront /ə'frʌnt/ n afrenta f, ofensa f. ● vt afrentar, ofender

afield /ə'fiːld/ adv. far ~ muy lejos

aflame /ə'fleɪm/ adv & a en llamas

afloat /ə'fləʊt/ adv a flote

afoot /ə'fʊt/ adv. sth is ~ se está tramando algo

aforesaid /ə'fɔːsed/ a susodicho

afraid /ə'freɪd/ a. be ~ tener miedo (of a); (be sorry) sentir, lamentar

afresh /ə'freʃ/ adv de nuevo

Africa /'æfrɪkə/ n África f. ~n a & n africano (m)

after /'ɑːftə(r)/ adv después; (behind) detrás. ● prep después de; (behind) detrás de. be ~ (seek) buscar, andar en busca de. ● conj después de que. ● a posterior

afterbirth /'ɑːftəbɜːθ/ n placenta f

after-effect /'ɑːftərfekt/ n consecuencia f, efecto m secundario

aftermath /'ɑːftəmæθ/ n secuelas fpl

afternoon /ɑːftə'nuːn/ n tarde f

aftershave /'ɑːftəʃeɪv/ n loción f para después del afeitado

afterthought /'ɑːftəθɔːt/ n ocurrencia f tardía

afterwards /'ɑːftəwədz/ adv después

again /ə'gen/ adv otra vez; (besides) además. ~ **and** ~ una y otra vez

against /ə'genst/ prep contra, en contra de

age /eɪdʒ/ n edad f. **of** ~ mayor de edad. **under** ~ menor de edad. ● vt/i (pres p ageing) envejecer. ~**d** /'eɪdʒd/ a de ... años. ~**d 10** de 10 años, que tiene 10 años. ~**d** /'eɪdʒɪd/ a viejo, anciano. ~**less** a siempre joven; (eternal) eterno, inmemorial. ~**s** (fam) siglos mpl

agency /'eɪdʒənsɪ/ n agencia f, organismo m, oficina f; (means) mediación f

agenda /ə'dʒendə/ npl orden m del día

agent /'eɪdʒənt/ n agente m & f; (representative) representante m & f

agglomeration /əglɒmə'reɪʃn/ n aglomeración f

aggravat|e /'ægrəveɪt/ vt agravar; (irritate, fam) irritar. ~**ion** /-'veɪʃn/ n agravación f; (irritation, fam) irritación f

aggregate /'ægrɪgət/ a total. ● n conjunto m. /'ægrɪgeɪt/ vt agregar. ● vi ascender a

aggress|ion /ə'greʃn/ n agresión f. ~**ive** a agresivo. ~**iveness** n agresividad f. ~**or** n agresor m

aggrieved /ə'griːvd/ a apenado, ofendido

aghast /ə'gɑːst/ a horrorizado

agil|e /'ædʒaɪl/ a ágil. ~**ity** /ə'dʒɪlətɪ/ n agilidad f

agitat|e /'ædʒɪteɪt/ vt agitar. ~**ion** /-'teɪʃn/ n agitación f, excitación f. ~**or** n agitador m

agnostic /æg'nɒstɪk/ a & n agnóstico (m). ~**ism** /-sɪzəm/ n agnosticismo m

ago /ə'gəʊ/ adv hace. **a long time** ~ hace mucho tiempo. **3 days** ~ hace 3 días

agog /ə'gɒg/ a ansioso

agon|ize /'ægənaɪz/ vi atormentarse. ~**izing** a atroz, angustioso, doloroso. ~**y** n dolor m (agudo); (mental) angustia f

agree /ə'griː/ vt acordar. ● vi estar de acuerdo; (of figures) concordar; (get on) entenderse. ~ **with** (of food etc) sentar bien a. ~**able** /ə'griːəbl/ a agradable. **be** ~**able** (willing) estar de acuerdo. ~**d** a (time, place) convenido. ~**ment** /ə'griːmənt/ n acuerdo m. **in** ~**ment** de acuerdo

agricultur|al /ægrɪ'kʌltʃərəl/ a agrícola. ~**e** /'ægrɪkʌltʃə(r)/ n agricultura f

aground /ə'graʊnd/ adv. **run** ~ (of ship) varar, encallar

ahead /ə'hed/ adv delante; (of time) antes de. **be** ~ ir delante

aid /eɪd/ vt ayudar. ● n ayuda f. **in** ~ **of** a beneficio de

aide /eɪd/ n (Amer) ayudante m & f

AIDS /eɪdz/ n (med) SIDA m

ail /eɪl/ vt afligir. ~**ing** a enfermo. ~**ment** n enfermedad f

aim /eɪm/ vt apuntar; (fig) dirigir. ● vi apuntar; (fig) pretender. ● n puntería f; (fig) propósito m. ~**less** a, ~**lessly** adv sin objeto, sin rumbo

air /eə(r)/ n aire m. **be on the** ~ estar en el aire. **put on** ~**s** darse aires. ● vt airear. ● a (base etc) aéreo. ~**borne** a en el aire; (mil) aerotransportado. ~**conditioned** a climatizado, con aire acondicionado. ~**craft** /'eəkrɑːft/ n (pl invar) avión m. ~**field** /'eəfiːld/ n aeródromo m. **A**~ **Force** fuerzas fpl aéreas. ~**gun** /'eəgʌn/ n escopeta f de aire comprimido. ~**lift** /'eəlɪft/ n puente m aéreo. ~**line** /'eəlaɪn/ n línea f aérea. ~**lock** /'eəlɒk/ n (in pipe) burbuja f de aire; (chamber) esclusa f de aire. ~ **mail** n correo m aéreo. ~**man** /'eəmən/ n (pl -men) n aviador m. ~**port** /'eəpɔːt/ n aeropuerto m. ~**tight** /'eətaɪt/ a hermético. ~**worthy** /'eəwɜːðɪ/ a en condiciones de vuelo. ~**y** /'eərɪ/ a (-ier, -iest) aireado; (manner) ligero

aisle /aɪl/ n nave f lateral; (gangway) pasillo m

ajar /ə'dʒɑː(r)/ adv & a entreabierto

akin /ə'kɪn/ a semejante (**a** to)

alabaster /'æləbɑːstə(r)/ n alabastro m

alacrity /ə'lækrətɪ/ n prontitud f

alarm /ə'lɑːm/ n alarma f; (clock) despertador m. ● vt asustar. ~**ist** n alarmista m & f

alas /ə'læs/ int ¡ay!, ¡ay de mí!

albatross /'ælbətrɒs/ n albatros m

albino /æl'biːnəʊ/ a & n albino (m)

album /'ælbəm/ n álbum m

alchem|ist /'ælkəmɪst/ n alquimista m & f. ~**y** n alquimia f

alcohol /'ælkəhɒl/ n alcohol m. ~**ic** /-'hɒlɪk/ a & n alcohólico (m). ~**ism** n alcoholismo m

alcove /'ælkəʊv/ n nicho m

ale /eɪl/ n cerveza f

alert /ə'lɜːt/ a vivo; (*watchful*) vigilante. ● n alerta f. **on the ~** alerta. ● vt avisar. **~ness** n vigilancia f

algebra /'ældʒɪbrə/ n álgebra f

Algeria /æl'dʒɪərɪə/ n Argelia f. **~n** a & n argelino (m)

alias /'eɪlɪəs/ n (pl **-ases**) alias m invar. ● adv alias

alibi /'ælɪbaɪ/ (pl **-is**) coartada f

alien /'eɪlɪən/ n extranjero m. ● a ajeno

alienat|e /'eɪlɪəneɪt/ vt enajenar. **~ion** /-'neɪʃn/ n enajenación f

alight[1] /ə'laɪt/ vi bajar; ⟨bird⟩ posarse

alight[2] /ə'laɪt/ a ardiendo; ⟨light⟩ encendido

align /ə'laɪn/ vt alinear. **~ment** n alineación f

alike /ə'laɪk/ a parecido, semejante. **look** or **be ~** parecerse. ● adv de la misma manera

alimony /'ælɪmənɪ/ n pensión f alimenticia

alive /ə'laɪv/ a vivo. **~ to** sensible a. **~ with** lleno de

alkali /'ælkəlaɪ/ n (pl **-is**) álcali m. **~ne** a alcalino

all /ɔːl/ a & pron todo. **~ but one** todos excepto uno. **~ of it** todo. ● adv completamente. **~ but** casi. **~ in** (*fam*) rendido. **~ of a sudden** de pronto. **~ over** (*finished*) acabado; (*everywhere*) por todas partes. **~ right!** ¡vale! **be ~ for** estar a favor de. **not at ~** de ninguna manera; (*after thanks!*) ¡no hay de qué!

allay /ə'leɪ/ vt aliviar ⟨pain⟩; aquietar ⟨fears etc⟩

all-clear /ɔːl'klɪə(r)/ n fin m de (la) alarma

allegation /ælɪ'geɪʃn/ n alegato m

allege /ə'ledʒ/ vt alegar. **~dly** /-ɪdlɪ/ adv según se dice, supuestamente

allegiance /ə'liːdʒəns/ n lealtad f

allegor|ical /ælɪ'gɒrɪkl/ a alegórico. **~y** /'ælɪgərɪ/ n alegoría f

allerg|ic /ə'lɜːdʒɪk/ a alérgico. **~y** /'ælədʒɪ/ n alergia f

alleviat|e /ə'liːvɪeɪt/ vt aliviar. **~ion** /-'eɪʃn/ n alivio m

alley /'ælɪ/ (pl **-eys**) n callejuela f; (for bowling) bolera f

alliance /ə'laɪəns/ n alianza f

allied /'ælaɪd/ a aliado

alligator /'ælɪgeɪtə(r)/ n caimán m

allocat|e /'æləkeɪt/ vt asignar; (*share out*) repartir. **~ion** /-'keɪʃn/ n asignación f, (*share*) ración f, (*distribution*) reparto m

allot /ə'lɒt/ vt (pt **allotted**) asignar. **~ment** n asignación f; (*share*) ración f; (*land*) parcela f

all-out /ɔːl'aʊt/ a máximo

allow /ə'laʊ/ vt permitir; (*grant*) conceder; (*reckon on*) prever; (*agree*) admitir. **~ for** tener en cuenta. **~ance** /ə'laʊəns/ n concesión f, (*pension*) pensión f; (*com*) rebaja f. **make ~ances for** ser indulgente con; (*take into account*) tener en cuenta

alloy /'ælɔɪ/ n aleación f. /ə'lɔɪ/ vt alear

all-round /ɔːl'raʊnd/ a completo

allude /ə'luːd/ vi aludir

allure /ə'lʊə(r)/ vt atraer. ● n atractivo m

allusion /ə'luːʒn/ n alusión f

ally /'ælaɪ/ n aliado m. /ə'laɪ/ vt aliarse

almanac /'ɔːlmənæk/ n almanaque m

almighty /ɔːl'maɪtɪ/ a todopoderoso; (*big, fam*) enorme. ● n. **the A~** el Todopoderoso m

almond /'ɑːmənd/ n almendra f; (*tree*) almendro (m)

almost /'ɔːlməʊst/ adv casi

alms /ɑːmz/ n limosna f

alone /ə'ləʊn/ a solo. ● adv sólo, solamente

along /ə'lɒŋ/ prep por, a lo largo de. ● adv. **~ with** junto con. **all ~** todo el tiempo. **come ~** venga

alongside /əlɒŋ'saɪd/ adv (*naut*) al costado. ● prep al lado de

aloof /ə'luːf/ adv apartado. ● a reservado. **~ness** n reserva f

aloud /ə'laʊd/ adv en voz alta

alphabet /'ælfəbet/ n alfabeto m. **~ical** /-'betɪkl/ a alfabético

alpine /'ælpaɪn/ a alpino

Alps /ælps/ npl. **the ~** los Alpes mpl

already /ɔːl'redɪ/ adv ya

Alsatian /æl'seɪʃn/ n (*geog*) alsaciano m; (*dog*) pastor m alemán

also /'ɔːlsəʊ/ adv también; (*moreover*) además

altar /'ɔːltə(r)/ n altar m

alter /'ɔːltə(r)/ vt cambiar. ● vi cambiarse. **~ation** /-'reɪʃn/ n modificación f; (*to garment*) arreglo m

alternate /ɔːl'tɜːnət/ a alterno. /'ɔːltəneɪt/ vt/i alternar. **~ly** adv alternativamente

alternative /ɔːlˈtɜːnətɪv/ *a* alternativo. ● *n* alternativa *f*. ~**ly** *adv* en cambio, por otra parte

although /ɔːlˈðəʊ/ *conj* aunque

altitude /ˈæltɪtjuːd/ *n* altitud *f*

altogether /ɔːltəˈɡeðə(r)/ *adv* completamente; (*on the whole*) en total

altruis|m /ˈæltruːɪzəm/ *n* altruismo *m*. ~**t** /ˈæltruːɪst/ *n* altruista *m & f*. ~**tic** /-ˈɪstɪk/ *a* altruista

aluminium /æljʊˈmɪnɪəm/ *n* aluminio *m*

always /ˈɔːlweɪz/ *adv* siempre

am /æm/ *see* **be**

a.m. /ˈeɪem/ *abbr* (*ante meridiem*) de la mañana

amalgamate /əˈmælɡəmeɪt/ *vt* amalgamar. ● *vi* amalgamarse

amass /əˈmæs/ *vt* amontonar

amateur /ˈæmətə(r)/ *n* aficionado *m*. ● *a* no profesional; (*in sports*) amateur. ~**ish** *a* (*pej*) torpe, chapucero

amaz|e /əˈmeɪz/ *vt* asombrar. ~**ed** *a* asombrado, estupefacto. **be** ~**ed at** quedarse asombrado de, asombrarse de. ~**ement** *n* asombro *m*. ~**ingly** *adv* extraordinariamente

ambassador /æmˈbæsədə(r)/ *n* embajador *m*

amber /ˈæmbə(r)/ *n* ámbar *m*; (*auto*) luz *f* amarilla

ambidextrous /æmbɪˈdekstrəs/ *a* ambidextro

ambience /ˈæmbɪəns/ *n* ambiente *m*

ambigu|ity /æmbɪˈɡjuːətɪ/ *n* ambigüedad *f*. ~**ous** /æmˈbɪɡjʊəs/ *a* ambiguo

ambit /ˈæmbɪt/ *n* ámbito *m*

ambiti|on /æmˈbɪʃn/ *n* ambición *f*. ~**ous** *a* ambicioso

ambivalen|ce /æmˈbɪvələns/ *n* ambivalencia *f*. ~**t** *a* ambivalente

amble /ˈæmbl/ *vi* andar despacio, andar sin prisa

ambulance /ˈæmbjʊləns/ *n* ambulancia *f*

ambush /ˈæmbʊʃ/ *n* emboscada *f*. ● *vt* tender una emboscada a

amen /ɑːˈmen/ *int* amén

amenable /əˈmiːnəbl/ *a*. ~ **to** (*responsive*) sensible a, flexible a

amend /əˈmend/ *vt* enmendar. ~**ment** *n* enmienda *f*. ~**s** *npl*. **make** ~**s** reparar

amenities /əˈmiːnətɪz/ *npl* atractivos *mpl*, comodidades *fpl*, instalaciones *fpl*

America /əˈmerɪkə/ *n* América; (*North America*) Estados *mpl* Unidos. ~**n** *a & n* americano (*m*); (*North American*) estadounidense (*m & f*). ~**nism** *n* americanismo *m*. ~**nize** *vt* americanizar

amethyst /ˈæmɪθɪst/ *n* amatista *f*

amiable /ˈeɪmɪəbl/ *a* simpático

amicabl|e /ˈæmɪkəbl/ *a* amistoso. ~**y** *adv* amistosaménte

amid(st) /əˈmɪd(st)/ *prep* entre, en medio de

amiss /əˈmɪs/ *a* malo. ● *adv* mal. **sth** ~ algo que no va bien. **take sth** ~ llevar algo a mal

ammonia /əˈməʊnɪə/ *n* amoníaco *m*, amoniaco *m*

ammunition /æmjʊˈnɪʃn/ *n* municiones *fpl*

amnesia /æmˈniːzɪə/ *n* amnesia *f*

amnesty /ˈæmnəstɪ/ *n* amnistía *f*

amok /əˈmɒk/ *adv*. **run** ~ volverse loco

among(st) /əˈmʌŋ(st)/ *prep* entre

amoral /eɪˈmɒrəl/ *a* amoral

amorous /ˈæmərəs/ *a* amoroso

amorphous /əˈmɔːfəs/ *a* amorfo

amount /əˈmaʊnt/ *n* cantidad *f*; (*total*) total *m*, suma *f*. ● *vi*. ~ **to** sumar; (*fig*) equivaler a, significar

amp(ere) /ˈæmp(eə(r))/ *n* amperio *m*

amphibi|an /æmˈfɪbɪən/ *n* anfibio *m*. ~**ous** *a* anfibio

amphitheatre /ˈæmfɪθɪətə(r)/ *n* anfiteatro *m*

ampl|e /ˈæmpl/ *a* (**-er**, **-est**) amplio; (*enough*) suficiente; (*plentiful*) abundante. ~**y** *adv* ampliamente, bastante

amplif|ier /ˈæmplɪfaɪə(r)/ *n* amplificador *m*. ~**y** *vt* amplificar

amputat|e /ˈæmpjʊteɪt/ *vt* amputar. ~**ion** /-ˈteɪʃn/ *n* amputación *f*

amus|e /əˈmjuːz/ *vt* divertir. ~**ement** *n* diversión *f*. ~**ing** *a* divertido

an /ən, æn/ *see* **a**

anachronism /əˈnækrənɪzəm/ *n* anacronismo *m*

anaemi|a /əˈniːmɪə/ *n* anemia *f*. ~**c** *a* anémico

anaesthe|sia /ænɪsˈθiːzɪə/ *n* anestesia *f*. ~**tic** /ænɪsˈθetɪk/ *n* anestésico *m*. ~**tist** /əˈniːsθɪtɪst/ *n* anestesista *m & f*

anagram /ˈænəɡræm/ *n* anagrama *m*

analogy /əˈnælədʒɪ/ *n* analogía *f*

analys|e /ˈænəlaɪz/ *vt* analizar. ~**is** /əˈnæləsɪs/ *n* (*pl* **-yses** /-siːz/) *n* análisis *m*. ~**t** /ˈænəlɪst/ *n* analista *m & f*

analytic(al) /ænə'lıtık(əl)/ *a* analítico

anarch|ist /'ænəkıst/ *n* anarquista *m* & *f*. **~y** *n* anarquía *f*

anathema /ə'næθəmə/ *n* anatema *m*

anatom|ical /ænə'tɒmıkl/ *a* anatómico. **~y** /ə'nætəmı/ *n* anatomía *f*

ancest|or /'ænsestə(r)/ *n* antepasado *m*. **~ral** /-'sestrəl/ *a* ancestral. **~ry** /'ænsestrı/ *n* ascendencia *f*

anchor /'æŋkə(r)/ *n* ancla *f*. ● *vt* anclar; (*fig*) sujetar. ● *vi* anclar

anchovy /'æntʃəvı/ *n* (*fresh*) boquerón *m*; (*tinned*) anchoa *f*

ancient /'eınʃənt/ *a* antiguo, viejo

ancillary /æn'sılərı/ *a* auxiliar

and /ənd, ænd/ *conj* y; (*before* i- *and* hi-) e. **go ~ see him** vete a verle. **more ~ more** siempre más, cada vez más. **try ~ come** ven si puedes, trata de venir

Andalusia /ændə'lu:zjə/ *f* Andalucía *f*

anecdote /'ænıkdəʊt/ *n* anécdota *f*

anew /ə'nju:/ *adv* de nuevo

angel /'eındʒl/ *n* ángel *m*. **~ic** /æn'dʒelık/ *a* angélico

anger /'æŋgə(r)/ *n* ira *f*. ● *vt* enojar

angle[1] /'æŋgl/ *n* ángulo *m*; (*fig*) punto *m* de vista

angle[2] /'æŋgl/ *vi* pescar con caña. **~ for** (*fig*) buscar. **~r** /-ə(r)/ *n* pescador *m*

Anglican /'æŋglıkən/ *a* & *n* anglicano (*m*)

Anglo-... /'æŋgləʊ/ *pref* anglo...

Anglo-Saxon /'æŋgləʊ'sæksn/ *a* & *n* anglosajón (*m*)

angr|ily /'æŋgrılı/ *adv* con enojo. **~y** /'æŋgrı/ *a* (**-ier, -iest**) enojado. **get ~y** enfadarse

anguish /'æŋgwıʃ/ *n* angustia *f*

angular /'æŋgjʊlə(r)/ *a* angular; (*face*) anguloso

animal /'ænıməl/ *a* & *n* animal (*m*)

animat|e /'ænımət/ *a* vivo. /'ænımeıt/ *vt* animar. **~ion** /-'meıʃn/ *n* animación *f*

animosity /ænı'mɒsətı/ *n* animosidad *f*

aniseed /'ænısi:d/ *n* anís *m*

ankle /'æŋkl/ *n* tobillo *m*. **~ sock** escarpín *m*, calcetín *m*

annals /'ænlz/ *npl* anales *mpl*

annex /ə'neks/ *vt* anexionar. **~ation** /ænek'seıʃn/ *n* anexión *f*

annexe /'æneks/ *n* anexo *m*, dependencia *f*

annihilat|e /ə'naıəleıt/ *vt* aniquilar. **~ion** /-'leıʃn/ *n* aniquilación *f*

anniversary /ænı'vɜ:sərı/ *n* aniversario *m*

annotat|e /'ænəteıt/ *vt* anotar. **~ion** /-'teıʃn/ *n* anotación *f*

announce /ə'naʊns/ *vt* anunciar, comunicar. **~ment** *n* anuncio *m*, aviso *m*, declaración *f*. **~r** /-ə(r)/ *n* (*radio, TV*) locutor *m*

annoy /ə'nɔı/ *vt* molestar. **~ance** *n* disgusto *m*. **~ed** *a* enfadado. **~ing** *a* molesto

annual /'ænjʊəl/ *a* anual. ● *n* anuario *m*. **~ly** *adv* cada año

annuity /ə'nju:ətı/ *n* anualidad *f*. **life ~** renta *f* vitalicia

annul /ə'nʌl/ *vt* (*pt* **annulled**) anular. **~ment** *n* anulación *f*

anoint /ə'nɔınt/ *vt* ungir

anomal|ous /ə'nɒmələs/ *a* anómalo. **~y** *n* anomalía *f*

anon /ə'nɒn/ *adv* (*old use*) dentro de poco

anonymous /ə'nɒnıməs/ *a* anónimo

anorak /'ænəræk/ *n* anorac *m*

another /ə'nʌðə(r)/ *a* & *pron* otro (*m*). **~ 10 minutes** 10 minutos más. **in ~ way** de otra manera. **one ~** unos a otros

answer /'ɑ:nsə(r)/ *n* respuesta *f*; (*solution*) solución *f*. ● *vt* contestar a; escuchar, oír (*prayer*). **~ the door** abrir la puerta. ● *vi* contestar. **~ back** replicar. **~ for** ser responsable de. **~able** *a* responsable. **~ing-machine** *n* contestador *m* automático

ant /ænt/ *n* hormiga *f*

antagoni|sm /æn'tægənızəm/ *n* antagonismo *m*. **~stic** /-'nıstık/ *a* antagónico, opuesto. **~ze** /æn'tægənaız/ *vt* provocar la enemistad de

Antarctic /æn'tɑ:ktık/ *a* antártico. ● *n* Antártico *m*

ante-... /'æntı/ *pref* ante...

antecedent /æntı'si:dnt/ *n* antecedente *m*

antelope /'æntıləʊp/ *n* antílope *m*

antenatal /'æntıneıtl/ *a* prenatal

antenna /æn'tenə/ *n* antena *f*

anthem /'ænθəm/ *n* himno *m*

anthill /'ænthıl/ *n* hormiguero *m*

anthology /æn'θɒlədʒı/ *n* antología *f*

anthropolog|ist /ænθrə'pɒlədʒıst/ *n* antropológo *m*. **~y** *n* antropología *f*

anti-... /'æntı/ *pref* anti... **~aircraft** *a* antiaéreo

antibiotic /ˌæntɪbaɪˈɒtɪk/ *a & n* antibiótico (*m*)

antibody /ˈæntɪbɒdɪ/ *n* anticuerpo *m*

antic /ˈæntɪk/ *n* payasada *f*, travesura *f*

anticipat|e /ænˈtɪsɪpeɪt/ *vt* anticiparse a; (*foresee*) prever; (*forestall*) prevenir. **~ion** /-ˈpeɪʃn/ *n* anticipación *f*; (*expectation*) esperanza *f*

anticlimax /æntɪˈklaɪmæks/ *n* decepción *f*

anticlockwise /æntɪˈklɒkwaɪz/ *adv & a* en sentido contrario al de las agujas del reloj, hacia la izquierda

anticyclone /æntɪˈsaɪkləʊn/ *n* anticiclón *m*

antidote /ˈæntɪdəʊt/ *m* antídoto *m*

antifreeze /ˈæntɪfriːz/ *n* anticongelante *m*

antipathy /ænˈtɪpəθɪ/ *n* antipatía *f*

antiquarian /æntɪˈkweərɪən/ *a & n* anticuario (*m*)

antiquated /ˈæntɪkweɪtɪd/ *a* anticuado

antique /ænˈtiːk/ *a* antiguo. ● *n* antigüedad *f*. **~ dealer** anticuario *m*. **~ shop** tienda *f* de antigüedades

antiquity /ænˈtɪkwətɪ/ *n* antigüedad *f*

anti-Semitic /æntɪsɪˈmɪtɪk/ *a* antisemítico

antiseptic /æntɪˈseptɪk/ *a & n* antiséptico (*m*)

antisocial /æntɪˈsəʊʃl/ *a* antisocial

antithesis /ænˈtɪθəsɪs/ *n* (*pl* **-eses** /-siːz/) antítesis *f*

antler /ˈæntlər/ *n* cornamenta *f*

anus /ˈeɪnəs/ *n* ano *m*

anvil /ˈænvɪl/ *n* yunque *m*

anxiety /æŋˈzaɪətɪ/ *n* ansiedad *f*; (*worry*) inquietud *f*; (*eagerness*) anhelo *m*

anxious /ˈæŋkʃəs/ *a* inquieto; (*eager*) deseoso. **~ly** *adv* con inquietud; (*eagerly*) con impaciencia

any /ˈenɪ/ *a* algún *m*; (*negative*) ningún *m*; (*whatever*) cualquier; (*every*) todo. **at ~ moment** en cualquier momento. **have you ~ wine?** ¿tienes vino? ● *pron* alguno; (*negative*) ninguno. **have we ~?** ¿tenemos algunos? **not ~** ninguno. ● *adv* (*a little*) un poco, algo. **is it ~ better?** ¿está algo mejor? **it isn't ~ good** no sirve para nada

anybody /ˈenɪbɒdɪ/ *pron* alguien; (*after negative*) nadie. **~ can do it**

cualquiera sabe hacerlo, cualquiera puede hacerlo

anyhow /ˈenɪhaʊ/ *adv* de todas formas; (*in spite of all*) a pesar de todo; (*badly*) de cualquier modo

anyone /ˈenɪwʌn/ *pron* alguien; (*after negative*) nadie

anything /ˈenɪθɪŋ/ *pron* algo; (*whatever*) cualquier cosa; (*after negative*) nada. **~ but** todo menos

anyway /ˈenɪweɪ/ *adv* de todas formas

anywhere /ˈenɪweə(r)/ *adv* en cualquier parte; (*after negative*) en ningún sitio; (*everywhere*) en todas partes. **~ else** en cualquier otro lugar. **~ you go** dondequiera que vayas

apace /əˈpeɪs/ *adv* rápidamente

apart /əˈpɑːt/ *adv* aparte; (*separated*) apartado, separado. **~ from** aparte de. **come ~** romperse. **take ~** desmontar

apartheid /əˈpɑːtheɪt/ *n* segregación *f* racial, apartheid *m*

apartment /əˈpɑːtmənt/ *n* (*Amer*) apartamento *m*

apath|etic /æpəˈθetɪk/ *a* apático, indiferente. **~y** /ˈæpəθɪ/ *n* apatía *f*

ape /eɪp/ *n* mono *m*. ● *vt* imitar

aperient /əˈpɪərɪənt/ *a & n* laxante (*m*)

aperitif /əˈperətɪf/ *n* aperitivo *m*

aperture /ˈæpətʃʊə(r)/ *n* abertura *f*

apex /ˈeɪpeks/ *n* ápice *m*

aphorism /ˈæfərɪzəm/ *n* aforismo *m*

aphrodisiac /æfrəˈdɪzɪæk/ *a & n* afrodisíaco (*m*), afrodisiaco (*m*)

apiece /əˈpiːs/ *adv* cada uno

aplomb /əˈplɒm/ *n* aplomo *m*

apolog|etic /əpɒləˈdʒetɪk/ *a* lleno de disculpas. **be ~etic** disculparse. **~ize** /əˈpɒlədʒaɪz/ *vi* disculparse (**for** de). **~y** /əˈpɒlədʒɪ/ *n* disculpa *f*; (*poor specimen*) birria *f*

apople|ctic /æpəˈplektɪk/ *a* apoplético. **~xy** /ˈæpəpleksɪ/ *n* apoplejía *f*

apostle /əˈpɒsl/ *n* apóstol *m*

apostrophe /əˈpɒstrəfɪ/ *n* (*punctuation mark*) apóstrofo *m*

appal /əˈpɔːl/ *vt* (*pt* **appalled**) horrorizar. **~ling** *a* espantoso

apparatus /æpəˈreɪtəs/ *n* aparato *m*

apparel /əˈpærəl/ *n* ropa *f*, indumentaria *f*

apparent /əˈpærənt/ *a* aparente; (*clear*) evidente. **~ly** *adv* por lo visto

apparition /æpəˈrɪʃn/ *n* aparición *f*

appeal /ə'pi:l/ *vi* apelar; (*attract*) atraer. ● *n* llamamiento *m*; (*attraction*) atractivo *m*; (*jurid*) apelación *f*. ~**ing** *a* atrayente

appear /ə'pɪə(r)/ *vi* aparecer; (*arrive*) llegar; (*seem*) parecer; (*on stage*) actuar. ~**ance** *n* aparición *f*; (*aspect*) aspecto *m*

appease /ə'pi:z/ *vt* aplacar; (*pacify*) apaciguar

append /ə'pend/ *vt* adjuntar. ~**age** /ə'pendɪdʒ/ *n* añadidura *f*

appendicitis /əpendɪ'saɪtɪs/ *n* apendicitis *f*

appendix /ə'pendɪks/ *n* (*pl* -ices /-si:z/) (*of book*) apéndice *m*. (*pl* -ixes) (*anat*) apéndice *m*

appertain /æpə'teɪn/ *vi* relacionarse (**to** con)

appetite /'æpɪtaɪt/ *n* apetito *m*

appetiz|er /'æpɪtaɪzə(r)/ *n* aperitivo *m*. ~**ing** *a* apetitoso

applau|d /ə'plɔ:d/ *vt/i* aplaudir. ~**se** *n* aplausos *mpl*

apple /'æpl/ *n* manzana *f*. ~**tree** *n* manzano *m*

appliance /ə'plaɪəns/ *n* aparato *m*. **electrical** ~ electrodoméstico *m*

applicable /'æplɪkəbl/ *a* aplicable; (*relevant*) pertinente

applicant /'æplɪkənt/ *n* candidato *m*, solicitante *m* & *f*

application /æplɪ'keɪʃn/ *n* aplicación *f*; (*request*) solicitud *f*. ~ **form** formulario *m* (de solicitud)

appl|ied /ə'plaɪd/ *a* aplicado. ~**y** /ə'plaɪ/ *vt* aplicar. ● *vi* aplicarse; (*ask*) dirigirse. ~**y for** solicitar 〈*job etc*〉

appoint /ə'pɔɪnt/ *vt* nombrar; (*fix*) señalar. ~**ment** *n* cita *f*; (*job*) empleo *m*

apportion /ə'pɔ:ʃn/ *vt* repartir

apposite /'æpəzɪt/ *a* apropiado

apprais|al /ə'preɪzl/ *n* evaluación *f*. ~**e** *vt* evaluar

appreciable /ə'pri:ʃəbl/ *a* sensible; (*considerable*) considerable

appreciat|e /ə'pri:ʃɪeɪt/ *vt* apreciar; (*understand*) comprender; (*be grateful for*) agradecer. ● *vi* (*increase value*) aumentar en valor. ~**ion** /-'eɪʃn/ *n* aprecio *m*; (*gratitude*) agradecimiento *m*. ~**ive** /ə'pri:ʃɪətɪv/ *a* (*grateful*) agradecido

apprehen|d /æprɪ'hend/ *vt* detener; (*understand*) comprender. ~**sion** /-ʃn/ *n* detención *f*; (*fear*) recelo *m*

apprehensive /æprɪ'hensɪv/ *a* aprensivo

apprentice /ə'prentɪs/ *n* aprendiz *m*. ● *vt* poner de aprendiz. ~**ship** *n* aprendizaje *m*

approach /ə'prəʊtʃ/ *vt* acercarse a. ● *vi* acercarse. ● *n* acercamiento *m*; (*to problem*) enfoque *m*; (*access*) acceso *m*. **make** ~**es to** dirigirse a. ~**able** *a* accesible

approbation /æprə'beɪʃn/ *n* aprobación *f*

appropriate /ə'prəʊprɪət/ *a* apropiado. /ə'prəʊprɪeɪt/ *vt* apropiarse de. ~**ly** *adv* apropiadamente

approval /ə'pru:vl/ *n* aprobación *f*. **on** ~ a prueba

approv|e /ə'pru:v/ *vt/i* aprobar. ~**ingly** *adv* con aprobación

approximat|e /ə'prɒksɪmət/ *a* aproximado. /ə'prɒksɪmeɪt/ *vt* aproximarse a. ~**ely** *adv* aproximadamente. ~**ion** /-'meɪʃn/ *n* aproximación *f*

apricot /'eɪprɪkɒt/ *n* albaricoque *m*, chabacano *m* (*Mex*). ~**tree** *n* albaricoquero *m*, chabacano *m* (*Mex*)

April /'eɪprəl/ *n* abril *m*. ~ **fool!** ¡inocentón!

apron /'eɪprən/ *n* delantal *m*

apropos /'æprəpəʊ/ *adv* a propósito

apse /æps/ *n* ábside *m*

apt /æpt/ *a* apropiado; 〈*pupil*〉 listo. **be** ~ **to** tener tendencia a

aptitude /'æptɪtju:d/ *n* aptitud *f*

aptly /'æptlɪ/ *adv* acertadamente

aqualung /'ækwəlʌŋ/ *n* pulmón *m* acuático

aquarium /ə'kweərɪəm/ *n* (*pl* -ums) acuario *m*

Aquarius /ə'kweərɪəs/ *n* Acuario *m*

aquatic /ə'kwætɪk/ *a* acuático

aqueduct /'ækwɪdʌkt/ *n* acueducto *m*

aquiline /'ækwɪlaɪn/ *a* aquilino

Arab /'ærəb/ *a* & *n* árabe *m*. ~**ian** /ə'reɪbɪən/ *a* árabe. ~**ic** /'ærəbɪk/ *a* & *n* árabe (*m*). ~**ic numerals** números *mpl* arábigos

arable /'ærəbl/ *a* cultivable

arbiter /'ɑ:bɪtə(r)/ *n* árbitro *m*

arbitrary /'ɑ:bɪtrərɪ/ *a* arbitrario

arbitrat|e /'ɑ:bɪtreɪt/ *vi* arbitrar. ~**ion** /-'treɪʃn/ *n* arbitraje *m*. ~**or** *n* árbitro *m*

arc /ɑ:k/ *n* arco *m*

arcade /ɑ:'keɪd/ *n* arcada *f*; (*around square*) soportales *mpl*; (*shops*) galería f. **amusement** ~ galería f de atracciones

arcane /ɑːˈkeɪn/ a misterioso

arch[1] /ɑːtʃ/ n arco m. ● vt arquear. ● vi arquearse

arch[2] /ɑːtʃ/ a malicioso

archaeolog|ical /ɑːkɪəˈlodʒɪkl/ a arqueológico. **~ist** /ɑːkɪˈɒlədʒɪst/ n arqueólogo m. **~y** /ɑːkɪˈɒlədʒɪ/ n arqueología f

archaic /ɑːˈkeɪɪk/ a arcaico

archbishop /ɑːtʃˈbɪʃəp/ n arzobispo m

arch-enemy /ɑːtʃˈenəmɪ/ n enemigo m jurado

archer /ˈɑːtʃə(r)/ n arquero m. **~y** n tiro m al arco

archetype /ˈɑːkɪtaɪp/ n arquetipo m

archipelago /ɑːkɪˈpeləgəʊ/ n (pl -os) archipiélago m

architect /ˈɑːkɪtekt/ n arquitecto m. **~ure** /ˈɑːkɪtektʃə(r)/ n arquitectura f. **~ural** /-ˈtektʃərəl/ a arquitectónico

archiv|es /ˈɑːkaɪvz/ npl archivo m. **~ist** /-ɪvɪst/ n archivero m

archway /ˈɑːtʃweɪ/ n arco m

Arctic /ˈɑːktɪk/ a ártico. ● n Ártico m

arctic /ˈɑːktɪk/ a glacial

ardent /ˈɑːdənt/ a ardiente, fervoroso, apasionado. **~ly** adv ardientemente

ardour /ˈɑːdə(r)/ n ardor m, fervor m, pasión f

arduous /ˈɑːdjʊəs/ a arduo

are /ɑː(r)/ see **be**

area /ˈeərɪə/ n (surface) superficie f; (region) zona f; (fig) campo m

arena /əˈriːnə/ n arena f; (in circus) pista f; (in bullring) ruedo m

aren't /ɑːnt/ = **are not**

Argentin|a /ɑːdʒənˈtiːnə/ n Argentina f. **~ian** /-ˈtɪnɪən/ a & n argentino (m)

arguable /ˈɑːgjʊəbl/ a discutible

argue /ˈɑːgjuː/ vi discutir; (reason) razonar

argument /ˈɑːgjʊmənt/ n disputa f; (reasoning) argumento m. **~ative** /-ˈmentətɪv/ a discutidor

arid /ˈærɪd/ a árido

Aries /ˈeəriːz/ n Aries m

arise /əˈraɪz/ vi (pt arose, pp arisen) levantarse; (fig) surgir. ~ **from** resultar de

aristocra|cy /ærɪˈstɒkrəsɪ/ n aristocracia f. **~t** /ˈærɪstəkræt/ n aristócrata m & f. **~tic** /-ˈkrætɪk/ a aristocrático

arithmetic /əˈrɪθmətɪk/ n aritmética f

ark /ɑːk/ n (relig) arca f

arm[1] /ɑːm/ n brazo m. ~ **in** ~ cogidos del brazo

arm[2] /ɑːm/ n. **~s** npl armas fpl. ● vt armar

armada /ɑːˈmɑːdə/ n armada f

armament /ˈɑːməmənt/ n armamento m

armchair /ˈɑːmtʃeə(r)/ n sillón m

armed robbery /ɑːmdˈrɒbərɪ/ n robo m a mano armada

armful /ˈɑːmfʊl/ n brazada f

armistice /ˈɑːmɪstɪs/ n armisticio m

armlet /ˈɑːmlɪt/ n brazalete m

armour /ˈɑːmə(r)/ n armadura f. **~ed** a blindado

armoury /ˈɑːmərɪ/ n arsenal m

armpit /ˈɑːmpɪt/ n sobaco m, axila f

army /ˈɑːmɪ/ n ejército m

aroma /əˈrəʊmə/ n aroma m. **~tic** /ærəˈmætɪk/ a aromático

arose /əˈrəʊz/ see **arise**

around /əˈraʊnd/ adv alrededor; (near) cerca. **all** ~ por todas partes. ● prep alrededor de; (with time) a eso de

arouse /əˈraʊz/ vt despertar

arpeggio /ɑːˈpedʒɪəʊ/ n arpegio m

arrange /əˈreɪndʒ/ vt arreglar; (fix) fijar. **~ment** n arreglo m; (agreement) acuerdo m; (pl, plans) preparativos mpl

array /əˈreɪ/ vt (dress) ataviar; (mil) formar. ● n atavío m; (mil) orden m; (fig) colección f, conjunto m

arrears /əˈrɪəz/ npl atrasos mpl. **in** ~ atrasado en pagos

arrest /əˈrest/ vt detener; llamar (attention). ● n detención f. **under** ~ detenido

arriv|al /əˈraɪvl/ n llegada f. **new ~al** recien llegado m. **~e** /əˈraɪv/ vi llegar

arrogan|ce /ˈærəgəns/ n arrogancia f. **~t** a arrogante. **~tly** adv con arrogancia

arrow /ˈærəʊ/ n flecha f

arsenal /ˈɑːsənl/ n arsenal m

arsenic /ˈɑːsnɪk/ n arsénico m

arson /ˈɑːsn/ n incendio m provocado. **~ist** n incendiario m

art[1] /ɑːt/ n arte m. **A~s** npl (Univ) Filosofía y Letras fpl. **fine ~s** bellas artes fpl

art[2] /ɑːt/ (old use, with thou) = **are**

artefact /ˈɑːtɪfækt/ n artefacto m

arterial /ɑːˈtɪərɪəl/ a arterial. ~ **road** n carretera f nacional

artery /ˈɑːtərɪ/ n arteria f

artesian /ɑːˈtiːzjən/ a. ∼ **well** pozo m artesiano

artful /ˈɑːtfʊl/ a astuto. ∼**ness** n astucia f

art gallery /ˈɑːtgælərɪ/ n museo m de pinturas, pinacoteca f, galería f de arte

arthriti|c /ɑːˈθrɪtɪk/ a artrítico. ∼**s** /ɑːˈθraɪtɪs/ n artritis f

artichoke /ˈɑːtɪtʃəʊk/ n alcachofa f. **Jerusalem** ∼ pataca f

article /ˈɑːtɪkl/ n artículo m. ∼ **of clothing** prenda f de vestir. **leading** ∼ artículo de fondo

articulat|e /ɑːˈtɪkjʊlət/ a articulado; ⟨person⟩ elocuente. /ɑːˈtɪkjʊleɪt/ vt/i articular. ∼**ed lorry** n camión m con remolque. ∼**ion** /-ˈleɪʃn/ n articulación f

artifice /ˈɑːtɪfɪs/ n artificio m

artificial /ɑːtɪˈfɪʃl/ a artificial; ⟨hair etc⟩ postizo

artillery /ɑːˈtɪlərɪ/ n artillería f

artisan /ɑːtɪˈzæn/ n artesano m

artist /ˈɑːtɪst/ n artista m & f

artiste /ɑːˈtiːst/ n (in theatre) artista m & f

artist|ic /ɑːˈtɪstɪk/ a artístico. ∼**ry** n arte m, habilidad f

artless /ˈɑːtlɪs/ a ingenuo

arty /ˈɑːtɪ/ a (fam) que se las da de artista

as /æz, əz/ adv & conj como; (since) ya que; (while) mientras. ∼ **big** ∼ tan grande como. ∼ **far** ∼ (distance) hasta; (qualitative) en cuanto a. ∼ **far** ∼ **I know** que yo sepa. ∼ **if** como si. ∼ **long** ∼ mientras. ∼ **much** ∼ tanto como. ∼ **soon** ∼ tan pronto como. ∼ **well** también

asbestos /æzˈbestɒs/ n amianto m, asbesto m

ascen|d /əˈsend/ vt/i subir. ∼**t** /əˈsent/ n subida f

ascertain /æsəˈteɪn/ vt averiguar

ascetic /əˈsetɪk/ a ascético. ● n asceta m & f

ascribe /əˈskraɪb/ vt atribuir

ash[1] /æʃ/ n ceniza f

ash[2] /æʃ/ n. ∼**(-tree)** fresno m

ashamed /əˈʃeɪmd/ a avergonzado. **be** ∼ avergonzarse

ashen /ˈæʃn/ a ceniciento

ashore /əˈʃɔː(r)/ adv a tierra. **go** ∼ desembarcar

ash: ∼tray /ˈæʃtreɪ/ n cenicero m. **A∼ Wednesday** n Miércoles m de Ceniza

Asia /ˈeɪʃə/ n Asia f. ∼**n** a & n asiático (m). ∼**tic** /-ˈætɪk/ a asiático

aside /əˈsaɪd/ adv a un lado. ● n (in theatre) aparte m

asinine /ˈæsɪnaɪn/ a estúpido

ask /ɑːsk/ vt pedir; preguntar ⟨question⟩; (invite) invitar. ∼ **about** enterarse de. ∼ **after** pedir noticias de. ∼ **for help** pedir ayuda. ∼ **for trouble** buscarse problemas. ∼ **s.o. in** invitar a uno a pasar

askance /əˈskæns/ adv. **look** ∼ **at** mirar de soslayo

askew /əˈskjuː/ adv & a ladeado

asleep /əˈsliːp/ adv & a dormido. **fall** ∼ dormirse, quedar dormido

asparagus /əˈspærəgəs/ n espárrago m

aspect /ˈæspekt/ n aspecto m; (of house etc) orientación f

aspersions /əˈspɜːʃnz/ npl. **cast** ∼ **on** difamar

asphalt /ˈæsfælt/ n asfalto m. ● vt asfaltar

asphyxia /æsˈfɪksɪə/ n asfixia f. ∼**te** /əsˈfɪksɪeɪt/ vt asfixiar. ∼**tion** /-ˈeɪʃn/ n asfixia f

aspic /ˈæspɪk/ n gelatina f

aspir|ation /æspəˈreɪʃn/ n aspiración f. ∼**e** /əsˈpaɪə(r)/ vi aspirar

aspirin /ˈæsprɪn/ n aspirina f

ass /æs/ n asno m; (fig, fam) imbécil m

assail /əˈseɪl/ vt asaltar. ∼**ant** n asaltador m

assassin /əˈsæsɪn/ n asesino m. ∼**ate** /əˈsæsɪneɪt/ vt asesinar. ∼**ation** /-ˈeɪʃn/ n asesinato m

assault /əˈsɔːlt/ n (mil) ataque m; (jurid) atentado m. ● vt asaltar

assemblage /əˈsemblɪdʒ/ n (of things) colección f; (of people) reunión f; (mec) montaje m

assemble /əˈsembl/ vt reunir; (mec) montar. ● vi reunirse

assembly /əˈsemblɪ/ n reunión f; (pol etc) asamblea f. ∼ **line** n línea f de montaje

assent /əˈsent/ n asentimiento m. ● vi asentir

assert /əˈsɜːt/ vt afirmar; hacer valer ⟨one's rights⟩. ∼**ion** /-ʃn/ n afirmación f. ∼**ive** a positivo, firme

assess /əˈses/ vt valorar; (determine) determinar; fijar ⟨tax etc⟩. ∼**ment** n valoración f

asset /ˈæset/ n (advantage) ventaja f; (pl, com) bienes mpl

assiduous /əˈsɪdjʊəs/ a asiduo

assign /əˈsaɪn/ vt asignar; (appoint) nombrar

assignation /æsɪgˈneɪʃn/ n asignación f; (meeting) cita f

assignment /əˈsaɪnmənt/ n asignación f, misión f; (task) tarea f

assimilat|e /əˈsɪmɪleɪt/ vt asimilar. ● vi asimilarse. ~ion /-ˈeɪʃn/ n asimilación f

assist /əˈsɪst/ vt/i ayudar. ~ance n ayuda f. ~ant /əˈsɪstənt/ n ayudante m & f; (shop) dependienta f, dependiente m. ● a auxiliar, adjunto

associat|e /əˈsəʊʃɪeɪt/ vt asociar. ● vi asociarse. /əˈsəʊʃɪət/ a asociado. ● n colega m & f; (com) socio m. ~ion /-ˈeɪʃn/ n asociación f. A~ion football n fútbol m

assort|ed /əˈsɔːtɪd/ a surtido. ~ment n surtido m

assume /əˈsjuːm/ vt suponer; tomar ⟨power, attitude⟩; asumir ⟨role, burden⟩

assumption /əˈsʌmpʃn/ n suposición f. the A~ la Asunción f

assur|ance /əˈʃʊərəns/ n seguridad f; (insurance) seguro m. ~e /əˈʃʊə(r)/ vt asegurar. ~ed a seguro. ~edly /-rɪdlɪ/ adv seguramente

asterisk /ˈæstərɪsk/ n asterisco m

astern /əˈstɜːn/ adv a popa

asthma /ˈæsmə/ n asma f. ~tic /-ˈmætɪk/ a & n asmático (m)

astonish /əˈstɒnɪʃ/ vt asombrar. ~ing a asombroso. ~ment n asombro m

astound /əˈstaʊnd/ vt asombrar

astray /əˈstreɪ/ adv & a. go ~ extraviarse. lead ~ llevar por mal camino

astride /əˈstraɪd/ adv a horcajadas. ● prep a horcajadas sobre

astringent /əˈstrɪndʒənt/ a astringente; (fig) austero. ● n astringente m

astrolog|er /əˈstrɒlədʒə(r)/ n astrólogo m. ~y n astrología f

astronaut /ˈæstrənɔːt/ n astronauta m & f

astronom|er /əˈstrɒnəmə(r)/ n astrónomo m. ~ical /æstrəˈnɒmɪkl/ a astronómico. ~y /əˈstrɒnəmɪ/ n astronomía f

astute /əˈstjuːt/ a astuto. ~ness n astucia f

asunder /əˈsʌndə(r)/ adv en pedazos; (in two) en dos

asylum /əˈsaɪləm/ n asilo m. lunatic ~ manicomio m

at /ət, æt/ prep a. ~ home en casa. ~ night por la noche. ~ Robert's en casa de Roberto. ~ once en seguida; (simultaneously) a la vez. ~ sea en el mar. ~ the station en la estación. ~ times a veces. not ~ all nada; (after thanks) ¡de nada!

ate /et/ see eat

atheis|m /ˈeɪθɪzəm/ n ateísmo m. ~t /ˈeɪθɪɪst/ n ateo m

athlet|e /ˈæθliːt/ n atleta m & f. ~ic /-ˈletɪk/ a atlético. ~ics /-ˈletɪks/ npl atletismo m

Atlantic /ətˈlæntɪk/ a & n atlántico (m). ● n. ~ (Ocean) (Océano m) Atlántico m

atlas /ˈætləs/ n atlas m

atmospher|e /ˈætməsfɪə(r)/ n atmósfera f; (fig) ambiente m. ~ic /-ˈferɪk/ a atmosférico. ~ics /-ˈferɪks/ npl parásitos mpl

atom /ˈætəm/ n átomo m. ~ic /əˈtɒmɪk/ a atómico

atomize /ˈætəmaɪz/ vt atomizar. ~r /ˈætəmaɪzə(r)/ n atomizador m

atone /əˈtəʊn/ vi. ~ for expiar. ~ment n expiación f

atroci|ous /əˈtrəʊʃəs/ a atroz. ~ty /əˈtrɒsətɪ/ n atrocidad f

atrophy /ˈætrəfɪ/ n atrofia f

attach /əˈtætʃ/ vt sujetar; adjuntar ⟨document etc⟩. be ~ed to (be fond of) tener cariño a

attaché /əˈtæʃeɪ/ n agregado m. ~ case maletín m

attachment /əˈtætʃmənt/ n (affection) cariño m; (tool) accesorio m

attack /əˈtæk/ n ataque m. ● vt/i atacar. ~er n agresor m

attain /əˈteɪn/ vt conseguir. ~able a alcanzable. ~ment n logro m. ~ments npl conocimientos mpl, talento m

attempt /əˈtempt/ vt intentar. ● n tentativa f; (attack) atentado m

attend /əˈtend/ vt asistir a; (escort) acompañar. ● vi prestar atención. ~ to (look after) ocuparse de. ~ance n asistencia f; (people present) concurrencia f. ~ant /əˈtendənt/ a concomitante. ● n encargado m; (servant) sirviente m

attention /əˈtenʃn/ n atención f. ~! (mil) ¡firmes! pay ~ prestar atención

attentive /əˈtentɪv/ a atento. ~ness n atención f

attenuate /əˈtenjʊeɪt/ vt atenuar

attest /ə'test/ vt atestiguar. ● vi dar testimonio. **~ation** /æte'steɪʃn/ n testimonio m

attic /'ætɪk/ n desván m

attire /ə'taɪə(r)/ n atavío m. ● vt vestir

attitude /'ætɪtjuːd/ n postura f

attorney /ə'tɜːnɪ/ n (pl **-eys**) apoderado m; (Amer) abogado m

attract /ə'trækt/ vt atraer. **~ion** /-ʃn/ n atracción f; (charm) atractivo m

attractive /ə'træktɪv/ a atractivo; (interesting) atrayente. **~ness** n atractivo m

attribute /ə'trɪbjuːt/ vt atribuir. /'ætrɪbjuːt/ n atributo m

attrition /ə'trɪʃn/ n desgaste m

aubergine /'əʊbəʒiːn/ n berenjena f

auburn /'ɔːbən/ a castaño

auction /'ɔːkʃn/ n subasta f. ● vt subastar. **~eer** /-ə'nɪə(r)/ n subastador m

audaci|ous /ɔː'deɪʃəs/ a audaz. **~ty** /-æsətɪ/ n audacia f

audible /'ɔːdəbl/ a audible

audience /'ɔːdɪəns/ n (interview) audiencia f; (teatro, radio) público m

audio-visual /ɔːdɪəʊ'vɪʒʊəl/ a audio-visual

audit /'ɔːdɪt/ n revisión f de cuentas. ● vt revisar

audition /ɔː'dɪʃn/ n audición f. ● vt dar audición a

auditor /'ɔːdɪtə(r)/ n interventor m de cuentas

auditorium /ɔːdɪ'tɔːrɪəm/ n sala f, auditorio m

augment /ɔːg'ment/ vt aumentar

augur /'ɔːgə(r)/ vt augurar. it **~s well** es de buen agüero

august /ɔː'gʌst/ a augusto

August /'ɔːgəst/ n agosto m

aunt /ɑːnt/ n tía f

au pair /əʊ'peə(r)/ n chica f au pair

aura /'ɔːrə/ n atmósfera f, halo m

auspices /'ɔːspɪsɪz/ npl auspicios mpl

auspicious /ɔː'spɪʃəs/ a propicio

auster|e /ɔː'stɪə(r)/ a austero. **~ity** /-erətɪ/ n austeridad f

Australia /ɒ'streɪlɪə/ n Australia f. **~n** a & n australiano (m)

Austria /'ɒstrɪə/ n Austria f. **~n** a & n austríaco (m)

authentic /ɔː'θentɪk/ a auténtico. **~ate** /ɔː'θentɪkeɪt/ vt autenticar. **~ity** /-ən'tɪsətɪ/ n autenticidad f

author /'ɔːθə(r)/ n autor m. **~ess** n autora f

authoritarian /ɔːθɒrɪ'teərɪən/ a autoritario

authoritative /ɔː'θɒrɪtətɪv/ a autorizado; (manner) autoritario

authority /ɔː'θɒrətɪ/ n autoridad f; (permission) autorización f

authoriz|ation /ɔːθəraɪ'zeɪʃn/ n autorización f. **~e** /'ɔːθəraɪz/ vt autorizar

authorship /'ɔːθəʃɪp/ n profesión f de autor; (origin) paternidad f literaria

autistic /ɔː'tɪstɪk/ a autista

autobiography /ɔːtəʊbaɪ'ɒgrəfɪ/ n autobiografía f

autocra|cy /ɔː'tɒkrəsɪ/ n autocracia f. **~t** /'ɔːtəkræt/ n autócrata m & f. **~tic** /-'krætɪk/ a autocrático

autograph /'ɔːtəgrɑːf/ n autógrafo m. ● vt firmar

automat|e /'ɔːtəmeɪt/ vt automatizar. **~ic** /ɔːtə'mætɪk/ a automático. **~ion** /-'meɪʃn/ n automatización f. **~on** /ɔː'tɒmətən/ n autómata m

automobile /'ɔːtəməbiːl/ n (Amer) coche m, automóvil m

autonom|ous /ɔː'tɒnəməs/ a autónomo. **~y** n autonomía f

autopsy /'ɔːtɒpsɪ/ n autopsia f

autumn /'ɔːtəm/ n otoño m. **~al** /-'tʌmnəl/ a de otoño, otoñal

auxiliary /ɔːg'zɪlɪərɪ/ a auxiliar. ● n asistente m; (verb) verbo m auxiliar; (pl, troops) tropas fpl auxiliares

avail /ə'veɪl/ vt/i servir. **~ o.s. of** aprovecharse de. ● n ventaja f. **to no ~** inútil

availab|ility /əveɪlə'bɪlətɪ/ n disponibilidad f. **~le** /ə'veɪləbl/ a disponible

avalanche /'ævəlɑːnʃ/ n avalancha f

avaric|e /'ævərɪs/ n avaricia f. **~ious** /-'rɪʃəs/ a avaro

avenge /ə'vendʒ/ vt vengar

avenue /'ævənjuː/ n avenida f; (fig) vía f

average /'ævərɪdʒ/ n promedio m. **on ~** por término medio. ● a medio. ● vt calcular el promedio de. ● vi alcanzar un promedio de

averse /ə'vɜːs/ a enemigo (to de). be **~e to** sentir repugnancia por, no gustarle. **~ion** /-ʃn/ n repugnancia f

avert /ə'vɜːt/ *vt* (*turn away*) apartar; (*ward off*) desviar

aviary /'eɪvɪərɪ/ *n* pajarera *f*

aviation /eɪvɪ'eɪʃn/ *n* aviación *f*

aviator /'eɪvɪeɪtə(r)/ *n* (*old use*) aviador *m*

avid /'ævɪd/ *a* ávido. ~**ity** /-'vɪdətɪ/ *n* avidez *f*

avocado /ævə'kɑːdəʊ/ *n* (*pl* -os) aguacate *m*

avoid /ə'vɔɪd/ *vt* evitar. ~**able** *a* evitable. ~**ance** *n* el evitar *m*

avuncular /ə'vʌŋkjʊlə(r)/ *a* de tío

await /ə'weɪt/ *vt* esperar

awake /ə'weɪk/ *vt/i* (*pt* **awoke**, *pp* **awoken**) despertar. ● *a* despierto. **wide** ~ completamente despierto; (*fig*) despabilado. ~**n** /ə'weɪkən/ *vt/i* despertar. ~**ning** *n* el despertar *m*

award /ə'wɔːd/ *vt* otorgar; (*jurid*) adjudicar. ● *n* premio *m*; (*jurid*) adjudicación *f*; (*scholarship*) beca *f*

aware /ə'weə(r)/ *a* consciente. **are you** ~ **that?** ¿te das cuenta de que? ~**ness** *n* conciencia *f*

awash /ə'wɒʃ/ *a* inundado

away /ə'weɪ/ *adv* (*absent*) fuera; (*far*) lejos; (*persistently*) sin parar. ● *a* & *n*. ~ (**match**) partido *m* fuera de casa

awe /ɔː/ *n* temor *m*. ~**some** *a* imponente. ~**struck** *a* atemorizado

awful /'ɔːfʊl/ *a* terrible, malísimo. ~**ly** *adv* terriblemente

awhile /ə'waɪl/ *adv* un rato

awkward /'ɔːkwəd/ *a* difícil; (*inconvenient*) inoportuno; (*clumsy*) desmañado; (*embarrassed*) incómodo. ~**ly** *adv* con dificultad; (*clumsily*) de manera torpe. ~**ness** *n* dificultad *f*; (*discomfort*) molestia *f*; (*clumsiness*) torpeza *f*

awning /'ɔːnɪŋ/ *n* toldo *m*

awoke, awoken /ə'wəʊk, ə'wəʊkən/ *see* **awake**

awry /ə'raɪ/ *adv* & *a* ladeado. **go** ~ salir mal

axe /æks/ *n* hacha *f*. ● *vt* (*pres p* **axing**) cortar con hacha; (*fig*) recortar

axiom /'æksɪəm/ *n* axioma *m*

axis /'æksɪs/ *n* (*pl* **axes** /-iːz/) eje *m*

axle /'æksl/ *n* eje *m*

ay(e) /aɪ/ *adv* & *n* sí (*m*)

B

BA *abbr see* **bachelor**

babble /'bæbl/ *vi* balbucir; (*chatter*) parlotear; (*of stream*) murmullar. ● *n* balbuceo *m*; (*chatter*) parloteo *m*; (*of stream*) murmullo *m*

baboon /bə'buːn/ *n* mandril *m*

baby /'beɪbɪ/ *n* niño *m*, bebé *m*; (*Amer, sl*) chica *f*. ~**ish** /'beɪbɪɪʃ/ *a* infantil. ~**sit** *vi* cuidar a los niños, hacer de canguro. ~**sitter** *n* persona *f* que cuida a los niños, canguro *m*

bachelor /'bætʃələ(r)/ *n* soltero *m*. **B~ of Arts (BA)** licenciado *m* en filosofía y letras. **B~ of Science (BSc)** licenciado *m* en ciencias

back /bæk/ *n* espalda *f*; (*of car*) parte *f* trasera; (*of chair*) respaldo *m*; (*of cloth*) revés *m*; (*of house*) parte *f* de atrás; (*of animal, book*) lomo *m*; (*of hand, document*) dorso *m*; (*football*) defensa *m* & *f*. ~ **of beyond** en el quinto pino. ● *a* trasero; (*taxes*) atrasado. ● *adv* atrás; (*returned*) de vuelta. ● *vt* apoyar; (*betting*) apostar a; dar marcha atrás a ⟨*car*⟩. ● *vi* retroceder; ⟨*car*⟩ dar marcha atrás. ~ **down** *vi* volverse atrás. ~ **out** *vi* retirarse. ~ **up** *vi* (*auto*) retroceder. ~**ache** /'bækeɪk/ *n* dolor *m* de espalda. ~**bencher** *n* (*pol*) diputado *m* sin poder ministerial. ~**biting** /'bækbaɪtɪŋ/ *n* maledicencia *f*. ~**bone** /'bækbəʊn/ *n* columna *f* vertebral; (*fig*) pilar *m*. ~**chat** /'bæktʃæt/ *n* impertinencias *fpl*. ~**date** /bæk'deɪt/ *vt* antedatar. ~**er** /'bækə(r)/ *n* partidario *m*; (*com*) financiador *m*. ~**fire** /bæk'faɪə(r)/ *vi* (*auto*) petardear; (*fig*) fallar, salir el tiro por la culata. ~**gammon** /bæk'gæmən/ *n* backgamon *m*. ~**ground** /'bækgraʊnd/ *n* fondo *m*; (*environment*) antecedentes *mpl*. ~**hand** /'bækhænd/ *n* (*sport*) revés *m*. ~**handed** *a* dado con el dorso de la mano; (*fig*) equívoco, ambiguo. ~**hander** *n* (*sport*) revés *m*; (*fig*) ataque *m* indirecto; (*bribe, sl*) soborno *m*. ~**ing** /'bækɪŋ/ *n* apoyo *m*. ~**lash** /'bæklæʃ/ *n* reacción *f*. ~**log** /'bæklɒg/ *n* atrasos *mpl*. ~**side** /bæk'saɪd/ *n* (*fam*) trasero *m*. ~**stage** /bæk'steɪdʒ/ *a* de bastidores. ● *adv* entre bastidores. ~**stroke** /'bækstrəʊk/ *n* (*tennis etc*) revés *m*; (*swimming*) braza *f* de espaldas. ~**up** *n* apoyo *m*. ~**ward** /'bækwəd/ *a* ⟨*step etc*⟩ hacia atrás;

(*retarded*) atrasado. **~wards**
/'bækwədz/ *adv* hacia atrás; (*fall*) de
espaldas; (*back to front*) al revés. **go
~wards and forwards** ir de acá
para allá. **~water** /'bækwɔːtə(r)/ *n*
agua *f* estancada; (*fig*) lugar *m*
apartado

bacon /'beɪkən/ *n* tocino *m*

bacteria /bæk'tɪərɪə/ *npl* bacterias
fpl. **~l** *a* bacteriano

bad /bæd/ *a* (**worse, worst**) malo;
(*serious*) grave; (*harmful*) nocivo;
(*language*) indecente. **feel ~** sentirse mal

bade /beɪd/ *see* bid

badge /bædʒ/ *n* distintivo *m*, chapa *f*

badger /'bædʒə(r)/ *n* tejón *m*. ● *vt*
acosar

bad: ~ly *adv* mal. **want ~ly** desear
muchísimo. **~ly off** mal de dinero.
~mannered *a* mal educado

badminton /'bædmɪntən/ *n* bádminton *m*

bad-tempered /bæd'tempəd/ *a*
(*always*) de mal genio; (*temporarily*) de mal humor

baffle /'bæfl/ *vt* desconcertar

bag /bæg/ *n* bolsa *f*; (*handbag*) bolso
m. ● *vt* (*pt* **bagged**) ensacar; (*take*)
coger (*not LAm*), agarrar (*LAm*). **~s**
npl (*luggage*) equipaje *m*. **~s of**
(*fam*) montones de

baggage /'bægɪdʒ/ *n* equipaje *m*

baggy /'bægɪ/ *a* (*clothes*) holgado

bagpipes /'bægpaɪps/ *npl* gaita *f*

Bahamas /bə'hɑːməz/ *npl*. **the ~** las
Bahamas *fpl*

bail¹ /beɪl/ *n* caución *f*, fianza *f*. ● *vt*
poner en libertad bajo fianza. **~ s.o.
out** obtener la libertad de uno bajo
fianza

bail² /beɪl/ *n* (*cricket*) travesaño *m*

bail³ /beɪl/ *vt* (*naut*) achicar

bailiff /'beɪlɪf/ *n* alguacil *m*; (*estate*)
administrador *m*

bait /beɪt/ *n* cebo *m*. ● *vt* cebar; (*torment*) atormentar

bak|e /beɪk/ *vt* cocer al horno. ● *vi*
cocerse. **~er** *n* panadero *m*. **~ery**
/'beɪkərɪ/ *n* panadería *f*. **~ing** *n*
cocción *f*; (*batch*) hornada *f*. **~ing-
powder** *n* levadura *f* en polvo

balance /'bæləns/ *n* equilibrio *m*;
(*com*) balance *m*; (*sum*) saldo *m*;
(*scales*) balanza *f*; (*remainder*) resto
m. ● *vt* equilibrar; (*com*) saldar; nivelar (*budget*). ● *vi* equilibrarse;
(*com*) saldarse. **~d** *a* equilibrado

balcony /'bælkənɪ/ *n* balcón *m*

bald /bɔːld/ *a* (**-er, -est**) calvo; (*tyre*)
desgastado

balderdash /'bɔːldədæʃ/ *n* tonterías
fpl

bald: ~ly *adv* escuetamente. **~ness**
n calvicie *f*

bale /beɪl/ *n* bala *f*, fardo *m*. ● *vi*. **~
out** lanzarse en paracaídas

Balearic /bælɪ'ærɪk/ *a*. **~ Islands**
Islas *fpl* Baleares

baleful /'beɪlfʊl/ *a* funesto

balk /bɔːk/ *vt* frustrar. ● *vi*. **~ (at)**
resistirse (a)

ball¹ /bɔːl/ *n* bola *f*; (*tennis etc*) pelota
f; (*football etc*) balón *m*; (*of yarn*)
ovillo *m*

ball² /bɔːl/ (*dance*) baile *m*

ballad /'bæləd/ *n* balada *f*

ballast /'bæləst/ *n* lastre *m*

ball: ~bearing *n* cojinete *m* de
bolas. **~cock** *n* llave *f* de bola

ballerina /bælə'riːnə/ *f* bailarina *f*

ballet /'bæleɪ/ *n* ballet *m*

ballistic /bə'lɪstɪk/ *a* balístico. **~s** *n*
balística *f*

balloon /bə'luːn/ *n* globo *m*

balloonist /bə'luːnɪst/ *n* aeronauta
m & f

ballot /'bælət/ *n* votación *f*.
(-paper) *n* papeleta *f*. **~box** *n* urna
f

ball-point /'bɔːlpɔɪnt/ *n*. **~ (pen)**
bolígrafo *m*

ballroom /'bɔːlruːm/ *n* salón *m* de
baile

ballyhoo /bælɪ'huː/ *n* (*publicity*)
publicidad *f* sensacionalista;
(*uproar*) jaleo *m*

balm /bɑːm/ *n* bálsamo *m*. **~y** *a*
(*mild*) suave; (*sl*) chiflado

baloney /bə'ləʊnɪ/ *n* (*sl*) tonterías *fpl*

balsam /'bɔːlsəm/ *n* bálsamo *m*

balustrade /bælə'streɪd/ *n* barandilla *f*

bamboo /bæm'buː/ *n* bambú *m*

bamboozle /bæm'buːzl/ *vt*
engatusar

ban /bæn/ *vt* (*pt* **banned**) prohibir. **~
from** excluir de. ● *n* prohibición *f*

banal /bə'nɑːl/ *a* banal. **~ity** /-ælətɪ/ *n*
banalidad *f*

banana /bə'nɑːnə/ *n* plátano *m*,
banana *f* (*LAm*). **~tree** plátano *m*,
banano *m*

band¹ /bænd/ *n* banda *f*

band² /bænd/ *n* (*mus*) orquesta *f*;
(*military, brass*) banda *f*. ● *vi*. **~
together** juntarse

bandage /'bændɪdʒ/ *n* venda *f*. ● *vt* vendar

b & b *abbr* (*bed and breakfast*) cama *f* y desayuno

bandit /'bændɪt/ *n* bandido *m*

bandstand /'bændstænd/ *n* quiosco *m* de música

bandwagon /'bændwægən/ *n*. **jump on the** ~ (*fig*) subirse al carro

bandy¹ /'bændɪ/ *a* (**-ier**, **-iest**) patizambo

bandy² /'bændɪ/ *vt*. ~ **about** repetir. **be bandied about** estar en boca de todos

bandy-legged /'bændɪlegd/ *a* patizambo

bane /beɪn/ *n* (*fig*) perdición *f*. ~**ful** *a* funesto

bang /bæŋ/ *n* (*noise*) ruido *m*; (*blow*) golpe *m*; (*of gun*) estampido *m*; (*of door*) golpe *m*. ● *vt/i* golpear. ● *adv* exactamente. ● *int* ¡pum!

banger /'bæŋə(r)/ *n* petardo *m*; (*culin*, *sl*) salchicha *f*

bangle /'bæŋgl/ *n* brazalete *m*

banish /'bænɪʃ/ *vt* desterrar

banisters /'bænɪstəz/ *npl* barandilla *f*

banjo /'bændʒəʊ/ *n* (*pl* **-os**) banjo *m*

bank¹ /bæŋk/ *n* (*of river*) orilla *f*. ● *vt* cubrir ⟨*fire*⟩. ● *vi* (*aviat*) ladearse

bank² /bæŋk/ *n* banco *m*. ● *vt* depositar. ~ **on** *vt* contar con. ~ **with** tener una cuenta con. ~**er** *n* banquero *m*. ~ **holiday** *n* día *m* festivo, fiesta *f*. ~**ing** *n* (*com*) banca *f*. ~**note** /'bæŋknəʊt/ *n* billete *m* de banco

bankrupt /'bæŋkrʌpt/ *a* & *n* quebrado (*m*). ● *vt* hacer quebrar. ~**cy** *n* bancarrota *f*, quiebra *f*

banner /'bænə(r)/ *n* bandera *f*; (*in demonstration*) pancarta *f*

banns /bænz/ *npl* amonestaciones *fpl*

banquet /'bæŋkwɪt/ *n* banquete *m*

bantamweight /'bæntəmweɪt/ *n* peso *m* gallo

banter /'bæntə(r)/ *n* chanza *f*. ● *vi* chancearse

bap /bæp/ *n* panecillo *m* blando

baptism /'bæptɪzəm/ *n* bautismo *m*; (*act*) bautizo *m*

Baptist /'bæptɪst/ *n* bautista *m* & *f*

baptize /bæp'taɪz/ *vt* bautizar

bar /bɑː(r)/ *n* barra *f*; (*on window*) reja *f*; (*of chocolate*) tableta *f*; (*of soap*) pastilla *f*; (*pub*) bar *m*; (*mus*) compás *m*; (*jurid*) abogacía *f*; (*fig*)

obstáculo *m*. ● *vt* (*pt* **barred**) atrancar ⟨*door*⟩; (*exclude*) excluir; (*prohibit*) prohibir. ● *prep* excepto

barbar|ian /bɑː'beərɪən/ *a* & *n* bárbaro (*m*). ~**ic** /bɑː'bærɪk/ *a* bárbaro. ~**ity** /-ətɪ/ *n* barbaridad *f*. ~**ous** *a* /'bɑːbərəs/ *a* bárbaro

barbecue /'bɑːbɪkjuː/ *n* barbacoa *f*. ● *vt* asar a la parrilla

barbed /bɑːbd/ *a*. ~ **wire** alambre *m* de espinas

barber /'bɑːbə(r)/ *n* peluquero *m*, barbero *m*

barbiturate /bɑː'bɪtjʊrət/ *n* barbitúrico *m*

bare /beə(r)/ *a* (**-er**, **est**) desnudo; ⟨*room*⟩ con pocos muebles; (*mere*) simple; (*empty*) vacío. ● *vt* desnudar; (*uncover*) descubrir. ~ **one's teeth** mostrar los dientes. ~**back** /'beəbæk/ *adv* a pelo. ~**faced** /'beəfeɪst/ *a* descarado. ~**foot** *a* descalzo. ~**headed** /'beəhedɪd/ *a* descubierto. ~**ly** *adv* apenas. ~**ness** *n* desnudez *f*

bargain /'bɑːgɪn/ *n* (*agreement*) pacto *m*; (*good buy*) ganga *f*. ● *vi* negociar; (*haggle*) regatear. ~ **for** esperar, contar con

barge /bɑːdʒ/ *n* barcaza *f*. ● *vi*. ~ **in** irrumpir

baritone /'bærɪtəʊn/ *n* barítono *m*

barium /'beərɪəm/ *n* bario *m*

bark¹ /bɑːk/ *n* (*of dog*) ladrido *m*. ● *vi* ladrar

bark² /bɑːk/ *n* (*of tree*) corteza *f*

barley /'bɑːlɪ/ *n* cebada *f*. ~**water** *n* hordiate *m*

bar: ~**maid** /'bɑːmeɪd/ *n* camarera *f*. ~**man** /'bɑːmən/ *n* (*pl* **-men**) camarero *m*

barmy /'bɑːmɪ/ *a* (*sl*) chiflado

barn /bɑːn/ *n* granero *m*

barometer /bə'rɒmɪtə(r)/ *n* barómetro *m*

baron /'bærən/ *n* barón *m*. ~**ess** *n* baronesa *f*

baroque /bə'rɒk/ *a* & *n* barroco (*m*)

barracks /'bærəks/ *npl* cuartel *m*

barrage /'bærɑːʒ/ *n* (*mil*) barrera *f*; (*dam*) presa *f*; (*of questions*) bombardeo *m*

barrel /'bærəl/ *n* tonel *m*; (*of gun*) cañón *m*. ~**organ** *n* organillo *m*

barren /'bærən/ *a* estéril. ~**ness** *n* esterilidad *f*, aridez *f*

barricade /bærɪ'keɪd/ *n* barricada *f*. ● *vt* cerrar con barricadas

barrier /'bærɪə(r)/ *n* barrera *f*

barring /'bɑːrɪŋ/ *prep* salvo

barrister /'bærɪstə(r)/ *n* abogado *m*

barrow /'bærəʊ/ *n* carro *m*; (*wheelbarrow*) carretilla *f*

barter /'bɑːtə(r)/ *n* trueque *m*. ● *vt* trocar

base /beɪs/ *n* base *f*. ● *vt* basar. ● *a* vil

baseball /'beɪsbɔːl/ *n* béisbol *m*

baseless /'beɪslɪs/ *a* infundado

basement /'beɪsmənt/ *n* sótano *m*

bash /bæʃ/ *vt* golpear. ● *n* golpe *m*. **have a ~** (*sl*) probar

bashful /'bæʃfl/ *a* tímido

basic /'beɪsɪk/ *a* básico, fundamental. **~ally** *adv* fundamentalmente

basil /'bæzl/ *n* albahaca *f*

basilica /bə'zɪlɪkə/ *n* basílica *f*

basin /'beɪsn/ *n* (*for washing*) palangana *f*; (*for food*) cuenco *m*; (*geog*) cuenca *f*

basis /'beɪsɪs/ *n* (*pl* **bases** /-siːz/) base *f*

bask /bɑːsk/ *vi* asolearse; (*fig*) gozar (**in** de)

basket /'bɑːskɪt/ *n* cesta *f*; (*big*) cesto *m*. **~ball** /'bɑːskɪtbɔːl/ *n* baloncesto *m*

Basque /bɑːsk/ *a* & *n* vasco (*m*). **~ Country** *n* País *m* Vasco. **~ Provinces** *npl* Vascongadas *fpl*

bass[1] /beɪs/ *a* bajo. ● *n* (*mus*) bajo *m*

bass[2] /bæs/ *n* (*marine fish*) róbalo *m*; (*freshwater fish*) perca *f*

bassoon /bə'suːn/ *n* fagot *m*

bastard /'bɑːstəd/ *a* & *n* bastardo (*m*). **you ~!** (*fam*) ¡cabrón!

baste /beɪst/ *vt* (*sew*) hilvanar; (*culin*) lard(e)ar

bastion /'bæstɪən/ *n* baluarte *m*

bat[1] /bæt/ *n* bate *m*; (*for table tennis*) raqueta *f*. **off one's own ~** por sí solo. ● *vt* (*pt* **batted**) golpear. ● *vi* batear

bat[2] /bæt/ *n* (*mammal*) murciélago *m*

bat[3] /bæt/ *vt*. **without ~ting an eyelid** sin pestañear

batch /bætʃ/ *n* (*of people*) grupo *m*; (*of papers*) lío *m*; (*of goods*) remesa *f*; (*of bread*) hornada *f*

bated /'beɪtɪd/ *a*. **with ~ breath** con aliento entrecortado

bath /bɑːθ/ *n* (*pl* **-s** /bɑːðz/) baño *m*; (*tub*) bañera *f*; (*pl*, *swimming pool*) piscina *f*. ● *vt* bañar. ● *vi* bañarse

bathe /beɪð/ *vt* bañar. ● *vi* bañarse. ● *n* baño *m*. **~r** /-ə(r)/ *n* bañista *m* & *f*

bathing /'beɪðɪŋ/ *n* baños *mpl*. **~-costume** *n* traje *m* de baño

bathroom /'bɑːθrʊm/ *n* cuarto *m* de baño

batman /'bætmən/ *n* (*pl* **-men**) (*mil*) ordenanza *f*

baton /'bætən/ *n* (*mil*) bastón *m*; (*mus*) batuta *f*

batsman /'bætsmən/ *n* (*pl* **-men**) bateador *m*

battalion /bə'tælɪən/ *n* batallón *m*

batter[1] /'bætə(r)/ *vt* apalear

batter[2] /'bætə(r)/ *n* batido *m* para rebozar, albardilla *f*

batter: **~ed** *a* (*car etc*) estropeado; (*wife etc*) golpeado. **~ing** *n* (*fam*) bombardeo *m*

battery /'bætərɪ/ *n* (*mil*, *auto*) batería *f*; (*of torch*, *radio*) pila *f*

battle /'bætl/ *n* batalla *f*; (*fig*) lucha *f*. ● *vi* luchar. **~axe** /'bætlæks/ *n* (*woman*, *fam*) arpía *f*. **~field** /'bætlfiːld/ *n* campo *m* de batalla. **~ments** /'bætlmənts/ *npl* almenas *fpl*. **~ship** /'bætlʃɪp/ *n* acorazado *m*

batty /'bætɪ/ *a* (*sl*) chiflado

baulk /bɔːlk/ *vt* frustrar. ● *vi*. **~ (at)** resistirse (a)

bawd|iness /'bɔːdɪnəs/ *n* obscenidad *f*. **~y** /'bɔːdɪ/ *a* (**-ier, -iest**) obsceno, verde

bawl /bɔːl/ *vt/i* gritar

bay[1] /beɪ/ *n* (*geog*) bahía *f*

bay[2] /beɪ/ *n* (*bot*) laurel *m*

bay[3] /beɪ/ *n* (*of dog*) ladrido *m*. **keep at ~** mantener a raya. ● *vi* ladrar

bayonet /'beɪənet/ *n* bayoneta *f*

bay window /beɪ'wɪndəʊ/ *n* ventana *f* salediza

bazaar /bə'zɑː(r)/ *n* bazar *m*

BC /biː'siː/ *abbr* (*before Christ*) a. de C., antes de Cristo

be /biː/ *vi* (*pres* **am**, **are**, **is**; *pt* **was**, **were**; *pp* **been**) (*position or temporary*) estar; (*permanent*) ser. **~ cold/hot, etc** tener frío/calor, etc. **~ reading/singing, etc** (*aux*) leer/cantar, etc. **~ that as it may** sea como fuere. **he is 30** (*age*) tiene 30 años. **he is to come** (*must*) tiene que venir. **how are you?** ¿cómo estás? **how much is it?** ¿cuánto vale?, ¿cuánto es? **have been to** haber estado en. **it is cold/hot, etc** (*weather*) hace frío/calor, etc

beach /biːtʃ/ *n* playa *f*

beachcomber /'biːtʃkəʊmə(r)/ *n* raquero *m*

beacon /'biːkən/ *n* faro *m*

bead /biːd/ n cuenta f; (of glass) abalorio m

beak /biːk/ n pico m

beaker /ˈbiːkə(r)/ n jarra f, vaso m

beam /biːm/ n viga f; (of light) rayo m; (naut) bao m. ● vt emitir. ● vi irradiar; (smile) sonreír. **~ends** npl. **be on one's ~ends** no tener más dinero. **~ing** a radiante

bean /biːn/ n judía f; (broad bean) haba f; (of coffee) grano m

beano /ˈbiːnəʊ/ n (pl -os) (fam) juerga f

bear[1] /beə(r)/ vt (pt bore, pp borne) llevar; parir ⟨niño⟩; (endure) soportar. **~ right** torcer a la derecha. **~ in mind** tener en cuenta. **~ with** tener paciencia con

bear[2] /beə(r)/ n oso m

bearable /ˈbeərəbl/ a soportable

beard /bɪəd/ n barba f. **~ed** a barbudo

bearer /ˈbeərə(r)/ n portador m; (of passport) poseedor m

bearing /ˈbeərɪŋ/ n comportamiento m; (relevance) relación f; (mec) cojinete m. **get one's ~s** orientarse

beast /biːst/ n bestia f; (person) bruto m. **~ly** /ˈbiːstlɪ/ a (-ier, -iest) bestial; (fam) horrible

beat /biːt/ vt (pt beat, pp beaten) golpear; (culin) batir; (defeat) derrotar; (better) sobrepasar; (baffle) dejar perplejo. **~ a retreat** (mil) batirse en retirada. **~ it** (sl) largarse. ● vi ⟨heart⟩ latir. ● n latido m; (mus) ritmo m; (of policeman) ronda f. **~ up** dar una paliza a; (culin) batir. **~er** n batidor m. **~ing** n paliza f

beautician /bjuːˈtɪʃn/ n esteticista m & f

beautiful /ˈbjuːtɪfl/ a hermoso. **~ly** adv maravillosamente

beautify /ˈbjuːtɪfaɪ/ vt embellecer

beauty /ˈbjuːtɪ/ n belleza f. **~ parlour** n salón m de belleza. **~ spot** (on face) lunar m; (site) lugar m pintoresco

beaver /ˈbiːvə(r)/ n castor m

became /bɪˈkeɪm/ see **become**

because /bɪˈkɒz/ conj porque. ● adv. **~ of** a causa de

beck /bek/ n. **be at the ~ and call of** estar a disposición de

beckon /ˈbekən/ vt/i. **~ (to)** hacer señas (a)

become /bɪˈkʌm/ vt (pt became, pp become) ⟨clothes⟩ sentar bien. ● vi hacerse, llegar a ser, volverse, convertirse en. **what has ~ of her?** ¿qué es de ella?

becoming /bɪˈkʌmɪŋ/ a ⟨clothes⟩ favorecedor

bed /bed/ n cama f; (layer) estrato m; (of sea, river) fondo m; (of flowers) macizo m. ● vi (pt bedded). **~ down** acostarse. **~ and breakfast (b & b)** cama y desayuno. **~bug** /ˈbedbʌg/ n chinche f. **~clothes** /ˈbedkləʊðz/ npl, **~ding** n ropa f de cama

bedevil /bɪˈdevl/ vt (pt bedevilled) (torment) atormentar

bedlam /ˈbedləm/ n confusión f, manicomio m

bed: **~pan** /ˈbedpæn/ n orinal m de cama. **~post** /ˈbedpəʊst/ n columna f de la cama

bedraggled /bɪˈdrægld/ a sucio

bed: **~ridden** /ˈbedrɪdn/ a encamado. **~room** /ˈbedrʊm/ n dormitorio m, habitación f. **~side** /ˈbedsaɪd/ n cabecera f. **~sitting-room** /bedˈsɪtɪŋruːm/ n salón m con cama, estudio m. **~spread** /ˈbedspred/ n colcha f. **~time** /ˈbedtaɪm/ n hora f de acostarse

bee /biː/ n abeja f. **make a ~line for** ir en línea recta hacia

beech /biːtʃ/ n haya f

beef /biːf/ n carne f de vaca, carne f de res (LAm). ● vi (sl) quejarse. **~burger** /ˈbiːfbɜːgə(r)/ n hamburguesa f

beefeater /ˈbiːfiːtə(r)/ n alabardero m de la torre de Londres

beefsteak /biːfˈsteɪk/ n filete m, bistec m, bife m (Arg)

beefy /ˈbiːfɪ/ a (-ier, -iest) musculoso

beehive /ˈbiːhaɪv/ n colmena f

been /biːn/ see **be**

beer /bɪə(r)/ n cerveza f

beet /biːt/ n remolacha f

beetle /ˈbiːtl/ n escarabajo m

beetroot /ˈbiːtruːt/ n invar remolacha f

befall /bɪˈfɔːl/ vt (pt befell, pp befallen) acontecer a. ● vi acontecer

befit /bɪˈfɪt/ vt (pt befitted) convenir a

before /bɪˈfɔː(r)/ prep (time) antes de; (place) delante de. **~ leaving** antes de marcharse. ● adv (place) delante; (time) antes. **a week ~** una semana antes. **the week ~** la semana anterior. ● conj (time) antes de que. **~ he leaves** antes de que se vaya. **~hand** /bɪˈfɔːhænd/ *adv* de antemano

befriend /bɪˈfrend/ *vt* ofrecer amistad a

beg /beg/ *vt/i* (*pt* **begged**) mendigar; (*entreat*) suplicar; (*ask*) pedir. **~ s.o.'s pardon** pedir perdón a uno. **I ~ your pardon!** ¡perdone Vd! **I ~ your pardon?** ¿cómo? **it's going ~ging** no lo quiere nadie

began /bɪˈgæn/ *see* **begin**

beget /bɪˈget/ *vt* (*pt* **begot**, *pp* **begotten**, *pres p* **begetting**) engendrar

beggar /ˈbegə(r)/ *n* mendigo *m*; (*sl*) individuo *m*, tío *m* (*fam*)

begin /bɪˈgɪn/ *vt/i* (*pt* **began**, *pp* **begun**, *pres p* **beginning**) comenzar, empezar. **~ner** *n* principiante *m & f*. **~ning** *n* principio *m*

begot, begotten /bɪˈgot, bɪˈgotn/ *see* **beget**

begrudge /bɪˈgrʌdʒ/ *vt* envidiar; (*give*) dar de mala gana

beguile /bɪˈgaɪl/ *vt* engañar, seducir; (*entertain*) entretener

begun /bɪˈgʌn/ *see* **begin**

behalf /bɪˈhɑːf/ *n*. **on ~ of** de parte de, en nombre de

behav|e /bɪˈheɪv/ *vi* comportarse, portarse. **~ (o.s.)** portarse bien. **~iour** /bɪˈheɪvjə(r)/ *n* comportamiento *m*

behead /bɪˈhed/ *vt* decapitar

beheld /bɪˈheld/ *see* **behold**

behind /bɪˈhaɪnd/ *prep* detrás de. ● *adv* detrás; (*late*) atrasado. ● *n* (*fam*) trasero *m*

behold /bɪˈhəʊld/ *vt* (*pt* **beheld**) (*old use*) mirar, contemplar

beholden /bɪˈhəʊldən/ *a* agradecido

being /ˈbiːɪŋ/ *n* ser *m*. **come into ~** nacer

belated /bɪˈleɪtɪd/ *a* tardío

belch /beltʃ/ *vi* eructar. ● *vt*. **~ out** arrojar (*smoke*)

belfry /ˈbelfrɪ/ *n* campanario *m*

Belgi|an /ˈbeldʒən/ *a & n* belga (*m & f*). **~um** /ˈbeldʒəm/ *n* Bélgica *f*

belie /bɪˈlaɪ/ *vt* desmentir

belie|f /bɪˈliːf/ *n* (*trust*) fe *f*; (*opinion*) creencia *f*. **~ve** /bɪˈliːv/ *vt/i* creer. **make ~ve** fingir. **~ver** /-ə(r)/ *n* creyente *m & f*; (*supporter*) partidario *m*

belittle /bɪˈlɪtl/ *vt* empequeñecer; (*fig*) despreciar

bell /bel/ *n* campana *f*; (*on door*) timbre *m*

belligerent /bɪˈlɪdʒərənt/ *a & n* beligerante (*m & f*)

bellow /ˈbeləʊ/ *vt* gritar. ● *vi* bramar

bellows /ˈbeləʊz/ *npl* fuelle *m*

belly /ˈbelɪ/ *n* vientre *m*. **~ful** /ˈbelɪfʊl/ *n* panzada *f*. **have a ~ful of** (*sl*) estar harto de

belong /bɪˈlɒŋ/ *vi* pertenecer; (*club*) ser socio (**to** de)

belongings /bɪˈlɒŋɪŋz/ *npl* pertenencias *fpl*. **personal ~** efectos *mpl* personales

beloved /bɪˈlʌvɪd/ *a & n* querido (*m*)

below /bɪˈləʊ/ *prep* debajo de; (*fig*) inferior a. ● *adv* abajo

belt /belt/ *n* cinturón *m*; (*area*) zona *f*. ● *vt* (*fig*) rodear; (*sl*) pegar

bemused /bɪˈmjuːzd/ *a* perplejo

bench /bentʃ/ *n* banco *m*. **the B~** (*jurid*) la magistratura *f*

bend /bend/ *vt* (*pt & pp* **bent**) doblar; torcer (*arm, leg*). ● *vi* doblarse; (*road*) torcerse. ● *n* curva *f*. **~ down/over** inclinarse

beneath /bɪˈniːθ/ *prep* debajo de; (*fig*) inferior a. ● *adv* abajo

benediction /benɪˈdɪkʃn/ *n* bendición *f*

benefactor /ˈbenɪfæktə(r)/ *n* bienhechor *m*, benefactor *m*

beneficial /benɪˈfɪʃl/ *a* provechoso

beneficiary /benɪˈfɪʃərɪ/ *a & n* beneficiario (*m*)

benefit /ˈbenɪfɪt/ *n* provecho *m*, ventaja *f*; (*allowance*) subsidio *m*; (*financial gain*) beneficio *m*. ● *vt* (*pt* **benefited**, *pres p* **benefiting**) aprovechar. ● *vi* aprovecharse

benevolen|ce /bɪˈnevələns/ *n* benevolencia *f*. **~t** *a* benévolo

benign /bɪˈnaɪn/ *a* benigno

bent /bent/ *see* **bend**. ● *n* inclinación *f*. ● *a* encorvado; (*sl*) corrompido

bequeath /bɪˈkwiːð/ *vt* legar

bequest /bɪˈkwest/ *n* legado *m*

bereave|d /bɪˈriːvd/ *n*. **the ~d** la familia *f* del difunto. **~ment** *n* pérdida *f*; (*mourning*) luto *m*

bereft /bɪˈreft/ *a*. **~ of** privado de

beret /ˈbereɪ/ *n* boina *f*

Bermuda /bəˈmjuːdə/ *n* Islas *fpl* Bermudas

berry /ˈberɪ/ *n* baya *f*

berserk /bəˈsɜːk/ *a*. **go ~** volverse loco, perder los estribos

berth /bɜːθ/ *n* litera *f*; (*anchorage*) amarradero *m*. **give a wide ~ to** evitar. ● *vi* atracar

beseech /bɪˈsiːtʃ/ vt (pt **besought**) suplicar

beset /bɪˈset/ vt (pt **beset**, pres p **besetting**) acosar

beside /bɪˈsaɪd/ prep al lado de. **be ~ o.s.** estar fuera de sí

besides /bɪˈsaɪdz/ prep además de; (except) excepto. ● adv además

besiege /bɪˈsiːdʒ/ vt asediar; (fig) acosar

besought /bɪˈsɔːt/ see **beseech**

bespoke /bɪˈspəʊk/ a ⟨tailor⟩ que confecciona a la medida

best /best/ a (el) mejor. **the ~ thing is to...** lo mejor es... ● adv (lo) mejor. **like ~** preferir. ● n lo mejor. **at ~** a lo más. **do one's ~** hacer todo lo posible. **make the ~ of** contentarse con. **~ man** n padrino m (de boda)

bestow /bɪˈstəʊ/ vt conceder

bestseller /bestˈselə(r)/ n éxito m de librería, bestseller m

bet /bet/ n apuesta f. ● vt/i (pt **bet** or **betted**) apostar

betray /bɪˈtreɪ/ vt traicionar. **~al** n traición f

betroth|al /bɪˈtrəʊðəl/ n esponsales mpl. **~ed** a prometido

better /ˈbetə(r)/ a & adv mejor. **~ off** en mejores condiciones; (richer) más rico. **get ~** mejorar. **all the ~** tanto mejor. **I'd ~** más vale que. **the ~ part of** la mayor parte de. **the sooner the ~** cuanto antes mejor. ● vt mejorar; (beat) sobrepasar. ● n superior m. **get the ~ of** vencer a. **one's ~s** sus superiores mpl

between /bɪˈtwiːn/ prep entre. ● adv en medio

beverage /ˈbevərɪdʒ/ n bebida f

bevy /ˈbevɪ/ n grupo m

beware /bɪˈweə(r)/ vi tener cuidado. ● int ¡cuidado!

bewilder /bɪˈwɪldə(r)/ vt desconcertar. **~ment** n aturdimiento m

bewitch /bɪˈwɪtʃ/ vt hechizar

beyond /bɪˈjɒnd/ prep más allá de; (fig) fuera de. **~ doubt** sin lugar a duda. **~ reason** irrazonable. ● adv más allá

bias /ˈbaɪəs/ n predisposición f; (prejudice) prejuicio m; (sewing) sesgo m. ● vt (pt **biased**) influir en. **~ed** a parcial

bib /bɪb/ n babero m

Bible /ˈbaɪbl/ n Biblia f

biblical /ˈbɪblɪkl/ a bíblico

bibliography /bɪblɪˈɒɡrəfɪ/ n bibliografía f

biceps /ˈbaɪseps/ n bíceps m

bicker /ˈbɪkə(r)/ vi altercar

bicycle /ˈbaɪsɪkl/ n bicicleta f. ● vi ir en bicicleta

bid /bɪd/ n (offer) oferta f; (attempt) tentativa f. ● vi hacer una oferta. ● vt (pt **bid**, pres p **bidding**) ofrecer; (pt **bid**, pp **bidden**, pres p **bidding**) mandar; dar ⟨welcome, good-day etc⟩. **~der** n postor m. **~ding** n (at auction) ofertas fpl; (order) mandato m

bide /baɪd/ vt. **~ one's time** esperar el momento oportuno

biennial /baɪˈenɪəl/ a bienal. ● n (event) bienal f; (bot) planta f bienal

bifocals /baɪˈfəʊklz/ npl gafas fpl bifocales, anteojos mpl bifocales (LAm)

big /bɪɡ/ a (**bigger**, **biggest**) grande; (generous, sl) generoso. ● adv. **talk ~** fanfarronear

bigam|ist /ˈbɪɡəmɪst/ n bígamo m. **~ous** a bígamo. **~y** n bigamia f

big-headed /bɪɡˈhedɪd/ a engreído

bigot /ˈbɪɡət/ n fanático m. **~ed** a fanático. **~ry** n fanatismo m

bigwig /ˈbɪɡwɪɡ/ n (fam) pez m gordo

bike /baɪk/ n (fam) bicicleta f, bici f (fam)

bikini /bɪˈkiːnɪ/ n (pl **-is**) biquini m, bikini m

bilberry /ˈbɪlbərɪ/ n arándano m

bile /baɪl/ n bilis f

bilingual /baɪˈlɪŋɡwəl/ a bilingüe

bilious /ˈbɪlɪəs/ a (med) bilioso

bill[1] /bɪl/ n cuenta f; (invoice) factura f; (notice) cartel m; (Amer, banknote) billete m; (pol) proyecto m de ley. ● vt pasar la factura; (in theatre) anunciar

bill[2] /bɪl/ n (of bird) pico m

billet /ˈbɪlɪt/ n (mil) alojamiento m. ● vt alojar

billiards /ˈbɪlɪədz/ n billar m

billion /ˈbɪlɪən/ n billón m; (Amer) mil millones mpl

billy-goat /ˈbɪlɪɡəʊt/ n macho m cabrío

bin /bɪn/ n recipiente m; (for rubbish) cubo m; (for waste paper) papelera f

bind /baɪnd/ vt (pt **bound**) atar; encuadernar ⟨book⟩; (jurid) obligar. ● n (sl) lata f. **~ing**

/'baɪndɪŋ/ *n* (*of books*) encuadernación *f*; (*braid*) ribete *m*

binge /bɪndʒ/ *n* (*sl*) (*of food*) comilona *f*; (*of drink*) borrachera *f*. **go on a ~** ir de juerga

bingo /'bɪŋɡəʊ/ *n* bingo *m*

binoculars /bɪ'nɒkjʊləz/ *npl* prismáticos *mpl*

biochemistry /baɪəʊ'kemɪstrɪ/ *n* bioquímica *f*

biograph|er /baɪ'ɒɡrəfə(r)/ *n* biógrafo *m*. **~y** *n* biografía *f*

biolog|ical /baɪə'lɒdʒɪkl/ *a* biológico. **~ist** *n* biólogo *m*. **~** /baɪ'ɒlədʒɪ/ *n* biología *f*

biped /'baɪped/ *n* bípedo *m*

birch /bɜːtʃ/ *n* (*tree*) abedul *m*; (*whip*) férula *f*

bird /bɜːd/ *n* ave *f*; (*small*) pájaro *m*; (*fam*) tipo *m*; (*girl, sl*) chica *f*

Biro /'baɪərəʊ/ *n* (*pl* **-os**) (P) bolígrafo *m*, biromen *m* (*Arg*)

birth /bɜːθ/ *n* nacimiento *m*. **~certificate** *n* partida *f* de nacimiento. **~control** *n* control *m* de la natalidad. **~day** /'bɜːθdeɪ/ *n* cumpleaños *m invar*. **~mark** /'bɜːθmɑːk/ *n* marca *f* de nacimiento. **~rate** *n* natalidad *f*. **~right** /'bɜːθraɪt/ *n* derechos *mpl* de nacimiento

biscuit /'bɪskɪt/ *n* galleta *f*

bisect /baɪ'sekt/ *vt* bisecar

bishop /'bɪʃəp/ *n* obispo *m*

bit¹ /bɪt/ *n* trozo *m*; (*quantity*) poco *m*

bit² /bɪt/ *see* **bite**

bit³ /bɪt/ *n* (*of horse*) bocado *m*; (*mec*) broca *f*

bitch /bɪtʃ/ *n* perra *f*; (*woman, fam*) mujer *f* maligna, bruja *f* (*fam*). ● *vi* (*fam*) quejarse (**about** de). **~y** *a* malintencionado

bit|e /baɪt/ *vt/i* (*pt* **bit**, *pp* **bitten**) morder. **~e one's nails** morderse las uñas. ● *n* mordisco *m*; (*mouthful*) bocado *m*; (*of insect etc*) picadura *f*. **~ing** /'baɪtɪŋ/ *a* mordaz

bitter /'bɪtə(r)/ *a* amargo; (*of weather*) glacial. **to the ~ end** hasta el final. ● *n* cerveza *f* amarga. **~ly** *adv* amargamente. **it's ~ly cold** hace un frío glacial. **~ness** *n* amargor *m*; (*resentment*) amargura *f*

bizarre /bɪ'zɑː(r)/ *a* extraño

blab /blæb/ *vi* (*pt* **blabbed**) chismear

black /blæk/ *a* (**-er**, **-est**) negro. **~ and blue** amoratado. ● *n* negro *m*. ● *vt* ennegrecer; limpiar ⟨shoes⟩. **~**

out desmayarse; (*make dark*) apagar las luces de

blackball /'blækbɔːl/ *vt* votar en contra de

blackberry /'blækbərɪ/ *n* zarzamora *f*

blackbird /'blækbɜːd/ *n* mirlo *m*

blackboard /'blækbɔːd/ *n* pizarra *f*

blackcurrant /blæk'kʌrənt/ *n* casis *f*

blacken /'blækən/ *vt* ennegrecer. ● *vi* ennegrecerse

blackguard /'blægɑːd/ *n* canalla *m*

blackleg /'blækleg/ *n* esquirol *m*

blacklist /'blæklɪst/ *vt* poner en la lista negra

blackmail /'blækmeɪl/ *n* chantaje *m*. ● *vt* chantajear. **~er** *n* chantajista *m & f*

black-out /'blækaʊt/ *n* apagón *m*; (*med*) desmayo *m*; (*of news*) censura *f*

blacksmith /'blæksmɪθ/ *n* herrero *m*

bladder /'blædə(r)/ *n* vejiga *f*

blade /bleɪd/ *n* hoja *f*; (*razor-blade*) cuchilla *f*. **~ of grass** brizna *f* de hierba

blame /bleɪm/ *vt* echar la culpa a. **be to ~** tener la culpa. ● *n* culpa *f*. **~less** *a* inocente

bland /blænd/ *a* (**-er**, **-est**) suave

blandishments /'blændɪʃmənts/ *npl* halagos *mpl*

blank /blæŋk/ *a* en blanco; (*cartridge*) sin bala; (*fig*) vacío. **~ verse** *n* verso *m* suelto. ● *n* blanco *m*

blanket /'blæŋkɪt/ *n* manta *f*; (*fig*) capa *f*. ● *vt* (*pt* **blanketed**) (*fig*) cubrir (**in, with** de)

blare /bleə(r)/ *vi* sonar muy fuerte. ● *n* estrépito *m*

blarney /'blɑːnɪ/ *n* coba *f*. ● *vt* dar coba

blasé /'blɑːzeɪ/ *a* hastiado

blasphem|e /blæs'fiːm/ *vt/i* blasfemar. **~er** *n* blasfemador *m*. **~ous** /'blæsfəməs/ *a* blasfemo. **~y** /'blæsfəmɪ/ *n* blasfemia *f*

blast /blɑːst/ *n* explosión *f*; (*gust*) ráfaga *f*; (*sound*) toque *m*. ● *vt* volar. **~ed** *a* maldito. **~furnace** *n* alto horno *m*. **~off** *n* (*of missile*) despegue *m*

blatant /'bleɪtnt/ *a* patente; (*shameless*) descarado

blaze /bleɪz/ *n* llamarada *f*; (*of light*) resplandor *m*; (*fig*) arranque *m*. ● *vi* arder en llamas; (*fig*) brillar. **~ a trail** abrir un camino

blazer /'bleɪzə(r)/ *n* chaqueta *f*

bleach /bli:tʃ/ n lejía f; (for hair) decolorante m. ● vt blanquear; decolorar ⟨hair⟩. ● vi blanquearse

bleak /bli:k/ a (-er, -est) desolado; (fig) sombrío

bleary /'blɪərɪ/ a ⟨eyes⟩ nublado; (indistinct) indistinto

bleat /bli:t/ n balido m. ● vi balar

bleed /bli:d/ vt/i (pt bled) sangrar

bleep /bli:p/ n pitido m. ~er n busca m, buscapersonas m

blemish /'blemɪʃ/ n tacha f

blend /blend/ n mezcla f. ● vt mezclar. ● vi combinarse

bless /bles/ vt bendecir. ~ you! (on sneezing) ¡Jesús! ~ed a bendito. be ~ed with estar dotado de. ~ing n bendición f; (advantage) ventaja f

blew /blu:/ see **blow**[1]

blight /blaɪt/ n añublo m, tizón m; (fig) plaga f. ● vt añublar, atizonar; (fig) destrozar

blighter /'blaɪtə(r)/ n (sl) tío m (fam), sinvergüenza m

blind /blaɪnd/ a ciego. ~ alley n callejón m sin salida. ● n persiana f; (fig) pretexto m. ● vt cegar. ~fold /'blaɪndfəʊld/ a & adv con los ojos vendados. ● n venda f. ● vt vendar los ojos. ~ly adv a ciegas. ~ness n ceguera f

blink /blɪŋk/ vi parpadear; (of light) centellear

blinkers /'blɪŋkəz/ npl anteojeras fpl; (auto) intermitente m

bliss /blɪs/ n felicidad f. ~ful a feliz. ~fully adv felizmente; (completely) completamente

blister /'blɪstə(r)/ n ampolla f. ● vi formarse ampollas

blithe /blaɪð/ a alegre

blitz /blɪts/ n bombardeo m aéreo. ● vt bombardear

blizzard /'blɪzəd/ n ventisca f

bloated /'bləʊtɪd/ a hinchado (with de)

bloater /'bləʊtə(r)/ n arenque m ahumado

blob /blɒb/ n gota f; (stain) mancha f

bloc /blɒk/ n (pol) bloque m

block /blɒk/ n bloque m; (of wood) zoquete m; (of buildings) manzana f, cuadra f (LAm); (in pipe) obstrucción f. in ~ letters en letra de imprenta. **traffic** ~ embotellamiento m. ● vt obstruir. ~ade /blɒ'keɪd/ n bloqueo m. ● vt bloquear. ~age n obstrucción f

blockhead /'blɒkhed/ n (fam) zopenco m

bloke /bləʊk/ n (fam) tío m (fam), tipo m

blond /blɒnd/ a & n rubio (m). ~e a & n rubia (f)

blood /blʌd/ n sangre f. ~ count n recuento m sanguíneo. ~curdling a horripilante

bloodhound /'blʌdhaʊnd/ n sabueso m

blood: ~ **pressure** n tensión f arterial. **high** ~ **pressure** hipertensión f. ~shed /'blʌdʃed/ n efusión f de sangre, derramamiento m de sangre, matanza f. ~shot /'blʌdʃɒt/ a sanguinolento; ⟨eye⟩ inyectado de sangre. ~stream /'blʌdstri:m/ n sangre f

bloodthirsty /'blʌdθɜ:stɪ/ a sanguinario

bloody /'blʌdɪ/ a (-ier, -iest) sangriento; (stained) ensangrentado; (sl) maldito. ~y-minded a (fam) terco

bloom /blu:m/ n flor f. ● vi florecer

bloomer /'blu:mə(r)/ n (sl) metedura f de pata

blooming a floreciente; (fam) maldito

blossom /'blɒsəm/ n flor f. ● vi florecer. ~ out (into) (fig) llegar a ser

blot /blɒt/ n borrón m. ● vt (pt blotted) manchar; (dry) secar. ~ out oscurecer

blotch /blɒtʃ/ n mancha f. ~y a lleno de manchas

blotter /'blɒtə(r)/ n, **blotting-paper** /'blɒtɪŋpeɪpə(r)/ n papel m secante

blouse /blaʊz/ n blusa f

blow[1] /bləʊ/ vt (pt blew, pp blown) soplar; fundir ⟨fuse⟩; tocar ⟨trumpet⟩. ● vi soplar; ⟨fuse⟩ fundirse; (sound) sonar. ● n (puff) soplo m. ~ **down** vt derribar. ~ **out** apagar ⟨candle⟩. ~ **over** pasar. ~ **up** vt inflar; (explode) volar; (photo) ampliar. ● vi (explode) estallar; (burst) reventar

blow[2] /bləʊ/ n (incl fig) golpe m

blow-dry /'bləʊdraɪ/ vt secar con secador

blowlamp /'bləʊlæmp/ n soplete m

blow: ~out n (of tyre) reventón m. ~up n (photo) ampliación f

blowzy /'blaʊzɪ/ a desaliñado

blubber /'blʌbə(r)/ n grasa f de ballena

bludgeon /'blʌdʒən/ n cachiporra f.
● vt aporrear

blue /bluː/ a (-er, -est) azul; ⟨joke⟩
verde. ● n azul m. **out of the ~**
totalmente inesperado. **~s** npl.
have the ~s tener tristeza

bluebell /'bluːbel/ n campanilla f

bluebottle /'bluːbɒtl/ n moscarda f

blueprint /'bluːprɪnt/ n ferro-
prusiato m; ⟨fig, plan⟩ anteproyecto
m

bluff /blʌf/ a ⟨person⟩ brusco. ● n
⟨poker⟩ farol m. ● vt engañar. ● vi
⟨poker⟩ tirarse un farol

blunder /'blʌndə(r)/ vi cometer un
error. ● n metedura f de pata

blunt /blʌnt/ a desafilado; ⟨person⟩
directo, abrupto. ● vt desafilar. **~ly**
adv francamente. **~ness** n embot-
adura f; ⟨fig⟩ franqueza f, brusquedad f

blur /blɜː(r)/ n impresión f indis-
tinta. ● vt ⟨pt blurred⟩ hacer
borroso

blurb /blɜːb/ n resumen f
publicitario

blurt /blɜːt/ vt. **~ out** dejar escapar

blush /blʌʃ/ vi ruborizarse. ● n
sonrojo m

bluster /'blʌstə(r)/ vi ⟨weather⟩ bramar; ⟨person⟩ fanfarronear. **~y** a
tempestuoso

boar /bɔː(r)/ n verraco m

board /bɔːd/ n tabla f, tablero m; ⟨for
notices⟩ tablón m; ⟨food⟩ pensión f;
⟨admin⟩ junta f. **~ and lodging** casa
y comida. **above ~** correcto. **full ~**
pensión f completa. **go by the ~** ser
abandonado. ● vt alojar; ⟨naut⟩
embarcar en. ● vi alojarse (**with** en
casa de); ⟨at school⟩ ser interno. **~er**
n huésped m; ⟨schol⟩ interno m.
~ing-house n casa f de huéspedes,
pensión f. **~ing-school** n internado
m

boast /bəʊst/ vt enorgullecerse de.
● vi jactarse. ● n jactancia f. **~er** n
jactancioso m. **~ful** a jactancioso

boat /bəʊt/ n barco m; ⟨large⟩ navío
m; ⟨small⟩ barca f

boater /'bəʊtə(r)/ n ⟨hat⟩ canotié m

boatswain /'bəʊsn/ n con-
tramaestre m

bob[1] /bɒb/ vi ⟨pt bobbed⟩ menearse,
subir y bajar. **~ up** presentarse
súbitamente

bob[2] /bɒb/ n invar ⟨sl⟩ chelín m

bobbin /'bɒbɪn/ n carrete m; ⟨in sewing machine⟩ canilla f

bobby /'bɒbɪ/ n ⟨fam⟩ policía m, poli
m ⟨fam⟩

bobsleigh /'bɒbsleɪ/ n bob(sleigh) m

bode /bəʊd/ vi presagiar. **~ well/ill**
ser de buen/mal agüero

bodice /'bɒdɪs/ n corpiño m

bodily /'bɒdɪlɪ/ a físico, corporal.
● adv físicamente; ⟨in person⟩ en
persona

body /'bɒdɪ/ n cuerpo m. **~guard**
/'bɒdɪgɑːd/ n guardaespaldas m
invar. **~work** n carrocería f

boffin /'bɒfɪn/ n ⟨sl⟩ científico m

bog /bɒg/ n ciénaga f. ● vt ⟨pt
bogged⟩. **get ~ged down**
empantanarse

bogey /'bəʊgɪ/ n duende m; ⟨nuis-
ance⟩ pesadilla f

boggle /'bɒgl/ vi sobresaltarse. **the
mind ~s** ¡no es posible!

bogus /'bəʊgəs/ a falso

bogy /'bəʊgɪ/ n duende m; ⟨nuis-
ance⟩ pesadilla f

boil[1] /bɔɪl/ vt/i hervir. **be ~ing hot**
estar ardiendo; ⟨weather⟩ hacer
mucho calor. **~ away** evaporarse.
~ down to reducirse a. **~ over**
rebosar

boil[2] /bɔɪl/ n furúnculo m

boiled /'bɔɪld/ a hervido; ⟨egg⟩ pasado por agua

boiler /'bɔɪlə(r)/ n caldera f. **~ suit** n
mono m

boisterous /'bɔɪstərəs/ a ruidoso,
bullicioso

bold /bəʊld/ a (-er, -est) audaz.
~ness n audacia f

Bolivia /bə'lɪvɪə/ n Bolivia f. **~n** a &
n boliviano (m)

bollard /'bɒləd/ n ⟨naut⟩ noray m;
⟨Brit, auto⟩ poste m

bolster /'bəʊlstə(r)/ n cabezal m.
● vt. **~ up** sostener

bolt /bəʊlt/ n cerrojo m; ⟨for nut⟩
perno m; ⟨lightning⟩ rayo m; ⟨leap⟩
fuga f. ● vt echar el cerrojo a ⟨door⟩;
engullir ⟨food⟩. ● vi fugarse. ● adv.
~ upright rígido

bomb /bɒm/ n bomba f. ● vt bombardear. **~ard** /bɒm'bɑːd/ vt
bombardear

bombastic /bɒm'bæstɪk/ a ampuloso

bomb: **~er** /'bɒmə(r)/ n bom-
bardero m. **~ing** n bombardeo m.
~shell n bomba f

bonanza /bə'nænzə/ n bonanza f

bond /bɒnd/ n ⟨agreement⟩ obligación f; ⟨link⟩ lazo m; ⟨com⟩ bono m

bondage /'bɒndɪdʒ/ n esclavitud f

bone /bəʊn/ n hueso m; (of fish) espina f. ● vt deshuesar. ~-dry a completamente seco. ~ idle a holgazán

bonfire /'bɒnfaɪə(r)/ n hoguera f

bonnet /'bɒnɪt/ n gorra f; (auto) capó m, tapa f del motor (Mex)

bonny /'bɒnɪ/ a (-ier, -iest) bonito

bonus /'bəʊnəs/ n prima f; (fig) plus m

bony /'bəʊnɪ/ a (-ier, -iest) huesudo; ⟨fish⟩ lleno de espinas

boo /buː/ int ¡bu! ● vt/i abuchear

boob /buːb/ n (mistake, sl) metedura f de pata. ● vi (sl) meter la pata

booby /'buːbɪ/ n bobo m. ~ trap trampa f; (mil) trampa f explosiva

book /bʊk/ n libro m; (of cheques etc) talonario m; (notebook) libreta f; (exercise book) cuaderno m; (pl, com) cuentas fpl. ● vt (enter) registrar; (reserve) reservar. ● vi reservar. ~able a que se puede reservar. ~case /'bʊkkeɪs/ n estantería f, librería f. ~ing-office (in theatre) taquilla f; (rail) despacho m de billetes. ~let /'bʊklɪt/ n folleto m

bookkeeping /'bʊkkiːpɪŋ/ n contabilidad f

bookmaker /'bʊkmeɪkə(r)/ n corredor m de apuestas

book: ~mark /'bʊkmɑː(r)k/ n señal f. ~seller /'bʊksələ(r)/ n librero m. ~shop /'bʊkʃɒp/ n librería f. ~stall /'bʊkstɔːl/ n quiosco m de libros. ~worm /'bʊkwɜːm/ n (fig) ratón m de biblioteca

boom /buːm/ vi retumbar; (fig) prosperar. ● n estampido m; (com) auge m

boon /buːn/ n beneficio m

boor /bʊə(r)/ n patán m. ~ish a grosero

boost /buːst/ vt estimular; reforzar ⟨morale⟩; aumentar ⟨price⟩; (publicize) hacer publicidad por. ● n empuje m. ~er n (med) revacunación f

boot /buːt/ n bota f; (auto) maletero m, baúl m (LAm). get the ~ (sl) ser despedido

booth /buːð/ n cabina f; (at fair) puesto m

booty /'buːtɪ/ n botín m

booze /buːz/ vi (fam) beber mucho. ● n (fam) alcohol m; (spree) borrachera f

border /'bɔːdə(r)/ n borde m; (frontier) frontera f; (in garden) arriate m. ● vi. ~ on lindar con

borderline /'bɔːdəlaɪn/ n línea f divisoria. ~ case n caso m dudoso

bore[1] /bɔː(r)/ vt (tec) taladrar. ● vi taladrar

bore[2] /bɔː(r)/ vt (annoy) aburrir. ● n (person) pelmazo m; (thing) lata f

bore[3] /bɔː(r)/ see **bear**[1]

boredom /'bɔːdəm/ n aburrimiento m

boring /'bɔːrɪŋ/ a aburrido, pesado

born /bɔːn/ a nato. be ~ nacer

borne /bɔːn/ see **bear**[1]

borough /'bʌrə/ n municipio m

borrow /'bɒrəʊ/ vt pedir prestado

Borstal /'bɔːstl/ n reformatorio m

bosh /bɒʃ/ int & n (sl) tonterías (fpl)

bosom /'bʊzəm/ n seno m. ~ friend n amigo m íntimo

boss /bɒs/ n (fam) jefe m. ● vt. ~ (about) (fam) dar órdenes a. ~y /'bɒsɪ/ a mandón

botan|ical /bə'tænɪkl/ a botánico. ~ist /'bɒtənɪst/ n botánico m. ~y /'bɒtənɪ/ n botánica f

botch /bɒtʃ/ vt chapucear. ● n chapuza f

both /bəʊθ/ a & pron ambos (mpl), los dos (mpl). ● adv al mismo tiempo, a la vez

bother /'bɒðə(r)/ vt molestar; (worry) preocupar. ~ it! int ¡caramba! ● vi molestarse. ~ about preocuparse de. ~ doing tenerse la molestia de hacer. ● n molestia f

bottle /'bɒtl/ n botella f; (for baby) biberón m. ● vt embotellar. ~ up (fig) reprimir. ~neck /'bɒtlnek/ n (traffic jam) embotellamiento m. ~opener n destapaoor m, abrebotellas m invar; (corkscrew) sacacorchos m invar

bottom /'bɒtəm/ n fondo m; (of hill) pie m; (buttocks) trasero m. ● a último, inferior. ~less a sin fondo

bough /baʊ/ n rama f

bought /bɔːt/ see **buy**

boulder /'bəʊldə(r)/ n canto m

boulevard /'buːləvɑːd/ n bulevar m

bounc|e /baʊns/ vt hacer rebotar. ● vi rebotar; (person) saltar; ⟨cheque, sl⟩ ser rechazado. ● n rebote m. ~ing /'baʊnsɪŋ/ a robusto

bound[1] /baʊnd/ vi saltar. ● n salto m

bound[2] /baʊnd/ n. out of ~s zona f prohibida

bound³ /baʊnd/ a. be ∼ for dirigirse a

bound⁴ /baʊnd/ see **bind**. ∼ **to** obligado a; (certain) seguro de

boundary /'baʊndərɪ/ n límite m

boundless /'baʊndləs/ a ilimitado

bountiful /'baʊntɪfl/ a abundante

bouquet /bʊ'keɪ/ n ramo m; (perfume) aroma m; (of wine) buqué m, nariz f

bout /baʊt/ n período m; (med) ataque m; (sport) encuentro m

bow¹ /bəʊ/ n (weapon, mus) arco m; (knot) lazo m

bow² /baʊ/ n reverencia f. ● vi inclinarse. ● vt inclinar

bow³ /baʊ/ n (naut) proa f

bowels /'baʊəlz/ npl intestinos mpl; (fig) entrañas fpl

bowl¹ /bəʊl/ n cuenco m; (for washing) palangana f; (of pipe) cazoleta f

bowl² /bəʊl/ n (ball) bola f. ● vt (cricket) arrojar. ● vi (cricket) arrojar la pelota. ∼ **over** derribar

bow-legged /bəʊ'legɪd/ a estevado

bowler¹ /'bəʊlə(r)/ n (cricket) lanzador m

bowler² /'bəʊlə(r)/ n. ∼ **(hat)** hongo m, bombín m

bowling /'bəʊlɪŋ/ n bolos mpl

bow-tie /bəʊ'taɪ/ n corbata f de lazo, pajarita f

box¹ /bɒks/ n caja f; (for jewels etc) estuche m; (in theatre) palco m

box² /bɒks/ vt boxear contra. ∼ **s.o.'s ears** dar una manotada a uno. ● vi boxear. ∼**er** n boxeador m. ∼**ing** n boxeo m

box: B∼**ing Day** n el 26 de diciembre. ∼**-office** n taquilla f. ∼**-room** n trastero m

boy /bɔɪ/ n chico m, muchacho m; (young) niño m

boycott /'bɔɪkɒt/ vt boicotear. ● n boicoteo m

boy: ∼**friend** n novio m. ∼**hood** n niñez f. ∼**ish** a de muchacho; (childish) infantil

bra /brɑː/ n sostén m, sujetador m

brace /breɪs/ n abrazadera f; (dental) aparato m. ● vt asegurar. ∼ **o.s.** prepararse. ∼**s** npl tirantes mpl

bracelet /'breɪslɪt/ n pulsera f

bracing /'breɪsɪŋ/ a vigorizante

bracken /'brækən/ n helecho m

bracket /'brækɪt/ n soporte m; (group) categoría f; (typ) paréntesis m invar. **square** ∼**s** corchetes mpl.

● vt poner entre paréntesis; (join together) agrupar

brag /bræg/ vi (pt bragged) jactarse (**about** de)

braid /breɪd/ n galón m; (of hair) trenza f

brain /breɪn/ n cerebro m. ● vt romper la cabeza

brain-child /'breɪntʃaɪld/ n invento m

brain: ∼ **drain** (fam) fuga f de cerebros. ∼**less** a estúpido. ∼**s** npl (fig) inteligencia f

brainstorm /'breɪnstɔːm/ n ataque m de locura; (Amer, brainwave) idea f genial

brainwash /'breɪnwɒʃ/ vt lavar el cerebro

brainwave /'breɪnweɪv/ n idea f genial

brainy /'breɪnɪ/ a (-ier, -iest) inteligente

braise /breɪz/ vt cocer a fuego lento

brake /breɪk/ n freno m. **disc** ∼ freno de disco. **hand** ∼ freno de mano. ● vt/i frenar. ∼ **fluid** n líquido m de freno. ∼ **lining** n forro m del freno. ∼ **shoe** n zapata f del freno

bramble /'bræmbl/ n zarza f

bran /bræn/ n salvado m

branch /brɑːntʃ/ n rama f; (of road) bifurcación f; (com) sucursal m; (fig) ramo m. ● vi. ∼ **off** bifurcarse. ∼ **out** ramificarse

brand /brænd/ n marca f; (iron) hierro m. ● vt marcar; (reputation) tildar de

brandish /'brændɪʃ/ vt blandir

brand-new /brænd'njuː/ a flamante

brandy /'brændɪ/ n coñac m

brash /bræʃ/ a descarado

brass /brɑːs/ n latón m. **get down to** ∼ **tacks** (fig) ir al grano. **top** ∼ (sl) peces mpl gordos. ∼**y** a (-ier, -iest) descarado

brassière /'bræsjeə(r)/ n sostén m, sujetador m

brat /bræt/ n (pej) mocoso m

bravado /brə'vɑːdəʊ/ n bravata f

brave /breɪv/ a (-er, -est) valiente. ● n (Red Indian) guerrero m indio. ● vt afrontar. ∼**ry** /-ərɪ/ n valentía f, valor m

brawl /brɔːl/ n alboroto m. ● vi pelearse

brawn /brɔːn/ n músculo m; (strength) fuerza f muscular. ∼**y** a musculoso

bray /breɪ/ n rebuzno m. ● vi rebuznar

brazen /'breɪzn/ a descarado

brazier /'breɪzɪə(r)/ n brasero m

Brazil /brə'zɪl/ n el Brasil m. ~ian a & n brasileño (m)

breach /briːtʃ/ n violación f; (of contract) incumplimiento m; (gap) brecha f. ● vt abrir una brecha en

bread /bred/ n pan m. loaf of ~ pan. ~crumbs /'bredkrʌmz/ npl migajas fpl; (culin) pan rallado. ~line n. on the ~line en la miseria

breadth /bredθ/ n anchura f

bread-winner /'bredwɪnə(r)/ n sostén m de la familia, cabeza f de familia

break /breɪk/ vt (pt **broke**, pp **broken**) romper; quebrantar ⟨law⟩; batir ⟨record⟩; comunicar ⟨news⟩; interrumpir ⟨journey⟩. ● vi romperse; ⟨news⟩ divulgarse. ● n ruptura f; (interval) intervalo m; (chance, fam) oportunidad f; (in weather) cambio m. ~ away escapar. ~ down vt derribar; analizar ⟨figures⟩. ● vi estropearse; (auto) averiarse; (med) sufrir un colapso; (cry) deshacerse en lágrimas. ~ into forzar ⟨house etc⟩; (start doing) ponerse a. ~ off interrumpirse. ~ out ⟨war, disease⟩ estallar; (run away) escaparse. ~ up romperse; ⟨schools⟩ terminar. ~able a frágil. ~age n rotura f

breakdown /'breɪkdaʊn/ n (tec) falla f; (med) colapso m, crisis f nerviosa; (of figures) análisis f

breaker /'breɪkə(r)/ n (wave) cachón m

breakfast /'brekfəst/ n desayuno m

breakthrough /'breɪkθruː/ n adelanto m

breakwater /'breɪkwɔːtə(r)/ n rompeolas m invar

breast /brest/ n pecho m; (of chicken etc) pechuga f. ~-stroke n braza f de pecho

breath /breθ/ n aliento m, respiración f. out of ~ sin aliento. under one's ~ a media voz. ~alyser /'breθəlaɪzə(r)/ n alcoholímetro m

breathe /briːð/ vt/i respirar. ~er /'briːðə(r)/ n descanso m, pausa f. ~ing n respiración f

breathtaking /'breθteɪkɪŋ/ a impresionante

bred /bred/ see **breed**

breeches /'brɪtʃɪz/ npl calzones mpl

breed /briːd/ vt/i (pt **bred**) reproducirse; (fig) engendrar. ● n raza f. ~er n criador m. ~ing n cría f; (manners) educación f

breez|e /briːz/ n brisa f. ~y a de mucho viento; (person) despreocupado. **it is ~y** hace viento

Breton /'bretn/ a & n bretón (m)

brew /bruː/ vt hacer. ● vi fermentar; ⟨tea⟩ reposar; (fig) prepararse. ● n infusión f. ~er n cervecero m. ~ery n fábrica f de cerveza, cervecería f

bribe /braɪb/ n soborno m. ● vt sobornar. ~ry /-ərɪ/ n soborno m

brick /brɪk/ n ladrillo m. ● vt. ~ up tapar con ladrillos. ~layer /'brɪkleɪə(r)/ n albañil m

bridal /'braɪdl/ a nupcial

bride /braɪd/ n novia f. ~groom /'braɪdgrʊm/ n novio m. ~smaid /'braɪdzmeɪd/ n dama f de honor

bridge[1] /brɪdʒ/ n puente m; (of nose) caballete m. ● vt tender un puente sobre. ~ **a gap** llenar un vacío

bridge[2] /brɪdʒ/ n (cards) bridge m

bridle /'braɪdl/ n brida f. ● vt embridar. ~-path n camino m de herradura

brief /briːf/ a (-er, -est) breve. ● n (jurid) escrito m. ● vt dar instrucciones a. ~case /'briːfkeɪs/ n maletín m. ~ly adv brevemente. ~s npl (man's) calzoncillos mpl; (woman's) bragas fpl

brigad|e /brɪ'geɪd/ n brigada f. ~ier /-ə'dɪə(r)/ n general m de brigada

bright /braɪt/ a (-er, -est) brillante, claro; (clever) listo; (cheerful) alegre. ~en /'braɪtn/ vt aclarar; hacer más alegre ⟨house etc⟩. ● vi ⟨weather⟩ aclararse; (face) animarse. ~ly adv brillantemente. ~ness n claridad f

brillian|ce /'brɪljəns/ n brillantez f, brillo m. ~t a brillante

brim /brɪm/ n borde m; (of hat) ala f. ● vi (pt **brimmed**). ~ **over** desbordar

brine /braɪn/ n salmuera f

bring /brɪŋ/ vt (pt **brought**) traer ⟨thing⟩; conducir ⟨person, vehicle⟩. ~ **about** causar. ~ **back** devolver. ~ **down** derribar; rebajar ⟨price⟩. ~ **off** lograr. ~ **on** causar. ~ **out** sacar; lanzar ⟨product⟩; publicar ⟨book⟩. ~ **round/to** hacer volver en sí ⟨unconscious person⟩. ~ **up** (med) vomitar; educar ⟨children⟩; plantear ⟨question⟩

brink /brɪŋk/ n borde m

brisk /brɪsk/ a (-er, -est) enérgico, vivo. **~ness** n energía f

bristl|e /'brɪsl/ n cerda f. ● vi erizarse. **~ing with** erizado de

Brit|ain /'brɪtən/ n Gran Bretaña f. **~ish** /'brɪtɪʃ/ a británico. **the ~ish** los británicos. **~on** /'brɪtən/ n británico m

Brittany /'brɪtənɪ/ n Bretaña f

brittle /'brɪtl/ a frágil, quebradizo

broach /brəʊtʃ/ vt abordar ‹subject›; espitar ‹cask›

broad /brɔːd/ a (-er, -est) ancho. **in ~ daylight** en pleno día. **~ bean** n haba f

broadcast /'brɔːdkɑːst/ n emisión f. ● vt (pt broadcast) emitir. ● vi hablar por la radio. **~ing** a de radio-difusión. ● n radio-difusión f

broad: **~en** /'brɔːdn/ vt ensanchar. ● vi ensancharse. **~ly** adv en general. **~-minded** a de miras amplias, tolerante, liberal

brocade /brə'keɪd/ n brocado m

broccoli /'brɒkəlɪ/ n invar brécol m

brochure /'brəʊʃə(r)/ n folleto m

brogue /brəʊg/ n abarca f; (accent) acento m regional

broke /brəʊk/ see **break**. ● a (sl) sin blanca

broken /'brəʊkən/ see **break**. ● a. **~ English** inglés m chapurreado. **~-hearted** a con el corazón destrozado

broker /'brəʊkə(r)/ n corredor m

brolly /'brɒlɪ/ n (fam) paraguas m invar

bronchitis /brɒŋ'kaɪtɪs/ n bronquitis f

bronze /brɒnz/ n bronce m. ● vt broncear. ● vi broncearse

brooch /brəʊtʃ/ n broche m

brood /bruːd/ n cría f; (joc) prole m. ● vi empollar; (fig) meditar. **~y** a contemplativo

brook[1] /brʊk/ n arroyo m

brook[2] /brʊk/ vt soportar

broom /bruːm/ n hiniesta f; (brush) escoba f. **~stick** /'bruːmstɪk/ n palo m de escoba

broth /brɒθ/ n caldo m

brothel /'brɒθl/ n burdel m

brother /'brʌðə(r)/ n hermano m. **~hood** n fraternidad f, (relig) hermandad f. **~-in-law** n cuñado m. **~ly** a fraternal

brought /brɔːt/ see **bring**

brow /braʊ/ n frente f; (of hill) cima f

browbeat /'braʊbiːt/ vt (pt -beat, pp -beaten) intimidar

brown /braʊn/ a (-er, -est) marrón; ‹skin› moreno; ‹hair› castaño. ● n marrón m. ● vt poner moreno; (culin) dorar. ● vi ponerse moreno; (culin) dorarse. **be ~ed off** (sl) estar hasta la coronilla

Brownie /'braʊnɪ/ n niña f exploradora

browse /braʊz/ vi (in a shop) curiosear; ‹animal› pacer

bruise /bruːz/ n magulladura f. ● vt magullar; machucar ‹fruit›. ● vi magullarse; ‹fruit› machacarse

brunch /brʌntʃ/ n (fam) desayuno m tardío

brunette /bruː'net/ n morena f

brunt /brʌnt/ n. **the ~ of** lo más fuerte de

brush /brʌʃ/ n cepillo m; (large) escoba f, (for decorating) brocha f; ‹artist's› pincel; (skirmish) escaramuza f. ● vt cepillar. **~ against** rozar. **~ aside** rechazar. **~ off** (rebuff) desairar. **~ up (on)** refrescar

brusque /bruːsk/ a brusco. **~ly** adv bruscamente

Brussels /'brʌslz/ n Bruselas f. **~ sprout** col m de Bruselas

brutal /'bruːtl/ a brutal. **~ity** /-'tælətɪ/ n brutalidad f

brute /bruːt/ n bestia f. **~ force** fuerza f bruta

BSc abbr see **bachelor**

bubble /'bʌbl/ n burbuja f. ● vi burbujear. **~ over** desbordarse

bubbly /'bʌblɪ/ a burbujeante. ● n (fam) champaña m, champán m (fam)

buck[1] /bʌk/ a macho. ● n (deer) ciervo m. ● vi (of horse) corcovear. **~ up** (hurry, sl) darse prisa; (cheer up, sl) animarse

buck[2] /bʌk/ (Amer, sl) dólar m

buck[3] /bʌk/ n. **pass the ~ to** s.o. echarle a uno el muerto

bucket /'bʌkɪt/ n cubo m

buckle /'bʌkl/ n hebilla f. ● vt abrochar. ● vi torcerse. **~ down to** dedicarse con empeño a

bud /bʌd/ n brote m. ● vi (pt budded) brotar

Buddhis|m /'bʊdɪzəm/ n budismo m. **~t** /'bʊdɪst/ a & n budista (m & f)

budding /'bʌdɪŋ/ a (fig) en ciernes

buddy /'bʌdɪ/ n (fam) compañero m, amigote m (fam)

budge /bʌdʒ/ vt mover. ● vi moverse

budgerigar /'bʌdʒərɪgɑː(r)/ n periquito m

budget /'bʌdʒɪt/ n presupuesto m. ● vi (pt **budgeted**) presupuestar

buff /bʌf/ n (colour) color m de ante; (fam) aficionado m. ● vt pulir

buffalo /'bʌfələʊ/ n (pl **-oes** or **-o**) búfalo m

buffer /'bʌfə(r)/ n parachoques m invar. ~ **state** n estado m tapón

buffet /'bʊfeɪ/ n (meal, counter) bufé m. /'bʌfɪt/ n golpe m; (slap) bofetada f. ● vt (pt **buffeted**) golpear

buffoon /bə'fuːn/ n payaso m, bufón m

bug /bʌg/ n bicho m; (germ, sl) microbio m; (device, sl) micrófono m oculto. ● vt (pt **bugged**) ocultar un micrófono en; intervenir ‹telephone›; (Amer, sl) molestar

bugbear /'bʌgbeə(r)/ n pesadilla f

buggy /'bʌgɪ/ n. **baby** ~ (esp Amer) cochecito m de niño

bugle /'bjuːgl/ n corneta f

build /bɪld/ vt/i (pt **built**) construir. ~ **up** vt urbanizar; (increase) aumentar. ● n (of person) figura f, tipo m. ~**er** n constructor m. ~**up** n aumento m; (of gas etc) acumulación f; (fig) propaganda f

built /bɪlt/ see **build**. ~**in** a empotrado. ~**up area** n zona f urbanizada

bulb /bʌlb/ n bulbo m; (elec) bombilla f. ~**ous** a bulboso

Bulgaria /bʌl'geərɪə/ n Bulgaria f. ~**n** a & n búlgaro (m)

bulge /bʌldʒ/ n protuberancia f. ● vi pandearse; (jut out) sobresalir. ~**ing** a abultado; ‹eyes› saltón

bulk /bʌlk/ n bulto m, volumen m. in ~ a granel; (loose) suelto. the ~ of la mayor parte de. ~**y** a voluminoso

bull /bʊl/ n toro m

bulldog /'bʊldɒg/ n buldog m

bulldozer /'bʊldəʊzə(r)/ n oruga f aplanadora, bulldozer m

bullet /'bʊlɪt/ n bala f

bulletin /'bʊlɪtɪn/ n anuncio m; (journal) boletín m

bullet-proof /'bʊlɪtpruːf/ a a prueba de balas

bullfight /'bʊlfaɪt/ n corrida f (de toros). ~**er** n torero m

bullion /'bʊljən/ n (gold) oro m en barras; (silver) plata f en barras

bull: ~**ring** /'bʊlrɪŋ/ n plaza f de toros. ~**'s-eye** n centro m del blanco, diana f

bully /'bʊlɪ/ n matón m. ● vt intimidar. ~**ing** n intimidación f

bum[1] /bʌm/ n (bottom, sl) trasero m

bum[2] /bʌm/ n (Amer, sl) holgazán m

bumble-bee /'bʌmblbiː/ n abejorro m

bump /bʌmp/ vt chocar contra. ● vi dar sacudidas. ● n choque m; (swelling) chichón m. ~ **into** chocar contra; (meet) encontrar

bumper ·/'bʌmpə(r)/ n parachoques m invar. ● a abundante. ~ **edition** n edición f especial

bumpkin /'bʌmpkɪn/ n patán m, paleto m (fam)

bumptious /'bʌmpʃəs/ a presuntuoso

bun /bʌn/ n bollo m; (hair) moño m

bunch /bʌntʃ/ n manojo m; (of people) grupo m; (of bananas, grapes) racimo m, (of flowers) ramo m

bundle /'bʌndl/ n bulto m; (of papers) legajo m; (of nerves) manojo m. ● vt. ~ **up** atar

bung /bʌŋ/ n tapón m. ● vt tapar; (sl) tirar

bungalow /'bʌŋgələʊ/ n casa f de un solo piso, chalé m, bungalow m

bungle /'bʌŋgl/ vt chapucear

bunion /'bʌnjən/ n juanete m

bunk /bʌŋk/ n litera f

bunker /'bʌŋkə(r)/ n carbonera f; (golf) obstáculo m; (mil) refugio m, búnker m

bunkum /'bʌŋkəm/ n tonterías fpl

bunny /'bʌnɪ/ n conejito m

buoy /bɔɪ/ n boya f. ● vt. ~ **up** hacer flotar; (fig) animar

buoyan|**cy** /'bɔɪənsɪ/ n flotabilidad f; (fig) optimismo m. ~**t** /'bɔɪənt/ a boyante; (fig) alegre

burden /'bɜːdn/ n carga f. ● vt cargar (**with** de). ~**some** a pesado

bureau /'bjʊərəʊ/ n (pl **-eaux** /-əʊz/) escritorio m; (office) oficina f

bureaucra|**cy** /bjʊə'rɒkrəsɪ/ n burocracia f. ~**t** /'bjʊərəkræt/ n burócrata m & f. ~**tic** /-'krætɪk/ a burocrático

burgeon /'bɜːdʒən/ vi brotar; (fig) crecer

burgl|**ar** /'bɜːglə(r)/ n ladrón m. ~**ary** n robo m con allanamiento de morada. **~e** /'bɜːgl/ vt robar con allanamiento

Burgundy /'bɜːgəndɪ/ n Borgoña f; (wine) vino m de Borgoña

burial /'berɪəl/ n entierro m

burlesque /bɜːˈlesk/ n burlesco m

burly /'bɜːlɪ/ a (-ier, -iest) corpulento

Burm|a /'bɜːmə/ Birmania f. **~ese** /-'miːz/ a & n birmano (m)

burn /bɜːn/ vt (pt burned or burnt) quemar. ● vi quemarse. **~ down** vt destruir con fuego. ● n quemadura f. **~er** n quemador m. **~ing** a ardiente; (food) que quema; (question) candente

burnish /'bɜːnɪʃ/ vt lustrar, pulir

burnt /bɜːnt/ see **burn**

burp /bɜːp/ n (fam) eructo m. ● vi (fam) eructar

burr /bɜː(r)/ n (bot) erizo m

burrow /'bʌrəʊ/ n madriguera f. ● vt excavar

bursar /'bɜːsə(r)/ n tesorero m. **~y** /'bɜːsərɪ/ n beca f

burst /bɜːst/ vt (pt burst) reventar. ● vi reventarse; (tyre) pincharse. ● n reventón m; (mil) ráfaga f; (fig) explosión f. **~ of laughter** carcajada f

bury /'berɪ/ vt enterrar; (hide) ocultar

bus /bʌs/ n (pl buses) autobús m, camión m (Mex). ● vi (pt bussed) ir en autobús

bush /bʊʃ/ n arbusto m; (land) monte m. **~y** a espeso

busily /'bɪzɪlɪ/ adv afanosamente

business /'bɪznɪs/ n negocio m; (com) negocios mpl; (profession) ocupación f; (fig) asunto m. **mind one's own ~** ocuparse de sus propios asuntos. **~like** a práctico, serio. **~man** n hombre m de negocios

busker /'bʌskə(r)/ n músico m ambulante

bus-stop /'bʌsstɒp/ n parada f de autobús

bust[1] /bʌst/ n busto m; (chest) pecho m

bust[2] /bʌst/ vt (pt busted or bust) (sl) romper. ● vi romperse. ● a roto. **go ~** (sl) quebrar

bustle /'bʌsl/ vi apresurarse. ● n bullicio m

bust-up /'bʌstʌp/ n (sl) riña f

busy /'bɪzɪ/ a (-ier, -iest) ocupado; (street) concurrido. ● vt. **~ o.s. with** ocuparse de

busybody /'bɪzɪbɒdɪ/ n entrometido m

but /bʌt/ conj pero; (after negative) sino. ● prep menos. **~ for** si no fuera por. **last ~ one** penúltimo. ● adv solamente

butane /'bjuːteɪn/ n butano m

butcher /'bʊtʃə(r)/ n carnicero m. ● vt matar; (fig) hacer una carnicería con. **~y** n carnicería f, matanza f

butler /'bʌtlə(r)/ n mayordomo m

butt /bʌt/ n (of gun) culata f; (of cigarette) colilla f; (target) blanco m. ● vi topar. **~ in** interrumpir

butter /'bʌtə(r)/ n mantequilla f. ● vt untar con mantequilla. **~ up** vt (fam) lisonjear, dar jabón a. **~bean** n judía f

buttercup /'bʌtəkʌp/ n ranúnculo m

butter-fingers /'bʌtəfɪŋgəz/ n manazas m invar, torpe m

butterfly /'bʌtəflaɪ/ n mariposa f

buttock /'bʌtək/ n nalga f

button /'bʌtn/ n botón m. ● vt abotonar. ● vi abotonarse. **~hole** /'bʌtnhəʊl/ n ojal m. ● vt (fig) detener

buttress /'bʌtrɪs/ n contrafuerte m. ● vt apoyar

buxom /'bʌksəm/ a (woman) rollizo

buy /baɪ/ vt (pt bought) comprar. ● n compra f. **~er** n comprador m

buzz /bʌz/ n zumbido m; (phone call, fam) llamada f. ● vi zumbar. **~ off** (sl) largarse. **~er** n timbre m

by /baɪ/ prep por; (near) cerca de; (before) antes de; (according to) según. **~ and large** en conjunto, en general. **~ car** en coche. **~ oneself** por sí solo

bye-bye /'baɪbaɪ/ int (fam) ¡adiós!

by-election /'baɪɪlekʃn/ n elección f parcial

bygone /'baɪgɒn/ a pasado

by-law /'baɪlɔː/ n reglamento m (local)

bypass /'baɪpaːs/ n carretera f de circunvalación. ● vt evitar

by-product /'baɪprɒdʌkt/ n subproducto m

bystander /'baɪstændə(r)/ n espectador m

byword /'baɪwɜːd/ n sinónimo m. **be a ~ for** ser conocido por

C

cab /kæb/ *n* taxi *m*; (*of lorry, train*) cabina *f*

cabaret /'kæbəreɪ/ *n* espectáculo *m*

cabbage /'kæbɪdʒ/ *n* col *m*, repollo *m*

cabin /'kæbɪn/ *n* cabaña *f*; (*in ship*) camarote *m*; (*in plane*) cabina *f*

cabinet /'kæbɪnɪt/ *n* (*cupboard*) armario *m*; (*for display*) vitrina *f*. **C~** (*pol*) gabinete *m*. **~maker** *n* ebanista *m & f*

cable /'keɪbl/ *n* cable *m*. ● *vt* cablegrafiar. **~ railway** *n* funicular *m*

cache /kæʃ/ *n* (*place*) escondrijo *m*; (*things*) reservas *fpl* escondidas. ● *vt* ocultar

cackle /'kækl/ *n* (*of hen*) cacareo *m*; (*laugh*) risotada *f*. ● *vi* cacarear; (*laugh*) reírse a carcajadas

cacophon|ous /kə'kɒfənəs/ *a* cacofónico. **~y** *n* cacofonía *f*

cactus /'kæktəs/ *n* (*pl* **-ti** /-taɪ/) cacto *m*

cad /kæd/ *n* sinvergüenza *m*. **~dish** *a* desvergonzado

caddie /'kædɪ/ *n* (*golf*) portador *m* de palos

caddy /'kædɪ/ *n* cajita *f*

cadence /'keɪdəns/ *n* cadencia *f*

cadet /kə'det/ *n* cadete *m*

cadge /kædʒ/ *vt/i* gorronear. **~r** /-ə(r)/ *n* gorrón *m*

Caesarean /sɪ'zeərɪən/ *a* cesáreo. **~ section** *n* cesárea *f*

café /'kæfeɪ/ *n* cafetería *f*

cafeteria /kæfɪ'tɪərɪə/ *n* autoservicio *m*

caffeine /'kæfiːn/ *n* cafeína *f*

cage /keɪdʒ/ *n* jaula *f*. ● *vt* enjaular

cagey /'keɪdʒɪ/ *a* (*fam*) evasivo

Cairo /'kaɪərəʊ/ *n* el Cairo *m*

cajole /kə'dʒəʊl/ *vt* engatusar. **~ry** *n* engatusamiento *m*

cake /keɪk/ *n* pastel *m*, tarta *f*; (*sponge*) bizcocho *m*. **~ of soap** pastilla *f* de jabón. **~d** *a* incrustado

calamit|ous /kə'læmɪtəs/ *a* desastroso. **~y** /kə'læmətɪ/ *n* calamidad *f*

calcium /'kælsɪəm/ *n* calcio *m*

calculat|e /'kælkjʊleɪt/ *vt/i* calcular; (*Amer*) suponer. **~ing** *a* calculador. **~ion** /-'leɪʃn/ *n* cálculo *m*. **~or** *n* calculadora *f*

calculus /'kælkjʊləs/ *n* (*pl* **-li**) cálculo *m*

calendar /'kælɪndə(r)/ *n* calendario *m*

calf[1] /kɑːf/ *n* (*pl* **calves**) ternero *m*

calf[2] /kɑːf/ *n* (*pl* **calves**) (*of leg*) pantorrilla *f*

calibre /'kælɪbə(r)/ *n* calibre *m*

calico /'kælɪkəʊ/ *n* calicó *m*

call /kɔːl/ *vt/i* llamar. ● *n* llamada *f*; (*shout*) grito *m*; (*visit*) visita *f*. **be on ~** estar de guardia. **long distance ~** conferencia *f*. **~ back** *vt* hacer volver; (*on phone*) volver a llamar. ● *vi* volver; (*on phone*) volver a llamar. **~ for** pedir; (*fetch*) ir a buscar. **~ off** cancelar. **~ on** visitar. **~ out** dar voces. **~ together** convocar. **~ up** (*mil*) llamar al servicio militar; (*phone*) llamar. **~box** *n* cabina *f* telefónica. **~er** *n* visita *f*; (*phone*) el que llama *m*. **~ing** *n* vocación *f*

callous /'kæləs/ *a* insensible, cruel. **~ness** *n* crueldad *f*

callow /'kæləʊ/ *a* (**-er, -est**) inexperto

calm /kɑːm/ *a* (**-er, -est**) tranquilo; (*weather*) calmoso. ● *n* tranquilidad *f*, calma *f*. ● *vt* calmar. ● *vi* calmarse. **~ness** *n* tranquilidad *f*, calma *f*

calorie /'kælərɪ/ *n* caloría *f*

camber /'kæmbə(r)/ *n* curvatura *f*

came /keɪm/ *see* **come**

camel /'kæml/ *n* camello *m*

camellia /kə'miːljə/ *n* camelia *f*

cameo /'kæmɪəʊ/ *n* (*pl* **-os**) camafeo *m*

camera /'kæmərə/ *n* máquina *f* (fotográfica); (*TV*) cámara *f*. **~man** *n* (*pl* **-men**) operador *m*, cámara *m*

camouflage /'kæməflɑːʒ/ *n* camuflaje *m*. ● *vt* encubrir; (*mil*) camuflar

camp[1] /kæmp/ *n* campamento *m*. ● *vi* acamparse

camp[2] /kæmp/ *a* (*affected*) amanerado

campaign /kæm'peɪn/ *n* campaña *f*. ● *vi* hacer campaña

camp: ~bed *n* catre *m* de tijera. **~er** *n* campista *m & f*; (*vehicle*) caravana *f*. **~ing** *n* camping *m*. **go ~ing** hacer camping. **~site** /'kæmpsaɪt/ *n* camping *m*

campus /'kæmpəs/ *n* (*pl* **-puses**) ciudad *f* universitaria

can[1] /kæn/ *v aux* (*pt* **could**) (*be able to*) poder; (*know how to*) saber. **~not** (*neg*), **~'t** (*neg, fam*). **I ~not/ ~'t go** no puedo ir

can² /kæn/ *n* lata *f*. ● *vt* (*pt* **canned**) enlatar. **∼ned music** música *f* grabada

Canad|a /'kænədə/ *n* el Canadá *m*. **∼ian** /kə'neɪdɪən/ *a & n* canadiense (*m & f*)

canal /kə'næl/ *n* canal *m*

canary /kə'neərɪ/ *n* canario *m*

cancel /'kænsl/ *vt/i* (*pt* **cancelled**) anular; cancelar ⟨*contract etc*⟩; suspender ⟨*appointment etc*⟩; (*delete*) tachar. **∼lation** /-'leɪʃn/ *n* cancelación *f*

cancer /'kænsə(r)/ *n* cáncer *m*. **C∼** *n* (*Astr*) Cáncer *m*. **∼ous** *a* canceroso

candid /'kændɪd/ *a* franco

candida|cy /'kændɪdəsɪ/ *n* candidatura *f*. **∼te** /'kændɪdeɪt/ *n* candidato *m*

candle /'kændl/ *n* vela *f*. **∼stick** /'kændlstɪk/ *n* candelero *m*

candour /'kændə(r)/ *n* franqueza *f*

candy /'kændɪ/ *n* (*Amer*) caramelo *m*. **∼floss** *n* algodón *m* de azúcar

cane /keɪn/ *n* caña *f*; (*for baskets*) mimbre *m*; (*stick*) bastón *m*. ● *vt* (*strike*) castigar con palmeta

canine /'keɪnaɪn/ *a* canino

canister /'kænɪstə(r)/ *n* bote *m*

cannabis /'kænəbɪs/ *n* cáñamo *m* índico, hachís *m*, mariguana *f*

cannibal /'kænɪbl/ *n* caníbal *m*. **∼ism** *n* canibalismo *m*

cannon /'kænən/ *n invar* cañón *m*. **∼ shot** cañonazo *m*

cannot /'kænɒt/ *see* **can¹**

canny /'kænɪ/ *a* astuto

canoe /kə'nu:/ *n* canoa *f*, piragua *f*. ● *vi* ir en canoa. **∼ist** *n* piragüista *m & f*

canon /'kænən/ *n* canon *m*; (*person*) canónigo *m*. **∼ize** /'kænənaɪz/ *vt* canonizar

can-opener /'kænəʊpnə(r)/ *n* abrelatas *m invar*

canopy /'kænəpɪ/ *n* dosel *m*; (*of parachute*) casquete *m*

cant /kænt/ *n* jerga *f*

can't /kɑ:nt/ *see* **can¹**

cantankerous /kæn'tæŋkərəs/ *a* malhumorado

canteen /kæn'ti:n/ *n* cantina *f*; (*of cutlery*) juego *m*; (*flask*) cantimplora *f*

canter /'kæntə(r)/ *n* medio galope *m*. ● *vi* ir a medio galope

canvas /'kænvəs/ *n* lona *f*, (*artist's*) lienzo *m*

canvass /'kænvəs/ *vi* hacer campaña, solicitar votos. **∼ing** *n* solicitación *f* (de votos)

canyon /'kænjən/ *n* cañón *m*

cap /kæp/ *n* gorra *f*; (*lid*) tapa *f*; (*of cartridge*) cápsula *f*; (*academic*) birrete *m*; (*of pen*) capuchón *m*; (*mec*) casquete *m*. ● *vt* (*pt* **capped**) tapar, poner cápsula a; (*outdo*) superar

capab|ility /keɪpə'bɪlətɪ/ *n* capacidad *f*. **∼le** /'keɪpəbl/ *a* capaz. **∼ly** *adv* competentemente

capacity /kə'pæsətɪ/ *n* capacidad *f*; (*function*) calidad *f*

cape¹ /keɪp/ *n* (*cloak*) capa *f*

cape² /keɪp/ *n* (*geog*) cabo *m*

caper¹ /'keɪpə(r)/ *vi* brincar. ● *n* salto *m*; (*fig*) travesura *f*

caper² /'keɪpə(r)/ *n* (*culin*) alcaparra *f*

capital /'kæpɪtl/ *a* capital. **∼ letter** *n* mayúscula *f*. ● *n* (*town*) capital *f*; (*money*) capital *m*

capitalis|m /'kæpɪtəlɪzəm/ *n* capitalismo *m*. **∼t** *a & n* capitalista (*m & f*)

capitalize /'kæpɪtəlaɪz/ *vt* capitalizar; (*typ*) escribir con mayúsculas. **∼ on** aprovechar

capitulat|e /kə'pɪtʃʊleɪt/ *vi* capitular. **∼ion** /-'leɪʃn/ *n* capitulación *f*

capon /'keɪpən/ *n* capón *m*

capricious /kə'prɪʃəs/ *a* caprichoso

Capricorn /'kæprɪkɔ:n/ *n* Capricornio *m*

capsicum /'kæpsɪkəm/ *n* pimiento *m*

capsize /kæp'saɪz/ *vt* hacer zozobrar. ● *vi* zozobrar

capsule /'kæpsju:l/ *n* cápsula *f*

captain /'kæptɪn/ *n* capitán *m*. ● *vt* capitanear

caption /'kæpʃn/ *n* (*heading*) título *m*; (*of cartoon etc*) leyenda *f*

captivate /'kæptɪveɪt/ *vt* encantar

captiv|e /'kæptɪv/ *a & n* cautivo (*m*). **∼ity** /-'tɪvətɪ/ *n* cautiverio *m*, cautividad *f*

capture /'kæptʃə(r)/ *vt* prender; llamar ⟨*attention*⟩; (*mil*) tomar. ● *n* apresamiento *m*; (*mil*) toma *f*

car /kɑ:(r)/ *n* coche *m*, carro *m* (*LAm*)

carafe /kə'ræf/ *n* jarro *m*, garrafa *f*

caramel /'kærəmel/ *n* azúcar *m* quemado; (*sweet*) caramelo *m*

carat /'kærət/ *n* quilate *m*

caravan /'kærəvæn/ *n* caravana *f*

carbohydrate /kɑ:bəʊ'haɪdreɪt/ *n* hidrato *m* de carbono

carbon /'kɑːbən/ *n* carbono *m*; (*paper*) carbón *m*. ~ **copy** copia *f* al carbón

carburettor /kɑːbjʊ'retə(r)/ *n* carburador *m*

carcass /'kɑːkəs/ *n* cadáver *m*, esqueleto *m*

card /kɑːd/ *n* tarjeta *f*; (*for games*) carta *f*; (*membership*) carnet *m*; (*records*) ficha *f*

cardboard /'kɑːdbɔːd/ *n* cartón *m*

cardiac /'kɑːdiæk/ *a* cardíaco

cardigan /'kɑːdigən/ *n* chaqueta *f* de punto, rebeca *f*

cardinal /'kɑːdinəl/ *a* cardinal. ● *n* cardenal *m*

card-index /'kɑːdindeks/ *n* fichero *m*

care /keə(r)/ *n* cuidado *m*; (*worry*) preocupación *f*; (*protection*) cargo *m*. ~ **of** a cuidado de, en casa de. **take** ~ **of** cuidar de (*person*); ocuparse de (*matter*). ● *vi* interesarse. **I don't** ~ me es igual. ~ **about** interesarse por. ~ **for** cuidar de; (*like*) querer

career /kə'riə(r)/ *n* carrera *f*. ● *vi* correr a toda velocidad

carefree /'keəfriː/ *a* despreocupado

careful /'keəfʊl/ *a* cuidadoso; (*cautious*) prudente. ~**ly** *adv* con cuidado

careless /'keəlis/ *a* negligente; (*not worried*) indiferente. ~**ly** *adv* descuidadamente. ~**ness** *n* descuido *m*

caress /kə'res/ *n* caricia *f*. ● *vt* acariciar

caretaker /'keəteikə(r)/ *n* vigilante *m*; (*of flats etc*) portero *m*

car-ferry /'kɑːferi/ *n* transbordador *m* de coches

cargo /'kɑːgəʊ/ *n* (*pl* -**oes**) carga *f*

Caribbean /kærɪ'biːən/ *a* caribe. ~ **Sea** *n* mar *m* Caribe

caricature /'kærɪkətʃʊə(r)/ *n* caricatura *f*. ● *vt* caricaturizar

carnage /'kɑːnidʒ/ *n* carnicería *f*, matanza *f*

carnal /'kɑːnl/ *a* carnal

carnation /kɑː'neiʃn/ *n* clavel *m*

carnival /'kɑːnivl/ *n* carnaval *m*

carol /'kærəl/ *n* villancico *m*

carouse /kə'raʊz/ *vi* correrse una juerga

carousel /kærə'sel/ *n* tiovivo *m*

carp[1] /kɑːp/ *n* invar carpa *f*

carp[2] /kɑːp/ *vi*. ~ **at** quejarse de

car park /'kɑːpɑːk/ *n* aparcamiento *m*

carpenter /'kɑːpintə(r)/ *n* carpintero *m*. ~**ry** *n* carpintería *f*

carpet /'kɑːpit/ *n* alfombra *f*. **be on the** ~ (*fam*) recibir un rapapolvo; (*under consideration*) estar sobre el tapete. ● *vt* alfombrar. ~**-sweeper** *n* escoba *f* mecánica

carriage /'kærɪdʒ/ *n* coche *m*; (*mec*) carro *m*; (*transport*) transporte *m*; (*cost, bearing*) porte *m*

carriageway /'kærɪdʒwei/ *n* calzada *f*, carretera *f*

carrier /'kærɪə(r)/ *n* transportista *m* & *f*; (*company*) empresa *f* de transportes; (*med*) portador *m*. ~**-bag** bolsa *f*

carrot /'kærət/ *n* zanahoria *f*

carry /'kæri/ *vt* llevar; transportar (*goods*); (*involve*) llevar consigo, implicar. ● *vi* (*sounds*) llegar, oírse. ~ **off** llevarse. ~ **on** continuar; (*complain, fam*) quejarse. ~ **out** realizar; cumplir (*promise, threat*). ~**-cot** *n* capazo *m*

cart /kɑːt/ *n* carro *m*. ● *vt* acarrear; (*carry, fam*) llevar

cartilage /'kɑːtɪlɪdʒ/ *n* cartílago *m*

carton /'kɑːtən/ *n* caja *f* (de cartón)

cartoon /kɑː'tuːn/ *n* caricatura *f*, chiste *m*; (*strip*) historieta *f*; (*film*) dibujos *mpl* animados. ~**ist** *n* caricaturista *m* & *f*

cartridge /'kɑːtridʒ/ *n* cartucho *m*

carve /kɑːv/ *vt* tallar; trinchar (*meat*)

cascade /kæs'keid/ *n* cascada *f*. ● *vi* caer en cascadas

case /keis/ *n* caso *m*; (*jurid*) proceso *m*; (*crate*) cajón *m*; (*box*) caja *f*; (*suitcase*) maleta *f*. **in any** ~ en todo caso. **in** ~ **he comes** por si viene. **in** ~ **of** en caso de. **lower** ~ caja *f* baja, minúscula *f*. **upper** ~ caja *f* alta, mayúscula *f*

cash /kæʃ/ *n* dinero *m* efectivo. **pay (in)** ~ pagar al contado. ● *vt* cobrar. ~ **in (on)** aprovecharse de. ~ **desk** *n* caja *f*

cashew /'kæʃuː/ *n* anacardo *m*

cashier /kæ'ʃiə(r)/ *n* cajero *m*

cashmere /kæʃ'mɪə(r)/ *n* casimir *m*, cachemir *m*

casino /kə'siːnəʊ/ *n* (*pl* -**os**) casino *m*

cask /kɑːsk/ *n* barril *m*

casket /'kɑːskit/ *n* cajita *f*

casserole /'kæsərəʊl/ *n* cacerola *f*; (*stew*) cazuela *f*

cassette /kə'set/ *n* casete *m*

cast /kɑːst/ *vt* (*pt* **cast**) arrojar; fundir (*metal*); dar (*vote*); (*in theatre*) repartir. ● *n* lanzamiento *m*; (*in play*) reparto *m*; (*mould*) molde *m*

castanets /kæstə'nets/ *npl* castañuelas *fpl*

castaway /'kɑːstəweɪ/ *n* náufrago *m*

caste /kɑːst/ *n* casta *f*

cast: ~ **iron** *n* hierro *m* fundido. ~**iron** *a* de hierro fundido; (*fig*) sólido

castle /'kɑːsl/ *n* castillo *m*; (*chess*) torre *f*

cast-offs /'kɑːstɒfs/ *npl* desechos *mpl*

castor /'kɑːstə(r)/ *n* ruedecilla *f*

castor oil /kɑːstər'ɔɪl/ *n* aceite *m* de ricino

castor sugar /'kɑːstəʃʊgə(r)/ *n* azúcar *m* extrafino

castrat|e /kæ'streɪt/ *vt* castrar. ~**ion** /-ʃn/ *n* castración *f*

casual /'kæʒʊəl/ *a* casual; (*meeting*) fortuito; (*work*) ocasional; (*attitude*) despreocupado; (*clothes*) informal, de sport. ~**ly** *adv* de paso

casualt|y /'kæʒʊəltɪ/ *n* accidente *m*; (*injured*) víctima *f*, herido *m*; (*dead*) víctima *f*, muerto *m*. ~**ies** *npl* (*mil*) bajas *fpl*

cat /kæt/ *n* gato *m*

cataclysm /'kætəklɪzəm/ *n* cataclismo *m*

catacomb /'kætəkuːm/ *n* catacumba *f*

catalogue /'kætəlɒg/ *n* catálogo *m*. ● *vt* catalogar

catalyst /'kætəlɪst/ *n* catalizador *m*

catamaran /kætəmə'ræn/ *n* catamarán *m*

catapult /'kætəpʌlt/ *n* catapulta *f*; (*child's*) tirador *m*, tirachinos *m invar*

cataract /'kætərækt/ *n* catarata *f*

catarrh /kə'tɑː(r)/ *n* catarro *m*

catastroph|e /kə'tæstrəfɪ/ *n* catástrofe *m*. ~**ic** /kætə'strɒfɪk/ *a* catastrófico

catch /kætʃ/ *vt* (*pt* **caught**) coger (*not LAm*), agarrar; (*grab*) asir; tomar (*train, bus*); (*unawares*) sorprender; (*understand*) comprender; contraer (*disease*). ~ **a cold** resfriarse. ~ **sight of** avistar. ● *vi* (*get stuck*) engancharse; (*fire*) prenderse. ● *n* cogida *f*, (*of fish*) pesca *f*; (*on door*) pestillo *m*; (*on window*) cerradura *f*. ~ **on** (*fam*) hacerse popular. ~ **up** poner al día. ~ **up with** alcanzar; ponerse al corriente de (*news etc*)

catching /'kætʃɪŋ/ *a* contagioso

catchment /'kætʃmənt/ *n*. ~ **area** *n* zona *f* de captación

catch-phrase /'kætʃfreɪz/ *n* eslogan *m*

catchword /'kætʃwɜːd/ *n* eslogan *m*, consigna *f*

catchy /'kætʃɪ/ *a* pegadizo

catechism /'kætɪkɪzəm/ *n* catecismo *m*

categorical /kætɪ'gɒrɪkl/ *a* categórico

category /'kætɪgərɪ/ *n* categoría *f*

cater /'keɪtə(r)/ *vi* proveer comida a. ~ **for** proveer a (*needs*). ~**er** *n* proveedor *m*

caterpillar /'kætəpɪlə(r)/ *n* oruga *f*

cathedral /kə'θiːdrəl/ *n* catedral *f*

catholic /'kæθəlɪk/ *a* universal. **C**~ *a* & *n* católico (*m*). **C**~**ism** /kəθɒlɪsɪzəm/ *n* catolicismo *m*

catnap /'kætnæp/ *n* sueñecito *m*

cat's eyes /'kætsaɪz/ *npl* catafotos *mpl*

cattle /'kætl/ *npl* ganado *m* (vacuno)

cat|ty /'kætɪ/ *a* malicioso. ~**walk** /'kætwɔːk/ *n* pasarela *f*

caucus /'kɔːkəs/ *n* comité *m* electoral

caught /kɔːt/ *see* **catch**

cauldron /'kɔːldrən/ *n* caldera *f*

cauliflower /'kɒlɪflaʊə(r)/ *n* coliflor *f*

cause /kɔːz/ *n* causa *f*, motivo *m*. ● *vt* causar

causeway /'kɔːzweɪ/ *n* calzada *f* elevada, carretera *f* elevada

caustic /'kɔːstɪk/ *a* & *n* cáustico (*m*)

cauterize /'kɔːtəraɪz/ *vt* cauterizar

caution /'kɔːʃn/ *n* cautela *f*; (*warning*) advertencia *f*. ● *vt* advertir; (*jurid*) amonestar

cautious /'kɔːʃəs/ *a* cauteloso, prudente. ~**ly** *adv* con precaución, cautelosamente

cavalcade /kævəl'keɪd/ *n* cabalgata *f*

cavalier /kævə'lɪə(r)/ *a* arrogante

cavalry /'kævəlrɪ/ *n* caballería *f*

cave /keɪv/ *n* cueva *f*. ● *vi*. ~ **in** hundirse. ~**man** *n* (*pl* -**men**) troglodita *m*

cavern /'kævən/ *n* caverna *f*, cueva *f*

caviare /'kævɪɑː(r)/ *n* caviar *m*

caving /'keɪvɪŋ/ *n* espeleología *f*

cavity /'kævətɪ/ *n* cavidad *f*; (*in tooth*) caries *f*

cavort /kə'vɔːt/ *vi* brincar

cease /siːs/ *vt/i* cesar. ● *n*. **without** ~ sin cesar. ~**fire** *n* tregua *f*, alto *m* el fuego. ~**less** *a* incesante

cedar /'siːdə(r)/ *n* cedro *m*

cede /si:d/ vt ceder

cedilla /sɪ'dɪlə/ n cedilla f

ceiling /'si:lɪŋ/ n techo m

celebrat|e /'selɪbreɪt/ vt celebrar.
● vi divertirse. ∼ed /'selɪbreɪtɪd/ a
célebre. ∼ion /-'breɪʃn/ n cele-
bración f; (party) fiesta f

celebrity /sɪ'lebrətɪ/ n celebridad f

celery /'selərɪ/ n apio m

celestial /sɪ'lestjəl/ a celestial

celiba|cy /'selɪbəsɪ/ n celibato m.
∼te /'selɪbət/ a & n célibe (m & f)

cell /sel/ n celda f; (biol) célula f;
(elec) pila f

cellar /'selə(r)/ n sótano m; (for wine)
bodega f

cell|ist /'tʃelɪst/ n violonc(h)elo m &
f, violonc(h)elista m & f. ∼o
/'tʃeləʊ/ n (pl -os) violonc(h)elo m

Cellophane /'seləfeɪn/ n (P) celofán
m (P)

cellular /'seljʊlə(r)/ a celular

celluloid /'seljʊlɔɪd/ n celuloide m

cellulose /'seljʊləʊs/ n celulosa f

Celt /kelt/ n celta m & f. ∼ic a céltico

cement /sɪ'ment/ n cemento m. ● vt
cementar; (fig) consolidar

cemetery /'semətrɪ/ n cementerio m

cenotaph /'senətɑ:f/ n cenotafio m

censor /'sensə(r)/ n censor m. ● vt
censurar. ∼ship n censura f

censure /'senʃə(r)/ n censura f. ● vt
censurar

census /'sensəs/ n censo m

cent /sent/ n centavo m

centenary /sen'ti:nərɪ/ n centenario
m

centigrade /'sentɪgreɪd/ a centí-
grado

centilitre /'sentɪli:tə(r)/ n centilitro
m

centimetre /'sentɪmi:tə(r)/ n centí-
metro m

centipede /'sentɪpi:d/ n ciempiés m
invar

central /'sentrəl/ a central; (of town)
céntrico. ∼ heating n calefacción f
central. ∼ize vt centralizar. ∼ly
adv (situated) en el centro

centre /'sentə(r)/ n centro m. ● vt (pt
centred) vi concentrarse

centrifugal /sen'trɪfjʊgəl/ a
centrífugo

century /'sentʃərɪ/ n siglo m

ceramic /sɪ'ræmɪk/ a cerámico. ∼s
npl cerámica f

cereal /'sɪərɪəl/ n cereal m

cerebral /'serɪbrəl/ a cerebral

ceremon|ial /serɪ'məʊnɪəl/ a & n
ceremonial (m). ∼ious /-'məʊnɪəs/
a ceremonioso. ∼y /'serɪmənɪ/ n
ceremonia f

certain /'sɜ:tn/ a cierto. for ∼
seguro. make ∼ of asegurarse de.
∼ly adv desde luego. ∼ty n certeza
f

certificate /sə'tɪfɪkət/ n certificado
m; (of birth, death etc) partida f

certify /'sɜ:tɪfaɪ/ vt certificar

cessation /se'seɪʃən/ n cesación f

cesspit /'sespɪt/ n, **cesspool** /'sespu:l/
n pozo m negro; (fig) sentina f

chafe /tʃeɪf/ vt rozar. ● vi rozarse;
(fig) irritarse

chaff /tʃæf/ vt zumbarse de

chaffinch /'tʃæfɪntʃ/ n pinzón m

chagrin /'ʃægrɪn/ n disgusto m

chain /tʃeɪn/ n cadena f. ● vt encadenar. ∼ reaction n reacción f en
cadena. ∼smoker n fumador m que
siempre tiene un cigarillo encendido. ∼ store n sucursal m

chair /tʃeə(r)/ n silla f; (univ) cátedra
f. ● vt presidir. ∼lift n telesilla m

chairman /'tʃeəmən/ n (pl -men) presidente m

chalet /'ʃæleɪ/ n chalé m

chalice /'tʃælɪs/ n cáliz m

chalk /tʃɔ:k/ n creta f; (stick) tiza f.
∼y a cretáceo

challeng|e /'tʃælɪndʒ/ n desafío m;
(fig) reto m. ● vt desafiar; (question)
poner en duda. ∼ing a estimulante

chamber /'tʃeɪmbə(r)/ n (old use)
cámara f. ∼maid /'tʃeɪmbəmeɪd/ n
camarera f. ∼pot n orinal m. ∼s
npl despacho m, bufete m

chameleon /kə'mi:ljən/ n camaleón
m

chamois /'ʃæmɪ/ n gamuza f

champagne /ʃæm'peɪn/ n champaña m, champán m (fam)

champion /'tʃæmpɪən/ n campeón
m. ● vt defender. ∼ship n campeonato m

chance /tʃɑ:ns/ n casualidad f; (likelihood) probabilidad f; (opportunity) oportunidad f; (risk) riesgo
m. by ∼ por casualidad. ● a fortuito. ● vt arriesgar. ● vi suceder. ∼
upon tropezar con

chancellor /'tʃɑ:nsələ(r)/ n canciller
m; (univ) rector m. C∼ of the
Exchequer Ministro m de Hacienda

chancy /'tʃɑ:nsɪ/ a arriesgado; (uncertain) incierto

chandelier /ˌʃændəˈlɪə(r)/ n araña f (de luces)

change /tʃeɪndʒ/ vt cambiar; (substitute) reemplazar. **~ one's mind** cambiar de idea. ● vi cambiarse. ● n cambio m; (small coins) suelto m. **~ of life** menopausia f. **~able** a cambiable; ⟨weather⟩ variable. **~over** n cambio m

channel /ˈtʃænl/ n canal m; (fig) medio m. **the C~ Islands** npl las islas fpl Anglonormandas. **the (English) C~** el canal de la Mancha. ● vt (pt **channelled**) acanalar; (fig) encauzar

chant /tʃɑːnt/ n canto m. ● vt/i cantar; (fig) salmodiar

chao|s /ˈkeɪɒs/ n caos m, desorden m. **~tic** /-ˈɒtɪk/ a caótico, desordenado

chap[1] /tʃæp/ n (crack) grieta f. ● vt (pt **chapped**) agrietar. ● vi agrietarse

chap[2] /tʃæp/ n (fam) hombre m, tío m (fam)

chapel /ˈtʃæpl/ n capilla f

chaperon /ˈʃæpərəʊn/ n acompañanta f. ● vt acompañar

chaplain /ˈtʃæplɪn/ n capellán m

chapter /ˈtʃæptə(r)/ n capítulo m

char[1] /tʃɑː(r)/ vt (pt **charred**) carbonizar

char[2] /tʃɑː(r)/ n asistenta f

character /ˈkærəktə(r)/ n carácter m; (in play) personaje m. **in ~** característico

characteristic /kærəktəˈrɪstɪk/ a característico. **~ally** adv típicamente

characterize /ˈkærəktəraɪz/ vt caracterizar

charade /ʃəˈrɑːd/ n charada f, farsa f

charcoal /ˈtʃɑːkəʊl/ n carbón m vegetal; (for drawing) carboncillo m

charge /tʃɑːdʒ/ n precio m; (elec, mil) carga f; (jurid) acusación f; (task, custody) encargo m; (responsibility) responsabilidad f. **in ~ of** responsable de, encargado de. **take ~ of** encargarse de. ● vt pedir; (elec, mil) cargar; (jurid) acusar; (entrust) encargar. ● vi cargar; (money) cobrar. **~able** a a cargo (de)

chariot /ˈtʃærɪət/ n carro m

charisma /kəˈrɪzmə/ n carisma m. **~tic** /-ˈmætɪk/ a carismático

charitable /ˈtʃærɪtəbl/ a caritativo

charity /ˈtʃærɪtɪ/ n caridad f; (society) institución f benéfica

charlatan /ˈʃɑːlətən/ n charlatán m

charm /tʃɑːm/ n encanto m; (spell) hechizo m; (on bracelet) dije m, amuleto m. ● vt encantar. **~ing** a encantador

chart /tʃɑːt/ n (naut) carta f de marear; (table) tabla f. ● vt poner en una carta de marear

charter /ˈtʃɑːtə(r)/ n carta f. ● vt conceder carta a, estatuir; alquilar ⟨bus, train⟩; fletar ⟨plane, ship⟩. **~ed accountant** n contador m titulado. **~ flight** n vuelo m charter

charwoman /ˈtʃɑːwʊmən/ n (pl -women) asistenta f

chary /ˈtʃeərɪ/ a cauteloso

chase /tʃeɪs/ vt perseguir. ● vi correr. ● n persecución f. **~ away**, **~ off** ahuyentar

chasm /ˈkæzəm/ n abismo m

chassis /ˈʃæsɪ/ n chasis m

chaste /tʃeɪst/ a casto

chastise /tʃæsˈtaɪz/ vt castigar

chastity /ˈtʃæstətɪ/ n castidad f

chat /tʃæt/ n charla f. **have a ~** charlar. ● vi (pt **chatted**) charlar

chattels /ˈtʃætlz/ n bienes mpl muebles

chatter /ˈtʃætə(r)/ n charla f. ● vi charlar. **his teeth are ~ing** le castañetean los dientes. **~box** /ˈtʃætəbɒks/ n parlanchín m

chatty a hablador; ⟨style⟩ familiar

chauffeur /ˈʃəʊfə(r)/ n chófer m

chauvinis|m /ˈʃəʊvɪnɪzəm/ n patriotería f; (male) machismo m. **~t** /ˈʃəʊvɪnɪst/ n patriotero m; (male) machista m & f

cheap /tʃiːp/ a (-er, -est) barato; (poor quality) de baja calidad; ⟨rate⟩ económico. **~en** /ˈtʃiːpən/ vt abaratar. **~(ly)** adv barato, a bajo precio. **~ness** n baratura f

cheat /tʃiːt/ vt defraudar; (deceive) engañar. ● vi (at cards) hacer trampas. ● n trampa f; (person) tramposo m

check[1] /tʃek/ vt comprobar; (examine) inspeccionar; (curb) detener; (chess) dar jaque a. ● vi comprobar. ● n comprobación f; (of tickets) control m; (curb) freno m; (chess) jaque m; (bill, Amer) cuenta f. **~ in** registrarse; (at airport) facturar el equipaje. **~ out** pagar la cuenta y marcharse. **~ up** comprobar. **~ up on** investigar

check[2] /tʃek/ n (pattern) cuadro m. **~ed** a a cuadros

checkmate /'tʃekmeɪt/ n jaque m
mate. ● vt dar mate a
check-up /'tʃekʌp/ n examen m
cheek /tʃiːk/ n mejilla f; (fig) descaro
m. ~**bone** n pómulo m. ~**y** a
descarado
cheep /tʃiːp/ vi piar
cheer /tʃɪə(r)/ n alegría f; (applause)
viva m. ● vt alegrar; (applaud)
aplaudir. ● vi alegrarse; (applaud)
aplaudir. ~ **up!** ¡anímate! ~**ful** a
alegre. ~**fulness** n alegría f
cheerio /tʃɪərɪ'əʊ/ int (fam) ¡adiós!,
¡hasta luego!
cheer: ~**less** /'tʃɪəlɪs/ a triste. ~**s!**
¡salud!
cheese /tʃiːz/ n queso m
cheetah /'tʃiːtə/ n guepardo m
chef /ʃef/ n cocinero m
chemical /'kemɪkl/ a químico. ● n
producto m químico
chemist /'kemɪst/ n farmacéutico m;
(scientist) químico m. ~**ry** n quí-
mica f. ~**'s (shop)** n farmacia f
cheque /tʃek/ n cheque m, talón m.
~**book** n talonario m
chequered /'tʃekəd/ a a cuadros;
(fig) con altibajos
cherish /'tʃerɪʃ/ vt cuidar; (love)
querer; abrigar ⟨hope⟩
cherry /'tʃerɪ/ n cereza f. ~**tree** n
cerezo m
cherub /'tʃerəb/ n (pl -im) (angel)
querubín m
chess /tʃes/ n ajedrez m. ~**board** n
tablero m de ajedrez
chest /tʃest/ n pecho m; (box) cofre
m, cajón m. ~ **of drawers** n cómoda
f
chestnut /'tʃesnʌt/ n castaña f.
~**tree** n castaño m
chew /tʃuː/ vt masticar; (fig) rumiar.
~**ing-gum** n chicle m
chic /ʃiːk/ a elegante. ● n elegancia f
chick /tʃɪk/ n polluelo m. ~**en**
/'tʃɪkɪn/ n pollo m. ● a (sl) cobarde.
● vi. ~**en out** (sl) retirarse. ~**en-
pox** n varicela f
chicory /'tʃɪkərɪ/ n (in coffee) achicoria f; (in salad) escarola f
chide /tʃaɪd/ vt (pt **chided**)
reprender
chief /tʃiːf/ n jefe m. ● a principal.
~**ly** adv principalmente
chilblain /'tʃɪlbleɪn/ n sabañón m
child /tʃaɪld/ n (pl **children**
/'tʃɪldrən/) niño m; (offspring) hijo
m. ~**birth** /'tʃaɪldbɜːθ/ n parto m.
~**hood** n niñez f. ~**ish** a infantil.

~**less** a sin hijos. ~**like** a inocente,
infantil
Chile /'tʃɪlɪ/ n Chile m. ~**an** a & n
chileno (m)
chill /tʃɪl/ n frío m; (illness) resfriado
m. ● a frío. ● vt enfriar; refrigerar
⟨food⟩
chilli /'tʃɪlɪ/ n (pl -ies) chile m
chilly /'tʃɪlɪ/ a frío
chime /tʃaɪm/ n carillón m. ● vt
tocar ⟨bells⟩; dar ⟨hours⟩. ● vi
repicar
chimney /'tʃɪmnɪ/ n (pl -eys) chimenea f. ~**pot** n cañón m de chimenea. ~**sweep** n deshollinador m
chimpanzee /tʃɪmpæn'ziː/ n chimpancé m
chin /tʃɪn/ n barbilla f
china /'tʃaɪnə/ n porcelana f
Chin|a /'tʃaɪnə/ n China f. ~**ese** /-'niː-
z/ a & n chino (m)
chink[1] /tʃɪŋk/ n (crack) grieta f
chink[2] /tʃɪŋk/ n (sound) tintín m. ● vt
hacer tintinear. ● vi tintinear
chip /tʃɪp/ n pedacito m; (splinter)
astilla f; (culin) patata f frita;
(gambling) ficha f. **have a ~ on
one's shoulder** guardar rencor. ● vt
(pt **chipped**) desportillar. ● vi
desportillarse. ~ **in** (fam) interrumpir; (with money) contribuir
chiropodist /kɪ'rɒpədɪst/ n callista
m & f
chirp /tʃɜːp/ n pío m. ● vi piar
chirpy /'tʃɜːpɪ/ a alegre
chisel /'tʃɪzl/ n formón m. ● vt (pt
chiselled) cincelar
chit /tʃɪt/ n vale m, nota f
chit-chat /'tʃɪttʃæt/ n cháchara f
chivalr|ous a /'ʃɪvəlrəs/ a caba-
lleroso. ~**y** /'ʃɪvəlrɪ/ n caba-
llerosidad f
chive /tʃaɪv/ n cebollino m
chlorine /'klɔːriːn/ n cloro m
chock /tʃɒk/ n calzo m. ~**a-block** a,
~**full** a atestado
chocolate /'tʃɒklɪt/ n chocolate m;
(individual sweet) bombón m
choice /tʃɔɪs/ n elección f; (pref-
erence) preferencia f. ● a escogido
choir /'kwaɪə(r)/ n coro m. ~**boy**
/'kwaɪəbɔɪ/ n niño m de coro
choke /tʃəʊk/ vt sofocar. ● vi
sofocarse. ● n (auto) estrangulador
m, estárter m
cholera /'kɒlərə/ n cólera m
cholesterol /kə'lestərɒl/ n colesterol
m

choose /tʃuːz/ vt/i (pt **chose**, pp **chosen**) elegir. **~y** /'tʃuːzi/ a (fam) exigente

chop /tʃɒp/ vt (pt **chopped**) cortar. ● n (culin) chuleta f. **~ down** talar. **~ off** cortar. **~per** n hacha f; (butcher's) cuchilla f; (sl) helicóptero m

choppy /'tʃɒpɪ/ a picado

chopstick /'tʃɒpstɪk/ n palillo m (chino)

choral /'kɔːrəl/ a coral

chord /kɔːd/ n cuerda f; (mus) acorde m

chore /tʃɔː(r)/ n tarea f, faena f. **household ~s** npl faenas fpl domésticas

choreographer /kɒrɪ'ɒgrəfə(r)/ n coreógrafo m

chorister /'kɒrɪstə(r)/ n (singer) corista m & f

chortle /'tʃɔːtl/ n risita f alegre. ● vi reírse alegremente

chorus /'kɔːrəs/ n coro m; (of song) estribillo m

chose, chosen /tʃəuz, 'tʃəuzn/ see **choose**

Christ /kraɪst/ n Cristo m

christen /'krɪsn/ vt bautizar. **~ing** n bautizo m

Christian /'krɪstjən/ a & n cristiano (m). **~ name** n nombre m de pila

Christmas /'krɪsməs/ n Navidad f; (period) Navidades fpl. ● a de Navidad, navideño. **~box** n aguinaldo m. **~ day** n día m de Navidad. **~ Eve** n Nochebuena f. **Father ~** n Papá m Noel. **Happy ~!** ¡Felices Pascuas!

chrom|e /krəum/ n cromo m. **~ium** /'krəumɪəm/ n cromo m. **~ium plating** n cromado m

chromosome /'krəuməsəum/ n cromosoma m

chronic /'krɒnɪk/ a crónico; (bad, fam) terrible

chronicle /'krɒnɪkl/ n crónica f. ● vt historiar

chronolog|ical /krɒnə'lɒdʒɪkl/ a cronológico. **~y** /krə'nɒlədʒɪ/ n cronología f

chrysanthemum /krɪ'sænθəməm/ n crisantemo m

chubby /'tʃʌbɪ/ a (-ier, -iest) regordete; ⟨face⟩ mofletudo

chuck /tʃʌk/ vt (fam) arrojar. **~ out** tirar

chuckle /'tʃʌkl/ n risa f ahogada. ● vi reírse entre dientes

chuffed /tʃʌft/ a (sl) contento

chug /tʃʌg/ vi (pt **chugged**) (of motor) traquetear

chum /tʃʌm/ n amigo m, compinche m. **~my** a. **be ~my** ⟨2 people⟩ ser muy amigos. **be ~my with** ser muy amigo de

chump /tʃʌmp/ n (sl) tonto m. **~ chop** n chuleta f

chunk /tʃʌŋk/ n trozo m grueso. **~y** /tʃʌŋkɪ/ a macizo

church /tʃɜːtʃ/ n iglesia f. **~yard** /'tʃɜːtʃjɑːd/ n cementerio m

churlish /'tʃɜːlɪʃ/ a grosero

churn /tʃɜːn/ n (for milk) lechera f, cántara f; (for butter) mantequera f. ● vt agitar. **~ out** producir en profusión

chute /ʃuːt/ n tobogán m

chutney /'tʃʌtnɪ/ n (pl -eys) condimento m agridulce

cider /'saɪdə(r)/ n sidra f

cigar /sɪ'gɑː(r)/ n puro m

cigarette /sɪgə'ret/ n cigarillo m. **~-holder** n boquilla f

cine-camera /'sɪnɪkæmərə/ n cámara f, tomavistas m invar

cinema /'sɪnəmə/ n cine m

cinnamon /'sɪnəmən/ n canela f

cipher /'saɪfə(r)/ n (math, fig) cero m; (secret system) cifra f

circle /'sɜːkl/ n círculo m; (in theatre) anfiteatro m. ● vt girar alrededor de. ● vi dar vueltas

circuit /'sɜːkɪt/ n circuito m; (chain) cadena f

circuitous /sɜː'kjuːɪtəs/ a indirecto

circular /'sɜːkjulə(r)/ a & n circular (f)

circularize /'sɜːkjuləraɪz/ vt enviar circulares a

circulat|e /'sɜːkjuleɪt/ vt hacer circular. ● vi circular. **~ion** /-'leɪʃn/ n circulación f; (of journals) tirada f

circumcis|e /'sɜːkəmsaɪz/ vt circuncidar. **~ion** /-'sɪʒn/ n circuncisión f

circumference /sə'kʌmfərəns/ n circunferencia f

circumflex /'sɜːkəmfleks/ a & n circunflejo (m)

circumspect /'sɜːkəmspekt/ a circunspecto

circumstance /'sɜːkəmstəns/ n circunstancia f. **~s** (means) npl situación f económica

circus /'sɜːkəs/ n circo m

cistern /'sɪstən/ n depósito m; (of WC) cisterna f

citadel /'sɪtədl/ n ciudadela f

citation /saɪˈteɪʃn/ n citación f

cite /saɪt/ vt citar

citizen /ˈsɪtɪzn/ n ciudadano m; (inhabitant) habitante m & f. **~ship** n ciudadanía f

citrus /ˈsɪtrəs/ n. **~ fruits** cítricos mpl

city /ˈsɪtɪ/ n ciudad f; **the C~** el centro m financiero de Londres

civic /ˈsɪvɪk/ a cívico. **~s** npl cívica f

civil /ˈsɪvl/ a civil, cortés

civilian /sɪˈvɪlɪən/ a & n civil (m & f). **~ clothes** npl traje m de paisano

civility /sɪˈvɪlətɪ/ n cortesía f

civiliz|ation /sɪvɪlaɪˈzeɪʃn/ n civilización f. **~e** /ˈsɪvɪlaɪz/ vt civilizar.

civil: **~ servant** n funcionario m. **~ service** n administración f pública

civvies /ˈsɪvɪz/ npl. **in ~** (sl) en traje m de paisano

clad /klæd/ see **clothe**

claim /kleɪm/ vt reclamar; (assert) pretender. ● n reclamación f; (right) derecho m; (jurid) demanda f. **~ant** n demandante m & f; (to throne) pretendiente m

clairvoyant /kleəˈvɔɪənt/ n clarividente m & f

clam /klæm/ n almeja f

clamber /ˈklæmbə(r)/ vi trepar a gatas

clammy /ˈklæmɪ/ a (-ier, -iest) húmedo

clamour /ˈklæmə(r)/ n clamor m. ● vi. **~ for** pedir a voces

clamp /klæmp/ n abrazadera f; (auto) cepo m. ● vt sujetar con abrazadera. **~ down on** reprimir

clan /klæn/ n clan m

clandestine /klænˈdestɪn/ a clandestino

clang /klæŋ/ n sonido m metálico

clanger /ˈklæŋə(r)/ n (sl) metedura f de pata

clap /klæp/ vt (pt **clapped**) aplaudir; batir ⟨hands⟩. ● vi aplaudir. ● n palmada f; (of thunder) trueno m

claptrap /ˈklæptræp/ n charlatanería f, tonterías fpl

claret /ˈklærət/ n clarete m

clarif|ication /klærɪfɪˈkeɪʃn/ n aclaración f. **~y** /ˈklærɪfaɪ/ vt aclarar. ● vi aclararse

clarinet /klærɪˈnet/ n clarinete m

clarity /ˈklærətɪ/ n claridad f

clash /klæʃ/ n choque m; (noise) estruendo m; (contrast) contraste m; (fig) conflicto m. ● vt golpear. ● vi encontrarse; ⟨dates⟩ coincidir;

⟨opinions⟩ estar en desacuerdo; ⟨colours⟩ desentonar

clasp /klɑːsp/ n cierre m. ● vt agarrar; apretar ⟨hand⟩; (fasten) abrochar

class /klɑːs/ n clase f. **evening ~** n clase nocturna. ● vt clasificar

classic /ˈklæsɪk/ a & n clásico (m). **~al** a clásico. **~s** npl estudios mpl clásicos

classif|ication /klæsɪfɪˈkeɪʃn/ n clasificación f. **~y** /ˈklæsɪfaɪ/ vt clasificar

classroom /ˈklɑːsruːm/ n aula f

classy /ˈklɑːsɪ/ a (sl) elegante

clatter /ˈklætə(r)/ n estrépito m. ● vi hacer ruido

clause /klɔːz/ n cláusula f; (gram) oración f

claustrophobia /klɔːstrəˈfəʊbɪə/ n claustrofobia f

claw /klɔː/ n garra f; (of cat) uña f; (of crab) pinza f; (device) garfio m. ● vt arañar

clay /kleɪ/ n arcilla f

clean /kliːn/ a (-er, -est) limpio; ⟨stroke⟩ neto. ● adv completamente. ● vt limpiar. ● vi hacer la limpieza. **~ up** hacer la limpieza. **~-cut** a bien definido. **~er** n mujer f de la limpieza. **~liness** /ˈklenlɪnɪs/ n limpieza f

cleans|e /klenz/ vt limpiar; (fig) purificar. **~ing cream** n crema f desmaquilladora

clear /klɪə(r)/ a (-er, -est) claro; (transparent) transparente; (without obstacles) libre; ⟨profit⟩ neto; ⟨sky⟩ despejado. **keep ~ of** evitar. ● adv claramente. ● vt despejar; liquidar ⟨goods⟩; (jurid) absolver; (jump over) saltar por encima de; quitar ⟨table⟩. ● vi ⟨weather⟩ despejarse; ⟨fog⟩ disolverse. **~ off** vi (sl), **~ out** vi (sl) largarse. **~ up** vt (tidy) poner en orden; aclarar ⟨mystery⟩. ● vi ⟨weather⟩ despejarse

clearance /ˈklɪərəns/ n espacio m libre; (removal of obstructions) despeje m; (authorization) permiso m; (by customs) despacho m; (by security) acreditación f. **~ sale** n liquidación f

clearing /ˈklɪərɪŋ/ n claro m

clearly /ˈklɪəlɪ/ adv evidentemente

clearway /ˈklɪəweɪ/ n carretera f en la que no se permite parar

cleavage /ˈkliːvɪdʒ/ n escote m; (fig) división f

cleave /kliːv/ vt (pt **cleaved**, **clove** or **cleft**; pp **cloven** or **cleft**) hender. ● vi henderse

clef /klef/ n (mus) clave f

cleft /kleft/ see **cleave**

clemen|cy /'klemənsɪ/ n clemencia f. ~**t** a clemente

clench /klentʃ/ vt apretar

clergy /'klɜ:dʒɪ/ n clero m. ~**man** n (pl **-men**) clérigo m

cleric /'klerɪk/ n clérigo m. ~**al** a clerical; (of clerks) de oficina

clerk /klɑ:k/ n empleado m; (jurid) escribano m

clever /'klevə(r)/ a (**-er, -est**) listo; (skilful) hábil. ~**ly** adv inteligentemente; (with skill) hábilmente. ~**ness** n inteligencia f

cliché /'kli:ʃeɪ/ n tópico m, frase f hecha

click /klɪk/ n golpecito m. ● vi chascar; (sl) llevarse bien

client /'klaɪənt/ n cliente m & f

clientele /kli:ən'tel/ n clientela f

cliff /klɪf/ n acantilado m

climat|e /'klaɪmɪt/ n clima m. ~**ic** /-'mætɪk/ a climático

climax /'klaɪmæks/ n punto m culminante

climb /klaɪm/ vt subir ⟨stairs⟩; trepar ⟨tree⟩; escalar ⟨mountain⟩. ● vi subir. ● n subida f. ~ **down** bajar; (fig) volverse atrás, rajarse. ~**er** n (sport) alpinista m & f; (plant) trepadora f

clinch /klɪntʃ/ vt cerrar ⟨deal⟩

cling /klɪŋ/ vi (pt **clung**) agarrarse; (stick) pegarse

clinic /'klɪnɪk/ n clínica f. ~**al** /'klɪnɪkl/ a clínico

clink /klɪŋk/ n sonido m metálico. ● vt hacer tintinear. ● vi tintinear

clinker /'klɪŋkə(r)/ n escoria f

clip /klɪp/ n (for paper) sujetapapeles m invar; (for hair) horquilla f. ● vt (pt **clipped**) (join) sujetar

clip² /klɪp/ n (with scissors) tijeretada f; (blow, fam) golpe m. ● vt (pt **clipped**) (cut) cortar; (fam) golpear. ~**pers** /'klɪpəz/ npl (for hair) maquinilla f para cortar el pelo; (for nails) cortauñas m invar. ~**ping** n recorte m

clique /kli:k/ n pandilla f

cloak /kləuk/ n capa f. ~**room** /'kləukru:m/ n guardarropa m; (toilet) servicios mpl

clobber /'klɒbə(r)/ n (sl) trastos mpl. ● vt (sl) dar una paliza a

clock /klɒk/ n reloj m. **grandfather** ~ reloj de caja. ● vi. ~ **in** fichar,

registrar la llegada. ~**wise** /'klɒkwaɪz/ a & adv en el sentido de las agujas del reloj, a la derecha. ~**work** /'klɒkwɜ:k/ n mecanismo m de relojería. **like** ~**work** con precisión

clod /klɒd/ n terrón m

clog /klɒg/ n zueco m. ● vt (pt **clogged**) atascar. ● vi atascarse

cloister /'klɔɪstə(r)/ n claustro m

close¹ /kləus/ a (**-er, -est**) cercano; (together) apretado; (friend) íntimo; (weather) bochornoso; (link etc) estrecho; (game, battle) reñido. **have a** ~ **shave** (fig) escaparse de milagro. ● adv cerca. ● n recinto m

close² /kləuz/ vt cerrar. ● vi cerrarse; (end) terminar. ● n fin m. ~**d shop** n empresa f que emplea solamente a miembros del sindicato

close: ~**ly** adv de cerca; (with attention) atentamente; (exactly) exactamente. ~**ness** n proximidad f; (togetherness) intimidad f

closet /'klɒzɪt/ n (Amer) armario m

close-up /'kləusʌp/ n (cinema etc) primer plano m

closure /'kləuʒə(r)/ n cierre m

clot /klɒt/ n (culin) grumo m; (med) coágulo m; (sl) tonto m. ● vi (pt **clotted**) cuajarse

cloth /klɒθ/ n tela f; (duster) trapo m; (table-cloth) mantel m

cloth|e /kləuð/ vt (pt **clothed** or **clad**) vestir. ~**es** /kləuðz/ npl, ~**ing** n ropa f

cloud /klaud/ n nube f. ● vi nublarse. ~**burst** /'klaudbɜ:st/ n chaparrón m. ~**y** a (**-ier, -iest**) nublado; (liquid) turbio

clout /klaut/ n bofetada f. ● vt abofetear

clove¹ /kləuv/ n clavo m

clove² /kləuv/ n. ~ **of garlic** n diente m de ajo

clove³ /kləuv/ see **cleave**

clover /'kləuvə(r)/ n trébol m

clown /klaun/ n payaso m. ● vi hacer el payaso

cloy /klɔɪ/ vt empalagar

club /klʌb/ n club m; (weapon) porra f; (at cards) trébol m. ● vt (pt **clubbed**) aporrear. ● vi. ~ **together** reunirse, pagar a escote

cluck /klʌk/ vi cloquear

clue /klu:/ n pista f; (in crosswords) indicación f. **not to have a** ~ no tener la menor idea

clump /klʌmp/ n grupo m. ● vt agrupar. ● vi pisar fuertemente

clums|iness /'klʌmzınıs/ n torpeza f. ~y /'klʌmzı/ a (-ier, -iest) torpe

clung /klʌŋ/ see **cling**

cluster /'klʌstə(r)/ n grupo m. ● vi agruparse

clutch /klʌtʃ/ vt agarrar. ● n (auto) embrague m

clutter /'klʌtə(r)/ n desorden m. ● vt llenar desordenadamente

coach /kəʊtʃ/ n autocar m; (of train) vagón m; (horse-drawn) coche m; (sport) entrenador m. ● vt dar clases particulares; (sport) entrenar

coagulate /kəʊ'ægjʊleɪt/ vt coagular. ● vi coagularse

coal /kəʊl/ n carbón m. ~field /'kəʊlfi:ld/ n yacimiento m de carbón

coalition /kəʊə'lıʃn/ n coalición f

coarse /kɔ:s/ a (-er, -est) grosero; (material) basto. ~ness n grosería f; (texture) basteza f

coast /kəʊst/ n costa f. ● vi (with cycle) deslizarse cuesta abajo; (with car) ir en punto muerto. ~al a costero. ~er /'kəʊstə(r)/ n (ship) barco m de cabotaje; (for glass) posavasos m invar. ~guard /'kəʊstgɑ:d/ n guardacostas m invar. ~line /'kəʊstlaın/ n litoral m

coat /kəʊt/ n abrigo m; (jacket) chaqueta f; (of animal) pelo m; (of paint) mano f. ● vt cubrir, revestir. ~ing n capa f. ~ of arms n escudo m de armas

coax /kəʊks/ vt engatusar

cob /kɒb/ n (of corn) mazorca f

cobble¹ /'kɒbl/ n guijarro m, adoquín m. ● vt empedrar con guijarros, adoquinar

cobble² /'kɒbl/ vt (mend) remendar. ~r /'kɒblə(r)/ n (old use) remendón m

cobweb /'kɒbweb/ n telaraña f

cocaine /kə'keɪn/ n cocaína f

cock /kɒk/ n gallo m; (mec) grifo m; (of gun) martillo m. ● vt amartillar (gun); aguzar (ears). ~-and-bull story n patraña f. ~erel /'kɒkərəl/ n gallo m. ~-eyed a (sl) torcido

cockle /'kɒkl/ n berberecho m

cockney /'kɒknı/ a & n (pl -eys) londinense (m & f) (del este de Londres)

cockpit /'kɒkpıt/ n (in aircraft) cabina f del piloto

cockroach /'kɒkrəʊtʃ/ n cucaracha f

cocksure /kɒk'ʃʊə(r)/ a presuntuoso

cocktail /'kɒkteɪl/ n cóctel m. **fruit ~** macedonia f de frutas

cock-up /'kɒkʌp/ n (sl) lío m

cocky /'kɒkı/ a (-ier, -iest) engreído

cocoa /'kəʊkəʊ/ n cacao m; (drink) chocolate m

coconut /'kəʊkənʌt/ n coco m

cocoon /kə'ku:n/ n capullo m

cod /kɒd/ n (pl cod) bacalao m, abadejo m

coddle /'kɒdl/ vt mimar; (culin) cocer a fuego lento

code /kəʊd/ n código m; (secret) cifra f

codify /'kəʊdıfaı/ vt codificar

cod-liver oil /'kɒdlıvə(r)ɒıl/ n aceite m de hígado de bacalao

coeducational /kəʊedʒʊ'keıʃənl/ a mixto

coerc|e /kəʊ'з:s/ vt obligar. ~ion /-ʃn/ n coacción f

coexist /kəʊıg'zıst/ vi coexistir. ~ence n coexistencia f

coffee /'kɒfı/ n café m. ~mill n molinillo m de café. ~pot n cafetera f

coffer /'kɒfə(r)/ n cofre m

coffin /'kɒfın/ n ataúd m

cog /kɒg/ n diente m; (fig) pieza f

cogent /'kəʊdʒənt/ a convincente

cohabit /kəʊ'hæbıt/ vi cohabitar

coherent /kəʊ'hıərənt/ a coherente

coil /kɔıl/ vt enrollar. ● n rollo m; (one ring) vuelta f

coin /kɔın/ n moneda f. ● vt acuñar. ~age n sistema m monetario

coincide /kəʊın'saıd/ vi coincidir

coinciden|ce /kəʊ'ınsıdəns/ n casualidad f. ~tal /-'dentl/ a casual; (coinciding) coincidente

coke /kəʊk/ n (coal) coque m

colander /'kʌləndə(r)/ n colador m

cold /kəʊld/ a (-er, -est) frío. **be ~** tener frío. **it is ~** hace frío. ● n frío m; (med) resfriado m. **have a ~** estar constipado. ~-blooded a insensible. **~ cream** n crema f. ~ **feet** (fig) miedits f. ~ness n frialdad f. **~shoulder** vt tratar con frialdad. **~ sore** n herpes m labial. **~ storage** n conservación f en frigorífico

coleslaw /'kəʊlslɔ:/ n ensalada f de col

colic /'kɒlık/ n cólico m

collaborat|e /kə'læbəreıt/ vi colaborar. ~ion /-'reıʃn/ n colaboración f. ~or n colaborador m

collage /'kɒlɑːʒ/ n collage m

collaps|e /kə'læps/ vi derrumbarse; (med) sufrir un colapso. ● n derrumbamiento m; (med) colapso m. ~ible /kə'læpsəbl/ a plegable

collar /'kɒlə(r)/ n cuello m; (for animals) collar m. ● vt (fam) hurtar. ~bone n clavícula f

colleague /'kɒliːg/ n colega m & f

collect /kə'lekt/ vt reunir; (hobby) coleccionar; (pick up) recoger; recaudar (rent). ● vi (people) reunirse; (things) acumularse. ~ed /kə'lektɪd/ a reunido; (person) tranquilo. ~ion /-ʃn/ n colección f; (in church) colecta f; (of post) recogida f. ~ive /kə'lektɪv/ a colectivo. ~or n coleccionista m & f; (of taxes) recaudador m

college /'kɒlɪdʒ/ n colegio m; (of art, music etc) escuela f; (univ) colegio m mayor

collide /kə'laɪd/ vi chocar

colliery /'kɒliərɪ/ n mina f de carbón

collision /kə'lɪʒn/ n choque m

colloquial /kə'ləʊkwɪəl/ a familiar. ~ism n expresión f familiar

collusion /kə'luːʒn/ n connivencia f

colon /'kəʊlən/ n (gram) dos puntos mpl; (med) colon m

colonel /'kɜːnl/ n coronel m

colon|ial /kə'ləʊnɪəl/ a colonial. ~ize /'kɒlənaɪz/ vt colonizar. ~y /'kɒlənɪ/ n colonia f

colossal /kə'lɒsl/ a colosal

colour /'kʌlə(r)/ n color m. off ~ (fig) indispuesto. ● a de color(es), en color(es). ● vt colorar; (dye) teñir. ● vi (blush) sonrojarse. ~ bar n barrera f racial. ~-blind a daltoniano. ~ed /'kʌləd/ a de color. ~ful a lleno de color; (fig) pintoresco. ~less a incoloro. ~s npl (flag) bandera f

colt /kəʊlt/ n potro m

column /'kɒləm/ n columna f. ~ist /'kɒləmnɪst/ n columnista m & f

coma /'kəʊmə/ n coma m

comb /kəʊm/ n peine m. ● vt peinar; (search) registrar

combat /'kɒmbæt/ n combate m. ● vt (pt combated) combatir. ~ant /-ətənt/ n combatiente m & f

combination /kɒmbɪ'neɪʃn/ n combinación f

combine /kəm'baɪn/ vt combinar. ● vi combinarse. /'kɒmbaɪn/ n asociación f. ~harvester n cosechadora f

combustion /kəm'bʌstʃən/ n combustión f

come /kʌm/ vi (pt came, pp come) venir; (occur) pasar. ~ about ocurrir. ~ across encontrarse con (person); encontrar (object). ~ apart deshacerse. ~ away marcharse. ~ back volver. ~ by obtener; (pass) pasar. ~ down bajar. ~ in entrar. ~ in for recibir. ~ into heredar (money). ~ off desprenderse; (succeed) tener éxito. ~ off it! (fam) ¡no me vengas con eso! ~ out salir; (result) resultar. ~ round (after fainting) volver en sí; (be converted) cambiar de idea. ~ to llegar a (decision etc). ~ up subir; (fig) salir. ~ up with proponer (idea)

comeback /'kʌmbæk/ n retorno m; (retort) réplica f

comedian /kə'miːdɪən/ n cómico m

comedown /'kʌmdaʊn/ n revés m

comedy /'kɒmədɪ/ n comedia f

comely /'kʌmlɪ/ a (-ier, -iest) (old use) bonito

comet /'kɒmɪt/ n cometa m

comeuppance /kʌm'ʌpəns/ n (Amer) merecido m

comf|ort /'kʌmfət/ n bienestar m; (consolation) consuelo m. ● vt consolar. ~ortable a cómodo; (wealthy) holgado. ~y /'kʌmfɪ/ a (fam) cómodo

comic /'kɒmɪk/ a cómico. ● n cómico m; (periodical) tebeo m. ~al a cómico. ~ strip n historieta f

coming /'kʌmɪŋ/ n llegada f. ● a próximo; (week, month etc) que viene. ~ and going ir y venir

comma /'kɒmə/ n coma f

command /kə'mɑːnd/ n orden f; (mastery) dominio m. ● vt mandar; (deserve) merecer

commandeer /kɒmən'dɪə(r)/ vt requisar

commander /kə'mɑːndə(r)/ n comandante m

commanding /kə'mɑːndɪŋ/ a imponente

commandment /kə'mɑːndmənt/ n mandamiento m

commando /kə'mɑːndəʊ/ n (pl -os) comando m

commemorat|e /kə'meməreɪt/ vt conmemorar. ~ion /-'reɪʃn/ n conmemoración f. ~ive /-ətɪv/ a conmemorativo

commence /kə'mens/ vt/i empezar. ~ment n principio m

commend /kə'mend/ *vt* alabar; (*entrust*) encomendar. **~able** *a* loable. **~ation** /kɒmen'deɪʃn/ *n* elogio *m*

commensurate /kə'menʃərət/ *a* proporcionado

comment /'kɒment/ *n* observación *f*. ● *vi* hacer observaciones

commentary /'kɒməntrɪ/ *n* comentario *m*; (*radio*, *TV*) reportaje *m*

commentat|e /'kɒmənteɪt/ *vi* narrar. **~or** *n* (*radio*, *TV*) locutor *m*

commerc|e /'kɒmɜːs/ *n* comercio *m*. **~ial** /kə'mɜːʃl/ *a* comercial. ● *n* anuncio *m*. **~ialize** *vt* comercializar

commiserat|e /kə'mɪzəreɪt/ *vt* compadecer. ● *vi* compadecerse (**with** de). **~ion** /-'reɪʃn/ *n* conmiseración *f*

commission /kə'mɪʃn/ *n* comisión *f*. **out of** **~** fuera de servicio. ● *vt* encargar; (*mil*) nombrar

commissionaire /kəmɪʃə'neə(r)/ *n* portero *m*

commissioner /kə'mɪʃənə(r)/ *n* comisario *m*; (*of police*) jefe *m*

commit /kə'mɪt/ *vt* (*pt* **committed**) cometer; (*entrust*) confiar. **~ o.s.** comprometerse. **~ to memory** aprender de memoria. **~ment** *n* compromiso *m*

committee /kə'mɪtɪ/ *n* comité *m*

commodity /kə'mɒdətɪ/ *n* producto *m*, artículo *m*

common /'kɒmən/ *a* (**-er**, **-est**) común; (*usual*) corriente; (*vulgar*) ordinario. ● *n* ejido *m*

commoner /'kɒmənə(r)/ *n* plebeyo *m*

common: **~ law** *n* derecho *m* consuetudinario. **~ly** *adv* comúnmente. **C~ Market** *n* Mercado *m* Común

commonplace /'kɒmənpleɪs/ *a* banal. ● *n* banalidad *f*

common: **~-room** *n* sala *f* común, salón *m* común. **~ sense** *n* sentido *m* común

Commonwealth /'kɒmənwelθ/ *n*. **the ~** la Mancomunidad *f* Británica

commotion /kə'məʊʃn/ *n* confusión *f*

communal /'kɒmjʊnl/ *a* comunal

commune[1] /'kɒmjuːn/ *n* comuna *f*

commune[2] /kə'mjuːn/ *vi* comuñicarse

communicat|e /kə'mjuːnɪkeɪt/ *vt* comunicar. ● *vi* comunicarse. **~ion** /-'keɪʃn/ *n* comunicación *f*. **~ive** /-ətɪv/ *a* comunicativo

communion /kə'mjuːnɪən/ *n* comunión *f*

communiqué /kə'mjuːnɪkeɪ/ *n* comunicado *m*

communis|m /'kɒmjʊnɪsəm/ *n* comunismo *m*. **~t** /'kɒmjʊnɪst/ *n* comunista *m & f*

community /kə'mjuːnətɪ/ *n* comunidad *f*. **~ centre** *n* centro *m* social

commute /kə'mjuːt/ *vi* viajar diariamente. ● *vt* (*jurid*) conmutar. **~r** /-ə(r)/ *n* viajero *m* diario

compact /kəm'pækt/ *a* compacto. /'kɒmpækt/ *n* (*for powder*) polvera *f*. **~ disc** /'kɒm-/ *n* disco *m* compacto

companion /kəm'pænɪən/ *n* compañero *m*. **~ship** *n* compañerismo *m*

company /'kʌmpənɪ/ *n* compañía *f*; (*guests*, *fam*) visita *f*; (*com*) sociedad *f*

compar|able /'kɒmpərəbl/ *a* comparable. **~ative** /kəm'pærətɪv/ *a* comparativo; (*fig*) relativo. ● *n* (*gram*) comparativo *m*. **~e** /kəm'peə(r)/ *vt* comparar. ● *vi* poderse comparar. **~ison** /kəm'pærɪsn/ *n* comparación *f*

compartment /kəm'pɑːtmənt/ *n* compartimiento *m*; (*on train*) departamento *m*

compass /'kʌmpəs/ *n* brújula *f*. **~es** *npl* compás *m*

compassion /kəm'pæʃn/ *n* compasión *f*. **~ate** *a* compasivo

compatib|ility /kəmpætə'bɪlətɪ/ *n* compatibilidad *f*. **~le** /kəm'pætəbl/ *a* compatible

compatriot /kəm'pætrɪət/ *n* compatriota *m & f*

compel /kəm'pel/ *vt* (*pt* **compelled**) obligar. **~ling** *a* irresistible

compendium /kəm'pendɪəm/ *n* compendio *m*

compensat|e /'kɒmpənseɪt/ *vt* compensar; (*for loss*) indemnizar. ● *vi* compensar. **~ion** /-'seɪʃn/ *n* compensación *f*; (*financial*) indemnización *f*

compère /'kɒmpeə(r)/ *n* presentador *m*. ● *vt* presentar

compete /kəm'piːt/ *vi* competir

competen|ce /'kɒmpətəns/ *n* competencia *f*, aptitud *f*. **~t** /'kɒmpɪtənt/ *a* competente, capaz

competit|ion /kɒmpə'tɪʃn/ *n* (*contest*) concurso *m*; (*com*) competencia *f*. **~ive** /kəm'petətɪv/ *a*

competidor; ⟨price⟩ competitivo.
~or /kəm'petɪtə(r)/ n competidor
m; (in contest) concursante m & f
compile /kəm'paɪl/ vt compilar. **~r**
/-ə(r)/ n recopilador m, compilador
m
complacen|cy /kəm'pleɪsənsɪ/ n
satisfacción f de sí mismo. **~t**
/kəm'pleɪsnt/ a satisfecho de sí
mismo
complain /kəm'pleɪn/ vi. **~ (about)**
quejarse (de). **~ of** (med) sufrir de.
~t /kəm'pleɪnt/ n queja f; (med)
enfermedad f
complement /'kɒmplɪmənt/ n complemento m. ● vt complementar.
~ary /-'mentrɪ/ a complementario
complet|e /kəm'pli:t/ a completo;
(finished) acabado; (downright)
total. ● vt acabar; llenar ⟨a form⟩.
~ely adv completamente. **~ion**
/-ʃn/ n conclusión f
complex /'kɒmpleks/ a complejo.
● n complejo m
complexion /kəm'plekʃn/ n tez f;
(fig) aspecto m
complexity /kəm'pleksətɪ/ n com-
plejidad f
complian|ce /kəm'plaɪəns/ n sumi-
sión f. **in ~ce with** de acuerdo con.
~t a sumiso
complicat|e /'kɒmplɪkeɪt/ vt com-
plicar. **~ed** a complicado. **~ion**
/-'keɪʃn/ n complicación f
complicity /kəm'plɪsətɪ/ n com-
plicidad f
compliment /'kɒmplɪmənt/ n cumplido m; (amorous) piropo m. ● vt
felicitar. **~ary** /-'mentrɪ/ a hal-
agador; (given free) de favor. **~s** npl
saludos mpl
comply /kəm'plaɪ/ vi. **~ with** conformarse con
component /kəm'pəʊnənt/ a & n
componente (m)
compose /kəm'pəʊz/ vt componer.
~ o.s. tranquilizarse. **~d** a sereno
compos|er /kəm'pəʊzə(r)/ n com-
positor m. **~ition** /kɒmpə'zɪʃn/ n
composición f
compost /'kɒmpɒst/ n abono m
composure /kəm'pəʊʒə(r)/ n ser-
enidad f
compound[1] /'kɒmpaʊnd/ n compuesto m. ● a compuesto; ⟨fracture⟩
complicado. /kəm'paʊnd/ vt componer; agravar ⟨problem etc⟩. ● vi
(settle) arreglarse

compound[2] /'kɒmpaʊnd/ n (enclosure) recinto m
comprehen|d /kɒmprɪ'hend/ vt
comprender. **~sion** /kɒmprɪ'henʃn/
n comprensión f
comprehensive /kɒmprɪ'hensɪv/ a
extenso; ⟨insurance⟩ a todo riesgo.
~ school n instituto m
compress /'kɒmpres/ n (med) compresa f. /kəm'pres/ vt comprimir;
(fig) condensar. **~ion** /-ʃn/ n com-
presión f
comprise /kəm'praɪz/ vt comprender
compromise /'kɒmprəmaɪz/ n
acuerdo m, acomodo m, arreglo m.
● vt comprometer. ● vi llegar a un
acuerdo
compuls|ion /kəm'pʌlʃn/ n obli-
gación f, impulso m. **~ive**
/kəm'pʌlsɪv/ a compulsivo. **~ory**
/kəm'pʌlsərɪ/ a obligatorio
compunction /kəm'pʌŋkʃn/ n
remordimiento m
computer /kəm'pju:tə(r)/ n ordenador m. **~ize** vt instalar ord-
enadores en. **be ~ized** tener
ordenador
comrade /'kɒmreɪd/ n camarada m
& f. **~ship** n camaradería f
con[1] /kɒn/ vt (pt conned) (fam)
estafar. ● n (fam) estafa f
con[2] /kɒn/ see pro and con
concave /'kɒŋkeɪv/ a cóncavo
conceal /kən'si:l/ vt ocultar. **~ment**
n encubrimiento m
concede /kən'si:d/ vt conceder
conceit /kən'si:t/ n vanidad f. **~ed** a
engreído
conceiv|able /kən'si:vəbl/ a con-
cebible. **~ably** adv. **may ~ably** es
concebible que. **~e** /kən'si:v/ vt/i
concebir
concentrat|e /'kɒnsəntreɪt/ vt con-
centrar. ● vi concentrarse. **~ion**
/-'treɪʃn/ n concentración f. **~ion
camp** n campo m de concentración
concept /'kɒnsept/ n concepto m
conception /kən'sepʃn/ n con-
cepción f
conceptual /kən'septʃʊəl/ a conceptual
concern /kən'sɜ:n/ n asunto m;
(worry) preocupación f; (com)
empresa f. ● vt tener que ver con;
(deal with) tratar de. **as far as I'm
~ed** en cuanto a mí. **be ~ed about**
preocuparse por. **~ing** prep acerca
de

concert /'kɒnsət/ n concierto m. **in ~ de** común acuerdo. **~ed** /kən'sɜːtɪd/ a concertado

concertina /kɒnsə'tiːnə/ n concertina f

concerto /kən'tʃɜːtəʊ/ n (pl -os) concierto m

concession /kən'seʃn/ n concesión f

conciliat|e /kən'sɪlɪeɪt/ vt conciliar. **~ion** /-'eɪʃn/ n conciliación f

concise /kən'saɪs/ a conciso. **~ly** adv concisamente. **~ness** n concisión f

conclu|de /kən'kluːd/ vt concluir. ● vi concluirse. **~ding** a final. **~sion** n conclusión f

conclusive /kən'kluːsɪv/ a decisivo. **~ly** adv concluyentemente

concoct /kən'kɒkt/ vt confeccionar; (fig) inventar. **~ion** /-ʃn/ n mezcla f; (drink) brebaje m

concourse /'kɒŋkɔːs/ n (rail) vestíbulo m

concrete /'kɒŋkriːt/ n hormigón m. ● a concreto. ● vt cubrir con hormigón

concur /kən'kɜː(r)/ vi (pt concurred) estar de acuerdo

concussion /kən'kʌʃn/ n conmoción f cerebral

condemn /kən'dem/ vt condenar. **~ation** /kɒndem'neɪʃn/ n condenación f, condena f; (censure) censura f

condens|ation /kɒnden'seɪʃn/ n condensación f. **~e** /kən'dens/ vt condensar. ● vi condensarse

condescend /kɒndɪ'send/ vi dignarse (to a). **~ing** a superior

condiment /'kɒndɪmənt/ n condimento m

condition /kən'dɪʃn/ n condición f. **on ~ that** a condición de que. ● vt condicionar. **~al** a condicional. **~er** n acondicionador m; (for hair) suavizante m

condolences /kən'dəʊlənsɪz/ npl pésame m

condom /'kɒndɒm/ n condón m

condone /kən'dəʊn/ vt condonar

conducive /kən'djuːsɪv/ a. **be ~ to** ser favorable a

conduct /kən'dʌkt/ vt conducir; dirigir ⟨orchestra⟩. /'kɒndʌkt/ n conducta f. **~or** /kən'dʌktə(r)/ n director m; (of bus) cobrador m. **~ress** n cobradora f

cone /kəʊn/ n cono m; (for icecream) cucurucho m

confectioner /kən'fekʃənə(r)/ n pastelero m. **~y** n dulces mpl, golosinas fpl

confederation /kənfedə'reɪʃn/ n confederación f

confer /kən'fɜː(r)/ vt (pt conferred) conferir. ● vi consultar

conference /'kɒnfərəns/ n congreso m

confess /kən'fes/ vt confesar. ● vi confesarse. **~ion** /-ʃn/ n confesión f. **~ional** n confes(i)onario m. **~or** n confesor m

confetti /kən'fetɪ/ n confeti m, confetis mpl

confide /kən'faɪd/ vt/i confiar

confiden|ce /'kɒnfɪdəns/ n confianza f; (secret) confidencia f. **~ce trick** n estafa f, timo m. **~t** /'kɒnfɪdənt/ a seguro

confidential /kɒnfɪ'denʃl/ a confidencial

confine /kən'faɪn/ vt confinar; (limit) limitar. **~ment** n (imprisonment) prisión f; (med) parto m

confines /'kɒnfaɪnz/ npl confines mpl

confirm /kən'fɜːm/ vt confirmar. **~ation** /kɒnfə'meɪʃn/ n confirmación f. **~ed** a inveterado

confiscat|e /'kɒnfɪskeɪt/ vt confiscar. **~ion** /-'keɪʃn/ n confiscación f

conflagration /kɒnflə'greɪʃn/ n conflagración f

conflict /'kɒnflɪkt/ n conflicto m. /kən'flɪkt/ vi chocar. **~ing** /kən-/ a contradictorio

conform /kən'fɔːm/ vt conformar. ● vi conformarse. **~ist** n conformista m & f

confound /kən'faʊnd/ vt confundir. **~ed** a (fam) maldito

confront /kən'frʌnt/ vt hacer frente a; (face) enfrentarse con. **~ation** /kɒnfrʌn'teɪʃn/ n confrontación f

confus|e /kən'fjuːz/ vt confundir. **~ing** a desconcertante. **~ion** /-ʒn/ n confusión f

congeal /kən'dʒiːl/ vt coagular. ● vi coagularse

congenial /kən'dʒiːnɪəl/ a simpático

congenital /kən'dʒenɪtl/ a congénito

congest|ed /kən'dʒestɪd/ a congestionado. **~ion** /-'tʃən/ n congestión f

congratulat|e /kən'grætjʊleɪt/ vt felicitar. **~ions** /-'leɪʃnz/ npl felicitaciones fpl

congregat|e /'kɒŋgrɪgeɪt/ vi congregarse. **~ion** /-'geɪʃn/ n asamblea f; (relig) fieles mpl, feligreses mpl

congress /'kɒŋgres/ n congreso m. **C~** (Amer) el Congreso

conic(al) /'kɒnɪk(l)/ a cónico

conifer /'kɒnɪfə(r)/ n conífera f

conjecture /kən'dʒektʃə(r)/ n conjetura f. ● vt conjeturar. ● vi hacer conjeturas

conjugal /'kɒndʒʊgl/ a conyugal

conjugat|e /'kɒndʒʊgeɪt/ vt conjugar. **~ion** /-'geɪʃn/ n conjugación f

conjunction /kən'dʒʌŋkʃn/ n conjunción f

conjur|e /'kʌndʒə(r)/ vi hacer juegos de manos. ● vt. **~e up** evocar. **~or** n prestidigitador m

conk /kɒŋk/ vi. **~ out** (sl) fallar; ⟨person⟩ desmayarse

conker /'kɒŋkə(r)/ n (fam) castaña f de Indias

conman /'kɒnmæn/ n (fam) estafador m, timador m

connect /kə'nekt/ vt juntar; (elec) conectar. ● vi unirse; (elec) conectarse. **~ with** ⟨train⟩ enlazar con. **~ed** a unido; (related) relacionado. **be ~ed with** tener que ver con, estar emparentado con

connection /kə'nekʃn/ n unión f; (rail) enlace m; (elec, mec) conexión f; (fig) relación f. **in ~ with** a propósito de, con respecto a. **~s** npl relaciones fpl

conniv|ance /kə'naɪvəns/ n connivencia f. **~e** /kə'naɪv/ vi. **~e at** hacer la vista gorda a

connoisseur /kɒnə'sɜː(r)/ n experto m

connot|ation /kɒnə'teɪʃn/ n connotación f. **~e** /kə'nəʊt/ vt connotar; (imply) implicar

conquer /'kɒŋkə(r)/ vt conquistar; (fig) vencer. **~or** n conquistador m

conquest /'kɒŋkwest/ n conquista f

conscience /'kɒnʃəns/ n conciencia f

conscientious /kɒnʃɪ'enʃəs/ a concienzudo

conscious /'kɒnʃəs/ a consciente; (deliberate) intencional. **~ly** adv a sabiendas. **~ness** n consciencia f; (med) conocimiento m

conscript /'kɒnskrɪpt/ n recluta m. /kən'skrɪpt/ vt reclutar. **~ion** /kən'skrɪpʃn/ n reclutamiento m

consecrat|e /'kɒnsɪkreɪt/ vt consagrar. **~ion** /-'kreɪʃn/ n consagración f

consecutive /kən'sekjʊtɪv/ a sucesivo

consensus /kən'sensəs/ n consenso m

consent /kən'sent/ vi consentir. ● n consentimiento m

consequen|ce /'kɒnsɪkwəns/ n consecuencia f. **~t** /'kɒnsɪkwənt/ a consiguiente. **~tly** adv por consiguiente

conservation /kɒnsə'veɪʃn/ n conservación f, preservación f. **~ist** /kɒnsə'veɪʃənɪst/ n conservacionista m & f

conservative /kən'sɜːvətɪv/ a conservador; (modest) prudente, moderado. **C~** a & n conservador (m)

conservatory /kən'sɜːvətrɪ/ n (greenhouse) invernadero m

conserve /kən'sɜːv/ vt conservar

consider /kən'sɪdə(r)/ vt considerar; (take into account) tomar en cuenta. **~able** /kən'sɪdərəbl/ a considerable. **~ably** adv considerablemente

considerat|e /kən'sɪdərət/ a considerado. **~ion** /-'reɪʃn/ n consideración f

considering /kən'sɪdərɪŋ/ prep en vista de

consign /kən'saɪn/ vt consignar; (send) enviar. **~ment** n envío m

consist /kən'sɪst/ vi. **~ of** consistir en

consistency /kən'sɪstənsɪ/ n consistencia f; (fig) coherencia f

consistent /kən'sɪstənt/ a coherente; (unchanging) constante. **~ with** compatible con. **~ly** adv constantemente

consolation /kɒnsə'leɪʃn/ n consuelo m

console /kən'səʊl/ vt consolar

consolidat|e /kən'sɒlɪdeɪt/ vt consolidar. ● vi consolidarse. **~ion** /-'deɪʃn/ n consolidación f

consonant /'kɒnsənənt/ n consonante f

consort /'kɒnsɔːt/ n consorte m & f. /kən'sɔːt/ vi. **~ with** asociarse con

consortium /kən'sɔːtɪəm/ n (pl -tia) consorcio m

conspicuous /kən'spɪkjʊəs/ a (easily seen) visible; (showy) llamativo; (noteworthy) notable

conspir|acy /kən'spɪrəsɪ/ n complot m, conspiración f. **~e** /kən'spaɪə(r)/ vi conspirar

constab|le /'kʌnstəbl/ n policía m, guardia m. **~ulary** /kən'stæbjʊlərɪ/ n policía f

constant /'kɒnstənt/ a constante. **~ly** adv constantemente

constellation /kɒnstə'leɪʃn/ n constelación f

consternation /kɒnstə'neɪʃn/ n consternación f

constipat|ed /'kɒnstɪpeɪtɪd/ a estreñido. **~ion** /-'peɪʃn/ n estreñimiento m

constituen|cy /kən'stɪtjʊənsɪ/ n distrito m electoral. **~t** /kən'stɪtjʊənt/ n componente m; (pol) elector m

constitut|e /'kɒnstɪtjuːt/ vt constituir. **~ion** /-'tjuːʃn/ n constitución f. **~ional** /-'tjuːʃənl/ a constitucional. ● n paseo m

constrain /kən'streɪn/ vt forzar, obligar, constreñir. **~t** /kən'streɪnt/ n fuerza f

constrict /kən'strɪkt/ vt apretar. **~ion** /-ʃn/ n constricción f

construct /kən'strʌkt/ vt construir. **~ion** /-ʃn/ n construcción f. **~ive** /kən'strʌktɪv/ a constructivo

construe /kən'struː/ vt interpretar; (gram) construir

consul /'kɒnsl/ n cónsul m. **~ar** /-jʊlə(r)/ a consular. **~ate** /-ət/ n consulado m

consult /kən'sʌlt/ vt/i consultar. **~ant** /kən'sʌltənt/ n asesor m; (med) especialista m & f; (tec) consejero m técnico. **~ation** /kɒnsəl'teɪʃn/ n consulta f

consume /kən'sjuːm/ vt consumir; (eat) comer; (drink) beber. **~r** /-ə(r)/ n consumidor m. ● a de consumo. **~rism** /kən'sjuːmərɪzəm/ n protección f del consumidor, consumismo m

consummat|e /'kɒnsəmeɪt/ vt consumar. **~ion** /-'meɪʃn/ n consumación f

consumption /kən'sʌmpʃn/ n consumo m; (med) tisis f

contact /'kɒntækt/ n contacto m. ● vt ponerse en contacto con

contagious /kən'teɪdʒəs/ a contagioso

contain /kən'teɪn/ vt contener. **~ o.s.** contenerse. **~er** n recipiente m; (com) contenedor m

contaminat|e /kən'tæmɪneɪt/ vt contaminar. **~ion** /-'neɪʃn/ n contaminación f

contemplat|e /'kɒntəmpleɪt/ vt contemplar; (consider) considerar. **~ion** /-'pleɪʃn/ n contemplación f

contemporary /kən'tempərərɪ/ a & n contemporáneo (m)

contempt /kən'tempt/ n desprecio m. **~ible** a despreciable. **~uous** /-tjʊəs/ a desdeñoso

contend /kən'tend/ vt sostener. ● vi contender. **~er** n contendiente m & f

content¹ /kən'tent/ a satisfecho. ● vt contentar

content² /'kɒntent/ n contenido m

contented /kən'tentɪd/ a satisfecho

contention /kən'tenʃn/ n contienda f; (opinion) opinión f, argumento m

contentment /kən'tentmənt/ n contento m

contest /'kɒntest/ n (competition) concurso m; (fight) contienda f. /kən'test/ vt disputar. **~ant** n contendiente m & f, concursante m & f

context /'kɒntekst/ n contexto m

continent /'kɒntɪnənt/ n continente m. **the C~** Europa f. **~al** /-'nentl/ a continental

contingency /kən'tɪndʒənsɪ/ n contingencia f

contingent /kən'tɪndʒənt/ a & n contingente (m)

continu|al /kən'tɪnjʊəl/ a continuo. **~ance** /kən'tɪnjʊəns/ n continuación f. **~ation** /kən'tɪnjʊ'eɪʃn/ n continuación f. **~e** /kən'tɪnjuː/ vt/i continuar; (resume) seguir. **~ed** a continuo. **~ity** /kɒntɪ'njuːətɪ/ n continuidad f. **~ity girl** (cinema, TV) secretaria f de rodaje. **~ous** /kən'tɪnjʊəs/ a continuo. **~ously** adv continuamente

contort /kən'tɔːt/ vt retorcer. **~ion** /-ʃn/ n contorsión f. **~ionist** /-ʃənɪst/ n contorsionista m & f

contour /'kɒntʊə(r)/ n contorno m. **~ line** n curva f de nivel

contraband /'kɒntrəbænd/ n contrabando m

contracepti|on /kɒntrə'sepʃn/ n contracepción f. **~ve** /kɒntrə'septɪv/ a & n anticonceptivo (m)

contract /'kɒntrækt/ n contrato m. /kən'trækt/ vt contraer. ● vi contraerse. **~ion** /kən'trækʃn/ n contracción f. **~or** /kən'træktə(r)/ n contratista m & f

contradict /kɒntrə'dɪkt/ vt contradecir. **~ion** /-ʃn/ n contradicción f. **~ory** a contradictorio

contraption /kən'træpʃn/ n (fam) artilugio m

contrary /'kɒntrəri/ a & n contrario (m). **on the ~** al contrario. ● adv. **~ to** contrariamente a. /kən'treəri/ a terco

contrast /'kɒntrɑːst/ n contraste m. /kən'trɑːst/ vt poner en contraste. ● vi contrastar. **~ing** a contrastante

contraven|e /kɒntrə'viːn/ vt contravenir. **~tion** /-'venʃn/ n contravención f

contribut|e /kən'trɪbjuːt/ vt/i contribuir. **~e to** escribir para (newspaper). **~ion** /kɒntrɪ'bjuːʃn/ n contribución f; (from salary) cotización f. **~or** n contribuyente m & f; (to newspaper) colaborador m

contrite /'kɒntraɪt/ a arrepentido, pesaroso

contriv|ance /kən'traɪvəns/ n invención f. **~e** /kən'traɪv/ vt idear. **~e to** conseguir

control /kən'trəul/ vt (pt controlled) controlar. ● n control m. **~s** npl (mec) mandos mpl

controvers|ial /kɒntrə'vɜːʃl/ a polémico, discutible. **~y** /'kɒntrəvɜːsɪ/ n controversia f

conundrum /kə'nʌndrəm/ n adivinanza f; (problem) enigma m

conurbation /kɒnɜː'beɪʃn/ n conurbación f

convalesce /kɒnvə'les/ vi convalecer. **~nce** n convalecencia f. **~nt** a & n convaleciente (m & f). **~nt home** n casa f de convalecencia

convector /kən'vektə(r)/ n estufa f de convección

convene /kən'viːn/ vt convocar. ● vi reunirse

convenien|ce /kən'viːnɪəns/ n conveniencia f, comodidad f. **all modern ~ces** todas las comodidades. **at your ~ce** según le convenga. **~ces** npl servicios mpl. **~t** /kən'viːnɪənt/ a cómodo; (place) bien situado; (time) oportuno. **be ~t** convenir. **~tly** adv convenientemente

convent /'kɒnvənt/ n convento m

convention /kən'venʃn/ n convención f; (meeting) congreso m. **~al** a convencional

converge /kən'vɜːdʒ/ vi convergir

conversant /kən'vɜːsənt/ a. **~ with** versado en

conversation /kɒnvə'seɪʃn/ n conversación f. **~al** a de la conversación. **~alist** n hábil conversador m

converse¹ /kən'vɜːs/ vi conversar

converse² /'kɒnvɜːs/ a inverso. ● n lo contrario. **~ly** adv a la inversa

conver|sion /kən'vɜːʃn/ n conversión f. **~t** /kən'vɜːt/ vt convertir. /'kɒnvɜːt/ n converso m. **~tible** /kən'vɜːtɪbl/ a convertible. ● n (auto) descapotable m

convex /'kɒnveks/ a convexo

convey /kən'veɪ/ vt llevar; transportar (goods); comunicar (idea, feeling). **~ance** n transporte m. **~or belt** n cinta f transportadora

convict /kən'vɪkt/ vt condenar. /'kɒnvɪkt/ n presidiario m. **~ion** /kən'vɪkʃn/ n condena f; (belief) creencia f

convinc|e /kən'vɪns/ vt convencer. **~ing** a convincente

convivial /kən'vɪvɪəl/ a alegre

convoke /kən'vəuk/ vt convocar

convoluted /'kɒnvəluːtɪd/ a enrollado; (argument) complicado

convoy /'kɒnvɔɪ/ n convoy m

convuls|e /kən'vʌls/ vt convulsionar. **be ~ed with laughter** desternillarse de risa. **~ion** /-ʃn/ n convulsión f

coo /kuː/ vi arrullar

cook /kuk/ vt cocinar; (alter, fam) falsificar. **~ up** (fam) inventar. ● n cocinero m

cooker /'kukə(r)/ n cocina f

cookery /'kukərɪ/ n cocina f

cookie /'kukɪ/ n (Amer) galleta f

cool /kuːl/ a (-er, -est) fresco; (calm) tranquilo; (unfriendly) frío. ● n fresco m; (sl) calma f. ● vt enfriar. ● vi enfriarse. **~ down** (person) calmarse. **~ly** adv tranquilamente. **~ness** n frescura f

coop /kuːp/ n gallinero m. ● vt. **~ up** encerrar

co-operat|e /kəu'ɒpəreɪt/ vi cooperar. **~ion** /-'reɪʃn/ n cooperación f

cooperative /kəu'ɒpərətɪv/ a cooperativo. ● n cooperativa f

co-opt /kəu'ɒpt/ vt cooptar

co-ordinat|e /kəu'ɔːdɪneɪt/ vt coordinar. **~ion** /-'neɪʃn/ n coordinación f

cop /kɒp/ vt (pt copped) (sl) prender. ● n (sl) policía m

cope /kəʊp/ vi (fam) arreglárselas. ~ **with** enfrentarse con

copious /ˈkəʊpɪəs/ a abundante

copper[1] /ˈkɒpə(r)/ n cobre m; (coin) perra f. ● a de cobre

copper[2] /ˈkɒpə(r)/ n (sl) policía m

coppice /ˈkɒpɪs/ n, **copse** /kɒps/ n bosquecillo m

Coptic /ˈkɒptɪk/ a copto

copulat|e /ˈkɒpjʊleɪt/ vi copular. ~**ion** /-ˈleɪʃn/ n cópula f

copy /ˈkɒpɪ/ n copia f; (typ) material m. ● vt copiar

copyright /ˈkɒpɪraɪt/ n derechos mpl de autor

copy-writer /ˈkɒpɪraɪtə(r)/ n redactor m de textos publicitarios

coral /ˈkɒrəl/ n coral m

cord /kɔ:d/ n cuerda f; (fabric) pana f. ~**s** npl pantalones mpl de pana

cordial /ˈkɔ:dɪəl/ a & n cordial (m)

cordon /ˈkɔ:dn/ n cordón m. ● vt. ~ **off** acordonar

corduroy /ˈkɔ:dərɔɪ/ n pana f

core /kɔ:(r)/ n (of apple) corazón m; (fig) meollo m

cork /kɔ:k/ n corcho m. ● vt taponar. ~**screw** /ˈkɔ:kskru:/ n sacacorchos m invar

corn[1] /kɔ:n/ n (wheat) trigo m; (Amer) maíz m; (seed) grano m

corn[2] /kɔ:n/ n (hard skin) callo m

corned /kɔ:nd/ a. ~ **beef** n carne f de vaca en lata

corner /ˈkɔ:nə(r)/ n ángulo m; (inside) rincón m; (outside) esquina f; (football) saque m de esquina. ● vt arrinconar; (com) acaparar. ~**stone** n piedra f angular

cornet /ˈkɔ:nɪt/ n (mus) corneta f; (for ice-cream) cucurucho m

cornflakes /ˈkɔ:nfleɪks/ npl copos mpl de maíz

cornflour /ˈkɔ:nflaʊə(r)/ n harina f de maíz

cornice /ˈkɔ:nɪs/ n cornisa f

cornucopia /kɔ:njʊˈkəʊpɪə/ n cuerno m de la abundancia

Corn|ish /ˈkɔ:nɪʃ/ a de Cornualles. ~**wall** /ˈkɔ:nwəl/ n Cornualles m

corny /ˈkɔ:nɪ/ a (trite, fam) gastado; (mawkish) sentimental, sensiblero

corollary /kəˈrɒlərɪ/ n corolario m

coronary /ˈkɒrənərɪ/ n trombosis f coronaria

coronation /kɒrəˈneɪʃn/ n coronación f

coroner /ˈkɒrənə(r)/ n juez m de primera instancia

corporal[1] /ˈkɔ:pərəl/ n cabo m

corporal[2] /ˈkɔ:pərəl/ a corporal

corporate /ˈkɔ:pərət/ a corporativo

corporation /kɔ:pəˈreɪʃn/ n corporación f; (of town) ayuntamiento m

corps /kɔ:(r)/ n (pl **corps** /kɔ:z/) cuerpo m

corpse /kɔ:ps/ n cadáver m

corpulent /ˈkɔ:pjʊlənt/ a gordo, corpulento

corpuscle /ˈkɔ:pʌsl/ n glóbulo m

corral /kəˈrɑ:l/ n (Amer) corral m

correct /kəˈrekt/ a correcto; ⟨time⟩ exacto. ● vt corregir. ~**ion** /-ʃn/ n corrección f

correlat|e /ˈkɒrəleɪt/ vt poner en correlación. ~**ion** /-ˈleɪʃn/ n correlación f

correspond /kɒrɪˈspɒnd/ vi corresponder; (write) escribirse. ~**ence** n correspondencia f. ~**ent** n corresponsal m & f

corridor /ˈkɒrɪdɔ:(r)/ n pasillo m

corroborate /kəˈrɒbəreɪt/ vt corroborar

corro|de /kəˈrəʊd/ vt corroer. ● vi corroerse. ~**sion** n corrosión f

corrugated /ˈkɒrəgeɪtɪd/ a ondulado. ~ **iron** n hierro m ondulado

corrupt /kəˈrʌpt/ a corrompido. ● vt corromper. ~**ion** /-ʃn/ n corrupción f

corset /ˈkɔ:sɪt/ n corsé m

Corsica /ˈkɔ:sɪkə/ n Córcega f. ~**n** a & n corso (m)

cortège /ˈkɔ:teɪʒ/ n cortejo m

cos /kɒs/ n lechuga f romana

cosh /kɒʃ/ n cachiporra f. ● vt aporrear

cosiness /ˈkəʊzɪnɪs/ n comodidad f

cosmetic /kɒzˈmetɪk/ a & n cosmético (m)

cosmic /ˈkɒzmɪk/ a cósmico

cosmonaut /ˈkɒzmənɔ:t/ n cosmonauta m & f

cosmopolitan /kɒzməˈpɒlɪtən/ a & n cosmopolita (m & f)

cosmos /ˈkɒzmɒs/ n cosmos m

Cossack /ˈkɒsæk/ a & n cosaco (m)

cosset /ˈkɒsɪt/ vt (pt **cosseted**) mimar

cost /kɒst/ vi (pt **cost**) costar, valer. ● vt (pt **costed**) calcular el coste de. ● n precio m. **at all** ~**s** cueste lo que cueste. **to one's** ~ a sus expensas. ~**s** npl (jurid) costas fpl

Costa Rica /kɒstəˈri:kə/ n Costa Rica. ~**n** a & n costarricense (m & f), costarriqueño (m)

costly /'kɒstlɪ/ a (**-ier, -iest**) caro, costoso

costume /'kɒstjuːm/ n traje m

cosy /'kəʊzɪ/ a (**-ier, -iest**) cómodo; ⟨place⟩ acogedor. • n cubierta f (de tetera)

cot /kɒt/ n cuna f

cottage /'kɒtɪdʒ/ n casita f de campo. ~ **cheese** n requesón m. ~ **industry** n industria f casera. ~ **pie** n carne f picada con puré de patatas

cotton /'kɒtn/ n algodón m. • vi. ~ **on** (sl) comprender. ~ **wool** n algodón hidrófilo

couch /kaʊtʃ/ n sofá m. • vt expresar

couchette /kuː'ʃet/ n litera f

cough /kɒf/ vi toser. • n tos f. ~ **up** (sl) pagar. ~ **mixture** n jarabe m para la tos

could /kʊd, kəd/ pt of **can**

couldn't /'kʊdnt/ = **could not**

council /'kaʊnsl/ n consejo m; (of town) ayuntamiento m. ~ **house** n vivienda f protegida. ~**lor** /'kaʊnsələ(r)/ n concejal m

counsel /'kaʊnsl/ n consejo m; (pl invar) (jurid) abogado m. ~**lor** n consejero m

count[1] /kaʊnt/ n recuento m. • vt/i contar

count[2] /kaʊnt/ n (nobleman) conde m

countdown /'kaʊntdaʊn/ n cuenta f atrás

countenance /'kaʊntɪnəns/ n semblante m. • vt aprobar

counter /'kaʊntə(r)/ n (in shop etc) mostrador m; (token) ficha f. • adv. ~ **to** en contra de. • a opuesto. • vt oponerse a; parar ⟨blow⟩. • vi contraatacar

counter... /'kaʊntə(r)/ pref contra...

counteract /kaʊntər'ækt/ vt contrarrestar

counter-attack /'kaʊntərətæk/ n contraataque m. • vt/i contraatacar

counterbalance /'kaʊntəbæləns/ n contrapeso m. • vt/i contrapesar

counterfeit /'kaʊntəfɪt/ a falsificado. • n falsificación f. • vt falsificar

counterfoil /'kaʊntəfɔɪl/ n talón m

counterpart /'kaʊntəpɑːt/ n equivalente m; (person) homólogo m

counter-productive /'kaʊntəprə'dʌktɪv/ a contraproducente

countersign /'kaʊntəsaɪn/ vt refrendar

countess /'kaʊntɪs/ n condesa f

countless /'kaʊntlɪs/ a innumerable

countrified /'kʌntrɪfaɪd/ a rústico

country /'kʌntrɪ/ n (native land) país m; (countryside) campo m. ~ **folk** n gente f del campo. **go to the** ~ ir al campo; (pol) convocar elecciones generales

countryman /'kʌntrɪmən/ n (pl **-men**) campesino m; (of one's own country) compatriota m

countryside /'kʌntrɪsaɪd/ n campo m

county /'kaʊntɪ/ n condado m, provincia f

coup /kuː/ n golpe m

coupé /'kuːpeɪ/ n cupé m

couple /'kʌpl/ n (of things) par m; (of people) pareja f; (married) matrimonio m. **a** ~ **of** un par de. • vt unir; (tec) acoplar. • vi copularse

coupon /'kuːpɒn/ n cupón m

courage /'kʌrɪdʒ/ n valor m. ~**ous** /kə'reɪdʒəs/ a valiente. ~**ously** adv valientemente

courgette /kʊə'ʒet/ n calabacín m

courier /'kʊrɪə(r)/ n mensajero m; (for tourists) guía m & f

course /kɔːs/ n curso m; (behaviour) conducta f; (aviat, naut) rumbo m; (culin) plato m; (for golf) campo m. **in due** ~ a su debido tiempo. **in the** ~ **of** en el transcurso de, durante. **of** ~ desde luego, por supuesto

court /kɔːt/ n corte f; (tennis) pista f; (jurid) tribunal m. • vt cortejar; buscar ⟨danger⟩

courteous /'kɜːtɪəs/ a cortés

courtesan /kɔːtɪ'zæn/ n (old use) cortesana f

courtesy /'kɜːtəsɪ/ n cortesía f

court: ~**ier** /'kɔːtɪə(r)/ n (old use) cortesano m. ~ **martial** n (pl **courts martial**) consejo m de guerra. ~-**martial** vt (pt ~-**martialled**) juzgar en consejo de guerra. ~**ship** /'kɔːtʃɪp/ n cortejo m

courtyard /'kɔːtjɑːd/ n patio m

cousin /'kʌzn/ n primo m. **first** ~ primo carnal. **second** ~ primo segundo

cove /kəʊv/ n cala f

covenant /'kʌvənənt/ n acuerdo m

Coventry /'kɒvntrɪ/ n. **send to** ~ hacer el vacío

cover /'kʌvə(r)/ vt cubrir; (journalism) hacer un reportaje sobre. ~

up cubrir; (*fig*) ocultar. ● *n* cubierta
f; (*shelter*) abrigo *m*; (*lid*) tapa *f*; (*for furniture*) funda *f*; (*pretext*) pretexto
m; (*of magazine*) portada *f*. ~age
/ˈkʌvərɪdʒ/ *n* reportaje *m*. ~ charge
n precio *m* del cubierto. ~ing *n*
cubierta *f*. ~ing letter *n* carta *f*
explicatoria, carta *f* adjunta

covet /ˈkʌvɪt/ *vt* codiciar

cow /kaʊ/ *n* vaca *f*

coward /ˈkaʊəd/ *n* cobarde *m*. ~ly *a*
cobarde. ~ice /ˈkaʊədɪs/ *n* cobardía
f

cowboy /ˈkaʊbɔɪ/ *n* vaquero *m*

cower /ˈkaʊə(r)/ *vi* encogerse,
acobardarse

cowl /kaʊl/ *n* capucha *f*; (*of chimney*)
sombrerete *m*

cowshed /ˈkaʊʃed/ *n* establo *m*

coxswain /ˈkɒksn/ *n* timonel *m*

coy /kɔɪ/ *a* (-er, -est) (falsamente)
tímido, remilgado

crab¹ /kræb/ *n* cangrejo *m*

crab² /kræb/ *vi* (*pt* crabbed) quejarse

crab-apple /ˈkræbæpl/ *n* manzana *f*
silvestre

crack /kræk/ *n* grieta *f*; (*noise*) crujido *m*; (*of whip*) chasquido *m*; (*joke*,
sl) chiste *m*. ● *a* (*fam*) de primera.
● *vt* agrietar; chasquear ⟨*whip*,
fingers⟩; cascar ⟨*nut*⟩; gastar ⟨*joke*⟩;
resolver ⟨*problem*⟩. ● *vi* agrietarse.
get ~ing (*fam*) darse prisa. ~ down
on (*fam*) tomar medidas enérgicas
contra. ~ up *vi* fallar; ⟨*person*⟩ volverse loco. ~ed /krækt/ *a* (*sl*)
chiflado

cracker /ˈkrækə(r)/ *n* petardo *m*;
(*culin*) galleta *f* (soso); (*culin*, *Amer*)
galleta *f*

crackers /ˈkrækəz/ *a* (*sl*) chiflado

crackl|e /ˈkrækl/ *vi* crepitar. ● *n* crepitación *f*, crujido *m*. ~ing
/ˈkræklɪŋ/ *n* crepitación *f*, crujido
m; (*of pork*) chicharrón *m*

crackpot /ˈkrækpɒt/ *n* (*sl*) chiflado *m*

cradle /ˈkreɪdl/ *n* cuna *f*. ● *vt* acunar

craft /krɑːft/ *n* destreza *f*; (*technique*)
arte *f*; (*cunning*) astucia *f*. ● *n invar*
(*boat*) barco *m*

craftsman /ˈkrɑːftsmən/ *n* (*pl* -men)
artesano *m*. ~ship *n* artesanía *f*

crafty /ˈkrɑːftɪ/ *a* (-ier, -iest) astuto

crag /kræg/ *n* despeñadero *m*. ~gy *a*
peñascoso

cram /kræm/ *vt* (*pt* crammed)
rellenar. ~ with llenar de. ● *vi* (*for exams*) empollar. ~full *a* atestado

cramp /kræmp/ *n* calambre *m*

cramped /kræmpt/ *a* apretado

cranberry /ˈkrænbərɪ/ *n* arándano *m*

crane /kreɪn/ *n* grúa *f*; (*bird*) grulla
f. ● *vt* estirar ⟨*neck*⟩

crank¹ /kræŋk/ *n* manivela *f*

crank² /kræŋk/ *n* (*person*) excéntrico
m. ~y *a* excéntrico

cranny /ˈkrænɪ/ *n* grieta *f*

crash /kræʃ/ *n* accidente *m*; (*noise*)
estruendo *m*; (*collision*) choque *m*;
(*com*) quiebra *f*. ● *vt* estrellar. ● *vi*
quebrar con estrépito; (*have accident*) tener un accidente; ⟨*car etc*⟩
chocar; (*fail*) fracasar. ~ course *n*
curso *m* intensivo. ~helmet *n*
casco *m* protector. ~land *vi* hacer
un aterrizaje de emergencia, hacer
un aterrizaje forzoso

crass /kræs/ *a* craso, burdo

crate /kreɪt/ *n* cajón *m*. ● *vt* embalar

crater /ˈkreɪtə(r)/ *n* cráter *m*

cravat /krəˈvæt/ *n* corbata *f*, fular *m*

crav|e /kreɪv/ *vi*. ~e for anhelar.
~ing *n* ansia *f*

crawl /krɔːl/ *vi* andar a gatas; (*move slowly*) avanzar lentamente; (*drag o.s.*) arrastrarse. ● *n* (*swimming*)
crol *m*. at a ~ a paso lento. ~ to
humillarse ante. ~ with hervir de

crayon /ˈkreɪən/ *n* lápiz *m* de color

craze /kreɪz/ *n* manía *f*

craz|iness /ˈkreɪzɪnɪs/ *n* locura *f*. ~y
/ˈkreɪzɪ/ *a* (-ier, -iest) loco. be ~y
about andar loco por. ~y paving *n*
enlosado *m* irregular

creak /kriːk/ *n* crujido *m*; (*of hinge*)
chirrido *m*. ● *vi* crujir; ⟨*hinge*⟩
chirriar

cream /kriːm/ *n* crema *f*; (*fresh*) nata
f. ● *a* (*colour*) color de crema. ● *vt*
(*remove*) desnatar; (*beat*) batir. ~
cheese *n* queso *m* de nata. ~y *a*
cremoso

crease /kriːs/ *n* pliegue *m*; (*crumple*)
arruga *f*. ● *vt* plegar; (*wrinkle*) arrugar. ● *vi* arrugarse

creat|e /kriːˈeɪt/ *vt* crear. ~ion /-ʃn/
n creación *f*. ~ive *a* creativo. ~or *n*
creador *m*

creature /ˈkriːtʃə(r)/ *n* criatura *f*,
bicho *m*, animal *m*

crèche /kreɪʃ/ *n* guardería *f* infantil

credence /ˈkriːdns/ *n* creencia *f*, fe *f*

credentials /krɪˈdenʃlz/ *npl* credenciales *mpl*

credib|ility /kredəˈbɪlətɪ/ *n* credibilidad *f*. ~le /ˈkredəbl/ *a* creíble

credit /ˈkredɪt/ *n* crédito *m*; (*honour*)
honor *m*. take the ~ for atribuirse

el mérito de. ● *vt* (*pt* **credited**) acreditar; (*believe*) creer. ~ **s.o. with** atribuir a uno. ~**able** *a* loable. ~ **card** *n* tarjeta *f* de crédito. ~**or** *n* acreedor *m*

credulous /'krɔdjʊləs/ *a* crédulo

creed /kri:d/ *n* credo *m*

creek /kri:k/ *n* ensenada *f*. **up the** ~ (*sl*) en apuros

creep /kri:p/ *vi* (*pt* **crept**) arrastrarse; (*plant*) trepar. ● *n* (*sl*) persona *f* desagradable. ~**er** *n* enredadera *f*. ~**s** /kri:ps/ *npl*. **give s.o. the** ~**s** dar repugnancia a uno

cremat|e /krɪ'meɪt/ *vt* incinerar. ~**ion** /-ʃn/ *n* cremación *f*. ~**orium** /kremə'tɔ:rɪəm/ *n* (*pl* **-ia**) crematorio *m*

Creole /'krɪəʊl/ *a* & *n* criollo (*m*)

crêpe /kreɪp/ *n* crespón *m*

crept /krept/ *see* **creep**

crescendo /krɪ'ʃendəʊ/ *n* (*pl* **-os**) crescendo *m*

crescent /'kresnt/ *n* media luna *f*; (*street*) calle *f* en forma de media luna

cress /kres/ *n* berro *m*

crest /krest/ *n* cresta *f*; (*coat of arms*) blasón *m*

Crete /kri:t/ *n* Creta *f*

cretin /'kretɪn/ *n* cretino *m*

crevasse /krɪ'væs/ *n* grieta *f*

crevice /'krevɪs/ *n* grieta *f*

crew[1] /kru:/ *n* tripulación *f*; (*gang*) pandilla *f*

crew[2] /kru:/ *see* **crow**[2]

crew: ~ **cut** *n* corte *m* al rape. ~ **neck** *n* cuello *m* redondo

crib /krɪb/ *n* cuna *f*; (*relig*) belén *m*; (*plagiarism*) plagio *m*. ● *vt/i* (*pt* **cribbed**) plagiar

crick /krɪk/ *n* calambre *m*; (*in neck*) tortícolis *f*

cricket[1] /'krɪkɪt/ *n* criquet *m*

cricket[2] /'krɪkɪt/ *n* (*insect*) grillo *m*

cricketer /'krɪkɪtə(r)/ *n* jugador *m* de criquet

crim|e /kraɪm/ *n* crimen *m*; (*acts*) criminalidad *f*. ~**inal** /'krɪmɪnl/ *a* & *n* criminal (*m*)

crimp /krɪmp/ *vt* rizar

crimson /'krɪmzn/ *a* & *n* carmesí (*m*)

cringe /krɪndʒ/ *vi* encogerse; (*fig*) humillarse

crinkle /'krɪŋkl/ *vt* arrugar. ● *vi* arrugarse. ● *n* arruga *f*

crinoline /'krɪnəlɪn/ *n* miriñaque *m*

cripple /'krɪpl/ *n* lisiado *m*, mutilado *m*. ● *vt* lisiar; (*fig*) paralizar

crisis /'kraɪsɪs/ *n* (*pl* **crises** /'kraɪsi:z/) crisis *f*

crisp /krɪsp/ *a* (**-er, -est**) (*culin*) crujiente; (*air*) vigorizador. ~**s** *npl* patatas *fpl* fritas a la inglesa

criss-cross /'krɪskrɒs/ *a* entrecruzado. ● *vt* entrecruzar. ● *vi* entrecruzarse

criterion /kraɪ'tɪərɪən/ *n* (*pl* **-ia**) criterio *m*

critic /'krɪtɪk/ *n* crítico *m*

critical /'krɪtɪkl/ *a* crítico. ~**ly** *adv* críticamente; (*ill*) gravemente

critici|sm /'krɪtɪsɪzəm/ *n* crítica *f*. ~**ze** /'krɪtɪsaɪz/ *vt/i* criticar

croak /krəʊk/ *n* (*of person*) gruñido *m*; (*of frog*) canto *m*. ● *vi* gruñir; (*frog*) croar

crochet /'krəʊʃeɪ/ *n* croché *m*, ganchillo *m*. ● *vt* hacer ganchillo

crock[1] /krɒk/ *n* (*person, fam*) vejancón *m*; (*old car*) cacharro *m*

crock[2] /krɒk/ *n* vasija *f* de loza

crockery /'krɒkərɪ/ *n* loza *f*

crocodile /'krɒkədaɪl/ *n* cocodrilo *m*. ~ **tears** *npl* lágrimas *fpl* de cocodrilo

crocus /'krəʊkəs/ *n* (*pl* **-es**) azafrán *m*

crony /'krəʊnɪ/ *n* amigote *m*

crook /krʊk/ *n* (*fam*) maleante *m* & *f*, estafador *m*, criminal *m*; (*stick*) cayado *m*; (*of arm*) pliegue *m*

crooked /'krʊkɪd/ *a* torcido; (*winding*) tortuoso; (*dishonest*) poco honrado

croon /kru:n/ *vt/i* canturrear

crop /krɒp/ *n* cosecha *f*; (*fig*) montón *m*. ● *vt* (*pt* **cropped**) *vi* cortar. ~ **up** surgir

cropper /'krɒpə(r)/ *n*. **come a** ~ (*fall, fam*) caer; (*fail, fam*) fracasar

croquet /'krəʊkeɪ/ *n* croquet *m*

croquette /krə'ket/ *n* croqueta *f*

cross /krɒs/ *n* cruz *f*; (*of animals*) cruce *m*. ● *vt/i* cruzar; (*oppose*) contrariar. ~ **off** tachar. ~ **o.s.** santiguarse. ~ **out** tachar. ~ **s.o.'s mind** ocurrírsele a uno. ● *a* enfadado. **talk at** ~ **purposes** hablar sin entenderse

crossbar /'krɒsbɑ:(r)/ *n* travesaño *m*

cross-examine /krɒsɪg'zæmɪn/ *vt* interrogar

cross-eyed /'krɒsaɪd/ *a* bizco

crossfire /'krɒsfaɪə(r)/ *n* fuego *m* cruzado

crossing /'krɒsɪŋ/ *n* (*by boat*) travesía *f*; (*on road*) paso *m* para peatones

crossly /'krɒslɪ/ *adv* con enfado
cross-reference /krɒs'refrəns/ *n* referencia *f*
crossroads /'krɒsrəʊdz/ *n* cruce *m* (de carreteras)
cross-section /krɒs'sekʃn/ *n* sección *f* transversal; (*fig*) muestra *f* representativa
crosswise /'krɒswaɪz/ *adv* al través
crossword /'krɒswɜːd/ *n* crucigrama *m*
crotch /krɒtʃ/ *n* entrepiernas *fpl*
crotchety /'krɒtʃɪtɪ/ *a* de mal genio
crouch /kraʊtʃ/ *vi* agacharse
crow[1] /krəʊ/ *n* cuervo *m*. **as the ~ flies** en línea recta
crow[2] /krəʊ/ *vi* (*pt* **crew**) cacarear
crowbar /'krəʊbɑː(r)/ *n* palanca *f*
crowd /kraʊd/ *n* muchedumbre *f*. ● *vt* amontonar; (*fill*) llenar. ● *vi* amontonarse; (*gather*) reunirse. **~ed** *a* atestado
crown /kraʊn/ *n* corona *f*; (*of hill*) cumbre *f*; (*of head*) coronilla *f*. ● *vt* coronar; poner una corona a (*tooth*). **C~ Court** *n* tribunal *m* regional. **C~ prince** *n* príncipe *m* heredero
crucial /'kruːʃl/ *a* crucial
crucifix /'kruːsɪfɪks/ *n* crucifijo *m*. **~ion** /-'fɪkʃn/ *n* crucifixión *f*
crucify /'kruːsɪfaɪ/ *vt* crucificar
crude /kruːd/ *a* (**-er, -est**) (*raw*) crudo; (*rough*) tosco; (*vulgar*) ordinario
cruel /krʊəl/ *a* (**crueller, cruellest**) cruel. **~ty** *n* crueldad *f*
cruet /'kruːɪt/ *n* vinagreras *fpl*
cruise /kruːz/ *n* crucero *m*. ● *vi* hacer un crucero; (*of car*) circular lentamente. **~r** *n* crucero *m*
crumb /krʌm/ *n* migaja *f*
crumble /'krʌmbl/ *vt* desmenuzar. ● *vi* desmenuzarse; (*collapse*) derrumbarse
crummy /'krʌmɪ/ *a* (**-ier, -iest**) (*sl*) miserable
crumpet /'krʌmpɪt/ *n* bollo *m* blando
crumple /'krʌmpl/ *vt* arrugar; estrujar (*paper*). ● *vi* arrugarse
crunch /krʌntʃ/ *vt* hacer crujir; (*bite*) ronzar, morder, masticar. ● *n* crujido *m*; (*fig*) momento *m* decisivo
crusade /kruː'seɪd/ *n* cruzada *f*. **~r** /-ə(r)/ *n* cruzado *m*
crush /krʌʃ/ *vt* aplastar; arrugar (*clothes*); estrujar (*paper*). ● *n* (*crowd*) aglomeración *f*. **have a ~**

on (*sl*) estar perdido por. **orange ~** *n* naranjada *f*
crust /krʌst/ *n* corteza *f*. **~y** *a* (*bread*) de corteza dura; (*person*) malhumorado
crutch /krʌtʃ/ *n* muleta *f*; (*anat*) entrepiernas *fpl*
crux /krʌks/ *n* (*pl* **cruxes**) punto *m* más importante, quid *m*, busilis *m*
cry /kraɪ/ *n* grito *m*. **be a far ~ from** (*fig*) distar mucho de. ● *vi* llorar; (*call out*) gritar. **~ off** rajarse. **~-baby** *n* llorón *m*
crypt /krɪpt/ *n* cripta *f*
cryptic /'krɪptɪk/ *a* enigmático
crystal /'krɪstl/ *n* cristal *m*. **~lize** *vt* cristalizar. ● *vi* cristalizarse
cub /kʌb/ *n* cachorro *m*. **C~ (Scout)** *n* niño *m* explorador
Cuba /'kjuːbə/ *n* Cuba *f*. **~n** *a* & *n* cubano (*m*)
cubby-hole /'kʌbɪhəʊl/ *n* casilla *f*; (*room*) chiribitil *m*, cuchitril *m*
cub|e /kjuːb/ *n* cubo *m*. **~ic** *a* cúbico
cubicle /'kjuːbɪkl/ *n* cubículo *m*; (*changing room*) caseta *f*
cubis|m /'kjuːbɪzm/ *n* cubismo *m*. **~t** *a* & *n* cubista (*m* & *f*)
cuckold /'kʌkəʊld/ *n* cornudo *m*
cuckoo /'kʊkuː/ *n* cuco *m*, cuclillo *m*
cucumber /'kjuːkʌmbə(r)/ *n* pepino *m*
cuddl|e /'kʌdl/ *vt* abrazar. ● *vi* abrazarse. ● *n* abrazo *m*. **~y** *a* mimoso
cudgel /'kʌdʒl/ *n* porra *f*. ● *vt* (*pt* **cudgelled**) aporrear
cue[1] /kjuː/ *n* indicación *f*; (*in theatre*) pie *m*
cue[2] /kjuː/ *n* (*in billiards*) taco *m*
cuff /kʌf/ *n* puño *m*; (*blow*) bofetada *f*. **speak off the ~** hablar de improviso. ● *vt* abofetear. **~-link** *n* gemelo *m*
cul-de-sac /'kʌldəsæk/ *n* callejón *m* sin salida
culinary /'kʌlɪnərɪ/ *a* culinario
cull /kʌl/ *vt* coger (*flowers*); entresacar (*animals*)
culminat|e /'kʌlmɪneɪt/ *vi* culminar. **~ion** /-'neɪʃn/ *n* culminación *f*
culottes /kʊ'lɒts/ *npl* falda *f* pantalón
culprit /'kʌlprɪt/ *n* culpable *m*
cult /kʌlt/ *n* culto *m*
cultivat|e /'kʌltɪveɪt/ *vt* cultivar. **~ion** /-'veɪʃn/ *n* cultivo *m*; (*fig*) cultura *f*

cultur|al /'kʌltʃərəl/ a cultural. **~e** /'kʌltʃə(r)/ n cultura f; (bot etc) cultivo m. **~ed** a cultivado; ⟨person⟩ culto

cumbersome /'kʌmbəsəm/ a incómodo; (heavy) pesado

cumulative /'kju:mjʊlətɪv/ a cumulativo

cunning /'kʌnɪŋ/ a astuto. ● n astucia f

cup /kʌp/ n taza f; (prize) copa f

cupboard /'kʌbəd/ n armario m

Cup Final /kʌp'faɪnl/ n final f del campeonato

cupful /'kʌpfʊl/ n taza f

cupidity /kju:'pɪdɪtɪ/ n codicia f

curable /'kjʊərəbl/ a curable

curate /'kjʊərət/ n coadjutor m

curator /kjʊə'reɪtə(r)/ n (of museum) conservador m

curb /kɜ:b/ n freno m. ● vt refrenar

curdle /'kɜ:dl/ vt cuajar. ● vi cuajarse; ⟨milk⟩ cortarse

curds /kɜ:dz/ npl cuajada f, requesón m

cure /kjʊə(r)/ vt curar. ● n cura f

curfew /'kɜ:fju:/ n queda f; (signal) toque m de queda

curio /'kjʊərɪəʊ/ n (pl -os) curiosidad f

curio|us /'kjʊərɪəs/ a curioso. **~sity** /-'ɒsətɪ/ n curiosidad f

curl /kɜ:l/ vt rizar ⟨hair⟩. **~ o.s. up** acurrucarse. ● vi ⟨hair⟩ rizarse; ⟨paper⟩ arrollarse. ● n rizo m. **~er** /'kɜ:lə(r)/ n bigudí m, rulo m. **~y** /'kɜ:lɪ/ a (-ier, -iest) rizado

currant /'kʌrənt/ n pasa f de Corinto

currency /'kʌrənsɪ/ n moneda f; (acceptance) uso m (corriente)

current /'kʌrənt/ a & n corriente (f). **~ events** asuntos mpl de actualidad. **~ly** adv actualmente

curriculum /kə'rɪkjʊləm/ n (pl -la) programa m de estudios. **~ vitae** n curriculum m vitae

curry[1] /'kʌrɪ/ n curry m

curry[2] /'kʌrɪ/ vt. **~ favour with** congraciarse con

curse /kɜ:s/ n maldición f; (oath) palabrota f. ● vt maldecir. ● vi decir palabrotas

cursory /'kɜ:sərɪ/ a superficial

curt /kɜ:t/ a brusco

curtail /kɜ:'teɪl/ vt abreviar; reducir ⟨expenses⟩

curtain /'kɜ:tn/ n cortina f; (in theatre) telón m

curtsy /'kɜ:tsɪ/ n reverencia f. ● vi hacer una reverencia

curve /kɜ:v/ n curva f. ● vt encurvar. ● vi encorvarse; ⟨road⟩ torcerse

cushion /'kʊʃn/ n cojín m. ● vt amortiguar ⟨a blow⟩; (fig) proteger

cushy /'kʊʃɪ/ a (-ier, -iest) (fam) fácil

custard /'kʌstəd/ n natillas fpl

custodian /kʌ'stəʊdɪən/ n custodio m

custody /'kʌstədɪ/ n custodia f. **be in ~** (jurid) estar detenido

custom /'kʌstəm/ n costumbre f; (com) clientela f

customary /'kʌstəmərɪ/ a acostumbrado

customer /'kʌstəmə(r)/ n cliente m

customs /'kʌstəmz/ npl aduana f. **~ officer** n aduanero m

cut /kʌt/ vt/i (pt cut, pres p cutting) cortar; reducir ⟨prices⟩. ● n corte m; (reduction) reducción f. **~ across** atravesar. **~ back, ~ down** reducir. **~ in** interrumpir. **~ off** cortar; (phone) desconectar; (fig) aislar. **~ out** recortar; (omit) suprimir. **~ through** atravesar. **~ up** cortar en pedazos. **be ~ up about** (fig) afligirse por

cute /kju:t/ a (-er, -est) (fam) listo; (Amer) mono

cuticle /'kju:tɪkl/ n cutícula f

cutlery /'kʌtlərɪ/ n cubiertos mpl

cutlet /'kʌtlɪt/ n chuleta f

cut-price /'kʌtpraɪs/ a a precio reducido

cut-throat /'kʌtθrəʊt/ a despiadado

cutting /'kʌtɪŋ/ a cortante; ⟨remark⟩ mordaz. ● n (from newspaper) recorte m; (of plant) esqueje m

cyanide /'saɪənaɪd/ n cianuro m

cybernetics /saɪbə'netɪks/ n cibernética f

cyclamen /'sɪkləmən/ n ciclamen m

cycle /'saɪkl/ n ciclo m; (bicycle) bicicleta f. ● vi ir en bicicleta

cyclic(al) /'saɪklɪk(l)/ a cíclico

cycli|ng /'saɪklɪŋ/ n ciclismo m. **~st** n ciclista m & f

cyclone /'saɪkləʊn/ n ciclón m

cylind|er /'sɪlɪndə(r)/ n cilindro m. **~er head** (auto) n culata f. **~rical** /-'lɪndrɪkl/ a cilíndrico

cymbal /'sɪmbl/ n címbalo m

cynic /'sɪnɪk/ n cínico m. **~al** a cínico. **~ism** /-sɪzəm/ n cinismo m

cypress /'saɪprəs/ n ciprés m

Cypr|iot /'sɪprɪət/ *a* & *n* chipriota (*m* & *f*). **~us** /'saɪprəs/ *n* Chipre *f*

cyst /sɪst/ *n* quiste *m*

czar /zɑ:(r)/ *n* zar *m*

Czech /tʃek/ *a* & *n* checo (*m*). **the ~ Republic** *n* la república *f* Checa

Czechoslovak /tʃekəʊ'sləʊvæk/ *a* & *n* (*history*) checoslovaco (*m*). **~ia** /-ə'vækiə/ *n* (*history*) Checoslovaquia *f*

D

dab /dæb/ *vt* (*pt* dabbed) tocar ligeramente. ● *n* toque *m* suave. **a ~ of** un poquito de

dabble /'dæbl/ *vi*. **~ in** meterse (superficialmente) en. **~r** /ə(r)/ *n* aficionado *m*

dad /dæd/ *n* (*fam*) papá *m*. **~dy** *n* (*children's use*) papá *m*. **~dy-long-legs** *n* típula *f*

daffodil /'dæfədɪl/ *n* narciso *m*

daft /dɑ:ft/ *a* (**-er, -est**) tonto

dagger /'dægə(r)/ *n* puñal *m*

dahlia /'deɪlɪə/ *n* dalia *f*

daily /'deɪlɪ/ *a* diario. ● *adv* diariamente, cada día. ● *n* diario *m*; (*cleaner, fam*) asistenta *f*

dainty /'deɪntɪ/ *a* (**-ier, -iest**) delicado

dairy /'deərɪ/ *n* vaquería *f*; (*shop*) lechería *f*. ● *a* lechero

dais /deɪs/ *n* estrado *m*

daisy /'deɪzɪ/ *n* margarita *f*

dale /deɪl/ *n* valle *m*

dally /'dælɪ/ *vi* tardar; (*waste time*) perder el tiempo

dam /dæm/ *n* presa *f*. ● *vt* (*pt* dammed) embalsar

damage /'dæmɪdʒ/ *n* daño *m*; (*pl*, *jurid*) daños *mpl* y perjuicios *mpl*. ● *vt* (*fig*) dañar, estropear. **~ing** *a* perjudicial

damask /'dæməsk/ *n* damasco *m*

dame /deɪm/ *n* (*old use*) dama *f*; (*Amer, sl*) chica *f*

damn /dæm/ *vt* condenar; (*curse*) maldecir. ● *int* ¡córcholis! ● *a* maldito. ● *n*. **I don't care a ~** (no) me importa un comino. **~ation** /-'neɪʃn/ *n* condenación *f*, perdición *f*

damp /dæmp/ *n* humedad *f*. ● *a* (**-er, -est**) húmedo. ● *vt* mojar; (*fig*) ahogar. **~er** /'dæmpə(r)/ *n* apagador *m*, sordina *f*; (*fig*) aguafiestas *m invar*. **~ness** *n* humedad *f*

damsel /'dæmzl/ *n* (*old use*) doncella *f*

dance /dɑ:ns/ *vt/i* bailar. ● *n* baile *m*. **~-hall** *n* salón *m* de baile. **~r** /-ə(r)/ *n* bailador *m*; (*professional*) bailarín *m*

dandelion /'dændɪlaɪən/ *n* diente *m* de león

dandruff /'dændrʌf/ *n* caspa *f*

dandy /'dændɪ/ *n* petimetre *m*

Dane /deɪn/ *n* danés *m*

danger /'deɪndʒə(r)/ *n* peligro *m*; (*risk*) riesgo *m*. **~ous** *a* peligroso

dangle /'dæŋgl/ *vt* balancear. ● *vi* suspender, colgar

Danish /'deɪnɪʃ/ *a* danés. ● *m* (*lang*) danés *m*

dank /dæŋk/ *a* (**-er, -est**) húmedo, malsano

dare /deə(r)/ *vt* desafiar. ● *vi* atreverse a. **I ~ say** probablemente. ● *n* desafío *m*

daredevil /'deədevl/ *n* atrevido *m*

daring /'deərɪŋ/ *a* atrevido

dark /dɑ:k/ *a* (**-er, -est**) oscuro; (*gloomy*) sombrío; ⟨*skin, hair*⟩ moreno. ● *n* oscuridad *f*; (*nightfall*) atardecer. **in the ~** a oscuras. **~en** /'dɑ:kən/ *vt* oscurecer. ● *vi* oscurecerse. **~ horse** *n* persona *f* de talentos desconocidos. **~ness** *n* oscuridad *f*. **~-room** *n* cámara *f* oscura

darling /'dɑ:lɪŋ/ *a* querido. ● *n* querido *m*

darn /dɑ:n/ *vt* zurcir

dart /dɑ:t/ *n* dardo *m*. ● *vi* lanzarse; (*run*) precipitarse. **~board** /'dɑ:tbɔ:d/ *n* blanco *m*. **~s** *npl* los dardos *mpl*

dash /dæʃ/ *vi* precipitarse. **~ off** marcharse apresuradamente. **~ out** salir corriendo. ● *vt* lanzar; (*break*) romper; defraudar ⟨*hopes*⟩. ● *n* carrera *f*; (*small amount*) poquito *m*; (*stroke*) raya *f*. **cut a ~** causar sensación

dashboard /'dæʃbɔ:d/ *n* tablero *m* de mandos

dashing /'dæʃɪŋ/ *a* vivo; (*showy*) vistoso

data /'deɪtə/ *npl* datos *mpl*. **~ processing** *n* proceso *m* de datos

date[1] /deɪt/ *n* fecha *f*; (*fam*) cita *f*. **to ~** hasta la fecha. ● *vt* fechar; (*go out with, fam*) salir con. ● *vi* datar; (*be old-fashioned*) quedar anticuado

date[2] /deɪt/ *n* (*fruit*) dátil *m*

dated /'deɪtɪd/ *a* pasado de moda

daub /dɔːb/ vt embadurnar

daughter /'dɔːtə(r)/ n hija f. **~-in-law** n nuera f

daunt /dɔːnt/ vt intimidar

dauntless /'dɔːntlɪs/ a intrépido

dawdle /'dɔːdl/ vi andar despacio; (waste time) perder el tiempo. **~r** /-ə(r)/ n rezagado m

dawn /dɔːn/ n amanecer m. ● vi amanecer; (fig) nacer. **it ~ed on me that** caí en la cuenta de que, comprendí que

day /deɪ/ n día m; (whole day) jornada f; (period) época f. **~break** n amanecer m. **~dream** n ensueño m. ● vi soñar despierto. **~light** /'deɪlaɪt/ n luz f del día. **~time** /'deɪtaɪm/ n día m

daze /deɪz/ vt aturdir. ● n aturdimiento m. **in a ~** aturdido

dazzle /'dæzl/ vt deslumbrar

deacon /'diːkən/ n diácono m

dead /ded/ a muerto; (numb) entumecido. **~ centre** justo en medio. ● adv completamente. **~ beat** rendido. **~ on time** justo a tiempo. **~ slow** muy lento. **stop ~** parar en seco. ● n muertos mpl. **in the ~ of night** en plena noche. **the ~** los muertos mpl. **~en** /'dedn/ vt amortiguar (sound, blow); calmar (pain). **~ end** n callejón m sin salida. **~ heat** n empate m

deadline /'dedlaɪn/ n fecha f tope, fin m de plazo

deadlock /'dedlɒk/ n punto m muerto

deadly /'dedlɪ/ a (-ier, -iest) mortal; (harmful) nocivo; (dreary) aburrido

deadpan /'dedpæn/ a impasible

deaf /def/ a (-er, -est) sordo. **~-aid** n audífono m m. **~en** /'defn/ vt ensordecer. **~ening** a ensordecedor. **~-mute** n sordomudo m. **~ness** n sordera f

deal /diːl/ n (transaction) negocio m; (agreement) pacto m; (of cards) reparto m; (treatment) trato m; (amount) cantidad f. **a great ~** muchísimo. ● vt (pt dealt) distribuir; dar (a blow, cards). ● vi. **~ in** comerciar en. **~ with** tratar con (person); tratar de (subject etc); ocuparse de (problem etc). **~er** n comerciante m. **~ings** /'diːlɪŋz/ npl trato m

dean /diːn/ n deán m; (univ) decano m

dear /dɪə(r)/ a (-er, -est) querido; (expensive) caro. ● n querido m; (child) pequeño m. ● adv caro. ● int ¡Dios mío! **~ me!** ¡Dios mío! **~ly** adv tiernamente; (pay) caro; (very much) muchísimo

dearth /dɜːθ/ n escasez f

death /deθ/ n muerte f. **~ duty** n derechos mpl reales. **~ly** a mortal; (silence) profundo. ● adv como la muerte. **~'s head** n calavera f. **~-trap** n lugar m peligroso.

débâcle /deɪ'bɑːkl/ n fracaso m, desastre m

debar /dɪ'bɑː(r)/ vt (pt debarred) excluir

debase /dɪ'beɪs/ vt degradar

debat|able /dɪ'beɪtəbl/ a discutible. **~e** /dɪ'beɪt/ n debate m. ● vt debatir, discutir. ● vi discutir; (consider) considerar

debauch /dɪ'bɔːtʃ/ vt corromper. **~ery** n libertinaje m

debilit|ate /dɪ'bɪlɪteɪt/ vt debilitar. **~y** /dɪ'bɪlɪtɪ/ n debilidad f

debit /'debɪt/ n debe m. ● vt. **~ s.o.'s account** cargar en cuenta a uno

debonair /debə'neə(r)/ a alegre

debris /'debriː/ n escombros mpl

debt /det/ n deuda f. **be in ~** tener deudas. **~or** n deudor m

debutante /'debjuːtɑːnt/ n (old use) debutante f

decade /'dekeɪd/ n década f

decaden|ce /'dekədəns/ n decadencia f. **~t** /'dekədənt/ a decadente

decant /dɪ'kænt/ vt decantar. **~er** /-ə(r)/ n garrafa f

decapitate /dɪ'kæpɪteɪt/ vt decapitar

decay /dɪ'keɪ/ vi decaer; (tooth) cariarse. ● n decadencia f; (of tooth) caries f

deceased /dɪ'siːst/ a difunto

deceit /dɪ'siːt/ n engaño m. **~ful** a falso. **~fully** adv falsamente

deceive /dɪ'siːv/ vt engañar

December /dɪ'sembə(r)/ n diciembre m

decen|cy /'diːsənsɪ/ n decencia f. **~t** /'diːsnt/ a decente; (good, fam) bueno; (kind, fam) amable. **~tly** adv decentemente

decentralize /diː'sentrəlaɪz/ vt descentralizar

decepti|on /dɪ'sepʃn/ n engaño m. **~ve** /dɪ'septɪv/ a engañoso

decibel /'desɪbel/ n decibel(io) m

decide /dɪ'saɪd/ vt/i decidir. **~d** /-ɪd/ a resuelto; (unquestionable) indudable. **~dly** /-ɪdlɪ/ adv decididamente; (unquestionably) indudablemente

decimal /'desɪml/ a & n decimal (f). **~ point** n coma f (decimal)

decimate /'desɪmeɪt/ vt diezmar

decipher /dɪ'saɪfə(r)/ vt descifrar

decision /dɪ'sɪʒn/ n decisión f

decisive /dɪ'saɪsɪv/ a decisivo; (manner) decidido. **~ly** adv de manera decisiva

deck /dek/ n cubierta f; (of cards, Amer) baraja f. **top ~** (of bus) imperial m. ● vt adornar. **~chair** n tumbona f

declaim /dɪ'kleɪm/ vt declamar

declar|ation /deklə'reɪʃn/ n declaración f. **~e** /dɪ'kleə(r)/ vt declarar

decline /dɪ'klaɪn/ vt rehusar; (gram) declinar. ● vi disminuir; (deteriorate) deteriorarse; (fall) bajar. ● n decadencia f; (decrease) disminución f; (fall) baja f

decode /di:'kəʊd/ vt descifrar

decompos|e /di:kəm'pəʊz/ vt descomponer. ● vi descomponerse. **~ition** /-ɒmpə'zɪʃn/ n descomposición f

décor /'deɪkɔ:(r)/ n decoración f

decorat|e /'dekəreɪt/ vt decorar; empapelar y pintar (room). **~ion** /-'reɪʃn/ n (act) decoración f; (ornament) adorno m. **~ive** /-ətɪv/ a decorativo. **~or** /'dekəreɪtə(r)/ n pintor m decorador. **interior ~or** decorador m de interiores

decorum /dɪ'kɔ:rəm/ n decoro m

decoy /'di:kɔɪ/ n señuelo m. /dɪ'kɔɪ/ vt atraer con señuelo

decrease /dɪ'kri:s/ vt disminuir. ● vi disminuirse. /'di:kri:s/ n disminución f

decree /dɪ'kri:/ n decreto m; (jurid) sentencia f. ● vt (pt decreed) decretar

decrepit /dɪ'krepɪt/ a decrépito

decry /dɪ'kraɪ/ vt denigrar

dedicat|e /'dedɪkeɪt/ vt dedicar. **~ion** /-'keɪʃn/ n dedicación f; (in book) dedicatoria f

deduce /dɪ'dju:s/ vt deducir

deduct /dɪ'dʌkt/ vt deducir. **~ion** /-ʃn/ n deducción f

deed /di:d/ n hecho m; (jurid) escritura f

deem /di:m/ vt juzgar, considerar

deep /di:p/ a (-er, est) adv profundo. **get into ~ waters** meterse en honduras. **go off the ~ end** enfadarse. ● adv profundamente. **be ~ in thought** estar absorto en sus pensamientos. **~en** /'di:pən/ vt profundizar. ● vi hacerse más profundo. **~freeze** n congelador m. **~ly** adv profundamente

deer /dɪə(r)/ n invar ciervo m

deface /dɪ'feɪs/ vt desfigurar

defamation /defə'meɪʃn/ n difamación f

default /dɪ'fɔ:lt/ vi faltar. ● n. **by ~** en rebeldía. **in ~ of** en ausencia de

defeat /dɪ'fi:t/ vt vencer; (frustrate) frustrar. ● n derrota f; (of plan etc) fracaso m. **~ism** /dɪ'fi:tɪzm/ n derrotismo m. **~ist** /dɪ'fi:tɪst/ n derrotista m & f

defect /'di:fekt/ n defecto m. /dɪ'fekt/ vi desertar. **~ to** pasar a. **~ion** /dɪ'fekʃn/ n deserción f. **~ive** /dɪ'fektɪv/ a defectuoso

defence /dɪ'fens/ n defensa f. **~less** a indefenso

defend /dɪ'fend/ vt defender. **~ant** n (jurid) acusado m

defensive /dɪ'fensɪv/ a defensivo. ● n defensiva f

defer /dɪ'fɜ:(r)/ vt (pt deferred) aplazar

deferen|ce /'defərəns/ n deferencia f. **~tial** /-'renʃl/ a deferente

defian|ce /dɪ'faɪəns/ n desafío m. **in ~ce of** a despecho de. **~t** a desafiante. **~tly** adv con tono retador

deficien|cy /dɪ'fɪʃənsɪ/ n falta f. **~t** /dɪ'fɪʃnt/ a deficiente. **be ~t in** carecer de

deficit /'defɪsɪt/ n déficit m

defile /dɪ'faɪl/ vt ensuciar; (fig) deshonrar

define /dɪ'faɪn/ vt definir

definite /'defɪnɪt/ a determinado; (clear) claro; (firm) categórico. **~ly** adv claramente; (certainly) seguramente

definition /defɪ'nɪʃn/ n definición f

definitive /dɪ'fɪnɪtɪv/ a definitivo

deflat|e /dɪ'fleɪt/ vt desinflar. ● vi desinflarse. **~ion** /-ʃn/ n (com) deflación f

deflect /dɪ'flekt/ vt desviar. ● vi desviarse

deform /dɪ'fɔ:m/ vt deformar. **~ed** a deforme. **~ity** n deformidad f

defraud /dɪ'frɔ:d/ vt defraudar

defray /dɪ'freɪ/ vt pagar

defrost /diːˈfrɒst/ vt descongelar

deft /deft/ a (-er, -est) hábil. ∼ness n destreza f

defunct /dɪˈfʌŋkt/ a difunto

defuse /diːˈfjuːz/ vt desactivar ⟨bomb⟩; (fig) calmar

defy /dɪˈfaɪ/ vt desafiar; (resist) resistir

degenerate /dɪˈdʒenəreɪt/ vi degenerar. /dɪˈdʒenərət/ a & n degenerado (m)

degrad|ation /degrəˈdeɪʃn/ n degradación f. ∼e /dɪˈgreɪd/ vt degradar

degree /dɪˈgriː/ n grado m; (univ) licenciatura f; (rank) rango m. **to a certain** ∼ hasta cierto punto. **to a** ∼ (fam) sumamente

dehydrate /diːˈhaɪdreɪt/ vt deshidratar

de-ice /diːˈaɪs/ vt descongelar

deign /deɪn/ vi. ∼ **to** dignarse

deity /ˈdiːɪtɪ/ n deidad f

deject|ed /dɪˈdʒektɪd/ a desanimado. ∼ion /-ʃn/ n abatimiento m

delay /dɪˈleɪ/ vt retardar; (postpone) aplazar. ● vi demorarse. ● n demora f

delectable /dɪˈlektəbl/ a deleitable

delegat|e /ˈdelɪgeɪt/ vt delegar. /ˈdelɪgət/ n delegado m. ∼ion /-ˈgeɪʃn/ n delegación f

delet|e /dɪˈliːt/ vt tachar. ∼ion /-ʃn/ n tachadura f

deliberat|e /dɪˈlɪbəreɪt/ vt/i deliberar. /dɪˈlɪbərət/ a intencionado; ⟨steps etc⟩ pausado. ∼ely adv a propósito. ∼ion /-ˈreɪʃn/ n deliberación f

delica|cy /ˈdelɪkəsɪ/ n delicadeza f; (food) manjar m; (sweet food) golosina f. ∼te /ˈdelɪkət/ a delicado

delicatessen /delɪkəˈtesn/ n charcutería f fina

delicious /dɪˈlɪʃəs/ a delicioso

delight /dɪˈlaɪt/ n placer m. ● vt encantar. ● vi deleitarse. ∼ed a encantado. ∼ful a delicioso

delineat|e /dɪˈlɪnɪeɪt/ vt delinear. ∼ion /-ˈeɪʃn/ n delineación f

delinquen|cy /dɪˈlɪŋkwənsɪ/ n delincuencia f. ∼t /dɪˈlɪŋkwənt/ a & n delincuente (m & f)

deliri|ous /dɪˈlɪrɪəs/ a delirante. ∼um n delirio m

deliver /dɪˈlɪvə(r)/ vt entregar; (utter) pronunciar; (aim) lanzar; (set free) librar; (med) asistir al parto de. ∼ance n liberación f. ∼y n

entrega f; (of post) reparto m; (med) parto m

delta /ˈdeltə/ n (geog) delta m

delude /dɪˈluːd/ vt engañar. ∼ **o.s.** engañarse

deluge /ˈdeljuːdʒ/ n diluvio m

delusion /dɪˈluːʒn/ n ilusión f

de luxe /dɪˈlʌks/ a de lujo

delve /delv/ vi cavar. ∼ **into** (investigate) investigar

demagogue /ˈdeməgɒg/ n demagogo m

demand /dɪˈmɑːnd/ vt exigir. ● n petición f; (claim) reclamación f; (com) demanda f. **in** ∼ muy popular, muy solicitado. **on** ∼ a solicitud. ∼**ing** a exigente. ∼**s** npl exigencias fpl

demarcation /diːmɑːˈkeɪʃn/ n demarcación f

demean /dɪˈmiːn/ vt. ∼ **o.s.** degradarse. ∼**our** /dɪˈmiːnə(r)/ n conducta f

demented /dɪˈmentɪd/ a demente

demerara /deməˈreərə/ n. ∼ (**sugar**) n azúcar m moreno

demise /dɪˈmaɪz/ n fallecimiento m

demo /ˈdeməʊ/ n (pl **-os**) (fam) manifestación f

demobilize /diːˈməʊbəlaɪz/ vt desmovilizar

democra|cy /dɪˈmɒkrəsɪ/ n democracia f. ∼**t** /ˈdeməkræt/ n demócrata m & f. ∼**tic** /-ˈkrætɪk/ a democrático

demoli|sh /dɪˈmɒlɪʃ/ vt derribar. ∼**tion** /deməˈlɪʃn/ n demolición f

demon /ˈdiːmən/ n demonio m

demonstrat|e /ˈdemənstreɪt/ vt demostrar. ● vi manifestarse, hacer una manifestación. ∼**ion** /-ˈstreɪʃn/ n demostración f; (pol etc) manifestación f

demonstrative /dɪˈmɒnstrətɪv/ a demostrativo

demonstrator /ˈdemənstreɪtə(r)/ n demostrador m; (pol etc) manifestante m & f

demoralize /dɪˈmɒrəlaɪz/ vt desmoralizar

demote /dɪˈməʊt/ vt degradar

demure /dɪˈmjʊə(r)/ a recatado

den /den/ n (of animal) guarida f, madriguera f

denial /dɪˈnaɪəl/ n denegación f; (statement) desmentimiento m

denigrate /ˈdenɪgreɪt/ vt denigrar

denim /ˈdenɪm/ n dril m (de algodón azul grueso). ∼**s** npl pantalón m vaquero

Denmark /'denmɑ:k/ n Dinamarca f

denomination /dɪnɒmɪ'neɪʃn/ n denominación f; (relig) secta f

denote /dɪ'nəʊt/ vt denotar

denounce /dɪ'naʊns/ vt denunciar

dens|e /dens/ a (-er, -est) espeso; ⟨person⟩ torpe. **~ely** adv densamente. **~ity** n densidad f

dent /dent/ n abolladura f. ● vt abollar

dental /'dentl/ a dental. **~ surgeon** n dentista m & f

dentist /'dentɪst/ n dentista m & f. **~ry** n odontología f

denture /'dentʃə(r)/ n dentadura f postiza

denude /dɪ'nju:d/ vt desnudar; (fig) despojar

denunciation /dɪnʌnsɪ'eɪʃn/ n denuncia f

deny /dɪ'naɪ/ vt negar; desmentir ⟨rumour⟩; (disown) renegar

deodorant /di:'əʊdərənt/ a & n desodorante (m)

depart /dɪ'pɑ:t/ vi marcharse; ⟨train etc⟩ salir. **~ from** apartarse de

department /dɪ'pɑ:tment/ n departamento m; (com) sección f. **~ store** n grandes almacenes mpl

departure /dɪ'pɑ:tʃə(r)/ n partida f; (of train etc) salida f. **~ from** (fig) desviación f

depend /dɪ'pend/ vi depender. **~ on** depender de; (rely) contar con. **~able** a seguro. **~ant** /dɪ'pendənt/ n familiar m & f dependiente. **~ence** n dependencia f. **~ent** a dependiente. **be ~ent on** depender de

depict /dɪ'pɪkt/ vt pintar; (in words) describir

deplete /dɪ'pli:t/ vt agotar

deplor|able /dɪ'plɔ:rəbl/ a lamentable. **~e** /dɪ'plɔ:(r)/ vt lamentar

deploy /dɪ'plɔɪ/ vt desplegar. ● vi desplegarse

depopulate /di:'pɒpjʊleɪt/ vt despoblar

deport /dɪ'pɔ:t/ vt deportar. **~ation** /di:pɔ:'teɪʃn/ n deportación f

depose /dɪ'pəʊz/ vt deponer

deposit /dɪ'pɒzɪt/ vt (pt deposited) depositar. ● n depósito m. **~or** n depositante m & f

depot /'depəʊ/ n depósito m; (Amer) estación f

deprav|e /dɪ'preɪv/ vt depravar. **~ity** /-'prævətɪ/ n depravación f

deprecate /'deprɪkeɪt/ vt desaprobar

depreciat|e /dɪ'pri:ʃɪeɪt/ vt depreciar. ● vi depreciarse. **~ion** /-'eɪʃn/ n depreciación f

depress /dɪ'pres/ vt deprimir; (press down) apretar. **~ion** /-ʃn/ n depresión f

depriv|ation /deprɪ'veɪʃn/ n privación f. **~e** /dɪ'praɪv/ vt. **~ of** privar de

depth /depθ/ n profundidad f. **be out of one's ~** perder pie; (fig) meterse en honduras. **in the ~s of** en lo más hondo de

deputation /depjʊ'teɪʃn/ n diputación f

deputize /'depjʊtaɪz/ vi. **~ for** sustituir a

deputy /'depjʊtɪ/ n sustituto m. **~ chairman** n vicepresidente m

derail /dɪ'reɪl/ vt hacer descarrilar. **~ment** n descarrilamiento m

deranged /dɪ'reɪndʒd/ a ⟨mind⟩ trastornado

derelict /'derəlɪkt/ a abandonado

deri|de /dɪ'raɪd/ vt mofarse de. **~sion** /-'rɪʒn/ n mofa f. **~sive** a burlón. **~sory** /dɪ'raɪsərɪ/ a mofador; (offer etc) irrisorio

deriv|ation /derɪ'veɪʃn/ n derivación f. **~ative** /dɪ'rɪvətɪv/ a & n derivado (m). **~e** /dɪ'raɪv/ vt/i derivar

derogatory /dɪ'rɒgətrɪ/ a despectivo

derv /dɜ:v/ n gasóleo m

descen|d /dɪ'send/ vt/i descender, bajar. **~dant** n descendiente m & f. **~t** /dɪ'sent/ n descenso m; (lineage) descendencia f

descri|be /dɪs'kraɪb/ vt describir. **~ption** /-'krɪpʃn/ n descripción f. **~ptive** /-'krɪptɪv/ a descriptivo

desecrat|e /'desɪkreɪt/ vt profanar. **~ion** /-'kreɪʃn/ n profanación f

desert[1] /dɪ'zɜ:t/ vt abandonar. ● vi (mil) desertar

desert[2] /'dezət/ a & n desierto (m)

deserter /dɪ'zɜ:tə(r)/ n desertor m

deserts /dɪ'zɜ:ts/ npl lo merecido. **get one's ~** llevarse su merecido

deserv|e /dɪ'zɜ:v/ vt merecer. **~edly** adv merecidamente. **~ing** a ⟨person⟩ digno de; ⟨action⟩ meritorio

design /dɪ'zaɪn/ n diseño m; (plan) proyecto m; (pattern) modelo m; (aim) propósito m. **have ~s on**

poner la mira en. ● *vt* diseñar; (*plan*) proyectar

designat|e /'dezigneit/ *vt* designar; (*appoint*) nombrar. ~**ion** /-'neiʃn/ *n* denominación *f*; (*appointment*) nombramiento *m*

designer /di'zainə(r)/ *n* diseñador *m*; (*of clothing*) modisto *m*; (*in theatre*) escenógrafo *m*

desirab|ility /dizaiərə'biləti/ *n* conveniencia *f*. ~**le** /di'zairəbl/ *a* deseable

desire /di'zaiə(r)/ *n* deseo *m*. ● *vt* desear

desist /di'zist/ *vi* desistir

desk /desk/ *n* escritorio *m*; (*at school*) pupitre *m*; (*in hotel*) recepción *f*; (*com*) caja *f*

desolat|e /'desələt/ *a* desolado; (*uninhabited*) deshabitado. ~**ion** /-'leiʃn/ *n* desolación *f*

despair /di'speə(r)/ *n* desesperación *f*. ● *vi*. ~ **of** desesperarse de

desperat|e /'despərət/ *a* desesperado; (*dangerous*) peligroso. ~**ely** *adv* desesperadamente. ~**ion** /-'reiʃn/ *n* desesperación *f*

despicable /di'spikəbl/ *a* despreciable

despise /di'spaiz/ *vt* despreciar

despite /di'spait/ *prep* a pesar de

desponden|cy /di'spɒndənsi/ *n* abatimiento *m*. ~**t** /di'spɒndənt/ *a* desanimado

despot /'despɒt/ *n* déspota *m*

dessert /di'zɜ:t/ *n* postre *m*. ~**spoon** *n* cuchara *f* de postre

destination /desti'neiʃn/ *n* destino *m*

destine /'destin/ *vt* destinar

destiny /'destini/ *n* destino *m*

destitute /'destitju:t/ *a* indigente. ~ **of** desprovisto de

destroy /di'stroi/ *vt* destruir

destroyer /di'stroiə(r)/ *n* (*naut*) destructor *m*

destructi|on /di'strʌkʃn/ *n* destrucción *f*. ~**ve** *a* destructivo

desultory /'desəltri/ *a* irregular

detach /di'tætʃ/ *vt* separar. ~**able** *a* separable. ~**ed** *a* separado. ~**ed house** *n* chalet *m*. ~**ment** /di'tætʃmənt/ *n* separación *f*; (*mil*) destacamento *m*; (*fig*) indiferencia *f*

detail /'di:teil/ *n* detalle *m*. ● *vt* detallar; (*mil*) destacar. ~**ed** *a* detallado

detain /di'tein/ *vt* detener; (*delay*) retener. ~**ee** /di:tei'ni:/ *n* detenido *m*

detect /di'tekt/ *vt* percibir; (*discover*) descubrir. ~**ion** /-ʃn/ *n* descubrimiento *m*, detección *f*. ~**or** *n* detector *m*

detective /di'tektiv/ *n* detective *m*. ~ **story** *n* novela *f* policíaca

detention /di'tenʃn/ *n* detención *f*

deter /di'tɜ:(r)/ *vt* (*pt* **deterred**) disuadir; (*prevent*) impedir

detergent /di'tɜ:dʒənt/ *a* & *n* detergente (*m*)

deteriorat|e /di'tiəriəreit/ *vi* deteriorarse. ~**ion** /-'reiʃn/ *n* deterioro *m*

determination /ditɜ:mi'neiʃn/ *n* determinación *f*

determine /di'tɜ:min/ *vt* determinar; (*decide*) decidir. ~**d** *a* determinado; (*resolute*) resuelto

deterrent /di'terənt/ *n* fuerza *f* de disuasión

detest /di'test/ *vt* aborrecer. ~**able** *a* odioso

detonat|e /'detəneit/ *vt* hacer detonar. ● *vi* detonar. ~**ion** /-'neiʃn/ *n* detonación *f*. ~**or** *n* detonador *m*

detour /'di:tʊə(r)/ *n* desviación *f*

detract /di'trækt/ *vi*. ~ **from** (*lessen*) disminuir

detriment /'detrimənt/ *n* perjuicio *m*. ~**al** /-'mentl/ *a* perjudicial

devalu|ation /di:vælju:'eiʃn/ *n* desvalorización *f*. ~**e** /di:'vælju:/ *vt* desvalorizar

devastat|e /'devəsteit/ *vt* devastar. ~**ing** *a* devastador; (*fig*) arrollador

develop /di'veləp/ *vt* desarrollar; contraer ⟨*illness*⟩; urbanizar ⟨*land*⟩. ● *vi* desarrollarse; (*show*) aparecerse. ~**er** *n* (*foto*) revelador *m*. ~**ing country** *n* país *m* en vías de desarrollo. ~**ment** *n* desarrollo *m*. (**new**) ~**ment** novedad *f*

deviant /'di:viənt/ *a* desviado

deviat|e /'di:vieit/ *vi* desviarse. ~**ion** /-'eiʃn/ *n* desviación *f*

device /di'vais/ *n* dispositivo *m*; (*scheme*) estratagema *f*

devil /'devl/ *n* diablo *m*. ~**ish** *a* diabólico

devious /'di:viəs/ *a* tortuoso

devise /di'vaiz/ *vt* idear

devoid /di'void/ *a*. ~ **of** desprovisto de

devolution /di:və'lu:ʃn/ *n* descentralización *f*; (*of power*) delegación *f*

devot|e /di'vəut/ *vt* dedicar. ~**ed** *a* leal. ~**edly** *adv* con devoción *f*. ~**ee**

/devə'ti:/ n partidario m. ~ion /-ʃn/ n dedicación f. ~ions npl (relig) oraciones fpl

devour /dɪ'vaʊə(r)/ vt devorar

devout /dɪ'vaʊt/ a devoto

dew /dju:/ n rocío m

dext|erity /dek'sterətɪ/ n destreza f. ~(e)rous 'dekstrəs/ a diestro

diabet|es /daɪə'bi:ti:z/ n diabetes f. ~ic /-'betɪk/ a & n diabético (m)

diabolical /daɪə'bɒlɪkl/ a diabólico

diadem /'daɪədem/ n diadema f

diagnos|e /'daɪəgnəʊz/ vt diagnosticar. ~is /daɪəg'nəʊsɪs/ n (pl -oses /-si:z/) diagnóstico m

diagonal /daɪ'ægənl/ a & n diagonal (f)

diagram /'daɪəgræm/ n diagrama m

dial /'daɪəl/ n cuadrante m; (on phone) disco m. ● vt (pt dialled) marcar

dialect /'daɪəlekt/ n dialecto m

dial: ~ling code n prefijo m. ~ling tone n señal f para marcar

dialogue /'daɪəlɒg/ n diálogo m

diameter /daɪ'æmɪtə(r)/ n diámetro m

diamond /'daɪəmənd/ n diamante m; (shape) rombo m. ~s npl (cards) diamantes mpl

diaper /'daɪəpə(r)/ n (Amer) pañal m

diaphanous /daɪ'æfənəs/ a diáfano

diaphragm /'daɪəfræm/ n diafragma m

diarrhoea /daɪə'rɪə/ n diarrea f

diary /'daɪərɪ/ n diario m; (book) agenda f

diatribe /'daɪətraɪb/ n diatriba f

dice /daɪs/ n invar dado m. ● vt (culin) cortar en cubitos

dicey /'daɪsɪ/ a (sl) arriesgado

dictat|e /dɪk'teɪt/ vt/i dictar. ~es /'dɪkteɪts/ npl dictados mpl. ~ion /dɪk'teɪʃn/ n dictado m

dictator /dɪk'teɪtə(r)/ n dictador m. ~ship n dictadura f

diction /'dɪkʃn/ n dicción f

dictionary /'dɪkʃənərɪ/ n diccionario m

did /dɪd/ see **do**

didactic /daɪ'dæktɪk/ a didáctico

diddle /'dɪdl/ vt (sl) estafar

didn't /'dɪdnt/ = **did not**

die[1] /daɪ/ vi (pres p **dying**) morir. **be dying to** morirse por. ~ **down** disminuir. ~ **out** extinguirse

die[2] /daɪ/ n (tec) cuño m

die-hard /'daɪhɑ:d/ n intransigente m & f

diesel /'di:zl/ n (fuel) gasóleo m. ~ **engine** n motor m diesel

diet /'daɪət/ n alimentación f; (restricted) régimen m. ● vi estar a régimen. ~etic /daɪə'tetɪk/ a dietético. ~itian n dietético m

differ /'dɪfə(r)/ vi ser distinto; (disagree) no estar de acuerdo. ~ence /'dɪfrəns/ n diferencia f; (disagreement) desacuerdo m. ~ent /'dɪfrənt/ a distinto, diferente

differentia|l /dɪfə'renʃl/ a & n diferencial (f). ~te /dɪfə'renʃɪeɪt/ vt diferenciar. ● vi diferenciarse

differently /'dɪfrəntlɪ/ adv de otra manera

difficult /'dɪfɪkəlt/ a difícil. ~y n dificultad f

diffiden|ce /'dɪfɪdəns/ n falta f de confianza. ~t /'dɪfɪdənt/ a que falta confianza

diffus|e /dɪ'fju:s/ a difuso. /dɪ'fju:z/ vt difundir. ● vi difundirse. ~ion /-ʒn/ n difusión f

dig /dɪg/ n (poke) empujón m; (poke with elbow) codazo m; (remark) indirecta f; (archaeol) excavación f. ● vt (pt **dug**, pres p **digging**) cavar; (thrust) empujar. ● vi cavar. ~ **out** extraer. ~ **up** desenterrar. ~s npl (fam) alojamiento m

digest /'daɪdʒest/ n resumen m. ● vt digerir. ~ible a digerible. ~ion /-ʃn/ n digestión f. ~ive a digestivo

digger /'dɪgə(r)/ n (mec) excavadora f

digit /'dɪdʒɪt/ n cifra f; (finger) dedo m. ~al /'dɪdʒɪtl/ a digital

dignif|ied /'dɪgnɪfaɪd/ a solemne. ~y /'dɪgnɪfaɪ/ vt dignificar

dignitary /'dɪgnɪtərɪ/ n dignatario m

dignity /'dɪgnətɪ/ n dignidad f

digress /daɪ'gres/ vi divagar.. ~ **from** apartarse de. ~ion /-ʃn/ n digresión f

dike /daɪk/ n dique m

dilapidated /dɪ'læpɪdeɪtɪd/ a ruinoso

dilat|e /daɪ'leɪt/ vt dilatar. ● vi dilatarse. ~ion /-ʃn/ n dilatación f

dilatory /'dɪlətərɪ/ a dilatorio, lento

dilemma /daɪ'lemə/ n dilema m

diligen|ce /'dɪlɪdʒəns/ n diligencia f. ~t /'dɪlɪdʒənt/ a diligente

dilly-dally /'dɪlɪdælɪ/ vi (fam) perder el tiempo

dilute /daɪ'lju:t/ vt diluir

dim /dɪm/ a (**dimmer**, **dimmest**) (weak) débil; (dark) oscuro; (stupid, *fam*) torpe. ● *vt* (*pt* **dimmed**) amortiguar. ● *vi* apagarse. ~ **the headlights** bajar los faros

dime /daɪm/ *n* (*Amer*) moneda *f* de diez centavos

dimension /daɪ'menʃn/ *n* dimensión *f*

diminish /dɪ'mɪnɪʃ/ *vt/i* disminuir

diminutive /dɪ'mɪnjʊtɪv/ *a* diminuto. ● *n* diminutivo *m*

dimness /'dɪmnɪs/ *n* debilidad *f*; (*of room etc*) oscuridad *f*

dimple /'dɪmpl/ *n* hoyuelo *m*

din /dɪn/ *n* jaleo *m*

dine /daɪn/ *vi* cenar. ~**r** /-ɔ(r)/ *n* comensal *m* & *f*; (*rail*) coche *m* restaurante

dinghy /'dɪŋgɪ/ *n* (*inflatable*) bote *m* neumático

ding|iness /'dɪndʒɪnɪs/ *n* suciedad *f*. ~**y** /'dɪndʒɪ/ *a* (**-ier**, **-iest**) miserable, sucio

dining-room /'daɪnɪŋruːm/ *n* comedor *m*

dinner /'dɪnə(r)/ *n* cena *f*. ~**jacket** esmoquin *m*. ~ **party** *n* cena *f*

dinosaur /'daɪnəsɔ:(r)/ *n* dinosaurio *m*

dint /dɪnt/ *n*. **by** ~ **of** a fuerza de

diocese /'daɪəsɪs/ *n* diócesis *f*

dip /dɪp/ *vt* (*pt* **dipped**) sumergir. ● *vi* bajar. ~ **into** hojear ⟨*book*⟩. ● *n* (*slope*) inclinación *f*; (*in sea*) baño *m*

diphtheria /dɪf'θɪərɪə/ *n* difteria *f*

diphthong /'dɪfθɒŋ/ *n* diptongo *m*

diploma /dɪ'pləʊmə/ *n* diploma *m*

diplomacy /dɪ'pləʊməsɪ/ *n* diplomacia *f*

diplomat /'dɪpləmæt/ *n* diplomático *m*. ~**ic** /-'mætɪk/ *a* diplomático

dipstick /'dɪpstɪk/ *n* (*auto*) varilla *f* del nivel de aceite

dire /daɪə(r)/ *a* (**-er**, **-est**) terrible; ⟨*need, poverty*⟩ extremo

direct /dɪ'rekt/ *a* directo. ● *adv* directamente. ● *vt* dirigir; (*show the way*) indicar

direction /dɪ'rekʃn/ *n* dirección *f*. ~**s** *npl* instrucciones *fpl*

directly /dɪ'rektlɪ/ *adv* directamente; (*at once*) en seguida. ● *conj* (*fam*) en cuanto

director /dɪ'rektə(r)/ *n* director *m*

directory /dɪ'rektərɪ/ *n* guía *f*

dirge /dɜ:dʒ/ *n* canto *m* fúnebre

dirt /dɜ:t/ *n* suciedad *f*. ~**-track** (*sport*) pista *f* de ceniza. ~**y** /'dɜ:tɪ/ *a* (**-ier**, **-iest**) sucio. ~**y trick** *n* mala jugada *f*. ~**y word** *n* palabrota *f*. ● *vt* ensuciar

disability /dɪsə'bɪlətɪ/ *n* invalidez *f*

disable /dɪs'eɪbl/ *vt* incapacitar. ~**d** *a* minusválido

disabuse /dɪsə'bju:z/ *vt* desengañar

disadvantage /dɪsəd'vɑ:ntɪdʒ/ *n* desventaja *f*. ~**d** *a* desventajado

disagree /dɪsə'gri:/ *vi* no estar de acuerdo; ⟨*food, climate*⟩ sentar mal a. ~**able** /dɪsə'gri:əbl/ *a* desagradable. ~**ment** *n* desacuerdo *m*; (*quarrel*) riña *f*

disappear /dɪsə'pɪə(r)/ *vi* desaparecer. ~**ance** *n* desaparición *f*

disappoint /dɪsə'pɔɪnt/ *vt* desilusionar, decepcionar. ~**ment** *n* desilusión *f*, decepción *f*

disapprov|al /dɪsə'pru:vl/ *n* desaprobación *f*. ~**e** /dɪsə'pru:v/ *vi*. ~ **of** desaprobar

disarm /dɪs'ɑ:m/ *vt/i* desarmar. ~**ament** *n* desarme *m*

disarray /dɪsə'reɪ/ *n* desorden *m*

disast|er /dɪ'zɑ:stə(r)/ *n* desastre *m*. ~**rous** *a* catastrófico

disband /dɪs'bænd/ *vt* disolver. ● *vi* disolverse

disbelief /dɪsbɪ'li:f/ *n* incredulidad *f*

disc /dɪsk/ *n* disco *m*

discard /dɪs'kɑ:d/ *vt* descartar; abandonar ⟨*beliefs etc*⟩

discern /dɪ'sɜ:n/ *vt* percibir. ~**ible** *a* perceptible. ~**ing** *a* perspicaz

discharge /dɪs'tʃɑ:dʒ/ *vt* descargar; cumplir ⟨*duty*⟩; (*dismiss*) despedir; poner en libertad ⟨*prisoner*⟩; (*mil*) licenciar. /'dɪstʃɑ:dʒ/ *n* descarga *f*; (*med*) secreción *f*; (*mil*) licenciamiento *m*; (*dismissal*) despedida *f*

disciple /dɪ'saɪpl/ *n* discípulo *m*

disciplin|arian /dɪsəplɪ'neərɪən/ *n* ordenancista *m* & *f*. ~**ary** *a* disciplinario. ~**e** /'dɪsɪplɪn/ *n* disciplina *f*. ● *vt* disciplinar; (*punish*) castigar

disc jockey /'dɪskdʒɒkɪ/ *n* (*on radio*) pinchadiscos *m* & *f invar*

disclaim /dɪs'kleɪm/ *vt* desconocer. ~**er** *n* renuncia *f*

disclos|e /dɪs'kləʊz/ *vt* revelar. ~**ure** /-ʒə(r)/ *n* revelación *f*

disco /'dɪskəʊ/ *n* (*pl* **-os**) (*fam*) discoteca *f*

discolo|ur /dɪs'kʌlə(r)/ *vt* decolorar. ● *vi* decolorarse. ~**ration** /-'reɪʃn/ *n* decoloración *f*

discomfort /dɪsˈkʌmfət/ *n* malestar *m*; (*lack of comfort*) incomodidad *f*

disconcert /dɪskənˈsɜːt/ *vt* desconcertar

disconnect /dɪskəˈnekt/ *vt* separar; (*elec*) desconectar

disconsolate /dɪsˈkɒnsələt/ *a* desconsolado

discontent /dɪskənˈtent/ *n* descontento *m*. ~**ed** *a* descontento

discontinue /dɪskənˈtɪnjuː/ *vt* interrumpir

discord /ˈdɪskɔːd/ *n* discordia *f*; (*mus*) disonancia *f*. ~**ant** /-ˈskɔːdənt/ *a* discorde; (*mus*) disonante

discothèque /ˈdɪskətek/ *n* discoteca *f*

discount /ˈdɪskaʊnt/ *n* descuento *m*. /dɪsˈkaʊnt/ *vt* hacer caso omiso de; (*com*) descontar

discourage /dɪsˈkʌrɪdʒ/ *vt* desanimar; (*dissuade*) disuadir

discourse /ˈdɪskɔːs/ *n* discurso *m*

discourteous /dɪsˈkɜːtɪəs/ *a* descortés

discover /dɪsˈkʌvə(r)/ *vt* descubrir. ~**y** *n* descubrimiento *m*

discredit /dɪsˈkredɪt/ *vt* (*pt* **discredited**) desacreditar. ● *n* descrédito *m*

discreet /dɪsˈkriːt/ *a* discreto. ~**ly** *adv* discretamente

discrepancy /dɪˈskrepənsɪ/ *n* discrepancia *f*

discretion /dɪˈskreʃn/ *n* discreción *f*

discriminat|e /dɪsˈkrɪmɪneɪt/ *vt/i* discriminar. ~**e between** distinguir entre. ~**ing** *a* perspicaz. ~**ion** /-ˈneɪʃn/ *n* discernimiento *m*; (*bias*) discriminación *f*

discus /ˈdɪskəs/ *n* disco *m*

discuss /dɪˈskʌs/ *vt* discutir. ~**ion** /-ʃn/ *n* discusión *f*

disdain /dɪsˈdeɪn/ *n* desdén *m*. ● *vt* desdeñar. ~**ful** *a* desdeñoso

disease /dɪˈziːz/ *n* enfermedad *f*. ~**d** *a* enfermo

disembark /dɪsɪmˈbɑːk/ *vt/i* desembarcar

disembodied /dɪsɪmˈbɒdɪd/ *a* incorpóreo

disenchant /dɪsɪnˈtʃɑːnt/ *vt* desencantar. ~**ment** *n* desencanto *m*

disengage /dɪsɪnˈgeɪdʒ/ *vt* soltar. ~ **the clutch** desembragar. ~**ment** *n* soltura *f*

disentangle /dɪsɪnˈtæŋgl/ *vt* desenredar

disfavour /dɪsˈfeɪvə(r)/ *n* desaprobación *f*. **fall into** ~ (*person*) caer en desgracia; (*custom, word*) caer en desuso

disfigure /dɪsˈfɪgə(r)/ *vt* desfigurar

disgorge /dɪsˈgɔːdʒ/ *vt* arrojar; (*river*) descargar; (*fig*) restituir

disgrace /dɪsˈgreɪs/ *n* deshonra *f*; (*disfavour*) desgracia *f*. ● *vt* deshonrar. ~**ful** *a* vergonzoso

disgruntled /dɪsˈgrʌntld/ *a* descontento

disguise /dɪsˈgaɪz/ *vt* disfrazar. ● *n* disfraz *m*. **in** ~ disfrazado

disgust /dɪsˈgʌst/ *n* repugnancia *f*, asco *m*. ● *vt* repugnar, dar asco. ~**ing** *a* repugnante, asqueroso

dish /dɪʃ/ *n* plato *m*. ● *vt*. ~ **out** (*fam*) distribuir. ~ **up** servir. ~**cloth** /ˈdɪʃklɒθ/ *n* bayeta *f*

dishearten /dɪsˈhɑːtn/ *vt* desanimar

dishevelled /dɪˈʃevld/ *a* desaliñado; (*hair*) despeinado

dishonest /dɪsˈɒnɪst/ *a* (*person*) poco honrado; (*means*) fraudulento. ~**y** *n* falta *f* de honradez

dishonour /dɪsˈɒnə(r)/ *n* deshonra *f*. ● *vt* deshonrar. ~**able** *a* deshonroso. ~**ably** *adv* deshonrosamente

dishwasher /ˈdɪʃwɒʃə(r)/ *n* lavaplatos *m & f*

disillusion /dɪsɪˈluːʒn/ *vt* desilusionar. ~**ment** *n* desilusión

disincentive /dɪsɪnˈsentɪv/ *n* freno *m*

disinclined /dɪsɪnˈklaɪnd/ *a* poco dispuesto

disinfect /dɪsɪnˈfekt/ *vt* desinfectar. ~**ant** *n* desinfectante *m*

disinherit /dɪsɪnˈherɪt/ *vt* desheredar

disintegrate /dɪsˈɪntɪgreɪt/ *vt* desintegrar. ● *vi* desintegrarse

disinterested /dɪsˈɪntrəstɪd/ *a* desinteresado

disjointed /dɪsˈdʒɔɪntɪd/ *a* inconexo

disk /dɪsk/ *n* disco *m*

dislike /dɪsˈlaɪk/ *n* aversión *f*. ● *vt* tener aversión a

dislocat|e /ˈdɪsləkeɪt/ *vt* dislocar(se) (*limb*). ~**ion** /-ˈkeɪʃn/ *n* dislocación *f*

dislodge /dɪsˈlɒdʒ/ *vt* sacar; (*oust*) desalojar

disloyal /dɪsˈlɔɪəl/ *a* desleal. ~**ty** *n* deslealtad *f*

dismal /ˈdɪzməl/ *a* triste; (*bad*) fatal

dismantle /dɪsˈmæntl/ *vt* desarmar

dismay /dɪsˈmeɪ/ n consternación f.
● vt consternar

dismiss /dɪsˈmɪs/ vt despedir; (reject)
rechazar. ~**al** n despedida f; (of
idea) abandono m

dismount /dɪsˈmaʊnt/ vi apearse

disobedien|ce /dɪsəˈbiːdɪəns/ n
desobediencia f. ~**t** /dɪsəˈbiːdɪənt/ a
desobediente

disobey /dɪsəˈbeɪ/ vt/i desobedecer

disorder /dɪsˈɔːdə(r)/ n desorden m;
(ailment) trastorno m. ~**ly** a
desordenado

disorganize /dɪsˈɔːgənaɪz/ vt desorganizar

disorientate /dɪsˈɔːrɪənteɪt/ vt des-
orientar

disown /dɪsˈəʊn/ vt repudiar

disparaging /dɪsˈpærɪdʒɪŋ/ a
despreciativo. ~**ly** adv con
desprecio

disparity /dɪsˈpærətɪ/ n disparidad f

dispassionate /dɪsˈpæʃənət/ a
desapasionado

dispatch /dɪsˈpætʃ/ vt enviar. ● n
envío m; (report) despacho m.
~**rider** n correo m

dispel /dɪsˈpel/ vt (pt dispelled)
disipar

dispensable /dɪsˈpensəbl/ a
prescindible

dispensary /dɪsˈpensərɪ/ n farmacia
f

dispensation /dɪspenˈseɪʃn/ n distribución f; (relig) dispensa f

dispense /dɪsˈpens/ vt distribuir;
(med) preparar; (relig) dispensar;
administrar (justice). ~ **with** prescindir de. ~**r** /-ə(r)/ n (mec) distribuidor m automático; (med) farmacéutico m

dispers|al /dɪˈspɜːsl/ n dispersión f.
~**e** /dɪˈspɜːs/ vt dispersar. ● vi
dispersarse

dispirited /dɪsˈpɪrɪtɪd/ a desani-
mado

displace /dɪsˈpleɪs/ vt desplazar

display /dɪsˈpleɪ/ vt mostrar; exhibir
(goods); manifestar (feelings). ● n
exposición f; (of feelings) manifestación f; (pej) ostentación f

displeas|e /dɪsˈpliːz/ vt desagradar.
be ~**ed with** estar disgustado con.
~**ure** /-ˈpleʒə(r)/ n desagrado m

dispos|able /dɪsˈpəʊzəbl/ a dese-
chable. ~**al** n (of waste) eliminación
f. at s.o.'s ~**al** a la disposición de
uno. ~**e** /dɪsˈpəʊz/ vt disponer. be

well ~**ed towards** estar bien dispuesto hacia. ● vi. ~**e of** deshacerse de

disposition /dɪspəˈzɪʃn/ n disposición f

disproportionate /dɪsprəˈpɔːʃənət/
a desproporcionado

disprove /dɪsˈpruːv/ vt refutar

dispute /dɪsˈpjuːt/ vt disputar. ● n
disputa f. in ~ disputado

disqualif|ication /dɪskwɒlɪfɪˈkeɪʃn/
n descalificación f. ~**y**
/dɪsˈkwɒlɪfaɪ/ vt incapacitar; (sport)
descalificar

disquiet /dɪsˈkwaɪət/ n inquietud f

disregard /dɪsrɪˈgɑːd/ vt no hacer
caso de. ● n indiferencia f (for a)

disrepair /dɪsrɪˈpeə(r)/ n mal estado
m

disreputable /dɪsˈrepjʊtəbl/ a de
mala fama

disrepute /dɪsrɪˈpjuːt/ n descrédito
m

disrespect /dɪsrɪsˈpekt/ n falta f de
respeto

disrobe /dɪsˈrəʊb/ vt desvestir. ● vi
desvestirse

disrupt /dɪsˈrʌpt/ vt interrumpir;
trastornar (plans). ~**ion** /-ʃn/ n
interrupción f; (disorder) desor-
ganización f. ~**ive** a desbaratador

dissatisfaction /dɪsætɪsˈfækʃn/ n
descontento m

dissatisfied /dɪˈsætɪsfaɪd/ a
descontento

dissect /dɪˈsekt/ vt disecar. ~**ion**
/-ʃn/ n disección f

disseminat|e /dɪˈsemɪneɪt/ vt dis-
eminar. ~**ion** /-ˈneɪʃn/ n di-
seminación f

dissent /dɪˈsent/ vi disentir. ● n dis-
entimiento m

dissertation /dɪsəˈteɪʃn/ n disertación f; (univ) tesis f

disservice /dɪsˈsɜːvɪs/ n mal servicio
m

dissident /ˈdɪsɪdənt/ a & n disidente
(m & f)

dissimilar /dɪˈsɪmɪlə(r)/ a distinto

dissipate /ˈdɪsɪpeɪt/ vt disipar; (fig)
desvanecer. ~**d** a disoluto

dissociate /dɪˈsəʊʃɪeɪt/ vt disociar

dissolut|e /ˈdɪsəluːt/ a disoluto.
~**ion** /dɪsəˈluːʃn/ n disolución f

dissolve /dɪˈzɒlv/ vt disolver. ● vi
disolverse

dissuade /dɪˈsweɪd/ vt disuadir

distan|ce /ˈdɪstəns/ n distancia f.
from a ~**ce** desde lejos. **in the** ~**ce** a

lo lejos. **~t** /'dɪstənt/ a lejano; (*aloof*) frío

distaste /dɪs'teɪst/ n aversión f. **~ful** a desagradable

distemper[1] /dɪ'stempə(r)/ n (*paint*) temple m. ● vt pintar al temple

distemper[2] /dɪ'stempə(r)/ n (*of dogs*) moquillo m

distend /dɪs'tend/ vt dilatar. ● vi dilatarse

distil /dɪs'tɪl/ vt (*pt* **distilled**) destilar. **~lation** /-'leɪʃn/ n destilación f. **~lery** /dɪs'tɪlərɪ/ n destilería f

distinct /dɪs'tɪŋkt/ a distinto; (*clear*) claro; (*marked*) marcado. **~ion** /-ʃn/ n distinción f; (*in exam*) sobresaliente m. **~ive** a distintivo. **~ly** adv claramente

distinguish /dɪs'tɪŋgwɪʃ/ vt/i distinguir. **~ed** a distinguido

distort /dɪs'tɔ:t/ vt torcer. **~ion** /-ʃn/ n deformación f

distract /dɪs'trækt/ vt distraer. **~ed** a aturdido. **~ing** a molesto. **~ion** /-ʃn/ n distracción f; (*confusion*) aturdimiento m

distraught /dɪs'trɔ:t/ a aturdido

distress /dɪs'tres/ n angustia f; (*poverty*) miseria f; (*danger*) peligro m. ● vt afligir. **~ing** a penoso

distribut|e /dɪs'trɪbju:t/ vt distribuir. **~ion** /-'bju:ʃn/ n distribución f. **~or** n distribuidor m; (*auto*) distribuidor m de encendido

district /'dɪstrɪkt/ n distrito m; (*of town*) barrio m

distrust /dɪs'trʌst/ n desconfianza f. ● vt desconfiar de

disturb /dɪs'tɜ:b/ vt molestar; (*perturb*) inquietar; (*move*) desordenar; (*interrupt*) interrumpir. **~ance** n disturbio m; (*tumult*) alboroto m. **~ed** a trastornado. **~ing** a inquietante

disused /dɪs'ju:zd/ a fuera de uso

ditch /dɪtʃ/ n zanja f; (*for irrigation*) acequia f. ● vt (*sl*) abandonar

dither /'dɪðə(r)/ vi vacilar

ditto /'dɪtəʊ/ adv ídem

divan /dɪ'væn/ n diván m

dive /daɪv/ vi tirarse de cabeza; (*rush*) meterse (precipitadamente); (*underwater*) bucear. ● n salto m; (*of plane*) picado m; (*place, fam*) taberna f. **~r** n saltador m; (*underwater*) buzo m

diverge /daɪ'vɜ:dʒ/ vi divergir. **~nt** /daɪ'vɜ:dʒənt/ a divergente

divers|e /daɪ'vɜ:s/ a diverso. **~ify** /daɪ'vɜ:sɪfaɪ/ vt diversificar. **~ity** /daɪ'vɜ:sətɪ/ n diversidad f

diver|sion /daɪ'vɜ:ʃn/ n desvío m; (*distraction*) diversión f. **~t** /daɪ'vɜ:t/ vt desviar; (*entertain*) divertir

divest /daɪ'vest/ vt. **~ of** despojar de

divide /dɪ'vaɪd/ vt dividir. ● vi dividirse

dividend /'dɪvɪdend/ n dividendo m

divine /dɪ'vaɪn/ a divino

diving-board /'daɪvɪŋbɔ:d/ n trampolín m

diving-suit /'daɪvɪŋsu:t/ n escafandra f

divinity /dɪ'vɪnɪtɪ/ n divinidad f

division /dɪ'vɪʒn/ n división f

divorce /dɪ'vɔ:s/ n divorcio m. ● vt divorciarse de; (*judge*) divorciar. ● vi divorciarse. **~e** /dɪvɔ:'si:/ n divorciado m

divulge /daɪ'vʌldʒ/ vt divulgar

DIY abbr see **do-it-yourself**

dizz|iness /'dɪzɪnɪs/ n vértigo m. **~y** /'dɪzɪ/ a (**-ier, -iest**) mareado; (*speed*) vertiginoso. **be** or **feel ~y** marearse

do /du:/ vt (3 sing pres **does**, pt **did**, pp **done**) hacer; (*swindle*, sl) engañar. ● vi hacer; (*fare*) ir; (*be suitable*) convenir; (*be enough*) bastar. ● n (pl **dos** or **do's**) (*fam*) fiesta f. ● v aux. **~ you speak Spanish? Yes I ~** ¿habla Vd español? Sí. **doesn't he?, don't you?** ¿verdad? **~ come in!** (*emphatic*) ¡pase Vd! **~ away with** abolir. **~ in** (*exhaust, fam*) agotar; (*kill, sl*) matar. **~ out** (*clean*) limpiar. **~ up** abotonar (*coat etc*); renovar (*house*). **~ with** tener que ver con; (*need*) necesitar. **~ without** prescindir de. **~ne for** (*fam*) arruinado. **~ne in** (*fam*) agotado. **well ~ne** (*culin*) bien hecho. **well ~ne!** ¡muy bien!

docile /'dəʊsaɪl/ a dócil

dock[1] /dɒk/ n dique m. ● vt poner en dique. ● vi atracar al muelle

dock[2] /dɒk/ n (*jurid*) banquillo m de los acusados

dock: **~er** n estibador m. **~yard** /'dɒkjɑ:d/ n astillero m

doctor /'dɒktə(r)/ n médico m, doctor m; (*univ*) doctor m. ● vt castrar (*cat*); (*fig*) adulterar

doctorate /'dɒktərət/ n doctorado m

doctrine /'dɒktrɪn/ n doctrina f

document /'dɒkjʊmənt/ n documento m. **~ary** /-'mentrɪ/ a & n documental (m)

doddering /'dɒdərɪŋ/ a chocho

dodge /dɒdʒ/ vt esquivar. ● vi esquivarse. ● n regate m; (fam) truco m

dodgems /'dɒdʒəmz/ npl autos mpl de choque

dodgy /'dɒdʒɪ/ a (-ier, -iest) (awkward) difícil

does /dʌz/ see do

doesn't /'dʌznt/ = does not

dog /dɒɡ/ n perro m. ● vt (pt dogged) perseguir. ~collar n (relig, fam) alzacuello m. ~eared a ⟨book⟩ sobado

dogged /'dɒɡɪd/ a obstinado

doghouse /'dɒɡhaʊs/ n (Amer) perrera f. in the ~ (sl) en desgracia

dogma /'dɒɡmə/ n dogma m. ~tic /-'mætɪk/ a dogmático

dogsbody /'dɒɡzbɒdɪ/ n (fam) burro m de carga

doh /dəʊ/ n (mus, first note of any musical scale) do m

doily /'dɔɪlɪ/ n tapete m

doings /'duːɪŋz/ npl (fam) actividades fpl

do-it-yourself /'duːɪtjɔː'self/ (abbr DIY) n bricolaje m. ~ enthusiast n manitas m

doldrums /'dɒldrəmz/ npl. be in the ~ estar abatido

dole /dəʊl/ vt. ~ out distribuir. ● n (fam) subsidio m de paro. on the ~ (fam) parado

doleful /'dəʊlfl/ a triste

doll /dɒl/ n muñeca f. ● vt. ~ up (fam) emperejilar

dollar /'dɒlə(r)/ n dólar m

dollop /'dɒləp/ n (fam) masa f

dolphin /'dɒlfɪn/ n delfín m

domain /dəʊ'meɪn/ n dominio m; (fig) campo m

dome /dəʊm/ n cúpula f. ~d a abovedado

domestic /də'mestɪk/ a doméstico; ⟨trade, flights, etc⟩ nacional

domesticated a ⟨animal⟩ domesticado

domesticity /dɒme'stɪsətɪ/ n domesticidad f

domestic: ~ **science** n economía f doméstica. ~ **servant** n doméstico m

dominant /'dɒmɪnənt/ a dominante

dominat|e /'dɒmɪneɪt/ vt/i dominar. ~ion /-'neɪʃn/ n dominación f

domineer /dɒmɪ'nɪə(r)/ vi tiranizar

Dominican Republic /dəmɪnɪkən rɪ'pʌblɪk/ n República f Dominicana

dominion /də'mɪnjən/ n dominio m

domino /'dɒmɪnəʊ/ n (pl ~es) ficha f de dominó. ~es npl (game) dominó m

don¹ /dɒn/ n profesor m

don² /dɒn/ vt (pt donned) ponerse

donat|e /dəʊ'neɪt/ vt donar. ~ion /-ʃn/ n donativo m

done /dʌn/ see do

donkey /'dɒŋkɪ/ n burro m. ~work n trabajo m penoso

donor /'dəʊnə(r)/ n donante m & f

don't /dəʊnt/ = do not

doodle /'duːdl/ vi garrapatear

doom /duːm/ n destino m; (death) muerte f. ● vt. be ~ed to ser condenado a

doomsday /'duːmzdeɪ/ n día m del juicio final

door /dɔː(r)/ n puerta f. ~man /'dɔːmən/ n (pl -men) portero m. ~mat /'dɔːmæt/ n felpudo m. ~step /'dɔːstep/ n peldaño m. ~way /'dɔːweɪ/ n entrada f

dope /dəʊp/ n (fam) droga f; (idiot, sl) imbécil m. ● vt (fam) drogar. ~y a (sl) torpe

dormant /'dɔːmənt/ a inactivo

dormer /'dɔːmə(r)/ n. ~ (window) buhardilla f

dormitory /'dɔːmɪtrɪ/ n dormitorio m

dormouse /'dɔːmaʊs/ n (pl -mice) lirón m

dos|age /'dəʊsɪdʒ/ n dosis f. ~e /dəʊs/ n dosis f

doss /dɒs/ vi (sl) dormir. ~house n refugio m

dot /dɒt/ n punto m. on the ~ en punto. ● vt (pt dotted) salpicar. be ~ted with estar salpicado de

dote /dəʊt/ vi. ~ on adorar

dotted line /dɒtɪd'laɪn/ n línea f de puntos

dotty /'dɒtɪ/ a (-ier, -iest) (fam) chiflado

double /'dʌbl/ a doble. ● adv doble, dos veces. ● n doble m; (person) doble m & f. at the ~ corriendo. ● vt doblar; redoblar ⟨efforts etc⟩. ● vi doblarse. ~bass n contrabajo m. ~bed n cama f de matrimonio. ~breasted a cruzado. ~chin n papada f. ~cross vt traicionar. ~dealing n doblez m & f. ~decker n autobús m de dos pisos. ~ Dutch n galimatías *m.* **~-jointed** *a* con articulaciones dobles. **~s** *npl* (*tennis*) doble *m*

doubt /daʊt/ *n* duda *f.* ● *vt* dudar; (*distrust*) dudar de, desconfiar de. **~ful** *a* dudoso. **~less** *adv* sin duda

doubly /'dʌblɪ/ *adv* doblemente

dough /dəʊ/ *n* masa *f;* (*money, sl*) dinero *m,* pasta *f* (*sl*)

doughnut /'dəʊnʌt/ *n* buñuelo *m*

douse /daʊs/ *vt* mojar; apagar (*fire*)

dove /dʌv/ *n* paloma *f*

dowager /'daʊədʒə(r)/ *n* viuda *f* (con bienes o título del marido)

dowdy /'daʊdɪ/ *a* (**-ier, -iest**) poco atractivo

down[1] /daʊn/ *adv* abajo. **~ with** abajo. **come ~** bajar. **go ~** bajar; (*sun*) ponerse. ● *prep* abajo. ● *a* (*sad*) triste. ● *vt* derribar; (*drink, fam*) beber

down[2] /daʊn/ *n* (*feathers*) plumón *m*

down-and-out /'daʊnənd'aʊt/ *n* vagabundo *m*

downcast /'daʊnkɑːst/ *a* abatido

downfall /'daʊnfɔːl/ *n* caída *f;* (*fig*) perdición *f*

downgrade /daʊn'greɪd/ *vt* degradar

down-hearted /daʊn'hɑːtɪd/ *a* abatido

downhill /daʊn'hɪl/ *adv* cuesta abajo

down payment /'daʊnpeɪmənt/ *n* depósito *m*

downpour /'daʊnpɔː(r)/ *n* aguacero *m*

downright /'daʊnraɪt/ *a* completo; (*honest*) franco. ● *adv* completamente

downs /daʊnz/ *npl* colinas *fpl*

downstairs /daʊn'steəz/ *adv* abajo. /'daʊnsteəz/ *a* de abajo

downstream /'daʊnstriːm/ *adv* río abajo

down-to-earth /daʊntʊ'ɜːθ/ *a* práctico

downtrodden /'daʊntrɒdn/ *a* oprimido

down: ~ under en las antípodas; (*in Australia*) en Australia. **~ward** /'daʊnwəd/ *a & adv,* **~wards** *adv* hacia abajo

dowry /'daʊərɪ/ *n* dote *f*

doze /dəʊz/ *vi* dormitar. **~ off** dormirse, dar una cabezada. ● *n* sueño *m* ligero

dozen /'dʌzn/ *n* docena *f.* **~s of** (*fam*) miles de, muchos

Dr *abbr* (*Doctor*) Dr, Doctor *m.* **~ Broadley** (el) Doctor Broadley

drab /dræb/ *a* monótono

draft /drɑːft/ *n* borrador *m;* (*outline*) bosquejo *m;* (*com*) letra *f* de cambio; (*Amer, mil*) reclutamiento *m;* (*Amer, of air*) corriente *f* de aire. ● *vt* bosquejar; (*mil*) destacar; (*Amer, conscript*) reclutar

drag /dræg/ *vt* (*pt* **dragged**) arrastrar; rastrear (*river*). ● *vi* arrastrarse por el suelo. ● *n* (*fam*) lata *f.* **in ~** (*man, sl*) vestido de mujer

dragon /'drægən/ *n* dragón *m*

dragon-fly /'drægənflaɪ/ *n* libélula *f*

drain /dreɪn/ *vt* desaguar; apurar (*tank, glass*); (*fig*) agotar. ● *vi* escurrirse. ● *n* desaguadero *m.* **be a ~ on** agotar. **~ing-board** *n* escurridero *m*

drama /'drɑːmə/ *n* drama *m;* (*art*) arte *m* teatral. **~tic** /drə'mætɪk/ *a* dramático. **~tist** /'dræmətɪst/ *n* dramaturgo *m.* **~tize** /'dræmətaɪz/ *vt* adaptar al teatro; (*fig*) dramatizar

drank /dræŋk/ *see* **drink**

drape /dreɪp/ *vt* cubrir; (*hang*) colgar. **~s** *npl* (*Amer*) cortinas *fpl*

drastic /'dræstɪk/ *a* drástico

draught /drɑːft/ *n* corriente *f* de aire. **~ beer** *n* cerveza *f* de barril. **~s** *n pl* (*game*) juego *m* de damas

draughtsman /'drɑːftsmən/ *n* (*pl* -men) diseñador *m*

draughty /'drɑːftɪ/ *a* lleno de corrientes de aire

draw /drɔː/ *vt* (*pt* **drew,** *pp* **drawn**) tirar; (*attract*) atraer; dibujar (*picture*); trazar (*line*); retirar (*money*). **~ the line at** trazar el límite. ● *vi* (*sport*) empatar; dibujar (*pictures*); (*in lottery*) sortear. ● *n* (*sport*) empate *m;* (*in lottery*) sorteo *m.* **~ in** (*days*) acortarse. **~ out** sacar (*money*). **~ up** pararse; redactar (*document*); acercar (*chair*)

drawback /'drɔːbæk/ *n* desventaja *f*

drawbridge /'drɔːbrɪdʒ/ *n* puente *m* levadizo

drawer /drɔː(r)/ *n* cajón *m.* **~s** /drɔːz/ *npl* calzoncillos *mpl;* (*women's*) bragas *fpl*

drawing /'drɔːɪŋ/ *n* dibujo *m.* **~-pin** *n* chinche *m,* chincheta *f*

drawing-room /'drɔːɪŋruːm/ *n* salón *m*

drawl /drɔːl/ *n* habla *f* lenta

drawn /drɔːn/ *see* **draw**. ● *a* (*face*) ojeroso

dread /dred/ *n* terror *m*. ● *vt* temer. **~ful** /'dredfl/ *a* terrible. **~fully** *adv* terriblemente

dream /dri:m/ *n* sueño *m*. ● *vt/i* (*pt* **dreamed** *or* **dreamt**) soñar. ● *a* ideal. **~ up** idear. **~er** *n* soñador *m*. **~y** *a* soñador

drear|iness /'drɪərɪnɪs/ *n* tristeza *f*; (*monotony*) monotonía *f*. **~y** /'drɪərɪ/ *a* (**-ier, -iest**) triste; (*boring*) monótono

dredge[1] /dredʒ/ *n* draga *f*. ● *vt* dragar

dredge[2] /dredʒ/ *n* (*culin*) espolvorear

dredger[1] /'dredʒə(r)/ *n* draga *f*

dredger[2] /'dredʒə(r)/ *n* (*for sugar*) espolvoreador *m*

dregs /dregz/ *npl* heces *fpl*; (*fig*) hez *f*

drench /drentʃ/ *vt* empapar

dress /dres/ *n* vestido *m*; (*clothing*) ropa *f*. ● *vt* vestir; (*decorate*) adornar; (*med*) vendar; (*culin*) aderezar, aliñar. ● *vi* vestirse. **~ circle** *n* primer palco *m*

dresser[1] /'dresə(r)/ *n* (*furniture*) aparador *m*

dresser[2] /'dresə(r)/ *n* (*in theatre*) camarero *m*

dressing /'dresɪŋ/ *n* (*sauce*) aliño *m*; (*bandage*) vendaje *m*. **~case** *n* neceser *m*. **~down** *n* rapapolvo *m*, reprensión *f*. **~gown** *n* bata *f*. **~room** *n* tocador *m*; (*in theatre*) camarín *m*. **~table** *n* tocador *m*

dressmak|er /'dresmeɪkə(r)/ *n* modista *m & f*. **~ing** *n* costura *f*

dress rehearsal /'dresrɪhɜːsl/ *n* ensayo *m* general

dressy /'dresɪ/ *a* (**-ier, -iest**) elegante

drew /dru:/ *see* **draw**

dribble /'drɪbl/ *vi* gotear; (*baby*) babear; (*in football*) regatear

dribs and drabs /drɪbzn'dræbz/ *npl*. **in ~** poco a poco, en cantidades pequeñas

drie|d /draɪd/ *a* (*food*) seco; (*fruit*) paso. **~r** /'draɪə(r)/ *n* secador *m*

drift /drɪft/ *vi* ir a la deriva; (*snow*) amontonarse. ● *n* (*movement*) dirección *f*; (*of snow*) montón *m*; (*meaning*) significado *m*. **~er** *n* persona *f* sin rumbo. **~wood** /'drɪftwʊd/ *n* madera *f* flotante

drill /drɪl/ *n* (*tool*) taladro *m*; (*training*) ejercicio *m*; (*fig*) lo normal. ● *vt* taladrar, perforar; (*train*) entrenar. ● *vi* entrenarse

drily /'draɪlɪ/ *adv* secamente

drink /drɪŋk/ *vt/i* (*pt* **drank**, *pp* **drunk**) beber. ● *n* bebida *f*. **~able** *a* bebible; (*water*) potable. **~er** *n* bebedor *m*. **~ing-water** *n* agua *f* potable

drip /drɪp/ *vi* (*pt* **dripped**) gotear. ● *n* gota *f*; (*med*) goteo *m* intravenoso; (*person, sl*) mentecato *m*. **~dry** *a* que no necesita plancharse

dripping /'drɪpɪŋ/ *n* (*culin*) pringue *m*

drive /draɪv/ *vt* (*pt* **drove**, *pp* **driven**) empujar; conducir, manejar (*LAm*) (*car etc*). **~ in** clavar (*nail*). **~ s.o. mad** volver loco a uno. ● *vi* conducir. **~ in** (*in car*) entrar en coche. ● *n* paseo *m*; (*road*) calle *f*; (*private road*) camino *m* de entrada; (*fig*) energía *f*; (*pol*) campaña *f*. **~ at** querer decir. **~r** /'draɪvə(r)/ *n* conductor *m*, chófer *m* (*LAm*)

drivel /'drɪvl/ *n* tonterías *fpl*

driving /'draɪvɪŋ/ *n* conducción *f*. **~licence** *n* carné *m* de conducir. **~ school** *n* autoescuela *f*

drizzl|e /'drɪzl/ *n* llovizna *f*. ● *vi* lloviznar. **~y** *a* lloviznoso

dromedary /'drɒmədərɪ/ *n* dromedario *m*

drone /drəʊn/ *n* (*noise*) zumbido *m*; (*bee*) zángano *m*. ● *vi* zumbar; (*fig*) hablar en voz monótona; (*idle, fam*) holgazanear

drool /dru:l/ *vi* babear

droop /dru:p/ *vt* inclinar. ● *vi* inclinarse; (*flowers*) marchitarse

drop /drɒp/ *n* gota *f*; (*fall*) caída *f*; (*decrease*) baja *f*; (*of cliff*) precipicio *m*. ● *vt* (*pt* **dropped**) dejar caer; (*lower*) bajar. ● *vi* caer. **~ in on** pasar por casa de. **~ off** (*sleep*) dormirse. **~ out** retirarse; (*student*) abandonar los estudios. **~-out** *n* marginado *m*

droppings /'drɒpɪŋz/ *npl* excremento *m*

dross /drɒs/ *n* escoria *f*

drought /draʊt/ *n* sequía *f*

drove[1] /drəʊv/ *see* **drive**

drove[2] /drəʊv/ *n* manada *f*

drown /draʊn/ *vt* ahogar. ● *vi* ahogarse

drowsy /'draʊzɪ/ *a* soñoliento

drudge /drʌdʒ/ *n* esclavo *m* del trabajo. **~ry** /-ərɪ/ *n* trabajo *m* pesado

drug /drʌg/ *n* droga *f*; (*med*) medicamento *m*. ● *vt* (*pt* **drugged**) drogar. **~ addict** *n* toxicómano *m*

drugstore /'drʌgstɔ:(r)/ n (*Amer*) farmacia f (que vende otros artículos también)

drum /drʌm/ n tambor m; (*for oil*) bidón m. ● vi (*pt* **drummed**) tocar el tambor. ● vt. ~ **into s.o.** inculcar en la mente de uno. ~**mer** n tambor m; (*in group*) batería f. ~**s** npl batería f. ~**stick** /'drʌmstɪk/ n baqueta f; (*culin*) pierna f (de pollo)

drunk /drʌŋk/ see **drink**. ● a borracho. **get** ~ emborracharse. ~**ard** n borracho m. ~**en** a borracho. ~**enness** n embriaguez f

dry /draɪ/ a (**drier, driest**) seco. ● vt secar. ● vi secarse. ~ **up** (*fam*) secar los platos. ~**clean** vt limpiar en seco. ~**cleaner** n tintorero m. ~**cleaner's** (*shop*) tintorería f. ~**ness** n sequedad f

dual /'dju:əl/ a doble. ~ **carriageway** n autovía f, carretera f de doble calzada. ~**purpose** a de doble uso

dub /dʌb/ vt (*pt* **dubbed**) doblar (*film*); (*nickname*) apodar

dubious /'dju:bɪəs/ a dudoso; (*person*) sospechoso

duchess /'dʌtʃɪs/ n duquesa f

duck[1] /dʌk/ n pato m

duck[2] /dʌk/ vt sumergir; bajar (*head etc*). ● vi agacharse

duckling /'dʌklɪŋ/ n patito m

duct /dʌkt/ n conducto m

dud /dʌd/ a inútil; (*cheque*) sin fondos; (*coin*) falso

due /dju:/ a debido; (*expected*) esperado. ~ **to** debido a. ● adv. ~ **north** n derecho hacia el norte. ~**s** npl derechos mpl

duel /'dju:əl/ n duelo m

duet /dju:'et/ n dúo m

duffle /'dʌfl/ a. ~ **bag** n bolsa f de lona. ~**coat** n trenca f

dug /dʌg/ see **dig**

duke /dju:k/ n duque m

dull /dʌl/ a (**-er, -est**) (*weather*) gris; (*colour*) apagado; (*person, play, etc*) pesado; (*sound*) sordo; (*stupid*) torpe. ● vt aliviar (*pain*); entorpecer (*mind*)

duly /'dju:lɪ/ adv debidamente

dumb /dʌm/ a (**-er, -est**) mudo; (*fam*) estúpido

dumbfound /dʌm'faʊnd/ vt pasmar

dummy /'dʌmɪ/ n muñeco m; (*of tailor*) maniquí m; (*of baby*) chupete m. ● a falso. ~ **run** n prueba f

dump /dʌmp/ vt descargar; (*fam*) deshacerse de. ● n vertedero m; (*mil*) depósito m; (*fam*) lugar m desagradable. **be down in the** ~**s** estar deprimido

dumpling /'dʌmplɪŋ/ n bola f de masa hervida

dumpy /'dʌmpɪ/ a (**-ier, -iest**) regordete

dunce /dʌns/ n burro m

dung /dʌŋ/ n excremento m; (*manure*) estiércol m

dungarees /dʌŋgə'ri:z/ npl mono m, peto m

dungeon /'dʌndʒən/ n calabozo m

dunk /dʌŋk/ vt remojar

duo /'dju:əʊ/ n dúo m

dupe /dju:p/ vt engañar. ● n inocentón m

duplicat|e /'dju:plɪkət/ a & n duplicado (m). /'dju:plɪkeɪt/ vt duplicar; (*on machine*) reproducir. ~**or** n multicopista f

duplicity /dju:'plɪsətɪ/ n doblez f

durable /'djʊərəbl/ a resistente; (*enduring*) duradero

duration /djʊ'reɪʃn/ n duración f

duress /djʊ'res/ n coacción f

during /'djʊərɪŋ/ prep durante

dusk /dʌsk/ n crepúsculo m

dusky /'dʌskɪ/ a (**-ier, -iest**) oscuro

dust /dʌst/ n polvo m. ● vt quitar el polvo a; (*sprinkle*) espolvorear

dustbin /'dʌstbɪn/ n cubo m de la basura

dust-cover /'dʌstkʌvə(r)/ n sobrecubierta f

duster /'dʌstə(r)/ n trapo m

dust-jacket /'dʌstdʒækɪt/ n sobrecubierta f

dustman /'dʌstmən/ n (*pl* **-men**) basurero m

dustpan /'dʌstpæn/ n recogedor m

dusty /'dʌstɪ/ a (**-ier, -iest**) polvoriento

Dutch /dʌtʃ/ a & n holandés (m). **go** ~ pagar a escote. ~**man** m holandés m. ~**woman** n holandesa f

dutiful /'dju:tɪfl/ a obediente

duty /'dju:tɪ/ n deber m; (*tax*) derechos mpl de aduana. **on** ~ de servicio. ~**free** a libre de impuestos

duvet /'dju:veɪ/ n edredón m

dwarf /dwɔ:f/ n (*pl* **-s**) enano m. ● vt empequeñecer

dwell /dwel/ vi (*pt* **dwelt**) morar. ~ **on** dilatarse. ~**er** n habitante m & f. ~**ing** n morada f

dwindle /'dwɪndl/ vi disminuir

dye /daɪ/ vt (pres p **dyeing**) teñir. ● n tinte m

dying /'daɪɪŋ/ see **die**

dynamic /daɪ'næmɪk/ a dinámico. ~**s** npl dinámica f

dynamite /'daɪnəmaɪt/ n dinamita f. ● vt dinamitar

dynamo /'daɪnəməʊ/ n dinamo f, dínamo f

dynasty /'dɪnəstɪ/ n dinastía f

dysentery /'dɪsəntrɪ/ n disentería f

dyslexia /dɪs'leksɪə/ n dislexia f

E

each /iːtʃ/ a cada. ● pron cada uno. ~ **one** cada uno. ~ **other** uno a otro, el uno al otro. **they love** ~ **other** se aman

eager /'iːgə(r)/ a impaciente; (enthusiastic) ávido. ~**ly** adv con impaciencia. ~**ness** n impaciencia f, ansia f

eagle /'iːgl/ n águila f

ear[1] /ɪə(r)/ n oído m; (outer) oreja f

ear[2] /ɪə(r)/ n (of corn) espiga f

ear: ~**ache** /'ɪəreɪk/ n dolor m de oído. ~**drum** n tímpano m

earl /ɜːl/ n conde m

early /'ɜːlɪ/ a (-ier, -iest) temprano; (before expected time) prematuro. **in the** ~ **spring** a principios de la primavera. ● adv temprano; (ahead of time) con anticipación

earmark /'ɪəmɑːk/ vt. ~ **for** destinar a

earn /ɜːn/ vt ganar; (deserve) merecer

earnest /'ɜːnɪst/ a serio. **in** ~ en serio

earnings /'ɜːnɪŋz/ npl ingresos mpl; (com) ganacias fpl

ear: ~**phones** /'ɪəfəʊnz/ npl auricular m. ~**ring** n pendiente m

earshot /'ɪəʃɒt/ n. **within** ~ al alcance del oído

earth /ɜːθ/ n tierra f. ● vt (elec) conectar a tierra. ~**ly** a terrenal

earthenware /'ɜːθnweə(r)/ n loza f de barro

earthquake /'ɜːθkweɪk/ n terremoto m

earthy /'ɜːθɪ/ a terroso; (coarse) grosero

earwig /'ɪəwɪg/ n tijereta f

ease /iːz/ n facilidad f; (comfort) tranquilidad f. **at** ~ a gusto; (mil)

en posición de descanso. **ill at** ~ molesto. **with** ~ fácilmente. ● vt calmar; aliviar ⟨pain⟩; tranquilizar ⟨mind⟩; (loosen) aflojar. ● vi calmarse; (lessen) disminuir

easel /'iːzl/ n caballete m

east /iːst/ n este m, oriente m. ● a del este, oriental. ● adv hacia el este.

Easter /'iːstə(r)/ n Semana f Santa; (relig) Pascua f de Resurrección. ~ **egg** n huevo m de Pascua

east: ~**erly** a este; ⟨wind⟩ del este. ~**ern** a del este, oriental. ~**ward** adv, ~**wards** adv hacia el este

easy /'iːzɪ/ a (-ier, -iest) fácil; (relaxed) tranquilo. **go** ~ **on** (fam) tener cuidado con. **take it** ~ no preocuparse. ● int ¡despacio! ~ **chair** n sillón m. ~**going** a acomodadizo

eat /iːt/ vt/i (pt **ate**, pp **eaten**) comer. ~ **into** corroer. ~**able** a comestible. ~**er** n comedor m

eau-de-Cologne /əʊdəkə'ləʊn/ n agua f de colonia

eaves /iːvz/ npl alero m

eavesdrop /'iːvzdrɒp/ vi (pt -**dropped**) escuchar a escondidas

ebb /eb/ n reflujo m. ● vi bajar; (fig) decaer

ebony /'ebənɪ/ n ébano m

ebullient /ɪ'bʌlɪənt/ a exuberante

EC /iː'siː/ abbr (European Community) CE (Comunidad f Europea)

eccentric /ɪk'sentrɪk/ a & n excéntrico (m). ~**ity** /eksen'trɪsətɪ/ n excentricidad f

ecclesiastical /ɪkliːzɪ'æstɪkl/ a eclesiástico

echelon /'eʃəlɒn/ n escalón m

echo /'ekəʊ/ n (pl -**oes**) eco m. ● vt (pt **echoed**, pres p **echoing**) repetir; (imitate) imitar. ● vi hacer eco

eclectic /ɪk'lektɪk/ a & n ecléctico (m)

eclipse /ɪ'klɪps/ n eclipse m. ● vt eclipsar

ecology /ɪ'kɒlədʒɪ/ n ecología f

econom|**ic** /iːkə'nɒmɪk/ a económico. ~**ical** a económico. ~**ics** n economía f. ~**ist** /ɪ'kɒnəmɪst/ n economista m & f. ~**ize** /ɪ'kɒnəmaɪz/ vi economizar. ~**y** /ɪ'kɒnəmɪ/ n economía f

ecsta|**sy** /'ekstəsɪ/ n éxtasis f. ~**tic** /ɪk'stætɪk/ a extático. ~**tically** adv con éxtasis

Ecuador /'ekwədɔː(r)/ n el Ecuador m

ecumenical /iːkjuːˈmenɪkl/ a
ecuménico (m)

eddy /ˈedɪ/ n remolino m

edge /edʒ/ n borde m, margen m; (of
knife) filo m; (of town) afueras fpl.
have the ~ on (fam) llevar la ventaja a. **on ~** nervioso. ● vt ribetear;
(move) mover poco a poco. ● vi
avanzar cautelosamente. **~ways**
adv de lado

edging /ˈedʒɪŋ/ n borde m; (sewing)
ribete m

edgy /ˈedʒɪ/ a nervioso

edible /ˈedɪbl/ a comestible

edict /ˈiːdɪkt/ n edicto m

edifice /ˈedɪfɪs/ n edificio m

edify /ˈedɪfaɪ/ vt edificar

edit /ˈedɪt/ vt dirigir ⟨newspaper⟩;
preparar una edición de ⟨text⟩;
(write) redactar; montar ⟨film⟩.
~ed by a cargo de. **~ion** /ɪˈdɪʃn/ n
edición f. **~or** /ˈedɪtə(r)/ n (of newspaper) director m; (of text) redactor
m. **~orial** /edɪˈtɔːrɪəl/ a editorial.
● n artículo m de fondo. **~or in chief**
n jefe m de redacción

educat|e /ˈedʒʊkeɪt/ vt instruir, edu-
car. **~ed** a culto. **~ion** /-ˈkeɪʃn/ n
enseñanza f; (culture) cultura f;
(upbringing) educación f. **~ional**
/-ˈkeɪʃənl/ a instructivo

EEC /iːiːˈsiː/ abbr (European Economic Community) CEE (Comunidad f Económica Europea)

eel /iːl/ n anguila f

eerie /ˈɪərɪ/ a (-ier, -iest) misterioso

efface /ɪˈfeɪs/ vt borrar

effect /ɪˈfekt/ n efecto m. **in ~** efectivamente. **take ~** entrar en vigor.
● vt efectuar

effective /ɪˈfektɪv/ a eficaz; (striking) impresionante; (mil) efectivo.
~ly adv eficazmente. **~ness** n efi-
cacia f

effeminate /ɪˈfemɪnət/ a afeminado

effervescent /efəˈvesnt/ a efervescente

effete /ɪˈfiːt/ a agotado

efficien|cy /ɪˈfɪʃənsɪ/ n eficiencia f;
(mec) rendimiento m. **~t** /ɪˈfɪʃnt/ a
eficiente. **~tly** adv eficientemente

effigy /ˈefɪdʒɪ/ n efigie f

effort /ˈefət/ n esfuerzo m. **~less** a
fácil

effrontery /ɪˈfrʌntərɪ/ n descaro m

effusive /ɪˈfjuːsɪv/ a efusivo

e.g. /iːˈdʒiː/ abbr (exempli gratia)
p.ej., por ejemplo

egalitarian /ɪgælɪˈteərɪən/ a & n igu-
alitario (m)

egg¹ /eg/ n huevo m

egg² /eg/ vt. **~ on** (fam) incitar

egg-cup /ˈegkʌp/ n huevera f

egg-plant /ˈegplɑːnt/ n berenjena f

eggshell /ˈegʃel/ n cáscara f de
huevo

ego /ˈiːgəʊ/ n (pl -os) yo m. **~ism** n
egoísmo m. **~ist** n egoísta m & f.
~centric /iːgəʊˈsentrɪk/ a egocéntrico. **~tism** n egotismo m. **~tist**
n egotista m & f

Egypt /ˈiːdʒɪpt/ n Egipto m. **~ian**
/ɪˈdʒɪpʃn/ a & n egipcio (m)

eh /eɪ/ int (fam) ¡eh!

eiderdown /ˈaɪdədaʊn/ n edredón m

eight /eɪt/ a & n ocho (m)

eighteen /eɪˈtiːn/ a & n dieciocho
(m). **~th** a & n decimoctavo (m)

eighth /eɪtθ/ a & n octavo (m)

eight|ieth /ˈeɪtɪəθ/ a & n ochenta
(m), octogésimo (m). **~y** /ˈeɪtɪ/ a &
n ochenta (m)

either /ˈaɪðə(r)/ a cualquiera de los
dos; (negative) ninguno de los dos;
(each) cada. ● pron uno u otro; (with
negative) ni uno ni otro. ● adv (negative) tampoco. ● conj o. **~ he or** o
él o; (with negative) ni él ni

ejaculate /ɪˈdʒækjʊleɪt/ vt/i
(exclaim) exclamar

eject /ɪˈdʒekt/ vt expulsar, echar

eke /iːk/ vt. **~ out** hacer bastar;
(increase) complementar

elaborate /ɪˈlæbərət/ a complicado.
/ɪˈlæbəreɪt/ vt elaborar. ● vi explicarse

elapse /ɪˈlæps/ vi (of time) transcurrir

elastic /ɪˈlæstɪk/ a & n elástico (m).
~ band n goma f (elástica)

elasticity /ɪlæˈstɪsətɪ/ n elasticidad f

elat|ed /ɪˈleɪtɪd/ a regocijado. **~ion**
/-ʃn/ n regocijo m

elbow /ˈelbəʊ/ n codo m

elder¹ /ˈeldə(r)/ a & n mayor (m)

elder² /ˈeldə(r)/ n (tree) saúco m

elderly /ˈeldəlɪ/ a mayor, anciano

eldest /ˈeldɪst/ a & n el mayor (m)

elect /ɪˈlekt/ vt elegir. **~ to do** decidir hacer. ● a electo. **~ion** /-ʃn/ n
elección f

elector /ɪˈlektə(r)/ n elector m. **~al** a
electoral. **~ate** n electorado m

electric /ɪˈlektrɪk/ a eléctrico. **~al** a
eléctrico. **~ blanket** n manta f eléctrica. **~ian** /ɪlekˈtrɪʃn/ n electricista

m & f. **∼ity** /ɪlek'trɪsətɪ/ *n* electricidad *f*

electrify /ɪ'lektrɪfaɪ/ *vt* electrificar; *(fig)* electrizar

electrocute /ɪ'lektrəkju:t/ *vt* electrocutar

electrolysis /ɪlek'trɒlɪsɪs/ *n* electrólisis *f*

electron /ɪ'lektrɒn/ *n* electrón *m*

electronic /ɪlek'trɒnɪk/ *a* electrónico. **∼s** *n* electrónica *f*

elegan|ce /'elɪɡəns/ *n* elegancia *f*. **∼t** /'elɪɡənt/ *a* elegante. **∼tly** *adv* elegantemente

element /'elɪmənt/ *n* elemento *m*. **∼ary** /-'mentrɪ/ *a* elemental

elephant /'elɪfənt/ *n* elefante *m*

elevat|e /'elɪveɪt/ *vt* elevar. **∼ion** /-'veɪʃn/ *n* elevación *f*. **∼or** /'elɪveɪtə(r)/ *n* (*Amer*) ascensor *m*

eleven /ɪ'levn/ *a & n* once (*m*). **∼th** *a & n* undécimo (*m*)

elf /elf/ *n* (*pl* **elves**) duende *m*

elicit /ɪ'lɪsɪt/ *vt* sacar

eligible /'elɪdʒəbl/ *a* elegible. **be ∼ for** tener derecho a

eliminat|e /ɪ'lɪmɪneɪt/ *vt* eliminar. **∼ion** /-'neɪʃn/ *n* eliminación *f*

élite /eɪ'li:t/ *n* elite *f*, élite *m*

elixir /ɪ'lɪksɪə(r)/ *n* elixir *m*

ellip|se /ɪ'lɪps/ *n* elipse *f*. **∼tical** *a* elíptico

elm /elm/ *n* olmo *m*

elocution /elə'kju:ʃn/ *n* elocución *f*

elongate /'i:lɒŋɡeɪt/ *vt* alargar

elope /ɪ'ləʊp/ *vi* fugarse con el amante. **∼ment** *n* fuga *f*

eloquen|ce /'eləkwəns/ *n* elocuencia *f*. **∼t** /'eləkwənt/ *a* elocuente. **∼tly** *adv* con elocuencia

El Salvador /el'sælvədɔ:(r)/ *n* El Salvador *m*

else /els/ *adv* más. **everybody ∼** todos los demás. **nobody ∼** ningún otro, nadie más. **nothing ∼** nada más. **or ∼** o bien. **somewhere ∼** en otra parte

elsewhere /els'weə(r)/ *adv* en otra parte

elucidate /ɪ'lu:sɪdeɪt/ *vt* aclarar

elude /ɪ'lu:d/ *vt* eludir

elusive /ɪ'lu:sɪv/ *a* esquivo

emaciated /ɪ'meɪʃɪeɪtɪd/ *a* esquelético

emanate /'eməneɪt/ *vi* emanar

emancipat|e /ɪ'mænsɪpeɪt/ *vt* emancipar. **∼ion** /-'peɪʃn/ *n* emancipación *f*

embalm /ɪm'bɑ:m/ *vt* embalsamar

embankment /ɪm'bæŋkmənt/ *n* terraplén *m*; (*of river*) dique *m*

embargo /ɪm'bɑ:ɡəʊ/ *n* (*pl* **-oes**) prohibición *f*

embark /ɪm'bɑ:k/ *vt* embarcar. • *vi* embarcarse. **∼ on** (*fig*) emprender. **∼ation** /emba:'keɪʃn/ *n* (*of people*) embarco *m*; (*of goods*) embarque *m*

embarrass /ɪm'bærəs/ *vt* desconcertar; (*shame*) dar vergüenza. **∼ment** *n* desconcierto *m*; (*shame*) vergüenza *f*

embassy /'embəsɪ/ *n* embajada *f*

embed /ɪm'bed/ *vt* (*pt* **embedded**) embutir; (*fig*) fijar

embellish /ɪm'belɪʃ/ *vt* embellecer. **∼ment** *n* embellecimiento *m*

embers /'embəz/ *npl* ascua *f*

embezzle /ɪm'bezl/ *vt* desfalcar. **∼ment** *n* desfalco *m*

embitter /ɪm'bɪtə(r)/ *vt* amargar

emblem /'embləm/ *n* emblema *m*

embod|iment /ɪm'bɒdɪmənt/ *n* encarnación *f*. **∼y** /ɪm'bɒdɪ/ *vt* encarnar; (*include*) incluir

emboss /ɪm'bɒs/ *vt* grabar en relieve, repujar. **∼ed** *a* en relieve, repujado

embrace /ɪm'breɪs/ *vt* abrazar; (*fig*) abarcar. • *vi* abrazarse. • *n* abrazo *m*

embroider /ɪm'brɔɪdə(r)/ *vt* bordar. **∼y** *n* bordado *m*

embroil /ɪm'brɔɪl/ *vt* enredar

embryo /'embrɪəʊ/ *n* (*pl* **-os**) embrión *m*. **∼nic** /-'ɒnɪk/ *a* embrionario

emend /ɪ'mend/ *vt* enmendar

emerald /'emərəld/ *n* esmeralda *f*

emerge /ɪ'mɜ:dʒ/ *vi* salir. **∼nce** /-əns/ *n* aparición *f*

emergency /ɪ'mɜ:dʒənsɪ/ *n* emergencia *f*. **in an ∼** en caso de emergencia. **∼ exit** *n* salida *f* de emergencia

emery /'emərɪ/ *n* esmeril *m*. **∼board** *n* lima *f* de uñas

emigrant /'emɪɡrənt/ *n* emigrante *m & f*

emigrat|e /'emɪɡreɪt/ *vi* emigrar. **∼ion** /-'ɡreɪʃn/ *n* emigración *f*

eminen|ce /'emɪnəns/ *n* eminencia *f*. **∼t** /'emɪnənt/ *a* eminente. **∼tly** *adv* eminentemente

emissary /'emɪsərɪ/ *n* emisario *m*

emission /ɪ'mɪʃn/ *n* emisión *f*

emit /ɪ'mɪt/ *vt* (*pt* **emitted**) emitir

emollient /ɪ'mɒlɪənt/ *a & n* emoliente (*m*)

emoti|on /ɪˈməʊʃn/ *n* emoción *f*. **~onal** *a* emocional; ⟨*person*⟩ emotivo; ⟨*moving*⟩ conmovedor. **~ve** /ɪˈməʊtɪv/ *a* emotivo

empathy /ˈempəθɪ/ *n* empatía *f*

emperor /ˈempərə(r)/ *n* emperador *m*

emphasi|s /ˈemfəsɪs/ *n* (*pl* **~ses** /-siːz/) énfasis *m*. **~ze** /ˈemfəsaɪz/ *vt* subrayar; ⟨*single out*⟩ destacar

emphatic /ɪmˈfætɪk/ *a* categórico; ⟨*resolute*⟩ decidido

empire /ˈempaɪə(r)/ *n* imperio *m*

empirical /ɪmˈpɪrɪkl/ *a* empírico

employ /ɪmˈplɔɪ/ *vt* emplear. **~ee** /emplɔɪˈiː/ *n* empleado *m*. **~er** *n* patrón *m*. **~ment** *n* empleo *m*. **~ment agency** *n* agencia *f* de colocaciones

empower /ɪmˈpaʊə(r)/ *vt* autorizar (**to do** a hacer)

empress /ˈempris/ *n* emperatriz *f*

empt|ies /ˈemptiz/ *npl* envases *mpl*. **~iness** *n* vacío *m*. **~y** /ˈemptɪ/ *a* vacío; ⟨*promise*⟩ vano. **on an ~y stomach** con el estómago vacío. ● *vt* vaciar. ● *vi* vaciarse

emulate /ˈemjʊleɪt/ *vt* emular

emulsion /ɪˈmʌlʃn/ *n* emulsión *f*

enable /ɪˈneɪbl/ *vt*. **~ s.o. to** permitir a uno

enact /ɪˈnækt/ *vt* (*jurid*) decretar; (*in theatre*) representar

enamel /ɪˈnæml/ *n* esmalte *m*. ● *vt* (*pt* **enamelled**) esmaltar

enamoured /ɪˈnæməd/ *a*. **be ~ of** estar enamorado de

encampment /ɪnˈkæmpmənt/ *n* campamento *m*

encase /ɪnˈkeɪs/ *vt* encerrar

enchant /ɪnˈtʃɑːnt/ *vt* encantar. **~ing** *a* encantador. **~ment** *n* encanto *m*

encircle /ɪnˈsɜːkl/ *vt* rodear

enclave /ˈenkleɪv/ *n* enclave *m*

enclos|e /ɪnˈkləʊz/ *vt* cercar ⟨*land*⟩; (*with letter*) adjuntar; (*in receptacle*) encerrar. **~ed** *a* ⟨*space*⟩ encerrado; (*com*) adjunto. **~ure** /ɪnˈkləʊʒə(r)/ *n* cercamiento *m*; (*area*) recinto *m*; (*com*) documento *m* adjunto

encompass /ɪnˈkʌmpəs/ *vt* cercar; (*include*) incluir, abarcar

encore /ˈɒŋkɔː(r)/ *int* ¡bis! ● *n* bis *m*, repetición *f*

encounter /ɪnˈkaʊntə(r)/ *vt* encontrar. ● *n* encuentro *m*

encourage /ɪnˈkʌrɪdʒ/ *vt* animar; (*stimulate*) estimular. **~ment** *n* estímulo *m*

encroach /ɪnˈkrəʊtʃ/ *vi*. **~ on** invadir ⟨*land*⟩; quitar ⟨*time*⟩. **~ment** *n* usurpación *f*

encumb|er /ɪnˈkʌmbə(r)/ *vt* (*hamper*) estorbar; (*burden*) cargar. **be ~ered with** estar cargado de. **~rance** *n* estorbo *m*; (*burden*) carga *f*

encyclical /ɪnˈsɪklɪkl/ *n* encíclica *f*

encyclopaedi|a /ɪnsaɪklə'piːdɪə/ *n* enciclopedia *f*. **~c** *a* enciclopédico

end /end/ *n* fin *m*; (*furthest point*) extremo *m*. **in the ~** por fin. **make ~s meet** poder llegar a fin de mes. **no ~** (*fam*) muy. **no ~ of** muchísimos. **on ~** de pie; (*consecutive*) seguido. ● *vt/i* terminar, acabar

endanger /ɪnˈdeɪndʒə(r)/ *vt* arriesgar

endear|ing /ɪnˈdɪərɪŋ/ *a* simpático. **~ment** *n* palabra *f* cariñosa

endeavour /ɪnˈdevə(r)/ *n* tentativa *f*. ● *vi*. **~ to** esforzarse por

ending /ˈendɪŋ/ *n* fin *m*

endive /ˈendɪv/ *n* escarola *f*, endibia *f*

endless /ˈendlɪs/ *a* interminable; ⟨*patience*⟩ infinito

endorse /ɪnˈdɔːs/ *vt* endosar; (*fig*) aprobar. **~ment** *n* endoso *m*; (*fig*) aprobación *f*; (*auto*) nota *f* de inhabilitación

endow /ɪnˈdaʊ/ *vt* dotar

endur|able /ɪnˈdjʊərəbl/ *a* aguantable. **~ance** *n* resistencia *f*. **~e** /ɪnˈdjʊə(r)/ *vt* aguantar. ● *vi* durar. **~ing** *a* perdurable

enemy /ˈenəmɪ/ *n* & *a* enemigo (*m*)

energ|etic /enəˈdʒetɪk/ *a* enérgico. **~y** /ˈenədʒɪ/ *n* energía *f*

enervat|e /ˈenəveɪt/ *vt* debilitar. **~ing** *a* debilitante

enfold /ɪnˈfəʊld/ *vt* envolver; (*in arms*) abrazar

enforce /ɪnˈfɔːs/ *vt* aplicar; (*impose*) imponer; hacer cumplir ⟨*law*⟩. **~d** *a* forzado

engage /ɪnˈgeɪdʒ/ *vt* emplear ⟨*staff*⟩; (*reserve*) reservar; ocupar ⟨*attention*⟩; (*mec*) hacer engranar. ● *vi* (*mec*) engranar. **~d** *a* prometido; (*busy*) ocupado. **get ~d** prometerse. **~ment** *n* compromiso *m*; (*undertaking*) obligación *f*

engaging /ɪnˈgeɪdʒɪŋ/ *a* atractivo

engender /ɪnˈdʒendə(r)/ *vt* engendrar

engine /ˈendʒɪn/ *n* motor *m*; (*of train*) locomotora *f*. **~-driver** *n* maquinista *m*

engineer /endʒɪ'nɪə(r)/ n ingeniero m; (*mechanic*) mecánico m. ● vt (*contrive*, *fam*) lograr. ~**ing** n ingeniería f

England /'ɪŋɡlənd/ n Inglaterra f

English /'ɪŋɡlɪʃ/ a inglés. ● n (*lang*) inglés m; (*people*) ingleses mpl. ~**man** n inglés m. ~**woman** n inglesa f. **the ~ Channel** n el canal m de la Mancha

engrav|e /ɪn'ɡreɪv/ vt grabar. ~**ing** n grabado m

engrossed /ɪn'ɡrəʊst/ a absorto

engulf /ɪn'ɡʌlf/ vt tragar(se)

enhance /ɪn'haːns/ vt aumentar

enigma /ɪ'nɪɡmə/ n enigma m. ~**tic** /enɪɡ'mætɪk/ a enigmático

enjoy /ɪn'dʒɔɪ/ vt gozar de. ~ **o.s.** divertirse. **I ~ reading** me gusta la lectura. ~**able** a agradable. ~**ment** n placer m

enlarge /ɪn'lɑːdʒ/ vt agrandar; (*foto*) ampliar. ● vi agrandarse. ~ **upon** extenderse sobre. ~**ment** n (*foto*) ampliación f

enlighten /ɪn'laɪtn/ vt aclarar; (*inform*) informar. ~**ment** n aclaración f. **the E~ment** el siglo m de la luces

enlist /ɪn'lɪst/ vt alistar; (*fig*) conseguir. ● vi alistarse

enliven /ɪn'laɪvn/ vt animar

enmity /'enmətɪ/ n enemistad f

ennoble /ɪ'nəʊbl/ vt ennoblecer

enorm|ity /ɪ'nɔːmətɪ/ n enormidad f. ~**ous** /ɪ'nɔːməs/ a enorme

enough /ɪ'nʌf/ a & adv bastante. ● n bastante m, suficiente m. ● int ¡basta!

enquir|e /ɪn'kwaɪə(r)/ vt/i preguntar. ~ **about** informarse de. ~**y** n pregunta f, (*investigation*) investigación f

enrage /ɪn'reɪdʒ/ vt enfurecer

enrapture /ɪn'ræptʃə(r)/ vt extasiar

enrich /ɪn'rɪtʃ/ vt enriquecer

enrol /ɪn'rəʊl/ vt (*pt* **enrolled**) inscribir; matricular (*student*). ● vi inscribirse; (*student*) matricularse. ~**ment** n inscripción f; (*of student*) matrícula f

ensconce /ɪn'skɒns/ vt. ~ **o.s.** arrellanarse

ensemble /ɒn'sɒmbl/ n conjunto m

enshrine /ɪn'ʃraɪn/ vt encerrar

ensign /'ensaɪn/ n enseña f

enslave /ɪn'sleɪv/ vt esclavizar

ensue /ɪn'sjuː/ vi resultar, seguirse

ensure /ɪn'ʃʊə(r)/ vt asegurar

entail /ɪn'teɪl/ vt suponer; acarrear (*trouble etc*)

entangle /ɪn'tæŋɡl/ vt enredar. ~**ment** n enredo m; (*mil*) alambrada f

enter /'entə(r)/ vt entrar en; (*write*) escribir; matricular (*school etc*); hacerse socio de (*club*). ● vi entrar

enterprise /'entəpraɪz/ n empresa f; (*fig*) iniciativa f

enterprising /'entəpraɪzɪŋ/ a emprendedor

entertain /entə'teɪn/ vt divertir; recibir (*guests*); abrigar (*ideas*, *hopes*); (*consider*) considerar. ~**ment** n diversión f; (*performance*) espectáculo m; (*reception*) recepción f

enthral /ɪn'θrɔːl/ vt (*pt* **enthralled**) cautivar

enthuse /ɪn'θjuːz/ vi. ~ **over** entusiasmarse por

enthusias|m /ɪn'θjuːzɪæzəm/ n entusiasmo m. ~**tic** /-'æstɪk/ a entusiasta; (*thing*) entusiástico. ~**tically** /-'æstɪklɪ/ adv con entusiasmo. ~**t** /ɪn'θjuːzɪæst/ n entusiasta m & f

entice /ɪn'taɪs/ vt atraer. ~**ment** n atracción f

entire /ɪn'taɪə(r)/ a entero. ~**ly** adv completamente. ~**ty** /ɪn'taɪərətɪ/ n. **in its ~ty** en su totalidad

entitle /ɪn'taɪtl/ vt titular; (*give a right*) dar derecho a. **be ~d to** tener derecho a. ~**ment** n derecho m

entity /'entətɪ/ n entidad f

entomb /ɪn'tuːm/ vt sepultar

entrails /'entreɪlz/ npl entrañas fpl

entrance¹ /'entrəns/ n entrada f; (*right to enter*) admisión f

entrance² /ɪn'trɑːns/ vt encantar

entrant /'entrənt/ n participante m & f; (*in exam*) candidato m

entreat /ɪn'triːt/ vt suplicar. ~**y** n súplica f

entrench /ɪn'trentʃ/ vt atrincherar

entrust /ɪn'trʌst/ vt confiar

entry /'entrɪ/ n entrada f; (*of street*) bocacalle f; (*note*) apunte m

entwine /ɪn'twaɪn/ vt entrelazar

enumerate /ɪ'njuːməreɪt/ vt enumerar

enunciate /ɪ'nʌnsɪeɪt/ vt pronunciar; (*state*) enunciar

envelop /ɪn'veləp/ vt (*pt* **enveloped**) envolver

envelope /'envələʊp/ n sobre m

enviable /'envɪəbl/ a envidiable

envious /ˈenvɪəs/ *a* envidioso. **~ly** *adv* con envidia

environment /ɪnˈvaɪərənmənt/ *n* medio *m* ambiente. **~al** /-ˈmentl/ *a* ambiental

envisage /ɪnˈvɪzɪdʒ/ *vt* prever; (*imagine*) imaginar

envoy /ˈenvɔɪ/ *n* enviado *m*

envy /ˈenvɪ/ *n* envidia *f*. ● *vt* envidiar

enzyme /ˈenzaɪm/ *n* enzima *f*

epaulette /ˈepɔʊlet/ *n* charretera *f*

ephemeral /ɪˈfemərəl/ *a* efímero

epic /ˈepɪk/ *n* épica *f*. ● *a* épico

epicentre /ˈepɪsentə(r)/ *n* epicentro *m*

epicure /ˈepɪkjʊə(r)/ *n* sibarita *m* & *f*; (*gourmet*) gastrónomo *m*

epidemic /epɪˈdemɪk/ *n* epidemia *f*. ● *a* epidémico

epilep|sy /ˈepɪlepsɪ/ *n* epilepsia *f*. **~tic** /-ˈleptɪk/ *a* & *n* epiléptico (*m*)

epilogue /ˈepɪlɒg/ *n* epílogo *m*

episode /ˈepɪsəʊd/ *n* episodio *m*

epistle /ɪˈpɪsl/ *n* epístola *f*

epitaph /ˈepɪtɑːf/ *n* epitafio *m*

epithet /ˈepɪθet/ *n* epíteto *m*

epitom|e /ɪˈpɪtəmɪ/ *n* epítome *m*, personificación *f*. **~ize** *vt* epitomar, personificar, ser la personificación de

epoch /ˈiːpɒk/ *n* época *f*. **~-making** *a* que hace época

equal /ˈiːkwəl/ *a* & *n* igual (*m* & *f*). **~ to** (*a task*) a la altura de. ● *vt* (*pt* **equalled**) ser igual a; (*math*) ser. **~ity** /ɪˈkwɒlətɪ/ *n* igualdad *f*. **~ize** /ˈiːkwəlaɪz/ *vt/i* igualar. **~izer** /-ə(r)/ *n* (*sport*) tanto *m* de empate. **~ly** *adv* igualmente

equanimity /ekwəˈnɪmətɪ/ *n* ecuanimidad *f*

equate /ɪˈkweɪt/ *vt* igualar

equation /ɪˈkweɪʒn/ *n* ecuación *f*

equator /ɪˈkweɪtə(r)/ *n* ecuador *m*. **~ial** /ekwəˈtɔːrɪəl/ *a* ecuatorial

equestrian /ɪˈkwestrɪən/ *a* ecuestre

equilateral /iːkwɪˈlætərəl/ *a* equilátero

equilibrium /iːkwɪˈlɪbrɪəm/ *n* equilibrio *m*

equinox /ˈiːkwɪnɒks/ *n* equinoccio *m*

equip /ɪˈkwɪp/ *vt* (*pt* **equipped**) equipar. **~ment** *n* equipo *m*

equitable /ˈekwɪtəbl/ *a* equitativo

equity /ˈekwətɪ/ *n* equidad *f*; (*pl, com*) acciones *fpl* ordinarias

equivalen|ce /ɪˈkwɪvələns/ *n* equivalencia *f*. **~t** /ɪˈkwɪvələnt/ *a* & *n* equivalente (*m*)

equivocal /ɪˈkwɪvəkl/ *a* equívoco

era /ˈɪərə/ *n* era *f*

eradicate /ɪˈrædɪkeɪt/ *vt* extirpar

erase /ɪˈreɪz/ *vt* borrar. **~r** /-ə(r)/ *n* borrador *m*

erect /ɪˈrekt/ *a* erguido. ● *vt* levantar. **~ion** /-ʃn/ *n* erección *f*, montaje *m*

ermine /ˈɜːmɪn/ *n* armiño *m*

ero|de /ɪˈrəʊd/ *vt* desgastar. **~sion** /-ʒn/ *n* desgaste *m*

erotic /ɪˈrɒtɪk/ *a* erótico. **~ism** /-sɪzəm/ *n* erotismo *m*

err /ɜː(r)/ *vi* errar; (*sin*) pecar

errand /ˈerənd/ *n* recado *m*

erratic /ɪˈrætɪk/ *a* irregular; ⟨*person*⟩ voluble

erroneous /ɪˈrəʊnɪəs/ *a* erróneo

error /ˈerə(r)/ *n* error *m*

erudit|e /ˈeruːdaɪt/ *a* erudito. **~ion** /-ˈdɪʃn/ *n* erudición *f*

erupt /ɪˈrʌpt/ *vi* estar en erupción; (*fig*) estallar. **~ion** /-ʃn/ *n* erupción *f*

escalat|e /ˈeskəleɪt/ *vt* intensificar. ● *vi* intensificarse. **~ion** /-ˈleɪʃn/ *n* intensificación *f*

escalator /ˈeskəleɪtə(r)/ *n* escalera *f* mecánica

escapade /eskəˈpeɪd/ *n* aventura *f*

escap|e /ɪˈskeɪp/ *vi* escaparse. ● *vt* evitar. ● *n* fuga *f*; (*avoidance*) evasión *f*. **have a narrow ~e** escapar por un pelo. **~ism** /ɪˈskeɪpɪzəm/ *n* escapismo *m*

escarpment /ɪsˈkɑːpmənt/ *n* escarpa *f*

escort /ˈeskɔːt/ *n* acompañante *m*; (*mil*) escolta *f*. /ɪˈskɔːt/ *vt* acompañar; (*mil*) escoltar

Eskimo /ˈeskɪməʊ/ *n* (*pl* **-os**, **-o**) esquimal (*m* & *f*)

especial /ɪˈspeʃl/ *a* especial. **~ly** *adv* especialmente

espionage /ˈespɪɒnɑːʒ/ *n* espionaje *m*

esplanade /espləˈneɪd/ *n* paseo *m* marítimo

Esq. /ɪˈskwaɪə(r)/ *abbr* (*Esquire*) (*in address*). **E. Ashton,** **~** Sr. D. E. Ashton

essay /ˈeseɪ/ *n* ensayo *m*; (*at school*) composición *f*

essence /ˈesns/ *n* esencia *f*. **in ~** esencialmente

essential /ɪˈsenʃl/ *a* esencial. ● *n* lo esencial. **~ly** *adv* esencialmente

establish /ɪ'stæblɪʃ/ *vt* establecer; (*prove*) probar. **~ment** *n* establecimiento *m*. **the E~ment** los que mandan, el sistema *m*

estate /ɪ'steɪt/ *n* finca *f*; (*possessions*) bienes *mpl*. **~ agent** *n* agente *m* inmobiliario. **~ car** *n* furgoneta *f*

esteem /ɪ'sti:m/ *vt* estimar. ● *n* estimación *f*, estima *f*

estimat|e /'estɪmət/ *n* cálculo *m*; (*com*) presupuesto *m*. /'estɪmeɪt/ *vt* calcular. **~ion** /-'meɪʃn/ *n* estima *f*, estimación *f*; (*opinion*) opinión *f*

estranged /ɪs'treɪndʒd/ *a* alejado

estuary /'estʃʊərɪ/ *n* estuario *m*

etc. /et'setrə/ *abbr* (*et cetera*) etc., etcétera

etching /'etʃɪŋ/ *n* aguafuerte *m*

eternal /ɪ'tɜ:nl/ *a* eterno

eternity /ɪ'tɜ:nətɪ/ *n* eternidad *f*

ether /'i:θə(r)/ *n* éter *m*

ethereal /ɪ'θɪərɪəl/ *a* etéreo

ethic /'eθɪk/ *n* ética *f*. **~s** *npl* ética *f*. **~al** *a* ético

ethnic /'eθnɪk/ *a* étnico

ethos /'i:θɒs/ *n* carácter *m* distintivo

etiquette /'etɪket/ *n* etiqueta *f*

etymology /etɪ'mɒlədʒɪ/ *n* etimología *f*

eucalyptus /ju:kə'lɪptəs/ *n* (*pl* **-tuses**) eucalipto *m*

eulogy /'ju:lədʒɪ/ *n* encomio *m*

euphemism /'ju:fəmɪzəm/ *n* eufemismo *m*

euphoria /ju:'fɔ:rɪə/ *n* euforia *f*

Europe /'jʊərəp/ *n* Europa *f*. **~an** /-'pɪən/ *a* & *n* europeo (*m*)

euthanasia /ju:θə'neɪzɪə/ *n* eutanasia *f*

evacuat|e /ɪ'vækjʊeɪt/ *vt* evacuar; desocupar ⟨*building*⟩. **~ion** /-'eɪʃn/ *n* evacuación *f*

evade /ɪ'veɪd/ *vt* evadir

evaluate /ɪ'væljʊeɪt/ *vt* evaluar

evangeli|cal /i:væn'dʒelɪkl/ *a* evangélico. **~st** /ɪ'vændʒəlɪst/ *n* evangelista *m* & *f*

evaporat|e /ɪ'væpəreɪt/ *vi* evaporarse. **~ion** /-'reɪʃn/ *n* evaporación *f*

evasion /ɪ'veɪʒn/ *n* evasión *f*

evasive /ɪ'veɪsɪv/ *a* evasivo

eve /i:v/ *n* víspera *f*

even /'i:vn/ *a* regular; (*flat*) llano; ⟨*surface*⟩ liso; ⟨*amount*⟩ igual; (*number*) par. **get ~ with** desquitarse con. ● *vt* nivelar. **~ up** igualar. ● *adv* aun, hasta, incluso. **~ if**

aunque. **~ so** aun así. **not ~** ni siquiera

evening /'i:vnɪŋ/ *n* tarde *f*; (*after dark*) noche *f*. **~ class** *n* clase *f* nocturna. **~ dress** *n* (*man's*) traje *m* de etiqueta; (*woman's*) traje *m* de noche

evensong /'i:vənsɒŋ/ *n* vísperas *fpl*

event /ɪ'vent/ *n* acontecimiento *m*; (*sport*) prueba *f*. **in the ~ of** en caso de. **~ful** *a* lleno de acontecimientos

eventual /ɪ'ventʃʊəl/ *a* final, definitivo. **~ity** /-'ælətɪ/ *n* eventualidad *f*. **~ly** *adv* finalmente

ever /'evə(r)/ *adv* jamás, nunca; (*at all times*) siempre. **~ after** desde entonces. **~ since** desde entonces. ● *conj* después de que. **~ so** (*fam*) muy. **for ~** para siempre. **hardly ~** casi nunca

evergreen /'evəgri:n/ *a* de hoja perenne. ● *n* árbol *m* de hoja perenne

everlasting /'evəlɑ:stɪŋ/ *a* eterno

every /'evrɪ/ *a* cada, todo. **~ child** todos los niños. **~ one** cada uno. **~ other day** cada dos días

everybody /'evrɪbɒdɪ/ *pron* todo el mundo

everyday /'evrɪdeɪ/ *a* todos los días

everyone /'evrɪwʌn/ *pron* todo el mundo. **~ else** todos los demás

everything /'evrɪθɪŋ/ *pron* todo

everywhere /'evrɪweə(r)/ *adv* en todas partes

evict /ɪ'vɪkt/ *vt* desahuciar. **~ion** /-ʃn/ *n* desahucio *m*

eviden|ce /'evɪdəns/ *n* evidencia *f*; (*proof*) pruebas *fpl*; (*jurid*) testimonio *m*. **~ce of** señales de. in **~ce** visible. **~t** /'evɪdənt/ *a* evidente. **~tly** *adv* evidentemente

evil /'i:vl/ *a* malo. ● *n* mal *m*, maldad *f*

evocative /ɪ'vɒkətɪv/ *a* evocador

evoke /ɪ'vəʊk/ *vt* evocar

evolution /i:və'lu:ʃn/ *n* evolución *f*

evolve /ɪ'vɒlv/ *vt* desarrollar. ● *vi* desarrollarse, evolucionar

ewe /ju:/ *n* oveja *f*

ex... /eks/ *pref* ex...

exacerbate /ɪg'zæsəbeɪt/ *vt* exacerbar

exact /ɪg'zækt/ *a* exacto. ● *vt* exigir (**from** a). **~ing** *a* exigente. **~itude** *n* exactitud *f*. **~ly** *adv* exactamente

exaggerat|e /ɪg'zædʒəreɪt/ *vt* exagerar. **~ion** /-'reɪʃn/ *n* exageración *f*

exalt /ɪg'zɔ:lt/ *vt* exaltar

exam /ɪg'zæm/ n (fam) examen m.
~ination /ɪgzæmɪ'neɪʃn/ n examen m. **~ine** /ɪg'zæmɪn/ vt examinar; interrogar ‹witness›. **~iner** /-ə(r)/ n examinador m

example /ɪg'zɑ:mpl/ n ejemplo m. **make an ~ of** infligir castigo ejemplar a

exasperat|e /ɪg'zæspəreɪt/ vt exasperar. **~ion** /-'reɪʃn/ n exasperación f

excavat|e /'ekskəveɪt/ vt excavar. **~ion** /-'veɪʃn/ n excavación f

exceed /ɪk'si:d/ vt exceder. **~ingly** adv extremadamente

excel /ɪk'sel/ vi (pt excelled) sobresalir. ● vt superar

excellen|ce /'eksələns/ n excelencia f. **~t** /'eksələnt/ a excelente. **~tly** adv excelentemente

except /ɪk'sept/ prep excepto, con excepción de. **~ for** con excepción de. ● vt exceptuar. **~ing** prep con excepción de

exception /ɪk'sepʃən/ n excepción f. **take ~ to** ofenderse por. **~al** /ɪk'sepʃənl/ a excepcional. **~ally** adv excepcionalmente

excerpt /'eksɜ:pt/ n extracto m

excess /ɪk'ses/ n exceso m. /'ekses/ a excedente. **~ fare** n suplemento m. **~ luggage** n exceso m de equipaje

excessive /ɪk'sesɪv/ a excesivo. **~ly** adv excesivamente

exchange /ɪk'stʃeɪndʒ/ vt cambiar. ● n cambio m. **(telephone) ~** central f telefónica

exchequer /ɪks'tʃekə(r)/ n (pol) erario m, hacienda f

excise¹ /'eksaɪz/ n impuestos mpl indirectos

excise² /ek'saɪz/ vt quitar

excit|able /ɪk'saɪtəbl/ a excitable. **~e** /ɪk'saɪt/ vt emocionar; (stimulate) excitar. **~ed** a entusiasmado. **~ement** n emoción f; (enthusiasm) entusiasmo m. **~ing** a emocionante

excla|im /ɪk'skleɪm/ vi exclamar. **~mation** /eksklə'meɪʃn/ n exclamación f. **~mation mark** n signo m de admiración f, punto m de exclamación

exclu|de /ɪk'sklu:d/ vt excluir. **~sion** /-ʒn/ n exclusión f

exclusive /ɪk'sklu:sɪv/ a exclusivo; ‹club› selecto. **~ of** excluyendo. **~ly** adv exclusivamente

excomunicate /ekskə'mju:nɪkeɪt/ vt excomulgar

excrement /'ekskrɪmənt/ n excremento m

excruciating /ɪk'skru:ʃɪeɪtɪŋ/ a atroz, insoportable

excursion /ɪk'skɜ:ʃn/ n excursión f

excus|able a /ɪk'skju:zəbl/ a perdonable. **~e** /ɪk'skju:z/ vt perdonar. **~e from** dispensar de. **~e me!** ¡perdón! /ɪk'skju:s/ n excusa f

ex-directory /eksdɪ'rektərɪ/ a que no está en la guía telefónica

execrable /'eksɪkrəbl/ a execrable

execut|e /'eksɪkju:t/ vt ejecutar. **~ion** /eksɪ'kju:ʃn/ n ejecución f. **~ioner** n verdugo m

executive /ɪg'zekjʊtɪv/ a & n ejecutivo (m)

executor /ɪg'zekjʊtə(r)/ n (jurid) testamentario m

exemplary /ɪg'zemplərɪ/ a ejemplar

exemplify /ɪg'zemplɪfaɪ/ vt ilustrar

exempt /ɪg'zempt/ a exento. ● vt dispensar. **~ion** /-ʃn/ n exención f

exercise /'eksəsaɪz/ n ejercicio m. ● vt ejercer. ● vi hacer ejercicios. **~ book** n cuaderno m

exert /ɪg'zɜ:t/ vt ejercer. **~ o.s.** esforzarse. **~ion** /-ʃn/ n esfuerzo m

exhal|ation /ekshə'leɪʃn/ n exhalación f. **~e** /eks'heɪl/ vt/i exhalar

exhaust /ɪg'zɔ:st/ vt agotar. ● n (auto) tubo m de escape. **~ed** a agotado. **~ion** /-stʃən/ n agotamiento m. **~ive** /ɪg'zɔ:stɪv/ a exhaustivo

exhibit /ɪg'zɪbɪt/ vt exponer; (jurid) exhibir; (fig) mostrar. ● n objeto m expuesto; (jurid) documento m

exhibition /eksɪ'bɪʃn/ n exposición f; (act of showing) demostración f; (univ) beca f. **~ist** n exhibicionista m & f

exhibitor /ɪg'zɪbɪtə(r)/ n expositor m

exhilarat|e /ɪg'zɪləreɪt/ vt alegrar. **~ion** /-'reɪʃn/ n regocijo m

exhort /ɪg'zɔ:t/ vt exhortar

exile /'eksaɪl/ n exilio m; (person) exiliado m. ● vt desterrar

exist /ɪg'zɪst/ vi existir. **~ence** n existencia f. **in ~ence** existente

existentialism /egzɪs'tenʃəlɪzəm/ n existencialismo m

exit /'eksɪt/ n salida f

exodus /'eksədəs/ n éxodo m

exonerate /ɪg'zɒnəreɪt/ vt disculpar

exorbitant /ɪg'zɔ:bɪtənt/ a exorbitante

exorcis|e /ˈeksɔːsaɪz/ *vt* exorcizar.
~m /-sɪzəm/ *n* exorcismo *m*
exotic /ɪgˈzɒtɪk/ *a* exótico
expand /ɪkˈspænd/ *vt* extender; dilatar 〈metal〉; (develop) desarrollar.
● *vi* extenderse; (develop) desarrollarse; 〈metal〉 dilatarse
expanse /ɪkˈspæns/ *n* extensión *f*
expansion /ɪkˈspænʃn/ *n* extensión *f*; (of metal) dilatación *f*
expansive /ɪkˈspænsɪv/ *a* expansivo
expatriate /eksˈpætrɪət/ *a & n* expatriado (*m*)
expect /ɪkˈspekt/ *vt* esperar; (suppose) suponer; (demand) contar con. **I ~ so** supongo que sí
expectan|cy /ɪkˈspektənsɪ/ *n* esperanza *f*. **life ~cy** esperanza *f* de vida. **~t** /ɪkˈspektənt/ *a* expectante. **~t mother** *n* futura madre *f*
expectation /ekspekˈteɪʃn/ *n* esperanza *f*
expedien|cy /ɪkˈspiːdɪənsɪ/ *n* conveniencia *f*. **~t** /ɪkˈspiːdɪənt/ *a* conveniente
expedite /ˈekspɪdaɪt/ *vt* acelerar
expedition /ekspɪˈdɪʃn/ *n* expedición *f*. **~ary** *a* expedicionario
expel /ɪkˈspel/ *vt* (pt **expelled**) expulsar
expend /ɪkˈspend/ *vt* gastar. **~able** *a* prescindible
expenditure /ɪkˈspendɪtʃə(r)/ *n* gastos *mpl*
expens|e /ɪkˈspens/ *n* gasto *m*; (fig) costa *f*. **at s.o.'s ~e** a costa de uno. **~ive** /ɪkˈspensɪv/ *a* caro. **~ively** *adv* costosamente
experience /ɪkˈspɪərɪəns/ *n* experiencia. ● *vt* experimentar. **~d** *a* experto
experiment /ɪkˈsperɪmənt/ *n* experimento *m*. ● *vi* experimentar. **~al** /-ˈmentl/ *a* experimental
expert /ˈekspɜːt/ *a & n* experto (*m*). **~ise** /ekspɜːˈtiːz/ *n* pericia *f*. **~ly** *adv* hábilmente
expir|e /ɪkˈspaɪə(r)/ *vi* expirar. **~y** *n* expiración *f*
expla|in /ɪkˈspleɪn/ *vt* explicar. **~nation** /eksplə'neɪʃn/ *n* explicación *f*. **~natory** /ɪksˈplænətərɪ/ *a* explicativo
expletive /ɪkˈspliːtɪv/ *n* palabrota *f*
explicit /ɪkˈsplɪsɪt/ *a* explícito
explode /ɪkˈspləʊd/ *vt* hacer explotar; (tec) explosionar. ● *vi* estallar
exploit /ˈeksplɔɪt/ *n* hazaña *f*. /ɪkˈsplɔɪt/ *vt* explotar. **~ation** /eksplɔɪ'teɪʃn/ *n* explotación *f*

explor|ation /eksplə'reɪʃn/ *n* exploración *f*. **~atory** /ɪkˈsplɒrətrɪ/ *a* exploratorio. **~e** /ɪkˈsplɔː(r)/ *vt* explorar. **~er** *n* explorador *m*
explosi|on /ɪkˈspləʊʒn/ *n* explosión *f*. **~ve** *a & n* explosivo (*m*)
exponent /ɪkˈspəʊnənt/ *n* exponente *m*
export /ɪkˈspɔːt/ *vt* exportar. /ˈekspɔːt/ *n* exportación *f*. **~er** /ɪksˈpɔːtə(r)/ *n* exportador *m*
expos|e /ɪkˈspəʊz/ *vt* exponer; (reveal) descubrir. **~ure** /-ʒə(r)/ *n* exposición *f*. **die of ~ure** morir de frío
expound /ɪkˈspaʊnd/ *vt* exponer
express[1] /ɪkˈspres/ *vt* expresar
express[2] /ɪkˈspres/ *a* expreso; 〈letter〉 urgente. ● *adv* (by express post) por correo urgente. ● *n* (train) rápido *m*, expreso *m*
expression /ɪkˈspreʃn/ *n* expresión *f*
expressive /ɪkˈspresɪv/ *a* expresivo
expressly /ɪkˈspreslɪ/ *adv* expresamente
expulsion /ɪkˈspʌlʃn/ *n* expulsión *f*
expurgate /ˈekspəgeɪt/ *vt* expurgar
exquisite /ˈekskwɪzɪt/ *a* exquisito. **~ly** *adv* primorosamente
ex-serviceman /eksˈsɜːvɪsmən/ *n* (pl **-men**) excombatiente *m*
extant /ekˈstænt/ *a* existente
extempore /ekˈstempərɪ/ *a* improvisado. ● *adv* de improviso
exten|d /ɪkˈstend/ *vt* extender; (prolong) prolongar; ensanchar 〈house〉. ● *vi* extenderse. **~sion** *n* extensión *f*; (of road, time) prolongación *f*; (building) anejo *m*; (com) prórroga *f*
extensive /ɪkˈstensɪv/ *a* extenso. **~ly** *adv* extensamente
extent /ɪkˈstent/ *n* extensión *f*; (fig) alcance. **to a certain ~** hasta cierto punto
extenuate /ɪkˈstenjʊeɪt/ *vt* atenuar
exterior /ɪkˈstɪərɪə(r)/ *a & n* exterior (*m*)
exterminat|e /ɪkˈstɜːmɪneɪt/ *vt* exterminar. **~ion** /-ˈneɪʃn/ *n* exterminio *m*
external /ɪkˈstɜːnl/ *a* externo. **~ly** *adv* externamente
extinct /ɪkˈstɪŋkt/ *a* extinto. **~ion** /-ʃn/ *n* extinción *f*
extinguish /ɪkˈstɪŋgwɪʃ/ *vt* extinguir. **~er** *n* extintor *m*
extol /ɪkˈstəʊl/ *vt* (pt **extolled**) alabar

extort /ɪkˈstɔːt/ vt sacar por la fuerza. **~ion** /-ʃn/ n exacción f. **~ionate** /ɪkˈstɔːʃənət/ a exorbitante

extra /ˈekstrə/ a suplementario. ● adv extraordinariamente. ● n suplemento m; (cinema) extra m & f

extract /ˈekstrækt/ n extracto m. /ɪkˈstrækt/ vt extraer; (fig) arrancar. **~ion** /-ʃn/ n extracción f; (lineage) origen m

extradit|e /ˈekstrədaɪt/ vt extraditar. **~ion** /-ˈdɪʃn/ n extradición f

extramarital /ekstrəˈmærɪtl/ a fuera del matrimonio

extramural /ekstrəˈmjʊərəl/ a fuera del recinto universitario; (for external students) para estudiantes externos

extraordinary /ɪkˈstrɔːdnrɪ/ a extraordinario

extra-sensory /ekstrəˈsensərɪ/ a extrasensorial

extravagan|ce /ɪkˈstrævəgəns/ n prodigalidad f, extravagancia f. **~t** /ɪkˈstrævəgənt/ a pródigo, extravagante

extrem|e /ɪkˈstriːm/ a & n extremo (m). **~ely** adv extremadamente. **~ist** n extremista m & f. **~ity** /ɪkˈstreməti/ n extremidad f

extricate /ˈekstrɪkeɪt/ vt desenredar, librar

extrovert /ˈekstrəvɜːt/ n extrovertido m

exuberan|ce /ɪgˈzjuːbərəns/ n exuberancia f. **~t** /ɪgˈzjuːbərənt/ a exuberante

exude /ɪgˈzjuːd/ vt rezumar

exult /ɪgˈzʌlt/ vi exultar

eye /aɪ/ n ojo m. **keep an ~ on** no perder de vista. **see ~ to ~** estar de acuerdo con. ● vt (pt **eyed**, pres p **eyeing**) mirar. **~ball** /ˈaɪbɔːl/ n globo m del ojo. **~brow** /ˈaɪbraʊ/ n ceja f. **~ful** /ˈaɪfʊl/ n (fam) espectáculo m sorprendente. **~lash** /ˈaɪlæʃ/ n pestaña f. **~let** /ˈaɪlɪt/ n ojete m. **~lid** /ˈaɪlɪd/ n párpado m. **~opener** n (fam) revelación f. **~shadow** n sombra f de ojos, sombreador m. **~sight** /ˈaɪsaɪt/ n vista f. **~sore** /ˈaɪsɔː(r)/ n (fig, fam) monstruosidad f, horror m. **~witness** /ˈaɪwɪtnɪs/ n testigo m ocular

F

fable /ˈfeɪbl/ n fábula f

fabric /ˈfæbrɪk/ n tejido m, tela f

fabrication /fæbrɪˈkeɪʃn/ n invención f

fabulous /ˈfæbjʊləs/ a fabuloso

façade /fəˈsɑːd/ n fachada f

face /feɪs/ n cara f, rostro m; (of watch) esfera f; (aspect) aspecto m. **~ down(wards)** boca abajo. **~ up(wards)** boca arriba. **in the ~ of** frente a. **lose ~** quedar mal. **pull ~s** hacer muecas. ● vt mirar hacia; ⟨house⟩ dar a; (confront) enfrentarse con. ● vi volverse. **~ up to** enfrentarse con. **~ flannel** n paño m (para lavarse la cara). **~less** a anónimo. **~-lift** n cirugía f estética en la cara

facet /ˈfæsɪt/ n faceta f

facetious /fəˈsiːʃəs/ a chistoso, gracioso

facial /ˈfeɪʃl/ a facial. ● n masaje m facial

facile /ˈfæsaɪl/ a fácil

facilitate /fəˈsɪlɪteɪt/ vt facilitar

facility /fəˈsɪlɪtɪ/ n facilidad f

facing /ˈfeɪsɪŋ/ n revestimiento m. **~s** npl (on clothes) vueltas fpl

facsimile /fækˈsɪmɪlɪ/ n facsímile m

fact /fækt/ n hecho m. **as a matter of ~, in ~** en realidad, a decir verdad

faction /ˈfækʃn/ n facción f

factor /ˈfæktə(r)/ n factor m

factory /ˈfæktərɪ/ n fábrica f

factual /ˈfæktʃʊəl/ a basado en hechos, factual

faculty /ˈfækltɪ/ n facultad f

fad /fæd/ n manía f, capricho m

fade /feɪd/ vi descolorarse; ⟨colour⟩ descolorarse; ⟨flowers⟩ marchitarse; ⟨light⟩ apagarse; ⟨memory, sound⟩ desvanecerse

faeces /ˈfiːsiːz/ npl excrementos mpl

fag[1] /fæg/ n (chore, fam) faena f; (cigarette, sl) cigarrillo m, pitillo m

fag[2] /fæg/ n (homosexual, Amer, sl) marica m

fagged /fægd/ a. **~ (out)** rendido

fah /fɑː/ n (mus, fourth note of any musical scale) fa m

fail /feɪl/ vi fallar; (run short) acabarse. **he ~ed to arrive** no llegó. ● vt no aprobar ⟨exam⟩; suspender ⟨candidate⟩; (disappoint) fallar. **~ s.o.** ⟨words etc⟩ faltarle a uno. ● n. **without ~** sin falta

failing /ˈfeɪlɪŋ/ n defecto m. ● prep a falta de

failure /'feɪljə(r)/ n fracaso m; (person) fracasado m; (med) ataque m; (mec) fallo m. ~ **to do** dejar m de hacer

faint /feɪnt/ a (-er, -est) (weak) débil; (indistinct) indistinto. ~ **estar** mareado. **the** ~**est idea** la más remota idea. ● vi desmayarse. ● n desmayo m. ~**-hearted** a pusilánime, cobarde. ~**ly** adv (weakly) débilmente; (indistinctly) indistintamente. ~**ness** n debilidad f

fair[1] /feə(r)/ a (-er, -est) (just) justo; ⟨weather⟩ bueno; ⟨amount⟩ razonable; ⟨hair⟩ rubio; ⟨skin⟩ blanco. ~ **play** n juego m limpio. ● adv limpio

fair[2] /feə(r)/ n feria f

fair: ~**ly** adv (justly) justamente; (rather) bastante. ~**ness** n justicia f

fairy /'feərɪ/ n hada f. ~**land** n país m de las hadas. ~ **story**, ~**-tale** cuento m de hadas

fait accompli /feɪtə'kɒmpli/ n hecho m consumado

faith /feɪθ/ n (trust) confianza f; (relig) fe f. ~**ful** a fiel. ~**fully** adv fielmente. ~**fulness** n fidelidad f. ~**healing** n curación f por la fe

fake /feɪk/ n falsificación f; (person) impostor m. ● a falso. ● vt falsificar; (pretend) fingir

fakir /'feɪkɪə(r)/ n faquir m

falcon /'fɔ:lkən/ n halcón m

Falkland /'fɔ:klənd/ n. **the** ~ **Islands** npl las islas fpl Malvinas

fall /fɔ:l/ vi (pt **fell**, pp **fallen**) caer. ● n caída f; (autumn, Amer) otoño m; (in price) baja f. ~ **back on** recurrir a. ~ **down** (fall) caer; (be unsuccessful) fracasar. ~ **for** (fam) enamorarse de ⟨person⟩; (fam) dejarse engañar por ⟨trick⟩. ~ **in** (mil) formar filas. ~ **off** (diminish) disminuir. ~ **out** (quarrel) reñir (with con); (drop out) caer. ~ **over** caer(se). ~ **over sth** tropezar con algo. ~ **short** ser insuficiente. ~ **through** fracasar

fallacy /'fæləsɪ/ n error m

fallible /'fælɪbl/ a falible

fallout /'fɔ:laʊt/ n lluvia f radiactiva

fallow /'fæləʊ/ a en barbecho

false /fɔ:ls/ a falso. ~**hood** n mentira f. ~**ly** adv falsamente. ~**ness** n falsedad f

falsetto /fɔ:l'setəʊ/ n (pl -os) falsete m

falsify /'fɔ:lsɪfaɪ/ vt falsificar

falter /'fɔ:ltə(r)/ vi vacilar

fame /feɪm/ n fama f. ~**d** a famoso

familiar /fə'mɪlɪə(r)/ a familiar. **be** ~ **with** conocer. ~**ity** /-'ærətɪ/ n familiaridad f. ~**ize** vt familiarizar

family /'fæmɪlɪ/ n familia f. ● a de (la) familia, familiar

famine /'fæmɪn/ n hambre f, hambruna f (Amer)

famished /'fæmɪʃt/ a hambriento

famous /'feɪməs/ a famoso. ~**ly** adv (fam) a las mil maravillas

fan[1] /fæn/ n abanico m; (mec) ventilador m. ● vt (pt **fanned**) abanicar; soplar ⟨fire⟩. ● vi. ~ **out** desparramarse en forma de abanico

fan[2] /fæn/ n (of person) admirador m; (enthusiast) aficionado m, entusiasta m & f

fanatic /fə'nætɪk/ n fanático m. ~**al** a fanático. ~**ism** /-sɪzəm/ n fanatismo m

fan belt /'fænbelt/ n correa f de ventilador

fancier /'fænsɪə(r)/ n aficionado m

fanciful /'fænsɪfl/ a (imaginative) imaginativo; (unreal) imaginario

fancy /'fænsɪ/ n fantasía f; (liking) gusto m. **take a** ~ **to** tomar cariño a ⟨person⟩; aficionarse a ⟨thing⟩. ● a de lujo; (extravagant) excesivo. ● vt (imagine) imaginar; (believe) creer; (want, fam) apetecer a. ~ **dress** n disfraz m

fanfare /'fænfeə(r)/ n fanfarria f

fang /fæŋ/ n (of animal) colmillo m; (of snake) diente m

fanlight /'fænlaɪt/ n montante m

fantasize /'fæntəsaɪz/ vi fantasear

fantastic /fæn'tæstɪk/ a fantástico

fantasy /'fæntəsɪ/ n fantasía f

far /fɑ:(r)/ adv lejos; (much) mucho. **as** ~ **as** hasta. **as** ~ **as I know** que yo sepa. **by** ~ con mucho. ● a (further, furthest or farther, farthest) lejano

far-away /'fɑ:rəweɪ/ a lejano

farc|e /fɑ:s/ n farsa f. ~**ical** a ridículo

fare /feə(r)/ n (for transport) tarifa f; (food) comida f. ● vi irle. **how did you** ~? ¿qué tal te fue?

Far East /fɑ:(r)'i:st/ n Extremo/Lejano Oriente m

farewell /feə'wel/ int & n adiós (m)

far-fetched /fɑ:'fetʃt/ a improbable

farm /fɑ:m/ n granja f. ● vt cultivar. ~ **out** arrendar. ● vi ser agricultor. ~**er** n agricultor m. ~**house** n granja f. ~**ing** n agricultura f. ~**yard** n corral m

far: **~off** *a* lejano. **~reaching** *a* trascendental. **~seeing** *a* clarividente. **~sighted** *a* hipermétrope; (*fig*) clarividente

farther, farthest /'fɑːðə(r), 'fɑːðəst/ *see* **far**

fascinat|e /'fæsɪneɪt/ *vt* fascinar. **~ion** /-'neɪʃn/ *n* fascinación *f*

fascis|m /'fæʃɪzəm/ *n* fascismo *m*. **~t** /'fæʃɪst/ *a & n* fascista (*m & f*)

fashion /'fæʃn/ *n* (*manner*) manera *f*; (*vogue*) moda *f*. **~able** *a* de moda

fast¹ /fɑːst/ *a* (**-er, -est**) rápido; ‹*clock*› adelantado; (*secure*) fijo; ‹*colours*› sólido. ● *adv* rápidamente; (*securely*) firmemente. **~ asleep** profundamente dormido

fast² /fɑːst/ *vi* ayunar. ● *n* ayuno *m*

fasten /'fɑːsn/ *vt/i* sujetar; cerrar ‹*windows, doors*›; abrochar ‹*belt etc*›. **~er** *n*, **~ing** *n* (*on box, window*) cierre *m*; (*on door*) cerrojo *m*

fastidious /fə'stɪdɪəs/ *a* exigente, minucioso

fat /fæt/ *n* grasa *f*. ● *a* (**fatter, fattest**) gordo; ‹*meat*› que tiene mucha grasa; (*thick*) grueso. **a ~ lot of** (*sl*) muy poco

fatal /'feɪtl/ *a* mortal; (*fateful*) fatídico

fatalis|m /'feɪtəlɪzəm/ *n* fatalismo *m*. **~t** *n* fatalista *m & f*

fatality /fə'tælətɪ/ *n* calamidad *f*; (*death*) muerte *f*

fatally /'feɪtəlɪ/ *adv* mortalmente; (*by fate*) fatalmente

fate /feɪt/ *n* destino *m*; (*one's lot*) suerte *f*. **~d** *a* predestinado. **~ful** *a* fatídico

fat-head /'fæthed/ *n* imbécil *m*

father /'fɑːðə(r)/ *n* padre *m*. **~hood** *m* paternidad *f*. **~-in-law** *m* (*pl* **fathers-in-law**) *m* suegro *m*. **~ly** *a* paternal

fathom /'fæðəm/ *n* braza *f*. ● *vt*. **~ (out)** comprender

fatigue /fə'tiːg/ *n* fatiga *f*. ● *vt* fatigar

fat: **~ness** *n* gordura *f*. **~ten** *vt/i* engordar. **~tening** *a* que engorda. **~ty** *a* graso. ● *n* (*fam*) gordinflón *m*

fatuous /'fætjʊəs/ *a* fatuo

faucet /'fɔːsɪt/ *n* (*Amer*) grifo *m*

fault /fɔːlt/ *n* defecto *m*; (*blame*) culpa *f*; (*tennis*) falta *f*; (*geol*) falla *f*. **at ~** culpable. ● *vt* criticar. **~less** *a* impecable. **~y** *a* defectuoso

fauna /'fɔːnə/ *n* fauna *f*

faux pas /fəʊ'pɑː/ *n* (*pl* **faux pas** /fəʊ'pɑː /*) *n* metedura *f* de pata, paso *m* en falso

favour /'feɪvə(r)/ *n* favor *m*. ● *vt* favorecer; (*support*) estar a favor de; (*prefer*) preferir. **~able** *a* favorable. **~ably** *adv* favorablemente

favourit|e /'feɪvərɪt/ *a & n* preferido (*m*). **~ism** *n* favoritismo *m*

fawn¹ /fɔːn/ *n* cervato *m*. ● *a* color de cervato, beige, beis

fawn² /fɔːn/ *vi*. **~ on** adular

fax /fæks/ *n* telefacsímil *m*, fax *m*

fear /fɪə(r)/ *n* miedo *m*. ● *vt* temer. **~ful** *a* (*frightening*) espantoso; (*frightened*) temeroso. **~less** *a* intrépido. **~lessness** *n* intrepidez *f*. **~some** *a* espantoso

feasib|ility /fiːzə'bɪlətɪ/ *n* viabilidad *f*. **~le** /'fiːzəbl/ *a* factible; (*likely*) posible

feast /fiːst/ *n* (*relig*) fiesta *f*; (*meal*) banquete *m*, comilona *f*. ● *vt* banquetear, festejar. **~ on** regalarse con

feat /fiːt/ *n* hazaña *f*

feather /'feðə(r)/ *n* pluma *f*. ● *vt*. **~ one's nest** hacer su agosto. **~-brained** *a* tonto. **~weight** *n* peso *m* pluma

feature /'fiːtʃə(r)/ *n* (*on face*) facción *f*; (*characteristic*) característica *f*; (*in newspaper*) artículo *m*; ~ (**film**) película *f* principal, largometraje *m*. ● *vt* presentar; (*give prominence to*) destacar. ● *vi* figurar

February /'februərɪ/ *n* febrero *m*

feckless /'feklɪs/ *a* inepto; (*irresponsible*) irreflexivo

fed /fed/ *see* **feed**. ● *a*. **~ up** (*sl*) harto (**with** de)

federal /'fedərəl/ *a* federal

federation /fedə'reɪʃn/ *n* federación *f*

fee /fiː/ *n* (*professional*) honorarios *mpl*; (*enrolment*) derechos *mpl*; (*club*) cuota *f*

feeble /'fiːbl/ *a* (**-er, -est**) débil. **~-minded** *a* imbécil

feed /fiːd/ *vt* (*pt* **fed**) dar de comer a; (*supply*) alimentar. ● *vi* comer. ● *n* (*for animals*) pienso *m*; (*for babies*) comida *f*. **~back** *n* reacciones *fpl*, comentarios *mpl*

feel /fiːl/ *vt* (*pt* **felt**) sentir; (*touch*) tocar; (*think*) parecerle. **do you ~ it's a good idea?** te parece buena idea? **I ~ it is necessary** me parece necesario. **~ as if** tener la impresión de que. **~ hot/hungry** tener calor/hambre. **~ like** (*want, fam*) tener ganas de. ~ **up to** sentirse capaz de

feeler /ˈfiːlə(r)/ n (of insects) antena f. **put out a** ~ (fig) hacer un sondeo

feeling /ˈfiːlɪŋ/ n sentimiento m; (physical) sensación f

feet /fiːt/ see **foot**

feign /feɪn/ vt fingir

feint /feɪnt/ n finta f

felicitous /fəˈlɪsɪtəs/ a feliz, oportuno

feline /ˈfiːlaɪn/ a felino

fell[1] /fel/ see **fall**

fell[2] /fel/ vt derribar

fellow /ˈfeləʊ/ n (fam) tipo m; (comrade) compañero m; (society) socio m. ~**countryman** n compatriota m & f. ~ **passenger/traveller** n compañero m de viaje. ~**ship** n compañerismo m; (group) asociación f

felony /ˈfeləni/ n crimen m

felt[1] /felt/ n fieltro m

felt[2] /felt/ see **feel**

female /ˈfiːmeɪl/ a hembra; (voice, sex etc) femenino. ● n mujer f; (animal) hembra f

femini|ne /ˈfemənɪn/ a & n femenino (m). ~**nity** /-ˈnɪnəti/ n feminidad f. ~**st** n feminista m & f

fenc|e /fens/ n cerca f; (person, sl) perista m & f (fam). ● vt. ~**e** (**in**) encerrar, cercar. ● vi (sport) practicar la esgrima. ~**er** n esgrimidor m. ~**ing** n (sport) esgrima f

fend /fend/ vi. ~ **for o.s.** valerse por sí mismo. ● vt. ~ **off** defenderse de

fender /ˈfendə(r)/ n guardafuego m; (mudguard, Amer) guardabarros m invar; (naut) defensa f

fennel /ˈfenl/ n hinojo m

ferment /ˈfɜːment/ n fermento m; (fig) agitación f. /fəˈment/ vt/i fermentar. ~**ation** /-ˈteɪʃn/ n fermentación f

fern /fɜːn/ n helecho m

feroci|ous /fəˈrəʊʃəs/ a feroz. ~**ty** /fəˈrɒsəti/ n ferocidad f

ferret /ˈferɪt/ n hurón m. ● vi (pt ferreted) huronear. ● vt. ~ **out** descubrir

ferry /ˈferi/ n ferry m. ● vt transportar

fertil|e /ˈfɜːtaɪl/ a fértil; (biol) fecundo. ~**ity** /-ˈtɪləti/ n fertilidad f; (biol) fecundidad f

fertilize /ˈfɜːtəlaɪz/ vt abonar; (biol) fecundar. ~**r** n abono m

fervent /ˈfɜːvənt/ a ferviente

fervour /ˈfɜːvə(r)/ n fervor m

fester /ˈfestə(r)/ vi enconarse

festival /ˈfestəvl/ n fiesta f; (of arts) festival m

festive /ˈfestɪv/ a festivo. ~ **season** n temporada f de fiestas

festivity /feˈstɪvəti/ n festividad f

festoon /feˈstuːn/ vi. ~ **with** adornar de

fetch /fetʃ/ vt (go for) ir a buscar; (bring) traer; (be sold for) venderse por

fetching /ˈfetʃɪŋ/ a atractivo

fête /feɪt/ n fiesta f. ● vt festejar

fetid /ˈfetɪd/ a fétido

fetish /ˈfetɪʃ/ n fetiche m; (psych) obsesión f

fetter /ˈfetə(r)/ vt encadenar. ~**s** npl grilletes mpl

fettle /ˈfetl/ n condición f

feud /fjuːd/ n enemistad f (inveterada)

feudal /ˈfjuːdl/ a feudal. ~**ism** n feudalismo m

fever /ˈfiːvə(r)/ n fiebre f. ~**ish** a febril

few /fjuː/ a pocos. ● n pocos mpl. a ~ unos (pocos). **a good** ~, **quite a** ~ (fam) muchos. ~**er** a & n menos. ~**est** a & n el menor número de

fiancé /fɪˈɒnseɪ/ n novio m. ~**e** /fɪˈɒnseɪ/ n novia f

fiasco /fɪˈæskəʊ/ n (pl -os) fiasco m

fib /fɪb/ n mentirijilla f. ~**ber** n mentiroso m

fibre /ˈfaɪbə(r)/ n fibra f. ~**glass** n fibra f de vidrio

fickle /ˈfɪkl/ a inconstante

fiction /ˈfɪkʃn/ n ficción f. (**works of**) ~ novelas fpl. ~**al** a novelesco

fictitious /fɪkˈtɪʃəs/ a ficticio

fiddle /ˈfɪdl/ n (fam) violín m; (swindle, sl) trampa f. ● vt (sl) falsificar. ~ **with** juguetear con, toquetear, manosear. ~**r** n (fam) violinista m & f; (cheat, sl) tramposo m

fidelity /fɪˈdeləti/ n fidelidad f

fidget /ˈfɪdʒɪt/ vi (pt fidgeted) moverse, ponerse nervioso. ~ **with** juguetear con. ● n azogado m. ~**y** a azogado

field /fiːld/ n campo m. ~ **day** n gran ocasión f. ~ **glasses** npl gemelos mpl. **F**~ **Marshal** n mariscal m de campo, capitán m general. ~**work** n investigaciones fpl en el terreno

fiend /fiːnd/ n demonio m. ~**ish** a diabólico

fierce /fɪəs/ a (-er, -est) feroz; ⟨attack⟩ violento. **~ness** n ferocidad f, violencia f

fiery /ˈfaɪərɪ/ a (-ier, -iest) ardiente

fifteen /fɪfˈtiːn/ a & n quince (m). **~th** a & n quince (m), decimoquinto (m). ● n (fraction) quinzavo m

fifth /fɪfθ/ a & n quinto (m). **~ column** n quinta columna f

fift|ieth /ˈfɪftɪəθ/ a & n cincuenta (m). **~y** a & n cincuenta (m). **~y-~y** mitad y mitad, a medias. **a ~y-~y chance** una posibilidad f de cada dos

fig /fɪg/ n higo m

fight /faɪt/ vt/i (pt fought) luchar; ⟨quarrel⟩ disputar. **~ shy of** evitar. ● n lucha f; ⟨quarrel⟩ disputa f; ⟨mil⟩ combate m. **~ back** defenderse. **~ off** rechazar ⟨attack⟩; luchar contra ⟨illness⟩. **~er** n luchador m; ⟨mil⟩ combatiente m & f; ⟨aircraft⟩ avión m de caza. **~ing** n luchas fpl

figment /ˈfɪgmənt/ n invención f

figurative /ˈfɪgjʊrətɪv/ a figurado

figure /ˈfɪgə(r)/ n ⟨number⟩ cifra f; ⟨diagram⟩ figura f; ⟨shape⟩ forma f; ⟨of woman⟩ tipo m. ● vt imaginar. ● vi figurar. **that ~s** (Amer, fam) es lógico. **~ out** explicarse. **~head** n testaferro m, mascarón m de proa. **~ of speech** n tropo m, figura f. **~s** npl (arithmetic) aritmética f

filament /ˈfɪləmənt/ n filamento m

filch /fɪltʃ/ vt hurtar

file[1] /faɪl/ n carpeta f; ⟨set of papers⟩ expediente m. ● vt archivar ⟨papers⟩

file[2] /faɪl/ n ⟨row⟩ fila f. ● vi. **~ in** entrar en fila. **~ past** desfilar ante

file[3] /faɪl/ n ⟨tool⟩ lima f. ● vt limar

filings /ˈfaɪlɪŋz/ npl limaduras fpl

fill /fɪl/ vt llenar. **~ oneself. ~ in** rellenar ⟨form⟩. **~ out** ⟨get fatter⟩ engordar. **~ up** ⟨auto⟩ llenar, repostar. ● n. **eat one's ~** hartarse de comer. **have had one's ~ of** estar harto de

fillet /ˈfɪlɪt/ n filete m. ● vt (pt filleted) cortar en filetes

filling /ˈfɪlɪŋ/ n ⟨in tooth⟩ empaste m. **~ station** n estación f de servicio

film /fɪlm/ n película f. ● vt filmar. **~ star** n estrella f de cine. **~strip** n tira f de película

filter /ˈfɪltə(r)/ n filtro m. ● vt filtrar. ● vi filtrarse. **~tipped** a con filtro

filth /fɪlθ/ n inmundicia f. **~iness** n inmundicia f. **~y** a inmundo

fin /fɪn/ n aleta f

final /ˈfaɪnl/ a último; ⟨conclusive⟩ decisivo. ● n ⟨sport⟩ final f. **~s** npl ⟨schol⟩ exámenes mpl de fin de curso

finale /fɪˈnɑːlɪ/ n final m

final: ~ist n finalista m & f. **~ize** vt concluir. **~ly** adv ⟨lastly⟩ finalmente, por fin; ⟨once and for all⟩ definitivamente

financ|e /ˈfaɪnæns/ n finanzas fpl. ● vt financiar. **~ial** /faɪˈnænʃl/ a financiero. **~ially** adv económicamente. **~ier** /faɪˈnænsɪə(r)/ n financiero m

finch /fɪntʃ/ n pinzón m

find /faɪnd/ vt (pt found) encontrar. **~ out** enterarse de. **~er** n el m que encuentra, descubridor m. **~ings** npl resultados mpl

fine[1] /faɪn/ a (-er, -est) fino; ⟨excellent⟩ excelente. ● adv muy bien; ⟨small⟩ en trozos pequeños

fine[2] /faɪn/ n multa f. ● vt multar

fine: ~ arts npl bellas artes fpl. **~ly** adv ⟨admirably⟩ espléndidamente; ⟨cut⟩ en trozos pequeños. **~ry** /ˈfaɪnərɪ/ n galas fpl

finesse /fɪˈnes/ n tino m

finger /ˈfɪŋgə(r)/ n dedo m. ● vt tocar. **~nail** n uña f. **~print** n huella f dactilar. **~stall** n dedil m. **~tip** n punta f del dedo

finicking /ˈfɪnɪkɪŋ/ a, **finicky** /ˈfɪnɪkɪ/ a melindroso

finish /ˈfɪnɪʃ/ vt/i terminar. **~ doing** terminar de hacer. **~ up doing** terminar por hacer. ● n fin m; ⟨of race⟩ llegada f, meta f; ⟨appearance⟩ acabado m

finite /ˈfaɪnaɪt/ a finito

Fin|land /ˈfɪnlənd/ n Finlandia f. **~n** n finlandés m. **~nish** a & n finlandés (m)

fiord /fjɔːd/ n fiordo m

fir /fɜː(r)/ n abeto m

fire /faɪə(r)/ n fuego m; ⟨conflagration⟩ incendio m. ● vt disparar ⟨bullet etc⟩; ⟨dismiss⟩ despedir; ⟨fig⟩ excitar, enardecer, inflamar. ● vi tirar. **~arm** n arma f de fuego. **~ brigade** n cuerpo m de bomberos. **~cracker** n (Amer) petardo m. **~ department** n (Amer) cuerpo m de bomberos. **~engine** n coche m de bomberos. **~escape** n escalera f de incendios. **~light** n

lumbre f. **~man** n bombero m.
~place n chimenea f. **~side** n hogar
m. **~ station** n parque m de bomberos. **~wood** n leña f. **~work** n
fuego m artificial

firing-squad /'faɪərɪŋskwɒd/ n pelotón m de ejecución

firm¹ /fɜːm/ n empresa f

firm² /fɜːm/ a (**-er, -est**) firme. **~ly**
adv firmemente. **~ness** n firmeza f

first /fɜːst/ a primero. **at ~ hand** directamente. **at ~ sight** a primera
vista. ● n primero m. ● adv primero; (first time) por primera vez.
~ of all ante todo. **~ aid** n primeros
auxilios mpl. **~-born** a primogénito. **~-class** a de primera clase.
~ floor n primer piso m; (Amer)
planta f baja. **F~ Lady** n (Amer)
Primera Dama f. **~-ly** adv en primer
lugar. **~ name** n nombre m de pila.
~-rate a excelente

fiscal /'fɪskl/ a fiscal

fish /fɪʃ/ n (usually invar) (alive in
water) pez m; (food) pescado m. ● vi
pescar. **~ for** pescar. **~ out** (take
out, fam) sacar. **go ~ing** ir de pesca.
~erman /'fɪʃəmən/ n pescador m.
~ing n pesca f. **~ing-rod** n caña f
de pesca. **~monger** n pescadero m.
~shop n pescadería f. **~y** a (smell)
a pescado; (questionable, fam)
sospechoso

fission /'fɪʃn/ n fisión f

fist /fɪst/ n puño m

fit¹ /fɪt/ a (**fitter, fittest**) con-
veniente; (healthy) sano; (good
enough) adecuado; (able) capaz. ● n
(of clothes) corte m. ● vt (pt **fitted**)
(adapt) adaptar; (be the right size
for) sentar bien a; (install) colocar.
● vi encajar; (in certain space)
caber; (clothes) sentar. **~ out**
equipar. **~ up** equipar

fit² /fɪt/ n ataque m

fitful /'fɪtfl/ a irregular

fitment /'fɪtmənt/ n mueble m

fitness /'fɪtnɪs/ n (buena) salud f; (of
remark) conveniencia f

fitting /'fɪtɪŋ/ a apropiado. ● n (of
clothes) prueba f. **~s** /'fɪtɪŋz/ npl (in
house) accesorios mpl

five /faɪv/ a & n cinco (m). **~r**
/'faɪvə(r)/ n (fam) billete m de cinco
libras

fix /fɪks/ vt (make firm, attach,
decide) fijar; (mend, deal with) arreglar. ● n. **in a ~** en un aprieto.

~ation /-eɪʃn/ n fijación f. **~ed** a
fijo

fixture /'fɪkstʃə(r) n (sport) partido m.
~s (in house) accesorios mpl

fizz /fɪz/ vi burbujear. ● n efer-
vescencia f. **~le** /fɪzl/ vi burbujear.
~le out fracasar. **~y** a efervescente; (water) con gas

flab /flæb/ n (fam) flaccidez f

flabbergast /'flæbəgɑːst/ vt pasmar

flabby /'flæbɪ/ a flojo

flag /flæg/ n bandera f. ● vt (pt
flagged). **~ down** hacer señales de
parada a. ● vi (pt **flagged**) (weaken)
flaquear; (interest) decaer; (conversation) languidecer

flagon /'flægən/ n botella f grande,
jarro m

flag-pole /'flægpəʊl/ n asta f de
bandera

flagrant /'fleɪgrənt/ a (glaring)
flagrante; (scandalous) escandaloso

flagstone /'flægstəʊn/ n losa f

flair /fleə(r)/ n don m (for de)

flak|e /fleɪk/ n copo m; (of paint,
metal) escama f. ● vi desconcharse.
~e out (fam) caer rendido. **~y** a
escamoso

flamboyant /flæm'bɔɪənt/ a (clothes) vistoso; (manner) extravagante

flame /fleɪm/ n llama f. ● vi llamear

flamingo /flə'mɪŋgəʊ/ n (pl **-o(e)s**)
flamenco m

flammable /'flæməbl/ a inflamable

flan /flæn/ n tartaleta f, tarteleta f

flank /flæŋk/ n (of animal) ijada f,
flanco m; (of person) costado m; (of
mountain) falda f; (mil) flanco m

flannel /'flænl/ n franela f (de lana);
(for face) paño m (para lavarse la
cara). **~ette** n franela f (de
algodón), muletón m

flap /flæp/ vi (pt **flapped**) ondear;
(wings) aletear; (become agitated,
fam) ponerse nervioso. ● vt sacudir; batir (wings). ● n (of pocket)
cartera f; (of table) ala f. **get into a
~** ponerse nervioso

flare /fleə(r)/ ● n llamarada f; (mil)
bengala f; (in skirt) vuelo m. ● vi. **~
up** llamear; (fighting) estallar; (person) encolerizarse. **~d** a (skirt)
acampanado

flash /flæʃ/ ● vi brillar; (on and off)
destellar. ● vt despedir; (aim torch)
dirigir; (flaunt) hacer ostentación
de. **~ past** pasar como un rayo. ● n
relámpago m; (of news, camera)

flash *m.* **~back** *n* escena *f* retrospectiva. **~light** *n* (*torch*) linterna *f*

flashy /'flæʃɪ/ *a* ostentoso

flask /flɑːsk/ *n* frasco *m*; (*vacuum flask*) termo *m*

flat[1] /flæt/ *a* (**flatter, flattest**) llano; (*tyre*) desinflado; (*refusal*) categórico; (*fare, rate*) fijo; (*mus*) desafinado. ● *adv.* **~ out** (*at top speed*) a toda velocidad

flat[2] /flæt/ *n* (*rooms*) piso *m*, apartamento *m*; (*tyre*) (*fam*) pinchazo *m*; (*mus*) bemol *m*

flat: **~ly** *adv* categóricamente. **~ness** *n* llanura *f*. **~ten** /'flætn/ *vt* allanar, aplanar. ● *vi* allanarse, aplanarse

flatter /flætə(r)/ *vt* adular. **~er** *n* adulador *m.* **~ing** *a* (*person*) lisonjero; (*clothes*) favorecedor. **~y** *n* adulación *f*

flatulence /'flætjʊləns/ *n* flatulencia *f*

flaunt /flɔːnt/ *vt* hacer ostentación de

flautist /'flɔːtɪst/ *n* flautista *m* & *f*

flavour /'fleɪvə(r)/ *n* sabor *m.* ● *vt* condimentar. **~ing** *n* condimento *m*

flaw /flɔː/ *n* defecto *m.* **~less** *a* perfecto

flax /flæks/ *n* lino *m.* **~en** *a* de lino; (*hair*) rubio

flea /fliː/ *n* pulga *f*

fleck /flek/ *n* mancha *f*, pinta *f*

fled /fled/ *see* **flee**

fledged /fledʒd/ *a.* **fully ~** (*doctor etc*) hecho y derecho; (*member*) de pleno derecho

fledg(e)ling /'fledʒlɪŋ/ *n* pájaro *m* volantón

flee /fliː/ *vi* (*pt* **fled**) huir. ● *vt* huir de

fleece /fliːs/ *n* vellón *m.* ● *vt* (*rob*) desplumar

fleet /fliːt/ *n* (*naut, aviat*) flota *f*; (*of cars*) parque *m*

fleeting /'fliːtɪŋ/ *a* fugaz

Flemish /'flemɪʃ/ *a* & *n* flamenco (*m*)

flesh /fleʃ/ *n* carne *f*. **in the ~** en persona. **one's own ~ and blood** los de su sangre. **~y** *a* (*fruit*) carnoso

flew /fluː/ *see* **fly**[1]

flex /fleks/ *vt* doblar; flexionar (*muscle*). ● *n* (*elec*) cable *m*, flexible *m*

flexib|ility /fleksə'bɪlɪtɪ/ *n* flexibilidad *f*. **~le** /'fleksəbl/ *a* flexible

flexitime /'fleksɪ'taɪm/ *n* horario *m* flexible

flick /flɪk/ *n* golpecito *m.* ● *vt* dar un golpecito a. **~ through** hojear

flicker /'flɪkə(r)/ *vi* temblar; (*light*) parpadear. ● *n* temblor *m*; (*of hope*) resquicio *m*; (*of light*) parpadeo *m*

flick: **~knife** *n* navaja *f* de muelle. **~s** *npl* cine *m*

flier /'flaɪə(r)/ *n* aviador *m*; (*circular, Amer*) prospecto *m*, folleto *m*

flies /flaɪz/ *npl* (*on trousers, fam*) bragueta *f*

flight /flaɪt/ *n* vuelo *m*; (*fleeing*) huida *f*, fuga *f*. **~ of stairs** tramo *m* de escalera *f.* **put to ~** poner en fuga. **take (to) ~** darse a la fuga. **~deck** *n* cubierta *f* de vuelo

flighty /'flaɪtɪ/ *a* (**-ier, -iest**) frívolo

flimsy /'flɪmzɪ/ *a* (**-ier, -iest**) flojo, débil, poco substancioso

flinch /flɪntʃ/ *vi* (*draw back*) retroceder (**from** ante). **without ~ing** (*without wincing*) sin pestañear

fling /flɪŋ/ *vt* (*pt* **flung**) arrojar. ● *n.* **have a ~** echar una cana al aire

flint /flɪnt/ *n* pedernal *m*; (*for lighter*) piedra *f*

flip /flɪp/ *vt* (*pt* **flipped**) dar un golpecito a. **~ through** hojear. ● *n* golpecito *m.* **~ side** *n* otra cara *f*

flippant /'flɪpənt/ *a* poco serio; (*disrespectful*) irrespetuoso

flipper /'flɪpə(r)/ *n* aleta *f*

flirt /flɜːt/ *vi* coquetear. ● *n* (*woman*) coqueta *f*; (*man*) mariposón *m*, coqueto *m.* **~ation** /-'teɪʃn/ *n* coqueteo *m*

flit /flɪt/ *vi* (*pt* **flitted**) revolotear

float /fləʊt/ *vi* flotar. ● *vt* hacer flotar. ● *n* flotador *m*; (*on fishing line*) corcho *m*; (*cart*) carroza *f*

flock /flɒk/ *n* (*of birds*) bandada *f*; (*of sheep*) rebaño *m*; (*of people*) muchedumbre *f*, multitud *f.* ● *vi* congregarse

flog /flɒg/ *vt* (*pt* **flogged**) (*beat*) azotar; (*sell, sl*) vender

flood /flʌd/ *n* inundación *f*; (*fig*) torrente *m.* ● *vt* inundar. ● *vi* (*building etc*) inundarse; (*river*) desbordar

floodlight /'flʌdlaɪt/ *n* foco *m.* ● *vt* (*pt* **floodlit**) iluminar (con focos)

floor /flɔː(r)/ *n* suelo *m*; (*storey*) piso *m*; (*for dancing*) pista *f.* ● *vt* (*knock down*) derribar; (*baffle*) confundir

flop /flɒp/ *vi* (*pt* **flopped**) dejarse caer pesadamente; (*fail, sl*) fracasar. ● *n* (*sl*) fracaso *m*. ~**py** *a* flojo

flora /'flɔːrə/ *n* flora *f*

floral /'flɔːrəl/ *a* floral

florid /'flɒrɪd/ *a* florido

florist /'flɒrɪst/ *n* florista *m & f*

flounce /flaʊns/ *n* volante *m*

flounder[1] /'flaʊndə(r)/ *vi* avanzar con dificultad, no saber qué hacer

flounder[2] /'flaʊndə(r)/ *n* (*fish*) platija *f*

flour /flaʊə(r)/ *n* harina *f*

flourish /'flʌrɪʃ/ *vi* prosperar. ● *vt* blandir. ● *n* ademán *m* elegante; (*in handwriting*) rasgo *m*. ~**ing** *a* próspero

floury /'flaʊərɪ/ *a* harinoso

flout /flaʊt/ *vt* burlarse de

flow /fləʊ/ *vi* correr; (*hang loosely*) caer. ~ **into** ⟨*river*⟩ desembocar en. ● *n* flujo *m*; (*jet*) chorro *m*; (*stream*) corriente *f*; (*of words, tears*) torrente *m*. ~ **chart** *n* organigrama *m*

flower /'flaʊə(r)/ *n* flor *f*. ~**bed** *n* macizo *m* de flores. ~**ed** *a* floreado, de flores. ~**y** *a* florido

flown /fləʊn/ *see* fly[1]

flu /fluː/ *n* (*fam*) gripe *f*

fluctuat|e /'flʌktjʊeɪt/ *vi* fluctuar. ~**ion** /-eɪʃn/ *n* fluctuación *f*

flue /fluː/ *n* humero *m*

fluen|cy /'fluːənsɪ/ *n* facilidad *f*. ~**t** *a* ⟨*style*⟩ fluido; ⟨*speaker*⟩ elocuente. **be** ~**t (in a language)** hablar (un idioma) con soltura. ~**tly** *adv* con fluidez; (*lang*) con soltura

fluff /flʌf/ *n* pelusa *f*. ~**y** *a* (**-ier, -iest**) velloso

fluid /'fluːɪd/ *a & n* fluido (*m*)

fluke /fluːk/ *n* (*stroke of luck*) chiripa *f*

flung /flʌŋ/ *see* fling

flunk /flʌŋk/ *vt* (*Amer, fam*) ser suspendido en ⟨*exam*⟩; suspender ⟨*person*⟩. ● *vi* (*fam*) ser suspendido

fluorescent /flʊəˈresnt/ *a* fluorescente

fluoride /'flʊəraɪd/ *n* fluoruro *m*

flurry /'flʌrɪ/ *n* (*squall*) ráfaga *f*; (*fig*) agitación *f*

flush[1] /flʌʃ/ *vi* ruborizarse. ● *vt* limpiar con agua. ~ **the toilet** tirar de la cadena. ● *n* (*blush*) rubor *m*; (*fig*) emoción *f*

flush[2] /flʌʃ/ *a*. ~ **(with)** a nivel (con)

flush[3] /flʌʃ/ *vt/i*. ~ **out** (*drive out*) echar fuera

fluster /'flʌstə(r)/ *vt* poner nervioso

flute /fluːt/ *n* flauta *f*

flutter /'flʌtə(r)/ *vi* ondear; ⟨*bird*⟩ revolotear. ● *n* (*of wings*) revoloteo *m*; (*fig*) agitación *f*

flux /flʌks/ *n* flujo *m*. **be in a state of** ~ estar siempre cambiando

fly[1] /flaɪ/ *vi* (*pt* **flew**, *pp* **flown**) volar; ⟨*passenger*⟩ ir en avión; ⟨*flag*⟩ flotar; (*rush*) correr. ● *vt* pilotar ⟨*aircraft*⟩; transportar en avión ⟨*passengers, goods*⟩; izar ⟨*flag*⟩. ● *n* (*of trousers*) bragueta *f*

fly[2] /flaɪ/ *n* mosca *f*

flyer /'flaɪə(r)/ *n* aviador *m*; (*circular, Amer*) prospecto *m*, folleto *m*

flying /'flaɪɪŋ/ *a* volante; (*hasty*) relámpago *invar*. ● *n* (*activity*) aviación *f*. ~ **visit** *n* visita *f* relámpago

fly: ~**leaf** *n* guarda *f*. ~**over** *n* paso *m* elevado. ~**weight** *n* peso *m* mosca

foal /fəʊl/ *n* potro *m*

foam /fəʊm/ *n* espuma *f*. ~**(rubber)** *n* goma *f* espuma. ● *vi* espumar

fob /fɒb/ *vt* (*pt* **fobbed**). ~ **off on s.o.** (*palm off*) encajar a uno

focal /'fəʊkl/ *a* focal

focus /'fəʊkəs/ *n* (*pl* **-cuses** *or* **-ci** /-saɪ/) foco *m*; (*fig*) centro *m*. **in** ~ enfocado. **out of** ~ desenfocado. ● *vt/i* (*pt* **focused**) enfocar(se); (*fig*) concentrar

fodder /'fɒdə(r)/ *n* forraje *m*

foe /fəʊ/ *n* enemigo *m*

foetus /'fiːtəs/ *n* (*pl* **-tuses**) feto *m*

fog /fɒg/ *n* niebla *f*. ● *vt* (*pt* **fogged**) envolver en niebla; (*photo*) velar. ● *vi*. ~ **(up)** empañarse; (*photo*) velarse

fog(e)y /'fəʊgɪ/ *n*. **be an old** ~ estar chapado a la antigua

foggy /'fɒgɪ/ *a* (**-ier, -iest**) nebuloso. **it is** ~ hay niebla

foghorn /'fɒghɔːn/ *n* sirena *f* de niebla

foible /'fɔɪbl/ *n* punto *m* débil

foil[1] /fɔɪl/ *vt* (*thwart*) frustrar

foil[2] /fɔɪl/ *n* papel *m* de plata; (*fig*) contraste *m*

foist /fɔɪst/ *vt* encajar (on a)

fold[1] /fəʊld/ *vt* doblar; cruzar ⟨*arms*⟩. ● *vi* doblarse; (*fail*) fracasar. ● *n* pliegue *m*

fold[2] /fəʊld/ *n* (*for sheep*) redil *m*

folder /'fəʊldə(r)/ *n* (*file*) carpeta *f*; (*leaflet*) folleto *m*

folding /'fəʊldɪŋ/ *a* plegable

foliage /'fəʊlɪdʒ/ *n* follaje *m*

folk /fəʊk/ n gente f. ● a popular. ∼**lore** n folklore m. ∼**s** npl (one's relatives) familia f

follow /'fɒləʊ/ vt/i seguir. ∼ **up** seguir; (investigate further) investigar. ∼**er** n seguidor m. ∼**ing** n partidarios mpl. ● a siguiente. ● prep después de

folly /'fɒlɪ/ n locura f

foment /fə'ment/ vt fomentar

fond /fɒnd/ a (-er, -est) (loving) cariñoso; ⟨hope⟩ vivo. be ∼ of s.o. tener(le) cariño a uno. be ∼ of sth ser aficionado a algo

fondle /'fɒndl/ vt acariciar

fondness /'fɒndnɪs/ n cariño m; (for things) afición f

font /fɒnt/ n pila f bautismal

food /fuːd/ n alimento m, comida f. ∼ **processor** n robot m de cocina, batidora f

fool /fuːl/ n tonto m. ● vt engañar. ● vi hacer el tonto

foolhardy /'fuːlhɑːdɪ/ a temerario

foolish /'fuːlɪʃ/ a tonto. ∼**ly** adv tontamente. ∼**ness** n tontería f

foolproof /'fuːlpruːf/ a infalible, a toda prueba, a prueba de tontos

foot /fʊt/ n (pl feet) pie m; (measure) pie m (= 30,48 cm); (of animal, furniture) pata f. get under s.o.'s feet estorbar a uno. on ∼ a pie. on/to one's feet de pie. put one's ∼ in it meter la pata. ● vt pagar ⟨bill⟩. ∼ it ir andando

footage /'fʊtɪdʒ/ n (of film) secuencia f

football /'fʊtbɔːl/ n (ball) balón m; (game) fútbol m. ∼**er** n futbolista m & f

footbridge /'fʊtbrɪdʒ/ n puente m para peatones

foothills /'fʊthɪlz/ npl estribaciones fpl

foothold /'fʊthəʊld/ n punto m de apoyo m

footing /'fʊtɪŋ/ n pie m

footlights /'fʊtlaɪts/ npl candilejas fpl

footloose /'fʊtluːs/ a libre

footman /'fʊtmən/ n lacayo m

footnote /'fʊtnəʊt/ n nota f (al pie de la página)

foot: ∼**path** n (in country) senda f; (in town) acera f, vereda f (Arg), banqueta f (Mex). ∼**print** n huella f. ∼**sore** a. be ∼**sore** tener los pies doloridos. ∼**step** n paso m. ∼**stool** n escabel m. ∼**wear** n calzado m

for /fɔː(r)/, unstressed /fə(r)/ prep (expressing purpose) para; (on behalf of) por; (in spite of) a pesar de; (during) durante; (in favour of) a favor de. **he has been in Madrid ∼ two months** hace dos meses que está en Madrid. ● conj ya que

forage /'fɒrɪdʒ/ vi forrajear. ● n forraje m

foray /'fɒreɪ/ n incursión f

forbade /fə'bæd/ see **forbid**

forbear /fɔː'beər/ vt/i (pt **forbore**, pp **forborne**) contenerse. ∼**ance** n paciencia f

forbid /fə'bɪd/ vt (pt **forbade**, pp **forbidden**) prohibir (**s.o. to do** a uno hacer). ∼ **s.o. sth** prohibir algo a uno

forbidding /fə'bɪdɪŋ/ a imponente

force /fɔːs/ n fuerza f. **come into ∼** entrar en vigor. **the ∼s** las fuerzas fpl armadas. ● vt forzar. ∼ **on** imponer a. ∼**d** a forzado. ∼**feed** vt alimentar a la fuerza. ∼**ful** /'fɔːsfʊl/ a enérgico

forceps /'fɔːseps/ n invar tenazas fpl; (for obstetric use) fórceps m invar; (for dental use) gatillo m

forcible /'fɔːsəbl/ a a la fuerza. ∼**y** adv a la fuerza

ford /fɔːd/ n vado m, botadero m (Mex). ● vt vadear

fore /fɔː(r)/ a anterior. ● n. **come to the ∼** hacerse evidente

forearm /'fɔːrɑːm/ n antebrazo m

foreboding /fɔː'bəʊdɪŋ/ n presentimiento m

forecast /'fɔːkɑːst/ vt (pt **forecast**) pronosticar. ● n pronóstico m

forecourt /'fɔːkɔːt/ n patio m

forefathers /'fɔːfɑːðəz/ npl antepasados mpl

forefinger /'fɔːfɪŋɡə(r)/ n (dedo m) índice m

forefront /'fɔːfrʌnt/ n vanguardia f. **in the ∼** a/en vanguardia, en primer plano

foregone /'fɔːɡɒn/ a. ∼ **conclusion** resultado m previsto

foreground /'fɔːɡraʊnd/ n primer plano m

forehead /'fɒrɪd/ n frente f

foreign /'fɒrən/ a extranjero; ⟨trade⟩ exterior; ⟨travel⟩ al extranjero, en el extranjero. ∼**er** n extranjero m. **F∼ Secretary** n ministro m de Asuntos Exteriores

foreman /'fɔːmən/ n capataz m, caporal m

foremost /'fɔːməʊst/ *a* primero.
● *adv.* **first and ~** ante todo

forensic /fə'rensɪk/ *a* forense

forerunner /'fɔːrʌnə(r)/ *n* precursor *m*

foresee /fɔː'siː/ *vt* (*pt* -**saw**, *pp* -**seen**) prever. **~able** *a* previsible

foreshadow /fɔː'ʃædəʊ/ *vt* presagiar

foresight /'fɔːsaɪt/ *n* previsión *f*

forest /'fɒrɪst/ *n* bosque *m*

forestall /fɔː'stɔːl/ *vt* anticiparse a

forestry /'fɒrɪstrɪ/ *n* silvicultura *f*

foretaste /'fɔːteɪst/ *n* anticipación *f*

foretell /fɔː'tel/ *vt* (*pt* **foretold**) predecir

forever /fə'revə(r)/ *adv* para siempre

forewarn /fɔː'wɔːn/ *vt* prevenir

foreword /'fɔːwɜːd/ *n* prefacio *m*

forfeit /'fɔːfɪt/ *n* (*penalty*) pena *f*; (*in game*) prenda *f*; (*fine*) multa *f*. ● *vt* perder

forgave /fə'geɪv/ *see* **forgive**

forge[1] /fɔːdʒ/ *n* fragua *f*. ● *vt* fraguar; (*copy*) falsificar

forge[2] /fɔːdʒ/ *vi* avanzar. **~ahead** adelantarse rápidamente

forge: **~r** /'fɔːdʒə(r)/ *n* falsificador *m*. **~ry** *n* falsificación *f*

forget /fə'get/ *vt* (*pt* **forgot**, *pp* **forgotten**) olvidar. **~ o.s.** propasarse, extralimitarse. ● *vi* olvidar(se). **I forgot** se me olvidó. **~ful** *a* olvidadizo. **~ful of** olvidando. **~me-not** *n* nomeolvides *f invar*

forgive /fə'gɪv/ *vt* (*pt* **forgave**, *pp* **forgiven**) perdonar. **~ness** *n* perdón *m*

forgo /fɔː'gəʊ/ *vt* (*pt* **forwent**, *pp* **forgone**) renunciar a

fork /fɔːk/ *n* tenedor *m*; (*for digging*) horca *f*; (*in road*) bifurcación *f*. ● *vi* ⟨*road*⟩ bifurcarse. **~ out** (*sl*) aflojar la bolsa (*fam*), pagar. **~ed** *a* ahorquillado; ⟨*road*⟩ bifurcado. **~lift truck** *n* carretilla *f* elevadora

forlorn /fə'lɔːn/ *a* (*hopeless*) desesperado; (*abandoned*) abandonado. **~ hope** *n* empresa *f* desesperada

form /fɔːm/ *n* forma *f*; (*document*) impreso *m*, formulario *m*; (*schol*) clase *f*. ● *vt* formar. ● *vi* formarse

formal /'fɔːml/ *a* formal; ⟨*person*⟩ formalista; ⟨*dress*⟩ de etiqueta. **~ity** /-'mælətɪ/ *n* formalidad *f*. **~ly** *adv* oficialmente

format /'fɔːmæt/ *n* formato *m*

formation /fɔː'meɪʃn/ *n* formación *f*

formative /'fɔːmətɪv/ *a* formativo

former /'fɔːmə(r)/ *a* anterior; (*first of two*) primero. **~ly** *adv* antes

formidable /'fɔːmɪdəbl/ *a* formidable

formless /'fɔːmlɪs/ *a* informe

formula /'fɔːmjʊlə/ *n* (*pl* -**ae** /-iː/ *or* -**as**) fórmula *f*

formulate /'fɔːmjʊleɪt/ *vt* formular

fornicat|e /'fɔːnɪkeɪt/ *vi* fornicar. **~ion** /-'keɪʃn/ *n* fornicación *f*

forsake /fə'seɪk/ *vt* (*pt* **forsook**, *pp* **forsaken**) abandonar

fort /fɔːt/ *n* (*mil*) fuerte *m*

forte /'fɔːteɪ/ *n* (*talent*) fuerte *m*

forth /fɔːθ/ *adv* en adelante. **and so ~** y así sucesivamente. **go back and ~** ir y venir

forthcoming /fɔːθ'kʌmɪŋ/ *a* próximo, venidero; (*sociable*, *fam*) comunicativo

forthright /'fɔːθraɪt/ *a* directo

forthwith /fɔːθ'wɪθ/ *adv* inmediatamente

fortieth /'fɔːtɪɪθ/ *a* cuarenta, cuadragésimo. ● *n* cuadragésima parte *f*

fortification /fɔːtɪfɪ'keɪʃn/ *n* fortificación *f*. **~y** /'fɔːtɪfaɪ/ *vt* fortificar

fortitude /'fɔːtɪtjuːd/ *n* valor *m*

fortnight /'fɔːtnaɪt/ *n* quince días *mpl*, quincena *f*. **~ly** *a* bimensual. ● *adv* cada quince días

fortress /'fɔːtrɪs/ *n* fortaleza *f*

fortuitous /fɔː'tjuːɪtəs/ *a* fortuito

fortunate /'fɔːtʃənət/ *a* afortunado. **be ~** tener suerte. **~ly** *adv* afortunadamente

fortune /'fɔːtʃuːn/ *n* fortuna *f*. **have the good ~ to** tener la suerte de. **~teller** *n* adivino *m*

forty /'fɔːtɪ/ *a & n* cuarenta (*m*). **~ winks** un sueñecito *m*

forum /'fɔːrəm/ *n* foro *m*

forward /'fɔːwəd/ *a* delantero; (*advanced*) precoz; (*pert*) impertinente. ● *n* (*sport*) delantero *m*. ● *adv* adelante. **come ~** presentarse. **go ~** avanzar. ● *vt* hacer seguir ⟨*letter*⟩; enviar ⟨*goods*⟩; (*fig*) favorecer. **~ness** *n* precocidad *f*

forwards /'fɔːwədz/ *adv* adelante

fossil /'fɒsl/ *a & n* fósil (*m*)

foster /'fɒstə(r)/ *vt* (*promote*) fomentar; criar ⟨*child*⟩. **~child** *n* hijo *m* adoptivo. **~mother** *n* madre *f* adoptiva

fought /fɔːt/ *see* **fight**

foul /faʊl/ a (**-er, -est**) ⟨smell, weather⟩ asqueroso; (dirty) sucio; ⟨language⟩ obsceno; ⟨air⟩ viciado. ~ **play** n jugada f sucia; (crime) delito m. ● n (sport) falta f. ● vt ensuciar; manchar ⟨reputation⟩. ~**-mouthed** a obsceno

found[1] /faʊnd/ see **find**

found[2] /faʊnd/ vt fundar

found[3] /faʊnd/ vt (tec) fundir

foundation /faʊn'deɪʃn/ n fundación f; (basis) fundamento. ~**s** npl (archit) cimientos mpl

founder[1] /'faʊndə(r)/ n fundador m

founder[2] /'faʊndə(r)/ vi ⟨ship⟩ hundirse

foundry /'faʊndrɪ/ n fundición f

fountain /'faʊntɪn/ n fuente f. ~**-pen** n estilográfica f

four /fɔː(r)/ a & n cuatro (m). ~**fold** a cuádruple. ● adv cuatro veces. ~**-poster** n cama f con cuatro columnas

foursome /'fɔːsəm/ n grupo m de cuatro personas

fourteen /'fɔː'tiːn/ a & n catorce (m). ~**th** a & n catorce (m), decimocuarto (m). ● n (fraction) catorceavo m

fourth /fɔːθ/ a & n cuarto (m)

fowl /faʊl/ n ave f

fox /fɒks/ n zorro m, zorra f. ● vt (baffle) dejar perplejo; (deceive) engañar

foyer /'fɔɪeɪ/ n (hall) vestíbulo m

fraction /'frækʃn/ n fracción f

fractious /'frækʃəs/ a díscolo

fracture /'fræktʃə(r)/ n fractura f. ● vt fracturar. ● vi fracturarse

fragile /'frædʒaɪl/ a frágil

fragment /'frægmənt/ n fragmento m. ~**ary** a fragmentario

fragran|ce /'freɪɡrəns/ n fragancia f. ~**t** a fragante

frail /freɪl/ a (**-er, -est**) frágil

frame /freɪm/ n (of picture, door, window) marco m; (of spectacles) montura f; (fig, structure) estructura f; (temporary state) estado m. ~ **of mind** estado m de ánimo. ● vt enmarcar; (fig) formular; (jurid, sl) incriminar falsamente. ~**-up** n (sl) complot m

framework /'freɪmwɜːk/ n estructura f; (context) marco m

France /frɑːns/ n Francia f

franchise /'fræntʃaɪz/ n (pol) derecho m a votar; (com) concesión f

Franco... /'fræŋkəʊ/ pref franco...

frank /fræŋk/ a sincero. ● vt franquear. ~**ly** adv sinceramente. ~**ness** n sinceridad f

frantic /'fræntɪk/ a frenético. ~ **with** loco de

fraternal /frə'tɜːnl/ a fraternal

fraternity /frə'tɜːnɪtɪ/ n fraternidad f; (club) asociación f

fraternize /'frætənaɪz/ vi fraternizar

fraud /frɔːd/ n (deception) fraude m; (person) impostor m. ~**ulent** a fraudulento

fraught /frɔːt/ a (tense) tenso. ~ **with** cargado de

fray[1] /freɪ/ vt desgastar. ● vi deshilacharse

fray[2] /freɪ/ n riña f

freak /friːk/ n (caprice) capricho m; (monster) monstruo m; (person) chalado m. ● a anormal. ~**ish** a anormal

freckle /'frekl/ n peca f. ~**d** a pecoso

free /friː/ a (**freer** /'friːə(r)/, **freest** /'friːɪst/) libre; (gratis) gratis; (lavish) generoso. ~ **kick** n golpe m franco. ~ **of charge** gratis. ~ **speech** n libertad f de expresión. **give a ~ hand** dar carta blanca. ● vt (pt **freed**) (set at liberty) poner en libertad; (relieve from) liberar (from/of de); (untangle) desenredar; (loosen) soltar

freedom /'friːdəm/ n libertad f

freehold /'friːhəʊld/ n propiedad f absoluta

freelance /'friːlɑːns/ a independiente

freely /'friːlɪ/ adv libremente

Freemason /'friːmeɪsn/ n masón m. ~**ry** n masonería f

free-range /'friːreɪndʒ/ a ⟨eggs⟩ de granja

freesia /'friːzjə/ n fresia f

freeway /'friːweɪ/ n (Amer) autopista f

freez|e /'friːz/ vt (pt **froze**, pp **frozen**) helar; congelar ⟨food, wages⟩. ● vi helarse; congelarse; (become motionless) quedarse inmóvil. ● n helada f; (of wages, prices) congelación f. ~**er** n congelador m. ~**ing** a glacial. ● n congelación f. **below** ~**ing** bajo cero

freight /freɪt/ n (goods) mercancías fpl; (hire of ship etc) flete m. ~**er** n (ship) buque m de carga

French /frentʃ/ a francés. ● n (lang) francés m. ~**man** n francés m. ~**-speaking** a francófono. ~ **window** n puertaventana f. ~**woman** n francesa f

frenz|ied /'frenzɪd/ *a* frenético. **~y** *n* frenesí *m*

frequency /'fri:kwənsɪ/ *n* frecuencia *f*

frequent /frɪ'kwent/ *vt* frecuentar. /'fri:kwənt/ *a* frecuente. **~ly** *adv* frecuentemente

fresco /'freskəʊ/ *n* (*pl* **-o(e)s**) fresco *m*

fresh /freʃ/ *a* (**-er, -est**) fresco; (*different, additional*) nuevo; (*cheeky*) fresco, descarado; ⟨*water*⟩ dulce. **~en** *vi* refrescar. **~en up** ⟨*person*⟩ refrescarse. **~ly** *adv* recientemente. **~man** *n* estudiante *m* de primer año. **~ness** *n* frescura *f*

fret /fret/ *vi* (*pt* **fretted**) inquietarse. **~ful** *a* (*discontented*) quejoso; (*irritable*) irritable

Freudian /'frɔɪdjən/ *a* freudiano

friar /'fraɪə(r)/ *n* fraile *m*

friction /'frɪkʃn/ *n* fricción *f*

Friday /'fraɪdeɪ/ *n* viernes *m*. **Good ~** Viernes Santo

fridge /frɪdʒ/ *n* (*fam*) nevera *f*, refrigerador *m*, refrigeradora *f*

fried /fraɪd/ *see* **fry**. ● *a* frito

friend /frend/ *n* amigo *m*. **~liness** /'frendlɪnɪs/ *n* simpatía *f*. **~ly** *a* (**-ier, -iest**) simpático. **F~ly Society** *n* mutualidad *f*. **~ship** /'frendʃɪp/ *n* amistad *f*

frieze /fri:z/ *n* friso *m*

frigate /'frɪgət/ *n* fragata *f*

fright /fraɪt/ *n* susto *m*; (*person*) espantajo *m*; (*thing*) horror *m*

frighten /'fraɪtn/ *vt* asustar. **~ off** ahuyentar. **~ed** *a* asustado. **be ~ed** tener miedo (**of** de)

frightful /'fraɪtfl/ *a* espantoso, horrible. **~ly** *adv* terriblemente

frigid /'frɪdʒɪd/ *a* frío; (*psych*) frígido. **~ity** /-'dʒɪdətɪ/ *n* frigidez *f*

frill /frɪl/ *n* volante *m*. **~s** *npl* (*fig*) adornos *mpl*. **with no ~s** sencillo

fringe /frɪndʒ/ *n* (*sewing*) fleco *m*; (*ornamental border*) franja *f*; (*of hair*) flequillo *m*; (*of area*) periferia *f*; (*of society*) margen *m*. **~ benefits** *npl* beneficios *mpl* suplementarios. **~ theatre** *n* teatro *m* de vanguardia

frisk /frɪsk/ *vt* (*search*) cachear

frisky /'frɪskɪ/ *a* (**-ier, -iest**) retozón; ⟨*horse*⟩ fogoso

fritter[1] /'frɪtə(r)/ *vt*. **~ away** desperdiciar

fritter[2] /'frɪtə(r)/ *n* buñuelo *m*

frivol|ity /frɪ'vɒlətɪ/ *n* frivolidad *f*. **~ous** /'frɪvələs/ *a* frívolo

frizzy /'frɪzɪ/ *a* crespo

fro /frəʊ/ *see* **to and fro**

frock /frɒk/ *n* vestido *m*; (*of monk*) hábito *m*

frog /frɒg/ *n* rana *f*. **have a ~ in one's throat** tener carraspera

frogman /'frɒgmən/ *n* hombre *m* rana

frolic /'frɒlɪk/ *vi* (*pt* **frolicked**) retozar. ● *n* broma *f*

from /frɒm/, *unstressed* /frəm/ *prep* de; (*with time, prices, etc*) a partir de; (*habit, conviction*) por; (*according to*) según. **take ~** (*away from*) quitar a

front /frʌnt/ *n* parte *f* delantera; (*of building*) fachada *f*; (*of clothes*) delantera *f*; (*mil, pol*) frente *f*; (*of book*) principio *m*; (*fig, appearance*) apariencia *f*; (*sea front*) paseo *m* marítimo. **in ~ of** delante de. **put a bold ~ on** hacer de tripas corazón, mostrar firmeza. ● *a* delantero; (*first*) primero. **~age** *n* fachada *f*. **~al** *a* frontal; ⟨*attack*⟩ de frente. **~ door** *n* puerta *f* principal. **~ page** *n* (*of newspaper*) primera plana *f*

frontier /'frʌntɪə(r)/ *n* frontera *f*

frost /frɒst/ *n* (*freezing*) helada *f*; (*frozen dew*) escarcha *f*. **~bite** *n* congelación *f*. **~bitten** *a* congelado. **~ed** *a* ⟨*glass*⟩ esmerilado

frosting /'frɒstɪŋ/ *n* (*icing, Amer*) azúcar *m* glaseado

frosty *a* ⟨*weather*⟩ de helada; ⟨*window*⟩ escarchado; (*fig*) glacial

froth /frɒθ/ *n* espuma *f*. ● *vi* espumar. **~y** *a* espumoso

frown /fraʊn/ *vi* fruncir el entrecejo. **~ on** desaprobar. ● *n* ceño *m*

froze /frəʊz/, **frozen** /'frəʊzn/ *see* **freeze**

frugal /'fru:gl/ *a* frugal. **~ly** *adv* frugalmente

fruit /fru:t/ *n* (*bot, on tree, fig*) fruto *m*; (*as food*) fruta *f*. **~erer** *n* frutero *m*. **~ful** /'fru:tfl/ *a* fértil; (*fig*) fructífero. **~less** *a* infructuoso. **~ machine** *n* (máquina *f*) tragaperras *m*. **~ salad** *n* macedonia *f* de frutas. **~y** /'fru:tɪ/ *a* ⟨*taste*⟩ que sabe a fruta

fruition /fru:'ɪʃn/ *n*. **come to ~** realizarse

frump /frʌmp/ *n* espantajo *m*

frustrat|e /frʌ'streɪt/ *vt* frustrar. **~ion** /-ʃn/ *n* frustración *f*; (*disappointment*) decepción *f*

fry[1] /fraɪ/ *vt* (*pt* **fried**) freír. ● *vi* freírse

fry² /fraɪ/ n (pl **fry**). **small ~** gente f de poca monta

frying-pan /'fraɪɪŋpæn/ n sartén f

fuchsia /'fjuːʃə/ n fucsia f

fuddy-duddy /'fʌdɪdʌdɪ/ n. **be a ~** (sl) estar chapado a la antigua

fudge /fʌdʒ/ n dulce m de azúcar

fuel /'fjuːəl/ n combustible m; (for car engine) carburante m; (fig) pábulo m. ● vt (pt **fuelled**) alimentar de combustible

fugitive /'fjuːdʒɪtɪv/ a & n fugitivo (m)

fugue /fjuːg/ n (mus) fuga f

fulfil /fʊl'fɪl/ vt (pt **fulfilled**) cumplir (con) ‹promise, obligation›; satisfacer ‹condition›; realizar ‹hopes, plans›; llevar a cabo ‹task›. **~ment** n (of promise, obligation) cumplimiento m; (of conditions) satisfacción f; (of hopes, plans) realización f; (of task) ejecución f

full /fʊl/ a (**-er, -est**) lleno; ‹bus, hotel› completo; ‹skirt› amplio; ‹account› detallado. **at ~ speed** a máxima velocidad. **be ~ (up)** (with food) no poder más. **in ~ swing** en plena marcha. ● n. **in ~** sin quitar nada. **to the ~** completamente. **write in ~** escribir con todas las letras. **~ back** n (sport) defensa m & f. **~-blooded** a vigoroso. **~ moon** n plenilunio m. **~-scale** a ‹drawing› de tamaño natural; (fig) amplio. **~ stop** n punto m; (at end of paragraph, fig) punto m final. **~ time** a de jornada completa. **~y** adv completamente

fulsome /'fʊlsəm/ a excesivo

fumble /'fʌmbl/ vi buscar (torpemente)

fume /fjuːm/ vi humear; (fig, be furious) estar furioso. **~s** npl humo m

fumigate /'fjuːmɪgeɪt/ vt fumigar

fun /fʌn/ n (amusement) diversión f; (merriment) alegría f. **for ~** en broma. **have ~** divertirse. **make ~ of** burlarse de

function /'fʌŋkʃn/ n (purpose, duty) función f; (reception) recepción f. ● vi funcionar. **~al** a funcional

fund /fʌnd/ n fondo m. ● vt proveer fondos para

fundamental /fʌndə'mentl/ a fundamental

funeral /'fjuːnərəl/ n funeral m, funerales mpl. ● a fúnebre

fun-fair /'fʌnfeə(r)/ n parque m de atracciones

fungus /'fʌŋgəs/ n (pl **-gi** /-gaɪ/) hongo m

funicular /fjuː'nɪkjʊlə(r)/ n funicular m

funk /fʌŋk/ m (fear, sl) miedo m; (state of depression, Amer, sl) depresión f. **be in a (blue) ~** tener (mucho) miedo; (Amer) estar (muy) deprimido. ● vi rajarse

funnel /'fʌnl/ n (for pouring) embudo m; (of ship) chimenea f

funn|ily /'fʌnɪlɪ/ adv graciosamente; (oddly) curiosamente. **~y** a (**-ier, -iest**) divertido, gracioso; (odd) curioso, raro. **~y-bone** n cóndilo m del húmero. **~y business** n engaño m

fur /fɜː(r)/ n pelo m; (pelt) piel f; (in kettle) sarro m

furbish /'fɜːbɪʃ/ vt pulir; (renovate) renovar

furious /'fjʊərɪəs/ a furioso. **~ly** adv furiosamente

furnace /'fɜːnɪs/ n horno m

furnish /'fɜːnɪʃ/ vt (with furniture) amueblar; (supply) proveer. **~ings** npl muebles mpl, mobiliario m

furniture /'fɜːnɪtʃə(r)/ n muebles mpl, mobiliario m

furrier /'fʌrɪə(r)/ n peletero m

furrow /'fʌrəʊ/ n surco m

furry /'fɜːrɪ/ a peludo

furthe|r /'fɜːðə(r)/ a más lejano; (additional) nuevo. ● adv más lejos; (more) además. ● vt fomentar. **~rmore** adv además. **~rmost** a más lejano. **~st** a más lejano. ● adv más lejos

furtive /'fɜːtɪv/ a furtivo

fury /'fjʊərɪ/ n furia f

fuse¹ /fjuːz/ vt (melt) fundir; (fig, unite) fusionar. **~ the lights** fundir los plomos. ● vi fundirse; (fig) fusionarse. ● n fusible m, plomo m

fuse² /fjuːz/ n (of bomb) mecha f

fuse-box /'fjuːzbɒks/ n caja f de fusibles

fuselage /'fjuːzəlɑːʒ/ n fuselaje m

fusion /'fjuːʒn/ n fusión f

fuss /fʌs/ n (commotion) jaleo m. **kick up a ~** armar un lío, armar una bronca, protestar. **make a ~ of** tratar con mucha atención. **~y** a (**-ier, -iest**) (finicky) remilgado; (demanding) exigente; (ornate) recargado

fusty /'fʌstɪ/ a (**-ier, -iest**) que huele a cerrado

futile /'fjuːtaɪl/ a inútil, vano

future /'fjuːtʃə(r)/ a futuro. ● n futuro m, porvenir m; (gram) futuro m. **in ~** en lo sucesivo, de ahora en adelante

futuristic /fjuːtʃə'rɪstɪk/ a futurista

fuzz /fʌz/ n (fluff) pelusa f; (police, sl) policía f, poli f (fam)

fuzzy /'fʌzɪ/ a ⟨hair⟩ crespo; ⟨photograph⟩ borroso

G

gab /gæb/ n charla f. **have the gift of the ~** tener un pico de oro

gabardine /gæbə'diːn/ n gabardina f

gabble /'gæbl/ vt decir atropelladamente. ● vi hablar atropelladamente. ● n torrente m de palabras

gable /'geɪbl/ n aguilón m

gad /gæd/ vi (pt gadded). **~ about** callejear

gadget /'gædʒɪt/ n chisme m

Gaelic /'geɪlɪk/ a & n gaélico (m)

gaffe /gæf/ n plancha f, metedura f de pata

gag /gæg/ n mordaza f; (joke) chiste m. ● vt (pt gagged) amordazar

gaga /'gɑːgɑː/ a (sl) chocho

gaiety /'geɪətɪ/ n alegría f

gaily /'geɪlɪ/ adv alegremente

gain /geɪn/ vt ganar; (acquire) adquirir; (obtain) conseguir. ● vi ⟨clock⟩ adelantar. ● n ganancia f; (increase) aumento m. **~ful** a lucrativo

gainsay /geɪn'seɪ/ vt (pt gainsaid) (formal) negar

gait /geɪt/ n modo m de andar

gala /'gɑːlə/ n fiesta f; (sport) competición f

galaxy /'gæləksɪ/ n galaxia f

gale /geɪl/ n vendaval m; (storm) tempestad f

gall /gɔːl/ n bilis f; (fig) hiel f; (impudence) descaro m

gallant /'gælənt/ a (brave) valiente; (chivalrous) galante. **~ry** n valor m

gall-bladder /'gɔːlblædə(r)/ n vesícula f biliar

galleon /'gælɪən/ n galeón m

gallery /'gælərɪ/ n galería f

galley /'gælɪ/ n (ship) galera f; (ship's kitchen) cocina f. **~ (proof)** n (typ) galerada f

Gallic /'gælɪk/ a gálico. **~ism** n galicismo m

gallivant /'gælɪvænt/ vi (fam) callejear

gallon /'gælən/ n galón m (imperial = 4,546l; Amer = 3,785l)

gallop /'gæləp/ n galope m. ● vi (pt galloped) galopar

gallows /'gæləʊz/ n horca f

galore /gə'lɔː(r)/ adv en abundancia

galosh /gə'lɒʃ/ n chanclo m

galvanize /'gælvənaɪz/ vt galvanizar

gambit /'gæmbɪt/ n (in chess) gambito m; (fig) táctica f

gambl|e /'gæmbl/ vt/i jugar. **~e on** contar con. ● n (venture) empresa f arriesgada; (bet) jugada f; (risk) riesgo m. **~er** n jugador m. **~ing** n juego m

game[1] /geɪm/ n juego m; (match) partido m; (animals, birds) caza f. ● a valiente. **~ for** listo para

game[2] /geɪm/ a (lame) cojo

gamekeeper /'geɪmkiːpə(r)/ n guardabosque m

gammon /'gæmən/ n jamón m ahumado

gamut /'gæmət/ n gama f

gamy /'geɪmɪ/ a manido

gander /'gændə(r)/ n ganso m

gang /gæŋ/ n pandilla f; (of workmen) equipo m. ● vi. **~ up** unirse (on contra)

gangling /'gæŋglɪŋ/ a larguirucho

gangrene /'gæŋgriːn/ n gangrena f

gangster /'gæŋstə(r)/ n bandido m, gángster m

gangway /'gæŋweɪ/ n pasillo m; (of ship) pasarela f

gaol /dʒeɪl/ n cárcel f. **~bird** n criminal m empedernido. **~er** n carcelero m

gap /gæp/ n vacío m; (breach) brecha f; (in time) intervalo m; (deficiency) laguna f; (difference) diferencia f

gap|e /'geɪp/ vi quedarse boquiabierto; (be wide open) estar muy abierto. **~ing** a abierto; (person) boquiabierto

garage /'gærɑːʒ/ n garaje m; (petrol station) gasolinera f; (for repairs) taller m. ● vt dejar en (el) garaje

garb /gɑːb/ n vestido m

garbage /'gɑːbɪdʒ/ n basura f

garble /'gɑːbl/ vt mutilar

garden /'gɑːdn/ n (of flowers) jardín m; (of vegetables/fruit) huerto m. ● vi trabajar en el jardín/huerto. **~er** n jardinero/hortelano m. **~ing** n jardinería/horticultura f

gargantuan /gɑːˈgæntjʊən/ a gigantesco

gargle /ˈgɑːgl/ vi hacer gárgaras. n gargarismo m

gargoyle /ˈgɑːgɔɪl/ n gárgola f

garish /ˈgeərɪʃ/ a chillón

garland /ˈgɑːlənd/ n guirnalda f

garlic /ˈgɑːlɪk/ n ajo m

garment /ˈgɑːmənt/ n prenda f (de vestir)

garnet /ˈgɑːnɪt/ n granate m

garnish /ˈgɑːnɪʃ/ vt aderezar. ● n aderezo m

garret /ˈgærət/ n guardilla f, buhardilla f

garrison /ˈgærɪsn/ n guarnición f

garrulous /ˈgærələs/ a hablador

garter /ˈgɑːtə(r)/ n liga f

gas /gæs/ n (pl **gases**) gas m; (med) anestésico m; (petrol, Amer, fam) gasolina f. ● vt (pt **gassed**) asfixiar con gas. ● vi (fam) charlar. ~ **fire** n estufa f de gas

gash /gæʃ/ n cuchillada f. ● vt acuchillar

gasket /ˈgæskɪt/ n junta f

gas: ~ **mask** n careta f antigás a invar. ~ **meter** n contador m de gas

gasoline /ˈgæsəliːn/ n (petrol, Amer) gasolina f

gasometer /gæˈsɒmɪtə(r)/ n gasómetro m

gasp /gɑːsp/ vi jadear; (with surprise) quedarse boquiabierto. ● n jadeo m

gas: ~ **ring** n hornillo m de gas. ~ **station** n (Amer) gasolinera f

gastric /ˈgæstrɪk/ a gástrico

gastronomy /gæˈstrɒnəmɪ/ n gastronomía f

gate /geɪt/ n puerta f; (of metal) verja f; (barrier) barrera f

gateau /ˈgætəʊ/ n (pl **gateaux**) tarta f

gate: ~**crasher** n intruso m (que ha entrado sin ser invitado o sin pagar). ~**way** n puerta f

gather /ˈgæðə(r)/ vt reunir ‹people, things›; (accumulate) acumular; (pick up) recoger; recoger ‹flowers›; (fig, infer) deducir; (sewing) fruncir. ~ **speed** acelerar. ● vi ‹people› reunirse; ‹things› acumularse. ~**ing** n reunión f

gauche /gəʊʃ/ a torpe

gaudy /ˈgɔːdɪ/ a (-ier, -iest) chillón

gauge /geɪdʒ/ n (measurement) medida f; (rail) entrevía f; (instrument) indicador m. ● vt medir; (fig) estimar

gaunt /gɔːnt/ a macilento; (grim) lúgubre

gauntlet /ˈgɔːntlɪt/ n. **run the** ~ **of** estar sometido a

gauze /gɔːz/ n gasa f

gave /geɪv/ see **give**

gawk /gɔːk/ vi. ~ **at** mirar como un tonto

gawky /ˈgɔːkɪ/ a (-ier, -iest) torpe

gawp /gɔːp/ vi. ~ **at** mirar como un tonto

gay /geɪ/ a (-er, -est) (joyful) alegre; (homosexual, fam) homosexual, gay (fam)

gaze /geɪz/ vi. ~ **(at)** mirar (fijamente). ● n mirada f (fija)

gazelle /gəˈzel/ n gacela f

gazette /gəˈzet/ n boletín m oficial, gaceta f

gazump /gəˈzʌmp/ vt aceptar un precio más elevado de otro comprador

GB abbr see **Great Britain**

gear /gɪə(r)/ n equipo m; (tec) engranaje m; (auto) marcha f. **in** ~ engranado. **out of** ~ desengranado. ● vt adaptar. ~**box** n (auto) caja f de cambios

geese /giːs/ see **goose**

geezer /ˈgiːzə(r)/ n (sl) tipo m

gelatine /ˈdʒelətiːn/ n gelatina f

gelignite /ˈdʒelɪgnaɪt/ n gelignita f

gem /dʒem/ n piedra f preciosa

Gemini /ˈdʒemɪnaɪ/ n (astr) Gemelos mpl, Géminis mpl

gen /dʒen/ n (sl) información f

gender /ˈdʒendə(r)/ n género m

gene /dʒiːn/ n gene m

genealogy /dʒiːnɪˈælədʒɪ/ n genealogía f

general /ˈdʒenərəl/ a general. ● n general m. **in** ~ generalmente. ~ **election** n elecciones fpl generales

generaliz|ation /dʒenərəlaɪˈzeɪʃn/ n generalización f. ~**e** vt/i generalizar

generally /ˈdʒenərəlɪ/ adv generalmente

general practitioner /ˈdʒenərəl prækˈtɪʃənə(r)/ n médico m de cabecera

generate /ˈdʒenəreɪt/ vt producir; (elec) generar

generation /dʒenəˈreɪʃn/ n generación f

generator /ˈdʒenəreɪtə(r)/ n (elec) generador m

genero|sity /dʒenəˈrɒsətɪ/ n generosidad f. ~**us** /ˈdʒenərəs/ a generoso; (plentiful) abundante

genetic /dʒɪ'netɪk/ *a* genético. **~s** *n* genética *f*

Geneva /dʒɪ'niːvə/ *n* Ginebra *f*

genial /'dʒiːnɪəl/ *a* simpático, afable; ⟨*climate*⟩ suave, templado

genital /'dʒenɪtl/ *a* genital. **~s** *npl* genitales *mpl*

genitive /'dʒenɪtɪv/ *a & n* genitivo (*m*)

genius /'dʒiːnɪəs/ *n* (*pl* **-uses**) genio *m*

genocide /'dʒenəsaɪd/ *n* genocidio *m*

genre /ʒɑːŋr/ *n* género *m*

gent /dʒent/ *n* (*sl*) señor *m*. **~s** *n* aseo *m* de caballeros

genteel /dʒen'tiːl/ *a* distinguido; (*excessively refined*) cursi

gentle /'dʒentl/ *a* (**-er, -est**) (*mild, kind*) amable, dulce; (*slight*) ligero; ⟨*hint*⟩ discreto

gentlefolk /'dʒentlfəʊk/ *npl* gente *f* de buena familia

gentleman /'dʒentlmən/ *n* señor *m*; (*well-bred*) caballero *m*

gentleness /'dʒentlnɪs/ *n* amabilidad *f*

gentlewoman /'dʒentlwʊmən/ *n* señora *f* (de buena familia)

gently /'dʒentlɪ/ *adv* amablemente; (*slowly*) despacio

gentry /'dʒentrɪ/ *npl* pequeña aristocracia *f*

genuflect /'dʒenjuːflekt/ *vi* doblar la rodilla

genuine /'dʒenjʊɪn/ *a* verdadero; ⟨*person*⟩ sincero

geograph|er /dʒɪ'ɒɡrəfə(r)/ *n* geógrafo *m*. **~ical** /dʒɪə'ɡræfɪkl/ *a* geográfico. **~y** /dʒɪ'ɒɡrəfɪ/ *n* geografía *f*

geolog|ical /dʒɪə'lɒdʒɪkl/ *a* geológico. **~ist** *n* geólogo *m*. **~y** /dʒɪ'ɒlədʒɪ/ *n* geología *f*

geometr|ic(al) /dʒɪə'metrɪk(l)/ *a* geométrico. **~y** /dʒɪ'ɒmətrɪ/ *n* geometría *f*

geranium /dʒə'reɪnɪəm/ *n* geranio *m*

geriatrics /dʒerɪ'ætrɪks/ *n* geriatría *f*

germ /dʒɜːm/ *n* (*rudiment, seed*) germen *m*; (*med*) microbio *m*

German /'dʒɜːmən/ *a & n* alemán (*m*). **~ic** /dʒə'mænɪk/ *a* germánico. **~ measles** *n* rubéola *f*. **~ shepherd (dog)** *n* (perro *m*) pastor *m* alemán. **~y** *n* Alemania *f*

germicide /'dʒɜːmɪsaɪd/ *n* germicida *m*

germinate /'dʒɜːmɪneɪt/ *vi* germinar. ● *vt* hacer germinar

gerrymander /'dʒerɪmændə(r)/ *n* falsificación *f* electoral

gestation /dʒe'steɪʃn/ *n* gestación *f*

gesticulate /dʒe'stɪkjʊleɪt/ *vi* hacer ademanes, gesticular

gesture /'dʒestʃə(r)/ *n* ademán *m*; (*fig*) gesto *m*

get /get/ *vt* (*pt & pp* **got**, *pp Amer* **gotten**, *pres p* **getting**) obtener, tener; (*catch*) coger (*not LAm*), agarrar (*esp LAm*); (*buy*) comprar; (*find*) encontrar; (*fetch*) buscar, traer; (*understand, sl*) comprender, caer (*fam*). **~ s.o. to do sth** conseguir que uno haga algo. ● *vi* (*go*) ir; (*become*) hacerse; (*start to*) empezar a; (*manage*) conseguir. **~ married** casarse. **~ ready** prepararse. **~ about** ⟨*person*⟩ salir mucho; (*after illness*) levantarse. **~ along** (*manage*) ir tirando; (*progress*) hacer progresos. **~ along with** llevarse bien con. **~ at** (*reach*) llegar a; (*imply*) querer decir. **~ away** salir; (*escape*) escaparse. **~ back** *vi* volver. ● *vt* (*recover*) recobrar. **~ by** (*manage*) ir tirando; (*pass*) pasar. **~ down** bajar; (*depress*) deprimir. **~ in** entrar; subir ⟨*vehicle*⟩; (*arrive*) llegar. **~ off** bajar de ⟨*train, car etc*⟩; (*leave*) irse; (*jurid*) salir absuelto. **~ on** (*progress*) hacer progresos; (*succeed*) tener éxito. **~ on with** (*be on good terms with*) llevarse bien con; (*continue*) seguir. **~ out** ⟨*person*⟩ salir; (*take out*) sacar. **~ out of** (*fig*) librarse de. **~ over** reponerse de ⟨*illness*⟩. **~ round** soslayar ⟨*difficulty etc*⟩; engatusar ⟨*person*⟩. **~ through** (*pass*) pasar; (*finish*) terminar; (*on phone*) comunicar con. **~ up** levantarse; (*climb*) subir; (*organize*) preparar. **~away** *n* huida *f*. **~up** *n* traje *m*

geyser /'giːzə(r)/ *n* calentador *m* de agua; (*geog*) géiser *m*

Ghana /'ɡɑːnə/ *n* Ghana *f*

ghastly /'ɡɑːstlɪ/ *a* (**-ier, -iest**) horrible; (*pale*) pálido

gherkin /'ɡɜːkɪn/ *n* pepinillo *m*

ghetto /'ɡetəʊ/ *n* (*pl* **-os**) (*Jewish quarter*) judería *f*; (*ethnic settlement*) barrio *m* pobre habitado por un grupo étnico

ghost /ɡəʊst/ *n* fantasma *m*. **~ly** *a* espectral

ghoulish /'ɡuːlɪʃ/ *a* macabro

giant /'dʒaɪənt/ *n* gigante *m*. ● *a* gigantesco

gibberish /'dʒibərɪʃ/ n jerigonza f

gibe /dʒaɪb/ n mofa f

giblets /'dʒɪblɪts/ npl menudillos mpl

Gibraltar /dʒɪ'brɔːltə(r)/ n Gibraltar m

gidd|iness /'gɪdɪnɪs/ n vértigo m. ~y a (-ier, -iest) mareado; ‹speed› vertiginoso. **be/feel ~y** estar/sentirse mareado

gift /gɪft/ n regalo m; (ability) don m. ~**ed** a dotado de talento. ~**wrap** vt envolver para regalo

gig /gɪg/ n (fam) concierto m

gigantic /dʒaɪ'gæntɪk/ a gigantesco

giggle /'gɪgl/ vi reírse tontamente. ● n risita f. **the ~s** la risa f tonta

gild /gɪld/ vt dorar

gills /gɪlz/ npl agallas fpl

gilt /gɪlt/ a dorado. ~**edged** a (com) de máxima garantía

gimmick /'gɪmɪk/ n truco m

gin /dʒɪn/ n ginebra f

ginger /'dʒɪndʒə(r)/ n jengibre m. ● a rojizo. ● vt. ~ **up** animar. ~ **ale** n, ~ **beer** n cerveza f de jengibre. ~**bread** n pan m de jengibre

gingerly /'dʒɪndʒəlɪ/ adv cautelosamente

gingham /'gɪŋəm/ n guinga f

gipsy /'dʒɪpsɪ/ n gitano m

giraffe /dʒɪ'rɑːf/ n jirafa f

girder /'gɜːdə(r)/ n viga f

girdle /'gɜːdl/ n (belt) cinturón m; (corset) corsé m

girl /gɜːl/ n chica f, muchacha f; (child) niña f. ~**friend** n amiga f; (of boy) novia f. ~**hood** n (up to adolescence) niñez f; (adolescence) juventud f. ~**ish** a de niña; ‹boy› afeminado

giro /'dʒaɪrəʊ/ n (pl -os) giro m (bancario)

girth /gɜːθ/ n circunferencia f

gist /dʒɪst/ n lo esencial invar

give /gɪv/ vt (pt gave, pp given) dar; (deliver) entregar; regalar ‹present›; prestar ‹aid, attention›; (grant) conceder; (yield) ceder; (devote) dedicar. ~ **o.s. to** darse a. ● vi dar; (yield) ceder; (stretch) estirarse. ● n elasticidad f. ~ **away** regalar; descubrir ‹secret›. ~ **back** devolver. ~ **in** (yield) rendirse. ~ **off** emitir. ~ **o.s. up** entregarse (a). ~ **out** distribuir; (announce) anunciar; (become used up) agotarse. ~ **over** (devote) dedicar; (stop, fam)

dejar (de). ~ **up** (renounce) renunciar a; (yield) ceder

given /'gɪvn/ see **give**. ● a dado. ~ **name** n nombre m de pila

glacier /'glæsɪə(r)/ n glaciar m

glad /glæd/ a contento. ~**den** vt alegrar

glade /gleɪd/ n claro m

gladiator /'glædɪeɪtə(r)/ n gladiador m

gladiolus /glædɪ'əʊləs/ n (pl -li /-laɪ/) estoque m, gladiolo m, gladíolo m

gladly /'glædlɪ/ adv alegremente; (willingly) con mucho gusto

glamo|rize /'glæmərɪaɪz/ vt embellecer. ~**rous** a atractivo. ~**ur** n encanto m

glance /glɑːns/ n ojeada f. ● vi. ~ **at** dar un vistazo a

gland /glænd/ n glándula f

glar|e /gleə(r)/ vi deslumbrar; (stare angrily) mirar airadamente. ● n deslumbramiento m; (stare, fig) mirada f airada. ~**ing** a deslumbrador; (obvious) manifiesto

glass /glɑːs/ n (material) vidrio m; (without stem or for wine) vaso m; (with stem) copa f; (for beer) caña f; (mirror) espejo m. ~**es** npl (spectacles) gafas fpl, anteojos (LAm) mpl. ~**y** a vítreo

glaze /gleɪz/ vt poner cristales a ‹windows, doors›; vidriar ‹pottery›. ● n barniz m; (for pottery) esmalte m. ~**d** a ‹object› vidriado; ‹eye› vidrioso

gleam /gliːm/ n destello m. ● vi destellar

glean /gliːn/ vt espigar

glee /gliː/ n regocijo m. ~ **club** n orfeón m. ~**ful** a regocijado

glen /glen/ n cañada f

glib /glɪb/ a de mucha labia; ‹reply› fácil. ~**ly** adv con poca sinceridad

glid|e /glaɪd/ vi deslizarse; ‹plane› planear. ~**er** n planeador m. ~**ing** n planeo m

glimmer /'glɪmə(r)/ n destello m. ● vi destellar

glimpse /glɪmps/ n vislumbre f. **catch a ~ of** vislumbrar. ● vt vislumbrar

glint /glɪnt/ n destello m. ● vi destellar

glisten /'glɪsn/ vi brillar

glitter /'glɪtə(r)/ vi brillar. ● n brillo m

gloat /gləʊt/ vi. ~ **on/over** regodearse

global /'glɔʊbl/ a (world-wide)
mundial; (all-embracing) global
globe /glɔʊb/ n globo m
globule /'glɒbjuːl/ n glóbulo m
gloom /gluːm/ n oscuridad f; (sadness, fig) tristeza f. ~y a (-ier, -iest)
triste; (pessimistic) pesimista
glorify /'glɔːrɪfaɪ/ vt glorificar
glorious /'glɔːrɪəs/ a espléndido;
⟨deed, hero etc⟩ glorioso
glory /'glɔːrɪ/ n gloria f; (beauty)
esplendor m. ● vi. ~ in enorgullecerse de. ~hole n (untidy
room) leonera f
gloss /glɒs/ n lustre m. ● a brillante.
● vi. ~ over (make light of) minimizar; (cover up) encubrir
glossary /'glɒsərɪ/ n glosario m
glossy /'glɒsɪ/ a brillante
glove /glʌv/ n guante m. ~ compartment n (auto) guantera f, gaveta f. ~d a enguantado
glow /glɔʊ/ vi brillar; (with health)
rebosar de; (with passion) enar-
decerse. ● n incandescencia f; (of
cheeks) rubor m
glower /'glaʊə(r)/ vi. ~ (at) mirar
airadamente
glowing /'glɔʊɪŋ/ a incandescente;
⟨account⟩ entusiasta; ⟨complexion⟩
rojo; (with health) rebosante de
glucose /'gluːkəʊs/ n glucosa f
glue /gluː/ n cola f. ● vt (pres p glu-
ing) pegar
glum /glʌm/ a (glummer, glum-
mest) triste
glut /glʌt/ n superabundancia f
glutton /'glʌtn/ n glotón m. ~ous a
glotón. ~y n glotonería f
glycerine /'glɪsəriːn/ n glicerina f
gnarled /nɑːld/ a nudoso
gnash /næʃ/ vt. ~ one's teeth
rechinar los dientes
gnat /næt/ n mosquito m
gnaw /nɔː/ vt/i roer
gnome /nɔʊm/ n gnomo m
go /gɔʊ/ vi (pt went, pp gone) ir;
(leave) irse; (work) funcionar;
(become) hacerse; (be sold) venderse; (vanish) desaparecer. ~
ahead! ¡adelante! ● bad pasarse. ~
riding montar a caballo. ~ shopping ir de compras. be ~ing to do ir
a hacer. ● n (pl goes) (energy) energía f. be on the ~ trabajar sin cesar.
have a ~ intentar. it's your ~ te
toca a ti. make a ~ of tener éxito
en. ~ across cruzar. ~ away irse.
~ back volver. ~ back on faltar a

⟨promise etc⟩. ~ by pasar. ~ down
bajar; ⟨sun⟩ ponerse. ~ for buscar,
traer; (like) gustar; (attack, sl)
atacar. ~ in entrar. ~ in for presentarse para ⟨exam⟩. ~ off (leave)
irse; (go bad) pasarse; (explode)
estallar. ~ on seguir; (happen)
pasar. ~ out salir; ⟨light, fire⟩ apagarse. ~ over (check) examinar. ~
round (be enough) ser bastante. ~
through (suffer) sufrir; (check)
examinar. ~ under hundirse. ~ up
subir. ~ without pasarse sin
goad /gɔʊd/ vt aguijonear
go-ahead /'gɔʊəhed/ n luz f verde.
● a dinámico
goal /gɔʊl/ n fin m, objeto m; (sport)
gol m. ~ie n (fam) portero m.
~keeper n portero m. ~post n
poste m (de la portería)
goat /gɔʊt/ n cabra f
goatee /gɔʊ'tiː/ n perilla f, barbas
fpl de chivo
gobble /'gɒbl/ vt engullir
go-between /'gɔʊbɪtwiːn/ n intermediario m
goblet /'gɒblɪt/ n copa f
goblin /'gɒblɪn/ n duende m
God /gɒd/ n Dios m. ~-forsaken a
olvidado de Dios
god /gɒd/ n dios m. ~child n ahijado
m. ~daughter n ahijada f. ~dess
/'gɒdɪs/ n diosa f. ~father n padrino
m. ~ly a devoto. ~mother n madrina f. ~send n beneficio m inesperado. ~son n ahijado m
go-getter /gɔʊ'getə(r)/ n persona f
ambiciosa
goggle /'gɒgl/ vi. ~ (at) mirar con
los ojos desmesuradamente
abiertos
goggles /'gɒglz/ npl gafas fpl
protectoras
going /'gɔʊɪŋ/ n camino m; (racing)
(estado m del) terreno m. it is slow/
hard ~ es lento/difícil. ● a (price)
actual; ⟨concern⟩ en funcionamiento. ~s-on npl actividades fpl
anormales, tejemaneje m
gold /gɔʊld/ n oro m. ● a de oro. ~en
/'gɔʊldən/ a de oro; (in colour) dorado; ⟨opportunity⟩ único. ~en wedding n bodas fpl de oro. ~fish n
invar pez m de colores, carpa f
dorada. ~mine n mina f de oro;
(fig) fuente f de gran riqueza.
~-plated a chapado en oro.
~smith n orfebre m

golf /gɒlf/ n golf m. **~course** n campo m de golf. **~er** n jugador m de golf

golly /'gɒlɪ/ int ¡caramba!

golosh /gə'lɒʃ/ n chanclo m

gondol|a /'gɒndələ/ n góndola f. **~ier** /gɒndə'lɪə(r)/ n gondolero m

gone /gɒn/ see **go**. ● a pasado. **~ six o'clock** después de las seis

gong /gɒŋ/ n gong(o) m

good /gʊd/ a (**better, best**) bueno, (*before masculine singular noun*) buen. **~ afternoon!** ¡buenas tardes! **~ evening!** (*before dark*) ¡buenas tardes!; (*after dark*) ¡buenas noches! G**~ Friday** n Viernes m Santo. **~ morning!** ¡buenos días! **~ name** n (buena) reputación f. **~ night!** ¡buenas noches! **a ~ deal** bastante. **as ~ as** (*almost*) casi. **be ~ with** entender. **do ~** hacer bien. **feel ~** sentirse bien. **have a ~ time** divertirse. **it is ~ for you** le sentará bien. ● n bien m. **for ~** para siempre. **it is no ~ shouting/etc** es inútil gritar/etc.

goodbye /gʊd'baɪ/ int ¡adiós! ● n adiós m. **say ~ to** despedirse de

good: ~for-nothing a & n inútil (m). **~looking** a guapo

goodness /'gʊdnɪs/ n bondad f. **~!**, **~ gracious!**, **~ me!**, **my ~!** ¡Dios mío!

goods /gʊdz/ npl (*merchandise*) mercancías fpl

goodwill /gʊd'wɪl/ n buena voluntad f

goody /'gʊdɪ/ n (*culin, fam*) golosina f; (*in film*) bueno m. **~goody** n mojigato m

gooey /'guːɪ/ a (**gooier, gooiest**) (*sl*) pegajoso; (*fig*) sentimental

goof /guːf/ vi (*Amer, blunder*) cometer una pifia. **~y** a (*sl*) necio

goose /guːs/ n (pl **geese**) oca f

gooseberry /'gʊzbərɪ/ n uva f espina, grosella f

goose-flesh /'guːsfleʃ/ n, **goose-pimples** /'guːspɪmplz/ n carne f de gallina

gore /gɔː(r)/ n sangre f. ● vt cornear

gorge /gɔːdʒ/ n (*geog*) garganta f. ● vt. **~ o.s.** hartarse (**on** de)

gorgeous /'gɔːdʒəs/ a magnífico

gorilla /gə'rɪlə/ n gorila m

gormless /'gɔːmlɪs/ a (*sl*) idiota

gorse /gɔːs/ n aulaga f

gory /'gɔːrɪ/ a (**-ier, -iest**) (*covered in blood*) ensangrentado; (*horrific, fig*) horrible

gosh /gɒʃ/ int ¡caramba!

go-slow /gəʊ'sləʊ/ n huelga f de celo

gospel /'gɒspl/ n evangelio m

gossip /'gɒsɪp/ n (*idle chatter*) charla f, (*tittle-tattle*) comadreo m; (*person*) chismoso m. ● vi (pt **gossiped**) (*chatter*) charlar; (*repeat scandal*) comadrear. **~y** a chismoso

got /gɒt/ see **get**. **have ~** tener. **have ~ to do** tener que hacer

Gothic /'gɒθɪk/ a (*archit*) gótico; ⟨*people*⟩ godo

gouge /gaʊdʒ/ vt. **~ out** arrancar

gourmet /'gʊəmeɪ/ n gastrónomo m

gout /gaʊt/ n (*med*) gota f

govern /'gʌvn/ vt/i gobernar

governess /'gʌvənɪs/ n institutriz f

government /'gʌvənmənt/ n gobierno m. **~al** /gʌvən'mentl/ a gubernamental

governor /'gʌvənə(r)/ n gobernador m

gown /gaʊn/ n vestido m; (*of judge, teacher*) toga f

GP abbr see **general practitioner**

grab /græb/ vt (pt **grabbed**) agarrar

grace /greɪs/ n gracia f. **~ful** a elegante

gracious /'greɪʃəs/ a (*kind*) amable; (*elegant*) elegante

gradation /grə'deɪʃn/ n gradación f

grade /greɪd/ n clase f, categoría f; (*of goods*) clase f, calidad f; (*on scale*) grado m; (*school mark*) nota f; (*class, Amer*) curso m. **~ school** n (*Amer*) escuela f primaria. ● vt clasificar; (*schol*) calificar

gradient /'greɪdɪənt/ n (*slope*) pendiente f

gradual /'grædʒʊəl/ a gradual. **~ly** adv gradualmente

graduat|e /'grædjʊət/ n (*univ*) licenciado. ● vi /'grædjʊeɪt/ licenciarse. ● vt graduar. **~ion** /-'eɪʃn/ n entrega f de títulos

graffiti /grə'fiːtɪ/ npl pintada f

graft[1] /grɑːft/ n (*med, bot*) injerto m. ● vt injertar

graft[2] /grɑːft/ n (*bribery, fam*) corrupción f

grain /greɪn/ n grano m

gram /græm/ n gramo m

gramma|r /'græmə(r)/ n gramática f. **~tical** /grə'mætɪkl/ a gramatical

gramophone /'græməfəʊn/ n tocadiscos m invar

grand /grænd/ a (**-er, -est**) magnífico; (*excellent, fam*) estupendo. **~child** n nieto m. **~daughter** n nieta f

grandeur /'grændʒə(r)/ n grandiosidad f

grandfather /'grændfɑːðə(r)/ n abuelo m

grandiose /'grændɪəʊs/ a grandioso

grand: ~**mother** n abuela f. ~**parents** npl abuelos mpl. ~ **piano** n piano m de cola. ~**son** n nieto m

grandstand /'grænstænd/ n tribuna f

granite /'grænɪt/ n granito m

granny /'grænɪ/ n (fam) abuela f, nana f (fam)

grant /grɑːnt/ vt conceder; (give) donar; (admit) admitir (**that** que). **take for** ~**ed** dar por sentado. ● n concesión f; (univ) beca f

granulated /'grænjʊleɪtɪd/ a. ~ **sugar** n azúcar m granulado

granule /'grænuːl/ n gránulo m

grape /greɪp/ n uva f

grapefruit /'greɪpfruːt/ n invar toronja f, pomelo m

graph /grɑːf/ n gráfica f

graphic /'græfɪk/ a gráfico

grapple /'græpl/ vi. ~ **with** intentar vencer

grasp /grɑːsp/ vt agarrar. ● n (hold) agarro m; (strength of hand) apretón m; (reach) alcance m; (fig) comprensión f

grasping /'grɑːspɪŋ/ a avaro

grass /grɑːs/ n hierba f. ~**hopper** n saltamontes m invar. ~**land** n pradera f. ~ **roots** npl base f popular. ● a popular. ~**y** a cubierto de hierba

grate /greɪt/ n (fireplace) parrilla f. ● vt rallar. ~ **one's teeth** hacer rechinar los dientes. ● vi rechinar

grateful /'greɪtfl/ a agradecido. ~**ly** adv con gratitud

grater /'greɪtə(r)/ n rallador m

gratif|ied /'grætɪfaɪd/ a contento. ~**y** vt satisfacer; (please) agradar a. ~**ying** a agradable

grating /'greɪtɪŋ/ n reja f

gratis /'grɑːtɪs/ a & adv gratis (a invar)

gratitude /'grætɪtjuːd/ n gratitud f

gratuitous /grə'tjuːɪtəs/ a gratuito

gratuity /grə'tjuːətɪ/ n (tip) propina f; (gift of money) gratificación f

grave[1] /greɪv/ n sepultura f

grave[2] /greɪv/ a (-er, -est) (serious) serio. /grɑːv/ a. ~ **accent** n acento m grave

grave-digger /'greɪvdɪgə(r)/ n sepulturero m

gravel /'grævl/ n grava f

gravely /'greɪvlɪ/ a (seriously) seriamente

grave: ~**stone** n lápida f. ~**yard** n cementerio m

gravitat|e /'grævɪteɪt/ vi gravitar. ~**ion** n /·'teɪʃn/ n gravitación f

gravity /'grævətɪ/ n gravedad f

gravy /'greɪvɪ/ n salsa f

graze[1] /greɪz/ vt/i (eat) pacer

graze[2] /greɪz/ vt (touch) rozar; (scrape) raspar. ● n rozadura f

greas|e /griːs/ n grasa f. ● vt engrasar. ~**e-paint** n maquillaje m. ~**e-proof paper** n papel m a prueba de grasa, apergaminado m. ~**y** a grasiento

great /greɪt/ a (-er, -est) grande, (before singular noun) gran; (very good, fam) estupendo. **G~ Britain** n Gran Bretaña f. ~**grandfather** n bisabuelo m. ~**grandmother** n bisabuela f. ~**ly** /'greɪtlɪ/ adv (very) muy; (much) mucho. ~**ness** n grandeza f

Greece /griːs/ n Grecia f

greed /griːd/ n avaricia f; (for food) glotonería f. ~**y** a avaro; (for food) glotón

Greek /griːk/ a & n griego (m)

green /griːn/ a (-er, -est) verde; (fig) crédulo. ● n verde m; (grass) césped m. ~ **belt** n zona f verde. ~**ery** n verdor m. ~ **fingers** npl habilidad f con las plantas

greengage /'griːngeɪdʒ/ n (plum) claudia f

greengrocer /'griːngrəʊsə(r)/ n verdulero m

greenhouse /'griːnhaʊs/ n invernadero m

green: ~ **light** n luz f verde. ~**s** npl verduras fpl

Greenwich Mean Time /grenɪtʃ'miː ntaɪm/ n hora f media de Greenwich

greet /griːt/ vt saludar; (receive) recibir. ~**ing** n saludo m. ~**ings** npl (in letter) recuerdos mpl

gregarious /grɪ'geərɪəs/ a gregario

grenade /grɪ'neɪd/ n granada f

grew /gruː/ see **grow**

grey /greɪ/ a & n (-er, -est) gris (m). ● vi ⟨hair⟩ encanecer

greyhound /'greɪhaʊnd/ n galgo m

grid /grɪd/ n reja f; (network, elec) red f; (culin) parrilla f; (on map) cuadrícula f

grief /griːf/ n dolor m. **come to ~** ⟨person⟩ sufrir un accidente; ⟨fail⟩ fracasar

grievance /ˈgriːvns/ n queja f

grieve /griːv/ vt afligir. • vi afligirse. **~ for** llorar

grievous /ˈgriːvəs/ a doloroso; ⟨serious⟩ grave

grill /grɪl/ n ⟨cooking device⟩ parrilla f; ⟨food⟩ parrillada f, asado m, asada f. • vt asar a la parrilla; ⟨interrogate⟩ interrogar

grille /grɪl/ n rejilla f

grim /grɪm/ a (**grimmer**, **grimmest**) severo

grimace /ˈgrɪməs/ n mueca f. • vi hacer muecas

grim|e /graɪm/ n mugre f. **~y** a mugriento

grin /grɪn/ vt (pt **grinned**) sonreír. • n sonrisa f (abierta)

grind /graɪnd/ vt (pt **ground**) moler ⟨coffee, corn etc⟩; ⟨pulverize⟩ pulverizar; ⟨sharpen⟩ afilar. **~ one's teeth** hacer rechinar los dientes. • n faena f

grip /grɪp/ vt (pt **gripped**) agarrar; ⟨interest⟩ captar la atención de. • n ⟨hold⟩ agarro m; ⟨strength of hand⟩ apretón m. **come to ~s** encararse (**with** a/con)

gripe /graɪp/ n. **~s** npl ⟨med⟩ cólico m

grisly /ˈgrɪzlɪ/ a (**-ier**, **-iest**) horrible

gristle /ˈgrɪsl/ n cartílago m

grit /grɪt/ n arena f; ⟨fig⟩ valor m, aguante m. • vt (pt **gritted**) echar arena en ⟨road⟩. **~ one's teeth** ⟨fig⟩ acorazarse

grizzle /ˈgrɪzl/ vi lloriquear

groan /grəʊn/ vi gemir. • n gemido m

grocer /ˈgrəʊsə(r)/ n tendero m. **~ies** npl comestibles mpl. **~y** n tienda f de comestibles

grog /grɒg/ n grog m

groggy /ˈgrɒgɪ/ a ⟨weak⟩ débil; ⟨unsteady⟩ inseguro; ⟨ill⟩ malucho

groin /grɔɪn/ n ingle f

groom /gruːm/ n mozo m de caballos; ⟨bridegroom⟩ novio m. • vt almohazar ⟨horses⟩; ⟨fig⟩ preparar. **well-~ed** a bien arreglado

groove /gruːv/ n ranura f; ⟨in record⟩ surco m

grope /grəʊp/ vi ⟨find one's way⟩ moverse a tientas. **~ for** buscar a tientas

gross /grəʊs/ a (**-er**, **-est**) ⟨coarse⟩ grosero; ⟨com⟩ bruto; ⟨fat⟩ grueso; ⟨flagrant⟩ grave. • n invar gruesa f. **~ly** adv groseramente; ⟨very⟩ enormemente

grotesque /grəʊˈtesk/ a grotesco

grotto /ˈgrɒtəʊ/ n (pl **-oes**) gruta f

grotty /ˈgrɒtɪ/ a ⟨sl⟩ desagradable; ⟨dirty⟩ sucio

grouch /graʊtʃ/ vi ⟨grumble, fam⟩ rezongar

ground[1] /graʊnd/ n suelo m; ⟨area⟩ terreno m; ⟨reason⟩ razón f; ⟨elec, Amer⟩ toma f de tierra. • vt varar ⟨ship⟩; prohibir despegar ⟨aircraft⟩. **~s** npl jardines mpl; ⟨sediment⟩ poso m

ground[2] /graʊnd/ see **grind**

ground: ~ floor n planta f baja. **~ rent** n alquiler m del terreno

grounding /ˈgraʊndɪŋ/ n base f, conocimientos mpl (**in** de)

groundless /ˈgraʊndlɪs/ a infundado

ground: ~sheet n tela f impermeable. **~swell** n mar m de fondo. **~work** n trabajo m preparatorio

group /gruːp/ n grupo m. • vt agrupar. • vi agruparse

grouse[1] /graʊs/ n invar ⟨bird⟩ urogallo m. **red ~** lagópodo m escocés

grouse[2] /graʊs/ vi ⟨grumble, fam⟩ rezongar

grove /grəʊv/ n arboleda f. **lemon ~** n limonar m. **olive ~** n olivar m. **orange ~** n naranjal m. **pine ~** n pinar m

grovel /ˈgrɒvl/ vi (pt **grovelled**) arrastrarse, humillarse. **~ling** a servil

grow /grəʊ/ vi (pt **grew**, pp **grown**) crecer; ⟨cultivated plant⟩ cultivarse; ⟨become⟩ volverse, ponerse. • vt cultivar. **~ up** hacerse mayor. **~er** n cultivador m

growl /graʊl/ vi gruñir. • n gruñido m

grown /grəʊn/ see **grow**. • a adulto. **~-up** a & n adulto (m)

growth /grəʊθ/ n crecimiento m; ⟨increase⟩ aumento m; ⟨development⟩ desarrollo m; ⟨med⟩ tumor m

grub /grʌb/ n ⟨larva⟩ larva f; ⟨food, sl⟩ comida f

grubby /ˈgrʌbɪ/ a (**-ier**, **-iest**) mugriento

grudg|e /grʌdʒ/ vt dar de mala gana; ⟨envy⟩ envidiar. **~e doing** molestarle hacer. **he ~ed paying** le molestó pagar. ● *n* rencor *m*. **bear/ have a ~e against s.o.** guardar rencor a alguien. **~ingly** *adv* de mala gana

gruelling /'gru:əlɪŋ/ *a* agotador

gruesome /'gru:səm/ *a* horrible

gruff /grʌf/ *a* (**-er, -est**) ⟨*manners*⟩ brusco; ⟨*voice*⟩ ronco

grumble /'grʌmbl/ *vi* rezongar

grumpy /'grʌmpɪ/ *a* (**-ier, -iest**) malhumorado

grunt /grʌnt/ *vi* gruñir. ● *n* gruñido *m*

guarant|ee /gærən'ti:/ *n* garantía *f*. ● *vt* garantizar. **~or** *n* garante *m* & *f*

guard /gɑ:d/ *vt* proteger; ⟨*watch*⟩ vigilar. ● *vi*. **~ against** guardar de. ● *n* (*vigilance, mil group*) guardia *f*; (*person*) guardia *m*; (*on train*) jefe *m* de tren

guarded /'gɑ:dɪd/ *a* cauteloso

guardian /'gɑ:dɪən/ *n* guardián *m*; (*of orphan*) tutor *m*

guer(r)illa /gə'rɪlə/ *n* guerrillero *m*. **~ warfare** *n* guerra *f* de guerrillas

guess /ges/ *vt/i* adivinar; (*suppose, Amer*) creer. ● *n* conjetura *f*. **~work** *n* conjetura(s) *f(pl)*

guest /gest/ *n* invitado *m*; (*in hotel*) huésped *m*. **~house** *n* casa *f* de huéspedes

guffaw /gʌ'fɔ:/ *n* carcajada *f*. ● *vi* reírse a carcajadas

guidance /'gaɪdəns/ *n* (*advice*) consejos *mpl*; (*information*) información *f*

guide /gaɪd/ *n* (*person*) guía *m* & *f*; (*book*) guía *f*. **Girl G~** exploradora *f*, guía *f* (*fam*). ● *vt* guiar. **~book** *n* guía *f*. **~d missile** *n* proyectil *m* teledirigido. **~lines** *npl* pauta *f*

guild /gɪld/ *n* gremio *m*

guile /gaɪl/ *n* astucia *f*

guillotine /'gɪləti:n/ *n* guillotina *f*

guilt /gɪlt/ *n* culpabilidad *f*. **~y** *a* culpable

guinea-pig /'gɪnɪpɪg/ *n* (*including fig*) cobaya *f*

guise /gaɪz/ *n* (*external appearance*) apariencia *f*; (*style*) manera *f*

guitar /gɪ'tɑ:(r)/ *n* guitarra *f*. **~ist** *n* guitarrista *m* & *f*

gulf /gʌlf/ *n* (*part of sea*) golfo *m*; (*hollow*) abismo *m*

gull /gʌl/ *n* gaviota *f*

gullet /'gʌlɪt/ *n* esófago *m*

gullible /'gʌləbl/ *a* crédulo

gully /'gʌlɪ/ *n* (*ravine*) barranco *m*

gulp /gʌlp/ *vt*. **~ down** tragarse de prisa. ● *vi* tragar; (*from fear etc*) sentir dificultad para tragar. ● *n* trago *m*

gum¹ /gʌm/ *n* goma *f*; (*for chewing*) chicle *m*. ● *vt* (*pt* **gummed**) engomar

gum² /gʌm/ *n* (*anat*) encía *f*. **~boil** /'gʌmbɔɪl/ *n* flemón *m*

gumboot /'gʌmbu:t/ *n* bota *f* de agua

gumption /'gʌmpʃn/ *n* (*fam*) iniciativa *f*; (*common sense*) sentido *m* común

gun /gʌn/ *n* (*pistol*) pistola *f*; (*rifle*) fusil *m*; (*large*) cañón *m*. ● *vt* (*pt* **gunned**). **~ down** abatir a tiros. **~fire** *n* tiros *mpl*

gunge /gʌndʒ/ *n* (*sl*) materia *f* sucia (y pegajosa)

gun: ~man /'gʌnmən/ *n* pistolero *m*. **~ner** /'gʌnə(r)/ *n* artillero *m*. **~powder** *n* pólvora *f*. **~shot** *n* disparo *m*

gurgle /'gɜ:gl/ *n* (*of liquid*) gorgoteo *m*; (*of baby*) gorjeo *m*. ● *vi* ⟨*liquid*⟩ gorgotear; ⟨*baby*⟩ gorjear

guru /'goru:/ *n* (*pl* **-us**) mentor *m*

gush /gʌʃ/ *vi*. **~ (out)** salir a borbotones. ● *n* (*of liquid*) chorro *m*; (*fig*) torrente *m*. **~ing** *a* efusivo

gusset /'gʌsɪt/ *n* escudete *m*

gust /gʌst/ *n* ráfaga *f*; (*of smoke*) bocanada *f*

gusto /'gʌstəʊ/ *n* entusiasmo *m*

gusty /'gʌstɪ/ *a* borrascoso

gut /gʌt/ *n* tripa *f*, intestino *m*. ● *vt* (*pt* **gutted**) destripar; ⟨*fire*⟩ destruir. **~s** *npl* tripas *fpl*; (*courage, fam*) valor *m*

gutter /'gʌtə(r)/ *n* (*on roof*) canalón *m*; (*in street*) cuneta *f*; (*slum, fig*) arroyo *m*. **~snipe** *n* golfillo *m*

guttural /'gʌtərəl/ *a* gutural

guy /gaɪ/ *n* (*man, fam*) hombre *m*, tío *m* (*fam*)

guzzle /'gʌzl/ *vt/i* soplarse, tragarse

gym /dʒɪm/ *n* (*gymnasium, fam*) gimnasio *m*; (*gymnastics, fam*) gimnasia *f*

gymkhana /dʒɪm'kɑ:nə/ *n* gincana *f*, gymkhana *f*

gymnasium /dʒɪm'neɪzɪəm/ *n* gimnasio *m*

gymnast /'dʒɪmnæst/ *n* gimnasta *m* & *f*. **~ics** *npl* gimnasia *f*

gym-slip /'dʒɪmslɪp/ *n* túnica *f* (de gimnasia)

gynaecolog|ist /gaɪnɪ'kɒlədʒɪst/ *n* ginecólogo *m*. **~y** *n* ginecología *f*

gypsy /'dʒɪpsɪ/ *n* gitano *m*

gyrate /dʒaɪəˈreɪt/ *vi* girar

gyroscope /ˈdʒaɪərəskəʊp/ *n* giroscopio *m*

H

haberdashery /hæbəˈdæʃərɪ/ *n* mercería *f*

habit /ˈhæbɪt/ *n* costumbre *f*; (*costume, relig*) hábito *m*. **be in the ∼ of** (+ *gerund*) tener la costumbre de (+ *infintive*), soler (+ *infinitive*). **get into the ∼ of** (+ *gerund*) acostumbrarse a (+ *infinitive*)

habitable /ˈhæbɪtəbl/ *a* habitable

habitat /ˈhæbɪtæt/ *n* hábitat *m*

habitation /hæbɪˈteɪʃn/ *n* habitación *f*

habitual /həˈbɪtjʊəl/ *a* habitual; ⟨*smoker, liar*⟩ inveterado. **∼ly** *adv* de costumbre

hack /hæk/ *n* (*old horse*) jamelgo *m*; (*writer*) escritorzuelo *m*. ● *vt* cortar. **∼ to pieces** cortar en pedazos

hackney /ˈhæknɪ/ *a*. **∼ carriage** *n* coche *m* de alquiler, taxi *m*

hackneyed /ˈhæknɪd/ *a* manido

had /hæd/ *see* **have**

haddock /ˈhædək/ *n invar* eglefino *m*. **smoked ∼** *n* eglefino *m* ahumado

haemorrhage /ˈhemərɪdʒ/ *n* hemorragia *f*

haemorrhoids /ˈhemərɔɪdz/ *npl* hemorroides *fpl*, almorranas *fpl*

hag /hæg/ *n* bruja *f*

haggard /ˈhægəd/ *a* ojeroso

haggle /ˈhægl/ *vi* regatear

Hague /heɪg/ *n*. **The ∼** La Haya *f*

hail¹ /heɪl/ *n* granizo *m*. ● *vi* granizar

hail² /heɪl/ *vt* (*greet*) saludar; llamar ⟨*taxi*⟩. ● *vi*. **∼ from** venir de

hailstone /ˈheɪlstəʊn/ *n* grano *m* de granizo

hair /heə(r)/ *n* pelo *m*. **∼brush** *n* cepillo *m* para el pelo. **∼cut** *n* corte *m* de pelo. **have a ∼cut** cortarse el pelo. **∼do** *n* (*fam*) peinado *m*. **∼dresser** *n* peluquero *m*. **∼dresser's (shop)** *n* peluquería *f*. **∼dryer** *n* secador *m*. **∼pin** *n* horquilla *f*. **∼pin bend** *n* curva *f* cerrada. **∼raising** *a* espeluznante. **∼style** *n* peinado *m*

hairy /ˈheərɪ/ *a* (**-ier, -iest**) peludo; (*terrifying, sl*) espeluznante

hake /heɪk/ *n invar* merluza *f*

halcyon /ˈhælsɪən/ *a* sereno. **∼ days** *npl* época *f* feliz

hale /heɪl/ *a* robusto

half /hɑːf/ *n* (*pl* **halves**) mitad *f*. ● *a* medio. **∼ a dozen** media docena *f*. **∼ an hour** media hora *f*. ● *adv* medio, a medias. **∼back** *n* (*sport*) medio *m*. **∼caste** *a & n* mestizo (*m*). **∼hearted** *a* poco entusiasta. **∼term** *n* vacaciones *fpl* de medio trimestre. **∼time** *n* (*sport*) descanso *m*. **∼way** *a* medio. ● *adv* a medio camino. **∼wit** *n* imbécil *m & f*. **at ∼mast** a media asta

halibut /ˈhælɪbət/ *n invar* hipogloso *m*, halibut *m*

hall /hɔːl/ *n* (*room*) sala *f*; (*mansion*) casa *f* solariega; (*entrance*) vestíbulo *m*. **∼ of residence** *n* colegio *m* mayor

hallelujah /hælɪˈluːjə/ *int & n* aleluya (*f*)

hallmark /ˈhɔːlmɑːk/ *n* (*on gold etc*) contraste *m*; (*fig*) sello *m* (distintivo)

hallo /həˈləʊ/ *int* = **hello**

hallow /ˈhæləʊ/ *vt* santificar. **H∼e'en** *n* víspera *f* de Todos los Santos

hallucination /həluːsɪˈneɪʃn/ *n* alucinación *f*

halo /ˈheɪləʊ/ *n* (*pl* **-oes**) aureola *f*

halt /hɔːlt/ *n* alto *m*. ● *vt* parar. ● *vi* pararse

halve /hɑːv/ *vt* dividir por mitad

ham /hæm/ *n* jamón *m*; (*theatre, sl*) racionista *m & f*

hamburger /ˈhæmbɜːgə(r)/ *n* hamburguesa *f*

hamlet /ˈhæmlɪt/ *n* aldea *f*, caserío *m*

hammer /ˈhæmə(r)/ *n* martillo *m*. ● *vt* martill(e)ar; (*defeat, fam*) machacar

hammock /ˈhæmək/ *n* hamaca *f*

hamper¹ /ˈhæmpə(r)/ *n* cesta *f*

hamper² /ˈhæmpə(r)/ *vt* estorbar, poner trabas

hamster /ˈhæmstə(r)/ *n* hámster *m*

hand /hænd/ *n* (*including cards*) mano *f*; (*of clock*) manecilla *f*; (*writing*) escritura *f*, letra *f*; (*worker*) obrero *m*. **at ∼** a mano. **by ∼** a mano. **lend a ∼** echar una mano. **on ∼** a mano. **on one's ∼s** (*fig*) en (las) manos de uno. **on the one ∼... on the other ∼** por un lado... por otro.

out of ~ fuera de control. **to** ~ a mano. ● *vt* dar. ~ **down** pasar. ~ **in** entregar. ~ **over** entregar. ~ **out** distribuir. ~**bag** *n* bolso *m*, cartera *f* (*LAm*). ~**book** *n* (*manual*) manual *m*; (*guidebook*) guía *f*. ~**cuffs** *npl* esposas *fpl*. ~**ful** /'hændfʊl/ *n* puñado *m*; (*person, fam*) persona *f* difícil. ~**luggage** *n* equipaje *m* de mano. ~**out** *n* folleto *m*; (*money*) limosna *f*

handicap /'hændɪkæp/ *n* desventaja *f*; (*sport*) handicap *m*. ● *vt* (*pt* **handicapped**) imponer impedimentos a

handicraft /'hændɪkrɑːft/ *n* artesanía *f*

handiwork /'hændɪwɜːk/ *n* obra *f*, trabajo *m* manual

handkerchief /'hæŋkətʃɪf/ *n* (*pl* **-fs**) pañuelo *m*

handle /'hændl/ *n* (*of door etc*) tirador *m*; (*of implement*) mango *m*; (*of cup, bag, basket etc*) asa *f*. ● *vt* manejar; (*touch*) tocar; (*control*) controlar

handlebar /'hændlbɑː(r)/ *n* (*on bicycle*) manillar *m*

handshake /'hændʃeɪk/ *n* apretón *m* de manos

handsome /'hænsəm/ *a* (*good-looking*) guapo; (*generous*) generoso; (*large*) considerable

handwriting /'hændraɪtɪŋ/ *n* escritura *f*, letra *f*

handy /'hændɪ/ *a* (**-ier, -iest**) (*useful*) cómodo; ‹*person*› diestro; (*near*) a mano. ~**man** *n* hombre *m* habilidoso

hang /hæŋ/ *vt* (*pt* **hung**) colgar; (*pt* **hanged**) (*capital punishment*) ahorcar. ● *vi* colgar; ‹*hair*› caer. ● *n*. **get the** ~ **of sth** coger el truco de algo. ~ **about** holgazanear. ~ **on** (*hold out*) resistir; (*wait, sl*) esperar. ~ **out** *vi* tender; (*live, sl*) vivir. ~ **up** (*telephone*) colgar

hangar /'hæŋə(r)/ *n* hangar *m*

hanger /'hæŋə(r)/ *n* (*for clothes*) percha *f*. ~**on** *n* parásito *m*, pegote *m*

hang-gliding /'hæŋglaɪdɪŋ/ *n* vuelo *m* libre

hangman /'hæŋmən/ *n* verdugo *m*

hangover /'hæŋəʊvə(r)/ *n* (*after drinking*) resaca *f*

hang-up /'hæŋʌp/ *n* (*sl*) complejo *m*

hanker /'hæŋkə(r)/ *vi*. ~ **after** anhelar. ~**ing** *n* anhelo *m*

hanky-panky /'hæŋkɪpæŋkɪ/ *n* (*trickery, sl*) trucos *mpl*

haphazard /hæp'hæzəd/ *a* fortuito. ~**ly** *adv* al azar

hapless /'hæplɪs/ *a* desafortunado

happen /'hæpən/ *vi* pasar, suceder, ocurrir. **if he** ~**s to come** si acaso viene. ~**ing** *n* acontecimiento *m*

happ|ily /'hæpɪlɪ/ *adv* felizmente; (*fortunately*) afortunadamente. ~**iness** *n* felicidad *f*. ~**y** *a* (**-ier, -iest**) feliz. ~**y-go-lucky** *a* despreocupado. ~**y medium** *n* término *m* medio

harangue /hə'ræŋ/ *n* arenga *f*. ● *vt* arengar

harass /'hærəs/ *vt* acosar. ~**ment** *n* tormento *m*

harbour /'hɑːbə(r)/ *n* puerto *m*. ● *vt* encubrir ‹*criminal*›; abrigar ‹*feelings*›

hard /hɑːd/ *a* (**-er, -est**) duro; (*difficult*) difícil. ~ **of hearing** duro de oído. ● *adv* mucho; (*pull*) fuerte. ~ **by** (muy) cerca. ~ **done by** tratado injustamente. ~ **up** (*fam*) sin un cuarto. ~**board** *n* chapa *f* de madera, tabla *f*. ~**boiled egg** *n* huevo *m* duro. ~**en** /'hɑːdn/ *vt* endurecer. ● *vi* endurecerse. ~**headed** *a* realista

hardly /'hɑːdlɪ/ *adv* apenas. ~ **ever** casi nunca

hardness /'hɑːdnɪs/ *n* dureza *f*

hardship /'hɑːdʃɪp/ *n* apuro *m*

hard: ~ **shoulder** *n* arcén *m*. ~**ware** *n* ferretería *f*; ‹*computer*› hardware *m*. ~**working** *a* trabajador

hardy /'hɑːdɪ/ *a* (**-ier, -iest**) (*bold*) audaz; (*robust*) robusto; (*bot*) resistente

hare /heə(r)/ *n* liebre *f*. ~**brained** *a* aturdido

harem /'hɑːriːm/ *n* harén *m*

haricot /'hærɪkəʊ/ *n*. ~ **bean** alubia *f*, judía *f*

hark /hɑːk/ *vi* escuchar. ~ **back to** volver a

harlot /'hɑːlət/ *n* prostituta *f*

harm /hɑːm/ *n* daño *m*. **there is no** ~ **in** (+ *gerund*) no hay ningún mal en (+ *infinitive*). ● *vt* hacer daño a ‹*person*›; dañar ‹*thing*›; perjudicar ‹*interests*›. ~**ful** *a* perjudical. ~**less** *a* inofensivo

harmonica /hɑː'mɒnɪkə/ *n* armónica *f*

harmon|ious /hɑː'məʊnɪəs/ *a* armonioso. ~**ize** *vt/i* armonizar. ~**y** *n* armonía *f*

harness /'hɑːnɪs/ n (*for horses*) guarniciones *fpl*; (*for children*) andadores *mpl*. ● *vt* poner guarniciones a ‹*horse*›; (*fig*) aprovechar

harp /hɑːp/ n arpa *f*. ● *vi*. ~ **on** (**about**) machacar. ~**ist** /'hɑːpɪst/ n arpista *m & f*

harpoon /hɑːˈpuːn/ n arpón *m*

harpsichord /'hɑːpsɪkɔːd/ n clavicémbalo *m*, clave *m*

harrowing /'hærəʊɪŋ/ a desgarrador

harsh /hɑːʃ/ a (**-er**, **-est**) duro, severo; ‹*taste, sound*› áspero. ~**ly** adv severamente. ~**ness** n severidad *f*

harvest /'hɑːvɪst/ n cosecha *f*. ● *vt* cosechar. ~**er** n (*person*) segador; (*machine*) cosechadora *f*

has /hæz/ *see* **have**

hash /hæʃ/ n picadillo *m*. **make a ~ of sth** hacer algo con los pies, estropear algo

hashish /'hæʃiːʃ/ n hachís *m*

hassle /'hæsl/ n (*quarrel*) pelea *f*; (*difficulty*) problema *m*, dificultad *f*; (*bother, fam*) pena *f*, follón *m*, lío *m*. ● *vt* (*harass*) acosar, dar la lata

haste /heɪst/ n prisa *f*. **in ~** de prisa. **make ~** darse prisa

hasten /'heɪsn/ *vt* apresurar. ● *vi* apresurarse, darse prisa

hast|ily /'heɪstɪlɪ/ adv de prisa. ~**y** a (**-ier**, **-iest**) precipitado; (*rash*) irreflexivo

hat /hæt/ n sombrero *m*. **a ~ trick** n tres victorias *fpl* consecutivas

hatch[1] /hætʃ/ n (*for food*) ventanilla *f*; (*naut*) escotilla *f*

hatch[2] /hætʃ/ *vt* empollar ‹*eggs*›; tramar ‹*plot*›. ● *vi* salir del cascarón

hatchback /'hætʃbæk/ n (*coche m*) cincopuertas *m invar*, coche *m* con puerta trasera

hatchet /'hætʃɪt/ n hacha *f*

hate /heɪt/ n odio *m*. ● *vt* odiar. ~**ful** a odioso

hatred /'heɪtrɪd/ n odio *m*

haughty /'hɔːtɪ/ a (**-ier**, **-iest**) altivo

haul /hɔːl/ *vt* arrastrar; transportar ‹*goods*›. ● n (*catch*) redada *f*; (*stolen goods*) botín *m*; (*journey*) recorrido *m*. ~**age** n transporte *m*. ~**ier** n transportista *m & f*

haunch /hɔːntʃ/ n anca *f*

haunt /hɔːnt/ *vt* frecuentar. ● n sitio *m* preferido. ~**ed house** n casa *f* frecuentada por fantasmas

Havana /həˈvænə/ n La Habana *f*

have /hæv/ *vt* (*3 sing pres tense* **has**, *pt* **had**) tener; (*eat, drink*) tomar. ~ **it out with** resolver el asunto. ~ **sth done** hacer hacer algo. ~ **to do** tener que hacer. ● *v aux* haber. ~ **just done** acabar de hacer. ● n. **the ~s and ~nots** los ricos *mpl* y los pobres *mpl*

haven /'heɪvn/ n puerto *m*; (*refuge*) refugio *m*

haversack /'hævəsæk/ n mochila *f*

havoc /'hævək/ n estragos *mpl*

haw /hɔː/ *see* **hum**

hawk[1] /hɔːk/ n halcón *m*

hawk[2] /hɔːk/ *vt* vender por las calles. ~**er** n vendedor *m* ambulante

hawthorn /'hɔːθɔːn/ n espino *m* (blanco)

hay /heɪ/ n heno *m*. ~ **fever** n fiebre *f* del heno. ~**stack** n almiar *m*

haywire /'heɪwaɪə(r)/ a. **go ~** ‹*plans*› desorganizarse; ‹*machine*› estropearse

hazard /'hæzəd/ n riesgo *m*. ● *vt* arriesgar; aventurar ‹*guess*›. ~**ous** a arriesgado

haze /heɪz/ n neblina *f*

hazel /'heɪzl/ n avellano *m*. ~**nut** n avellana *f*

hazy /'heɪzɪ/ a (**-ier**, **-iest**) nebuloso

he /hiː/ pron él. ● n (*animal*) macho *m*; (*man*) varón *m*

head /hed/ n cabeza *f*; (*leader*) jefe *m*; (*of beer*) espuma *f*. ~**s or tails** cara o cruz. ● a principal. ~ **waiter** n jefe *m* de comedor. ● *vt* encabezar. ~ **the ball** dar un cabezazo. ~ **for** dirigirse a. ~**ache** n dolor *m* de cabeza. ~**dress** n tocado *m*. ~**er** n (*football*) cabezazo *m*. ~ **first** adv de cabeza. ~**gear** n tocado *m*

heading /'hedɪŋ/ n título *m*, encabezamiento *m*

headlamp /'hedlæmp/ n faro *m*

headland /'hedlənd/ n promontorio *m*

headlight /'hedlaɪt/ n faro *m*

headline /'hedlaɪn/ n titular *m*

headlong /'hedlɒŋ/ adv de cabeza; (*precipitately*) precipitadamente

head: ~**master** n director *m*. ~**mistress** n directora *f*. ~**-on** a & adv de frente. ~**phone** n auricular *m*, audífono *m* (*LAm*)

headquarters /hed'kwɔːtəz/ n (*of organization*) sede *f*; (*of business*) oficina *f* central; (*mil*) cuartel *m* general

headstrong /'hedstrɒŋ/ a testarudo

headway /'hedweɪ/ n progreso m. **make ~** hacer progresos

heady /'hedɪ/ a (**-ier, -iest**) (*impetuous*) impetuoso; (*intoxicating*) embriagador

heal /hiːl/ vt curar. ● vi (*wound*) cicatrizarse; (*fig*) curarse

health /helθ/ n salud f. **~y** a sano

heap /hiːp/ n montón m. ● vt amontonar. **~s of** (*fam*) montones de, muchísimos

hear /hɪə(r)/ vt/i (pt **heard** /hɜːd/) oír. **~, ~!** ¡bravo! **not ~ of** (*refuse to allow*) no querer oír. **~ about** oír hablar de. **~ from** recibir noticias de. **~ of** oír hablar de

hearing /'hɪərɪŋ/ n oído m; (*of witness*) audición f. **~-aid** n audífono m

hearsay /'hɪəseɪ/ n rumores mpl. **from ~** según los rumores

hearse /hɜːs/ n coche m fúnebre

heart /hɑːt/ n corazón m. **at ~** en el fondo. **by ~** de memoria. **lose ~** descorazonarse. **~ache** n pena f. **~ attack** n ataque m al corazón. **~-break** n pena f. **~-breaking** a desgarrador. **~-broken** a. **be ~-broken** partírsele el corazón

heartburn /'hɑːtbɜːn/ n acedía f

hearten /'hɑːtn/ vt animar

heartfelt /'hɑːtfelt/ a sincero

hearth /hɑːθ/ n hogar m

heartily /'hɑːtɪlɪ/ adv de buena gana; (*sincerely*) sinceramente

heart: ~less a cruel. **~-searching** n examen m de conciencia. **~-to-~** a abierto

hearty /'hɑːtɪ/ a (*sincere*) sincero; (*meal*) abundante

heat /hiːt/ n calor m; (*contest*) eliminatoria f. ● vt calentar. ● vi calentarse. **~ed** a (*fig*) acalorado. **~er** /'hiːtə(r)/ n calentador m

heath /hiːθ/ n brezal m, descampado m, terreno m baldío

heathen /'hiːðn/ n & a pagano (m)

heather /'heðə(r)/ n brezo m

heat: ~ing n calefacción f. **~-stroke** n insolación f. **~-wave** n ola f de calor

heave /hiːv/ vt (*lift*) levantar; exhalar (*sigh*); (*throw, fam*) lanzar. ● vi (*retch*) sentir náuseas

heaven /'hevn/ n cielo m. **~ly** a celestial; (*astronomy*) celeste; (*excellent, fam*) divino

heav|ily /'hevɪlɪ/ adv pesadamente; (*smoke, drink*) mucho. **~y** a (**-ier,**

-iest) pesado; (*sea*) grueso; (*traffic*) denso; (*work*) duro. **~yweight** n peso m pesado

Hebrew /'hiːbruː/ a & n hebreo (m)

heckle /'hekl/ vt interrumpir (*speaker*)

hectic /'hektɪk/ a febril

hedge /hedʒ/ n seto m vivo. ● vt rodear con seto vivo. ● vi escaparse por la tangente

hedgehog /'hedʒhɒg/ n erizo m

heed /hiːd/ vt hacer caso de. ● n atención f. **pay ~ to** hacer caso de. **~less** a desatento

heel /hiːl/ n talón m; (*of shoe*) tacón m. **down at ~, down at the ~s** (*Amer*) desharrapado

hefty /'heftɪ/ a (**-ier, -iest**) (*sturdy*) fuerte; (*heavy*) pesado

heifer /'hefə(r)/ n novilla f

height /haɪt/ n altura f; (*of person*) estatura f; (*of fame, glory*) cumbre f; (*of joy, folly, pain*) colmo m

heighten /'haɪtn/ vt (*raise*) elevar; (*fig*) aumentar

heinous /'heɪnəs/ a atroz

heir /eə(r)/ n heredero m. **~ess** n heredera f. **~loom** /'eəluːm/ n reliquia f heredada

held /held/ see **hold**[1]

helicopter /'helɪkɒptə(r)/ n helicóptero m

heliport /'helɪpɔːt/ n helipuerto m

hell /hel/ n infierno m. **~-bent** a resuelto. **~ish** a infernal

hello /hə'ləʊ/ int ¡hola!; (*telephone, caller*) ¡oiga!, ¡bueno! (*Mex*), ¡hola! (*Arg*); (*telephone, person answering*) ¡diga!, ¡bueno! (*Mex*), ¡hola! (*Arg*); (*surprise*) ¡vaya! **say ~ to** saludar

helm /helm/ n (*of ship*) timón m

helmet /'helmɪt/ n casco m

help /help/ vt/i ayudar. **he cannot ~ laughing** no puede menos de reír. **~ o.s. to** servirse. **it cannot be ~ed** no hay más remedio. ● n ayuda f; (*charwoman*) asistenta f. **~er** n ayudante m. **~ful** a útil; (*person*) amable

helping /'helpɪŋ/ n porción f

helpless /'helplɪs/ a (*unable to manage*) incapaz; (*powerless*) impotente

helter-skelter /heltə'skeltə(r)/ n tobogán m. ● adv atropelladamente

hem /hem/ n dobladillo m. ● vt (pt **hemmed**) hacer un dobladillo. **~ in** encerrar

hemisphere /'hemɪsfɪə(r)/ n hemisferio m

hemp /hemp/ n (plant) cáñamo m; (hashish) hachís m

hen /hen/ n gallina f

hence /hens/ adv de aquí. ~forth adv de ahora en adelante

henchman /'hentʃmən/ n secuaz m

henna /'henə/ n alheña f

hen-party /'henpɑːtɪ/ n (fam) reunión f de mujeres

henpecked /'henpekt/ a dominado por su mujer

her /hɜː(r)/ pron (accusative) la; (dative) le; (after prep) ella. **I know ~** la conozco. ● a su, sus pl

herald /'herəld/ vt anunciar

heraldry /'herəldrɪ/ n heráldica f

herb /hɜːb/ n hierba f. ~s npl hierbas fpl finas

herbaceous /hɜːˈbeɪʃəs/ a herbáceo

herbalist /'hɜːbəlɪst/ n herbolario m

herculean /hɜːkjʊˈliːən/ a hercúleo

herd /hɜːd/ n rebaño m. ● vt. ~ together reunir

here /hɪə(r)/ adv aquí. ~! (take this) ¡tenga! ~abouts adv por aquí. ~after adv en el futuro. ~by adv por este medio; (in letter) por la presente

heredit|ary /hɪˈredɪtərɪ/ a hereditario. ~y /hɪˈredətɪ/ n herencia f

here|sy /'herəsɪ/ n herejía f. ~tic n hereje m & f

herewith /hɪəˈwɪð/ adv adjunto

heritage /'herɪtɪdʒ/ n herencia f; (fig) patrimonio m

hermetic /hɜːˈmetɪk/ a hermético

hermit /'hɜːmɪt/ n ermitaño m

hernia /'hɜːnɪə/ n hernia f

hero /'hɪərəʊ/ n (pl -oes) héroe m. ~ic a heroico

heroin /'herəʊɪn/ n heroína f

hero: ~ine /'herəʊɪn/ n heroína f. ~ism /'herəʊɪzm/ n heroísmo m

heron /'herən/ n garza f real

herring /'herɪŋ/ n arenque m

hers /hɜːz/ poss pron suyo m, suya f, suyos mpl, suyas fpl, de ella

herself /hɜːˈself/ pron ella misma; (reflexive) se; (after prep) sí

hesitant /'hezɪtənt/ a vacilante

hesitat|e /'hezɪteɪt/ vi vacilar. ~ion /-'teɪʃn/ n vacilación f

hessian /'hesɪən/ n arpillera f

het /het/ a. ~ up (sl) nervioso

heterogeneous /hetərəʊˈdʒiːnɪəs/ a heterogéneo

heterosexual /hetərəʊˈseksjʊəl/ a heterosexual

hew /hjuː/ vt (pp hewn) cortar; (cut into shape) tallar

hexagon /'heksəgən/ n hexágono m. ~al /-ˈægənl/ a hexagonal

hey /heɪ/ int ¡eh!

heyday /'heɪdeɪ/ n apogeo m

hi /haɪ/ int (fam) ¡hola!

hiatus /haɪˈeɪtəs/ n (pl -tuses) hiato m

hibernat|e /'haɪbəneɪt/ vi hibernar. ~ion n hibernación f

hibiscus /hɪˈbɪskəs/ n hibisco m

hiccup /'hɪkʌp/ n hipo m. **have (the) ~s** tener hipo. ● vi tener hipo

hide[1] /haɪd/ vt (pt hid, pp hidden) esconder. ● vi esconderse

hide[2] /haɪd/ n piel f, cuero m

hideous /'hɪdɪəs/ a (dreadful) horrible; (ugly) feo

hide-out /'haɪdaʊt/ n escondrijo m

hiding[1] /'haɪdɪŋ/ n (thrashing) paliza f

hiding[2] /'haɪdɪŋ/ n. **go into ~** esconderse

hierarchy /'haɪərɑːkɪ/ n jerarquía f

hieroglyph /'haɪərəɡlɪf/ n jeroglífico m

hi-fi /'haɪfaɪ/ a de alta fidelidad. ● n (equipo m de) alta fidelidad (f)

higgledy-piggledy /hɪɡldɪˈpɪɡldɪ/ adv en desorden

high /haɪ/ a (-er, -est) alto; (price) elevado; (number; speed) grande; (wind) fuerte; (intoxicated, fam) ebrio; (voice) agudo; (meat) manido. **in the ~ season** en plena temporada. ● n alto nivel m. **a (new) ~** un récord m. ● adv alto

highbrow /'haɪbraʊ/ a & n intelectual (m & f)

higher education /haɪər edʒʊˈkeɪʃn/ n enseñanza f superior

high-falutin /haɪfəˈluːtɪn/ a pomposo

high-handed /haɪˈhændɪd/ a despótico

high jump /'haɪdʒʌmp/ n salto m de altura

highlight /'haɪlaɪt/ n punto m culminante. ● vt destacar

highly /'haɪlɪ/ adv muy; (paid) muy bien. ~ strung a nervioso

highness /'haɪnɪs/ n (title) alteza f

high: ~rise building n rascacielos m. ~ school n instituto m. ~speed a de gran velocidad. ~ spot n (fam) punto m culminante. ~ street n calle *f* mayor. **~strung** *a* (*Amer*) nervioso. **~ tea** *n* merienda *f* substanciosa

highway /'haɪweɪ/ *n* carretera *f*. **~man** *n* salteador *m* de caminos

hijack /'haɪdʒæk/ *vt* secuestrar. ● *n* secuestro *m*. **~er** *n* secuestrador

hike /haɪk/ *n* caminata *f*. ● *vi* darse la caminata. **~r** *n* excursionista *m* & *f*

hilarious /hɪ'leərɪəs/ *a* (*funny*) muy divertido

hill /hɪl/ *n* colina *f*; (*slope*) cuesta *f*. **~billy** *n* rústico *m*. **~side** *n* ladera *f*. **~y** *a* montuoso

hilt /hɪlt/ *n* (*of sword*) puño *m*. **to the ~** totalmente

him /hɪm/ *pron* le, lo; (*after prep*) él. **I know ~** le/lo conozco

himself /hɪm'self/ *pron* él mismo; (*reflexive*) se

hind /haɪnd/ *a* trasero

hinder /'hɪndə(r)/ *vt* estorbar; (*prevent*) impedir

hindrance /'hɪndrəns/ *n* obstáculo *m*

hindsight /'haɪnsaɪt/ *n*. **with ~** retrospectivamente

Hindu /hɪn'duː/ *n* & *a* hindú (*m* & *f*). **~ism** *n* hinduismo *m*

hinge /hɪndʒ/ *n* bisagra *f*. ● *vi*. **~ on** (*depend on*) depender de

hint /hɪnt/ *n* indirecta *f*; (*advice*) consejo *m*. ● *vt* dar a entender. ● *vi* soltar una indirecta. **~ at** hacer alusión a

hinterland /'hɪntəlænd/ *n* interior *m*

hip /hɪp/ *n* cadera *f*

hippie /'hɪpɪ/ *n* hippie *m* & *f*

hippopotamus /hɪpə'pɒtəməs/ *n* (*pl* **-muses** *or* **-mi**) hipopótamo *m*

hire /haɪə(r)/ *vt* alquilar ‹thing›; contratar ‹person›. ● *n* alquiler *m*. **~-purchase** *n* compra *f* a plazos

hirsute /'hɜːsjuːt/ *a* hirsuto

his /hɪz/ *a* su, sus *pl*. ● *poss pron* el suyo *m*, la suya *f*, los suyos *mpl*, las suyas *fpl*

Hispan|ic /hɪ'spænɪk/ *a* hispánico. **~ist** /'hɪspənɪst/ *n* hispanista *m* & *f*. **~o...** *pref* hispano...

hiss /hɪs/ *n* silbido. ● *vt/i* silbar

histor|ian /hɪ'stɔːrɪən/ *n* historiador *m*. **~ic(al)** /hɪ'stɒrɪkl/ *a* histórico. **~y** /'hɪstərɪ/ *n* historia *f*. **make ~y** pasar a la historia

histrionic /hɪstrɪ'ɒnɪk/ *a* histriónico

hit /hɪt/ *vt* (*pt* **hit**, *pres p* **hitting**) golpear; (*collide with*) chocar con;

(*find*) dar con; (*affect*) afectar. **~ it off with** hacer buenas migas con. ● *n* (*blow*) golpe *m*; (*fig*) éxito *m*. **~ on** *vi* encontrar, dar con

hitch /hɪtʃ/ *vt* (*fasten*) atar. ● *n* (*snag*) problema *m*. **~ a lift, ~-hike** *vi* hacer autostop, hacer dedo (*Arg*), pedir aventón (*Mex*). **~-hiker** *n* autostopista *m* & *f*

hither /'hɪðə(r)/ *adv* acá. **~ and thither** acá y allá

hitherto /'hɪðətuː/ *adv* hasta ahora

hit-or-miss /'hɪtɔː'mɪs/ *a* (*fam*) a la buena de Dios, a ojo

hive /haɪv/ *n* colmena *f*. ● *vt*. **~off** separar; (*industry*) desnacionalizar

hoard /hɔːd/ *vt* acumular. ● *n* provisión *f*; (*of money*) tesoro *m*

hoarding /'hɔːdɪŋ/ *n* cartelera *f*, valla *f* publicitaria

hoar-frost /'hɔːfrɒst/ *n* escarcha *f*

hoarse /hɔːs/ *a* (**-er**, **-est**) ronco. **~ness** *n* (*of voice*) ronquera *f*; (*of sound*) ronquedad *f*

hoax /həʊks/ *n* engaño *m*. ● *vt* engañar

hob /hɒb/ *n* repisa *f*; (*of cooker*) fogón *m*

hobble /'hɒbl/ *vi* cojear

hobby /'hɒbɪ/ *n* pasatiempo *m*

hobby-horse /'hɒbɪhɔːs/ *n* (*toy*) caballito *m* (de niño); (*fixation*) caballo *m* de batalla

hobnail /'hɒbneɪl/ *n* clavo *m*

hob-nob /'hɒbnɒb/ *vi* (*pt* **hobnobbed**). **~ with** codearse con

hock[1] /hɒk/ *n* vino *m* del Rin

hock[2] /hɒk/ *vt* (*pawn*, *sl*) empeñar

hockey /'hɒkɪ/ *n* hockey *m*

hodgepodge /'hɒdʒpɒdʒ/ *n* mezcolanza *f*

hoe /həʊ/ *n* azada *f*. ● *vt* (*pres p* **hoeing**) azadonar

hog /hɒg/ *n* cerdo *m*. ● *vt* (*pt* **hogged**) (*fam*) acaparar

hoist /hɔɪst/ *vt* levantar; izar ‹flag›. ● *n* montacargas *m invar*

hold[1] /həʊld/ *vt* (*pt* **held**) tener; (*grasp*) coger (*not LAm*), agarrar; (*contain*) contener; mantener ‹interest›; (*believe*) creer; contener ‹breath›. **~ one's tongue** callarse. ● *vi* mantenerse. ● *n* asidero *m*; (*influence*) influencia *f*. **get ~ of** agarrar; (*fig*, *acquire*) adquirir. **~ back** (*contain*) contener; (*conceal*) ocultar. **~ on** (*stand firm*) resistir; (*wait*) esperar. **~ on to** (*keep*) guardar; (*cling to*) agarrarse a. **~**

out vt (offer) ofrecer. ● vi (resist) resistir. ~ **over** aplazar. ~ **up** (support) sostener; (delay) retrasar; (rob) atracar. ~ **with** aprobar

hold² /həʊld/ n (of ship) bodega f

holdall /'həʊldɔːl/ n bolsa f (de viaje)

holder /'həʊldə(r)/ n tenedor m; (of post) titular m; (for object) soporte m

holding /'həʊldɪŋ/ n (land) propiedad f

hold-up /'həʊldʌp/ n atraco m

hole /həʊl/ n agujero m; (in ground) hoyo m; (in road) bache m. ● vt agujerear

holiday /'hɒlɪdeɪ/ n vacaciones fpl; (public) fiesta f. ● vi pasar las vacaciones. ~**maker** n veraneante m

holiness /'həʊlɪnɪs/ n santidad f

Holland /'hɒlənd/ n Holanda f

hollow /'hɒləʊ/ a & n hueco (m). ● vt ahuecar

holly /'hɒlɪ/ n acebo m. ~**hock** n malva f real

holocaust /'hɒləkɔːst/ n holocausto m

holster /'həʊlstə(r)/ n pistolera f

holy /'həʊlɪ/ a (-ier, -iest) santo, sagrado. H~ **Ghost** n, H~ **Spirit** n Espíritu m Santo. ~ **water** n agua f bendita

homage /'hɒmɪdʒ/ n homenaje m

home /həʊm/ n casa f; (institution) asilo m; (for soldiers) hogar m; (native land) patria f. feel at ~ with sentirse como en su casa. ● a casera, de casa; (of family) de familia; (pol) interior; (match) de casa. ● adv. (at) ~ en casa. H~ **Counties** npl región f alrededor de Londres. ~**land** n patria f. ~**less** a sin hogar. ~**ly** /'həʊmlɪ/ a (-ier, -iest) casero; (ugly) feo. H~ **Office** n Ministerio m del Interior. H~ **Secretary** n Ministro m del Interior. ~**sick** a. be ~**sick** tener morriña. ~ **town** n ciudad f natal. ~ **truths** npl las verdades fpl del barquero, las cuatro verdades fpl. ~**ward** /'həʊmwəd/ a (journey) de vuelta. ● adv hacia casa. ~**work** n deberes mpl

homicide /'hɒmɪsaɪd/ n homicidio m

homoeopath|ic /həʊmɪəʊ'pæθɪk/ a homeopático. ~**y** /-'ɒpəθɪ/ n homeopatía f

homogeneous /həʊməʊ'dʒiːnɪəs/ a homogéneo

homosexual /həʊməʊ'seksjʊəl/ a & n homosexual (m)

hone /həʊn/ vt afilar

honest /'ɒnɪst/ a honrado; (frank) sincero. ~**ly** adv honradamente. ~**y** n honradez f

honey /'hʌnɪ/ n miel f; (person, fam) cielo m, cariño m. ~**comb** /'hʌnɪkəʊm/ n panal m

honeymoon /'hʌnɪmuːn/ n luna f de miel

honeysuckle /'hʌnɪsʌkl/ n madreselva f

honk /hɒŋk/ vi tocar la bocina

honorary /'ɒnərərɪ/ a honorario

honour /'ɒnə(r)/ n honor m. ● vt honrar. ~**able** a honorable

hood /hʊd/ n capucha f; (car roof) capota f; (car bonnet) capó m

hoodlum /'huːdləm/ n gamberro m, matón m

hoodwink /'hʊdwɪŋk/ vt engañar

hoof /huːf/ n (pl hoofs or hooves) casco m

hook /hʊk/ n gancho m; (on garment) corchete m; (for fishing) anzuelo m. **by** ~ **or by crook** por fas o por nefas, por las buenas o por las malas. **get s.o. off the** ~ sacar a uno de un apuro. **off the** ~ (telephone) descolgado. ● vt enganchar. ● vi engancharse

hooked /hʊkt/ a ganchudo. ~ **on** (sl) adicto a

hooker /'hʊkə(r)/ n (rugby) talonador m; (Amer, sl) prostituta f

hookey /'hʊkɪ/ n. **play** ~ (Amer, sl) hacer novillos

hooligan /'huːlɪgən/ n gamberro m

hoop /huːp/ n aro m

hooray /hʊ'reɪ/ int & n ¡viva! (m)

hoot /huːt/ n (of horn) bocinazo m; (of owl) ululato m. ● vi tocar la bocina; (owl) ulular

hooter /'huːtə(r)/ n (of car) bocina f; (of factory) sirena f

Hoover /'huːvə(r)/ n (P) aspiradora f. ● vt pasar la aspiradora

hop¹ /hɒp/ vi (pt hopped) saltar a la pata coja. ~ **in** (fam) subir. ~ **it** (sl) largarse. ~ **out** (fam) bajar. ● n salto m; (flight) etapa f

hop² /hɒp/ n. ~(**s**) lúpulo m

hope /həʊp/ n esperanza f. ● vt/i esperar. ~ **for** esperar. ~**ful** a esperanzador. ~**fully** adv con optimismo; (it is hoped) se espera. ~**less** a desesperado. ~**lessly** adv sin esperanza

hopscotch /'hɒpskɒtʃ/ n tejo m

horde /hɔːd/ n horda f

horizon /həˈraɪzn/ n horizonte m
horizontal /hɒrɪˈzɒntl/ a horizontal.
~**ly** adv horizontalmente
hormone /ˈhɔːməʊn/ n hormona f
horn /hɔːn/ n cuerno m; (of car) bocina f; (mus) trompa f. ● vt. ~ **in** (sl) entrometerse. ~**ed** a con cuernos
hornet /ˈhɔːnɪt/ n avispón m
horny /ˈhɔːnɪ/ a ⟨hands⟩ calloso
horoscope /ˈhɒrəskəʊp/ n horóscopo m
horri|ble /ˈhɒrəbl/ a horrible. ~**d** /ˈhɒrɪd/ a horrible
horrif|ic /həˈrɪfɪk/ a horroroso. ~**y** /ˈhɒrɪfaɪ/ vt horrorizar
horror /ˈhɒrə(r)/ n horror m. ~ **film** n película f de miedo
hors-d'oevre /ɔːˈdɜːvr/ n entremés m
horse /hɔːs/ n caballo m. ~**back** n. **on** ~**back** a caballo
horse chestnut /hɔːsˈtʃesnʌt/ n castaña f de Indias
horse: ~**man** n jinete m. ~**play** n payasadas fpl. ~**power** n (unit) caballo m (de fuerza). ~**racing** n carreras fpl de caballos
horseradish /ˈhɔːsrædɪʃ/ n rábano m picante
horse: ~ **sense** n (fam) sentido m común. ~**shoe** /ˈhɔːsʃuː/ n herradura f
horsy /ˈhɔːsɪ/ a ⟨face etc⟩ caballuno
horticultur|al /hɔːtɪˈkʌltʃərəl/ a hortícola. ~**e** /ˈhɔːtɪkʌltʃə(r)/ n horticultura f
hose /həʊz/ n (tube) manga f. ● vt (water) regar con una manga; (clean) limpiar con una manga. ~**pipe** n manga f
hosiery /ˈhəʊzɪərɪ/ n calcetería f
hospice /ˈhɒspɪs/ n hospicio m
hospitabl|e /hɒˈspɪtəbl/ a hospitalario. ~**y** adv con hospitalidad
hospital /ˈhɒspɪtl/ n hospital m
hospitality /hɒspɪˈtælətɪ/ n hospitalidad f
host[1] /həʊst/ n. **a** ~ **of** un montón de
host[2] /həʊst/ n (master of house) huésped m, anfitrión m
host[3] /həʊst/ n (relig) hostia f
hostage /ˈhɒstɪdʒ/ n rehén m
hostel /ˈhɒstl/ n (for students) residencia f. **youth** ~ albergue m juvenil
hostess /ˈhəʊstɪs/ n huéspeda f, anfitriona f
hostil|e /ˈhɒstaɪl/ a hostil. ~**ity** n hostilidad f

hot /hɒt/ a (**hotter, hottest**) caliente; (culin) picante; ⟨news⟩ de última hora. **be/feel** ~ tener calor. **in** ~ **water** (fam) en un apuro. **it is** ~ hace calor. ● vt/i. ~ **up** (fam) calentarse
hotbed /ˈhɒtbed/ n (fig) semillero m
hotchpotch /ˈhɒtʃpɒtʃ/ n mezcolanza f
hot dog /hɒtˈdɒg/ n perrito m caliente
hotel /həʊˈtel/ n hotel m. ~**ier** n hotelero m
hot: ~**head** n impetuoso m. ~**headed** a impetuoso. ~**house** n invernadero m. ~**line** n teléfono m rojo. ~**plate** n calentador m. ~**water bottle** n bolsa f de agua caliente
hound /haʊnd/ n perro m de caza. ● vt perseguir
hour /aʊə(r)/ n hora f. ~**ly** a & adv cada hora. ~**ly pay** n sueldo m por hora. **paid** ~**ly** pagado por hora
house /haʊs/ n (pl -s /ˈhaʊzɪz/) casa f; (theatre building) sala f; (theatre audience) público m; (pol) cámara f. /haʊz/ vt alojar; (keep) guardar. ~**boat** n casa f flotante. ~**breaking** n robo m de casa. ~**hold** /ˈhaʊshəʊld/ n casa f, familia f. ~**holder** n dueño m de una casa; (head of household) cabeza f de familia. ~**keeper** n ama f de llaves. ~**keeping** n gobierno m de la casa. ~**maid** n criada f, mucama f (LAm). **H~ of Commons** n Cámara f de los Comunes. ~**proud** a meticuloso. ~**warming** n inauguración f de una casa. ~**wife** /ˈhaʊswaɪf/ n ama f de casa. ~**work** n quehaceres mpl domésticos
housing /ˈhaʊzɪŋ/ n alojamiento m. ~ **estate** n urbanización f
hovel /ˈhɒvl/ n casucha f
hover /ˈhɒvə(r)/ vi ⟨bird, threat etc⟩ cernerse; (loiter) rondar. ~**craft** n aerodeslizador m
how /haʊ/ adv cómo. ~ **about a walk?** ¿qué le parece si damos un paseo? ~ **are you?** ¿cómo está Vd? ~ **do you do?** (in introduction) mucho gusto. ~ **long?** ¿cuánto tiempo? ~ **many?** ¿cuántos? ~ **much?** ¿cuánto? ~ **often?** ¿cuántas veces? **and** ~! ¡y cómo!
however /haʊˈevə(r)/ adv (with verb) de cualquier manera que (+ subjunctive); (with adjective or adverb) por... que (+ subjunctive);

howl (*nevertheless*) no obstante, sin embargo. **~ much it rains** por mucho que llueva

howl /haʊl/ *n* aullido. ● *vi* aullar

howler /ˈhaʊlə(r)/ *n* (*fam*) plancha *f*

HP *abbr see* **hire-purchase**

hp *abbr see* **horsepower**

hub /hʌb/ *n* (*of wheel*) cubo *m*; (*fig*) centro *m*

hubbub /ˈhʌbʌb/ *n* barahúnda *f*

hub-cap /ˈhʌbkæp/ *n* tapacubos *m invar*

huddle /ˈhʌdl/ *vi* apiñarse

hue[1] /hjuː/ *n* (*colour*) color *m*

hue[2] /hjuː/ *n*. **~ and cry** clamor *m*

huff /hʌf/ *n*. **in a ~** enojado

hug /hʌg/ *vt* (*pt* hugged) abrazar; (*keep close to*) no apartarse de. ● *n* abrazo *m*

huge /hjuːdʒ/ *a* enorme. **~ly** *adv* enormemente

hulk /hʌlk/ *n* (*of ship*) barco *m* viejo; (*person*) armatoste *m*

hull /hʌl/ *n* (*of ship*) casco *m*

hullabaloo /hʌləbəˈluː/ *n* tumulto *m*

hullo /həˈləʊ/ *int* = **hello**

hum /hʌm/ *vt/i* (*pt* hummed) (*person*) canturrear; (*insect, engine*) zumbar. ● *n* zumbido *m*. **~ (or hem) and haw (or ha)** vacilar

human /ˈhjuːmən/ *a & n* humano (*m*). **~ being** *n* ser *m* humano

humane /hjuːˈmeɪn/ *a* humano

humanism /ˈhjuːmənɪzəm/ *n* humanismo *m*

humanitarian /hjuːmænɪˈteərɪən/ *a* humanitario

humanity /hjuːˈmænətɪ/ *n* humanidad *f*

humbl|e /ˈhʌmbl/ *a* (-er, -est) humilde. ● *vt* humillar. **~y** *adv* humildemente

humbug /ˈhʌmbʌg/ *n* (*false talk*) charlatanería *f*; (*person*) charlatán *m*; (*sweet*) caramelo *m* de menta

humdrum /ˈhʌmdrʌm/ *a* monótono

humid /ˈhjuːmɪd/ *a* húmedo. **~ifier** *n* humedecedor *m*. **~ity** /hjuːˈmɪdətɪ/ *n* humedad *f*

humiliat|e /hjuːˈmɪlɪeɪt/ *vt* humillar. **~ion** /-ˈeɪʃn/ *n* humillación *f*

humility /hjuːˈmɪlətɪ/ *n* humildad *f*

humorist /ˈhjuːmərɪst/ *n* humorista *m & f*

humo|rous /ˈhjuːmərəs/ *a* divertido. **~rously** *adv* con gracia. **~ur** *n* humorismo *m*; (*mood*) humor *m*. **sense of ~ur** *n* sentido *m* del humor

hump /hʌmp/ *n* montecillo *m*; (*of the spine*) joroba *f*. **the ~** (*sl*) malhumor *m*. ● *vt* encorvarse; (*hoist up*) llevar al hombro

hunch /hʌntʃ/ *vt* encorvar. **~ed up** encorvado. ● *n* presentimiento *m*; (*lump*) joroba *f*. **~back** /ˈhʌntʃbæk/ *n* jorobado *m*

hundred /ˈhʌndrəd/ *a* ciento, (*before noun*) cien. ● *n* ciento *m*. **~fold** *a* céntuplo. ● *adv* cien veces. **~s** of centenares de. **~th** *a* centésimo. ● *n* centésimo *m*, centésima parte *f*

hundredweight /ˈhʌndrədweɪt/ *n* 50,8kg; (*Amer*) 45,36kg

hung /hʌŋ/ *see* **hang**

Hungar|ian /hʌŋˈgeərɪən/ *a & n* húngaro (*m*). **~y** /ˈhʌŋgərɪ/ *n* Hungría *f*

hunger /ˈhʌŋgə(r)/ *n* hambre *f*. ● *vi*. **~ for** tener hambre de. **~-strike** *n* huelga *f* de hambre

hungr|ily /ˈhʌŋgrəlɪ/ *adv* ávidamente. **~y** *a* (-ier, -iest) hambriento. **be ~y** tener hambre

hunk /hʌŋk/ *n* (buen) pedazo *m*

hunt /hʌnt/ *vt/i* cazar. **~ for** buscar. ● *n* caza *f*. **~er** *n* cazador *m*. **~ing** *n* caza *f*

hurdle /ˈhɜːdl/ *n* (*sport*) valla *f*; (*fig*) obstáculo *m*

hurdy-gurdy /ˈhɜːdɪgɜːdɪ/ *n* organillo *m*

hurl /hɜːl/ *vt* lanzar

hurly-burly /ˈhɜːlɪbɜːlɪ/ *n* tumulto *m*

hurrah /huˈrɑː/, **hurray** /huˈreɪ/ *int & n* ¡viva! *m*

hurricane /ˈhʌrɪkən/ *n* huracán *m*

hurried /ˈhʌrɪd/ *a* apresurado. **~ly** *adv* apresuradamente

hurry /ˈhʌrɪ/ *vi* apresurarse, darse prisa. ● *vt* apresurar, dar prisa a. ● *n* prisa *f*. **be in a ~** tener prisa

hurt /hɜːt/ *vt/i* (*pt* hurt) herir. ● *n* (*injury*) herida *f*; (*harm*) daño *m*. **~ful** *a* hiriente; (*harmful*) dañoso

hurtle /ˈhɜːtl/ *vt* lanzar. ● *vi*. **~ along** mover rápidamente

husband /ˈhʌzbənd/ *n* marido *m*

hush /hʌʃ/ *vt* acallar. ● *n* silencio *m*. **~ up** ocultar (*affair*). **~~~** *a* (*fam*) muy secreto

husk /hʌsk/ *n* cáscara *f*

husky /ˈhʌskɪ/ *a* (-ier, -iest) (*hoarse*) ronco; (*burly*) fornido

hussy /ˈhʌsɪ/ *n* desvergonzada *f*

hustle /ˈhʌsl/ *vt* (*jostle*) empujar. ● *vi* (*hurry*) darse prisa. ● *n* empuje *m*. **~ and bustle** *n* bullicio *m*

hut /hʌt/ *n* cabaña *f*

hutch /hʌtʃ/ n conejera f
hyacinth /'haɪəsɪnθ/ n jacinto m
hybrid /'haɪbrɪd/ a & n híbrido (m)
hydrangea /haɪ'dreɪndʒə/ n hortensia f
hydrant /'haɪdrənt/ n. (fire) ~ n boca f de riego
hydraulic /haɪ'drɔːlɪk/ a hidráulico
hydroelectric /haɪdrəʊɪ'lektrɪk/ a hidroeléctrico
hydrofoil /'haɪdrəfɔɪl/ n aerodeslizador m
hydrogen /'haɪdrədʒən/ n hidrógeno m. ~ **bomb** n bomba f de hidrógeno. ~ **peroxide** n peróxido m de hidrógeno
hyena /haɪ'iːnə/ n hiena f
hygien|e /'haɪdʒiːn/ n higiene f. ~**ic** a higiénico
hymn /hɪm/ n himno m
hyper... /'haɪpə(r)/ pref hiper...
hypermarket /'haɪpəmɑːkɪt/ n hipermercado m
hyphen /'haɪfn/ n guión m. ~**ate** vt escribir con guión
hypno|sis /hɪp'nəʊsɪs/ n hipnosis f. ~**tic** /-'nɒtɪk/ a hipnótico. ~**tism** /'hɪpnə'tɪzəm/ n hipnotismo m. ~**tist** n hipnotista m & f. ~**tize** vt hipnotizar
hypochondriac /haɪpə'kɒndrɪæk/ n hipocondríaco m
hypocrisy /hɪ'pɒkrəsɪ/ n hipocresía f
hypocrit|e /'hɪpəkrɪt/ n hipócrita m & f. ~**ical** a hipócrita
hypodermic /haɪpə'dɜːmɪk/ a hipodérmico. ● n jeringa f hipodérmica
hypothe|sis /haɪ'pɒθəsɪs/ n (pl -theses /-siːz/) hipótesis f. ~**tical** /-ə'θetɪkl/ a hipotético
hysteri|a /hɪ'stɪərɪə/ n histerismo m. ~**cal** /-'terɪkl/ a histérico. ~**cs** /hɪ'sterɪks/ npl histerismo m. **have** ~**cs** ponerse histérico; (laugh) morir de risa

I

I /aɪ/ pron yo
ice /aɪs/ n hielo m. ● vt helar; glasear ‹cake›. ● vi. ~ **(up)** helarse. ~**berg** n iceberg m, témpano m. ~**cream** n helado m. ~**cube** n cubito m de hielo. ~ **hockey** n hockey m sobre hielo

Iceland /'aɪslənd/ n Islandia f. ~**er** n islandés m. ~**ic** /-'lændɪk/ a islandés
ice lolly /aɪs'lɒlɪ/ polo m, paleta f (LAm)
icicle /'aɪsɪkl/ n carámbano m
icing /'aɪsɪŋ/ n (sugar) azúcar m glaseado
icon /'aɪkɒn/ n icono m
icy /'aɪsɪ/ a (-ier, -iest) glacial
idea /aɪ'dɪə/ n idea f
ideal /aɪ'dɪəl/ a ideal. ● n ideal m. ~**ism** n idealismo m. ~**ist** n idealista m & f. ~**istic** /-'lɪstɪk/ a idealista. ~**ize** vt idealizar. ~**ly** adv idealmente
identical /aɪ'dentɪkl/ a idéntico
identif|ication /aɪdentɪfɪ'keɪʃn/ n identificación f. ~**y** /aɪ'dentɪfaɪ/ vt identificar. ● vi. ~**y with** identificarse con
identikit /aɪ'dentɪkɪt/ n retratorobot m
identity /aɪ'dentɪtɪ/ n identidad f
ideolog|ical /aɪdɪə'lɒdʒɪkl/ a ideológico. ~**y** /aɪdɪ'ɒlədʒɪ/ n ideología f
idiocy /'ɪdɪəsɪ/ n idiotez f
idiom /'ɪdɪəm/ n locución f. ~**atic** /-'mætɪk/ a idiomático
idiosyncrasy /ɪdɪəʊ'sɪnkrəsɪ/ n idiosincrasia f
idiot /'ɪdɪət/ n idiota m & f. ~**ic** /-'ɒtɪk/ a idiota
idle /'aɪdl/ a (-er, -est) ocioso; (lazy) holgazán; (out of work) desocupado; ‹machine› parado. ● vi ‹engine› marchar en vacío. ● vt. ~ **away** perder. ~**ness** n ociosidad f. ~**r** /-ə(r)/ n ocioso m
idol /'aɪdl/ n ídolo m. ~**ize** vt idolatrar
idyllic /ɪ'dɪlɪk/ a idílico
i.e. /aɪ'iː/ abbr (id est) es decir
if /ɪf/ conj si
igloo /'ɪgluː/ n iglú m
ignite /ɪg'naɪt/ vt encender. ● vi encenderse
ignition /ɪg'nɪʃn/ n ignición f; (auto) encendido m. ~ **(switch)** n contacto m
ignoramus /ɪgnə'reɪməs/ n (pl -muses) ignorante
ignoran|ce /'ɪgnərəns/ n ignorancia f. ~**t** a ignorante. ~**tly** adv por ignorancia
ignore /ɪg'nɔː(r)/ vt no hacer caso de
ilk /ɪlk/ n ralea f
ill /ɪl/ a enfermo; (bad) malo. ~ **will** n mala voluntad f. ● adv mal. ~ **at**

ease inquieto. ● *n* mal *m*. ∼**advised** *a* imprudente. ∼**bred** *a* mal educado

illegal /ɪ'liːgl/ *a* ilegal

illegible /ɪ'ledʒəbl/ *a* ilegible

illegitima|cy /ɪlɪ'dʒɪtɪməsɪ/ *n* ilegitimidad *f*. ∼**te** *a* ilegítimo

ill: ∼**-fated** *a* malogrado. ∼**gotten** *a* mal adquirido

illitera|cy /ɪ'lɪtərəsɪ/ *n* analfabetismo *m*. ∼**te** *a* & *n* analfabeto (*m*)

ill: ∼**natured** *a* poco afable. ∼**ness** *n* enfermedad *f*

illogical /ɪ'lɒdʒɪkl/ *a* ilógico

ill: ∼**starred** *a* malogrado. ∼**treat** *vt* maltratar

illuminat|e /ɪ'luːmɪneɪt/ *vt* iluminar. ∼**ion** /-'neɪʃn/ *n* iluminación *f*

illus|ion /ɪ'luːʒn/ *n* ilusión *f*. ∼**sory** *a* ilusorio

illustrat|e /'ɪləstreɪt/ *vt* ilustrar. ∼**ion** *n* (*example*) ejemplo *m*; (*picture in book*) grabado *m*, lámina *f*. ∼**ive** *a* ilustrativo

illustrious /ɪ'lʌstrɪəs/ *a* ilustre

image /'ɪmɪdʒ/ *n* imagen *f*. ∼**ry** *n* imágenes *fpl*

imagin|able /ɪ'mædʒɪnəbl/ *a* imaginable. ∼**ary** *a* imaginario. ∼**ation** /-'neɪʃn/ *n* imaginación *f*. ∼**ative** *a* imaginativo. ∼**e** *vt* imaginar(se)

imbalance /ɪm'bæləns/ *n* desequilibrio *m*

imbecil|e /'ɪmbəsiːl/ *a* & *n* imbécil (*m* & *f*). ∼**ity** /-'sɪlətɪ/ *n* imbecilidad *f*

imbibe /ɪm'baɪb/ *vt* embeber; (*drink*) beber

imbue /ɪm'bjuː/ *vt* empapar (**with** de)

imitat|e /'ɪmɪteɪt/ *vt* imitar. ∼**ion** /-'teɪʃn/ *n* imitación *f*. ∼**or** *n* imitador *m*

immaculate /ɪ'mækjʊlət/ *a* inmaculado

immaterial /ɪmə'tɪərɪəl/ *a* inmaterial; (*unimportant*) insignificante

immature /ɪmə'tjʊə(r)/ *a* inmaduro

immediate /ɪ'miːdɪət/ *a* inmediato. ∼**ly** *adv* inmediatamente. ∼**ly you hear me** en cuanto me oigas. ● *conj* en cuanto (+ *subj*)

immens|e /ɪ'mens/ *a* inmenso. ∼**ely** *adv* inmensamente; (*very much*, *fam*) muchísimo. ∼**ity** *n* inmensidad *f*

immers|e /ɪ'mɜːs/ *vt* sumergir. ∼**ion** /ɪ'mɜːʃn/ *n* inmersión *f*. ∼**ion heater** *n* calentador *m* de inmersión

immigra|nt /'ɪmɪgrənt/ *a* & *n* inmigrante (*m* & *f*). ∼**te** *vi* inmigrar. ∼**tion** /-'greɪʃn/ *n* inmigración *f*

imminen|ce /'ɪmɪnəns/ *n* inminencia *f*. ∼**t** *a* inminente

immobil|e /ɪ'məʊbaɪl/ *a* inmóvil. ∼**ize** /-bɪlaɪz/ *vt* inmovilizar

immoderate /ɪ'mɒdərət/ *a* inmoderado

immodest /ɪ'mɒdɪst/ *a* inmodesto

immoral /ɪ'mɒrəl/ *a* inmoral. ∼**ity** /ɪmə'rælətɪ/ *n* inmoralidad *f*

immortal /ɪ'mɔːtl/ *a* inmortal. ∼**ity** /-'tælətɪ/ *n* inmortalidad *f*. ∼**ize** *vt* inmortalizar

immun|e /ɪ'mjuːn/ *a* inmune (**from**, **to** a, contra). ∼**ity** *n* inmunidad *f*. ∼**ization** /ɪmjʊnaɪ'zeɪʃn/ *n* inmunización *f*. ∼**ize** *vt* inmunizar

imp /ɪmp/ *n* diablillo *m*

impact /'ɪmpækt/ *n* impacto *m*

impair /ɪm'peə(r)/ *vt* perjudicar

impale /ɪm'peɪl/ *vt* empalar

impart /ɪm'pɑːt/ *vt* comunicar

impartial /ɪm'pɑːʃl/ *a* imparcial. ∼**ity** /-ɪ'ælətɪ/ *n* imparcialidad *f*

impassable /ɪm'pɑːsəbl/ *a* ‹*barrier etc*› infranqueable; ‹*road*› impracticable

impasse /æm'pɑːs/ *n* callejón *m* sin salida

impassioned /ɪm'pæʃnd/ *a* apasionado

impassive /ɪm'pæsɪv/ *a* impasible

impatien|ce /ɪm'peɪʃəns/ *n* impaciencia *f*. ∼**t** *a* impaciente. ∼**tly** *adv* con impaciencia

impeach /ɪm'piːtʃ/ *vt* acusar

impeccable /ɪm'pekəbl/ *a* impecable

impede /ɪm'piːd/ *vt* estorbar

impediment /ɪm'pedɪmənt/ *n* obstáculo *m*. (**speech**) ∼ *n* defecto *m* del habla

impel /ɪm'pel/ *vt* (*pt* **impelled**) impeler

impending /ɪm'pendɪŋ/ *a* inminente

impenetrable /ɪm'penɪtrəbl/ *a* impenetrable

imperative /ɪm'perətɪv/ *a* imprescindible. ● *n* (*gram*) imperativo *m*

imperceptible /ɪmpə'septəbl/ *a* imperceptible

imperfect /ɪm'pɜːfɪkt/ *a* imperfecto. ∼**ion** /ə-'fekʃn/ *n* imperfección *f*

imperial /ɪm'pɪərɪəl/ *a* imperial. ∼**ism** *n* imperialismo *m*

imperil /ɪmˈperəl/ *vt* (*pt* **imperilled**) poner en peligro

imperious /ɪmˈpɪərɪəs/ *a* imperioso

impersonal /ɪmˈpɜːsənl/ *a* impersonal

impersonat|e /ɪmˈpɜːsəneɪt/ *vt* hacerse pasar por; (*mimic*) imitar. **~ion** /-ˈneɪʃn/ *n* imitación *f*. **~or** *n* imitador *m*

impertinen|ce /ɪmˈpɜːtɪnəns/ *n* impertinencia *f*. **~t** *a* impertinente. **~tly** *adv* impertinentemente

impervious /ɪmˈpɜːvɪəs/ *a*. **~ to** impermeable a; (*fig*) insensible a

impetuous /ɪmˈpetjʊəs/ *a* impetuoso

impetus /ˈɪmpɪtəs/ *n* ímpetu *m*

impinge /ɪmˈpɪndʒ/ *vi*. **~ on** afectar a

impish /ˈɪmpɪʃ/ *a* travieso

implacable /ɪmˈplækəbl/ *a* implacable

implant /ɪmˈplɑːnt/ *vt* implantar

implement /ˈɪmplɪmənt/ *n* herramienta *f*. /ˈɪmplɪment/ *vt* realizar

implicat|e /ˈɪmplɪkeɪt/ *vt* implicar. **~ion** /-ˈkeɪʃn/ *n* implicación *f*

implicit /ɪmˈplɪsɪt/ *a* (*implied*) implícito; (*unquestioning*) absoluto

implied /ɪmˈplaɪd/ *a* implícito

implore /ɪmˈplɔː(r)/ *vt* implorar

imply /ɪmˈplaɪ/ *vt* implicar; (*mean*) querer decir; (*insinuate*) dar a entender

impolite /ɪmpəˈlaɪt/ *a* mal educado

imponderable /ɪmˈpɒndərəbl/ *a & n* imponderable (*m*)

import /ɪmˈpɔːt/ *vt* importar. /ˈɪmpɔːt/ *n* (*article*) importación *f*; (*meaning*) significación *f*

importan|ce /ɪmˈpɔːtəns/ *n* importancia *f*. **~t** *a* importante

importation /ɪmpɔːˈteɪʃn/ *n* importación *f*

importer /ɪmˈpɔːtə(r)/ *n* importador *m*

impose /ɪmˈpəʊz/ *vt* imponer. ● *vi*. **~ on** abusar de la amabilidad de

imposing /ɪmˈpəʊzɪŋ/ *a* imponente

imposition /ɪmpəˈzɪʃn/ *n* imposición *f*; (*fig*) molestia *f*

impossib|ility /ɪmpɒsəˈbɪlətɪ/ *n* imposibilidad *f*. **~le** *a* imposible

impostor /ɪmˈpɒstə(r)/ *n* impostor *m*

impoten|ce /ˈɪmpətəns/ *n* impotencia *f*. **~t** *a* impotente

impound /ɪmˈpaʊnd/ *vt* confiscar

impoverish /ɪmˈpɒvərɪʃ/ *vt* empobrecer

impracticable /ɪmˈpræktɪkəbl/ *a* impracticable

impractical /ɪmˈpræktɪkl/ *a* poco práctico

imprecise /ɪmprɪˈsaɪs/ *a* impreciso

impregnable /ɪmˈpregnəbl/ *a* inexpugnable

impregnate /ˈɪmpregneɪt/ *vt* impregnar (**with** de)

impresario /ɪmprɪˈsɑːrɪəʊ/ *n* (*pl* **-os**) empresario *m*

impress /ɪmˈpres/ *vt* impresionar; (*imprint*) imprimir. **~ on s.o.** hacer entender a uno

impression /ɪmˈpreʃn/ *n* impresión *f*. **~able** *a* impresionable

impressive /ɪmˈpresɪv/ *a* impresionante

imprint /ˈɪmprɪnt/ *n* impresión *f*. /ɪmˈprɪnt/ *vt* imprimir

imprison /ɪmˈprɪzn/ *vt* encarcelar. **~ment** *n* encarcelamiento *m*

improbab|ility /ɪmprɒbəˈbɪlətɪ/ *n* improbabilidad *f*. **~le** *a* improbable

impromptu /ɪmˈprɒmptjuː/ *a* improvisado. ● *adv* de improviso

improper /ɪmˈprɒpə(r)/ *a* impropio; (*incorrect*) incorrecto

impropriety /ɪmprəˈpraɪətɪ/ *n* inconveniencia *f*

improve /ɪmˈpruːv/ *vt* mejorar. ● *vi* mejorar(se). **~ment** *n* mejora *f*

improvis|ation /ɪmprəvaɪˈzeɪʃn/ *n* improvisación *f*. **~e** *vt/i* improvisar

imprudent /ɪmˈpruːdənt/ *a* imprudente

impuden|ce /ˈɪmpjʊdəns/ *n* insolencia *f*. **~t** *a* insolente

impulse /ˈɪmpʌls/ *n* impulso *m*. **on ~** sin reflexionar

impulsive /ɪmˈpʌlsɪv/ *a* irreflexivo. **~ly** *adv* sin reflexionar

impunity /ɪmˈpjuːnɪtɪ/ *n* impunidad *f*. **with ~** impunemente

impur|e /ɪmˈpjʊə(r)/ *a* impuro. **~ity** *n* impureza *f*

impute /ɪmˈpjuːt/ *vt* imputar

in /ɪn/ *prep* en, dentro de. **~ a firm manner** de una manera terminante. **~ an hour('s time)** dentro de una hora. **~ doing** al hacer. **~ so far as** en cuanto que. **~ the evening** por la tarde. **~ the main** por la mayor parte. **~ the rain** bajo la lluvia. **~ the sun** al sol. **one ~ ten** uno de cada diez. **the best ~** el mejor de. ● *adv* (*inside*) dentro; (*at home*) en casa; (*in fashion*) de moda. ● *n.* the ~s and outs of los detalles *mpl* de

inability /ɪnə'bɪlətɪ/ *n* incapacidad *f*

inaccessible /ɪnæk'sesəbl/ *a* inaccesible

inaccura|cy /ɪn'ækjʊrəsɪ/ *n* inexactitud *f*. ~te *a* inexacto

inaction /ɪn'ækʃn/ *n* inacción *f*

inactiv|e /ɪn'æktɪv/ *a* inactivo. ~ity /-'tɪvətɪ/ *n* inactividad *f*

inadequa|cy /ɪn'ædɪkwəsɪ/ *n* insuficiencia *f*. ~te *a* insuficiente

inadmissible /ɪnəd'mɪsəbl/ *a* inadmisible

inadvertently /ɪnəd'vɜ:təntlɪ/ *adv* por descuido

inadvisable /ɪnəd'vaɪzəbl/ *a* no aconsejable

inane /ɪ'neɪn/ *a* estúpido

inanimate /ɪn'ænɪmət/ *a* inanimado

inappropriate /ɪnə'prəʊprɪət/ *a* inoportuno

inarticulate /ɪnɑ:'tɪkjʊlət/ *a* incapaz de expresarse claramente

inasmuch as /ɪnəz'mʌtʃəz/ *adv* ya que

inattentive /ɪnə'tentɪv/ *a* desatento

inaudible /ɪn'ɔ:dəbl/ *a* inaudible

inaugural /ɪ'nɔ:gjʊrəl/ *a* inaugural

inaugurat|e /ɪ'nɔ:gjʊreɪt/ *vt* inaugurar. ~ion /-'reɪʃn/ *n* inauguración *f*

inauspicious /ɪnɔ:'spɪʃəs/ *a* poco propicio

inborn /'ɪnbɔ:n/ *a* innato

inbred /ɪn'bred/ *a* (*inborn*) innato

incalculable /ɪn'kælkjʊləbl/ *a* incalculable

incapab|ility /ɪnkeɪpə'bɪlətɪ/ *n* incapacidad *f*. ~le *a* incapaz

incapacit|ate /ɪnkə'pæsɪteɪt/ *vt* incapacitar. ~y *n* incapacidad *f*

incarcerat|e /ɪn'kɑ:səreɪt/ *vt* encarcelar. ~ion /-'reɪʃn/ *n* encarcelamiento *m*

incarnat|e /ɪn'kɑ:nət/ *a* encarnado. ~ion /-'neɪʃn/ *n* encarnación *f*

incautious /ɪn'kɔ:ʃəs/ *a* incauto. ~ly *adv* incautamente

incendiary /ɪn'sendɪərɪ/ *a* incendiario. ● *n* (*person*) incendiario *m*; (*bomb*) bomba *f* incendiaria

incense[1] /'ɪnsens/ *n* incienso *m*

incense[2] /ɪn'sens/ *vt* enfurecer

incentive /ɪn'sentɪv/ *n* incentivo *m*; (*payment*) prima *f* de incentivo

inception /ɪn'sepʃn/ *n* principio *m*

incertitude /ɪn'sɜ:tɪtju:d/ *n* incertidumbre *f*

incessant /ɪn'sesnt/ *a* incesante. ~ly *adv* sin cesar

incest /'ɪnsest/ *n* incesto *m*. ~uous /-'sestjʊəs/ *a* incestuoso

inch /ɪntʃ/ *n* pulgada *f* (= 2,54cm). ● *vi* avanzar palmo a palmo

incidence /'ɪnsɪdəns/ *n* frecuencia *f*

incident /'ɪnsɪdənt/ *n* incidente *m*

incidental /ɪnsɪ'dentl/ *a* fortuito. ~ly *adv* incidentemente; (*by the way*) a propósito

incinerat|e /ɪn'sɪnəreɪt/ *vt* incinerar. ~or *n* incinerador *m*

incipient /ɪn'sɪpɪənt/ *a* incipiente

incision /ɪn'sɪʒn/ *n* incisión *f*

incisive /ɪn'saɪsɪv/ *a* incisivo

incite /ɪn'saɪt/ *vt* incitar. ~ment *n* incitación *f*

inclement /ɪn'klemənt/ *a* inclemente

inclination /ɪnklɪ'neɪʃn/ *n* inclinación *f*

incline[1] /ɪn'klaɪn/ *vt* inclinar. ● *vi* inclinarse. be ~d to tener tendencia a

incline[2] /'ɪnklaɪn/ *n* cuesta *f*

inclu|de /ɪn'klu:d/ *vt* incluir. ~ding *prep* incluso. ~sion /-ʒn/ *n* inclusión *f*

inclusive /ɪn'klu:sɪv/ *a* inclusivo. be ~ of incluir. ● *adv* inclusive

incognito /ɪnkɒg'ni:təʊ/ *adv* de incógnito

incoherent /ɪnkəʊ'hɪərənt/ *a* incoherente

income /'ɪnkʌm/ *n* ingresos *mpl*. ~ tax *n* impuesto *m* sobre la renta

incoming /'ɪnkʌmɪŋ/ *a* (*tide*) ascendente; (*tenant etc*) nuevo

incomparable /ɪn'kɒmpərəbl/ *a* incomparable

incompatible /ɪnkəm'pætəbl/ *a* incompatible

incompeten|ce /ɪn'kɒmpɪtəns/ *n* incompetencia *f*. ~t *a* incompetente

incomplete /ɪnkəm'pli:t/ *a* incompleto

incomprehensible /ɪnkɒmprɪ'hensəbl/ *a* incomprensible

inconceivable /ɪnkən'si:vəbl/ *a* inconcebible

inconclusive /ɪnkən'klu:sɪv/ *a* poco concluyente

incongruous /ɪn'kɒngrʊəs/ *a* incongruente

inconsequential /ɪnkɒnsɪ'kwenʃl/ *a* sin importancia

inconsiderate /ɪnkən'sɪdərət/ *a* desconsiderado

inconsisten|cy /ɪnkən'sɪstənsɪ/ *n* inconsecuencia *f*. ∼**t** *a* inconsecuente. **be** ∼**t with** no concordar con

inconspicuous /ɪnkən'spɪkjʊəs/ *a* que no llama la atención. ∼**ly** *adv* sin llamar la atención

incontinen|ce /ɪn'kɒntɪnəns/ *a* incontinencia *f*. ∼**t** *a* incontinente

inconvenien|ce /ɪnkən'viːnɪəns/ *n* incomodidad *f*; (*drawback*) inconveniente *m*. ∼**t** *a* incómodo; (*time*) inoportuno

incorporat|e /ɪn'kɔːpəreɪt/ *vt* incorporar; (*include*) incluir. ∼**ion** /-'reɪʃn/ *n* incorporación *f*

incorrect /ɪnkə'rekt/ *a* incorrecto

incorrigible /ɪn'kɒrɪdʒəbl/ *a* incorregible

incorruptible /ɪnkə'rʌptəbl/ *a* incorruptible

increase /'ɪnkriːs/ *n* aumento *m* (**in**, **of** de). /ɪn'kriːs/ *vt/i* aumentar

increasing /ɪn'kriːsɪŋ/ *a* creciente. ∼**ly** *adv* cada vez más

incredible /ɪn'kredəbl/ *a* increíble

incredulous /ɪn'kredjʊləs/ *a* incrédulo

increment /'ɪnkrɪmənt/ *n* aumento *m*

incriminat|e /ɪn'krɪmɪneɪt/ *vt* acriminar. ∼**ing** *a* acriminador

incubat|e /'ɪŋkjʊbeɪt/ *vt* incubar. ∼**ion** /-'beɪʃn/ *n* incubación *f*. ∼**or** *n* incubadora *f*

inculcate /'ɪnkʌlkeɪt/ *vt* inculcar

incumbent /ɪn'kʌmbənt/ *n* titular. ● *a*. **be** ∼ **on** incumbir a

incur /ɪn'kɜː(r)/ *vt* (*pt* **incurred**) incurrir en; contraer (*debts*)

incurable /ɪn'kjʊərəbl/ *a* incurable

incursion /ɪn'kɜːʃn/ *n* incursión *f*

indebted /ɪn'detɪd/ *a*. ∼ **to s.o.** estar en deuda con uno

indecen|cy /ɪn'diːsnsɪ/ *n* indecencia *f*. ∼**t** *a* indecente

indecisi|on /ɪndɪ'sɪʒn/ *n* indecisión *f*. ∼**ve** /ɪndɪ'saɪsɪv/ *a* indeciso

indeed /ɪn'diːd/ *adv* en efecto; (*really?*) ¿de veras?

indefatigable /ɪndɪ'fætɪgəbl/ *a* incansable

indefinable /ɪndɪ'faɪnəbl/ *a* indefinible

indefinite /ɪn'defɪnət/ *a* indefinido. ∼**ly** *adv* indefinidamente

indelible /ɪn'delɪbl/ *a* indeleble

indemni|fy /ɪn'demnɪfaɪ/ *vt* indemnizar. ∼**ty** /-ətɪ/ *n* indemnización *f*

indent /ɪn'dent/ *vt* endentar (*text*). ∼**ation** /-'teɪʃn/ *n* mella *f*

independen|ce /ɪndɪ'pendəns/ *n* independencia *f*. ∼**t** *a* independiente. ∼**tly** *adv* independientemente. ∼**tly of** independientemente de

indescribable /ɪndɪ'skraɪbəbl/ *a* indescriptible

indestructible /ɪndɪ'strʌktəbl/ *a* indestructible

indeterminate /ɪndɪ'tɜːmɪnət/ *a* indeterminado

index /'ɪndeks/ *n* (*pl* **indexes**) índice *m*. ● *vt* poner índice a; (*enter in the/ an index*) poner en el/un índice. ∼ **finger** *n* (dedo *m*) índice *m*. ∼**linked** *a* indexado

India /'ɪndɪə/ *n* la India *f*. ∼**n** *a* & *n* indio (*m*). ∼**n summer** *n* veranillo *m* de San Martín

indicat|e /'ɪndɪkeɪt/ *vt* indicar. ∼**ion** /-'keɪʃn/ *n* indicación *f*. ∼**ive** /ɪn'dɪkətɪv/ *a* & *n* indicativo (*m*). ∼**or** /'ɪndɪkeɪtə(r)/ *n* indicador *m*

indict /ɪn'daɪt/ *vt* acusar. ∼**ment** *n* acusación *f*

indifferen|ce /ɪn'dɪfrəns/ *n* indiferencia *f*. ∼**t** *a* indiferente; (*not good*) mediocre

indigenous /ɪn'dɪdʒɪnəs/ *a* indígena

indigesti|ble /ɪndɪ'dʒestəbl/ *a* indigesto. ∼**on** /-tʃən/ *n* indigestión *f*

indigna|nt /ɪn'dɪgnənt/ *a* indignado. ∼**tion** /-'neɪʃn/ *n* indignación *f*

indignity /ɪn'dɪgnətɪ/ *n* indignidad *f*

indigo /'ɪndɪgəʊ/ *n* añil (*m*)

indirect /ɪndɪ'rekt/ *a* indirecto. ∼**ly** *adv* indirectamente

indiscre|et /ɪndɪ'skriːt/ *a* indiscreto. ∼**tion** /-'kreʃn/ *n* indiscreción *f*

indiscriminate /ɪndɪ'skrɪmɪnət/ *a* indistinto. ∼**ly** *adv* indistintamente

indispensable /ɪndɪ'spensəbl/ *a* imprescindible

indispos|ed /ɪndɪ'spəʊzd/ *a* indispuesto. ∼**ition** /-ə'zɪʃn/ *n* indisposición *f*

indisputable /ɪndɪ'spjuːtəbl/ *a* indiscutible

indissoluble /ɪndɪ'sɒljʊbl/ *a* indisoluble

indistinct /ɪndɪ'stɪŋkt/ *a* indistinto

indistinguishable /ɪndɪ'stɪŋgwɪʃəbl/ *a* indistinguible

individual /ɪndɪ'vɪdjʊəl/ *a* individual. ● *n* individuo *m*. ∼**ist** *n* individualista *m* & *f*. ∼**ity** *n* individualidad *f.* **~ly** *adv* individualmente

indivisible /ˌɪndɪ'vɪzəbl/ *a* indivisible

Indo-China /ˌɪndəʊ'tʃaɪnə/ *n* Indo-china *f*

indoctrinat|e /ɪn'dɒktrɪneɪt/ *vt* adoctrinar. **~ion** /-'neɪʃn/ *n* adoctrinamiento *m*

indolen|ce /'ɪndələns/ *n* indolencia *f*. **~t** *a* indolente

indomitable /ɪn'dɒmɪtəbl/ *a* indomable

Indonesia /ˌɪndəʊ'niːzɪə/ *n* Indonesia *f*. **~n** *a & n* indonesio (*m*)

indoor /'ɪndɔː(r)/ *a* interior; ⟨*clothes etc*⟩ de casa; (*covered*) cubierto. **~s** *adv* dentro; (*at home*) en casa

induce /ɪn'djuːs/ *vt* inducir; (*cause*) provocar. **~ment** *n* incentivo *m*

induct /ɪn'dʌkt/ *vt* instalar; (*mil, Amer*) incorporar

indulge /ɪn'dʌldʒ/ *vt* satisfacer ⟨*desires*⟩; complacer ⟨*person*⟩. ● *vi.* **~ in** entregarse a. **~nce** /ɪn'dʌldʒəns/ *n* (*of desires*) satisfacción *f*; (*relig*) indulgencia *f*. **~nt** *a* indulgente

industrial /ɪn'dʌstrɪəl/ *a* industrial; ⟨*unrest*⟩ laboral. **~ist** *n* industrial *m & f*. **~ized** *a* industrializado

industrious /ɪn'dʌstrɪəs/ *a* trabajador

industry /'ɪndəstrɪ/ *n* industria *f*; (*zeal*) aplicación *f*

inebriated /ɪ'niːbrɪeɪtɪd/ *a* borracho

inedible /ɪn'edɪbl/ *a* incomible

ineffable /ɪn'efəbl/ *a* inefable

ineffective /ˌɪnɪ'fektɪv/ *a* ineficaz; ⟨*person*⟩ incapaz

ineffectual /ˌɪnɪ'fektjʊəl/ *a* ineficaz

inefficien|cy /ˌɪnɪ'fɪʃnsɪ/ *n* ineficacia *f*; (*of person*) incompetencia *f*. **~t** *a* ineficaz; ⟨*person*⟩ incompetente

ineligible /ɪn'elɪdʒəbl/ *a* inelegible. **be ~ for** no tener derecho a

inept /ɪ'nept/ *a* inepto

inequality /ˌɪnɪ'kwɒlətɪ/ *n* desigualdad *f*

inert /ɪ'nɜːt/ *a* inerte

inertia /ɪ'nɜːʃə/ *n* inercia *f*

inescapable /ˌɪnɪ'skeɪpəbl/ *a* ineludible

inestimable /ɪn'estɪməbl/ *a* inestimable

inevitabl|e /ɪn'evɪtəbl/ *a* inevitable. **~ly** *adv* inevitablemente

inexact /ˌɪnɪg'zækt/ *a* inexacto

inexcusable /ˌɪnɪk'skjuːsəbl/ *a* imperdonable

inexhaustible /ˌɪnɪg'zɔːstəbl/ *a* inagotable

inexorable /ɪn'eksərəbl/ *a* inexorable

inexpensive /ˌɪnɪk'spensɪv/ *a* económico, barato

inexperience /ˌɪnɪk'spɪərɪəns/ *n* falta *f* de experiencia. **~d** *a* inexperto

inexplicable /ˌɪnɪk'splɪkəbl/ *a* inexplicable

inextricable /ˌɪnɪk'strɪkəbl/ *a* inextricable

infallib|ility /ɪn'fæləbɪlətɪ/ *n* infalibilidad *f*. **~le** *a* infalible

infam|ous /'ɪnfəməs/ *a* infame. **~y** *n* infamia *f*

infan|cy /'ɪnfənsɪ/ *n* infancia *f*. **~t** *n* niño *m*. **~tile** /'ɪnfəntaɪl/ *a* infantil

infantry /'ɪnfəntrɪ/ *n* infantería *f*

infatuat|ed /ɪn'fætjʊeɪtɪd/ *a.* **be ~ed with** encapricharse por. **~ion** /-'eɪʃn/ *n* encaprichamiento *m*

infect /ɪn'fekt/ *vt* infectar; (*fig*) contagiar. **~ s.o. with** contagiar a uno. **~ion** /-'fekʃn/ *n* infección *f*; (*fig*) contagio *m*. **~ious** /ɪn'fekʃəs/ *a* contagioso

infer /ɪn'fɜː(r)/ *vt* (*pt* inferred) deducir. **~ence** /'ɪnfərəns/ *n* deducción *f*

inferior /ɪn'fɪərɪə(r)/ *a* inferior. ● *n* inferior *m & f*. **~ity** /-'ɒrətɪ/ *n* inferioridad *f*

infernal /ɪn'fɜːnl/ *a* infernal. **~ly** *adv* (*fam*) atrozmente

inferno /ɪn'fɜːnəʊ/ *n* (*pl* **-os**) infierno *m*

infertil|e /ɪn'fɜːtaɪl/ *a* estéril. **~ity** /-'tɪlətɪ/ *n* esterilidad *f*

infest /ɪn'fest/ *vt* infestar. **~ation** /-'steɪʃn/ *n* infestación *f*

infidelity /ˌɪnfɪ'delətɪ/ *n* infidelidad *f*

infighting /'ɪnfaɪtɪŋ/ *n* lucha *f* cuerpo a cuerpo; (*fig*) riñas *fpl* (internas)

infiltrat|e /ɪnfɪl'treɪt/ *vt* infiltrar. ● *vi* infiltrarse. **~ion** /-'treɪʃn/ *n* infiltración *f*

infinite /ɪn'fɪnət/ *a* infinito. **~ly** *adv* infinitamente

infinitesimal /ˌɪnfɪnɪ'tesɪml/ *a* infinitesimal

infinitive /ɪn'fɪnɪtɪv/ *n* infinitivo *m*

infinity /ɪn'fɪnɪtɪ/ *n* (*infinite distance*) infinito *m*; (*infinite quantity*) infinidad *f*

infirm /ɪn'fɜːm/ *a* enfermizo

infirmary /ɪn'fɜːmərɪ/ *n* hospital *m*; (*sick bay*) enfermería *f*

infirmity /ɪnˈfɜːmətɪ/ n enfermedad f; (weakness) debilidad f

inflam|e /ɪnˈfleɪm/ vt inflamar. **~mable** /ɪnˈflæməbl/ a inflamable. **~mation** /-əˈmeɪʃn/ n inflamación f. **~matory** /ɪnˈflæmətərɪ/ a inflamatorio

inflate /ɪnˈfleɪt/ vt inflar

inflation /ɪnˈfleɪʃn/ n inflación f. **~ary** a inflacionario

inflection /ɪnˈflekʃn/ n inflexión f

inflexible /ɪnˈfleksəbl/ a inflexible

inflict /ɪnˈflɪkt/ vt infligir (**on** a)

inflow /ˈɪnfləʊ/ n afluencia f

influence /ˈɪnfluəns/ n influencia f. **under the ~** (drunk, fam) borracho. ● vt influir, influenciar (esp LAm)

influential /ɪnfluˈenʃl/ a influyente

influenza /ɪnfluˈenzə/ n gripe f

influx /ˈɪnflʌks/ n afluencia f

inform /ɪnˈfɔːm/ vt informar. **keep ~ed** tener al corriente

informal /ɪnˈfɔːml/ a (simple) sencillo, sin ceremonia; (unofficial) oficioso. **~ity** /ˈmælətɪ/ n falta f de ceremonia. **~ly** adv sin ceremonia

inform|ant /ɪnˈfɔːmənt/ n informador m. **~ation** /ɪnfəˈmeɪʃn/ n información f. **~ative** /ɪnˈfɔːmətɪv/ a informativo. **~er** /ɪnˈfɔːmə(r)/ n denunciante m

infra-red /ɪnfrəˈred/ a infrarrojo

infrequent /ɪnˈfriːkwənt/ a poco frecuente. **~ly** adv raramente

infringe /ɪnˈfrɪndʒ/ vt infringir. **~ on** usurpar. **~ment** n infracción f

infuriate /ɪnˈfjʊərɪeɪt/ vt enfurecer

infus|e /ɪnˈfjuːz/ vt infundir. **~ion** /-ʒn/ n infusión f

ingen|ious /ɪnˈdʒiːnɪəs/ a ingenioso. **~uity** /ɪndʒɪˈnjuːətɪ/ n ingeniosidad f

ingenuous /ɪnˈdʒenjʊəs/ a ingenuo

ingest /ɪnˈdʒest/ vt ingerir

ingot /ˈɪŋɡət/ n lingote m

ingrained /ɪnˈɡreɪnd/ a arraigado

ingratiate /ɪnˈɡreɪʃɪeɪt/ vt. **~ o.s. with** congraciarse con

ingratitude /ɪnˈɡrætɪtjuːd/ n ingratitud f

ingredient /ɪnˈɡriːdɪənt/ n ingrediente m

ingrowing /ˈɪnɡrəʊɪŋ/ a. **~ nail** uñero m, uña f encarnada

inhabit /ɪnˈhæbɪt/ vt habitar. **~able** a habitable. **~ant** n habitante m

inhale /ɪnˈheɪl/ vt aspirar. ● vi (tobacco) aspirar el humo

inherent /ɪnˈhɪərənt/ a inherente. **~ly** adv intrínsecamente

inherit /ɪnˈherɪt/ vt heredar. **~ance** n herencia f

inhibit /ɪnˈhɪbɪt/ vt inhibir. **be ~ed** tener inhibiciones. **~ion** /-ˈbɪʃn/ n inhibición f

inhospitable /ɪnhəˈspɪtəbl/ a ⟨place⟩ inhóspito; ⟨person⟩ inhospitalario

inhuman /ɪnˈhjuːmən/ a inhumano. **~e** /ɪnhjuːˈmeɪn/ a inhumano. **~ity** /ɪnhjuːˈmænətɪ/ n inhumanidad f

inimical /ɪˈnɪmɪkl/ a hostil

inimitable /ɪˈnɪmɪtəbl/ a inimitable

iniquit|ous /ɪˈnɪkwɪtəs/ a inicuo. **~y** /-ətɪ/ n iniquidad f

initial /ɪˈnɪʃl/ n inicial f. ● vt (pt **initialled**) firmar con iniciales. **he ~led the document** firmó el documento con sus iniciales. ● a inicial. **~ly** adv al principio

initiat|e /ɪˈnɪʃɪeɪt/ vt iniciar; promover ⟨scheme etc⟩. **~ion** /-ˈeɪʃn/ n iniciación f

initiative /ɪˈnɪʃətɪv/ n iniciativa f

inject /ɪnˈdʒekt/ vt inyectar; (fig) injertar ⟨new element⟩. **~ion** /-ʃn/ n inyección f

injunction /ɪnˈdʒʌŋkʃn/ n (court order) entredicho m

injur|e /ˈɪndʒə(r)/ vt (wound) herir; (fig, damage) perjudicar. **~y** /ˈɪndʒərɪ/ n herida f; (damage) perjuicio m

injustice /ɪnˈdʒʌstɪs/ n injusticia f

ink /ɪŋk/ n tinta f

inkling /ˈɪŋklɪŋ/ n atisbo m

ink: ~well n tintero m. **~y** a manchado de tinta

inland /ˈɪnlənd/ a interior. ● adv tierra adentro. **I~ Revenue** n Hacienda f

in-laws /ˈɪnlɔːz/ npl parientes mpl políticos

inlay /ɪnˈleɪ/ vt (pt **inlaid**) taracear, incrustar. /ˈɪnleɪ/ n taracea f, incrustación f

inlet /ˈɪnlet/ n ensenada f; (tec) entrada f

inmate /ˈɪnmeɪt/ n (of asylum) internado m; (of prison) preso m

inn /ɪn/ n posada f

innards /ˈɪnədz/ npl tripas fpl

innate /ɪˈneɪt/ a innato

inner /ˈɪnə(r)/ a interior; (fig) íntimo. **~most** a más íntimo. **~ tube** n cámara f de aire, llanta f (LAm)

innings /ˈɪnɪŋz/ n invar turno m

innkeeper /ˈɪnkiːpə(r)/ n posadero m

innocen|ce /'ɪnəsns/ n inocencia f.
~**t** a & n inocente (m & f)

innocuous /ɪ'nɒkjʊəs/ a inocuo

innovat|e /'ɪnəveɪt/ vi innovar.
~**ion** /-'veɪʃn/ n innovación f. ~**or** n
innovador m

innuendo /ɪnju:'endəʊ/ n (pl -oes)
insinuación f

innumerable /ɪ'nju:mərəbl/ a innumerable

inoculat|e /ɪ'nɒkjʊleɪt/ vt inocular.
~**ion** /-'leɪʃn/ n inoculación f

inoffensive /ɪnə'fensɪv/ a inofensivo

inoperative /ɪn'ɒpərətɪv/ a inop-
erante

inopportune /ɪn'ɒpətjuːn/ a inoportuno

inordinate /ɪ'nɔːdɪnət/ a excesivo.
~**ly** adv excesivamente

in-patient /'ɪnpeɪʃnt/ n paciente m
interno

input /'ɪnpʊt/ n (data) datos mpl;
(comput process) entrada f, input m;
(elec) energía f

inquest /'ɪnkwest/ n investigación f
judicial

inquir|e /ɪn'kwaɪə(r)/ vi preguntar.
~**y** n (question) pregunta f; (invest-
igation) investigación f

inquisition /ɪnkwɪ'zɪʃn/ n inqui-
sición f

inquisitive /ɪn'kwɪzətɪv/ a inquis-
itivo

inroad /'ɪnrəʊd/ n incursión f

inrush /'ɪnrʌʃ/ n irrupción f

insan|e /ɪn'seɪn/ a loco. ~**ity**
/-'sænətɪ/ n locura f

insanitary /ɪn'sænɪtərɪ/ a insalubre

insatiable /ɪn'seɪʃəbl/ a insaciable

inscri|be /ɪn'skraɪb/ vt inscribir;
dedicar ⟨book⟩. ~**ption** /-ɪpʃn/ n
inscripción f; (in book) dedicatoria f

inscrutable /ɪn'skruːtəbl/ a
inescrutable

insect /'ɪnsekt/ n insecto m. ~**icide**
/ɪn'sektɪsaɪd/ n insecticida f

insecur|e /ɪnsɪ'kjʊə(r)/ a inseguro.
~**ity** n inseguridad f

insemination /ɪnsemɪ'neɪʃn/ n inse-
minación f

insensible /ɪn'sensəbl/ a insensible;
(unconscious) sin conocimiento

insensitive /ɪn'sensətɪv/ a insensible

inseparable /ɪn'sepərəbl/ a inseparable

insert /'ɪnsɜːt/ n materia f insertada.
/ɪn'sɜːt/ vt insertar. ~**ion** /-ʃn/ n
inserción f

inshore /ɪn'ʃɔː(r)/ a costero

inside /ɪn'saɪd/ n interior m. ~ **out**
al revés; (thoroughly) a fondo. ● a
interior. ● adv dentro. ● prep
dentro de. ~**s** npl tripas fpl

insidious /ɪn'sɪdɪəs/ a insidioso

insight /'ɪnsaɪt/ n (perception) pene-
tración f, revelación f

insignia /ɪn'sɪgnɪə/ npl insignias fpl

insignificant /ɪnsɪg'nɪfɪkənt/ a insignificante

insincer|e /ɪnsɪn'sɪə(r)/ a poco
sincero. ~**ity** /-'serətɪ/ n falta f de
sinceridad f

insinuat|e /ɪn'sɪnjʊeɪt/ vt insinuar.
~**ion** /-'eɪʃn/ n insinuación f

insipid /ɪn'sɪpɪd/ a insípido

insist /ɪn'sɪst/ vt/i insistir. ~ **on**
insistir en; (demand) exigir

insisten|ce /ɪn'sɪstəns/ n insistencia
f. ~**t** a insistente. ~**tly** adv con
insistencia

insolen|ce /'ɪnsələns/ n insolencia f.
~**t** a insolente

insoluble /ɪn'sɒljʊbl/ a insoluble

insolvent /ɪn'sɒlvənt/ a insolvente

insomnia /ɪn'sɒmnɪə/ n insomnio m.
~**c** /-ɪæk/ n insomne m & f

inspect /ɪn'spekt/ vt inspeccionar;
revisar ⟨ticket⟩. ~**ion** /-ʃn/ n inspección f. ~**or** n inspector m; (on train,
bus) revisor m

inspir|ation /ɪnspə'reɪʃn/ n inspi-
ración f. ~**e** /ɪn'spaɪə(r)/ vt inspirar

instability /ɪnstə'bɪlətɪ/ n ines-
tabilidad f

install /ɪn'stɔːl/ vt instalar. ~**ation**
/-ə'leɪʃn/ n instalación f

instalment /ɪn'stɔːlmənt/ n (payment) plazo m; (of serial) entrega f

instance /'ɪnstəns/ n ejemplo m;
(case) caso m. **for** ~ por ejemplo. **in
the first** ~ en primer lugar

instant /'ɪnstənt/ a inmediato;
⟨food⟩ instantáneo. ● n instante m.
~**aneous** /ɪnstən'teɪnɪəs/ a instantáneo. ~**ly** /'ɪnstəntlɪ/ adv inmediatamente

instead /ɪn'sted/ adv en cambio. ~
of doing en vez de hacer. ~ **of s.o.**
en lugar de uno

instep /'ɪnstep/ n empeine m

instigat|e /'ɪnstɪgeɪt/ vt instigar.
~**ion** /-'geɪʃn/ n instigación f. ~**or** n
instigador m

instil /ɪn'stɪl/ vt (pt **instilled**) in-
fundir

instinct /'ɪnstɪŋkt/ n instinto m.
~**ive** /ɪn'stɪŋktɪv/ a instintivo

institut|e /'ɪnstɪtjuːt/ n instituto m.
● vt instituir; iniciar ‹enquiry etc›.
~**ion** /-'tjuːʃn/ n institución f
instruct /ɪn'strʌkt/ vt instruir;
(order) mandar. ~ **s.o. in sth**
enseñar algo a uno. ~**ion** /-ʃn/ n
instrucción f. ~**ions** /-ʃnz/ npl (for
use) modo m de empleo. ~**ive** a
instructivo
instrument /'ɪnstrəmənt/ n instrumento m. ~**al** /ɪnstrə'mentl/ a
instrumental. **be ~al in** contribuir
a. ~**alist** n instrumentalista m & f
insubordinat|e /ɪnsə'bɔːdɪnət/ a
insubordinado. ~**ion** /-'neɪʃn/ n
insubordinación f
insufferable /ɪn'sʌfərəbl/ a insufrible, insoportable
insufficient /ɪnsə'fɪʃnt/ a insuficiente. ~**ly** adv insuficientemente
insular /'ɪnsjʊlə(r)/ a insular;
(narrow-minded) de miras
estrechas
insulat|e /'ɪnsjʊleɪt/ vt aislar. ~**ing
tape** n cinta f aisladora/aislante.
~**ion** /-'leɪʃn/ n aislamiento m
insulin /'ɪnsjʊlɪn/ n insulina f
insult /ɪn'sʌlt/ vt insultar. /'ɪnsʌlt/ n
insulto m
insuperable /ɪn'sjuːpərəbl/ a
insuperable
insur|ance /ɪn'ʃʊərəns/ n seguro m.
~**e** vt asegurar. ~**e that** asegurarse
de que
insurgent /ɪn'sɜːdʒənt/ a & n insur-
recto (m)
insurmountable /ɪnsə'maʊntəbl/ a
insuperable
insurrection /ɪnsə'rekʃn/ n in-
surrección f
intact /ɪn'tækt/ a intacto
intake /'ɪnteɪk/ n (quantity) número
m; (mec) admisión f; (of food) consumo m
intangible /ɪn'tændʒəbl/ a
intangible
integral /'ɪntɪgrəl/ a íntegro. **be an
~ part of** ser parte integrante de
integrat|e /'ɪntɪgreɪt/ vt integrar.
● vi integrarse. ~**ion** /-'greɪʃn/ n
integración f
integrity /ɪn'tegrətɪ/ n integridad f
intellect /'ɪntəlekt/ n intelecto m.
~**ual** a & n intelectual (m)
intelligen|ce /ɪn'telɪdʒəns/ n inte-
ligencia f; (information) información f. ~**t** a inteligente. ~**tly**

adv inteligentemente. ~**tsia**
/ɪntelɪ'dʒentsɪə/ n intelectualidad f
intelligible /ɪn'telɪdʒəbl/ a inteligible
intemperance /ɪn'tempərəns/ n in-
moderación f
intend /ɪn'tend/ vt destinar. ~ **to do**
tener la intención de hacer. ~**ed** a
intencionado. ● n (future spouse)
novio m
intense /ɪn'tens/ a intenso; ‹person›
apasionado. ~**ly** adv intensamente;
(very) sumamente
intensif|ication /ɪntensɪfɪ'keɪʃn/ n
intensificación f. ~**y** /-faɪ/ vt
intensificar
intensity /ɪn'tensətɪ/ n intensidad f
intensive /ɪn'tensɪv/ a intensivo. ~
care n asistencia f intensiva, cui-
dados mpl intensivos
intent /ɪn'tent/ n propósito m. ● a
atento. ~ **on** absorto en. ~ **on
doing** resuelto a hacer
intention /ɪn'tenʃn/ n intención f.
~**al** a intencional
intently /ɪn'tentlɪ/ adv atentamente
inter /ɪn'tɜː(r)/ vt (pt **interred**)
enterrar
inter... /ɪntə(r)/ pref inter..., entre...
interact /ɪntər'ækt/ vi obrar reci-
procamente. ~**ion** /-ʃn/ n interacción f
intercede /ɪntə'siːd/ vi interceder
intercept /ɪntə'sept/ vt interceptar.
~**ion** /-ʃn/ n interceptación f; (in
geometry) intersección f
interchange /'ɪntətʃeɪndʒ/ n (road
junction) cruce m. ~**able**
/-'tʃeɪndʒəbl/ a intercambiable
intercom /'ɪntəkɒm/ n inter-
comunicador m
interconnected /ɪntəkə'nektɪd/ a
relacionado
intercourse /'ɪntəkɔːs/ n trato m;
(sexual) trato m sexual
interest /'ɪntrest/ n interés m;
(advantage) ventaja f. ● vt inter-
esar. ~**ed** a interesado. **be ~ed in**
interesarse por. ~**ing** a interesante
interfere /ɪntə'fɪə(r)/ vi entrometerse. ~ **in** entrometerse en. ~
with entrometerse en, interferir en;
interferir ‹radio›. ~**nce** n inter-
ferencia f
interim a provisional. ● n. **in the ~**
entre tanto
interior /ɪn'tɪərɪə(r)/ a & n interior
(m)

interjection /ɪntə'dʒekʃn/ n interjección f

interlock /ɪntə'lɒk/ vt/i (tec) engranar

interloper /'ɪntələʊpə(r)/ n intruso m

interlude /'ɪntəluːd/ n intervalo m; (theatre, music) interludio m

intermarr|iage /ɪntə'mærɪdʒ/ n matrimonio m entre personas de distintas razas. ~y vi casarse (con personas de distintas razas)

intermediary /ɪntə'miːdɪərɪ/ a & n intermediario (m)

intermediate /ɪntə'miːdɪət/ a intermedio

interminable /ɪn'tɜːmɪnəbl/ a interminable

intermission /ɪntə'mɪʃn/ n pausa f; (theatre) descanso m

intermittent /ɪntə'mɪtnt/ a intermitente. ~ly adv con discontinuidad

intern /ɪn'tɜːn/ vt internar. /'ɪntɜːn/ n (doctor, Amer) interno m

internal /ɪn'tɜːnl/ a interior. ~ly adv interiormente

international /ɪntə'næʃnl/ a & n internacional (m)

internee /ˌɪntɜː'niː/ n internado m

internment /ɪn'tɜːnmənt/ n internamiento m

interplay /'ɪntəpleɪ/ n interacción f

interpolate /ɪn'tɜːpəleɪt/ vt interpolar

interpret /ɪn'tɜːprɪt/ vt/i interpretar. ~ation /-'teɪʃn/ n interpretación f. ~er n intérprete m & f

interrelated /ɪntərɪ'leɪtɪd/ a interrelacionado

interrogat|e /ɪn'terəgeɪt/ vt interrogar. ~ion /-'geɪʃn/ n interrogación f; (session of questions) interrogatorio m

interrogative /ɪntə'rɒgətɪv/ a & n interrogativo (m)

interrupt /ɪntə'rʌpt/ vt interrumpir. ~ion /-ʃn/ n interrupción f

intersect /ɪntə'sekt/ vt cruzar. ● vi (roads) cruzarse; (geometry) intersecarse. ~ion /-ʃn/ n (roads) cruce m; (geometry) intersección f

interspersed /ɪntə'spɜːst/ a disperso. ~ with salpicado de

intertwine /ɪntə'twaɪn/ vt entrelazar. ● vi entrelazarse

interval /'ɪntəvl/ n intervalo m; (theatre) descanso m. at ~s a intervalos

interven|e /ɪntə'viːn/ vi intervenir. ~tion /-'venʃn/ n intervención f

interview /'ɪntəvjuː/ n entrevista f. ● vt entrevistarse con. ~er n entrevistador m

intestin|al /ɪnte'staɪnl/ a intestinal. ~e /ɪn'testɪn/ n intestino m

intimacy /'ɪntɪməsɪ/ n intimidad f

intimate[1] /'ɪntɪmət/ a íntimo

intimate[2] /'ɪntɪmeɪt/ vt (state) anunciar; (imply) dar a entender

intimately /'ɪntɪmətlɪ/ adv íntimamente

intimidat|e /ɪn'tɪmɪdeɪt/ vt intimidar. ~ion /-'deɪʃn/ n intimidación f

into /'ɪntuː/, unstressed /'ɪntə/ prep en; (translate) a

intolerable /ɪn'tɒlərəbl/ a intolerable

intoleran|ce /ɪn'tɒlərəns/ n intolerancia f. ~t a intolerante

intonation /ɪntə'neɪʃn/ n entonación f

intoxicat|e /ɪn'tɒksɪkeɪt/ vt embriagar; (med) intoxicar. ~ed a ebrio. ~ion /-'keɪʃn/ n embriaguez f; (med) intoxicación f

intra... /'ɪntrə/ pref intra...

intractable /ɪn'træktəbl/ a (person) intratable; (thing) muy difícil

intransigent /ɪn'trænsɪdʒənt/ a intransigente

intransitive /ɪn'trænsɪtɪv/ a intransitivo

intravenous /ɪntrə'viːnəs/ a intravenoso

intrepid /ɪn'trepɪd/ a intrépido

intrica|cy /'ɪntrɪkəsɪ/ n complejidad f. ~te a complejo

intrigu|e /ɪn'triːg/ vt/i intrigar. ● n intriga f. ~ing a intrigante

intrinsic /ɪn'trɪnsɪk/ a intrínseco. ~ally adv intrínsecamente

introduc|e /ɪntrə'djuːs/ vt introducir; presentar (person). ~tion /ɪntrə'dʌkʃn/ n introducción f; (to person) presentación f. ~tory /-tərɪ/ a preliminar

introspective /ɪntrə'spektɪv/ a introspectivo

introvert /'ɪntrəvɜːt/ n introvertido m

intru|de /ɪn'truːd/ vi entrometerse; (disturb) molestar. ~der n intruso m. ~sion n intrusión f

intuiti|on /ɪntjuː'ɪʃn/ n intuición f. ~ve /ɪn'tjuːɪtɪv/ a intuitivo

inundat|e /'ɪnʌndeɪt/ *vt* inundar. **~ion** /-'deɪʃn/ *n* inundación *f*

invade /ɪn'veɪd/ *vt* invadir. **~r** /-ə(r)/ *n* invasor *m*

invalid¹ /'ɪnvəlɪd/ *n* enfermo *m*, inválido *m*

invalid² /ɪn'vælɪd/ *a* nulo. **~ate** *vt* invalidar

invaluable /ɪn'væljʊəbl/ *a* inestimable

invariabl|e /ɪn'veərɪəbl/ *a* invariable. **~y** *adv* invariablemente

invasion /ɪn'veɪʒn/ *n* invasión *f*

invective /ɪn'vektɪv/ *n* invectiva *f*

inveigh /ɪn'veɪ/ *vi* dirigir invectivas (**against** contra)

inveigle /ɪn'veɪgl/ *vt* engatusar, persuadir

invent /ɪn'vent/ *vt* inventar. **~ion** /-'venʃn/ *n* invención *f*. **~ive** *a* inventivo. **~or** *n* inventor *m*

inventory /'ɪnvəntərɪ/ *n* inventario *m*

invers|e /ɪn'vɜːs/ *a & n* inverso (*m*). **~ely** *adv* inversamente. **~ion** /ɪn'vɜːʃn/ *n* inversión *f*

invert /ɪn'vɜːt/ *vt* invertir. **~ed commas** *npl* comillas *fpl*

invest /ɪn'vest/ *vt* invertir. ● *vi.* **~ in** hacer una inversión *f*

investigat|e /ɪn'vestɪgeɪt/ *vt* investigar. **~ion** /-'geɪʃn/ *n* investigación *f*. **under ~ion** sometido a examen. **~or** *n* investigador *m*

inveterate /ɪn'vetərət/ *a* inveterado

invidious /ɪn'vɪdɪəs/ *a* (*hateful*) odioso; (*unfair*) injusto

invigilat|e /ɪn'vɪdʒɪleɪt/ *vi* vigilar. **~or** *n* celador *m*

invigorate /ɪn'vɪgəreɪt/ *vt* vigorizar; (*stimulate*) estimular

invincible /ɪn'vɪnsɪbl/ *a* invencible

invisible /ɪn'vɪzəbl/ *a* invisible

invit|ation /ɪnvɪ'teɪʃn/ *n* invitación *f*. **~e** /ɪn'vaɪt/ *vt* invitar; (*ask for*) pedir. **~ing** *a* atrayente

invoice /'ɪnvɔɪs/ *n* factura *f*. ● *vt* facturar

invoke /ɪn'vəʊk/ *vt* invocar

involuntary /ɪn'vɒləntərɪ/ *a* involuntario

involve /ɪn'vɒlv/ *vt* enredar. **~d** *a* (*complex*) complicado. **~d in** embrollado en. **~ment** *n* enredo *m*

invulnerable /ɪn'vʌlnərəbl/ *a* invulnerable

inward /'ɪnwəd/ *a* interior. ● *adv* interiormente. **~s** *adv* hacia/para dentro

iodine /'aɪədiːn/ *n* yodo *m*

iota /aɪ'əʊtə/ *n* (*amount*) pizca *f*

IOU /aɪəʊ'juː/ *abbr* (*I owe you*) pagaré *m*

IQ /aɪ'kjuː/ *abbr* (*intelligence quotient*) cociente *m* intelectual

Iran /ɪ'rɑːn/ *n* Irán *m*. **~ian** /ɪ'reɪnɪən/ *a & n* iraní (*m*)

Iraq /ɪ'rɑːk/ *n* Irak *m*. **~i** *a & n* iraquí (*m*)

irascible /ɪ'ræsəbl/ *a* irascible

irate /aɪ'reɪt/ *a* colérico

ire /aɪə(r)/ *n* ira *f*

Ireland /'aɪələnd/ *n* Irlanda *f*

iris /'aɪərɪs/ *n* (*anat*) iris *m*; (*bot*) lirio *m*

Irish /'aɪərɪʃ/ *a* irlandés. ● *n* (*lang*) irlandés *m*. **~man** *n* irlandés *m*. **~woman** *n* irlandesa *f*

irk /ɜːk/ *vt* fastidiar. **~some** *a* fastidioso

iron /'aɪən/ *n* hierro *m*; (*appliance*) plancha *f*. ● *a* de hierro. ● *vt* planchar. **~ out** allanar. **I~ Curtain** *n* telón *m* de acero

ironic(al) /aɪ'rɒnɪk(l)/ *a* irónico

ironing-board /'aɪənɪŋ'bɔːd/ *n* tabla *f* de planchar

ironmonger /'aɪənmʌŋgə(r)/ *n* ferretero *m*. **~y** *n* ferretería *f*

ironwork /'aɪənwɜːk/ *n* herraje *m*

irony /'aɪərənɪ/ *n* ironía *f*

irrational /ɪ'ræʃənl/ *a* irracional

irreconcilable /ɪrekən'saɪləbl/ *a* irreconciliable

irrefutable /ɪrɪ'fjuːtəbl/ *a* irrefutable

irregular /ɪ'regjʊlə(r)/ *a* irregular. **~ity** /-'lærətɪ/ *n* irregularidad *f*

irrelevan|ce /ɪ'reləvəns/ *n* inoportunidad *f*, impertinencia *f*. **~t** *a* no pertinente

irreparable /ɪ'repərəbl/ *a* irreparable

irreplaceable /ɪrɪ'pleɪsəbl/ *a* irreemplazable

irrepressible /ɪrɪ'presəbl/ *a* irreprimible

irresistible /ɪrɪ'zɪstəbl/ *a* irresistible

irresolute /ɪ'rezəluːt/ *a* irresoluto, indeciso

irrespective /ɪrɪ'spektɪv/ *a.* **~ of** sin tomar en cuenta

irresponsible /ɪrɪ'spɒnsəbl/ *a* irresponsable

irretrievable /ɪrɪ'triːvəbl/ *a* irrecuperable

irreverent /ɪ'revərənt/ *a* irreverente

irreversible /ɪrɪ'vɜːsəbl/ *a* irreversible; ⟨*decision*⟩ irrevocable

irrevocable /ɪ'revəkəbl/ *a* irrevocable

irrigat|e /'ɪrɪgeɪt/ *vt* regar; (*med*) irrigar. **~ion** /-'geɪʃn/ *n* riego *m*; (*med*) irrigación *f*

irritable /'ɪrɪtəbl/ *a* irritable

irritat|e /'ɪrɪteɪt/ *vt* irritar. **~ion** /-'teɪʃn/ *n* irritación *f*

is /ɪz/ *see* **be**

Islam /'ɪzlɑːm/ *n* Islam *m*. **~ic** /ɪz'læmɪk/ *a* islámico

island /'aɪlənd/ *n* isla *f*. **traffic ~** *n* refugio *m* (en la calle). **~er** *n* isleño *m*

isle /aɪl/ *n* isla *f*

isolat|e /'aɪsəleɪt/ *vt* aislar. **~ion** /-'leɪʃn/ *n* aislamiento *m*

isotope /'aɪsətəʊp/ *n* isotopo *m*

Israel /'ɪzreɪl/ *n* Israel *m*. **~i** /ɪz'reɪlɪ/ *a & n* israelí (*m*)

issue /'ɪʃuː/ *n* asunto *m*; (*outcome*) resultado *m*; (*of magazine etc*) número *m*; (*of stamps*) emisión *f*; (*offspring*) descendencia *f*. **at ~** en cuestión. **take ~ with** oponerse a. ● *vt* distribuir; emitir ⟨*stamps etc*⟩; publicar ⟨*book*⟩. ● *vi*. **~ from** salir de

isthmus /'ɪsməs/ *n* istmo *m*

it /ɪt/ *pron* (*subject*) el, ella, ello; (*direct object*) lo, la; (*indirect object*) le; (*after preposition*) él, ella, ello. **~ is hot** hace calor. **~ is me** soy yo. **far from ~** ni mucho menos. **that's ~** eso es. **who is ~?** ¿quién es?

italic /ɪ'tælɪk/ *a* bastardillo *m*. **~s** *npl* (letra *f*) bastardilla *f*

ital|ian /ɪ'tæljən/ *a & n* italiano (*m*). **I~y** /'ɪtəlɪ/ *n* Italia *f*

itch /ɪtʃ/ *n* picazón *f*. ● *vi* picar. **I'm ~ing to** rabio por. **my arm ~es** me pica el brazo. **~y** *a* que pica

item /'aɪtəm/ *n* artículo *m*; (*on agenda*) asunto *m*. **news ~** *n* noticia *f*. **~ize** *vt* detallar

itinerant /aɪ'tɪnərənt/ *a* ambulante

itinerary /aɪ'tɪnərərɪ/ *n* itinerario *m*

its /ɪts/ *a* su, sus (*pl*). ● *pron* (el) suyo *m*, (la) suya *f*, (los) suyos *mpl*, (las) suyas *fpl*

it's /ɪts/ = **it is, it has**

itself /ɪt'self/ *pron* él mismo, ella misma, ello mismo; (*reflexive*) se; (*after prep*) sí mismo, sí misma

ivory /'aɪvərɪ/ *n* marfil *m*. **~ tower** *n* torre *f* de marfil

ivy /'aɪvɪ/ *n* hiedra *f*

J

jab /dʒæb/ *vt* (*pt* **jabbed**) pinchar; (*thrust*) hurgonear. ● *n* pinchazo *m*

jabber /'dʒæbə(r)/ *vi* barbullar. ● *n* farfulla *f*

jack /dʒæk/ *n* (*mec*) gato *m*; (*cards*) sota *f*. ● *vt*. **~ up** alzar con gato

jackal /'dʒækl/ *n* chacal *m*

jackass /'dʒækæs/ *n* burro *m*

jackdaw /'dʒækdɔː/ *n* grajilla *f*

jacket /'dʒækɪt/ *n* chaqueta *f*, saco *m* (*LAm*); (*of book*) sobrecubierta *f*, camisa *f*

jack-knife /'dʒæknaɪf/ *n* navaja *f*

jackpot /'dʒækpɒt/ *n* premio *m* gordo. **hit the ~** sacar el premio gordo

jade /dʒeɪd/ *n* (*stone*) jade *m*

jaded /'dʒeɪdɪd/ *a* cansado

jagged /'dʒægɪd/ *a* dentado

jaguar /'dʒægjʊə(r)/ *n* jaguar *m*

jail /dʒeɪl/ *n* cárcel *m*. **~bird** *n* criminal *m* emperdernido. **~er** *n* carcelero *m*

jalopy /dʒə'lɒpɪ/ *n* cacharro *m*

jam¹ /dʒæm/ *vt* (*pt* **jammed**) interferir con ⟨*radio*⟩; ⟨*traffic*⟩ embotellar; ⟨*people*⟩ agolparse en. ● *vi* obstruirse; ⟨*mechanism etc*⟩ atascarse. ● *n* (*of people*) agolpamiento *m*; (*of traffic*) embotellamiento *m*; (*situation, fam*) apuro *m*

jam² /dʒæm/ *n* mermelada *f*

Jamaica /dʒə'meɪkə/ *n* Jamaica *f*

jamboree /dʒæmbə'riː/ *n* reunión *f*

jam-packed /'dʒæm'pækt/ *a* atestado

jangle /'dʒæŋgl/ *n* sonido *m* metálico (y áspero). ● *vt/i* sonar discordemente

janitor /'dʒænɪtə(r)/ *n* portero *m*

January /'dʒænjʊərɪ/ *n* enero *m*

Japan /dʒə'pæn/ *n* el Japón *m*. **~ese** /dʒæpə'niːz/ *a & n* japonés (*m*)

jar¹ /dʒɑː(r)/ *n* tarro *m*, frasco *m*

jar² /dʒɑː(r)/ *vi* (*pt* **jarred**) ⟨*sound*⟩ sonar mal; ⟨*colours*⟩ chillar. ● *vt* sacudir

jar³ /dʒɑː(r)/ *n*. **on the ~** (*ajar*) entreabierto

jargon /'dʒɑːgən/ *n* jerga *f*

jarring /'dʒɑːrɪŋ/ *a* discorde

jasmine /'dʒæsmɪn/ *n* jazmín *m*

jaundice /'dʒɔːndɪs/ *n* ictericia *f*. **~d** *a* (*envious*) envidioso; (*bitter*) amargado

jaunt /dʒɔːnt/ *n* excursión *f*

jaunty /'dʒɔːntɪ/ a (**-ier**, **-iest**) garboso

javelin /'dʒævəlɪn/ n jabalina f

jaw /dʒɔː/ n mandíbula f. ● vi (talk lengthily, sl) hablar por los codos

jay /dʒeɪ/ n arrendajo m. **~-walk** vi cruzar la calle descuidadamente

jazz /dʒæz/ n jazz m. ● vt. **~ up** animar. **~y** a chillón

jealous /'dʒeləs/ a celoso. **~y** n celos mpl

jeans /dʒiːnz/ npl (pantalones mpl) vaqueros mpl

jeep /dʒiːp/ n jeep m

jeer /dʒɪə(r)/ vt/i. **~ at** mofarse de, befar; (boo) abuchear. ● n mofa f; (boo) abucheo m

jell /dʒel/ vi cuajar. **~ied** a en gelatina

jelly /'dʒelɪ/ n jalea f. **~fish** n medusa f

jeopard|ize /'dʒepədaɪz/ vt arriesgar. **~y** n peligro m

jerk /dʒɜːk/ n sacudida f; (fool, sl) idiota m & f. ● vt sacudir. **~ily** adv a sacudidas. **~y** a espasmódico

jersey /'dʒɜːzɪ/ n (pl **-eys**) jersey m

jest /dʒest/ n broma f. ● vi bromear. **~er** n bufón m

Jesus /'dʒiːzəs/ n Jesús m

jet[1] /dʒet/ n (stream) chorro m; (plane) yet m, avión m de propulsión por reacción

jet[2] /dʒet/ n (mineral) azabache m. **~-black** a de azabache, como el azabache

jet: ~ lag n cansancio m retardado después de un vuelo largo. **have ~ lag** estar desfasado. **~-propelled** a (de propulsión) a reacción

jettison /'dʒetɪsn/ vt echar al mar; (fig, discard) deshacerse de

jetty /'dʒetɪ/ n muelle m

Jew /dʒuː/ n judío m

jewel /'dʒuːəl/ n joya f. **~led** a enjoyado. **~ler** n joyero m. **~lery** n joyas fpl

Jew: ~ess n judía f. **~ish** a judío. **~ry** /dʒʊərɪ/ n los judíos mpl

jib[1] /dʒɪb/ n (sail) foque m

jib[2] /dʒɪb/ vi (pt **jibbed**) rehusar. **~ at** oponerse a.

jiffy /'dʒɪfɪ/ n momentito m. **do sth in a ~** hacer algo en un santiamén

jig /dʒɪg/ n (dance) giga f

jiggle /'dʒɪgl/ vt zangolotear

jigsaw /'dʒɪgsɔː/ n rompecabezas m invar

jilt /dʒɪlt/ vt plantar, dejar plantado

jingle /'dʒɪŋgl/ vt hacer sonar. ● vi tintinear. ● n tintineo m; (advert) anuncio m cantado

jinx /dʒɪŋks/ n (person) gafe m; (spell) maleficio m

jitter|s /'dʒɪtəz/ npl. **have the ~s** estar nervioso. **~y** /-ərɪ/ a nervioso. **be ~y** estar nervioso.

job /dʒɒb/ n trabajo m; (post) empleo m, puesto m. **have a ~ doing** costar trabajo hacer. **it is a good ~ that** menos mal que. **~centre** n bolsa f de trabajo. **~less** a sin trabajo.

jockey /'dʒɒkɪ/ n jockey m. ● vi (manoeuvre) maniobrar (for para)

jocular /'dʒɒkjʊlə(r)/ a jocoso

jog /dʒɒg/ vt (pt **jogged**) empujar; refrescar (memory). ● vi hacer footing. **~ging** n jogging m

join /dʒɔɪn/ vt unir, juntar; hacerse socio de (club); hacerse miembro de (political group); alistarse en (army); reunirse con (another person). ● vi (roads etc) empalmar; (rivers) confluir. **~ in** participar (en). **~ up** (mil) alistarse. ● n juntura f

joiner /'dʒɔɪnə(r)/ n carpintero m

joint /dʒɔɪnt/ a común. **~ author** n coautor m. ● n (join) juntura f; (anat) articulación f; (culin) asado m; (place, sl) garito m; (marijuana, sl) cigarillo m de marijuana. **out of ~** descoyuntado. **~ly** adv conjuntamente

joist /dʒɔɪst/ n viga f

jok|e /dʒəʊk/ n broma f; (funny story) chiste m. ● vi bromear. **~er** n bromista m & f; (cards) comodín m. **~ingly** adv en broma

joll|ification /dʒɒlɪfɪ'keɪʃn/ n jolgorio m. **~ity** n jolgorio m. **~y** a (**-ier**, **-iest**) alegre. ● adv (fam) muy

jolt /dʒɒlt/ vt sacudir. ● vt (vehicle) traquetear. ● n sacudida f

Jordan /'dʒɔːdən/ n Jordania f. **~ian** a & n /-'deɪnɪən/ jordano (m)

jostle /'dʒɒsl/ vt/i empujar(se)

jot /dʒɒt/ n pizca f. ● vt (pt **jotted**) apuntar. **~ter** n bloc m

journal /'dʒɜːnl/ n (diary) diario m; (newspaper) periódico m; (magazine) revista f. **~ese** /dʒɜːnə'liːz/ n jerga f periodística. **~ism** n periodismo m. **~ist** n periodista m & f

journey /'dʒɜːnɪ/ n viaje m. ● vi viajar

jovial /'dʒəʊvɪəl/ a jovial

jowl /dʒaʊl/ n (jaw) quijada f; (cheek) mejilla f. **cheek by ~** muy cerca

joy /dʒɔɪ/ n alegría f. **~ful** a alegre. **~ride** n paseo m en coche sin permiso del dueño. **~ous** a alegre

jubila|nt /'dʒuːbɪlənt/ a jubiloso. **~tion** /-'leɪʃn/ n júbilo m

jubilee /'dʒuːbɪliː/ n aniversario m especial

Judaism /'dʒuːdeɪɪzəm/ n judaísmo m

judder /'dʒʌdə(r)/ vi vibrar. ● n vibración f

judge /dʒʌdʒ/ n juez m. ● vt juzgar. **~ment** n juicio m

judicia|l /dʒuː'dɪʃl/ a judicial. **~ry** n magistratura f

judicious /dʒuː'dɪʃəs/ a juicioso

judo /'dʒuːdəʊ/ n judo m

jug /dʒʌg/ n jarra f

juggernaut /'dʒʌgənɔːt/ n (lorry) camión m grande

juggle /'dʒʌgl/ vt/i hacer juegos malabares (con). **~r** n malabarista m & f

juic|e /dʒuːs/ n jugo m, zumo m. **~y** a jugoso, zumoso; ⟨story etc⟩ (fam) picante

juke-box /'dʒuːkbɒks/ n tocadiscos m invar tragaperras

July /dʒuː'laɪ/ n julio m

jumble /'dʒʌmbl/ vt mezclar. ● n (muddle) revoltijo m. **~ sale** n venta f de objetos usados, mercadillo m

jumbo /'dʒʌmbəʊ/ a. **~ jet** n jumbo m

jump /dʒʌmp/ vt/i saltar. **~ the gun** obrar prematuramente. **~ the queue** colarse. ● vi saltar; (start) asustarse; (prices) alzarse. **~ at** apresurarse a aprovechar. ● n salto m; (start) susto m; (increase) aumento m

jumper /'dʒʌmpə(r)/ n jersey m; (dress, Amer) mandil m, falda f con peto

jumpy /'dʒʌmpɪ/ a nervioso

junction /'dʒʌŋkʃn/ n juntura f; (of roads) cruce m, entronque m (LAm); (rail) empalme m, entronque m (LAm)

juncture /'dʒʌŋktʃə(r)/ n momento m; (state of affairs) coyuntura f

June /dʒuːn/ n junio m

jungle /'dʒʌŋgl/ n selva f

junior /'dʒuːnɪə(r)/ a (in age) más joven (to que); (in rank) subalterno. ● n menor m. **~ school** n escuela f

junk /dʒʌŋk/ n trastos mpl viejos. ● vt (fam) tirar

junkie /'dʒʌŋkɪ/ n (sl) drogadicto m

junk shop /'dʒʌŋkʃɒp/ n tienda f de trastos viejos

junta /'dʒʌntə/ n junta f

jurisdiction /dʒʊərɪs'dɪkʃn/ n jurisdicción f

jurisprudence /dʒʊərɪs'pruːdəns/ n jurisprudencia f

juror /'dʒʊərə(r)/ n jurado m

jury /'dʒʊərɪ/ n jurado m

just /dʒʌst/ a (fair) justo. ● adv exactamente; (slightly) apenas; (only) sólo, solamente. **~ as tall** tan alto (as como). **~ listen!** ¡escucha! **he has ~ left** acaba de marcharse

justice /'dʒʌstɪs/ n justicia f. **J~ of the Peace** juez m de paz

justif|iable /dʒʌstɪ'faɪəbl/ a justificable. **~iably** adv con razón. **~ication** /dʒʌstɪfɪ'keɪʃn/ n justificación f. **~y** /'dʒʌstɪfaɪ/ vt justificar

justly /'dʒʌstlɪ/ adv con justicia

jut /dʒʌt/ vi (pt jutted). **~ out** sobresalir

juvenile /'dʒuːvənaɪl/ a juvenil; (childish) infantil. ● n joven m & f. **~ court** n tribunal m de menores

juxtapose /dʒʌkstə'pəʊz/ vt yuxtaponer

K

kaleidoscope /kə'laɪdəskəʊp/ n caleidoscopio m

kangaroo /kæŋgə'ruː/ n canguro m

kapok /'keɪpɒk/ n miraguano m

karate /kə'rɑːtɪ/ n karate m

kebab /kɪ'bæb/ n broqueta f

keel /kiːl/ n (of ship) quilla f. ● vi. **~ over** volcarse

keen /kiːn/ a (-er, -est) ⟨interest, feeling⟩ vivo; ⟨wind, mind, analysis⟩ penetrante; ⟨edge⟩ afilado; ⟨appetite⟩ bueno; ⟨eyesight⟩ agudo; ⟨eager⟩ entusiasta. **be ~ on** gustarle a uno. **he's ~ on Shostakovich** le gusta Shostakovich. **~ly** adv vivamente; (enthusiastically) con entusiasmo. **~ness** n intensidad f; (enthusiasm) entusiasmo m.

keep /kiːp/ vt (pt kept) guardar; cumplir ⟨promise⟩; tener ⟨shop, animals⟩; mantener ⟨family⟩; observar ⟨rule⟩; (celebrate) celebrar; (delay) detener; (prevent) impedir. ● vi ⟨food⟩ conservarse; (remain) quedarse. ● n subsistencia f; (of castle) torreón *m*. **for ~s** (*fam*) para siempre. **~ back** *vt* retener. ● *vi* no acercarse. **~ in** no dejar salir. **~ in with** mantenerse en buenas relaciones con. **~ out** no dejar entrar. **~ up** mantener. **~ up (with)** estar al día (en). **~er** *n* guarda *m*

keeping /'ki:pɪŋ/ *n* cuidado *m*. **in ~ with** de acuerdo con

keepsake /'ki:pseɪk/ *n* recuerdo *m*

keg /keg/ *n* barrilete *m*

kennel /'kenl/ *n* perrera *f*

Kenya /'kenjə/ *n* Kenia *f*

kept /kept/ *see* **keep**

kerb /kɜːb/ *n* bordillo *m*

kerfuffle /kə'fʌfl/ *n* (*fuss, fam*) lío *m*

kernel /'kɜːnl/ *n* almendra *f*; (*fig*) meollo *m*

kerosene /'kerəsiːn/ *n* queroseno *m*

ketchup /'ketʃʌp/ *n* salsa *f* de tomate

kettle /'ketl/ *n* hervidor *m*

key /kiː/ *n* llave *f*; (*of typewriter, piano etc*) tecla *f*. ● *a* clave. ● *vt*. **~ up** excitar. **~board** *n* teclado *m*. **~hole** *n* ojo *m* de la cerradura. **~note** *n* (*mus*) tónica *f*; (*speech*) idea *f* fundamental. **~ring** *n* llavero *m*. **~stone** *n* piedra *f* clave

khaki /'kɑːkɪ/ *a* caqui

kibbutz /kɪ'buts/ *n* (*pl* **-im** /-iːm/ *or* **-es**) kibbutz *m*

kick /kɪk/ *vt* dar una patada a; ⟨*animals*⟩ tirar una coz a. ● *vi* dar patadas; ⟨*firearm*⟩ dar culatazo. ● *n* patada *f*; (*of animal*) coz *f*; (*of firearm*) culatazo *m*; (*thrill, fam*) placer *m*. **~ out** (*fam*) echar a patadas. **~ up** armar ⟨*fuss etc*⟩. **~back** *n* culatazo *m*; (*payment*) soborno *m*. **~off** *n* (*sport*) saque *m* inicial

kid /kɪd/ *n* (*young goat*) cabrito *m*; (*leather*) cabritilla *f*; (*child, sl*) chaval *m*. ● *vt* (*pt* **kidded**) tomar el pelo a. ● *vi* bromear

kidnap /'kɪdnæp/ *vt* (*pt* **kidnapped**) secuestrar. **~ping** *n* secuestro *m*

kidney /'kɪdnɪ/ *n* riñón *m*. ● *a* renal

kill /kɪl/ *vt* matar; (*fig*) acabar con. ● *n* matanza *f*; (*in hunt*) pieza(s) *f(pl)*. **~er** *n* matador *m*; (*murderer*) asesino *m*. **~ing** *n* matanza *f*; (*murder*) asesinato *m*. ● *a* (*funny, fam*) para morirse de risa; (*tiring, fam*) agotador. **~joy** *n* aguafiestas *m* & *f* invar

kiln /kɪln/ *n* horno *m*

kilo /'kiːləʊ/ *n* (*pl* **-os**) kilo *m*

kilogram(me) /'kɪləɡræm/ *n* kilogramo *m*

kilohertz /'kɪləhɜːts/ *n* kilohercio *m*

kilometre /'kɪləmiːtə(r)/ *n* kilómetro *m*

kilowatt /'kɪləwɒt/ *n* kilovatio *m*

kilt /kɪlt/ *n* falda *f* escocesa

kin /kɪn/ *n* parientes *mpl*. **next of ~** pariente *m* más próximo, parientes *mpl* más próximos

kind¹ /kaɪnd/ *n* clase *f*. **~ of** (*somewhat, fam*) un poco. **in ~** en especie. **be two of a ~** ser tal para cual

kind² /kaɪnd/ *a* amable

kindergarten /'kɪndəɡɑːtn/ *n* escuela *f* de párvulos

kind-hearted /kaɪnd'hɑːtɪd/ *a* bondadoso

kindle /'kɪndl/ *vt/i* encender(se)

kind: ~liness *n* bondad *f*. **~ly** *a* (**-ier, -iest**) bondadoso. ● *adv* bondadosamente; (*please*) haga el favor de. **~ness** *n* bondad *f*

kindred /'kɪndrɪd/ *a* emparentado. **~ spirits** *npl* almas *fpl* afines

kinetic /kɪ'netɪk/ *a* cinético

king /kɪŋ/ *n* rey *m*

kingdom /'kɪŋdəm/ *n* reino *m*

kingpin /'kɪŋpɪn/ *n* (*person*) persona *f* clave; (*thing*) piedra *f* angular

king-size(d) /'kɪŋsaɪz(d)/ *a* extraordinariamente grande

kink /kɪŋk/ *n* (*in rope*) retorcimiento *m*; (*fig*) manía *f*. **~y** *a* (*fam*) pervertido

kiosk /'kiːɒsk/ *n* quiosco *m*. **telephone ~** cabina *f* telefónica

kip /kɪp/ *n* (*sl*) sueño *m*. ● *vi* (*pt* **kipped**) dormir

kipper /'kɪpə(r)/ *n* arenque *m* ahumado

kiss /kɪs/ *n* beso *m*. ● *vt/i* besar(se)

kit /kɪt/ *n* avíos *mpl*; (*tools*) herramientos *mpl*. ● *vt* (*pt* **kitted**). **~ out** equipar de. **~bag** *n* mochila *f*

kitchen /'kɪtʃɪn/ *n* cocina *f*. **~ette** /kɪtʃɪ'net/ *n* cocina *f* pequeña. **~ garden** *n* huerto *m*

kite /kaɪt/ *n* (*toy*) cometa *f*

kith /kɪθ/ *n*. **~ and kin** amigos *mpl* y parientes *mpl*

kitten /'kɪtn/ *n* gatito *m*

kitty /'kɪtɪ/ *n* (*fund*) fondo *m* común

kleptomaniac /kleptəʊ'meɪnɪæk/ *n* cleptómano *m*

knack /næk/ *n* truco *m*

knapsack /'næpsæk/ *n* mochila *f*

knave /neɪv/ *n* (*cards*) sota *f*

knead /niːd/ *vt* amasar

knee /niː/ *n* rodilla *f*. **~cap** *n* rótula *f*

kneel /niːl/ vi (pt **knelt**). ~ (**down**) arrodillarse

knees-up /'niːzʌp/ n (fam) baile m

knell /nel/ n toque m de difuntos

knelt /nelt/ see **kneel**

knew /njuː/ see **know**

knickerbockers /'nɪkəbɒkəz/ npl pantalón m bombacho

knickers /'nɪkəz/ npl bragas fpl

knick-knack /'nɪknæk/ n chuchería f

knife /naɪf/ n (pl **knives**) cuchillo m. ● vt acuchillar

knight /naɪt/ n caballero m; (chess) caballo m. ● vt conceder el título de Sir a. **~hood** n título m de Sir

knit /nɪt/ vt (pt **knitted** or **knit**) tejer. ● vi hacer punto. ~ **one's brow** fruncir el ceño. **~ting** n labor f de punto. **~wear** n artículos mpl de punto

knob /nɒb/ n botón m; (of door, drawer etc) tirador m. **~bly** a nudoso

knock /nɒk/ vt golpear; (criticize) criticar. ● vi golpear; (at door) llamar. ● n golpe m. ~ **about** vt maltratar. ● vi rodar. ~ **down** derribar; atropellar ⟨person⟩; rebajar ⟨prices⟩. ~ **off** vt hacer caer; (complete quickly, fam) despachar; (steal, sl) birlar. ● vi (finish work, fam) terminar, salir del trabajo. ~ **out** (by blow) dejar sin conocimiento; (eliminate) eliminar; (tire) agotar. ~ **over** tirar; atropellar ⟨person⟩. ~ **up** preparar de prisa ⟨meal etc⟩. **~down** a ⟨price⟩ de saldo. **~er** n aldaba f. **~kneed** a patizambo. **~out** n (boxing) knock-out m

knot /nɒt/ n nudo m. ● vt (pt **knotted**) anudar. **~ty** /'nɒtɪ/ a nudoso

know /nəʊ/ vt (pt **knew**) saber; (be acquainted with) conocer. ● vi saber. ● n. **be in the** ~ estar al tanto. ~ **about** entender de ⟨cars etc⟩. ~ **of** saber de. **~all** n, **~-it-all** (Amer) n sabelotodo m & f. **~-how** n habilidad f. **~ingly** adv deliberadamente

knowledge /'nɒlɪdʒ/ n conocimiento m; (learning) conocimientos mpl. **~able** a informado

known /nəʊn/ see **know**. ● a conocido

knuckle /'nʌkl/ n nudillo m. ● vi. ~ **under** someterse

Koran /kə'rɑːn/ n Corán m, Alcorán m

Korea /kə'rɪə/ n Corea f

kosher /'kəʊʃə(r)/ a preparado según la ley judía

kowtow /kaʊ'taʊ/ vi humillarse (**to** ante)

kudos /'kjuːdɒs/ n prestigio m

L

lab /læb/ n (fam) laboratorio m

label /'leɪbl/ n etiqueta f. ● vt (pt **labelled**) poner etiqueta a; (fig, describe as) describir como

laboratory /lə'bɒrətərɪ/ n laboratorio m

laborious /lə'bɔːrɪəs/ a penoso

labour /'leɪbə(r)/ n trabajo m; (workers) mano f de obra. **in** ~ de parto. ● vi trabajar. ● vt insistir en

Labour /'leɪbə(r)/ n el partido m laborista. ● a laborista

laboured /'leɪbəd/ a penoso

labourer /'leɪbərə(r)/ n obrero m; (on farm) labriego m

labyrinth /'læbərɪnθ/ n laberinto m

lace /leɪs/ n encaje m; (of shoe) cordón m, agujeta f (Mex). ● vt (fasten) atar. ~ **with** echar a ⟨a drink⟩

lacerate /'læsəreɪt/ vt lacerar

lack /læk/ n falta f. **for** ~ **of** por falta de. ● vt faltarle a uno. **he ~s money** carece de dinero. **be ~ing** faltar

lackadaisical /lækə'deɪzɪkl/ a indolente, apático

lackey /'lækɪ/ n lacayo m

laconic /lə'kɒnɪk/ a lacónico

lacquer /'lækə(r)/ n laca f

lad /læd/ n muchacho m

ladder /'lædə(r)/ n escalera f (de mano); (in stocking) carrera f. ● vt hacer una carrera en. ● vi hacerse una carrera

laden /'leɪdn/ a cargado (**with** de)

ladle /'leɪdl/ n cucharón m

lady /'leɪdɪ/ n señora f; (title) señora f. **young** ~ señorita f. **~bird** n, **~bug** n (Amer) mariquita f. ~ **friend** n amiga f. **~-in-waiting** n dama f de honor. **~like** a distinguido. **~ship** n Señora f

lag[1] /læg/ vi (pt **lagged**). ~ (**behind**) retrasarse. ● n (interval) intervalo m

lag[2] /læg/ vt (pt **lagged**) revestir ⟨pipes⟩

lager /'lɑːgə(r)/ n cerveza f dorada

laggard /'lægəd/ n holgazán m

lagging /'lægɪŋ/ n revestimiento m calorífugo
lagoon /lə'gu:n/ n laguna f
lah /lɑ:/ n (mus, sixth note of any musical scale) la m
laid /leɪd/ see lay¹
lain /leɪn/ see lie¹
lair /leə(r)/ n guarida f
laity /'leɪətɪ/ n laicado m
lake /leɪk/ n lago m
lamb /læm/ n cordero m. ~swool n lana f de cordero
lame /leɪm/ a (-er, -est) cojo; ⟨excuse⟩ poco convincente. ~ly adv ⟨argue⟩ con poca convicción f
lament /lə'ment/ n lamento m. ● vt/i lamentarse (de). ~able /'læməntəbl/ a lamentable
laminated /'læmɪneɪtɪd/ a laminado
lamp /læmp/ n lámpara f. ~post n farol m. ~shade n pantalla f
lance /lɑ:ns/ n lanza f. ● vt (med) abrir con lanceta. ~corporal n cabo m interino
lancet /'lɑ:nsɪt/ n lanceta f
land /lænd/ n tierra f; ⟨country⟩ país m; ⟨plot⟩ terreno m. ● a terrestre; ⟨breeze⟩ de tierra; ⟨policy, reform⟩ agrario. ● vt desembarcar; ⟨obtain⟩ conseguir; dar ⟨blow⟩; ⟨put⟩ meter. ● vi ⟨from ship⟩ desembarcar; ⟨aircraft⟩ aterrizar; ⟨fall⟩ caer. ~ up ir a parar
landed /'lændɪd/ a hacendado
landing /'lændɪŋ/ n desembarque m; ⟨aviat⟩ aterrizaje m; ⟨top of stairs⟩ descanso m. ~stage n desembarcadero m
landlady /'lændleɪdɪ/ n propietaria f; ⟨of inn⟩ patrona f
land-locked /'lændlɒkt/ a rodeado de tierra
landlord /'lændlɔːd/ n propietario m; ⟨of inn⟩ patrón m
land: ~mark n punto m destacado. ~scape /'lændskeɪp/ n paisaje m. ● vt ajardinar. ~slide n desprendimiento m de tierras; ⟨pol⟩ victoria f arrolladora
lane /leɪn/ n ⟨path, road⟩ camino m; ⟨strip of road⟩ carril m; ⟨aviat⟩ ruta f
language /'læŋgwɪdʒ/ n idioma m; ⟨speech, style⟩ lenguaje m
langu|id /'læŋgwɪd/ a lánguido. ~ish /'læŋgwɪʃ/ vi languidecer. ~or /'læŋgə(r)/ n languidez f
lank /læŋk/ a larguirucho; ⟨hair⟩ lacio. ~y /'læŋkɪ/ a (-ier, -iest) larguirucho

lantern /'læntən/ n linterna f
lap¹ /læp/ n regazo m
lap² /læp/ n ⟨sport⟩ vuelta f. ● vt/i (pt lapped). ~ over traslapar(se)
lap³ /læp/ vt (pt lapped). ~ up beber a lengüetazos; ⟨fig⟩ aceptar con entusiasmo. ● vi ⟨waves⟩ chapotear
lapel /lə'pel/ n solapa f
lapse /læps/ vi ⟨decline⟩ degradarse; ⟨expire⟩ caducar; ⟨time⟩ transcurrir. ~ into recaer en. ● n error m; ⟨of time⟩ intervalo m
larceny /'lɑːsənɪ/ n robo m
lard /lɑːd/ n manteca f de cerdo
larder /'lɑːdə(r)/ n despensa f
large /lɑːdʒ/ a (-er, -est) grande, ⟨before singular noun⟩ gran. ● n. at ~ en libertad. ~ly adv en gran parte. ~ness n ⟨gran⟩ tamaño m
largesse /lɑː'ʒes/ n generosidad f
lark¹ /lɑːk/ n alondra f
lark² /lɑːk/ n broma f; ⟨bit of fun⟩ travesura f. ● vi andar de juerga
larva /'lɑːvə/ n (pl -vae /-viː/) larva f
laryn|gitis /lærɪn'dʒaɪtɪs/ n laringitis f. ~x /'lærɪŋks/ n laringe f
lascivious /lə'sɪvɪəs/ a lascivo
laser /'leɪzə(r)/ n láser m
lash /læʃ/ vt azotar. ~ out ⟨spend⟩ gastar. ~ out against atacar. ● n latigazo m; ⟨eyelash⟩ pestaña f
lashings /'læʃɪŋz/ npl. ~ of ⟨cream etc, sl⟩ montones de
lass /læs/ n muchacha f
lassitude /'læsɪtjuːd/ n lasitud f
lasso /læ'suː/ n (pl -os) lazo m
last¹ /lɑːst/ a último; ⟨week etc⟩ pasado. ~ Monday n el lunes pasado. have the ~ word decir la última palabra. the ~ straw n el colmo m. ● adv por último; ⟨most recently⟩ la última vez. he came ~ llegó el último. ● n último m; ⟨remainder⟩ lo que queda. ~ but one penúltimo. at (long) ~ en fin.
last² /lɑːst/ vi durar. ~ out sobrevivir
last³ /lɑːst/ n horma f
lasting /'lɑːstɪŋ/ a duradero
last: ~ly adv por último. ~ night n anoche m
latch /lætʃ/ n picaporte m
late /leɪt/ a (-er, -est) ⟨not on time⟩ tarde; ⟨recent⟩ reciente; ⟨former⟩ antiguo, ex; ⟨fruit⟩ tardío; ⟨hour⟩ avanzado; ⟨deceased⟩ difunto. in ~ July a fines de julio. the ~ Dr Phillips el difunto Dr. Phillips. ● adv tarde. of ~ últimamente. ~ly adv últimamente. ~ness n ⟨delay⟩ retraso m; ⟨of hour⟩ lo avanzado

latent /'leɪtnt/ a latente

lateral /'lætərəl/ a lateral

latest /'leɪtɪst/ a último. **at the ~** a más tardar

lathe /leɪð/ n torno m

lather /'lɑːðə(r)/ n espuma f. ● vt enjabonar. ● vi hacer espuma

Latin /'lætɪn/ n (lang) latín m. ● a latino

latitude /'lætɪtjuːd/ n latitud m

latrine /lə'triːn/ n letrina f

latter /'lætə(r)/ a último; (of two) segundo. ● n. **the ~** éste m, ésta f, éstos mpl, éstas fpl. **~day** a moderno. **~ly** adv últimamente

lattice /'lætɪs/ n enrejado m

laudable /'lɔːdəbl/ a laudable

laugh /lɑːf/ vi reír(se) (**at** de). ● n risa f. **~able** a ridículo. **~ing-stock** n hazmerreír m invar. **~ter** /'lɑːftə(r)/ n (act) risa f; (sound of laughs) risas fpl

launch¹ /lɔːntʃ/ vt lanzar. ● n lanzamiento m. **~ (out) into** lanzarse a

launch² /lɔːntʃ/ n (boat) lancha f

launching pad /'lɔːntʃɪŋpæd/ n plataforma f de lanzamiento

laund|er /'lɔːndə(r)/ vt lavar (y planchar). **~erette** n lavandería f automática. **~ress** n lavandera f. **~ry** /'lɔːndrɪ/ n (place) lavandería f; (dirty clothes) ropa f sucia; (clean clothes) colada f

laurel /'lɒrəl/ n laurel m

lava /'lɑːvə/ n lava f

lavatory /'lævətərɪ/ n retrete m. **public ~** servicios mpl

lavender /'lævəndə(r)/ n lavanda f

lavish /'lævɪʃ/ a ⟨person⟩ pródigo; (plentiful) abundante; (lush) suntuoso. ● vt prodigar. **~ly** adv profusamente

law /lɔː/ n ley f; (profession, subject of study) derecho m. **~abiding** a observante de la ley. **~ and order** n orden m público. **~ court** n tribunal m. **~ful** a (permitted by law) lícito; (recognized by law) legítimo. **~fully** adv legalmente. **~less** a sin leyes

lawn /lɔːn/ n césped m. **~mower** n cortacésped f. **~ tennis** n tenis m (sobre hierba)

lawsuit /'lɔːsuːt/ n pleito m

lawyer /'lɔɪə(r)/ n abogado m

lax /læks/ a descuidado; ⟨morals etc⟩ laxo

laxative /'læksətɪv/ n laxante m

laxity /'læksətɪ/ n descuido m

lay¹ /leɪ/ vt (pt **laid**) poner ⟨incl table, eggs⟩; tender ⟨trap⟩; formar ⟨plan⟩. **~ hands on** echar mano a. **~ hold of** agarrar. **~ waste** asolar. **~ aside** dejar a un lado. **~ down** dejar a un lado; imponer ⟨condition⟩. **~ into** (sl) dar una paliza a. **~ off** vt despedir ⟨worker⟩; ● vi (fam) terminar. **~ on** (provide) proveer. **~ out** (design) disponer; (display) exponer; desembolsar ⟨money⟩. **~ up** (store) guardar; obligar a guardar cama ⟨person⟩

lay² /leɪ/ a (non-clerical) laico; ⟨opinion etc⟩ profano

lay³ /leɪ/ see **lie**

layabout /'leɪəbaʊt/ n holgazán m

lay-by /'leɪbaɪ/ n apartadero m

layer /'leɪə(r)/ n capa f

layette /leɪ'et/ n canastilla f

layman /'leɪmən/ n lego m

lay-off /'leɪɒf/ n paro m forzoso

layout /'leɪaʊt/ n disposición f

laze /leɪz/ vi holgazanear; (relax) descansar

laz|iness /'leɪzɪnɪs/ n pereza f. **~y** a perezoso. **~y-bones** n holgazán m

lb. abbr (pound) libra f

lead¹ /liːd/ vt (pt **led**) conducir; dirigir ⟨team⟩; llevar ⟨life⟩; (induce) inducir a. ● vi (go first) ir delante; ⟨road⟩ ir, conducir; (in cards) salir. ● n mando m; (clue) pista f; (leash) correa f; (in theatre) primer papel m; (wire) cable m; (example) ejemplo m. **in the ~** en cabeza. **~ away** llevar. **~ up to** preparar el terreno para

lead² /led/ n plomo m; (of pencil) mina f. **~en** /'ledn/ a de plomo

leader /'liːdə(r)/ n jefe m; (leading article) editorial m. **~ship** n dirección f

leading /'liːdɪŋ/ a principal; (in front) delantero. **~ article** n editorial m

leaf /liːf/ n (pl **leaves**) hoja f. ● vi. **~ through** hojear

leaflet /'liːflɪt/ n folleto m

leafy /'liːfɪ/ a frondoso

league /liːg/ n liga f. **be in ~ with** conchabarse con

leak /liːk/ n (hole) agujero m; (of gas, liquid) escape m; (of information) filtración f; (in roof) gotera f; (in boat) vía f de agua. ● vi ⟨receptacle, gas, liquid⟩ salirse; ⟨information⟩ filtrarse; (drip) gotear; ⟨boat⟩ hacer agua. ● vt dejar escapar; filtrar ⟨in-

formation⟩. ~age n = leak. ~y a ⟨re-
ceptacle⟩ agujereado; ⟨roof⟩ que
tiene goteras; ⟨boat⟩ que hace agua
lean[1] /liːn/ vt (pt **leaned** or **leant**
/lent/) apoyar. ● vi inclinarse. ~
against apoyarse en. ~ **on** apoyarse
en. ~**out** asomarse (of a). ~ **over**
inclinarse
lean[2] /liːn/ a (**-er, -est**) magro. ● n
carne f magra
leaning /ˈliːnɪŋ/ a inclinado. ● n
inclinación f
leanness /ˈliːnnɪs/ n (of meat) mag-
rez f; (of person) flaqueza f
lean-to /ˈliːntuː/ n colgadizo m
leap /liːp/ vi (pt **leaped** or **leapt**
/lept/) saltar. ● n salto m. ~**frog** n
salto m, saltacabrilla f. ● vi (pt
-frogged) jugar a saltacabrilla. ~
year n año m bisiesto
learn /lɜːn/ vt/i (pt **learned** or **learnt**)
aprender (**to do** a hacer). ~**ed** /ˈlɜː-
nɪd/ a culto. ~**er** /ˈlɜːnə(r)/ n principiante m; (apprentice) aprendiz m;
(student) estudiante m & f. ~**ing** n
saber m
lease /liːs/ n arriendo m. ● vt
arrendar
leash /liːʃ/ n correa f
least /liːst/ a. **the** ~ (smallest
amount of) mínimo; (slightest)
menor; (smallest) más pequeño. ● n
lo menos. **at** ~ por lo menos. **not in
the** ~ en absoluto. ● adv menos
leather /ˈleðə(r)/ n piel f, cuero m
leave /liːv/ vt (pt **left**) dejar; (depart
from) marcharse de. ~ **alone** dejar
de tocar ⟨thing⟩; dejar en paz ⟨per-
son⟩. **be left (over)** quedar. ● vi
marcharse; ⟨train⟩ salir. ● n permiso m. **on** ~ (mil) de permiso. **take
one's** ~ **of** despedirse de. ~ **out**
omitir
leavings /ˈliːvɪŋz/ npl restos mpl
Leban|on /ˈlebənən/ n el Líbano m.
~**ese** /-ˈniːz/ a & n libanés (m)
lecher /ˈletʃə(r)/ n libertino m. ~**ous**
a lascivo. ~**y** n lascivia f
lectern /ˈlektɜːn/ n atril m; (in
church) facistol m
lecture /ˈlektʃə(r)/ n conferencia f;
(univ) clase f; (rebuke) sermón m.
● vt/i dar una conferencia (a);
(univ) dar clases (a); (rebuke) ser-
monear. ~**r** n conferenciante m;
(univ) profesor m
led /led/ see **lead**[1]
ledge /ledʒ/ n repisa f; (of window)
antepecho m

ledger /ˈledʒə(r)/ n libro m mayor
lee /liː/ n sotavento m; (fig) abrigo m
leech /liːtʃ/ n sanguijuela f
leek /liːk/ n puerro m
leer /ˈlɪə(r)/ vi. ~ (**at**) mirar
impúdicamente. ● n mirada f
impúdica
leeway /ˈliːweɪ/ n deriva f; (fig, freedom of action) libertad f de acción.
make up ~ recuperar los atrasos
left[1] /left/ a izquierdo. ● adv a la
izquierda. ● n izquierda f
left[2] /left/ see **leave**
left: ~**hand** a izquierdo. ~**handed**
a zurdo. ~**ist** n izquierdista m & f.
~ **luggage** n consigna f. ~**overs**
npl restos mpl
left-wing /ˈleftˈwɪŋ/ a izquierdista
leg /leg/ n pierna f; (of animal, furniture) pata f; (of pork) pernil m; (of
lamb) pierna f; (of journey) etapa f.
on its last ~**s** en las últimas
legacy /ˈlegəsɪ/ n herencia f
legal /ˈliːgl/ a (permitted by law)
lícito; (recognized by law) legítimo;
⟨affairs etc⟩ jurídico. ~ **aid** n abogacía f de pobres. ~**ity** /-ˈgælətɪ/ n
legalidad f. ~**ize** vt legalizar. ~**ly**
adv legalmente
legation /lɪˈgeɪʃn/ n legación f
legend /ˈledʒənd/ n leyenda f. ~**ary**
a legendario
leggings /ˈlegɪŋz/ npl polainas fpl
legib|ility /ledʒəbɪlətɪ/ n legibilidad
f. ~**le** a legible. ~**ly** a legiblemente
legion /ˈliːdʒən/ n legión f
legislat|e /ˈledʒɪsleɪt/ vi legislar.
~**ion** /-ˈleɪʃn/ n legislación f. ~**ive** a
legislativo. ~**ure** /-eɪtʃə(r)/ n
cuerpo m legislativo
legitima|cy /lɪˈdʒɪtɪməsɪ/ f legit-
imidad f. ~**te** a legítimo
leisure /ˈleʒə(r)/ n ocio m. **at one's** ~
cuando tenga tiempo. ~**ly** adv sin
prisa
lemon /ˈlemən/ n limón m. ~**ade**
/leməˈneɪd/ n (fizzy) gaseosa f (de
limón); (still) limonada f
lend /lend/ vt (pt **lent**) prestar. ~
itself to prestarse a. ~**er** n pres-
tador m; (moneylender) prestamista m & f. ~**ing** n préstamo m.
~**ing library** n biblioteca f de
préstamo
length /leŋθ/ n largo m; (in time)
duración f; (of cloth) largo m; (of
road) tramo m. **at** ~ (at last) por fin.
at (great) ~ detalladamente. ~**en**

/'leŋθən/ vt alargar. ● vi alargarse. ~ways adv a lo largo. ~y a largo

lenien|cy /'li:nɪənsɪ/ n indulgencia f. ~t a indulgente. ~tly adv con indulgencia

lens /lens/ n lente f. **contact ~es** npl lentillas fpl

lent /lent/ see **lend**

Lent /lent/ n cuaresma f

lentil /'lentl/ n (bean) lenteja f

Leo /'li:əʊ/ n (astr) Leo m

leopard /'lepəd/ n leopardo m

leotard /'li:əta:d/ n leotardo m

lep|er /'lepə(r)/ n leproso m. ~rosy /'leprəsɪ/ n lepra f

lesbian /'lezbɪən/ n lesbiana f. ● a lesbiano

lesion /'li:ʒn/ n lesión f

less /les/ a (in quantity) menos; (in size) menor. ● adv & prep menos. ~ **than** menos que; (with numbers) menos de. ● n menor m. ~ **and** ~ cada vez menos. **none the** ~ sin embargo. ~en /'lesn/ vt/i disminuir. ~er /'lesə(r)/ a menor

lesson /'lesn/ n clase f

lest /lest/ conj por miedo de que

let /let/ vt (pt let, pres p letting) dejar; (lease) alquilar. ~ **me do it** déjame hacerlo. ● v aux. ~'s go! ¡vamos!, ¡vámonos! ~'s see (vamos) a ver. ~'s talk/drink hablemos/ bebamos. ● n alquiler m. ~ **down** bajar; (deflate) desinflar; (fig) defraudar. ~ **go** soltar. ~ **in** dejar entrar. ~ **off** disparar ⟨gun⟩; (cause to explode) hacer explotar; hacer estallar ⟨firework⟩; (excuse) perdonar. ~ **off steam** (fig) desfogarse. ~ **on** (sl) revelar. ~ **o.s. in for** meterse en. ~ **out** dejar salir. ~ **through** dejar pasar. ~ **up** disminuir. ~down n desilusión f

lethal /'li:θl/ a ⟨dose, wound⟩ mortal; ⟨weapon⟩ mortífero

letharg|ic /lɪ'tɑ:dʒɪk/ a letárgico. ~y /'leθədʒɪ/ n letargo m

letter /'letə(r)/ n (of alphabet) letra f; (written message) carta f. ~bomb n carta f explosiva. ~box n buzón m. ~head n membrete m. ~ing n letras fpl

lettuce /'letɪs/ n lechuga f

let-up /'letʌp/ n (fam) descanso m

leukaemia /lu:'ki:mɪə/ n leucemia f

level /'levl/ a (flat) llano; (on surface) horizontal; (in height) a nivel; (in score) igual; ⟨spoonful⟩ raso. ● n

nivel m. **be on the** ~ (fam) ser honrado. ● vt (pt **levelled**) nivelar; (aim) apuntar. ~ **crossing** n paso m a nivel. ~headed a juicioso

lever /'li:və(r)/ n palanca f. ● vt apalancar. ~age /'li:vərɪdʒ/ n apalancamiento m

levity /'levətɪ/ n ligereza f

levy /'levɪ/ vt exigir ⟨tax⟩. ● n impuesto m

lewd /lu:d/ a (-er, -est) lascivo

lexicography /leksɪ'kɒɡrəfɪ/ n lexicografía f

lexicon /'leksɪkən/ n léxico m

liable /'laɪəbl/ a. **be** ~ **to do** tener tendencia a hacer. ~ **for** responsable de. ~ **to** susceptible de; expuesto a ⟨fine⟩

liability /laɪə'bɪlətɪ/ n responsabilidad f; (disadvantage, fam) inconveniente m. **liabilities** npl (debts) deudas fpl

liais|e /lɪ'eɪz/ vi hacer un enlace, enlazar. ~on /lɪ'eɪzɒn/ n enlace m; (love affair) lío m

liar /'laɪə(r)/ n mentiroso m

libel /'laɪbl/ n libelo m. ● vt (pt **libelled**) difamar (por escrito)

Liberal /'lɪbərəl/ a & n liberal (m & f)

liberal /'lɪbərəl/ a liberal; (generous) generoso; (tolerant) tolerante. ~ly adv liberalmente; (generously) generosamente; (tolerantly) tolerantemente

liberat|e /'lɪbəreɪt/ vt liberar. ~ion /-'reɪʃn/ n liberación f

libertine /'lɪbəti:n/ n libertino m

liberty /'lɪbətɪ/ n libertad f. **be at** ~ **to** estar autorizado para. **take liberties** tomarse libertades. **take the** ~ **of** tomarse la libertad de

libido /lɪ'bi:dəʊ/ n (pl -os) libido m

Libra /'li:brə/ n (astr) Libra f

librar|ian /laɪ'breərɪən/ n bibliotecario m. ~y /'laɪbrərɪ/ n biblioteca f

libretto /lɪ'bretəʊ/ n (pl -os) libreto m

Libya /'lɪbɪə/ n Libia f. ~n a & n libio (m)

lice /laɪs/ see **louse**

licence /'laɪsns/ n licencia f, permiso m; (fig, liberty) libertad f. ~ **plate** n (placa f de) matrícula f. **driving** ~ carné m de conducir

license /'laɪsns/ vt autorizar

licentious /laɪ'senʃəs/ a licencioso

lichen /'laɪkən/ n liquen m

lick /lɪk/ vt lamer; (*defeat, sl*) dar una paliza a. ~ **one's chops** relamerse. • n lametón m

licorice /ˈlɪkərɪs/ n (*Amer*) regaliz m

lid /lɪd/ n tapa f; (*of pan*) cobertera f

lido /ˈliːdəʊ/ n (*pl -os*) piscina f

lie[1] /laɪ/ vi (*pt* lay, *pp* lain, *pres p* lying) echarse; (*state*) estar echado; (*remain*) quedarse; (*be*) estar, encontrarse; (*in grave*) yacer. **be lying** estar echado. ~ **down** acostarse. ~ **low** quedarse escondido

lie[2] /laɪ/ n mentira f. • vi (*pt* lied, *pres p* lying) mentir. **give the ~ to** desmentir

lie-in /laɪˈɪn/ n. **have a ~in** quedarse en la cama

lieu /ljuː/ n. **in ~ of** en lugar de

lieutenant /lefˈtenənt/ n (*mil*) teniente m

life /laɪf/ n (*pl* lives) vida f. ~**belt** n cinturón m salvavidas. ~**boat** n lancha f de salvamento; (*on ship*) bote m salvavidas. ~**buoy** n boya f salvavidas. ~ **cycle** n ciclo m vital. ~**guard** n bañero m. ~**jacket** n chaleco m salvavidas. ~**less** a sin vida. ~**like** a natural. ~**line** n cuerda f salvavidas; (*fig*) cordón m umbilical. ~**long** a de toda la vida. ~**size(d)** a de tamaño natural. ~**time** n vida f

lift /lɪft/ vt levantar; (*steal, fam*) robar. • vi (*fog*) disiparse. • n ascensor m, elevador m (*LAm*). **give a ~ to s.o.** llevar a uno en su coche, dar aventón a uno (*LAm*). ~**off** n (*aviat*) despegue m

ligament /ˈlɪgəmənt/ n ligamento m

light[1] /laɪt/ n luz f; (*lamp*) lámpara f, luz f; (*flame*) fuego m; (*headlight*) faro m. **bring to ~** sacar a luz. **come to ~** salir a luz. **have you got a ~?** ¿tienes fuego? **the ~s** npl (*auto, traffic signals*) el semáforo m. • a claro. • vt (*pt* lit *or* lighted) encender; (*illuminate*) alumbrar. ~ **up** vt/i iluminar(se)

light[2] /laɪt/ a (*-er, -est*) (*not heavy*) ligero

lighten[1] /ˈlaɪtn/ vt (*make less heavy*) aligerar

lighten[2] /ˈlaɪtn/ vt (*give light to*) iluminar; (*make brighter*) aclarar

lighter /ˈlaɪtə(r)/ n (*for cigarettes*) mechero m

light-fingered /laɪtˈfɪŋgəd/ a largo de uñas

light-headed /laɪtˈhedɪd/ a (*dizzy*) mareado; (*frivolous*) casquivano

light-hearted /laɪtˈhɑːtɪd/ a alegre

lighthouse /ˈlaɪthaʊs/ n faro m

lighting /ˈlaɪtɪŋ/ n (*system*) alumbrado m; (*act*) iluminación f

light: ~**ly** adv ligeramente. ~**ness** n ligereza f

lightning /ˈlaɪtnɪŋ/ n relámpago m. • a relámpago

lightweight /ˈlaɪtweɪt/ a ligero. • n (*boxing*) peso m ligero

light-year /ˈlaɪtjɪə(r)/ n año m luz

like[1] /laɪk/ a parecido. • prep como. • conj (*fam*) como. • n igual. **the ~s of you** la gente como tú

like[2] /laɪk/ vt gustarle (a uno). **I ~ chocolate** me gusta el chocolate. **I should ~** quisiera. **they ~ swimming** (a ellos) les gusta nadar. **would you ~?** ¿quieres? ~**able** a simpático. ~**s** npl gustos mpl

likelihood /ˈlaɪklɪhʊd/ n probabilidad f

likely a (*-ier, -iest*) probable. **he is ~ to come** es probable que venga. • adv probablemente. **not ~!** ¡ni hablar!

like-minded /laɪkˈmaɪndɪd/ a. **be ~** tener las mismas opiniones

liken /ˈlaɪkən/ vt comparar

likeness /ˈlaɪknɪs/ n parecido m. **be a good ~** parecerse mucho

likewise /ˈlaɪkwaɪz/ adv (*also*) también; (*the same way*) lo mismo

liking /ˈlaɪkɪŋ/ n (*for thing*) afición f; (*for person*) simpatía f

lilac /ˈlaɪlək/ n lila f. • a color de lila

lilt /lɪlt/ n ritmo m

lily /ˈlɪlɪ/ n lirio m. ~ **of the valley** lirio m de los valles

limb /lɪm/ n miembro m. **out on a ~** aislado

limber /ˈlɪmbə(r)/ vi. ~ **up** hacer ejercicios preliminares

limbo /ˈlɪmbəʊ/ n limbo m. **be in ~** (*forgotten*) estar olvidado

lime[1] /laɪm/ n (*white substance*) cal f

lime[2] /laɪm/ n (*fruit*) lima f

lime[3] /laɪm/ n. ~**(-tree)** (*linden tree*) tilo m

limelight /ˈlaɪmlaɪt/ n. **be in the ~** estar muy a la vista

limerick /ˈlɪmərɪk/ n quintilla f humorística

limestone /ˈlaɪmstəʊn/ n caliza f

limit /ˈlɪmɪt/ n límite m. • vt limitar. ~**ation** /-ˈteɪʃn/ n limitación f. ~**ed**

a limitado. **~ed company** *n* sociedad *f* anónima

limousine /'lɪməziːn/ *n* limusina *f*

limp[1] /lɪmp/ *vi* cojear. ● *n* cojera *f*. **have a ~** cojear

limp[2] /lɪmp/ *a* (**-er, -est**) flojo

limpid /'lɪmpɪd/ *a* límpido

linctus /'lɪŋktəs/ *n* jarabe *m* (para la tos)

line[1] /laɪn/ *n* línea *f*; (*track*) vía *f*; (*wrinkle*) arruga *f*; (*row*) fila *f*; (*of poem*) verso *m*; (*rope*) cuerda *f*; (*of goods*) surtido *m*; (*queue*, *Amer*) cola *f*. **in ~ with** de acuerdo con. ● *vt* (*on paper etc*) rayar; bordear ‹*streets etc*›. **~ up** alinearse; (*in queue*) hacer cola

line[2] /laɪn/ *vt* forrar; (*fill*) llenar

lineage /'lɪnɪɪdʒ/ *n* linaje *m*

linear /'lɪnɪə(r)/ *a* lineal

linen /'lɪnɪn/ *n* (*sheets etc*) ropa *f* blanca; (*material*) lino *m*

liner /'laɪnə(r)/ *n* transatlántico *m*

linesman /'laɪnzmən/ *n* (*football*) juez *m* de línea

linger /'lɪŋɡə(r)/ *vi* tardar en marcharse; ‹*smells etc*› persistir. **~ over** dilatarse en

lingerie /'lænʒərɪ/ *n* ropa *f* interior, lencería *f*

lingo /'lɪŋɡəʊ/ *n* (*pl* **-os**) idioma *m*; (*specialized vocabulary*) jerga *f*

linguist /'lɪŋɡwɪst/ *n* (*specialist in languages*) políglota *m & f*; (*specialist in linguistics*) lingüista *m & f*. **~ic** /lɪŋ'ɡwɪstɪk/ *a* lingüístico. **~ics** *n* lingüística *f*

lining /'laɪnɪŋ/ *n* forro *m*; (*auto, of brakes*) guarnición *f*

link /lɪŋk/ *n* (*of chain*) eslabón *m*; (*fig*) lazo *m*. ● *vt* eslabonar; (*fig*) enlazar. **~ up with** reunirse con. **~age** *n* enlace *m*

links /lɪŋks/ *n invar* campo *m* de golf

lino /'laɪnəʊ/ *n* (*pl* **-os**) linóleo *m*. **~leum** /lɪ'nəʊlɪəm/ *n* linóleo *m*

lint /lɪnt/ *n* (*med*) hilas *fpl*; (*fluff*) pelusa *f*

lion /'laɪən/ *n* león *m*. **the ~'s share** la parte *f* del león. **~ess** *n* leona *f*

lionize /'laɪənaɪz/ *vt* tratar como una celebridad

lip /lɪp/ *n* labio *m*; (*edge*) borde *m*. **pay ~ service to** aprobar de boquilla. **stiff upper ~** *n* imperturbabilidad *f*. **~-read** *vt/i* leer en los labios. **~salve** *n* crema *f* para los labios. **~stick** *n* lápiz *m* de labios.

liquefy /'lɪkwɪfaɪ/ *vt/i* licuar(se)

liqueur /lɪ'kjʊə(r)/ *n* licor *m*

liquid /'lɪkwɪd/ *a & n* líquido (*m*)

liquidat|e /'lɪkwɪdeɪt/ *vt* liquidar. **~ion** /-'deɪʃn/ *n* liquidación *f*

liquidize /'lɪkwɪdaɪz/ *vt* licuar. **~r** *n* licuadora *f*

liquor /'lɪkə(r)/ *n* bebida *f* alcohólica

liquorice /'lɪkərɪs/ *n* regaliz *m*

lira /'lɪərə/ *n* (*pl* **lire** /'lɪəreɪ/ *or* **liras**) lira *f*

lisle /laɪl/ *n* hilo *m* de Escocia

lisp /lɪsp/ *n* ceceo *m*. **speak with a ~** cecear. ● *vi* cecear

lissom /'lɪsəm/ *a* flexible, ágil

list[1] /lɪst/ *n* lista *f*. ● *vt* hacer una lista de; (*enter in a list*) inscribir

list[2] /lɪst/ *vi* ‹*ship*› escorar

listen /'lɪsn/ *vi* escuchar. **~ in (to)** escuchar. **~ to** escuchar. **~er** *n* oyente *m & f*

listless /'lɪstlɪs/ *a* apático

lit /lɪt/ *see* **light**[1]

litany /'lɪtənɪ/ *n* letanía *f*

literacy /'lɪtərəsɪ/ *n* capacidad *f* de leer y escribir

literal /'lɪtərəl/ *a* literal; (*fig*) prosaico. **~ly** *adv* al pie de la letra, literalmente

literary /'lɪtərərɪ/ *a* literario

literate /'lɪtərət/ *a* que sabe leer y escribir

literature /'lɪtərətʃə(r)/ *n* literatura *f*; (*fig*) impresos *mpl*

lithe /laɪð/ *a* ágil

lithograph /'lɪθəɡrɑːf/ *n* litografía *f*

litigation /lɪtɪ'ɡeɪʃn/ *n* litigio *m*

litre /'liːtə(r)/ *n* litro *m*

litter /'lɪtə(r)/ *n* basura *f*; (*of animals*) camada *f*. ● *vt* ensuciar; (*scatter*) esparcir. **~ed with** lleno de. **~bin** *n* papelera *f*

little /'lɪtl/ *a* pequeño; (*not much*) poco de. ● *n* poco *m*. **a ~** un poco. **a ~ water** un poco de agua. ● *adv* poco. **~ by ~** poco a poco. **~ finger** *n* meñique *m*

liturgy /'lɪtədʒɪ/ *n* liturgia *f*

live[1] /lɪv/ *vt/i* vivir. **~ down** lograr borrar. **~ it up** echar una cana al aire. **~ on** (*feed o.s. on*) vivir de; (*continue*) perdurar. **~ up to** vivir de acuerdo con; cumplir ‹*a promise*›

live[2] /laɪv/ *a* vivo; ‹*wire*› con corriente; ‹*broadcast*› en directo. **be a ~ wire** ser una persona enérgica

livelihood /'laɪvlɪhʊd/ *n* sustento *m*

livel|iness /'laɪvlɪnɪs/ *n* vivacidad *f*. **~y** *a* (**-ier, -iest**) vivo

liven /'laɪvn/ *vt/i.* ~ **up** animar(se); (*cheer up*) alegrar(se)

liver /'lɪvə(r)/ *n* hígado *m*

livery /'lɪvərɪ/ *n* librea *f*

livestock /'laɪvstɒk/ *n* ganado *m*

livid /'lɪvɪd/ *a* lívido; (*angry, fam*) furioso

living /'lɪvɪŋ/ *a* vivo. ● *n* vida *f*. ~**-room** *n* cuarto *m* de estar, cuarto *m* de estancia (*LAm*)

lizard /'lɪzəd/ *n* lagartija *f*; (*big*) lagarto *m*

llama /'lɑːmə/ *n* llama *f*

load /ləʊd/ *n* (*incl elec*) carga *f*; (*quantity*) cantidad *f*; (*weight, strain*) peso *m*. ● *vt* cargar. ~**ed** *a* ⟨*incl dice*⟩ cargado; (*wealthy, sl*) muy rico. ~**s of** (*fam*) montones de

loaf[1] /ləʊf/ *n* (*pl* **loaves**) pan *m*; (*stick of bread*) barra *f*

loaf[2] /ləʊf/ *vi.* ~ (**about**) holgazanear. ~**er** *n* holgazán *m*

loam /ləʊm/ *n* marga *f*

loan /ləʊn/ *n* préstamo *m*. **on** ~ prestado. ● *vt* prestar

loath /ləʊθ/ *a* poco dispuesto (**to** a)

loath|e /ləʊð/ *vt* odiar. ~**ing** *n* odio *m* (**of** a). ~**some** *a* odioso

lobby /'lɒbɪ/ *n* vestíbulo *m*; (*pol*) grupo *m* de presión. ● *vt* hacer presión sobre

lobe /ləʊb/ *n* lóbulo *m*

lobster /'lɒbstə(r)/ *n* langosta *f*

local /'ləʊkl/ *a* local. ● *n* (*pub, fam*) bar *m*. **the** ~**s** los vecinos *mpl*

locale /ləʊ'kɑːl/ *n* escenario *m*

local government /ləʊkl-'gʌvənmənt/ *n* gobierno *m* municipal

locality /ləʊ'kælətɪ/ *n* localidad *f*

localized /'ləʊkəlaɪzd/ *a* localizado

locally /'ləʊkəlɪ/ *adv* localmente; (*nearby*) en la localidad

locate /ləʊ'keɪt/ *vt* (*situate*) situar; (*find*) encontrar

location /ləʊ'keɪʃn/ *n* colocación *f*; (*place*) situación *f*. **on** ~ fuera del estudio. **to film on** ~ **in Andalusia** rodar en Andalucía

lock[1] /lɒk/ *n* (*of door etc*) cerradura *f*; (*on canal*) esclusa *f*. ● *vt/i* cerrar(se) con llave. ~ **in** encerrar. ~ **out** cerrar la puerta a. ~ **up** encerrar

lock[2] /lɒk/ *n* (*of hair*) mechón *m*. ~**s** *npl* pelo *m*

locker /'lɒkə(r)/ *n* armario *m*

locket /'lɒkɪt/ *n* medallón *m*

lock-out /'lɒkaʊt/ *n* lock-out *m*

locksmith /'lɒksmɪθ/ *n* cerrajero *m*

locomotion /ləʊkə'məʊʃn/ *n* locomoción *f*

locomotive /ləʊkə'məʊtɪv/ *n* locomotora *f*

locum /'ləʊkəm/ *n* interino *m*

locust /'ləʊkəst/ *n* langosta *f*

lodge /lɒdʒ/ *n* (*in park*) casa *f* del guarda; (*of porter*) portería *f*. ● *vt* alojar; presentar ⟨*complaint*⟩; depositar ⟨*money*⟩. ● *vi* alojarse. ~**r** /-ə(r)/ *n* huésped *m*

lodgings /'lɒdʒɪŋz/ *n* alojamiento *m*; (*room*) habitación *f*

loft /lɒft/ *n* desván *m*

lofty /'lɒftɪ/ *a* (**-ier, -iest**) elevado; (*haughty*) altanero

log /lɒg/ *n* (*of wood*) leño *m*; (*naut*) cuaderno *m* de bitácora. **sleep like a** ~ dormir como un lirón. ● *vt* (*pt* **logged**) apuntar; (*travel*) recorrer

logarithm /'lɒgərɪðəm/ *n* logaritmo *m*

log-book /'lɒgbʊk/ *n* cuaderno *m* de bitácora; (*aviat*) diario *m* de vuelo

loggerheads /'lɒgəhedz/ *npl.* **be at** ~ **with** estar a matar con

logic /'lɒdʒɪk/ *a* lógica *f*. ~**al** *a* lógico. ~**ally** *adv* lógicamente

logistics /lə'dʒɪstɪks/ *n* logística *f*

logo /'ləʊgəʊ/ *n* (*pl* **-os**) logotipo *m*

loin /lɔɪn/ *n* (*culin*) solomillo *m*. ~**s** *npl* ijadas *fpl*

loiter /'lɔɪtə(r)/ *vi* holgazanear

loll /lɒl/ *vi* repantigarse

loll|ipop /'lɒlɪpɒp/ *n* (*boiled sweet*) pirulí *m*. ~**y** *n* (*iced*) polo *m*; (*money, sl*) dinero *m*

London /'lʌndən/ *n* Londres *m*. ● *a* londinense. ~**er** *n* londinense *m* & *f*

lone /ləʊn/ *a* solitario. ~**ly** /'ləʊnlɪ/ *a* (**-ier, -iest**) solitario. **feel** ~**ly** sentirse muy solo. ~**r** /'ləʊnə(r)/ *n* solitario *m*. ~**some** *a* solitario

long[1] /lɒŋ/ *a* (**-er, -est**) largo. **a** ~ **time** mucho tiempo. **how** ~ **is it?** ¿cuánto tiene de largo? **in the** ~ **run** a la larga. ● *adv* largo/mucho tiempo. **as** ~ **as** (*while*) mientras; (*provided that*) con tal que (+ *subjunctive*). **before** ~ dentro de poco. **so** ~**!** ¡hasta luego! **so** ~ **as** (*provided that*) con tal que (+ *subjunctive*)

long[2] /lɒŋ/ *vi.* ~ **for** anhelar

long-distance /lɒŋ'dɪstəns/ *a* de larga distancia. ~ **(tele)phone call** *n* conferencia *f*

longer /'lɒŋgə(r)/ *adv.* **no** ~**er** ya no

longevity /lɒn'dʒevətɪ/ n longe-vidad f

long: ~ face n cara f triste. **~hand** n escritura f a mano. **~ johns** npl (fam) calzoncillos mpl largos. **~ jump** n salto m de longitud

longing /'lɒŋɪŋ/ n anhelo m, ansia f

longitude /'lɒŋɡɪtjuːd/ n longitud f

long: ~playing record n elepé m. **~range** a de gran alcance. **~sigh-ted** a présbita. **~standing** a de mucho tiempo. **~suffering** a sufrido. **~term** a a largo plazo. **~ wave** n onda f larga. **~winded** a ⟨speaker etc⟩ prolijo

loo /luː/ n (fam) servicios mpl

look /lʊk/ vt mirar; (seem) parecer; representar ⟨age⟩. ● vi mirar; (seem) parecer; (search) buscar. ● n mirada f, (appearance) aspecto m. **~ after** ocuparse de; cuidar ⟨person⟩. **~ at** mirar. **~ down on** despreciar. **~ for** buscar. **~ for-ward to** esperar con ansia. **~ in** pasar por casa de. **~ into** inves-tigar. **~ like** (resemble) parecerse a. **~ on to** ⟨room, window⟩ dar a. **~ out** tener cuidado. **~ out for** bus-car; (watch) tener cuidado con. **~ round** volver la cabeza. **~ through** hojear. **~ up** buscar ⟨word⟩; (visit) ir a ver. **~ up to** respetar. **~er-on** n espectador m. **~ing-glass** n espejo m. **~out** n (mil) atalaya f; (person) vigía m. **~s** npl belleza f. **good ~s** mpl belleza f

loom¹ /luːm/ n telar m

loom² /luːm/ vi aparecerse

loony /'luːnɪ/ a & n (sl) chiflado (m) (fam), loco (m). **~ bin** n (sl) manic-omio m

loop /luːp/ n lazo m. ● vt hacer pre-silla con

loophole /'luːphəʊl/ n (in rule) esca-patoria f

loose /luːs/ a (-er, -est) (untied) suelto; (not tight) flojo; (inexact) vago; (immoral) inmoral; (not packed) suelto. **be at a ~ end, be at ~ ends** (Amer) no tener nada que hacer. **~ly** adv sueltamente; (roughly) aproximadamente. **~n** /'luːsn/ vt (slacken) aflojar; (untie) desatar

loot /luːt/ n botín m. ● vt saquear. **~er** n saqueador m. **~ing** n saqueo m

lop /lɒp/ vt (pt lopped). **~ off** cortar

lop-sided /lɒp'saɪdɪd/ a ladeado

loquacious /ləʊ'kweɪʃəs/ a locuaz

lord /lɔːd/ n señor m; (British title) lord m. **(good) L~!** ¡Dios mío! **the L~** el Señor m. **the (House of) L~s** la Cámara f de los Lores. **~ly** señor-ial; (haughty) altivo. **~ship** n señoría f

lore /lɔː(r)/ n tradiciones fpl

lorgnette /lɔː'njet/ n impertinentes mpl

lorry /'lɒrɪ/ n camión m

lose /luːz/ vt/i (pt lost) perder. **~r** n perdedor m

loss /lɒs/ n pérdida f. **be at a ~** estar perplejo. **be at a ~ for words** no encontrar palabras. **be at a ~ to** no saber cómo

lost /lɒst/ see **lose**. ● a perdido. **~ property** n, **~ and found** (Amer) n oficina f de objetos perdidos. **get ~** perderse

lot /lɒt/ n (fate) suerte f, (at auction) lote m; (land) solar m. **a ~ (of)** muchos. **quite a ~ of** (fam) bastante. **~s (of)** (fam) muchos. **the ~** todos mpl

lotion /'ləʊʃn/ n loción f

lottery /'lɒtərɪ/ n lotería f

lotto /'lɒtəʊ/ n lotería f

lotus /'ləʊtəs/ n (pl -uses) loto m

loud /laʊd/ a (-er, -est) fuerte; (noisy) ruidoso; (gaudy) chillón. **out ~** en voz alta. **~ hailer** n megáfono m. **~ly** adv (speak etc) en voz alta; (noisily) ruidosamente. **~speaker** n altavoz m

lounge /laʊndʒ/ vi repantigarse. ● n salón m. **~ suit** n traje m de calle

louse /laʊs/ n (pl lice) piojo m

lousy /'laʊzɪ/ a (-ier, -iest) piojoso; (bad, sl) malísimo

lout /laʊt/ n patán m

lovable /'lʌvəbl/ a adorable

love /lʌv/ n amor m; (tennis) cero m. **be in ~ with** estar enamorado de. **fall in ~ with** enamorarse de. ● vt querer ⟨person⟩; gustarle mucho a uno, encantarle a uno ⟨things⟩. **I ~ milk** me encanta la leche. **~ affair** n amores mpl

lovely /'lʌvlɪ/ a (-ier, -iest) hermoso; (delightful, fam) precioso. **have a ~ time** divertirse

lover /'lʌvə(r)/ n amante m & f

lovesick /'lʌvsɪk/ a atortolado

loving /'lʌvɪŋ/ a cariñoso

low¹ /ləʊ/ a & adv (-er, -est) bajo. ● n (low pressure) área f de baja presión

low² /ləʊ/ vi mugir

lowbrow /'ləʊbraʊ/ *a* poco culto

low-cut /'ləʊkʌt/ *a* escotado

low-down /'ləʊdaʊn/ *a* bajo. ● *n* (*sl*) informes *mpl*

lower /'ləʊə(r)/ *a & adv see* **low²**. ● *vt* bajar. ~ **o.s.** envilecerse

low-key /'ləʊ'ki:/ *a* moderado

lowlands /'ləʊləndz/ *npl* tierra *f* baja

lowly /'ləʊlɪ/ *a* (**-ier, -iest**) humilde

loyal /'lɔɪəl/ *a* leal. ~**ly** *adv* lealmente. ~**ty** *n* lealtad *f*

lozenge /'lɒzɪndʒ/ *n* (*shape*) rombo *m*; (*tablet*) pastilla *f*

LP /el'pi:/ *abbr* (*long-playing record*) elepé *m*

Ltd /'lɪmɪtɪd/ *abbr* (*Limited*) S.A., Sociedad Anónima

lubrica|nt /'lu:brɪkənt/ *n* lubricante *m*. ~**te** /-'keɪt/ *vt* lubricar. ~**tion** /-'keɪʃn/ *n* lubricación *f*

lucid /'lu:sɪd/ *a* lúcido. ~**ity** /-'sɪdətɪ/ *n* lucidez *f*

luck /lʌk/ *n* suerte *f*. **bad** ~ *n* mala suerte *f*. ~**ily** /'lʌkɪlɪ/ *adv* afortunadamente. ~**y** *a* (**-ier, -iest**) afortunado

lucrative /'lu:krətɪv/ *a* lucrativo

lucre /'lu:kə(r)/ *n* (*pej*) dinero *m*. **filthy** ~ vil metal *m*

ludicrous /'lu:dɪkrəs/ *a* ridículo

lug /lʌg/ *vt* (*pt* **lugged**) arrastrar

luggage /'lʌgɪdʒ/ *n* equipaje *m*. ~**-rack** *n* rejilla *f*. ~**van** *n* furgón *m*

lugubrious /lu:'gu:brɪəs/ *a* lúgubre

lukewarm /'lu:kwɔ:m/ *a* tibio

lull /lʌl/ *vt* (*soothe, send to sleep*) adormecer; (*calm*) calmar. ● *n* periodo *m* de calma

lullaby /'lʌləbaɪ/ *n* canción *f* de cuna

lumbago /lʌm'beɪgəʊ/ *n* lumbago *m*

lumber /'lʌmbə(r)/ *n* trastos *mpl* viejos; (*wood*) maderos *mpl*. ● *vt*. ~ **s.o. with** hacer que uno cargue con. ~**jack** *n* leñador *m*

luminous /'lu:mɪnəs/ *a* luminoso

lump¹ /'lʌmp/ *n* protuberancia *f*; (*in liquid*) grumo *m*; (*of sugar*) terrón *m*; (*in throat*) nudo *m*. ● *vt*. ~ **together** agrupar

lump² /lʌmp/ *vt*. ~ **it** (*fam*) aguantarlo

lump: ~ **sum** *n* suma *f* global. ~**y** *a* ⟨*sauce*⟩ grumoso; (*bumpy*) cubierto de protuberancias

lunacy /'lu:nəsɪ/ *n* locura *f*

lunar /'lu:nə(r)/ *a* lunar

lunatic /'lu:nətɪk/ *n* loco *m*

lunch /lʌntʃ/ *n* comida *f*, almuerzo *m*. ● *vi* comer

luncheon /'lʌntʃən/ *n* comida *f*, almuerzo *m*. ~ **meat** *n* carne *f* en lata. ~ **voucher** *n* vale *m* de comida

lung /lʌŋ/ *n* pulmón *m*

lunge /lʌndʒ/ *n* arremetida *f*

lurch¹ /lɜ:tʃ/ *vi* tambalearse

lurch² /lɜ:tʃ/ *n*. **leave in the** ~ dejar en la estacada

lure /ljʊə(r)/ *vt* atraer. ● *n* (*attraction*) atractivo *m*

lurid /'ljʊərɪd/ *a* chillón; (*shocking*) espeluznante

lurk /lɜ:k/ *vi* esconderse; (*in ambush*) estar al acecho; (*prowl*) rondar

luscious /'lʌʃəs/ *a* delicioso

lush /lʌʃ/ *a* exuberante. ● *n* (*Amer, sl*) borracho *m*

lust /lʌst/ *n* lujuria *f*; (*fig*) ansia *f*. ● *vi*. ~ **after** codiciar. ~**ful** *a* lujurioso

lustre /'lʌstə(r)/ *n* lustre *m*

lusty /'lʌstɪ/ *a* (**-ier, -iest**) fuerte

lute /lu:t/ *n* laúd *m*

Luxemburg /'lʌksəmbɜ:g/ *n* Luxemburgo *m*

luxuriant /lʌg'zjʊərɪənt/ *a* exuberante

luxur|ious /lʌg'zjʊərɪəs/ *a* lujoso. ~**y** /'lʌkʃərɪ/ *n* lujo *m*. ● *a* de lujo

lye /laɪ/ *n* lejía *f*

lying /'laɪɪŋ/ *see* **lie¹**, **lie²**. ● *n* mentiras *fpl*

lynch /lɪntʃ/ *vt* linchar

lynx /lɪŋks/ *n* lince *m*

lyre /'laɪə(r)/ *n* lira *f*

lyric /'lɪrɪk/ *a* lírico. ~**al** *a* lírico. ~**ism** /-sɪzəm/ *n* lirismo *m*. ~**s** *npl* letra *f*

M

MA *abbr* (*Master of Arts*) Master *m*, grado *m* universitario entre el de licenciado y doctor

mac /mæk/ *n* (*fam*) impermeable *m*

macabre /mə'kɑ:brə/ *a* macabro

macaroni /mækə'rəʊnɪ/ *n* macarrones *mpl*

macaroon /mækə'ru:n/ *n* mostachón *m*

mace¹ /meɪs/ *n* (*staff*) maza *f*

mace² /meɪs/ *n* (*spice*) macis *f*

Mach /mɑ:k/ *n*. ~ (**number**) *n* (número *m* de) Mach (*m*)

machiavellian /mækɪə'velɪən/ *a* maquiavélico

machinations /mækɪ'neɪʃnz/ *npl* maquinaciones *fpl*

machine /mə'ʃiːn/ *n* máquina *f*. ● *vt* (*sew*) coser a máquina; (*tec*) trabajar a máquina. **~gun** *n* ametralladora *f*. **~ry** /mə'ʃiːnərɪ/ *n* maquinaria *f*; (*working parts, fig*) mecanismo *m*. **~ tool** *n* máquina *f* herramienta

machinist /mə'ʃiːnɪst/ *n* maquinista *m & f*

mach|ismo /mæ'tʃɪzməʊ/ *n* machismo *m*. **~o** *a* macho

mackerel /'mækrəl/ *n invar* (*fish*) caballa *f*

mackintosh /'mækɪntɒʃ/ *n* impermeable *m*

macrobiotic /mækrəʊbaɪ'ɒtɪk/ *a* macrobiótico

mad /mæd/ *a* (**madder, maddest**) loco; (*foolish*) insensato; (*dog*) rabioso; (*angry, fam*) furioso. **be ~ about** estar loco por. **like ~** como un loco; (*a lot*) muchísimo

Madagascar /mædə'gæskə(r)/ *n* Madagascar *m*

madam /'mædəm/ *n* señora *f*; (*unmarried*) señorita *f*

madcap /'mædkæp/ *a* atolondrado. ● *n* locuelo *m*

madden /'mædn/ *vt* (*make mad*) enloquecer; (*make angry*) enfurecer

made /meɪd/ *see* **make**. **~ to measure** hecho a la medida

Madeira /mə'dɪərə/ *n* (*wine*) vino *m* de Madera

mad: ~house *n* manicomio *m*. **~ly** *adv* (*interested, in love etc*) locamente; (*frantically*) como un loco. **~man** *n* loco *m*. **~ness** *n* locura *f*

madonna /mə'dɒnə/ *n* Virgen *f* María

madrigal /'mædrɪgl/ *n* madrigal *m*

maelstrom /'meɪlstrəm/ *n* remolino *m*

maestro /'maɪstrəʊ/ *n* (*pl* **maestri** /-striː/ *or* **os**) maestro *m*

Mafia /'mæfɪə/ *n* mafia *f*

magazine /mægə'ziːn/ *n* revista *f*; (*of gun*) recámara *f*

magenta /mə'dʒentə/ *a* rojo purpúreo

maggot /'mægət/ *n* gusano *m*. **~y** *a* agusanado

Magi /'meɪdʒaɪ/ *npl*. **the ~** los Reyes *mpl* Magos

magic /'mædʒɪk/ *n* magia *f*. ● *a* mágico. **~al** *a* mágico. **~ian** /mə'dʒɪʃn/ *n* mago *m*

magisterial /mædʒɪ'stɪərɪəl/ *a* magistral; (*imperious*) autoritario

magistrate /'mædʒɪstreɪt/ *n* magistrado *m*, juez *m*

magnanim|ity /mægnə'nɪmətɪ/ *n* magnanimidad *f*. **~ous** /-'nænɪməs/ *a* magnánimo

magnate /'mægneɪt/ *n* magnate *m*

magnesia /mæg'niːʒə/ *n* magnesia *f*

magnet /'mægnɪt/ *n* imán *m*. **~ic** /-'netɪk/ *a* magnético. **~ism** *n* magnetismo *m*. **~ize** *vt* magnetizar

magnificen|ce /mæg'nɪfɪsns/ *a* magnificencia *f*. **~t** *a* magnífico

magnif|ication /mægnɪfɪ'keɪʃn/ *n* aumento *m*. **~ier** /-'faɪə(r)/ *n* lupa *f*, lente *f* de aumento. **~y** /-faɪ/ *vt* aumentar. **~ying-glass** *n* lupa *f*, lente *f* de aumento

magnitude /'mægnɪtjuːd/ *n* magnitud *f*

magnolia /mæg'nəʊlɪə/ *n* magnolia *f*

magnum /'mægnəm/ *n* botella *f* de litro y medio

magpie /'mægpaɪ/ *n* urraca *f*

mahogany /mə'hɒgənɪ/ *n* caoba *f*

maid /meɪd/ *n* (*servant*) criada *f*; (*girl, old use*) doncella *f*. **old ~** solterona *f*

maiden /'meɪdn/ *n* doncella *f*. ● *a* (*aunt*) soltera; (*voyage*) inaugural. **~hood** *n* doncellez *f*, virginidad *f*, soltería *f*. **~ly** *adv* virginal. **~ name** *n* apellido *m* de soltera

mail[1] /meɪl/ *n* correo *m*; (*letters*) cartas *fpl*. ● *a* postal, de correos. ● *vt* (*post*) echar al correo; (*send*) enviar por correo

mail[2] /meɪl/ *n* (*armour*) (cota *f* de) malla *f*

mail: ~ing list *n* lista *f* de direcciones. **~man** *n* (*Amer*) cartero *m*. **~ order** *n* venta *f* por correo

maim /meɪm/ *vt* mutilar

main /meɪn/ *n*. (**waterúgas**) **~** cañería *f* principal. **in the ~** en su mayor parte. **the ~s** *npl* (*elec*) la red *f* eléctrica. ● *a* principal. **a ~ road** *n* una carretera *f*. **~land** *n* continente *m*. **~ly** *adv* principalmente. **~spring** *n* muelle *m* real; (*fig, motive*) móvil *m* principal. **~stay** *n* sostén *m*. **~stream** *n* corriente *f* principal. **~ street** *n* calle *f* principal

maintain /meɪn'teɪn/ *vt* mantener

maintenance /'meɪntənəns/ *n* mantenimiento *m*; (*allowance*) pensión *f* alimenticia

maisonette /meɪzə'net/ n (small house) casita f; (part of house) dúplex m

maize /meɪz/ n maíz m

majestic /mə'dʒestɪk/ a majestuoso

majesty /'mædʒəstɪ/ n majestad f

major /'meɪdʒə(r)/ a mayor. **a ~ road** una calle f prioritaria. ● n comandante m. ● vi. **~ in** (univ, Amer) especializarse en

Majorca /mə'jɔːkə/ n Mallorca f

majority /mə'dʒɒrətɪ/ n mayoría f. **the ~ of people** la mayoría f de la gente. ● a mayoritario

make /meɪk/ vt/i (pt made) hacer; (manufacture) fabricar; ganar (money); tomar (decision); llegar a (destination). ~ **s.o. do sth** obligar a uno a hacer algo. **be made of** estar hecho de. **I cannot ~ anything of it** no me lo explico. **I ~ it two o'clock** yo tengo las dos. ● n fabricación f; (brand) marca f. ~ **as if to** estar a punto de. ~ **believe** fingir. ~ **do** (manage) arreglarse. ~ **do with** (content o.s.) contentarse con. ~ **for** dirigirse a. ~ **good** vi tener éxito. ● vt compensar; (repair) reparar. ~ **it** llegar; (succeed) tener éxito. ~ **it up** (become reconciled) hacer las paces. ~ **much of** dar mucha importancia a. ~ **off** escaparse (**with** con). ~ **out** vt distinguir; (understand) entender; (draw up) extender; (assert) dar a entender. ● vi arreglárselas. ~ **over** ceder (**to** a). ~ **up** formar; (prepare) preparar; inventar (story); (compensate) compensar. ● vi hacer las paces. ~ **up (one's face)** maquillarse. ~ **up for** compensar; recuperar (time). ~ **up to** congraciarse con. **~believe** a fingido, simulado. ● n ficción f

maker /'meɪkə(r)/ n fabricante m & f. **the M~** el Hacedor m, el Creador m

makeshift /'meɪkʃɪft/ n expediente m. ● a (temporary) provisional; (improvised) improvisado

make-up /'meɪkʌp/ n maquillaje m

makeweight /'meɪkweɪt/ n complemento m

making /'meɪkɪŋ/ n. **be the ~ of** ser la causa del éxito de. **he has the ~s of** tiene madera de. **in the ~** en vías de formación

maladjust|ed /mælə'dʒʌstɪd/ a inadaptado. **~ment** n inadaptación f

maladministration /mæləd-mɪnɪ'streɪʃn/ n mala administración f

malady /'mælədɪ/ n enfermedad f

malaise /mæ'leɪz/ n malestar m

malaria /mə'leərɪə/ n paludismo m

Malay /mə'leɪ/ a & n malayo (m). **~sia** n Malasia f

male /meɪl/ a masculino; (bot, tec) macho. ● n macho m; (man) varón m

malefactor /'mælɪfæktə(r)/ n malhechor m

malevolen|ce /mə'levəlns/ n malevolencia f. **~t** a malévolo

malform|ation /mælfɔː'meɪʃn/ n malformación f. **~ed** a deforme

malfunction /mæl'fʌŋkʃn/ n funcionamiento m defectuoso. ● vi funcionar mal

malic|e /'mælɪs/ n rencor m. **bear s.o. ~e** guardar rencor a uno. **~ious** /mə'lɪʃəs/ a malévolo. **~iously** adv con malevolencia

malign /mə'laɪn/ a maligno. ● vt calumniar

malignan|cy /mə'lɪgnənsɪ/ n malignidad f. **~t** a maligno

malinger /mə'lɪŋgə(r)/ vi fingirse enfermo. **~er** n enfermo m fingido

malleable /'mælɪəbl/ a maleable

mallet /'mælɪt/ n mazo m

malnutrition /mælnju:'trɪʃn/ n desnutrición f

malpractice /mæl'præktɪs/ n falta f profesional

malt /mɔːlt/ n malta f

Malt|a /'mɔːltə/ n Malta f. **~ese** /-'ti:z/ a & n maltés (m)

maltreat /mæl'tri:t/ vt maltratar. **~ment** n maltrato m

malt whisky /mɔːlt'wɪskɪ/ n güisqui m de malta

mammal /'mæml/ n mamífero m

mammoth /'mæməθ/ n mamut m. ● a gigantesco

man /mæn/ n (pl men) hombre m; (in sports team) jugador m; (chess) pieza f. ~ **in the street** hombre m de la calle. ~ **to** ~ de hombre a hombre. ● vt (pt **manned**) guarnecer (de hombres); tripular (ship); servir (guns)

manacle /'mænəkl/ n manilla f. ● vt poner esposas a

manage /'mænɪdʒ/ vt dirigir; llevar (shop, affairs); (handle) manejar. ● vi arreglárselas. ~ **to do** lograr

hacer. **~able** a manejable. **~ment**
n dirección f

manager /'mænɪdʒə(r)/ n director m;
(of actor) empresario m. **~ess**
/-'res/ n directora f. **~ial** /-'dʒɪərɪəl/
a directivo. **~ial staff** n personal m
dirigente

managing director /'mænɪdʒɪŋ
daɪ'rektə(r)/ n director m gerente

mandarin /'mændərɪn/ n mandarín
m; (orange) mandarina f

mandate /'mændeɪt/ n mandato m

mandatory /'mændətərɪ/ a obligatorio

mane /meɪn/ n (of horse) crin f; (of
lion) melena f

manful /'mænfl/ a valiente

manganese /'mæŋgəniːz/ n man-
ganeso m

manger /'meɪndʒə(r)/ n pesebre m

mangle[1] 'mæŋgl/ n (for wringing)
exprimidor m; (for smoothing)
máquina f de planchar

mangle[2] /'mæŋgl/ vt destrozar

mango /'mæŋgəʊ/ n (pl **-oes**) mango
m

mangy /'meɪndʒɪ/ a sarnoso

man: **~handle** vt maltratar. **~hole**
n registro m. **~hole cover** n tapa f
de registro. **~hood** n edad f viril;
(quality) virilidad f. **~hour** n ho-
ra-hombre f. **~hunt** n persecución
f

mania /'meɪnɪə/ n manía f. **~c** /-ræk/
n maníaco m

manicur|e /'mænɪkjʊə(r)/ n manic-
ura f. ● vt hacer la manicura a (person). **~ist** n manicuro m

manifest /'mænɪfest/ a manifiesto.
● vt mostrar. **~ation** /-'steɪʃn/ n
manifestación f

manifesto /mænɪ'festəʊ/ n (pl **-os**)
manifiesto m

manifold /'mænɪfəʊld/ a múltiple

manipulat|e /mə'nɪpjʊleɪt/ vt man-
ipular. **~ion** /-'leɪʃn/ n mani-
pulación f

mankind /mæn'kaɪnd/ n la humanidad f

man: **~ly** adv viril. **~made** a
artificial

mannequin /'mænɪkɪn/ n maniquí
m

manner /'mænə(r)/ n manera f;
(behaviour) comportamiento m;
(kind) clase f. **~ed** a amanerado.
bad-~ed a mal educado. **~s** npl
(social behaviour) educación f. **have
no ~s** no tener educación

mannerism /'mænərɪzəm/ n peculiaridad f

mannish /'mænɪʃ/ a (woman)
hombruna

manoeuvre /mə'nuːvə(r)/ n maniobra
f. ● vt/i maniobrar

man-of-war /mænəv'wɔː(r)/ n buque
m de guerra

manor /'mænə(r)/ n casa f solariega

manpower /'mænpaʊə(r)/ n mano f
de obra

manservant /'mænsɜːvənt/ n criado
m

mansion /'mænʃn/ n mansión f

man: **~size(d)** a grande. **~slaugh-
ter** n homicidio m impremeditado

mantelpiece /'mæntlpiːs/ n repisa f
de chimenea

mantilla /mæn'tɪlə/ n mantilla f

mantle /'mæntl/ n manto m

manual /'mænjʊəl/ a manual. ● n
(handbook) manual m

manufacture /mænju'fæktʃə(r)/ vt
fabricar. ● n fabricación f. **~r** /-ə(r)/
n fabricante m

manure /mə'njʊə(r)/ n estiércol m

manuscript /'mænjʊskrɪpt/ n manuscrito m

many /'menɪ/ a & n muchos (mpl).
~ people mucha gente f. **~ a time**
muchas veces. **a great/good ~**
muchísimos

map /mæp/ n mapa m; (of streets etc)
plano m. ● vt (pt **mapped**) levantar
un mapa de. **~ out** organizar

maple /'meɪpl/ n arce m

mar /mɑː/ vt (pt **marred**) estropear;
aguar (enjoyment)

marathon /'mærəθən/ n maratón m

maraud|er /mə'rɔːdə(r)/ n mer-
odeador m. **~ing** a merodeador

marble /'mɑːbl/ n mármol m; (for
game) canica f

March /mɑːtʃ/ n marzo m

march /mɑːtʃ/ vi (mil) marchar. **~ off**
irse. ● vt. **~ off** (lead away)
llevarse. ● n marcha f

marchioness /mɑːʃə'nes/ n marquesa
f

march-past /'mɑːtʃpɑːst/ n desfile m

mare /meə(r)/ n yegua f

margarine /mɑːdʒə'riːn/ n margarina
f

margin /'mɑːdʒɪn/ n margen f. **~al** a
marginal. **~al seat** n (pol) escaño m
inseguro. **~ally** adv muy poco

marguerite /mɑːgə'riːt/ n margarita f

marigold /'mærɪgəʊld/ n caléndula f

marijuana /mærɪ'hwɑ:nə/ n marihuana f

marina /mə'ri:nə/ n puerto m deportivo

marina|de /mærɪ'neɪd/ n escabeche m. **~te** /'mærɪneɪt/ vt escabechar

marine /mə'ri:n/ a marino. ● n (sailor) soldado m de infantería de marina; (shipping) marina f

marionette /mærɪə'net/ n marioneta f

marital /'mærɪtl/ a marital, matrimonial. **~ status** n estado m civil

maritime /'mærɪtaɪm/ a marítimo

marjoram /'mɑ:dʒərəm/ n mejorana f

mark[1] /mɑ:k/ n marca f; (trace) huella f; (schol) nota f; (target) blanco m. ● vt marcar; poner nota a ⟨exam⟩. **~ time** marcar el paso. **~ out** trazar; escoger ⟨person⟩

mark[2] /mɑ:k/ n (currency) marco m

marked /mɑ:kt/ a marcado. **~ly** /-kɪdlɪ/ adv marcadamente

marker /'mɑ:kə(r)/ n marcador m; (for book) registro m

market /'mɑ:kɪt/ n mercado m. **on the ~** en venta. ● vt (sell) vender; (launch) comercializar. **~ garden** n huerto m. **~ing** n marketing m

marking /'mɑ:kɪŋ/ n (marks) marcas fpl

marksman /'mɑ:ksmən/ n tirador m. **~ship** n puntería f

marmalade /'mɑ:məleɪd/ n mermelada f de naranja

marmot /'mɑ:mət/ n marmota f

maroon /mə'ru:n/ n granate m. ● a de color granate

marooned /mə'ru:nd/ a abandonado; (snow-bound etc) aislado

marquee /mɑ:ki:/ n tienda de campaña f grande; (awning, Amer) marquesina f

marquetry /'mɑ:kɪtrɪ/ n marquetería f

marquis /'mɑ:kwɪs/ n marqués m

marriage /'mærɪdʒ/ n matrimonio m; (wedding) boda f. **~able** a casadero

married /'mærɪd/ a casado; ⟨life⟩ conjugal

marrow /'mærəʊ/ n (of bone) tuétano m; (vegetable) calabacín m

marry /'mærɪ/ vt casarse con; (give or unite in marriage) casar. ● vi casarse. **get married** casarse

marsh /mɑ:ʃ/ n pantano m

marshal /'mɑ:ʃl/ n (mil) mariscal m; (master of ceremonies) maestro m de

ceremonias; (at sports events) oficial m. ● vt (pt **marshalled**) ordenar; formar ⟨troops⟩

marsh mallow /mɑ:ʃ'mæləʊ/ n (plant) malvavisco m

marshmallow /mɑ:ʃ'mæləʊ/ n (sweet) caramelo m blando

marshy /'mɑ:ʃɪ/ a pantanoso

martial /'mɑ:ʃl/ a marcial. **~ law** n ley f marcial

Martian /'mɑ:ʃn/ a & n marciano (m)

martinet /mɑ:tɪ'net/ n ordenancista m & f

martyr /'mɑ:tə(r)/ n mártir m & f. ● vt martirizar. **~dom** n martirio m

marvel /'mɑ:vl/ n maravilla f. ● vi (pt **marvelled**) maravillarse (at con, de). **~lous** /'mɑ:vələs/ a maravilloso

Marxis|m /'mɑ:ksɪzəm/ n marxismo m. **~t** a & n marxista (m & f)

marzipan /'mɑ:zɪpæn/ n mazapán m

mascara /mæ'skɑ:rə/ n rimel m

mascot /'mæskɒt/ n mascota f

masculin|e /'mæskjʊlɪn/ a & n masculino (m). **~ity** /-'lɪnətɪ/ n masculinidad f

mash /mæʃ/ n mezcla f; (potatoes, fam) puré m de patatas. ● vt (crush) machacar; (mix) mezclar. **~ed potatoes** n puré m de patatas

mask /mɑ:sk/ n máscara f. ● vt enmascarar

masochis|m /'mæsəkɪzəm/ n masoquismo m. **~t** n masoquista m & f

mason /'meɪsn/ n (builder) albañil m

Mason /'meɪsn/ n. **~** masón m. **~ic** /mə'sɒnɪk/ a masónico

masonry /'meɪsnrɪ/ n albañilería f

masquerade /mɑ:skə'reɪd/ n mascarada f. ● vi. **~ as** hacerse pasar por

mass[1] /mæs/ n masa f; (large quantity) montón m. **the ~es** npl las masas fpl. ● vt/i agrupar(se)

mass[2] /mæs/ n (relig) misa f. **high ~** misa f mayor

massacre /'mæsəkə(r)/ n masacre f, matanza f. ● vt masacrar

massage /'mæsɑ:ʒ/ n masaje m. ● vt dar masaje a

masseu|r /mæ'sɜ:(r)/ n masajista m. **~se** /mæ'sɜ:z/ n masajista f

massive /'mæsɪv/ a masivo; (heavy) macizo; (huge) enorme

mass: ~ media n medios mpl de comunicación. **~-produce** vt fabricar en serie

mast /mɑːst/ *n* mástil *m*; (*for radio*, *TV*) torre *f*

master /ˈmɑːstə(r)/ *n* maestro *m*; (*in secondary school*) profesor *m*; (*of ship*) capitán *m*. ● *vt* dominar. ~**-key** *n* llave *f* maestra. ~**ly** *a* magistral. ~**mind** *n* cerebro *m*. ● *vt* dirigir. **M~ of Arts** master *m*, grado *m* universitario entre el de licenciado y el de doctor

masterpiece /ˈmɑːstəpiːs/ *n* obra *f* maestra

master-stroke /ˈmɑːstəstrəʊk/ *n* golpe *m* maestro

mastery /ˈmɑːstərɪ/ *n* dominio *m*; (*skill*) maestría *f*

masturbat|e /ˈmæstəbeɪt/ *vi* masturbarse. ~**ion** /-ˈbeɪʃn/ *n* masturbación *f*

mat /mæt/ *n* estera *f*; (*at door*) felpudo *m*

match[1] /mætʃ/ *n* (*sport*) partido *m*; (*equal*) igual *m*; (*marriage*) matrimonio *m*; (*s.o. to marry*) partido *m*. ● *vt* emparejar; (*equal*) igualar; ⟨*clothes, colours*⟩ hacer juego con. ● *vi* hacer juego

match[2] /mætʃ/ *n* (*of wood*) fósforo *m*; (*of wax*) cerilla *f*. ~**box** /ˈmætʃbɒks/ *n* (*for wooden matches*) caja *f* de fósforos; (*for wax matches*) caja *f* de cerillas

matching /ˈmætʃɪŋ/ *a* que hace juego

mate[1] /meɪt/ *n* compañero *m*; (*of animals*) macho *m*, hembra *f*; (*assistant*) ayudante *m*. ● *vt/i* acoplar(se)

mate[2] /meɪt/ *n* (*chess*) mate *m*

material /məˈtɪərɪəl/ *n* material *m*; (*cloth*) tela *f*. ● *a* material; (*fig*) importante. ~**istic** /-ˈlɪstɪk/ *a* materialista. ~**s** *npl* materiales *mpl*. **raw ~s** *npl* materias *fpl* primas

materialize /məˈtɪərɪəlaɪz/ *vi* materializarse

maternal /məˈtɜːnl/ *a* maternal; ⟨*relation*⟩ materno

maternity /məˈtɜːnɪtɪ/ *n* maternidad *f*. ● *a* de maternidad. ~ **clothes** *npl* vestido *m* pre-mamá. ~ **hospital** *n* maternidad *f*

matey /ˈmeɪtɪ/ *a* (*fam*) simpático

mathematic|ian /ˌmæθəməˈtɪʃn/ *n* matemático *m*. ~**al** /-ˈmætɪkl/ *a* matemático. ~**s** /-ˈmætɪks/ *n & npl* matemáticas *fpl*

maths /mæθs/, **math** (*Amer*) *n & npl* matemáticas *fpl*

matinée /ˈmætɪneɪ/ *n* función *f* de tarde

matriculat|e /məˈtrɪkjʊleɪt/ *vt/i* matricular(se). ~**ion** /-ˈleɪʃn/ *n* matriculación *f*

matrimon|ial /ˌmætrɪˈməʊnɪəl/ *a* matrimonial. ~**y** /ˈmætrɪmənɪ/ *n* matrimonio *m*

matrix /ˈmeɪtrɪks/ *n* (*pl* **matrices** /-siːz/) matriz *f*

matron /ˈmeɪtrən/ *n* (*married, elderly*) matrona *f*; (*in school*) ama *f* de llaves; (*former use, in hospital*) enfermera *f* jefe. ~**ly** *a* matronil

matt /mæt/ *a* mate

matted /ˈmætɪd/ *a* enmarañado

matter /ˈmætə(r)/ *n* (*substance*) materia *f*; (*affair*) asunto *m*; (*pus*) pus *m*. **as a ~ of fact** en realidad. **no ~** no importa. **what is the ~?** ¿qué pasa? ● *vi* importar. **it does not ~** no importa. ~**-of-fact** *a* realista

matting /ˈmætɪŋ/ *n* estera *f*

mattress /ˈmætrɪs/ *n* colchón *m*

matur|e /məˈtjʊə(r)/ *a* maduro. ● *vt/i* madurar. ~**ity** *n* madurez *f*

maul /mɔːl/ *vt* maltratar

Mauritius /məˈrɪʃəs/ *n* Mauricio *m*

mausoleum /ˌmɔːsəˈlɪəm/ *n* mausoleo *m*

mauve /məʊv/ *a & n* color (*m*) de malva

mawkish /ˈmɔːkɪʃ/ *a* empalagoso

maxim /ˈmæksɪm/ *n* máxima *f*

maxim|ize /ˈmæksɪmaɪz/ *vt* llevar al máximo. ~**um** *a & n* (*pl* **-ima**) máximo (*m*)

may /meɪ/ *v aux* (*pt* **might**) poder. ~ **I smoke?** ¿se permite fumar? ~ **he be happy** ¡que sea feliz! **he ~/might come** puede que venga. **I ~/might as well stay** más vale quedarme. **it ~/might be true** puede ser verdad

May /meɪ/ *n* mayo *m*. ~ **Day** *n* el primero *m* de mayo

maybe /ˈmeɪbɪ/ *adv* quizá(s)

mayhem /ˈmeɪhem/ *n* (*havoc*) alboroto *m*

mayonnaise /ˌmeɪəˈneɪz/ *n* mayonesa *f*

mayor /meə(r)/ *n* alcalde *m*, alcaldesa *f*. ~**ess** *n* alcaldesa *f*

maze /meɪz/ *n* laberinto *m*

me[1] /miː/ *pron* me; (*after prep*) mí. **he knows ~** me conoce. **it's ~** soy yo

me[2] /miː/ *n* (*mus, third note of any musical scale*) mi *m*

meadow /ˈmedəʊ/ *n* prado *m*

meagre /'miːgə(r)/ a escaso

meal¹ /miːl/ n comida f

meal² /miːl/ n (grain) harina f

mealy-mouthed /miːlɪ'maʊðd/ a hipócrita

mean¹ /miːn/ vt (pt meant) (intend) tener la intención de, querer; (signify) querer decir, significar. ~ **to do** tener la intención de hacer. ~ **well** tener buenas intenciones. **be meant for** estar destinado a

mean² /miːn/ a (-er, -est) (miserly) tacaño; (unkind) malo; (poor) pobre

mean³ /miːn/ a medio. ● n medio m; (average) promedio m

meander /mɪ'ændə(r)/ vi (river) serpentear; (person) vagar

meaning /'miːnɪŋ/ n sentido m. ~**ful** a significativo. ~**less** a sin sentido

meanness /'miːnnɪs/ n (miserliness) tacañería f; (unkindness) maldad f

means /miːnz/ n medio m. **by all** ~ por supuesto. **by no** ~ de ninguna manera. ● npl (wealth) recursos mpl. ~ **test** n investigación f financial

meant /ment/ see **mean¹**

meantime /'miːntaɪm/ adv entretanto. **in the** ~ entretanto

meanwhile /'miːnwaɪl/ adv entretanto

measles /'miːzlz/ n sarampión m

measly /'miːzlɪ/ a (sl) miserable

measurable /'meʒərəbl/ a mensurable

measure /'meʒə(r)/ n medida f; (ruler) regla f. ● vt/i medir. ~ **up to** estar a la altura de. ~**d** a (rhythmical) acompasado; (carefully considered) prudente. ~**ment** n medida f

meat /miːt/ n carne f. ~**y** a carnoso; (fig) sustancioso

mechanic /mɪ'kænɪk/ n mecánico m. ~**al** /mɪ'kænɪkl/ a mecánico. ~**s** n mecánica f

mechani|sm /'mekənɪzəm/ n mecanismo m. ~**ze** vt mecanizar

medal /'medl/ n medalla f

medallion /mɪ'dælɪən/ n medallón m

medallist /'medəlɪst/ n ganador m de una medalla. **be a gold** ~ ganar una medalla de oro

meddle /'medl/ vi entrometerse (**in** en); (tinker) tocar. ~ **with** (tinker) tocar. ~**some** a entrometido

media /'miːdɪə/ see **medium**. ● npl. **the** ~ npl los medios mpl de comunicación

mediat|e /'miːdɪeɪt/ vi mediar. ~**ion** /-eɪʃn/ n mediación f. ~**or** n mediador m

medical /'medɪkl/ a médico; (student) de medicina. ● n (fam) reconocimiento m médico

medicat|ed /'medɪkeɪtɪd/ a medicinal. ~**ion** /-'keɪʃn/ n medicación f

medicin|e /'medsɪn/ n medicina f. ~**al** /mɪ'dɪsɪnl/ a medicinal

medieval /medɪ'iːvl/ a medieval

mediocr|e /miːdɪ'əʊkə(r)/ a mediocre. ~**ity** /-'ɒkrətɪ/ n mediocridad f

meditat|e /'medɪteɪt/ vt/i meditar. ~**ion** /-'teɪʃn/ n meditación f

Mediterranean /medɪtə'reɪnɪən/ a mediterráneo. ● n. **the** ~ el Mediterráneo m

medium /'miːdɪəm/ n (pl **media**) medio m; (pl **mediums**) (person) médium m. ● a mediano

medley /'medlɪ/ n popurrí m

meek /miːk/ a (-er, -est) manso

meet /miːt/ vt (pt met) encontrar; (bump into s.o.) encontrarse con; (see again) ver; (fetch) ir a buscar; (get to know, be introduced to) conocer. ~ **the bill** pagar la cuenta. ● vi encontrarse; (get to know) conocerse; (in session) reunirse. ~ **with** tropezar con (obstacles)

meeting /'miːtɪŋ/ n reunión f; (accidental between two people) encuentro m; (arranged between two people) cita f

megalomania /megələʊ'meɪnɪə/ n megalomanía f

megaphone /'megəfəʊn/ n megáfono m

melanchol|ic /melən'kɒlɪk/ a melancólico. ~**y** /'melənkɒlɪ/ n melancolía f. ● a melancólico

mêlée /'meleɪ/ n pelea f confusa

mellow /'meləʊ/ a (-er, -est) (fruit, person) maduro; (sound, colour) dulce. ● vt/i madurar(se)

melodi|c /mɪ'lɒdɪk/ a melódico. ~**ous** /mɪ'ləʊdɪəs/ a melodioso

melodrama /'melədrɑːmə/ n melodrama m. ~**tic** /-ə'mætɪk/ a melodramático

melody /'melədɪ/ n melodía f

melon /'melən/ n melón m

melt /melt/ vt (make liquid) derretir; fundir (metals). ● vi (become liquid) derretirse; (metals) fundirse. ~**ing-pot** n crisol m

member /'membə(r)/ n miembro m. **M~ of Parliament** n diputado m.

~**ship** *n* calidad *f* de miembro; (*members*) miembros *mpl*

membrane /'membreɪn/ *n* membrana *f*

memento /mɪ'mentəʊ/ *n* (*pl* **-oes**) recuerdo *m*

memo /'meməʊ/ *n* (*pl* **-os**) (*fam*) nota *f*

memoir /'memwɑ:(r)/ *n* memoria *f*

memorable /'memərəbl/ *a* memorable

memorandum /memə'rændəm/ *n* (*pl* **-ums**) nota *f*

memorial /mɪ'mɔ:rɪəl/ *n* monumento *m*. ● *a* conmemorativo

memorize /'meməraɪz/ *vt* aprender de memoria

memory /'memərɪ/ *n* (*faculty*) memoria *f*; (*thing remembered*) recuerdo *m*. **from** ~ de memoria. **in** ~ **of** en memoria de

men /men/ *see* **man**

menac|e /'menəs/ *n* amenaza *f*; (*nuisance*) pesado *m*. ● *vt* amenazar. ~**ingly** *adv* de manera amenazadora

menagerie /mɪ'nædʒərɪ/ *n* casa *f* de fieras

mend /mend/ *vt* reparar; (*darn*) zurcir. ~ **one's ways** enmendarse. ● *n* remiendo *m*. **be on the** ~ ir mejorando

menfolk /'menfəʊk/ *n* hombres *mpl*

menial /'mi:nɪəl/ *a* servil

meningitis /menɪn'dʒaɪtɪs/ *n* meningitis *f*

menopause /'menəpɔ:z/ *n* menopausia *f*

menstruat|e /'menstrʊeɪt/ *vi* menstruar. ~**ion** /-eɪʃn/ *n* menstruación *f*

mental /'mentl/ *a* mental; (*hospital*) psiquiátrico

mentality /men'tælətɪ/ *n* mentalidad *f*

menthol /'menθɒl/ *n* mentol *m*. ~**ated** *a* mentolado

mention /'menʃn/ *vt* mencionar. **don't** ~ **it!** ¡no hay de qué! ● *n* mención *f*

mentor /'mentɔ:(r)/ *n* mentor *m*

menu /'menju:/ *n* (*set meal*) menú *m*; (*a la carte*) lista *f* (de platos)

mercantile /'mɜ:kəntaɪl/ *a* mercantil

mercenary /'mɜ:sɪnərɪ/ *a* & *n* mercenario (*m*)

merchandise /'mɜ:tʃəndaɪz/ *n* mercancías *fpl*

merchant /'mɜ:tʃənt/ *n* comerciante *m*. ● *a* (*ship, navy*) mercante. ~ **bank** *n* banco *m* mercantil

merci|ful /'mɜ:sɪfl/ *a* misericordioso. ~**fully** *adv* (*fortunately, fam*) gracias a Dios. ~**less** /'mɜ:sɪlɪs/ *a* despiadado

mercur|ial /mɜ:'kjʊərɪəl/ *a* mercurial; (*fig, active*) vivo. ~**y** /'mɜ:kjʊrɪ/ *n* mercurio *m*

mercy /'mɜ:sɪ/ *n* compasión *f*. **at the** ~ **of** a merced de

mere /mɪə(r)/ *a* simple. ~**ly** *adv* simplemente

merest /'mɪərɪst/ *a* mínimo

merge /mɜ:dʒ/ *vt* unir; fusionar (*companies*). ● *vi* unirse; (*companies*) fusionarse. ~**r** /-ə(r)/ *n* fusión *f*

meridian /mə'rɪdɪən/ *n* meridiano *m*

meringue /mə'ræŋ/ *n* merengue *m*

merit /'merɪt/ *n* mérito *m*. ● *vt* (*pt* **merited**) merecer. ~**orious** /-'tɔ:rɪəs/ *a* meritorio

mermaid /'mɜ:meɪd/ *n* sirena *f*

merr|ily /'merəlɪ/ *adv* alegremente. ~**iment** /'merɪmənt/ *n* alegría *f*. ~**y** /'merɪ/ *a* (**-ier**, **-iest**) alegre. **make** ~ divertirse. ~**y-go-round** *n* tiovivo *m*. ~**y-making** *n* holgorio *m*

mesh /meʃ/ *n* malla *f*; (*network*) red *f*

mesmerize /'mezməraɪz/ *vt* hipnotizar

mess /mes/ *n* desorden *m*; (*dirt*) suciedad *f*; (*mil*) rancho *m*. **make a** ~ **of** chapucear, estropear. ● *vt*. ~ **up** desordenar; (*dirty*) ensuciar. ● *vi*. ~ **about** entretenerse. ~ **with** (*tinker with*) manosear

message /'mesɪdʒ/ *n* recado *m*

messenger /'mesɪndʒə(r)/ *n* mensajero *m*

Messiah /mɪ'saɪə/ *n* Mesías *m*

Messrs /'mesəz/ *npl*. ~ **Smith** los señores *mpl* or Sres. Smith

messy /'mesɪ/ *a* (**-ier**, **-iest**) en desorden; (*dirty*) sucio

met /met/ *see* **meet**

metabolism /mɪ'tæbəlɪzəm/ *n* metabolismo *m*

metal /'metl/ *n* metal. ● *a* de metal. ~**lic** /mɪ'tælɪk/ *a* metálico

metallurgy /mɪ'tælədʒɪ/ *n* metalurgia *f*

metamorphosis /metə'mɔ:fəsɪs/ *n* (*pl* **-phoses** /-sɪ:z/) metamorfosis *f*

metaphor /'metəfə(r)/ *n* metáfora *f*. ~**ical** /-'fɒrɪkl/ *a* metafórico

mete /miːt/ *vt.* ~ **out** repartir; dar ⟨*punishment*⟩

meteor /'miːtɪə(r)/ *n* meteoro *m*

meteorite /'miːtɪəraɪt/ *n* meteorito *m*

meteorolog|ical /miːtɪərə'lɒdʒɪkl/ *a* meteorológico. ~**y** /-'rɒlədʒɪ/ *n* meteorología *f*

meter[1] /'miːtə(r)/ *n* contador *m*

meter[2] /'miːtə(r)/ *n* (*Amer*) = **metre**

method /'meθəd/ *n* método *m*

methodical /mɪ'θɒdɪkl/ *a* metódico

Methodist /'meθədɪst/ *a & n* metodista (*m & f*)

methylated /'meθɪleɪtɪd/ *a.* ~ **spirit** *n* alcohol *m* desnaturalizado

meticulous /mɪ'tɪkjʊləs/ *a* meticuloso

metre /'miːtə(r)/ *n* metro *m*

metric /'metrɪk/ *a* métrico. ~**ation** /-'keɪʃn/ *n* cambio *m* al sistema métrico

metropolis /mɪ'trɒpəlɪs/ *n* metrópoli *f*

metropolitan /metrə'pɒlɪtən/ *a* metropolitano

mettle /'metl/ *n* valor *m*

mew /mjuː/ *n* maullido *m.* ● *vi* maullar

mews /mjuːz/ *npl* casas *fpl* pequeñas (que antes eran caballerizas)

Mexic|an /'meksɪkən/ *a & n* mejicano (*m*); (*in Mexico*) mexicano (*m*). ~**o** /-kəʊ/ *n* Méjico *m*; (*in Mexico*) México *m*

mezzanine /'metsəniːn/ *n* entresuelo *m*

mi /miː/ *n* (*mus, third note of any musical scale*) mi *m*

miaow /miːˈaʊ/ *n & vi* = **mew**

mice /maɪs/ *see* **mouse**

mickey /'mɪkɪ/ *n.* **take the** ~ **out of** (*sl*) tomar el pelo a

micro... /'maɪkrəʊ/ *pref* micro...

microbe /'maɪkrəʊb/ *n* microbio *m*

microchip /'maɪkrəʊtʃɪp/ *n* pastilla *f*

microfilm /'maɪkrəʊfɪlm/ *n* microfilme *m*

microphone /'maɪkrəfəʊn/ *n* micrófono *m*

microprocessor /maɪkrəʊ'prəʊsesə(r)/ *n* microprocesador *m*

microscop|e /'maɪkrəskəʊp/ *n* microscopio *m.* ~**ic** /-'skɒpɪk/ *a* microscópico

microwave /'maɪkrəʊweɪv/ *n* microonda *f.* ~ **oven** *n* horno *m* de microondas

mid /mɪd/ *a.* **in** ~ **air** en pleno aire. **in** ~ **March** a mediados de marzo. **in** ~ **ocean** en medio del océano

midday /mɪd'deɪ/ *n* mediodía *m*

middle /'mɪdl/ *a* de en medio; ⟨*quality*⟩ mediano. ● *n* medio *m.* **in the** ~ **of** en medio de. ~**aged** *a* de mediana edad. **M**~ **Ages** *npl* Edad *f* Media. ~ **class** *n* clase *f* media. ~**class** *a* de la clase media. **M**~ **East** *n* Oriente *m* Medio. ~**man** *n* intermediario *m*

middling /'mɪdlɪŋ/ *a* regular

midge /mɪdʒ/ *n* mosquito *m*

midget /'mɪdʒɪt/ *n* enano *m.* ● *a* minúsculo

Midlands /'mɪdləndz/ *npl* región *f* central de Inglaterra

midnight /'mɪdnaɪt/ *n* medianoche *f*

midriff /'mɪdrɪf/ *n* diafragma *m*; (*fam*) vientre *m*

midst /mɪdst/ *n.* **in our** ~ entre nosotros. **in the** ~ **of** en medio de

midsummer /mɪd'sʌmə(r)/ *n* pleno verano *m*; (*solstice*) solsticio *m* de verano

midway /mɪd'weɪ/ *adv* a medio camino

midwife /'mɪdwaɪf/ *n* comadrona *f*

midwinter /mɪd'wɪntə(r)/ *n* pleno invierno *m*

might[1] /maɪt/ *see* **may**

might[2] /maɪt/ *n* (*strength*) fuerza *f*; (*power*) poder *m.* ~**y** *a* (*strong*) fuerte; (*powerful*) poderoso; (*very great, fam*) enorme. ● *adv* (*fam*) muy

migraine /'miːgreɪn/ *n* jaqueca *f*

migrant /'maɪgrənt/ *a* migratorio. ● *n* (*person*) emigrante *m & f*

migrat|e /maɪ'greɪt/ *vi* emigrar. ~**ion** /-ʃn/ *n* migración *f*

mike /maɪk/ *n* (*fam*) micrófono *m*

mild /maɪld/ *a* (-er, -est) ⟨*person*⟩ apacible; ⟨*climate*⟩ templado; (*slight*) ligero; ⟨*taste*⟩ suave; ⟨*illness*⟩ benigno

mildew /'mɪldjuː/ *n* moho *m*

mild: ~**ly** *adv* (*slightly*) ligeramente. ~**ness** *n* (*of person*) apacibilidad *f*; (*of climate, illness*) benignidad *f*; (*of taste*) suavidad *f*

mile /maɪl/ *n* milla *f.* ~**s better** (*fam*) mucho mejor. ~**s too big** (*fam*) demasiado grande. ~**age** *n* (*loosely*) kilometraje *m.* ~**stone** *n* mojón *m*; (*event, stage, fig*) hito *m*

milieu /mɪ'ljɜː/ *n* ambiente *m*

militant /'mɪlɪtənt/ *a & n* militante (*m & f*)

military /'mɪlɪtərɪ/ *a* militar

militate /'mɪlɪteɪt/ *vi* militar (**against** contra)

militia /mɪ'lɪʃə/ *n* milicia *f*

milk /mɪlk/ *n* leche *f*. ● *a* (*product*) lácteo; (*chocolate*) con leche. ● *vt* ordeñar (*cow*); (*exploit*) chupar. **~man** *n* repartidor *m* de leche. **~ shake** *n* batido *m* de leche. **~y** *a* lechoso. **M~y Way** *n* Vía *f* Láctea

mill /mɪl/ *n* molino *m*; (*for coffee, pepper*) molinillo *m*; (*factory*) fábrica *f*. ● *vt* moler. ● *vi*. **~ about/around** apiñarse, circular

millennium /mɪ'lenɪəm/ *n* (*pl* **-ia** or **-iums**) milenio *m*

miller /'mɪlə(r)/ *n* molinero *m*

millet /'mɪlɪt/ *n* mijo *m*

milli... /'mɪlɪ/ *pref* mili...

milligram(me) /'mɪlɪgræm/ *n* miligramo *m*

millimetre /'mɪlɪmiːtə(r)/ *n* milímetro *m*

milliner /'mɪlɪnə(r)/ *n* sombrerero *m*

million /'mɪljən/ *n* millón *m*. **a ~ pounds** un millón *m* de libras. **~aire** *n* millonario *m*

millstone /'mɪlstəʊn/ *n* muela *f* (de molino); (*fig, burden*) losa *f*

mime /maɪm/ *n* pantomima *f*. ● *vt* hacer en pantomima. ● *vi* actuar de mimo

mimic /'mɪmɪk/ *vt* (*pt* **mimicked**) imitar. ● *n* imitador *m*. **~ry** *n* imitación *f*

mimosa /mɪ'məʊzə/ *n* mimosa *f*

minaret /mɪnə'ret/ *n* alminar *m*

mince /mɪns/ *vt* desmenuzar; picar (*meat*). **not to ~ matters/words** no tener pelos en la lengua. ● *n* carne *f* picada. **~meat** *n* conserva *f* de fruta picada. **make ~meat of s.o.** hacer trizas a uno. **~ pie** *n* pastel *m* con frutas picadas. **~r** *n* máquina *f* de picar carne

mind /maɪnd/ *n* mente *f*; (*sanity*) juicio *m*; (*opinion*) parecer *m*; (*intention*) intención *f*. **be on one's ~** preocuparle a uno. ● *vt* (*look after*) cuidar; (*heed*) hacer caso de. **I don't ~** me da igual. **I don't ~ the noise** no me molesta el ruido. **never ~** no te preocupes, no se preocupe. **~er** *n* cuidador *m*. **~ful** *a* atento (**of** a). **~less** *a* estúpido

mine[1] /maɪn/ *poss pron* (el) mío *m*, (la) mía *f*, (los) míos *mpl*, (las) mías *fpl*. **it is ~** es mío

mine[2] /maɪn/ *n* mina *f*. ● *vt* extraer. **~field** *n* campo *m* de minas. **~r** *n* minero *m*

mineral /'mɪnərəl/ *a & n* mineral (*m*). **~ (water)** *n* (*fizzy soft drink*) gaseosa *f*. **~ water** *n* (*natural*) agua *f* mineral

minesweeper /'maɪnswiːpə(r)/ *n* (*ship*) dragaminas *m invar*

mingle /'mɪŋgl/ *vt/i* mezclar(se)

mingy /'mɪndʒɪ/ *a* tacaño

mini... /'mɪnɪ/ *pref* mini...

miniature /'mɪnɪtʃə(r)/ *a & n* miniatura (*f*)

mini: ~bus *n* microbús *m*. **~cab** *n* taxi *m*

minim /'mɪnɪm/ *n* (*mus*) blanca *f*

minim|al /'mɪnɪml/ *a* mínimo. **~ize** *vt* minimizar. **~um** *a & n* (*pl* **-ima**) mínimo (*m*)

mining /'maɪnɪŋ/ *n* explotación *f*. ● *a* minero

miniskirt /'mɪnɪskɜːt/ *n* minifalda *f*

minist|er /'mɪnɪstə(r)/ *n* ministro *m*; (*relig*) pastor *m*. **~erial** /-'stɪərɪəl/ *a* ministerial. **~ry** *n* ministerio *m*

mink /mɪŋk/ *n* visón *m*

minor /'maɪnə(r)/ *a* (*incl mus*) menor; (*of little importance*) sin importancia. ● *n* menor *m & f* de edad

minority /maɪ'nɒrətɪ/ *n* minoría *f*. ● *a* minoritario

minster /'mɪnstə(r)/ *n* catedral *f*

minstrel /'mɪnstrəl/ *n* juglar *m*

mint[1] /mɪnt/ *n* (*plant*) menta *f*; (*sweet*) caramelo *m* de menta

mint[2] /mɪnt/ *n*. **the M~** *n* casa *f* de la moneda. **a ~** un dineral *m*. ● *vt* acuñar. **in ~ condition** como nuevo

minuet /mɪnjʊ'et/ *n* minué *m*

minus /'maɪnəs/ *prep* menos; (*without, fam*) sin. ● *n* (*sign*) menos *m*. **~ sign** *n* menos *m*

minuscule /'mɪnəskjuːl/ *a* minúsculo

minute[1] /'mɪnɪt/ *n* minuto *m*. **~s** *npl* (*of meeting*) actas *fpl*

minute[2] /maɪ'njuːt/ *a* minúsculo; (*detailed*) minucioso

minx /mɪŋks/ *n* chica *f* descarada

mirac|le /'mɪrəkl/ *n* milagro *m*. **~ulous** /mɪ'rækjʊləs/ *a* milagroso

mirage /'mɪrɑːʒ/ *n* espejismo *m*

mire /'maɪə(r)/ *n* fango *m*

mirror /'mɪrə(r)/ *n* espejo *m*. ● *vt* reflejar

mirth /mɜːθ/ *n* (*merriment*) alegría *f*; (*laughter*) risas *fpl*

misadventure /ˌmɪsədˈventʃə(r)/ n desgracia f

misanthropist /mɪˈzænθrəpɪst/ n misántropo m

misapprehension /ˌmɪsæprɪˈhenʃṇ/ n malentendido m

misbehav|e /ˌmɪsbɪˈheɪv/ vi portarse mal. **~iour** n mala conducta f

miscalculat|e /ˌmɪsˈkælkjʊleɪt/ vt/i calcular mal. **~ion** /-ˈleɪʃn/ n desacierto m

miscarr|iage /ˈmɪskærɪdʒ/ n aborto m. **~iage of justice** n error m judicial. **~y** vi abortar

miscellaneous /ˌmɪsəˈleɪnɪəs/ a vario

mischief /ˈmɪstʃɪf/ n (foolish conduct) travesura f; (harm) daño m. **get into ~** cometer travesuras. **make ~** armar un lío

mischievous /ˈmɪstʃɪvəs/ a travieso; (malicious) perjudicial

misconception /ˌmɪskənˈsepʃn/ n equivocación f

misconduct /mɪsˈkɒndʌkt/ n mala conducta f

misconstrue /ˌmɪskənˈstruː/ vt interpretar mal

misdeed /mɪsˈdiːd/ n fechoría f

misdemeanour /ˌmɪsdɪˈmiːnə(r)/ n fechoría f

misdirect /ˌmɪsdɪˈrekt/ vt dirigir mal ⟨person⟩

miser /ˈmaɪzə(r)/ n avaro m

miserable /ˈmɪzərəbl/ a (sad) triste; (wretched) miserable; (weather) malo

miserly /ˈmaɪzəlɪ/ a avariento

misery /ˈmɪzərɪ/ n (unhappiness) tristeza f; (pain) sufrimiento m; (poverty) pobreza f; (person, fam) aguafiestas m & f

misfire /mɪsˈfaɪə(r)/ vi fallar

misfit /ˈmɪsfɪt/ n (person) inadaptado m; (thing) cosa f mal ajustada

misfortune /mɪsˈfɔːtʃuːn/ n desgracia f

misgiving /mɪsˈɡɪvɪŋ/ n (doubt) duda f; (apprehension) presentimiento m

misguided /mɪsˈɡaɪdɪd/ a equivocado. **be ~** equivocarse

mishap /ˈmɪshæp/ n desgracia f

misinform /ˌmɪsɪnˈfɔːm/ vt informar mal

misinterpret /ˌmɪsɪnˈtɜːprɪt/ vt interpretar mal

misjudge /mɪsˈdʒʌdʒ/ vt juzgar mal

mislay /mɪsˈleɪ/ vt (pt **mislaid**) extraviar

mislead /mɪsˈliːd/ vt (pt **misled**) engañar. **~ing** a engañoso

mismanage /mɪsˈmænɪdʒ/ vt administrar mal. **~ment** n mala administración f

misnomer /mɪsˈnəʊmə(r)/ n nombre m equivocado

misplace /mɪsˈpleɪs/ vt colocar mal; (lose) extraviar

misprint /ˈmɪsprɪnt/ n errata f

misquote /mɪsˈkwəʊt/ vt citar mal

misrepresent /ˌmɪsreprɪˈzent/ vt describir engañosamente

miss[1] /mɪs/ vt (fail to hit) errar; (notice absence of) echar de menos; perder ⟨train⟩. **~ the point** no comprender. ● n fallo m. **~ out** omitir

miss[2] /mɪs/ n (pl **misses**) señorita f

misshapen /mɪsˈʃeɪpən/ a deforme

missile /ˈmɪsaɪl/ n proyectil m

missing /ˈmɪsɪŋ/ a ⟨person⟩ (absent) ausente; ⟨person⟩ (after disaster) desaparecido; (lost) perdido. **be ~** faltar

mission /ˈmɪʃn/ n misión f. **~ary** /ˈmɪʃənərɪ/ n misionero m

missive /ˈmɪsɪv/ n misiva f

misspell /mɪsˈspel/ vt (pt **misspelt** or **misspelled**) escribir mal

mist /mɪst/ n neblina f; (at sea) bruma f. ● vt/i empañar(se)

mistake /mɪsˈteɪk/ n error m. ● vt (pt **mistook**, pp **mistaken**) equivocarse de; (misunderstand) entender mal. **~ for** tomar por. **~n** /-ən/ a equivocado. **be ~n** equivocarse. **~nly** adv equivocadamente

mistletoe /ˈmɪsltəʊ/ n muérdago m

mistreat /mɪsˈtriːt/ vt maltratar

mistress /ˈmɪstrɪs/ n (of house) señora f; (primary school teacher) maestra f; (secondary school teacher) profesora f; (lover) amante f

mistrust /mɪsˈtrʌst/ vt desconfiar de. ● n desconfianza f

misty /ˈmɪstɪ/ a (**-ier, -iest**) nebuloso; ⟨day⟩ de niebla; ⟨glass⟩ empañado. **it is ~** hay neblina

misunderstand /ˌmɪsʌndəˈstænd/ vt (pt **-stood**) entender mal. **~ing** n malentendido m

misuse /mɪsˈjuːz/ vt emplear mal; abusar de ⟨power etc⟩. /mɪsˈjuːs/ n mal uso m; (unfair use) abuso m

mite /maɪt/ n (insect) ácaro m, garrapata f; (child) niño m pequeño

mitigate /ˈmɪtɪɡeɪt/ vt mitigar

mitre /'maɪtə(r)/ n (*head-dress*) mitra f

mitten /'mɪtn/ n manopla f; (*leaving fingers exposed*) mitón m

mix /mɪks/ vt/i mezclar(se). ~ **up** mezclar; (*confuse*) confundir. ~ **with** frecuentar ⟨*people*⟩. ● n mezcla f

mixed /mɪkst/ a ⟨*school etc*⟩ mixto; (*assorted*) variado. **be ~ up** estar confuso

mixer /'mɪksə(r)/ n (*culin*) batidora f. **be a good ~** tener don de gentes

mixture /'mɪkstʃə(r)/ n mezcla f

mix-up /'mɪksʌp/ n lío m

moan /məʊn/ n gemido m. ● vi gemir; (*complain*) quejarse (**about** de). ~**er** n refunfuñador m

moat /məʊt/ n foso m

mob /mɒb/ n (*crowd*) muchedumbre f; (*gang*) pandilla f; (*masses*) populacho m. ● vt (*pt* **mobbed**) acosar

mobil|e /'məʊbaɪl/ a móvil. ~**e home** n caravana f. ● n móvil m. ~**ity** /mə'bɪlətɪ/ n movilidad f

mobiliz|ation /məʊbɪlaɪ'zeɪʃn/ n movilización f. ~**e** /'məʊbɪlaɪz/ vt/i movilizar

moccasin /'mɒkəsɪn/ n mocasín m

mocha /'mɒkə/ n moca m

mock /mɒk/ vt burlarse de. ● vi burlarse. ● a fingido

mockery /'mɒkərɪ/ n burla f. **a ~ of** una parodia f de

mock-up /'mɒkʌp/ n maqueta f

mode /məʊd/ n (*way, method*) modo m; (*fashion*) moda f

model /'mɒdl/ n modelo m; (*mock-up*) maqueta f; (*for fashion*) maniquí m. ● a (*exemplary*) ejemplar; ⟨*car etc*⟩ en miniatura. ● vt (*pt* **modelled**) modelar; presentar ⟨*clothes*⟩. ● vi ser maniquí; (*pose*) posar. ~**ling** n profesión f de maniquí

moderate /'mɒdərət/ a & n moderado (m). /'mɒdəreɪt/ vt/i moderar(se). ~**ly** /'mɒdərətlɪ/ adv (*in moderation*) moderadamente; (*fairly*) medianamente

moderation /mɒdə'reɪʃn/ n moderación f. **in ~** con moderación

modern /'mɒdn/ a moderno. ~**ize** vt modernizar

modest /'mɒdɪst/ a modesto. ~**y** n modestia f

modicum /'mɒdɪkəm/ n. **a ~ of** un poquito m de

modif|ication /mɒdɪfɪ'keɪʃn/ n modificación f. ~**y** /-faɪ/ vt/i modificar(se)

modulat|e /'mɒdjʊleɪt/ vt/i modular. ~**ion** /-'leɪʃn/ n modulación f

module /'mɒdjuːl/ n módulo m

mogul /'məʊgəl/ n (*fam*) magnate m

mohair /'məʊheə(r)/ n mohair m

moist /mɔɪst/ a (**-er**, **-est**) húmedo. ~**en** /'mɔɪsn/ vt humedecer

moistur|e /'mɔɪstʃə(r)/ n humedad f. ~**ize** /'mɔɪstʃəraɪz/ vt humedecer. ~**izer** n crema f hidratante

molar /'məʊlə(r)/ n muela f

molasses /mə'læsɪz/ n melaza f

mold /məʊld/ (*Amer*) = **mould**

mole¹ /məʊl/ n (*animal*) topo m

mole² /məʊl/ n (*on skin*) lunar m

mole³ /məʊl/ n (*breakwater*) malecón m

molecule /'mɒlɪkjuːl/ n molécula f

molehill /'məʊlhɪl/ n topera f

molest /mə'lest/ vt importunar

mollify /'mɒlɪfaɪ/ vt apaciguar

mollusc /'mɒləsk/ n molusco m

mollycoddle /'mɒlɪkɒdl/ vt mimar

molten /'məʊltən/ a fundido

mom /mɒm/ n (*Amer*) mamá f

moment /'məʊmənt/ n momento m. ~**arily** /'məʊməntərɪlɪ/ adv momentáneamente. ~**ary** a momentáneo

momentous /mə'mentəs/ a importante

momentum /mə'mentəm/ n momento m; (*speed*) velocidad f; (*fig*) ímpetu m

Monaco /'mɒnəkəʊ/ n Mónaco m

monarch /'mɒnək/ n monarca m. ~**ist** n monárquico m. ~**y** n monarquía f

monast|ery /'mɒnəstərɪ/ n monasterio m. ~**ic** /mə'næstɪk/ a monástico

Monday /'mʌndeɪ/ n lunes m

monetar|ist /'mʌnɪtərɪst/ n monetarista m & f. ~**y** a monetario

money /'mʌnɪ/ n dinero m. ~**-box** n hucha f. ~**ed** a adinerado. ~**-lender** n prestamista m & f. ~**-order** n giro m postal. ~**s** npl cantidades fpl de dinero. ~**-spinner** n mina f de dinero

mongol /'mɒŋgl/ n & a (*med*) mongólico (m)

mongrel /'mʌŋgrəl/ n perro m mestizo

monitor /'mɒnɪtə(r)/ n (*pupil*) monitor m & f; (*tec*) monitor m. ● vt controlar; escuchar ⟨*a broadcast*⟩

monk /mʌŋk/ n monje m

monkey /'mʌŋkɪ/ n mono m. **~-nut** n cacahuete m, maní m (LAm). **~-wrench** n llave f inglesa

mono /'mɒnəʊ/ a monofónico m

monocle /'mɒnəkl/ n monóculo m

monogram /'mɒnəgræm/ n monograma m

monologue /'mɒnəlɒg/ n monólogo m

monopol|ize /məˈnɒpəlaɪz/ vt monopolizar. **~y** n monopolio m

monosyllab|ic /mɒnəsɪˈlæbɪk/ a monosilábico. **~le** /-ˈsɪləbl/ n monosílabo m

monotone /'mɒnətəʊn/ n monotonía f. **speak in a ~** hablar con una voz monótona

monoton|ous /məˈnɒtənəs/ a monótono. **~y** n monotonía f

monsoon /mɒnˈsuːn/ n monzón m

monster /'mɒnstə(r)/ n monstruo m

monstrosity /mɒnˈstrɒsətɪ/ n monstruosidad f

monstrous /'mɒnstrəs/ a monstruoso

montage /mɒnˈtɑːʒ/ n montaje m

month /mʌnθ/ n mes m. **~ly** /'mʌnθlɪ/ a mensual. ● adv mensualmente. ● n (periodical) revista f mensual

monument /'mɒnjʊmənt/ n monumento m. **~al** /-ˈmentl/ a monumental

moo /muː/ n mugido m. ● vi mugir

mooch /muːtʃ/ vi (sl) haraganear. ● vt (Amer, sl) birlar

mood /muːd/ n humor m. **be in the ~ for** tener ganas de. **in a good/bad ~** de buen/mal humor. **~y** a (-ier, -iest) de humor cambiadizo; (bad-tempered) malhumorado

moon /muːn/ n luna f. **~light** n luz f de la luna. **~lighting** n (fam) pluriempleo m. **~lit** a iluminado por la luna; (night) de luna

moor¹ /mʊə(r)/ n (open land) páramo m

moor² /mʊə(r)/ vt amarrar. **~ings** npl (ropes) amarras fpl; (place) amarradero m

Moor /mʊə(r)/ n moro m

moose /muːs/ n invar alce m

moot /muːt/ a discutible. ● vt proponer (question)

mop /mɒp/ n fregona f. **~ of hair** pelambrera f. ● vt (pt mopped) fregar. **~ (up)** limpiar

mope /məʊp/ vi estar abatido

moped /'məʊped/ n ciclomotor m

moral /'mɒrəl/ a moral. ● n moraleja f. **~s** npl moralidad f

morale /məˈrɑːl/ n moral f

moral|ist /'mɒrəlɪst/ n moralista m & f. **~ity** /məˈræləti/ n moralidad f. **~ize** vi moralizar. **~ly** adv moralmente

morass /məˈræs/ n (marsh) pantano m; (fig, entanglement) embrollo m

morbid /'mɔːbɪd/ a morboso

more /mɔː(r)/ a & n & adv más. **~ and ~** cada vez más. **~ or less** más o menos. **once ~** una vez más. **some ~** más

moreover /mɔːˈrəʊvə(r)/ adv además

morgue /mɔːg/ n depósito m de cadáveres

moribund /'mɒrɪbʌnd/ a moribundo

morning /'mɔːnɪŋ/ n mañana f; (early hours) madrugada f. **at 11 o'clock in the ~** a las once de la mañana. **in the ~** por la mañana

Morocc|an /məˈrɒkən/ a & n marroquí (m & f). **~o** /-kəʊ/ n Marruecos mpl

moron /'mɔːrɒn/ n imbécil m & f

morose /məˈrəʊs/ a malhumorado

morphine /'mɔːfiːn/ n morfina f

Morse /mɔːs/ n Morse m. **~ (code)** n alfabeto m Morse

morsel /'mɔːsl/ n pedazo m; (mouthful) bocado m

mortal /'mɔːtl/ a & n mortal (m). **~ity** /-ˈtæləti/ n mortalidad f

mortar /'mɔːtə(r)/ n (all senses) mortero m

mortgage /'mɔːgɪdʒ/ n hipoteca f. ● vt hipotecar

mortify /'mɔːtɪfaɪ/ vt mortificar

mortuary /'mɔːtjʊərɪ/ n depósito m de cadáveres

mosaic /məʊˈzeɪk/ n mosaico m

Moscow /'mɒskəʊ/ n Moscú m

Moses /'məʊzɪz/ a. **~ basket** n moisés m

mosque /mɒsk/ n mezquita f

mosquito /mɒsˈkiːtəʊ/ n (pl -oes) mosquito m

moss /mɒs/ n musgo m. **~y** a musgoso

most /məʊst/ a más. **for the ~ part** en su mayor parte. ● n la mayoría f. **~ of** la mayor parte de. **at ~** a lo más. **make the ~ of** aprovechar al máximo. ● adv más; (very) muy. **~ly** adv principalmente

MOT *abbr* (*Ministry of Transport*). ~ (*test*) ITV, inspección *f* técnica de vehículos

motel /məʊˈtel/ *n* motel *m*

moth /mɒθ/ *n* mariposa *f* (nocturna); (*in clothes*) polilla *f*. **~ball** *n* bola *f* de naftalina. **~eaten** *a* apolillado

mother /ˈmʌðə(r)/ *n* madre *f*. ● *vt* cuidar como a un hijo. **~hood** *n* maternidad *f*. **~-in-law** *n* (*pl* **~s-in-law**) suegra *f*. **~land** *n* patria *f*. **~ly** *adv* maternalmente. **~-of-pearl** *n* nácar *m*. **M~'s Day** *n* el día *m* de la Madre. **~-to-be** *n* futura madre *f*. ~ **tongue** *n* lengua *f* materna

motif /məʊˈtiːf/ *n* motivo *m*

motion /ˈməʊʃn/ *n* movimiento *m*; (*proposal*) moción *f*. ● *vt/i*. ~ (**to**) **s.o. to** hacer señas a uno para que. **~less** *a* inmóvil

motivat|e /ˈməʊtɪveɪt/ *vt* motivar. **~ion** /-ˈveɪʃn/ *n* motivación *f*

motive /ˈməʊtɪv/ *n* motivo *m*

motley /ˈmɒtlɪ/ *a* abigarrado

motor /ˈməʊtə(r)/ *n* motor *m*; (*car*) coche *m*. ● *a* motor; (*fem*) motora, motriz. ● *vi* ir en coche. **~ bike** *n* (*fam*) motocicleta *f*, moto *f* (*fam*). **~boat** *n* lancha *f* motora. **~cade** /ˈməʊtəkeɪd/ *n* (*Amer*) desfile *m* de automóviles. **~ car** *n* coche *m*, automóvil *m*. **~ cycle** *n* motocicleta *f*. **~cyclist** *n* motociclista *m* & *f*. **~ing** *n* automovilismo *m*. **~ist** *n* automovilista *m* & *f*. **~ize** *vt* motorizar. **~way** *n* autopista *f*

mottled /ˈmɒtld/ *a* abigarrado

motto /ˈmɒtəʊ/ *n* (*pl* -**oes**) lema *m*

mould[1] /məʊld/ *n* molde *m*. ● *vt* moldear

mould[2] /məʊld/ *n* (*fungus*, *rot*) moho *m*

moulding /ˈməʊldɪŋ/ *n* (*on wall etc*) moldura *f*

mouldy /ˈməʊldɪ/ *a* mohoso

moult /məʊlt/ *vi* mudar

mound /maʊnd/ *n* montículo *m*; (*pile*, *fig*) montón *m*

mount[1] /maʊnt/ *vt/i* subir. ● *n* montura *f*. ~ **up** aumentar

mount[2] /maʊnt/ *n* (*hill*) monte *m*

mountain /ˈmaʊntɪn/ *n* montaña *f*. **~eer** /maʊntɪˈnɪə(r)/ *n* alpinista *m* & *f*. **~eering** *n* alpinismo *m*. **~ous** /ˈmaʊntɪnəs/ *a* montañoso

mourn /mɔːn/ *vt* llorar. ● *vi* lamentarse. ~ **for** llorar la muerte de. **~er** *n* persona *f* que acompaña el cortejo fúnebre. **~ful** *a* triste. **~ing** *n* luto *m*

mouse /maʊs/ *n* (*pl* **mice**) ratón *m*. **~trap** *n* ratonera *f*

mousse /muːs/ *n* (*dish*) crema *f* batida

moustache /məˈstɑːʃ/ *n* bigote *m*

mousy /ˈmaʊsɪ/ *a* ⟨*hair*⟩ pardusco; (*fig*) tímido

mouth /maʊð/ *vt* formar con los labios. /maʊθ/ *n* boca *f*. **~ful** *n* bocado *m*. **~organ** *n* armónica *f*. **~piece** *n* (*mus*) boquilla *f*; (*fig*, *person*) portavoz *f*, vocero *m* (*LAm*). **~wash** *n* enjuague *m*

movable /ˈmuːvəbl/ *a* móvil, movible

move /muːv/ *vt* mover; mudarse de ⟨*house*⟩; (*with emotion*) conmover; (*propose*) proponer. ● *vi* moverse; (*be in motion*) estar en movimiento; (*progress*) hacer progresos; (*take action*) tomar medidas; (*depart*) irse. ~ (**out**) irse. ● *n* movimiento *m*; (*in game*) jugada *f*; (*player's turn*) turno *m*; (*removal*) mudanza *f*. **on the** ~ en movimiento. ~ **along** (hacer) circular. ~ **away** alejarse. ~ **back** (hacer) retroceder. ~ **forward** (hacer) avanzar. ~ **in** instalarse. ~ **on** (hacer) circular. ~ **over** apartarse. **~ment** /ˈmuːvmənt/ *n* movimiento *m*

movie /ˈmuːvɪ/ *n* (*Amer*) película *f*. **the ~s** *npl* el cine *m*

moving /ˈmuːvɪŋ/ *a* en movimiento; (*touching*) conmovedor

mow /məʊ/ *vt* (*pt* **mowed** *or* **mown**) segar. ~ **down** derribar. **~er** *n* (*for lawn*) cortacésped *m* *inv*

MP *abbr see* **Member of Parliament**

Mr /ˈmɪstə(r)/ *abbr* (*pl* **Messrs**) (*Mister*) señor *m*. ~ **Coldbeck** (el) Sr. Coldbeck

Mrs /ˈmɪsɪz/ *abbr* (*pl* **Mrs**) (*Missis*) señora *f*. ~ **Andrews** (la) Sra. Andrews. **the** ~ **Andrews** (las) Sras. Andrews

Ms /mɪz/ *abbr* (*title of married or unmarried woman*) señora *f*, señorita. **Ms Lawton** (la) Sra. Lawton

much /mʌtʃ/ *a* & *n* mucho (*m*). ● *adv* mucho; (*before pp*) muy. ~ **as** por mucho que. ~ **the same** más o menos lo mismo. **so** ~ tanto. **too** ~ demasiado

muck /mʌk/ *n* estiércol *m*; (*dirt*, *fam*) suciedad *f*. ● *vi*. ~ **about** (*sl*) perder el tiempo. ~ **about with** (*sl*) juguetear con. ● *vt.* ~ **up** (*sl*) echar a perder. ~ **in** (*sl*) participar. ~**y** *a* sucio.

mucus /'mjuːkəs/ *n* moco *m*

mud /mʌd/ *n* lodo *m*, barro *m*

muddle /'mʌdl/ *vt* embrollar. ● *vi.* ~ **through** salir del paso. ● *n* desorden *m*; (*mix-up*) lío *m*

muddy /'mʌdɪ/ *a* lodoso; ‹*hands etc*› cubierto de lodo

mudguard /'mʌdgɑːd/ *n* guardabarros *m invar*

muff /mʌf/ *n* manguito *m*

muffin /'mʌfɪn/ *n* mollete *m*

muffle /'mʌfl/ *vt* tapar; amortiguar ‹*a sound*›. ~**r** *n* (*scarf*) bufanda *f*

mug /mʌg/ *n* tazón *m*; (*for beer*) jarra *f*; (*face, sl*) cara *f*, jeta *f* (*sl*); (*fool, sl*) primo *m*. ● *vt* (*pt* **mugged**) asaltar. ~**ger** *n* asaltador *m*. ~**ging** *n* asalto *m*

muggy /'mʌgɪ/ *a* bochornoso

Muhammadan /mə'hæmɪdən/ *a & n* mahometano (*m*)

mule[1] /mjuːl/ *n* mula *f*, mulo *m*

mule[2] /mjuːl/ *n* (*slipper*) babucha *f*

mull[1] /mʌl/ *vt.* ~ **over** reflexionar sobre

mull[2] /mʌl/ *vt* calentar con especias ‹*wine*›

multi... /'mʌltɪ/ *pref* multi...

multicoloured /mʌltɪ'kʌləd/ *a* multicolor

multifarious /mʌltɪ'feərɪəs/ *a* múltiple

multinational /mʌltɪ'næʃənl/ *a & n* multinacional (*f*)

multipl|e /'mʌltɪpl/ *a & n* múltiplo (*m*). ~**ication** /mʌltɪplɪ'keɪʃn/ *n* multiplicación *f*. ~**y** /'mʌltɪplaɪ/ *vt/i* multiplicar(se)

multitude /'mʌltɪtjuːd/ *n* multitud *f*

mum[1] /mʌm/ *n* (*mother, fam*) mamá *f* (*fam*)

mum[2] /mʌm/ *a.* **keep** ~ (*fam*) guardar silencio

mumble /'mʌmbl/ *vt* decir entre dientes. ● *vi* hablar entre dientes

mummify /'mʌmɪfaɪ/ *vt/i* momificar(se)

mummy[1] /'mʌmɪ/ *n* (*mother, fam*) mamá *f* (*fam*)

mummy[2] /'mʌmɪ/ *n* momia *f*

mumps /mʌmps/ *n* paperas *fpl*

munch /mʌntʃ/ *vt/i* mascar

mundane /mʌn'deɪn/ *a* mundano

municipal /mjuː'nɪsɪpl/ *a* municipal. ~**ity** /-'pælətɪ/ *n* municipio *m*

munificent /mjuː'nɪfɪsənt/ *a* munífico

munitions /mjuː'nɪʃnz/ *npl* municiones *fpl*

mural /'mjʊərəl/ *a & n* mural (*f*)

murder /'mɜːdə(r)/ *n* asesinato *m*. ● *vt* asesinar. ~**er** *n* asesino *m*. ~**ess** *n* asesina *f*. ~**ous** *a* homicida

murky /'mɜːkɪ/ *a* (-**ier, -iest**) oscuro

murmur /'mɜːmə(r)/ *n* murmullo *m*. ● *vt/i* murmurar

muscle /'mʌsl/ *n* músculo *m*. ● *vi.* ~ **in** (*Amer, sl*) meterse por fuerza en

muscular /'mʌskjʊlə(r)/ *a* muscular; (*having well-developed muscles*) musculoso

muse /mjuːz/ *vi* meditar

museum /mjuː'zɪəm/ *n* museo *m*

mush /mʌʃ/ *n* pulpa *f*

mushrom /'mʌʃrʊm/ *n* champiñón *m*; (*bot*) seta *f*. ● *vi* (*appear in large numbers*) crecer como hongos

mushy /'mʌʃɪ/ *a* pulposo

music /'mjuːzɪk/ *n* música *f*. ~**al** *a* musical; ‹*instrument*› de música; (*talented*) que tiene don de música. ● *n* comedia *f* musical. ~ **hall** *n* teatro *m* de variedades. ~**ian** /mjuː'zɪʃn/ *n* músico *m*

musk /mʌsk/ *n* almizcle *m*

Muslim /'mʊzlɪm/ *a & n* musulmán (*m*)

muslin /'mʌzlɪn/ *n* muselina *f*

musquash /'mʌskwɒʃ/ *n* ratón *m* almizclero

mussel /'mʌsl/ *n* mejillón *m*

must /mʌst/ *v aux* deber, tener que. **he** ~ **be old** debe ser viejo. **I** ~ **have done it** debo haberlo hecho. **you** ~ **go** debes marcharte. ● *n.* **be a** ~ ser imprescindible

mustard /'mʌstəd/ *n* mostaza *f*

muster /'mʌstə(r)/ *vt/i* reunir(se)

musty /'mʌstɪ/ *a* (-**ier, -iest**) que huele a cerrado

mutation /mjuː'teɪʃn/ *n* mutación *f*

mute /mjuːt/ *a & n* mudo (*m*). ~**d** *a* ‹*sound*› sordo; ‹*criticism*› callado

mutilat|e /'mjuːtɪleɪt/ *vt* mutilar. ~**ion** /-'leɪʃn/ *n* mutilación *f*

mutin|ous /'mjuːtɪnəs/ *a* ‹*sailor etc*› amotinado; (*fig*) rebelde. ~**y** *n* motín *m*. ● *vi* amotinarse

mutter /'mʌtə(r)/ *vt/i* murmurar

mutton /'mʌtn/ *n* cordero *m*

mutual /'mjuːtʃʊəl/ *a* mutuo; (*common, fam*) común. ~**ly** *adv* mutuamente

muzzle /'mʌzl/ *n* (*snout*) hocico *m*; (*device*) bozal *m*; (*of gun*) boca *f*. ● *vt* poner el bozal a

my /maɪ/ *a* mi, mis *pl*

myopic /maɪˈɒpɪk/ *a* miope

myriad /ˈmɪrɪəd/ *n* miríada *f*

myself /maɪˈself/ *pron* yo mismo *m*, yo misma *f*; (*reflexive*) me; (*after prep*) mí (mismo), mí (misma) *f*

myster|ious /mɪˈstɪərɪəs/ *a* misterioso. ~y /ˈmɪstərɪ/ *n* misterio *m*

mystic /ˈmɪstɪk/ *a* & *n* místico (*m*). ~al *a* místico. ~ism /-sɪzəm/ *n* misticismo *m*

mystif|ication /mɪstɪfɪˈkeɪʃn/ *n* confusión *f*. ~y /-faɪ/ *vt* dejar perplejo

mystique /mɪˈstiːk/ *n* mística *f*

myth /mɪθ/ *n* mito *m*. ~ical *a* mítico. ~ology /mɪˈθɒlədʒɪ/ *n* mitología *f*

N

N *abbr* (*north*) norte *m*

nab /næb/ *vt* (*pt* **nabbed**) (*arrest, sl*) coger (*not LAm*), agarrar (*esp LAm*)

nag /næg/ *vt* (*pt* **nagged**) fastidiar; (*scold*) regañar. ● *vi* criticar

nagging /ˈnægɪŋ/ *a* persistente, regañón

nail /neɪl/ *n* clavo *m*; (*of finger, toe*) uña *f*. **pay on the** ~ pagar a tocateja. ● *vt* clavar. ~ **polish** *n* esmalte *m* para las uñas

naïve /naɪˈiːv/ *a* ingenuo

naked /ˈneɪkɪd/ *a* desnudo. **to the** ~ **eye** a simple vista. ~**ly** *adv* desnudamente. ~**ness** *n* desnudez *f*

namby-pamby /næmbɪˈpæmbɪ/ *a* & *n* ñoño (*m*)

name /neɪm/ *n* nombre *m*; (*fig*) fama *f*. ● *vt* nombrar; (*fix*) fijar. **be** ~**d after** llevar el nombre de. ~**less** *a* anónimo. ~**ly** /ˈneɪmlɪ/ *adv* a saber. ~**sake** /ˈneɪmseɪk/ *n* (*person*) tocayo *m*

nanny /ˈnænɪ/ *n* niñera *f*. ~**goat** *n* cabra *f*

nap¹ /næp/ *n* (*sleep*) sueñecito *m*; (*after lunch*) siesta *f*. ● *vi* (*pt* **napped**) echarse un sueño. **catch s.o.** ~**ping** coger a uno desprevenido

nap² /næp/ *n* (*fibres*) lanilla *f*

nape /neɪp/ *n* nuca *f*

napkin /ˈnæpkɪn/ *n* (*at meals*) servilleta *f*; (*for baby*) pañal *m*

nappy /ˈnæpɪ/ *n* pañal *m*

narcotic /nɑːˈkɒtɪk/ *a* & *n* narcótico (*m*)

narrat|e /nəˈreɪt/ *vt* contar. ~**ion** /-ʃn/ *n* narración *f*. ~**ive** /ˈnærətɪv/ *n* relato *m*. ~**or** /nəˈreɪtə(r)/ *n* narrador *m*

narrow /ˈnærəʊ/ *a* (**-er, -est**) estrecho. **have a** ~ **escape** escaparse por los pelos. ● *vt* estrechar; (*limit*) limitar. ● *vi* estrecharse. ~**ly** *adv* estrechamente; (*just*) por poco. ~**-minded** *a* de miras estrechas. ~**ness** *n* estrechez *f*

nasal /ˈneɪzl/ *a* nasal

nast|ily /ˈnɑːstɪlɪ/ *adv* desagradablemente; (*maliciously*) con malevolencia. ~**iness** *n* (*malice*) malevolencia *f*. ~**y** *a* /ˈnɑːstɪ/ (**-ier, -iest**) desagradable; (*malicious*) malévolo; (*weather*) malo; (*taste, smell*) asqueroso; (*wound*) grave; (*person*) antipático

natal /ˈneɪtl/ *a* natal

nation /ˈneɪʃn/ *n* nación *f*

national /ˈnæʃənl/ *a* nacional. ● *n* súbdito *m*. ~ **anthem** *n* himno *m* nacional. ~**ism** *n* nacionalismo *m*. ~**ity** /næʃəˈnælətɪ/ *n* nacionalidad *f*. ~**ize** *vt* nacionalizar. ~**ly** *adv* a nivel nacional

nationwide /ˈneɪʃnwaɪd/ *a* nacional

native /ˈneɪtɪv/ *n* natural *m* & *f*. **be a** ~ **of** ser natural de. ● *a* nativo; (*country, town*) natal; (*inborn*) innato. ~ **speaker of Spanish** hispanohablante *m* & *f*. ~ **language** *n* lengua *f* materna

Nativity /nəˈtɪvətɪ/ *n*. **the** ~ la Natividad *f*

NATO /ˈneɪtəʊ/ *abbr* (*North Atlantic Treaty Organization*) OTAN *f*, Organización *f* del Tratado del Atlántico Norte

natter /ˈnætə(r)/ *vi* (*fam*) charlar. ● *n* (*fam*) charla *f*

natural /ˈnætʃərəl/ *a* natural. ~ **history** *n* historia *f* natural. ~**ist** *n* naturalista *m* & *f*

naturaliz|ation /nætʃərəlaɪˈzeɪʃn/ *n* naturalización *f*. ~**e** *vt* naturalizar

naturally /ˈnætʃərəlɪ/ *adv* (*of course*) naturalmente; (*by nature*) por naturaleza

nature /ˈneɪtʃə(r)/ *n* naturaleza *f*; (*kind*) género *m*; (*of person*) carácter *m*

naught /nɔːt/ *n* (*old use*) nada *f*; (*maths*) cero *m*

naught|ily /ˈnɔːtɪlɪ/ *adv* mal. ~**y** *a* (**-ier, -iest**) malo; (*child*) travieso; (*joke*) verde

nause|a /'nɔːzɪə/ n náusea f. ~ate vt dar náuseas a. ~ous a nauseabundo

nautical /'nɔːtɪkl/ a náutico. ~ mile n milla f marina

naval /'neɪvl/ a naval; (officer) de marina

Navarre /nə'vɑː(r)/ n Navarra f. ~se a navarro

nave /neɪv/ n (of church) nave f

navel /'neɪvl/ n ombligo m

navigable /'nævɪgəbl/ a navegable

navigat|e /'nævɪgeɪt/ vt navegar por ‹sea etc›; gobernar ‹ship›. ● vi navegar. ~ion n navegación f. ~or n navegante m

navvy /'nævɪ/ n peón m caminero

navy /'neɪvɪ/ n marina f. ~ (blue) azul m marino

NE abbr (north-east) noreste m

near /nɪə(r)/ adv cerca. ~ at hand muy cerca. ~ by adv cerca. draw ~ acercarse. ● prep. ~ (to) cerca de. ● a cercano. ● vt acercarse a. ~by a cercano. N~ East n Oriente m Próximo. ~ly /'nɪəlɪ/ adv casi. not ~ly as pretty as no es ni con mucho tan guapa como. ~ness /'nɪənɪs/ n proximidad f

neat /niːt/ a (-er, -est) pulcro; ‹room etc› bien arreglado; (clever) diestro; (ingenious) hábil; ‹whisky, brandy etc› solo. ~ly adv pulcramente. ~ness n pulcritud f

nebulous /'nebjʊləs/ a nebuloso

necessar|ies /'nesəsərɪz/ npl lo indispensable. ~ily /nesə'serɪlɪ/ adv necesariamente. ~y a necesario, imprescindible

necessit|ate /nə'sesɪteɪt/ vt necesitar. ~y /nɪ'sesətɪ/ n necesidad f; (thing) cosa f indispensable

neck /nek/ n (of person, bottle, dress) cuello m; (of animal) pescuezo m. ~ and ~ parejos. ~lace /'nekləs/ n collar m. ~line n escote m. ~tie n corbata f

nectar /'nektə(r)/ n néctar m

nectarine /nektə'riːn/ n nectarina f

née /neɪ/ a de soltera

need /niːd/ n necesidad f. ● vt necesitar; (demand) exigir. you ~ not speak no tienes que hablar

needle /'niːdl/ n aguja f. ● vt (annoy, fam) pinchar

needless /'niːdlɪs/ a innecesario. ~ly adv innecesariamente

needlework /'niːdlwɜːk/ n costura f; (embroidery) bordado m

needy /'niːdɪ/ a (-ier, -iest) necesitado

negation /nɪ'geɪʃn/ n negación f

negative /'negətɪv/ a negativo. ● n (of photograph) negativo m; (word, gram) negativa f. ~ly adv negativamente

neglect /nɪ'glekt/ vt descuidar; no cumplir con ‹duty›. ~ to do dejar de hacer. ● n descuido m, negligencia f. (state of) ~ abandono m. ~ful a descuidado

négligé /'neglɪʒeɪ/ n bata f, salto m de cama

negligen|ce /'neglɪdʒəns/ n negligencia f, descuido m. ~t a descuidado

negligible /'neglɪdʒəbl/ a insignificante

negotiable /nɪ'gəʊʃəbl/ a negociable

negotiat|e /nɪ'gəʊʃɪeɪt/ vt/i negociar. ~ion /-'eɪʃn/ n negociación f. ~or n negociador m

Negr|ess /'niːgrɪs/ n negra f. ~o n (pl -oes) negro m. ● a negro

neigh /neɪ/ n relincho m. ● vi relinchar

neighbour /'neɪbə(r)/ n vecino m. ~hood n vecindad f, barrio m. in the ~hood of alrededor de. ~ing a vecino. ~ly /'neɪbəlɪ/ a amable

neither /'naɪðə(r)/ a & pron ninguno m de los dos, ni el uno m ni el otro m. ● adv ni. ~ big nor small ni grande ni pequeño. ~ shall I come no voy yo tampoco. ● conj tampoco

neon /'niːɒn/ n neón m. ● a ‹lamp etc› de neón

nephew /'nevjuː/ n sobrino m

nepotism /'nepətɪzəm/ m nepotismo m

nerve /nɜːv/ n nervio m; (courage) valor m; (calm) sangre f fría; (impudence, fam) descaro m. ~-racking a exasperante. ~s npl (before exams etc) nervios mpl

nervous /'nɜːvəs/ a nervioso. be/feel ~ (afraid) tener miedo (of a). ~ly adv (tensely) nerviosamente; (timidly) tímidamente. ~ness n nerviosidad f; (fear) miedo m

nervy /'nɜːvɪ/ a see nervous; (Amer, fam) descarado

nest /nest/ n nido m. ● vi anidar. ~-egg n (money) ahorros mpl

nestle /'nesl/ vi acomodarse. ~ up to arrimarse a

net /net/ n red f. ● vt (pt **netted**) coger (not LAm), agarrar (esp LAm). ● a (weight etc) neto

netball /'netbɔ:l/ n baloncesto m

Netherlands /'neðələndz/ npl. the ~ los Países mpl Bajos

netting /'netɪŋ/ n (nets) redes fpl; (wire) malla f; (fabric) tul m

nettle /'netl/ n ortiga f

network /'netwɜ:k/ n red f

neuralgia /njʊə'rældʒɪə/ n neuralgia f

neuro|sis /njʊə'rəʊsɪs/ n (pl -oses /-si:z/) neurosis f. ~**tic** a & n neurótico (m)

neuter /'nju:tə(r)/ a & n neutro (m). ● vt castrar ⟨animals⟩

neutral /'nju:trəl/ a neutral; ⟨colour⟩ neutro; (elec) neutro. ~ (**gear**) (auto) punto m muerto. ~**ity** /-'trælətɪ/ n neutralidad f

neutron /'nju:trɒn/ n neutrón m. ~ **bomb** n bomba f de neutrones

never /'nevə(r)/ adv nunca, jamás; (not, fam) no. ~ **again** nunca más. ~ **mind** (don't worry) no te preocupes, no se preocupe; (it doesn't matter) no importa. **he** ~ **smiles** no sonríe nunca. **I** ~ **saw him** (fam) no le vi. ~**ending** a interminable

nevertheless /nevəðə'les/ adv sin embargo, no obstante

new /nju:/ a (-er, -est) (new to owner) nuevo (placed before noun); (brand new) nuevo (placed after noun). ~**born** a recién nacido. ~**comer** n recién llegado m. ~**fangled** a (pej) moderno. ~**laid egg** n huevo m fresco. ~**ly** adv nuevamente; (recently) recién. ~**ly-weds** npl recién casados mpl. ~ **moon** n luna f nueva. ~**ness** n novedad f

news /nju:z/ n noticias fpl; (broadcasting, press) informaciones fpl; (on TV) telediario m; (on radio) diario m hablado. ~**agent** n vendedor m de periódicos. ~**caster** n locutor m. ~**letter** n boletín m. ~**paper** n periódico m. ~**reader** n locutor m. ~**reel** n noticiario m, nodo m (in Spain)

newt /nju:t/ n tritón m

new year /nju:'jɪə(r)/ n año m nuevo. **N**~**'s Day** n día m de Año Nuevo. **N**~**'s Eve** n noche f vieja

New Zealand /nju:'zi:lənd/ n Nueva Zelanda f. ~**er** n neozelandés m

next /nekst/ a próximo; ⟨week, month etc⟩ que viene, próximo; (adjoining) vecino; (following) siguiente. ● adv la próxima vez; (afterwards) después. ● n siguiente m. ~ **to** junto a. ~ **to nothing** casi nada. ~ **door** al lado (**to** de). ~**door** de al lado. ~**best** mejor alternativa f. ~ **of kin** n pariente m más próximo, parientes mpl más próximos

nib /nɪb/ n (of pen) plumilla f

nibble /'nɪbl/ vt/i mordisquear. ● n mordisco m

nice /naɪs/ a (-er, -est) agradable; (likeable) simpático; (kind) amable; (pretty) bonito; ⟨weather⟩ bueno; (subtle) sutil. ~**ly** adv agradablemente; (kindly) amablemente; (well) bien

nicety /'naɪsətɪ/ n (precision) precisión f; (detail) detalle. **to a** ~ exactamente

niche /nɪtʃ, ni:ʃ/ n (recess) nicho m; (fig) buena posición f

nick /nɪk/ n corte m pequeño; (prison, sl) cárcel f. **in the** ~ **of time** justo a tiempo. ● vt (steal, arrest, sl) birlar

nickel /'nɪkl/ n níquel m; (Amer) moneda f de cinco centavos

nickname /'nɪkneɪm/ n apodo m; (short form) diminutivo m. ● vt apodar

nicotine /'nɪkəti:n/ n nicotina f

niece /ni:s/ n sobrina f

nifty /'nɪftɪ/ a (sl) (smart) elegante

Nigeria /naɪ'dʒɪərɪə/ n Nigeria f. ~**n** a & n nigeriano (m)

niggardly /'nɪgədlɪ/ a ⟨person⟩ tacaño; ⟨thing⟩ miserable

niggling /'nɪglɪŋ/ a molesto

night /naɪt/ n noche f; (evening) tarde f. ● a nocturno, de noche. ~**cap** n (hat) gorro m de dormir; (drink) bebida f (tomada antes de acostarse). ~**club** n sala f de fiestas, boîte f. ~**dress** n camisón m. ~**fall** n anochecer m. ~**gown** n camisón m

nightingale /'naɪtɪŋgeɪl/ n ruiseñor m

night: ~life n vida f nocturna. ~**ly** adv todas las noches. ~**mare** n pesadilla f. ~**school** n escuela f nocturna. ~**time** n noche f. ~**watchman** n sereno m

nil /nɪl/ n nada f; (sport) cero m

nimble /'nɪmbl/ a (-er, -est) ágil

nine /naɪn/ a & n nueve (m)

nineteen /naɪn'ti:n/ a & n diecinueve (m). ~**th** a & n diecinueve (m), decimonoveno (m)

ninet|ieth /'naɪntɪəθ/ *a* noventa, nonagésimo. **~y** *a* & *n* noventa (*m*)

ninth /'naɪnθ/ *a* & *n* noveno (*m*)

nip[1] /nɪp/ *vt* (*pt* **nipped**) (*pinch*) pellizcar; (*bite*) mordisquear. ● *vi* (*rush*, *sl*) correr. ● *n* (*pinch*) pellizco *m*; (*cold*) frío *m*

nip[2] /nɪp/ *n* (*of drink*) trago *m*

nipper /'nɪpə(r)/ *n* (*sl*) chaval *m*

nipple /'nɪpl/ *n* pezón *m*; (*of baby's bottle*) tetilla *f*

nippy /'nɪpɪ/ *a* (**-ier, -iest**) (*nimble*, *fam*) ágil; (*quick*, *fam*) rápido; (*chilly*, *fam*) fresquito

nitrogen /'naɪtrədʒən/ *n* nitrógeno *m*

nitwit /'nɪtwɪt/ *n* (*fam*) imbécil *m* & *f*

no /nəʊ/ *a* ninguno. **~ entry** prohibido el paso. **~ man's land** *n* tierra *f* de nadie. **~ smoking** se prohibe fumar. **~ way!** (*Amer*, *fam*) ¡ni hablar! ● *adv* no. ● *n* (*pl* **noes**) no *m*

nobility /nəʊ'bɪlətɪ/ *n* nobleza *f*

noble /'nəʊbl/ *a* (**-er, -est**) noble. **~man** *n* noble *m*

nobody /'nəʊbədɪ/ *pron* nadie *m*. ● *n* nadie *m*. **~ is there** no hay nadie. **he knows ~** no conoce a nadie

nocturnal /nɒk'tɜːnl/ *a* nocturno

nod /nɒd/ *vt* (*pt* **nodded**). **~ one's head** asentir con la cabeza. ● *vi* (*in agreement*) asentir con la cabeza; (*in greeting*) saludar; (*be drowsy*) dar cabezadas. ● *n* inclinación *f* de cabeza

nodule /'nɒdjuːl/ *n* nódulo *m*

nois|e /nɔɪz/ *n* ruido *m*. **~eless** *a* silencioso. **~ily** /'nɔɪzɪlɪ/ *adv* ruidosamente. **~y** *a* (**-ier, -iest**) ruidoso

nomad /'nəʊmæd/ *n* nómada *m* & *f*. **~ic** /-'mædɪk/ *a* nómada

nominal /'nɒmɪnl/ *a* nominal

nominat|e /'nɒmɪneɪt/ *vt* nombrar; (*put forward*) proponer. **~ion** /-'neɪʃn/ *n* nombramiento *m*

non-... /nɒn/ *pref* no ...

nonagenarian /nəʊnədʒɪ'neərɪən/ *a* & *n* nonagenario (*m*), noventón (*m*)

nonchalant /'nɒnʃələnt/ *a* imperturbable

non-commissioned /nɒnkə'mɪʃnd/ *a*. **~ officer** *n* suboficial *m*

non-comittal /nɒnkə'mɪtl/ *a* evasivo

nondescript /'nɒndɪskrɪpt/ *a* inclasificable, anodino

none /nʌn/ *pron* (*person*) nadie, ninguno; (*thing*) ninguno, nada. **~ of**

nada de. **~ of us** ninguno de nosotros. **I have ~** no tengo nada. ● *adv* no, de ninguna manera. **he is ~ the happier** no está más contento

non-existent /nɒnɪg'zɪstənt/ *a* inexistente

nonplussed /nɒn'plʌst/ *a* perplejo

nonsens|e /'nɒnsns/ *n* tonterías *fpl*, disparates *mpl*. **~ical** /-'sensɪkl/ *a* absurdo

non-smoker /nɒn'sməʊkə(r)/ *n* persona *f* que no fuma; (*rail*) departamento *m* de no fumadores

non-starter /nɒn'stɑːtə(r)/ *n* (*fam*) proyecto *m* imposible

non-stop /nɒn'stɒp/ *a* (*train*) directo; (*flight*) sin escalas. ● *adv* sin parar; (*by train*) directamente; (*by air*) sin escalas

noodles /'nuːdlz/ *npl* fideos *mpl*

nook /nʊk/ *n* rincón *m*

noon /nuːn/ *n* mediodía *m*

no-one /'nəʊwʌn/ *pron* nadie. *see* **nobody**

noose /nuːs/ *n* nudo *m* corredizo

nor /nɔː(r)/ *conj* ni, tampoco. **neither blue ~ red** ni azul ni rojo. **he doesn't play the piano, ~ do I** no sabe tocar el piano, ni yo tampoco

Nordic /'nɔːdɪk/ *a* nórdico

norm /nɔːm/ *n* norma *f*; (*normal*) lo normal

normal /'nɔːml/ *a* normal. **~cy** *n* (*Amer*) normalidad *f*. **~ity** /-'mælətɪ/ *n* normalidad *f*. **~ly** *adv* normalmente

Norman /'nɔːmən/ *a* & *n* normando (*m*)

Normandy /'nɔːməndɪ/ *n* Normandía *f*

north /nɔːθ/ *n* norte *m*. ● *a* del norte, norteño. ● *adv* hacia el norte. **N~ America** *n* América *f* del Norte, Norteamérica *f*. **N~ American** *a* & *n* norteamericano (*m*). **~-east** *n* nordeste *m*. **~erly** /'nɔːðəlɪ/ *a* del norte. **~ern** /'nɔːðən/ *a* del norte. **~erner** *n* norteño *m*. **N~ Sea** *n* mar *m* del Norte. **~ward** *a* hacia el norte. **~wards** *adv* hacia el norte. **~west** *n* noroeste *m*

Norw|ay /'nɔːweɪ/ *n* Noruega *f*. **~egian** *a* & *n* noruego (*m*)

nose /nəʊz/ *n* nariz *f*. ● *vi*. **~ about** curiosear. **~bleed** *n* hemorragia *f* nasal. **~dive** *n* picado *m*

nostalgi|a /nɒ'stældʒə/ *n* nostalgia *f*. **~c** *a* nostálgico

nostril /'nɒstrɪl/ n nariz f; (of horse) ollar m

nosy /'nəʊzɪ/ a (-ier, -iest) (fam) entrometido

not /nɒt/ adv no. ~ **at all** no... nada; (after thank you) de nada. ~ **yet** aún no. **I do** ~ **know** no sé. **I suppose** ~ supongo que no

notabl|e /'nəʊtəbl/ a notable. ● n (person) notabilidad f. ~**y** /'nəʊtəblɪ/ adv notablemente

notary /'nəʊtərɪ/ n notario m

notation /nəʊ'teɪʃn/ n notación f

notch /nɒtʃ/ n muesca f. ● vt. ~ **up** apuntar ‹score etc›

note /nəʊt/ n nota f; (banknote) billete m. **take** ~s tomar apuntes. ● vt notar. ~**book** n libreta f. ~**d** a célebre. ~**paper** n papel m de escribir. ~**worthy** a notable

nothing /'nʌθɪŋ/ pron nada. **he eats** ~ no come nada. **for** ~ (free) gratis; (in vain) inútilmente. ● n nada f; (person) nulidad f; (thing of no importance) fruslería f; (zero) cero m. ● adv de ninguna manera. ~ **big** nada grande. ~ **else** nada más. ~ **much** poca cosa

notice /'nəʊtɪs/ n (attention) atención f; (advert) anuncio m; (sign) letrero m; (poster) cartel m; (termination of employment) despido m; (warning) aviso m. **(advance)** ~ previo aviso m. ~ **(of dismissal)** despido m. **take** ~ **of** prestar atención a, hacer caso a ‹person›; hacer caso de ‹thing›. ● vt notar. ~**able** a evidente. ~**ably** adv visiblemente. ~**board** n tablón m de anuncios

notif|ication /nəʊtɪfɪ'keɪʃn/ n aviso m, notificación f. ~**y** vt avisar

notion /'nəʊʃn/ n (concept) concepto m; (idea) idea f. ~**s** npl (sewing goods etc, Amer) artículos mpl de mercería

notori|ety /nəʊtə'raɪətɪ/ n notoriedad f; (pej) mala fama f. ~**ous** /nəʊ'tɔ:rɪəs/ a notorio. ~**ously** adv notoriamente

notwithstanding /nɒtwɪθ'stændɪŋ/ prep a pesar de. ● adv sin embargo

nougat /'nu:gɑ:/ n turrón m

nought /nɔ:t/ n cero m

noun /naʊn/ n sustantivo m, nombre m

nourish /'nʌrɪʃ/ vt alimentar; (incl fig) nutrir. ~**ment** n alimento m

novel /'nɒvl/ n novela f. ● a nuevo. ~**ist** n novelista m & f. ~**ty** n novedad f

November /nəʊ'vembə(r)/ n noviembre m

novice /'nɒvɪs/ n principiante m & f

now /naʊ/ adv ahora. ~ **and again**, ~ **and then** de vez en cuando. **just** ~ ahora mismo; (a moment ago) hace poco. ● conj ahora que

nowadays /'naʊədeɪz/ adv hoy (en) día

nowhere /'nəʊweə(r)/ adv en/por ninguna parte; (after motion towards) a ninguna parte

noxious /'nɒkʃəs/ a nocivo

nozzle /'nɒzl/ n boquilla f; (tec) tobera f

nuance /'nju:ɑ:ns/ n matiz m

nuclear /'nju:klɪə(r)/ a nuclear

nucleus /'nju:klɪəs/ n (pl **-lei** /-lɪaɪ/) núcleo m

nude /nju:d/ a & n desnudo (m). **in the** ~ desnudo

nudge /nʌdʒ/ vt dar un codazo a. ● n codazo m

nudi|sm /'nju:dɪzəm/ n desnudismo m. ~**st** n nudista m & f. ~**ty** /'nju:dətɪ/ n desnudez f

nuisance /'nju:sns/ n (thing, event) fastidio m; (person) pesado m. **be a** ~ dar la lata

null /nʌl/ a nulo. ~**ify** vt anular

numb /nʌm/ a entumecido. ● vt entumecer

number /'nʌmbə(r)/ n número m. ● vt numerar; (count, include) contar. ~**plate** n matrícula f

numeracy /'nju:mərəsɪ/ n conocimientos mpl de matemáticas

numeral /'nju:mərəl/ n número m

numerate /'nju:mərət/ a que tiene buenos conocimientos de matemáticas

numerical /nju:'merɪkl/ a numérico

numerous /'nju:mərəs/ a numeroso

nun /nʌn/ n monja f

nurse /nɜ:s/ n enfermera f, enfermero m; (nanny) niñera f. **wet** ~ n nodriza f. ● vt cuidar; abrigar ‹hope etc›. ~**maid** n niñera f

nursery /'nɜ:sərɪ/ n cuarto m de los niños; (for plants) vivero m. **(day)** ~ n guardería f infantil. ~ **rhyme** n canción f infantil. ~ **school** n escuela f de párvulos

nursing home /'nɜ:sɪŋhəʊm/ n (for old people) asilo m de ancianos

nurture /'nɜ:tʃə(r)/ vt alimentar

nut /nʌt/ n (walnut, Brazil nut etc) nuez f; (hazlenut) avellana f; (peanut) cacahuete m; (tec) tuerca f;

(*crazy person, sl*) chiflado *m*.
~crackers *npl* cascanueces *m invar*
nutmeg /'nʌtmeg/ *n* nuez *f* moscada
nutrient /'nju:trɪənt/ *n* alimento *m*
nutrit|ion /nju:'trɪʃn/ *n* nutrición *f*.
~ious *a* nutritivo
nuts /nʌtz/ *a* (*crazy, sl*) chiflado
nutshell /'nʌtʃel/ *n* cáscara *f* de
nuez. **in a ~** en pocas palabras
nuzzle /'nʌzl/ *vt* acariciar con el
hocico
NW *abbr* (*north-west*) noroeste *m*
nylon /'naɪlɒn/ *n* nailon *m*. **~s** *npl*
medias *fpl* de nailon
nymph /nɪmf/ *n* ninfa *f*

O

oaf /əʊf/ *n* (*pl* **oafs**) zoquete *m*
oak /əʊk/ *n* roble *m*
OAP /əʊeɪ'pi:/ *abbr* (*old-age pensioner*) *n* pensionista *m & f*
oar /ɔ:(r)/ *n* remo *m*. **~sman** /'ɔ:zmən/ *n* (*pl* **-men**) remero *m*
oasis /əʊ'eɪsɪs/ *n* (*pl* **oases** /-si:z/) oasis *m invar*
oath /əʊθ/ *n* juramento *m*; (*swearword*) palabrota *f*
oat|meal /'əʊtmi:l/ *n* harina *f* de avena. **~s** /əʊts/ *npl* avena *f*
obedien|ce /əʊ'bi:dɪəns/ *n* obediencia *f*. **~t** /əʊ'bi:dɪənt/ *a* obediente.
~tly *adv* obedientemente
obelisk /'ɒbəlɪsk/ *n* obelisco *m*
obes|e /əʊ'bi:s/ *a* obeso. **~ity** *n* obesidad *f*
obey /əʊ'beɪ/ *vt* obedecer; cumplir
⟨*instructions etc*⟩
obituary /ə'bɪtʃʊərɪ/ *n* necrología *f*
object /'ɒbdʒɪkt/ *n* objeto *m*. /əb'dʒekt/ *vi* oponerse
objection /əb'dʒekʃn/ *n* objeción *f*.
~able /əb'dʒekʃnəbl/ *a* censurable;
(*unpleasant*) desagradable
objective /əb'dʒektɪv/ *a & n* objetivo
(*m*). **~ively** *adv* objetivamente
objector /əb'dʒektə(r)/ *n* objetante
m & f
oblig|ation /ɒblɪ'geɪʃn/ *n* obligación
f. **be under an ~ation to** tener obligación de. **~atory** /ə'blɪgətrɪ/ *a* obligatorio. **~e** /ə'blaɪdʒ/ *vt* obligar; (*do a small service*) hacer un favor a.
~ed *a* agradecido. **much ~ed!** ¡muchas gracias! **~ing** *a* atento
oblique /ə'bli:k/ *a* oblicuo

obliterat|e /ə'blɪtəreɪt/ *vt* borrar.
~ion /-'reɪʃn/ *n* borradura *f*
oblivio|n /ə'blɪvɪən/ *n* olvido *m*. **~us**
/ə'blɪvɪəs/ *a* (*unaware*) inconsciente
(**to, of** de)
oblong /'ɒblɒŋ/ *a & n* oblongo (*m*)
obnoxious /əb'nɒkʃəs/ *a* odioso
oboe /'əʊbəʊ/ *n* oboe *m*
obscen|e /əb'si:n/ *a* obsceno. **~ity**
/-enətɪ/ *n* obscenidad *f*
obscur|e /əb'skjʊə(r)/ *a* oscuro. ● *vt*
oscurecer; (*conceal*) esconder; (*confuse*) confundir. **~ity** *n* oscuridad *f*
obsequious /əb'si:kwɪəs/ *a* obsequioso
observan|ce /əb'zɜ:vəns/ *n* observancia *f*. **~t** /əb'zɜ:vənt/ *a* observador
observation /ɒbzə'veɪʃn/ *n* observación *f*
observatory /əb'zɜ:vətrɪ/ *n* observatorio *m*
observe /əb'zɜ:v/ *vt* observar. **~r** *n* observador *m*
obsess /əb'ses/ *vt* obsesionar. **~ion**
/-ʃn/ *n* obsesión *f*. **~ive** *a* obsesivo
obsolete /'ɒbsəli:t/ *a* desusado
obstacle /'ɒbstəkl/ *n* obstáculo *m*
obstetrics /əb'stetrɪks/ *n* obstetricia
f
obstina|cy /'ɒbstɪnəsɪ/ *n* obstinación *f*. **~te** /'ɒbstɪnət/ *a* obstinado. **~tely** *adv* obstinadamente
obstreperous /ɒb'strepərəs/ *a* turbulento, ruidoso, protestón
obstruct /əb'strʌkt/ *vt* obstruir.
~ion /-ʃn/ *n* obstrucción *f*
obtain /əb'teɪn/ *vt* obtener. ● *vi* prevalecer. **~able** *a* asequible
obtrusive /əb'tru:sɪv/ *a* importuno
obtuse /əb'tju:s/ *a* obtuso
obviate /'ɒbvɪeɪt/ *vt* evitar
obvious /'ɒbvɪəs/ *a* obvio. **~ly**
obviamente
occasion /ə'keɪʒn/ *n* ocasión *f*, oportunidad *f*. **on ~** de vez en cuando.
● *vt* ocasionar. **~al** /ə'keɪʒənl/ *a*
poco frecuente. **~ally** *adv* de vez en cuando
occult /ɒ'kʌlt/ *a* oculto
occup|ant /'ɒkjʊpənt/ *n* ocupante *m*
& f. **~ation** /ɒkjʊ'peɪʃn/ *n* ocupación *f*; (*job*) trabajo *m*, profesión *f*. **~ational** *a* profesional. **~ier** *n* ocupante *m & f*. **~y** /'ɒkjʊpaɪ/ *vt* ocupar
occur /ə'kɜ:(r)/ *vi* (*pt* **occurred**) ocurrir, suceder; (*exist*) encontrarse. **it**
~red to me that se me ocurrió que.

~**rence** /ə'kʌrəns/ n suceso m, acontecimiento m

ocean /'əʊʃn/ n océano m

o'clock /ə'klɒk/ adv. **it is 7 ~** son las siete

octagon /'ɒktəgən/ n octágono m

octane /'ɒkteɪn/ n octano m

octave /'ɒktɪv/ n octava f

October /ɒk'təʊbə(r)/ n octubre m

octopus /'ɒktəpəs/ n (pl **-puses**) pulpo m

oculist /'ɒkjʊlɪst/ n oculista m & f

odd /ɒd/ a (**-er, -est**) extraño, raro; ⟨number⟩ impar; (one of pair) sin pareja; (occasional) poco frecuente; (left over) sobrante. **fifty-~** unos cincuenta, cincuenta y pico. **the ~ one out** la excepción f. ~**ity** n (thing) curiosidad f; (person) excéntrico m. ~**ly** adv extrañamente. ~**ly enough** por extraño que parezca. ~**ment** /'ɒdmənt/ n retazo m. ~**s** /ɒdz/ npl probabilidades fpl; (in betting) apuesta f. ~**s and ends** retazos mpl. **at ~s** de punta, de malas

ode /əʊd/ n oda f

odious /'əʊdɪəs/ a odioso

odour /'əʊdə(r)/ n olor m. ~**less** a inodoro

of /əv, ɒv/ prep de. **a friend ~ mine** un amigo mío. **how kind ~ you** es Vd muy amable

off /ɒf/ adv lejos; ⟨light etc⟩ apagado; ⟨tap⟩ cerrado; ⟨food⟩ pasado. ● prep de, desde; (away from) fuera de; (distant from) lejos de. **be better ~** estar mejor. **be ~** marcharse. **day ~** n día m de asueto, día m libre

offal /'ɒfl/ n menudos mpl, asaduras fpl

off: ~**beat** a insólito. **~ chance** n posibilidad f remota. **~ colour** a indispuesto

offen|ce /ə'fens/ n ofensa f; (illegal act) delito m. **take ~ce** ofenderse. ~**d** /ə'fend/ vt ofender. ~**der** n delincuente m & f. ~**sive** /ə'fensɪv/ a ofensivo; (disgusting) repugnante. ● n ofensiva f

offer /'ɒfə(r)/ vt ofrecer. ● n oferta f. **on ~** en oferta

offhand /ɒf'hænd/ a (casual) desenvuelto; (brusque) descortés. ● adv de improviso

office /'ɒfɪs/ n oficina f; (post) cargo m

officer /'ɒfɪsə(r)/ n oficial m; (policeman) policía f, guardia m; (of organization) director m

official /ə'fɪʃl/ a & n oficial (m). ~**ly** adv oficialmente

officiate /ə'fɪʃɪeɪt/ vi oficiar. **~ as** desempeñar las funciones de

officious /ə'fɪʃəs/ a oficioso

offing /'ɒfɪŋ/ n. **in the ~** en perspectiva

off: ~**licence** n tienda f de bebidas alcohólicas. ~**load** vt descargar. ~**putting** a (disconcerting, fam) desconcertante; (repellent) repugnante. ~**set** /'ɒfset/ vt (pt **-set**, pres p **-setting**) contrapesar. ~**shoot** /'ɒfʃuːt/ n retoño m; (fig) ramificación f. ~**side** /ɒf'saɪd/ a (sport) fuera de juego. ~**spring** /'ɒfsprɪŋ/ invar progenie f. ~**stage** a entre bastidores. ~**white** a blancuzco, color hueso

often /'ɒfn/ adv muchas veces, con frecuencia, a menudo. **how ~?** ¿cuántas veces?

ogle /'əʊgl/ vt comerse con los ojos

ogre /'əʊgə(r)/ n ogro m

oh /əʊ/ int ¡oh!, ¡ay!

oil /ɔɪl/ n aceite m; (petroleum) petróleo m. ● vt lubricar. ~**field** /'ɔɪlfiːld/ n yacimiento m petrolífero. ~**painting** n pintura f al óleo. ~**rig** /'ɔɪlrɪg/ n plataforma f de perforación. ~**skins** /'ɔɪlskɪnz/ npl chubasquero m. ~**y** a aceitoso; ⟨food⟩ grasiento

ointment /'ɔɪntmənt/ n ungüento m

OK /əʊ'keɪ/ int ¡vale!, ¡de acuerdo! ● a bien; (satisfactory) satisfactorio. ● adv muy bien

old /əʊld/ a (**-er, -est**) viejo; (not modern) anticuado; (former) antiguo. **how ~ is she?** ¿cuántos años tiene? **she is ten years ~** tiene diez años. **of ~** de antaño. **~ age** n vejez f. ~**fashioned** a anticuado. ~**maid** n solterona f. ~**world** a antiguo

oleander /əʊlɪ'ændə(r)/ n adelfa f

olive /'ɒlɪv/ n (fruit) aceituna f; (tree) olivo m. ● a de oliva; (colour) aceitunado

Olympic /ə'lɪmpɪk/ a olímpico. ~**s** npl, ~ **Games** npl Juegos mpl Olímpicos

omelette /'ɒmlɪt/ n tortilla f, tortilla f de huevos (Mex)

om|en /'əʊmen/ n agüero m. ~**inous** /'ɒmɪnəs/ a siniestro

omi|ssion /ə'mɪʃn/ n omisión f. ~**t** /ə'mɪt/ vt (pt **omitted**) omitir

omnipotent /ɒm'nɪpətənt/ a omnipotente

on /ɒn/ *prep* en, sobre. **~ foot** a pie. **~ Monday** el lunes. **~ Mondays** los lunes. **~ seeing** al ver. **~ the way** de camino. ● *adv* (*light etc*) encendido; (*put on*) puesto, poco natural; (*machine*) en marcha; (*tap*) abierto. **~ and off** de vez en cuando. **~ and ~** sin cesar. **and so ~** y así sucesivamente. **be ~ at** (*fam*) criticar. **go ~** continuar. **later ~** más tarde

once /wʌns/ *adv* una vez; (*formerly*) antes. ● *conj* una vez que. **at ~** en seguida. **~over** *n* (*fam*) ojeada *f*

oncoming /ˈɒnkʌmɪŋ/ *a* que se acerca; (*traffic*) que viene en sentido contrario, de frente

one /wʌn/ *a* & *n* uno (*m*). ● *pron* uno. **~ another** el uno al otro. **~ by ~** uno a uno. **~ never knows** nunca se sabe. **the blue ~** el azul. **this ~** éste. **~off** *a* (*fam*) único

onerous /ˈɒnərəs/ *a* oneroso

one: ~self /wʌnˈself/ *pron* (*subject*) uno mismo; (*object*) se; (*after prep*) sí (mismo). **by ~self** solo. **~sided** *a* unilateral. **~way** *a* (*street*) de dirección única; (*ticket*) de ida

onion /ˈʌnɪən/ *n* cebolla *f*

onlooker /ˈɒnlʊkə(r)/ *n* espectador *m*

only /ˈəʊnlɪ/ *a* único. **~ son** *n* hijo *m* único. ● *adv* sólo, solamente. **~ just** apenas. **~ too** de veras. ● *conj* pero, sólo que

onset /ˈɒnset/ *n* principio *m*; (*attack*) ataque *m*

onslaught /ˈɒnslɔ:t/ *n* ataque *m* violento

onus /ˈəʊnəs/ *n* responsabilidad *f*

onward(s) /ˈɒnwəd(z)/ *a* & *adv* hacia adelante

onyx /ˈɒnɪks/ *n* ónice *f*

ooze /u:z/ *vt/i* rezumar

opal /ˈəʊpl/ *n* ópalo *m*

opaque /əʊˈpeɪk/ *a* opaco

open /ˈəʊpən/ *a* abierto; (*free to all*) público; (*undisguised*) manifiesto; (*question*) discutible; (*view*) despejado. **~ sea** *n* alta mar *f*. **~ secret** *n* secreto *m* a voces. **O~ University** *n* Universidad *f* a Distancia. **half-~** *a* medio abierto. **in the ~** *n* al aire libre. ● *vt/i* abrir. **~ended** *a* abierto. **~er** /ˈəʊpənə(r)/ *n* (*for tins*) abrelatas *m invar*; (*for bottles with caps*) abrebotellas *m invar*; (*corkscrew*) sacacorchos *m invar*. **eye~er** *n* (*fam*) revelación *f*. **~ing** /ˈəʊpənɪŋ/ *n* abertura *f*; (*beginning*)

principio *m*; (*job*) vacante *m*. **~ly** /ˈəʊpənlɪ/ *adv* abiertamente. **~minded** *a* imparcial

opera /ˈɒprə/ *n* ópera *f*. **~glasses** *npl* gemelos *mpl* de teatro

operate /ˈɒpəreɪt/ *vt* hacer funcionar. ● *vi* funcionar; (*medicine etc*) operar. **~ on** (*med*) operar a

operatic /ɒpəˈrætɪk/ *a* operístico

operation /ɒpəˈreɪʃn/ *n* operación *f*; (*mec*) funcionamiento *m*. **in ~** en vigor. **~al** /ɒpəˈreɪʃnl/ *a* operacional

operative /ˈɒpərətɪv/ *a* operativo; (*law etc*) en vigor

operator *n* operario *m*; (*telephonist*) telefonista *m* & *f*

operetta /ɒpəˈretə/ *n* opereta *f*

opinion /əˈpɪnɪən/ *n* opinión *f*. **in my ~** a mi parecer. **~ated** *a* dogmático

opium /ˈəʊpɪəm/ *n* opio *m*

opponent /əˈpəʊnənt/ *n* adversario *m*

opportun|e /ˈɒpətjuːn/ *a* oportuno. **~ist** /ɒpəˈtjuːnɪst/ *n* oportunista *m* & *f*. **~ity** /ɒpəˈtjuːnətɪ/ *n* oportunidad *f*

oppos|e /əˈpəʊz/ *vt* oponerse a. **~ed to** en contra de. **be ~ed to** oponerse a. **~ing** *a* opuesto

opposite /ˈɒpəzɪt/ *a* opuesto; (*facing*) de enfrente. **~** *n* contrario *m*. ● *adv* enfrente. ● *prep* enfrente de. **~ number** *n* homólogo *m*

opposition /ɒpəˈzɪʃn/ *n* oposición *f*; (*resistence*) resistencia *f*

oppress /əˈpres/ *vt* oprimir. **~ion** /-ʃn/ *n* opresión *f*. **~ive** *a* (*cruel*) opresivo; (*heat*) sofocante. **~or** *n* opresor *m*

opt /ɒpt/ *vi*. **~ for** elegir. **~ out** negarse a participar

optic|al /ˈɒptɪkl/ *a* óptico. **~ian** /ɒpˈtɪʃn/ *n* óptico *m*

optimis|m /ˈɒptɪmɪzəm/ *n* optimismo *m*. **~t** /ˈɒptɪmɪst/ *n* optimista *m* & *f*. **~tic** /-ˈmɪstɪk/ *a* optimista

optimum /ˈɒptɪməm/ *n* lo óptimo *m* mejor

option /ˈɒpʃn/ *n* opción *f*. **~al** /ˈɒpʃənl/ *a* facultativo

opulen|ce /ˈɒpjʊləns/ *n* opulencia *f*. **~t** /ˈɒpjʊlənt/ *a* opulento

or /ɔ:(r)/ *conj* o; (*before Spanish o- and ho-*) u; (*after negative*) ni. **~ else** si no, o bien

oracle /ˈɒrəkl/ *n* oráculo *m*

oral /'ɔːrəl/ a oral. ● n (fam) examen m oral

orange /'ɒrɪndʒ/ n naranja f; (tree) naranjo m; (colour) color m naranja. ● a de color naranja. ~ade n naranjada f

orator /'ɒrətə(r)/ n orador m

oratorio /ɒrə'tɔːrɪəʊ/ n (pl -os) oratorio m

oratory /'ɒrətrɪ/ n oratoria f

orb /ɔːb/ n orbe m

orbit /'ɔːbɪt/ n órbita f. ● vt orbitar

orchard /'ɔːtʃəd/ n huerto m

orchestra /'ɔːkɪstrə/ n orquesta f. ~l /-'kestrəl/ a orquestal. ~te /'ɔːkɪstreɪt/ vt orquestar

orchid /'ɔːkɪd/ n orquídea f

ordain /ɔː'deɪn/ vt ordenar

ordeal /ɔː'diːl/ n prueba f dura

order /'ɔːdə(r)/ n orden m; (com) pedido m. **in** ~ **that** para que. **in** ~ **to** para. ● vt (command) mandar; (com) pedir

orderly /'ɔːdəlɪ/ a ordenado. ● n asistente m & f

ordinary /'ɔːdɪnrɪ/ a corriente; (average) medio; (mediocre) ordinario

ordination /ɔːdɪ'neɪʃn/ n ordenación f

ore /ɔː(r)/ n mineral m

organ /'ɔːgən/ n órgano m

organic /ɔː'gænɪk/ a orgánico

organism /'ɔːgənɪzəm/ n organismo m

organist /'ɔːgənɪst/ n organista m & f

organiz|ation /ɔːgənaɪ'zeɪʃn/ n organización f. ~e /'ɔːgənaɪz/ vt organizar. ~er n organizador m

orgasm /'ɔːgæzəm/ n orgasmo m

orgy /'ɔːdʒɪ/ n orgía f

Orient /'ɔːrɪənt/ n Oriente m. ~al /-'entl/ a & n oriental (m & f)

orientat|e /'ɔːrɪənteɪt/ vt orientar. ~ion /-'teɪʃn/ n orientación f

orifice /'ɒrɪfɪs/ n orificio m

origin /'ɒrɪdʒɪn/ n origen m. ~al /ə'rɪdʒənl/ a original. ~ality /-'nælətɪ/ n originalidad f. ~ally adv originalmente. ~ate /ə'rɪdʒɪneɪt/ vi. ~ate from provenir de. ~ator n autor m

ormolu /'ɔːməluː/ n similor m

ornament /'ɔːnəmənt/ n adorno m. ~al /-'mentl/ a de adorno. ~ation /-en'teɪʃn/ n ornamentación f

ornate /ɔː'neɪt/ a adornado; (style) florido

ornithology /ɔːnɪ'θɒlədʒɪ/ n ornitología f

orphan /'ɔːfn/ n huérfano m. ● vt dejar huérfano. ~age n orfanato m

orthodox /'ɔːθədɒks/ a ortodoxo. ~y n ortodoxia f

orthopaedic /ɔːθə'piːdɪk/ a ortopédico. ~s n ortopedia f

oscillate /'ɒsɪleɪt/ vi oscilar

ossify /'ɒsɪfaɪ/ vt osificar. ● vi osificarse

ostensibl|e /ɒs'tensɪbl/ a aparente. ~y adv aparentemente

ostentat|ion /ɒsten'teɪʃn/ n ostentación f. ~ious a ostentoso

osteopath /'ɒstɪəpæθ/ n osteópata m & f. ~y /-'ɒpəθɪ/ n osteopatía f

ostracize /'ɒstrəsaɪz/ vt excluir

ostrich /'ɒstrɪtʃ/ n avestruz m

other /'ʌðə(r)/ a & n & pron otro (m). ~ **than** de otra manera que. **the** ~ **one** el otro. ~wise /'ʌðəwaɪz/ adv de otra manera; (or) si no

otter /'ɒtə(r)/ n nutria f

ouch /aʊtʃ/ int ¡ay!

ought /ɔːt/ v aux deber. **I** ~ **to see it** debería verlo. **he** ~ **to have done it** debería haberlo hecho

ounce /aʊns/ n onza f (= 28.35 gr.)

our /'aʊə(r)/ a nuestro. ~s /'aʊəz/ poss pron el nuestro, la nuestra, los nuestros, las nuestras. ~selves /aʊə'selvz/ pron (subject) nosotros mismos, nosotras mismas; (reflexive) nos; (after prep) nosotros (mismos), nosotras (mismas)

oust /aʊst/ vt expulsar, desalojar

out /aʊt/ adv fuera; (light) apagado; (in blossom) en flor; (in error) equivocado. ~-**and**-~ a cien por cien. ~ **of date** anticuado; (not valid) caducado. ~ **of doors** fuera. ~ **of order** estropeado; (sign) no funciona. ~ **of pity** por compasión. ~ **of place** fuera de lugar; (fig) inoportuno. ~ **of print** agotado. ~ **of sorts** indispuesto. ~ **of stock** agotado. ~ **of tune** desafinado. ~ **of work** parado, desempleado. **be** ~ equivocarse. **be** ~ **of** quedarse sin. **be** ~ **to** estar resuelto a. **five** ~ **of six** cinco de cada seis. **made** ~ **of** hecho de

outbid /aʊt'bɪd/ vt (pt -bid, pres p -bidding) ofrecer más que

outboard /'aʊtbɔːd/ a fuera borda

outbreak /'aʊtbreɪk/ n (of anger) arranque m; (of war) comienzo m; (of disease) epidemia f

outbuilding /'aʊtbɪldɪŋ/ *n* dependencia *f*

outburst /'aʊtbɜːst/ *n* explosión *f*

outcast /'aʊtkɑːst/ *n* paria *m* & *f*

outcome /'aʊtkʌm/ *n* resultado *m*

outcry /'aʊtkraɪ/ *n* protesta *f*

outdated /aʊt'deɪtɪd/ *a* anticuado

outdo /aʊt'duː/ *vt* (*pt* **-did**, *pp* **-done**) superar

outdoor /'aʊtdɔː(r)/ *a* al aire libre. **~s** /-'dɔːz/ *adv* al aire libre

outer /'aʊtə(r)/ *a* exterior

outfit /'aʊtfɪt/ *n* equipo *m*; (*clothes*) traje *m*. **~ter** *n* camisero *m*

outgoing /'aʊtgəʊɪŋ/ *a* (*minister etc*) saliente; (*sociable*) abierto. **~s** *npl* gastos *mpl*

outgrow /aʊt'grəʊ/ *vt* (*pt* **-grew**, *pp* **-grown**) crecer más que (*person*); hacerse demasiado grande para (*clothes*). **he's ~n his trousers** le quedan pequeños los pantalones

outhouse /'aʊthaʊs/ *n* dependencia *f*

outing /'aʊtɪŋ/ *n* excursión *f*

outlandish /aʊt'lændɪʃ/ *a* extravagante

outlaw /'aʊtlɔː/ *n* proscrito *m*. ● *vt* proscribir

outlay /'aʊtleɪ/ *n* gastos *mpl*

outlet /'aʊtlet/ *n* salida *f*

outline /'aʊtlaɪn/ *n* contorno *m*; (*summary*) resumen *m*. ● *vt* trazar; (*describe*) dar un resumen de

outlive /aʊt'lɪv/ *vt* sobrevivir a

outlook /'aʊtlʊk/ *n* perspectiva *f*

outlying /'aʊtlaɪɪŋ/ *a* remoto

outmoded /aʊt'məʊdɪd/ *a* anticuado

outnumber /aʊt'nʌmbə(r)/ *vt* sobrepasar en número

outpatient /aʊt'peɪʃnt/ *n* paciente *m* externo

outpost /'aʊtpəʊst/ *n* avanzada *f*

output /'aʊtpʊt/ *n* producción *f*

outrage /'aʊtreɪdʒ/ *n* ultraje *m*. ● *vt* ultrajar. **~ous** /aʊt'reɪdʒəs/ *a* escandaloso, atroz

outright /'aʊtraɪt/ *adv* completamente; (*at once*) inmediatamente; (*frankly*) francamente. ● *a* completo; (*refusal*) rotundo

outset /'aʊtset/ *n* principio *m*

outside /'aʊtsaɪd/ *a* & *n* exterior (*m*). /aʊt'saɪd/ *adv* fuera. ● *prep* fuera de. **~r** /aʊt'saɪdə(r)/ *n* forastero *m*; (*in race*) caballo *m* no favorito

outsize /'aʊtsaɪz/ *a* de tamaño extraordinario

outskirts /'aʊtskɜːts/ *npl* afueras *fpl*

outspoken /aʊt'spəʊkn/ *a* franco. **be ~** no tener pelos en la lengua

outstanding /aʊt'stændɪŋ/ *a* excepcional; (*not settled*) pendiente; (*conspicuous*) sobresaliente

outstretched /aʊt'stretʃt/ *a* extendido

outstrip /aʊt'strɪp/ *vt* (*pt* **-stripped**) superar

outward /'aʊtwəd/ *a* externo; (*journey*) de ida. **~ly** *adv* por fuera, exteriormente. **~(s)** *adv* hacia fuera

outweigh /aʊt'weɪ/ *vt* pesar más que; (*fig*) valer más que

outwit /aʊt'wɪt/ *vt* (*pt* **-witted**) ser más listo que

oval /'əʊvl/ *a* oval(ado). ● *n* óvalo *m*

ovary /'əʊvərɪ/ *n* ovario *m*

ovation /əʊ'veɪʃn/ *n* ovación *f*

oven /'ʌvn/ *n* horno *m*

over /'əʊvə(r)/ *prep* por encima de; (*across*) al otro lado de; (*during*) durante; (*more than*) más de. **~ and above** por encima de. ● *adv* por encima; (*ended*) terminado; (*more*) más; (*in excess*) de sobra. **~ again** otra vez. **~ and ~** una y otra vez. **~ here** por aquí. **~ there** por allí. **all ~** por todas partes

over... /'əʊvə(r)/ *pref* sobre..., super...

overall /əʊvər'ɔːl/ *a* global; (*length, cost*) total. ● *adv* en conjunto. /'əʊvərɔːl/ *n*, **~s** *npl* mono *m*

overawe /əʊvər'ɔː/ *vt* intimidar

overbalance /əʊvə'bæləns/ *vt* hacer perder el equilibrio. ● *vi* perder el equilibrio

overbearing /əʊvə'beərɪŋ/ *a* dominante

overboard /'əʊvəbɔːd/ *adv* al agua

overbook /əʊvə'bʊk/ *vt* aceptar demasiadas reservaciones para

overcast /əʊvə'kɑːst/ *a* nublado

overcharge /əʊvə'tʃɑːdʒ/ *vt* (*fill too much*) sobrecargar; (*charge too much*) cobrar demasiado

overcoat /'əʊvəkəʊt/ *n* abrigo *m*

overcome /əʊvə'kʌm/ *vt* (*pt* **-came**, *pp* **-come**) superar, vencer. **be ~ by** estar abrumado de

overcrowded /əʊvə'kraʊdɪd/ *a* atestado (de gente)

overdo /əʊvə'duː/ *vt* (*pt* **-did**, *pp* **-done**) exagerar; (*culin*) cocer demasiado

overdose /'əʊvədəʊs/ n sobredosis f

overdraft /'əʊvədrɑːft/ n giro m en descubierto

overdraw /əʊvə'drɔː/ vt (pt **-drew**, pp **-drawn**) girar en descubierto. **be ~n** tener un saldo deudor

overdue /əʊvə'djuː/ a retrasado; (belated) tardío; ⟨bill⟩ vencido y no pagado

overestimate /əʊvər'estɪmeɪt/ vt sobrestimar

overflow /əʊvə'fləʊ/ vi desbordarse. /'əʊvəfləʊ/ n (excess) exceso m; (outlet) rebosadero m

overgrown /əʊvə'grəʊn/ a demasiado grande; ⟨garden⟩ cubierto de hierbas

overhang /əʊvə'hæŋ/ vt (pt **-hung**) sobresalir por encima de; (fig) amenazar. ● vi sobresalir. /'əʊvəhæŋ/ n saliente f

overhaul /əʊvə'hɔːl/ vt revisar. /'əʊvəhɔːl/ n revisión f

overhead /əʊvə'hed/ adv por encima. /'əʊvəhed/ a de arriba. **~s** npl gastos mpl generales

overhear /əʊvə'hɪə(r)/ vt (pt **-heard**) oír por casualidad

overjoyed /əʊvə'dʒɔɪd/ a muy contento. **he was ~** rebosaba de alegría

overland /'əʊvəlænd/ a terrestre. ● adv por tierra

overlap /əʊvə'læp/ vt (pt **-lapped**) traslapar. ● vi traslaparse

overleaf /əʊvə'liːf/ adv a la vuelta. **see ~** véase al dorso

overload /əʊvə'ləʊd/ vt sobrecargar

overlook /əʊvə'lʊk/ vt dominar; ⟨building⟩ dar a; (forget) olvidar; (oversee) inspeccionar; (forgive) perdonar

overnight /əʊvə'naɪt/ adv por la noche, durante la noche; (fig, instantly) de la noche a la mañana. **stay ~** pasar la noche. ● a de noche

overpass /'əʊvəpɑːs/ n paso m a desnivel, paso m elevado

overpay /əʊvə'peɪ/ vt (pt **-paid**) pagar demasiado

overpower /əʊvə'paʊə(r)/ vt subyugar; dominar ⟨opponent⟩; (fig) abrumar. **~ing** a abrumador

overpriced /əʊvə'praɪst/ a demasiado caro

overrate /əʊvə'reɪt/ vt supervalorar

overreach /əʊvə'riːtʃ/ vr. **~ o.s.** extralimitarse

overreact /əʊvərɪ'ækt/ vi reaccionar excesivamente

overrid|e /əʊvə'raɪd/ vt (pt **-rode**, pp **-ridden**) pasar por encima de. **~ing** a dominante

overripe /'əʊvəraɪp/ a pasado, demasiado maduro

overrule /əʊvə'ruːl/ vt anular; denegar ⟨claim⟩

overrun /əʊvə'rʌn/ vt (pt **-ran**, pp **-run**, pres p **-running**) invadir; exceder ⟨limit⟩

overseas /əʊvə'siːz/ a de ultramar. ● adv al extranjero, en ultramar

oversee /əʊvə'siː/ vt (pt **-saw**, pp **-seen**) vigilar. **~r** /'əʊvəsɪə(r)/ n supervisor m

overshadow /əʊvə'ʃædəʊ/ vt (darken) sombrear; (fig) eclipsar

overshoot /əʊvə'ʃuːt/ vt (pt **-shot**) excederse. **~ the mark** pasarse de la raya

oversight /'əʊvəsaɪt/ n descuido m

oversleep /əʊvə'sliːp/ vi (pt **-slept**) despertarse tarde. **I overslept** se me pegaron las sábanas

overstep /əʊvə'step/ vt (pt **-stepped**) pasar de. **~ the mark** pasarse de la raya

overt /'əʊvɜːt/ a manifiesto

overtak|e /əʊvə'teɪk/ vt/i (pt **-took**, pp **-taken**) sobrepasar; (auto) adelantar. **~ing** n adelantamiento m

overtax /əʊvə'tæks/ vt exigir demasiado

overthrow /əʊvə'θrəʊ/ vt (pt **-threw**, pp **-thrown**) derrocar. /'əʊvəθrəʊ/ n derrocamiento m

overtime /'əʊvətaɪm/ n horas fpl extra

overtone /'əʊvətəʊn/ n (fig) matiz m

overture /'əʊvətjʊə(r)/ n obertura f. **~s** npl (fig) propuestas fpl

overturn /əʊvə'tɜːn/ vt/i volcar

overweight /əʊvə'weɪt/ a demasiado pesado. **be ~** pesar demasiado, ser gordo

overwhelm /əʊvə'welm/ vt aplastar; (with emotion) abrumar. **~ing** a aplastante; (fig) abrumador

overwork /əʊvə'wɜːk/ vt hacer trabajar demasiado. ● vi trabajar demasiado. ● n trabajo m excesivo

overwrought /əʊvə'rɔːt/ a agotado, muy nervioso

ovulation /ɒvjʊ'leɪʃn/ n ovulación f

ow|e /əʊ/ vt deber. **~ing** a debido. **~ing to** a causa de

owl /aʊl/ n lechuza f, búho m

own /əʊn/ a propio. **get one's ~ back** (fam) vengarse. **hold one's ~**

mantenerse firme, saber defenderse. **on one's ~** por su cuenta.
● *vt* poseer, tener. ● *vi*. **~ up (to)**
(*fam*) confesar. **~er** *n* propietario
m, dueño *m*. **~ership** *n* posesión *f*;
(*right*) propiedad *f*
ox /ɒks/ *n* (*pl* **oxen**) buey *m*
oxide /'ɒksaɪd/ *n* óxido *m*
oxygen /'ɒksɪdʒən/ *n* oxígeno *m*
oyster /'ɔɪstə(r)/ *n* ostra *f*

P

p /piː/ *abbr* (*pence, penny*)
penique(s) (*m*(*pl*))
pace /peɪs/ *n* paso *m*. ● *vi*. **~ up and
down** pasearse de aquí para allá.
~-maker *n* (*runner*) el que marca el
paso; (*med*) marcapasos *m invar*.
keep ~ with andar al mismo paso
que
Pacific /pə'sɪfɪk/ *a* pacífico. ● *n*. **~
(Ocean)** (Océano *m*) Pacífico *m*
pacif|ist /'pæsɪfɪst/ *n* pacifista *m & f*.
~y /'pæsɪfaɪ/ *vt* apaciguar
pack /pæk/ *n* fardo *m*; (*of cards*)
baraja *f*; (*of hounds*) jauría *f*; (*of
wolves*) manada *f*; (*large amount*)
montón *m*. ● *vt* empaquetar; hacer
⟨*suitcase*⟩; (*press down*) apretar.
● *vi* hacer la maleta. **~age**
/'pækɪdʒ/ *n* paquete *m*. ● *vt* empaquetar. **~age deal** *n* acuerdo *m*
global. **~age tour** *n* viaje *m* organizado. **~ed lunch** *n* almuerzo *m* frío.
~ed out (*fam*) de bote en bote. **~et**
/'pækɪt/ *n* paquete *m*. **send ~ing**
echar a paseo
pact /pækt/ *n* pacto *m*, acuerdo *m*
pad /pæd/ *n* almohadilla *f*; (*for writing*) bloc *m*; (*for ink*) tampón *m*;
(*flat, fam*) piso *m*. ● *vt* (*pt* **padded**)
rellenar. **~ding** *n* relleno *m*. ● *vi*
andar a pasos quedos. **launching ~**
plataforma *f* de lanzamiento
paddle¹ /'pædl/ *n* canalete *m*
paddle² /'pædl/ *vi* mojarse los pies
paddle-steamer /'pædlstiːmə(r)/ *n*
vapor *m* de ruedas
paddock /'pædək/ *n* recinto *m*; (*field*)
prado *m*
paddy /'pædɪ/ *n* arroz *m* con
cáscara. **~field** *n* arrozal *m*
padlock /'pædlɒk/ *n* candado *m*. ● *vt*
cerrar con candado
paediatrician /piːdɪə'trɪʃn/ *n* pediatra *m & f*

pagan /'peɪgən/ *a & n* pagano (*m*)
page¹ /peɪdʒ/ *n* página *f*. ● *vt*
paginar
page² /peɪdʒ/ (*in hotel*) botones *m
invar*. ● *vt* llamar
pageant /'pædʒənt/ *n* espectáculo *m*
(*histórico*). **~ry** *n* boato *m*
pagoda /pə'gəʊdə/ *n* pagoda *f*
paid /peɪd/ *see* **pay**. ● *a.* **put ~ to**
(*fam*) acabar con
pail /peɪl/ *n* cubo *m*
pain /peɪn/ *n* dolor *m*. **~ in the neck**
(*fam*) ⟨*persona*⟩ pesado *m*; ⟨*thing*⟩
lata *f*. **be in ~** tener dolores. **~s** *npl*
(*effort*) esfuerzos *mpl*. **be at ~s**
esmerarse. ● *vt* doler. **~ful** /'peɪnfl/
a doloroso; (*laborious*) penoso.
~-killer *n* calmante *m*. **~less** *a*
indoloro. **~staking** /'peɪnzteɪkɪŋ/ *a*
esmerado
paint /peɪnt/ *n* pintura *f*. ● *vt/i*
pintar. **~er** *n* pintor *m*. **~ing** *n* pintura *f*
pair /peə(r)/ *n* par *m*; (*of people*)
pareja *f*. **~ of trousers** pantalón *m*,
pantalones *mpl*. ● *vi* emparejarse.
~ off emparejarse
pajamas /pə'dʒɑːməz/ *npl* pijama *m*
Pakistan /pɑːkɪ'stɑːn/ *n* el Pakistán *m*.
~i *a & n* paquistaní (*m & f*)
pal /pæl/ *n* (*fam*) amigo *m*
palace /'pælɪs/ *n* palacio *m*
palat|able /'pælətəbl/ *a* sabroso; (*fig*)
aceptable. **~e** /'pælət/ *n* paladar *m*
palatial /pə'leɪʃl/ *a* suntuoso
palaver /pə'lɑːvə(r)/ *n* (*fam*) lío *m*
pale¹ /peɪl/ *a* (**-er, -est**) pálido; ⟨*colour*⟩ claro. ● *vi* palidecer
pale² /peɪl/ *n* estaca *n*
paleness /'peɪlnɪs/ *n* palidez *f*
Palestin|e /'pælɪstaɪn/ *n* Palestina *f*.
~ian /-'stɪnɪən/ *a & n* palestino (*m*)
palette /'pælɪt/ *n* paleta *f*. **~-knife** *n*
espátula *f*
pall¹ /pɔːl/ *n* paño *m* mortuorio; (*fig*)
capa *f*
pall² /pɔːl/ *vi*. **~ (on)** perder su sabor
(para)
pallid /'pælɪd/ *a* pálido
palm /pɑːm/ *n* palma *f*. ● *vt*. **~ off**
encajar (**on** a). **~ist** /'pɑːmɪst/ *n* quiromántico *m*. **P~ Sunday** *n*
Domingo *m* de Ramos
palpable /'pælpəbl/ *a* palpable
palpitat|e /'pælpɪteɪt/ *vi* palpitar.
~ion /-'teɪʃn/ *n* palpitación *f*
paltry /'pɔːltrɪ/ *a* (**-ier, -iest**)
insignificante
pamper /'pæmpə(r)/ *vt* mimar

pamphlet /'pæmflɪt/ *n* folleto *m*

pan /pæn/ *n* cacerola *f*; (*for frying*) sartén *f*; (*of scales*) platillo *m*; (*of lavatory*) taza *f*

panacea /pænə'sɪə/ *n* panacea *f*

panache /pæ'næʃ/ *n* brío *m*

pancake /'pænkeɪk/ *n* hojuela *f*, crêpe *f*

panda /'pændə/ *n* panda *m*. ~ **car** *n* coche *m* de la policía

pandemonium /pændɪ'məʊnɪəm/ *n* pandemonio *m*

pander /'pændə(r)/ *vi*. ~ **to** complacer

pane /peɪn/ *n* (*of glass*) vidrio *m*

panel /'pænl/ *n* panel *m*; (*group of people*) jurado *m*. ~**ling** *n* paneles *mpl*

pang /pæŋ/ *n* punzada *f*

panic /'pænɪk/ *n* pánico *m*. ● *vi* (*pt* **panicked**) ser preso de pánico. ~-**stricken** *a* preso de pánico.

panoram|a /pænə'rɑːmə/ *n* panorama *m*. ~**ic** /-'ræmɪk/ *a* panorámico

pansy /'pænzɪ/ *n* pensamiento *m*; (*effeminate man*, *fam*) maricón *m*

pant /pænt/ *vi* jadear

pantechnicon /pæn'teknɪkən/ *n* camión *m* de mudanzas

panther /'pænθə(r)/ *n* pantera *f*

panties /'pæntɪz/ *npl* bragas *fpl*

pantomime /'pæntəmaɪm/ *n* pantomima *f*

pantry /'pæntrɪ/ *n* despensa *f*

pants /pænts/ *npl* (*man's underwear*, *fam*) calzoncillos *mpl*; (*woman's underwear*, *fam*) bragas *fpl*; (*trousers*, *fam*) pantalones *mpl*

papa|cy /'peɪpəsɪ/ *n* papado *m*. ~**l** *a* papal

paper /'peɪpə(r)/ *n* papel *m*; (*newspaper*) periódico *m*; (*exam*) examen *m*; (*document*) documento *m*. **on** ~ en teoría. ● *vt* empapelar, tapizar (*LAm*). ~**back** /'peɪpəbæk/ *a* en rústica. ● *n* libro *m* en rústica. ~**clip** *n* sujetapapeles *m invar*, clip *m*. ~**weight** /'peɪpəweɪt/ *n* pisapapeles *m invar*. ~**work** *n* papeleo *m*, trabajo *m* de oficina

papier mâché /pæpɪeɪ'mæʃeɪ/ *n* cartón *m* piedra

par /pɑː(r)/ *n* par *f*; (*golf*) par *m*. **feel below** ~ no estar en forma. **on a** ~ **with** a la par con

parable /'pærəbl/ *n* parábola *f*

parachut|e /'pærəʃuːt/ *n* paracaídas *m invar*. ● *vi* lanzarse en paracaídas. ~**ist** *n* paracaidista *m* & *f*

parade /pə'reɪd/ *n* desfile *m*; (*street*) paseo *m*; (*display*) alarde *m*. ● *vi* desfilar. ● *vt* hacer alarde de

paradise /'pærədaɪs/ *n* paraíso *m*

paradox /'pærədɒks/ *n* paradoja *f*. ~**ical** /-'dɒksɪkl/ *a* paradójico

paraffin /'pærəfɪn/ *n* queroseno *m*

paragon /'pærəgən/ *n* dechado *m*

paragraph /'pærəgrɑːf/ *n* párrafo *m*

parallel /'pærəlel/ *a* paralelo. ● *n* paralelo *m*; (*line*) paralela *f*. ● *vt* ser paralelo a

paraly|se /'pærəlaɪz/ *vt* paralizar. ~**sis** /pə'ræləsɪs/ *n* (*pl* **-ses** /-siːz/) parálisis *f*. ~**tic** /pærə'lɪtɪk/ *a* & *n* paralítico (*m*)

parameter /pə'ræmɪtə(r)/ *n* parámetro *m*

paramount /'pærəmaʊnt/ *a* supremo

paranoia /pærə'nɔɪə/ *n* paranoia *f*

parapet /'pærəpɪt/ *n* parapeto *m*

paraphernalia /pærəfə'neɪlɪə/ *n* trastos *mpl*

paraphrase /'pærəfreɪz/ *n* paráfrasis *f*. ● *vt* parafrasear

paraplegic /pærə'pliːdʒɪk/ *n* parapléjico *m*

parasite /'pærəsaɪt/ *n* parásito *m*

parasol /'pærəsɒl/ *n* sombrilla *f*

paratrooper /'pærətruːpə(r)/ *n* paracaidista *m*

parcel /'pɑːsl/ *n* paquete *m*

parch /pɑːtʃ/ *vt* resecar. **be** ~**ed** tener mucha sed

parchment /'pɑːtʃmənt/ *n* pergamino *m*

pardon /'pɑːdn/ *n* perdón *m*; (*jurid*) indulto *m*. **I beg your** ~! ¡perdone Vd! **I beg your** ~? ¿cómo?, ¿mande? (*Mex*). ● *vt* perdonar

pare /peə(r)/ *vt* cortar ⟨*nails*⟩; (*peel*) pelar, mondar

parent /'peərənt/ *n* (*father*) padre *m*; (*mother*) madre *f*; (*source*) origen *m*. ~**s** *npl* padres *mpl*. ~**al** /pə'rentl/ *a* de los padres

parenthesis /pə'renθəsɪs/ *n* (*pl* **-theses** /-siːz/) paréntesis *m invar*

parenthood /'peərənthʊd/ *n* paternidad *f*, maternidad *f*

Paris /'pærɪs/ *n* París *m*

parish /'pærɪʃ/ *n* parroquia *f*; (*municipal*) municipio *m*. ~**ioner** /pə'rɪʃənə(r)/ *n* feligrés *m*

Parisian /pə'rɪzɪən/ *a* & *n* parisino (*m*)

parity /'pærtɪ/ *n* igualdad *f*

park /pɑːk/ n parque m. ● vt/i aparcar. ~ **oneself** vr (fam) instalarse

parka /'pɑːkə/ n anorak m

parking-meter /'pɑːkɪŋmiːtə(r)/ n parquímetro m

parliament /'pɑːləmənt/ n parlamento m. ~**ary** /-'mentrɪ/ a parlamentario

parlour /'pɑːlə(r)/ n salón m

parochial /pə'rəʊkɪəl/ a parroquial; (fig) pueblerino

parody /'pærədɪ/ n parodia f. ● vt parodiar

parole /pə'rəʊl/ n libertad f bajo palabra, libertad f provisional. on ~ libre bajo palabra. ● vt liberar bajo palabra

paroxysm /'pærəksɪzəm/ n paroxismo m

parquet /'pɑːkeɪ/ n. ~ **floor** n parqué m

parrot /'pærət/ n papagayo m

parry /'pærɪ/ vt parar; (avoid) esquivar. ● n parada f

parsimonious /pɑːsɪ'məʊnɪəs/ a parsimonioso

parsley /'pɑːslɪ/ n perejil m

parsnip /'pɑːsnɪp/ n pastinaca f

parson /'pɑːsn/ n cura m, párroco m

part /pɑːt/ n parte f; (of machine) pieza f; (of serial) entrega f; (in play) papel m; (side in dispute) partido m. on the ~ of por parte de. ● adv en parte. ● vt separar. ~ **with** vt separarse de. ● vi separarse

partake /pɑː'teɪk/ vt (pt -took, pp -taken) participar. ~ **of** compartir

partial /'pɑːʃl/ a parcial. be ~ to ser aficionado a. ~**ity** /-ɪ'ælətɪ/ n parcialidad f. ~**ly** adv parcialmente

participa|nt /pɑː'tɪsɪpənt/ n participante m & f. ~**te** /pɑː'tɪsɪpeɪt/ vi participar. ~**tion** /-'peɪʃn/ n participación f

participle /'pɑːtɪsɪpl/ n participio m

particle /'pɑːtɪkl/ n partícula f

particular /pə'tɪkjʊlə(r)/ a particular; (precise) meticuloso; (fastidious) quisquilloso. ● n. in ~ especialmente. ~**ly** adv especialmente. ~**s** npl detalles mpl

parting /'pɑːtɪŋ/ n separación f; (in hair) raya f. ● a de despedida

partisan /pɑːtɪ'zæn/ n partidario m

partition /pɑː'tɪʃn/ n partición f; (wall) tabique m. ● vt dividir

partly /'pɑːtlɪ/ adv en parte

partner /'pɑːtnə(r)/ n socio m; (sport) pareja f. ~**ship** n asociación f; (com) sociedad f

partridge /'pɑːtrɪdʒ/ n perdiz f

part-time /pɑːt'taɪm/ a & adv a tiempo parcial

party /'pɑːtɪ/ n reunión f, fiesta f; (group) grupo m; (pol) partido m; (jurid) parte f. ~ **line** n (telephone) línea f colectiva

pass /pɑːs/ vt pasar; (in front of) pasar por delante de; (overtake) adelantar; (approve) aprobar ⟨exam, bill, law⟩; hacer ⟨remark⟩; pronunciar ⟨judgement⟩. ~ **down** transmitir. ~ **over** pasar por alto de. ~ **round** distribuir. ~ **through** pasar por; (cross) atravesar. ~ **up** (fam) dejar pasar. ● vi pasar; (in exam) aprobar. ~ **away** morir. ~ **out** (fam) desmayarse. ● n (permit) permiso m; (in mountains) puerto m, desfiladero m; (sport) pase m; (in exam) aprobado m. make a ~ at (fam) hacer proposiciones amorosas a. ~**able** /'pɑːsəbl/ a pasable; ⟨road⟩ transitable

passage /'pæsɪdʒ/ n paso m; (voyage) travesía f; (corridor) pasillo m; (in book) pasaje m

passenger /'pæsɪndʒə(r)/ n pasajero m

passer-by /pɑːsə'baɪ/ n (pl passers-by) transeúnte m & f

passion /'pæʃn/ n pasión f. ~**ate** a apasionado. ~**ately** adv apasionadamente

passive /'pæsɪv/ a pasivo. ~**ness** n pasividad f

passmark /'pɑːsmɑːk/ n aprobado m

Passover /'pɑːsəʊvə(r)/ n Pascua f de los hebreos

passport /'pɑːspɔːt/ n pasaporte m

password /'pɑːswɜːd/ n contraseña f

past /pɑːst/ a & n pasado (m). in times ~ en tiempos pasados. the ~ week n la semana f pasada. ● prep por delante de; (beyond) más allá de. ● adv por delante. drive ~ pasar en coche. go ~ pasar

paste /peɪst/ n pasta f; (adhesive) engrudo m. ● vt (fasten) pegar; (cover) engrudar. ~**board** /'peɪstbɔːd/ n cartón m. ~ **jewellery** n joyas fpl de imitación

pastel /'pæstl/ a & n pastel (m)

pasteurize /'pæstʃəraɪz/ vt pasteurizar

pastiche /pæ'stiːʃ/ n pastiche m

pastille /'pæstɪl/ n pastilla f

pastime /'pɑːstaɪm/ n pasatiempo m

pastoral /'pɑːstərəl/ a pastoral

pastr|ies npl pasteles mpl, pastas fpl. ~**y** /'peɪstrɪ/ n pasta f

pasture /'pɑːstʃə(r)/ n pasto m

pasty[1] /'pæstɪ/ n empanada f

pasty[2] /'peɪstɪ/ a pastoso; (pale) pálido

pat[1] /pæt/ vt (pt **patted**) dar palmaditas en; acariciar ⟨dog etc⟩. ● n palmadita f; (of butter) porción f

pat[2] /pæt/ adv en el momento oportuno

patch /pætʃ/ n pedazo m; (period) período m; (repair) remiendo m; (piece of ground) terreno m. **not a** ~ **on** (fam) muy inferior a. ● vt remendar. ~ **up** arreglar. ~**work** n labor m de retazos; (fig) mosaico m. ~**y** a desigual

pâté /'pæteɪ/ n pasta f, paté m

patent /'peɪtnt/ a patente. ● n patente f. ● vt patentar. ~ **leather** n charol m. ~**ly** adv evidentemente

patern|al /pə'tɜːnl/ a paterno. ~**ity** /pə'tɜːnətɪ/ n paternidad f

path /pɑːθ/ n (pl -s /pɑːðz/) sendero m; (sport) pista f; (of rocket) trayectoria f; (fig) camino m

pathetic /pə'θetɪk/ a patético, lastimoso

pathology /pə'θɒlədʒɪ/ n patología f

pathos /'peɪθɒs/ n patetismo m

patien|ce /'peɪʃns/ n paciencia f. ~**t** /'peɪʃnt/ a & n paciente (m & f). ~**tly** adv con paciencia

patio /'pætɪəʊ/ n (pl -os) patio m

patriarch /'peɪtrɪɑːk/ n patriarca m

patrician /pə'trɪʃn/ a & n patricio (m)

patriot /'pætrɪət/ n patriota m & f. ~**ic** /-'ɒtɪk/ a patriótico. ~**ism** n patriotismo m

patrol /pə'trəʊl/ n patrulla f. ● vt/i patrullar

patron /'peɪtrən/ n (of the arts etc) mecenas m & f; (customer) cliente m & f; (of charity) patrocinador m. ~**age** /'pætrənɪdʒ/ n patrocinio m; (of shop etc) clientela f. ~**ize** vt ser cliente de; (fig) tratar con condescendencia

patter[1] /'pætə(r)/ n (of steps) golpeteo m; (of rain) tamborileo m. ● vi correr con pasos ligeros; ⟨rain⟩ tamborilear

patter[2] /'pætə(r)/ (speech) jerga f; (chatter) parloteo m

pattern /'pætn/ n diseño m; (model) modelo m; (sample) muestra f; (manner) modo m; (in dressmaking) patrón m

paunch /pɔːntʃ/ n panza f

pauper /'pɔːpə(r)/ n indigente m & f, pobre m & f

pause /pɔːz/ n pausa f. ● vi hacer una pausa

pave /peɪv/ vt pavimentar. ~ **the way for** preparar el terreno para

pavement /'peɪvmənt/ n pavimento m; (at side of road) acera f

pavilion /pə'vɪlɪən/ n pabellón m

paving-stone /'peɪvɪŋstəʊn/ n losa f

paw /pɔː/ n pata f, (of cat) garra f. ● vi tocar con la pata; ⟨person⟩ manosear

pawn[1] /pɔːn/ n (chess) peón m; (fig) instrumento m

pawn[2] /pɔːn/ vt empeñar. ● n. **in** ~ en prenda. ~**broker** /'pɔːnbrəʊkə(r)/ n prestamista m & f. ~**shop** n monte m de piedad

pawpaw /'pɔːpɔː/ n papaya f

pay /peɪ/ vt (pt **paid**) pagar; prestar ⟨attention⟩; hacer ⟨compliment, visit⟩. ~ **back** devolver. ~ **cash** pagar al contado. ~ **in** ingresar. ~ **off** pagar. ~ **out** pagar. ● vi pagar; (be profitable) rendir. ● n paga f. **in the** ~ **of** al servicio de. ~**able** /'peɪəbl/ a pagadero. ~**ment** /'peɪmənt/ n pago m. ~**off** n (sl) liquidación f; (fig) ajuste m de cuentas. ~**roll** /'peɪrəʊl/ n nómina f. ~ **up** pagar

pea /piː/ n guisante m

peace /piːs/ n paz f. ~ **of mind** tranquilidad f. ~**able** a pacífico. ~**ful** /'piːsfl/ a tranquilo. ~**maker** /'piːsmeɪkə(r)/ n pacificador m

peach /piːtʃ/ n melocotón m, durazno m (LAm); (tree) melocotonero m, duraznero m (LAm)

peacock /'piːkɒk/ n pavo m real

peak /piːk/ n cumbre f; (maximum) máximo m. ~ **hours** npl horas fpl punta. ~**ed cap** n gorra f de visera

peaky /'piːkɪ/ a pálido

peal /piːl/ n repique m. ~**s of laughter** risotadas fpl

peanut /'piːnʌt/ n cacahuete m, maní m (Mex). ~**s** (sl) una bagatela f

pear /peə(r)/ n pera f; (tree) peral m

pearl /pɜːl/ n perla f. ~**y** a nacarado

peasant /'peznt/ n campesino m

peat /piːt/ n turba f

pebble /'pebl/ n guijarro m

peck /pek/ *vt* picotear; (*kiss, fam*) dar un besito a. ● *n* picotazo *m*; (*kiss*) besito *m*. **~ish** /'pekɪʃ/ *a*. be **~ish** (*fam*) tener hambre, tener gazuza (*fam*)

peculiar /pɪ'kjuːlɪə(r)/ *a* raro; (*special*) especial. **~ity** /-'ærətɪ/ *n* rareza *f*; (*feature*) particularidad *f*

pedal /'pedl/ *n* pedal *m*. ● *vi* pedalear

pedantic /pɪ'dæntɪk/ *a* pedante

peddle /'pedl/ *vt* vender por las calles

pedestal /'pedɪstl/ *n* pedestal *m*

pedestrian /pɪ'destrɪən/ *n* peatón *m*. ● *a* de peatones; (*dull*) prosaico. **~ crossing** *n* paso *m* de peatones

pedigree /'pedɪgriː/ *n* linaje *m*; (*of animal*) pedigrí *m*. ● *a* ‹*animal*› de raza

pedlar /'pedlə(r)/ *n* buhonero *m*, vendedor *m* ambulante

peek /piːk/ *vi* mirar a hurtadillas

peel /piːl/ *n* cáscara *f*. ● *vt* pelar ‹*fruit, vegetables*›. ● *vi* pelarse. **~ings** *npl* peladuras *fpl*, monda *f*

peep[1] /piːp/ *vi* mirar a hurtadillas. ● *n* mirada *f* furtiva

peep[2] /piːp/ ‹*bird*› piar. ● *n* pío *m*

peep-hole /'piːphəʊl/ *n* mirilla *f*

peer[1] /pɪə(r)/ *vi* mirar. **~ at** escudriñar

peer[2] /pɪə(r)/ *n* par *m*, compañero *m*. **~age** *n* pares *mpl*

peev|ed /piːvd/ *a* (*sl*) irritado. **~ish** /'piːvɪʃ/ *a* picajoso

peg /peg/ *n* clavija *f*; (*for washing*) pinza *f*; (*hook*) gancho *m*; (*for tent*) estaca *f*. off the **~** de percha. ● *vt* (*pt* **pegged**) fijar ‹*precios*›. **~ away at** afanarse por

pejorative /pɪ'dʒɒrətɪv/ *a* peyorativo, despectivo

pelican /'pelɪkən/ *n* pelícano *m*. **~ crossing** *n* paso *m* de peatones (con semáforo)

pellet /'pelɪt/ *n* pelotilla *f*; (*for gun*) perdigón *m*

pelt[1] /pelt/ *n* pellejo *m*

pelt[2] /pelt/ *vt* tirar. ● *vi* llover a cántaros

pelvis /'pelvɪs/ *n* pelvis *f*

pen[1] /pen/ *n* (*enclosure*) recinto *m*

pen[2] /pen/ (*for writing*) pluma *f*, estilográfica *f*; (*ball-point*) bolígrafo *m*

penal /'piːnl/ *a* penal. **~ize** *vt* castigar. **~ty** /'penltɪ/ *n* castigo *m*; (*fine*)

multa *f*. **~ty kick** *n* (*football*) penalty *m*

penance /'penəns/ *n* penitencia *f*

pence /pens/ *see* **penny**

pencil /'pensl/ *n* lápiz *m*. ● *vt* (*pt* **pencilled**) escribir con lápiz. **~-sharpener** *n* sacapuntas *m invar*

pendant /'pendənt/ *n* dije *m*, medallón *m*

pending /'pendɪŋ/ *a* pendiente. ● *prep* hasta

pendulum /'pendjʊləm/ *n* péndulo *m*

penetrat|e /'penɪtreɪt/ *vt/i* penetrar. **~ing** *a* penetrante. **~ion** /-'treɪʃn/ *n* penetración *f*

penguin /'peŋgwɪn/ *n* pingüino *m*

penicillin /penɪ'sɪlɪn/ *n* penicilina *f*

peninsula /pə'nɪnsjʊlə/ *n* península *f*

penis /'piːnɪs/ *n* pene *m*

peniten|ce /'penɪtəns/ *n* penitencia *f*. **~t** /'penɪtənt/ *a* & *n* penitente (*m* & *f*). **~tiary** /penɪ'tenʃərɪ/ *n* (*Amer*) cárcel *m*

pen: ~knife /'pennaɪf/ *n* (*pl* **penknives**) navaja *f*; (*small*) cortaplumas *m invar*. **~name** *n* seudónimo *m*

pennant /'penənt/ *n* banderín *m*

penn|iless /'penɪlɪs/ *a* sin un céntimo. **~y** /'penɪ/ *n* (*pl* **pennies** *or* **pence**) penique *m*

pension /'penʃn/ *n* pensión *f*; (*for retirement*) jubilación *f*. ● *vt* pensionar. **~able** *a* con derecho a pensión; ‹*age*› de la jubilación. **~er** *n* jubilado *m*. **~ off** jubilar

pensive /'pensɪv/ *a* pensativo

pent-up /pent'ʌp/ *a* reprimido; (*confined*) encerrado

pentagon /'pentəgən/ *n* pentágono *m*

Pentecost /'pentɪkɒst/ *n* Pentecostés *m*

penthouse /'penthaʊs/ *n* ático *m*

penultimate /pen'ʌltɪmət/ *a* penúltimo

penury /'penjʊərɪ/ *n* penuria *f*

peony /'piːənɪ/ *n* peonía *f*

people /'piːpl/ *npl* gente *f*; (*citizens*) pueblo *m*. **~ say** se dice. English **~** los ingleses *mpl*. my **~** (*fam*) mi familia *f*. ● *vt* poblar

pep /pep/ *n* vigor *m*. ● *vt*. **~ up** animar

pepper /'pepə(r)/ *n* pimienta *f*; (*vegetable*) pimiento *m*. ● *vt* sazonar con pimienta. **~y** *a* picante. **~corn**

/'pepəkɔ:n/ *n* grano *m* de pimienta. **∼corn rent** *n* alquiler *m* nominal

peppermint /'pepəmɪnt/ *n* menta *f*; (*sweet*) pastilla *f* de menta

pep talk /'peptɔ:k/ *n* palabras *fpl* animadoras

per /pɜ:(r)/ *prep* por. **∼ annum** al año. **∼ cent** por ciento. **∼ head** por cabeza, por persona. **ten miles ∼ hour** diez millas por hora

perceive /pə'si:v/ *vt* percibir; (*notice*) darse cuenta de

percentage /pə'sentɪdʒ/ *n* porcentaje *m*

percepti|ble /pə'septəbl/ *a* perceptible. **∼on** /pə'sepʃn/ *n* percepción *f*. **∼ve** *a* perspicaz

perch¹ /pɜ:tʃ/ *n* (*of bird*) percha *f*. ● *vi* posarse

perch² /pɜ:tʃ/ (*fish*) perca *f*

percolat|e /'pɜ:kəleɪt/ *vt* filtrar. ● *vi* filtrarse. **∼or** *n* cafetera *f*

percussion /pə'kʌʃn/ *n* percusión *f*

peremptory /pə'remptərɪ/ *a* perentorio

perennial /pə'renɪəl/ *a* & *n* perenne (*m*)

perfect /'pɜ:fɪkt/ *a* perfecto. /pə'fekt/ *vt* perfeccionar. **∼ion** /pə'fekʃn/ *n* perfección *f*. **to ∼ion** a la perfección. **∼ionist** *n* perfeccionista *m* & *f*. **∼ly** /'pɜ:fɪktlɪ/ *adv* perfectamente

perforat|e /'pɜ:fəreɪt/ *vt* perforar. **∼ion** /-'reɪʃn/ *n* perforación *f*

perform /pə'fɔ:m/ *vt* hacer, realizar; representar ⟨play⟩; desempeñar ⟨role⟩; (*mus*) interpretar. **∼ an operation** (*med*) operar. **∼ance** *n* ejecución *f*; (*of play*) representación *f*; (*of car*) rendimiento *m*; (*fuss, fam*) jaleo *m*. **∼er** *n* artista *m* & *f*

perfume /'pɜ:fju:m/ *n* perfume *m*

perfunctory /pə'fʌŋktərɪ/ *a* superficial

perhaps /pə'hæps/ *adv* quizá(s), tal vez

peril /'perəl/ *n* peligro *m*. **∼ous** *a* arriesgado, peligroso

perimeter /pə'rɪmɪtə(r)/ *n* perímetro *m*

period /'pɪərɪəd/ *n* período *m*; (*lesson*) clase *f*; (*gram*) punto *m*. ● *a* de (la) época. **∼ic** /-'ɒdɪk/ *a* periódico. **∼ical** /pɪərɪ'ɒdɪkl/ *n* revista *f*. **∼ically** /-'ɒdɪklɪ/ *adv* periódico

peripher|al /pə'rɪfərəl/ *a* periférico. **∼y** /pə'rɪfərɪ/ *n* periferia *f*

periscope /'perɪskəʊp/ *n* periscopio *m*

perish /'perɪʃ/ *vi* perecer; (*rot*) estropearse. **∼able** *a* perecedero. **∼ing** *a* (*fam*) glacial

perjur|e /'pɜ:dʒə(r)/ *vr*. **∼e o.s.** perjurarse. **∼y** *n* perjurio *m*

perk¹ /pɜ:k/ *n* gaje *m*

perk² /pɜ:k/ *vt/i*. **∼ up** *vt* reanimar. ● *vi* reanimarse. **∼y** *a* alegre

perm /pɜ:m/ *n* permanente *f*. ● *vt* hacer una permanente a

permanen|ce /'pɜ:mənəns/ *n* permanencia *f*. **∼t** /'pɜ:mənənt/ *a* permanente. **∼tly** *adv* permanentemente

permea|ble /'pɜ:mɪəbl/ *a* permeable. **∼te** /'pɜ:mɪeɪt/ *vt* penetrar; (*soak*) empapar

permissible /pə'mɪsəbl/ *a* permisible

permission /pə'mɪʃn/ *n* permiso *m*

permissive /pə'mɪsɪv/ *a* indulgente. **∼ness** *n* tolerancia *f*. **∼ society** *n* sociedad *f* permisiva

permit /pə'mɪt/ *vt* (*pt* **permitted**) permitir. /'pɜ:mɪt/ *n* permiso *m*

permutation /pɜ:mju:'teɪʃn/ *n* permutación *f*

pernicious /pə'nɪʃəs/ *a* pernicioso

peroxide /pə'rɒksaɪd/ *n* peróxido *m*

perpendicular /pɜ:pən'dɪkjʊlə(r)/ *a* & *n* perpendicular (*f*)

perpetrat|e /'pɜ:pɪtreɪt/ *vt* cometer. **∼or** *n* autor *m*

perpetua|l /pə'petʃʊəl/ *a* perpetuo. **∼te** /pə'petʃʊeɪt/ *vt* perpetuar. **∼tion** /-'eɪʃn/ *n* perpetuación *f*

perplex /pə'pleks/ *vt* dejar perplejo. **∼ed** *a* perplejo. **∼ing** *a* desconcertante. **∼ity** *n* perplejidad *f*

persecut|e /'pɜ:sɪkju:t/ *vt* perseguir. **∼ion** /-'kju:ʃn/ *n* persecución *f*

persever|ance /pɜ:sɪ'vɪərəns/ *n* perseverancia *f*. **∼e** /pɜ:sɪ'vɪə(r)/ *vi* perseverar, persistir

Persian /'pɜ:ʃn/ *a* persa. **the ∼ Gulf** *n* el golfo *m* Pérsico. ● *n* persa (*m* & *f*); (*lang*) persa *m*

persist /pə'sɪst/ *vi* persistir. **∼ence** *n* persistencia *f*. **∼ent** *a* persistente; (*continual*) continuo. **∼ently** *adv* persistentemente

person /'pɜ:sn/ *n* persona *f*

personal /'pɜ:sənl/ *a* personal

personality /pɜ:sə'næləti/ *n* personalidad *f*; (*on TV*) personaje *m*

personally /'pɜ:sənəlɪ/ *adv* personalmente; (*in person*) en persona

personify /pə'sɒnɪfaɪ/ *vt* personificar

personnel /pɜːsə'nel/ *n* personal *m*

perspective /pə'spektɪv/ *n* perspectiva *f*

perspicacious /pɜːspɪ'keɪʃəs/ *a* perspicaz

perspir|ation /pɜːspə'reɪʃn/ *n* sudor *m*. **~e** /pəs'paɪə(r)/ *vi* sudar

persua|de /pə'sweɪd/ *vt* persuadir. **~sion** *n* persuasión *f*. **~sive** /pə'sweɪsɪv/ *a* persuasivo. **~sively** *adv* de manera persuasiva

pert /pɜːt/ *a* (*saucy*) impertinente; (*lively*) animado

pertain /pə'teɪn/ *vi*. **~ to** relacionarse con

pertinent /pɜːtɪnənt/ *a* pertinente. **~ly** *adv* pertinentemente

pertly /'pɜːtlɪ/ *adv* impertinentemente

perturb /pə'tɜːb/ *vt* perturbar

Peru /pə'ruː/ *n* el Perú *m*

perus|al /pə'ruːzl/ *n* lectura *f* cuidadosa. **~e** /pə'ruːz/ *vt* leer cuidadosamente

Peruvian /pə'ruːvɪən/ *a & n* peruano (*m*)

perva|de /pə'veɪd/ *vt* difundirse por. **~sive** *a* penetrante

perver|se /pə'vɜːs/ *a* (*stubborn*) terco; (*wicked*) perverso. **~sity** *n* terquedad *f*; (*wickedness*) perversidad *f*. **~sion** *n* perversión *f*. **~t** /pə'vɜːt/ *vt* pervertir. /'pɜːvɜːt/ *n* pervertido *m*

pessimis|m /'pesɪmɪzəm/ *n* pesimismo *m*. **~t** /'pesɪmɪst/ *n* pesimista *m & f*. **~tic** /-'mɪstɪk/ *a* pesimista

pest /pest/ *n* insecto *m* nocivo, plaga *f*; (*person*) pelma *m*; (*thing*) lata *f*

pester /'pestə(r)/ *vt* importunar

pesticide /'pestɪsaɪd/ *n* pesticida *f*

pet /pet/ *n* animal *m* doméstico; (*favourite*) favorito *m*. ● *a* preferido. ● *vt* (*pt* petted) acariciar

petal /'petl/ *n* pétalo *m*

peter /'piːtə(r)/ *vi*. **~ out** (*supplies*) agotarse; (*disappear*) desparecer

petite /pə'tiːt/ *a* (*of woman*) chiquita

petition /pɪ'tɪʃn/ *n* petición *f*. ● *vt* dirigir una petición a

pet name /'petneɪm/ *n* apodo *m* cariñoso

petrify /'petrɪfaɪ/ *vt* petrificar. ● *vi* petrificarse

petrol /'petrəl/ *n* gasolina *f*. **~eum** /pɪ'trəʊlɪəm/ *n* petróleo *m*. **~ gauge** *n* indicador *m* de nivel de gasolina. **~ pump** *n* (*in car*) bomba *f* de gasolina; (*at garage*) surtidor *m* de gasolina. **~ station** *n* gasolinera *f*. **~ tank** *n* depósito *m* de gasolina

petticoat /'petɪkəʊt/ *n* enaguas *fpl*

pett|iness /'petɪnɪs/ *n* mezquindad *f*. **~y** /'petɪ/ *a* (**-ier, -iest**) insignificante; (*mean*) mezquino. **~y cash** *n* dinero *m* para gastos menores. **~y officer** *n* suboficial *m* de marina

petulan|ce /'petjʊləns/ *n* irritabilidad *f*. **~t** /'petjʊlənt/ *a* irritable

pew /pjuː/ *n* banco *m* (de iglesia)

pewter /'pjuːtə(r)/ *n* peltre *m*

phallic /'fælɪk/ *a* fálico

phantom /'fæntəm/ *n* fantasma *m*

pharmaceutical /fɑːmə'sjuːtɪkl/ *a* farmacéutico

pharmac|ist /'fɑːməsɪst/ *n* farmacéutico *m*. **~y** /'fɑːməsɪ/ *n* farmacia *f*

pharyngitis /færɪn'dʒaɪtɪs/ *n* faringitis *f*

phase /feɪz/ *n* etapa *f*. ● *vt*. **~ in** introducir progresivamente. **~ out** retirar progresivamente

PhD *abbr* (*Doctor of Philosophy*) *n* Doctor *m* en Filosofía

pheasant /'feznt/ *n* faisán *m*

phenomenal /fɪ'nɒmɪnl/ *a* fenomenal

phenomenon /fɪ'nɒmɪnən/ *n* (*pl* **-ena**) fenómeno *m*

phew /fjuː/ *int* ¡uy!

phial /'faɪəl/ *n* frasco *m*

philanderer /fɪ'lændərə(r)/ *n* mariposón *m*

philanthrop|ic /fɪlən'θrɒpɪk/ *a* filantrópico. **~ist** /fɪ'lænθrəpɪst/ *n* filántropo *m*

philatel|ist /fɪ'lætəlɪst/ *n* filatelista *m & f*. **~y** /fɪ'lætəlɪ/ *n* filatelia *f*

philharmonic /fɪlhɑː'mɒnɪk/ *a* filarmónico

Philippines /'fɪlɪpiːnz/ *npl* Filipinas *fpl*

philistine /'fɪlɪstaɪn/ *a & n* filisteo (*m*)

philosoph|er /fɪ'lɒsəfə(r)/ *n* filósofo *m*. **~ical** /-ə'sɒfɪkl/ *a* filosófico. **~y** /fɪ'lɒsəfɪ/ *n* filosofía *f*

phlegm /flem/ *n* flema *f*. **~atic** /fleg'mætɪk/ *a* flemático

phobia /'fəʊbɪə/ *n* fobia *f*

phone /fəʊn/ *n* (*fam*) teléfono *m*. ● *vt/i* llamar por teléfono. **~ back**

‹caller› volver a llamar; ‹person called› llamar. ~ **box** n cabina f telefónica

phonetic /fə'netɪk/ a fonético. ~**s** n fonética f

phoney /'fəʊnɪ/ a (**-ier, -iest**) (sl) falso. ● n (sl) farsante m & f

phosphate /'fɒsfeɪt/ n fosfato m

phosphorus /'fɒsfərəs/ n fósforo m

photo /'fəʊtəʊ/ n (pl **-os**) (fam) fotografía f, foto f (fam)

photocopy /'fəʊtəʊkɒpɪ/ n fotocopia f. ● vt fotocopiar

photogenic /fəʊtəʊ'dʒenɪk/ a fotogénico

photograph /'fəʊtəɡrɑːf/ n fotografía f. ● vt hacer una fotografía de, sacar fotos de. ~**er** /fə'tɒɡrəfə(r)/ n fotógrafo m. ~**ic** /-'ɡræfɪk/ a fotográfico ~**y** /fə'tɒɡrəfɪ/ n fotografía f

phrase /freɪz/ n frase f, locución f, expresión f. ● vt expresar. ~**book** n libro m de frases

physical /'fɪzɪkl/ a físico

physician /fɪ'zɪʃn/ n médico m

physic|ist /'fɪzɪsɪst/ n físico m. ~**s** /'fɪzɪks/ n física f

physiology /fɪzɪ'ɒlədʒɪ/ n fisiología f

physiotherap|ist /fɪzɪəʊ'θerəpɪst/ n fisioterapeuta m & f. ~**y** /fɪzɪəʊ'θerəpɪ/ n fisioterapia f

physique /fɪ'ziːk/ n constitución f; (appearance) físico m

pian|ist /'pɪənɪst/ n pianista m & f. ~**o** /pɪ'ænəʊ/ n (pl **-os**) piano m

piccolo /'pɪkələʊ/ n flautín m, píccolo m

pick[1] /pɪk/ (tool) pico m

pick[2] /pɪk/ vt escoger; recoger ‹flowers etc›; forzar ‹a lock›; (dig) picar. ~ **a quarrel** buscar camorra. ~ **holes in** criticar. ● n (choice) selección f; (the best) lo mejor. ~ **on** vt (nag) meterse con. ~ **out** vt escoger; (identify) identificar; destacar ‹colour›. ~ **up** vt recoger; (lift) levantar; (learn) aprender; adquirir ‹habit, etc›; obtener ‹information›; contagiarse de ‹illness›. ● vi mejorar; (med) reponerse

pickaxe /'pɪkæks/ n pico m

picket /'pɪkɪt/ n (striker) huelguista m & f; (group of strikers) piquete m; (stake) estaca f. ~ **line** n piquete m. ● vt vigilar por piquetes. ● vi estar de guardia

pickle /'pɪkl/ n (in vinegar) encurtido m; (in brine) salmuera f. **in a** ~

(fam) en un apuro. ● vt encurtir. ~**s** npl encurtido m

pick: ~pocket /'pɪkpɒkɪt/ n ratero m. ~**up** n (sl) ligue m; (truck) camioneta f; (stylus-holder) fonocaptor m, brazo m

picnic /'pɪknɪk/ n comida f campestre. ● vi (pt **picnicked**) merendar en el campo

pictorial /pɪk'tɔːrɪəl/ a ilustrado

picture /'pɪktʃə(r)/ n (painting) cuadro m; (photo) fotografía f; (drawing) dibujo m; (beautiful thing) preciosidad f; (film) película f; (fig) descripción f. **the** ~**s** npl el cine m. ● vt imaginarse; (describe) describir

picturesque /pɪktʃə'resk/ a pintoresco

piddling /'pɪdlɪŋ/ a (fam) insignificante

pidgin /'pɪdʒɪn/ a. ~ **English** n inglés m corrompido

pie /paɪ/ n empanada f; (sweet) pastel m, tarta f

piebald /'paɪbɔːld/ a pío

piece /piːs/ n pedazo m; (coin) moneda f; (in game) pieza f. **a** ~ **of advice** un consejo m. **a** ~ **of news** una noticia f. **take to** ~**s** desmontar. ● vt. ~ **together** juntar. ~**meal** /'piːsmiːl/ a gradual; (unsystematic) poco sistemático. —adv poco a poco. ~**work** n trabajo m a destajo

pier /pɪə(r)/ n muelle m

pierce /pɪəs/ vt perforar. ~**ing** a penetrante

piety /'paɪətɪ/ n piedad f

piffl|e /'pɪfl/ n (sl) tonterías fpl. ~**ing** a (sl) insignificante

pig /pɪg/ n cerdo m

pigeon /'pɪdʒɪn/ n paloma f; (culin) pichón m. ~**hole** n casilla f

pig: ~gy /'pɪgɪ/ a (greedy, fam) glotón. ~**gy-back** adv a cuestas. ~**gy bank** n hucha f. ~**headed** a terco

pigment /'pɪɡmənt/ n pigmento m. ~**ation** /-'teɪʃn/ n pigmentación f

pig: ~skin /'pɪɡskɪn/ n piel m de cerdo. ~**sty** /'pɪɡstaɪ/ n pocilga f

pigtail /'pɪɡteɪl/ n (plait) trenza f

pike /paɪk/ n invar (fish) lucio m

pilchard /'pɪltʃəd/ n sardina f

pile[1] /paɪl/ n (heap) montón m. ● vt amontonar. ~ **it on** exagerar. ● vi amontonar. ~ **up** vt amontonar. ● vi amontonarse. ~**s** /paɪlz/ npl (med) almorranas fpl

pile[2] /paɪl/ n (of fabric) pelo m

pile-up /'paɪlʌp/ n accidente m múltiple

pilfer /'pɪlfə(r)/ vt/i hurtar. **~age** n, **~ing** n hurto m

pilgrim /'pɪlgrɪm/ n peregrino. **~age** n peregrinación f

pill /pɪl/ n píldora f

pillage /'pɪlɪdʒ/ n saqueo m. ● vt saquear

pillar /'pɪlə(r)/ n columna f. **~box** n buzón m

pillion /'pɪlɪən/ n asiento m trasero. **ride ~** ir en el asiento trasero

pillory /'pɪlərɪ/ n picota f

pillow /'pɪləʊ/ n almohada f. **~case** /'pɪləʊkeɪs/ n funda f de almohada

pilot /'paɪlət/ n piloto m. ● vt pilotar. **~light** n fuego m piloto

pimp /pɪmp/ n alcahuete m

pimple /'pɪmpl/ n grano m

pin /pɪn/ n alfiler m; (mec) perno m. **~s and needles** hormigueo m. ● vt (pt **pinned**) prender con alfileres; (hold down) enclavijar; (fix) sujetar. **~ s.o. down** obligar a uno a que se decida. **~ up** fijar

pinafore /'pɪnəfɔ:(r)/ n delantal m. **~ dress** n mandil m

pincers /'pɪnsəz/ npl tenazas fpl

pinch /pɪntʃ/ vt pellizcar; (steal, sl) hurtar. ● vi (shoe) apretar. ● n pellizco m; (small amount) pizca f. **at a ~** en caso de necesidad

pincushion /'pɪnkʊʃn/ n acerico m

pine[1] /paɪn/ n pino m

pine[2] /paɪn/ vi. **~ away** consumirse. **~ for** suspirar por

pineapple /'paɪnæpl/ n piña f, ananás m

ping /pɪŋ/ n sonido m agudo. **~pong** /'pɪŋpɒŋ/ n pimpón m, ping-pong m

pinion /'pɪnjən/ vt maniatar

pink /pɪŋk/ a & n color (m) de rosa

pinnacle /'pɪnəkl/ n pináculo m

pin: ~point vt determinar con precisión f. **~stripe** /'pɪnstraɪp/ n raya f fina

pint /paɪnt/ n pinta f (= 0.57 litre)

pin-up /'pɪnʌp/ n (fam) fotografía f de mujer

pioneer /paɪə'nɪə(r)/ n pionero m. ● vt ser el primero, promotor de, promover

pious /'paɪəs/ a piadoso

pip[1] /pɪp/ n (seed) pepita f

pip[2] /pɪp/ (time signal) señal f

pip[3] /pɪp/ (on uniform) estrella f

pipe /paɪp/ n tubo m; (mus) caramillo m; (for smoking) pipa f. ● vt conducir por tuberías. **~down** (fam) bajar la voz, callarse. **~cleaner** n limpiapipas m invar. **~dream** n ilusión f. **~line** /'paɪplaɪn/ n tubería f; (for oil) oleoducto m. **in the ~line** en preparación f. **~r** n flautista m & f

piping /'paɪpɪŋ/ n tubería f. **~ hot** muy caliente, hirviendo

piquant /'pi:kənt/ a picante

pique /pi:k/ n resentimiento m

pira|cy /'paɪərəsɪ/ n piratería f. **~te** /'paɪərət/ n pirata m

pirouette /pɪrʊ'et/ n pirueta f. ● vi piruetear

Pisces /'paɪsi:z/ n (astr) Piscis m

pistol /'pɪstl/ n pistola f

piston /'pɪstən/ n pistón m

pit /pɪt/ n foso m; (mine) mina f; (of stomach) boca f. ● vt (pt **pitted**) marcar con hoyos; (fig) oponer. **~ o.s. against** medirse con

pitch[1] /pɪtʃ/ n brea f

pitch[2] /pɪtʃ/ n (degree) grado m; (mus) tono m; (sport) campo m. ● vt lanzar; armar (tent). **~ into** (fam) atacar. ● vi caerse; (ship) cabecear. **~ in** (fam) contribuir. **~ed battle** n batalla f campal

pitch-black /pɪtʃ'blæk/ a oscuro como boca de lobo

pitcher /'pɪtʃə(r)/ n jarro m

pitchfork /'pɪtʃfɔ:k/ n horca f

piteous /'pɪtɪəs/ a lastimoso

pitfall /'pɪtfɔ:l/ n trampa f

pith /pɪθ/ n (of orange, lemon) médula f; (fig) meollo m

pithy /'pɪθɪ/ a (-ier, -iest) conciso

piti|ful /'pɪtɪfl/ a lastimoso. **~less** a despiadado

pittance /'pɪtns/ n sueldo m irrisorio

pity /'pɪtɪ/ n piedad f; (regret) lástima f. ● vt compadecerse de

pivot /'pɪvət/ n pivote m. ● vt montonar sobre un pivote. ● vi girar sobre un pivote; (fig) depender (on de)

pixie /'pɪksɪ/ n duende m

placard /'plækɑ:d/ n pancarta f; (poster) cartel m

placate /plə'keɪt/ vt apaciguar

place /pleɪs/ n lugar m; (seat) asiento m; (post) puesto m; (house, fam) casa f. **take ~** tener lugar. ● vt poner, colocar; (remember) recordar; (identify) identificar. **be**

~d (*in race*) colocarse. ~mat *n* salvamanteles *m invar*. ~ment /'pleɪsmənt/ *n* colocación *f*

placid /'plæsɪd/ *a* plácido

plagiari|sm /'pleɪdʒərɪzm/ *n* plagio *m*. ~ze /'pleɪdʒəraɪz/ *vt* plagiar

plague /pleɪg/ *n* peste *f*; (*fig*) plaga *f*. ● *vt* atormentar

plaice /pleɪs/ *n invar* platija *f*

plaid /plæd/ *n* tartán *m*

plain /pleɪn/ *a* (-er, -est) claro; (*simple*) sencillo; (*candid*) franco; (*ugly*) feo. in ~ **clothes** en traje de paisano. ● *adv* claramente. ● *n* llanura *f*. ~ly *adv* claramente; (*frankly*) francamente; (*simply*) sencillamente. ~ness *n* claridad *f*; (*simplicity*) sencillez *f*

plaintiff /'pleɪntɪf/ *n* demandante *m & f*

plait /plæt/ *vt* trenzar. ● *n* trenza *f*

plan /plæn/ *n* proyecto *m*; (*map*) plano *m*. ● *vt* (*pt* planned) planear, proyectar; (*intend*) proponerse

plane[1] /pleɪn/ *n* (*tree*) plátano *m*

plane[2] /pleɪn/ (*level*) nivel *m*; (*aviat*) avión *m*. ● *a* plano

plane[3] /pleɪn/ (*tool*) cepillo *m*. ● *vt* cepillar

planet /'plænɪt/ *n* planeta *m*. ~ary *a* planetario

plank /plæŋk/ *n* tabla *f*

planning /'plænɪŋ/ *n* planificación *f*. **family** ~ *n* planificación familiar. **town** ~ *n* urbanismo *m*

plant /plɑːnt/ *n* planta *f*; (*mec*) maquinaria *f*; (*factory*) fábrica *f*. ● *vt* plantar; (*place in position*) colocar. ~ation /plæn'teɪʃn/ *n* plantación *f*

plaque /plæk/ *n* placa *f*

plasma /'plæzmə/ *n* plasma *m*

plaster /'plɑːstə(r)/ *n* yeso *m*; (*adhesive*) esparadrapo *m*; (*for setting bones*) escayola *f*. ~ **of Paris** *n* yeso *m* mate. ● *vt* enyesar; (*med*) escayolar (*broken bone*); (*cover*) cubrir (**with** de). ~ed *a* (*fam*) borracho

plastic /'plæstɪk/ *a & n* plástico (*m*)

Plasticine /'plæstɪsiːn/ *n* (P) pasta *f* de modelar, plastilina *f* (P)

plastic surgery /plæstɪk'sɜːdʒərɪ/ *n* cirugía *f* estética

plate /pleɪt/ *n* plato *m*; (*of metal*) chapa *f*; (*silverware*) vajilla *f* de plata; (*in book*) lámina *f*. ● *vt* (*cover with metal*) chapear

plateau /'plætəʊ/ *n* (*pl* plateaux) meseta *f*

plateful /'pleɪtfl/ *n* (*pl* -fuls) plato *m*

platform /'plætfɔːm/ *n* plataforma *f*; (*rail*) andén *m*

platinum /'plætɪnəm/ *n* platino *m*

platitude /'plætɪtjuːd/ *n* tópico *m*, perogrullada *f*, lugar *m* común

platonic /plə'tɒnɪk/ *a* platónico

platoon /plə'tuːn/ *n* pelotón *m*

platter /'plætə(r)/ *n* fuente *f*, plato *m* grande

plausible /'plɔːzəbl/ *a* plausible; (*person*) convincente

play /pleɪ/ *vt* jugar; (*act role*) desempeñar el papel de; tocar (*instrument*). ~ **safe** no arriesgarse. ~ **up** to halagar. ● *vi* jugar. ~ed out agotado. ● *n* juego *m*; (*drama*) obra *f* de teatro. ~ **on words** *n* juego *m* de palabras. ~ **down** *vt* minimizar. ~ **on** *vt* aprovecharse de. ~ **up** *vi* (*fam*) causar problemas. ~ **up** *vi* hacer la comedia. ~boy /'pleɪbɔɪ/ *n* calavera *m*. ~er *n* jugador *m*; (*mus*) músico *m*. ~ful /'pleɪfl/ *a* juguetón. ~fully *adv* jugando; (*jokingly*) en broma. ~ground /'pleɪgraʊnd/ *n* parque *m* de juegos infantiles; (*in school*) campo *m* de recreo. ~group *n* jardín *m* de la infancia. ~ing /'pleɪɪŋ/ *n* juego *m*. ~ing-card *n* naipe *m*. ~ing-field *n* campo *m* de deportes. ~mate /'pleɪmeɪt/ *n* compañero *m* (de juego). ~pen *n* corralito *m*. ~thing *n* juguete *m*. ~wright /'pleɪraɪt/ *n* dramaturgo *m*

plc /piːel'siː/ *abbr* (*public limited company*) S.A., sociedad *f* anónima

plea /pliː/ *n* súplica *f*; (*excuse*) excusa *f*; (*jurid*) defensa *f*

plead /pliːd/ *vt* (*jurid*) alegar; (*as excuse*) pretextar. ● *vi* suplicar; (*jurid*) abogar. ~ **with** suplicar

pleasant /'pleznt/ *a* agradable

pleas|e /pliːz/ *int* por favor. ● *vt* agradar, dar gusto a. ● *vi* agradar; (*wish*) querer. ~ o.s. hacer lo que quiera. do as you ~e haz lo que quieras. ~ed *a* contento. ~ed with satisfecho de. ~ing *a* agradable

pleasur|e /'pleʒə(r)/ *n* placer *m*. ~able *a* agradable

pleat /pliːt/ *n* pliegue *m*. ● *vt* hacer pliegues en

plebiscite /'plebɪsɪt/ *n* plebiscito *m*

plectrum /'plektrəm/ *n* plectro *m*

pledge /pledʒ/ *n* prenda *f*; (*promise*) promesa *f*. ● *vt* empeñar; (*promise*) prometer

plent|iful /'plentɪfl/ *a* abundante. ~y /'plentɪ/ *n* abundancia *f*. ~y (of) muchos (de)

pleurisy /'plʊərəsɪ/ n pleuresía f

pliable /'plaɪəbl/ a flexible

pliers /'plaɪəz/ npl alicates mpl

plight /plaɪt/ n situación f (difícil)

plimsolls /'plɪmsəlz/ npl zapatillas fpl de lona

plinth /plɪnθ/ n plinto m

plod /plɒd/ vi (pt **plodded**) caminar con paso pesado; (work hard) trabajar laboriosamente. **~der** n empollón m

plonk /plɒŋk/ n (sl) vino m peleón

plop /plɒp/ n paf m. ● vi (pt **plopped**) caerse con un paf

plot /plɒt/ n complot m; (of novel etc) argumento m; (piece of land) parcela f. ● vt (pt **plotted**) tramar; (mark out) trazar. ● vi conspirar

plough /plaʊ/ n arado m. ● vt/i arar. **~ through** avanzar laboriosamente por

ploy /plɔɪ/ n (fam) estratagema f, truco m

pluck /plʌk/ vt arrancar; depilarse (eyebrows); desplumar (bird); recoger (flowers). **~ up courage** hacer de tripas corazón. ● n valor m. **~y** a (-ier, -iest) valiente

plug /plʌg/ n tapón m; (elec) enchufe m; (auto) bujía f. ● vt (pt **plugged**) tapar; (advertise, fam) dar publicidad a. **~ in** (elec) enchufar

plum /plʌm/ n ciruela f; (tree) ciruelo m

plumage /'pluːmɪdʒ/ n plumaje m

plumb /plʌm/ a vertical. ● n plomada f. ● adv verticalmente; (exactly) exactamente. ● vt sondar

plumb|er /'plʌmə(r)/ n fontanero m. **~ing** n instalación f sanitaria, instalación f de cañerías

plume /pluːm/ n pluma f

plum job /plʌm'dʒɒb/ n (fam) puesto m estupendo

plummet /'plʌmɪt/ n plomada f. ● vi caer a plomo, caer en picado

plump /plʌmp/ a (-er, -est) rechoncho. ● vt. **~ for** elegir. **~ness** n gordura f

plum pudding /plʌm'pʊdɪŋ/ n budín m de pasas

plunder /'plʌndə(r)/ n (act) saqueo m; (goods) botín m. ● vt saquear

plung|e /plʌndʒ/ vt hundir; (in water) sumergir. ● vi zambullirse; (fall) caer. ● n salto m. **~er** n (for sink) desatascador m; (mec) émbolo m. **~ing** a (neckline) bajo, escotado

plural /'plʊərəl/ a & n plural (m)

plus /plʌs/ prep más. ● a positivo. ● n signo m más; (fig) ventaja f. **five ~** más de cinco

plush /plʌʃ/ n felpa f. ● a de felpa, afelpado; (fig) lujoso. **~y** a lujoso

plutocrat /'pluːtəkræt/ n plutócrata m & f

plutonium /pluː'təʊnjəm/ n plutonio m

ply /plaɪ/ vt manejar (tool); ejercer (trade). **~ s.o. with drink** dar continuamente de beber a uno. **~wood** n contrachapado m

p.m. /piː'em/ abbr (post meridiem) de la tarde

pneumatic /njuː'mætɪk/ a neumático

pneumonia /njuː'məʊnjə/ n pulmonía f

PO /piː'əʊ/ abbr (Post Office) oficina f de correos

poach /pəʊtʃ/ vt escalfar (egg); cocer (fish etc); (steal) cazar en vedado. **~er** n cazador m furtivo

pocket /'pɒkɪt/ n bolsillo m; (of air, resistance) bolsa f. **be in ~** salir ganado. **be out of ~** salir perdiendo. ● vt poner en el bolsillo. **~book** n (notebook) libro m de bolsillo; (purse, Amer) cartera f; (handbag, Amer) bolso m. **~money** n dinero m para los gastos personales

pock-marked /'pɒkmɑːkt/ a (face) picado de viruelas

pod /pɒd/ n vaina f

podgy /'pɒdʒɪ/ a (-ier, -iest) rechoncho

poem /'pəʊɪm/ n poesía f

poet /'pəʊɪt/ n poeta m. **~ess** n poetisa f. **~ic** /-'etɪk/ a, **~ical** /-'etɪkl/ a poético. **P~ Laureate** n poeta laureado. **~ry** /'pəʊɪtrɪ/ n poesía f

poignant /'pɔɪnjənt/ a conmovedor

point /pɔɪnt/ n punto m; (sharp end) punta f; (significance) lo importante; (elec) toma f de corriente. **good ~s** cualidades fpl. **to the ~** pertinente. **up to a ~** hasta cierto punto. **what is the ~?** ¿para qué?, ¿a qué fin? ● vt (aim) apuntar; (show) indicar. **~ out** señalar. ● vi señalar. **~-blank** a & adv a boca de jarro, a quemarropa. **~ed** /'pɔɪntɪd/ a puntiagudo; (fig) mordaz. **~er** /'pɔɪntə(r)/ n indicador m; (dog) perro m de muestra; (clue, fam) indicación f. **~less** /'pɔɪntlɪs/ a inútil

poise /pɔɪz/ n equilibrio m; (elegance) elegancia f; (fig) aplomo m. ∼d a en equilibrio. ∼d for listo para

poison /'pɔɪzn/ n veneno m. ● vt envenenar. ∼ous a venenoso; (chemical etc) tóxico

poke /pəʊk/ vt empujar; atizar (fire). ∼ fun at burlarse de. ∼ out asomar (head). ● vi hurgar; (pry) meterse. ∼ about fisgonear. ● n empuje m

poker[1] /'pəʊkə(r)/ n atizador m

poker[2] /'pəʊkə(r)/ (cards) póquer m. ∼-face n cara f inmutable

poky /'pəʊki/ a (-ier, -iest) estrecho

Poland /'pəʊlənd/ n Polonia f

polar /'pəʊlə(r)/ a polar. ∼ bear n oso m blanco

polarize /'pəʊləraɪz/ vt polarizar

Pole /pəʊl/ n polaco n

pole[1] /pəʊl/ n palo m; (for flag) asta f

pole[2] /pəʊl/ (geog) polo m. ∼-star n estrella f polar

polemic /pə'lemɪk/ a polémico. ● n polémica f

police /pə'li:s/ n policía f. ● vt vigilar. ∼man /pə'li:smən/ n (pl -men) policía m, guardia m. ∼ record n antecedentes mpl penales. ∼ state n estado m policíaco. ∼ station n comisaría f. ∼woman /-wʊmən/ n (pl -women) mujer m policía

policy[1] /'pɒlɪsɪ/ n política f

policy[2] /'pɒlɪsɪ/ (insurance) póliza f (de seguros)

polio(myelitis) /'pəʊlɪəʊ(maɪə'laɪtɪs)/ n polio(mielitis) f

polish /'pɒlɪʃ/ n (for shoes) betún m; (for floor) cera f; (for nails) esmalte m de uñas; (shine) brillo m; (fig) finura f. nail ∼ esmalte m de uñas. ● vt pulir; limpiar (shoes); encerar (floor). ∼ off despachar. ∼ed a pulido; (manner) refinado. ∼er n pulidor m; (machine) pulidora f

Polish /'pəʊlɪʃ/ a & n polaco (m)

polite /pə'laɪt/ a cortés. ∼ly adv cortésmente. ∼ness n cortesía f

politic|al /pə'lɪtɪkl/ a político. ∼ian /pɒlɪ'tɪʃn/ n político m. ∼s /'pɒlɪtɪks/ n política f

polka /'pɒlkə/ n polca f. ∼ dots npl diseño m de puntos

poll /pəʊl/ n elección f; (survey) encuesta f. ● vt obtener (votes)

pollen /'pɒlən/ n polen m

polling-booth /'pəʊlɪŋbu:ð/ n cabina f de votar

pollut|e /pə'lu:t/ vt contaminar. ∼ion /-ʃn/ n contaminación f

polo /'pəʊləʊ/ n polo m. ∼-neck n cuello m vuelto

poltergeist /'pɒltəgaɪst/ n duende m

polyester /pɒlɪ'estə(r)/ n poliéster m

polygam|ist /pə'lɪgəmɪst/ n polígamo m. ∼ous a polígamo. ∼y /pə'lɪgəmɪ/ n poligamia f

polyglot /'pɒlɪglɒt/ a & n políglota (m & f)

polygon /'pɒlɪgən/ n polígono m

polyp /'pɒlɪp/ n pólipo m

polystyrene /pɒlɪ'staɪri:n/ n poliestireno m

polytechnic /pɒlɪ'teknɪk/ n escuela f politécnica

polythene /'pɒlɪθi:n/ n polietileno m. ∼ bag n bolsa f de plástico

pomegranate /'pɒmɪgrænɪt/ n (fruit) granada f

pommel /'pʌml/ n pomo m

pomp /pɒmp/ n pompa f

pompon /'pɒmpɒn/ n pompón m

pompo|sity /pɒm'pɒsətɪ/ n pomposidad f. ∼us /'pɒmpəs/ a pomposo

poncho /'pɒntʃəʊ/ n (pl -os) poncho m

pond /pɒnd/ n charca f; (artificial) estanque m

ponder /'pɒndə(r)/ vt considerar. ● vi reflexionar. ∼ous /'pɒndərəs/ a pesado

pong /pɒŋ/ n (sl) hedor m. ● vi (sl) apestar

pontif|f /'pɒntɪf/ n pontífice m. ∼ical /-'tɪfɪkl/ a pontifical; (fig) dogmático. ∼icate /pɒn'tɪfɪkeɪt/ vi pontificar

pontoon /pɒn'tu:n/ n pontón m. ∼ bridge n puente m de pontones

pony /'pəʊnɪ/ n poni m. ∼-tail n cola f de caballo. ∼-trekking n excursionismo m en poni

poodle /'pu:dl/ n perro m de lanas, caniche m

pool[1] /pu:l/ n charca f; (artificial) estanque m. (swimming-)∼ n piscina f

pool[2] /pu:l/ (common fund) fondos mpl comunes; (snooker) billar m americano. ● vt aunar. ∼s npl quinielas fpl

poor /pʊə(r)/ a (-er, -est) pobre; (not good) malo. be in ∼ health estar mal de salud. ∼ly a (fam) indispuesto. ● adv pobremente; (badly) mal

pop[1] /pɒp/ n ruido m seco; (of bottle) taponazo m. ● vt (pt **popped**) hacer reventar; (put) poner. ~ **in** vi entrar; (visit) pasar por. ~ **out** vi saltar; ⟨person⟩ salir un rato. ~ **up** vi surgir, aparecer

pop[2] /pɒp/ a (popular) pop invar. ● n (fam) música f pop. ~ **art** n arte m pop

popcorn /ˈpɒpkɔːn/ n palomitas fpl

pope /pəʊp/ n papa m

popgun /ˈpɒpɡʌn/ n pistola f de aire comprimido

poplar /ˈpɒplə(r)/ n chopo m

poplin /ˈpɒplɪn/ n popelina f

poppy /ˈpɒpɪ/ n amapola f

popular /ˈpɒpjʊlə(r)/ a popular. ~**ity** /-ˈlærətɪ/ n popularidad f. ~**ize** vt popularizar

populat|e /ˈpɒpjʊleɪt/ vt poblar. ~**ion** /-ˈleɪʃn/ n población f; (number of inhabitants) habitantes mpl

porcelain /ˈpɔːsəlɪn/ n porcelana f

porch /pɔːtʃ/ n porche m

porcupine /ˈpɔːkjʊpaɪn/ n puerco m espín

pore[1] /pɔː(r)/ n poro m

pore[2] /pɔː(r)/ vi. ~ **over** estudiar detenidamente

pork /pɔːk/ n cerdo m

porn /pɔːn/ n (fam) pornografía f. ~**ographic** /-əˈɡræfɪk/ a pornográfico. ~**ography** /pɔːˈnɒɡrəfɪ/ n pornografía f

porous /ˈpɔːrəs/ a poroso

porpoise /ˈpɔːpəs/ n marsopa f

porridge /ˈpɒrɪdʒ/ n gachas fpl de avena

port[1] /pɔːt/ n puerto m; (porthole) portilla f. ~ **of call** puerto de escala

port[2] /pɔːt/ n (naut, left) babor m. ● a de babor

port[3] /pɔːt/ n (wine) oporto m

portable /ˈpɔːtəbl/ a portátil

portal /ˈpɔːtl/ n portal m

portent /ˈpɔːtent/ n presagio m

porter /ˈpɔːtə(r)/ n portero m; (for luggage) mozo m. ~**age** n porte m

portfolio /pɔːtˈfəʊljəʊ/ n (pl **-os**) cartera f

porthole /ˈpɔːthəʊl/ n portilla f

portico /ˈpɔːtɪkəʊ/ n (pl **-oes**) pórtico m

portion /ˈpɔːʃn/ n porción f. ● vt repartir

portly /ˈpɔːtlɪ/ a (**-ier**, **-iest**) corpulento

portrait /ˈpɔːtrɪt/ n retrato m

portray /pɔːˈtreɪ/ vt retratar; (represent) representar. ~**al** n retrato m

Portug|al /ˈpɔːtjʊɡl/ n Portugal m. ~**uese** /-ˈɡiːz/ a & n portugués (m)

pose /pəʊz/ n postura f. ● vt colocar; hacer ⟨question⟩; plantear ⟨problem⟩. ● vi posar. ~ **as** hacerse pasar por. ~**r** /ˈpəʊzə(r)/ n pregunta f difícil

posh /pɒʃ/ a (sl) elegante

position /pəˈzɪʃn/ n posición f; (job) puesto m; (status) rango m. ● vt colocar

positive /ˈpɒzətɪv/ a positivo; (real) verdadero; (certain) seguro. ● n (foto) positiva f. ~**ly** adv positivamente

possess /pəˈzes/ vt poseer. ~**ion** /pəˈzeʃn/ n posesión f. **take** ~**ion of** tomar posesión de. ~**ions** npl posesiones fpl; (jurid) bienes mpl. ~**ive** /pəˈzesɪv/ a posesivo. ~**or** n poseedor m

possib|ility /pɒsəˈbɪlətɪ/ n posibilidad f. ~**le** /ˈpɒsəbl/ a posible. ~**ly** adv posiblemente

post[1] /pəʊst/ n (pole) poste m. ● vt fijar ⟨notice⟩

post[2] /pəʊst/ n (place) puesto m

post[3] /pəʊst/ n (mail) correo m. ● vt echar ⟨letter⟩. **keep s.o.** ~**ed** tener a uno al corriente

post... /pəʊst/ pref post

post: ~**age** /ˈpəʊstɪdʒ/ n franqueo m. ~**al** /ˈpəʊstl/ a postal. ~**al order** n giro m postal. ~**box** n buzón m. ~**card** /ˈpəʊstkɑːd/ n (tarjeta f) postal f. ~**code** n código m postal

post-date /pəʊstˈdeɪt/ vt poner fecha posterior a

poster /ˈpəʊstə(r)/ n cartel m

poste restante /pəʊstˈresta:nt/ n lista f de correos

posteri|or /pɒˈstɪərɪə(r)/ a posterior. ● n trasero m. ~**ty** /pɒsˈterətɪ/ n posteridad f

posthumous /ˈpɒstjʊməs/ a póstumo. ~**ly** adv después de la muerte

post: ~**man** /ˈpəʊstmən/ n (pl **-men**) cartero m. ~**mark** /ˈpəʊstmɑːk/ n matasellos m invar. ~**master** /ˈpəʊstmɑːstə(r)/ n administrador m de correos. ~**mistress** /ˈpəʊstmɪstrɪs/ n administradora f de correos

post-mortem /ˈpəʊstmɔːtəm/ n autopsia f

Post Office /ˈpəʊstɒfɪs/ n oficina f de correos, correos mpl

postpone /pəʊst'pəʊn/ vt aplazar. **~ment** n aplazamiento m

postscript /'pəʊstskrɪpt/ n posdata f

postulant /'pɒstjʊlənt/ n postulante m & f

postulate /'pɒstjʊleɪt/ vt postular

posture /'pɒstʃə(r)/ n postura f. ● vi adoptar una postura

posy /'pəʊzɪ/ n ramillete m

pot /pɒt/ n (for cooking) olla f; (for flowers) tiesto m; (marijuana, sl) mariguana f. **go to ~** (sl) echarse a perder. ● vt (pt **potted**) poner en tiesto

potassium /pə'tæsjəm/ n potasio m

potato /pə'teɪtəʊ/ n (pl -oes) patata f, papa f (LAm)

pot: **~belly** n barriga f. **~boiler** n obra f literaria escrita sólo para ganar dinero

poten|cy /'pəʊtənsɪ/ n potencia f. **~t** /'pəʊtnt/ a potente; ⟨drink⟩ fuerte

potentate /'pəʊtənteɪt/ n potentado m

potential /pəʊ'tenʃl/ a & n potencial (m). **~ity** /-ʃɪ'ælətɪ/ n potencialidad f. **~ly** adv potencialmente

pot-hole /'pɒthəʊl/ n caverna f; (in road) bache m. **~r** n espeleólogo m

potion /'pəʊʃn/ n poción f

pot: **~ luck** n lo que haya. **~shot** n tiro m al azar. **~ted** /'pɒtɪd/ see **pot**. ● a ⟨food⟩ en conserva

potter[1] /'pɒtə(r)/ n alfarero m

potter[2] /'pɒtə(r)/ vi hacer pequeños trabajos agradables, no hacer nada de particular

pottery /'pɒtərɪ/ n cerámica f

potty /'pɒtɪ/ a (-ier, -iest) (sl) chiflado. ● n orinal m

pouch /paʊtʃ/ n bolsa f pequeña

pouffe /puːf/ n (stool) taburete m

poulterer /'pəʊltərə(r)/ n pollero m

poultice /'pəʊltɪs/ n cataplasma f

poultry /'pəʊltrɪ/ n aves fpl de corral

pounce /paʊns/ vi saltar, atacar de repente. ● n salto m, ataque m repentino

pound[1] /paʊnd/ n (weight) libra f (= 454g); (money) libra f (esterlina)

pound[2] /paʊnd/ n (for cars) depósito m

pound[3] /paʊnd/ vt (crush) machacar; (bombard) bombardear. ● vi golpear; ⟨heart⟩ palpitar; ⟨walk⟩ ir con pasos pesados

pour /pɔː(r)/ vt verter. **~ out** servir ⟨drink⟩. ● vi fluir; (rain) llover a cántaros. **~ in** ⟨people⟩ entrar en tropel. **~ing rain** n lluvia f torrencial. **~ out** ⟨people⟩ salir en tropel

pout /paʊt/ vi hacer pucheros. ● n puchero m, mala cara f

poverty /'pɒvətɪ/ n pobreza f

powder /'paʊdə(r)/ n polvo m; (cosmetic) polvos mpl. ● vt polvorear; (pulverize) pulverizar. **~ one's face** ponerse polvos en la cara. **~ed** a en polvo. **~y** a polvoriento

power /'paʊə(r)/ n poder m; (elec) corriente f; (energy) energía f; (nation) potencia f. **~ cut** n apagón m. **~ed** a con motor. **~ed by** impulsado por. **~ful** a poderoso. **~less** a impotente. **~station** n central f eléctrica

practicable /'præktɪkəbl/ a practicable

practical /'præktɪkl/ a práctico. **~ joke** n broma f pesada. **~ly** adv prácticamente

practi|ce /'præktɪs/ n práctica f; (custom) costumbre f; (exercise) ejercicio m; (sport) entrenamiento m; (clients) clientela f. **be in ~ce** ⟨doctor, lawyer⟩ ejercer. **be out of ~ce** no estar en forma. **in ~ce** (in fact) en la práctica; (on form) en forma. **~se** /'præktɪs/ vt hacer ejercicios en; (put into practice) poner en práctica; (sport) entrenarse en; ejercer ⟨profession⟩. ● vi ejercitarse; ⟨professional⟩ ejercer. **—~sed** a experto

practitioner /præk'tɪʃənə(r)/ n profesional m & f. **general ~** médico m de cabecera. **medical ~** médico m

pragmatic /præg'mætɪk/ a pragmático

prairie /'preərɪ/ n pradera f

praise /preɪz/ vt alabar. ● n alabanza f. **~worthy** a loable

pram /præm/ n cochecito m de niño

prance /prɑːns/ vi ⟨horse⟩ hacer cabriolas; ⟨person⟩ pavonearse

prank /præŋk/ n travesura f

prattle /'prætl/ vi parlotear. ● n parloteo m

prawn /prɔːn/ n gamba f

pray /preɪ/ vi rezar. **~er** /preə(r)/ n oración f. **~ for** rogar

pre.. /priː/ pref pre...

preach /priːtʃ/ vt/i predicar. **~er** n predicador m

preamble /priː'æmbl/ n preámbulo m

pre-arrange /priːəˈreɪndʒ/ *vt* arreglar de antemano. **~ment** *n* arreglo *m* previo

precarious /prɪˈkeərɪəs/ *a* precario. **~ly** *adv* precariamente

precaution /prɪˈkɔːʃn/ *n* precaución *f*. **~ary** *a* de precaución; (*preventive*) preventivo

precede /prɪˈsiːd/ *vt* preceder

preceden|ce /ˈpresɪdəns/ *n* precedencia *f*. **~t** /ˈpresɪdənt/ *n* precedente *m*

preceding /prɪˈsiːdɪŋ/ *a* precedente

precept /ˈpriːsept/ *n* precepto *m*

precinct /ˈpriːsɪŋkt/ *n* recinto *m*. **pedestrian ~** zona *f* peatonal. **~s** *npl* contornos *mpl*

precious /ˈpreʃəs/ *a* precioso. ● *adv* (*fam*) muy

precipice /ˈpresɪpɪs/ *n* precipicio *m*

precipitat|e /prɪˈsɪpɪteɪt/ *vt* precipitar. /prɪˈsɪpɪtət/ *n* precipitado *m*. ● *a* precipitado. **~ion** /-ˈteɪʃn/ *n* precipitación *f*

precipitous /prɪˈsɪpɪtəs/ *a* escarpado

précis /ˈpreɪsiː/ *n* (*pl* **précis** /-siːz/) resumen *m*

precis|e /prɪˈsaɪs/ *a* preciso; (*careful*) meticuloso. **~ely** *adv* precisamente. **~ion** /-ˈsɪʒn/ *n* precisión *f*

preclude /prɪˈkluːd/ *vt* (*prevent*) impedir; (*exclude*) excluir

precocious /prɪˈkəʊʃəs/ *a* precoz. **~ly** *adv* precozmente

preconce|ived /priːkənˈsiːvd/ *a* preconcebido. **~ption** /-ˈsepʃn/ *n* preconcepción *f*

precursor /priːˈkɜːsə(r)/ *n* precursor *m*

predator /ˈpredətə(r)/ *n* animal *m* de rapiña. **~y** *a* de rapiña

predecessor /ˈpriːdɪsesə(r)/ *n* predecesor *m*, antecesor *m*

predestin|ation /prɪdestɪˈneɪʃn/ *n* predestinación *f*. **~e** /priːˈdestɪn/ *vt* predestinar

predicament /prɪˈdɪkəmənt/ *n* apuro *m*

predicat|e /ˈpredɪkət/ *n* predicado *m*. **~ive** /prɪˈdɪkətɪv/ *a* predicativo

predict /prɪˈdɪkt/ *vt* predecir. **~ion** /-ʃn/ *n* predicción *f*

predilection /priːdɪˈlekʃn/ *n* predilección *f*

predispose /priːdɪˈspəʊz/ *vt* predisponer

predomina|nt /prɪˈdɒmɪnənt/ *a* predominante. **~te** /prɪˈdɒmɪneɪt/ *vi* predominar

pre-eminent /priːˈemɪnənt/ *a* preeminente

pre-empt /priːˈempt/ *vt* adquirir por adelantado, adelantarse a

preen /priːn/ *vt* limpiar, arreglar. **~ o.s.** atildarse

prefab /ˈpriːfæb/ *n* (*fam*) casa *f* prefabricada. **~ricated** /-ˈfæbrɪkeɪtɪd/ *a* prefabricado

preface /ˈprefəs/ *n* prólogo *m*

prefect /ˈpriːfekt/ *n* monitor *m*; (*official*) prefecto *m*

prefer /prɪˈfɜː(r)/ *vt* (*pt* **preferred**) preferir. **~able** /ˈprefrəbl/ *a* preferible. **~ence** /ˈprefrəns/ *n* preferencia *f*. **~ential** /-əˈrenʃl/ *a* preferente

prefix /ˈpriːfɪks/ *n* (*pl* **-ixes**) prefijo *m*

pregnan|cy /ˈpregnənsɪ/ *n* embarazo *m*. **~t** /ˈpregnənt/ *a* embarazada

prehistoric /priːhɪˈstɒrɪk/ *a* prehistórico

prejudge /priːˈdʒʌdʒ/ *vt* prejuzgar

prejudice /ˈpredʒʊdɪs/ *n* prejuicio *m*; (*harm*) perjuicio *m*. ● *vt* predisponer; (*harm*) perjudicar. **~d** *a* parcial

prelate /ˈprelət/ *n* prelado *m*

preliminar|ies /prɪˈlɪmɪnərɪz/ *npl* preliminares *mpl*. **~y** /prɪˈlɪmɪnərɪ/ *a* preliminar

prelude /ˈpreljuːd/ *n* preludio *m*

pre-marital /priːˈmærɪtl/ *a* prematrimonial

premature /ˈpremətjʊə(r)/ *a* prematuro

premeditated /priːˈmedɪteɪtɪd/ *a* premeditado

premier /ˈpremɪə(r)/ *a* primero. ● *n* (*pol*) primer ministro

première /ˈpremɪə(r)/ *n* estreno *m*

premises /ˈpremɪsɪz/ *npl* local *m*. **on the ~** en el local

premiss /ˈpremɪs/ *n* premisa *f*

premium /ˈpriːmɪəm/ *n* premio *m*. **at a ~** muy solicitado

premonition /priːməˈnɪʃn/ *n* presentimiento *m*

preoccup|ation /priːɒkjʊˈpeɪʃn/ *n* preocupación *f*. **~ied** /-ˈɒkjʊpaɪd/ *a* preocupado

prep /prep/ *n* deberes *mpl*

preparation /prepəˈreɪʃn/ *n* preparación *f*. **~s** *npl* preparativos *mpl*

preparatory /prɪˈpærətrɪ/ a preparatorio. ~ **school** n escuela f primaria privada

prepare /prɪˈpeə(r)/ vt preparar. ● vi prepararse. ~d to dispuesto a

prepay /priːˈpeɪ/ vt (pt **-paid**) pagar por adelantado

preponderance /prɪˈpɒndərəns/ n preponderancia f

preposition /prepəˈzɪʃn/ n preposición f

prepossessing /priːpəˈzesɪŋ/ a atractivo

preposterous /prɪˈpɒstərəs/ a absurdo

prep school /ˈprepskuːl/ n escuela f primaria privada

prerequisite /priːˈrekwɪzɪt/ n requisito m previo

prerogative /prɪˈrɒɡətɪv/ n prerrogativa f

Presbyterian /prezbɪˈtɪərɪən/ a & n presbiteriano (m)

prescri|be /prɪˈskraɪb/ vt prescribir; (med) recetar. ~ption /-ˈɪpʃn/ n prescripción f; (med) receta f

presence /ˈprezns/ n presencia f; (attendance) asistencia f. ~ of mind presencia f de ánimo

present¹ /ˈpreznt/ a & n presente (m & f). at ~ actualmente. for the ~ por ahora

present² /ˈpreznt/ n (gift) regalo m

present³ /prɪˈzent/ vt presentar; (give) obsequiar. ~ s.o. with obsequiar a uno con. ~able a presentable. ~ation /prezn̩ˈteɪʃn/ n presentación f; (ceremony) ceremonia f de entrega

presently /ˈprezntlɪ/ adv dentro de poco

preserv|ation /prezəˈveɪʃn/ n conservación f. ~ative /prɪˈzɜːvətɪv/ n preservativo m. ~e /prɪˈzɜːv/ vt conservar; (maintain) mantener; (culin) poner en conserva. ● n coto m; (jam) confitura f

preside /prɪˈzaɪd/ vi presidir. ~ over presidir

presiden|cy /ˈprezɪdənsɪ/ n presidencia f. ~t /ˈprezɪdənt/ n presidente m. ~tial /-ˈdenʃl/ a presidencial

press /pres/ vt apretar; exprimir (fruit etc); (insist on) insistir en; (iron) planchar. be ~ed for tener poco. ● vi apretar; (time) apremiar; (fig) urgir. ~ on seguir adelante. ● n presión f; (mec, newspapers)

prensa f; (printing) imprenta f. ~ **conference** n rueda f de prensa. ~ **cutting** n recorte m de periódico. ~ing /ˈpresɪŋ/ a urgente. ~**stud** n automático m. ~**up** n plancha f

pressure /ˈpreʃə(r)/ n presión f. ● vt hacer presión sobre. ~**cooker** n olla f a presión. ~ **group** n grupo m de presión

pressurize /ˈpreʃəraɪz/ vt hacer presión sobre

prestig|e /preˈstiːʒ/ n prestigio m. ~**ious** /preˈstɪdʒəs/ a prestigioso

presum|ably /prɪˈzjuːməblɪ/ adv presumiblemente, probablemente. ~**e** /prɪˈzjuːm/ vt presumir. ~**e (up)on** vi abusar de. ~**ption** /-ˈzʌmpʃn/ n presunción f. ~**ptuous** /prɪˈzʌmptʃʊəs/ a presuntuoso

presuppose /priːsəˈpəʊz/ vt presuponer

preten|ce /prɪˈtens/ n fingimiento m; (claim) pretensión f; (pretext) pretexto m. ~**d** /prɪˈtend/ vt/i fingir. ~**d to** (lay claim) pretender

pretentious /prɪˈtenʃəs/ a pretencioso

pretext /ˈpriːtekst/ n pretexto m

pretty /ˈprɪtɪ/ a (-ier, -iest) adv bonito, lindo (esp LAm); (person) guapo

prevail /prɪˈveɪl/ vi predominar; (win) prevalecer. ~ on persuadir

prevalen|ce /ˈprevələns/ n costumbre f. ~**t** /ˈprevələnt/ a extendido

prevaricate /prɪˈværɪkeɪt/ vi despistar

prevent /prɪˈvent/ vt impedir. ~**able** a evitable. ~**ion** /-ʃn/ n prevención f. ~**ive** a preventivo

preview /ˈpriːvjuː/ n preestreno m, avance m

previous /ˈpriːvɪəs/ a anterior. ~ **to** antes de. ~**ly** adv anteriormente, antes

pre-war /priːˈwɔː(r)/ a de antes de la guerra

prey /preɪ/ n presa f; (fig) víctima f. **bird of** ~ n ave f de rapiña. ● vi. ~ **on** alimentarse de; (worry) atormentar

price /praɪs/ n precio m. ● vt fijar el precio de. ~**less** a inapreciable; (amusing, fam) muy divertido. ~**y** a (fam) caro

prick /prɪk/ vt/i pinchar. ~ **up one's ears** aguzar las orejas. ● n pinchazo m

prickl|e /ˈprɪkl/ n (bot) espina f; (of animal) púa f; (sensation) picor m. **~y** a espinoso; ⟨animal⟩ lleno de púas; ⟨person⟩ quisquilloso

pride /praɪd/ n orgullo m. **~ of place** n puesto m de honor. ● vr. **~ o.s. on** enorgullecerse de

priest /priːst/ n sacerdote m. **~hood** n sacerdocio m. **~ly** a sacerdotal

prig /prɪg/ n mojigato m. **~gish** a mojigato

prim /prɪm/ a (**primmer, primmest**) estirado; (prudish) gazmoño

primarily /ˈpraɪmərɪlɪ/ adv en primer lugar

primary /ˈpraɪmərɪ/ a primario; (chief) principal. **~ school** n escuela f primaria

prime[1] /praɪm/ vt cebar ⟨gun⟩; (prepare) preparar; aprestar ⟨surface⟩

prime[2] /praɪm/ a principal; (first rate) excelente. **~ minister** n primer ministro m. ● n. **be in one's ~** estar en la flor de la vida

primer[1] /ˈpraɪmə(r)/ n (of paint) primera mano f

primer[2] /ˈpraɪmə(r)/ (book) silabario m

primeval /praɪˈmiːvl/ a primitivo

primitive /ˈprɪmɪtɪv/ a primitivo

primrose /ˈprɪmrəʊz/ n primavera f

prince /prɪns/ n príncipe m. **~ly** a principesco. **~ss** /prɪnˈses/ n princesa f

principal /ˈprɪnsəpl/ a principal. ● n (of school etc) director m

principality /prɪnsɪˈpælətɪ/ n principado m

principally /ˈprɪnsɪpəlɪ/ adv principalmente

principle /ˈprɪnsəpl/ n principio m. **in ~** en principio. **on ~** por principio

print /prɪnt/ vt imprimir; (write in capitals) escribir con letras de molde. ● n (of finger, foot) huella f; (letters) caracteres mpl; (of design) estampado m; (picture) grabado m; (photo) copia f. **in ~** ⟨book⟩ disponible. **out of ~** agotado. **~ed matter** n impresos mpl. **~er** /ˈprɪntə(r)/ n impresor m; (machine) impresora f. **~ing** n tipografía f. **~-out** n listado m

prior /ˈpraɪə(r)/ n prior m. ● a anterior. **~ to** antes de

priority /praɪˈɒrətɪ/ n prioridad f

priory /ˈpraɪərɪ/ n priorato m

prise /praɪz/ vt apalancar. **~ open** abrir por fuerza

prism /ˈprɪzəm/ n prisma m

prison /ˈprɪzn/ n cárcel m. **~er** n prisionero m; (in prison) preso m; (under arrest) detenido m. **~ officer** n carcelero m

pristine /ˈprɪstiːn/ a prístino

privacy /ˈprɪvəsɪ/ n intimidad f; (private life) vida f privada. **in ~** en la intimidad

private /ˈpraɪvət/ a privado; (confidential) personal; ⟨lessons, house⟩ particular; ⟨ceremony⟩ en la intimidad. ● n soldado m raso. **in ~** en privado; (secretly) en secreto. **~ eye** n (fam) detective m privado. **~ly** adv en privado; (inwardly) interiormente

privation /praɪˈveɪʃn/ n privación f

privet /ˈprɪvɪt/ n alheña f

privilege /ˈprɪvəlɪdʒ/ n privilegio m. **~d** a privilegiado

privy /ˈprɪvɪ/ a. **~ to** al corriente de

prize /praɪz/ n premio m. ● a ⟨idiot etc⟩ de remate. ● vt estimar. **~fighter** n boxeador m profesional. **~giving** n reparto m de premios. **~winner** n premiado m

pro /prəʊ/ n. **~s and cons** el pro m y el contra m

probab|ility /prɒbəˈbɪlətɪ/ n probabilidad f. **~le** /ˈprɒbəbl/ a probable. **~ly** adv probablemente

probation /prəˈbeɪʃn/ n prueba f; (jurid) libertad f condicional. **~ary** a de prueba

probe /prəʊb/ n sonda f; (fig) encuesta f. ● vt sondar. ● vi. **~ into** investigar

problem /ˈprɒbləm/ n problema m. ● a difícil. **~atic** /-ˈmætɪk/ a problemático

procedure /prəˈsiːdʒə(r)/ n procedimiento m

proceed /prəˈsiːd/ vi proceder. **~ing** n procedimiento m. **~ings** /prəˈsiːdɪŋz/ npl (report) actas fpl; (jurid) proceso m

proceeds /ˈprəʊsiːdz/ npl ganancias fpl

process /ˈprəʊsesɪz/ n proceso m. **in ~ of** en vías de. **in the ~ of time** con el tiempo. ● vt tratar; revelar ⟨photo⟩. **~ion** /prəˈseʃn/ n desfile m

procla|im /prəˈkleɪm/ vt proclamar. **~mation** /prɒkləˈmeɪʃn/ n proclamación f

procrastinate /prəʊˈkræstɪneɪt/ *vi* aplazar, demorar, diferir

procreation /prəʊkrɪˈeɪʃn/ *n* procreación *f*

procure /prəˈkjʊə(r)/ *vt* obtener

prod /prɒd/ *vt* (*pt* **prodded**) empujar; (*with elbow*) dar un codazo a. ● *vi* dar con el dedo. ● *n* empuje *m*; (*with elbow*) codazo *m*

prodigal /ˈprɒdɪɡl/ *a* pródigo

prodigious /prəˈdɪdʒəs/ *a* prodigioso

prodigy /ˈprɒdɪdʒɪ/ *n* prodigio *m*

produce /prəˈdjuːs/ *vt* (*show*) presentar; (*bring out*) sacar; poner en escena ⟨*play*⟩ causar; (*manufacture*) producir. /ˈprɒdjuːs/ *n* productos *mpl*. ∼**er** /prəˈdjuːsə(r)/ *n* productor *m*; (*in theatre*) director *m*

product /ˈprɒdʌkt/ *n* producto *m*. ∼**ion** /prəˈdʌkʃn/ *n* producción *f*; (*of play*) representación *f*

productiv|e /prəˈdʌktɪv/ *a* productivo. ∼**ity** /prɒdʌkˈtɪvətɪ/ *n* productividad *f*

profan|e /prəˈfeɪn/ *a* profano; (*blasphemous*) blasfemo. ∼**ity** /-ˈfænətɪ/ *n* profanidad *f*

profess /prəˈfes/ *vt* profesar; (*pretend*) pretender

profession /prəˈfeʃn/ *n* profesión *f*. ∼**al** *a & n* profesional (*m & f*)

professor /prəˈfesə(r)/ *n* catedrático *m*; (*Amer*) profesor *m*

proffer /ˈprɒfə(r)/ *vt* ofrecer

proficien|cy /prəˈfɪʃənsɪ/ *n* competencia *f*. ∼**t** /prəˈfɪʃnt/ *a* competente

profile /ˈprəʊfaɪl/ *n* perfil *m*

profit /ˈprɒfɪt/ *n* (*com*) ganancia *f*; (*fig*) provecho *m*. ● *vi*. ∼ **from** sacar provecho de. ∼**able** *a* provechoso

profound /prəˈfaʊnd/ *a* profundo. ∼**ly** *adv* profundamente

profus|e /prəˈfjuːs/ *a* profuso. ∼**ely** *adv* profusamente. ∼**ion** /-ʒn/ *n* profusión *f*

progeny /ˈprɒdʒənɪ/ *n* progenie *f*

prognosis /prɒɡˈnəʊsɪs/ *n* (*pl* -**oses**) pronóstico *m*

program(|me) /ˈprəʊɡræm/ *n* programa *m*. ● *vt* (*pt* **programmed**) programar. ∼**mer** *n* programador *m*

progress /ˈprəʊɡres/ *n* progreso *m*, progresos *mpl*; (*development*) desarrollo *m*. **in** ∼ en curso. /prəˈɡres/ *vi* hacer progresos; (*develop*) desarrollarse. ∼**ion** /prəˈɡreʃn/ *n* progresión *f*

progressive /prəˈɡresɪv/ *a* progresivo; (*reforming*) progresista. ∼**ly** *adv* progresivamente

prohibit /prəˈhɪbɪt/ *vt* prohibir. ∼**ive** /-bətɪv/ *a* prohibitivo

project /prəˈdʒekt/ *vt* proyectar. ● *vi* (*stick out*) sobresalir. /ˈprɒdʒekt/ *n* proyecto *m*

projectile /prəˈdʒektaɪl/ *n* proyectil *m*

projector /prəˈdʒektə(r)/ *n* proyector *m*

proletari|an /prəʊlɪˈteərɪən/ *a & n* proletario (*m*). ∼**at** /prəʊlɪˈteərɪət/ *n* proletariado *m*

prolif|erate /prəˈlɪfəreɪt/ *vi* proliferar. ∼**eration** /-ˈreɪʃn/ *n* proliferación *f*. ∼**ic** /prəˈlɪfɪk/ *a* prolífico

prologue /ˈprəʊlɒɡ/ *n* prólogo *m*

prolong /prəˈlɒŋ/ *vt* prolongar

promenade /prɒməˈnɑːd/ *n* paseo *m*; (*along beach*) paseo *m* marítimo. ● *vt* pasear. ● *vi* pasearse. ∼ **concert** *n* concierto *m* (que forma parte de un festival de música clásica en Londres, en que no todo el público tiene asientos)

prominen|ce /ˈprɒmɪnəns/ *n* prominencia *f*; (*fig*) importancia *f*. ∼**t** /ˈprɒmɪnənt/ *a* prominente; (*important*) importante; (*conspicuous*) conspicuo

promiscu|ity /prɒmɪˈskjuːətɪ/ *n* libertinaje *m*. ∼**ous** /prəˈmɪskjʊəs/ *a* libertino

promis|e /ˈprɒmɪs/ *n* promesa *f*. ● *vt/i* prometer. ∼**ing** *a* prometedor; ⟨*person*⟩ que promete

promontory /ˈprɒməntrɪ/ *n* promontorio *m*

promot|e /prəˈməʊt/ *vt* promover. ∼**ion** /-ˈməʊʃn/ *n* promoción *f*

prompt /prɒmpt/ *a* pronto; (*punctual*) puntual. ● *adv* en punto. ● *vt* incitar; apuntar ⟨*actor*⟩. ∼**er** *n* apuntador *m*. ∼**ly** *adv* puntualmente. ∼**ness** *n* prontitud *f*

promulgate /ˈprɒməlɡeɪt/ *vt* promulgar

prone /prəʊn/ *a* echado boca abajo. ∼ **to** propenso a

prong /prɒŋ/ *n* (*of fork*) diente *m*

pronoun /ˈprəʊnaʊn/ *n* pronombre *m*

pronounc|e /prəˈnaʊns/ *vt* pronunciar; (*declare*) declarar. ∼**ement** *n* declaración *f*. ∼**ed**

/prə'naʊnst/ *a* pronunciado; (*noticeable*) marcado

pronunciation /prənʌnsɪ'eɪʃn/ *n* pronunciación *f*

proof /pruːf/ *n* prueba *f*; (*of alcohol*) graduación *f* normal. ● *a.* ~ **against** a prueba de. ~**reading** *n* corrección *f* de pruebas

prop[1] /prɒp/ *n* puntal *m*; (*fig*) apoyo *m*. ● *vt* (*pt* **propped**) apoyar. ~ **against** (*lean*) apoyar en

prop[2] /prɒp/ (*in theatre, fam*) accesorio *m*

propaganda /prɒpə'gændə/ *n* propaganda *f*

propagat|e /'prɒpəgeɪt/ *vt* propagar. ● *vi* propagarse. ~**ion** /-'geɪʃn/ *n* propagación *f*

propel /prə'pel/ *vt* (*pt* **propelled**) propulsar. ~**ler** /prə'pelə(r)/ *n* hélice *f*

propensity /prə'pensətɪ/ *n* propensión *f*

proper /'prɒpə(r)/ *a* correcto; (*suitable*) apropiado; (*gram*) propio; (*real, fam*) verdadero. ~**ly** *adv* correctamente

property /'prɒpətɪ/ *n* propiedad *f*; (*things owned*) bienes *mpl*. ● *a* inmobiliario

prophe|cy /'prɒfəsɪ/ *n* profecía *f*. ~**sy** /'prɒfɪsaɪ/ *vt/i* profetizar. ~**t** /'prɒfɪt/ *n* profeta *m*. ~**tic** /prə'fetɪk/ *a* profético

propitious /prə'pɪʃəs/ *a* propicio

proportion /prə'pɔːʃn/ *n* proporción *f*. ~**al** *a*, ~**ate** *a* proporcional

propos|al /prə'pəʊzl/ *n* propuesta *f*. ~**al of marriage** oferta *f* de matrimonio. ~**e** /prə'pəʊz/ *vt* proponer. ● *vi* hacer una oferta de matrimonio

proposition /prɒpə'zɪʃn/ *n* proposición *f*; (*project, fam*) asunto *m*

propound /prə'paʊnd/ *vt* proponer

proprietor /prə'praɪətə(r)/ *n* propietario *m*

propriety /prə'praɪətɪ/ *n* decoro *m*

propulsion /prə'pʌlʃn/ *n* propulsión *f*

prosaic /prə'zeɪk/ *a* prosaico

proscribe /prə'skraɪb/ *vt* proscribir

prose /prəʊz/ *n* prosa *f*

prosecut|e /'prɒsɪkjuːt/ *vt* procesar; (*carry on*) proseguir. ~**ion** /-'kjuːʃn/ *n* proceso *m*. ~**or** *n* acusador *m*. **Public P~or** fiscal *m*

prospect /'prɒspekt/ *n* vista *f*; (*expectation*) perspectiva *f*. /prə'spekt/ *vi* prospectar

prospective /prə'spektɪv/ *a* probable; (*future*) futuro

prospector /prə'spektə(r)/ *n* prospector *m*, explorador *m*

prospectus /prə'spektəs/ *n* prospecto *m*

prosper /'prɒspə(r)/ *vi* prosperar. ~**ity** /-'sperətɪ/ *n* prosperidad *f*. ~**ous** /'prɒspərəs/ *a* próspero

prostitut|e /'prɒstɪtjuːt/ *n* prostituta *f*. ~**ion** /-'tjuːʃn/ *n* prostitución *f*

prostrate /'prɒstreɪt/ *a* echado boca abajo; (*fig*) postrado

protagonist /prə'tægənɪst/ *n* protagonista *m & f*

protect /prə'tekt/ *vt* proteger. ~**ion** /-ʃn/ *n* protección *f*. ~**ive** /prə'tektɪv/ *a* protector. ~**or** *n* protector *m*

protégé /'prɒtɪʒeɪ/ *n* protegido *m*. ~**e** *n* protegida *f*

protein /'prəʊtiːn/ *n* proteína *f*

protest /'prəʊtest/ *n* protesta *f*. **under** ~ bajo protesta. /prə'test/ *vt/i* protestar. ~**er** *n* (*demonstrator*) manifestante *m & f*

Protestant /'prɒtɪstənt/ *a & n* protestante (*m & f*)

protocol /'prəʊtəkɒl/ *n* protocolo *m*

prototype /'prəʊtətaɪp/ *n* prototipo *m*

protract /prə'trækt/ *vt* prolongar

protractor /prə'træktə(r)/ *n* transportador *m*

protrude /prə'truːd/ *vi* sobresalir

protuberance /prə'tjuːbərəns/ *n* protuberancia *f*

proud /praʊd/ *a* orgulloso. ~**ly** *adv* orgullosamente

prove /pruːv/ *vt* probar. ● *vi* resultar. ~**n** *a* probado

provenance /'prɒvənəns/ *n* procedencia *f*

proverb /'prɒvɜːb/ *n* proverbio *m*. ~**ial** /prə'vɜːbɪəl/ *a* proverbial

provide /prə'vaɪd/ *vt* proveer. ● *vi*. ~ **against** precaverse de. ~ **for** (*allow for*) prever; mantener (*person*). ~**d** /prə'vaɪdɪd/ *conj*. ~ (**that**) con tal que

providen|ce /'prɒvɪdəns/ *n* providencia *f*. ~**t** *a* providente. ~**tial** /prɒvɪ'denʃl/ *a* providencial

providing /prə'vaɪdɪŋ/ *conj*. ~ **that** con tal que

provinc|e /'prɒvɪns/ *n* provincia *f*; (*fig*) competencia *f*. ~**ial** /prə'vɪnʃl/ *a* provincial

provision /prə'vɪʒn/ n provisión f;
(*supply*) suministro m; (*stipulation*)
condición f. **~s** npl comestibles mpl

provisional /prə'vɪʒənl/ a provisional. **~ly** adv provisionalmente

proviso /prə'vaɪzəʊ/ n (pl **-os**) condición f

provo|cation /prɒvə'keɪʃn/ n provo-
cación f. **~cative** /-'vɒkətɪv/ a
provocador. **~ke** /prə'vəʊk/ vt
provocar

prow /praʊ/ n proa f

prowess /'praʊɪs/ n habilidad f;
(*valour*) valor m

prowl /praʊl/ vi merodear. ● n
ronda f. **be on the ~** merodear. **~er**
n merodeador m

proximity /prɒk'sɪmətɪ/ n proximidad f

proxy /'prɒksɪ/ n poder m. **by ~** por
poder

prude /pruːd/ n mojigato m

pruden|ce /'pruːdəns/ n prudencia f.
~t /'pruːdənt/ a prudente. **~tly** adv
prudentemente

prudish /'pruːdɪʃ/ a mojigato

prune[1] /pruːn/ n ciruela f pasa

prune[2] /pruːn/ vt podar

pry /praɪ/ vi entrometerse

psalm /sɑːm/ n salmo m

pseudo... /'sjuːdəʊ/ pref seudo...

pseudonym /'sjuːdənɪm/ n seudónimo m

psychiatr|ic /saɪkɪ'ætrɪk/ a psi-
quiátrico. **~ist** /saɪ'kaɪətrɪst/ n
psiquiatra m & f. **~y** /saɪ'kaɪətrɪ/ n
psiquiatría f

physic /'saɪkɪk/ a psíquico

psycho-analys|e /saɪkəʊ'ænəlaɪz/ vt
psicoanalizar. **~is** /saɪkəʊə'næləsɪs/
n psicoanálisis m. **~t** /-ɪst/ n psico-
analista m & f

psycholog|ical /saɪkə'lɒdʒɪkl/ a psi-
cológico. **~ist** /saɪ'kɒlədʒɪst/ n psicólogo m. **~y** /saɪ'kɒlədʒɪ/ n
psicología f

psychopath /'saɪkəpæθ/ n psicópata
m & f

pub /pʌb/ n bar m

puberty /'pjuːbətɪ/ n pubertad f

pubic /'pjuːbɪk/ a pubiano, púbico

public /'pʌblɪk/ a público

publican /'pʌblɪkən/ n tabernero m

publication /pʌblɪ'keɪʃn/ n publicación f

public house /pʌblɪk'haʊs/ n bar m

publicity /pʌb'lɪsətɪ/ n publicidad f

publicize /'pʌblɪsaɪz/ vt publicar,
anunciar

publicly /'pʌblɪklɪ/ adv públic-
amente

public school /pʌblɪk'skuːl/ n colegio m privado; (*Amer*) instituto m

public-spirited /pʌblɪk'spɪrɪtɪd/ a
cívico

publish /'pʌblɪʃ/ vt publicar. **~er** n
editor m. **~ing** n publicación f

puck /pʌk/ n (*ice hockey*) disco m

pucker /'pʌkə(r)/ vt arrugar. ● vi
arrugarse

pudding /'pʊdɪŋ/ n postre m;
(*steamed*) budín m

puddle /'pʌdl/ n charco m

pudgy /'pʌdʒɪ/ a (**-ier**, **-iest**)
rechoncho

puerile /'pjʊəraɪl/ a pueril

puff /pʌf/ n soplo m; (*for powder*)
borla f. ● vt/i soplar. **~ at** chupar
(*pipe*). **~ out** apagar (*candle*); (*swell
up*) hinchar. **~ed** a (*out of breath*)
sin aliento. **~ pastry** n hojaldre m.
~y /'pʌfɪ/ a hinchado

pugnacious /pʌg'neɪʃəs/ a belicoso

pug-nosed /'pʌgnəʊzd/ a chato

pull /pʊl/ vt tirar de; sacar (*tooth*);
torcer (*muscle*). **~ a face** hacer una
mueca. **~ a fast one** hacer una
mala jugada. **~ down** derribar
(*building*). **~ off** quitarse; (*fig*)
lograr. **~ one's weight** poner de su
parte. **~ out** sacar. **~ s.o.'s leg** tom-
arle el pelo a uno. **~ up** (*uproot*) desarraigar; (*reprimand*) reprender. ● vi
tirar (at de). **~ away** (*auto*) alejarse.
~ back retirarse. **~ in** (*enter*) entrar;
(*auto*) parar. **~ o.s. together** tranquilizarse. **~ out** (*auto*) salirse. **~
through** recobrar la salud. **~ up**
(*auto*) parar. ● n tirón m; (*fig*) atracción f; (*influence*) influencia f. **give a
~** tirar

pulley /'pʊlɪ/ n polea f

pullover /'pʊləʊvə(r)/ n jersey m

pulp /pʌlp/ n pulpa f; (*for paper*)
pasta f

pulpit /'pʊlpɪt/ n púlpito m

pulsate /'pʌlseɪt/ vi pulsar

pulse /pʌls/ n (*med*) pulso m

pulverize /'pʌlvəraɪz/ vt pulverizar

pumice /'pʌmɪs/ n piedra f pómez

pummel /'pʌml/ vt (pt **pummelled**)
aporrear

pump[1] /pʌmp/ n bomba f; ● vt sacar
con una bomba; (*fig*) sonsacar. **~
up** inflar

pump[2] /pʌmp/ (*plimsoll*) zapatilla f
de lona; (*dancing shoe*) escarpín m

pumpkin /'pʌmpkɪn/ n calabaza f

pun /pʌn/ n juego m de palabras

punch[1] /pʌntʃ/ vt dar un puñetazo a; (perforate) perforar; hacer ⟨hole⟩. ● n puñetazo m; (vigour, sl) empuje m; (device) punzón m

punch[2] /pʌntʃ/ (drink) ponche m

punch: ~**-drunk** a aturdido a golpes. ~ **line** n gracia f. ~**up** n riña f

punctilious /pʌŋk'tɪlɪəs/ a meticuloso

punctual /pʌŋktʃʊəl/ a puntual. ~**ity** /-'ælətɪ/ n puntualidad f. ~**ly** adv puntualmente

punctuat|e /pʌŋktʃʊeɪt/ vt puntuar. ~**ion** /-'eɪʃn/ n puntuación f

puncture /pʌŋktʃə(r)/ n (in tyre) pinchazo m. ● vt pinchar. ● vi pincharse

pundit /pʌndɪt/ n experto m

pungen|cy /pʌndʒənsɪ/ n acritud f; (fig) mordacidad f. ~**t** /pʌndʒənt/ a acre; ⟨remark⟩ mordaz

punish /pʌnɪʃ/ vt castigar. ~**able** a castigable. ~**ment** n castigo m

punitive /pju:nɪtɪv/ a punitivo

punk /pʌŋk/ a ⟨music, person⟩ punk

punnet /pʌnɪt/ n canastilla f

punt[1] /pʌnt/ n (boat) batea f

punt[2] /pʌnt/ vi apostar. ~**er** n apostante m & f

puny /pju:nɪ/ a (-ier, -iest) diminuto; (weak) débil; (petty) insignificante

pup /pʌp/ n cachorro m

pupil[1] /pju:pl/ n alumno m

pupil[2] /pju:pl/ (of eye) pupila f

puppet /pʌpɪt/ n títere m

puppy /pʌpɪ/ n cachorro m

purchase /pɜ:tʃəs/ vt comprar. ● n compra f. ~**r** n comprador m

pur|e /pjʊə(r)/ a (-er, -est) puro. ~**ely** adv puramente. ~**ity** n pureza f

purée /pjʊəreɪ/ n puré m

purgatory /pɜ:gətrɪ/ n purgatorio m

purge /pɜ:dʒ/ vt purgar. ● n purga f

purif|ication /pjʊərɪfɪ'keɪʃn/ n purificación f. ~**y** /pjʊərɪfaɪ/ vt purificar

purist /pjʊərɪst/ n purista m & f

puritan /pjʊərɪtən/ n puritano m. ~**ical** /-'tænɪkl/ a puritano

purl /pɜ:l/ n (knitting) punto m del revés

purple /pɜ:pl/ a purpúreo, morado. ● n púrpura f

purport /pə'pɔ:t/ vt. ~ **to be** pretender ser

purpose /pɜ:pəs/ n propósito m; (determination) resolución f. **on** ~ a propósito. **to no** ~ en vano. ~**-built** a construido especialmente. ~**ful** a (resolute) resuelto. ~**ly** adv a propósito

purr /pɜ:(r)/ vi ronronear

purse /pɜ:s/ n monedero m; (Amer) bolso m, cartera f (LAm). ● vt fruncir

pursu|e /pə'sju:/ vt perseguir, seguir. ~**er** n perseguidor m. ~**it** /pə'sju:t/ n persecución f; (fig) ocupación f

purveyor /pə'veɪə(r)/ n proveedor m

pus /pʌs/ n pus m

push /pʊʃ/ vt empujar; apretar ⟨button⟩. ● vi empujar. ● n empuje m; (effort) esfuerzo m; (drive) dinamismo m. **at a** ~ en caso de necesidad. **get the** ~ (sl) ser despedido. ~ **aside** vt apartar. ~ **back** vt hacer retroceder. ~ **off** vi (sl) marcharse. ~ **on** vi seguir adelante. ~ **up** vt levantar. ~**-button telephone** n teléfono m de teclas. ~**-chair** n sillita f con ruedas. ~**ing** /pʊʃɪŋ/ a ambicioso. ~**over** n (fam) cosa f muy fácil, pan comido. ~**y** a (pej) ambicioso

puss /pʊs/ n minino m

put /pʊt/ vt (pt put, pres p putting) poner; (express) expresar; (say) decir; (estimate) estimar; hacer ⟨question⟩. ~ **across** comunicar. (deceive) engañar. ~ **aside** poner aparte. ~ **away** guardar. ~ **back** devolver; retrasar ⟨clock⟩. ~ **by** guardar; ahorrar ⟨money⟩. ~ **down** depositar; (suppress) suprimir; (write) apuntar; (kill) sacrificar. ~ **forward** avanzar. ~ **in** introducir; (submit) presentar. ~ **in for** pedir. ~ **off** aplazar; (disconcert) desconcertar. ~ **on** (wear) ponerse; cobrar ⟨speed⟩; encender ⟨light⟩. ~ **one's foot down** mantenerse firme. ~ **out** (extinguish) apagar; (inconvenience) incomodar; extender ⟨hand⟩; (disconcert) desconcertar. ~ **to sea** hacerse a la mar. ~ **through** (phone) poner. ~ **up** levantar; subir ⟨price⟩; alojar ⟨guest⟩. ~ **up with** soportar. **stay** ~ (fam) no moverse

putrefy /pju:trɪfaɪ/ vi pudrirse

putt /pʌt/ n (golf) golpe m suave

putty /pʌtɪ/ n masilla f

put-up /pʊtʌp/ a. ~ **job** n confabulación f

puzzl|e /'pʌzl/ n enigma m; (game) rompecabezas m invar. ● vt dejar perplejo. ● vi calentarse los sesos. **~ing** a incomprensible; (odd) curioso

pygmy /'pɪgmɪ/ n pigmeo m

pyjamas /pə'dʒɑːməz/ npl pijama m

pylon /'paɪlɒn/ n pilón m

pyramid /'pɪrəmɪd/ n pirámide f

python /'paɪθn/ n pitón m

Q

quack[1] /kwæk/ n (of duck) graznido m

quack[2] /kwæk/ (person) charlatán m. **~ doctor** n curandero m

quadrangle /'kwɒdræŋgl/ n cuadrilátero m; (court) patio m

quadruped /'kwɒdrʊped/ n cuadrúpedo m

quadruple /'kwɒdrʊpl/ a & n cuádruplo (m). ● vt cuadruplicar. **~t** /-plət/ n cuatrillizo m

quagmire /'kwæɡmaɪə(r)/ n ciénaga f; (fig) atolladero m

quail /kweɪl/ n codorniz f

quaint /kweɪnt/ a (-er, -est) pintoresco; (odd) curioso

quake /kweɪk/ vi temblar. ● n (fam) terremoto m

Quaker /'kweɪkə(r)/ n cuáquero (m)

qualification /kwɒlɪfɪ'keɪʃn/ n título m; (requirement) requisito m; (ability) capacidad f; (fig) reserva f

qualif|ied /'kwɒlɪfaɪd/ a cualificado; (limited) limitado; (with degree, diploma) titulado. **~y** /'kwɒlɪfaɪ/ vt calificar; (limit) limitar. ● vi sacar el título; (sport) clasificarse; (fig) llenar los requisitos

qualitative /'kwɒlɪtətɪv/ a cualitativo

quality /'kwɒlɪtɪ/ n calidad f; (attribute) cualidad f

qualm /kwɑːm/ n escrúpulo m

quandary /'kwɒndrɪ/ n. **in a ~** en un dilema

quantitative /'kwɒntɪtətɪv/ a cuantitativo

quantity /'kwɒntɪtɪ/ n cantidad f

quarantine /'kwɒrəntiːn/ n cuarentena f

quarrel /'kwɒrəl/ n riña f. ● vi (pt **quarrelled**) reñir. **~some** a pendenciero

quarry[1] /'kwɒrɪ/ n (excavation) cantera f

quarry[2] /'kwɒrɪ/ n (animal) presa f

quart /kwɔːt/ n (poco más de un) litro m

quarter /'kwɔːtə(r)/ n cuarto m; (of year) trimestre m; (district) barrio m. **from all ~s** de todas partes. ● vt dividir en cuartos; (mil) acuartelar. **~s** npl alojamiento m

quartermaster /'kwɔːtəmɑːstə(r)/ n intendente m

quarter: ~-final n cuarto m de final. **~ly** a trimestral. ● adv cada tres meses

quartet /kwɔː'tet/ n cuarteto m

quartz /kwɔːts/ n cuarzo m. ● a ⟨watch etc⟩ de cuarzo

quash /kwɒʃ/ vt anular

quasi.. /'kweɪsaɪ/ pref cuasi...

quaver /'kweɪvə(r)/ vi temblar. ● n (mus) corchea f

quay /kiː/ n muelle m

queasy /'kwiːzɪ/ a ⟨stomach⟩ delicado

queen /kwiːn/ n reina f. **~ mother** n reina f madre

queer /kwɪə(r)/ a (-er, -est) extraño; (dubious) sospechoso; (ill) indispuesto. ● n (sl) homosexual m

quell /kwel/ vt reprimir

quench /kwentʃ/ vt apagar; sofocar ⟨desire⟩

querulous /'kwerʊləs/ a quejumbroso

query /'kwɪərɪ/ n pregunta f. ● vt preguntar; (doubt) poner en duda

quest /kwest/ n busca f

question /'kwestʃən/ n pregunta f; (for discussion) cuestión f. **in ~** en cuestión. **out of the ~** imposible. **without ~** sin duda. ● vt preguntar; ⟨police etc⟩ interrogar; (doubt) poner en duda. **~able** /'kwestʃənəbl/ a discutible. **~ mark** n signo m de interrogación. **~naire** /kwestʃə'neə(r)/ n cuestionario m

queue /kjuː/ n cola f. ● vi (pres p **queuing**) hacer cola

quibble /'kwɪbl/ vi discutir; (split hairs) sutilizar

quick /kwɪk/ a (-er, -est) rápido. **be ~!** ¡date prisa! ● adv rápidamente. ● n. **to the ~** en lo vivo. **~en** /'kwɪkən/ vt acelerar. ● vi acelerarse. **~ly** adv rápidamente. **~sand** /'kwɪksænd/ n arena f movediza. **~-tempered** a irascible

quid /kwɪd/ n invar (sl) libra f (esterlina)

quiet /'kwaɪət/ a (-er, -est) tranquilo; (silent) callado; (discreet) discreto. ● n tranquilidad f. **on the ~** a escondidas. **~en** /'kwaɪətn/ vt calmar. ● vi calmarse. **~ly** adv tranquilamente; (silently) silenciosamente; (discreetly) discretamente. **~ness** n tranquilidad f

quill /kwɪl/ n pluma f

quilt /kwɪlt/ n edredón m. ● vt acolchar

quince /kwɪns/ n membrillo m

quinine /kwɪ'niːn/ n quinina f

quintessence /kwɪn'tesns/ n quintaesencia f

quintet /kwɪn'tet/ n quinteto m

quintuplet /'kwɪntjuːplət/ n quintillizo m

quip /kwɪp/ n ocurrencia f

quirk /kwɜːk/ n peculiaridad f

quit /kwɪt/ vt (pt quitted) dejar. ● vi abandonar; (leave) marcharse; (resign) dimitir. **~ doing** (cease, Amer) dejar de hacer

quite /kwaɪt/ adv bastante; (completely) totalmente; (really) verdaderamente. **~ (so)!** ¡claro! **~ a few** bastante

quits /kwɪts/ a a la par. **call it ~** darlo por terminado

quiver /'kwɪvə(r)/ vi temblar

quixotic /kwɪk'sɒtɪk/ a quijotesco

quiz /kwɪz/ n (pl quizzes) serie f de preguntas; (game) concurso m. ● vt (pt quizzed) interrogar. **~zical** /'kwɪzɪkl/ a burlón

quorum /'kwɔːrəm/ n quórum m

quota /'kwəʊtə/ n cuota f

quot|ation /kwəʊ'teɪʃn/ n cita f; (price) presupuesto m. **~ation marks** npl comillas fpl. **~e** /kwəʊt/ vt citar; (com) cotizar. ● n (fam) cita f; (price) presupuesto m. **in ~es** npl entre comillas

quotient /'kwəʊʃnt/ n cociente m

R

rabbi /'ræbaɪ/ n rabino m

rabbit /'ræbɪt/ n conejo m

rabble /'ræbl/ n gentío m. **the ~** (pej) el populacho m

rabi|d /'ræbɪd/ a feroz; (dog) rabioso. **~es** /'reɪbiːz/ n rabia f

race[1] /reɪs/ n carrera f. ● vt hacer correr (horse); acelerar (engine). ● vi (run) correr, ir corriendo; (rush) ir de prisa

race[2] /reɪs/ n (group) raza f

race: ~course /'reɪskɔːs/ n hipódromo m. **~horse** /'reɪshɔːs/ n caballo m de carreras. **~riots** /'reɪsraɪəts/ npl disturbios mpl raciales. **~track** /'reɪstræk/ n hipódromo m

racial /'reɪʃl/ a racial. **~ism** /-ɪzəm/ n racismo m

racing /'reɪsɪŋ/ n carreras fpl. **~ car** n coche m de carreras

racis|m /'reɪsɪzəm/ n racismo m. **~t** /'reɪsɪst/ a & n racista (m & f)

rack[1] /ræk/ n (shelf) estante m; (for luggage) rejilla f; (for plates) escurreplatos m invar. ● vt. **~ one's brains** devanarse los sesos

rack[2] /ræk/ n. **go to ~ and ruin** quedarse en la ruina

racket[1] /'rækɪt/ n (for sports) raqueta

racket[2] /'rækɪt/ (din) alboroto m; (swindle) estafa f. **~eer** /-ə'tɪə(r)/ n estafador m

raconteur /rækɒn'tɜː/ n anecdotista m & f

racy /'reɪsɪ/ a (-ier, -iest) vivo

radar /'reɪdɑː(r)/ n radar m

radian|ce /'reɪdɪəns/ n resplandor m. **~t** /'reɪdɪənt/ a radiante. **~tly** adv con resplandor

radiat|e /'reɪdɪeɪt/ vt irradiar. ● vi divergir. **~ion** /-'eɪʃn/ n radiación f. **~or** /'reɪdɪeɪtə(r)/ n radiador m

radical /'rædɪkl/ a & n radical (m)

radio /'reɪdɪəʊ/ n (pl -os) radio f. ● vt transmitir por radio

radioactiv|e /reɪdɪəʊ'æktɪv/ a radiactivo. **~ity** /-'tɪvətɪ/ n radiactividad f

radiograph|er /reɪdɪ'ɒgrəfə(r)/ n radiógrafo m. **~y** n radiografía f

radish /'rædɪʃ/ n rábano m

radius /'reɪdɪəs/ n (pl -dii /-dɪaɪ/) radio m

raffish /'ræfɪʃ/ a disoluto

raffle /ræfl/ n rifa f

raft /rɑːft/ n balsa f

rafter /'rɑːftə(r)/ n cabrio m

rag[1] /ræg/ n andrajo m; (for wiping) trapo m; (newspaper) periodicucho m. **in ~s** (person) andrajoso; (clothes) hecho jirones

rag[2] /ræg/ n (univ) festival m estudiantil; (prank, fam) broma f pesada. ● *vt* (*pt* **ragged**) (*sl*) tomar el pelo a

ragamuffin /'rægəmʌfɪn/ *n* granuja *m*, golfo *m*

rage /reɪdʒ/ *n* rabia *f*; (*fashion*) moda *f*. ● *vi* estar furioso; (*storm*) bramar

ragged /'rægɪd/ *a* (*person*) andrajoso; (*clothes*) hecho jirones; (*edge*) mellado

raid /reɪd/ *n* (*mil*) incursión *f*; (*by police, etc*) redada *f*; (*by thieves*) asalto *m*. ● *vt* (*mil*) atacar; (*police*) hacer una redada en; (*thieves*) asaltar. **~er** *n* invasor *m*; (*thief*) ladrón *m*

rail[1] /reɪl/ *n* barandilla *f*; (*for train*) riel *m*; (*rod*) barra *f*. **by ~** por ferrocarril

rail[2] /reɪl/ *vi*. **~ against**, **~ at** insultar

railing /'reɪlɪŋ/ *n* barandilla *f*; (*fence*) verja *f*

rail|road /'reɪlrəʊd/ *n* (*Amer*), **~way** /'reɪlweɪ/ *n* ferrocarril *m*. **~wayman** *n* (*pl* **-men**) ferroviario *m*. **~way station** *n* estación *f* de ferrocarril

rain /reɪn/ *n* lluvia *f*. ● *vi* llover. **~bow** /'reɪnbəʊ/ *n* arco *m* iris. **~coat** /'reɪnkəʊt/ *n* impermeable *m*. **~fall** /'reɪnfɔːl/ *n* precipitación *f*. **~water** *n* agua *f* de lluvia. **~y** /'reɪnɪ/ *a* (**-ier**, **-iest**) lluvioso

raise /reɪz/ *vt* levantar; (*breed*) criar; obtener (*money etc*); hacer (*question*); plantear (*problem*); subir (*price*). **~ one's glass to** brindar por. **~ one's hat** descubrirse. ● *n* (*Amer*) aumento *m*

raisin /'reɪzn/ *n* (*uva f*) pasa *f*

rake[1] /reɪk/ *n* rastrillo *m*. ● *vt* rastrillar; (*search*) buscar en. **~ up** remover

rake[2] /reɪk/ *n* (*man*) calavera *m*

rake-off /'reɪkɒf/ *n* (*fam*) comisión *f*

rally /'rælɪ/ *vt* reunir; (*revive*) reanimar. ● *vi* reunirse; (*in sickness*) recuperarse. ● *n* reunión *f*; (*recovery*) recuperación *f*; (*auto*) rallye *m*

ram /ræm/ *n* carnero *m*. ● *vt* (*pt* **rammed**) (*thrust*) meter por la fuerza; (*crash into*) chocar con

rambl|e /'ræmbl/ *n* excursión *f* a pie. ● *vi* ir de paseo; (*in speech*) divagar. **~e on** divagar. **~er** *n* excursionista *m & f*. **~ing** *a* (*speech*) divagador

ramification /ræmɪfɪ'keɪʃn/ *n* ramificación *f*

ramp /ræmp/ *n* rampa *f*

rampage /ræm'peɪdʒ/ *vi* alborotarse. /'ræmpeɪdʒ/ *n*. **go on the ~** alborotarse

rampant /'ræmpənt/ *a*. **be ~** (*disease etc*) estar extendido

rampart /'ræmpɑːt/ *n* muralla *f*

ramshackle /'ræmʃækl/ *a* desvencijado

ran /ræn/ *see* **run**

ranch /rɑːntʃ/ *n* hacienda *f*

rancid /'rænsɪd/ *a* rancio

rancour /'ræŋkə(r)/ *n* rencor *m*

random /'rændəm/ *a* hecho al azar; (*chance*) fortuito. ● *n*. **at ~** al azar

randy /'rændɪ/ *a* (**-ier**, **-iest**) lujurioso, cachondo (*fam*)

rang /ræŋ/ *see* **ring**[2]

range /reɪndʒ/ *n* alcance *m*; (*distance*) distancia *f*; (*series*) serie *f*; (*of mountains*) cordillera *f*; (*extent*) extensión *f*; (*com*) surtido *m*; (*open area*) dehesa *f*; (*stove*) cocina *f* económica. ● *vi* extenderse; (*vary*) variar

ranger /'reɪndʒə(r)/ *n* guardabosque *m*

rank[1] /ræŋk/ *n* posición *f*, categoría *f*; (*row*) fila *f*; (*for taxis*) parada *f*. **the ~ and file** la masa *f*. ● *vt* clasificar. ● *vi* clasificarse. **~s** *npl* soldados *mpl* rasos

rank[2] /ræŋk/ *a* (**-er**, **-est**) exuberante; (*smell*) fétido; (*fig*) completo

rankle /ræŋkl/ *vi* (*fig*) causar rencor

ransack /'rænsæk/ *vt* registrar; (*pillage*) saquear

ransom /'rænsəm/ *n* rescate *m*. **hold s.o. to ~** exigir rescate por uno; (*fig*) hacer chantaje a uno. ● *vt* rescatar; (*redeem*) redimir

rant /rænt/ *vi* vociferar

rap /ræp/ *n* golpe *m* seco. ● *vt/i* (*pt* **rapped**) golpear

rapacious /rə'peɪʃs/ *a* rapaz

rape /reɪp/ *vt* violar. ● *n* violación *f*

rapid /'ræpɪd/ *a* rápido. **~ity** /rə'pɪdətɪ/ *n* rapidez *f*. **~s** /'ræpɪdz/ *npl* rápido *m*

rapist /'reɪpɪst/ *n* violador *m*

rapport /ræ'pɔː(r)/ *n* armonía *f*, relación *f*

rapt /ræpt/ *a* (*attention*) profundo. **~ in** absorto en

raptur|e /'ræptʃə(r)/ *n* éxtasis *m*. **~ous** *a* extático

rare[1] /reə(r)/ *a* (**-er**, **-est**) raro

rare[2] /reə(r)/ *a* (*culin*) poco hecho

rarefied /'reərɪfaɪd/ *a* enrarecido

rarely /'reəlɪ/ adv raramente

rarity /'reərətɪ/ n rareza f

raring /'reərɪŋ/ a (fam). ~ **to** impaciente por

rascal /'rɑːskl/ n tunante m & f

rash[1] /ræʃ/ a (-er, -est) imprudente, precipitado

rash[2] /ræʃ/ n erupción f

rasher /'ræʃə(r)/ n loncha f

rash|ly /'ræʃlɪ/ adv imprudentemente, a la ligera. ~ness n imprudencia f

rasp /rɑːsp/ n (file) escofina f

raspberry /'rɑːzbrɪ/ n frambuesa f

rasping /'rɑːspɪŋ/ a áspero

rat /ræt/ n rata f. ● vi (pt ratted). ~ **on** (desert) desertar; (inform on) denunciar, chivarse

rate /reɪt/ n (ratio) proporción f; (speed) velocidad f; (price) precio m; (of interest) tipo m. **at any** ~ de todas formas. **at the** ~ **of** (on the basis of) a razón de. **at this** ~ así. ● vt valorar; (consider) considerar; (deserve, Amer) merecer. ● vi ser considerado. ~able value n valor m imponible. ~payer /'reɪtpeɪə(r)/ n contribuyente m & f. ~s npl (taxes) impuestos mpl municipales

rather /'rɑːðə(r)/ adv mejor dicho; (fairly) bastante; (a little) un poco. ● int claro. **I would** ~ **not** prefiero no

ratif|ication /rætɪfɪ'keɪʃn/ n ratificación f. ~y /'rætɪfaɪ/ vt ratificar

rating /'reɪtɪŋ/ n clasificación f; (sailor) marinero m; (number, TV) índice m

ratio /'reɪʃɪəʊ/ n (pl -os) proporción f

ration /'ræʃn/ n ración f. ● vt racionar

rational /'ræʃənəl/ a racional. ~ize /'ræʃənəlaɪz/ vt racionalizar

rat race /'rætreɪs/ n lucha f incesante para triunfar

rattle /'rætl/ vi traquetear. ● vt (shake) agitar; (sl) desconcertar. ● n traqueteo m; (toy) sonajero m. ~ **off** (fig) decir de corrida

rattlesnake /'rætlsneɪk/ n serpiente f de cascabel

ratty /'rætɪ/ a (-ier, -iest) (sl) irritable

raucous /'rɔːkəs/ a estridente

ravage /'rævɪdʒ/ vt estragar. ~s /'rævɪdʒɪz/ npl estragos mpl

rave /reɪv/ vi delirar; (in anger) enfurecerse. ~ **about** entusiasmarse por

raven /'reɪvn/ n cuervo m. ● a (hair) negro

ravenous /'rævənəs/ a voraz; (person) hambriento. **be** ~ morirse de hambre

ravine /rə'viːn/ n barranco m

raving /'reɪvɪŋ/ a. ~ **mad** loco de atar. ~s npl divagaciones fpl

ravish /'rævɪʃ/ vt (rape) violar. ~ing a (enchanting) encantador

raw /rɔː/ a (-er, -est) crudo; (not processed) bruto; (wound) en carne viva; (inexperienced) inexperto; (weather) crudo. ~ **deal** n tratamiento m injusto, injusticia f. ~ **materials** npl materias fpl primas

ray /reɪ/ n rayo m

raze /reɪz/ vt arrasar

razor /'reɪzə(r)/ n navaja f de afeitar; (electric) maquinilla f de afeitar

Rd abbr (Road) C/, Calle f

re[1] /riː/ prep con referencia a. ● pref re...

re[2] /reɪ/ n (mus, second note of any musical scale) re m

reach /riːtʃ/ vt alcanzar; (extend) extender; (arrive at) llegar a; (achieve) lograr; (hand over) pasar, dar. ● vi extenderse. ● n alcance m; (of river) tramo m recto. **within** ~ **of** al alcance de; (close to) a corta distancia de

react /rɪ'ækt/ vi reaccionar. ~ion /rɪ'ækʃn/ n reacción f. ~ionary a & n reaccionario (m)

reactor /rɪ'æktə(r)/ n reactor m

read /riːd/ vt (pt read /red/) leer; (study) estudiar; (interpret) interpretar. ● vi leer; (instrument) indicar. ● n (fam) lectura f. ~ **out** vt leer en voz alta. ~able a interesante, agradable; (clear) legible. ~er /'riːdə(r)/ n lector m. ~ership n lectores m

readi|ly /'redɪlɪ/ adv (willingly) de buena gana; (easily) fácilmente. ~ness /'redɪnɪs/ n prontitud f. **in** ~ness preparado, listo

reading /'riːdɪŋ/ n lectura f

readjust /riːə'dʒʌst/ vt reajustar. ● vi readaptarse (**to** a)

ready /'redɪ/ a (-ier, -iest) listo, preparado; (quick) pronto. ~-made a confeccionado. ~ **money** n dinero m contante. ~ **reckoner** n baremo m. **get** ~ prepararse

real /rɪəl/ a verdadero. ● adv (Amer, fam) verdaderamente. ~ **estate** n bienes mpl raíces

realis|m /'rɪəlɪzəm/ n realismo m. ~**t** /'rɪəlɪst/ n realista m & f. ~**tic** /-'lɪstɪk/ a realista. ~**tically** /-'lɪstɪklɪ/ adv de manera realista

reality /rɪ'ælətɪ/ n realidad f

realiz|ation /rɪəlaɪ'zeɪʃn/ n comprensión f; (com) realización f. ~**e** /'rɪəlaɪz/ vt darse cuenta de; (fulfil, com) realizar

really /'rɪəlɪ/ adv verdaderamente

realm /relm/ n reino m

ream /riːm/ n resma f

reap /riːp/ vt segar; (fig) cosechar

re: ~appear /riːə'pɪə(r)/ vi reaparecer. ~**appraisal** /riːə'preɪzl/ n revaluación f

rear[1] /rɪə(r)/ n parte f de atrás. ● a posterior, trasero

rear[2] /rɪə(r)/ vt (bring up, breed) criar. ~ **one's head** levantar la cabeza. ● vi ⟨horse⟩ encabritarse. ~ **up** ⟨horse⟩ encabritarse

rear: ~admiral n contraalmirante m. ~**guard** /'rɪəgɑːd/ n retaguardia f

re: ~arm /riː'ɑːm/ vt rearmar. ● vi rearmarse. ~**arrange** /riːə'reɪndʒ/ vt arreglar de otra manera

reason /'riːzn/ n razón f, motivo m. **within** ~ dentro de lo razonable. ● vi razonar

reasonable /'riːzənəbl/ a razonable

reasoning /'riːznɪŋ/ n razonamiento m

reassur|ance /riːə'ʃʊərəns/ n promesa f tranquilizadora; (guarantee) garantía f. ~**e** /riːə'ʃʊə(r)/ vt tranquilizar

rebate /'riːbeɪt/ n reembolso m; (discount) rebaja f

rebel /'rebl/ n rebelde m & f. /rɪ'bel/ vi (pt rebelled) rebelarse. ~**lion** n rebelión f. ~**lious** a rebelde

rebound /rɪ'baʊnd/ vi rebotar; (fig) recaer. /'riːbaʊnd/ n rebote m. **on the** ~ (fig) por reacción

rebuff /rɪ'bʌf/ vt rechazar. ● n desaire m

rebuild /riː'bɪld/ vt (pt rebuilt) reconstruir

rebuke /rɪ'bjuːk/ vt reprender. ● n represión f

rebuttal /rɪ'bʌtl/ n refutación f

recall /rɪ'kɔːl/ vt (call s.o. back) llamar; (remember) recordar. ● n llamada f

recant /rɪ'kænt/ vi retractarse

recap /'riːkæp/ vt/i (pt recapped) (fam) resumir. ● n (fam) resumen m

recapitulat|e /riːkə'pɪtʃʊleɪt/ vt/i resumir. ~**ion** /-'leɪʃn/ n resumen m

recapture /riː'kæptʃə(r)/ vt recobrar; (recall) hacer revivir

reced|e /rɪ'siːd/ vi retroceder. ~**ing** a ⟨forehead⟩ huidizo

receipt /rɪ'siːt/ n recibo m. ~**s** npl (com) ingresos mpl

receive /rɪ'siːv/ vt recibir. ~**r** /-ə(r)/ n (of stolen goods) perista m & f; (of phone) auricular m

recent /'riːsnt/ a reciente. ~**ly** adv recientemente

receptacle /rɪ'septəkl/ n recipiente m

reception /rɪ'sepʃn/ n recepción f; (welcome) acogida f. ~**ist** n recepcionista m & f

receptive /rɪ'septɪv/ a receptivo

recess /rɪ'ses/ n hueco m; (holiday) vacaciones fpl; (fig) parte f recóndita

recession /rɪ'seʃn/ n recesión f

recharge /riː'tʃɑːdʒ/ vt cargar de nuevo, recargar

recipe /'resəpɪ/ n receta f

recipient /rɪ'sɪpɪənt/ n recipiente m & f; (of letter) destinatario m

reciprocal /rɪ'sɪprəkl/ a recíproco

reciprocate /rɪ'sɪprəkeɪt/ vt corresponder a

recital /rɪ'saɪtl/ n (mus) recital m

recite /rɪ'saɪt/ vt recitar; (list) enumerar

reckless /'reklɪs/ a imprudente. ~**ly** adv imprudentemente. ~**ness** n imprudencia f

reckon /'rekən/ vt/i calcular; (consider) considerar; (think) pensar. ~ **on** (rely) contar con. ~**ing** n cálculo m

reclaim /rɪ'kleɪm/ vt reclamar; recuperar ⟨land⟩

reclin|e /rɪ'klaɪn/ vi recostarse. ~**ing** a acostado; ⟨seat⟩ reclinable

recluse /rɪ'kluːs/ n solitario m

recogni|tion /rekəg'nɪʃn/ n reconocimiento m. **beyond** ~**tion** irreconocible. ~**ze** /'rekəgnaɪz/ vt reconocer

recoil /rɪ'kɔɪl/ vi retroceder. ● n (of gun) culatazo m

recollect /rekə'lekt/ vt recordar. ~**ion** /-ʃn/ n recuerdo m

recommend /rekə'mend/ vt recomendar. ~**ation** /-'deɪʃn/ n recomendación f

recompense /'rekəmpens/ *vt* recompensar. ● *n* recompensa *f*

reconcil|e /'rekənsaɪl/ *vt* reconciliar ⟨*people*⟩; conciliar ⟨*facts*⟩. ∼**e o.s.** resignarse (**to** a). ∼**iation** /-sɪlɪ'eɪʃn/ *n* reconciliación *f*

recondition /ri:kən'dɪʃn/ *vt* reacondicionar, arreglar

reconnaissance /rɪ'kɒnɪsns/ *n* reconocimiento *m*

reconnoitre /rekə'nɔɪtə(r)/ *vt* (*pres p* -**tring**) (*mil*) reconocer. ● *vi* hacer un reconocimiento

re: ∼consider /ri:kən'sɪdə(r)/ *vt* volver a considerar. ∼**construct** /ri:kən'strʌkt/ *vt* reconstruir. ∼**construction** /-ʃn/ *n* reconstrucción *f*

record /rɪ'kɔ:d/ *vt* (*in register*) registrar; (*in diary*) apuntar; (*mus*) grabar. /'rekɔ:d/ *n* (*file*) documentación *f*, expediente *m*; (*mus*) disco *m*; (*sport*) récord *m*. **off the** ∼ en confianza. ∼**er** /rɪ'kɔ:də(r)/ *n* registrador *m*; (*mus*) flauta *f* dulce. ∼**ing** *n* grabación *f*. ∼**player** *n* tocadiscos *m invar*

recount /rɪ'kaʊnt/ *vt* contar, relatar, referir

re-count /ri:'kaʊnt/ *vt* recontar. /'ri:kaʊnt/ *n* (*pol*) recuento *m*

recoup /rɪ'ku:p/ *vt* recuperar

recourse /rɪ'kɔ:s/ *n* recurso *m*. **have** ∼ **to** recurrir a

recover /rɪ'kʌvə(r)/ *vt* recuperar. ● *vi* reponerse. ∼**y** *n* recuperación *f*

recreation /rekrɪ'eɪʃn/ *n* recreo *m*. ∼**al** *a* de recreo

recrimination /rɪkrɪmɪ'neɪʃn/ *n* recriminación *f*

recruit /rɪ'kru:t/ *n* recluta *m*. ● *vt* reclutar. ∼**ment** *n* reclutamiento *m*

rectang|le /'rektæŋgl/ *n* rectángulo *m*. ∼**ular** /-'tæŋgjʊlə(r)/ *a* rectangular

rectif|ication /rektɪfɪ'keɪʃn/ *n* rectificación *f*. ∼**y** /'rektɪfaɪ/ *vt* rectificar

rector /'rektə(r)/ *n* párroco *m*; (*of college*) rector *m*. ∼**y** *n* rectoría *f*

recumbent /rɪ'kʌmbənt/ *a* recostado

recuperat|e /rɪ'ku:pəreɪt/ *vt* recuperar. ● *vi* reponerse. ∼**ion** /-'reɪʃn/ *n* recuperación *f*

recur /rɪ'kɜ:(r)/ *vi* (*pt* **recurred**) repetirse. ∼**rence** /rɪ'kʌrns/ *n* repetición *f*. ∼**rent** /rɪ'kʌrənt/ *a* repetido

recycle /ri:'saɪkl/ *vt* reciclar

red /red/ *a* (**redder**, **reddest**) rojo. ● *n* rojo. **in the** ∼ ⟨*account*⟩ en descubierto. ∼**breast** /'redbrest/ *n* petirrojo *m*. ∼**brick** /'redbrɪk/ *a* ⟨*univ*⟩ de reciente fundación. ∼**den** /'redn/ *vt* enrojecer. ● *vi* enrojecerse. ∼**dish** *a* rojizo

redecorate /ri:'dekəreɪt/ *vt* pintar de nuevo

rede|em /rɪ'di:m/ *vt* redimir. ∼**eming quality** *n* cualidad *f* compensadora. ∼**mption** /-'dempʃn/ *n* redención *f*

redeploy /ri:dɪ'plɔɪ/ *vt* disponer de otra manera; (*mil*) cambiar de frente

red: ∼handed *a* en flagrante. ∼ **herring** *n* (*fig*) pista *f* falsa. ∼**hot** *a* al rojo; ⟨*news*⟩ de última hora

Red Indian /red'ɪndjən/ *n* piel *m* & *f* roja

redirect /ri:daɪ'rekt/ *vt* reexpedir

red: ∼letter day *n* día *m* señalado, día *m* memorable. ∼ **light** *n* luz *f* roja. ∼**ness** *n* rojez *f*

redo /ri:'du:/ *vt* (*pt* **redid**, *pp* **redone**) rehacer

redouble /rɪ'dʌbl/ *vt* redoblar

redress /rɪ'dres/ *vt* reparar. ● *n* reparación *f*

red tape /red'teɪp/ *n* (*fig*) papeleo *m*

reduc|e /rɪ'dju:s/ *vt* reducir. ● *vi* reducirse; (*slim*) adelgazar. ∼**tion** /'dʌkʃn/ *n* reducción *f*

redundan|cy /rɪ'dʌndənsɪ/ *n* superfluidad *f*, (*unemployment*) desempleo *m*. ∼**t** /rɪ'dʌndənt/ superfluo. **be made** ∼**t** perder su empleo

reed /ri:d/ *n* caña *f*; (*mus*) lengüeta *f*

reef /ri:f/ *n* arrecife *m*

reek /ri:k/ *n* mal olor *m*. ● *vi*. ∼ (**of**) apestar a

reel /ri:l/ *n* carrete *m*. ● *vi* dar vueltas; (*stagger*) tambalearse. ● *vt*. ∼ **off** (*fig*) enumerar

refectory /rɪ'fektərɪ/ *n* refectorio *m*

refer /rɪ'fɜ:(r)/ *vt* (*pt* **referred**) remitir. ● *vi* referirse. ∼ **to** referirse a; (*consult*) consultar

referee /refə'ri:/ *n* árbitro *m*; (*for job*) referencia *f*. ● *vi* (*pt* **refereed**) arbitrar

reference /'refrəns/ *n* referencia *f*. ∼ **book** *n* libro *m* de consulta. **in** ∼ **to, with** ∼ **to** en cuanto a; (*com*) respecto a

referendum /refə'rendəm/ *n* (*pl* **-ums**) referéndum *m*

refill /ri:'fɪl/ *vt* rellenar. /'ri:fɪl/ *n* recambio *m*

refine /rɪ'faɪn/ *vt* refinar. **~d** *a* refinado. **~ment** *n* refinamiento *m*; (*tec*) refinación *f*. **~ry** /-ərɪ/ *n* refinería *f*

reflect /rɪ'flekt/ *vt* reflejar. ● *vi* reflejar; (*think*) reflexionar. **~ upon** perjudicar. **~ion** /-ʃn/ *n* reflexión *f*; (*image*) reflejo *m*. **~ive** /rɪ'flektɪv/ *a* reflector; (*thoughtful*) pensativo. **~or** *n* reflector *m*

reflex /'ri:fleks/ *a & n* reflejo (*m*)

reflexive /rɪ'fleksɪv/ *a* (*gram*) reflexivo

reform /rɪ'fɔ:m/ *vt* reformar. ● *vi* reformarse. ● *n* reforma *f*. **~er** *n* reformador *m*

refract /rɪ'frækt/ *vt* refractar

refrain[1] /rɪ'freɪn/ *n* estribillo *m*

refrain[2] /rɪ'freɪn/ *vi* abstenerse (**from** de)

refresh /rɪ'freʃ/ *vt* refrescar. **~er** /rɪ'freʃə(r)/ *a* ⟨*course*⟩ de repaso. **~ing** *a* refrescante. **~ments** *npl* (*food and drink*) refrigerio *m*

refrigerat|e /rɪ'frɪdʒəreɪt/ *vt* refrigerar. **~or** *n* nevera *f*, refrigeradora *f* (*LAm*)

refuel /ri:'fju:əl/ *vt/i* (*pt* **refuelled**) repostar

refuge /'refju:dʒ/ *n* refugio *m*. **take ~** refugiarse. **~e** /refjʊ'dʒi:/ *n* refugiado *m*

refund /rɪ'fʌnd/ *vt* reembolsar. /'ri: fʌnd/ *n* reembolso *m*

refurbish /ri:'fɜ:bɪʃ/ *vt* renovar

refusal /rɪ'fju:zl/ *n* negativa *f*

refuse[1] /rɪ'fju:z/ *vt* rehusar. ● *vi* negarse

refuse[2] /'refju:s/ *n* basura *f*

refute /rɪ'fju:t/ *vt* refutar

regain /rɪ'geɪn/ *vt* recobrar

regal /'ri:gl/ *a* real

regale /rɪ'geɪl/ *vt* festejar

regalia /rɪ'geɪlɪə/ *npl* insignias *fpl*

regard /rɪ'gɑ:d/ *vt* mirar; (*consider*) considerar. **as ~s** en cuanto a. ● *n* mirada *f*; (*care*) atención *f*; (*esteem*) respeto *m*. **~ing** *prep* en cuanto a. **~less** /rɪ'gɑ:dlɪs/ *adv* a pesar de todo. **~less of** sin tener en cuenta. **~s** *npl* saludos *mpl*. **kind ~s** *npl* recuerdos *mpl*

regatta /rɪ'gætə/ *n* regata *f*

regency /'ri:dʒənsɪ/ *n* regencia *f*

regenerate /rɪ'dʒenəreɪt/ *vt* regenerar

regent /'ri:dʒənt/ *n* regente *m & f*

regime /reɪ'ʒi:m/ *n* régimen *m*

regiment /'redʒɪmənt/ *n* regimiento *m*. **~al** /-'mentl/ *a* del regimiento. **~ation** /-en'teɪʃn/ *n* reglamentación *f* rígida

region /'ri:dʒən/ *n* región *f*. **in the ~ of** alrededor de. **~al** *a* regional

register /'redʒɪstə(r)/ *n* registro *m*. ● *vt* registrar; matricular ⟨*vehicle*⟩; declarar ⟨*birth*⟩; certificar ⟨*letter*⟩; facturar ⟨*luggage*⟩; (*indicate*) indicar; (*express*) expresar. ● *vi* (*enrol*) inscribirse; (*fig*) producir impresión. **~ office** *n* registro *m* civil

registrar /redʒɪ'strɑ:(r)/ *n* secretario *m* del registro civil; (*univ*) secretario *m* general

registration /redʒɪ'streɪʃn/ *n* registración *f*; (*in register*) inscripción *f*; (*of vehicle*) matrícula *f*

registry /'redʒɪstrɪ/ *n*. **~ office** *n* registro *m* civil

regression /rɪ'greʃn/ *n* regresión *f*

regret /rɪ'gret/ *n* pesar *m*. ● *vt* (*pt* **regretted**) lamentar. **I ~ that** siento (que). **~fully** *adv* con pesar. **~table** *a* lamentable. **~tably** *adv* lamentablemente

regular /'regjʊlə(r)/ *a* regular; (*usual*) habitual. ● *n* (*fam*) cliente *m* habitual. **~ity** /-'lærətɪ/ *n* regularidad *f*. **~ly** *adv* regularmente

regulat|e /'regjʊleɪt/ *vt* regular. **~ion** /-'leɪʃn/ *n* arreglo *m*; (*rule*) regla *f*

rehabilitat|e /ri:hə'bɪlɪteɪt/ *vt* rehabilitar. **~ion** /-'teɪʃn/ *n* rehabilitación *f*

rehash /ri:'hæʃ/ *vt* volver a presentar. /'ri:hæʃ/ *n* refrito *m*

rehears|al /rɪ'hɜ:sl/ *n* ensayo *m*. **~e** /rɪ'hɜ:s/ *vt* ensayar

reign /reɪn/ *n* reinado *m*. ● *vi* reinar

reimburse /ri:ɪm'bɜ:s/ *vt* reembolsar

reins /reɪnz/ *npl* riendas *fpl*

reindeer /'reɪndɪə(r)/ *n invar* reno *m*

reinforce /ri:ɪn'fɔ:s/ *vt* reforzar. **~ment** *n* refuerzo *m*

reinstate /ri:ɪn'steɪt/ *vt* reintegrar

reiterate /ri:'ɪtəreɪt/ *vt* reiterar

reject /rɪ'dʒekt/ *vt* rechazar. /'ri: dʒekt/ *n* producto *m* defectuoso. **~ion** /'dʒekʃn/ *n* rechazamiento *m*, rechazo *m*

rejoic|e /rɪ'dʒɔɪs/ *vi* regocijarse. **~ing** *n* regocijo *m*

rejoin /rɪ'dʒɔɪn/ *vt* reunirse con; (*answer*) replicar. **~der** /rɪ'dʒɔɪndə(r)/ *n* réplica *f*

rejuvenate /rɪ'dʒu:vəneɪt/ vt rejuvenecer

rekindle /ri:'kɪndl/ vt reavivar

relapse /rɪ'læps/ n recaída f. ● vi recaer; (into crime) reincidir

relate /rɪ'leɪt/ vt contar; (connect) relacionar. ● vi relacionarse (to con). ~d a emparentado; (ideas etc) relacionado

relation /rɪ'leɪʃn/ n relación f; (person) pariente m & f. ~ship n relación f; (blood tie) parentesco m; (affair) relaciones fpl

relative /'relətɪv/ n pariente m & f. ● a relativo. ~ly adv relativamente

relax /rɪ'læks/ vt relajar. ● vi relajarse. ~ation /ri:læk'seɪʃn/ n relajación f; (rest) descanso m; (recreation) recreo m. ~ing a relajante

relay /'ri:leɪ/ n relevo m. ~ (race) n carrera f de relevos. /rɪ'leɪ/ vt retransmitir

release /rɪ'li:s/ vt soltar; poner en libertad ⟨prisoner⟩; lanzar ⟨bomb⟩; estrenar ⟨film⟩; (mec) desenganchar; publicar ⟨news⟩; emitir ⟨smoke⟩. ● n liberación f; (of film) estreno m; (record) disco m nuevo

relegate /'relɪgeɪt/ vt relegar

relent /rɪ'lent/ vi ceder. ~less a implacable; (continuous) incesante

relevan|ce /'reləvəns/ n pertinencia f. ~t /'reləvənt/ a pertinente

reliab|ility /rɪlaɪə'bɪlətɪ/ n fiabilidad f. ~le /rɪ'laɪəbl/ a seguro; ⟨person⟩ de fiar; (com) serio

relian|ce /rɪ'laɪəns/ n dependencia f; (trust) confianza f. ~t a confiado

relic /'relɪk/ n reliquia f. ~s npl restos mpl

relie|f /rɪ'li:f/ n alivio m; (assistance) socorro m; (outline) relieve m. ~ve /rɪ'li:v/ vt aliviar; (take over from) relevar

religio|n /rɪ'lɪdʒən/ n religión f. ~us /rɪ'lɪdʒəs/ a religioso

relinquish /rɪ'lɪŋkwɪʃ/ vt abandonar, renunciar

relish /'relɪʃ/ n gusto m; (culin) salsa f. ● vt saborear. **I don't ~ the idea** no me gusta la idea

relocate /ri:ləʊ'keɪt/ vt colocar de nuevo

reluctan|ce /rɪ'lʌktəns/ n desgana f. ~t /rɪ'lʌktənt/ a mal dispuesto. **be ~t to** no tener ganas de. ~tly adv de mala gana

rely /rɪ'laɪ/ vi. ~ **on** contar con; (trust) fiarse de; (depend) depender

remain /rɪ'meɪn/ vi quedar. ~der /rɪ'meɪndə(r)/ n resto m. ~s npl restos mpl; (left-overs) sobras fpl

remand /rɪ'mɑ:nd/ vt. ~ **in custody** mantener bajo custodia. ● n. **on ~** bajo custodia

remark /rɪ'mɑ:k/ n observación f. ● vt observar. ~able a notable

remarry /ri:'mærɪ/ vi volver a casarse

remedial /rɪ'mi:dɪəl/ a remediador

remedy /'remədɪ/ n remedio m. ● vt remediar

rememb|er /rɪ'membə(r)/ vt acordarse de. ● vi acordarse. ~rance n recuerdo m

remind /rɪ'maɪnd/ vt recordar. ~er n recordatorio m; (letter) notificación f

reminisce /remɪ'nɪs/ vi recordar el pasado. ~nces npl recuerdos mpl. ~nt /remɪ'nɪsnt/ a. **be ~nt of** recordar

remiss /rɪ'mɪs/ a negligente

remission /rɪ'mɪʃn/ n remisión f; (of sentence) reducción f de condena

remit /rɪ'mɪt/ vt (pt **remitted**) perdonar; enviar ⟨money⟩. ● vi moderarse. ~tance n remesa f

remnant /'remnənt/ n resto m; (of cloth) retazo m; (trace) vestigio m

remonstrate /'remənstreɪt/ vi protestar

remorse /rɪ'mɔ:s/ n remordimiento m. ~ful a lleno de remordimiento. ~less a implacable

remote /rɪ'məʊt/ a remoto; (slight) leve; ⟨person⟩ distante. ~ **control** n mando m a distancia. ~ly adv remotamente. ~ness n lejanía f; (isolation) aislamiento m, alejamiento m; (fig) improbabilidad f

remov|able /rɪ'mu:vəbl/ a movible; (detachable) de quita y pon, separable. ~al n eliminación f; (from house) mudanza f. ~e /rɪ'mu:v/ vt quitar; (dismiss) despedir; (get rid of) eliminar; (do away with) suprimir

remunerat|e /rɪ'mju:nəreɪt/ vt remunerar. ~ion /-'reɪʃn/ n remuneración f. ~ive a remunerador

Renaissance /rə'neɪsəns/ n Renacimiento m

rend /rend/ vt (pt **rent**) rasgar

render /'rendə(r)/ *vt* rendir; *(com)* presentar; *(mus)* interpretar; prestar ⟨*help etc*⟩. **~ing** *n* *(mus)* interpretación *f*

rendezvous /'rɒndɪvu:/ *n* (*pl* **-vous** /-vu:z/) cita *f*

renegade /'renɪgeɪd/ *n* renegado

renew /rɪ'nju:/ *vt* renovar; *(resume)* reanudar. **~able** *a* renovable. **~al** *n* renovación *f*

renounce /rɪ'naʊns/ *vt* renunciar a; *(disown)* repudiar

renovat|e /'renəveɪt/ *vt* renovar. **~ion** /-'veɪʃn/ *n* renovación *f*

renown /rɪ'naʊn/ *n* fama *f*. **~ed** *a* célebre

rent[1] /rent/ *n* alquiler *m*. ● *vt* alquilar

rent[2] /rent/ *see* **rend**

rental /rentl/ *n* alquiler *m*

renunciation /rɪnʌnsɪ'eɪʃn/ *n* renuncia *f*

reopen /ri:'əʊpən/ *vt* reabrir. ● *vi* reabrirse. **~ing** *n* reapertura *f*

reorganize /ri:'ɔ:gənaɪz/ *vt* reorganizar

rep[1] /rep/ *n* *(com, fam)* representante *m* & *f*

rep[2] /rep/ *(theatre, fam)* teatro *m* de repertorio

repair /rɪ'peə(r)/ *vt* reparar; remendar ⟨*clothes, shoes*⟩. ● *n* reparación *f*; *(patch)* remiendo *m*. **in good ~** en buen estado

repartee /repɑ:'ti:/ *n* ocurrencias *fpl*

repatriat|e /ri:'pætrɪeɪt/ *vt* repatriar. **~ion** /-'eɪʃn/ *n* repatriación *f*

repay /ri:'peɪ/ *vt* (*pt* **repaid**) reembolsar; pagar ⟨*debt*⟩; *(reward)* recompensar. **~ment** *n* reembolso *m*, pago *m*

repeal /rɪ'pi:l/ *vt* abrogar. ● *n* abrogación *f*

repeat /rɪ'pi:t/ *vt* repetir. ● *vi* repetir(se). ● *n* repetición *f*. **~edly** /rɪ'pi:tɪdlɪ/ *adv* repetidas veces

repel /rɪ'pel/ *vt* (*pt* **repelled**) repeler. **~lent** *a* repelente

repent /rɪ'pent/ *vi* arrepentirse. **~ance** *n* arrepentimiento *m*. **~ant** *a* arrepentido

repercussion /ri:pə'kʌʃn/ *n* repercusión *f*

reperto|ire /'repətwɑ:(r)/ *n* repertorio *m*. **~ry** /'repətrɪ/ *n* repertorio *m*. **~ry (theatre)** *n* teatro *m* de repertorio

repetit|ion /repɪ'tɪʃn/ *n* repetición *f*. **~ious** /-'tɪʃəs/ *a*, **~ive** /rɪ'petətɪv/ *a* que se repite; *(dull)* monótono

replace /rɪ'pleɪs/ *vt* reponer; *(take the place of)* sustituir. **~ment** *n* sustitución *f*; *(person)* sustituto *m*. **~ment part** *n* recambio *m*

replay /'ri:pleɪ/ *n* *(sport)* repetición *f* del partido; *(recording)* repetición *f* inmediata

replenish /rɪ'plenɪʃ/ *vt* reponer; *(refill)* rellenar

replete /rɪ'pli:t/ *a* repleto

replica /'replɪkə/ *n* copia *f*

reply /rɪ'plaɪ/ *vt/i* contestar. ● *n* respuesta *f*

report /rɪ'pɔ:t/ *vt* anunciar; *(denounce)* denunciar. ● *vi* presentar un informe; *(present o.s.)* presentarse. ● *n* informe *m*; *(schol)* boletín *m*; *(rumour)* rumor *m*; *(newspaper)* reportaje *m*; *(sound)* estallido *m*. **~age** /repɔ:'tɑ:ʒ/ *n* reportaje *m*. **~edly** *adv* según se dice. **~er** /rɪ'pɔ:tə(r)/ *n* reportero *m*, informador *m*

repose /rɪ'pəʊz/ *n* reposo *m*

repository /rɪ'pɒzɪtrɪ/ *n* depósito *m*

repossess /ri:pə'zes/ *vt* recuperar

reprehen|d /reprɪ'hend/ *vt* reprender. **~sible** /-səbl/ *a* reprensible

represent /reprɪ'zent/ *vt* representar. **~ation** /-'teɪʃn/ *n* representación *f*. **~ative** /reprɪ'zentətɪv/ *a* representativo. ● *n* representante *m* & *f*

repress /rɪ'pres/ *vt* reprimir. **~ion** /-ʃn/ *n* represión *f*. **~ive** *a* represivo

reprieve /rɪ'pri:v/ *n* indulto *m*; *(fig)* respiro *m*. ● *vt* indultar; *(fig)* aliviar

reprimand /'reprɪmɑ:nd/ *vt* reprender. ● *n* reprensión *f*

reprint /'ri:prɪnt/ *n* reimpresión *f*; *(offprint)* tirada *f* aparte. /ri:'prɪnt/ *vt* reimprimir

reprisal /rɪ'praɪzl/ *n* represalia *f*

reproach /rɪ'prəʊtʃ/ *vt* reprochar. ● *n* reproche *m*. **~ful** *a* de reproche, reprobador. **~fully** *adv* con reproche

reprobate /'reprəbeɪt/ *n* malvado *m*; *(relig)* réprobo *m*

reproduc|e /ri:prə'dju:s/ *vt* reproducir. ● *vi* reproducirse. **~tion** /-'dʌkʃn/ *n* reproducción *f*. **~tive** /-'dʌktɪv/ *a* reproductor

reprove /rɪ'pru:v/ *vt* reprender

reptile /'reptaɪl/ *n* reptil *m*

republic /rɪ'pʌblɪk/ n república f. **~an** a & n republicano (m)

repudiate /rɪ'pjuːdɪeɪt/ vt repudiar; (refuse to recognize) negarse a reconocer

repugnan|ce /rɪ'pʌgnəns/ n repugnancia f. **~t** /rɪ'pʌgnənt/ a repugnante

repuls|e /rɪ'pʌls/ vt rechazar, repulsar. **~ion** /-ʃn/ n repulsión f. **~ive** a repulsivo

reputable /'repjʊtəbl/ a acreditado, de confianza, honroso

reputation /repjʊ'teɪʃn/ n reputación f

repute /rɪ'pjuːt/ n reputación f. **~d** /-ɪd/ a supuesto. **~dly** adv según se dice

request /rɪ'kwest/ n petición f. ● vt pedir. **~ stop** n parada f discrecional

require /rɪ'kwaɪə(r)/ vt requerir; (need) necesitar; (demand) exigir. **~d** a necesario. **~ment** n requisito m

requisite /'rekwɪzɪt/ a necesario. ● n requisito m

requisition /rekwɪ'zɪʃn/ n requisición f. ● vt requisar

resale /'riːseɪl/ n reventa f

rescind /rɪ'sɪnd/ vt rescindir

rescue /'reskjuː/ vt salvar. ● n salvamento m. **~r** /-ə(r)/ n salvador m

research /rɪ'sɜːtʃ/ n investigación f. ● vt investigar. **~er** n investigador m

resembl|ance /rɪ'zembləns/ n parecido m. **~e** /rɪ'zembl/ vt parecerse a

resent /rɪ'zent/ vt resentirse por. **~ful** a resentido. **~ment** n resentimiento m

reservation /rezə'veɪʃn/ n reserva f; (booking) reservación f

reserve /rɪ'zɜːv/ vt reservar. ● n reserva f; (in sports) suplente m & f. **~d** a reservado

reservist /rɪ'zɜːvɪst/ n reservista m & f

reservoir /'rezəvwɑː(r)/ n embalse m; (tank) depósito m

reshape /riː'ʃeɪp/ vt formar de nuevo, reorganizar

reshuffle /riː'ʃʌfl/ vt (pol) reorganizar. ● n (pol) reorganización f

reside /rɪ'zaɪd/ vi residir

residen|ce /'rezɪdəns/ n residencia f. **~ce permit** n permiso m de residencia. be in **~ce** ⟨doctor etc⟩

interno. **~t** /'rezɪdənt/ a & n residente (m & f). **~tial** /rezɪ'denʃl/ a residencial

residue /'rezɪdjuː/ n residuo m

resign /rɪ'zaɪn/ vt/i dimitir. **~ o.s. to** resignarse a. **~ation** /rezɪg'neɪʃn/ n resignación f; (from job) dimisión f. **~ed** a resignado

resilien|ce /rɪ'zɪlɪəns/ n elasticidad f; (of person) resistencia f. **~t** /rɪ'zɪlɪənt/ a elástico; ⟨person⟩ resistente

resin /'rezɪn/ n resina f

resist /rɪ'zɪst/ vt resistir. ● vi resistirse. **~ance** n resistencia f. **~ant** a resistente

resolut|e /'rezəluːt/ a resuelto. **~ion** /-'luːʃn/ n resolución f

resolve /rɪ'zɒlv/ vt resolver. **~ to do** resolverse a hacer. ● n resolución f. **~d** a resuelto

resonan|ce /'rezənəns/ n resonancia f. **~t** /'rezənənt/ a resonante

resort /rɪ'zɔːt/ vi. **~ to** recurrir a. ● n recurso m; (place) lugar m turístico. in the last **~** como último recurso

resound /rɪ'zaʊnd/ vi resonar. **~ing** a resonante

resource /rɪ'sɔːs/ n recurso m. **~ful** a ingenioso. **~fulness** n ingeniosidad f

respect /rɪ'spekt/ n (esteem) respeto m; (aspect) respecto m. with **~ to** con respecto a. ● vt respetar

respectab|ility /rɪspektə'bɪlətɪ/ n respetabilidad f. **~le** /rɪ'spektəbl/ a respetable. **~ly** adv respetablemente

respectful /rɪ'spektfl/ a respetuoso

respective /rɪ'spektɪv/ a respectivo. **~ly** adv respectivamente

respiration /respə'reɪʃn/ n respiración f

respite /'respaɪt/ n respiro m, tregua f

resplendent /rɪ'splendənt/ a resplandeciente

respon|d /rɪ'spɒnd/ vi responder. **~se** /rɪ'spɒns/ n respuesta f; (reaction) reacción f

responsib|ility /rɪspɒnsə'bɪlətɪ/ n responsabilidad f. **~le** /rɪ'spɒnsəbl/ a responsable; ⟨job⟩ de responsabilidad. **~ly** adv con formalidad

responsive /rɪ'spɒnsɪv/ a que reacciona bien. **~ to** sensible a

rest[1] /rest/ vt descansar; (lean) apoyar; (place) poner, colocar. ● vi descansar; (*lean*) apoyarse. ● *n* descanso *m*; (*mus*) pausa *f*

rest[2] /rest/ *n* (*remainder*) resto *m*, lo demás; (*people*) los demás, los otros *mpl*. ● *vi* (*remain*) quedar

restaurant /ˈrestərɒnt/ *n* restaurante *m*

restful /ˈrestfl/ *a* sosegado

restitution /restɪˈtjuːʃn/ *n* restitución *f*

restive /ˈrestɪv/ *a* inquieto

restless /ˈrestlɪs/ *a* inquieto. ~ly *adv* inquietamente. ~ness *n* inquietud *f*

restor|ation /restəˈreɪʃn/ *n* restauración *f*. ~e /rɪˈstɔ:(r)/ *vt* restablecer; restaurar ⟨*building*⟩; (*put back in position*) reponer; (*return*) devolver

restrain /rɪˈstreɪn/ *vt* contener. ~ o.s. contenerse. ~ed *a* (*moderate*) moderado; (*in control of self*) comedido. ~t *n* restricción *f*; (*moderation*) moderación *f*

restrict /rɪˈstrɪkt/ *vt* restringir. ~ion /-ʃn/ *n* restricción *f*. ~ive /rɪˈstrɪktɪv/ *a* restrictivo

result /rɪˈzʌlt/ *n* resultado *m*. ● *vi*. ~ from resultar de. ~ in dar como resultado

resume /rɪˈzjuːm/ *vt* reanudar. ● *vi* continuar

résumé /ˈrezjʊmeɪ/ *n* resumen *m*

resumption /rɪˈzʌmpʃn/ *n* continuación *f*

resurgence /rɪˈsɜːdʒəns/ *n* resurgimiento *m*

resurrect /rezəˈrekt/ *vt* resucitar. ~ion /-ʃn/ *n* resurrección *f*

resuscitat|e /rɪˈsʌsɪteɪt/ *vt* resucitar. ~ion /-ˈteɪʃn/ *n* resucitación *f*

retail /ˈriːteɪl/ *n* venta *f* al por menor. ● *a & adv* al por menor. ● *vt* vender al por menor. ● *vi* venderse al por menor. ~er *n* minorista *m & f*

retain /rɪˈteɪn/ *vt* retener; (*keep*) conservar

retainer /rɪˈteɪnə(r)/ *n* (*fee*) anticipo *m*

retaliat|e /rɪˈtælɪeɪt/ *vi* desquitarse. ~ion /-ˈeɪʃn/ *n* represalias *fpl*

retarded /rɪˈtɑːdɪd/ *a* retrasado

retentive /rɪˈtentɪv/ *a* ⟨*memory*⟩ bueno

rethink /riːˈθɪŋk/ *vt* (*pt* **rethought**) considerar de nuevo

reticen|ce /ˈretɪsns/ *n* reserva *f*. ~t /ˈretɪsnt/ *a* reservado, callado

retina /ˈretɪnə/ *n* retina *f*

retinue /ˈretɪnjuː/ *n* séquito *m*

retir|e /rɪˈtaɪə(r)/ *vi* (*from work*) jubilarse; (*withdraw*) retirarse; (*go to bed*) acostarse. ● *vt* jubilar. ~ed *a* jubilado. ~ement *n* jubilación *f*. ~ing /rɪˈtaɪərɪŋ/ *a* reservado

retort /rɪˈtɔːt/ *vt/i* replicar. ● *n* réplica *f*

retrace /riːˈtreɪs/ *vt* repasar. ~ one's steps volver sobre sus pasos

retract /rɪˈtrækt/ *vt* retirar. ● *vi* retractarse

retrain /riːˈtreɪn/ *vt* reciclar, reeducar

retreat /rɪˈtriːt/ *vi* retirarse. ● *n* retirada *f*; (*place*) refugio *m*

retrial /riːˈtraɪəl/ *n* nuevo proceso *m*

retribution /retrɪˈbjuːʃn/ *n* justo castigo

retriev|al /rɪˈtriːvl/ *n* recuperación *f*. ~e /rɪˈtriːv/ *vt* (*recover*) recuperar; (*save*) salvar; (*put right*) reparar. ~er *n* (*dog*) perro *m* cobrador

retrograde /ˈretrəɡreɪd/ *a* retrógrado

retrospect /ˈretrəspekt/ *n* retrospección *f*. in ~ retrospectivamente. ~ive /-ˈspektɪv/ *a* retrospectivo

return /rɪˈtɜːn/ *vi* volver; (*reappear*) reaparecer. ● *vt* devolver; (*com*) declarar; (*pol*) elegir. ● *n* vuelta *f*; (*com*) ganancia *f*; (*restitution*) devolución *f*. ~ of income *n* declaración *f* de ingresos. in ~ for a cambio de. many happy ~s! ¡feliz cumpleaños! ~ing /rɪˈtɜːnɪŋ/ *a*. ~ing officer *n* escrutador *m*. ~ match *n* partido *m* de desquite. ~ ticket *n* billete *m* de ida y vuelta. ~s *npl* (*com*) ingresos *mpl*

reunion /riːˈjuːnɪən/ *n* reunión *f*

reunite /riːjuːˈnaɪt/ *vt* reunir

rev /rev/ *n* (*auto, fam*) revolución *f*. ● *vt/i*. ~ (up) (*pt* **revved**) (*auto, fam*) acelerar(se)

revamp /riːˈvæmp/ *vt* renovar

reveal /rɪˈviːl/ *vt* revelar. ~ing *a* revelador

revel /ˈrevl/ *vi* (*pt* **revelled**) jaranear. ~ in deleitarse en. ~ry *n* juerga *f*

revelation /revəˈleɪʃn/ *n* revelación *f*

revenge /rɪˈvendʒ/ *n* venganza *f*; (*sport*) desquite *m*. take ~ vengarse. ● *vt* vengar. ~ful *a* vindicativo, vengativo

revenue /ˈrevənjuː/ *n* ingresos *mpl*

reverberate /rɪ'vɜ:bəreɪt/ vi ⟨light⟩ reverberar; ⟨sound⟩ resonar

revere /rɪ'vɪə(r)/ vt venerar

reverence /'revərəns/ n reverencia f

reverend /'revərənd/ a reverendo

reverent /'revərənt/ a reverente

reverie /'revərɪ/ n ensueño m

revers /rɪ'vɪə/ n (pl **revers** /rɪ'vɪəz/) n solapa f

revers|al /rɪ'vɜ:sl/ n inversión f. ∼e /rɪ'vɜ:s/ a inverso. ● n contrario m; (back) revés m; (auto) marcha f atrás. ● vt invertir; anular ⟨decision⟩; (auto) dar marcha atrás a. ● vi (auto) dar marcha atrás

revert /rɪ'vɜ:t/ vi. ∼ **to** volver a

review /rɪ'vju:/ n repaso m; (mil) revista f; (of book, play, etc) crítica f. ● vt analizar ⟨situation⟩; reseñar ⟨book, play, etc⟩. ∼**er** n crítico m

revile /rɪ'vaɪl/ vt injuriar

revis|e /rɪ'vaɪz/ vt revisar; ⟨schol⟩ repasar. ∼**ion** /-ɪʒn/ n revisión f; ⟨schol⟩ repaso m

reviv|al /rɪ'vaɪvl/ n restablecimiento m; ⟨of faith⟩ despertar m; ⟨of play⟩ reestreno m. ∼**e** /rɪ'vaɪv/ vt restablecer; resucitar ⟨person⟩. ● vi restablecerse; ⟨person⟩ volver en sí

revoke /rɪ'vəʊk/ vt revocar

revolt /rɪ'vəʊlt/ vi sublevarse. ● vt dar asco a. ● n sublevación f

revolting /rɪ'vəʊltɪŋ/ a asqueroso

revolution /revə'lu:ʃn/ n revolución f. ∼**ary** a & n revolucionario (m). ∼**ize** vt revolucionar

revolve /rɪ'vɒlv/ vi girar

revolver /rɪ'vɒlvə(r)/ n revólver m

revolving /rɪ'vɒlvɪŋ/ a giratorio

revue /rɪ'vju:/ n revista f

revulsion /rɪ'vʌlʃn/ n asco m

reward /rɪ'wɔ:d/ n recompensa f. ● vt recompensar. ∼**ing** a remunerador; (worthwhile) que vale la pena

rewrite /ri:'raɪt/ vt (pt **rewrote**, pp **rewritten**) escribir de nuevo; (change) redactar de nuevo

rhapsody /'ræpsədɪ/ n rapsodia f

rhetoric /'retərɪk/ n retórica f. ∼**al** /rɪ'tɒrɪkl/ a retórico

rheumati|c /ru:'mætɪk/ a reumático. ∼**sm** /'ru:mətɪzəm/ n reumatismo m

rhinoceros /raɪ'nɒsərəs/ n (pl **-oses**) rinoceronte m

rhubarb /'ru:bɑ:b/ n ruibarbo m

rhyme /raɪm/ n rima f; (poem) poesía f. ● vt/i rimar

rhythm /'rɪðəm/ n ritmo m. ∼**ic(al)** /'rɪðmɪk(l)/ a rítmico

rib /rɪb/ n costilla f. —vt (pt **ribbed**) (fam) tomar el pelo a

ribald /'rɪbld/ a obsceno, verde

ribbon /'rɪbən/ n cinta f

rice /raɪs/ n arroz m. ∼ **pudding** n arroz con leche

rich /rɪtʃ/ a (-er, -est) rico. ● n ricos mpl. ∼**es** npl riquezas fpl. ∼**ly** adv ricamente. ∼**ness** n riqueza f

rickety /'rɪkətɪ/ a (shaky) cojo, desvencijado

ricochet /'rɪkəʃeɪ/ n rebote m. ● vi rebotar

rid /rɪd/ vt (pt **rid**, pres p **ridding**) librar (**of** de). **get** ∼ **of** deshacerse de. ∼**dance** /'rɪdns/ n. **good** ∼**dance!** ¡qué alivio!

ridden /'rɪdn/ see **ride**. ● a (infested) infestado. ∼ **by** (oppressed) agobiado de

riddle[1] /'rɪdl/ n acertijo m

riddle[2] /'rɪdl/ vt acribillar. **be** ∼**d with** estar lleno de

ride /raɪd/ vi (pt **rode**, pp **ridden**) (on horseback) montar; (go) ir (en bicicleta, a caballo etc). **take s.o. for a** ∼ (fam) engañarle a uno. ● vt montar a ⟨horse⟩; ir en ⟨bicycle⟩; recorrer ⟨distance⟩. ● n (on horse) cabalgata f; (in car) paseo m en coche. ∼**r** /-ə(r)/ n (on horse) jinete m; (cyclist) ciclista m & f; (in document) cláusula f adicional

ridge /rɪdʒ/ n línea f, arruga f; (of mountain) cresta f; (of roof) caballete m

ridicul|e /'rɪdɪkju:l/ n irrisión f. ● vt ridiculizar. ∼**ous** /rɪ'dɪkjʊləs/ a ridículo

riding /'raɪdɪŋ/ n equitación f

rife /raɪf/ a difundido. ∼ **with** lleno de

riff-raff /'rɪfræf/ n gentuza f

rifle[1] /'raɪfl/ n fusil m

rifle[2] /'raɪfl/ vt saquear

rifle-range /'raɪflreɪndʒ/ n campo m de tiro

rift /rɪft/ n grieta f; (fig) ruptura f

rig[1] /rɪg/ vt (pt **rigged**) aparejar. ● n (at sea) plataforma f de perforación. ∼ **up** vt improvisar

rig[2] /rɪg/ vt (pej) amañar

right /raɪt/ a (correct, fair) exacto, justo; (morally) bueno; (not left) derecho; (suitable) adecuado. ● n (entitlement) derecho m; (not left) derecha f; (not evil) bien m. ∼ **of**

way *n* (*auto*) prioridad *f*. **be in the ~** tener razón. **on the ~** a la derecha. **put ~** rectificar. ● *vt* enderezar; (*fig*) corregir. ● *adv* a la derecha; (*directly*) derecho; (*completely*) completamente; (*well*) bien. **~ away** *adv* inmediatamente. **~ angle** *n* ángulo *m* recto

righteous /'raɪtʃəs/ *a* recto; (*cause*) justo

right: **~ful** /'raɪtfl/ *a* legítimo. **~fully** *adv* legítimamente. **~hand man** *n* brazo *m* derecho. **~ly** *adv* justamente. **~ wing** *a* (*pol*) derechista

rigid /'rɪdʒɪd/ *a* rígido. **~ity** /-'dʒɪdətɪ/ *n* rigidez *f*

rigmarole /'rɪgmərəʊl/ *n* galimatías *m invar*

rig|orous /'rɪgərəs/ *a* riguroso. **~our** /'rɪgə(r)/ *n* rigor *m*

rig-out /'rɪgaʊt/ *n* (*fam*) atavío *m*

rile /raɪl/ *vt* (*fam*) irritar

rim /rɪm/ *n* borde *m*; (*of wheel*) llanta *f*; (*of glasses*) montura *f*. **~med** *a* bordeado

rind /raɪnd/ *n* corteza *f*; (*of fruit*) cáscara *f*

ring[1] /rɪŋ/ *n* (*circle*) círculo *m*; (*circle of metal etc*) aro *m*; (*on finger*) anillo *m*; (*on finger with stone*) sortija *f*; (*boxing*) cuadrilátero *m*; (*bullring*) ruedo *m*, redondel *m*, plaza *f*; (*for circus*) pista *f*; ● *vt* rodear

ring[2] /rɪŋ/ *n* (*of bell*) toque *m*; (*tinkle*) tintineo *m*; (*telephone call*) llamada *f*. ● *vt* (*pt* **rang**, *pp* **rung**) hacer sonar; (*telephone*) llamar por teléfono. **~ the bell** tocar el timbre. ● *v* sonar. **~ back** *vt/i* volver a llamar. **~ off** *vi* colgar. **~ up** *vt* llamar por teléfono

ring: **~leader** /'rɪŋliːdə(r)/ *n* cabecilla *f*. **~ road** *n* carretera *f* de circunvalación

rink /rɪŋk/ *n* pista *f*

rinse /rɪns/ *vt* enjuagar. ● *n* aclarado *m*; (*of dishes*) enjuague *m*; (*for hair*) reflejo *m*

riot /'raɪət/ *n* disturbio *m*; (*of colours*) profusión *f*. **run ~** desenfrenarse. ● *vi* amotinarse. **~er** *n* amotinador *m*. **~ous** *a* tumultuoso

rip /rɪp/ *vt* (*pt* **ripped**) rasgar. ● *vi* rasgarse. **let ~** (*fig*) soltar. ● *n* rasgadura *f*. **~ off** *vt* (*sl*) robar. **~cord** *n* (*of parachute*) cuerda *f* de abertura

ripe /raɪp/ *a* (**-er, -est**) maduro. **~n** /'raɪpən/ *vt/i* madurar. **~ness** *n* madurez *f*

rip-off /'rɪpɒf/ *n* (*sl*) timo *m*

ripple /'rɪpl/ *n* rizo *m*; (*sound*) murmullo *m*. ● *vt* rizar. ● *vi* rizarse

rise /raɪz/ *vi* (*pt* **rose**, *pp* **risen**) levantarse; (*rebel*) sublevarse; (*river*) crecer; (*prices*) subir. ● *n* subida *f*; (*land*) altura *f*; (*increase*) aumento *m*; (*to power*) ascenso *m*. **give ~ to** ocasionar. **~r** /-ə(r)/ *n*. **early ~r** *n* madrugador *m*

rising /'raɪzɪŋ/ *n* (*revolt*) sublevación *f*. ● *a* (*sun*) naciente. **~ generation** *n* nueva generación *f*

risk /rɪsk/ *n* riesgo *m*. ● *vt* arriesgar. **~y** *a* (**-ier, -iest**) arriesgado

risqué /'riːskeɪ/ *a* subido de color

rissole /'rɪsəʊl/ *n* croqueta *f*

rite /raɪt/ *n* rito *m*

ritual /'rɪtjʊəl/ *a & n* ritual (*m*)

rival /'raɪvl/ *a & n* rival (*m*). ● *vt* (*pt* **rivalled**) rivalizar con. **~ry** *n* rivalidad *f*

river /'rɪvə(r)/ *n* río *m*

rivet /'rɪvɪt/ *n* remache *m*. ● *vt* remachar. **~ing** *a* fascinante

Riviera /rɪvɪ'eərə/ *n*. **the (French) ~** la Costa *f* Azul. **the (Italian) ~** la Riviera *f* (Italiana)

rivulet /'rɪvjʊlɪt/ *n* riachuelo *m*

road /rəʊd/ *n* (*in town*) calle *f*; (*between towns*) carretera *f*, (*way*) camino *m*. **on the ~** en camino. **~hog** *n* conductor *m* descortés. **~house** *n* albergue *m*. **~map** *n* mapa *m* de carreteras. **~side** /'rəʊdsaɪd/ *n* borde *m* de la carretera. **~ sign** *n* señal *f* de tráfico. **~way** *n* /'rəʊdweɪ/ *n* calzada *f*. **~works** *npl* obras *fpl*. **~worthy** /'rəʊdwɜːðɪ/ *a* (*vehicle*) seguro

roam /rəʊm/ *vi* vagar

roar /rɔː(r)/ *n* rugido *m*; (*laughter*) carcajada *f*. ● *vt/i* rugir. **~ past** (*vehicles*) pasar con estruendo. **~ with laughter** reírse a carcajadas. **~ing** /'rɔːrɪŋ/ *a* (*trade etc*) activo

roast /rəʊst/ *vt* asar; tostar (*coffee*). ● *vi* asarse; (*person, coffee*) tostarse. ● *a & n* asado (*m*). **~ beef** *n* rosbif *m*

rob /rɒb/ *vt* (*pt* **robbed**) robar; asaltar (*bank*). **~ of** privar de. **~ber** *n* ladrón *m*; (*of bank*) atracador *m*. **~bery** *n* robo *m*

robe /rəʊb/ *n* manto *m*; (*univ etc*) toga *f*. **bath~** *n* albornoz *m*

robin /'rɒbɪn/ *n* petirrojo *m*

robot /'rəʊbɒt/ n robot m, autómata m

robust /rəʊ'bʌst/ a robusto

rock[1] /rɒk/ n roca f; (boulder) peñasco m; (sweet) caramelo m en forma de barra; (of Gibraltar) peñón m. **on the ~s** ⟨drink⟩ con hielo; (fig) arruinado. **be on the ~s** ⟨marriage etc⟩ andar mal

rock[2] /rɒk/ vt mecer; (shake) sacudir. ● vi mecerse; (shake) sacudirse. ● n (mus) música f rock

rock: ~bottom a (fam) bajísimo. **~ery** /'rɒkərɪ/ n cuadro m alpino, rocalla f

rocket /'rɒkɪt/ n cohete m

rock: ~ing-chair n mecedora f. **~ing-horse** n caballo m de balancín. **~y** /'rɒkɪ/ a (-ier, -iest) rocoso; (fig, shaky) bamboleante

rod /rɒd/ n vara f; (for fishing) caña f; (metal) barra f

rode /rəʊd/ see **ride**

rodent /'rəʊdnt/ n roedor m

rodeo /rə'deɪəʊ/ n (pl -os) rodeo m

roe[1] /rəʊ/ n (fish eggs) hueva f

roe[2] /rəʊ/ (pl **roe**, or **roes**) (deer) corzo m

rogu|e /rəʊg/ n pícaro m. **~ish** a picaresco

role /rəʊl/ n papel m

roll /rəʊl/ vt hacer rodar; (roll up) enrollar; (flatten lawn) allanar; aplanar ⟨pastry⟩. ● vi rodar; ⟨ship⟩ balancearse; (on floor) revolcarse. **be ~ing (in money)** (fam) nadar (en dinero). ● n rollo m; (of ship) balanceo m; (of drum) redoble m; (of thunder) retumbo m; (bread) panecillo m; (list) lista f. **~ over** vi (turn over) dar una vuelta. **~ up** vt enrollar; arremangar ⟨sleeve⟩. ● vi (fam) llegar. **~call** n lista f

roller /'rəʊlə(r)/ n rodillo m; (wheel) rueda f; (for hair) rulo m, bigudí m. **~-coaster** n montaña f rusa. **~-skate** n patín m de ruedas

rollicking /'rɒlɪkɪŋ/ a alegre

rolling /'rəʊlɪŋ/ a ondulado. **~-pin** n rodillo m

Roman /'rəʊmən/ a & n romano (m). **~ Catholic** a & n católico (m) (romano)

romance /rə'mæns/ n novela f romántica; (love) amor m; (affair) aventura f

Romania /rəʊ'meɪnɪə/ n Rumania f. **~n** a & n rumano (m)

romantic /rəʊ'mæntɪk/ a romántico. **~ism** n romanticismo m

Rome /rəʊm/ n Roma f

romp /rɒmp/ vi retozar. ● n retozo m

rompers /'rɒmpəz/ npl pelele m

roof /ru:f/ n techo m, tejado m; (of mouth) paladar m. ● vt techar. **~-garden** n jardín m en la azotea. **~-rack** n baca f. **~-top** n tejado m

rook[1] /rʊk/ n grajo m

rook[2] /rʊk/ (in chess) torre f

room /ru:m/ n cuarto m, habitación f; (bedroom) dormitorio m; (space) sitio m; (large hall) sala f. **~y** a espacioso; ⟨clothes⟩ holgado

roost /ru:st/ n percha f. ● vi descansar. **~er** n gallo m

root[1] /ru:t/ n raíz f. **take ~** echar raíces. ● vt hacer arraigar. ● vi echar raíces, arraigarse

root[2] /ru:t/ vt/i. **~ about** vi hurgar. **~ for** vi (Amer, sl) alentar. **~ out** vt extirpar

rootless /'ru:tlɪs/ a desarraigado

rope /rəʊp/ n cuerda f. **know the ~s** estar al corriente. ● vt atar. **~ in** vt agarrar

rosary /'rəʊzərɪ/ n (relig) rosario m

rose[1] /rəʊz/ n rosa f; (nozzle) roseta f

rose[2] /rəʊz/ see **rise**

rosé /'rəʊzeɪ/ n (vino m) rosado m

rosette /rəʊ'zet/ n escarapela f

roster /'rɒstə(r)/ n lista f

rostrum /'rɒstrəm/ n tribuna f

rosy /'rəʊzɪ/ a (-ier, -iest) rosado; ⟨skin⟩ sonrosado

rot /rɒt/ vt (pt **rotted**) pudrir. ● vi pudrirse. ● n putrefacción f; (sl) tonterías fpl

rota /'rəʊtə/ n lista f

rotary /'rəʊtərɪ/ a giratorio, rotativo

rotat|e /rəʊ'teɪt/ vt girar; (change round) alternar. ● vi girar; (change round) alternarse. **~ion** /-ʃn/ n rotación f

rote /rəʊt/ n. **by ~** maquinalmente, de memoria

rotten /'rɒtn/ a podrido; (fam) desagradable

rotund /rəʊ'tʌnd/ a redondo; ⟨person⟩ regordete

rouge /ru:ʒ/ n colorete m

rough /rʌf/ a (-er, -est) áspero; ⟨person⟩ tosco; (bad) malo; ⟨ground⟩ accidentado; (violent) brutal; (approximate) aproximado; ⟨diamond⟩ bruto. ● adv duro. **~ copy** n, **~ draft** n borrador m. ● n (*ruffian*) matón *m*. ● *vt*. ~ **it** vivir sin comodidades. ~ **out** *vt* esbozar

roughage /'rʌfɪdʒ/ *n* alimento *m* indigesto, afrecho *m*; (*for animals*) forraje *m*

rough: ~**and-ready** *a* improvisado. ~**and-tumble** *n* riña *f*. ~**ly** *adv* toscamente; (*more or less*) más o menos. ~**ness** *n* aspereza *f*; (*lack of manners*) incultura *f*; (*crudeness*) tosquedad *f*

roulette /ru:'let/ *n* ruleta *f*

round /raʊnd/ *a* (**-er, -est**) redondo. ● *n* círculo *m*; (*slice*) tajada *f*; (*of visits, drinks*) ronda *f*; (*of competition*) vuelta *f*; (*boxing*) asalto *m*. ● *prep* alrededor de. ● *adv* alrededor. ~ **about** (*approximately*) aproximadamente. **come** ~ **to, go** ~ **to** (*a friend etc*) pasar por casa de. ● *vt* redondear; doblar (*corner*). ~ **off** *vt* terminar. ~ **up** *vt* reunir; redondear (*price*)

roundabout /'raʊndəbaʊt/ *n* tiovivo *m*; (*for traffic*) glorieta *f*. ● *a* indirecto

rounders /'raʊndəz/ *n* juego *m* parecido al béisbol

round: ~**ly** *adv* (*bluntly*) francamente. ~ **trip** *n* viaje *m* de ida y vuelta. ~**up** *n* reunión *f*; (*of suspects*) redada *f*

rous|e /raʊz/ *vt* despertar. ~**ing** *a* excitante

rout /raʊt/ *n* derrota *f*. ● *vt* derrotar

route /ru:t/ *n* ruta *f*; (*naut, aviat*) rumbo *m*; (*of bus*) línea *f*

routine /ru:'ti:n/ *n* rutina *f*. ● *a* rutinario

rov|e /rəʊv/ *vt/i* vagar (por). ~**ing** *a* errante

row[1] /rəʊ/ *n* fila *f*

row[2] /rəʊ/ *n* (*in boat*) paseo *m* en bote (de remos). ● *vi* remar

row[3] /raʊ/ *n* (*noise, fam*) ruido *m*; (*quarrel*) pelea *f*. ● *vi* (*fam*) pelearse

rowdy /'raʊdɪ/ *a* (**-ier, -iest**) *n* ruidoso

rowing /'rəʊɪŋ/ *n* remo *m*. ~**boat** *n* bote *m* de remos

royal /'rɔɪəl/ *a* real. ~**ist** *a* & *n* monárquico (*m*). ~**ly** *adv* magníficamente. ~**ty** /'rɔɪəltɪ/ *n* familia *f* real; (*payment*) derechos *mpl* de autor

rub /rʌb/ *vt* (*pt* **rubbed**) frotar. ~ **it in** insistir en algo. ● *n* frotamiento *m*. ~ **off on s.o.** *vi* pegársele a uno. ~ **out** *vt* borrar

rubber /'rʌbə(r)/ *n* goma *f*. ~ **band** *n* goma *f* (elástica). ~ **stamp** *n* sello *m* de goma. ~**stamp** *vt* (*fig*) aprobar maquinalmente. ~**y** *a* parecido al caucho

rubbish /'rʌbɪʃ/ *n* basura *f*; (*junk*) trastos *mpl*; (*fig*) tonterías *fpl*. ~**y** *a* sin valor

rubble /'rʌbl/ *n* escombros; (*small*) cascajo *m*

ruby /'ru:bɪ/ *n* rubí *m*

rucksack /'rʌksæk/ *n* mochila *f*

rudder /'rʌdə(r)/ *n* timón *m*

ruddy /'rʌdɪ/ *a* (**-ier, -iest**) rubicundo; (*sl*) maldito

rude /ru:d/ *a* (**-er, -est**) descortés, mal educado; (*improper*) indecente; (*brusque*) brusco. ~**ly** *adv* con descortesía. ~**ness** *n* descortesía *f*

rudiment /'ru:dɪmənt/ *n* rudimento *m*. ~**ary** /-'mentrɪ/ *a* rudimentario

rueful /'ru:fl/ *a* triste

ruffian /'rʌfɪən/ *n* rufián *m*

ruffle /'rʌfl/ *vt* despeinar (*hair*); arrugar (*clothes*). ● *n* (*frill*) volante *m*, fruncido *m*

rug /rʌg/ *n* tapete *m*; (*blanket*) manta *f*

Rugby /'rʌgbɪ/ *n*. ~ (**football**) *n* rugby *m*

rugged /'rʌgɪd/ *a* desigual; (*landscape*) accidentado; (*fig*) duro

ruin /'ru:ɪn/ *n* ruina *f*. ● *vt* arruinar. ~**ous** *a* ruinoso

rule /ru:l/ *n* regla *f*; (*custom*) costumbre *f*; (*pol*) dominio *m*. **as a** ~ por regla general. ● *vt* gobernar; (*master*) dominar; (*jurid*) decretar; (*decide*) decidir. ~ **out** *vt* descartar. ~**d paper** *n* papel *m* rayado

ruler /'ru:lə(r)/ *n* (*sovereign*) soberano *m*; (*leader*) gobernante *m* & *f*; (*measure*) regla *f*

ruling /'ru:lɪŋ/ *a* (*class*) dirigente. ● *n* decisión *f*

rum /rʌm/ *n* ron *m*

rumble /'rʌmbl/ *vi* retumbar; (*stomach*) hacer ruidos. ● *n* retumbo *m*; (*of stomach*) ruido *m*

ruminant /'ru:mɪnənt/ *a* & *n* rumiante (*m*)

rummage /'rʌmɪdʒ/ *vi* hurgar

rumour /'ru:mə(r)/ *n* rumor *m*. ● *vt*. **it is ~ed that** se dice que

rump /rʌmp/ *n* (*of horse*) grupa *f*; (*of fowl*) rabadilla *f*. ~ **steak** *n* filete *m*

rumpus /'rʌmpəs/ *n* (*fam*) jaleo *m*

run /rʌn/ *vi* (*pt* **ran**, *pp* **run**, *pres p* **running**) correr; (*flow*) fluir; (*pass*) pasar; (*function*) funcionar; (*melt*) derretirse; (*bus etc*) circular; (*play*) representarse (continuamente); ⟨*colours*⟩ correrse; (*in election*) presentarse. ● *vt* tener ⟨*house*⟩; (*control*) dirigir; correr ⟨*risk*⟩; (*drive*) conducir; (*pass*) pasar; (*present*) presentar; forzar ⟨*blockade*⟩. ∼ **a temperature** tener fiebre. ● *n* corrida *f*, carrera *f*; (*journey*) viaje *m*; (*outing*) paseo *m*, excursión *f*; (*distance travelled*) recorrido *m*; (*ladder*) carrera *f*; (*ski*) pista *f*; (*series*) serie *f*. **at a** ∼ corriendo. **have the** ∼ **of** tener a su disposición. **in the long** ∼ a la larga. **on the** ∼ de fuga. ∼ **across** *vt* toparse con ⟨*friend*⟩. ∼ **away** *vi* escaparse. ∼ **down** *vi* bajar corriendo; ⟨*clock*⟩ quedarse sin cuerda. ● *vt* (*auto*) atropellar; (*belittle*) denigrar. ∼ **in** *vt* rodar ⟨*vehicle*⟩. ● *vi* entrar corriendo. ∼ **into** *vt* toparse con ⟨*friend*⟩; (*hit*) chocar con. ∼ **off** *vt* tirar ⟨*copies etc*⟩. ∼ **out** *vi* salir corriendo; ⟨*liquid*⟩ salirse; (*fig*) agotarse. ∼ **out of** quedar sin. ∼ **over** *vt* (*auto*) atropellar. ∼ **through** *vt* traspasar; (*revise*) repasar. ∼ **up** *vt* hacerse ⟨*bill*⟩. ● *vi* subir corriendo. ∼ **up against** tropezar con ⟨*difficulties*⟩. ∼**away** /'rʌnəweɪ/ *a* fugitivo; ⟨*success*⟩ decisivo; ⟨*inflation*⟩ galopante. ● *n* fugitivo *m*. ∼ **down** *a* ⟨*person*⟩ agotado. ∼**down** *n* informe *m* detallado

rung[1] /rʌŋ/ *n* (*of ladder*) peldaño *m*

rung[2] /rʌŋ/ *see* **ring**

run: ∼**ner** /'rʌnə(r)/ *n* corredor *m*; (*on sledge*) patín *m*. ∼**ner bean** *n* judía *f* escarlata. ∼**ner-up** *n* subcampeón *m*, segundo *m*. ∼**ning** /'rʌnɪŋ/ *n* (*race*) carrera *f*. **be in the** ∼**ning** tener posibilidades de ganar. ● *a* en marcha; ⟨*water*⟩ corriente; ⟨*commentary*⟩ en directo. **four times** ∼**ning** cuatro veces seguidas. ∼**ny** /'rʌnɪ/ *a* líquido; ⟨*nose*⟩ que moquea. ∼**-of-the-mill** *a* ordinario. ∼**up** *n* período *m* que precede. ∼**way** /'rʌnweɪ/ *n* pista *f*

rupture /'rʌptʃə(r)/ *n* ruptura *f*; (*med*) hernia *f*. ● *vt/i* quebrarse

rural /'rʊərəl/ *a* rural

ruse /ruːz/ *n* ardid *m*

rush[1] /rʌʃ/ *n* (*haste*) prisa *f*; (*crush*) bullicio *m*. ● *vi* precipitarse. ● *vt* apresurar; (*mil*) asaltar

rush[2] /rʌʃ/ *n* (*plant*) junco *m*

rush-hour /'rʌʃaʊə(r)/ *n* hora *f* punta

rusk /rʌsk/ *n* galleta *f*, tostada *f*

russet /'rʌsɪt/ *a* rojizo. ● *n* (*apple*) manzana *f* rojiza

Russia /'rʌʃə/ *n* Rusia *f*. ∼**n** *a* & *n* ruso (*m*)

rust /rʌst/ *n* orín *m*. ● *vt* oxidar. ● *vi* oxidarse

rustic /'rʌstɪk/ *a* rústico

rustle /'rʌsl/ *vt* hacer susurrar; (*Amer*) robar. ∼ **up** (*fam*) preparar. ● *vi* susurrar

rust: ∼**proof** *a* inoxidable. ∼**y** *a* (**-ier, -iest**) oxidado

rut /rʌt/ *n* surco *m*. **in a** ∼ en la rutina de siempre

ruthless /'ruːθlɪs/ *a* despiadado. ∼**ness** *n* crueldad *f*

rye /raɪ/ *n* centeno *m*

S

S *abbr* (*south*) sur *m*

sabbath /'sæbəθ/ *n* día *m* de descanso; (*Christian*) domingo *m*; (*Jewish*) sábado *m*

sabbatical /sə'bætɪkl/ *a* sabático

sabot|age /'sæbətɑːʒ/ *n* sabotaje *m*. ● *vt* sabotear. ∼**eur** /-'tɜː(r)/ *n* saboteador *m*

saccharin /'sækərɪn/ *n* sacarina *f*

sachet /'sæʃeɪ/ *n* bolsita *f*

sack[1] /sæk/ *n* saco *m*. **get the** ∼ (*fam*) ser despedido. ● *vt* (*fam*) despedir. ∼**ing** *n* arpillera *f*; (*fam*) despido *m*

sack[2] /sæk/ *vt* (*plunder*) saquear

sacrament /'sækrəmənt/ *n* sacramento *m*

sacred /'seɪkrɪd/ *a* sagrado

sacrifice /'sækrɪfaɪs/ *n* sacrificio *m*. ● *vt* sacrificar

sacrileg|e /'sækrɪlɪdʒ/ *n* sacrilegio *m*. ∼**ious** /-'lɪdʒəs/ *a* sacrílego

sacrosanct /'sækrəʊsæŋkt/ *a* sacrosanto

sad /sæd/ *a* (**sadder, saddest**) triste. ∼**den** /'sædn/ *vt* entristecer

saddle /'sædl/ *n* silla *f*. **be in the** ∼ (*fig*) tener las riendas. ● *vt* ensillar ⟨*horse*⟩. ∼ **s.o. with** (*fig*) cargar a uno con. ∼**bag** *n* alforja *f*

sad: ∼**ly** *adv* tristemente; (*fig*) desgraciadamente. ∼**ness** *n* tristeza *f*

sadis|m /'seɪdɪzəm/ *n* sadismo *m*. ∼**t** /'seɪdɪst/ *n* sádico *m*. ∼**tic** /sə'dɪstɪk/ *a* sádico

safari /sə'fɑːrɪ/ n safari m
safe /seɪf/ a (-er, -est) seguro; (out of danger) salvo; (cautious) prudente. **~ and sound** sano y salvo. ● n caja f fuerte. **~ deposit** n caja f de seguridad. **~guard** /'seɪfgɑːd/ n salvaguardia f. ● vt salvaguardar. **~ly** adv sin peligro; (in safe place) en lugar seguro. **~ty** /'seɪftɪ/ n seguridad f. **~ty belt** n cinturón m de seguridad. **~ty-pin** n imperdible m. **~ty-valve** n válvula f de seguridad
saffron /'sæfrən/ n azafrán m
sag /sæg/ vi (pt **sagged**) hundirse; (give) aflojarse
saga /'sɑːgə/ n saga f
sage¹ /seɪdʒ/ n (wise person) sabio m. ● a sabio
sage² /seɪdʒ/ n (herb) salvia f
sagging /'sægɪŋ/ a hundido; (fig) decaído
Sagittarius /sædʒɪ'teərɪəs/ n (astr) Sagitario m
sago /'seɪgəʊ/ n sagú m
said /sed/ see **say**
sail /seɪl/ n vela f; (trip) paseo m (en barco). ● vi navegar; (leave) partir; (sport) practicar la vela; (fig) deslizarse. ● vt manejar ‹boat›. **~ing** n (sport) vela f. **~ing-boat** n, **~ing-ship** n barco m de vela. **~or** /'seɪlə(r)/ n marinero m
saint /seɪnt, before name sənt/ n santo m. **~ly** a santo
sake /seɪk/ n. **for the ~ of** por, por el amor de
salacious /sə'leɪʃəs/ a salaz
salad /'sæləd/ n ensalada f. **~ bowl** n ensaladera f. **~ cream** n mayonesa f. **~-dressing** n aliño m
salar|ied /'sælərɪd/ a asalariado. **~y** /'sælərɪ/ n sueldo m
sale /seɪl/ n venta f; (at reduced prices) liquidación f. **for ~** (sign) se vende. **on ~** en venta. **~able** /'seɪləbl/ a vendible. **~sman** /'seɪlzmən/ n (pl -men) vendedor m; (in shop) dependiente m; (traveller) viajante m. **~swoman** n (pl -women) vendedora f; (in shop) dependienta f
salient /'seɪlɪənt/ a saliente, destacado
saliva /sə'laɪvə/ n saliva f
sallow /'sæləʊ/ a (-er, -est) amarillento
salmon /'sæmən/ n invar salmón m. **~ trout** n trucha f salmonada
salon /'sælɒn/ n salón m

saloon /sə'luːn/ n (on ship) salón m; (Amer, bar) bar m; (auto) turismo m
salt /sɔːlt/ n sal f. ● a salado. ● vt salar. **~cellar** n salero m. **~y** a salado
salutary /'sæljʊtrɪ/ a saludable
salute /sə'luːt/ n saludo m. ● vt saludar. ● vi hacer un saludo
salvage /'sælvɪdʒ/ n salvamento m; (goods) objetos mpl salvados. ● vt salvar
salvation /sæl'veɪʃn/ n salvación f
salve /sælv/ n ungüento m
salver /'sælvə(r)/ n bandeja f
salvo /'sælvəʊ/ n (pl -os) salva f
same /seɪm/ a igual (as que); (before noun) mismo (as que). **at the ~ time** al mismo tiempo. ● pron. **the ~** el mismo, la misma, los mismos, las mismas. **do the ~ as** hacer como. ● adv. **the ~** de la misma manera. **all the ~** de todas formas
sample /'sɑːmpl/ n muestra f. ● vt probar ‹food›
sanatorium /sænə'tɔːrɪəm/ n (pl -ums) sanatorio m
sanctify /'sæŋktɪfaɪ/ vt santificar
sanctimonious /sæŋktɪ'məʊnɪəs/ a beato
sanction /'sæŋkʃn/ n sanción f. ● vt sancionar
sanctity /'sæŋktətɪ/ n santidad f
sanctuary /'sæŋktʃʊərɪ/ n (relig) santuario m; (for wildlife) reserva f; (refuge) asilo m
sand /sænd/ n arena f. ● vt enarenar. **~s** npl (beach) playa f
sandal /'sændl/ n sandalia f
sand: ~castle n castillo m de arena. **~paper** /'sændpeɪpə(r)/ n papel m de lija. ● vt lijar. **~storm** /'sændstɔːm/ n tempestad f de arena
sandwich /'sænwɪdʒ/ n bocadillo m, sandwich m. ● vt. **~ed between** intercalado
sandy /'sændɪ/ a arenoso
sane /seɪn/ a (-er, -est) ‹person› cuerdo; ‹judgement, policy› razonable. **~ly** adv sensatamente
sang /sæŋ/ see **sing**
sanitary /'sænɪtrɪ/ a higiénico; ‹system etc› sanitario. **~ towel** n, **~ napkin** n (Amer) compresa f (higiénica)
sanitation /sænɪ'teɪʃn/ n higiene f; (drainage) sistema m sanitario
sanity /'sænɪtɪ/ n cordura f; (fig) sensatez f
sank /sæŋk/ see **sink**

Santa Claus /'sæntəklɔːz/ n Papá m Noel

sap /sæp/ n (in plants) savia f. ● vt (pt **sapped**) agotar

sapling /'sæplɪŋ/ n árbol m joven

sapphire /'sæfaɪə(r)/ n zafiro m

sarcas|m /'sɑːkæzəm/ n sarcasmo m. **~tic** /-'kæstɪk/ a sarcástico

sardine /sɑː'diːn/ n sardina f

Sardinia /sɑː'dɪnɪə/ n Cerdeña f. **~n** a & n sardo (m)

sardonic /sɑː'dɒnɪk/ a sardónico

sash /sæʃ/ n (over shoulder) banda f; (round waist) fajín m. **~-window** n ventana f de guillotina

sat /sæt/ see **sit**

satanic /sə'tænɪk/ a satánico

satchel /'sætʃl/ n cartera f

satellite /'sætəlaɪt/ n & a satélite (m)

satiate /'seɪʃɪeɪt/ vt saciar

satin /'sætɪn/ n raso m. ● a de raso; (like satin) satinado

satir|e /'sætaɪə(r)/ n sátira f. **~ical** /sə'tɪrɪkl/ a satírico. **~ist** /'sætərɪst/ n satírico m. **~ize** /'sætəraɪz/ vt satirizar

satisfaction /sætɪs'fækʃn/ n satisfacción f

satisfactor|ily /sætɪs'fæktərɪlɪ/ adv satisfactoriamente. **~y** /sætɪs'fæktərɪ/ a satisfactorio

satisfy /'sætɪsfaɪ/ vt satisfacer; (convince) convencer. **~ing** a satisfactorio

satsuma /sæt'suːmə/ n mandarina f

saturat|e /'sætʃəreɪt/ vt saturar, empapar. **~ed** a saturado, empapado. **~ion** /-'reɪʃn/ n saturación f

Saturday /'sætədeɪ/ n sábado m

sauce /sɔːs/ n salsa f; (cheek) descaro m. **~pan** /'sɔːspən/ n cazo m

saucer /'sɔːsə(r)/ n platillo m

saucy /'sɔːsɪ/ a (-ier, -iest) descarado

Saudi Arabia /saʊdɪə'reɪbɪə/ n Arabia f Saudí

sauna /'sɔːnə/ n sauna f

saunter /'sɔːntə(r)/ vi deambular, pasearse

sausage /'sɒsɪdʒ/ n salchicha f

savage /'sævɪdʒ/ a salvaje; (fierce) feroz; (furious, fam) rabioso. ● n salvaje m & f. ● vt atacar. **~ry** n ferocidad f

sav|e /seɪv/ vt salvar; ahorrar (money, time); (prevent) evitar. ● n (football) parada f. ● prep salvo, con excepción de. **~er** n ahorrador m. **~ing** n ahorro m. **~ings** npl ahorros mpl

saviour /'seɪvɪə(r)/ n salvador m

savour /'seɪvə(r)/ n sabor m. ● vt saborear. **~y** a (appetizing) sabroso; (not sweet) no dulce. ● n aperitivo m (no dulce)

saw[1] /sɔː/ see **see**[1]

saw[2] /sɔː/ n sierra f. ● vt (pt **sawed**, pp **sawn**) serrar. **~dust** /'sɔːdʌst/ n serrín m. **~n** /sɔːn/ see **saw**

saxophone /'sæksəfəʊn/ n saxófono m

say /seɪ/ vt/i (pt **said** /sed/) decir; rezar (prayer). **I ~!** ¡no me digas! ● n. **have a ~** expresar una opinión; (in decision) tener voz en capítulo. **have no ~** no tener ni voz ni voto. **~ing** /'seɪɪŋ/ n refrán m

scab /skæb/ n costra f; (blackleg, fam) esquirol m

scaffold /'skæfəʊld/ n (gallows) cadalso m, patíbulo m. **~ing** /'skæfəldɪŋ/ n (for workmen) andamio m

scald /skɔːld/ vt escaldar; calentar (milk etc). ● n escaldadura f

scale[1] /skeɪl/ n escala f

scale[2] /skeɪl/ n (of fish) escama f

scale[3] /skeɪl/ vt (climb) escalar. **~ down** vt reducir (proporcionalmente)

scales /skeɪlz/ npl (for weighing) balanza f, peso m

scallop /'skɒləp/ n venera f; (on dress) festón m

scalp /skælp/ n cuero m cabelludo. ● vt quitar el cuero cabelludo a

scalpel /'skælpəl/ n escalpelo m

scamp /skæmp/ n bribón m

scamper /'skæmpə(r)/ vi. **~ away** marcharse corriendo

scampi /'skæmpɪ/ npl gambas fpl grandes

scan /skæn/ vt (pt **scanned**) escudriñar; (quickly) echar un vistazo a; (radar) explorar. ● vi (poetry) estar bien medido

scandal /'skændl/ n escándalo m; (gossip) chismorreo m. **~ize** /'skændəlaɪz/ vt escandalizar. **~ous** a escandaloso

Scandinavia /skændɪ'neɪvɪə/ n Escandinavia f. **~n** a & n escandinavo (m)

scant /skænt/ a escaso. **~ily** adv insuficientemente. **~y** /'skæntɪ/ a (-ier, -iest) escaso

scapegoat /'skeɪpgəʊt/ n cabeza f de turco

scar /skɑ:(r)/ n cicatriz f. ● vt (pt **scarred**) dejar una cicatriz en. ● vi cicatrizarse

scarc|e /skeəs/ a (**-er**, **-est**) escaso. **make o.s. ~e** (fam) mantenerse lejos. **~ely** /'skeəslı/ adv apenas. **~ity** n escasez f

scare /'skeə(r)/ vt asustar. **be ~d** tener miedo. ● n susto m. **~crow** /'skeəkrəʊ/ n espantapájaros m invar. **~monger** /'skeəmʌŋgə(r)/ n alarmista m & f

scarf /skɑ:f/ n (pl **scarves**) bufanda f; (over head) pañuelo m

scarlet /'skɑ:lət/ a escarlata f. **~ fever** n escarlatina f

scary /'skeərı/ a (**-ier**, **-iest**) que da miedo

scathing /'skeɪðɪŋ/ a mordaz

scatter /'skætə(r)/ vt (throw) esparcir; (disperse) dispersar. ● vi dispersarse. **~brained** a atolondrado. **~ed** a disperso; (occasional) esporádico

scatty /'skætı/ a (**-ier**, **-iest**) (sl) atolondrado

scavenge /'skævɪndʒ/ vi buscar (en la basura). **~r** /-ə(r)/ n (vagrant) persona f que busca objetos en la basura

scenario /sɪ'nɑ:rɪəʊ/ n (pl **-os**) argumento; (of film) guión m

scen|e /si:n/ n escena f; (sight) vista f; (fuss) lío m. **behind the ~es** entre bastidores. **~ery** /'si:nərı/ n paisaje m; (in theatre) decorado m. **~ic** /'si:nɪk/ a pintoresco

scent /sent/ n olor m; (perfume) perfume m; (trail) pista f. ● vt presentir; (make fragrant) perfumar

sceptic /'skeptɪk/ n escéptico m. **~al** a escéptico. **~ism** /-sɪzəm/ n escepticismo m

sceptre /'septə(r)/ n cetro m

schedule /'ʃedju:l, 'skedju:l/ n programa f; (timetable) horario m. **behind ~** con retraso. **on ~** sin retraso. ● vt proyectar. **~d flight** n vuelo m regular

scheme /ski:m/ n proyecto m; (plot) intriga f. ● vi hacer proyectos; (pej) intrigar. **~r** n intrigante m & f

schism /'sɪzəm/ n cisma m

schizophrenic /skɪtsə'frenɪk/ a & n esquizofrénico (m)

scholar /'skɒlə(r)/ n erudito m. **~ly** a erudito. **~ship** n erudición f; (grant) beca f

scholastic /skə'læstɪk/ a escolar

school /sku:l/ n escuela f; (of univ) facultad f. ● a ⟨age, holidays, year⟩ escolar. ● vt enseñar; (discipline) disciplinar. **~boy** /'sku:lbɔɪ/ n colegial m. **~girl** /-gɜ:l/ n colegiala f. **~ing** n instrucción f. **~master** /'sku:lmɑ:stə(r)/ n (primary) maestro m; (secondary) profesor m. **~mistress** n (primary) maestra f; (secondary) profesora f. **~teacher** n (primary) maestro m; (secondary) profesor m

schooner /'sku:nə(r)/ n goleta f; (glass) vaso m grande

sciatica /saɪ'ætɪkə/ n ciática f

scien|ce /'saɪəns/ n ciencia f. **~ce fiction** n ciencia y ficción. **~tific** /-'tɪfɪk/ a científico. **~tist** /'saɪəntɪst/ n científico m

scintillate /'sɪntɪleɪt/ vi centellear

scissors /'sɪsəz/ npl tijeras fpl

sclerosis /sklə'rəʊsɪs/ n esclerosis f

scoff /skɒf/ vt (sl) zamparse. ● vi. **~ at** mofarse de

scold /skəʊld/ vt regañar. **~ing** n regaño m

scone /skɒn/ n (tipo m de) bollo m

scoop /sku:p/ n paleta f; (news) noticia f exclusiva. ● vt. **~ out** excavar. **~ up** recoger

scoot /sku:t/ vi (fam) largarse corriendo. **~er** /'sku:tə(r)/ n escúter m; (for child) patinete m

scope /skəʊp/ n alcance m; (opportunity) oportunidad f

scorch /skɔ:tʃ/ vt chamuscar. **~er** n (fam) día m de mucho calor. **~ing** a (fam) de mucho calor

score /skɔ:(r)/ n tanteo m; (mus) partitura f; (twenty) veintena f; (reason) motivo m. **on that ~** en cuanto a eso. ● vt marcar; (slash) rayar; (mus) instrumentar; conseguir ⟨success⟩. ● vi marcar un tanto; (keep score) tantear. **~ over s.o.** aventajar a. **~r** /-ə(r)/ n tanteador m

scorn /skɔ:n/ n desdén m. ● vt desdeñar. **~ful** a desdeñoso. **~fully** adv desdeñosamente

Scorpio /'skɔ:pɪəʊ/ n (astr) Escorpión m

scorpion /'skɔ:pɪən/ n escorpión m

Scot /skɒt/ n escocés m. **~ch** /skɒtʃ/ a escocés. ● n güisqui m

scotch /skɒtʃ/ vt frustrar; (suppress) suprimir

scot-free /skɒt'fri:/ a impune; (gratis) sin pagar

Scot: ~**land** /'skɒtlənd/ n Escocia f. ~**s** a escocés. ~**sman** n escocés m. ~**swoman** n escocesa f. ~**tish** a escocés

scoundrel /'skaʊndrəl/ n canalla f

scour /'skaʊə(r)/ vt estregar; (*search*) registrar. ~**er** n estropajo m

scourge /skɜːdʒ/ n azote m

scout /skaʊt/ n explorador m. **Boy S**~ explorador m. ● vi. ~ **(for)** buscar

scowl /skaʊl/ n ceño m. ● vi fruncir el entrecejo

scraggy /'skrægɪ/ a (**-ier, -iest**) descarnado

scram /skræm/ vi (sl) largarse

scramble /'skræmbl/ vi (*clamber*) gatear. ~ **for** pelearse para obtener. ● vt revolver (*eggs*). ● n (*difficult climb*) subida f difícil; (*struggle*) lucha f

scrap /skræp/ n pedacito m; (*fight, fam*) pelea f. ● vt (*pt* **scrapped**) desechar. ~**book** n álbum m de recortes. ~**s** npl sobras fpl

scrape /skreɪp/ n raspadura f; (*fig*) apuro m. ● vt raspar; (*graze*) arañar; (*rub*) frotar. ● vi. ~ **through** lograr pasar; aprobar por los pelos (*exam*). ~ **together** reunir. ~**r** /-ə(r)/ n raspador m

scrap: ~ **heap** n montón m de deshechos. ~**-iron** n chatarra f

scrappy /'skræpɪ/ a fragmentario, pobre, de mala calidad

scratch /skrætʃ/ vt rayar; (*with nail etc*) arañar; rascar (*itch*). ● vi arañar. ● n raya f; (*from nail etc*) arañazo m. **start from** ~ empezar sin nada, empezar desde el principio. **up to** ~ al nivel requerido

scrawl /skrɔːl/ n garrapato m. ● vt/i garrapatear

scrawny /'skrɔːnɪ/ a (**-ier, -iest**) descarnado

scream /skriːm/ vt/i gritar. ● n grito m

screech /skriːtʃ/ vi gritar; (*brakes etc*) chirriar. ● n grito m; (*of brakes etc*) chirrido m

screen /skriːn/ n pantalla f; (*folding*) biombo m. ● vt (*hide*) ocultar; (*protect*) proteger; proyectar (*film*); seleccionar (*candidates*)

screw /skruː/ n tornillo m. ● vt atornillar. ~**driver** /'skruːdraɪvə(r)/ n destornillador m. ~ **up** atornillar; entornar (*eyes*); torcer (*face*); (*ruin,*

sl) arruinar. ~**y** /'skruːɪ/ a (**-ier, -iest**) (*sl*) chiflado

scribble /'skrɪbl/ vt/i garrapatear. ● n garrapato m

scribe /skraɪb/ n copista m & f

script /skrɪpt/ n escritura f; (*of film etc*) guión m

Scriptures /'skrɪptʃəz/ npl Sagradas Escrituras fpl

script-writer /'skrɪptraɪtə(r)/ n guionista m & f

scroll /skrəʊl/ n rollo m (de pergamino)

scrounge /skraʊndʒ/ vt/i obtener de gorra; (*steal*) birlar. ~**r** /-ə(r)/ n gorrón m

scrub /skrʌb/ n (*land*) maleza f; (*clean*) fregado m. ● vt/i (*pt* **scrubbed**) fregar

scruff /skrʌf/ n. **the** ~ **of the neck** el cogote m

scruffy /'skrʌfɪ/ a (**-ier, -iest**) desaliñado

scrum /skrʌm/ n, **scrummage** /'skrʌmɪdʒ/ n (*Rugby*) melée f

scrup|le /'skruːpl/ n escrúpulo m. ~**ulous** /'skruːpjʊləs/ a escrupuloso. ~**ulously** adv escrupulosamente

scrutin|ize /'skruːtɪnaɪz/ vt escudriñar. ~**y** /'skruːtɪnɪ/ n examen minucioso

scuff /skʌf/ vt arañar (*shoes*)

scuffle /'skʌfl/ n pelea f

scullery /'skʌlərɪ/ n trascocina f

sculpt /skʌlpt/ vt/i esculpir. ~**or** n escultor m. ~**ure** /-tʃə(r)/ n escultura f. ● vt/i esculpir

scum /skʌm/ n espuma f; (*people, pej*) escoria f

scurf /skɜːf/ n caspa f

scurrilous /'skʌrɪləs/ a grosero

scurry /'skʌrɪ/ vi correr

scurvy /'skɜːvɪ/ n escorbuto m

scuttle[1] /'skʌtl/ n cubo m del carbón

scuttle[2] /'skʌtl/ vt barrenar (*ship*)

scuttle[3] /'skʌtl/ vi. ~ **away** correr, irse de prisa

scythe /saɪð/ n guadaña f

SE abbr (*south-east*) sudeste m

sea /siː/ n mar m. **at** ~ en el mar; (*fig*) confuso. **by** ~ por mar. ~**board** /'siːbɔːd/ n litoral m. ~**farer** /'siːfeərə(r)/ n marinero m. ~**food** /'siːfuːd/ n mariscos mpl. ~**gull** /'siːgʌl/ n gaviota f. ~**horse** n caballito m de mar, hipocampo m

seal[1] /siːl/ n sello m. ● vt sellar. ~ **off** acordonar (*area*)

seal² /si:l/ (*animal*) foca *f*

sea level /'si:levl/ *n* nivel *m* del mar

sealing-wax /'si:lɪŋwæks/ *n* lacre *m*

sea lion /'si:laɪən/ *n* león *m* marino

seam /si:m/ *n* costura *f*; (*of coal*) veta *f*

seaman /'si:mən/ *n* (*pl* **-men**) marinero *m*

seamy /'si:mɪ/ *a*. **the ~ side** *n* el lado *m* sórdido, el revés *m*

seance /'seɪɑ:ns/ *n* sesión *f* de espiritismo

sea: ~plane /'si:pleɪn/ *n* hidroavión *f*. **~port** /'si:pɔ:t/ *n* puerto *m* de mar

search /sɜ:tʃ/ *vt* registrar; (*examine*) examinar. ● *vi* buscar. ● *n* (*for sth*) búsqueda *f*; (*of sth*) registro *m*. **in ~ of** en busca de. **~ for** buscar. **~ing** *a* penetrante. **~party** *n* equipo *m* de salvamento. **~light** /'sɜ:tʃlaɪt/ *n* reflector *m*

sea: ~scape /'si:skeɪp/ *n* marina *f*. **~shore** *n* orilla *f* del mar. **~sick** /'si:sɪk/ *a* mareado. **be ~sick** marearse. **~side** /'si:saɪd/ *n* playa *f*

season /'si:zn/ *n* estación *f*; (*period*) temporada *f*. ● *vt* (*culin*) sazonar; secar ⟨*wood*⟩. **~able** *a* propio de la estación. **~al** *a* estacional. **~ed** /'si:znd/ *a* (*fig*) experto. **~ing** *n* condimento *m*. **~ticket** *n* billete *m* de abono

seat /si:t/ *n* asiento *m*; (*place*) lugar *m*; (*of trousers*) fondillos *mpl*; (*bottom*) trasero *m*. **take a ~** sentarse. ● *vt* sentar; (*have seats for*) tener asientos para. **~belt** *n* cinturón *m* de seguridad

sea: ~urchin *n* erizo *m* de mar. **~weed** /'si:wi:d/ *n* alga *f*. **~worthy** /'si:wɜ:ðɪ/ *a* en estado de navegar

secateurs /'sekətɜ:z/ *npl* tijeras *fpl* de podar

sece|de /sɪ'si:d/ *vi* separarse. **~ssion** /-eʃn/ *n* secesión *f*

seclu|de /sɪ'klu:d/ *vt* aislar. **~ded** *a* aislado. **~sion** /-ʒn/ *n* aislamiento *m*

second¹ /'sekənd/ *a* & *n* segundo (*m*). **on ~ thoughts** pensándolo bien. ● *adv* (*in race etc*) en segundo lugar. ● *vt* apoyar. **~s** *npl* (*goods*) artículos *mpl* de segunda calidad; (*more food, fam*) otra porción *f*

second² /sɪ'kɒnd/ *vt* (*transfer*) trasladar temporalmente

secondary /'sekəndrɪ/ *a* secundario. **~ school** *n* instituto *m*

second: ~best *a* segundo. **~class** *a* de segunda clase. **~hand** *a* de segunda mano. **~ly** *adv* en segundo lugar. **~rate** *a* mediocre

secre|cy /'si:krəsɪ/ *n* secreto *m*. **~t** /'si:krɪt/ *a* & *n* secreto (*m*). **in ~t** en secreto

secretar|ial /sekrə'teərɪəl/ *a* de secretario. **~iat** /sekrə'teərɪət/ *n* secretaría *f*. **~y** /'sekrətrɪ/ *n* secretario *m*. **S~y of State** ministro *m*: (*Amer*) Ministro *m* de Asuntos Exteriores

secret|e /sɪ'kri:t/ *vt* (*med*) secretar. **~ion** /-ʃn/ *n* secreción *f*

secretive /'si:krɪtɪv/ *a* reservado

secretly /'si:krɪtlɪ/ *adv* en secreto

sect /sekt/ *n* secta *f*. **~arian** /-'teərɪən/ *a* sectario

section /'sekʃn/ *n* sección *f*; (*part*) parte *f*

sector /'sektə(r)/ *n* sector *m*

secular /'sekjʊlə(r)/ *a* seglar

secur|e /sɪ'kjʊə(r)/ *a* seguro; (*fixed*) fijo. ● *vt* asegurar; (*obtain*) obtener. **~ely** *adv* seguramente. **~ity** /sɪ'kjʊərətɪ/ *n* seguridad *f*; (*for loan*) garantía *f*, fianza *f*

sedate /sɪ'deɪt/ *a* sosegado

sedat|ion /sɪ'deɪʃn/ *n* sedación *f*. **~ive** /'sedətɪv/ *a* & *n* sedante (*m*)

sedentary /'sedəntrɪ/ *a* sedentario

sediment /'sedɪmənt/ *n* sedimento *m*

seduc|e /sɪ'dju:s/ *vt* seducir. **~er** /-ə(r)/ *n* seductor *m*. **~tion** /sɪ'dʌkʃn/ *n* seducción *f*. **~tive** /-tɪv/ *a* seductor

see¹ /si:/ ● *vt* (*pt* **saw**, *pp* **seen**) ver; (*understand*) comprender; (*notice*) notar; (*escort*) acompañar. **~ing that** visto que. **~ you later!** ¡hasta luego! ● *vi* ver; (*understand*) comprender. **~ about** ocuparse de. **~ off** despedirse de. **~ through** llevar a cabo; descubrir el juego de ⟨*person*⟩. **~ to** ocuparse de

see² /si:/ *n* diócesis *f*

seed /si:d/ *n* semilla *f*; (*fig*) germen *m*; (*tennis*) preseleccionado *m*. **~ling** *n* plantón *m*. **go to ~** granar; (*fig*) echarse a perder. **~y** /'si:dɪ/ *a* (**-ier, -iest**) sórdido

seek /si:k/ *vt* (*pt* **sought**) buscar. **~ out** buscar

seem /si:m/ *vi* parecer. **~ingly** *adv* aparentemente

seemly /'si:mlɪ/ *a* (**-ier, -iest**) correcto

seen /siːn/ *see* **see**[1]

seep /siːp/ *vi* filtrarse. **~age** *n* filtración *f*

see-saw /ˈsiːsɔː/ *n* balancín *m*

seethe /siːð/ *vi* (*fig*) hervir. **be seething with anger** estar furioso

see-through /ˈsiːθruː/ *a* transparente

segment /ˈsegmənt/ *n* segmento *m*; (*of orange*) gajo *m*

segregat|e /ˈsegrɪgeɪt/ *vt* segregar. **~ion** /-ˈgeɪʃn/ *n* segregación *f*

seiz|e /siːz/ *vt* agarrar; (*jurid*) incautarse de. **~e on** *vi* valerse de. **~e up** *vi* (*tec*) agarrotarse. **~ure** /ˈsiːʒə(r)/ *n* incautación *f*; (*med*) ataque *m*

seldom /ˈseldəm/ *adv* raramente

select /sɪˈlekt/ *vt* escoger; (*sport*) seleccionar. ● *a* selecto; (*exclusive*) exclusivo. **~ion** /-ʃn/ *n* selección *f*. **~ive** *a* selectivo

self /self/ *n* (*pl* **selves**) sí mismo. **~-addressed** *a* con su propia dirección. **~-assurance** *n* confianza *f* en sí mismo. **~-assured** *a* seguro de sí mismo. **~-catering** *a* con facilidades para cocinar. **~-centred** *a* egocéntrico. **~-confidence** *n* confianza *f* en sí mismo. **~-confident** *a* seguro de sí mismo. **~-conscious** *a* cohibido. **~-contained** *a* independiente. **~-control** *n* dominio *m* de sí mismo. **~-defence** *n* defensa *f* propia. **~-denial** *n* abnegación *f*. **~-employed** *a* que trabaja por cuenta propia. **~-esteem** *n* amor *m* propio. **~-evident** *a* evidente. **~-government** *n* autonomía *f*. **~-important** *a* presumido. **~-indulgent** *a* inmoderado. **~-interest** *n* interés *m* propio. **~ish** /ˈselfɪʃ/ *a* egoísta. **~ishness** *n* egoísmo *m*. **~less** /ˈselflɪs/ *a* desinteresado. **~-made** *a* rico por su propio esfuerzo. **~-opinionated** *a* intransigente; (*arrogant*) engreído. **~-pity** *n* compasión *f* de sí mismo. **~-portrait** *n* autorretrato *m*. **~-possessed** *a* dueño de sí mismo. **~-reliant** *a* independiente. **~-respect** *n* amor *m* propio. **~-righteous** *a* santurrón. **~-sacrifice** *n* abnegación *f*. **~-satisfied** *a* satisfecho de sí mismo. **~-seeking** *a* egoísta. **~-service** *a* & *n* autoservicio (*m*). **~-styled** *a* sedicente, llamado. **~-sufficient** *a* independiente. **~-willed** *a* terco

sell /sel/ *vt* (*pt* **sold**) vender. **be sold on** (*fam*) entusiasmarse por. **be sold out** estar agotado. ● *vi* venderse. **~-by date** *n* fecha *f* de caducidad. **~ off** *vt* liquidar. **~ up** *vt* vender todo. **~er** *n* vendedor *m*

Sellotape /ˈseləteɪp/ *n* (*P*) (papel *m*) celo *m*, cinta *f* adhesiva

sell-out /ˈselaʊt/ *n* (*betrayal*, *fam*) traición *f*

semantic /sɪˈmæntɪk/ *a* semántico. **~s** *n* semántica *f*

semaphore /ˈseməfɔː(r)/ *n* semáforo *m*

semblance /ˈsembləns/ *n* apariencia *f*

semen /ˈsiːmən/ *n* semen *m*

semester /sɪˈmestə(r)/ *n* (*Amer*) semestre *m*

semi... /ˈsemɪ/ *pref* semi...

semi|breve /ˈsemɪbriːv/ *n* semibreve *f*, redonda *f*. **~circle** /ˈsemɪsɜːkl/ *n* semicírculo *m*. **~circular** /-ˈsɜːkjʊlə(r)/ *a* semicircular. **~colon** /semɪˈkəʊlən/ *n* punto *m* y coma. **~detached** /semɪdɪˈtætʃt/ *a* (*house*) adosado. **~final** /semɪˈfaɪnl/ *n* semifinal *f*

seminar /ˈsemɪnɑː(r)/ *n* seminario *m*

seminary /ˈsemɪnərɪ/ *n* (*college*) seminario *m*

semiquaver /ˈsemɪkweɪvə(r)/ *n* (*mus*) semicorchea *f*

Semit|e /ˈsiːmaɪt/ *n* semita *m* & *f*. **~ic** /sɪˈmɪtɪk/ *a* semítico

semolina /seməˈliːnə/ *n* sémola *f*

senat|e /ˈsenɪt/ *n* senado *m*. **~or** /-ətə(r)/ *n* senador *m*

send /send/ *vt/i* (*pt* **sent**) enviar. **~ away** despedir. **~ away for** pedir (por correo). **~ for** enviar a buscar. **~ off for** pedir (por correo). **~ up** (*fam*) parodiar. **~er** *n* remitente *m*. **~off** *n* despedida *f*

senil|e /ˈsiːnaɪl/ *a* senil. **~ity** /sɪˈnɪlətɪ/ *n* senilidad *f*

senior /ˈsiːnɪə(r)/ *a* mayor; (*in rank*) superior; (*partner etc*) principal. ● *n* mayor *m* & *f*. **~ citizen** *n* jubilado *m*. **~ity** /-ˈɒrətɪ/ *n* antigüedad *f*

sensation /senˈseɪʃn/ *n* sensación *f*. **~al** *a* sensacional

sense /sens/ *n* sentido *m*; (*common sense*) juicio *m*; (*feeling*) sensación *f*. **make ~** *vt* tener sentido. **make ~ of** comprender. **~less** *a* insensato; (*med*) sin sentido

sensibilities /sensɪˈbɪlətɪz/ *npl* susceptibilidad *f*. **~ibility** /sensɪˈbɪlətɪ/ *n* sensibilidad *f*

sensible /'sensəbl/ *a* sensato; ⟨*clothing*⟩ práctico

sensitiv|e /'sensɪtɪv/ *a* sensible; (*touchy*) susceptible. ~**ity** /-'tɪvəti/ *n* sensibilidad *f*

sensory /'sensərɪ/ *a* sensorio

sensual /'senʃʊəl/ *a* sensual. ~**ity** /-'ælətɪ/ *n* sensualidad *f*

sensuous /'sensʊəs/ *a* sensual

sent /sent/ *see* **send**

sentence /'sentəns/ *n* frase *f*; (*jurid*) sentencia *f*; (*punishment*) condena *f*. ● *vt.* ~ **to** condenar a

sentiment /'sentɪmənt/ *n* sentimiento *m*; (*opinion*) opinión *f*. ~**al** /sentɪ'mentl/ *a* sentimental. ~**ality** /-'tælətɪ/ *n* sentimentalismo *m*

sentry /'sentrɪ/ *n* centinela *f*

separable /'sepərəbl/ *a* separable

separate[1] /'sepərət/ *a* separado; (*independent*) independiente. ~**ly** *adv* por separado. ~**s** *npl* coordinados *mpl*

separat|e[2] /'sepəreɪt/ *vt* separar. ● *vi* separarse. ~**ion** /-'reɪʃn/ *n* separación *f*. ~**ist** /'sepərətɪst/ *n* separatista *m & f*

September /sep'tembə(r)/ *n* se(p)tiembre *m*

septic /'septɪk/ *a* séptico. ~ **tank** *n* fosa *f* séptica

sequel /'si:kwəl/ *n* continuación *f*; (*consequence*) consecuencia *f*

sequence /'si:kwəns/ *n* sucesión *f*; (*of film*) secuencia *f*

sequin /'si:kwɪn/ *n* lentejuela *f*

serenade /serə'neɪd/ *n* serenata *f*. ● *vt* dar serenata a

seren|e /sɪ'ri:n/ *a* sereno. ~**ity** /-enətɪ/ *n* serenidad *f*

sergeant /'sɑ:dʒənt/ *n* sargento *m*

serial /'sɪərɪəl/ *n* serial *m*. ● *a* de serie. ~**ize** *vt* publicar por entregas

series /'sɪərɪːz/ *n* serie *f*

serious /'sɪərɪəs/ *a* serio. ~**ly** *adv* seriamente; (*ill*) gravemente. **take** ~**ly** tomar en serio. ~**ness** *n* seriedad *f*

sermon /'sɜːmən/ *n* sermón *m*

serpent /'sɜːpənt/ *n* serpiente *f*

serrated /sɪ'reɪtɪd/ *a* serrado

serum /'sɪərəm/ *n* (*pl* -a) suero *m*

servant /'sɜːvənt/ *n* criado *m*; (*fig*) servidor *m*

serve /sɜːv/ *vt* servir; (*in the army etc*) prestar servicio; cumplir ⟨*sentence*⟩. ~ **as** servir de. ~ **its purpose** servir para el caso. **it** ~**s you right** ¡bien te lo mereces! ¡te está bien merecido! ● *vi* servir. ● *n* (*in tennis*) saque *m*

service /'sɜːvɪs/ *n* servicio *m*; (*maintenance*) revisión *f*. **of** ~ **to** útil a. ● *vt* revisar ⟨*car etc*⟩. ~**able** /'sɜːvɪsəbl/ *a* práctico; (*durable*) duradero. ~ **charge** *n* servicio *m*. ~**man** /'sɜːvɪsmən/ *n* (*pl* -**men**) militar *m*. ~**s** *npl* (*mil*) fuerzas *fpl* armadas. ~ **station** *n* estación *f* de servicio

serviette /sɜːvɪ'et/ *n* servilleta *f*

servile /'sɜːvaɪl/ *a* servil

session /'seʃn/ *n* sesión *f*; (*univ*) curso *m*

set /set/ *vt* (*pt* **set**, *pres p* **setting**) poner; poner en hora ⟨*clock etc*⟩; fijar ⟨*limit etc*⟩; (*typ*) componer. ~ **fire to** pegar fuego a. ~ **free** *vt* poner en libertad. ● *vi* ⟨*sun*⟩ ponerse; ⟨*jelly*⟩ cuajarse. ● *n* serie *f*; (*of cutlery etc*) juego *m*; (*tennis*) set *m*; (*TV, radio*) aparato *m*; (*of hair*) marcado *m*; (*in theatre*) decorado *m*; (*of people*) círculo *m*. ● *a* fijo. **be** ~ **on** estar resuelto a. ~ **about** *vi* empezar a. ~ **back** *vt* (*delay*) retardar; (*cost, sl*) costar. ~ **off** *vi* salir. ● *vt* (*make start*) poner en marcha; hacer estallar ⟨*bomb*⟩. ~ **out** *vi* (*declare*) declarar; (*leave*) salir. ~ **sail** salir. ~ **the table** poner la mesa. ~ **up** *vt* establecer. ~**back** *n* revés *m*. ~ **square** *n* escuadra *f* de dibujar

settee /se'ti:/ *n* sofá *m*

setting /'setɪŋ/ *n* (*of sun*) puesta *f*; (*of jewel*) engaste *m*; (*in theatre*) escenario *m*; (*typ*) composición *f*. ~**lotion** *n* fijador *m*

settle /'setl/ *vt* (*arrange*) arreglar; (*pay*) pagar; fijar ⟨*date*⟩; calmar ⟨*nerves*⟩. ● *vi* (*come to rest*) posarse; (*live*) instalarse. ~ **down** calmarse; (*become orderly*) sentar la cabeza. ~ **for** aceptar. ~ **up** ajustar cuentas. ~**ment** /'setlmənt/ *n* establecimiento *m*; (*agreement*) acuerdo *m*; (*com*) liquidación *f*; (*place*) colonia *f*. ~**r** /-ə(r)/ *n* colonizador *m*

set: ~**to** *n* pelea *f*. ~**up** *n* (*fam*) sistema *m*

seven /sevn/ *a & n* siete (*m*). ~**teen** /sevn'ti:n/ *a & n* diecisiete (*m*). ~**teenth** *a & n* decimoséptimo (*m*). ~**th** *a & n* séptimo (*m*). ~**tieth** *a & n* setenta (*m*), septuagésimo (*m*). ~**ty** /'sevntɪ/ *a & n* setenta (*m*)

sever /'sevə(r)/ *vt* cortar; (*fig*) romper

several /'sevrəl/ *a & pron* varios

severance /'sevərəns/ *n* (*breaking off*) ruptura *f*

sever|e /sɪ'vɪə(r)/ *a* (**-er, -est**) severo; (*violent*) violento; (*serious*) grave; (*weather*) riguroso. **~ely** *adv* severamente; (*seriously*) gravemente. **~ity** /-'verətɪ/ *n* severidad *f*; (*violence*) violencia *f*; (*seriousness*) gravedad *f*

sew /səʊ/ *vt/i* (*pt* **sewed**, *pp* **sewn**, *or* **sewed**) coser

sew|age /'suːɪdʒ/ *n* aguas *fpl* residuales. **~er** /'suːə(r)/ *n* cloaca *f*

sewing /'səʊɪŋ/ *n* costura *f*. **~machine** *n* máquina *f* de coser

sewn /səʊn/ *see* **sew**

sex /seks/ *n* sexo *m*. **have ~** tener relaciones sexuales. ● *a* sexual. **~ist** /'seksɪst/ *a & n* sexista (*m & f*)

sextet /seks'tet/ *n* sexteto *m*

sexual /'seksʊəl/ *a* sexual. **~ intercourse** *n* relaciones *fpl* sexuales. **~ity** /-'ælətɪ/ *n* sexualidad *f*

sexy /'seksɪ/ *a* (**-ier, -iest**) excitante, sexy, provocativo

shabb|ily /'ʃæbɪlɪ/ *adv* pobremente; (*act*) mezquinamente. **~iness** *n* pobreza *f*; (*meanness*) mezquindad *f*. **~y** /'ʃæbɪ/ *a* (**-ier, -iest**) (*clothes*) gastado; (*person*) pobremente vestido; (*mean*) mezquino

shack /ʃæk/ *n* choza *f*

shackles /'ʃæklz/ *npl* grillos *mpl*, grilletes *mpl*

shade /ʃeɪd/ *n* sombra *f*; (*of colour*) matiz *m*; (*for lamp*) pantalla *f*. **a ~ better** un poquito mejor. ● *vt* dar sombra a

shadow /'ʃædəʊ/ *n* sombra *f*. **S~ Cabinet** *n* gobierno *m* en la sombra. ● *vt* (*follow*) seguir. **~y** *a* (*fig*) vago

shady /'ʃeɪdɪ/ *a* (**-ier, -iest**) sombreado; (*fig*) dudoso

shaft /ʃɑːft/ *n* (*of arrow*) astil *m*; (*mec*) eje *m*; (*of light*) rayo *m*; (*of lift, mine*) pozo *m*

shaggy /'ʃægɪ/ *a* (**-ier, -iest**) peludo

shak|e /ʃeɪk/ *vt* (*pt* **shook**, *pp* **shaken**) sacudir; agitar (*bottle*); (*shock*) desconcertar. **~e hands with** estrechar la mano a. ● *vi* temblar. **~e off** *vi* deshacerse de. ● *n* sacudida *f*. **~e-up** *n* reorganización *f*. **~y** /'ʃeɪkɪ/ *a* (**-ier, -iest**) tembloroso; (*table etc*) inestable; (*unreliable*) incierto

shall /ʃæl/ *v, aux* (*first person in future tense*). **I ~ go** iré. **we ~ see** veremos

shallot /ʃə'lɒt/ *n* chalote *m*

shallow /'ʃæləʊ/ *a* (**-er, -est**) poco profundo; (*fig*) superficial

sham /ʃæm/ *n* farsa *f*; (*person*) impostor *m*. ● *a* falso; (*affected*) fingido. ● *vt* (*pt* **shammed**) fingir

shambles /'ʃæmblz/ *npl* (*mess, fam*) desorden *m* total

shame /ʃeɪm/ *n* vergüenza *f*. **what a ~!** ¡qué lástima! ● *vt* avergonzar. **~faced** /'ʃeɪmfeɪst/ *a* avergonzado. **~ful** *a* vergonzoso. **~fully** *adv* vergonzosamente. **~less** *a* desvergonzado

shampoo /ʃæm'puː/ *n* champú *m*. ● *vt* lavar

shamrock /'ʃæmrɒk/ *n* trébol *m*

shandy /'ʃændɪ/ *n* cerveza *f* con gaseosa, clara *f*

shan't /ʃɑːnt/ = **shall not**

shanty /'ʃæntɪ/ *n* chabola *f*. **~ town** *n* chabolas *fpl*

shape /ʃeɪp/ *n* forma *f*. ● *vt* formar; determinar (*future*). ● *vi* formarse. **~ up** prometer. **~less** *a* informe. **~ly** /'ʃeɪplɪ/ *a* (**-ier, -iest**) bien proporcionado

share /ʃeə(r)/ *n* porción *f*; (*com*) acción *f*. **go ~s** compartir. ● *vt* compartir; (*divide*) dividir. ● *vi* participar. **~ in** participar en. **~holder** /'ʃeəhəʊldə(r)/ *n* accionista *m & f*. **~out** *n* reparto *m*

shark /ʃɑːk/ *n* tiburón *m*; (*fig*) estafador *m*

sharp /ʃɑːp/ *a* (**-er, -est**) (*knife etc*) afilado; (*pin etc*) puntiagudo; (*pain, sound*) agudo; (*taste*) acre; (*sudden, harsh*) brusco; (*well defined*) marcado; (*dishonest*) poco escrupuloso; (*clever*) listo. ● *adv* en punto. **at seven o'clock ~** a las siete en punto. ● *n* (*mus*) sostenido *m*. **~en** /'ʃɑːpn/ *vt* afilar; sacar punta a (*pencil*). **~ener** *n* (*mec*) afilador *m*; (*for pencils*) sacapuntas *m invar*. **~ly** *adv* bruscamente

shatter /'ʃætə(r)/ *vt* hacer añicos; (*upset*) perturbar. ● *vi* hacerse añicos. **~ed** *a* (*exhausted*) agotado

shav|e /ʃeɪv/ *vt* afeitar. ● *vi* afeitarse. ● *n* afeitado *m*. **have a ~e** afeitarse. **~en** *a* (*face*) afeitado; (*head*) rapado. **~er** *n* maquinilla *f* (de afeitar). **~ing-brush** *n* brocha *f* de afietar. **~ing-cream** *n* crema *f* de afeitar

shawl /ʃɔːl/ *n* chal *m*

she /ʃiː/ *pron* ella. ● *n* hembra *f*

sheaf /ʃiːf/ *n* (*pl* **sheaves**) gavilla *f*

shear /ʃɪə(r)/ *vt* (*pp* **shorn**, *or* **sheared**) esquilar. **~s** /ʃɪəz/ *npl* tijeras *fpl* grandes

sheath /ʃiːθ/ *n* (*pl* **-s** /ʃiːðz/) vaina *f*; (*contraceptive*) condón *m*. **~e** /ʃiːð/ *vt* envainar

shed[1] /ʃed/ *n* cobertizo *m*

shed[2] /ʃed/ *vt* (*pt* **shed**, *pres p* **shedding**) perder; derramar (*tears*); despojarse de (*clothes*). **~ light on** aclarar

sheen /ʃiːn/ *n* lustre *m*

sheep /ʃiːp/ *n invar* oveja *f*. **~-dog** *n* perro *m* pastor. **~ish** /ʃiːpɪʃ/ *a* vergonzoso. **~ishly** *adv* timidamente. **~skin** /ʃiːpskɪn/ *n* piel *f* de carnero, zamarra *f*

sheer /ʃɪə(r)/ *a* puro; (*steep*) perpendicular; (*fabric*) muy fino. ● *adv* a pico

sheet /ʃiːt/ *n* sábana *f*; (*of paper*) hoja *f*; (*of glass*) lámina *f*; (*of ice*) capa *f*

sheikh /ʃeɪk/ *n* jeque *m*

shelf /ʃelf/ *n* (*pl* **shelves**) estante *m*. **be on the ~** quedarse para vestir santos

shell /ʃel/ *n* concha *f*; (*of egg*) cáscara *f*; (*of building*) casco *m*; (*explosive*) proyectil *m*. ● *vt* desgranar (*peas etc*); (*mil*) bombardear. **~fish** /ʃelfɪʃ/ *n invar* (*crustacean*) crustáceo *m*; (*mollusc*) marisco *m*

shelter /ʃeltə(r)/ *n* refugio *m*, abrigo *m*. ● *vt* abrigar; (*protect*) proteger; (*give lodging to*) dar asilo a. ● *vi* abrigarse. **~ed** *a* (*spot*) abrigado; (*life etc*) protegido

shelv|e /ʃelv/ *vt* (*fig*) dar carpetazo a. **~ing** /ʃelvɪŋ/ *n* estantería *f*

shepherd /ʃepəd/ *n* pastor *m*. ● *vt* guiar. **~ess** /-'des/ *n* pastora *f*. **~'s pie** *n* carne *f* picada con puré de patatas

sherbet /ʃɜːbət/ *n* (*Amer, water-ice*) sorbete *m*

sheriff /ʃerɪf/ *n* alguacil *m*, sheriff *m*

sherry /ʃerɪ/ *n* (vino *m* de) jerez *m*

shield /ʃiːld/ *n* escudo *m*. ● *vt* proteger

shift /ʃɪft/ *vt* cambiar; cambiar de sitio (*furniture etc*); echar (*blame etc*). ● *n* cambio *m*; (*work*) turno *m*;

(*workers*) tanda *f*. **make ~** arreglárselas. **~less** /ʃɪftlɪs/ *a* holgazán

shifty /ʃɪftɪ/ *a* (**-ier, -iest**) taimado

shilling /ʃɪlɪŋ/ *n* chelín *m*

shilly-shally /ʃɪlɪʃælɪ/ *vi* titubear

shimmer /ʃɪmə(r)/ *vi* rielar, relucir. ● *n* luz *f* trémula

shin /ʃɪn/ *n* espinilla *f*

shine /ʃaɪn/ *vi* (*pt* **shone**) brillar. ● *vt* sacar brillo a. **~ on** dirigir (*torch*). ● *n* brillo *m*

shingle /ʃɪŋgl/ *n* (*pebbles*) guijarros *mpl*

shingles /ʃɪŋglz/ *npl* (*med*) herpes *mpl & fpl*

shiny /ʃaɪnɪ/ *a* (**-ier, -iest**) brillante

ship /ʃɪp/ *n* buque *m*, barco *m*. ● *vt* (*pt* **shipped**) transportar; (*send*) enviar; (*load*) embarcar. **~building** /ʃɪpbɪldɪŋ/ *n* construcción *f* naval. **~ment** *n* envío *m*. **~per** *n* expedidor *m*. **~ping** *n* envío *m*; (*ships*) barcos *mpl*. **~shape** /ʃɪpʃeɪp/ *adv & a* en buen orden, en regla. **~wreck** /ʃɪprek/ *n* naufragio *m*. **~wrecked** *a* naufragado. **be ~wrecked** naufragar. **~yard** /ʃɪpjɑːd/ *n* astillero *m*

shirk /ʃɜːk/ *vt* esquivar. **~er** *n* gandul *m*

shirt /ʃɜːt/ *n* camisa *f*. **in ~-sleeves** en mangas de camisa. **~y** /ʃɜːtɪ/ *a* (*sl*) enfadado

shiver /ʃɪvə(r)/ *vi* temblar. ● *n* escalofrío *m*

shoal /ʃəʊl/ *n* banco *m*

shock /ʃɒk/ *n* sacudida *f*; (*fig*) susto *m*; (*elec*) descarga *f*; (*med*) choque *m*. ● *vt* escandalizar. **~ing** *a* escandaloso; (*fam*) espantoso. **~ingly** *adv* terriblemente

shod /ʃɒd/ *see* **shoe**

shodd|ily /ʃɒdɪlɪ/ *adv* mal. **~y** /ʃɒdɪ/ *a* (**-ier, -iest**) mal hecho, de pacotilla

shoe /ʃuː/ *n* zapato *m*; (*of horse*) herradura *f*. ● *vt* (*pt* **shod**, *pres p* **shoeing**) herrar (*horse*). **be well shod** estar bien calzado. **~horn** /ʃuːhɔːn/ *n* calzador *m*. **~lace** *n* cordón *m* de zapato. **~maker** /ʃuːmeɪkə(r)/ *n* zapatero *m*. **~ polish** *n* betún *m*. **~string** *n*. **on a ~string** con poco dinero. **~tree** *n* horma *f*

shone /ʃɒn/ *see* **shine**

shoo /ʃuː/ *vt* ahuyentar

shook /ʃʊk/ *see* **shake**

shoot /ʃuːt/ *vt* (*pt* **shot**) disparar; rodar (*film*). ● *vi* (*hunt*) cazar. ● *n* *(bot)* retoño *m*; *(hunt)* cacería *f*. **~ down** *vt* derribar. **~ out** *vi (rush)* salir disparado. **~ up** *(prices)* subir de repente; *(grow)* crecer. **~ing-range** *n* campo *m* de tiro

shop /ʃɒp/ *n* tienda *f*; *(work-shop)* taller *m*. **talk ~** hablar de su trabajo. ● *vi (pt* **shopping)** hacer compras. **~ around** buscar el mejor precio. **go ~ping** ir de compras. **~ assistant** *n* dependiente *m*. **~keeper** /'ʃɒpkiːpə(r)/ *n* tendero *m*. **~lifter** *n* ratero *m* (de tiendas). **~lifting** *n* ratería *f* (de tiendas). **~per** *n* comprador *m*. **~ping** /'ʃɒpɪŋ/ *n* compras *fpl*. **~ping bag** bolsa *f* de la compra. **~ping centre** *n* centro *m* comercial. **~ steward** *n* enlace *m* sindical. **~window** *n* escaparate *m*

shore /ʃɔː(r)/ *n* orilla *f*

shorn /ʃɔːn/ *see* **shear**

short /ʃɔːt/ *a* (**-er**, **-est**) corto; *(not lasting)* breve; *(person)* bajo; *(curt)* brusco. **a ~ time ago** hace poco. **be ~ of** necesitar. **Mick is ~ for Michael** Mick es el diminutivo de Michael. ● *adv (stop)* en seco. **~ of doing** a menos que no hagamos. **● n. in ~** en resumen. **~age** /'ʃɔːtɪdʒ/ *n* escasez *f*. **~bread** /'ʃɔːtbred/ *n* galleta *f* de mantequilla. **~change** *vt* estafar, engañar. **~ circuit** *n* cortocircuito *m*. **~coming** /'ʃɔːtkʌmɪŋ/ *n* deficiencia *f*. **~ cut** *n* atajo *m*. **~en** /'ʃɔːtn/ *vt* acortar. **~hand** /'ʃɔːthænd/ *n* taquigrafía *f*. **~hand typist** *n* taquimecanógrafo *m*, taquimeca *f (fam)*. **~lived** *a* efímero. **~ly** /'ʃɔːtlɪ/ *adv* dentro de poco. **~s** *npl* pantalón *m* corto. **~sighted** *a* miope. **~tempered** *a* de mal genio

shot /ʃɒt/ *see* **shoot**. ● *n* tiro *m*; *(person)* tirador *m*; *(photo)* foto *f*; *(injection)* inyección *f*. **like a ~** como una bala; *(willingly)* de buena gana. **~gun** *n* escopeta *f*

should /ʃʊd, ʃəd/ *v, aux*. **I ~ go** debería ir. **I ~ have seen him** debiera haberlo visto. **I ~ like** me gustaría. **if he ~ come** si viniese

shoulder /'ʃəʊldə(r)/ *n* hombro *m*. ● *vt* cargar con *(responsibility)*; llevar a hombros *(burden)*. **~blade** *n* omóplato *m*. **~strap** *n* correa *f* del hombro; *(of bra etc)* tirante *m*

shout /ʃaʊt/ *n* grito *m*. ● *vt/i* gritar. **~ at s.o.** gritarle a uno. **~ down** hacer callar a gritos

shove /ʃʌv/ *n* empujón *m*. ● *vt* empujar; *(put, fam)* poner. ● *vi* empujar. **~ off** *vi (fam)* largarse

shovel /'ʃʌvl/ *n* pala *f*. ● *vt (pt* **shovelled)** mover con la pala

show /ʃəʊ/ *vt (pt* **showed**, *pp* **shown)** mostrar; *(put on display)* exponer; poner *(film)*. ● *vi (be visible)* verse. ● *n* demostración *f*; *(exhibition)* exposición *f*; *(ostentation)* pompa *f*; *(in theatre)* espectáculo *m*; *(in cinema)* sesión *f*. **on ~** expuesto. **~** *vt* lucir; *(pej)* ostentar. ● *vi* presumir. **~ up** *vi* destacar; *(be present)* presentarse. ● *vt (unmask)* desenmascarar. **~case** *n* vitrina *f*. **~down** *n* confrontación *f*

shower /'ʃaʊə(r)/ *n* chaparrón *m*; *(of blows etc)* lluvia *f*; *(for washing)* ducha *f*. **have a ~** ducharse. ● *vi* ducharse. ● *vt*. **~ with** colmar de. **~proof** /'ʃaʊəpruːf/ *a* impermeable. **~y** *a* lluvioso

show: **~jumping** *n* concurso *m* hípico. **~manship** /'ʃəʊmənʃɪp/ *n* teatralidad *f*, arte *f* de presentar espectáculos

shown /ʃəʊn/ *see* **show**

show: **~off** *n* fanfarrón *m*. **~place** *n* lugar *m* de interés turístico. **~room** /'ʃəʊruːm/ *n* sala *f* de exposición *f*

showy /'ʃəʊɪ/ *a* (**-ier**, **-iest**) llamativo; *(person)* ostentoso

shrank /ʃræŋk/ *see* **shrink**

shrapnel /'ʃræpnəl/ *n* metralla *f*

shred /ʃred/ *n* pedazo *m*; *(fig)* pizca *f*. ● *vt (pt* **shredded)** hacer tiras; *(culin)* cortar en tiras. **~der** *n* desfibradora *f*, trituradora *f*

shrew /ʃruː/ *n* musaraña *f*; *(woman)* arpía *f*

shrewd /ʃruːd/ *a* (**-er**, **-est**) astuto. **~ness** *n* astucia *f*

shriek /ʃriːk/ *n* chillido *m*. ● *vt/i* chillar

shrift /ʃrɪft/ *n*. **give s.o. short ~** despachar a uno con brusquedad

shrill /ʃrɪl/ *a* agudo

shrimp /ʃrɪmp/ *n* camarón *m*

shrine /ʃraɪn/ *n (place)* lugar *m* santo; *(tomb)* sepulcro *m*

shrink /ʃrɪŋk/ *vt (pt* **shrank**, *pp* **shrunk)** encoger. ● *vi* encogerse; *(draw back)* retirarse; *(lessen)* disminuir. **~age** *n* encogimiento *m*

shrivel /'ʃrɪvl/ *vi (pt* **shrivelled)** *(dry up)* secarse; *(become wrinkled)* arrugarse

shroud /ʃraʊd/ n sudario m; (fig) velo m. ● vt (veil) velar

Shrove /ʃrəʊv/ n. ~ **Tuesday** n martes m de carnaval

shrub /ʃrʌb/ n arbusto m

shrug /ʃrʌg/ vt (pt **shrugged**) encogerse de hombros. ● n encogimiento m de hombros

shrunk /ʃrʌŋk/ see **shrink**

shrunken /ˈʃrʌŋkən/ a encogido

shudder /ˈʃʌdə(r)/ vi estremecerse. ● n estremecimiento m

shuffle /ˈʃʌfl/ vi arrastrar los pies. ● vt barajar ⟨cards⟩. ● n arrastramiento m de los pies; (of cards) barajadura f

shun /ʃʌn/ vt (pt **shunned**) evitar

shunt /ʃʌnt/ vt apartar, desviar

shush /ʃʊʃ/ int ¡chitón!

shut /ʃʌt/ vt (pt **shut**, pres p **shutting**) cerrar. ● vi cerrarse. ~ **down** cerrar. ~ **up** vt cerrar; (fam) hacer callar. ● vi callarse. ~**down** n cierre m. ~**ter** /ˈʃʌtə(r)/ n contraventana f; (photo) obturador m

shuttle /ˈʃʌtl/ n lanzadera f; (train) tren m de enlace. ● vt transportar. ● vi ir y venir. ~**cock** /ˈʃʌtlkɒk/ n volante m. ~ **service** n servicio m de enlace

shy /ʃaɪ/ a (-er, -est) tímido. ● vi (pt **shied**) asustarse. ~ **away from** huir. ~**ness** n timidez f

Siamese /saɪəˈmiːz/ a siamés

sibling /ˈsɪblɪŋ/ n hermano m, hermana f

Sicil|ian /sɪˈsɪljən/ a & n siciliano (m). ~**y** /ˈsɪsɪlɪ/ n Sicilia f

sick /sɪk/ a enfermo; ⟨humour⟩ negro; (fed up, fam) harto. **be** ~ (vomit) vomitar. **be** ~ **of** (fig) estar harto de. **feel** ~ sentir náuseas. ~**en** /ˈsɪkən/ vt dar asco. ● vi caer enfermo. **be** ~**ening for** incubar

sickle /ˈsɪkl/ n hoz f

sick: ~**ly** /ˈsɪklɪ/ a (-ier, -iest) enfermizo; ⟨taste, smell etc⟩ nauseabundo. ~**ness** /ˈsɪknɪs/ n enfermedad f. ~**room** n cuarto m del enfermo

side /saɪd/ n lado m; (of river) orilla f; (of hill) ladera f; (team) equipo m; (fig) parte f. ~ **by** ~ uno al lado del otro. **on the** ~ (sideline) como actividad secundaria; (secretly) a escondidas. ● a lateral. ● vi. ~ **with** tomar el partido de. ~**board** /ˈsaɪdbɔːd/ n aparador m. ~**boards** npl, ~**burns** npl (sl) patillas fpl.

~**car** n sidecar m. ~**effect** n efecto m secundario. ~**light** /ˈsaɪdlaɪt/ n luz f de posición. ~**line** /ˈsaɪdlaɪn/ n actividad f secundaria. ~**long** /-lɒŋ/ a & adv de soslayo. ~**road** n calle f secundaria. ~**saddle** n silla f de mujer. **ride** ~**saddle** adv a mujeriegas. ~**show** n atracción f secundaria. ~**step** vt evitar. ~**track** vt desviar del asunto. ~**walk** /ˈsaɪdwɔːk/ n (Amer) acera f, vereda f (LAm). ~**ways** /ˈsaɪdweɪz/ a & adv de lado. ~**whiskers** npl patillas fpl

siding /ˈsaɪdɪŋ/ n apartadero m

sidle /ˈsaɪdl/ vi avanzar furtivamente. ~ **up to** acercarse furtivamente

siege /siːdʒ/ n sitio m, cerco m

siesta /sɪˈestə/ n siesta f

sieve /sɪv/ n cernedor m. ● vt cerner

sift /sɪft/ vt cerner. ● vi. ~ **through** examinar

sigh /saɪ/ n suspiro. ● vi suspirar

sight /saɪt/ n vista f; (spectacle) espectáculo m; (on gun) mira f. **at (first)** ~ a primera vista. **catch** ~ **of** vislumbrar. **lose** ~ **of** perder de vista. **on** ~ a primera vista. **within** ~ **of** (near) cerca de. ● vt ver, divisar. ~**seeing** /ˈsaɪtsiːɪŋ/ n visita f turística. ~**seer** /-ə(r)/ n turista m & f

sign /saɪn/ n señal f. ● vt firmar. ~ **on**, ~ **up** vt inscribir. ● vi inscribirse

signal /ˈsɪgnəl/ n señal f. ● vt (pt **signalled**) comunicar; hacer señas a ⟨person⟩. ~**box** n casilla f del guardavía. ~**man** /ˈsɪgnəlmən/ n (pl -**men**) guardavía f

signatory /ˈsɪgnətrɪ/ n firmante m & f

signature /ˈsɪgnətʃə(r)/ n firma f. ~ **tune** n sintonía f

signet-ring /ˈsɪgnɪtrɪŋ/ n anillo m de sello

significan|ce /sɪgˈnɪfɪkəns/ n significado m. ~**t** /sɪgˈnɪfɪkənt/ a significativo; (important) importante. ~**tly** adv significativamente

signify /ˈsɪgnɪfaɪ/ vt significar. ● vi (matter) importar, tener importancia

signpost /ˈsaɪnpəʊst/ n poste m indicador

silen|ce /ˈsaɪləns/ n silencio m. ● vt hacer callar. ~**cer** /-ə(r)/ n silenciador m. ~**t** /ˈsaɪlənt/ a silencioso;

⟨film⟩ mudo. **∼tly** adv silenciosamente

silhouette /sɪluːˈet/ n silueta f. ● vt.
be . **∼d** perfilarse, destacarse
(**against** contra)

silicon /ˈsɪlɪkən/ n silicio m. **∼ chip** n
pastilla f de silicio

silk /sɪlk/ n seda f. **∼en** a, **∼y** a (of
silk) de seda; (like silk) sedoso.
∼worm n gusano m de seda

sill /sɪl/ n antepecho m; (of window)
alféizar m; (of door) umbral m

silly /ˈsɪlɪ/ a (-ier, -iest) tonto. ● n.
∼billy (fam) tonto m

silo /ˈsaɪləʊ/ n (pl -os) silo m

silt /sɪlt/ n sedimento m

silver /ˈsɪlvə(r)/ n plata f. ● a de
plata. **∼ plated** a bañado en plata,
plateado. **∼side** /ˈsɪlvəsaɪd/ n
(culin) contra f. **∼smith** /ˈsɪlvəsmɪθ/
n platero m. **∼ware** /ˈsɪlvəweə(r)/ n
plata f. **∼ wedding** n bodas fpl de
plata. **∼y** a plateado; ⟨sound⟩
argentino

simil|ar /ˈsɪmɪlə(r)/ a parecido. **∼ar-
ity** /-ˈlærətɪ/ n parecido m. **∼arly**
adv de igual manera

simile /ˈsɪmɪlɪ/ n símil m

simmer /ˈsɪmə(r)/ vt/i hervir a fuego
lento; (fig) hervir. **∼ down**
calmarse

simpl|e /ˈsɪmpl/ a (-er, -est) sencillo;
⟨person⟩ ingenuo. **∼e-minded** a
ingenuo. **∼eton** /ˈsɪmpltən/ n sim-
plón m. **∼icity** /-ˈplɪsetɪ/ n sencillez f.
∼ification n sim-
plificación f. **∼ify** /ˈsɪmplɪfaɪ/ vt
simplificar. **∼y** adv sencillamente;
(absolutely) absolutamente

simulat|e /ˈsɪmjʊleɪt/ vt simular.
∼ion /-ˈleɪʃn/ n simulación f

simultaneous /sɪmlˈteɪnɪəs/ a
simultáneo. **∼ly** adv simul-
táneamente

sin /sɪn/ n pecado m. ● vi (pt sinned)
pecar

since /sɪns/ prep desde. ● adv desde
entonces. ● conj desde que;
(because) ya que

sincer|e /sɪnˈsɪə(r)/ a sincero. **∼ely**
adv sinceramente. **∼ity** /-ˈserətɪ/ n
sinceridad f

sinew /ˈsɪnjuː/ n tendón m. **∼s** npl
músculos mpl

sinful /ˈsɪnfl/ a pecaminoso; (shocking) escandaloso

sing /sɪŋ/ vt/i (pt sang, pp sung)
cantar

singe /sɪndʒ/ vt (pres p singeing)
chamuscar

singer /ˈsɪŋə(r)/ n cantante m & f

singl|e /ˈsɪŋgl/ a único; (not double)
sencillo; (unmarried) soltero; ⟨bed,
room⟩ individual. ● n (tennis) juego
m individual; (ticket) billete m sencillo. ● vt. **∼e out** escoger; (distinguish) distinguir. **∼e-handed** a
& adv sin ayuda. **∼e-minded** a
resuelto

singlet /ˈsɪŋglɪt/ n camiseta f

singly /ˈsɪŋglɪ/ adv uno a uno

singsong /ˈsɪŋsɒŋ/ a monótono. ● n.
have a ∼ cantar juntos

singular /ˈsɪŋgjʊlə(r)/ n singular f.
● a singular; (uncommon) raro;
⟨noun⟩ en singular. **∼ly** adv
singularmente

sinister /ˈsɪnɪstə(r)/ a siniestro

sink /sɪŋk/ vt (pt sank, pp sunk) hun-
dir; perforar ⟨well⟩; invertir
⟨money⟩. ● vi hundirse; ⟨patient⟩
debilitarse. ● n fregadero m. **∼ in** vi
penetrar

sinner /ˈsɪnə(r)/ n pecador m

sinuous /ˈsɪnjʊəs/ a sinuoso

sinus /ˈsaɪnəs/ n (pl -uses) seno m

sip /sɪp/ n sorbo m. ● vt (pt sipped)
sorber

siphon /ˈsaɪfən/ n sifón m. vt. **∼ out**
sacar con sifón

sir /sɜː(r)/ n señor m. **S∼** n (title) sir
m

siren /ˈsaɪərən/ n sirena f

sirloin /ˈsɜːlɔɪn/ n solomillo m, lomo
m bajo

sirocco /sɪˈrɒkəʊ/ n siroco m

sissy /ˈsɪsɪ/ n hombre m afeminado,
marica m, mariquita m; (coward)
gallina m & f

sister /ˈsɪstə(r)/ n hermana f; (nurse)
enfermera f jefe. **S∼ Mary** Sor
María. **∼-in-law** n (pl **∼s-in-law**)
cuñada f. **∼ly** a de hermana; (like
sister) como hermana

sit /sɪt/ vt (pt sat, pres p sitting)
sentar. ● vi sentarse; ⟨committee
etc⟩ reunirse. **be ∼ting** estar
sentado. **∼ back** vi (fig) relajarse. **∼
down** vi sentarse. **∼ for** vi presentarse a ⟨exam⟩; posar para ⟨por-
trait⟩. **∼ up** vi enderezarse; (stay
awake) velar. **∼-in** n ocupación f

site /saɪt/ n sitio m. **building ∼** n
solar m. ● vt situar

sit: ∼ting n sesión f; (in restaurant)
turno m. **∼ting-room** n cuarto m de
estar

situat|e /'sɪtjʊeɪt/ *vt* situar. **~ed** *a* situado. **~ion** /-'eɪʃn/ *n* situación *f*; (*job*) puesto *m*

six /sɪks/ *a & n* seis (*m*). **~teen** /sɪk'stiːn/ *a & n* dieciséis (*m*). **~teenth** *a & n* decimosexto (*m*). **~th** *a & n* sexto (*m*). **~tieth** *a & n* sesenta (*m*), sexagésimo (*m*). **~ty** /'sɪkstɪ/ *a & n* sesenta (*m*)

size /saɪz/ *n* tamaño *m*; (*of clothes*) talla *f*; (*of shoes*) número *m*; (*extent*) magnitud *f*. ● *vt*. **~ up** (*fam*) juzgar. **~able** *a* bastante grande

sizzle /'sɪzl/ *vi* crepitar

skate[1] /skeɪt/ *n* patín *m*. ● *vi* patinar. **~board** /'skeɪtbɔːd/ *n* monopatín *m*. **~r** *n* patinador *m*

skate[2] /skeɪt/ *n invar* (*fish*) raya *f*

skating /'skeɪtɪŋ/ *n* patinaje *m*. **~-rink** *n* pista *f* de patinaje

skein /skeɪn/ *n* madeja *f*

skelet|al /'skelɪtl/ *a* esquelético. **~on** /'skelɪtn/ *n* esqueleto *m*. **~on staff** *n* personal *m* reducido

sketch /sketʃ/ *n* esbozo *m*; (*drawing*) dibujo *m*; (*in theatre*) pieza *f* corta y divertida. ● *vt* esbozar. ● *vi* dibujar. **~y** /'sketʃɪ/ *a* (**-ier, -iest**) incompleto

skew /skjuː/ *n*. **on the ~** sesgado

skewer /'skjuːə(r)/ *n* broqueta *f*

ski /skiː/ *n* (*pl* **skis**) esquí *m*. ● *vi* (*pt* **skied**, *pres p* **skiing**) esquiar. **go ~ing** ir a esquiar

skid /skɪd/ *vi* (*pt* **skidded**) patinar. ● *n* patinazo *m*

ski: **~er** *n* esquiador *m*. **~ing** *n* esquí *m*

skilful /'skɪlfl/ *a* diestro

ski-lift /'skiːlɪft/ *n* telesquí *m*

skill /skɪl/ *n* destreza *f*, habilidad *f*. **~ed** *a* hábil; (*worker*) cualificado

skim /skɪm/ *vt* (*pt* **skimmed**) espumar; desnatar (*milk*); (*glide over*) rozar. **~ over** *vt* rasar. **~ through** *vi* hojear

skimp /skɪmp/ *vt* escatimar. **~y** /'skɪmpɪ/ *a* (**-ier, -iest**) insuficiente; (*skirt, dress*) corto

skin /skɪn/ *n* piel *f*. ● *vt* (*pt* **skinned**) despellejar; pelar (*fruit*). **~-deep** *a* superficial. **~-diving** *n* natación *f* submarina. **~flint** /'skɪnflɪnt/ *n* tacaño *m*. **~ny** /'skɪnɪ/ *a* (**-ier, -iest**) flaco

skint /skɪnt/ *a* (*sl*) sin una perra

skip[1] /skɪp/ *vi* (*pt* **skipped**) *vi* saltar; (*with rope*) saltar a la comba. ● *vt* saltarse. ● *n* salto *m*

skip[2] /skɪp/ *n* (*container*) cuba *f*

skipper /'skɪpə(r)/ *n* capitán *m*

skipping-rope /'skɪpɪŋrəʊp/ *n* comba *f*

skirmish /'skɜːmɪʃ/ *n* escaramuza *f*

skirt /skɜːt/ *n* falda *f*. ● *vt* rodear; (*go round*) ladear

skirting-board /'skɜːtɪŋbɔːd/ *n* rodapié *m*, zócalo *m*

skit /skɪt/ *n* pieza *f* satírica

skittish /'skɪtɪʃ/ *a* juguetón; (*horse*) nervioso

skittle /'skɪtl/ *n* bolo *m*

skive /skaɪv/ *vi* (*sl*) gandulear

skivvy /'skɪvɪ/ *n* (*fam*) criada *f*

skulk /skʌlk/ *vi* avanzar furtivamente; (*hide*) esconderse

skull /skʌl/ *n* cráneo *m*; (*remains*) calavera *f*. **~-cap** *n* casquete *m*

skunk /skʌŋk/ *n* mofeta *f*; (*person*) canalla *f*

sky /skaɪ/ *n* cielo *m*. **~-blue** *a & n* azul (*m*) celeste. **~jack** /'skaɪdʒæk/ *vt* secuestrar. **~jacker** *n* secuestrador *m*. **~light** /'skaɪlaɪt/ *n* tragaluz *m*. **~scraper** /'skaɪskreɪpə(r)/ *n* rascacielos *m invar*

slab /slæb/ *n* bloque *m*; (*of stone*) losa *f*; (*of chocolate*) tableta *f*

slack /slæk/ *a* (**-er, -est**) flojo; (*person*) negligente; (*period*) de poca actividad. ● *n* (*of rope*) parte *f* floja. ● *vt* aflojar. ● *vi* aflojarse; (*person*) descansar. **~en** /'slækən/ *vt* aflojar. ● *vi* aflojarse; (*person*) descansar. **~en (off)** *vt* aflojar. **~ off** (*fam*) aflojar

slacks /slæks/ *npl* pantalones *mpl*

slag /slæg/ *n* escoria *f*

slain /sleɪn/ *see* **slay**

slake /sleɪk/ *vt* apagar

slam /slæm/ *vt* (*pt* **slammed**) golpear; (*throw*) arrojar; (*criticize, sl*) criticar. **~ the door** dar un portazo. ● *vi* cerrarse de golpe. ● *n* golpe *m*; (*of door*) portazo *m*

slander /'slɑːndə(r)/ *n* calumnia *f*. ● *vt* difamar. **~ous** *a* calumnioso

slang /slæŋ/ *n* jerga *f*, argot *m*. **~y** *a* vulgar

slant /slɑːnt/ *vt* inclinar; presentar con parcialidad (*news*). ● *n* inclinación *f*; (*point of view*) punto *m* de vista

slap /slæp/ *vt* (*pt* **slapped**) abofetear; (*on the back*) dar una palmada; (*put*) arrojar. ● *n* bofetada *f*; (*on back*) palmada *f*. ● *adv* de lleno. **~dash**

/'slæpdæʃ/ *a* descuidado. **~happy** *a* (*fam*) despreocupado; (*dazed*, *fam*) aturdido. **~stick** /'slæpstɪk/ *n* payasada *f.* **~up** *a* (*sl*) de primera categoría

slash /slæʃ/ *vt* acuchillar; (*fig*) reducir radicalmente. ● *n* cuchillada *f*

slat /slæt/ *n* tablilla *f*

slate /sleɪt/ *n* pizarra *f.* ● *vt* (*fam*) criticar

slaughter /'slɔːtə(r)/ *vt* masacrar; matar (*animal*). ● *n* carnicería *f*; (*of animals*) matanza *f.* **~house** /'slɔːtəhaʊs/ *n* matadero *m*

Slav /slɑːv/ *a* & *n* eslavo (*m*)

slav|e /sleɪv/ *n* esclavo *m.* ● *vi* trabajar como un negro. **~e-driver** *n* negrero *m.* **~ery** /-ərɪ/ *n* esclavitud *f.* **~ish** /'sleɪvɪʃ/ *a* servil

Slavonic /slə'vɒnɪk/ *a* eslavo

slay /sleɪ/ *vt* (*pt* **slew**, *pp* **slain**) matar

sleazy /'sliːzɪ/ *a* (**-ier, -iest**) (*fam*) sórdido

sledge /sledʒ/ *n* trineo *m.* **~hammer** *n* almádena *f*

sleek /sliːk/ *a* (**-er, -est**) liso, brillante; (*elegant*) elegante

sleep /sliːp/ *n* sueño *m.* **go to ~** dormirse. ● *vi* (*pt* **slept**) dormir. ● *vt* poder alojar. **~er** *n* durmiente *m* & *f*; (*on track*) traviesa *f*; (*berth*) coche-cama *m.* **~ily** *adv* soñolientamente. **~ing-bag** *n* saco *m* de dormir. **~ing-pill** *n* somnífero *m.* **~less** *a* insomne. **~lessness** *n* insomnio *m.* **~walker** *n* sonámbulo *m.* **~y** /'sliːpɪ/ *a* (**-ier, -iest**) soñoliento. **be ~y** tener sueño

sleet /sliːt/ *n* aguanieve *f.* ● *vi* caer aguanieve

sleeve /sliːv/ *n* manga *f*; (*for record*) funda *f.* **up one's ~** en reserva. **~less** *a* sin mangas

sleigh /sleɪ/ *n* trineo *m*

sleight /slaɪt/ *n.* **~ of hand** prestidigitación *f*

slender /'slendə(r)/ *a* delgado; (*fig*) escaso

slept /slept/ *see* **sleep**

sleuth /sluːθ/ *n* investigador *m*

slew[1] /sluː/ *see* **slay**

slew[2] /sluː/ *vi* (*turn*) girar

slice /slaɪs/ *n* lonja *f*; (*of bread*) rebanada *f*; (*of sth round*) rodaja *f*; (*implement*) paleta *f.* ● *vt* cortar; rebanar (*bread*)

slick /slɪk/ *a* liso; (*cunning*) astuto. ● *n.* **(oil)~** capa *f* de aceite

slid|e /slaɪd/ *vt* (*pt* **slid**) deslizar. ● *vi* resbalar. **~e over** pasar por alto de. ● *n* resbalón *m*; (*in playground*) tobogán *m*; (*for hair*) pasador *m*; (*photo*) diapositiva *f*; (*fig, fall*) baja *f.* **~e-rule** *n* regla *f* de cálculo. **~ing** *a* corredizo. **~ing scale** *n* escala *f* móvil

slight /slaɪt/ *a* (**-er, -est**) ligero; (*slender*) delgado. ● *vt* ofender. ● *n* desaire *m.* **~est** *a* mínimo. **not in the ~est** en absoluto. **~ly** *adv* un poco

slim /slɪm/ *a* (**slimmer, slimmest**) delgado. ● *vi* (*pt* **slimmed**) adelgazar

slime /slaɪm/ *n* légamo *m*, lodo *m*, fango *m*

slimness /'slɪmnɪs/ *n* delgadez *f*

slimy /'slaɪmɪ/ *a* legamoso, fangoso, viscoso; (*fig*) rastrero

sling /slɪŋ/ *n* honda *f*; (*toy*) tirador; (*med*) cabestrillo *m.* ● *vt* (*pt* **slung**) lanzar

slip /slɪp/ *vt* (*pt* **slipped**) deslizar. **~ s.o.'s mind** olvidársele a uno. ● *vi* deslizarse. ● *n* resbalón *m*; (*mistake*) error *m*; (*petticoat*) combinación *f*; (*paper*) trozo *m.* **~ of the tongue** *n* lapsus *m* linguae. **give the ~ to** zafarse de, dar esquinazo a. **~ away** *vi* escabullirse. **~ into** *vi* ponerse (*clothes*). **~ up** *vi* (*fam*) equivocarse

slipper /'slɪpə(r)/ *n* zapatilla *f*

slippery /'slɪpərɪ/ *a* resbaladizo

slip: **~road** *n* rampa *f* de acceso. **~shod** /'slɪpʃɒd/ *a* descuidado. **~up** *n* (*fam*) error *m*

slit /slɪt/ *n* raja *f*; (*cut*) corte *m.* ● *vt* (*pt* **slit**, *pres p* **slitting**) rajar; (*cut*) cortar

slither /'slɪðə(r)/ *vi* deslizarse

sliver /'slɪvə(r)/ *n* trocito *m*; (*splinter*) astilla *f*

slobber /'slɒbə(r)/ *vi* babear

slog /slɒg/ *vt* (*pt* **slogged**) golpear. ● *vi* trabajar como un negro. ● *n* golpetazo *m*; (*hard work*) trabajo *m* penoso

slogan /'sləʊgən/ *n* eslogan *m*

slop /slɒp/ *vt* (*pt* **slopped**) derramar. ● *vi* derramarse. **~s** *npl* (*fam*) agua *f* sucia

slop|e /sləʊp/ *vi* inclinarse. ● *vt* inclinar. ● *n* declive *m*, pendiente *m.* **~ing** *a* inclinado

sloppy /'slɒpɪ/ *a* (**-ier, -iest**) (*wet*) mojado; (*food*) líquido; (*work*) descuidado; ⟨person⟩ desaliñado; (fig) sentimental

slosh /slɒʃ/ vi (fam) chapotear. ● vt (hit, sl) pegar

slot /slɒt/ n ranura f. ● vt (pt **slotted**) encajar

sloth /sləʊθ/ n pereza f

slot-machine /'slɒtməʃiːn/ n distribuidor m automático; (for gambling) máquina f tragaperras

slouch /slaʊtʃ/ vi andar cargado de espaldas; (in chair) repanchigarse

Slovak /'sləʊvæk/ a & n eslovaco (m). **~ia** /sləʊ'vækiə/ n Eslovaquia f

sloven|liness /'slʌvnlinɪs/ n despreocupación f. **~y** /'slʌvnli/ a descuidado

slow /sləʊ/ a (-er, -est) lento. be **~** ⟨clock⟩ estar atrasado. in **~ motion** a cámara lenta. ● adv despacio. ● vt retardar. ● vi ir más despacio. **~ down, ~ up** vt retardar. ● vi ir más despacio. **~coach** /'sləʊkəʊtʃ/ n tardón m. **~ly** adv despacio. **~ness** n lentitud f

sludge /slʌdʒ/ n fango m; (sediment) sedimento m

slug /slʌg/ n babosa f; (bullet) posta f. **~gish** /'slʌgɪʃ/ a lento

sluice /sluːs/ n (gate) compuerta f; (channel) canal m

slum /slʌm/ n tugurio m

slumber /'slʌmbə(r)/ n sueño m. ● vi dormir

slump /slʌmp/ n baja f repentina; (in business) depresión f. ● vi bajar repentinamente; (flop down) dejarse caer pesadamente; (collapse) desplomarse

slung /slʌŋ/ see **sling**

slur /slɜː(r)/ vt/i (pt **slurred**) articular mal. ● n dicción f defectuosa; (discredit) calumnia f

slush /slʌʃ/ n nieve f medio derretida; (fig) sentimentalismo m. **~ fund** n fondos mpl secretos para fines deshonestos. **~y** a ⟨road⟩ cubierto de nieve medio derretida

slut /slʌt/ n mujer f desaseada

sly /slaɪ/ a (**slyer, slyest**) (crafty) astuto; (secretive) furtivo. ● n. on the **~** a escondidas. **~ly** adv astutamente

smack¹ /smæk/ n golpe m; (on face) bofetada f. ● adv (fam) de lleno. ● vt pegar

smack² /smæk/ vi. **~ of** saber a; (fig) oler a

small /smɔːl/ a (-er, -est) pequeño. ● n. the **~ of the back** la región f lumbar. **~ ads** npl anuncios mpl por palabras. **~ change** n cambio m. **~holding** /'smɔːlhəʊldɪŋ/ n parcela f. **~pox** /'smɔːlpɒks/ n viruela f. **~ talk** n charla f. **~-time** a (fam) de poca monta

smarmy /'smɑːmɪ/ a (-ier, -iest) (fam) zalamero

smart /smɑːt/ a (-er, -est) elegante; (clever) inteligente; (brisk) rápido. ● vi escocer. **~en** /'smɑːtn/ vt arreglar. ● vi arreglarse. **~en up** vi arreglarse. **~ly** adv elegantemente; (quickly) rápidamente. **~ness** n elegancia f

smash /smæʃ/ vt romper; (into little pieces) hacer pedazos; batir ⟨record⟩. ● vi romperse; (collide) chocar (**into** con). ● n (noise) estruendo m; (collision) choque m; (com) quiebra f. **~ing** /'smæʃɪŋ/ a (fam) estupendo

smattering /'smætərɪŋ/ n conocimientos mpl superficiales

smear /smɪə(r)/ vt untar (**with** de); (stain) manchar (**with** de); (fig) difamar. ● n mancha f; (med) frotis m

smell /smel/ n olor m; (sense) olfato m. ● vt/i (pt **smelt**) oler. **~y** a maloliente

smelt¹ /smelt/ see **smell**

smelt² /smelt/ vt fundir

smile /smaɪl/ n sonrisa f. ● vi sonreír(se)

smirk /smɜːk/ n sonrisa f afectada

smite /smaɪt/ vt (pt **smote**, pp **smitten**) golpear

smith /smɪθ/ n herrero m

smithereens /smɪðə'riːnz/ npl añicos mpl. **smash to ~** hacer añicos

smitten /'smɪtn/ see **smite**. ● a encaprichado (**with** por)

smock /smɒk/ n blusa f, bata f

smog /smɒg/ n niebla f con humo

smok|e /sməʊk/ n humo m. ● vt/i fumar. **~eless** a sin humo. **~er** /-ə(r)/ n fumador m. **~e-screen** n cortina f de humo. **~y** a ⟨room⟩ lleno de humo

smooth /smuːð/ a (-er, -est) liso; ⟨sound, movement⟩ suave; ⟨sea⟩ tranquilo; ⟨manners⟩ zalamero. ● vt alisar; (fig) allanar. **~ly** adv suavemente

smote /sməʊt/ see **smite**

smother /'smʌðə(r)/ vt sofocar; (*cover*) cubrir

smoulder /'sməʊldə(r)/ vi arder sin llama; (*fig*) arder

smudge /smʌdʒ/ n borrón m, mancha f. ● vt tiznarse

smug /smʌg/ a (**smugger, smuggest**) satisfecho de sí mismo

smuggl|e /'smʌgl/ vt pasar de contrabando. **~er** n contrabandista m & f. **~ing** n contrabando m

smug: ~ly adv con suficiencia. **~ness** n suficiencia f

smut /smʌt/ n tizne m; (*mark*) tiznajo m. **~ty** a (**-ier, -iest**) tiznado; (*fig*) obsceno

snack /snæk/ n tentempié m. **~bar** n cafetería f

snag /snæg/ n problema m; (*in cloth*) rasgón m

snail /sneɪl/ n caracol m. **~'s pace** n paso m de tortuga

snake /sneɪk/ n serpiente f

snap /snæp/ vt (pt **snapped**) (*break*) romper; castañetear (*fingers*). ● vi romperse; (*dog*) intentar morder; (*say*) contestar bruscamente; (*whip*) chasquear. **~ at** (*dog*) intentar morder; (*say*) contestar bruscamente. ● n chasquido m; (*photo*) foto f. ● a instantáneo. **~ up** vt agarrar. **~py** /'snæpɪ/ a (**-ier, -iest**) (*fam*) rápido. **make it ~py!** (*fam*) ¡date prisa! **~shot** /'snæpʃɒt/ n foto f

snare /sneə(r)/ n trampa f

snarl /snɑːl/ vi gruñir. ● n gruñido m

snatch /snætʃ/ vt agarrar; (*steal*) robar. ● n arrebatamiento m; (*short part*) trocito m; (*theft*) robo m

sneak /sniːk/ ● n soplón m. ● vi. **~ in** entrar furtivamente. **~ out** salir furtivamente

sneakers /'sniːkəz/ npl zapatillas fpl de lona

sneak|ing /'sniːkɪŋ/ a furtivo. **~y** a furtivo

sneer /snɪə(r)/ n sonrisa f de desprecio. ● vi sonreír con desprecio. **~ at** hablar con desprecio a

sneeze /sniːz/ n estornudo m. ● vi estornudar

snide /snaɪd/ a (*fam*) despreciativo

sniff /snɪf/ vt oler. ● vi aspirar por la nariz. ● n aspiración f

snigger /'snɪgə(r)/ n risa f disimulada. ● vi reír disimuladamente

snip /snɪp/ vt (pt **snipped**) tijeretear. ● n tijeretada f; (*bargain, sl*) ganga f

snipe /snaɪp/ vi disparar desde un escondite. **~r** /ə(r)/ n tirador m emboscado, francotirador m

snippet /'snɪpɪt/ n retazo m

snivel /'snɪvl/ vi (pt **snivelled**) lloriquear. **~ling** a llorón

snob /snɒb/ n esnob m. **~bery** n esnobismo m. **~bish** a esnob

snooker /'snuːkə(r)/ n billar m

snoop /snuːp/ vi (*fam*) curiosear

snooty /'snuːtɪ/ a (*fam*) desdeñoso

snooze /snuːz/ n sueñecito m. ● vi echarse un sueñecito

snore /snɔː(r)/ n ronquido m. ● vi roncar

snorkel /'snɔːkl/ n tubo m respiratorio

snort /snɔːt/ n bufido m. ● vi bufar

snout /snaʊt/ n hocico m

snow /snəʊ/ n nieve f. ● vi nevar. **be ~ed under with** estar inundado por. **~ball** /'snəʊbɔːl/ n bola f de nieve. **~drift** n nieve amontonada. **~drop** /'snəʊdrɒp/ n campanilla f de invierno. **~fall** /'snəʊfɔːl/ n nevada f. **~flake** /'snəʊfleɪk/ n copo m de nieve. **~man** /'snəʊmæn/ n (pl **-men**) muñeco m de nieve. **~plough** n quitanieves m invar. **~storm** /'snəʊstɔːm/ n nevasca f. **~y** a (*place*) de nieves abundantes; (*weather*) con nevadas seguidas

snub /snʌb/ vt (pt **snubbed**) desairar. ● n desaire m. **~-nosed** /'snʌbnəʊzd/ a chato

snuff /snʌf/ n rapé m. ● vt despabilar (*candle*). **~ out** apagar (*candle*)

snuffle /'snʌfl/ vi respirar ruidosamente

snug /snʌg/ a (**snugger, snuggest**) cómodo; (*tight*) ajustado

snuggle /'snʌgl/ vi acomodarse

so /səʊ/ adv (*before a or adv*) tan; (*thus*) así. ● conj así que. **~ am I** yo tambien. **~ as to** para. **~ far** adv (*time*) hasta ahora; (*place*) hasta aquí. **~ far as I know** que yo sepa. **~ long!** (*fam*) ¡hasta luego! **~ much** tanto. **~ that** conj para que. **and ~ forth, and ~ on** y así sucesivamente. **if ~** si es así. **I think ~** creo que sí. **or ~** más o menos

soak /səʊk/ vt remojar. ● vi remojarse. **~ in** penetrar. **~ up** absorber. **~ing** a empapado. ● n remojón m

so-and-so /'səʊənsəʊ/ n fulano m

soap /səʊp/ *n* jabón *m*. ● *vt* enjabonar. ~ **powder** *n* jabón en polvo. ~**y** *a* jabonoso

soar /sɔː(r)/ *vi* elevarse; ⟨*price etc*⟩ ponerse por las nubes

sob /sɒb/ *n* sollozo *m*. ● *vi* (*pt* **sobbed**) sollozar

sober /'səʊbə(r)/ *a* sobrio; ⟨*colour*⟩ discreto

so-called /'səʊkɔːld/ *a* llamado, supuesto

soccer /'sɒkə(r)/ *n* (*fam*) fútbol *m*

sociable /'səʊʃəbl/ *a* sociable

social /'səʊʃl/ *a* social; (*sociable*) sociable. ● *n* reunión *f*. ~**ism** /-zəm/ *n* socialismo *m*. ~**ist** /'səʊʃəlɪst/ *a* & *n* socialista *m* & *f*. ~**ize** /'səʊʃəlaɪz/ *vt* socializar. ~**ly** *adv* socialmente. ~ **security** *n* seguridad *f* social. ~ **worker** *n* asistente *m* social

society /sə'saɪətɪ/ *n* sociedad *f*

sociolog|ical /səʊsɪə'lɒdʒɪkl/ *a* sociológico. ~**ist** *n* sociólogo *m*. ~**y** /səʊsɪ'ɒlədʒɪ/ *n* sociología *f*

sock[1] /sɒk/ *n* calcetín *m*

sock[2] /sɒk/ *vt* (*sl*) pegar

socket /'sɒkɪt/ *n* hueco *m*; (*of eye*) cuenca *f*; (*wall plug*) enchufe *m*; (*for bulb*) portalámparas *m invar*, casquillo *m*

soda /'səʊdə/ *n* sosa *f*; (*water*) soda *f*. ~**water** *n* soda *f*

sodden /'sɒdn/ *a* empapado

sodium /'səʊdɪəm/ *n* sodio *m*

sofa /'səʊfə/ *n* sofá *m*

soft /sɒft/ *a* (**-er, -est**) blando; ⟨*sound, colour*⟩ suave; (*gentle*) dulce, tierno; (*silly*) estúpido. ~ **drink** *n* bebida *f* no alcohólica. ~ **spot** *n* debilidad *f*. ~**en** /'sɒfn/ *vt* ablandar; (*fig*) suavizar. ● *vi* ablandarse; (*fig*) suavizarse. ~**ly** *adv* dulcemente. ~**ness** *n* blandura *f*; (*fig*) dulzura *f*. ~**ware** /'sɒftweə(r)/ *n* programación *f*, software *m*

soggy /'sɒgɪ/ *a* (**-ier, -iest**) empapado

soh /səʊ/ *n* (*mus, fifth note of any musical scale*) sol *m*

soil[1] /sɔɪl/ *n* suelo *m*

soil[2] /sɔɪl/ *vt* ensuciar. ● *vi* ensuciarse

solace /'sɒləs/ *n* consuelo *m*

solar /'səʊlə(r)/ *a* solar. ~**ium** /sə'leərɪəm/ *n* (*pl* **-a**) solario *m*

sold /səʊld/ *see* **sell**

solder /'sɒldə(r)/ *n* soldadura *f*. ● *vt* soldar

soldier /'səʊldʒə(r)/ *n* soldado *m*. ● *vi*. ~ **on** (*fam*) perseverar

sole[1] /səʊl/ *n* (*of foot*) planta *f*; (*of shoe*) suela *f*

sole[2] /səʊl/ (*fish*) lenguado *m*

sole[3] /səʊl/ *a* único, solo. ~**ly** *adv* únicamente

solemn /'sɒləm/ *a* solemne. ~**ity** /sə'lemnətɪ/ *n* solemnidad *f*. ~**ly** *adv* solemnemente

solicit /sə'lɪsɪt/ *vt* solicitar. ● *vi* importunar

solicitor /sə'lɪsɪtə(r)/ *n* abogado *m*; (*notary*) notario *m*

solicitous /sə'lɪsɪtəs/ *a* solícito

solid /'sɒlɪd/ *a* sólido; ⟨*gold etc*⟩ macizo; (*unanimous*) unánime; ⟨*meal*⟩ sustancioso. ● *n* sólido *m*. ~**arity** /sɒlɪ'dærətɪ/ *n* solidaridad *f*. ~**ify** /sə'lɪdɪfaɪ/ *vt* solidificar. ● *vi* solidificarse. ~**ity** /sə'lɪdətɪ/ *n* solidez *f*. ~**ly** *adv* sólidamente. ~**s** *npl* alimentos *mpl* sólidos

soliloquy /sə'lɪləkwɪ/ *n* soliloquio *m*

solitaire /sɒlɪ'teə(r)/ *n* solitario *m*

solitary /'sɒlɪtrɪ/ *a* solitario

solitude /'sɒlɪtjuːd/ *n* soledad *f*

solo /'səʊləʊ/ *n* (*pl* **-os**) (*mus*) solo *m*. ~**ist** *n* solista *m* & *f*

solstice /'sɒlstɪs/ *n* solsticio *m*

soluble /'sɒljʊbl/ *a* soluble

solution /sə'luːʃn/ *n* solución *f*

solvable *a* soluble

solve /sɒlv/ *vt* resolver

solvent /'sɒlvənt/ *a* & *n* solvente (*m*)

sombre /'sɒmbə(r)/ *a* sombrío

some /sʌm/ *a* alguno; (*a little*) un poco de. ~ **day** algún día. ~ **two hours** unas dos horas. **will you have** ~ **wine?** ¿quieres vino? ● *pron* algunos; (*a little*) un poco. ~ **of us** algunos de nosotros. **I want** ~ quiero un poco. ● *adv* (*approximately*) unos. ~**body** /'sʌmbədɪ/ *pron* alguien. ● *n* personaje *m*. ~**how** /'sʌmhaʊ/ *adv* de algún modo. ~**how or other** de una manera u otra. ~**one** /'sʌmwʌn/ *pron* alguien. ● *n* personaje *m*

some: ~**thing** /'sʌmθɪŋ/ *pron* algo *m*. ~**thing like** algo como; (*approximately*) cerca de. ~**time** /'sʌmtaɪm/ *a* ex. ● *adv* algún día; (*in past*) durante. ~**time last summer** *a* (durante) el verano pasado. ~**times** /'sʌmtaɪmz/ *adv* de vez en cuando, a veces. ~**what** /'sʌmwɒt/ *adv* algo, un poco. ~**where** /'sʌmweə(r)/ *adv* en alguna parte

son /sʌn/ n hijo m

sonata /sə'nɑːtə/ n sonata f

song /sɒŋ/ n canción f. **sell for a ~** vender muy barato. **~-book** n cancionero m

sonic /'sɒnɪk/ a sónico

son-in-law /'sʌnɪnlɔː/ n (pl **sons-in-law**) yerno m

sonnet /'sɒnɪt/ n soneto m

sonny /'sʌnɪ/ n (fam) hijo m

soon /suːn/ adv (-er, -est) pronto; (in a short time) dentro de poco; (early) temprano. **~ after** poco después. **~er or later** tarde o temprano. **as ~ as** en cuanto; **as ~ as possible** lo antes posible. **I would ~er not go** prefiero no ir

soot /sʊt/ n hollín m

sooth|e /suːð/ vt calmar. **~ing** a calmante

sooty /'sʊtɪ/ a cubierto de hollín

sophisticated /sə'fɪstɪkeɪtɪd/ a sofisticado; (complex) complejo

soporific /sɒpə'rɪfɪk/ a soporífero

sopping /'sɒpɪŋ/ a. **~ (wet)** empapado

soppy /'sɒpɪ/ a (-ier, -iest) (fam) sentimental; (silly, fam) tonto

soprano /sə'prɑːnəʊ/ n (pl -os) (voice) soprano m; (singer) soprano f

sorcerer /'sɔːsərə(r)/ n hechicero m

sordid /'sɔːdɪd/ a sórdido

sore /sɔː(r)/ a (-er, -est) que duele, dolorido; (distressed) penoso; (vexed) enojado. ● n llaga f. **~ly** /'sɔːlɪ/ adv gravemente. **~ throat** n dolor m de garganta. **I've got a ~ throat** me duele la garganta

sorrow /'sɒrəʊ/ n pena f, tristeza f. **~ful** a triste

sorry /'sɒrɪ/ a (-ier, -ier) arrepentido; (wretched) lamentable; (sad) triste. **be ~** sentirlo; (repent) arrepentirse. **be ~ for s.o.** (pity) compadecerse de uno. **~!** ¡perdón!, ¡perdone!

sort /sɔːt/ n clase f; (person, fam) tipo m. **be out of ~s** estar indispuesto; (irritable) estar de mal humor. ● vt clasificar. **~ out** (choose) escoger; (separate) separar; resolver (problem)

so-so /'səʊsəʊ/ a & adv regular

soufflé /'suːfleɪ/ n suflé m

sought /sɔːt/ see **seek**

soul /səʊl/ n alma f. **~ful** /'səʊlfl/ a sentimental

sound[1] /saʊnd/ n sonido m; ruido m. ● vt sonar; (test) sondar. ● vi sonar; (seem) parecer (**as if** que)

sound[2] /saʊnd/ a (-er, -est) sano; (argument etc) lógico; (secure) seguro. **~ asleep** profundamente dormido

sound[3] /saʊnd/ (strait) estrecho m

sound barrier /'saʊndbæərɪə(r)/ n barrera f del sonido

soundly /'saʊndlɪ/ adv sólidamente; (asleep) profundamente

sound: **~-proof** a insonorizado. **~-track** n banda f sonora

soup /suːp/ n sopa f. **in the ~** (sl) en apuros

sour /'saʊə(r)/ a (-er, -est) agrio; (cream, milk) cortado. ● vt agriar. ● vi agriarse

source /sɔːs/ n fuente f

south /saʊθ/ n sur m. ● a del sur. ● adv hacia el sur. **S~ Africa** n Africa f del Sur. **S~ America** n América f (del Sur), Sudamérica f. **S~ American** a & n sudamericano (m). **~-east** n sudeste m. **~erly** /'sʌðəlɪ/ a sur; (wind) del sur. **~ern** /'sʌðən/ a del sur, meridional. **~erner** n meridional m. **~ward** a sur; ● adv hacia el sur. **~wards** adv hacia el sur. **~-west** n sudoeste m

souvenir /suːvə'nɪə(r)/ n recuerdo m

sovereign /'sɒvrɪn/ n & a soberano (m). **~ty** n soberanía f

Soviet /'səʊvɪət/ a (history) soviético. **the ~ Union** n la Unión f Soviética

sow[1] /səʊ/ vt (pt **sowed**, pp **sowed** or **sown**) sembrar

sow[2] /saʊ/ n cerda f

soya /'sɔɪə/ n. **~ bean** n soja f

spa /spɑː/ n balneario m

space /speɪs/ n espacio m; (room) sitio m; (period) período m. ● a (research etc) espacial. ● vt espaciar. **~ out** espaciar. **~craft** /'speɪskrɑːft/ n, **~ship** n nave f espacial. **~suit** n traje m espacial

spacious /'speɪʃəs/ a espacioso

spade /speɪd/ n pala f. **~s** npl (cards) picos mpl, picas fpl; (in Spanish pack) espadas fpl. **~work** /'speɪdwɜːk/ n trabajo m preparatorio

spaghetti /spə'getɪ/ n espaguetis mpl

Spain /speɪn/ n España f

span[1] /spæn/ n (of arch) luz f; (of time) espacio m; (of wings) envergadura f. ● vt (pt **spanned**) extenderse sobre

span[2] /spæn/ see **spick**

Spaniard /'spænjəd/ n español m

spaniel /'spænjəl/ *n* perro *m* de aguas

Spanish /'spænɪʃ/ *a & n* español (*m*)

spank /spæŋk/ *vt* dar un azote a. ~**ing** *n* azote *m*

spanner /'spænə(r)/ *n* llave *f*

spar /spɑː(r)/ *vi* (*pt* **sparred**) entrenarse en el boxeo; (*argue*) disputar

spare /speə(r)/ *vt* salvar; (*do without*) prescindir de; (*afford to give*) dar; (*use with restraint*) escatimar. ● *a* de reserva; (*surplus*) sobrante; 〈*person*〉 enjuto; 〈*meal etc*〉 frugal. ~ (**part**) *n* repuesto *m*. ~ **time** *n* tiempo *m* libre. ~ **tyre** *n* neumático *m* de repuesto

sparing /'speərɪŋ/ *a* frugal. ~**ly** *adv* frugalmente

spark /spɑːk/ *n* chispa *f*. ● *vt*. ~ **off** (*initiate*) provocar. ~**ing-plug** *n* (*auto*) bujía *f*

sparkle /'spɑːkl/ *vi* centellear. ● *n* centelleo *m*. ~**ing** *a* centelleante; 〈*wine*〉 espumoso

sparrow /'spærəʊ/ *n* gorrión *m*

sparse /spɑːs/ *a* escaso; 〈*population*〉 poco denso. ~**ly** *adv* escasamente

spartan /'spɑːtn/ *a* espartano

spasm /'spæzəm/ *n* espasmo *m*; (*of cough*) acceso *m*. ~**odic** /spæz'mɒdɪk/ *a* espasmódico

spastic /'spæstɪk/ *n* víctima *f* de parálisis cerebral

spat /spæt/ *see* **spit**

spate /speɪt/ *n* avalancha *f*

spatial /'speɪʃl/ *a* espacial

spatter /'spætə(r)/ *vt* salpicar (**with** de)

spatula /'spætjʊlə/ *n* espátula *f*

spawn /spɔːn/ *n* hueva *f*. ● *vt* engendrar. ● *vi* desovar

speak /spiːk/ *vt/i* (*pt* **spoke**, *pp* **spoken**) hablar. ~ **for** *vi* hablar en nombre de. ~ **up** *vi* hablar más fuerte. ~**er** /'spiːkə(r)/ *n* (*in public*) orador *m*; (*loudspeaker*) altavoz *m*. **be a Spanish** ~**er** hablar español

spear /spɪə(r)/ *n* lanza *f*. ~**head** /'spɪəhed/ *n* punta *f* de lanza. ● *vt* (*lead*) encabezar. ~**mint** /'spɪəmɪnt/ *n* menta *f* verde

spec /spek/ *n*. **on** ~ (*fam*) por si acaso

special /'speʃl/ *a* especial. ~**ist** /'speʃəlɪst/ *n* especialista *m & f*. ~**ity** /-ɪ'ælətɪ/ *n* especialidad *f*. ~**ization** /-'zeɪʃn/ *n* especialización *f*. ~**ize** /'speʃəlaɪz/ *vi* especializarse.

~**ized** *a* especializado. ~**ty** *n* especialidad *f*. ~**ly** *adv* especialmente

species /'spiːʃiːz/ *n* especie *f*

specific /spə'sɪfɪk/ *a* específico. ~**ically** *adv* específicamente. ~**ication** /-ɪ'keɪʃn/ *n* especificación *f*; (*details*) descripción *f*. ~**y** /'spesɪfaɪ/ *vt* especificar

specimen /'spesɪmɪn/ *n* muestra *f*

speck /spek/ *n* manchita *f*; (*particle*) partícula *f*

speckled /'spekld/ *a* moteado

specs /speks/ *npl* (*fam*) gafas *fpl*, anteojos *mpl* (*LAm*)

spectacle /'spektəkl/ *n* espectáculo *m*. ~**les** *npl* gafas *fpl*, anteojos *mpl* (*LAm*). ~**ular** /spek'tækjʊlə(r)/ *a* espectacular

spectator /spek'teɪtə(r)/ *n* espectador *m*

spectre /'spektə(r)/ *n* espectro *m*

spectrum /'spektrəm/ *n* (*pl* **-tra**) espectro *m*; (*of ideas*) gama *f*

speculate /'spekjʊleɪt/ *vi* especular. ~**ion** /-'leɪʃn/ *n* especulación *f*. ~**ive** /-lətɪv/ *a* especulativo. ~**or** *n* especulador *m*

sped /sped/ *see* **speed**

speech /spiːtʃ/ *n* (*faculty*) habla *f*; (*address*) discurso *m*. ~**less** *a* mudo

speed /spiːd/ *n* velocidad *f*; (*rapidity*) rapidez *f*; (*haste*) prisa *f*. ● *vi* (*pt* **sped**) apresurarse. (*pt* **speeded**) (*drive too fast*) ir a una velocidad excesiva. ~ **up** *vt* acelerar. ● *vi* acelerarse. ~**boat** /'spiːdbəʊt/ *n* lancha *f* motora. ~**ily** *adv* rápidamente. ~**ing** *n* exceso *m* de velocidad. ~**ometer** /spiː'dɒmɪtə(r)/ *n* velocímetro *m*. ~**way** /'spiːdweɪ/ *n* pista *f*; (*Amer*) autopista *f*. ~**y** /'spiːdɪ/ *a* (**-ier**, **-iest**) rápido

spell[1] /spel/ *n* (*magic*) hechizo *m*

spell[2] /spel/ *vt/i* (*pt* **spelled** *or* **spelt**) escribir; (*mean*) significar. ~ **out** *vt* deletrear; (*fig*) explicar. ~**ing** *n* ortografía *f*

spell[3] /spel/ (*period*) período *m*

spellbound /'spelbaʊnd/ *a* hechizado

spelt /spelt/ *see* **spell**[2]

spend /spend/ *vt* (*pt* **spent**) gastar; pasar 〈*time etc*〉; dedicar 〈*care etc*〉. ● *vi* gastar dinero. ~**thrift** /'spendθrɪft/ *n* derrochador *m*

spent /spent/ *see* **spend**

sperm /spɜːm/ *n* (*pl* **sperms** *or* **sperm**) esperma *f*

spew /spjuː/ *vt/i* vomitar

spher|e /ˈsfɪə(r)/ *n* esfera *f.* ~**ical** /ˈsferɪkl/ *a* esférico

sphinx /ˈsfɪŋks/ *n* esfinge *f*

spice /spaɪs/ *n* especia *f*; (*fig*) sabor *m*

spick /spɪk/ *a.* ~ **and span** impecable

spicy /ˈspaɪsɪ/ *a* picante

spider /ˈspaɪdə(r)/ *n* araña *f*

spik|e /spaɪk/ *n* (*of metal etc*) punta *f.* ~**y** *a* puntiagudo; (*person*) quisquilloso

spill /spɪl/ *vt* (*pt* **spilled** *or* **spilt**) derramar. ● *vi* derramarse. ~ **over** desbordarse

spin /spɪn/ *vt* (*pt* **spun**, *pres p* **spinning**) hacer girar; hilar (*wool etc*). ● *vi* girar. ● *n* vuelta *f*; (*short drive*) paseo *m*

spinach /ˈspɪnɪdʒ/ *n* espinacas *fpl*

spinal /ˈspaɪnl/ *a* espinal. ~ **cord** *n* médula *f* espinal

spindl|e /ˈspɪndl/ *n* (*for spinning*) huso *m.* ~**y** *a* larguirucho

spin-drier /spɪnˈdraɪə(r)/ *n* secador *m* centrífugo

spine /spaɪn/ *n* columna *f* vertebral; (*of book*) lomo *m.* ~**less** *a* (*fig*) sin carácter

spinning /ˈspɪnɪŋ/ *n* hilado *m.* ~**top** *n* trompa *f*, peonza *f.* ~**wheel** *n* rueca *f*

spin-off /ˈspɪnɒf/ *n* beneficio *m* incidental; (*by-product*) subproducto *m*

spinster /ˈspɪnstə(r)/ *n* soltera *f*; (*old maid, fam*) solterona *f*

spiral /ˈspaɪərəl/ *a* espiral, helicoidal. ● *n* hélice *f.* ● *vi* (*pt* **spiralled**) moverse en espiral. ~ **staircase** *n* escalera *f* de caracol

spire /ˈspaɪə(r)/ *n* (*archit*) aguja *f*

spirit /ˈspɪrɪt/ *n* espíritu *m*; (*boldness*) valor *m.* **in low** ~**s** abatido. ● *vt.* ~ **away** hacer desaparecer. ~**ed** /ˈspɪrɪtɪd/ *a* animado, fogoso. ~**lamp** *n* lamparilla *f* de alcohol. ~**level** *n* nivel *m* de aire. ~**s** *npl* (*drinks*) bebidas *fpl* alcohólicas

spiritual /ˈspɪrɪtjʊəl/ *a* espiritual. ● *n* canción *f* religiosa de los negros. ~**ualism** /-zəm/ *n* espiritismo *m.* ~**ualist** /ˈspɪrɪtjʊəlɪst/ *n* espiritista *m & f*

spit[1] /spɪt/ *vt* (*pt* **spat** *or* **spit**, *pres p* **spitting**) escupir. ● *vi* escupir; (*rain*) lloviznar. ● *n* esputo *m*; (*spittle*) saliva *f*

spit[2] /spɪt/ (*for roasting*) asador *m*

spite /spaɪt/ *n* rencor *m.* **in** ~ **of** a pesar de. ● *vt* fastidiar. ~**ful** *a* rencoroso. ~**fully** *adv* con rencor

spitting image /spɪtɪŋˈɪmɪdʒ/ *n* vivo retrato *m*

spittle /ˈspɪtl/ *n* saliva *f*

splash /splæʃ/ *vt* salpicar. ● *vi* esparcirse; (*person*) chapotear. ● *n* salpicadura *f*; (*sound*) chapoteo *m*; (*of colour*) mancha *f*; (*drop, fam*) gota *f.* ~ **about** *vi* chapotear. ~ **down** *vi* (*spacecraft*) amerizar

spleen /spliːn/ *n* bazo *m*; (*fig*) esplín *m*

splendid /ˈsplendɪd/ *a* espléndido

splendour /ˈsplendə(r)/ *n* esplendor *m*

splint /splɪnt/ *n* tablilla *f*

splinter /ˈsplɪntə(r)/ *n* astilla *f.* ● *vi* astillarse. ~ **group** *n* grupo *m* disidente

split /splɪt/ *vt* (*pt* **split**, *pres p* **splitting**) hender, rajar; (*tear*) rajar; (*divide*) dividir; (*share*) repartir. ~ **one's sides** caerse de risa. ● *vi* partirse; (*divide*) dividirse. ~ **on s.o.** (*sl*) traicionar. ● *n* hendidura *f*; (*tear*) desgarrón *m*; (*quarrel*) ruptura *f*; (*pol*) escisión *f.* ~ **up** *vi* separarse. ~ **second** *n* fracción *f* de segundo

splurge /splɜːdʒ/ *vi* (*fam*) derrochar

splutter /ˈsplʌtə(r)/ *vi* chisporrotear; (*person*) farfullar. ● *n* chisporroteo *m*; (*speech*) farfulla *f*

spoil /spɔɪl/ *vt* (*pt* **spoilt** *or* **spoiled**) estropear, echar a perder; (*ruin*) arruinar; (*indulge*) mimar. ● *n* botín *m.* ~**s** *npl* botín *m.* ~**sport** *n* aguafiestas *m invar*

spoke[1] /spəʊk/ *see* **speak**

spoke[2] /spəʊk/ *n* (*of wheel*) radio *m*

spoken /ˈspəʊkən/ *see* **speak**

spokesman /ˈspəʊksmən/ *n* (*pl* **-men**) portavoz *m*

spong|e /spʌndʒ/ *n* esponja *f.* ● *vt* limpiar con una esponja. ● *vi.* ~**e on** vivir a costa de. ~**e-cake** *n* bizcocho *m.* ~**er** /-ə(r)/ *n* gorrón *m.* ~**y** *a* esponjoso

sponsor /ˈspɒnsə(r)/ *n* patrocinador *m*; (*surety*) garante *m.* ● *vt* patrocinar. ~**ship** *n* patrocinio *m*

spontane|ity /spɒntəˈneɪɪtɪ/ *n* espontaneidad *f.* ~**ous** /spɒnˈteɪnjəs/ *a* espontáneo. ~**ously** *adv* espontáneamente

spoof /spuːf/ *n* (*sl*) parodia *f*

spooky /ˈspuːkɪ/ *a* (**-ier**, **-iest**) (*fam*) escalofriante

spool /spuːl/ n carrete m; (of sewing-machine) canilla f

spoon /spuːn/ n cuchara f. **~fed** a (fig) mimado. **~feed** vt (pt **-fed**) dar de comer con cuchara. **~ful** n (pl **-fuls**) cucharada f

sporadic /spəˈrædɪk/ a esporádico

sport /spɔːt/ n deporte m; (amusement) pasatiempo m; (person, fam) persona f alegre, buen chico m, buena chica f. **be a good ~** ser buen perdedor. ● vt lucir. **~ing** a deportivo. **~ing chance** n probabilidad f de éxito. **~s car** n coche m deportivo. **~s coat** n chaqueta f de sport. **~sman** /ˈspɔːtsmən/ n, (pl **-men**) **~swoman** /ˈspɔːtswʊmən/ n (pl **-women**) deportista m & f

spot /spɒt/ n mancha f; (pimple) grano m; (place) lugar m; (in pattern) punto m; (drop) gota f; (a little, fam) poquito m. **in a ~** (fam) en un apuro. **on the ~** en el lugar; (without delay) en el acto. ● vt (pt **spotted**) manchar; (notice, fam) observar, ver. **~ check** n control m hecho al azar. **~less** a inmaculado. **~light** /ˈspɒtlaɪt/ n reflector m. **~ted** a moteado; ⟨cloth⟩ a puntos. **~ty** a (**-ier, -iest**) manchado; ⟨skin⟩ con granos

spouse /spaʊz/ n cónyuge m & f

spout /spaʊt/ n pico m; (jet) chorro m. **up the ~** (ruined, sl) perdido. ● vi chorrear

sprain /spreɪn/ vt torcer. ● n torcedura f

sprang /spræŋ/ see spring

sprat /spræt/ n espadín m

sprawl /sprɔːl/ vi ⟨person⟩ repanchigarse; ⟨city etc⟩ extenderse

spray /spreɪ/ n (of flowers) ramo m; (water) rociada f; (from sea) espuma f; (device) pulverizador m. ● vt rociar. **~gun** n pistola f pulverizadora

spread /spred/ vt (pt **spread**) (stretch, extend) extender; untar ⟨jam etc⟩; difundir ⟨idea, news⟩. ● vi extenderse; ⟨disease⟩ propagarse; ⟨idea, news⟩ difundirse. ● n extensión f; (paste) pasta f; (of disease) propagación f; (feast, fam) comilona f. **~eagled** a con los brazos y piernas extendidos

spree /spriː/ n. **go on a ~** (have fun, fam) ir de juerga

sprig /sprɪg/ n ramito m

sprightly /ˈspraɪtlɪ/ a (**-ier, -iest**) vivo

spring /sprɪŋ/ n (season) primavera f; (device) muelle m; (elasticity) elasticidad f; (water) manantial m. ● a de primavera. ● vt (pt **sprang**, pp **sprung**) hacer inesperadamente. ● vi saltar; (issue) brotar. **~ from** vi provenir de. **~ up** vi surgir. **~board** n trampolín m. **~time** n primavera f. **~y** a (**-ier, -iest**) elástico

sprinkl|e /ˈsprɪŋkl/ vt salpicar; (with liquid) rociar. ● n salpicadura f; (of liquid) rociada f. **~ed with** salpicado de. **~er** /-ə(r)/ n regadera f. **~ing** /ˈsprɪŋklɪŋ/ n (fig, amount) poco m

sprint /sprɪnt/ n carrera f. ● vi correr. **~er** n corredor m

sprite /spraɪt/ n duende m, hada f

sprout /spraʊt/ vi brotar. ● n brote m. **(Brussels) ~s** npl coles fpl de Bruselas

spruce /spruːs/ a elegante

sprung /sprʌŋ/ see spring. ● a de muelles

spry /spraɪ/ a (**spryer, spryest**) vivo

spud /spʌd/ n (sl) patata f, papa f (LAm)

spun /spʌn/ see spin

spur /spɜː(r)/ n espuela f; (stimulus) estímulo m. **on the ~ of the moment** impulsivamente. ● vt (pt **spurred**). **~ (on)** espolear; (fig) estimular

spurious /ˈspjʊərɪəs/ a falso. **~ly** adv falsamente

spurn /spɜːn/ vt despreciar; (reject) rechazar

spurt /spɜːt/ vi chorrear; (make sudden effort) hacer un esfuerzo repentino. ● n chorro m; (effort) esfuerzo m repentino

spy /spaɪ/ n espía m & f. ● vt divisar. ● vi espiar. **~ out** vt reconocer. **~ing** n espionaje m

squabble /ˈskwɒbl/ n riña f. ● vi reñir

squad /skwɒd/ n (mil) pelotón m; (of police) brigada f; (sport) equipo m

squadron /ˈskwɒdrən/ n (mil) escuadrón m; (naut, aviat) escuadrilla f

squalid /ˈskwɒlɪd/ a asqueroso; (wretched) miserable

squall /skwɔːl/ n turbión m. ● vi chillar. **~y** a borrascoso

squalor /ˈskwɒlə(r)/ n miseria f

squander /ˈskwɒndə(r)/ vt derrochar

square /skweə(r)/ n cuadrado m;
(open space in town) plaza f; (for
drawing) escuadra f. ● a cuadrado;
(not owing) sin deudas, iguales;
(honest) honrado; ⟨meal⟩ satisfactorio; (old-fashioned, sl) chapado
a la antigua. **all** ~ iguales. ● vt
(settle) arreglar; (math) cuadrar.
● vi (agree) cuadrar. ~ **up to**
enfrentarse con. ~**ly** adv
directamente

squash /skwɒʃ/ vt aplastar; (suppress) suprimir. ● n apiñamiento
m; (drink) zumo m; (sport) squash
m. ~**y** a blando

squat /skwɒt/ vi (pt **squatted**)
ponerse en cuclillas; (occupy illeg-
ally) ocupar sin derecho. ● n casa
f ocupada sin derecho. ● a (dumpy)
achaparrado. ~**ter** /-ə(r)/ n ocupante m & f ilegal

squawk /skwɔ:k/ n graznido m. ● vi
graznar

squeak /skwi:k/ n chillido m; (of
door etc) chirrido m. ● vi chillar;
⟨door etc⟩ chirriar. ~**y** a chirriador

squeal /skwi:l/ n chillido m. ● vi
chillar. ~ **on** (inform on, sl)
denunciar

squeamish /ˈskwi:mɪʃ/ a delicado;
(scrupulous) escrupuloso. **be** ~
about snakes tener horror a las
serpientes

squeeze /skwi:z/ vt apretar; exprimir ⟨lemon etc⟩; (extort) extorsionar
(**from** de). ● vi (force one's way)
abrirse paso. ● n estrujón m; (of
hand) apretón m. **credit** ~ n restricción f de crédito

squelch /skweltʃ/ vi chapotear. ● n
chapoteo m

squib /skwɪb/ n (firework) buscapiés
m invar

squid /skwɪd/ n calamar m

squiggle /ˈskwɪɡl/ n garabato m

squint /skwɪnt/ vi ser bizco; (look
sideways) mirar de soslayo. ● n
estrabismo m

squire /ˈskwaɪə(r)/ n terrateniente
m

squirm /skwɜ:m/ vi retorcerse

squirrel /ˈskwɪrəl/ n ardilla f

squirt /skwɜ:t/ vt arrojar a chorros.
● vi salir a chorros. ● n chorro m

St abbr (saint) /sənt/ S, San(to);
(street) C/, Calle f

stab /stæb/ vt (pt **stabbed**) apuñalar.
● n puñalada f; (pain) punzada f;
(attempt, fam) tentativa f

stabili|ty /stəˈbɪlətɪ/ n estabilidad f.
~**ze** /ˈsteɪbɪlaɪz/ vt estabilizar. ~**zer**
/-ə(r)/ n estabilizador m

stable[1] /ˈsteɪbl/ a (-er, -est) estable

stable[2] /ˈsteɪbl/ n cuadra f. ● vt
poner en una cuadra. ~**boy** n mozo
m de cuadra

stack /stæk/ n montón m. ● vt
amontonar

stadium /ˈsteɪdjəm/ n estadio m

staff /sta:f/ n (stick) palo m; (employees) personal m; (mil) estado m
mayor; (in school) profesorado m.
● vt proveer de personal

stag /stæɡ/ n ciervo m. ~**party** n
reunión f de hombres, fiesta f de
despedida de soltero

stage /steɪdʒ/ n (in theatre) escena f;
(phase) etapa f; (platform) plataforma f. **go on the** ~ hacerse
actor. ● vt representar; (arrange)
organizar. ~**coach** n (hist) dili-
gencia f. ~ **fright** n miedo m al público. ~**manager** n director m de
escena. ~ **whisper** n aparte m

stagger /ˈstæɡə(r)/ vi tambalearse.
● vt asombrar; escalonar ⟨holidays
etc⟩. ● n tambaleo m. ~**ing** a
asombroso

stagna|nt /ˈstæɡnənt/ a estancado.
~**te** /stæɡˈneɪt/ vi estancarse. ~**tion**
/-ʃn/ n estancamiento m

staid /steɪd/ a serio, formal

stain /steɪn/ vt manchar; (colour)
teñir. ● n mancha f; (liquid) tinte m.
~**ed glass window** n vidriera f de
colores. ~**less** /ˈsteɪnlɪs/ a inmaculado. ~**less steel** n acero m inoxidable. ~ **remover** n quitamanchas
m invar

stair /steə(r)/ n escalón m. ~**s** npl
escalera f. **flight of** ~**s** tramo m de
escalera. ~**case** /ˈsteəkeɪs/ n, ~**way**
n escalera f

stake /steɪk/ n estaca f; (for exe-
cution) hoguera f; (wager) apuesta f;
(com) intereses mpl. **at** ~ en juego.
● vt estacar; (wager) apostar. ~ **a
claim** reclamar

stalactite /ˈstæləktaɪt/ n estalactita f

stalagmite /ˈstæləɡmaɪt/ n esta-
lagmita f

stale /steɪl/ a (-er, -est) no fresco;
⟨bread⟩ duro; ⟨smell⟩ viciado;
⟨news⟩ viejo; (uninteresting)
gastado. ~**mate** /ˈsteɪlmeɪt/ n
(chess) ahogado m; (deadlock) punto
m muerto

stalk[1] /stɔ:k/ n tallo m

stalk² /stɔːk/ *vi* andar majestuosamente. ● *vt* seguir; ⟨*animal*⟩ acechar

stall¹ /stɔːl/ *n* (*stable*) cuadra *f*; (*in stable*) casilla *f*; (*in theatre*) butaca *f*; (*in market*) puesto *m*; (*kiosk*) quiosco *m*

stall² /stɔːl/ *vt* parar ⟨*engine*⟩. ● *vi* ⟨*engine*⟩ pararse; (*fig*) andar con rodeos

stallion /'stæljən/ *n* semental *m*

stalwart /'stɔːlwət/ *n* partidario *m* leal

stamina /'stæminə/ *n* resistencia *f*

stammer /'stæmə(r)/ *vi* tartamudear. ● *n* tartamudeo *m*

stamp /stæmp/ *vt* (*with feet*) patear; (*press*) estampar; poner un sello en ⟨*envelope*⟩; (*with rubber stamp*) sellar; (*fig*) señalar. ● *vi* patear. ● *n* sello *m*; (*with foot*) patada *f*; (*mark*) marca *f*, señal *f*. ~ **out** (*fig*) acabar con

stampede /stæm'piːd/ *n* desbandada *f*; (*fam*) pánico *m*. ● *vi* huir en desorden

stance /stɑːns/ *n* postura *f*

stand /stænd/ *vi* (*pt* **stood**) estar de pie; (*rise*) ponerse de pie; (*be*) encontrarse; (*stay firm*) permanecer; (*pol*) presentarse como candidato (**for** en). ~ **to reason** ser lógico. ● *vt* (*endure*) soportar; (*place*) poner; (*offer*) ofrecer. ~ **a chance** tener una posibilidad. ~ **one's ground** mantenerse firme. **I'll** ~ **you a drink** te invito a una copa. ● *n* posición *f*, postura *f*; (*mil*) resistencia *f*; (*for lamp etc*) pie *m*, sostén *m*; (*at market*) puesto *m*; (*booth*) quiosco *m*; (*sport*) tribuna *f*. ~ **around** no hacer nada. ~ **back** retroceder. ~ **by** *vi* estar preparado. ● *vt* (*support*) apoyar. ~ **down** *vi* retirarse. ~ **for** *vt* representar. ~ **in for** suplir a. ~ **out** *vi* destacarse. ~ **up** *vi* ponerse de pie. ~ **up for** defender. ~ **up to** *vt* resistir a

standard /'stændəd/ *n* norma *f*; (*level*) nivel *m*; (*flag*) estandarte *m*. ● *a* normal, corriente. ~**ize** *vt* uniformar. ~ **lamp** *n* lámpara *f* de pie. ~**s** *npl* valores *mpl*

stand: ~**by** *n* (*person*) reserva *f*; (*at airport*) lista *f* de espera. ~**in** *n* suplente *m* & *f*. ~**ing** /'stændɪŋ/ *a* de pie; (*upright*) derecho. ● *n* posición *f*; (*duration*) duración *f*. ~**offish** *a* (*fam*) frío. ~**point** /'stændpɔɪnt/ *n*

punto *m* de vista. ~**still** /'stændstɪl/ *n*. **at a** ~**still** parado. **come to a** ~**still** pararse

stank /stæŋk/ *see* **stink**

staple¹ /'steɪpl/ *a* principal

staple² /'steɪpl/ *n* grapa *f*. ● *vt* sujetar con una grapa. ~**r** /-ə(r)/ *n* grapadora *f*

star /stɑː/ *n* (*incl cinema*, *theatre*) estrella *f*; (*asterisk*) asterisco *m*. ● *vi* (*pt* **starred**) ser el protagonista

starboard /'stɑːbəd/ *n* estribor *m*

starch /stɑːtʃ/ *n* almidón *m*; (*in food*) fécula *f*. ● *vt* almidonar. ~**y** *a* almidonado; (*food*) feculento; (*fig*) formal

stardom /'stɑːdəm/ *n* estrellato *m*

stare /steə(r)/ *n* mirada *f* fija. ● *vi*. ~ **at** mirar fijamente

starfish /'stɑːfɪʃ/ *n* estrella *f* de mar

stark /stɑːk/ *a* (**-er**, **-est**) rígido; (*utter*) completo. ● *adv* completamente

starlight /'stɑːlaɪt/ *n* luz *f* de las estrellas

starling /'stɑːlɪŋ/ *n* estornino *m*

starry /'stɑːrɪ/ *a* estrellado. ~**-eyed** *a* (*fam*) ingenuo, idealista

start /stɑːt/ *vt* empezar; poner en marcha ⟨*machine*⟩; (*cause*) provocar. ● *vi* empezar; (*jump*) sobresaltarse; (*leave*) partir; ⟨*car etc*⟩ arrancar. ● *n* principio *m*; (*leaving*) salida *f*; (*sport*) ventaja *f*; (*jump*) susto *m*. ~**er** *n* (*sport*) participante *m* & *f*; (*auto*) motor *m* de arranque; (*culin*) primer plato *m*. ~**ing-point** *n* punto *m* de partida

startle /'stɑːtl/ *vt* asustar

starv|ation /stɑː'veɪʃn/ *n* hambre *f*. ~**e** /stɑːv/ *vt* hacer morir de hambre; (*deprive*) privar. ● *vi* morir de hambre

stash /stæʃ/ *vt* (*sl*) esconder

state /steɪt/ *n* estado *m*; (*grand style*) pompa *f*. **S~** *n* Estado *m*. **be in a** ~ estar agitado. ● *vt* declarar; expresar ⟨*views*⟩; (*fix*) fijar. ● *a* del Estado; (*schol*) público; (*with ceremony*) de gala. ~**less** *a* sin patria

stately /'steɪtlɪ/ *a* (**-ier**, **-iest**) majestuoso

statement /'steɪtmənt/ *n* declaración *f*; (*account*) informe *m*. **bank** ~ *n* estado *m* de cuenta

stateroom /'steɪtrʊm/ *n* (*on ship*) camarote *m*

statesman /'steɪtsmən/ *n* (*pl* **-men**) estadista *m*

static /'stætɪk/ *a* inmóvil. ~s *n* estática *f*; *(rad, TV)* parásitos *mpl* atmosféricos, interferencias *fpl*

station /'steɪʃn/ *n* estación *f*; *(status)* posición *f* social. ● *vt* colocar; *(mil)* estacionar

stationary /'steɪʃənərɪ/ *a* estacionario

stationer /'steɪʃənə(r)/ *n* papelero *m*. ~'s (shop) *n* papelería *f*. ~y *n* artículos *mpl* de escritorio

station-wagon /'steɪʃnwægən/ *n* furgoneta *f*

statistic /stə'tɪstɪk/ *n* estadística *f*. ~al /stə'tɪstɪkl/ *a* estadístico. ~s /stə'tɪstɪks/ *n* *(science)* estadística *f*

statue /'stætʃu:/ *n* estatua *f*. ~sque /-ʊ'esk/ *a* escultural. ~tte /-ʊ'et/ *n* figurilla *f*

stature /'stætʃə(r)/ *n* talla *f*, estatura *f*

status /'steɪtəs/ *n* posición *f* social; *(prestige)* categoría *f*; *(jurid)* estado *m*

statut|e /'stætʃu:t/ *n* estatuto *m*. ~ory /-ʊtrɪ/ *a* estatutario

staunch /stɔ:nʃ/ *a* (-er, -est) leal. ~ly *adv* lealmente

stave /'steɪv/ *n* *(mus)* pentagrama *m*. ● *vt*. ~ off evitar

stay /steɪ/ *n* soporte *m*, sostén *m*; *(of time)* estancia *f*; *(jurid)* suspensión *f*. ● *vi* quedar; *(spend time)* detenerse; *(reside)* alojarse. ● *vt* matar ⟨hunger⟩. ~ the course terminar. ~ in quedar en casa. ~ put mantenerse firme. ~ up no acostarse. ~ing-power *n* resistencia *f*

stays /steɪz/ *npl* *(old use)* corsé *m*

stead /sted/ *n*. in s.o.'s ~ en lugar de uno. stand s.o. in good ~ ser útil a uno

steadfast /'stedfɑ:st/ *a* firme

stead|ily /'stedɪlɪ/ *adv* firmemente; *(regularly)* regularmente. ~y /'stedɪ/ *a* (-ier, -iest) firme; *(regular)* regular; *(dependable)* serio

steak /steɪk/ *n* filete *m*

steal /sti:l/ *vt* *(pt* stole, *pp* stolen) robar. ~ the show llevarse los aplausos. ~ in *vi* entrar a hurtadillas. ~ out *vi* salir a hurtadillas

stealth /stelθ/ *n*. by ~ sigilosamente. ~y *a* sigiloso

steam /sti:m/ *n* vapor *m*; *(energy)* energía *f*. ● *vt* *(cook)* cocer al vapor; empañar ⟨window⟩. ● *vi* echar vapor. ~ ahead *(fam)* hacer progresos. ~ up *vi* ⟨glass⟩ empañar.

~engine *n* máquina *f* de vapor. ~er /'sti:mə(r)/ *n* *(ship)* barco *m* de vapor. ~roller /'sti:mrəʊlə(r)/ *n* apisonadora *f*. ~y *a* húmedo

steel /sti:l/ *n* acero *m*. ● *vt*. ~ o.s. fortalecerse. ~ industry *n* industria *f* siderúrgica. ~ wool *n* estropajo *m* de acero. ~y *a* acerado; *(fig)* duro, inflexible

steep /sti:p/ *a* (-er, -est) escarpado; ⟨price⟩ *(fam)* exorbitante. ● *vt* *(soak)* remojar. ~ed in *(fig)* empapado de

steeple /'sti:pl/ *n* aguja *f*, campanario *m*. ~chase /'sti:pltʃeɪs/ *n* carrera *f* de obstáculos

steep: ~ly *adv* de modo empinado. ~ness *n* lo escarpado

steer /stɪə(r)/ *vt* guiar; gobernar ⟨ship⟩. ● *vi* *(in ship)* gobernar. ~ clear of evitar. ~ing *n* *(auto)* dirección *f*. ~ing-wheel *n* volante *m*

stem /stem/ *n* tallo *m*; *(of glass)* pie *m*; *(of word)* raíz *f*; *(of ship)* roda *f*. ● *vt* *(pt* stemmed) detener. ● *vi*. ~ from provenir de

stench /stentʃ/ *n* hedor *m*

stencil /'stensl/ *n* plantilla *f*; *(for typing)* cliché *m*. ● *vt* *(pt* stencilled) estarcir

stenographer /ste'nɒɡrəfə(r)/ *n* *(Amer)* estenógrafo *m*

step /step/ *vi* *(pt* stepped) ir. ~ down retirarse. ~ in entrar; *(fig)* intervenir. ~ up *vt* aumentar. ● *n* paso *m*; *(surface)* escalón *m*; *(fig)* medida *f*. in ~ *(fig)* de acuerdo con. out of ~ *(fig)* en desacuerdo con. ~brother /'stepbrʌðə(r)/ *n* hermanastro *m*. ~daughter *n* hijastra *f*. ~father *n* padrastro *m*. ~ladder *n* escalera *f* de tijeras. ~mother *n* madrastra *f*. ~ping-stone /'stepɪŋstəʊn/ *n* pasadera *f*; *(fig)* escalón *m*. ~sister *n* hermanastra *f*. ~son *n* hijastro *m*

stereo /'sterɪəʊ/ *n* *(pl* -os) cadena *f* estereofónica. ● *a* estereofónico. ~phonic /sterɪəʊ'fɒnɪk/ *a* estereofónico. ~type /'sterɪəʊtaɪp/ *n* estereotipo *m*. ~typed *a* estereotipado

steril|e /'steraɪl/ *a* estéril. ~ity /stə'rɪlətɪ/ *n* esterilidad *f*. ~ization /-'zeɪʃn/ *n* esterilización *f*. ~ize /'sterɪlaɪz/ *vt* esterilizar

sterling /'stɜ:lɪŋ/ *n* libras *fpl* esterlinas. ● *a* ⟨pound⟩ esterlina; *(fig)* excelente. ~ silver *n* plata *f* de ley

stern¹ /stɜ:n/ *n* (*of boat*) popa *f*

stern² /stɜ:n/ *a* (**-er, -est**) severo. **~ly** *adv* severamente

stethoscope /'steθəskəʊp/ *n* estetoscopio *m*

stew /stju:/ *vt/i* guisar. ● *n* guisado *m*. **in a ~** (*fam*) en un apuro

steward /stjʊəd/ *n* administrador *m*; (*on ship, aircraft*) camarero *m*. **~ess** /-'des/ *n* camarera *f*; (*on aircraft*) azafata *f*

stick /stɪk/ *n* palo *m*; (*for walking*) bastón *m*; (*of celery etc*) tallo *m*. ● *vt* (*pt* **stuck**) (*glue*) pegar; (*put, fam*) poner; (*thrust*) clavar; (*endure, sl*) soportar. ● *vi* pegarse; (*remain, fam*) quedarse; (*jam*) bloquearse. **~ at** (*fam*) perseverar en. **~ out** sobresalir; (*catch the eye, fam*) resaltar. **~ to** aferrarse a; cumplir ⟨*promise*⟩. **~ up for** (*fam*) defender. **~er** /'stɪkə(r)/ *n* pegatina *f*. **~ing-plaster** *n* esparadrapo *m*. **~in-the-mud** *n* persona *f* chapada a la antigua

stickler /'stɪklə(r)/ *n*. **be a ~ for** insistir en

sticky /'stɪkɪ/ *a* (**-ier, -iest**) pegajoso; ⟨*label*⟩ engomado; (*sl*) difícil

stiff /stɪf/ *a* (**-er, -est**) rígido; (*difficult*) difícil; ⟨*manner*⟩ estirado; ⟨*drink*⟩ fuerte; ⟨*price*⟩ subido; ⟨*joint*⟩ tieso; ⟨*muscle*⟩ con agujetas. **~en** /'stɪfn/ *vt* poner tieso. **~ly** *adv* rígidamente. **~ neck** *n* tortícolis *f*. **~ness** *n* rigidez *f*

stifl|e /'staɪfl/ *vt* sofocar. **~ing** *a* sofocante

stigma /'stɪgmə/ *n* (*pl* **-as**) estigma *m*. (*pl* **stigmata** /'stɪgmətə/) (*relig*) estigma *m*. **~tize** *vt* estigmatizar

stile /staɪl/ *n* portillo *m* con escalones

stiletto /stɪ'letəʊ/ *n* (*pl* **-os**) estilete *m*. **~ heels** *npl* tacones *mpl* aguja

still¹ /stɪl/ *a* inmóvil; (*peaceful*) tranquilo; ⟨*drink*⟩ sin gas. ● *n* silencio *m*. ● *adv* todavía; (*nevertheless*) sin embargo

still² /stɪl/ (*apparatus*) alambique *m*

still: ~born *a* nacido muerto. **~ life** *n* (*pl* **-s**) bodegón *m*. **~ness** *n* tranquilidad *f*

stilted /'stɪltɪd/ *a* artificial

stilts /stɪlts/ *npl* zancos *mpl*

stimul|ant /'stɪmjʊlənt/ *n* estimulante *m*. **~ate** /'stɪmjʊleɪt/ *vt* estimular. **~ation** /-'leɪʃn/ *n* estímulo *m*. **~us** /'stɪmjʊləs/ *n* (*pl* **-li** /-laɪ/) estímulo *m*

sting /stɪŋ/ *n* picadura *f*; (*organ*) aguijón *m*. ● *vt/i* (*pt* **stung**) picar

sting|iness /'stɪndʒɪnɪs/ *n* tacañería *f*. **~y** /'stɪndʒɪ/ *a* (**-ier, -iest**) tacaño

stink /stɪŋk/ *n* hedor *m*. ● *vi* (*pt* **stank** *or* **stunk**, *pp* **stunk**) oler mal. ● *vt*. **~ out** apestar ⟨*room*⟩; ahuyentar ⟨*person*⟩. **~er** /-ə(r)/ *n* (*sl*) problema *m* difícil; (*person*) mal bicho *m*

stint /stɪnt/ *n* (*work*) trabajo *m*. ● *vi*. **~ on** escatimar

stipple /'stɪpl/ *vt* puntear

stipulat|e /'stɪpjʊleɪt/ *vt/i* estipular. **~ion** /-'leɪʃn/ *n* estipulación *f*

stir /stɜ:(r)/ *vt* (*pt* **stirred**) remover, agitar; (*mix*) mezclar; (*stimulate*) estimular. ● *vi* moverse. ● *n* agitación *f*; (*commotion*) conmoción *f*

stirrup /'stɪrəp/ *n* estribo *m*

stitch /stɪtʃ/ *n* (*in sewing*) puntada *f*; (*in knitting*) punto *m*; (*pain*) dolor *m* de costado; (*med*) punto *m* de sutura. **be in ~es** (*fam*) desternillarse de risa. ● *vt* coser

stoat /stəʊt/ *n* armiño *m*

stock /stɒk/ *n* (*com, supplies*) existencias *fpl*; (*com, variety*) surtido *m*; (*livestock*) ganado *m*; (*lineage*) linaje *m*; (*finance*) acciones *fpl*; (*culin*) caldo *m*; (*plant*) alhelí *m*. **out of ~** agotado. **take ~** (*fig*) evaluar. ● *a* corriente; (*fig*) trillado. ● *vt* abastecer (**with** de). ● *vi*. **~ up** abastecerse (**with** de). **~broker** /'stɒkbrəʊkə(r)/ *n* corredor *m* de bolsa. **S~ Exchange** *n* bolsa *f*. **well-~ed** *a* bien provisto

stocking /'stɒkɪŋ/ *n* media *f*

stock: ~-in-trade /'stɒkɪntreɪd/ *n* existencias *fpl*. **~ist** /'stɒkɪst/ *n* distribuidor *m*. **~pile** /'stɒkpaɪl/ *n* reservas *fpl*. ● *vt* acumular. **~still** *a* inmóvil. **~taking** *n* (*com*) inventario *m*

stocky /'stɒkɪ/ *a* (**-ier, -iest**) achaparrado

stodg|e /stɒdʒ/ *n* (*fam*) comida *f* pesada. **~y** *a* pesado

stoic /'stəʊɪk/ *n* estoico. **~al** *a* estoico. **~ally** *adv* estoicamente. **~ism** /-sɪzm/ *n* estoicismo *m*

stoke /stəʊk/ *vt* alimentar. **~r** /'stəʊkə(r)/ *n* fogonero *m*

stole¹ /stəʊl/ *see* **steal**

stole² /stəʊl/ *n* estola *f*

stolen /'stəʊlən/ *see* **steal**

stolid /'stɒlɪd/ *a* impasible. **~ly** *adv* impasiblemente

stomach /'stʌmək/ *n* estómago *m*.
● *vt* soportar. **~ache** *n* dolor *m* de
estómago

ston|e /stəʊn/ *n* piedra *f*; (*med*) cálculo *m*; (*in fruit*) hueso *m*; (*weight*,
pl **stone**) peso *m* de 14 libras (=
6,348 *kg*). ● *a* de piedra. ● *vt* apedrear; deshuesar ⟨*fruit*⟩. **~e-deaf** *a*
sordo como una tapia. **~emason**
/'stəʊnmeɪsn/ *n* albañil *m*. **~ework**
/'stəʊnwɜːk/ *n* cantería *f*. **~y** *a* pedregoso; (*like stone*) pétreo

stood /stʊd/ *see* **stand**

stooge /stuːdʒ/ *n* (*in theatre*) compañero *m*; (*underling*) lacayo *m*

stool /stuːl/ *n* taburete *m*

stoop /stuːp/ *vi* inclinarse; (*fig*)
rebajarse. ● *n.* **have a ~** ser cargado de espaldas

stop /stɒp/ *vt* (*pt* **stopped**) parar;
(*cease*) terminar; tapar ⟨*a leak etc*⟩;
(*prevent*) impedir; (*interrupt*) interrumpir. ● *vi* pararse; (*stay, fam*)
quedarse. ● *n* (*bus etc*) parada *f*;
(*gram*) punto *m*; (*mec*) tope *m*. **~
dead** *vi* pararse en seco. **~cock**
/'stɒpkɒk/ *n* llave *f* de paso. **~gap**
/'stɒpgæp/ *n* remedio *m* provisional.
~(-over) *n* escala *f*. **~page**
/'stɒpɪdʒ/ *n* parada *f*; (*of work*) paro
m; (*interruption*) interrupción *f*.
~per /'stɒpə(r)/ *n* tapón *m*. **~press**
n noticias *fpl* de última hora. **~
light** *n* luz *f* de freno. **~watch** *n*
cronómetro *m*

storage /'stɔːrɪdʒ/ *n* almacenamiento *m*. **~ heater** *n* acumulador *m*. **in cold ~** almacenaje *m*
frigorífico

store /stɔː(r)/ *n* provisión *f*; (*shop*,
depot) almacén *m*; (*fig*) reserva *f*. **in
~** en reserva. **set ~ by** dar importancia a. ● *vt* (*for future*) poner en
reserva; (*in warehouse*) almacenar.
~ up *vt* acumular

storeroom /'stɔːruːm/ *n* despensa *f*

storey /'stɔːrɪ/ *n* (*pl* **-eys**) piso *m*

stork /stɔːk/ *n* cigüeña *f*

storm /stɔːm/ *n* tempestad *f*; (*mil*)
asalto *m*. ● *vi* rabiar. ● *vt* (*mil*) asaltar. **~y** *a* tempestuoso

story /'stɔːrɪ/ *n* historia *f*; (*in newspaper*) artículo *m*; (*fam*) mentira *f*,
cuento *m*. **~teller** *n* cuentista *m & f*

stout /staʊt/ *a* (**-er, -est**) (*fat*) gordo;
(*brave*) valiente. ● *n* cerveza *f*
negra. **~ness** *n* corpulencia *f*

stove /stəʊv/ *n* estufa *f*

stow /stəʊ/ *vt* guardar; (*hide*) esconder. ● *vi.* **~ away** viajar de polizón.
~away /'stəʊəweɪ/ *n* polizón *m*

straddle /'strædl/ *vt* estar a
horcajadas

straggl|e /'strægl/ *vi* rezagarse. **~y**
a desordenado

straight /streɪt/ *a* (**-er, -est**) derecho,
recto; (*tidy*) en orden; (*frank*)
franco; (*drink*) solo, puro; (*hair*)
lacio. ● *adv* derecho; (*direct*) directamente; (*without delay*)
inmediatamente. **~ on** todo recto.
~ out sin vacilar. **go ~** enmendarse. ● *n* recta *f*. **~ away**
inmediatamente. **~en** /'streɪtn/ *vt*
enderezar. ● *vi* enderezarse.
~forward /streɪt'fɔːwəd/ *a* franco;
(*easy*) sencillo. **~forwardly** *adv*
francamente. **~ness** *n* rectitud *f*

strain[1] /streɪn/ *n* (*tension*) tensión *f*;
(*injury*) torcedura *f*. ● *vt* estirar;
(*tire*) cansar; (*injure*) torcer; (*sieve*)
colar

strain[2] /streɪn/ *n* (*lineage*) linaje *m*;
(*streak*) tendencia *f*

strained /streɪnd/ *a* forzado; (*relations*) tirante

strainer /-ə(r)/ *n* colador *m*

strains /streɪnz/ *npl* (*mus*) acordes
mpl

strait /streɪt/ *n* estrecho *m*. **~jacket**
n camisa *f* de fuerza. **~laced** *a*
remilgado, gazmoño. **~s** *npl* apuro
m

strand /strænd/ *n* (*thread*) hebra *f*;
(*sand*) playa *f*. ● *vi* ⟨*ship*⟩ varar. **be
~ed** quedarse sin recursos

strange /streɪndʒ/ *a* (**-er, -est**)
extraño, raro; (*not known*) desconocido; (*unaccustomed*) nuevo. **~ly**
adv extrañamente. **~ness** *n* extrañeza *f*. **~r** /'streɪndʒə(r)/ *n* desconocido *m*

strangl|e /'stræŋgl/ *vt* estrangular; (*fig*) ahogar. **~lehold**
/'stræŋglhəʊld/ *n* (*fig*) dominio *m*
completo. **~ler** /-ə(r)/ *n* estrangulador *m*. **~ulation** /stræŋgjʊ'leɪʃn/
n estrangulación *f*

strap /stræp/ *n* correa *f*; (*of garment*)
tirante *m*. ● *vt* (*pt* **strapped**) atar
con correa; (*flog*) azotar

strapping /'stræpɪŋ/ *a* robusto

strata /'strɑːtə/ *see* **stratum**

strat|agem /'strætədʒəm/ *n* estratagema *f*. **~egic** /strə'tiːdʒɪk/ *a*
estratégico. **~egically** *adv* estratégicamente. **~egist** *n* estratega

m & f. **~egy** /'strætədʒɪ/ *n* estrategia *f*

stratum /'strɑːtəm/ *n* (*pl* **strata**) estrato *m*

straw /strɔː/ *n* paja *f.* **the last ~** el colmo

strawberry /'strɔːbərɪ/ *n* fresa *f*

stray /streɪ/ *vi* vagar; (*deviate*) desviarse (**from** de). ● *a* ⟨*animal*⟩ extraviado, callejero; (*isolated*) aislado. ● *n* animal *m* extraviado, animal *m* callejero

streak /striːk/ *n* raya *f*; (*of madness*) vena *f.* ● *vt* rayar. ● *vi* moverse como un rayo. **~y** *a* (**-ier, -iest**) rayado; ⟨*bacon*⟩ entreverado

stream /striːm/ *n* arroyo *m*; (*current*) corriente *f*; (*of people*) desfile *m*; (*schol*) grupo *m.* ● *vi* correr. **~ out** *vi* ⟨*people*⟩ salir en tropel

streamer /'striːmə(r)/ *n* (*paper*) serpentina *f*; (*flag*) gallardete *m*

streamline /'striːmlaɪn/ *vt* dar línea aerodinámica a; (*simplify*) simplificar. **~d** *a* aerodinámico

street /striːt/ *n* calle *f*. **~car** /'striːtkɑː/ *n* (*Amer*) tranvía *m.* **~ lamp** farol *m.* **~ map** *n*, **~ plan** *n* plano *m*

strength /streŋθ/ *n* fuerza *f*; (*of wall etc*) solidez *f.* **on the ~ of** a base de. **~en** /'streŋθn/ *vt* reforzar

strenuous /'strenjʊəs/ *a* enérgico; (*arduous*) arduo; (*tiring*) fatigoso. **~ly** *adv* enérgicamente

stress /stres/ *n* énfasis *f*; (*gram*) acento *m*; (*mec, med, tension*) tensión *f.* ● *vt* insistir en

stretch /stretʃ/ *vt* estirar; (*extend*) extender; (*exaggerate*) forzar. **~ a point** hacer una excepción. ● *vi* estirarse; (*extend*) extenderse. ● *n* estirón *m*; (*period*) período *m*; (*of road*) tramo *m.* **at a ~** seguido; (*in one go*) de un tirón. **~er** /'stretʃə(r)/ *n* camilla *f*

strew /struː/ *vt* (*pt* **strewed**, *pp* **strewn** *or* **strewed**) esparcir; (*cover*) cubrir

stricken /'strɪkən/ *a.* **~ with** afectado de

strict /strɪkt/ *a* (**-er, -est**) severo; (*precise*) estricto, preciso. **~ly** *adv* estrictamente. **~ly speaking** en rigor

stricture /'strɪktʃə(r)/ *n* crítica *f*; (*constriction*) constricción *f*

stride /straɪd/ *vi* (*pt* **strode**, *pp* **stridden**) andar a zancadas. ● *n* zancada

f. **take sth in one's ~** hacer algo con facilidad, tomarse las cosas con calma

strident /'straɪdnt/ *a* estridente

strife /straɪf/ *n* conflicto *m*

strike /straɪk/ *vt* (*pt* **struck**) golpear; encender ⟨*match*⟩; encontrar ⟨*gold etc*⟩; ⟨*clock*⟩ dar. ● *vi* golpear; (*go on strike*) declararse en huelga; (*be on strike*) estar en huelga; (*attack*) atacar; ⟨*clock*⟩ dar la hora. ● *n* (*of workers*) huelga *f*; (*attack*) ataque *m*; (*find*) descubrimiento *m.* **on ~** en huelga. **~ off**, **~ out** tachar. **~ up a friendship** trabar amistad. **~r** /'straɪkə(r)/ *n* huelguista *m & f*

striking /'straɪkɪŋ/ *a* impresionante

string /strɪŋ/ *n* cuerda *f*; (*of lies, pearls*) sarta *f.* **pull ~s** tocar todos los resortes. ● *vt* (*pt* **strung**) (*thread*) ensartar. **~ along** (*fam*) engañar. **~ out** extender(se). **~ed** *a* (*mus*) de cuerda

stringen|cy /'strɪndʒənsɪ/ *n* rigor *m.* **~t** /'strɪndʒənt/ *a* riguroso

stringy /'strɪŋɪ/ *a* fibroso

strip /strɪp/ *vt* (*pt* **stripped**) desnudar; (*tear away, deprive*) quitar; desmontar ⟨*machine*⟩. ● *vi* desnudarse. ● *n* tira *f.* **~ cartoon** *n* historieta *f*

stripe /straɪp/ *n* raya *f*; (*mil*) galón *m.* **~d** *a* a rayas, rayado

strip: **~ light** *n* tubo *m* fluorescente. **~per** /-ə(r)/ *n* artista *m & f* de striptease. **~tease** *n* número *m* del desnudo, striptease *m*

strive /straɪv/ *vi* (*pt* **strove**, *pp* **striven**). **~ to** esforzarse por

strode /strəʊd/ *see* **stride**

stroke /strəʊk/ *n* golpe *m*; (*in swimming*) brazada *f*; (*med*) apoplejía *f*; (*of pen etc*) rasgo *m*; (*of clock*) campanada *f*; (*caress*) caricia *f.* ● *vt* acariciar

stroll /strəʊl/ *vi* pasearse. ● *n* paseo *m*

strong /strɒŋ/ *a* (**-er, -est**) fuerte. **~-box** *n* caja *f* fuerte. **~hold** /'strɒŋhəʊld/ *n* fortaleza *f*; (*fig*) baluarte *m.* **~ language** *n* palabras *fpl* fuertes, palabras *fpl* subidas de tono. **~ly** *adv* (*greatly*) fuertemente; (*with energy*) enérgicamente; (*deeply*) profundamente. **~ measures** *npl* medidas *fpl* enérgicas. **~-minded** *a* resuelto. **~-room** *n* cámara *f* acorazada

stroppy /'strɒpɪ/ *a* (*sl*) irascible

strove /strəʊv/ *see* **strive**

struck /strʌk/ *see* **strike**. **~ on** (*sl*) entusiasta de

structur|al /'strʌktʃərəl/ *a* estructural. **~e** /'strʌktʃə(r)/ *n* estructura *f*

struggle /'strʌgl/ *vi* luchar. **~ to one's feet** levantarse con dificultad. ● *n* lucha *f*

strum /strʌm/ *vt/i* (*pt* **strummed**) rasguear

strung /strʌŋ/ *see* **string**. ● *a*. **~ up** (*tense*) nervioso

strut /strʌt/ *n* puntal *m*; (*walk*) pavoneo *m*. ● *vi* (*pt* **strutted**) pavonearse

stub /stʌb/ *n* cabo *m*; (*counterfoil*) talón *m*; (*of cigarette*) colilla *f*; (*of tree*) tocón *m*. ● *vt* (*pt* **stubbed**). **~ out** apagar

stubble /'stʌbl/ *n* rastrojo *m*; (*beard*) barba *f* de varios días

stubborn /'stʌbən/ *a* terco. **~ly** *adv* tercamente. **~ness** *n* terquedad *f*

stubby /'stʌbɪ/ *a* (**-ier, -iest**) achaparrado

stucco /'stʌkəʊ/ *n* (*pl* **-oes**) estuco *m*

stuck /stʌk/ *see* **stick**. ● *a* (*jammed*) bloqueado; (*in difficulties*) en un apuro. **~ on** (*sl*) encantado con. **~-up** *a* (*sl*) presumido

stud¹ /stʌd/ *n* tachón *m*; (*for collar*) botón *m*. ● *vt* (*pt* **studded**) tachonar. **~ded with** sembrado de

stud² /stʌd/ *n* (*of horses*) caballeriza *f*

student /'stjuːdənt/ *n* estudiante *m & f*

studied /'stʌdɪd/ *a* deliberado

studio /'stjuːdɪəʊ/ *n* (*pl* **-os**) estudio *m*. **~ couch** *n* sofá *m* cama. **~ flat** *n* estudio *m* de artista

studious /'stjuːdɪəs/ *a* estudioso; (*studied*) deliberado. **~ly** *adv* estudiosamente; (*carefully*) cuidadosamente

study /'stʌdɪ/ *n* estudio *m*; (*office*) despacho *m*. ● *vt/i* estudiar

stuff /stʌf/ *n* materia *f*, sustancia *f*; (*sl*) cosas *fpl*. ● *vt* rellenar; disecar ‹*animal*›; (*cram*) atiborrar; (*block up*) tapar; (*put*) meter de prisa. **~ing** *n* relleno *m*

stuffy /'stʌfɪ/ *a* (**-ier, -iest**) mal ventilado; (*old-fashioned*) chapado a la antigua

stumble /'stʌmbl/ *vi* tropezar. **~e across, ~e on** tropezar con. ● *n*

tropezón *m*. **~ing-block** *n* tropiezo *m*, impedimento *m*

stump /stʌmp/ *n* cabo *m*; (*of limb*) muñón *m*; (*of tree*) tocón *m*. **~ed** /stʌmpt/ *a* (*fam*) perplejo. **~y** /'stʌmpɪ/ *a* (**-ier, -iest**) achaparrado

stun /stʌn/ *vt* (*pt* **stunned**) aturdir; (*bewilder*) pasmar. **~ning** *a* (*fabulous, fam*) estupendo

stung /stʌŋ/ *see* **sting**

stunk /stʌŋk/ *see* **stink**

stunt¹ /stʌnt/ *n* (*fam*) truco *m* publicitario

stunt² /stʌnt/ *vt* impedir el desarrollo de. **~ed** *a* enano

stupefy /'stjuːpɪfaɪ/ *vt* dejar estupefacto

stupendous /stjuː'pendəs/ *a* estupendo. **~ly** *adv* estupendamente

stupid /'stjuːpɪd/ *a* estúpido. **~ity** /-'pɪdətɪ/ *n* estupidez *f*. **~ly** *adv* estúpidamente

stupor /'stjuːpə(r)/ *n* estupor *m*

sturd|iness /'stɜːdɪnɪs/ *n* robustez *f*. **~y** /'stɜːdɪ/ *a* (**-ier, -iest**) robusto

sturgeon /'stɜːdʒən/ *n* (*pl* **sturgeon**) esturión *m*

stutter /'stʌtə(r)/ *vi* tartamudear. ● *n* tartamudeo *m*

sty¹ /staɪ/ *n* (*pl* **sties**) pocilga *f*

sty² /staɪ/ *n* (*pl* **sties**) (*med*) orzuelo *m*

styl|e /staɪl/ *n* estilo *m*; (*fashion*) moda *f*. **in ~** con todo lujo. ● *vt* diseñar. **~ish** /'staɪlɪʃ/ *a* elegante. **~ishly** *adv* elegantemente. **~ist** /'staɪlɪst/ *n* estilista *m & f*. **hair ~ist** *n* peluquero *m*. **~ized** /'staɪlaɪzd/ *a* estilizado

stylus /'staɪləs/ *n* (*pl* **-uses**) aguja *f* (de tocadiscos)

suave /swɑːv/ *a* (*pej*) zalamero

sub... /sʌb/ *pref* sub...

subaquatic /sʌbə'kwætɪk/ *a* subacuático

subconscious /sʌb'kɒnʃəs/ *a & n* subconsciente (*m*). **~ly** *adv* de modo subconsciente

subcontinent /sʌb'kɒntɪnənt/ *n* subcontinente *m*

subcontract /sʌbkən'trækt/ *vt* subcontratar. **~or** /-ɔ(r)/ *n* subcontratista *m & f*

subdivide /sʌbdɪ'vaɪd/ *vt* subdividir

subdue /səb'djuː/ *vt* dominar (*feelings*); sojuzgar ‹*country*›. **~d** *a* (*depressed*) abatido; ‹*light*› suave

subhuman /sʌb'hjuːmən/ *a* infrahumano

subject /'sʌbdʒɪkt/ *a* sometido. **~ to** sujeto a. ● *n* súbdito *m*; (*theme*) asunto *m*; (*schol*) asignatura *f*; (*gram*) sujeto *m*; (*of painting, play, book etc*) tema *m*. /səb'dʒekt/ *vt* sojuzgar; (*submit*) someter. **~ion** /-ʃn/ *n* sometimiento *m*

subjective /səb'dʒektɪv/ *a* subjetivo. **~ly** *adv* subjetivamente

subjugate /'sʌbdʒʊɡeɪt/ *vt* subyugar

subjunctive /səb'dʒʌŋktɪv/ *a & n* subjuntivo (*m*)

sublet /sʌb'let/ *vt* (*pt* **sublet**, *pres p* **subletting**) subarrendar

sublimat|e /'sʌblɪmeɪt/ *vt* sublimar. **~ion** /-'meɪʃn/ *n* sublimación *f*

sublime /sə'blaɪm/ *a* sublime. **~ly** *adv* sublimemente

submarine /sʌbmə'riːn/ *n* submarino *m*

submerge /səb'mɜːdʒ/ *vt* sumergir. ● *vi* sumergirse

submi|ssion /səb'mɪʃn/ *n* sumisión *f*. **~ssive** /-sɪv/ *a* sumiso. **~t** /səb'mɪt/ *vt* (*pt* **submitted**) someter. ● *vi* someterse

subordinat|e /sə'bɔːdɪnət/ *a & n* subordinado (*m*). /sə'bɔːdɪneɪt/ *vt* subordinar. **~ion** /-'neɪʃn/ *n* subordinación *f*

subscri|be /səb'skraɪb/ *vi* suscribir. **~be to** suscribir (*fund*); (*agree*) estar de acuerdo con; abonarse a (*newspaper*). **~ber** /-ə(r)/ *n* abonado *m*. **~ption** /-rɪpʃn/ *n* suscripción *f*

subsequent /'sʌbsɪkwənt/ *a* subsiguiente. **~ly** *adv* posteriormente

subservient /səb'sɜːvjənt/ *a* servil

subside /səb'saɪd/ *vi* ⟨*land*⟩ hundirse; (*flood*) bajar; ⟨*storm, wind*⟩ amainar. **~nce** *n* hundimiento *m*

subsidiary /səb'sɪdɪərɪ/ *a* subsidiario. ● *n* (*com*) sucursal *m*

subsid|ize /'sʌbsɪdaɪz/ *vt* subvencionar. **~y** /'sʌbsədɪ/ *n* subvención *f*

subsist /səb'sɪst/ *vi* subsistir. **~ence** *n* subsistencia *f*

subsoil /'sʌbsɔɪl/ *n* subsuelo *m*

subsonic /sʌb'sɒnɪk/ *a* subsónico

substance /'sʌbstəns/ *n* substancia *f*

substandard /sʌb'stændəd/ *a* inferior

substantial /səb'stænʃl/ *a* sólido; ⟨*meal*⟩ substancial; (*considerable*) considerable. **~ly** *adv* considerablemente

substantiate /səb'stænʃɪeɪt/ *vt* justificar

substitut|e /'sʌbstɪtjuːt/ *n* substituto *m*. ● *vt/i* substituir. **~ion** /-'tjuːʃn/ *n* substitución *f*

subterfuge /'sʌbtəfjuːdʒ/ *n* subterfugio *m*

subterranean /sʌbtə'reɪnjən/ *a* subterráneo

subtitle /'sʌbtaɪtl/ *n* subtítulo *m*

subtle /'sʌtl/ *a* (**-er**, **-est**) sutil. **~ty** *n* sutileza *f*

subtract /səb'trækt/ *vt* restar. **~ion** /-ʃn/ *n* resta *f*

suburb /'sʌbɜːb/ *n* barrio *m*. **the ~s** las afueras *fpl*. **~an** /sə'bɜːbən/ *a* suburbano. **~ia** /sə'bɜːbɪə/ *n* las afueras *fpl*

subvention /səb'venʃn/ *n* subvención *f*

subver|sion /səb'vɜːʃn/ *n* subversión *f*. **~sive** /səb'vɜːsɪv/ *a* subversivo. **~t** /səb'vɜːt/ *vt* subvertir

subway /'sʌbweɪ/ *n* paso *m* subterráneo; (*Amer*) metro *m*

succeed /sək'siːd/ *vi* tener éxito. ● *vt* suceder a. **~ in doing** lograr hacer. **~ing** *a* sucesivo

success /sək'ses/ *n* éxito *m*. **~ful** *a* que tiene éxito; (*chosen*) elegido

succession /sək'seʃn/ *n* sucesión *f*. **in ~** sucesivamente, seguidos

successive /sək'sesɪv/ *a* sucesivo. **~ly** *adv* sucesivamente

successor /sək'sesə(r)/ *n* sucesor *m*

succinct /sək'sɪŋkt/ *a* sucinto

succour /'sʌkə(r)/ *vt* socorrer. ● *n* socorro *m*

succulent /'sʌkjʊlənt/ *a* suculento

succumb /sə'kʌm/ *vi* sucumbir

such /sʌtʃ/ *a* tal. ● *pron* los que, las que; (*so much*) tanto. **and ~** y tal. ● *adv* tan. **~ a big house** una casa tan grande. **~ and ~** tal o cual. **~ as it is** tal como es. **~like** *a* (*fam*) semejante, de ese tipo

suck /sʌk/ *vt* chupar; sorber ⟨*liquid*⟩. **~ up** absorber. **~ up to** (*sl*) dar coba a. **~er** /'sʌkə(r)/ *n* (*plant*) chupón *m*; (*person, fam*) primo *m*

suckle /sʌkl/ *vt* amamantar

suction /'sʌkʃn/ *n* succión *f*

sudden /'sʌdn/ *a* repentino. **all of a ~** de repente. **~ly** *adv* de repente. **~ness** *lo* repentino

suds /sʌds/ *npl* espuma *f* (de jabón)

sue /suː/ *vt* (*pres p* **suing**) demandar (**for** por)

suede /sweɪd/ *n* ante *m*

suet /'suːt/ *n* sebo *m*

suffer /'sʌfə(r)/ *vt* sufrir; (*tolerate*) tolerar. ● *vi* sufrir. **~ance** /'sʌfərəns/ *n*. **on ~ance** por tolerancia. **~ing** *n* sufrimiento *m*

suffic|e /sə'faɪs/ *vi* bastar. **~iency** /sə'fɪʃənsɪ/ *n* suficiencia *f*. **~ient** /sə'fɪʃnt/ *a* suficiente; (*enough*) bastante. **~iently** *adv* suficientemente, bastante

suffix /'sʌfɪks/ *n* (*pl* **-ixes**) sufijo *m*

suffocat|e /'sʌfəkeɪt/ *vt* ahogar. ● *vi* ahogarse. **~ion** /-'keɪʃn/ *n* asfixia *f*

sugar /'ʃʊgə(r)/ *n* azúcar *m & f*. ● *vt* azucarar. **~-bowl** *n* azucarero *m*. **~lump** *n* terrón *m* de azúcar. **~y** *a* azucarado

suggest /sə'dʒest/ *vt* sugerir. **~ible** /sə'dʒestɪbl/ *a* sugestionable. **~ion** /-tʃən/ *n* sugerencia *f*; (*trace*) traza *f*. **~ive** /sə'dʒestɪv/ *a* sugestivo. **be ~ive of** evocar, recordar. **~ively** *adv* sugestivamente

suicid|al /suːɪ'saɪdl/ *a* suicida. **~e** /'suːɪsaɪd/ *n* suicidio *m*; (*person*) suicida *m & f*. **commit ~e** suicidarse

suit /suːt/ *n* traje *m*; (*woman's*) traje *m* de chaqueta; (*cards*) palo *m*; (*jurid*) pleito *m*. ● *vt* convenir; (*clothes*) sentar bien a; (*adapt*) adaptar. **be ~ed for** ser apto para. **~ability** *n* conveniencia *f*. **~able** *a* adecuado. **~ably** *adv* convenientemente. **~case** /'suːtkeɪs/ *n* maleta *f*, valija *f* (*LAm*)

suite /swiːt/ *n* (*of furniture*) juego *m*; (*of rooms*) apartamento *m*; (*retinue*) séquito *m*

suitor /'suːtə(r)/ *n* pretendiente *m*

sulk /sʌlk/ *vi* enfurruñarse. **~s** *npl* enfurruñamiento *m*. **~y** *a* enfurruñado

sullen /'sʌlən/ *a* resentido. **~ly** *adv* con resentimiento

sully /'sʌlɪ/ *vt* manchar

sulphur /'sʌlfə(r)/ *n* azufre *m*. **~ic** /-'fjʊərɪk/ *a* sulfúrico. **~ic acid** *n* ácido *m* sulfúrico

sultan /'sʌltən/ *n* sultán *m*

sultana /sʌl'tɑːnə/ *n* pasa *f* gorrona

sultry /'sʌltrɪ/ *a* (**-ier, -iest**) (*weather*) bochornoso; (*fig*) sensual

sum /sʌm/ *n* suma *f*. ● *vt* (*pt* **summed**) **~ up** resumir (*situation*); (*assess*) evaluar

summar|ily /'sʌmərɪlɪ/ *adv* sumariamente. **~ize** *vt* resumir. **~y** /'sʌmərɪ/ *a* sumario. ● *n* resumen *m*

summer /'sʌmə(r)/ *n* verano *m*. **~house** *n* glorieta *f*, cenador *m*. **~time** *n* verano *m*. **~ time** *n* hora *f* de verano. **~y** *a* veraniego

summit /'sʌmɪt/ *n* cumbre *f*. **~ conference** *n* conferencia *f* cumbre

summon /'sʌmən/ *vt* llamar; convocar (*meeting, s.o. to meeting*); (*jurid*) citar. **~ up** armarse de. **~s** /'sʌmənz/ *n* llamada *f*; (*jurid*) citación *f*. ● *vt* citar

sump /sʌmp/ *n* (*mec*) cárter *m*

sumptuous /'sʌmptjʊəs/ *a* suntuoso. **~ly** *adv* suntuosamente

sun /sʌn/ *n* sol *m*. ● *vt* (*pt* **sunned**). **~ o.s.** tomar el sol. **~bathe** /'sʌnbeɪð/ *vi* tomar el sol. **~beam** /'sʌnbiːm/ *n* rayo *m* de sol. **~burn** /'sʌnbɜːn/ *n* quemadura *f* de sol. **~burnt** *a* quemado por el sol

sundae /'sʌndeɪ/ *n* helado *m* con frutas y nueces

Sunday /'sʌndeɪ/ *n* domingo *m*. **~ school** *n* catequesis *f*

sun: ~dial /'sʌndaɪl/ *n* reloj *m* de sol. **~down** /'sʌndaʊn/ *n* puesta *f* del sol

sundry /'sʌndrɪ/ *a* diversos. **all and ~** todo el mundo. **sundries** *npl* artículos *mpl* diversos

sunflower /'sʌnflaʊə(r)/ *n* girasol *m*

sung /sʌŋ/ *see* **sing**

sun-glasses /'sʌnglɑːsɪz/ *npl* gafas *fpl* de sol

sunk /sʌŋk/ *see* **sink**. **~en** /'sʌŋkən/ ● *a* hundido

sunlight /'sʌnlaɪt/ *n* luz *f* del sol

sunny /'sʌnɪ/ *a* (**-ier, -iest**) (*day*) de sol; (*place*) soleado. **it is ~** hace sol

sun: ~rise /'sʌnraɪz/ *n* amanecer *m*, salida *f* del sol. **~roof** *n* techo *m* corredizo. **~set** /'sʌnset/ *n* puesta *f* del sol. **~shade** /'sʌnʃeɪd/ *n* quitasol *m*, sombrilla *f*; (*awning*) toldo *m*. **~shine** /'sʌnʃaɪn/ *n* sol *m*. **~spot** /'sʌnspɒt/ *n* mancha *f* solar. **~stroke** /'sʌnstrəʊk/ *n* insolación *f*. **~tan** *n* bronceado *m*. **~tanned** *a* bronceado. **~tan lotion** *n* bronceador *m*

sup /sʌp/ *vt* (*pt* **supped**) sorber

super /'suːpə(r)/ *a* (*fam*) estupendo

superannuation /suːpərænjʊ'eɪʃn/ *n* jubilación *f*

superb /suː'pɜːb/ *a* espléndido. **~ly** *adv* espléndidamente

supercilious /suːpə'sɪlɪəs/ *a* desdeñoso

superficial /suːpə'fɪʃl/ *a* superficial. **~ity** /-ɪ'rælətɪ/ *n* superficialidad *f*. **~ly** *adv* superficialmente

superfluous /su:'pɜ:fluəs/ a superfluo

superhuman /su:pə'hju:mən/ a sobrehumano

superimpose /su:pərɪm'pəuz/ vt sobreponer

superintend /su:pərɪn'tend/ vt vigilar. ∼ence n dirección f. ∼ent n director m; (of police) comisario m

superior /su:'pɪərɪə(r)/ a & n superior (m). ∼ity /-'ɒrətɪ/ n superioridad f

superlative /su:'pɜ:lətɪv/ a & n superlativo (m)

superman /'su:pəmæn/ n (pl -men) superhombre m

supermarket /'su:pəma:kɪt/ n supermercado m

supernatural /su:pə'nætʃrəl/ a sobrenatural

superpower /'su:pəpauə(r)/ n superpotencia f

supersede /su:pə'si:d/ vt reemplazar, suplantar

supersonic /su:pə'sɒnɪk/ a supersónico

superstitio|n /su:pə'stɪʃn/ n superstición f. ∼us a supersticioso

superstructure /'su:pəstrʌktʃə(r)/ n superestructura f

supertanker /'su:pətæŋkə(r)/ n petrolero m gigante

supervene /su:pə'vi:n/ vi sobrevenir

supervis|e /'su:pəvaɪz/ vt supervisar. ∼ion /-'vɪʒn/ n supervisión f. ∼or /-zə(r)/ n supervisor m. ∼ory a de supervisión

supper /'sʌpə(r)/ n cena f

supplant /sə'plɑ:nt/ vt suplantar

supple /sʌpl/ a flexible. ∼ness n flexibilidad f

supplement /'sʌplɪmənt/ n suplemento m. ● vt completar; (increase) aumentar. ∼ary /-'mentərɪ/ a suplementario

suppl|ier /sə'plaɪə(r)/ n suministrador m; (com) proveedor m. ∼y /sə'plaɪ/ vt proveer; (feed) alimentar; satisfacer ⟨a need⟩. ∼y with abastecer de. ● n provisión f, suministro m. ∼y and demand oferta f y demanda

support /sə'pɔ:t/ vt sostener; (endure) soportar, aguantar; (fig) apoyar. ● n apoyo m; (tec) soporte m. ∼er /-ə(r)/ n soporte m; (sport) seguidor m, hincha m & f. ∼ive a alentador

suppos|e /sə'pəuz/ vt suponer; (think) creer. **be ∼ed to** deber. **not be ∼ed to** (fam) no tener permiso para, no tener derecho a. ∼edly adv según cabe suponer; (before adjective) presuntamente. ∼ition /sʌpə'zɪʃn/ n suposición f

suppository /sə'pɒzɪtərɪ/ n supositorio m

suppress /sə'pres/ vt suprimir. ∼ion n supresión f. ∼or /-ə(r)/ n supresor m

suprem|acy /su:'preməsɪ/ n supremacía f. ∼e /su:'pri:m/ a supremo

surcharge /'sɜ:tʃɑ:dʒ/ n sobreprecio m; (tax) recargo m

sure /ʃuə(r)/ a (-er, -est) seguro, cierto. **make ∼** asegurarse. ● adv (Amer, fam) ¡claro! ∼ **enough** efectivamente. ∼**footed** a de pie firme. ∼**ly** adv seguramente

surety /'ʃuərətɪ/ n garantía f

surf /sɜ:f/ n oleaje m; (foam) espuma f

surface /'sɜ:fɪs/ n superficie f. ● a superficial, de la superficie. ● vt (smoothe) alisar; (cover) recubrir (with de). ● vi salir a la superficie; (emerge) emerger. ∼ **mail** n por vía marítima

surfboard /'sɜ:fbɔ:d/ n tabla f de surf

surfeit /'sɜ:fɪt/ n exceso m

surfing /'sɜ:fɪŋ/ n, **surf-riding** /'sɜ:fraɪdɪŋ/ n surf m

surge /sɜ:dʒ/ vi ⟨crowd⟩ moverse en tropel; ⟨waves⟩ encresparse. ● n oleada f; (elec) sobretensión f

surgeon /'sɜ:dʒən/ n cirujano m

surgery /'sɜ:dʒərɪ/ n cirugía f; (consulting room) consultorio m; (consulting hours) horas fpl de consulta

surgical /'sɜ:rdʒɪkl/ a quirúrgico

surl|iness /'sɜ:lɪnɪs/ n aspereza f. ∼y /'sɜ:lɪ/ a (-ier, -iest) áspero

surmise /sə'maɪz/ vt conjeturar

surmount /sə'maunt/ vt superar

surname /'sɜ:neɪm/ n apellido m

surpass /sə'pɑ:s/ vt sobrepasar, exceder

surplus /'sɜ:pləs/ a & n excedente (m)

surpris|e /sə'praɪz/ n sorpresa f. ● vt sorprender. ∼**ing** a sorprendente. ∼**ingly** adv asombrosamente

surrealis|m /sə'rɪəlɪzəm/ n surrealismo m. ∼t n surrealista m & f

surrender /sə'rendə(r)/ vt entregar. ● vi entregarse. ● n entrega f; (mil) rendición f

surreptitious /sʌrəp'tɪʃəs/ a clandestino

surrogate /'sʌrəgət/ n substituto m

surround /sə'raʊnd/ vt rodear; (mil) cercar. ● n borde m. ~ing a circundante. ~ings npl alrededores mpl

surveillance /sɜ:'veɪləns/ n vigilancia f

survey /'sɜ:veɪ/ n inspección f; (report) informe m; (general view) vista f de conjunto. /sə'veɪ/ vt examinar, inspeccionar; (inquire into) hacer una encuesta de. ~or n topógrafo m, agrimensor

surviv|al /sə'vaɪvl/ n supervivencia f. ~e /sə'vaɪv/ vt/i sobrevivir. ~or /-ə(r)/ n superviviente m & f

susceptib|ility /səseptə'bɪlətɪ/ n susceptibilidad f. ~le /sə'septəbl/ a susceptible. ~le to propenso a

suspect /sə'spekt/ vt sospechar. /'sʌspekt/ a & n sospechoso (m)

suspend /sə'spend/ vt suspender. ~er /sə'pendə(r)/ n liga f. ~er belt n liguero m. ~ers npl (Amer) tirantes mpl

suspense /sə'spens/ n incertidumbre f; (in film etc) suspense m

suspension /sə'spenʃn/ n suspensión f. ~ bridge n puente m colgante

suspicion /sə'spɪʃn/ n sospecha f; (trace) pizca f

suspicious /sə'spɪʃəs/ a desconfiado; (causing suspicion) sospechoso

sustain /sə'steɪn/ vt sostener; (suffer) sufrir

sustenance /'sʌstɪnəns/ n sustento m

svelte /svelt/ a esbelto

SW abbr (south-west) sudoeste m

swab /swɒb/ n (med) tapón m

swagger /'swægə(r)/ vi pavonearse

swallow[1] /'swɒləʊ/ vt/i tragar. ● n trago m. ~ up tragar; consumir (savings etc)

swallow[2] /'swɒləʊ/ n (bird) golondrina f

swam /swæm/ see **swim**

swamp /swɒmp/ n pantano m. ● vt inundar; (with work) agobiar. ~y a pantanoso

swan /swɒn/ n cisne m

swank /swæŋk/ n (fam) ostentación f. ● vi (fam) fanfarronear

swap /swɒp/ vt/i (pt swapped) (fam) (inter)cambiar. ● n (fam) (inter)cambio m

swarm /swɔ:m/ n enjambre m. ● vi ⟨bees⟩ enjambrar; (fig) hormiguear

swarthy /'swɔ:ðɪ/ a (-ier, -iest) moreno

swastika /'swɒstɪkə/ n cruz f gamada

swat /swɒt/ vt (pt swatted) aplastar

sway /sweɪ/ vi balancearse. ● vt (influence) influir en. ● n balanceo m; (rule) imperio m

swear /sweə(r)/ vt/i (pt swore, pp sworn) jurar. ~ by (fam) creer ciegamente en. ~word n palabrota f

sweat /swet/ n sudor m. ● vi sudar

sweat|er /'swetə(r)/ n jersey m. ~shirt n sudadera f

swede /swi:d/ n naba f

Swede /swi:d/ n sueco m

Sweden /'swi:dn/ n Suecia f

Swedish /'swi:dɪʃ/ a & n sueco (m)

sweep /swi:p/ vt (pt swept) barrer; deshollinar ⟨chimney⟩. ~ the board ganar todo. ● vi barrer; ⟨road⟩ extenderse; (go majestically) moverse majestuosamente. ● n barrido m; (curve) curva f; (movement) movimiento m; (person) deshollinador m. ~ away vt barrer. ~ing a ⟨gesture⟩ amplio; ⟨changes etc⟩ radical; ⟨statement⟩ demasiado general. ~stake /'swi:psteɪk/ n lotería f

sweet /swi:t/ a (-er, -est) dulce; (fragrant) fragante; (pleasant) agradable. **have a ~ tooth** ser dulcero. ● n caramelo m; (dish) postre m. ~bread /'swi:tbred/ n lechecillas fpl. ~en /'swi:tn/ vt endulzar. ~ener /-ə(r)/ n dulcificante m. ~heart /'swi:thɑ:t/ n amor m. ~ly adv dulcemente. ~ness n dulzura f. ~ pea n guisante m de olor

swell /swel/ vt (pt swelled, pp swollen or swelled) hinchar; (increase) aumentar. ● vi hincharse; (increase) aumentarse; ⟨river⟩ crecer. ● a (fam) estupendo. ● n (of sea) oleaje m. ~ing n hinchazón m

swelter /'sweltə(r)/ vi sofocarse de calor

swept /swept/ see **sweep**

swerve /swɜ:v/ vi desviarse

swift /swɪft/ a (-er, -est) rápido. ● n (bird) vencejo m. ~ly adv rápidamente. ~ness n rapidez f

swig /swɪg/ vt (pt swigged) (fam) beber a grandes tragos. ● n (fam) trago m

swill /swɪl/ vt enjuagar; (drink) beber a grandes tragos. ● n (food for pigs) bazofia f

swim /swɪm/ vi (pt swam, pp swum) nadar; ⟨room, head⟩ dar vueltas. ● n baño m. **~mer** n nadador m. **~ming-bath** n piscina f. **~mingly** /'swɪmɪŋlɪ/ adv a las mil maravillas. **~ming-pool** n piscina f. **~ming-trunks** npl bañador m. **~suit** n traje m de baño

swindle /'swɪndl/ vt estafar. ● n estafa f. **~r** /-ə(r)/ n estafador m

swine /swaɪn/ npl cerdos mpl. ● n (pl swine) (person, fam) canalla m

swing /swɪŋ/ vt (pt swung) balancear. ● vi oscilar; ⟨person⟩ balancearse; (turn round) girar. ● n balanceo m, vaivén m; (seat) columpio m; (mus) ritmo m. **in full ~** en plena actividad. **~ bridge** n puente m giratorio

swingeing /'swɪndʒɪŋ/ a enorme

swipe /swaɪp/ vt golpear; (snatch, sl) birlar. ● n (fam) golpe m

swirl /swɜːl/ vi arremolinarse. ● n remolino m

swish /swɪʃ/ vt silbar. ● a (fam) elegante

Swiss /swɪs/ a & n suizo (m). **~ roll** n bizcocho m enrollado

switch /swɪtʃ/ n (elec) interruptor m; (change) cambio m. ● vt cambiar; (deviate) desviar. **~ off** (elec) desconectar; apagar ⟨light⟩. **~ on** (elec) encender; arrancar ⟨engine⟩. **~back** /'swɪtʃbæk/ n montaña f rusa. **~board** /'swɪtʃbɔːd/ n centralita f

Switzerland /'swɪtsələnd/ n Suiza f

swivel /'swɪvl/ ● vi (pt swivelled) girar

swollen /'swəʊlən/ see **swell**. ● a hinchado

swoon /swuːn/ vi desmayarse

swoop /swuːp/ vi ⟨bird⟩ calarse; ⟨plane⟩ bajar en picado. ● n calada f; (by police) redada f

sword /sɔːd/ n espada f. **~fish** /'sɔː-dfɪʃ/ n pez m espada

swore /swɔː(r)/ see **swear**

sworn /swɔːn/ see **swear**. ● a ⟨enemy⟩ jurado; ⟨friend⟩ leal

swot /swɒt/ vt/i (pt swotted) (schol, sl) empollar. ● n (schol, sl) empollón m

swum /swʌm/ see **swim**

swung /swʌŋ/ see **swing**

sycamore /'sɪkəmɔː(r)/ n plátano m falso

syllable /'sɪləbl/ n sílaba f

syllabus /'sɪləbəs/ n (pl -buses) programa m (de estudios)

symbol /'sɪmbl/ n símbolo m. **~ic(al)** /-'bɒlɪk(l)/ a simbólico. **~ism** n simbolismo m. **~ize** vt simbolizar

symmetr|ical /sɪ'metrɪkl/ a simétrico. **~y** /'sɪmətrɪ/ n simetría f

sympath|etic /sɪmpə'θetɪk/ a comprensivo; (showing pity) compasivo. **~ize** /-aɪz/ vi comprender; (pity) compadecerse (with de). **~izer** n (pol) simpatizante m & f. **~y** /'sɪmpəθɪ/ n comprensión f; (pity) compasión f; (condolences) pésame m. **be in ~y with** estar de acuerdo con

symphon|ic /sɪm'fɒnɪk/ a sinfónico. **~y** /'sɪmfənɪ/ n sinfonía f

symposium /sɪm'pəʊzɪəm/ n (pl -ia) simposio m

symptom /'sɪmptəm/ n síntoma m. **~atic** /-'mætɪk/ a sintomático

synagogue /'sɪnəgɒg/ n sinagoga f

synchroniz|ation /sɪŋkrənaɪ'zeɪʃn/ n sincronización f. **~e** /'sɪŋkrənaɪz/ vt sincronizar

syncopat|e /'sɪŋkəpeɪt/ vt sincopar. **~ion** /-'peɪʃn/ n síncopa f

syndicate /'sɪndɪkət/ n sindicato m

syndrome /'sɪndrəʊm/ n síndrome m

synod /'sɪnəd/ n sínodo m

synonym /'sɪnənɪm/ n sinónimo m. **~ous** /-'nɒnɪməs/ a sinónimo

synopsis /sɪ'nɒpsɪs/ n (pl -opses /-siːz/) sinopsis f, resumen m

syntax /'sɪntæks/ n sintaxis f invar

synthesi|s /'sɪnθəsɪs/ n (pl -theses /-siːz/) síntesis f. **~ze** vt sintetizar

synthetic /sɪn'θetɪk/ a sintético

syphilis /'sɪfɪlɪs/ n sífilis f

Syria /'sɪrɪə/ n Siria f. **~n** a & n sirio (m)

syringe /'sɪrɪndʒ/ n jeringa f. ● vt jeringar

syrup /'sɪrəp/ n jarabe m, almíbar m; (treacle) melaza f. **~y** a almibarado

system /'sɪstəm/ n sistema m; (body) organismo m; (order) método m. **~atic** /-ə'mætɪk/ a sistemático. **~at-ically** /-ə'mætɪklɪ/ adv sistemáticamente. **~s analyst** n analista m & f de sistemas

T

tab /tæb/ *n* (*flap*) lengüeta *f*; (*label*) etiqueta *f*. **keep ~s on** (*fam*) vigilar

tabby /'tæbɪ/ *n* gato *m* atigrado

tabernacle /'tæbənækl/ *n* tabernáculo *m*

table /'teɪbl/ *n* mesa *f*; (*list*) tabla *f*. **~ of contents** índice *m*. ● *vt* presentar; (*postpone*) aplazar. **~cloth** *n* mantel *m*. **~-mat** *n* salvamanteles *m invar*. **~spoon** /'teɪblspuːn/ *n* cucharón *m*, cuchara *f* sopera. **~spoonful** *n* (*pl* **-fuls**) cucharada *f*

tablet /'tæblɪt/ *n* (*of stone*) lápida *f*; (*pill*) tableta *f*; (*of soap etc*) pastilla *f*

table tennis /'teɪblteɪnɪs/ *n* tenis *m* de mesa, ping-pong *m*

tabloid /'tæblɔɪd/ *n* tabloide *m*

taboo /tə'buː/ *a & n* tabú (*m*)

tabulator /'tæbjʊleɪtə(r)/ *n* tabulador *m*

tacit /'tæsɪt/ *a* tácito

taciturn /'tæsɪtɜːn/ *a* taciturno

tack /tæk/ *n* tachuela *f*; (*stitch*) hilván *m*; (*naut*) virada *f*; (*fig*) línea *f* de conducta. ● *vt* sujetar con tachuelas; (*sew*) hilvanar. **~ on** añadir. ● *vi* virar

tackle /'tækl/ *n* (*equipment*) equipo *m*; (*football*) placaje *m*. ● *vt* abordar ⟨*problem etc*⟩; (*in rugby*) hacer un placaje a

tacky /'tækɪ/ *a* pegajoso; (*in poor taste*) vulgar, de pacotilla

tact /tækt/ *n* tacto *m*. **~ful** *a* discreto. **~fully** *adv* discretamente

tactic|al /'tæktɪkl/ *a* táctico. **~s** /'tæktɪks/ *npl* táctica *f*

tactile /'tæktaɪl/ *a* táctil

tact: ~less *a* indiscreto. **~lessly** *adv* indiscretamente

tadpole /'tædpəʊl/ *n* renacuajo *m*

tag /tæg/ *n* (*on shoe-lace*) herrete *m*; (*label*) etiqueta *f*. ● *vt* (*pt* **tagged**) poner etiqueta a; (*trail*) seguir. ● *vi*. **~ along** (*fam*) seguir

tail /teɪl/ *n* cola *f*. **~s** *npl* (*tailcoat*) frac *m*; (*of coin*) cruz *f*. ● *vt* (*sl*) seguir. ● *vi*. **~ off** disminuir. **~-end** *n* extremo *m* final, cola *f*

tailor /'teɪlə(r)/ *n* sastre *m*. ● *vt* confeccionar. **~-made** *n* hecho a la medida. **~-made for** (*fig*) hecho para

tailplane /'teɪlpleɪn/ *n* plano *m* de cola

taint /teɪnt/ *n* mancha *f*. ● *vt* contaminar

take /teɪk/ *vt* (*pt* **took**, *pp* **taken**) tomar, coger (*not LAm*), agarrar (*esp LAm*); (*contain*) contener; (*capture*) capturar; (*endure*) aguantar; (*require*) requerir; tomar ⟨*bath*⟩; dar ⟨*walk*⟩; (*carry*) llevar; (*accompany*) acompañar; presentarse para ⟨*exam*⟩; sacar ⟨*photo*⟩; ganar ⟨*prize*⟩. **~ advantage of** aprovechar. **~ after** parecerse a. **~ away** quitar. **~ back** retirar ⟨*statement etc*⟩. **~ in** achicar ⟨*garment*⟩; (*understand*) comprender; (*deceive*) engañar. **~ off** quitarse ⟨*clothes*⟩; (*mimic*) imitar; (*aviat*) despegar. **~ o.s. off** marcharse. **~ on** (*undertake*) emprender; contratar ⟨*employee*⟩. **~ out** (*remove*) sacar. **~ over** tomar posesión de; (*assume control*) tomar el poder. **~ part** participar. **~ place** tener lugar. **~ sides** tomar partido. **~ to** dedicarse a; (*like*) tomar simpatía a ⟨*person*⟩; (*like*) aficionarse a ⟨*thing*⟩. **~ up** dedicarse a ⟨*hobby*⟩; (*occupy*) ocupar; (*resume*) reanudar. **~ up with** trabar amistad con. **be ~n ill** ponerse enfermo. ● *n* presa *f*; (*photo, cinema, TV*) toma *f*

takings /'teɪkɪŋz/ *npl* ingresos *mpl*

take: ~-off *n* despegue *m*. **~-over** *n* toma *f* de posesión.

talcum /'tælkəm/ *n*. **~ powder** *n* (polvos *mpl* de) talco (*m*)

tale /teɪl/ *n* cuento *m*

talent /'tælənt/ *n* talento *m*. **~ed** *a* talentoso

talisman /'tælɪzmən/ *n* talismán *m*

talk /tɔːk/ *vt/i* hablar. **~ about** hablar de. **~ over** discutir. ● *n* conversación *f*; (*lecture*) conferencia *f*. **small ~** charla *f*. **~ative** *a* hablador. **~er** *n* hablador *m*; (*chatterbox*) parlanchín *m*. **~ing-to** *n* reprensión *f*

tall /tɔːl/ *a* (**-er**, **-est**) alto. **~ story** *n* (*fam*) historia *f* inverosímil. **that's a ~ order** *n* (*fam*) eso es pedir mucho

tallboy /'tɔːlbɔɪ/ *n* cómoda *f* alta

tally /'tælɪ/ *n* tarja *f*; (*total*) total *m*. ● *vi* corresponder (**with** a)

talon /'tælən/ *n* garra *f*

tambourine /tæmbə'riːn/ *n* pandereta *f*

tame /teɪm/ *a* (**-er**, **-est**) ⟨*animal*⟩ doméstico; ⟨*person*⟩ dócil; (*dull*) insípido. ● *vt* domesticar; domar

⟨*wild animal*⟩. **∼ly** *adv* dócilmente.
∼r /-ə(r)/ *n* domador *m*

tamper /'tæmpə(r)/ *vi*. **∼ with** manosear; (*alter*) alterar, falsificar

tampon /'tæmpən/ *n* tampón *m*

tan /tæn/ *vt* (*pt* **tanned**) curtir ⟨*hide*⟩; ⟨*sun*⟩ broncear. ● *vi* ponerse moreno. ● *n* bronceado *m*. ● *a* (*colour*) de color canela

tandem /'tændəm/ *n* tándem *m*

tang /tæŋ/ *n* sabor *m* fuerte; (*smell*) olor *m* fuerte

tangent /'tændʒənt/ *n* tangente *f*

tangerine /tændʒə'ri:n/ *n* mandarina *f*

tangibl|e /'tændʒəbl/ *a* tangible. **∼y** *adv* perceptiblemente

tangle /'tæŋgl/ *vt* enredar. ● *vi* enredarse. ● *n* enredo *m*

tango /'tæŋgəʊ/ *n* (*pl* -**os**) tango *m*

tank /tæŋk/ *n* depósito *m*; (*mil*) tanque *m*

tankard /'tæŋkəd/ *n* jarra *f*, bock *m*

tanker /'tæŋkə(r)/ *n* petrolero *m*; (*truck*) camión *m* cisterna

tantaliz|e /'tæntəlaiz/ *vt* atormentar. **∼ing** *a* atormentador; (*tempting*) tentador

tantamount /'tæntəmaʊnt/ *a*. **∼ to** equivalente a

tantrum /'tæntrəm/ *n* rabieta *f*

tap[1] /tæp/ *n* grifo *m*. **on ∼** disponible. ● *vt* explotar ⟨*resources*⟩; interceptar ⟨*phone*⟩

tap[2] /tæp/ *n* (*knock*) golpe *m* ligero. ● *vt* (*pt* **tapped**) golpear ligeramente. **∼-dance** *n* zapateado *m*

tape /teɪp/ *n* cinta *f*. ● *vt* atar con cinta; (*record*) grabar. **have sth ∼d** (*sl*) comprender perfectamente. **∼-measure** *n* cinta *f* métrica

taper /'teɪpə(r)/ *n* bujía *f*. ● *vt* ahusar. ● *vi* ahusarse. **∼ off** disminuir

tape: **∼ recorder** *n* magnetofón *m*, magnetófono *m*. **∼ recording** *n* grabación *f*

tapestry /'tæpɪstrɪ/ *n* tapicería *f*; (*product*) tapiz *m*

tapioca /tæpɪ'əʊkə/ *n* tapioca *f*

tar /tɑ:(r)/ *n* alquitrán *m*. ● *vt* (*pt* **tarred**) alquitranar

tard|ily /'tɑ:dɪlɪ/ *adv* lentamente; (*late*) tardíamente. **∼y** /'tɑ:dɪ/ *a* (-**ier**, -**iest**) (*slow*) lento; (*late*) tardío

target /'tɑ:gɪt/ *n* blanco *m*; (*fig*) objetivo *m*

tariff /'tærɪf/ *n* tarifa *f*

tarmac /'tɑ:mæk/ *n* pista *f* de aterrizaje. **T∼** *n* (*P*) macadán *m*

tarnish /'tɑ:nɪʃ/ *vt* deslustrar. ● *vi* deslustrarse

tarpaulin /tɑ:'pɔ:lɪn/ *n* alquitranado *m*

tarragon /'tærəgən/ *n* estragón *m*

tart[1] /tɑ:t/ *n* pastel *m*; (*individual*) pastelillo *m*

tart[2] /tɑ:t/ *n* (*sl*, *woman*) prostituta *f*, fulana *f* (*fam*). ● *vt*. **∼ o.s. up** (*fam*) engalanarse

tart[3] /tɑ:t/ *a* (-**er**, -**est**) ácido; (*fig*) áspero

tartan /'tɑ:tn/ *n* tartán *m*, tela *f* escocesa

tartar /'tɑ:tə(r)/ *n* tártaro *m*. **∼ sauce** *n* salsa *f* tártara

task /tɑ:sk/ *n* tarea *f*. **take to ∼** reprender. **∼ force** *n* destacamento *m* especial

tassel /'tæsl/ *n* borla *f*

tast|e /teɪst/ *n* sabor *m*, gusto *m*; (*small quantity*) poquito *m*. ● *vt* probar. ● *vi*. **∼e of** saber a. **∼eful** *a* de buen gusto. **∼eless** *a* soso; (*fig*) de mal gusto. **∼y** *a* (-**ier**, -**iest**) sabroso

tat /tæt/ *see* **tit**[2]

tatter|ed /'tætəd/ *a* hecho jirones. **∼s** /'tætəz/ *npl* andrajos *mpl*

tattle /'tætl/ *vi* charlar. ● *n* charla *f*

tattoo[1] /tə'tu:/ (*mil*) espectáculo *m* militar

tattoo[2] /tə'tu:/ *vt* tatuar. ● *n* tatuaje *m*

tatty /'tætɪ/ *a* (-**ier**, -**iest**) gastado, en mal estado

taught /tɔ:t/ *see* **teach**

taunt /tɔ:nt/ *vt* mofarse de. **∼ s.o. with sth** echar algo en cara a uno. ● *n* mofa *f*

Taurus /'tɔ:rəs/ *n* (*astr*) Tauro *m*

taut /tɔ:t/ *a* tenso

tavern /'tævən/ *n* taberna *f*

tawdry /'tɔ:drɪ/ *a* (-**ier**, -**iest**) charro

tawny /'tɔ:nɪ/ *a* bronceado

tax /tæks/ *n* impuesto *m*. ● *vt* imponer contribuciones a ⟨*person*⟩; gravar con un impuesto ⟨*thing*⟩; (*fig*) poner a prueba. **∼able** *a* imponible. **∼ation** /-'seɪʃn/ *n* impuestos *mpl*. **∼collector** *n* recaudador *m* de contribuciones. **∼-free** *a* libre de impuestos

taxi /'tæksɪ/ *n* (*pl* -**is**) taxi *m*. ● *vi* (*pt* **taxied**, *pres p* **taxiing**) ⟨*aircraft*⟩ rodar por la pista. **∼ rank** *n* parada *f* de taxis

taxpayer /'tækspeɪə(r)/ *n* contribuyente *m* & *f*

te /ti:/ *n* (*mus, seventh note of any musical scale*) si *m*

tea /ti:/ *n* té *m*. **~bag** *n* bolsita *f* de té. **~break** *n* descanso *m* para el té

teach /ti:tʃ/ *vt/i* (*pt* **taught**) enseñar. **~er** *n* profesor *m*; (*primary*) maestro *m*. **~in** *n* seminario *m*. **~ing** *n* enseñanza *f*. ● *a* docente. **~ing staff** *n* profesorado *m*

teacup /'ti:kʌp/ *n* taza *f* de té

teak /ti:k/ *n* teca *f*

tea-leaf /'ti:li:f/ *n* hoja *f* de té

team /ti:m/ *n* equipo *m*; (*of horses*) tiro *m*. ● *vi*. **~ up** unirse. **~work** *n* trabajo *m* en equipo

teapot /'ti:pɒt/ *n* tetera *f*

tear[1] /teə(r)/ *vt* (*pt* **tore**, *pp* **torn**) rasgar. ● *vi* rasgarse; (*run*) precipitarse. ● *n* rasgón *m*. **~ apart** desgarrar. **~ o.s. away** separarse

tear[2] /tɪə(r)/ *n* lágrima *f*. **in ~s** llorando

tearaway /'teərəweɪ/ *n* gamberro *m*

tear /tɪə(r)/: **~ful** *a* lloroso. **~gas** *n* gas *m* lacrimógeno

tease /ti:z/ *vt* tomar el pelo a; cardar ‹*cloth etc*›. ● *n* guasón *m*. **~r** /-ə(r)/ *n* (*fam*) problema *m* difícil

tea: **~set** *n* juego *m* de té. **~spoon** /'ti:spu:n/ *n* cucharilla *f*. **~spoonful** *n* (*pl* **-fuls**) (*amount*) cucharadita *f*

teat /ti:t/ *n* (*of animal*) teta *f*; (*for bottle*) tetilla *f*

tea-towel /'ti:tauəl/ *n* paño *m* de cocina

technical /'teknɪkl/ *a* técnico. **~ity** *n* /-'kælətɪ/ *n* detalle *m* técnico. **~ly** *adv* técnicamente

technician /tek'nɪʃn/ *n* técnico *m*

technique /tek'ni:k/ *n* técnica *f*

technolog|ist /tek'nɒlədʒɪst/ *n* tecnólogo *m*. **~y** /tek'nɒlədʒɪ/ *n* tecnología *f*

teddy bear /'tedɪbeə(r)/ *n* osito *m* de felpa, osito *m* de peluche

tedious /'ti:dɪəs/ *a* pesado. **~ly** *adv* pesadamente

tedium /'ti:dɪəm/ *n* aburrimiento *m*

tee /ti:/ *n* (*golf*) tee *m*

teem /ti:m/ *vi* abundar; (*rain*) llover a cántaros

teen|age /'ti:neɪdʒ/ *a* adolescente; (*for teenagers*) para jóvenes. **~ager** /-ə(r)/ *n* adolescente *m* & *f*, joven *m* & *f*. **~s** /ti:nz/ *npl*. **the ~s** la adolescencia *f*

teeny /'ti:nɪ/ *a* (**-ier**, **-iest**) (*fam*) chiquito

teeter /'ti:tə(r)/ *vi* balancearse

teeth /ti:θ/ *see* **tooth**. **~e** /ti:ð/ *vi* echar los dientes. **~ing troubles** *npl* (*fig*) dificultades *fpl* iniciales

teetotaller /ti:'təʊtələ(r)/ *n* abstemio *m*

telecommunications /telɪkəmju:nɪ'keɪʃnz/ *npl* telecomunicaciones *fpl*

telegram /'telɪgræm/ *n* telegrama *m*

telegraph /'telɪgrɑ:f/ *n* telégrafo *m*. ● *vt* telegrafiar. **~ic** /-'græfɪk/ *a* telegráfico

telepath|ic /telɪ'pæθɪk/ *a* telepático. **~y** /tɪ'lepəθɪ/ *n* telepatía *f*

telephon|e /'telɪfəʊn/ *n* teléfono *m*. ● *vt* llamar por teléfono. **~e booth** *n* cabina *f* telefónica. **~e directory** *n* guía *f* telefónica. **~e exchange** *n* central *f* telefónica. **~ic** /-'fɒnɪk/ *a* telefónico. **~ist** /tɪ'lefənɪst/ *n* telefonista *m* & *f*

telephoto /telɪ'fəʊtəʊ/ *a*. **~ lens** *n* teleobjetivo *m*

teleprinter /'telɪprɪntə(r)/ *n* teleimpresor *m*

telescop|e /'telɪskəʊp/ *n* telescopio *m*. **~ic** /-'kɒpɪk/ *a* telescópico

televis|e /'telɪvaɪz/ *vt* televisar. **~ion** /'telɪvɪʒn/ *n* televisión *f*. **~ion set** *n* televisor *m*

telex /'teleks/ *n* télex *m*. ● *vt* enviar por télex

tell /tel/ *vt* (*pt* **told**) decir; contar ‹*story*›; (*distinguish*) distinguir. ● *vi* (*produce an effect*) tener efecto; (*know*) saber. **~ off** *vt* reprender. **~er** /'telə(r)/ *n* (*in bank*) cajero *m*

telling /'telɪŋ/ *a* eficaz

tell-tale /'telteɪl/ *n* soplón *m*. ● *a* revelador

telly /'telɪ/ *n* (*fam*) televisión *f*, tele *f* (*fam*)

temerity /tɪ'merətɪ/ *n* temeridad *f*

temp /temp/ *n* (*fam*) empleado *m* temporal

temper /'tempə(r)/ *n* (*disposition*) disposición *f*; (*mood*) humor *m*; (*fit of anger*) cólera *f*; (*of metal*) temple *m*. **be in a ~** estar de mal humor. **keep one's ~** contenerse. **lose one's ~** enfadarse, perder la paciencia. ● *vt* templar ‹*metal*›

temperament /'temprəmənt/ *n* temperamento *m*. **~al** /-'mentl/ *a* caprichoso

temperance /'tempərəns/ *n* moderación *f*

temperate /'tempərət/ *a* moderado; ⟨*climate*⟩ templado

temperature /'temprɪtʃə(r)/ *n* temperatura *f*. **have a ∼** tener fiebre

tempest /'tempɪst/ *n* tempestad *f*. **∼uous** /-'pestjʊəs/ *a* tempestuoso

temple[1] /'templ/ *n* templo *m*

temple[2] /'templ/ (*anat*) sien *f*

tempo /'tempəʊ/ *n* (*pl* **-os** *or* **tempi**) ritmo *m*

temporar|ily /'tempərərəlɪ/ *adv* temporalmente. **∼y** /'tempərərɪ/ *a* temporal, provisional

tempt /tempt/ *vt* tentar. **∼ s.o. to** inducir a uno a. **∼ation** /-'teɪʃn/ *n* tentación *f*. **∼ing** *a* tentador

ten /ten/ *a* & *n* diez (*m*)

tenable /'tenəbl/ *a* sostenible

tenaci|ous /tɪ'neɪʃəs/ *a* tenaz. **∼ty** /-'æsəti/ *n* tenacidad *f*

tenan|cy /'tenənsɪ/ *n* alquiler *m*. **∼t** /'tenənt/ *n* inquilino *m*

tend[1] /tend/ *vi*. **∼ to** tener tendencia a

tend[2] /tend/ *vt* cuidar

tendency /'tendənsɪ/ *n* tendencia *f*

tender[1] /'tendə(r)/ *a* tierno; (*painful*) dolorido

tender[2] /'tendə(r)/ *n* (*com*) oferta *f*. **legal ∼** *n* curso *m* legal. ● *vt* ofrecer, presentar

tender: **∼ly** *adv* tiernamente. **∼ness** *n* ternura *f*

tendon /'tendən/ *n* tendón *m*

tenement /'tenəmənt/ *n* vivienda *f*

tenet /'tenɪt/ *n* principio *m*

tenfold /'tenfəʊld/ *a* diez veces mayor, décuplo. ● *adv* diez veces

tenner /'tenə(r)/ *n* (*fam*) billete *m* de diez libras

tennis /'tenɪs/ *n* tenis *m*

tenor /'tenə(r)/ *n* tenor *m*

tens|e /tens/ *a* (**-er**, **-est**) tieso; (*fig*) tenso. ● *n* (*gram*) tiempo *m*. ● *vi*. **∼ up** tensarse. **∼eness** *n*, **∼ion** /'tenʃn/ *n* tensión *f*

tent /tent/ *n* tienda *f*, carpa *f* (*LAm*)

tentacle /'tentəkl/ *n* tentáculo *m*

tentative /'tentətɪv/ *a* provisional; (*hesitant*) indeciso. **∼ly** *adv* provisionalmente; (*timidly*) tímidamente

tenterhooks /'tentəhʊks/ *npl*. **on ∼** en ascuas

tenth /tenθ/ *a* & *n* décimo (*m*)

tenuous /'tenjʊəs/ *a* tenue

tenure /'tenjʊə(r)/ *n* posesión *f*

tepid /'tepɪd/ *a* tibio

term /tɜːm/ *n* (*of time*) período *m*; (*schol*) trimestre *m*; (*word etc*) término *m*. ● *vt* llamar. **∼s** *npl* condiciones *fpl*; (*com*) precio *m*. **on bad ∼s** en malas relaciones. **on good ∼s** en buenas relaciones

terminal /'tɜːmɪnl/ *a* terminal, final. ● *n* (*rail*) estación *f* terminal; (*elec*) borne *m*. **(air) ∼** *n* término *m*, terminal *m*

terminat|e /'tɜːmɪneɪt/ *vt* terminar. ● *vi* terminarse. **∼tion** /-'neɪʃn/ *n* terminación *f*

terminology /tɜːmɪ'nɒlədʒɪ/ *n* terminología *f*

terrace /'terəs/ *n* terraza *f*; (*houses*) hilera *f* de casas. **the ∼s** *npl* (*sport*) las gradas *fpl*

terrain /tə'reɪn/ *n* terreno *m*

terrestrial /tɪ'restrɪəl/ *a* terrestre

terribl|e /'terəbl/ *a* terrible. **∼y** *adv* terriblemente

terrier /'terɪə(r)/ *n* terrier *m*

terrific /tə'rɪfɪk/ *a* (*excellent*, *fam*) estupendo; (*huge*, *fam*) enorme. **∼ally** *adv* (*fam*) terriblemente; (*very well*) muy bien

terrify /'terɪfaɪ/ *vt* aterrorizar. **∼ing** *a* espantoso

territor|ial /terɪ'tɔːrɪəl/ *a* territorial. **∼y** /'terɪtrɪ/ *n* territorio *m*

terror /'terə(r)/ *n* terror *m*. **∼ism** /-zəm/ *n* terrorismo *m*. **∼ist** /'terərɪst/ *n* terrorista *m* & *f*. **∼ize** /'terəraɪz/ *vt* aterrorizar

terse /tɜːs/ *a* conciso; (*abrupt*) brusco

test /test/ *n* prueba *f*, (*exam*) examen *m*. ● *vt* probar; (*examine*) examinar

testament /'testəmənt/ *n* testamento *m*. **New T∼** Nuevo Testamento. **Old T∼** Antiguo Testamento

testicle /'testɪkl/ *n* testículo *m*

testify /'testɪfaɪ/ *vt* atestiguar. ● *vi* declarar

testimon|ial /testɪ'məʊnɪəl/ *n* certificado *m*; (*of character*) recomendación *f*. **∼y** /'testɪmənɪ/ *n* testimonio *m*

test: **∼ match** *n* partido *m* internacional. **∼-tube** *n* tubo *m* de ensayo, probeta *f*

testy /'testɪ/ *a* irritable

tetanus /'tetənəs/ *n* tétanos *m invar*

tetchy /'tetʃɪ/ *a* irritable

tether /'teðə(r)/ *vt* atar. ● *n.* **be at the end of one's** ~ no poder más

text /tekst/ *n* texto *m*. ~**book** *n* libro *m* de texto

textile /'tekstaɪl/ *a & n* textil (*m*)

texture /'tekstʃə(r)/ *n* textura *f*

Thai /taɪ/ *a & n* tailandés (*m*). ~**land** *n* Tailandia *f*

Thames /temz/ *n* Támesis *m*

than /ðæn, ðən/ *conj* que; (*with numbers*) de

thank /θæŋk/ *vt* dar las gracias a, agradecer. ~ **you** gracias. ~**ful** /'θæŋkfl/ *a* agradecido. ~**fully** *adv* con gratitud; (*happily*) afortunadamente. ~**less** /'θæŋklɪs/ *a* ingrato. ~**s** *npl* gracias *fpl*. ~**s!** (*fam*) ¡gracias! ~ **to** gracias a

that /ðæt, ðət/ *a* (*pl* **those**) ese, aquel, esa, aquella. ● *pron* (*pl* **those**) ése, aquél, ésa, aquélla. ~ **is** es decir. ~**'s it!** ¡eso es! ~ **is why** por eso. **is** ~ **you?** ¿eres tú? **like** ~ así. ● *adv* tan. ● *rel pron* que; (*with prep*) el que, la que, el cual, la cual. ● *conj* que

thatch /θætʃ/ *n* techo *m* de paja. ~**ed** *a* con techo de paja

thaw /θɔː/ *vt* deshelar. ● *vi* deshelarse; ⟨*snow*⟩ derretirse. ● *n* deshielo *m*

the /ðə, ðiː/ *def art* el, la, los, las. **at** ~ al, a la, a los, a las. **from** ~ del, de la, de los, de las. **to** ~ al, a la, a los, a las. ● *adv*. **all** ~ **better** tanto mejor

theatr|e /'θɪətə(r)/ *n* teatro *m*. ~**ical** /-'ætrɪkl/ *a* teatral

theft /θeft/ *n* hurto *m*

their /ðeə(r)/ *a* su, sus

theirs /ðeəz/ *poss pron* (el) suyo, (la) suya, (los) suyos, (las) suyas

them /ðem, ðəm/ *pron* (*accusative*) los, las; (*dative*) les; (*after prep*) ellos, ellas

theme /θiːm/ *n* tema *m*. ~ **song** *n* motivo *m* principal

themselves /ðəm'selvz/ *pron* ellos mismos, ellas mismas; (*reflexive*) se; (*after prep*) sí mismos, sí mismas

then /ðen/ *adv* entonces; (*next*) luego, después. **by** ~ para entonces. **now and** ~ de vez en cuando. **since** ~ desde entonces. ● *a* de entonces

theolog|ian /θɪə'ləʊdʒən/ *n* teólogo *m*. ~**y** /θɪ'ɒlədʒɪ/ *n* teología *f*

theorem /'θɪərəm/ *n* teorema *m*

theor|etical /θɪə'retɪkl/ *a* teórico. ~**y** /'θɪərɪ/ *n* teoría *f*

therap|eutic /θerə'pjuːtɪk/ *a* terapéutico. ~**ist** *n* terapeuta *m & f*. ~**y** /'θerəpɪ/ *n* terapia *f*

there /ðeə(r)/ *adv* ahí, allí. ~ **are** hay. ~ **he is** ahí está. ~ **is** hay. ~ **it is** ahí está. **down** ~ ahí abajo. **up** ~ ahí arriba. ● *int* ¡vaya! ~, ~**!** ¡ya, ya! ~**abouts** *adv* por ahí. ~**after** *adv* después. ~**by** *adv* por eso. ~**fore** /'ðeəfɔː(r)/ *adv* por lo tanto.

thermal /'θɜːml/ *a* termal

thermometer /θə'mɒmɪtə(r)/ *n* termómetro *m*

thermonuclear /θɜːməʊ'njuːklɪə(r)/ *a* termonuclear

Thermos /'θɜːməs/ *n* (*P*) termo *m*

thermostat /'θɜːməstæt/ *n* termostato *m*

thesaurus /θɪ'sɔːrəs/ *n* (*pl* -**ri** /-raɪ/) diccionario *m* de sinónimos

these /ðiːz/ *a* estos, estas. ● *pron* éstos, éstas

thesis /'θiːsɪs/ *n* (*pl* **theses** /-siːz/) tesis *f*

they /ðeɪ/ *pron* ellos, ellas. ~ **say that** se dice que

thick /θɪk/ *a* (-**er**, -**est**) espeso; (*dense*) denso; (*stupid*, *fam*) torpe; (*close*, *fam*) íntimo. ● *adv* espesamente, densamente. ● *n*. **in the** ~ **of** en medio de. ~**en** /'θɪkən/ *vt* espesar. ● *vi* espesarse

thicket /'θɪkɪt/ *n* matorral *m*

thick: ~**ly** *adv* espesamente, densamente. ~**ness** *n* espesor *m*

thickset /θɪk'set/ *a* fornido

thick-skinned /θɪk'skɪnd/ *a* insensible

thief /θiːf/ *n* (*pl* **thieves**) ladrón *m*

thiev|e /θiːv/ *vt/i* robar. ~**ing** *a* ladrón

thigh /θaɪ/ *n* muslo *m*

thimble /'θɪmbl/ *n* dedal *m*

thin /θɪn/ *a* (**thinner**, **thinnest**) delgado; ⟨*person*⟩ flaco; (*weak*) débil; (*fine*) fino; (*sparse*) escaso. ● *adv* ligeramente. ● *vt* (*pt* **thinned**) adelgazar; (*dilute*) diluir. ~ **out** hacer menos denso. ● *vi* adelgazarse; (*diminish*) disminuir

thing /θɪŋ/ *n* cosa *f*. **for one** ~ en primer lugar. **just the** ~ exactamente lo que se necesita. **poor** ~**!** ¡pobrecito! ~**s** *npl* (*belongings*) efectos *mpl*; (*clothing*) ropa *f*

think /θɪŋk/ *vt* (*pt* **thought**) pensar, creer. ● *vi* pensar (**about**, **of** en); (*carefully*) reflexionar; (*imagine*) imaginarse. ~ **better of it** cambiar de idea. **I** ~ **so** creo que sí. ~ **over** *vt* pensar bien. ~ **up** *vt* idear,

inventar. **~er** n pensador m.
~tank grupo m de expertos

thin: **~ly** adv ligeramente. **~ness** n
delgadez f; (of person) flaqueza f

third /θɜːd/ a tercero. ● n tercio m,
tercera parte f. **~-rate** a muy
inferior. **T~ World** n Tercer Mundo
m

thirst /θɜːst/ n sed f. **~y** a sediento.
be ~y tener sed

thirteen /θɜːˈtiːn/ a & n trece (m).
~th a & n decimotercero (m)

thirt|ieth /ˈθɜːtɪəθ/ a & n trigésimo
(m). **~y** /ˈθɜːtɪ/ a & n treinta (m)

this /ðɪs/ a (pl these) este, esta. ~
one éste, ésta. ● pron (pl these)
éste, ésta, esto. **like ~** así

thistle /ˈθɪsl/ n cardo m

thong /θɒŋ/ n correa f

thorn /θɔːn/ n espina f. **~y** a
espinoso

thorough /ˈθʌrə/ a completo; (deep)
profundo; ⟨cleaning etc⟩ a fondo;
⟨person⟩ concienzudo

thoroughbred /ˈθʌrəbred/ a de pura
sangre

thoroughfare /ˈθʌrəfeə(r)/ n calle f.
no ~ prohibido el paso

thoroughly /ˈθʌrəlɪ/ adv
completamente

those /ðəʊz/ a esos, aquellos, esas,
aquellas. ● pron ésos, aquéllos,
ésas, aquéllas

though /ðəʊ/ conj aunque. ● adv sin
embargo. **as ~** como si

thought /θɔːt/ see **think**. ● n pensamiento m; (idea) idea f. **~ful** /ˈθɔː
tfl/ a pensativo; (considerate)
atento. **~fully** adv pensativamente;
(considerately) atentamente. **~less**
/ˈθɔːtlɪs/ a irreflexivo; (inconsiderate) desconsiderado

thousand /ˈθaʊznd/ a & n mil (m).
~th a & n milésimo (m)

thrash /θræʃ/ vt azotar; (defeat)
derrotar. **~ out** discutir a fondo

thread /θred/ n hilo m; (of screw)
rosca f. ● vt ensartar. **~ one's way**
abrirse paso. **~bare** /ˈθredbeə(r)/ a
raído

threat /θret/ n amenaza f. **~en**
/ˈθretn/ vt/i amenazar. **~ening** a
amenazador. **~eningly** adv de
modo amenazador

three /θriː/ a & n tres (m). **~fold** a
triple. ● adv tres veces. **~some**
/ˈθriːsəm/ n conjunto m de tres
personas

thresh /θreʃ/ vt trillar

threshold /ˈθreʃhəʊld/ n umbral m

threw /θruː/ see **throw**

thrift /θrɪft/ n economía f, ahorro m.
~y a frugal

thrill /θrɪl/ n emoción f. ● vt
emocionar. ● vi emocionarse;
(quiver) estremecerse. **be ~ed with**
estar encantado de. **~er** /ˈθrɪlə(r)/
n (book) libro m de suspense; (film)
película f de suspense. **~ing** a
emocionante

thriv|e /θraɪv/ vi prosperar. **~ing** a
próspero

throat /θrəʊt/ n garganta f. **have a
sore ~** dolerle la garganta

throb /θrɒb/ vi (pt throbbed) palpitar; (with pain) dar punzadas; (fig)
vibrar. ● n palpitación f; (pain)
punzada f; (fig) vibración f. **~bing** a
⟨pain⟩ punzante

throes /θrəʊz/ npl. **in the ~ of** en
medio de

thrombosis /θrɒmˈbəʊsɪs/ n trombosis f

throne /θrəʊn/ n trono m

throng /θrɒŋ/ n multitud f

throttle /ˈθrɒtl/ n (auto) acelerador
m. ● vt ahogar

through /θruː/ prep por, a través de;
(during) durante; (by means of) por
medio de; (thanks to) gracias a.
● adv de parte a parte, de un lado
a otro; (entirely) completamente; (to
the end) hasta el final. **be ~** (finished) haber terminado. ● a ⟨train
etc⟩ directo

throughout /θruːˈaʊt/ prep por
todo; (time) en todo. ● adv en todas
partes; (all the time) todo el tiempo

throve /θrəʊv/ see **thrive**

throw /θrəʊ/ vt (pt threw, pp
thrown) arrojar; (baffle etc)
desconcertar. **~ a party** (fam) dar
una fiesta. ● n tiro m; (of dice) lance
m. **~ away** vt tirar. **~ over** vt abandonar. **~ up** vi (vomit) vomitar. **~a-
way** a desechable

thrush /θrʌʃ/ n tordo m

thrust /θrʌst/ vt (pt thrust) empujar;
(push in) meter. ● n empuje m. ~
(up)on imponer a

thud /θʌd/ n ruido m sordo

thug /θʌg/ n bruto m

thumb /θʌm/ n pulgar m. **under the
~ of** dominado por. ● vt hojear
⟨book⟩. **~ a lift** hacer autostop. **~in-
dex** n uñeros mpl

thump /θʌmp/ vt golpear. ● vi
⟨heart⟩ latir fuertemente. ● n por-
razo m; (noise) ruido m sordo

thunder /'θʌndə(r)/ n trueno m. • vi tronar. ~ **past** pasar con estruendo. ~**bolt** /'θʌndəbəʊlt/ n rayo m. ~**clap** /'θʌndəklæp/ n trueno m. ~**storm** /'θʌndəstɔːm/ n tronada f. ~**y** a con truenos

Thursday /'θɜːzdeɪ/ n jueves m

thus /ðʌs/ adv así

thwart /θwɔːt/ vt frustrar

thyme /taɪm/ n tomillo m

thyroid /'θaɪrɔɪd/ n tiroides m invar

tiara /tɪ'ɑːrə/ n diadema f

tic /tɪk/ n tic m

tick[1] /tɪk/ n tictac m; (mark) señal f, marca f; (instant, fam) momentito m. • vi hacer tictac. • vt. ~ (**off**) marcar. ~ **off** vt (sl) reprender. ~ **over** vi ⟨of engine⟩ marchar en vacío

tick[2] /tɪk/ n (insect) garrapata f

tick[3] /tɪk/ n. **on** ~ (fam) a crédito

ticket /'tɪkɪt/ n billete m, boleto m (LAm); (label) etiqueta f; (fine) multa f. ~**collector** n revisor m. ~**office** n taquilla f

tickle /'tɪkl/ vt hacer cosquillas a; (amuse) divertir. • n cosquilleo m. ~**ish** /'tɪklɪʃ/ a cosquilloso; ⟨problem⟩ delicado. **be** ~**ish** tener cosquillas

tidal /'taɪdl/ a de marea. ~ **wave** n maremoto m

tiddly-winks /'tɪdlɪwɪŋks/ n juego m de pulgas

tide /taɪd/ n marea f; (of events) curso m. • vt. ~ **over** ayudar a salir de un apuro

tidings /'taɪdɪŋz/ npl noticias fpl

tid|**ily** /'taɪdɪlɪ/ adv en orden; (well) bien. ~**iness** n orden m. ~**y** /'taɪdɪ/ a (-ier, -iest) ordenado; ⟨amount, fam⟩ considerable. • vt/i. ~**y** (**up**) ordenar. ~**y o.s. up** arreglarse

tie /taɪ/ vt (pres p **tying**) atar; hacer ⟨a knot⟩; (link) vincular. • vi (sport) empatar. • n atadura f; (necktie) corbata f; (link) lazo m; (sport) empate m. ~ **in with** relacionar con. ~ **up** atar; (com) inmovilizar. **be** ~**d up** (busy) estar ocupado

tier /tɪə(r)/ n fila f; (in stadium etc) grada f; (of cake) piso m

tie-up /'taɪʌp/ n enlace m

tiff /tɪf/ n riña f

tiger /'taɪgə(r)/ n tigre m

tight /taɪt/ a (-er, -est) ⟨clothes⟩ ceñido; (taut) tieso; ⟨control etc⟩ riguroso; ⟨knot, nut⟩ apretado; (drunk, fam) borracho. • adv bien; (shut) herméticamente. ~ **corner** n (fig)

apuro m. ~**en** /'taɪtn/ vt apretar. • vi apretarse. ~**fisted** a tacaño. ~**ly** adv bien; (shut) herméticamente. ~**ness** n estrechez f. ~**rope** /'taɪtrəʊp/ n cuerda f floja. ~**s** /taɪts/ npl leotardos mpl

tile /taɪl/ n (decorative) azulejo m; (on roof) teja f; (on floor) baldosa f. • vt azulejar; tejar ⟨roof⟩; embaldosar ⟨floor⟩

till[1] /tɪl/ prep hasta. • conj hasta que

till[2] /tɪl/ n caja f

till[3] /tɪl/ vt cultivar

tilt /tɪlt/ vt inclinar. • vi inclinarse. • n inclinación f. **at full** ~ a toda velocidad

timber /'tɪmbə(r)/ n madera f (de construcción); (trees) árboles mpl

time /taɪm/ n tiempo m; (moment) momento m; (occasion) ocasión f; (by clock) hora f; (epoch) época f; (rhythm) compás m. ~ **off** tiempo libre. **at** ~**s** a veces. **behind the** ~**s** anticuado. **behind** ~ atrasado. **for the** ~ **being** por ahora. **from** ~ **to** ~ de vez en cuando. **have a good** ~ divertirse, pasarlo bien. **in a year's** ~ dentro de un año. **in no** ~ en un abrir y cerrar de ojos. **in** ~ a tiempo; (eventually) con el tiempo. **on** ~ a la hora, puntual. • vt elegir el momento; cronometrar ⟨race⟩. ~ **bomb** n bomba f de tiempo. ~**honoured** a consagrado. ~**lag** n intervalo m

timeless /'taɪmlɪs/ a eterno

timely /'taɪmlɪ/ a oportuno

timer /'taɪmə(r)/ n cronómetro m; (culin) avisador m; (with sand) reloj m de arena; (elec) interruptor m de reloj

timetable /'taɪmteɪbl/ n horario m

time zone /'taɪmzəʊn/ n huso m horario

timid /'tɪmɪd/ a tímido; (fearful) miedoso. ~**ly** adv tímidamente

timing /'taɪmɪŋ/ n medida f del tiempo; (moment) momento m; (sport) cronometraje m

timorous /'tɪmərəs/ a tímido; (fearful) miedoso. ~**ly** adv tímidamente

tin /tɪn/ n estaño m; (container) lata f. ~ **foil** n papel m de estaño. • vt (pt **tinned**) conservar en lata, enlatar

tinge /tɪndʒ/ vt teñir (**with** de); (fig) matizar (**with** de). • n matiz m

tingle /'tɪŋgl/ vi sentir hormigueo; (with excitement) estremecerse

tinker /'tɪŋkə(r)/ n hojalatero m.
● vi. ~ **(with)** jugar con; (repair)
arreglar

tinkle /'tɪŋkl/ n retintín m; (phone
call, fam) llamada f

tin /tɪn/ n lata a en la metálico.
~-**opener** n abrelatas m invar. ~
plate n hojalata f

tinpot /'tɪnpɒt/ a (pej) inferior

tinsel /'tɪnsl/ n oropel m

tint /tɪnt/ n matiz m

tiny /'taɪnɪ/ a (-ier, -iest) diminuto

tip¹ /tɪp/ n punta f

tip² /tɪp/ vt (pt **tipped**) (tilt) inclinar;
(overturn) volcar; (pour) verter● vi
inclinarse; (overturn) volcarse.● n
(for rubbish) vertedero m. ~ **out**
verter

tip³ /tɪp/ vt (reward) dar una propina a. ~ **off** advertir. ● n (reward)
propina f; (advice) consejo m

tip-off /'tɪpɒf/ n advertencia f

tipped /tɪpt/ a ‹cigarette› con filtro

tipple /'tɪpl/ vi beborrotear. ● n
bebida f alcohólica. **have a** ~ tomar
una copa

tipsy /'tɪpsɪ/ a achispado

tiptoe /'tɪptəʊ/ n. **on** ~ de puntillas

tiptop /'tɪptɒp/ a (fam) de primera

tirade /taɪ'reɪd/ n diatriba f

tire /'taɪə(r)/ vt cansar. ● vi
cansarse. ~**d** /'taɪəd/ a cansado. ~**d**
of harto de. ~**d out** agotado. ~**less**
a incansable

tiresome /'taɪəsəm/ a (annoying)
fastidioso; (boring) pesado

tiring /'taɪərɪŋ/ a cansado

tissue /'tɪʃuː/ n tisú m; (handkerchief) pañuelo m de papel. ~-**paper** n papel m de seda

tit¹ /tɪt/ n (bird) paro m

tit² /tɪt/ n. ~ **for tat** golpe por golpe

titbit /'tɪtbɪt/ n golosina f

titillate /'tɪtɪleɪt/ vt excitar

title /'taɪtl/ n título m. ~**d** a con título nobiliario. ~**deed** n título m de
propiedad. ~**role** n papel m
principal

tittle-tattle /'tɪtltætl/ n cháchara f

titular /'tɪtjʊlə(r)/ a nominal

tizzy /'tɪzɪ/ n (sl). **get in a** ~ ponerse
nervioso

to /tuː, tə/ prep a; (towards) hacia;
(in order to) para; (according to)
según; (as far as) hasta; (with times)
menos; (of) de. **give it** ~ **me** dámelo.
I don't want to no quiero. **twenty**
~ **seven** (by clock) las siete menos
veinte. ● adv. **push** ~, **pull** ~

cerrar. ~ **and fro** adv de aquí para
allá

toad /təʊd/ n sapo m

toadstool /'təʊdstuːl/ n seta f
venenosa

toast /təʊst/ n pan m tostado, tostada f; (drink) brindis m. **drink a** ~
to brindar por. ● vt brindar por.
~**er** n tostador m de pan

tobacco /tə'bækəʊ/ n tabaco m.
~**nist** n estanquero m. ~**nist's shop**
n estanco m

to-be /tə'biː/ a futuro

toboggan /tə'bɒgən/ n tobogán m

today /tə'deɪ/ n & adv hoy (m). ~
week dentro de una semana

toddler /'tɒdlə(r)/ n niño m que
empieza a andar

toddy /'tɒdɪ/ n ponche m

to-do /tə'duː/ n lío m

toe /təʊ/ n dedo m del pie; (of shoe)
punta f. **big** ~ dedo m gordo (del
pie). **on one's** ~**s** (fig) alerta. ● vt.
~ **the line** conformarse. ~**hold** n
punto m de apoyo

toff /tɒf/ n (sl) petimetre m

toffee /'tɒfɪ/ n caramelo m

together /tə'geðə(r)/ adv junto, juntos; (at same time) a la vez. ~ **with**
junto con. ~**ness** n compañerismo
m

toil /tɔɪl/ vi afanarse. ● n trabajo m

toilet /'tɔɪlɪt/ n servicio m, retrete m;
(grooming) arreglo m, tocado m.
~-**paper** n papel m higiénico. ~-**ries**
/'tɔɪlɪtrɪz/ npl artículos mpl de tocador. ~ **water** n agua f de Colonia

token /'təʊkən/ n señal f; (voucher)
vale m; (coin) ficha f. ● a simbólico

told /təʊld/ see **tell**. ● a. **all** ~ con
todo

tolerabl|e /'tɒlərəbl/ a tolerable;
(not bad) regular. ~**y** adv
pasablemente

toleran|ce /'tɒlərəns/ n tolerancia f.
~**t** /'tɒlərənt/ a tolerante. ~**tly** adv
con tolerancia

tolerate /'tɒləreɪt/ vt tolerar

toll¹ /təʊl/ n peaje m. **death** ~
número m de muertos. **take a heavy**
~ dejar muchas víctimas

toll² /təʊl/ vi doblar, tocar a muerto

tom /tɒm/ n gato m (macho)

tomato /tə'mɑːtəʊ/ n (pl ~**oes**)
tomate m

tomb /tuːm/ n tumba f, sepulcro m

tomboy /'tɒmbɔɪ/ n marimacho m

tombstone /'tuːmstəʊn/ n lápida f
sepulcral

tom-cat /'tɒmkæt/ *n* gato *m* (macho)

tome /təʊm/ *n* libroto *m*

tomfoolery /tɒm'fu:lərɪ/ *n* payasadas *fpl*, tonterías *fpl*

tomorrow /tə'mɒrəʊ/ *n & adv* mañana (*f*). **see you ~!** ¡hasta mañana!

ton /tʌn/ *n* tonelada *f* (= *1,016 kg*). **~s of** (*fam*) montones de. **metric ~** tonelada *f* (métrica) (= *1,000 kg*)

tone /təʊn/ *n* tono *m*. ● *vt*. **~ down** atenuar. ~ **up** tonificar ⟨*muscles*⟩. ● *vi*. ~ **in** armonizar. **~deaf** *a* que no tiene buen oído

tongs /tɒŋz/ *npl* tenazas *fpl*; (*for hair, sugar*) tenacillas *fpl*

tongue /tʌŋ/ *n* lengua *f*. ~ **in cheek** *adv* irónicamente. **~tied** a mudo. **get ~tied** trabársele la lengua. **~twister** *n* trabalenguas *m invar*

tonic /'tɒnɪk/ *a* tónico. ● *n* (*tonic water*) tónica *f*; (*med, fig*) tónico *m*. ~ **water** *n* tónica *f*

tonight /tə'naɪt/ *adv & n* esta noche (*f*); (*evening*) esta tarde (*f*)

tonne /tʌn/ *n* tonelada *f* (métrica)

tonsil /'tɒnsl/ *n* amígdala *f*. **~litis** /-'laɪtɪs/ *n* amigdalitis *f*

too /tu:/ *adv* demasiado; (*also*) también. ~ **many** *a* demasiados. ~ **much** *a & adv* demasiado

took /tʊk/ *see* **take**

tool /tu:l/ *n* herramienta *f*. **~bag** *n* bolsa *f* de herramientas

toot /tu:t/ *n* bocinazo *m*. ● *vi* tocar la bocina

tooth /tu:θ/ *n* (*pl* **teeth**) diente *m*; (*molar*) muela *f*. **~ache** /'tu:θeɪk/ *n* dolor *m* de muelas. **~brush** /'tu:θbrʌʃ/ *n* cepillo *m* de dientes. **~comb** /'tu:θkəʊm/ *n* peine *m* de púa fina. **~less** *a* desdentado, sin dientes. **~paste** /'tu:θpeɪst/ *n* pasta *f* dentífrica. **~pick** /'tu:θpɪk/ *n* palillo *m* de dientes

top[1] /tɒp/ *n* cima *f*; (*upper part*) parte *f* de arriba; (*upper surface*) superficie *f*; (*lid, of bottle*) tapa *f*; (*of list*) cabeza *f*. **from ~ to bottom** de arriba abajo. **on ~ (of)** encima de; (*besides*) además. ● *a* más alto; (*in rank*) superior, principal; (*maximum*) máximo. **~ floor** *n* último piso *m*. ● *vt* (*pt* **topped**) cubrir; (*exceed*) exceder. ~ **up** *vt* llenar

top[2] /tɒp/ *n* (*toy*) trompa *f*, peonza *f*

top: ~ hat *n* chistera *f*. **~heavy** *a* más pesado arriba que abajo

topic /'tɒpɪk/ *n* tema *m*. **~al** /'tɒpɪkl/ *a* de actualidad

top: ~less /'tɒplɪs/ *a* ⟨*bather*⟩ con los senos desnudos. **~most** /'tɒpməʊst/ *a* (el) más alto. **~notch** *a* (*fam*) excelente

topography /tə'pɒgrəfɪ/ *n* topografía *f*

topple /'tɒpl/ *vi* derribar; (*overturn*) volcar

top secret /tɒp'si:krɪt/ *a* sumamente secreto

topsy-turvy /tɒpsɪ'tɜ:vɪ/ *adv & a* patas arriba

torch /tɔ:tʃ/ *n* lámpara *f* de bolsillo; (*flaming*) antorcha *f*

tore /tɔ:(r)/ *see* **tear**[1]

toreador /'tɒrɪədɔ:(r)/ *n* torero *m*

torment /'tɔ:ment/ *n* tormento *m*. /tɔ:'ment/ *vt* atormentar

torn /tɔ:n/ *see* **tear**[1]

tornado /tɔ:'neɪdəʊ/ *n* (*pl* **-oes**) tornado *m*

torpedo /tɔ:'pi:dəʊ/ *n* (*pl* **-oes**) torpedo *m*. ● *vt* torpedear

torpor /'tɔ:pə(r)/ *n* apatía *f*

torrent /'tɒrənt/ *n* torrente *m*. **~ial** /tə'renʃl/ *a* torrencial

torrid /'tɒrɪd/ *a* tórrido

torso /'tɔ:səʊ/ *n* (*pl* **-os**) torso *m*

tortoise /'tɔ:təs/ *n* tortuga *f*. **~shell** *n* carey *m*

tortuous /'tɔ:tjʊəs/ *a* tortuoso

torture /'tɔ:tʃə(r)/ *n* tortura *f*, tormento *m*. ● *vt* atormentar. **~r** /-ə(r)/ *n* atormentador *m*, verdugo *m*

Tory /'tɔ:rɪ/ *a & n* (*fam*) conservador (*m*)

toss /tɒs/ *vt* echar; (*shake*) sacudir. ● *vi* agitarse. ~ **and turn** (*in bed*) revolverse. ~ **up** echar a cara o cruz

tot[1] /tɒt/ *n* nene *m*; (*of liquor, fam*) trago *m*

tot[2] /tɒt/ *vt* (*pt* **totted**). ~ **up** (*fam*) sumar

total /'təʊtl/ *a & n* total (*m*). ● *vt* (*pt* **totalled**) sumar

totalitarian /təʊtælɪ'teərɪən/ *a* totalitario

total: ~ity /təʊ'tælətɪ/ *n* totalidad *f*. **~ly** *adv* totalmente

totter /'tɒtə(r)/ *vi* tambalearse. **~y** *a* inseguro

touch /tʌtʃ/ *vt* tocar; (*reach*) alcanzar; (*move*) conmover. ● *vi* tocarse. ● *n* toque *m*; (*sense*) tacto *m*; (*contact*) contacto *m*; (*trace*) pizca *f*. **get in ~ with** ponerse en contacto con. ~ **down** ⟨*aircraft*⟩ aterrizar. ~ **off**

disparar ⟨gun⟩; (fig) desencadenar. **~ on** tratar levemente. **~ up** retocar. **~and-go** a incierto, dudoso

touching /'tʌtʃɪŋ/ a conmovedor

touchstone /'tʌtʃstəʊn/ n (fig) piedra f de toque

touchy /'tʌtʃɪ/ a quisquilloso

tough /tʌf/ a (-er, -est) duro; (strong) fuerte, resistente. **~en** /'tʌfn/ vt endurecer. **~ness** n dureza f; (strength) resistencia f

toupee /'tu:peɪ/ n postizo m, tupé m

tour /tʊə(r)/ n viaje m; (visit) visita f; (excursion) excursión f; (by team etc) gira f. ● vt recorrer; (visit) visitar

touris|m /'tʊərɪzəm/ n turismo m. **~t** /'tʊərɪst/ n turista m & f. ● a turístico. **~t office** n oficina f de turismo

tournament /'tɔ:nəmənt/ n torneo m

tousle /'taʊzl/ vt despeinar

tout /taʊt/ vi. **~ (for)** solicitar. ● n solicitador m

tow /təʊ/ vt remolcar. ● n remolque m. **on ~** a remolque. **with his family in ~** (fam) acompañado por su familia

toward(s) /tə'wɔ:d(z)/ prep hacia

towel /'taʊəl/ n toalla f. **~ling** n (fabric) toalla f

tower /'taʊə(r)/ n torre f. ● vi. **~ above** dominar. **~ block** n edificio m alto. **~ing** a altísimo; ⟨rage⟩ violento

town /taʊn/ n ciudad f, pueblo m. **go to ~** (fam) no escatimar dinero. **~ hall** n ayuntamiento m. **~ planning** n urbanismo m

tow-path /'təʊpɑːθ/ n camino m de sirga

toxi|c /'tɒksɪk/ a tóxico. **~n** /'tɒksɪn/ n toxina f

toy /tɔɪ/ n juguete m. ● vi. **~ with** jugar con ⟨object⟩; acariciar ⟨idea⟩. **~shop** n juguetería f

trac|e /treɪs/ n huella f; (small amount) pizca f. ● vt seguir la pista de; ⟨draw⟩ dibujar; (with tracing-paper) calcar; (track down) encontrar. **~ing** /'treɪsɪŋ/ n calco m. **~ing-paper** n papel m de calcar

track /træk/ n huella f; (path) sendero m; (sport) pista f; (of rocket etc) trayectoria f; (rail) vía f. **keep ~ of** vigilar. **make ~s** (sl) marcharse. ● vt seguir la pista de. **~ down** vt localizar. **~ suit** n traje m de deporte, chandal m

tract[1] /trækt/ n (land) extensión f; (anat) aparato m

tract[2] /trækt/ n (pamphlet) opúsculo m

traction /'trækʃn/ n tracción f

tractor /'træktə(r)/ n tractor m

trade /treɪd/ n comercio m; (occupation) oficio m; (exchange) cambio m; (industry) industria f. ● vt cambiar. ● vi comerciar. **~ in** (give in part-exchange) dar como parte del pago. **~ on** aprovecharse de. **~ mark** n marca f registrada. **~r** /-ə(r)/ n comerciante m & f. **~sman** /'treɪdzmən/ n (pl -men) (shopkeeper) tendero m. **~ union** n sindicato m. **~ unionist** n sindicalista m & f. **~ wind** n viento m alisio

trading /'treɪdɪŋ/ n comercio m. **~ estate** n zona f industrial

tradition /trə'dɪʃn/ n tradición f. **~al** a tradicional. **~alist** n tradicionalista m & f. **~ally** adv tradicionalmente

traffic /'træfɪk/ n tráfico m. ● vi (pt trafficked) comerciar (in en). **~ lights** npl semáforo m. **~ warden** n guardia m, controlador m de tráfico

trag|edy /'trædʒɪdɪ/ n tragedia f. **~ic** /'trædʒɪk/ a trágico. **~ically** adv trágicamente

trail /treɪl/ vi arrastrarse; (lag) rezagarse. ● vt (track) seguir la pista de. ● n estela f; (track) pista f. (path) sendero m. **~er** /'treɪlə(r)/ n remolque m; (film) avance m

train /treɪn/ n tren m; (of dress) cola f; (series) sucesión f; (retinue) séquito m. ● vt adiestrar; (sport) entrenar; educar ⟨child⟩; guiar ⟨plant⟩; domar ⟨animal⟩. ● vi adiestrarse; (sport) entrenarse. **~ed** a (skilled) cualificado; ⟨doctor⟩ diplomado. **~ee** n aprendiz m. **~er** n (sport) entrenador m; (of animals) domador m. **~ers** mpl zapatillas fpl de deporte. **~ing** n instrucción f; (sport) entrenamiento m

traipse /treɪps/ vi (fam) vagar

trait /treɪ(t)/ n característica f, rasgo m

traitor /'treɪtə(r)/ n traidor m

tram /træm/ n tranvía m

tramp /træmp/ vt recorrer a pie. ● vi andar en pasos pesados. ● n (vagrant) vagabundo m; (sound) ruido m de pasos; (hike) paseo m largo

trample /'træmpl/ *vt/i* pisotear. ~
(on) pisotear
trampoline /'træmpəli:n/ *n* trampolín *m*
trance /trɑ:ns/ *n* trance *m*
tranquil /'træŋkwɪl/ *a* tranquilo.
~**lity** /-'kwɪləti/ *n* tranquilidad *f*
tranquillize /'træŋkwɪlaɪz/ *vt* tranquilizar. ~**r** /-ə(r)/ *n* tranquilizante
m
transact /træn'zækt/ *vt* negociar.
~**ion** /-ʃn/ *n* transacción *f*
transatlantic /trænzət'læntɪk/ *a*
transatlántico
transcend /træn'send/ *vt* exceder.
~**ent** *a* sobresaliente
transcendental /trænsen'dentl/ *a*
trascendental
transcribe /træns'kraɪb/ *vt* transcribir; grabar ⟨recorded sound⟩
transcript /'trænskrɪpt/ *n* copia *f*.
~**ion** /-ɪpʃn/ *n* transcripción *f*
transfer /træns'fɜ:(r)/ *vt* (*pt* **transferred**) trasladar; calcar ⟨drawing⟩.
● *vi* trasladarse. ~ **the charges** (*on
telephone*) llamar a cobro revertido.
/'trænsfɜ:(r)/ *n* traslado *m*; (*paper*)
calcomanía *f*. ~**able** *a* transferible
transfigur|ation /trænsfɪgjʊ'reɪʃn/
n transfiguración *f*. ~**e**
/træns'fɪgə(r)/ *vt* transfigurar
transfix /træns'fɪks/ *vt* traspasar;
(*fig*) paralizar
transform /træns'fɔ:m/ *vt* transformar. ~**ation** /-ə'meɪʃn/ *n* transformación *f*. ~**er** /-ə(r)/ *n*
transformador *m*
transfusion /træns'fju:ʒn/ *n* transfusión *f*
transgress /træns'gres/ *vt* traspasar, infringir. ~**ion** /-ʃn/ *n* transgresión *f*; (*sin*) pecado *m*
transient /'trænzɪənt/ *a* pasajero
transistor /træn'zɪstə(r)/ *n* transistor *m*
transit /'trænsɪt/ *n* tránsito *m*
transition /træn'zɪʒn/ *n* transición *f*
transitive /'trænsɪtɪv/ *a* transitivo
transitory /'trænsɪtrɪ/ *a* transitorio
translat|e /trænz'leɪt/ *vt* traducir.
~**ion** /-ʃn/ *n* traducción *f*. ~**or**
/-ə(r)/ *n* traductor *m*
translucen|ce /trænz'lu:sns/ *n* traslucidez *f*. ~**t** /trænz'lu:snt/ *a*
traslúcido
transmission /trænz'mɪʃn/ *n* transmisión *f*
transmit /trænz'mɪt/ *vt* (*pt* **transmitted**) transmitir. ~**ter** /-ə(r)/ *n*

transmisor *m*; (*TV, radio*) emisora *f*
transparen|cy /træns'pærənsɪ/ *n*
transparencia *f*; (*photo*) diapositiva
f. ~**t** /træns'pærənt/ *a* transparente
transpire /træn'spaɪə(r)/ *vi* transpirar; (*happen, fam*) suceder,
revelarse
transplant /træns'plɑ:nt/ *vt* trasplantar. /'trænsplɑ:nt/ *n* trasplante *m*
transport /træn'spɔ:t/ *vt* transportar. /'trænspɔ:t/ *n* transporte *m*.
~**ation** /-'teɪʃn/ *n* transporte *m*
transpos|e /træn'spəʊz/ *vt* transponer; (*mus*) transportar. ~**ition**
/-pə'zɪʃn/ *n* transposición *f*; (*mus*)
transporte *m*
transverse /'trænzvɜ:s/ *a* transverso
transvestite /trænz'vestaɪt/ *n* travestido *m*
trap /træp/ *n* trampa *f*. ● *vt* (*pt*
trapped) atrapar; (*jam*) atascar;
(*cut off*) bloquear. ~**door** /'træpdɔ:
(r)/ *n* trampa *f*; (*in theatre*) escotillón *m*
trapeze /trə'pi:z/ *n* trapecio *m*
trappings /'træpɪŋz/ *npl* (*fig*) atavíos
mpl
trash /træʃ/ *n* pacotilla *f*; (*refuse*)
basura *f*; (*nonsense*) tonterías *fpl*. ~
can *n* (*Amer*) cubo *m* de la basura.
~**y** *a* de baja calidad
trauma /'trɔ:mə/ *n* trauma *m*. ~**tic**
/-'mætɪk/ *a* traumático
travel /'trævl/ *vi* (*pt* **travelled**)
viajar. ● *vt* recorrer. ● *n* viajar *m*.
~**ler** /-ə(r)/ *n* viajero *m*. ~**ler's
cheque** *n* cheque *m* de viaje. ~**ling**
n viajar *m*
traverse /træ'vɜ:s/ *vt* atravesar,
recorrer
travesty /'trævɪstɪ/ *n* parodia *f*
trawler /'trɔ:lə(r)/ *n* pesquero *m* de
arrastre
tray /treɪ/ *n* bandeja *f*
treacher|ous *a* traidor; (*deceptive*)
engañoso. ~**ously** *adv* traidoramente. ~**y** /'tretʃərɪ/ *n* traición
f
treacle /'tri:kl/ *n* melaza *f*
tread /tred/ *vi* (*pt* trod, *pp* **trodden**)
andar. ~ **on** pisar. ● *vt* pisar. ● *n*
(*step*) paso *m*; (*of tyre*) banda *f* de
rodadura. ~**le** /'tredl/ *n* pedal *m*.
~**mill** /'tredmɪl/ *n* rueda *f* de molino; (*fig*) rutina *f*
treason /'tri:zn/ *n* traición *f*
treasure /'treʒə(r)/ *n* tesoro *m*. ● *vt*
apreciar mucho; (*store*) guardar

treasur|er /'treʒərə(r)/ *n* tesorero *m*. **~y** /'treʒərɪ/ *n* tesorería *f*. **the T~y** *n* el Ministerio *m* de Hacienda

treat /triːt/ *vt* tratar; (*consider*) considerar. **~ s.o.** invitar a uno. ● *n* placer *m*; (*present*) regalo *m*

treatise /'triːtɪz/ *n* tratado *m*

treatment /'triːtmənt/ *n* tratamiento *m*

treaty /'triːtɪ/ *n* tratado *m*

treble /'trebl/ *a* triple; ‹*clef*› de sol; ‹*voice*› de tiple. ● *vt* triplicar. ● *vi* triplicarse. ● *n* tiple *m & f*

tree /triː/ *n* árbol *m*

trek /trek/ *n* viaje *m* arduo, caminata *f*. ● *vi* (*pt* **trekked**) hacer un viaje arduo

trellis /'trelɪs/ *n* enrejado *m*

tremble /'trembl/ *vi* temblar

tremendous /trɪ'mendəs/ *a* tremendo; (*huge, fam*) enorme. **~ly** *adv* tremendamente

tremor /'tremə(r)/ *n* temblor *m*

tremulous /'tremjʊləs/ *a* tembloroso

trench /trentʃ/ *n* foso *m*, zanja *f*; (*mil*) trinchera *f*. **~ coat** *n* trinchera *f*

trend /trend/ *n* tendencia *f*; (*fashion*) moda *f*. **~setter** *n* persona *f* que lanza la moda. **~y** *a* (**-ier, -iest**) (*fam*) a la última

trepidation /trepɪ'deɪʃn/ *n* inquietud *f*

trespass /'trespəs/ *vi*. **~ on** entrar sin derecho; (*fig*) abusar de. **~er** /-ə(r)/ *n* intruso *m*

tress /tres/ *n* trenza *f*

trestle /'tresl/ *n* caballete *m*. **~-table** *n* mesa *f* de caballete

trews /truːz/ *npl* pantalón *m*

trial /'traɪəl/ *n* prueba *f*; (*jurid*) proceso *m*; (*ordeal*) prueba *f* dura. **~ and error** tanteo *m*. **be on ~** estar a prueba; (*jurid*) ser procesado

triang|le /'traɪæŋgl/ *n* triángulo *m*. **~ular** /-'æŋgjʊlə(r)/ *a* triangular

trib|al /'traɪbl/ *a* tribal. **~e** /traɪb/ *n* tribu *f*

tribulation /trɪbjʊ'leɪʃn/ *n* tribulación *f*

tribunal /traɪ'bjuːnl/ *n* tribunal *m*

tributary /'trɪbjʊtrɪ/ *n* (*stream*) afluente *m*

tribute /'trɪbjuːt/ *n* tributo *m*. **pay ~ to** rendir homenaje a

trice /traɪs/ *n*. **in a ~** en un abrir y cerrar de ojos

trick /trɪk/ *n* trampa *f*; engaño *m*; (*joke*) broma *f*; (*at cards*) baza *f*; (*habit*) manía *f*. **do the ~** servir. **play a ~ on** gastar una broma a. ● *vt* engañar. **~ery** /'trɪkərɪ/ *n* engaño *m*

trickle /'trɪkl/ *vi* gotear. **~ in** (*fig*) entrar poco a póco. **~ out** (*fig*) salir poco a poco

trickster /'trɪkstə(r)/ *n* estafador *m*

tricky /'trɪkɪ/ *a* delicado, difícil

tricolour /'trɪkələ(r)/ *n* bandera *f* tricolor

tricycle /'traɪsɪkl/ *n* triciclo *m*

trident /'traɪdənt/ *n* tridente *m*

tried /traɪd/ *see* **try**

trifl|e /'traɪfl/ *n* bagatela *f*; (*culin*) bizcocho *m* con natillas, jalea, frutas y nata. ● *vi*. **~e with** jugar con. **~ing** *a* insignificante

trigger /'trɪgə(r)/ *n* (*of gun*) gatillo *m*. ● *vt*. **~ (off)** desencadenar

trigonometry /trɪgə'nɒmɪtrɪ/ *n* trigonometría *f*

trilby /'trɪlbɪ/ *n* sombrero *m* de fieltro

trilogy /'trɪlədʒɪ/ *n* trilogía *f*

trim /trɪm/ *a* (**trimmer, trimmest**) arreglado. ● *vt* (*pt* **trimmed**) cortar; recortar ‹*hair etc*›; (*adorn*) adornar. ● *n* (*cut*) recorte *m*; (*decoration*) adorno *m*; (*state*) estado *m*. **in ~** en buen estado; (*fit*) en forma. **~ming** *n* adorno *m*. **~mings** *npl* recortes *mpl*; (*decorations*) adornos *mpl*; (*culin*) guarnición *f*

trinity /'trɪnɪtɪ/ *n* trinidad *f*. **the T~** la Trinidad

trinket /'trɪŋkɪt/ *n* chuchería *f*

trio /'triːəʊ/ *n* (*pl* **-os**) trío *m*

trip /trɪp/ *vt* (*pt* **tripped**) hacer tropezar. ● *vi* tropezar; (*go lightly*) andar con paso ligero. ● *n* (*journey*) viaje *m*; (*outing*) excursión *f*; (*stumble*) traspié *m*. **~ up** *vi* tropezar. ● *vt* hacer tropezar

tripe /traɪp/ *n* callos *mpl*; (*nonsense, sl*) tonterías *fpl*

triple /'trɪpl/ *a* triple. ● *vt* triplicar. ● *vi* triplicarse. **~ts** /'trɪplɪts/ *npl* trillizos *mpl*

triplicate /'trɪplɪkət/ *a* triplicado. **in ~** por triplicado

tripod /'traɪpɒd/ *n* trípode *m*

tripper /'trɪpə(r)/ *n* (*on day trip etc*) excursionista *m & f*

triptych /'trɪptɪk/ *n* tríptico *m*

trite /traɪt/ *a* trillado

triumph /ˈtraɪʌmf/ n triunfo m. ● vi trinunfar (over sobre). ~al /-ˈʌmfl/ a triunfal. ~ant /-ˈʌmfnt/ a triunfante

trivial /ˈtrɪvɪəl/ a insignificante. ~ity /-ˈælətɪ/ n insignificancia f

trod, trodden /trɒd, trɒdn/ see tread

trolley /ˈtrɒlɪ/ n (pl -eys) carretón m. **tea ~** n mesita f de ruedas. ~**bus** n trolebús m

trombone /trɒmˈbəʊn/ n trombón m

troop /truːp/ n grupo m. ● vi. ~ **in** entrar en tropel. ~ **out** salir en tropel. ● vt. ~**ing the colour** saludo m a la bandera. ~**er** n soldado m de caballería. ~**s** npl (mil) tropas fpl

trophy /ˈtrəʊfɪ/ n trofeo m

tropic /ˈtrɒpɪk/ n trópico m. ~**al** a tropical. ~**s** npl trópicos mpl

trot /trɒt/ n trote m. **on the ~** (fam) seguidos. ● vi (pt trotted) trotar. ~ **out** (produce, fam) producir

trotter /ˈtrɒtə(r)/ n (culin) pie m de cerdo

trouble /ˈtrʌbl/ n problema m; (awkward situation) apuro m; (inconvenience) molestia f; (conflict) conflicto m; (med) enfermedad f; (mec) avería f. **be in ~** estar en un apuro. **make ~** armar un lío. **take ~** tomarse la molestia. ● vt (bother) molestar; (worry) preocupar. ● vi molestarse; (worry) preocuparse. **be ~d about** preocuparse por. ~**-maker** n alborotador m. ~**some** a molesto

trough /trɒf/ n (for drinking) abrevadero m; (for feeding) pesebre m; (of wave) seno m; (atmospheric) mínimo m de presión

trounce /traʊns/ vt (defeat) derrotar; (thrash) pegar

troupe /truːp/ n compañía f

trousers /ˈtraʊzəz/ npl pantalón m; pantalones mpl

trousseau /ˈtruːsəʊ/ n (pl -s /-əʊz/) ajuar m

trout /traʊt/ n (pl trout) trucha f

trowel /ˈtraʊəl/ n (garden) desplantador m; (for mortar) paleta f

truant /ˈtruːənt/ n. **play ~** hacer novillos

truce /truːs/ n tregua f

truck[1] /trʌk/ n carro m; (rail) vagón m; (lorry) camión m

truck[2] /trʌk/ n (dealings) trato m

truculent /ˈtrʌkjʊlənt/ a agresivo

trudge /trʌdʒ/ vi andar penosamente. ● n caminata f penosa

true /truː/ a (-er, -est) verdadero; (loyal) leal; (genuine) auténtico; (accurate) exacto. **come ~** realizarse

truffle /ˈtrʌfl/ n trufa f; (chocolate) trufa f de chocolate

truism /ˈtruːɪzəm/ n perogrullada f

truly /ˈtruːlɪ/ adv verdaderamente; (sincerely) sinceramente; (faithfully) fielmente. **yours ~** (in letters) le saluda atentamente

trump /trʌmp/ n (cards) triunfo m. ● vt fallar. ~ **up** inventar

trumpet /ˈtrʌmpɪt/ n trompeta f. ~**er** n -ə(r)/ n trompetero m, trompeta m & f

truncated /trʌŋˈkeɪtɪd/ a truncado

truncheon /ˈtrʌntʃən/ n porra f

trundle /ˈtrʌndl/ vt hacer rodar. ● vi rodar

trunk /trʌŋk/ n tronco m; (box) baúl m; (of elephant) trompa f. ~**call** n conferencia f. ~**road** n carretera f (nacional). ~**s** npl bañador m

truss /trʌs/ n (med) braguero m. ~ **up** vt (culin) espetar

trust /trʌst/ n confianza f; (association) trust m. **on ~** a ojos cerrados; (com) al fiado. ● vi confiar. ~ **to** confiar en. ● vt confiar en; (hope) esperar. ~**ed** a leal

trustee /trʌˈstiː/ n administrador m

trust: ~**ful** a confiado. ~**fully** adv confiadamente. ~**worthy** a, ~**y** a digno de confianza

truth /truːθ/ n (pl -s /truːðz/) verdad f. ~**ful** a veraz; (true) verídico. ~**fully** adv sinceramente

try /traɪ/ vt (pt tried) probar; (be a strain on) poner a prueba; (jurid) procesar. ~ **on** vt probarse (garment). ~ **out** vt probar. ● vi probar. ~ **for** vi intentar conseguir. ● n tentativa f, prueba f; (rugby) ensayo m. ~**ing** a difícil; (annoying) molesto. ~**out** n prueba f

tryst /trɪst/ n cita f

T-shirt /ˈtiːʃɜːt/ n camiseta f

tub /tʌb/ n tina f; (bath, fam) baño m

tuba /ˈtjuːbə/ n tuba f

tubby /ˈtʌbɪ/ a (-ier, -iest) rechoncho

tube /tjuːb/ n tubo m; (rail, fam) metro m. **inner ~** n cámara f de aire

tuber /ˈtjuːbə(r)/ n tubérculo m

tuberculosis /tjuːbɜːkjʊˈləʊsɪs/ n tuberculosis f

tub|ing /'tjuːbɪŋ/ n tubería f, tubos mpl. **~ular** a tubular

tuck /tʌk/ n pliegue m. ● vt plegar; (put) meter; (put away) remeter; (hide) esconder. ~ **up** vt arropar ⟨child⟩. ● vi. ~ **in(to)** (eat, sl) comer con buen apetito. **~shop** n confitería f

Tuesday /'tjuːzdeɪ/ n martes m

tuft /tʌft/ n (of hair) mechón m; (of feathers) penacho m; (of grass) manojo m

tug /tʌg/ vt (pt **tugged**) tirar de; (tow) remolcar. ● vi tirar fuerte. ● n tirón m; (naut) remolcador m. **~of-war** n lucha f de la cuerda; (fig) tira m y afloja

tuition /tjuː'ɪʃn/ n enseñanza f

tulip /'tjuːlɪp/ n tulipán m

tumble /'tʌmbl/ vi caerse. ~ **to** (fam) comprender. ● n caída f

tumbledown /'tʌmbldaʊn/ a ruinoso

tumble-drier /tʌmbl'draɪə(r)/ n secadora f (eléctrica con aire de salida)

tumbler /'tʌmblə(r)/ n (glass) vaso m

tummy /'tʌmɪ/ n (fam) estómago m

tumour /'tjuːmə(r)/ n tumor m

tumult /'tjuːmʌlt/ n tumulto m. **~uous** /-'mʌltjʊəs/ a tumultuoso

tuna /'tjuːnə/ n (pl tuna) atún m

tune /tjuːn/ n aire m. **be in** ~ estar afinado. **be out of** ~ estar desafinado. ● vt afinar; sintonizar ⟨radio, TV⟩; (mec) poner a punto. ● vi. ~ **in (to)** ⟨radio, TV⟩ sintonizarse. ~ **up** afinar. **~ful** a melodioso. **~r** /-ə(r)/ n afinador m; (radio, TV) sintonizador m

tunic /'tjuːnɪk/ n túnica f

tuning-fork /'tjuːnɪŋfɔːk/ n diapasón m

Tunisia /tjuː'nɪzɪə/ n Túnez m. **~n** a & n tunecino (m)

tunnel /'tʌnl/ n túnel m. ● vi (pt **tunnelled**) construir un túnel en

turban /'tɜːbən/ n turbante m

turbid /'tɜːbɪd/ a túrbido

turbine /'tɜːbaɪn/ n turbina f

turbo-jet /'tɜːbəʊdʒet/ n turborreactor m

turbot /'tɜːbət/ n rodaballo m

turbulen|ce /'tɜːbjʊləns/ n turbulencia f. **~t** /'tɜːbjʊlənt/ a turbulento

tureen /tjʊ'riːn/ n sopera f

turf /tɜːf/ n (pl turfs or turves) césped m; (segment) tepe m. **the** ~ n las carreras fpl de caballos. ● vt. ~ **out** (sl) echar

turgid /'tɜːdʒɪd/ a ⟨language⟩ pomposo

Turk /tɜːk/ n turco m

turkey /'tɜːkɪ/ n (pl -eys) pavo m

Turk|ey /'tɜːkɪ/ f Turquía f. **T~ish** a & n turco (m)

turmoil /'tɜːmɔɪl/ n confusión f

turn /tɜːn/ vt hacer girar, dar vueltas a; volver ⟨direction, page, etc⟩; cumplir ⟨age⟩; dar ⟨hour⟩; doblar ⟨corner⟩; (change) cambiar; (deflect) desviar. ~ **the tables** volver las tornas. ● vi girar, dar vueltas; (become) hacerse; (change) cambiar. ● n vuelta f; (in road) curva f; (change) cambio m; (sequence) turno m; (of mind) disposición f; (in theatre) número m; (fright) susto m; (of illness, fam) ataque m. **bad** ~ mala jugada f. **good** ~ favor m. **in** ~ a su vez. **out of** ~ fuera de lugar. **to a** ~ (culin) en su punto. ~ **against** vt volverse en contra de. ~ **down** vt (fold) doblar; (reduce) bajar; (reject) rechazar. ~ **in** vt entregar. ● vi (go to bed, fam) acostarse. ~ **off** vt cerrar ⟨tap⟩; apagar ⟨light, TV, etc⟩. ● vi desviarse. ~ **on** vt abrir ⟨tap⟩; encender ⟨light etc⟩; (attack) atacar; (attract, fam) excitar. ~ **out** vt expulsar; apagar ⟨light etc⟩; (produce) producir; (empty) vaciar. ● vi (result) resultar. ~ **round** vi dar la vuelta. ~ **up** vi aparecer. ● vt (find) encontrar; levantar ⟨collar⟩; poner más fuerte ⟨gas⟩. **~ed-up** a ⟨nose⟩ respingona. **~ing** /'tɜːnɪŋ/ n vuelta f; (road) bocacalle f. **~ing-point** n punto m decisivo.

turnip /'tɜːnɪp/ n nabo m

turn: **~out** n (of people) concurrencia f; (of goods) producción f. **~over** /'tɜːnəʊvə(r)/ n (culin) empanada f; (com) volumen m de negocios; (of staff) rotación f. **~pike** /'tɜːnpaɪk/ n (Amer) autopista f de peaje. **~stile** /'tɜːnstaɪl/ n torniquete m. **~table** /'tɜːnteɪbl/ n plataforma f giratoria; (on record-player) plato m giratorio. **~up** n (of trousers) vuelta f

turpentine /'tɜːpəntaɪn/ n trementina f

turquoise /'tɜːkwɔɪz/ a & n turquesa (f)

turret /'tʌrɪt/ n torrecilla f; (mil) torreta f

turtle /'tɜ:tl/ n tortuga f de mar. ~**neck** n cuello m alto

tusk /tʌsk/ n colmillo m

tussle /'tʌsl/ vi pelearse. ● n pelea f

tussock /'tʌsək/ n montecillo m de hierbas

tutor /'tju:tə(r)/ n preceptor m; (univ) director m de estudios, profesor m. ~**ial** /tju:'tɔ:rɪəl/ n clase f particular

tuxedo /tʌk'si:dəʊ/ n (pl -os) (Amer) esmoquin m

TV /ti:'vi:/ n televisión f

twaddle /'twɒdl/ n tonterías fpl

twang /twæŋ/ n tañido m; (in voice) gangueo m. ● vt hacer vibrar. ● vi vibrar

tweed /twi:d/ n tela f gruesa de lana

tweet /twi:t/ n piada f. ● vi piar

tweezers /'twi:zəz/ npl pinzas fpl

twel|fth /twelfθ/ a & n duodécimo (m). ~**ve** /twelv/ a & n doce (m)

twent|ieth /'twentɪəθ/ a & n vigésimo (m). ~**y** /'twentɪ/ a & n veinte (m)

twerp /twɜ:p/ n (sl) imbécil m

twice /twaɪs/ adv dos veces

twiddle /'twɪdl/ vt hacer girar. ~ **one's thumbs** (fig) no tener nada que hacer. ~ **with** jugar con

twig[1] /twɪg/ n ramita f

twig[2] /twɪg/ vt/i (pt **twigged**) (fam) comprender

twilight /'twaɪlaɪt/ n crepúsculo m

twin /twɪn/ a & n gemelo (m)

twine /twaɪn/ n bramante m. ● vt torcer. ● vi enroscarse

twinge /twɪndʒ/ n punzada f; (fig) remordimiento m (de conciencia)

twinkle /'twɪŋkl/ vi centellear. ● n centelleo m

twirl /twɜ:l/ vt dar vueltas a. ● vi dar vueltas. ● n vuelta f

twist /twɪst/ vt torcer; (roll) enrollar; (distort) deformar. ● vi torcerse; (coil) enroscarse; (road) serpentear. ● n torsión f; (curve) vuelta f; (of character) peculiaridad f

twit[1] /twɪt/ n (sl) imbécil m

twit[2] /twɪt/ vt (pt **twitted**) tomar el pelo a

twitch /twɪtʃ/ vt crispar. ● vi crisparse. ● n tic m; (jerk) tirón m

twitter /'twɪtə(r)/ vi gorjear. ● n gorjeo m

two /tu:/ a & n dos (m). **in** ~ **minds** indeciso. ~**faced** a falso, insincero. ~**piece (suit)** n traje m (de dos piezas). ~**some** /'tu:səm/ n pareja f. ~**way** a (traffic) de doble sentido

tycoon /taɪ'ku:n/ n magnate m

tying /'taɪɪŋ/ see **tie**

type /taɪp/ n tipo m. ● vt/i escribir a máquina. ~**cast** a (actor) encasillado. ~**script** /'taɪpskrɪpt/ n texto m escrito a máquina. ~**writer** /'taɪpraɪtə(r)/ n máquina f de escribir. ~**written** /-ɪtn/ a escrito a máquina, mecanografiado

typhoid /'taɪfɔɪd/ n. ~ (**fever**) fiebre f tifoidea

typhoon /taɪ'fu:n/ n tifón m

typical /'tɪpɪkl/ a típico. ~**ly** adv típicamente

typify /'tɪpɪfaɪ/ vt tipificar

typi|ng /'taɪpɪŋ/ n mecanografía f. ~**st** n mecanógrafo m

typography /taɪ'pɒgrəfɪ/ n tipografía f

tyran|nical /tɪ'rænɪkl/ a tiránico. ~**nize** vi tiranizar. ~**ny** /'tɪrənɪ/ n tiranía f. ~**t** /'taɪərənt/ n tirano m

tyre /'taɪə(r)/ n neumático m, llanta f (Amer)

U

ubiquitous /ju:'bɪkwɪtəs/ a omnipresente, ubicuo

udder /'ʌdə(r)/ n ubre f

UFO /'ju:fəʊ/ abbr (unidentified flying object) OVNI m, objeto m volante no identificado

ugl|iness /ʌglɪnɪs/ n fealdad f. ~**y** /'ʌglɪ/ a (-ier, -iest) feo

UK /ju:'keɪ/ abbr (United Kingdom) Reino m Unido

ulcer /'ʌlsə(r)/ n úlcera f. ~**ous** a ulceroso

ulterior /ʌl'tɪərɪə(r)/ a ulterior. ~ **motive** n segunda intención f

ultimate /'ʌltɪmət/ a último; (definitive) definitivo; (fundamental) fundamental. ~**ly** adv al final; (basically) en el fondo

ultimatum /ʌltɪ'meɪtəm/ n (pl -ums) ultimátum m invar

ultra... /'ʌltrə/ pref ultra...

ultramarine /ʌltrəmə'ri:n/ n azul m marino

ultrasonic /ʌltrə'sɒnɪk/ a ultrasónico

ultraviolet /ˌʌltrəˈvaɪələt/ a ultravioleta a invar

umbilical /ʌmˈbɪlɪkl/ a umbilical. ~ **cord** n cordón m umbilical

umbrage /ˈʌmbrɪdʒ/ n resentimiento m. **take** ~ ofenderse (**at** por)

umbrella /ʌmˈbrelə/ n paraguas m invar

umpire /ˈʌmpaɪə(r)/ n árbitro m. ● vt arbitrar

umpteen /ˈʌmptiːn/ a (sl) muchísimos. ~**th** a (sl) enésimo

UN /juːˈen/ abbr (United Nations) ONU f, Organización f de las Naciones Unidas

un... /ʌn/ pref in..., des..., no, poco, sin

unabated /ʌnəˈbeɪtɪd/ a no disminuido

unable /ʌnˈeɪbl/ a incapaz (**to** de). **be** ~ **to** no poder

unabridged /ʌnəˈbrɪdʒd/ a íntegro

unacceptable /ʌnəkˈseptəbl/ a inaceptable

unaccountabl|e /ʌnəˈkaʊntəbl/ a inexplicable. ~**y** adv inexplicablemente

unaccustomed /ʌnəˈkʌstəmd/ a insólito. **be** ~ **to** a no estar acostumbrado a

unadopted /ʌnəˈdɒptɪd/ a ⟨of road⟩ privado

unadulterated /ʌnəˈdʌltəreɪtɪd/ a puro

unaffected /ʌnəˈfektɪd/ a sin afectación, natural

unaided /ʌnˈeɪdɪd/ a sin ayuda

unalloyed /ʌnəˈlɔɪd/ a puro

unanimous /juːˈnænɪməs/ a unánime. ~**ly** adv unánimemente

unannounced /ʌnəˈnaʊnst/ a sin previo aviso; (unexpected) inesperado

unarmed /ʌnˈɑːmd/ a desarmado

unassuming /ʌnəˈsjuːmɪŋ/ a modesto, sin pretensiones

unattached /ʌnəˈtætʃt/ a suelto; (unmarried) soltero

unattended /ʌnəˈtendɪd/ a sin vigilar

unattractive /ʌnəˈtræktɪv/ a poco atractivo

unavoidabl|e /ʌnəˈvɔɪdəbl/ a inevitable. ~**y** adv inevitablemente

unaware /ʌnəˈweə(r)/ a ignorante (**of** de). **be** ~ **of** ignorar. ~**s** /-eəz/ adv desprevenido

unbalanced /ʌnˈbælənst/ a desequilibrado

unbearabl|e /ʌnˈbeərəbl/ a inaguantable. ~**y** adv inaguantablemente

unbeat|able /ʌnˈbiːtəbl/ a insuperable. ~**en** a no vencido

unbeknown /ʌnbɪˈnəʊn/ a desconocido. ~ **to me** (fam) sin saberlo yo

unbelievable /ʌnbɪˈliːvəbl/ a increíble

unbend /ʌnˈbend/ vt (pt unbent) enderezar. ● vi (relax) relajarse. ~**ing** a inflexible

unbiased /ʌnˈbaɪəst/ a imparcial

unbidden /ʌnˈbɪdn/ a espontáneo; (without invitation) sin ser invitado

unblock /ʌnˈblɒk/ vt desatascar

unbolt /ʌnˈbəʊlt/ vt desatrancar

unborn /ʌnˈbɔːn/ a no nacido todavía

unbounded /ʌnˈbaʊndɪd/ a ilimitado

unbreakable /ʌnˈbreɪkəbl/ a irrompible

unbridled /ʌnˈbraɪdld/ a desenfrenado

unbroken /ʌnˈbrəʊkən/ a (intact) intacto; (continuous) continuo

unburden /ʌnˈbɜːdn/ vt. ~ **o.s.** desahogarse

unbutton /ʌnˈbʌtn/ vt desabotonar, desabrochar

uncalled-for /ʌnˈkɔːldfɔː(r)/ a fuera de lugar; (unjustified) injustificado

uncanny /ʌnˈkænɪ/ a (-ier, -iest) misterioso

unceasing /ʌnˈsiːsɪŋ/ a incesante

unceremonious /ʌnserɪˈməʊnɪəs/ a informal; (abrupt) brusco

uncertain /ʌnˈsɜːtn/ a incierto; (changeable) variable. **be** ~ **whether** no saber exactamente si. ~**ty** n incertidumbre f

unchang|ed /ʌnˈtʃeɪndʒd/ a igual. ~**ing** a inmutable

uncharitable /ʌnˈtʃærɪtəbl/ a severo

uncivilized /ʌnˈsɪvɪlaɪzd/ a incivilizado

uncle /ˈʌŋkl/ n tío m

unclean /ʌnˈkliːn/ a sucio

unclear /ʌnˈklɪə(r)/ a poco claro

uncomfortable /ʌnˈkʌmfətəbl/ a incómodo; (unpleasant) desagradable. **feel** ~ no estar a gusto

uncommon /ʌnˈkɒmən/ a raro. ~**ly** adv extraordinariamente

uncompromising /ʌnˈkɒmprəmaɪzɪŋ/ a intransigente

unconcerned /ʌnkənˈsɜːnd/ a indiferente

unconditional /ʌnkən'dɪʃənl/ *a* incondicional. **~ly** *adv* incondicionalmente

unconscious /ʌn'kɒnʃəs/ *a* inconsciente; (*med*) sin sentido. **~ly** *adv* inconscientemente

unconventional /ʌnkən'venʃənl/ *a* poco convencional

uncooperative /ʌnkəʊ'ɒpərətɪv/ *a* poco servicial

uncork /ʌn'kɔːk/ *vt* descorchar, destapar

uncouth /ʌn'kuːθ/ *a* grosero

uncover /ʌn'kʌvə(r)/ *vt* descubrir

unctuous /'ʌŋktjʊəs/ *a* untuoso; (*fig*) empalagoso

undecided /ʌndɪ'saɪdɪd/ *a* indeciso

undeniabl|e /ʌndɪ'naɪəbl/ *a* innegable. **~y** *adv* indiscutiblemente

under /'ʌndə(r)/ *prep* debajo de; (*less than*) menos de; (*in the course of*) bajo, en. ● *adv* debajo, abajo. **~ age** *a* menor de edad. **~ way** *adv* en curso; (*on the way*) en marcha

under... *pref* sub...

undercarriage /'ʌndəkærɪdʒ/ *n* (*aviat*) tren *m* de aterrizaje

underclothes /'ʌndəkləʊðz/ *npl* ropa *f* interior

undercoat /'ʌndəkəʊt/ *n* (*of paint*) primera mano *f*

undercover /ʌndə'kʌvə(r)/ *a* secreto

undercurrent /'ʌndəkʌrənt/ *n* corriente *f* submarina; (*fig*) tendencia *f* oculta

undercut /'ʌndəkʌt/ *vt* (*pt* **undercut**) (*com*) vender más barato que

underdeveloped /ʌndədɪ'veləpt/ *a* subdesarrollado

underdog /'ʌndədɒg/ *n* perdedor *m*. **the ~s** *npl* los de abajo

underdone /ʌndə'dʌn/ *a* (*meat*) poco hecho

underestimate /ʌndər'estɪmeɪt/ *vt* subestimar

underfed /ʌndə'fed/ *a* desnutrido

underfoot /ʌndə'fʊt/ *adv* bajo los pies

undergo /'ʌndəgəʊ/ *vt* (*pt* **-went**, *pp* **-gone**) sufrir

undergraduate /ʌndə'grædjʊət/ *n* estudiante *m* & *f* universitario (no licenciado)

underground /ʌndə'graʊnd/ *adv* bajo tierra; (*in secret*) clandestinamente. /'ʌndəgraʊnd/ *a* subterráneo; (*secret*) clandestino. ● *n* metro *m*

undergrowth /'ʌndəgrəʊθ/ *n* maleza *f*

underhand /'ʌndəhænd/ *a* (*secret*) clandestino; (*deceptive*) fraudulento

underlie /ʌndə'laɪ/ *vt* (*pt* **-lay**, *pp* **-lain**, *pres p* **-lying**) estar debajo de; (*fig*) estar a la base de

underline /ʌndə'laɪn/ *vt* subrayar

underling /'ʌndəlɪŋ/ *n* subalterno *m*

underlying /ʌndə'laɪŋ/ *a* fundamental

undermine /ʌndə'maɪn/ *vt* socavar

underneath /ʌndə'niːθ/ *prep* debajo de. ● *adv* por debajo

underpaid /ʌndə'peɪd/ *a* mal pagado

underpants /'ʌndəpænts/ *npl* calzoncillos *mpl*

underpass /'ʌndəpaːs/ *n* paso *m* subterráneo

underprivileged /ʌndə'prɪvɪlɪdʒd/ *a* desvalido

underrate /ʌndə'reɪt/ *vt* subestimar

undersell /ʌndə'sel/ *vt* (*pt* **-sold**) vender más barato que

undersigned /'ʌndəsaɪnd/ *a* abajo firmante

undersized /ʌndə'saɪzd/ *a* pequeño

understand /ʌndə'stænd/ *vt/i* (*pt* **-stood**) entender, comprender. **~able** *a* comprensible. **~ing** /ʌndə'stændɪŋ/ *a* comprensivo. ● *n* comprensión *f*; (*agreement*) acuerdo *m*

understatement /ʌndə'steɪtmənt/ *n* subestimación *f*

understudy /'ʌndəstʌdɪ/ *n* sobresaliente *m* & *f* (en el teatro)

undertake /ʌndə'teɪk/ *vt* (*pt* **-took**, *pp* **-taken**) emprender; (*assume responsibility*) encargarse de

undertaker /'ʌndəteɪkə(r)/ *n* empresario *m* de pompas fúnebres

undertaking /ʌndə'teɪkɪŋ/ *n* empresa *f*; (*promise*) promesa *f*

undertone /'ʌndətəʊn/ *n*. **in an ~** en voz baja

undertow /'ʌndətəʊ/ *n* resaca *f*

undervalue /ʌndə'vælju:/ *vt* subvalorar

underwater /ʌndə'wɔːtə(r)/ *a* submarino. ● *adv* bajo el agua

underwear /'ʌndəweə(r)/ *n* ropa *f* interior

underweight /'ʌndəweɪt/ *a* de peso insuficiente. **be ~** estar flaco

underwent /ʌndə'went/ *see* **undergo**

underworld /'ʌndəwɜːld/ n (criminals) hampa f

underwrite /ʌndə'raɪt/ vt (pt -wrote, pp -written) (com) asegurar. ~r /-ə(r)/ n asegurador m

undeserved /ʌndɪ'zɜːvd/ a inmerecido

undesirable /ʌndɪ'zaɪərəbl/ a indeseable

undeveloped /ʌndɪ'veləpt/ a sin desarrollar

undies /'ʌndɪz/ npl (fam) ropa f interior

undignified /ʌn'dɪgnɪfaɪd/ a indecoroso

undisputed /ʌndɪs'pjuːtɪd/ a incontestable

undistinguished /ʌndɪs'tɪŋgwɪʃt/ a mediocre

undo /ʌn'duː/ vt (pt -did, pp -done) deshacer; (ruin) arruinar; reparar (wrong). **leave ~ne** dejar sin hacer

undoubted /ʌn'daʊtɪd/ a indudable. **~ly** adv indudablemente

undress /ʌn'dres/ vt desnudar. ● vi desnudarse

undue /ʌn'djuː/ a excesivo

undulate /'ʌndjʊleɪt/ vi ondular. ~ion /-'leɪʃn/ n ondulación f

unduly /ʌn'djuːlɪ/ adv excesivamente

undying /ʌn'daɪɪŋ/ a eterno

unearth /ʌn'ɜːθ/ vt desenterrar

unearthly /ʌn'ɜːθlɪ/ a sobrenatural; (impossible, fam) absurdo. **~ hour** n hora intempestiva

uneas|ily /ʌn'iːzɪlɪ/ adv inquietamente. **~y** /ʌn'iːzɪ/ a incómodo; (worrying) inquieto

uneconomic /ʌniːkə'nɒmɪk/ a poco rentable

uneducated /ʌn'edjʊkeɪtɪd/ a inculto

unemploy|ed /ʌnɪm'plɔɪd/ a parado, desempleado; (not in use) inutilizado. **~ment** n paro m, desempleo m

unending /ʌn'endɪŋ/ a interminable, sin fin

unequal /ʌn'iːkwəl/ a desigual

unequivocal /ʌnɪ'kwɪvəkl/ a inequívoco

unerring /ʌn'ɜːrɪŋ/ a infalible

unethical /ʌn'eθɪkl/ a sin ética, inmoral

uneven /ʌn'iːvn/ a desigual

unexceptional /ʌnɪk'sepʃənl/ a corriente

unexpected /ʌnɪk'spektɪd/ a inesperado

unfailing /ʌn'feɪlɪŋ/ a inagotable; (constant) constante; (loyal) leal

unfair /ʌn'feə(r)/ a injusto. **~ly** adv injustamente. **~ness** n injusticia f

unfaithful /ʌn'feɪθfl/ a infiel. **~ness** n infidelidad f

unfamiliar /ʌnfə'mɪlɪə(r)/ a desconocido. **be ~ with** desconocer

unfasten /ʌn'fɑːsn/ vt desabrochar (clothes); (untie) desatar

unfavourable /ʌn'feɪvərəbl/ a desfavorable

unfeeling /ʌn'fiːlɪŋ/ a insensible

unfit /ʌn'fɪt/ a inadecuado, no apto; (unwell) en mal estado físico; (incapable) incapaz

unflinching /ʌn'flɪntʃɪŋ/ a resuelto

unfold /ʌn'fəʊld/ vt desdoblar; (fig) revelar. ● vi (view etc) extenderse

unforeseen /ʌnfɔː'siːn/ a imprevisto

unforgettable /ʌnfə'getəbl/ a inolvidable

unforgivable /ʌnfə'gɪvəbl/ a imperdonable

unfortunate /ʌn'fɔːtʃənət/ a desgraciado; (regrettable) lamentable. **~ly** adv desgraciadamente

unfounded /ʌn'faʊndɪd/ a infundado

unfriendly /ʌn'frendlɪ/ a poco amistoso, frío

unfurl /ʌn'fɜːl/ vt desplegar

ungainly /ʌn'geɪnlɪ/ a desgarbado

ungodly /ʌn'gɒdlɪ/ a impío. **~ hour** n (fam) hora f intempestiva

ungrateful /ʌn'greɪtfl/ a desagradecido

unguarded /ʌn'gɑːdɪd/ a indefenso; (incautious) imprudente, incauto

unhapp|ily /ʌn'hæpɪlɪ/ adv infelizmente; (unfortunately) desgraciadamente. **~iness** n tristeza f. **~y** /ʌn'hæpɪ/ a (-ier, -iest) infeliz, triste; (unsuitable) inoportuno. **~y with** insatisfecho de (plans etc)

unharmed /ʌn'hɑːmd/ a ileso, sano y salvo

unhealthy /ʌn'helθɪ/ a (-ier, -iest) enfermizo; (insanitary) malsano

unhinge /ʌn'hɪndʒ/ vt desquiciar

unholy /ʌn'həʊlɪ/ a (-ier, -iest) impío; (terrible, fam) terrible

unhook /ʌn'hʊk/ vt desenganchar

unhoped /ʌn'həʊpt/ a. **~ for** inesperado

unhurt /ʌn'hɜːt/ a ileso

unicorn /'juːnɪkɔːn/ n unicornio m

unification /ju:nɪfɪ'keɪʃn/ n unificación f

uniform /'ju:nɪfɔ:m/ a & n uniforme (m). ~ity /-'fɔ:mətɪ/ n uniformidad f. ~ly adv uniformemente

unify /'ju:nɪfaɪ/ vt unificar

unilateral /ju:nɪ'lætərəl/ a unilateral

unimaginable /ʌnɪ'mædʒɪnəbl/ a inconcebible

unimpeachable /ʌnɪm'pi:tʃəbl/ a irreprensible

unimportant /ʌnɪm'pɔ:tnt/ a insignificante

uninhabited /ʌnɪn'hæbɪtɪd/ a inhabitado; (abandoned) despoblado

unintentional /ʌnɪn'tenʃənl/ a involuntario

union /'ju:njən/ n unión f; (trade union) sindicato m. ~ist n sindicalista m & f. U~ Jack n bandera f del Reino Unido

unique /ju:'ni:k/ a único. ~ly adv extraordinariamente

unisex /'ju:nɪseks/ a unisex(o)

unison /'ju:nɪsn/ n. in ~ al unísono

unit /'ju:nɪt/ n unidad f; (of furniture etc) elemento m

unite /ju:'naɪt/ vt unir. • vi unirse. U~d Kingdom (UK) n Reino m Unido. U~d Nations (UN) n Organización f de las Naciones Unidas (ONU). U~d States (of America) (USA) n Estados mpl Unidos (de América) (EE.UU.)

unity /'ju:nɪtɪ/ n unidad f; (fig) acuerdo m

univers|al /ju:nɪ'vɜ:sl/ a universal. ~e /'ju:nɪvɜ:s/ n universo m

university /ju:nɪ'vɜ:sətɪ/ n universidad f. • a universitario

unjust /ʌn'dʒʌst/ a injusto

unkempt /ʌn'kempt/ a desaseado

unkind /ʌn'kaɪnd/ a poco amable; (cruel) cruel. ~ly adv poco amablemente. ~ness n falta f de amabilidad; (cruelty) crueldad f

unknown /ʌn'nəʊn/ a desconocido

unlawful /ʌn'lɔ:fl/ a ilegal

unleash /ʌn'li:ʃ/ vt soltar; (fig) desencadenar

unless /ʌn'les, ən'les/ conj a menos que, a no ser que

unlike /ʌn'laɪk/ a diferente; (not typical) impropio de. • prep a diferencia de. ~lihood n improbabilidad f. ~ly /ʌn'laɪklɪ/ a improbable

unlimited /ʌn'lɪmɪtɪd/ a ilimitado

unload /ʌn'ləʊd/ vt descargar

unlock /ʌn'lɒk/ vt abrir (con llave)

unluck|ily /ʌn'lʌkɪlɪ/ adv desgraciadamente. ~y /ʌn'lʌkɪ/ a (-ier, -iest) desgraciado; (number) de mala suerte

unmanly /ʌn'mænlɪ/ a poco viril

unmanned /ʌn'mænd/ a no tripulado

unmarried /ʌn'mærɪd/ a soltero. ~ mother n madre f soltera

unmask /ʌn'mɑ:sk/ vt desenmascarar. • vi quitarse la máscara

unmentionable /ʌn'menʃənəbl/ a a que no se debe aludir

unmistakabl|e /ʌnmɪ'steɪkəbl/ a inconfundible. ~y adv claramente

unmitigated /ʌn'mɪtɪgeɪtɪd/ a (absolute) absoluto

unmoved /ʌn'mu:vd/ a (fig) indiferente (by a), insensible (by a)

unnatural /ʌn'nætʃərəl/ a no natural; (not normal) anormal

unnecessar|ily /ʌn'nesəsərɪlɪ/ adv innecesariamente. ~y /ʌn'nesəsərɪ/ a innecesario

unnerve /ʌn'nɜ:v/ vt desconcertar

unnoticed /ʌn'nəʊtɪst/ a inadvertido

unobtainable /ʌnəb'teɪnəbl/ a inasequible; (fig) inalcanzable

unobtrusive /ʌnəb'tru:sɪv/ a discreto

unofficial /ʌnə'fɪʃl/ a no oficial. ~ly adv extraoficialmente

unpack /ʌn'pæk/ vt desempaquetar (parcel); deshacer (suitcase). • vi deshacer la maleta

unpalatable /ʌn'pælətəbl/ a desagradable

unparalleled /ʌn'pærəleld/ a sin par

unpick /ʌn'pɪk/ vt descoser

unpleasant /ʌn'pleznt/ a desagradable. ~ness n lo desagradable

unplug /ʌn'plʌg/ vt (elec) desenchufar

unpopular /ʌn'pɒpjʊlə(r)/ a impopular

unprecedented /ʌn'presɪdentɪd/ a sin precedente

unpredictable /ʌnprɪ'dɪktəbl/ a imprevisible

unpremeditated /ʌnprɪ'medɪteɪtɪd/ a impremeditado

unprepared /ʌnprɪ'peəd/ a no preparado; (unready) desprevenido

unprepossessing /ʌnpri:pə'zesɪŋ/ a poco atractivo

unpretentious /ʌnprɪ'tenʃəs/ a sin pretensiones, modesto

unprincipled /ʌnˈprɪnsɪpld/ *a* sin principios

unprofessional /ʌnprəˈfeʃənəl/ *a* contrario a la ética profesional

unpublished /ʌnˈpʌblɪʃt/ *a* inédito

unqualified /ʌnˈkwɒlɪfaɪd/ *a* sin título; ⟨*fig*⟩ absoluto

unquestionabl|e /ʌnˈkwestʃənəbl/ *a* indiscutible. **~y** *adv* indiscutiblemente

unquote /ʌnˈkwəʊt/ *vi* cerrar comillas

unravel /ʌnˈrævl/ *vt* (*pt* **unravelled**) desenredar; deshacer ⟨*knitting etc*⟩. ● *vi* desenredarse

unreal /ʌnˈrɪəl/ *a* irreal. **~istic** *a* poco realista

unreasonable /ʌnˈriːzənəbl/ *a* irrazonable

unrecognizable /ʌnrekəgˈnaɪzəbl/ *a* irreconocible

unrelated /ʌnrɪˈleɪtɪd/ *a* ⟨*facts*⟩ inconexo, sin relación; ⟨*people*⟩ no emparentado

unreliable /ʌnrɪˈlaɪəbl/ *a* ⟨*person*⟩ poco formal; ⟨*machine*⟩ poco fiable

unrelieved /ʌnrɪˈliːvd/ *a* no aliviado

unremitting /ʌnrɪˈmɪtɪŋ/ *a* incesante

unrepentant /ʌnrɪˈpentənt/ *a* impenitente

unrequited /ʌnrɪˈkwaɪtɪd/ *a* no correspondido

unreservedly /ʌnrɪˈzɜːvɪdlɪ/ *adv* sin reserva

unrest /ʌnˈrest/ *n* inquietud *f*; ⟨*pol*⟩ agitación *f*

unrivalled /ʌnˈraɪvld/ *a* sin par

unroll /ʌnˈrəʊl/ *vt* desenrollar. ● *vi* desenrollarse

unruffled /ʌnˈrʌfld/ ⟨*person*⟩ imperturbable

unruly /ʌnˈruːlɪ/ *a* indisciplinado

unsafe /ʌnˈseɪf/ *a* peligroso; ⟨*person*⟩ en peligro

unsaid /ʌnˈsed/ *a* sin decir

unsatisfactory /ʌnsætɪsˈfæktərɪ/ *a* insatisfactorio

unsavoury /ʌnˈseɪvərɪ/ *a* desagradable

unscathed /ʌnˈskeɪðd/ *a* ileso

unscramble /ʌnˈskræmbl/ *vt* descifrar

unscrew /ʌnˈskruː/ *vt* destornillar

unscrupulous /ʌnˈskruːpjʊləs/ *a* sin escrúpulos

unseat /ʌnˈsiːt/ *vt* ⟨*pol*⟩ quitar el escaño a

unseemly /ʌnˈsiːmlɪ/ *a* indecoroso

unseen /ʌnˈsiːn/ *a* inadvertido. ● *n* ⟨*translation*⟩ traducción *f* a primera vista

unselfish /ʌnˈselfɪʃ/ *a* desinteresado

unsettle /ʌnˈsetl/ *vt* perturbar. **~d** *a* perturbado; ⟨*weather*⟩ variable; ⟨*bill*⟩ por pagar

unshakeable /ʌnˈʃeɪkəbl/ *a* firme

unshaven /ʌnˈʃeɪvn/ *a* sin afeitar

unsightly /ʌnˈsaɪtlɪ/ *a* feo

unskilled /ʌnˈskɪld/ *a* inexperto. **~ worker** *n* obrero *m* no cualificado

unsociable /ʌnˈsəʊʃəbl/ *a* insociable

unsolicited /ʌnsəˈlɪsɪtɪd/ *a* no solicitado

unsophisticated /ʌnsəˈfɪstɪkeɪtɪd/ *a* sencillo

unsound /ʌnˈsaʊnd/ *a* defectuoso, erróneo. **of ~ mind** demente

unsparing /ʌnˈspeərɪŋ/ *a* pródigo; ⟨*cruel*⟩ cruel

unspeakable /ʌnˈspiːkəbl/ *a* indecible

unspecified /ʌnˈspesɪfaɪd/ *a* no especificado

unstable /ʌnˈsteɪbl/ *a* inestable

unsteady /ʌnˈstedɪ/ *a* inestable; ⟨*hand*⟩ poco firme; ⟨*step*⟩ inseguro

unstinted /ʌnˈstɪntɪd/ *a* abundante

unstuck /ʌnˈstʌk/ *a* suelto. **come ~** despegarse; ⟨*fail, fam*⟩ fracasar

unstudied /ʌnˈstʌdɪd/ *a* natural

unsuccessful /ʌnsəkˈsesfʊl/ *a* fracasado. **be ~** no tener éxito, fracasar

unsuitable /ʌnˈsuːtəbl/ *a* inadecuado; (*inconvenient*) inconveniente

unsure /ʌnˈʃʊə(r)/ *a* inseguro

unsuspecting /ʌnsəˈspektɪŋ/ *a* confiado

unthinkable /ʌnˈθɪŋkəbl/ *a* inconcebible

untid|ily /ʌnˈtaɪdɪlɪ/ *adv* desordenadamente. **~iness** *n* desorden *m*. **~y** /ʌnˈtaɪdɪ/ *a* (**-ier, -iest**) desordenado; ⟨*person*⟩ desaseado

untie /ʌnˈtaɪ/ *vt* desatar

until /ənˈtɪl, ʌnˈtɪl/ *prep* hasta. ● *conj* hasta que

untimely /ʌnˈtaɪmlɪ/ *a* inoportuno; (*premature*) prematuro

untiring /ʌnˈtaɪərɪŋ/ *a* incansable

untold /ʌnˈtəʊld/ *a* incalculable

untoward /ʌntəˈwɔːd/ *a* (*inconvenient*) inconveniente

untried /ʌnˈtraɪd/ *a* no probado

untrue /ʌnˈtruː/ *a* falso

unused /ʌnˈjuːzd/ *a* nuevo. /ʌnˈjuːst/ *a*. **~ to** no acostumbrado a

unusual /ʌnˈjuːʒʊəl/ *a* insólito; *(exceptional)* excepcional. **~ly** *adv* excepcionalmente

unutterable /ʌnˈʌtərəbl/ *a* indecible

unveil /ʌnˈveɪl/ *vt* descubrir; *(disclose)* revelar

unwanted /ʌnˈwɒntɪd/ *a* superfluo; *‹child›* no deseado

unwarranted /ʌnˈwɒrəntɪd/ *a* injustificado

unwelcome /ʌnˈwelkəm/ *a* desagradable; *‹guest›* inoportuno

unwell /ʌnˈwel/ *a* indispuesto

unwieldy /ʌnˈwiːldɪ/ *a* difícil de manejar

unwilling /ʌnˈwɪlɪŋ/ *a* no dispuesto. **be ~** no querer. **~ly** *adv* de mala gana

unwind /ʌnˈwaɪnd/ *vt* (*pt* **unwound**) desenvolver. ● *vi* desenvolverse; *(relax, fam)* relajarse

unwise /ʌnˈwaɪz/ *a* imprudente

unwitting /ʌnˈwɪtɪŋ/ *a* inconsciente; *(involuntary)* involuntario. **~ly** *adv* involuntariamente

unworthy /ʌnˈwɜːðɪ/ *a* indigno

unwrap /ʌnˈræp/ *vt* (*pt* **unwrapped**) desenvolver, deshacer

unwritten /ʌnˈrɪtn/ *a* no escrito; *‹agreement›* tácito

up /ʌp/ *adv* arriba; *(upwards)* hacia arriba; *(higher)* más arriba; *(out of bed)* levantado; *(finished)* terminado. **~ here** aquí arriba. **~ in** *(fam)* versado en, fuerte en. **~ there** allí arriba. **~ to** hasta. **be one ~ on** llevar la ventaja a. **be ~ against** enfrentarse con. **be ~ to** tramar *‹plot›*; *(one's turn)* tocar a; a la altura de *‹task›*; *(reach)* llegar a. **come ~** subir. **feel ~ to it** sentirse capaz. **go ~** subir. **it's ~ to you** depende de tí. **what is ~?** ¿qué pasa? ● *prep* arriba; *(on top of)* en lo alto de. ● *vt* (*pt* **upped**) aumentar. ● *n.* **~s and downs** *npl* altibajos *mpl*

upbraid /ʌpˈbreɪd/ *vt* reprender

upbringing /ˈʌpbrɪŋɪŋ/ *n* educación *f*

update /ʌpˈdeɪt/ *vt* poner al día

upgrade /ʌpˈɡreɪd/ *vt* ascender *‹person›*; mejorar *‹equipment›*

upheaval /ʌpˈhiːvl/ *n* trastorno *m*

uphill /ˈʌphɪl/ *a* ascendente; *(fig)* arduo. ● *adv* /ʌpˈhɪl/ cuesta arriba. **go ~** subir

uphold /ʌpˈhəʊld/ *vt* (*pt* **upheld**) sostener

upholster /ʌpˈhəʊlstə(r)/ *vt* tapizar. **~er** /-rə(r)/ *n* tapicero *m.* **~y** *n* tapicería *f*

upkeep /ˈʌpkiːp/ *n* mantenimiento *m*

up-market /ʌpˈmɑːkɪt/ *a* superior

upon /əˈpɒn/ *prep* en; *(on top of)* encima de. **once ~ a time** érase una vez

upper /ˈʌpə(r)/ *a* superior. **~ class** *n* clases *fpl* altas. **~ hand** *n* dominio *m*, ventaja *f.* **~most** *a* (el) más alto. ● *n (of shoe)* pala *f*

uppish /ˈʌpɪʃ/ *a* engreído

upright /ˈʌpraɪt/ *a* derecho; *‹piano›* vertical. ● *n* montante *m*

uprising /ˈʌpraɪzɪŋ/ *n* sublevación *f*

uproar /ˈʌprɔː(r)/ *n* tumulto *m.* **~ious** /-ˈrɔːrɪəs/ *a* tumultuoso

uproot /ʌpˈruːt/ *vt* desarraigar

upset /ʌpˈset/ *vt* (*pt* **upset**, *presp* **upsetting**) trastornar; desbaratar *‹plan etc›*; *(distress)* alterar. /ˈʌpset/ *n* trastorno *m*

upshot /ˈʌpʃɒt/ *n* resultado *m*

upside-down /ʌpsaɪdˈdaʊn/ *adv* al revés; *(in disorder)* patas arriba. **turn ~** volver

upstairs /ʌpˈsteəz/ *adv* arriba. /ˈʌpsteəz/ *a* de arriba

upstart /ˈʌpstɑːt/ *n* arribista *m & f*

upstream /ˈʌpstriːm/ *adv* río arriba; *(against the current)* contra la corriente

upsurge /ˈʌpsɜːdʒ/ *n* aumento *m*; *(of anger etc)* arrebato *m*

uptake /ˈʌpteɪk/ *n.* **quick on the ~** muy listo

uptight /ˈʌptaɪt/ *a (fam)* nervioso

up-to-date /ʌptəˈdeɪt/ *a* al día; *‹news›* de última hora; *(modern)* moderno

upturn /ˈʌptɜːn/ *n* aumento *m*; *(improvement)* mejora *f*

upward /ˈʌpwəd/ *a* ascendente. ● *adv* hacia arriba. **~s** *adv* hacia arriba

uranium /jʊˈreɪnɪəm/ *n* uranio *m*

urban /ˈɜːbən/ *a* urbano

urbane /ɜːˈbeɪn/ *a* cortés

urbanize /ˈɜːbənaɪz/ *vt* urbanizar

urchin /ˈɜːtʃɪn/ *n* pilluelo *m*

urge /ɜːdʒ/ *vt* incitar, animar. ● *n* impulso *m.* **~ on** animar

urgen|cy /ˈɜːdʒənsɪ/ *n* urgencia *f.* **~t** /ˈɜːdʒənt/ *a* urgente. **~tly** *adv* urgentemente

urin|ate /ˈjʊərɪneɪt/ *vi* orinar. **~e** /ˈjʊərɪn/ *n* orina *f*

urn /ɜːn/ n urna f

Uruguay /jʊərəgwaɪ/ n el Uruguay m. **~an** a & n uruguayo (m)

us /ʌs, əs/ pron nos; (after prep) nosotros, nosotras

US(A) /juːes'eɪ/ abbr (United States (of America)) EE.UU., Estados mpl Unidos

usage /'juːzɪdʒ/ n uso m

use /juːz/ vt emplear. /juːs/ n uso m, empleo m. **be of ~** servir. **it is no ~** es inútil, no sirve para nada. **make ~ of** servirse de. **~ up** agotar, consumir. **~d** /juːzd/ a ⟨clothes⟩ gastado. /juːst/ pt. **he ~d to say** decía, solía decir. ● a. **~d to** acostumbrado a. **~ful** /'juːsfl/ a útil. **~fully** adv útilmente. **~less** a inútil; ⟨person⟩ incompetente. **~r** /-zə(r)/ n usuario m

usher /'ʌʃə(r)/ n ujier m; (in theatre etc) acomodador m. ● vt. **~ in** hacer entrar. **~ette** n acomodadora f

USSR abbr (history) (Union of Soviet Socialist Republics) URSS

usual /'juːʒʊəl/ a usual, corriente; (habitual) acostumbrado, habitual. **as ~** como de costumbre, como siempre. **~ly** adv normalmente. **he ~ly wakes up early** suele despertarse temprano

usurer /'juːʒərə(r)/ n usurero m

usurp /jʊ'zɜːp/ vt usurpar. **~er** /-ə(r)/ n usurpador m

usury /'juːʒərɪ/ n usura f

utensil /juː'tensl/ n utensilio m

uterus /'juːtərəs/ n útero m

utilitarian /juːtɪlɪ'teərɪən/ a utilitario

utility /juː'tɪlətɪ/ n utilidad f. **public ~** n servicio m público. ● a utilitario

utilize /'juːtɪlaɪz/ vt utilizar

utmost /'ʌtməʊst/ a extremo. ● n. **one's ~** todo lo posible

utter[1] /'ʌtə(r)/ a completo

utter[2] /'ʌtə(r)/ vt (speak) pronunciar; dar ⟨sigh⟩; emitir ⟨sound⟩. **~ance** n expresión f

utterly /'ʌtəlɪ/ adv totalmente

U-turn /'juːtɜːn/ n vuelta f

V

vacan|cy /'veɪkənsɪ/ n (job) vacante f; (room) habitación f libre. **~t** a libre; (empty) vacío; ⟨look⟩ vago

vacate /və'keɪt/ vt dejar

vacation /və'keɪʃn/ n (Amer) vacaciones fpl

vaccin|ate /'væksɪneɪt/ vt vacunar. **~ation** /-'neɪʃn/ n vacunación f. **~e** /'væksiːn/ n vacuna f

vacuum /'vækjʊəm/ n (pl **-cuums** or **-cua**) vacío m. **~ cleaner** n aspiradora f. **~ flask** n termo m

vagabond /'vægəbɒnd/ n vagabundo m

vagary /'veɪgərɪ/ n capricho m

vagina /və'dʒaɪnə/ n vagina f

vagrant /'veɪgrənt/ n vagabundo m

vague /veɪg/ a (-er, -est) vago; ⟨outline⟩ indistinto. **be ~ about** no precisar. **~ly** adv vagamente

vain /veɪn/ a (-er, -est) vanidoso; (useless) vano, inútil. **in ~** en vano. **~ly** adv vanamente

valance /'væləns/ n cenefa f

vale /veɪl/ n valle m

valentine /'væləntaɪn/ n (card) tarjeta f del día de San Valentín

valet /'vælɪt, 'væleɪ/ n ayuda m de cámara

valiant /'vælɪənt/ a valeroso

valid /'vælɪd/ a válido; ⟨ticket⟩ valedero. **~ate** vt dar validez a; (confirm) convalidar. **~ity** /-'ɪdətɪ/ n validez f

valley /'vælɪ/ n (pl **-eys**) valle m

valour /'vælə(r)/ n valor m

valuable /'væljʊəbl/ a valioso. **~s** npl objetos mpl de valor

valuation /vælju'eɪʃn/ n valoración f

value /'væljuː/ n valor m; (usefulness) utilidad f. **face ~** n valor m nominal; (fig) significado m literal. ● vt valorar; (cherish) apreciar. **~ added tax (VAT)** n impuesto m sobre el valor añadido (IVA). **~d** a (appreciated) apreciado, estimado. **~r** /-ə(r)/ n tasador m

valve /vælv/ n válvula f

vampire /'væmpaɪə(r)/ n vampiro m

van /væn/ n furgoneta f; (rail) furgón m

vandal /'vændl/ n vándalo m. **~ism** /-əlɪzəm/ n vandalismo m. **~ize** vt destruir

vane /veɪn/ n (weathercock) veleta f; (naut, aviat) paleta f

vanguard /'vængɑːd/ n vanguardia f

vanilla /və'nɪlə/ n vainilla f

vanish /'vænɪʃ/ vi desaparecer

vanity /'vænɪtɪ/ n vanidad f. **~ case** n neceser m

vantage /'vɑːntɪdʒ/ n ventaja f. ~ **point** n posición f ventajosa

vapour /'veɪpə(r)/ n vapor m

variable /'veərɪəbl/ a variable

varian|ce /'veərɪəns/ n. **at** ~ce en desacuerdo. ~t /'veərɪənt/ a diferente. • n variante m

variation /veərɪ'eɪʃn/ n variación f

varicoloured /'veərɪkʌləd/ a multicolor

varied /'veərɪd/ a variado

varicose /'værɪkəʊs/ a varicoso. ~ **veins** npl varices fpl

variety /və'raɪətɪ/ n variedad f. ~ **show** n espectáculo m de variedades

various /'veərɪəs/ a diverso. ~ly adv diversamente

varnish /'vɑːnɪʃ/ n barniz m; (for nails) esmalte m. • vt barnizar

vary /'veərɪ/ vt/i variar. ~ing a diverso

vase /vɑːz, Amer veɪs/ n jarrón m

vasectomy /və'sektəmɪ/ n vasectomía f

vast /vɑːst/ a vasto, enorme. ~ly adv enormemente. ~ness n inmensidad f

vat /væt/ n tina f

VAT /viːeɪ'tiː/ abbr (value added tax) IVA m, impuesto m sobre el valor añadido

vault /vɔːlt/ n (roof) bóveda f; (in bank) cámara f acorazada; (tomb) cripta f; (cellar) sótano m; (jump) salto m. • vt/i saltar

vaunt /vɔːnt/ vt jactarse de

veal /viːl/ n ternera f

veer /vɪə(r)/ vi cambiar de dirección; (naut) virar

vegetable /'vedʒɪtəbl/ a vegetal. • n legumbre m; (greens) verduras fpl

vegetarian /vedʒɪ'teərɪən/ a & n vegetariano (m)

vegetate /'vedʒɪteɪt/ vi vegetar

vegetation /vedʒɪ'teɪʃn/ n vegetación f

vehemen|ce /'viːəməns/ n vehemencia f. ~t /'viːəmənt/ a vehemente. ~tly adv con vehemencia

vehicle /'viːɪkl/ n vehículo m

veil /veɪl/ n velo m. **take the** ~ hacerse monja. • vt velar

vein /veɪn/ n vena f; (mood) humor m. ~ed a veteado

velocity /vɪ'lɒsɪtɪ/ n velocidad f

velvet /'velvɪt/ n terciopelo m. ~y a aterciopelado

venal /'viːnl/ a venal. ~ity /-'nælətɪ/ n venalidad f

vendetta /ven'detə/ n enemistad f prolongada

vending-machine /'vendɪŋ məʃiːn/ n distribuidor m automático

vendor /'vendə(r)/ n vendedor m

veneer /və'nɪə(r)/ n chapa f; (fig) barniz m, apariencia f

venerable /'venərəbl/ a venerable

venereal /və'nɪərɪəl/ a venéreo

Venetian /və'niːʃn/ a & n veneciano (m). **v~ blind** n persiana f veneciana

vengeance /'vendʒəns/ n venganza f. **with a** ~ (fig) con creces

venison /'venɪzn/ n carne f de venado

venom /'venəm/ n veneno m. ~ous a venenoso

vent /vent/ n abertura f; (for air) respiradero m. **give** ~ **to** dar salida a. • vt hacer un agujero en; (fig) desahogar

ventilat|e /'ventɪleɪt/ vt ventilar. ~ion /-'leɪʃn/ n ventilación f. ~or /-ə(r)/ n ventilador m

ventriloquist /ven'trɪləkwɪst/ n ventrílocuo m

venture /'ventʃə(r)/ n empresa f (arriesgada). **at a** ~ a la ventura. • vt arriesgar. • vi atreverse

venue /'venjuː/ n lugar m (de reunión)

veranda /və'rændə/ n terraza f

verb /vɜːb/ n verbo m

verbal /'vɜːbl/ a verbal. ~ly adv verbalmente

verbatim /vɜː'beɪtɪm/ adv palabra por palabra, al pie de la letra

verbose /vɜː'bəʊs/ a prolijo

verdant /'vɜːdənt/ a verde

verdict /'vɜːdɪkt/ n veredicto m; (opinion) opinión f

verge /vɜːdʒ/ n borde m. • vt. ~ **on** acercarse a

verger /'vɜːdʒə(r)/ n sacristán m

verif|ication /verɪfɪ'keɪʃn/ n verificación f. ~y /'verɪfaɪ/ vt verificar

veritable /'verɪtəbl/ a verdadero

vermicelli /vɜːmɪ'tʃelɪ/ n fideos mpl

vermin /'vɜːmɪn/ n sabandijas fpl

vermouth /'vɜːməθ/ n vermut m

vernacular /və'nækjʊlə(r)/ n lengua f; (regional) dialecto m

versatil|e /'vɜːsətaɪl/ a versátil. ~ity /-'tɪlətɪ/ n versatilidad f

verse /vɜːs/ n estrofa f; (poetry) poesías fpl; (of Bible) versículo m

versed /vɜːst/ a. ~ **in** versado en

version /'vɜːʃn/ n versión f

versus /'vɜːsəs/ prep contra

vertebra /'vɜːtɪbrə/ n (pl **-brae** /-briː/) vértebra f

vertical /'vɜːtɪkl/ a & n vertical (f). ~**ly** adv verticalmente

vertigo /'vɜːtɪgəʊ/ n vértigo m

verve /vɜːv/ n entusiasmo m, vigor m

very /'verɪ/ adv muy. ~ **much** muchísimo. ~ **well** muy bien. **the** ~ **first** el primero de todos. ● a mismo. **the** ~ **thing** exactamente lo que hace falta

vespers /'vespəz/ npl vísperas fpl

vessel /'vesl/ n (receptacle) recipiente m; (ship) buque m; (anat) vaso m

vest /vest/ n camiseta f; (Amer) chaleco m. ● vt conferir. ~**ed interest** n interés m personal; (jurid) derecho m adquirido

vestige /'vestɪdʒ/ n vestigio m

vestment /'vestmənt/ n vestidura f

vestry /'vestrɪ/ n sacristía f

vet /vet/ n (fam) veterinario m. ● vt (pt **vetted**) examinar

veteran /'vetərən/ n veterano m

veterinary /'vetərɪnərɪ/ a veterinario. ~ **surgeon** n veterinario m

veto /'viːtəʊ/ n (pl **-oes**) veto m. ● vt poner el veto a

vex /veks/ vt fastidiar. ~**ation** /-'seɪʃn/ n fastidio m. ~**ed question** n cuestión f controvertida. ~**ing** a fastidioso

via /'vaɪə/ prep por, por vía de

viab|ility /vaɪə'bɪlətɪ/ n viabilidad f. ~**le** /'vaɪəbl/ a viable

viaduct /'vaɪədʌkt/ n viaducto m

vibrant /'vaɪbrənt/ a vibrante

vibrat|e /vaɪ'breɪt/ vt/i vibrar. ~**ion** /-ʃn/ n vibración f

vicar /'vɪkə(r)/ n párroco m. ~**age** /-rɪdʒ/ n casa f del párroco

vicarious /vɪ'keərɪəs/ a indirecto

vice¹ /vaɪs/ n vicio m

vice² /vaɪs/ n (tec) torno m de banco

vice... /'vaɪs/ pref vice...

vice versa /vaɪsɪ'vɜːsə/ adv viceversa

vicinity /vɪ'sɪnɪtɪ/ n vecindad f. **in the** ~ **of** cerca de

vicious /'vɪʃəs/ a (spiteful) malicioso; (violent) atroz. ~ **circle** n círculo m vicioso. ~**ly** adv cruelmente

vicissitudes /vɪ'sɪsɪtjuːdz/ npl vicisitudes fpl

victim /'vɪktɪm/ n víctima f. ~**ization** /-aɪ'zeɪʃn/ n persecución f. ~**ize** vt victimizar

victor /'vɪktə(r)/ n vencedor m

Victorian /vɪk'tɔːrɪən/ a victoriano

victor|ious /vɪk'tɔːrɪəs/ a victorioso. ~**y** /'vɪktərɪ/ n victoria f

video /'vɪdɪəʊ/ a video. ● n (fam) magnetoscopio m. ~ **recorder** n magnetoscopio m. ~**tape** n video-cassette f

vie /vaɪ/ vi (pres p **vying**) rivalizar

view /vjuː/ n vista f; (mental survey) visión f de conjunto; (opinion) opinión f. **in my** ~ a mi juicio. **in** ~ **of** en vista de. **on** ~ expuesto. **with a** ~ **to** con miras a. ● vt ver; (visit) visitar; (consider) considerar. ~**er** /-ə(r)/ n espectador m; (TV) televidente m & f. ~**finder** /'vjuːfaɪndə(r)/ n visor m. ~**point** /'vjuːpɔɪnt/ n punto m de vista

vigil /'vɪdʒɪl/ n vigilia f. ~**ance** n vigilancia f. ~**ant** a vigilante. **keep** ~ velar

vigo|rous /'vɪgərəs/ a vigoroso. ~**ur** /'vɪgə(r)/ n vigor m

vile /vaɪl/ a (base) vil; (bad) horrible; (weather, temper) de perros

vilif|ication /vɪlɪfɪ'keɪʃn/ n difamación f. ~**y** /'vɪlɪfaɪ/ vt difamar

village /'vɪlɪdʒ/ n aldea f. ~**r** /-ə(r)/ n aldeano m

villain /'vɪlən/ n malvado m; (in story etc) malo m. ~**ous** a infame. ~**y** n infamia f

vim /vɪm/ n (fam) energía f

vinaigrette /vɪnɪ'gret/ n. ~ **sauce** n vinagreta f

vindicat|e /'vɪndɪkeɪt/ vt vindicar. ~**ion** /-'keɪʃn/ n vindicación f

vindictive /vɪn'dɪktɪv/ a vengativo. ~**ness** n carácter m vengativo

vine /vaɪn/ n vid f

vinegar /'vɪnɪgə(r)/ n vinagre m. ~**y** a (person) avinagrado

vineyard /'vɪnjəd/ n viña f

vintage /'vɪntɪdʒ/ n (year) cosecha f. ● a (wine) añejo; (car) de época

vinyl /'vaɪnɪl/ n vinilo m

viola /vɪ'əʊlə/ n viola f

violat|e /'vaɪəleɪt/ vt violar. ~**ion** /-'leɪʃn/ n violación f

violen|ce /'vaɪələns/ n violencia f. ~**t** /'vaɪələnt/ a violento. ~**tly** adv violentamente

violet /'vaɪələt/ a & n violeta (f)

violin /'vaɪəlɪn/ n violín m. ~**ist** n violinista m & f

VIP /viːaɪˈpiː/ abbr (very important person) personaje m

viper /ˈvaɪpə(r)/ n víbora f

virgin /ˈvɜːdʒɪn/ a & n virgen (f). ~al a virginal. ~ity /vəˈdʒɪnəti/ n virginidad f

Virgo /ˈvɜːgəʊ/ n (astr) Virgo f

viril|e /ˈvɪraɪl/ a viril. ~ity /-ˈrɪləti/ n virilidad f

virtual /ˈvɜːtʃʊəl/ a verdadero. a ~ failure prácticamente un fracaso. ~ly adv prácticamente

virtue /ˈvɜːtʃuː/ n virtud f. by ~ of, in ~ of en virtud de

virtuoso /vɜːtjʊˈəʊzəʊ/ n (pl -si /-ziː/) virtuoso m

virtuous /ˈvɜːtʃʊəs/ a virtuoso

virulent /ˈvɪrʊlənt/ a virulento

virus /ˈvaɪərəs/ n (pl -uses) virus m

visa /ˈviːzə/ n visado m, visa f (LAm)

vis-a-vis /viːzɑːˈviː/ adv frente a frente. ● prep respecto a; (opposite) en frente de

viscount /ˈvaɪkaʊnt/ n vizconde m. ~ess n vizcondesa f

viscous /ˈvɪskəs/ a viscoso

visib|ility /vɪzɪˈbɪləti/ n visibilidad f. ~le /ˈvɪzɪbl/ a visible. ~ly adv visiblemente

vision /ˈvɪʒn/ n visión f; (sight) vista f. ~ary /ˈvɪʒənəri/ a & n visionario (m)

visit /ˈvɪzɪt/ vt visitar; hacer una visita a ⟨person⟩. ● vi hacer visitas. ● n visita f. ~or n visitante m & f; (guest) visita f; (in hotel) cliente m & f

visor /ˈvaɪzə(r)/ n visera f

vista /ˈvɪstə/ n perspectiva f

visual /ˈvɪʒʊəl/ a visual. ~ize /ˈvɪʒʊəlaɪz/ vt imaginar(se); (foresee) prever. ~ly adv visualmente

vital /ˈvaɪtl/ a vital; (essential) esencial

vitality /vaɪˈtæləti/ n vitalidad f

vital: ~ly /ˈvaɪtəli/ adv extremadamente. ~s npl órganos mpl vitales. ~ statistics npl (fam) medidas fpl

vitamin /ˈvɪtəmɪn/ n vitamina f

vitiate /ˈvɪʃɪeɪt/ vt viciar

vitreous /ˈvɪtrɪəs/ a vítreo

vituperat|e /vɪˈtjuːpəreɪt/ vt vituperar. ~ion /-ˈreɪʃn/ n vituperación f

vivaci|ous /vɪˈveɪʃəs/ a animado, vivo. ~ously adv animadamente. ~ty /-ˈvæsəti/ n viveza f

vivid /ˈvɪvɪd/ a vivo. ~ly adv intensamente; (describe) gráficamente. ~ness n viveza f

vivisection /vɪvɪˈsekʃn/ n vivisección f

vixen /ˈvɪksn/ n zorra f

vocabulary /vəˈkæbjʊləri/ n vocabulario m

vocal /ˈvəʊkl/ a vocal; (fig) franco. ~ist n cantante m & f

vocation /vəʊˈkeɪʃn/ n vocación f. ~al a profesional

vociferat|e /vəˈsɪfəreɪt/ vt/i vociferar. ~ous a vociferador

vogue /vəʊg/ n boga f. in ~ de moda

voice /vɔɪs/ n voz f. ● vt expresar

void /vɔɪd/ a vacío; (not valid) nulo. ~ of desprovisto de. ● n vacío m. ● vt anular

volatile /ˈvɒlətaɪl/ a volátil; ⟨person⟩ voluble

volcan|ic /vɒlˈkænɪk/ a volcánico. ~o /vɒlˈkeɪnəʊ/ n (pl -oes) volcán m

volition /vəˈlɪʃn/ n. of one's own ~ de su propia voluntad

volley /ˈvɒli/ n (pl -eys) (of blows) lluvia f; (of gunfire) descarga f cerrada

volt /vəʊlt/ n voltio m. ~age n voltaje m

voluble /ˈvɒljʊbl/ a locuaz

volume /ˈvɒljuːm/ n volumen m; (book) tomo m

voluminous /vəˈljuːmɪnəs/ a voluminoso

voluntar|ily /ˈvɒləntərəli/ adv voluntariamente. ~y /ˈvɒləntəri/ a voluntario

volunteer /vɒlənˈtɪə(r)/ n voluntario m. ● vt ofrecer. ● vi ofrecerse voluntariamente; (mil) alistarse como voluntario

voluptuous /vəˈlʌptjʊəs/ a voluptuoso

vomit /ˈvɒmɪt/ vt/i vomitar. ● n vómito m

voracious /vəˈreɪʃəs/ a voraz

vot|e /vəʊt/ n voto m; (right) derecho m de votar. ● vi votar. ~er /-ə(r)/ n votante m & f. ~ing n votación f

vouch /vaʊtʃ/ vi. ~ for garantizar

voucher /ˈvaʊtʃə(r)/ n vale m

vow /vaʊ/ n voto m. ● vi jurar

vowel /ˈvaʊəl/ n vocal f

voyage /ˈvɔɪɪdʒ/ n viaje m (en barco)

vulgar /ˈvʌlgə(r)/ a vulgar. ~ity /-ˈgærəti/ n vulgaridad f. ~ize vt vulgarizar

vulnerab|ility /vʌlnərə'bɪlətɪ/ n vulnerabilidad f. **~le** /'vʌlnərəbl/ a vulnerable

vulture /'vʌltʃə(r)/ n buitre m

vying /'vaɪɪŋ/ see **vie**

W

wad /wɒd/ n (pad) tapón m; (bundle) lío m; (of notes) fajo m; (of cotton wool etc) bolita f

wadding /'wɒdɪŋ/ n relleno m

waddle /'wɒdl/ vi contonearse

wade /weɪd/ vt vadear. ● vi. **~ through** abrirse paso entre; leer con dificultad ⟨book⟩

wafer /'weɪfə(r)/ n barquillo m; (relig) hostia f

waffle[1] /'wɒfl/ n (fam) palabrería f. ● vi (fam) divagar

waffle[2] /'wɒfl/ n (culin) gofre m

waft /wɒft/ vt llevar por el aire. ● vi flotar

wag /wæg/ vt (pt **wagged**) menear. ● vi menearse

wage /weɪdʒ/ n. **~s** npl salario m. ● vt. **~ war** hacer la guerra. **~r** /'weɪdʒə(r)/ n apuesta f. ● vt apostar

waggle /'wægl/ vt menear. ● vi menearse

wagon /'wægən/ n carro m; (rail) vagón m. **be on the ~** (sl) no beber

waif /weɪf/ n niño m abandonado

wail /weɪl/ vi lamentarse. ● n lamento m

wainscot /'weɪnskət/ n revestimiento m, zócalo m

waist /weɪst/ n cintura f. **~band** n cinturón m

waistcoat /'weɪstkəʊt/ n chaleco m

waistline /'weɪstlaɪn/ n cintura f

wait /weɪt/ vt/i esperar; (at table) servir. **~ for** esperar. **~ on** servir. ● n espera f. **lie in ~** acechar

waiter /'weɪtə(r)/ n camarero m

wait: ~ing-list n lista f de espera. **~ing-room** n sala f de espera

waitress /'weɪtrɪs/ n camarera f

waive /weɪv/ vt renunciar a

wake[1] /weɪk/ vt (pt **woke**, pp **woken**) despertar. ● vi despertarse. ● n velatorio m. **~ up** vt despertar. ● vi despertarse

wake[2] /weɪk/ n (naut) estela f. **in the ~ of** como resultado de, tras

waken /'weɪkən/ vt despertar. ● vi despertarse

wakeful /'weɪkfl/ a insomne

Wales /weɪlz/ n País m de Gales

walk /wɔːk/ vi andar; (not ride) ir a pie; (stroll) pasearse. **~ out** salir; ⟨workers⟩ declararse en huelga. **~ out on** abandonar. ● vt andar por ⟨streets⟩; llevar de paseo ⟨dog⟩. ● n paseo m; (gait) modo m de andar; (path) sendero m. **~ of life** clase f social. **~about** /'wɔːkəbaʊt/ n (of royalty) encuentro m con el público. **~er** /-ə(r)/ n paseante m & f

walkie-talkie /wɔːkɪ'tɔːkɪ/ n transmisor-receptor m portátil

walking /'wɔːkɪŋ/ n paseo m. **~-stick** n bastón m

Walkman /'wɔːkmən/ n (P) estereo m personal, Walkman m (P), magnetófono m de bolsillo

walk: ~out n huelga f. **~over** n victoria f fácil

wall /wɔːl/ n (interior) pared f; (exterior) muro m; (in garden) tapia f; (of city) muralla f. **go to the ~** fracasar. **up the ~** (fam) loco. ● vt amurallar ⟨city⟩

wallet /'wɒlɪt/ n cartera f, billetera f (LAm)

wallflower /'wɔːlflaʊə(r)/ n alhelí m

wallop /'wɒləp/ vt (pt **walloped**) (sl) golpear con fuerza. ● n (sl) golpe m fuerte

wallow /'wɒləʊ/ vi revolcarse

wallpaper /'wɔːlpeɪpə(r)/ n papel m pintado

walnut /'wɔːlnʌt/ n nuez f; (tree) nogal m

walrus /'wɔːlrəs/ n morsa f

waltz /wɔːls/ n vals m. ● vi valsar

wan /wɒn/ a pálido

wand /wɒnd/ n varita f

wander /'wɒndə(r)/ vi vagar; (stroll) pasearse; (digress) divagar; ⟨road, river⟩ serpentear. ● n paseo m. **~er** /-ə(r)/ n vagabundo m. **~lust** /'wɒndəlʌst/ n pasión f por los viajes

wane /weɪn/ vi menguar. ● n. **on the ~** disminuyendo

wangle /'wæŋgl/ vt (sl) agenciarse

want /wɒnt/ vt querer; (need) necesitar; (require) exigir. ● vi. **~ for** carecer de. ● n necesidad f; (lack) falta f; (desire) deseo m. **~ed** a ⟨criminal⟩ buscado. **~ing** a (lacking) falto de. **be ~ing** carecer de

wanton /'wɒntən/ a (licentious) lascivo; (motiveless) sin motivo

war /wɔː(r)/ n guerra f. **at ~** en guerra

warble /'wɔːbl/ vt cantar trinando.
● vi gorjear. ● n gorjeo m. ~r /-ə(r)/
n curruca f
ward /wɔːd/ n (in hospital) sala f; (of
town) barrio m; (child) pupilo m.
● vt. ~ **off** parar
warden /'wɔːdn/ n guarda m
warder /'wɔːdə(r)/ n carcelero m
wardrobe /'wɔːdrəʊb/ n armario m;
(clothes) vestuario m
warehouse /'weəhaʊs/ n almacén m
wares /weəz/ npl mercancías fpl
war: ~**fare** /'wɔːfeə(r)/ n guerra f.
~**head** /'wɔːhed/ n cabeza f
explosiva
warily /'weərɪlɪ/ adv cautelosamente
warlike /'wɔːlaɪk/ a belicoso
warm /wɔːm/ a (-er, -est) caliente;
(hearty) caluroso. be ~ (person)
tener calor. it is ~ hace calor. ● vt.
~ (up) calentar; recalentar (food);
(fig) animar. ● vi. ~ (up) calentarse; (fig) animarse. ~ to tomar
simpatía a (person); ir entu-
siasmándose por (idea etc).
~**blooded** a de sangre caliente.
~**hearted** a simpático. ~**ly** adv
(heartily) calurosamente
warmonger /'wɔːmʌŋgə(r)/ n beli-
cista m & f
warmth /wɔːmθ/ n calor m
warn /wɔːn/ vt avisar, advertir.
~**ing** n advertencia f; (notice) aviso
m. ~ **off** (advise against) aconsejar
en contra de; (forbid) impedir
warp /wɔːp/ vt deformar; (fig) per-
vertir. ● vi deformarse
warpath /'wɔːpɑːθ/ n. be on the ~
buscar camorra
warrant /'wɒrənt/ n autorización f;
(for arrest) orden f. ● vt justificar.
~**officer** n suboficial m
warranty /'wɒrəntɪ/ n garantía f
warring /'wɔːrɪŋ/ a en guerra
warrior /'wɒrɪə(r)/ n guerrero m
warship /'wɔːʃɪp/ n buque m de
guerra
wart /wɔːt/ n verruga f
wartime /'wɔːtaɪm/ n tiempo m de
guerra
wary /'weərɪ/ a (-ier, -iest) cauteloso
was /wəz, wɒz/ see **be**
wash /wɒʃ/ vt lavar; (flow over)
bañar. ● vi lavarse. ● n lavado m;
(dirty clothes) ropa f sucia; (wet
clothes) colada f; (of ship) estela f.
have a ~ lavarse. ~ **out** vt enjuagar; (fig) cancelar. ~ **up** vi fregar

los platos. ~**able** a lavable. ~**basin**
n lavabo m. ~**ed-out** a (pale) pálido;
(tired) rendido. ~**er** /'wɒʃə(r)/ n
arandela f; (washing-machine) lavadora f. ~**ing** /'wɒʃɪŋ/ n lavado m;
(dirty clothes) ropa f sucia; (wet
clothes) colada f, ~**ing-machine** n
lavadora f. ~**ing-powder** n jabón m
en polvo. ~**ing-up** n fregado m;
(dirty plates etc) platos mpl para fregar. ~**out** n (sl) desastre m.
~**room** n (Amer) servicios mpl.
~**stand** n lavabo m. ~**tub** n tina f
de lavar
wasp /wɒsp/ n avispa f
wastage /'weɪstɪdʒ/ n desperdicios
mpl
waste /weɪst/ a de desecho; (land)
yermo. ● n derroche m; (rubbish)
desperdicio m; (of time) pérdida f.
● vt derrochar; (not use) desperdiciar; perder (time). ● vi. ~ **away**
consumirse. ~**disposal unit** n trituradora f de basuras. ~**ful** a dis-
pendioso; (person) derrochador.
~**paper basket** n papelera f. ~**s** npl
tierras fpl baldías
watch /wɒtʃ/ vt mirar; (keep an eye
on) vigilar; (take heed) tener cuidado con; ver (TV). ● vi mirar; (keep
an eye on) vigilar. ● n vigilancia f;
(period of duty) guardia f; (time-
piece) reloj m. on the ~ alerta. ~
out vi tener cuidado. ~**dog** n perro
m guardián; (fig) guardián m. ~**ful**
a vigilante. ~**maker**
/'wɒtʃmeɪkə(r)/ n relojero m. ~**man**
/'wɒtʃmən/ n (pl -men) vigilante m.
~**tower** n atalaya f. ~**word**
/'wɒtʃwɜːd/ n santo m y seña
water /'wɔːtə(r)/ n agua f. by ~ (of
travel) por mar. in hot ~ (fam) en
un apuro. ● vt regar (plants etc);
(dilute) aguar, diluir. ● vi (eyes) llorar. make s.o.'s mouth ~ hacérsele
la boca agua. ~ **down** vt diluir; (fig)
suavizar. ~**closet** n wáter m. ~**colour** n acuarela f. ~**course** /'wɔːtəkɔː-
s/ n arroyo m; (artificial) canal m.
~**cress** /'wɔːtəkres/ n berro m. ~**fall**
/'wɔːtəfɔːl/ n cascada f. ~**ice** n sorbete m. ~**ing-can** /'wɔːtərɪŋkæn/ n
regadera f. ~**lily** n nenúfar m.
~**line** n línea f de flotación. ~**logged** /'wɔːtəlɒgd/ a saturado de agua,
empapado. ~ **main** n cañería f principal. ~ **melon** n sandía f. ~**mill** n
molino m de agua. ~ **polo** n polo m

acuático. **~power** n energía f hidráulica. **~proof** /'wɔːtəpruːf/ a & n impermeable (m); ⟨watch⟩ sumergible. **~shed** /'wɔːtəʃed/ n punto m decisivo. **~skiing** n esquí m acuático. **~softener** n ablandador m de agua. **~tight** /'wɔːtətaɪt/ a hermético, estanco; (fig) irrecusable. **~way** n canal m navegable. **~wheel** n rueda f hidráulica. **~wings** npl flotadores mpl. **~works** /'wɔːtəwɜːks/ n sistema m de abastecimiento de agua. **~y** /'wɔːtəri/ a acuoso; ⟨colour⟩ pálido; ⟨eyes⟩ lloroso

watt /wɒt/ n vatio m

wave /weɪv/ n onda f; (of hand) señal f; (fig) oleada f. ● vt agitar; ondular ⟨hair⟩. ● vi (signal) hacer señales con la mano; ⟨flag⟩ flotar. **~band** /'weɪvbænd/ n banda f de ondas. **~length** /'weɪvleŋθ/ n longitud f de onda

waver /'weɪvə(r)/ vi vacilar

wavy /'weɪvɪ/ a (-ier, -iest) ondulado

wax[1] /wæks/ n. ● vt encerar

wax[2] /wæks/ vi ⟨moon⟩ crecer

wax: **~en** a céreo. **~work** /'wækswɜːk/ n figura f de cera. **~y** a céreo

way /weɪ/ n camino m; (distance) distancia f; (manner) manera f, modo m; (direction) dirección f; (means) medio m; (habit) costumbre f. **be in the ~** estorbar. **by the ~** a propósito. **by ~ of** a título de, por. **either ~** de cualquier modo. **in a ~** en cierta manera. **in some ~s** en ciertos modos. **lead the ~** mostrar el camino. **make ~** dejar paso a. **on the ~** en camino. **out of the ~** remoto; (extraordinary) fuera de lo común. **that ~** por allí. **this ~** por aquí. **under ~** en curso. **~bill** n hoja f de ruta. **~farer** /'weɪfeərə(r)/ n viajero m. **~in** n entrada f

waylay /weɪ'leɪ/ vt (pt -laid) acechar; (detain) detener

way: **~ out** n salida f. **~out** a ultramoderno, original. **~s** npl costumbres fpl. **~side** /'weɪsaɪd/ n borde m del camino

wayward /'weɪwəd/ a caprichoso

we /wiː/ pron nosotros, nosotras

weak /wiːk/ a (-er, -est) débil; ⟨liquid⟩ aguado, acuoso; (fig) flojo. **~en** vt debilitar. **~kneed** a irresoluto. **~ling** /'wiːklɪŋ/ n persona f débil. **~ly** adv débilmente. ● a enfermizo. **~ness** n debilidad f

weal /wiːl/ n verdugón m

wealth /welθ/ n riqueza f. **~y** a (-ier, -iest) rico

wean /wiːn/ vt destetar

weapon /'wepən/ n arma f

wear /weə(r)/ vt (pt wore, pp worn) llevar; (put on) ponerse; tener ⟨expression etc⟩; (damage) desgastar. ● vi desgastarse; (last) durar. ● n uso m; (damage) desgaste m; (clothing) ropa f. **~ down** vt desgastar; agotar ⟨opposition etc⟩. **~ off** vi desaparecer. **~ on** vi ⟨time⟩ pasar. **~ out** vt desgastar; (tire) agotar. **~able** a que se puede llevar. **~ and tear** desgaste·m

wear|ily /'wɪərɪlɪ/ adv cansadamente. **~iness** n cansancio m. **~isome** /'wɪərɪsəm/ a cansado. **~y** /'wɪərɪ/ a (-ier, -iest) cansado. ● vt cansar. ● vi cansarse. **~y of** cansarse de

weasel /'wiːzl/ n comadreja f

weather /'weðə(r)/ n tiempo m. **under the ~** (fam) indispuesto. ● a meteorológico. ● vt curar ⟨wood⟩; (survive) superar. **~beaten** a curtido. **~cock** /'weðəkɒk/ n, **~vane** n veleta f

weave /wiːv/ vt (pt wove, pp woven) tejer; entretejer ⟨story etc⟩; entrelazar ⟨flowers etc⟩. **~ one's way** abrirse paso. ● n tejido m. **~r** /-ə(r)/ n tejedor m

web /web/ n tela f; (of spider) telaraña f; (on foot) membrana f. **~bing** n cincha f

wed /wed/ vt (pt wedded) casarse con; ⟨priest etc⟩ casar. ● vi casarse. **~ded to** (fig) unido a

wedding /'wedɪŋ/ n boda f. **~cake** n pastel m de boda. **~ring** n anillo m de boda

wedge /wedʒ/ n cuña f; (space filler) calce m. ● vt acuñar; (push) apretar

wedlock /'wedlɒk/ n matrimonio m

Wednesday /'wenzdeɪ/ n miércoles m

wee /wiː/ a (fam) pequeñito

weed /wiːd/ n mala hierba f. ● vt desherbar. **~killer** n herbicida m. **~ out** eliminar. **~y** a ⟨person⟩ débil

week /wiːk/ n semana f. **~day** /'wiːkdeɪ/ n día m laborable. **~end** n fin m de semana. **~ly** /'wiːklɪ/ a semanal. ● n semanario m. ● adv semanalmente

weep /wiːp/ vi (pt wept) llorar. **~ing willow** n sauce m llorón

weevil /'wiːvɪl/ n gorgojo m

weigh /weɪ/ vt/i pesar. ~ **anchor** levar anclas. ~ **down** vt (fig) oprimir. ~ **up** vt pesar; (fig) considerar

weight /weɪt/ n peso m. ~**less** a ingrávido. ~**lessness** n ingravidez f. ~**lifting** n halterofilia f, levantamiento m de pesos. ~**y** a (-ier, -iest) pesado; (influential) influyente

weir /wɪə(r)/ n presa f

weird /wɪəd/ a (-er, -est) misterioso; (bizarre) extraño

welcome /'welkəm/ a bienvenido. ~ **to do** libre de hacer. **you're** ~**e!** (after thank you) ¡de nada! ● n bienvenida f; (reception) acogida f. ● vt dar la bienvenida a; (appreciate) alegrarse de

welcoming /'welkəmɪŋ/ a acogedor

weld /weld/ vt soldar. ● n soldadura f. ~**er** n soldador m

welfare /'welfeə(r)/ n bienestar m; (aid) asistencia f social. **W~ State** n estado m benefactor. ~ **work** n asistencia f social

well[1] /wel/ adv (better, best) bien. ~ **done!** ¡bravo! **as** ~ también. **as** ~ **as** tanto... como. **be** ~ estar bien. **do** ~ (succeed) tener éxito. **very** ~ muy bien. ● a bien. ● int bueno; (surprise) ¡vaya! ~ **I never!** ¡no me digas!

well[2] /wel/ n pozo m; (of staircase) caja f

well: ~**-appointed** a bien equipado. ~**-behaved** a bien educado. ~**-being** n bienestar m. ~**-bred** a bien educado. ~**-disposed** a benévolo. ~**-groomed** a bien aseado. ~**-heeled** a (fam) rico

wellington /'welɪŋtən/ n bota f de agua

well: ~**-knit** a robusto. ~**-known** a conocido. ~**-meaning** a, ~ **meant** a bienintencionado. ~ **off** a acomodado. ~**-read** a culto. ~**-spoken** a bienhablado. ~**-to-do** a rico. ~**-wisher** n bienqueriente m & f

Welsh /welʃ/ a & n galés (m). ~ **rabbit** n pan m tostado con queso

welsh /welʃ/ vi. ~ **on** no cumplir con

wench /wentʃ/ n (old use) muchacha f

wend /wend/ vt. ~ **one's way** encaminarse

went /went/ see **go**

wept /wept/ see **weep**

were /wɜː(r), wə(r)/ see **be**

west /west/ n oeste m. **the** ~ el Occidente m. ● a del oeste. ● adv hacia el oeste, al oeste. **go** ~ (sl) morir. **W~ Germany** n Alemania f Occidental. ~**erly** a del oeste. ~**ern** a occidental. ● n (film) película f del Oeste. ~**erner** /-ənə(r)/ n occidental m & f. **W~ Indian** a & n antillano (m). **W~ Indies** npl Antillas fpl. ~**ward** a, ~**ward(s)** adv hacia el oeste

wet /wet/ a (**wetter**, **wettest**) mojado; (rainy) lluvioso, de lluvia; (person, sl) soso. ~ **paint** recién pintado. **get** ~ mojarse. ● vt (pt wetted) mojar, humedecer. ~ **blanket** n aguafiestas m & f invar. ~ **suit** n traje m de buzo

whack /wæk/ vt (fam) golpear. ● n (fam) golpe m. ~**ed** /wækt/ a (fam) agotado. ~**ing** a (huge, sl) enorme. ● n paliza f

whale /weɪl/ n ballena f. **a** ~ **of a** (fam) maravilloso, enorme

wham /wæm/ int ¡zas!

wharf /wɔːf/ n (pl **wharves** or **wharfs**) muelle m

what /wɒt/ a el que, la que, lo que, los que, las que; (in questions & exclamations) qué. ● pron lo que; (interrogative) qué. ~ **about going?** ¿si fuésemos? ~ **about me?** ¿y yo? ~ **for?** ¿para qué? ~ **if?** ¿y si? ~ **is it?** ¿qué es? ~ **you need** lo que te haga falta. ● int ¡cómo! ~ **a fool!** ¡qué tonto!

whatever /wɒt'evə(r)/ a cualquiera. ● pron (todo) lo que, cualquier cosa que

whatnot /'wɒtnɒt/ n chisme m

whatsoever /wɒtsəʊ'evə(r)/ a & pron = **whatever**

wheat /wiːt/ n trigo m. ~**en** a de trigo

wheedle /'wiːdl/ vt engatusar

wheel /wiːl/ n rueda f. **at the** ~ al volante. **steering-**~ n volante m. ● vt empujar (bicycle etc). ● vi girar. ~ **round** girar. ~**barrow** /'wiːlbærəʊ/ n carretilla f. ~**chair** /'wiːltʃeə(r)/ n silla f de ruedas

wheeze /wiːz/ vi resollar. ● n resuello m

when /wen/ adv cuándo. ● conj cuando

whence /wens/ adv de dónde

whenever /wen'evə(r)/ adv en cualquier momento; (every time that) cada vez que

where /weə(r)/ *adv & conj* donde; (*interrogative*) dónde. **~ are you going?** ¿adónde vas? **~ are you from?** ¿de dónde eres?

whereabouts /'weərəbaʊts/ *adv* dónde. ● *n* paradero *m*

whereas /weər'æz/ *conj* por cuanto; (*in contrast*) mientras (que)

whereby /weə'baɪ/ *adv* por lo cual

whereupon /weərə'pɒn/ *adv* después de lo cual

wherever /weər'evə(r)/ *adv* (*in whatever place*) dónde (diablos). ● *conj* dondequiera que

whet /wet/ *vt* (*pt* **whetted**) afilar; (*fig*) aguzar

whether /'weðə(r)/ *conj* si. **~ you like it or not** que te guste o no te guste. **I don't know ~ she will like it** no sé si le gustará

which /wɪtʃ/ *a* (*in questions*) qué. **~ one** cuál. **~ one of you** cuál de vosotros. ● *pron* (*in questions*) cuál; (*relative*) que; (*object*) el cual, la cual, lo cual, los cuales, las cuales

whichever /wɪtʃ'evə(r)/ *a* cualquier. ● *pron* cualquiera que, el que, la que

whiff /wɪf/ *n* soplo *m*; (*of smoke*) bocanada *f*; (*smell*) olorcillo *m*

while /waɪl/ *n* rato *m*. ● *conj* mientras; (*although*) aunque. ● *vt*. **~ away** pasar ⟨*time*⟩

whilst /waɪlst/ *conj* = **while**

whim /wɪm/ *n* capricho *m*

whimper /'wɪmpə(r)/ *vi* lloriquear. ● *n* lloriqueo *m*

whimsical /'wɪmzɪkl/ *a* caprichoso; (*odd*) extraño

whine /waɪn/ *vi* gimotear. ● *n* gimoteo *m*

whip /wɪp/ *n* látigo *m*; (*pol*) oficial *m* disciplinario. ● *vt* (*pt* **whipped**) azotar; (*culin*) batir; (*seize*) agarrar. **~cord** tralla *f*. **~ped cream** *n* nata *f* batida. **~ping-boy** /'wɪpɪŋbɔɪ/ *n* cabeza *f* de turco. **~round** colecta *f*. **~ up** (*incite*) estimular

whirl /wɜːl/ *vt* hacer girar rápidamente. ● *vi* girar rápidamente; (*swirl*) arremolinarse. ● *n* giro *m*; (*swirl*) remolino *m*. **~pool** /'wɜːlpuːl/ *n* remolino *m*. **~wind** /'wɜːlwɪnd/ *n* torbellino *m*

whirr /wɜː(r)/ *n* zumbido *m*. ● *vi* zumbar

whisk /wɪsk/ *vt* (*culin*) batir. ● *n* (*culin*) batidor *m*. **~ away** llevarse

whisker /'wɪskə(r)/ *n* pelo *m*. **~s** *npl* (*of man*) patillas *fpl*; (*of cat etc*) bigotes *mpl*

whisky /'wɪskɪ/ *n* güisqui *m*

whisper /'wɪspə(r)/ *vt* decir en voz baja. ● *vi* cuchichear; ⟨*leaves etc*⟩ susurrar. ● *n* cuchicheo *m*; (*of leaves*) susurro *m*; (*rumour*) rumor *m*

whistle /'wɪsl/ *n* silbido *m*; (*instrument*) silbato *m*. ● *vi* silbar. **~-stop** *n* (*pol*) breve parada *f* (en gira electoral)

white /waɪt/ *a* (**-er, -est**) blanco. **go ~** ponerse pálido. ● *n* blanco; (*of egg*) clara *f*. **~bait** /'waɪtbeɪt/ *n* (*pl* **~bait**) chanquetes *mpl*. **~ coffee** *n* café *m* con leche. **~collar worker** *n* empleado *m* de oficina. **~ elephant** *n* objeto *m* inútil y costoso

Whitehall /'waɪthɔːl/ *n* el gobierno *m* británico

white: ~ horses *n* cabrillas *fpl*. **~-hot** *a* ⟨*metal*⟩ candente. **~ lie** *n* mentirijilla *f*. **~n** *vt/i* blanquear. **~ness** *n* blancura *f*. **W~ Paper** *n* libro *m* blanco. **~wash** /'waɪtwɒʃ/ *n* jalbegue *m*; (*fig*) encubrimiento *m*. ● *vt* enjalbegar; (*fig*) encubrir

whiting /'waɪtɪŋ/ *n* (*pl* **whiting**) (*fish*) pescadilla *f*

whitlow /'wɪtləʊ/ *n* panadizo *m*

Whitsun /'wɪtsn/ *n* Pentecostés *m*

whittle /'wɪtl/ *vt*. **~ (down)** tallar; (*fig*) reducir

whiz /wɪz/ *vi* (*pt* **whizzed**) silbar; (*rush*) ir a gran velocidad. **~ past** pasar como un rayo. **~-kid** *n* (*fam*) joven *m* prometedor, promesa *f*

who /huː/ *pron* que, quien; (*interrogative*) quién; (*particular person*) el que, la que, los que, las que

whodunit /huː'dʌnɪt/ *n* (*fam*) novela *f* policíaca

whoever /huː'evə(r)/ *pron* quienquera que; (*interrogative*) quién (diablos)

whole /həʊl/ *a* entero; (*not broken*) intacto. ● *n* todo *m*, conjunto *m*; (*total*) total *m*. **as a ~** en conjunto. **on the ~** por regla general. **~hearted** *a* sincero. **~meal** *a* integral

wholesale /'həʊlseɪl/ *n* venta *f* al por mayor. ● *a & adv* al por mayor. **~r** /-ə(r)/ *n* comerciante *m & f* al por mayor

wholesome /'həʊlsəm/ *a* saludable

wholly /'həʊlɪ/ *adv* completamente

whom /hu:m/ *pron* que, a quien; (*interrogative*) a quién

whooping cough /'hu:pɪŋkɒf/ *n* tos *f* ferina

whore /hɔ:(r)/ *n* puta *f*

whose /hu:z/ *pron* de quién. ● *a* de quién; (*relative*) cuyo

why /waɪ/ *adv* por qué. ● *int* ¡toma!

wick /wɪk/ *n* mecha *f*

wicked /'wɪkɪd/ *a* malo; (*mischievous*) travieso; (*very bad, fam*) malísimo. **~ness** *n* maldad *f*

wicker /'wɪkə(r)/ *n* mimbre *m & f*. ● *a* de mimbre. **~work** *n* artículos *mpl* de mimbre

wicket /'wɪkɪt/ *n* (*cricket*) rastrillo *m*

wide /waɪd/ *a* (**-er, -est**) ancho; (*fully opened*) de par en par; (*far from target*) lejano; ⟨*knowledge etc*⟩ amplio. ● *adv* lejos. **far and ~** por todas partes. **~ awake** *a* completamente despierto; (*fig*) despabilado. **~ly** *adv* extensamente; (*believed*) generalmente; (*different*) muy. **~n** *vt* ensanchar

widespread /'waɪdspred/ *a* extendido; (*fig*) difundido

widow /'wɪdəʊ/ *n* viuda *f*. **~ed** *a* viudo. **~er** *n* viudo *m*. **~hood** *n* viudez *f*

width /wɪdθ/ *n* anchura *f*. **in ~** de ancho

wield /wi:ld/ *vt* manejar; ejercer ⟨*power*⟩

wife /waɪf/ *n* (*pl* **wives**) mujer *f*, esposa *f*

wig /wɪg/ *n* peluca *f*

wiggle /'wɪgl/ *vt* menear. ● *vi* menearse

wild /waɪld/ *a* (**-er, -est**) salvaje; (*enraged*) furioso; ⟨*idea*⟩ extravagante; (*with joy*) loco; (*random*) al azar. ● *adv* en estado salvaje. **run ~** crecer en estado salvaje. **~s** *npl* regiones *fpl* salvajes

wildcat /'waɪldkæt/ *a*. **~ strike** *n* huelga *f* salvaje

wilderness /'wɪldənɪs/ *n* desierto *m*

wild: **~fire** /'waɪldfaɪ(r)/ *n*. **spread like ~fire** correr como un reguero de pólvora. **~goose chase** *n* empresa *f* inútil. **~life** /'waɪldlaɪf/ *n* fauna *f*. **~ly** *adv* violentamente; (*fig*) locamente

wilful /'wɪlfʊl/ *a* intencionado; (*self-willed*) terco. **~ly** *adv* intencionadamente; (*obstinately*) obstinadamente

will[1] /wɪl/ *v aux*. **~ you have some wine?** ¿quieres vino? **he ~ be** será. **you ~ be back soon, won't you?** volverás pronto, ¿no?

will[2] /wɪl/ *n* voluntad *f*; (*document*) testamento *m*

willing /'wɪlɪŋ/ *a* complaciente. **~ to** dispuesto a. **~ly** *adv* de buena gana. **~ness** *n* buena voluntad *f*

willow /'wɪləʊ/ *n* sauce *m*

will-power /'wɪlpaʊə(r)/ *n* fuerza *f* de voluntad

willy-nilly /wɪlɪ'nɪlɪ/ *adv* quieras que no

wilt /wɪlt/ *vi* marchitarse

wily /'waɪlɪ/ *a* (**-ier, -iest**) astuto

win /wɪn/ *vt* (*pt* **won**, *pres p* **winning**) ganar; (*achieve, obtain*) conseguir. ● *vi* ganar. ● *n* victoria *f*. **~ back** *vi* reconquistar. **~ over** *vt* convencer

wince /wɪns/ *vi* hacer una mueca de dolor. **without wincing** sin pestañear. ● *n* mueca *f* de dolor

winch /wɪntʃ/ *n* cabrestante *m*. ● *vt* levantar con el cabrestante

wind[1] /wɪnd/ *n* viento *m*; (*in stomach*) flatulencia *f*. **get the ~ up** (*sl*) asustarse. **get ~ of** enterarse de. **in the ~** en el aire. ● *vt* dejar sin aliento.

wind[2] /waɪnd/ *vt* (*pt* **wound**) (*wrap around*) enrollar; dar cuerda a ⟨*clock etc*⟩. ● *vi* ⟨*road etc*⟩ serpentear. **~ up** *vt* dar cuerda a ⟨*watch, clock*⟩; (*provoke*) agitar, poner nervioso; (*fig*) terminar, concluir

wind /wɪnd/: **~bag** *n* charlatán *m*. **~cheater** *n* cazadora *f*

winder /'waɪndə(r)/ *n* devanador *m*; (*of clock, watch*) llave *f*

windfall /'wɪndfɔ:l/ *n* fruta *f* caída; (*fig*) suerte *f* inesperada

winding /'waɪndɪŋ/ *a* tortuoso

wind instrument /'wɪndɪnstrəmənt/ *n* instrumento *m* de viento

windmill /'wɪndmɪl/ *n* molino *m* (de viento)

window /'wɪndəʊ/ *n* ventana *f*; (*in shop*) escaparate *m*; (*of vehicle, booking-office*) ventanilla *f*. **~box** *n* jardinera *f*. **~dresser** *n* escaparatista *m & f*. **~shop** *vi* mirar los escaparates

windpipe /'wɪndpaɪp/ *n* tráquea *f*

windscreen /'wɪndskri:n/ *n*, **windshield** *n* (*Amer*) parabrisas *m invar*. **~ wiper** *n* limpiaparabrisas *m invar*

wind /wɪnd/: ~**swept** a barrido por el viento. ~**y** a (-**ier**, -**iest**) ventoso, de mucho viento. **it is** ~**y** hace viento

wine /waɪn/ n vino m. ~**cellar** n bodega f. ~**glass** n copa f. ~**grower** n vinicultor m. ~**growing** n vinicultura f. ● a vinícola. ~ **list** n lista f de vinos. ~**tasting** n cata f de vinos

wing /wɪŋ/ n ala f; (auto) aleta f. **under one's** ~ bajo la protección de uno. ~**ed** a alado. ~**er** /-ə(r)/ n (sport) ala m & f. ~**s** npl (in theatre) bastidores mpl

wink /wɪŋk/ vi guiñar el ojo; ⟨light etc⟩ centellear. ● n guiño m. **not to sleep a** ~ no pegar ojo

winkle /'wɪŋkl/ n bígaro m

win: ~**ner** /-ə(r)/ n ganador m. ~**ning-post** n poste m de llegada. ~**ning smile** n sonrisa f encantadora. ~**nings** npl ganancias fpl

winsome /'wɪnsəm/ a atractivo

wint|er /'wɪntə(r)/ n invierno m. ● vi invernar. ~**ry** a invernal

wipe /waɪp/ vt limpiar; (dry) secar. ● n limpión m. **give sth a** ~ limpiar algo. ~ **out** (cancel) cancelar; (destroy) destruir; (obliterate) borrar. ~ **up** limpiar; (dry) secar

wire /'waɪə(r)/ n alambre m; (elec) cable m; (telegram, fam) telegrama m

wireless /'waɪəlɪs/ n radio f

wire netting /waɪə'netɪŋ/ n alambrera f, tela f metálica

wiring n instalación f eléctrica

wiry /'waɪərɪ/ a (-**ier**, -**iest**) ⟨person⟩ delgado

wisdom /'wɪzdəm/ n sabiduría f. ~ **tooth** n muela f del juicio

wise /waɪz/ a (-**er**, -**est**) sabio; (sensible) prudente. ~**crack** /'waɪzkræk/ n (fam) salida f. ~**ly** adv sabiamente; (sensibly) prudentemente

wish /wɪʃ/ n deseo m; (greeting) saludo m. **with best** ~**es** (in letters) un fuerte abrazo. ● vt desear. ~ **on** (fam) encajar a. ~ **s.o. well** desear buena suerte a uno. ~**bone** n espoleta f (de las aves). ~**ful** a deseoso. ~**ful thinking** n ilusiones fpl

wishy-washy /'wɪʃɪwɒʃɪ/ a soso; ⟨person⟩ sin convicciones, falto de entereza

wisp /wɪsp/ n manojito m; (of smoke) voluta f; (of hair) mechón m

wisteria /wɪs'tɪərɪə/ n glicina f

wistful /'wɪstfl/ a melancólico

wit /wɪt/ n gracia f; (person) persona f chistosa; (intelligence) ingenio m. **be at one's** ~**s' end** no saber qué hacer. **live by one's** ~**s** vivir de expedientes, vivir del cuento

witch /wɪtʃ/ n bruja f. ~**craft** n brujería f. ~**doctor** n hechicero m

with /wɪð/ prep con; (cause, having) de. **be** ~ **it** (fam) estar al día, estar al tanto. **the man** ~ **the beard** el hombre de la barba

withdraw /wɪð'drɔː/ vt (pt **withdrew**, pp **withdrawn**) retirar. ● vi apartarse. ~**al** n retirada f. ~**n** a ⟨person⟩ introvertido

wither /'wɪðə(r)/ vi marchitarse. ● vt (fig) fulminar

withhold /wɪð'həʊld/ vt (pt **withheld**) retener; (conceal) ocultar (**from** a)

within /wɪð'ɪn/ prep dentro de. ● adv dentro. ~ **sight** a la vista

without /wɪð'aʊt/ prep sin

withstand /wɪð'stænd/ vt (pt ~**stood**) resistir a

witness /'wɪtnɪs/ n testigo m; (proof) testimonio m. ● vt presenciar; firmar como testigo ⟨document⟩. ~**box** n tribuna f de los testigos

witticism /'wɪtɪsɪzəm/ n ocurrencia f

wittingly /'wɪtɪŋlɪ/ adv a sabiendas

witty /'wɪtɪ/ a (-**ier**, -**iest**) gracioso

wives /waɪvz/ see **wife**

wizard /'wɪzəd/ n hechicero m. ~**ry** n hechicería f

wizened /'wɪznd/ a arrugado

wobbl|e /'wɒbl/ vi tambalearse; ⟨voice, jelly, hand⟩ temblar; ⟨chair etc⟩ balancearse. ~**y** a ⟨chair etc⟩ cojo

woe /wəʊ/ n aflicción f. ~**ful** a triste. ~**begone** /'wəʊbɪgɒn/ a desconsolado

woke, woken /wəʊk, 'wəʊkən/ see **wake**[1]

wolf /wʊlf/ n (pl **wolves**) lobo m. **cry** ~ gritar al lobo. ● vt zamparse. ~**whistle** n silbido m de admiración

woman /'wʊmən/ n (pl **women**) mujer f. **single** ~ soltera f. ~**ize** /'wʊmənaɪz/ vi ser mujeriego. ~**ly** a femenino

womb /wuːm/ n matriz f

women /'wɪmɪn/ npl see **woman**. ~**folk** /'wɪmɪnfəʊk/ npl mujeres fpl.

~'s lib n movimiento m de liberación de la mujer

won /wʌn/ *see* win

wonder /ˈwʌndə(r)/ n maravilla f; (*bewilderment*) asombro m. **no** ~ no es de extrañarse (**that** que). ● vi admirarse; (*reflect*) preguntarse

wonderful /ˈwʌndəfl/ a maravilloso. ~**ly** adv maravillosamente

won't /wəʊnt/ = will not

woo /wuː/ vt cortejar

wood /wʊd/ n madera f; (*for burning*) leña f; (*area*) bosque m; (*in bowls*) bola f. **out of the** ~ (*fig*) fuera de peligro. ~**cutter** /ˈwʊdkʌtə(r)/ n leñador m. ~**ed** a poblado de árboles, boscoso. ~**en** a de madera. ~**land** n bosque m

woodlouse /ˈwʊdlaʊs/ n (pl **-lice**) cochinilla f

woodpecker /ˈwʊdpekə(r)/ n pájaro m carpintero

woodwind /ˈwʊdwɪnd/ n instrumentos mpl de viento de madera

woodwork /ˈwʊdwɜːk/ n carpintería f; (*in room etc*) maderaje m

woodworm /ˈwʊdwɜːm/ n carcoma f

woody /ˈwʊdɪ/ a leñoso

wool /wʊl/ n lana f. **pull the** ~ **over s.o.'s eyes** engañar a uno. ~**len** a de lana. ~**lens** npl ropa f de lana. ~**ly** a (**-ier, -iest**) de lana; (*fig*) confuso. ● n jersey m

word /wɜːd/ n palabra f; (*news*) noticia f. **by** ~ **of mouth** de palabra. **have** ~**s with** reñir con. **in one** ~ en una palabra. **in other** ~**s** es decir. ● vt expresar. ~**ing** n expresión f, términos mpl. ~**perfect** a. **be** ~**perfect** saber de memoria. ~ **processor** n procesador m de textos. ~**y** a prolijo

wore /wɔː(r)/ *see* wear

work /wɜːk/ n trabajo m; (*arts*) obra f. ● vt hacer trabajar; manejar (*machine*). ● vi trabajar; (*machine*) funcionar; (*student*) estudiar; (*drug etc*) tener efecto; (*be successful*) tener éxito. ~ **in** introducir(se). ~ **off** desahogar. ~ **out** vt resolver; (*calculate*) calcular; elaborar (*plan*). ● vi (*succeed*) salir bien; (*sport*) entrenarse. ~ **up** vt desarrollar. ● vi excitarse. ~**able** /ˈwɜːkəbl/ a (*project*) factible. ~**aholic** /wɜːkəˈhɒlɪk/ n trabajador m obsesivo. ~**ed up** a agitado. ~**er** /ˈwɜː-

ka(r)/ n trabajador m; (*manual*) obrero m

workhouse /ˈwɜːkhaʊs/ n asilo m de pobres

work: ~**ing** /ˈwɜːkɪŋ/ a (*day*) laborable; (*clothes etc*) de trabajo. ● n (*mec*) funcionamiento m. **in** ~**ing order** en estado de funcionamiento. ~**ing class** n clase f obrera. ~**ing-class** a de la clase obrera. ~**man** /ˈwɜːkmən/ n (pl **-men**) obrero m. ~**manlike** /ˈwɜːkmənlaɪk/ a concienzudo. ~**manship** n destreza f. ~**s** npl (*building*) fábrica f; (*mec*) mecanismo m. ~**shop** /ˈwɜːkʃɒp/ n taller m. ~**to-rule** n huelga f de celo

world /wɜːld/ n mundo m. **a** ~ **of** enorme. **out of this** ~ maravilloso. ● a mundial. ~**ly** a mundano. ~**wide** a universal

worm /wɜːm/ n lombriz f; (*grub*) gusano m. ● vi. ~ **one's way** insinuarse. ~**eaten** a carcomido

worn /wɔːn/ *see* wear. ● a gastado. ~**out** a gastado; (*person*) rendido

worr|ied /ˈwʌrɪd/ a preocupado. ~**ier** /-ə(r)/ n aprensivo m. ~**y** /ˈwʌrɪ/ vt preocupar; (*annoy*) molestar. ● vi preocuparse. ● n preocupación f. ~**ying** a inquietante

worse /wɜːs/ a peor. ● adv peor; (*more*) más. ● n lo peor. ~**n** vt/i empeorar

worship /ˈwɜːʃɪp/ n culto m; (*title*) señor, su señoría. ● vt (pt **worshipped**) adorar

worst /wɜːst/ a (el) peor. ● adv peor. ● n lo peor. **get the** ~ **of it** llevar la peor parte

worsted /ˈwʊstɪd/ n estambre m

worth /wɜːθ/ n valor m. ● a. **be** ~ valer. **it is** ~ **trying** vale la pena probarlo. **it was** ~ **my while** (me) valió la pena. ~**less** a sin valor. ~**while** /wɜːθˈwaɪl/ a que vale la pena

worthy /ˈwɜːðɪ/ a meritorio; (*respectable*) respetable; (*laudable*) loable

would /wʊd/ v aux. ~ **you come here please?** ¿quieres venir aquí? ~ **you go?** ¿irías tú? **he** ~ **come if he could** vendría si pudiese. **I** ~ **come every day** (*used to*) venía todos los días. **I** ~ **do it** lo haría yo. ~**be** a supuesto

wound¹ /wuːnd/ n herida f. ● vt herir

wound² /waʊnd/ *see* wind²

wove, woven /wəʊv, 'wəʊvn/ *see* **weave**

wow /waʊ/ *int* ¡caramba!

wrangle /'ræŋgl/ *vi* reñir. ● *n* riña *f*

wrap /ræp/ *vt* (*pt* **wrapped**) envolver. **be ~ped up in** (*fig*) estar absorto en. ● *n* bata *f*; (*shawl*) chal *m*. **~per** /-ə(r)/ *n*, **~ping** *n* envoltura *f*

wrath /rɒθ/ *n* ira *f*. **~ful** *a* iracundo

wreath /riːθ/ *n* (*pl* **-ths** /-ðz/) guirnalda *f*; (*for funeral*) corona *f*

wreck /rek/ *n* ruina *f*; (*sinking*) naufragio *m*; (*remains of ship*) buque *m* naufragado. **be a nervous ~** tener los nervios destrozados. ● *vt* hacer naufragar; (*fig*) arruinar. **~age** *n* restos *mpl*; (*of building*) escombros *mpl*

wren /ren/ *n* troglodito *m*

wrench /rentʃ/ *vt* arrancar; (*twist*) torcer. ● *n* arranque *m*; (*tool*) llave *f* inglesa

wrest /rest/ *vt* arrancar (**from** a)

wrestl|e /'resl/ *vi* luchar. **~er** /-ə(r)/ *n* luchador *m*. **~ing** *n* lucha *f*

wretch /retʃ/ *n* desgraciado *m*; (*rascal*) tunante *m & f*. **~ed** *a* miserable; (*weather*) horrible, de perros; (*dog etc*) maldito

wriggle /'rɪgl/ *vi* culebrear. **~ out of** escaparse de. **~ through** deslizarse por. ● *n* serpenteo *m*

wring /rɪŋ/ *vt* (*pt* **wrung**) retorcer. **~ out of** (*obtain from*) arrancar. **~ing wet** empapado

wrinkle /'rɪŋkl/ *n* arruga *f*. ● *vt* arrugar. ● *vi* arrugarse

wrist /rɪst/ *n* muñeca *f*. **~watch** *n* reloj *m* de pulsera

writ /rɪt/ *n* decreto *m* judicial

write /raɪt/ *vt/i* (*pt* **wrote**, *pp* **written**, *pres p* **writing**) escribir. **~ down** *vt* anotar. **~ off** *vt* cancelar; (*fig*) dar por perdido. **~ up** *vt* hacer un reportaje de; (*keep up to date*) poner al día. **~-off** *n* pérdida *f* total. **~r** /-ə(r)/ *n* escritor *m*; (*author*) autor *m*. **~-up** *n* reportaje *m*; (*review*) crítica *f*

writhe /raɪð/ *vi* retorcerse

writing /'raɪtɪŋ/ *n* escribir *m*; (*handwriting*) letra *f*. **in ~** por escrito. **~s** *npl* obras *fpl*. **~-paper** *n* papel *m* de escribir

written /'rɪtn/ *see* **write**

wrong /rɒŋ/ *a* incorrecto; (*not just*) injusto; (*mistaken*) equivocado. **be ~** no tener razón; (*be mistaken*) equivocarse. ● *adv* mal. **go ~** equivocarse; (*plan*) salir mal; (*car etc*) estropearse. ● *n* injusticia *f*; (*evil*) mal *m*. **in the ~** equivocado. ● *vt* ser injusto con. **~ful** *a* injusto. **~ly** *adv* mal; (*unfairly*) injustamente

wrote /rəʊt/ *see* **write**

wrought /rɔːt/ *a*. **~ iron** *n* hierro *m* forjado

wrung /rʌŋ/ *see* **wring**

wry /raɪ/ *a* (**wryer, wryest**) torcido; (*smile*) forzado. **~ face** *n* mueca *f*

X

xenophobia /zenə'fəʊbɪə/ *n* xenofobia *f*

Xerox /'zɪərɒks/ *n* (*P*) fotocopiadora *f*. **xerox** *n* fotocopia *f*

Xmas /'krɪsməs/ *n abbr* (*Christmas*) Navidad *f*, Navidades *fpl*

X-ray /'eksreɪ/ *n* radiografía *f*. **~s** *npl* rayos *mpl* X. ● *vt* radiografiar

xylophone /'zaɪləfəʊn/ *n* xilófono *m*

Y

yacht /jɒt/ *n* yate *m*. **~ing** *n* navegación *f* a vela

yam /jæm/ *n* ñame *m*, batata *f*

yank /jæŋk/ *vt* (*fam*) arrancar violentamente

Yankee /'jæŋkɪ/ *n* (*fam*) yanqui *m & f*

yap /jæp/ *vi* (*pt* **yapped**) (*dog*) ladrar

yard[1] /jɑːd/ *n* (*measurement*) yarda *f* (= 0.9144 *metre*)

yard[2] /jɑːd/ *n* patio *m*; (*Amer, garden*) jardín *m*

yardage /'jɑːdɪdʒ/ *n* metraje *m*

yardstick /'jɑːdstɪk/ *n* (*fig*) criterio *m*

yarn /jɑːn/ *n* hilo *m*; (*tale, fam*) cuento *m*

yashmak /'jæʃmæk/ *n* velo *m*

yawn /jɔːn/ *vi* bostezar. ● *n* bostezo *m*

year /jɪə(r)/ *n* año *m*. **be three ~s old** tener tres años. **~book** *n* anuario *m*. **~ling** /'jɜːlɪŋ/ *n* primal *m*. **~ly** *a* anual. ● *adv* anualmente

yearn /jɜːn/ *vi*. **~ for** anhelar. **~ing** *n* ansia *f*

yeast /jiːst/ *n* levadura *f*

yell /jel/ *vi* gritar. ● *n* grito *m*

yellow /'jeləʊ/ *a* & *n* amarillo (*m*). **~ish** *a* amarillento

yelp /jelp/ *n* gañido *m*. ● *vi* gañir

yen /jen/ *n* muchas ganas *fpl*

yeoman /'jəʊmən/ *n* (*pl* **-men**). **Y~ of the Guard** alabardero *m* de la Casa Real

yes /jes/ *adv* & *n* sí (*m*)

yesterday /'jestədeɪ/ *adv* & *n* ayer (*m*). **the day before ~** anteayer *m*

yet /jet/ *adv* todavía, aún; (*already*) ya. **as ~** hasta ahora. ● *conj* sin embargo

yew /ju:/ *n* tejo *m*

Yiddish /'jɪdɪʃ/ *n* judeoalemán *m*

yield /ji:ld/ *vt* producir. ● *vi* ceder. ● *n* producción *f*; (*com*) rendimiento *m*

yoga /'jəʊgə/ *n* yoga *m*

yoghurt /'jɒgət/ *n* yogur *m*

yoke /jəʊk/ *n* yugo *m*; (*of garment*) canesú *m*

yokel /'jəʊkl/ *n* patán *m*, palurdo *m*

yolk /jəʊk/ *n* yema *f* (de huevo)

yonder /'jɒndə(r)/ *adv* a lo lejos

you /ju:/ *pron* (*familiar form*) tú, vos (*Arg*), (*pl*) vosotros, vosotras, ustedes (*LAm*); (*polite form*) usted, (*pl*) ustedes; (*familiar, object*) te, (*pl*) os, les (*LAm*); (*polite, object*) le, la, (*pl*) les; (*familiar, after prep*) ti, (*pl*) vosotros, vosotras, ustedes (*LAm*); (*polite, after prep*) usted, (*pl*) ustedes. **with ~** (*familiar*) contigo, (*pl*) con vosotros, con vosotras, con ustedes (*LAm*); (*polite*) con usted, (*pl*) con ustedes; (*polite reflexive*) consigo. **I know ~** te conozco, le conozco a usted. **you can't smoke here** aquí no se puede fumar

young /jʌŋ/ *a* (-er, -est) joven. **~ lady** *n* señorita *f*. **~ man** *n* joven *m*. **her ~ man** (*boyfriend*) su novio *m*. **the ~** *npl* los jóvenes *mpl*; (*of animals*) la cría *f*. **~ster** /'jʌŋstə(r)/ *n* joven *m*

your /jɔ:(r)/ *a* (*familiar*) tu, (*pl*) vuestro; (*polite*) su

yours /jɔ:z/ *poss pron* (el) tuyo, (*pl*) (el) vuestro, el de ustedes (*LAm*); (*polite*) el suyo. **a book of ~s** un libro tuyo, un libro suyo. **Y~s faithfully, Y~s sincerely** le saluda atentamente

yourself /jɔ:'self/ *pron* (*pl* **yourselves**) (*familiar, subject*) tú mismo, tú misma, (*pl*) vosotros mismos, vosotras mismas, ustedes mismos (*LAm*), ustedes mismas (*LAm*);

(*polite, subject*) usted mismo, usted misma, (*pl*) ustedes mismos, ustedes mismas; (*familiar, object*) te, (*pl*) os, se (*LAm*); (*polite, object*) se; (*familiar, after prep*) ti, (*pl*) vosotros, vosotras, ustedes (*LAm*); (*polite, after prep*) sí

youth /ju:θ/ *n* (*pl* **youths** /ju:ðz/) juventud *f*; (*boy*) joven *m*; (*young people*) jóvenes *mpl*. **~ful** *a* joven, juvenil. **~hostel** *n* albergue *m* para jóvenes

yowl /jaʊl/ *vi* aullar. ● *n* aullido *m*

Yugoslav /'ju:gəslɑ:v/ *a* & *n* yugoslavo (*m*). **~ia** /-'slɑ:vɪə/ *n* Yugoslavia *f*

yule /ju:l/ *n*, **yule-tide** /'ju:ltaɪd/ *n* (*old use*) Navidades *fpl*

Z

zany /'zeɪnɪ/ *a* (-ier, -iest) estrafalario

zeal /zi:l/ *n* celo *m*

zealot /'zelət/ *n* fanático *m*

zealous /'zeləs/ *a* entusiasta. **~ly** /'zeləslɪ/ *adv* con entusiasmo

zebra /'zebrə/ *n* cebra *f*. **~ crossing** *n* paso *m* de cebra

zenith /'zenɪθ/ *n* cenit *m*

zero /'zɪərəʊ/ *n* (*pl* **-os**) cero *m*

zest /zest/ *n* gusto *m*; (*peel*) cáscara *f*

zigzag /'zɪgzæg/ *n* zigzag *m*. ● *vi* (*pt* **zigzagged**) zigzaguear

zinc /zɪŋk/ *n* cinc *m*

Zionis|m /'zaɪənɪzəm/ *n* sionismo *m*. **~t** *n* sionista *m* & *f*

zip /zɪp/ *n* cremallera *f*. ● *vt*. **~ (up)** cerrar (la cremallera)

Zip code /'zɪpkəʊd/ *n* (*Amer*) código *m* postal

zip fastener /zɪp'fɑ:snə(r)/ *n* cremallera *f*

zircon /'zɜ:kən/ *n* circón *m*

zither /'zɪðə(r)/ *n* cítara *f*

zodiac /'zəʊdɪæk/ *n* zodiaco *m*

zombie /'zɒmbɪ/ *n* (*fam*) autómata *m* & *f*

zone /zəʊn/ *n* zona *f*

zoo /zu:/ *n* (*fam*) zoo *m*, jardín *m* zoológico. **~logical** /zəʊə'lɒdʒɪkl/ *a* zoológico

zoolog|ist /zəʊ'ɒlədʒɪst/ *n* zoólogo *m*. **~y** /zəʊ'ɒlədʒɪ/ *n* zoología *f*

zoom /zu:m/ *vi* ir a gran velocidad. **~** (*photo*) acercarse rápidamente. **~ past** pasar zumbando. **~ lens** *n* zoom *m*

Zulu /'zu:lu:/ *n* zulú *m* & *f*

Grammar

| Introduction

Spanish is the main language of twenty-one countries and it will soon have 400 million speakers, so anyone who knows both it and English can communicate with a significant proportion of the Earth's inhabitants. Since each Spanish-speaking country has its own accents, colloquialisms and peculiarities of grammar and vocabulary, and since no one agrees about which country speaks the best Spanish, it is occasionally a problem to know which words foreign students should learn. For example, a ball-point pen is **un bolígrafo** in Spain, **una birome** in Argentina, **un lapicero** in Peru and Central America, **un esfero** in Colombia and **una pluma** or **una pluma atómica** in Mexico, although in this, as in many similar cases, the word used in Spain is understood by many people everywhere.

This problem should not be exaggerated. The problem of variety mainly affects familiar or popular vocabulary and slang. Variations in Spanish pronunciation are no great problem: they never amount to more than fairly minor regional differences of accent, so one does not run into the kind of problem that can face Americans or Englishmen in the countryside of Scotland or Ireland. The basic grammar of Spanish is moreover amazingly uniform considering the tremendous size of the Spanish-speaking world. And, above all, virtually everybody—except perhaps in remote villages—knows generally-used words. For example, Mexicans often say **cuate** for *friend*, but they all know and also use the word **amigo**, just as Americans who say *buddy* and Britons and Australians who say *chum*, *pal* or *mate* all share the common word *friend*—which is obviously the word any foreign learner of English would learn first.

As far as possible the examples given in this book avoid regional forms and reflect the sort of Spanish used in the media and by educated people when talking to people from other Spanish-speaking countries. Nevertheless, where differences are unavoidable the language used is that of Spain and important Latin-American variants are noted where they arise. As a result this basic grammar should be equally useful to students of the Spanish of Europe and of Latin America.

Grammatical terms written with capital letters (e.g. Subjunctive, Indicative, Mood) are explained in the Glossary on p.320. The description of pronunciation given on pp. 214–221 is rather more detailed than is usual in this kind of book, since many of the pocket grammars, dictionaries and phrase-books on sale in the English-speaking world contain badly misleading accounts of the sounds of Spanish.

Incorrect forms —i.e. forms that learners must avoid — appear in bold italics and are marked with an asterisk, e.g. *'*quizá viene mañana*' for the correct **quizá venga mañana** *perhaps he's coming tomorrow*.

The American-English spelling 'preterit' (British 'preterite') is used throughout the book. In other cases where American and British English spelling differs, both forms are shown, e.g. *flavor/*(British *flavour*).

Contents

| Contents

| Contents

Contents

Contents

Verbs

Spanish verbs have different forms that show *Tense*[1]
(Present, Future, various kinds of Past Tense,

[1] Grammatical terms beginning with a capital letter are defined in the Glossary on p. 320.

Conditional, etc.), *Mood* (Indicative, Imperative or Subjunctive), *Person* (first, second or third) and *Number* (singular or plural). There are also three Non-Finite Forms of verbs: the *Gerund*, the *Past Participle* and the *Infinitive*. The latter, which always ends in **-r**, is the Dictionary Form of the verb.

FORMS OF VERBS

The various forms of Spanish Regular and Irregular verbs are shown on pp. 239–302.

■ Tense

Spanish tenses are of two basic kinds: Simple Tenses, consisting of a single word, and Compound Tenses, consisting of an appropriate form of the verb **haber** plus a Past Participle:

Simple Tenses	**bebo**, **beberé**, **bebí** *I drink, I'll drink, I drank*
Compound Tenses	**he bebido**, **había bebido** *I have drunk, I had drunk*

All the various tenses of verbs can also appear in the Continuous Form, made from the verb **estar** *to be* plus the Gerund, which always ends in **-ndo**:

estoy bebiendo *I'm (in the middle of) drinking*
estaba bebiendo *I was drinking*
he estado bebiendo *I have been drinking*

The Continuous form is discussed further on pp.13–16.

■ Mood

Verbs appear either in the Indicative Mood, used for making statements as explained on p.18, the Subjunctive Mood, explained on pp.20–35, or the Imperative Mood, which is used for making orders or requests and is explained on pp. 36–40.

■ Person and Number

Spanish verbs are unlike English verbs in that their endings show the Person and Number of their Subject:

hablo *I speak*   **hablamos** *we speak*

hablas *you speak*   **habláis** (Spain only) *you (plural) speak*

habla *he/she speaks, you* (singular) *speak*   **hablan** *they/you* (plural) *speak*

As a result, a verb on its own can form a Spanish sentence: **voy** means *I'm going*, **duermen** means *they're sleeping*. The Spanish words for *I, you, he/she/it, we, they* have special uses that are discussed later (p.107).

TYPES OF VERB

As far as the task of learning their various forms is concerned, there are three broad types of Spanish verb:

■ Regular Verbs

The vast majority of Spanish verbs are regular. If one knows the endings of the various tense forms and the spelling rules shown on p.249, one can predict every form of every regular verb.

Regular verbs are divided into three Conjugations according to whether their Infinitive ends in **-ar**, **-er** or **-ir**. Three commonly encountered regular verbs are **hablar** *to speak* (first conjugation), **beber** *to drink* (second conjugation), **vivir** *to live* (third conjugation). The various forms of these three verbs in all their tenses are shown on pp.239–249, and these forms should be learned first.

■ Radical Changing Verbs

The endings of Radical Changing Verbs are the same as for regular verbs, but their stem vowels change in certain forms, cf. **dormir** *to sleep*, **duermo** *I sleep*, **durmió** *he slept*, etc. These irregularities appear only in the Present Tenses (Indicative and Subjunctive), in the **tú** Imperative and, in the case of some -**ir** verbs, in the Preterit, the Imperfect Subjunctive and the Gerund. Radical changing verbs are quite numerous and many are in everyday use. The most important are listed on pp.253–302.

■ Irregular verbs

Some Spanish verbs are truly irregular: some of their forms are unpredictable and must be learned separately. These verbs are not very numerous, but they include the most common verbs in the language like 'to go', 'to come', 'to be', 'to have', 'to put', and they must therefore be memorized thoroughly. The irregularities are usually most obvious in the Present Indicative and the Preterit: with some exceptions one can usually predict most of the other forms from these two sets of forms.

Irregular verbs are listed on pp.253–302.

USES OF THE INDICATIVE TENSES

Present Indicative Tense

Present Indicative forms like **hablo, bebes, vivimos** mean *I speak, you drink, we live* and also *I'm speaking, you're drinking, we're living*. They are also often used for future actions and occasionally for past ones as well. This imprecision can sometimes be removed by using the Present Continuous forms of the verb to stress the idea that an action is actually in progress in the present: see p.13.

The main uses of the simple Present Indicative tense are:

■ To show that an action happens habitually or is timeless (i.e. is an eternal truth):

> **Me peino todos los días** *I do my hair every day* (habit)
>
> **Los españoles comen mucho ajo** *The Spanish eat a lot of garlic* (habit)
>
> **Trabajas demasiado** *You work too much* (habit)
>
> **El carbón de piedra produce calor** *Coal produces heat* (timeless)

■ To show that something is happening in the present:

> **Hoy hace mucho calor** *It's very hot today*
>
> **¿Qué haces hoy?** *What are you doing today?*
>
> **¡Cómo llueve!** *Look at the rain!* (literally *how it's raining*)
>
> **Nos hospedamos en el Hotel Palace** *We're staying at the Palace Hotel*

It is more appropriate to use the Present Continuous if we need to stress the fact that the action is in progress *at this very moment*:

> **Roberto está pintando la puerta** *Roberto is (in the middle of) painting the door*

■ To show that an event is imminent, i.e. is just about to happen:

> **¡Socorro! ¡Que me caigo!** *Help! I'm falling!*
>
> **¿Le pago ahora?** *Do I pay you now?/Shall I pay you now?*
>
> **¡Que se va el tren!** *The train's leaving!*
>
> **¿Vienes conmigo?** *Are you coming with me?*

■ To show that an event in the future is scheduled or pre-arranged. In this case it is often like the English present form ending in *-ing* in *next year* **we're going** to Miami:

> **La fiesta es mañana a las ocho** *The party's tomorrow at eight o'clock*

Te llamo esta noche a las nueve *I'll call you tonight at nine*

En diciembre voy a París *In December I'm going to Paris*

El avión sale mañana a las ocho *The plane leaves tomorrow at eight*

■ As a past tense (the 'Historic Present'). The present is often used as an alternative to the Preterit tense to make narrative in the past sound exciting. This is found both in formal literary styles and in informal speech:

Unos días después empieza la Guerra Civil *A few days later the Civil War began* (literally *begins*)

Entra y me dice . . . *She/He comes in and says to me . . .* (familiar style)

■ The present tense is also used in sentences of the type '*I've spoken/been speaking French since I was a girl*', '*it's the first time we've seen her in years*'. See p.205.

The Preterit Tense

■ To look back on an event as completed in the past. It is therefore used to report the fact that event A happened and *finished*, *then* event B happened, *then* event C, and so on.

Se sentó, sacó un cigarrillo y lo encendió *He sat down, took out a cigarette and lit it*

Anoche vi dos veces a tu madre *I saw your mother twice last night*

Fue intérprete y después profesor *He was an interpreter and then a teacher*

El viernes estuve en casa de la abuela *on Friday I visited grandmother's house*

■ For events that lasted for a specific period of time and then ended:

Fue presidente durante ocho años *He was President for eight years*

Su enfermedad duró varios meses *Her/his illness lasted several months*

Estuve esperando varias horas or **Esperé varias horas** *I waited several hours* (the Continuous stresses the action as long drawn-out)

English speakers often have difficulty in distinguishing between the Preterit and the Imperfect (see next section), especially in sentences of the following kind:

Tuve que decírselo *I had to tell it to him* (and I did)

Tenía que decírselo *I had to tell it to him* (I may or may not have done)

Fue un día magnífico *It was a magnificent day* (all day)

Era un día magnífico *It was a lovely day* (at the time, but perhaps it rained later during the day)

The last example shows how the Preterit of *ser*—**fue**—indicates a different point of view compared with the Imperfect **era**. The Preterit looks back on the event after it finished, whereas the Imperfect describes an event while it was still going on. This is clear in English with most verbs other than *to be*. Compare *what **did you do** in the garden yesterday?* (looks back on the event as finished, therefore Preterit: **¿qué hiciste ayer en el jardín?**) and *what **were you doing** in the garden yesterday?* (the action is described as not yet finished at the time, therefore Imperfect: **¿qué hacías ayer en el jardín?**).

The Imperfect Tense

■ To show that an event was not yet completed. The Imperfect is therefore used for events that *were continuing* when something else happened:

Ignacio estaba en la habitación cuando se hundió el techo *Ignacio was in the room when the roof caved in*

Llovía muy fuerte, así que cerré la ventana *It was raining very hard, so I shut the window*

Esta puerta era azul *This door was blue* (i.e. at the time)

Ana tenía diecinueve años cuando se casó *Ana was nineteen when she got married*

Cuando yo era pequeño yo adoraba a mi madre *When I was little I adored my mother*

As these examples show, the Imperfect gives us no clear information about whether the event continued or when it ended: Ignacio probably left the room after the roof collapsed, but the point is that he was still there when it happened. As a general rule, if an English verb can be rewritten using *was* and the *-ing* form, Spanish will use the Imperfect: **Ana llevaba una falda azul cuando la vi** *Ana was wearing a blue skirt when I saw her*. But, as the examples above show, this rule does not usually apply to the verb *to be*.

■ To express habitual or timeless events in the past, i.e. events that had no clearly defined end even though they may no longer be happening now:

De niño yo tenía ojos azules *I had/used to have blue eyes as a child*

Mi madre era vegetariana *My mother was/used to be a vegetarian*

Yo iba todos los días a casa de mi amigo *I went/used to go to my friend's house every day*

Londres era más grande que Nueva York *London was/used to be bigger than New York*

As a general rule, if the meaning of the English verb can be expressed by the formula *used to . . .* Spanish will use the Imperfect Tense.

■ To denote something that was just going to happen (usually the same as **iba a . . .** *was going to*):

> **Yo me marchaba cuando sonó el teléfono** *I was leaving when the phone rang*

The Perfect Tense

Spanish distinguishes between the Perfect Tense and the Preterit, much the same as English does between the Perfect *I have seen* and the Simple Past *I saw*. The Perfect Tense is common in written styles everywhere and it is constantly heard in speech in Spain, but in some Latin-American varieties of spoken Spanish the Preterit may more or less completely replace the Perfect, although practice varies from country to country. The Perfect Tense is used:

■ For past events that have happened in a period of time that has not yet ended. Compare **fui dos veces el año pasado** *I went twice **last** year* and **he ido dos veces este año** *I **have been** twice **this** year* (this year hasn't ended yet):

> **La bolsa ha subido mucho hoy** *The stock market has gone up a lot today*
> **Ha llovido menos durante este siglo** *It has rained less this century*
> **No han contestado todavía** *They haven't replied yet*
> **Hemos estado trabajando toda la mañana** *We've been working all morning*

Latin Americans often use the Preterit in this context:

la bolsa subió mucho hoy, no contestaron todavía, estuvimos trabajando . . . , etc.

■ To show that the effects of a past event linger in or are relevant to the present. Compare **estuvo enfermo** *he was unwell* (in the past, but now he's recovered) and **ha estado enfermo** *he's been unwell* (that's why he's pale, late for work, irritable, etc.):

> **Alguien ha fumado/ha estado fumando en esta habitación. Huele a humo** *Someone has smoked/been smoking in this room. It smells of smoke*
>
> **Está contento porque lo/le² han ascendido** *He's pleased because they've promoted him*

Latin Americans may also prefer the Preterit tense in these cases.

■ In Spain, optionally, to show that an event happened today (i.e. since midnight). This is the 'Perfect of Recency':

> **Me he levantado temprano** *I got up early (today)*
>
> **Quién ha llamado?** *Who phoned (just now)?*
>
> **Perdona, no he podido hacerlo** *Sorry, I couldn't do it (today)*
>
> **Hemos ido al parque esta mañana** *We went to the park this morning*

If the event is very recent, the Perfect is usual in Spain, but for events earlier in the day the Preterit or the Perfect may be used. Latin Americans use the Preterit: **me levanté temprano, ¿Quién llamó?**, etc.

---

² **Lo/le** shows that either pronoun can be used here for *him*, **lo** being more common in Latin America, and **le** preferred in Spain (although **lo** is also widely used).

The Pluperfect Tense

In general, the same as the English Pluperfect form (*had* + Past Participle), i.e. to show that an event in the past had finished before the next one started:

> **Ya habían dejado dos mensajes en el contestador cuando yo llegué** *They had already left two messages on the answering machine when I arrived*
>
> **La policía encontró el revólver que el asesino había comprado dos días antes** *The police found the revolver that the murderer had bought two days before*

The Future Tense

As was mentioned earlier, future time can be expressed by the simple Present Tense when the event is felt to be pre-scheduled or pre-arranged: **la película empieza a las ocho** *The film starts at eight*. Furthermore, the Future Tense forms shown here are often replaced by **ir a** + the Infinitive in informal styles, especially in Latin-American speech, e.g. **si me habla de esa manera, me enojaré** *if he talks like that to me I'll get angry* becomes **si me habla de esa manera, me voy a enojar/voy a enojarme**[3].

The Future Tense is used:

■ For future events that are not pre-scheduled or fixtures:

> **Algún día se casará con ella** *He'll marry her one day*
>
> **Ya te cansarás** *You'll get tired eventually/in the end*

[3] In Spain **enfadarse** is the normal word for *to get angry*.

Para entonces yo ya no estaré aquí *By then I won't be here any more*

■ For approximations, guesses and suppositions:

Miguel tendrá unos cincuenta años *(I guess) Miguel's about fifty*

Estará durmiendo a estas horas *(I guess) he'll be sleeping at this time*

Latin Americans tend to prefer the construction **deber** or **deber de** + Infinitive (which is also used in Spain): **debe (de) tener unos cincuenta años, debe (de) estar durmiendo . . .** The **de** is often dropped, but learners should retain it so as to distinguish between suppositions and obligations. Compare **debes hacerlo** *you've got to do it* (obligation).

■ In questions, to express wonder or amazement:

¿Qué habrá sido de él? *What (on earth) can have happened to him?*

¿Quién será éste? *I wonder who this is?*

The Conditional Tense

■ As an equivalent of the English *would* form in conditions:

En ese caso te dejarían en paz *In that case they would leave you in peace*

El pastel estaría mejor con menos azúcar *The cake would be better with less sugar*

Eso sí costaría más! *That **would** cost more!*

■ With **poder, querer,** to make polite requests or express polite wishes:

¿Podría usted abrir la ventana un poquito? *Could you open the window a bit?*

> **Querría terminarlo antes de las ocho** *I'd like to finish it before eight*

■ To express the future in the past (i.e. the same as **iba a** + Infinitive):

> **Aquel día empezó la que sería su última película** *That day he began what would be his last film*
>
> **Yo sabía que no me devolvería el dinero** *I knew he wouldn't/wasn't going to give the money back to me*

■ To express guesses or suppositions about the past:

> **Aquella semana la habríamos visto más de cinco veces** *That week we must have seen her more than five times*
>
> **Pesaría unos cien kilos** *It must have weighed about 100 kilos*

Deber or (preferably) **deber de** + Infinitive is more usual in this construction: **debía de pesar más de cien kilos**.

Note: the **-ra** form of the Imperfect Subjunctive is constantly found as an alternative for the Conditional of **haber** and **querer**:

> **Te hubiera/habría ayudado antes** *I would have helped you sooner*
>
> **Quisiera/querría verte mañana** *I'd like to see you tomorrow*

Continuous Forms of the Tenses

Spanish Continuous forms of the tenses (all formed with **estar** + the Gerund) either (a) stress that an event is, was or will be actually in progress at the time spoken of, or (b) in the case of the Preterit and Perfect Tenses, show that it continued for a certain amount of time in the past before ending.

As far as the Present, Imperfect and Future Continuous Tenses are concerned, English-speakers must remember to use the Continuous only for events actually *in progress*. The following is definitely *not* good Spanish: **'mañana estoy viajando a Los Ángeles'* *tomorrow I'm (in the middle of) traveling* (British *travelling*) *to Los Angeles,* correctly **mañana viajo a Los Ángeles.**

The Continuous is used:

■ In all tenses except the Preterit, Perfect and Pluperfect, to stress that an event is, was or will be actually in progress. Usually the non-Continuous tenses can also be used, but the Continuous is preferred nowadays when the event is actually in progress at the time:

> **Esto se está convirtiendo en una pesadilla** *This is turning into a nightmare*
>
> **Yo estaba durmiendo cuando sonó el despertador** *I was sleeping when the alarm clock went off*
>
> **Miguel está leyendo** *Miguel's reading*
>
> **Lo que pasó fue que ella estaba deseando irse** *What happened was that she wanted/was wanting to leave*
>
> **No puedes ir a las cinco porque estarás haciendo tus deberes** *You can't go at five o'clock because you'll be doing you're homework*

■ To show that an event is surprising or temporary:

> **¡¿Pero qué tonterías le has estado contando?!** *But what nonsense have you been telling him?!*
>
> **Es una zapatería, pero últimamente están vendiendo periódicos** *It's a shoe-shop, but lately they're selling newspapers*

María estaba trabajando de intérprete *Maria was working as an interpreter* (at the time, temporarily)

■ To emphasize the idea of repetitive actions that are or were still continuing:

Está bebiendo mucho últimamente *He's drinking a lot lately*

Siempre estaba pensando en ella *He was always thinking of her*

■ In the Preterit, Perfect or Pluperfect Tenses, to show that an event (a) lasted a certain length of time and (b) that it finished:

Anoche estuvimos viendo la televisión *We watched TV last night*

Te he estado esperando toda la mañana *I've been waiting for you all morning*

Había estado leyendo durante horas *He had been reading for hours*

Here the non-Continuous forms **vimos, he esperado, había leído** would not emphasize the long drawn-out nature of the events.

The Spanish Continuous *cannot* be used (at least in standard forms of the language):

■ For events that are not actually in progress:

Yo creo que este libro defiende una postura revolucionaria *I think that this book is defending/defends a revolutionary position* (not **está defendiendo**, which means *is in the middle of defending*)

Yo iba a verme con ella al día siguiente *I was seeing her the following day* (it hadn't happened yet)

Vamos mañana *We're going tomorrow* (it hasn't happened yet)

> **Su padre⁴ está enfermo de muerte** *His father is dying* (i.e. he is fatally ill. **Está muriendo** would mean that he is actually dying at this moment)
>
> **Está sentado** *He's sitting down* (**está sentándose** has the unlikely meaning *he's in the middle of sitting down*)

■ Normally, for events that are not really actions but conditions or states:

> **Llevaba una pajarita de seda** *He was wearing a silk bow-tie*
>
> **Parecías más joven aquella noche** *You were looking younger that night*
>
> **Un aroma delicado flotaba en el aire** *A delicate smell was floating in the air*

■ Never with the verb **estar**. One cannot say *'*estar estando*', although **estar siendo** occasionally occurs:

> **Está siendo debatido en este momento** *It's being debated at this moment*

■ In standard varieties of Spanish, the Continuous is not used with the verbs **ir** *to go* and **venir** *to come*:

> **¿Adónde van ustedes?** *Where are you going?*
>
> **Ya vienen** *They're coming*

Less Common Tense Forms

The following forms are occasionally found, all of them (except for **tengo hecho**, etc.) being more common in writing than in speech:

■ **Tener** 'to have' is sometimes used to form compound tenses instead of **haber**. This is only possible if the verb

---

⁴ Latin Americans tend to use **papá** for *father* and **mamá** for *mother*, but these words mean *daddy* and *mummy* in Spain.

has a direct object, and the difference between **lo he ter-minado** and **lo tengo terminado** is about the same as between *I've finished it* and *I've **got it** finished*: the latter emphasizes successful completion or acquisition of something—

> **Ya tengo pintadas tres de las paredes** *I've got three of the walls painted*
>
> **Ya tenemos compradas las flores** *We've got the flowers bought/We've bought the flowers*

As the examples show, the past participle agrees in number and gender with the direct object of the verb.

■ The **-ra** form, used for the Imperfect Subjunctive in normal styles, is often found in flowery writing, but not in spoken Spanish, as an alternative for the Pluperfect in Relative Clauses. This is especially common in Latin America but is gaining ground in Spain:

> **Se casó con la que** *fuera* **la esposa de su padre** *He married the woman who had been his father's wife* (everyday style . . . **había sido la esposa . . .**)

■ **-ra** forms (and sometimes also **-se** forms) of verbs frequently appear after **después de que** *after* and **desde que** *since* instead of the Preterit tense:

> **Este es el primer discurso que pronuncia desde que lo/le nombraran presidente** *This is the first speech he has delivered since he was appointed President*

This use of the **-ra** forms rather than the Preterit after **desde que** and **después de que** is the preferred construction in Spain, but the Preterit is possible, as this example from the Colombian novelist Gabriel García Márquez shows:

> **. . . su simple evocación le causaba un estremecimiento de pavor hasta mucho después**

> **de que se casó, y tuvo hijos** . . . *the mere mention of him caused her a shudder of fear until long after she had married and had children*

However, the Subjunctive is obligatory after **después de que** and **desde que** when they point to events that are or were still in the future. See pp.29–30.

■ The Preterit of **haber** + the Past Participle is occasionally used to form the Anterior Preterit tense (**Pretérito anterior**). This is found only in literary styles before words meaning *as soon as* or *when*, to emphasize that an event *had just* finished before the next started. It can be replaced by the Pluperfect or, much more commonly, by the Preterit:

> **Apenas hubo terminado la cena, todos los invitados se fueron** *Scarcely had supper finished when all the guests departed* (more usually **apenas terminó** . . .)

MOOD

The Indicative Mood

The uses of the various tenses of the Indicative Mood have already been discussed. The Indicative Mood is overwhelmingly the most commonly used verbal mood: in most types of Spanish well over 85% of the verbs are in the Indicative mood.

The Indicative is used:

■ In all Main Clauses (see Glossary) other than those that give orders (which require the Imperative mood):

> **En invierno no hacía mucho frío** *It wasn't very cold in Winter*

> **No me gusta el sabor de la cerveza** *I don't like the taste of beer*
>
> **Me voy a comprar unos zapatos** *I'm going to buy some shoes*

■ In Subordinate Clauses after statements meaning *it is true/correct/a fact/certain* **that** . . .

> **Es verdad/cierto/correcto/un hecho que los limones son agrios** *It's true/certain/correct/a fact that lemons are sour*

But the Subjunctive is normally used when such statements are negated or denied: **no es cierto que los limones *sean* dulces** *It isn't true that lemons are sweet.*

■ After statements that express beliefs or opinions:

> **Creo que llegan el martes** *I think that they're coming on Tuesday*
>
> **Parece que no pudo solucionarlo** *It seems he didn't manage to solve it*

Again, the Subjunctive is normally used when such statements are denied: **no creo que *lleguen* el martes** *I don't think they're coming on Tuesday*

■ When the clause is introduced by a Subordinator (see Glossary) that refers to a time when the action has or had happened: compare **yo estaba viendo la televisión cuando llegaron**[5] *I was watching TV when they arrived.* This is discussed below on pp.29 ff.

■ In Relative Clauses, when the antecedent (the thing referred to by the Relative Pronoun) is known to exist (see p.34):

> **Conozco una cafetería donde sirven té inglés** *I know a café where they serve English tea*

[5] In Spain one usually says **ver la televisión** *to 'see' TV*, although **mirar** *'to watch'* is heard in Latin America

▣ After **si** *if* in 'open' conditions: **si llueve me quedo en casa** *if it rains I'm staying at home*. Conditional Sentences are explained on p.40.

The Subjunctive Mood

The basic function of the Subjunctive is not to make statements of fact, but either (a) to show that the speaker is reacting emotionally in some way to the event referred to or (b) that the event mentioned in a Subordinate Clause is still not a reality (e.g. because it hasn't happened yet). Most learners of Spanish postpone the Subjunctive until the last moment, but there are good reasons for tackling it early, since it is common in all styles of language.

The Subjunctive can be explained under five headings:

(a) Cases in which it appears in Subordinate Clauses (see Glossary) introduced by **que**, following some statement indicating want, necessity, possibility, emotional reaction, fear, doubt, etc.

(b) Cases in which it appears after a number of words which are mostly Subordinators (see Glossary), for example **cuando** *when*, **apenas** *scarcely*, **quizá** *perhaps*, **posiblemente** *possibly*, **antes de que** *before*, **después de que** *after*, **con tal de que** *provided that*, etc . . .

(c) Cases in which it appears in Relative Clauses, e.g. **quiero comprar una casa que** *tenga* **muchas ventanas** *I want to buy a house that has a lot of windows*.

(d) Cases in which the Subjunctive can appear in the Main Clause of a sentence, i.e. cases in which the Subjunctive could stand as the first word in a sentence (rare—the Imperative excepted).

(e) Cases in which it appears in the if-clause of Conditional Sentences, e.g. **si** *tuviera* **más tiempo lo**

haría mejor *if I had more time I'd do it better.* This is discussed on p.40.

Forms of the subjunctive

The Subjunctive has three simple tense forms (the fourth tense form, the Future Subjunctive, is virtually obsolete. See below).

Present:

> **(que) yo hable** *that I should speak . . .*
> **(que) él diga** *that he should say . . .*

-ra Past:

> **(que) yo fuera** *that I should have been . . .*
> **(que) usted pensara** *that you should have thought . . .*

-se Past:

> **(que) yo fuese** *that I should have been . . .*
> **(que) usted pensase** *that you should have thought . . .*

The Subjunctive can also appear in compound tenses:

Perfect:

> **(que) yo haya hablado** *that I should have spoken . . .*
> **(que) él haya dicho** *that he should have said . . .*

Pluperfect:

> **(que) yo hubiera/hubiese hablado** *that I should have spoken* (before then)
> **(que) él hubiera/hubiese dicho** *that he should have said* (before then)

Continuous forms are also possible, e.g. **(que) yo esté hablando** *that I should be (in the middle of) speaking,* etc.

These are formed from the appropriate tense of the Subjunctive of **estar** + the Gerund.

The English translations shown above are very approximate and misleading. The Spanish Subjunctive cannot usually be translated clearly into English since the latter language has lost most of its Subjunctive forms.

■ The Future Subjunctive

This is virtually obsolete. It is formed by replacing the last **a** in the -ra Imperfect Subjunctive by **e**: **hablare hablares hablare habláremos hablareis hablaren, comiere, comieres, comiere, comiéremos, comiereis, comieren**, etc.

It is nowadays rarely seen outside legal documents and similar very formal texts. In all other cases it is replaced by the Present or Imperfect Subjunctive, so foreign learners will not need to use it.

■ Equivalence of the **-ra** and **-se** Subjunctives

When they are used as Subjunctives, the -ra forms and the -se forms are interchangeable, the -ra forms being nowadays much more frequent than the -se forms:

> **Yo quería que me *llamaras* = Yo quería que me *llamases* I wanted you to call me**

In this book, unless otherwise stated, whenever the -ra form appears the -se form could have been used, and vice-versa.

Tense Agreement with the Subjunctive

The basic rules, which apply to ninety per cent of Spanish sentences, are:

Tense of verb in Main Clause	*Tense of Subjunctive in Subordinate Clause*
Present	Present
Future	" "
Perfect	Present (sometimes Imperfect)
Conditional	Imperfect (-ra or -se)
Imperfect	" "
Preterit	" "
Pluperfect	" "

Es/será/ha sido necesario que vengas *It is/will be/has been necessary for you to come*
Sería/era/fue/había sido necesario que vinieras/vinieses *It would be/was/had been necessary for you to come*

Replacement of a finite verb by an infinitive

When the subject of the Main Clause in a sentence and the subject of the Subordinate Clause refer to the same person or thing, the Infinitive is often used and not the Finite verb form: **quiero hacerlo** *I want to do it* (**yo** is the subject of both **querer** and **hacer**), but **quiero que él lo haga** *I want him to do it*.

In this respect English differs sharply from Spanish in allowing the Infinitive to refer to a new subject: *I prefer him to go*. The fact that Spanish does not allow this (with the few exceptions mentioned below) is the chief reason why it constantly uses the Subjunctive: **yo prefiero que él vaya**.

The use of the Infinitive is also found after certain Subordinators (note the appearance of **que** when the Infinitive is not used):

¿Te voy a ver antes de irme? *Will I see you before I go?*

¿Te voy a ver antes de que te vayas? *Will I see you before **you** go?*

Lo hizo sin darse cuenta *He did it without realizing*

Lo hizo sin que yo me diera cuenta *He did it without **my** realizing*

Other Subordinators that allow this are:

con tal de (que) *provided that*
después de (que) *after*
en caso de (que) *in the event of*
hasta (que) *until*
para (que)/a (que) *in order to*
a pesar de (que) *in spite of*

But most Subordinators require a Finite verb form (Subjunctive or Indicative) whether the subjects are the same or not:

Lo haré cuando termine esto *I'll do it when I finish (or he/she/you finish(es)) this* (never *'**lo haré cuando terminar esto**')

Nos vamos en cuanto/apenas terminemos esto *We're going as soon as we finish this*

No digo nada, aunque sé la verdad *I'm saying nothing although I know the truth*

Lo hace bien porque sabe mucho *He does it well because he knows a lot*

The rules that determine whether the Finite verb is in the Indicative or Subjunctive are discussed below.

Subjunctive in clauses introduced by *que*

The Subjunctive is required in Subordinate Clauses after the word **que** when this word is introduced by a statement meaning:

■ Wanting, wishing, requesting

> **Quiero que me contestes** *I want you to answer*
> **Estaba deseando que se fueran** *He was wanting them to go*
> **Mi sueño de que mi hijo fuera médico** *My dream that my son would be a doctor*
> **Pidió que lo/le dejaran en paz** *He asked them to leave him in peace*
> **Prefiero que ustedes me lo entreguen a domicilio** *I prefer you to deliver it to me at home*

■ Ordering, obliging, causing, recommending, insisting

> **Le dijeron que se quedara** *They told him to stay*
> **Les ordenó que cargasen sus fusiles** *He ordered them to load their rifles*
> **El médico le recomendó que dejara de fumar** *The doctor recommended him to stop smoking*
> **Hizo que se quedaran en casa** *He made them stay at home*
> **Insistió en que se hiciera así** *He insisted that it should be done like this*

The verbs **ordenar, mandar, hacer, recomendar, aconsejar** *to advise*, **obligar** *to oblige* can optionally take the Infinitive: **les ordenó/mandó apagar las luces** or **ordenó/mandó que apagaran las luces** *he ordered them to put out the lights*; **los hizo quedarse en casa** *he made them stay at home*; **te recomiendo no hacerlo** *I recommend you not to do it*.

Decir que with the indicative mood means *to tell (i.e. inform) someone that*: **le dijeron que se quedaba** *they told him he that he was staying*.

■ Allowing and forbidding

> **No permito que mi hija viaje sola** *I don't allow my daughter to travel alone*

Les prohíbe que fumen en casa *He forbids them to smoke at home*

And similarly **dejar** *to let*, **tolerar/aguantar** *to tolerate*, **oponerse a que** *to oppose*. However, **permitir, prohibir** and **dejar** also allow the infinitive construction: **no le permito/dejo a mi hija viajar sola, les prohíbe fumar en casa**

■ Needing

Es necesario/preciso que nos pongamos en contacto con ellos *It's necessary that we contact them*
Hace falta que trabajen más *They need to work more*

■ Possibility and impossibility

Es posible/probable/previsible que no lo terminen a tiempo *It's possible/probable/likely that they won't finish it on time*
No puede ser que tenga tanto dinero *It can't be (possible) that he's got so much money*

Use of the subjunctive with words meaning *perhaps* is discussed later in this section.

■ Emotional reactions, e.g. surprise, pleasure, displeasure, puzzlement

Me irrita que tengas esa actitud *It irritates me that you have that attitude*
Fue increíble que no se diesen cuenta *It was incredible that they didn't realize*
Estoy hasta la coronilla de que siempre tengamos tanto trabajo *I'm sick to death of the fact that we have so much work*
Siento mucho que no puedan venir *I'm sorry you/they can't come*

Nos extrañaba que no hubiese escrito *It puzzled us that he hadn't written*

■ The verb **quejarse de que** *to complain that* usually takes the Indicative: **siempre se queja de que tiene frío** *he's always complaining that he feels cold.*

■ Value judgments, i.e. any phrase meaning *it's good/bad that . . .* , *it's natural/logical/preferable/undesirable/satisfying that . . .* , etc.:

Conviene que llueva de vez en cuando *It's good that it rains from time to time*

Era absurdo que lo dejasen sin pintar *It was absurd for them to leave it unpainted*

Es natural que usted se sienta cansado *It's natural that you should feel tired*

Es importante que sepamos la verdad *It's important for us to know the truth*

The expression **menos mal que . . .** *it's a good thing that . . .* takes the Indicative: **menos mal que lo hiciste ayer** *it's a good thing you did it yesterday.*

■ Denial of truth, opinion, appearance or knowledge

No es verdad que la haya llamado *It isn't true that he called her*

No parece que esté dispuesta a hacerlo *It doesn't seem that she's prepared to do it*

No creo que sea posible *I don't think it's possible*

No sabía que fueras tan inteligente *I didn't know you were so intelligent*

No es que sea incorrecto, sino que es increíble *It isn't that it's incorrect but that it's incredible*

But these verbs take the indicative when they are positive: **es verdad que la ha llamado** *It's true that he called her*, etc. The indicative is also possible with **no saber que** when the thing referred to is not an opinion but a fact: **no**

sabía que ya había pagado *I didn't know that he'd already paid.*

■ Doubt

>
> **Dudo que sepas hacerlo** *I doubt you know how to do it*

■ Fear

>
> **Temo que la paz no sea posible** *I fear peace isn't possible*
>
> **Tengo miedo de que me muerda ese perro** *I'm scared that dog's going to bite me*

The indicative is usual after **temerse** when it expresses a regret: **me temo que he cometido un error** *I fear I've made a mistake.*

■ Hoping, depending on, sympathizing with, avoiding, explaining the cause of something:

>
> **Espero que ustedes estén bien** *I hope you're well*
>
> **Dependo de que me dé dinero periódicamente** *I depend on him giving me money regularly*
>
> **Esto sólo hacía que él se riera más** *This only made him laugh more*
>
> **Comprendo que no quieras hablar de ello** *I understand you not wanting to talk about it*
>
> **Intentaba evitar que su suegra se enterase** *He was trying to avoid his mother-in-law finding out*
>
> **Esto explicaba el que prefiriera quedarse en casa** *This explained the fact that he preferred to stay at home*

■ *The fact that . . .*

Use of the Subjunctive is common after **el hecho de que** *. . . the fact that*, and also after **el que . . .** or **que . . .** when they mean the same as **el hecho de que**. The question of when the Subjunctive is used after these words is complex, but the general rule is that the Subjunctive is usual except when **el hecho de que** is preceded by a preposition:

> **El hecho de que los gramáticos no siempre estén de acuerdo deja perplejos a muchos estudiantes** *The fact that the grammarians aren't always in agreement leaves many students perplexed*
>
> **El que lo hayamos visto tres veces no puede ser una coincidencia** *The fact that we've seen him/it three times can't be a coincidence*
>
> **Que fuera él quien lo hizo no debería sorprender a nadie** *The fact that he was the one who did it should surprise no one*

but

> **No quiso contestar por el hecho de que no se fiaba de la policía** *He refused to answer due to the fact that he didn't trust the police*

Use of the subjunctive after subordinators

The Subjunctive is required in certain cases after clauses introduced by Subordinators, e.g. words that introduce clauses and mean *when, as soon as, in order to, after, without, as long as*, etc. Most, but not all, of these are phrases that include the word **que**.

The Subjunctive is used after these words whenever the action that follows them has not or had not yet happened at the time referred to in the Main Clause. Compare **me acosté cuando llegó mamá** *I went to bed when* (i.e. *after*) *mother arrived* and **me acostaré cuando llegue mamá** *I'll go to bed when mother arrives* (she hasn't arrived yet).

With some subordinators the Subjunctive is always necessary: these include **antes de que** *before*, **sin que** *without*, **para que** and **a que** *in order to*, **con tal de que** and **a**

condición de que *provided that*. In a few cases the Indicative is always used, but with most subordinators either the Indicative or the Subjunctive is used, according to whether the event has or has not happened at the time:

> **Te llamaré en cuanto/apenas llegue** *I'll call you as soon as I arrive/he arrives*
>
> **Te llamé en cuanto/apenas llegó** *I called you as soon as he arrived*
>
> **Bebíamos champán siempre que nos traía una botella** *We drank champagne whenever he brought us a bottle*
>
> **Beberemos champán siempre que nos traigas una botella** *We'll drink champagne whenever/provided you bring us a bottle*
>
> **Lo compré después de que lo repararon**[6] *I bought it after they fixed it*
>
> **Lo compraré después de que lo reparen/hayan reparado** *I'll buy it after they've fixed it*

The following list includes the most common subordinators. Those marked 'variable' obey the rule just explained, while the others either always or never take the Subjunctive:

> **cuando** *when* (variable)
> **antes de que** *before* (always)
> **después de que** *after* (variable, but see p.17)
> **desde que** *since, from the moment that* (variable, but see p.17)
> **a partir del momento en que** *from the time that* (variable)

---

[6] However, as explained on page 17, the **-ra** form is common in Spain after **después de que** and **desde que** *since*, to refer to any event in the past: **después de que lo repararan, desde que la viera** *since he had seen her*.

según *as* (as in *he answered the letters as they arrived* **contestaba a las cartas según iban lle-gando**) (variable)

a medida que *as* (as **según**, but implies *without delay*; variable)

tan pronto como, nada más, en cuanto, nomás (the latter in Lat. Am. only), **apenas** all meaning *as soon as, scarcely* (variable)

a que, para que, a fin de que, con el objeto de que *in order to* (always)

no sea que, no fuera que *lest, in order that . . . not* (always)

de ahí que *hence the fact that* (always)

sin que *without* (always)

de manera que, de modo que, de forma que *in such a way that, so* (indicating manner or result) (variable)

en caso de que *in the event of . . .* (always)
por si *in case* (usually indicative)
suponiendo que *supposing that* (always)

hasta que *until* (variable)
siempre que *whenever, every time that* (variable)
mientras (que) when it means *provided that, as long as*, always takes the Subjunctive. When it means *while* and refers to some future event it optionally takes the Subjunctive **tú puedes des-cansar mientras que yo trabajo/trabaje** *you can rest while I work;* otherwise it takes the Indicative

con tal de que, siempre que, a condición de que *provided that* (always)

salvo que, excepto que, a menos que *unless* (nearly always take Subjunctive)

aunque *although* takes the Subjunctive when it refers to an uncertainty: **dile que venga aunque esté enfermo** *tell him to come even if he is sick.* It takes the indicative when it refers to past events: **fuimos al parque, aunque llovía a cántaros** *we went to the park although it was pouring with rain*

a pesar de que, pese a que *despite the fact that* (variable)

puesto que, ya que, en vista de que, debido a que *seeing that, in view of the fact that, due to the fact that* (never)

pues *because* (literary styles only; see p.189), *well . . . , in that case* (never)

como (see p. 187)

como si *as if* (always)

porque *because*. Only takes Subjunctive after the phrase **no porque** . . . *not because* . . . and also when it means an emphatic *simply because* or *just because*: **no voy a quedarme en casa sólo porque tú me lo digas** *I'm not staying at home simply because you tell me to* (you may not have said it yet, but even if you do . . .). **Porque** plus the subjunctive occasionally means *in order that* after a few verbs, especially those meaning *to make an effort*: **se esforzaba para que/porque todo el mundo lo aceptara** *he was making an effort to get everyone to accept it/him*

Subjunctive after words meaning 'perhaps'

■ After **a lo mejor**, which is colloquial (like *maybe* in British English), the appropriate tense of an Indicative verb form is used:

> **A lo mejor pensaba que no estabas en casa**
> *Maybe he thought you weren't at home*
> **A lo mejor es ella** *Maybe it's her*

■ After **quizá**[7], **tal vez** (Lat. Am. **talvez**), **acaso** (literary style) and **posiblemente** *possibly,* the Subjunctive is always correct. However, modern Spanish increasingly prefers the Indicative in certain circumstances, and the following remarks reflect current tendencies:

The Present Subjunctive must be used if the event refers to the future:

> **Quizá/tal vez/acaso llegue mañana** *Perhaps it'll arrive tomorrow* (not *"**quizá llega mañana**')
> **Quizá/tal vez/posiblemente sea mejor . . .**
> *Perhaps/possibly it would be better . . .*

Either the Present Subjunctive or Present Indicative can be used if the verb refers to the present, the Subjunctive being more formal or rather more hesitant or hypothetical:

> **Quizá/tal vez sea/es verdad que . . .** *Perhaps it's true that*

An Indicative past tense or the Imperfect Subjunctive may be used if the event is in the past, the Subjunctive being slightly more hesitant:

> **Quizá pensaba/pensara/haya pensado que
> nadie se enteraría** *Perhaps he thought no one would find out*

The Imperfect Subjunctive or the Imperfect of **ir a . . .** is used for a future in the past:

> **Quizá/posiblemente me lo diera/iba a dar
> cuando llegase al día siguiente** *Perhaps/*

---

[7] The form **quizás** is generally avoided in writing.

possibly he would give it to me when he arrived the next day (not **Quizá me lo daba'*)

■ The word **igual** is nowadays constantly heard in Spain with the meaning *maybe* or *probably*, but it is not used in writing or formal speech. It always takes the Indicative mood.

The subjunctive in relative clauses

The Subjunctive must be used in relative clauses when the thing referred to by the relative pronoun does not exist or is not yet known to exist. Compare **quiero vivir en un país donde nunca *haga* frío** *I want to live in a country where it's never cold* (we don't know yet which country) and **los guatemaltecos viven en un país donde nunca *hace* frío** *the Guatemalans live in a country where it's never cold*. Further examples:

> **Nunca hubo guerra que no fuera un desastre**
> *There was never a war that wasn't a disaster*
> **Tienes que hablar con alguien que te comprenda** *You have to talk to someone who understands you*
> **Dame algo que no tenga alcohol** *Give me something/anything that doesn't have alcohol in it*

This construction requires practice since English does not make the distinction clear. Compare **va a casarse con una mujer que *tiene* mucho dinero** *he's going to marry a woman who has a lot of money* (Indicative, because he has found her) and **quiere casarse con una mujer que *tenga* mucho dinero** *he wants to marry a woman who has a lot of money* (Subjunctive: he's still looking for her).

There are a number of words and phrases that correspond to English words ending in *-ever*, e.g. *whatever, whenever, however, whoever, wherever*. These take the Subjunctive and can be conveniently included under discussion of the Subjunctive in relative clauses:

> **sea lo que sea** *whatever it is*
> **Tome lo que usted quiera** *Take whatever you like*
> **Pueden comer cuando quieran** *You can eat
> whenever you like*
> **Hazlo como quieras** *Do it however you like*
> **sea quien sea/quienquiera que sea** *whoever it is*
> **sea cual sea** *whichever it is*
> **esté donde esté/dondequiera que esté** *wherever
> he is*

The Subjunctive is also found in relative clauses—at least in formal styles—after a superlative when the idea of *ever* is stressed:

> **la temperatura más alta que se haya registrado
> en treinta años** *the highest temperature that
> has **ever** been recorded in thirty years*

but

> **Éstos son los mejores zapatos que tengo** *These
> are the best shoes I've got*

The subjunctive in main clauses

The Subjunctive can also appear in Main Clauses, i.e. it is possible for a Subjunctive verb to be the only verb in the sentence. This occurs:

■ In all forms of the **usted/ustedes** imperative: **dígame** *tell me*, **dénmelo** *give it to me*, **no me diga** *don't tell me*.

■ In the *negative* form of the **tú** and **vosotros** imperatives: **no me digas (tú)**, **no me digáis (vosotros)** *don't tell me*.

■ In third and first-person imperatives: **que pasen** *let them come in*, **pensemos** *let's think*.

■ After **ojalá** *let's hope that . . .* and after **quién** when it means *if only*: **¡Ojalá no llueva!** *Let's hope it doesn't rain!*, **¡Quién tuviera tanto dinero como tú!** *If only I had as much money as you!*

The imperative

The Imperative mood is used for orders and requests.

There are four second-person forms of the Imperative corresponding to the four pronouns meaning *you*: **tú**, **usted**, **vosotros/vosotras** and **ustedes**. There are also first-person plural imperatives (*let's go, let's wait*) and third-person imperatives (*let him go, let it be*). These are discussed below.

Vosotros/vosotras is not used in Latin America, where the only form used for *you* in the plural, whether one is speaking to intimate friends, little children, strangers or even animals, is **ustedes**.

■ The **tú** imperative is formed by removing the **-s** of the second-person singular of the present indicative: **habla** *speak*, **cuenta** *count/tell* (from **contar**), **escribe** *write*. There are eight common exceptions:

decir *to say*	**di**
hacer *to make*	**haz**
ir *to go*	**ve**
poner *to put*	**pon**
salir *to go out*	**sal**
ser *to be*	**sé**[8]
tener *to have*	**ten**
venir *to come*	**ven**

The imperative of **estar** *to be* is usually formed (but not in every Latin-American region) from the Pronominal Form of the verb (see Glossary): **¡Estate quieto!**[9] *Sit still!*

These forms of the **tú** imperative are used only for *positive* orders. All *negative* orders in Spanish are based on the Present Subjunctive: **no hables** *don't speak!*, **no escribas**

---

[8] The accent distinguishes it from the pronoun **se**.

[9] **Quieto** = 'still', **callado** = 'quiet'.

don't write!; **sal** *leave!/get out!*, **no salgas** *don't leave/don't go out.*

In Argentina and in most of Central America (but not in Mexico) the pronoun **vos** replaces **tú** in ordinary speech. The imperative forms used vary from country to country, but in Argentina and in most other places they are created by dropping the **-d** from the standard Spanish **vosotros** imperative (see below): **decí, vení, contestame** (standard forms **di, ven, contéstame**). In the negative the standard Subjunctive forms should be used: **no digas, no vengas, no me contestes.**

■ The **vosotros/vosotras** Imperative is considered archaic in Latin America (and in the Canary Islands) and it is replaced by the **ustedes** form; but it is constantly heard in Spain. It is used for two or more close friends, children, family members or animals. It is formed by replacing the **-r** of the Infinitive by **-d**: **hablad** *speak!*, **venid** *come!*, **id** *go!* This form ending in **-d** is often nowadays replaced in familiar styles by the Infinitive: **hablar, venir, ir**, etc. However, careful speakers may consider this slovenly, so foreigners should use the **-d** forms.

All *negative* imperatives are based on the present Subjunctive, so one says **no habléis** *don't speak!*, **no vengáis** *don't come!*, **no vayáis** *don't go!*

■ The **usted** imperative is used when addressing a stranger (other than a child or another young person if you are also young), and the **ustedes** form is used for addressing more than one stranger (in Spain) or for more than one person, friend or stranger, in Latin America. All the **usted** and **ustedes** imperative forms, positive and negative, are identical to the third-person Present Subjunctive: **venga (usted)** *come!*, **contesten (ustedes)** *answer!*, **¡No se queden atrás!** *Don't fall behind!*

Object pronouns with the imperative

In the case of positive imperatives, Object Forms of
Personal Pronouns are attached to the imperative as
suffixes, in the order shown on page 113.

> **Dime la verdad** *Tell me the truth* (**tú**)
> **Llámala ahora** *Call her now* (**tú**)
> **Siéntate** *Sit down* (**tú**)
> **Decídnoslo** *Tell it to us* (**vosotros**)
> **Deme** *Give me*[10] (**usted**)
> **Déselo** *Give it to him/her/them* (**usted**)
> **Envíenmelos** *Send them to me* (**ustedes**)

Note that an accent is often necessary to show that the
stress is not shifted when the pronouns are added: **da** *give*
(**tú** form), **dame** *give me*, **dámelo** *give me it/give it to me*.

When the pronoun **os** is added to a **vosotros** imperative, the **d** is dropped: **lavad** + **os** = **lavaos** *get washed*;
also **callaos** *be quiet*, **decidíos** *make up your minds* (from
decidid + **os**; note accent). There is one exception: **idos**
go away (instead of **íos*). Familiar speech nowadays
usually avoids these forms by using the Infinitive—
lavaros, callaros, decidiros, iros—although non-fluent
foreigners should not do this. The **vosotros** form is
replaced by the **ustedes** form in Latin America: **lávense,
cállense, decídanse, váyanse**, etc.

Personal pronouns are put *before* negative imperatives in
the same order as above:

> **No me digas la verdad** *Don't tell me the truth* (**tú**)
> **No la llames ahora** *Don't call her now* (**tú**)
> **No te sientes** *Don't sit down* (**tú**)
> **No nos lo digáis** *Don't tell it to us* (**vosotros**)

---

[10] Or **déme**. There is some disagreement about whether the
accent of **dé**, the third-person present subjunctive of **dar**, should be
retained when one pronoun is attached to it. The accent is required
on the word **dé** when it stands alone to avoid confusion with **de** *of*.

No se lo dé *Don't give it to him/her/them* (**usted**)
No nos los envíen *Don't send them to us* (**ustedes**)

Third-person imperatives

These translate English forms like *let him . . .*, *tell him/her to . . .*, etc. They consist of **que** plus the third-person present Subjunctive:

> **Que diga quién es** *Tell him to say who he is*
> **Que vuelvan más tarde** *Tell them to come back later*

The Passive **se** construction (see p.73) used with the Subjunctive forms an imperative often used in recipes, instructions and official forms to give impersonal orders:

> **Pónganse en una cacerola las patatas** (Lat.-Am. **papas**) **y los tomates** *Put the potatoes and tomatoes in a saucepan*

Ponga en una cacerola las patatas, etc. would have meant the same thing.

First-person imperatives

The first-person plural of the Present Subjunctive translates the English *let's . . .*, *let us . . .*:

> **Pensemos un poco antes de hacerlo** *Let's think a bit before doing it*

When the pronoun **nos** is added to this imperative form, the final -**s** of the verb is dropped:

> **Sentémonos** *Let's sit down.*

The verb **ir** is unusual in that the Present Indicative is used for *let's go*: **vamos, vámonos**

Other forms of the imperative

■ There is a tendency to use the Infinitive for second-person Imperatives, singular and plural, especially in written instructions but also sometimes in speech: **re-llenar el cupón y enviarlo a . . .** *fill in the coupon and send it to . . .*, **no fumar** *no smoking*, **tirar** *pull!* Grammarians and schoolteachers disapprove of this, but it is becoming increasingly frequent.

■ The ordinary Present Indicative is often used for the Imperative, but it can sound angry: **¡Te duermes en seguida o me voy a enfadar!** (Lat-Am. **me voy a enojar**) *you're going to sleep right now or I'm going to get mad!*

■ The Imperative may be softened or replaced in polite speech by one of the following constructions, which are more friendly in tone:

> **¿Podría usted guardar mi maleta?** *Could you look after my suitcase?*
>
> **¿Le importaría llamar a mi mujer?** *Would you mind phoning my wife?*
>
> **¿Quisiera hacerme el favor de llamarme cuando sepa algo?** *Would you call me when you know something?*
>
> **Hagan el favor de permanecer sentados** *Please remain seated*
>
> **¿Me da una cerveza?** *Would you give me a beer, please?* (Question form used for polite request)

CONDITIONS

There are three basic kinds of Conditional Sentence in Spanish:

■ Conditions that do not require the Subjunctive in the *if*-clause[11]. These are conditions in which the condition is

---

[11] The Spanish for *if* is **si**. However, foreign learners are often confused by the widespread tendency to use **si** simply as a way of turning a remark into a protest: **¡Si te lo dije anoche!** *But I told you last night!*

equally likely or unlikely to be fulfilled. The verbs are in the Indicative Mood, and their tense is the same as in their English equivalents:

> **Si me das dinero, te compraré un helado** *If you give me some money I'll buy you an ice-cream*
> **Si te pones esa corbata, no voy contigo** *If you put that tie on, I'm not going with you*

The Imperfect Indicative is used if these conditions are reported by someone, but the Imperfect Indicative is not used in any other kinds of Conditional Sentence[12]:

> **Me dijo que no iría conmigo si me ponía esa corbata** *She said she wouldn't go with me if I put that tie on*

Como + Subjunctive is sometimes used instead of **si** in this kind of condition. This is particularly common in threats and apparently more frequent in Spain than Latin America:

> **Como vuelvas a hacerlo, llamo a la policía** *If you do it again, I'm calling the police*

■ Conditions that require the Imperfect Subjunctive in the *if*-clause and the Conditional in the other clause. The condition is less likely to be met or impossible to meet:

> **Si yo tuviera veinte años menos, sería feliz** *If I were twenty years younger, I'd be happy* (impossible)
> **Si trabajaras más te darían mejores notas** *If you worked harder they'd give you better grades/marks* (some doubt about whether it's possible)

The best styles of Spanish prefer the **-ra** form of the Imperfect Subjunctive in the *if*-clause of these sentences, although the **-se** form is common in speech.

[12] Except in familiar speech as an occasional alternative for the Conditional Tense, although beginners should avoid this.

■ Conditions that require the Pluperfect Subjunctive in the *if*-clause and the Pluperfect Conditional in the other clause. In this case the condition was not fulfilled:

> **Si se hubiera casado con ella, habría sido rico**
> *If he had married her he would have been rich*
> (but he didn't)
>
> **Si te hubiera visto, te habría saludado** *If I had*
> *seen you I would have said hello to you* (but I
> didn't)

Either the Conditional or the -**ra** form of **haber** can be used in the second clause (e.g. **hubiera saludado** or **habría saludado**).

The **si** and the Subjunctive in this kind of clause are occasionally replaced by **de** + Infinitive, but only if the verbs in each clause are in the same person:

> **De haberte visto, te habría saludado** *Had I seen*
> *you, I'd have said hello*

NON-FINITE VERB FORMS (SEE GLOSSARY)

The infinitive

This non-finite form always ends in -**ar**, -**er**, -**ir** or -**ír**: **andar** *to walk*, **convencer** *to convince*, **insistir** *to insist*, **reír** *to laugh*.

It is used:

■ After Modal Verbs (see p.60), e.g. **poder** *to be able*, **deber** *must*, **tener que** *to have to*, **hay que** *it's necessary to*, **saber** *to know how to*:

> **No puedo salir hoy** *I can't go out today*

Debiste llamarla *You should have called her*
Tenemos que esperar *We've got to wait*
Habrá que hacerlo *It'll be necessary to do it*
No sé nadar *I don't know how to swim*

■ After prepositions and prepositional phrases

Ha ido a América a estudiar *He's gone to study in America*
Tosía por haber fumado demasiado *He was coughing from having smoked too much*
Corrió hasta no poder más *He ran until he could (run) no more*
Roncaba sin darse cuenta *He was snoring without realizing*
lejos de pensar que . . . *far from thinking that . . .*
En lugar de ir a España . . . *Instead of going to Spain*

If the subject of the Infinitive and the subject of the Main Clause do not refer to the same thing or person, the Infinitive cannot be used (at least in careful Spanish): **tosía porque ella había fumado demasiado** *he was coughing because she had smoked too much* (not *'por ella haber fumado demasiado'*).

After some prepositions, the Spanish Infinitive may have a passive meaning: **una carta sin terminar** *an unfinished letter*, **cosas por hacer** *things to be done*.

■ After many other verbs

With some verbs no preposition is required before the Infinitive, and with other verbs a preposition is necessary. This list shows the construction with some of the most common verbs. Where no preposition is shown none is required, e.g. **quiero hacerlo** *I want to do it*:

abstenerse de *to abstain from*
acabar de: acabo de verla *I've just seen her*
acabar por *to end by*
acercarse a *to approach*
aconsejar *to advise*
acordarse de *to remember*
acostumbrar a *to be accustomed to*
acusar de *to accuse of*
admitir *to admit*
afirmar *to claim/state*
alegrarse de *to be happy at/to*
amenazar or **amenazar con** *to threaten*
anhelar *to long to*
animar a *to encourage to*
aparentar *to seem to, to have the look of . . .*
aprender a *to learn to*
arrepentirse de *to regret/repent*
asegurar *to assure/insure*
asombrarse de *to be surprised at*
asustarse de *to be frightened by*
atreverse a *to dare to*
autorizar a *to authorize to*
avergonzarse de *to be ashamed of*
ayudar a *to help to*
buscar *to seek to*
cansarse de *to tire of*
cesar de *to cease from*
comenzar a *to begin to*
comprometerse a *to undertake to*
condenar a *to condemn to*
conducir a *to lead to*
confesar *to confess*
conseguir *to succeed in*
consentir en *to consent to*
consistir en *to consist of*
contar con *count on*

contribuir a *to contribute to*
convenir en *to agree to*
convidar a *to invite to*
cuidar de *to take care to*
deber *must*
decidir *to decide to*
decidirse a *to make up one's mind to*
declarar *to declare*
dejar *to let/allow:* **me dejó hacerlo** *he let me do it*
dejar de *to stop/leave off, e.g.* **dejó de fumar** *he stopped smoking*
demostrar *to demonstrate*
depender de *depend on*
desafiar a *to challenge to*
desear *to desire/wish to*
desesperarse de *to despair of*
dignarse *to deign to*
disponerse a *to get ready to*
disuadir de *to dissuade from*
divertirse en *to amuse oneself by*
dudar *to doubt*
dudar en *to hesitate over*
echar(se) a *to begin to*
empeñarse en *to insist on*
empezar a *to begin to*
empezar por *to begin by*
enfadarse de *to get angry at*
enojarse de *to get angry at*
enseñar a *to show how to/teach how to*
escoger *to choose to*
esforzarse por *to strive to*
esperar *to hope/expect/wait*
evitar *to avoid*
fingir *to pretend to*
forzar a *to force to*

guardarse de *to take care not to*
habituarse a *to get used to*
hartarse de *to get tired of*
imaginar(se) *to imagine*
impedir *to prevent from*
incitar a *to incite to*
inclinar a *to incline to*
insistir en *to insist on*
intentar *to try to*
interesarse en (or **por**) *to be interested in*
invitar a *to invite to*[13]
jactarse de *to boast of*
jurar *to swear to*
juzgar *to judge*
limitarse a *to limit oneself to*
luchar por *to struggle to*
llevar a *to lead to*
lograr *to succeed in*
mandar *to order to*
mandar a *to send to*
maravillarse de *to marvel at*
merecer *to deserve to*
meterse a *to start to*
mover a *to move to*
necesitar *to need to*
negar *to deny*
negarse a *to refuse to*
obligar a *to oblige to*
ofrecerse a *to offer to*
olvidar, olvidarse de, olvidársele a uno[14] *to forget*
oponerse a *to oppose/resist*

[13] Note one special use of this verb in bars, restaurants etc.: **te invito** *I'm paying for you*, **¿Quién invita?** *Who's paying for us?*

[14] Note construction: **me olvidé de decirte** or **se me olvidó decirte** *I forgot to tell you.*

optar por *to opt to/for*
ordenar *to order to*
parar de[15] *to stop*
parecer *to seem to*
pasar a *to go on to*
pasar de *to pass from, to be uninterested in*
pedir *to ask to*
pensar: pienso hacerlo *I plan to do it*
pensar en *to think about*
permitir *to allow to*
poder *to be able to*
preferir *to prefer to*
prepararse a *to get ready to*
pretender *to claim to*
procurar *to try hard to*
prohibir *to prohibit from*
prometer *to promise to*
quedar en *to agree to*
querer *to want to*
recordar *to remember*[16]
renunciar a *to renounce*
resignarse a *to resign oneself to*
resistirse a *to resist*
resolver *to resolve to*
sentir *to regret/be sorry for*
soler: solía ir *he used to go*
solicitar *to apply to*
soñar con *to dream of*
sorprenderse de *to be surprised that*
tardar en *to be late in/be a long time*
temer *to fear to*
tender a *to tend to*

[15] **Pararse** means *to come to a halt* in Spain, *to stand up* in Latin America.
[16] Note alternatives: **recordar algo** or **acordarse de algo** *to remember something.*

> **tener que** *to have to*
> **terminar de** *to finish*
> **terminar por** *to finish by*
> **tratar de** *to try to*
> **vacilar en** *to hesitate over*
> **venir de** *to come from . . .*
> **volver a (hacer)** *to (do) again*

The Infinitive is normally only possible with the above verbs when the subject of both verbs is the same. Compare

and

> **Soñaba con ser bombero** *He dreamt of being a fireman*

> **Soñaba con que su hijo *fuese* bombero** *He dreamt of his son being a fireman.*

Verbs of permitting and forbidding allow either construction:

> **Te permito hacerlo/Te permito que lo hagas** *I allow you to do it*
> **Te prohibía ir/Te prohibía que fueses** *He forbade you to go.*

■ With verbs of stating, believing, claiming

In this case the Infinitive construction is *optionally* allowed when both verbs share the same subject:

> **Dice ser de Madrid/Dice que es de Madrid** *He says he's from Madrid (he is talking about himself)*
> **Afirmaba haberlos visto/que los había visto** *He claimed to have seen them*
> **Parecía conocerla/Parecía que la conocía** *He seemed to recognize her/It seemed that he recognized her*

Similarly with **pretender** *to claim*, **imaginar** *to imagine*, **creer** *to believe*, **recordar/acordarse de** *to remember*, **reconocer** *to recognize*, **admitir** *to admit*, **confesar** *to confess*.

▪ After **ver** *to see* and **oír** *to hear*

> **Le oí decir que tenía mucho dinero** *I heard him say that he had a lot of money*
> **Te vi entrar en su casa** *I saw you enter his/her house*

For the possible use of the Gerund as an alternative to the Infinitive in this construction, see p.53.

▪ In the common construction **al** + Infinitive, which translates *on doing something . . . , when . . .* **al llegar a Madrid** *. . . on arriving at Madrid . . .*

> **al levantarse** *. . . on getting up . . .*

▪ After Subordinators (other than **cuando** *when*, **en cuanto**, *as soon as*, **apenas** *as soon as/scarcely* and a few others mentioned on p.24) when the subject of the first verb is identical to the subject of the second verb: Compare **comí antes de salir de casa** *I ate before leaving home* and **comí antes de que tú salieras de casa** *I ate before **you** left home*:

> **Entró sin hacer ruido** *He entered without making any noise*
> **Redecoraremos la casa en lugar de venderla** *We'll redecorate the house instead of selling it*

▪ In combination with an adjective, and with noun phrases

> **Es difícil hacerlo** *It's difficult to do it*
> **Parecía imposible equivocarse** *It seemed impossible to make a mistake*
> **Cuesta trabajo pensar eso** *It's hard to think that*

If the Infinitive has no object and is not followed by **que**, **de** is required:

> **Es que ella es difícil *de* olvidar** *The fact is she's difficult to forget*
>
> **Sería imposible *de* probar** *It would be impossible to prove*

But this construction is usually avoided and **es que es difícil olvidarla, sería difícil probarlo**, etc. are used instead.

■ As a noun. In this case it often corresponds to the English form ending in *-ing*. When used as a noun, the Spanish Infinitive is masculine and singular:

> **No me gusta esperar** *I don't like waiting*
>
> **Cansa mucho viajar en avión** *Traveling* (British travelling) *in planes makes one very tired*
>
> **Sería mejor dejarlos aquí** *It would be better to leave them here*

This kind of sentence must never be translated using the Spanish Gerund: **'hablando da sed'* is definitely not possible for **(el) hablar da sed** *talking makes you thirsty*.

Use of the Definite Article with the Infinitive in such sentences is more or less optional, although it is common in literary styles at the head of a sentence or clause:

> **(El) decir esto le iba a causar muchos problemas** *Saying this was to cause him many problems*
>
> **Los médicos afirman que (el) comer mucho ajo es bueno para el corazón** *Doctors claim that eating a lot of garlic is good for the heart*

■ To make a quick answer to a question

> **—¿Qué hacemos? —Pensar** *'What are we going to do?' 'Think.'*

■ In familiar speech, as an alternative for the Imperative

This construction is discussed under the Imperative, p.36 ff.

■ In combination with **que**, or with the prepositions **por** or **a**, as an alternative for a relative clause.

The construction with **a** is commonly seen, but foreigners should use it only in set phrases like the ones shown:

> **Tengo mucho que hacer** *I've got a lot to do*
> **Queda mucho que/por hacer** *There's a lot left to do*
> **total a pagar** *total to pay/payable*
> **asuntos a tratar** *matters to be discussed*

> **Para** is used after verbs of wanting, needing:

> **Quieren algo para comer** *They want something to eat*
> **Necesito dinero para vivir** *I need money to live*

The gerund

The Gerund always ends in **-ndo**. It is formed:

In the case of all **-ar** verbs, by replacing the **-ar** by **-ando**: **hablar—hablando** *talking*, **andar—andando** *walking*.

In the case of most **-er** and **-ir** verbs, by replacing the Infinitive ending by **-iendo**: **comer—comiendo, vivir - viviendo, ser -siendo**, etc.

-iendo is written **-yendo** when it follows another vowel: **destruir—destruyendo** *destroying*, **creer— creyendo** *believing*, **caer—cayendo** *falling*, **oír—oyendo** *hearing*. The Gerund of **ir** is regularly formed: **yendo** *going*.

-iendo becomes **-endo** after **ñ** or **ll**: **gruñir— gruñendo** *growling*, **reñir—riñendo** *scolding*, **engullir— engullendo** *gobbling up, swallowing whole*.

Poder, venir, morir and **dormir,** and all verbs conjugated like **pedir, sentir** and **reír** base their Gerund on the stem of the third-person Preterit:

Infinitive	3rd-person Preterit	Gerund
poder	pudo	**pudiendo** *being able*
venir	vino	**viniendo** *coming*
repetir	repitió	**repitiendo** *repeating,*
pedir	pidió	**pidiendo** *asking for*
sentir	sintió	**sintiendo** *feeling*
corregir	corrigió	**corrigiendo** *correcting*
freír	frió	**friendo** *frying*
dormir	durmió	**durmiendo** *sleeping*
morir	murió	**muriendo** *dying*

The gerund of **decir** is not based on the preterite form (**dijo**): **diciendo** *saying*.

The Gerund is used:

■ To show that an action is simultaneous with another:

> **Entró riendo** *He came in laughing*
> **Se lo diré, pero no estando aquí este señor** *I'll tell you, but not while this gentleman is here*

■ To show the method by which something is done

> **Se hizo rico vendiendo vídeos ilegales** *He got rich selling illegal videos*
> **Verás el jardín asomándote al balcón** *You'll see the garden by looking out of the window*
> **Me molestaba cada cinco minutos diciéndome que no tenía dinero** *He bothered me every five minutes saying that he didn't have any money*

■ With **estar** to make the Continuous Form of verbs: **está trabajando** *he's (in the middle of) working*. This is discussed on p.13 ff.

■ With verbs meaning *see, imagine, paint, draw, photograph, meet, find, catch, surprise, remember*:

> **Los cogieron robando manzanas** *They caught them stealing apples*
> **Le sacaron una foto cenando con el presidente** *They took a photo of him/her having dinner with the President*
> **La vi jugando en el parque** *I saw her playing in the park*

Other verbs found with this construction are **recordar** *to remember*, **describir** *to describe*, **dibujar** *to sketch*, **pintar** *to paint*, **mostrar** *to show*, **representar** *to represent*.

With the verb **ver** *to see* the Infinitive is used if the action is complete: **lo/le vi bajarse del autobús** *I saw him get out of the bus* but **la vi jugando en el jardín** *I saw her (while she was) playing in the garden.*

The Infinitive is used after **oír** *to hear*: **te oyeron entrar** *they heard you come in.* The Infinitive is also always used with the verbs **venir** *to come* and **ir** *to go*: **la veíamos venir** *we could see her coming*, **lo/le vi ir hacia la puerta** *I saw him go towards the door.*

With **ver** and **oír** the idea of ongoing action can be stressed in colloquial language by using **que** + Imperfect Indicative: **la vi que iba en bicicleta** *I saw her riding a bicycle.*

■ With **venir** and **ir** to show that an event is drawn out over a period of time:

> **Iba apuntando todo lo que decían** *He was noting down everything they were saying*
> **Los problemas vienen siendo cada vez más complicados** *The problems are getting more and more complicated*

■ With **llevar** *to carry* to translate the idea of *to do something for n days/months/years*, etc.

> **Lleva varios días pintando la casa** *He's been painting his house for several days*

See page 205 for more remarks on this construction.

■ Occasionally as alternative for **aunque** *although* or **a pesar de que** *despite*

> **Un día se confesó que, amando inmensamente a su hija, le tenía envidia** *One day she admitted to herself that, despite loving her daughter immensely, she envied her*

■ As an alternative to **porque** *because* or **ya que** *since*:

> **Calló, viendo que el otro no le hacía caso** *He fell silent, seeing that the other was not paying attention to him*

■ In combination with **como**, as an alternative to **como si** *as if*

> **Se agachó como preparándose para saltar** *He squatted down, as if preparing to jump*
> **Emitió una tosecilla, como llamándonos al orden** *He made a slight cough, as if calling us to order*

The gerund as a participle

English regularly uses the *-ing* form of verbs to form an adjective: *an exhausting task, a surprising attitude, a freezing wind*. The Spanish Gerund is not possible in these cases: an adjective or a participle in **-nte** must be used (if one exists: see below): **una tarea agotadora, una actitud sorprendente, un viento helado**. The only exceptions are the two invariable adjectives **hirviendo** and **ardiendo**—**agua hirviendo** *boiling water*, **un árbol ardiendo** *a burning tree*.

English also constantly uses the *-ing* form to replace a relative pronoun plus a finite verb: *passengers waiting for* *the train*, *a woman driving a car*. In Spanish a Relative Pronoun and a Finite Verb must be used: **los pasajeros que esperan el tren, una mujer que conduce/con-ducía un coche**. The only exception that need concern beginners is captions to pictures: **una foto de una mujer dando de comer a un niño** *a photo of a woman feeding a child*.

In general, foreign students should respect the rule that the Spanish Gerund is basically a kind of adverb and must therefore modify a verb. If there is no verb, as in the phrase *a plane carrying passengers* there can be no Gerund: **un avión que lleva/llevaba pasajeros,** not **'un avión llevando pasajeros'*.

The past participle

Forms

from **-ar** verbs		by replacing the **-ar** by **-ado**	
from **-er** and **-ir** verbs		by replacing the ending by **-ido**	

hablar	*to speak*	**hablado**	*spoken*
comer	*to eat*	**comido**	*eaten*
ser	*to be*	**sido**	*been*
vivir	*to live*	**vivido**	*lived*
ir	*to go*	**ido**	*gone*

When the Infinitive ends in **-ír**, **-aer** or **-eer** the Past Participle ending is written with an accent: **reír—reído** *to laugh*, **traer—traído** *to bring*, **creer—creído** *to believe*. Verbs whose Infinitive ends in **-uir** do not have an accent: **construir—construido** *to build*.

The following forms are irregular:

abrir	*to open*	**abierto**	*opened*
absolver	*to absolve*	**absuelto**	*absolved*

cubrir	*to cover*	**cubierto**	*covered*
decir	*to say*	**dicho**	*said*
descomponer	*to put out of order*	**descompuesto**	*disordered*
describir	*to describe*	**descrito**	*described*
descubrir	*to discover*	**descubierto**	*discovered*
devolver	*to give back*	**devuelto**	*given back*
encubrir	*to cover up/ conceal*	**encubierto**	*concealed*
envolver	*to wrap up*	**envuelto**	*wrapped up*
escribir	*to write*	**escrito**	*written*
freír	*to fry*	**frito**	*fried*
hacer	*to make/do*	**hecho**	*made/done*
imponer	*to impose*	**impuesto**	*imposed*
inscribirse	*to sign on*	**inscrito**	*signed on*
morir	*to die*	**muerto**	*dead/died*
poner	*to put*	**puesto**	*put*
posponer	*to postpone*	**pospuesto**	*postponed*
prever	*to predict*	**previsto**	*foreseen*
resolver	*to resolve*	**resuelto**	*resolved*
revolver	*to turn over/ around*	**revuelto**	*turned over/ scrambled*
romper	*to break*	**roto**	*broken*
suponer	*to suppose*	**supuesto**	*supposed*
ver	*to see*	**visto**	*seen*
volver	*to return*	**vuelto**	*returned*

Another kind of irregularity involves a distinction between the verbal past participle and the past participle used as an adjective. The forms in the second column are used to form the Compound Tenses (e.g. **ha absorbido** *it has absorbed*, **habían soltado** *they had set free*), while the words in the third column form adjectives: **estaba absorto en su trabajo** *he was engrossed/absorbed in his work*, **unos papeles sueltos** *some loose sheets of paper*.

Infinitive	Verbal	Adjectival	
absorber	absorbido	absorto	*absorbed*
bendecir	bendecido	bendito	*blessed*
confesar	confesado	confeso	*confessed*
confundir	confundido	confuso	*confused*
despertar	despertado	despierto	*woken up*
elegir	elegido	electo	*chosen/elect*
imprimir	imprimido	impreso	*printed*
maldecir	maldecido	maldito	*cursed*
prender	prendido	preso	*taken prisoner*
presumir	presumido	presunto	*presumed*
proveer	proveído	provisto	*equipped with*
soltar	soltado	suelto	*let out*
suspender	suspendido	suspenso	*failed (exams)*

Uses of the past participle

The uses of the Spanish Past Participle resemble that of the English past participle. The main uses are:

■ In combination with the appropriate form of **haber**, to form Compound Tenses (e.g. the Perfect, Pluperfect, etc.):

> **Los científicos han descubierto una nueva droga** *Scientists have discovered a new drug*

> **No se habían dado cuenta** *They hadn't realized*

In these tenses the participle is invariable in form: it does not agree with either the subject or the object of the verb. The use of the Compound Tenses is discussed on p. 9 ff.

■ In combination with the verb **ser**, and also sometimes with the verb **estar**, to form the Passive Voice of verbs (which is discussed further on pp.64 ff):

> **El nuevo proyecto será presentado por el ministro de Obras Públicas** *The new project will be presented by the Minister for Public Works*

As in English, the passive participle frequently appears without the verb *to be:*

> **Han encontrado a las niñas perdidas** *They've found the lost girls (i.e. the girls that were lost)*
> **Preguntados sobre el aumento a los mínimos para este año, los portavoces contestaron que** . . . *Asked about the increase in minimum salaries for this year, the spokespersons replied that* . . .

As the examples show, the participle must agree in number and gender with the noun it refers to.

■ To form adverbial phrases which describe the manner or appearance of the subject of a verb. As the examples show, this construction is used with a much wider range of participles than in English:

> **Gritó alborozado** *He shouted in glee/gleefully*
> **Me miraba fascinada** *She looked at me in fascination*
> **Salió contrariado del cuarto** *He came/went out of the room in an upset state*
> **Llegados a este punto, podríamos preguntarnos si** . . . *Having got this far, we might ask ourselves whether* . . .
> **un autor nacido en España y muerto en Francia** *an author who was born in Spain and died in France*

■ To form absolute participle clauses, i.e. ones that do not depend on the finite verb in the sentence:

> **Cometido este acto de vandalismo, se guardó la navaja** *Having committed this act of vandalism, he put away his knife*

Pero, una vez compradas las flores y la tarjeta, me di cuenta de que me había olvidado de su dirección *But, having bought the flowers and the card, I realized that I'd forgotten her address*

Adjectival participles

Many Spanish verbs have an adjectival participle formed by adding -**ante** to -**ar** verbs, and -**iente** (or, in some cases, -**ente**) to -**er** and -**ir** verbs:

preocupar *to worry*	**preocupante** *worrying*
cambiar *to change*	**cambiante** *changing/fickle*
excitar *to arouse*	**excitante** *arousing*
crecer *to grow*	**creciente** *growing*
sorprender *to surprise*	**sorprendente** *surprising*
conducir *to lead/drive*	**conducente a** *leading to*
consistir en *to consist of*	**consisente en** *consisting of*
existir *to exist*	**existente** *existing*

There are a few irregular forms, the most common being

convencer *to convince*	**convincente** *convincing*
dormir *to sleep*	**durmiente** *sleeping*
herir *to wound*	**hiriente** *wounding*
provenir de *to come from*	**proveniente de** *coming from*
seguir *to follow*	**siguiente** *following*

The suffix -**nte** is very productive, although many of the new formations are seen only in newspaper and technical language. But foreigners should not attempt to invent new words by using it: many verbs, for no obvious reason, do not form adjectives in -**nte**, e.g.

aburrir *to bore*	**aburrido** *boring*
asombrar *to amaze*	**asombroso** *amazing*
aterrar *to terrify*	**aterrador** *terrifying*
cansar *to tire*	**cansado** *tiring*

confiar *to trust*
venir *to come*

confiado *trusting*
venidero *coming*

MODAL VERBS (SEE GLOSSARY)

These are **poder** *to be able*, **deber** *must*, **querer** *to want*, **tener que** *to have to*, **haber que** *to be necessary*, **saber** *to know how to*, **soler** *to be accustomed to*. They are followed by an Infinitive, although **poder + que** + Subjunctive is used to mean *it is possible that* and **querer** requires the Subjunctive when its subject is not the same as that of the following verb. **Saber** is also followed by **que** and an indicative tense when it means *to know* rather than *to know how to*.

■ Poder

This differs little in meaning and use from the English *can, may*:

> **No puedo ir hoy** *I can't go today*
> **Podría llover** *It might rain*
> **Puede que la situación mejore** *It may be that the situation will improve* (Lat. Am. also **pueda que . . .**)

The Preterit often means *managed to* (i.e. *could and did*) whereas the Imperfect means *was able* (but may not have)

> **No pudo abrir la puerta** *He didn't manage to get the door open*
> **Como no podía hacerlo, pidió ayuda** *Since he couldn't do it, he asked for help*

The Preterit can also refer to something that could have happened but definitely did not:

> **Tuviste suerte. Te pudiste matar** *You were lucky. You could have got killed*

■ Deber

This translates *must*. As in English, it may indicate obligation or likelihood: *you must do it/you've got to do it, he must be fifty*. The strict rule is that when it refers to likelihood it should be followed by **de**:

> **Debe de tener cincuenta años** *He must be fifty* (guess)
>
> **Debían de pensar que no era verdad** *They must have been thinking that it wasn't true* (guess)
>
> **Debes hacerlo ahora** *You've got to do it now* (obligation)
>
> **Deberías llamarlos ahora mismo** *You ought to call them right now* (obligation)

The form **deber de** is never used for obligations, but the form without **de** is constantly used nowadays for both meanings, which can be confusing for learners. When it is used for suppositions, **deber (de)** does not appear in the Future or Conditional tense: **deben (de) ser las cinco** *(I guess) it must be five o'clock,* not **'deberán (de) ser . . .'* or **'deberían (de) ser . . .'*

The Imperfect of **deber** either implies *was/were supposed to . . .* or it may be a familiar alternative for the Conditional: *ought to do it*: **debías hacerlo tú** *you were supposed to do it/you ought to do it* (i.e. **deberías hacerlo tú**). The Preterit of **deber** may mean *should have done it but didn't*, or *must have done it*:

> **Debí haberme ido, pero me quedé** *I should have left, but I stayed*
>
> **Debió de pensar que estamos todos locos** *He must have thought we're all mad*

The idea of *had to* (i.e. *was obliged to and did*) is translated by the Preterit of **tener que**:

> **Tuve que ponerme un suéter porque tenía frío** *I had to put on a sweater because I was cold*

■ Tener que

Tener que implies a strong obligation:

> **Tienes que decirnos la verdad** *You've got to tell us the truth*
>
> **Tuve que dárselo** *I was obliged to give it to him (and did)*

■ Haber que

Haber que (Present Indicative **hay que**) is an impersonal verb followed by the Infinitive and meaning *it is necessary to*:

> **Hay que añadir un poco de agua** *It's necessary to/We'll have to add a bit of water*
>
> **Hubo que encerrar al perro** *it was necessary to shut the dog in*

■ Haber de

Haber de is much used in Mexico for suppositions, where standard Spanish uses **deber de**, e.g. **ha de tener más de cincuenta años** for **debe de tener más de cincuenta años** or **tendrá más de cincuenta años** *he must be more than fifty*. In Spain **haber de** is a rather old-fashioned form that usually expresses a mild obligation: **si viene has de decirle lo que ha pasado** *if he comes you must tell him what has happened*; . . . **debes/tienes que decirle** . . . are more usual.

■ Querer

This verb translates *to want*. It also means *to love*, but in the latter sense it can refer only to human beings and animals: **quiero a mis padres, a mi perro** *I love my parents, my dog* but **adoro las novelas de amor** *I love novels about love*.

The conditional form, **querría** or, more commonly, **quisiera**, is used to make polite requests:

> **Quisiera/querría expresar mi agradecimiento a los organizadores . . .** *I'd like to express my gratitude to the organizers*

The Imperfect means *wanted to*. The Preterit has two mutually exclusive meanings that can only be clarified by context. It usually implies *tried to . . .* (i.e. *wanted to but couldn't*):

> **Quiso acercarse al Rey, pero no pudo** *He tried to get close to the King was, but he couldn't manage it*

However, it may imply *wanted to and did* when some idea of getting one's own way is involved: **lo dije porque quise, nada más** *I said it because I felt like it, and that's that*. The negative of the Preterit means *refused* (i.e. *didn't want to and didn't*): **no quiso decir su nombre** *he refused to give his name*.

■ Saber

The basic meaning of **saber** is *to know* (a fact); it must be distinguished from **conocer** *to know* (a person or place). Combined with an Infinitive it means *to know how to*, as in

> **Casi me ahogué por no saber nadar** *I nearly drowned because of not knowing how to swim*
> **Me despidieron porque no sabía escribir a máquina** *They fired me because I couldn't type*

■ Soler

This basically means *to be accustomed to, usually*. It is not used in the future or conditional tenses:

> **Solía limpiar mi coche** (Lat. Am. **carro/auto**) **todos los días** *I used to clean my car every day*
> **Suele hacer menos calor en septiembre** *It's usually less hot in September*

THE PASSIVE

The Passive construction makes the Direct Object of an Active sentence into the Subject of a Passive one. Active: *I chose the red one*. Passive: *the red one was chosen by me*.

The Spanish Passive is formed in one of two ways:

(a) In a way similar to English, by using the verb meaning *to be* (**ser,** or occasionally **estar**) + the Past Participle, which must agree in number and gender:

> **Mis dos novelas fueron publicadas el año
>   pasado** *My two novels were published last year*
> **El proyecto fue rechazado por el comité** *The
>   project was rejected by the committee*

(b) By using the Passive **se** construction:

> **Mis dos novelas se publicaron el año pasado**
>   *My two novels were published last year*

Construction (a) and construction (b) are usually interchangeable, but only if the preposition **por** does not appear. In other words, if **se** is used we cannot go on to say *by* whom or what the action was done. For this reason one should not say **'el proyecto se rechazó por el comité'*. The Passive with **se** is further discussed at pp. 73–4.

The following points about the Spanish Passive with **ser** should be noted:

■ It is only used in written Spanish (where it is common, especially in newspapers)

This is a bold generalization, but English-speaking learners of Spanish will do well to avoid the Passive with **ser** when speaking Spanish and to master first the use of the much more common Passive **se** (p.73). Usually a simple active construction produces the best and most idiomatic Spanish: passive sentences like **estoy muy con-**

tento porque *fui besado por* una actriz muy famosa
I'm really happy because I was kissed by a famous actress
sound natural to English-speakers but they are very
clumsy in Spanish. The active construction is more normal: . . . **porque me besó una actriz muy famosa** . . .
because a very famous actress kissed me.

Examples of the passive from written Spanish:

> **El derrumbamiento del edificio fue causado por
> un terremoto** *The collapse of the building was
> caused by an earthquake*
>
> **Los hechos serán investigados por las autori-
> dades** *The facts will be investigated by the
> authorities*
>
> **Varias personas han sido expulsadas del par-
> tido** *Several people have been expelled from the
> party*

■ It must *never* be used when the subject of the verb **ser**
would be the Indirect Object

English allows two passive versions of sentences like
they gave fifty dollars to me: *fifty dollars were given to me* or *I
was given fifty dollars*. The second of these two construction is *never* possible in Spanish and the best translation in
both cases is **me dieron cincuenta dólares** *they gave me
fifty dollars*. *'Fui dado cincuenta dólares'* is definitely
not Spanish. Further examples

> **Nunca me contaban la verdad** *I was never told
> the truth/They never told me the truth.*
>
> **Me preguntaron varias cosas** *I was asked sev-
> eral things/They asked me several things*
>
> **Le enviaron una carta** *He/She was sent a
> letter/They sent him/her a letter*

Fue enviada una carta can only mean *a letter was sent*.

■ *Never* with verbs combined with a preposition. Compare
this bed has been slept in and **alguien ha dormido en esta**

cama (*someone has slept in this bed*), never **'esta cama ha sido dormido en'* which is emphatically not Spanish.

■ Usually only with the Preterit, Perfect and Future tenses of **ser**

Sentences like **fue interrogado por la policía** *he was interrogated by the police*, **ha sido interrogado . . .** and **será interrogado . . .** sound more natural than **es interrogado por la policía** *he is interrogated . . .* or **era interrogado por la policía** *he was being interrogated . . .* (although **estaba siendo interrogado . . .** is not unusual). Use of the Present or Imperfect of **ser** with the Passive is rather more common in Latin America than in Spain.

Use of *estar* to form the passive

■ A passive construction may be formed with **estar**

Use of **estar** draws attention to the state something is in, whereas use of **ser** describes the event that caused the state. Compare

> **La ciudad estaba inundada por las lluvias** *The city was covered in water as a result of the rains* (describes the state the city was in)
>
> **La ciudad fue inundada por las lluvias** *The city was flooded by the rain* (describes an event)

PRONOMINAL ('REFLEXIVE') VERBS

Pronominal verbs are verbs like **llamarse** *to be called*, **defenderse** *to defend oneself/to 'get by'*, **inhibirse** *to be inhibited*, **irse** *to go away*. These verbs are often called 'reflexive verbs', but the name is inaccurate. 'Reflexive' refers to only one of the various meanings of the Pronominal forms of verbs.

Pronominal verbs have an object pronoun that is of the same person and number as the subject of the verb:

> **(Yo) me lavo** *I wash (myself)*
> **(Tú) te vas** *You go away*
> **(Él/ella/usted) se cayó** *He/she/you fell over*
> **(Nosotros) nos queremos** *We love one another*
> **(Vosotros) os arrepentisteis** *You repented*
> **(Ellos/ellas/ustedes) se imaginan** *They/you imagine*

As the examples show, the third-person pronoun used for singular and plural is **se**. This pronoun may variously be translated *himself/herself/itself/yourself/themselves/yourselves*, but it also has several other uses.

Pronominal verbs have many uses in Spanish—far more than in French—and some of them are rather subtle. The picture is made more complicated by the fact that, as explained on p. 114, the pronoun **le** becomes **se** before **lo/la/los/las**, as in **se lo dije a mi madre** *I told it to my mother* (instead of the impossible *'le lo dije a mi madre'*). This is an entirely different use of **se** not related to the issues discussed in this section.

The various uses of Pronominal verbs are best clarified by considering cases in which the subject of the verb is animate (human or some other animal) and cases in which the subject is inanimate.

Pronominal verbs with animate (human or animal) subjects

In this case the Pronominal form of verbs is used:

■ To show that the action is *not* done to someone or something else. Compare **asustas** *you frighten/you're frightening* (i.e. for someone else) and *te* **asustas** *you get frightened* (no one else involved). English often requires translation by *get . . .* + adjective or by *become*. Further examples:

Casó a su hija con un abogado *He married his daughter off to a lawyer*

Su hija se casó con un abogado *His daughter married/got married to a lawyer*

Convence cuando habla así *He's convincing (to others) when he talks like that*

Se convence cuando habla así *He gets convinced when he talks like that*

Se divorciaron al cabo de tres años *They got divorced after three years*

Me matriculé para el curso de inglés *I registered for the course of English*

Me canso fácilmente *I get tired easily*

Se irrita por nada *He gets irritable over nothing*

No te enojes/enfades *Don't get cross*

■ Simply to give the verb a different meaning altogether:

admirar *to admire*	**admirarse** *to be surprised*
despedir *to fire*	**despedirse** *to say good-bye*
dormir *to sleep*	**dormirse** *to go to sleep*
fumar *to smoke*	**fumarse** *to skip a class, meeting* (colloquial)
guardar *to guard*	**guardarse de** *to refrain from*

Some verbs are only found in the pronominal form. The following are common:

abstenerse *to abstain*
acatarrarse *to get a cold*
arrepentirse *to repent*
atreverse a *to dare*
enfermarse *to get ill* (but **enfermar** is used in Spain with the same meaning)
quejarse de *to complain about*
suicidarse *to commit suicide*

There are also certain commonly occurring verbs in which the pronominal form merely has a special nuance that needs separate explanation for each verb. A list of these appears on pp.75 ff.

■ To show that an action is done *to* or *for* oneself: this is the 'reflexive' use of pronominal verbs. The action can be accidental or deliberate. The subject is human or animal for the obvious reason that cups, doors etc. don't usually do things to themselves:

> **Me rasqué** *I scratched myself*
> **Te peinaste** *You did your hair* (literally *you combed yourself*)
> **Mario se ensució** *Mario got himself dirty*
> **Ustedes se van a matar haciendo eso** *You're going to kill yourselves doing that*
> **Se quitó el sombrero** *He took off his hat*
> **Se sacó el dinero del bolsillo** *He took the money out of his (own) pocket*

■ When the verb is plural, to mean *to do something to or for one another*:

This is the 'reciprocal' use of the pronominal form, and again the subjects are usually humans or other animals since doors or bricks don't usually do things to one another:

> **Se escriben todas las semanas** *They write to one another every week*
> **Se daban golpes** *They were hitting one another*
> **Nos respetamos el uno al otro** *We respect one another*

The phrase **el uno al otro** or (when more than two subjects are involved) **los unos a los otros** *one another* may be added to clarify the meaning. **La una a la otra** and **las unas a las otras** are used only when only females are involved.

■ To give the sentence a passive meaning. This is rare with animate subjects because of the clash of meanings with the other uses of the Pronominal form listed above. However, it occurs when the noun does not refer to specific individuals, as in **se ven muchos turistas en agosto** *a lot of tourists are seen in August*. This construction is very common with inanimate subjects (see below).

When the noun refers to specific individuals, a special construction exists which makes Passive **se** unambiguous with human subjects:

> **Se detuvo *a* un narcotraficante** *A drug-pusher was arrested*
>
> **Se admiraba mucho *a* estos profesores** *These teachers were much admired*

In this case the verb is always singular and the preposition **a** is put before the noun. This construction avoids the problem raised by **estos profesores se admiraban mucho**, which would mean *these teachers admired themselves a lot* or . . . *admired one another a lot*.

Students must not confuse this construction with Passive **se** used with nouns referring to inanimate things, as described on page 73. It is possible to rewrite **se admiraba mucho a estos profesores** as **se les**[17] **admiraba mucho** *they were admired a lot*. But this is not possible when the original sentence refers to an inanimate thing, as in **se venden manzanas** *apples are sold*, which can only be rewritten **se venden** *they are sold*, not ***'*se las vende'***. This is discussed in more detail in note (c) on page 74.

---

[17] There is a tendency everywhere to use **le/les** for *him/her/you* (i.e. **usted** or **ustedes**)/*them* in this construction rather than **lo/la/los/las**, although the latter is not incorrect.

■ With singular intransitive verbs (like *to go*, *to arrive*, *to be*), as an equivalent of English impersonal sentences that have the subject *one*, *people* or *you* used impersonally:

> **En España se duerme por la tarde** *In Spain people sleep in the afternoon*
>
> **Por esta carretera se llega al castillo medieval** *Along this road one arrives at the medieval castle*
>
> **Se está mejor al sol** *One's better off in the sun*

This construction cannot be used with a verb that already has **se** attached for some other reason. In this case the pronoun **uno** *one* is required or, in less formal language, **tú**:

> **Si uno se levanta tarde, se pierde lo mejor del día** *If one gets up late one misses the best part of the day* (**levantarse** *to get up* is already a pronominal verb)
>
> **Uno se olvida de esas cosas/Te olvidas de esas cosas** *One forgets such things/you forget such things* (**olvidarse de** *to forget*)

■ With singular transitive verbs which in English would have the pronoun *people*, *one*, *you*.

This construction is sometimes difficult to distinguish from the Passive use of **se** described later. If the sentence contains no noun or pronoun that could be understood as the subject, the impersonal meaning is intended. Thus, if we are talking about olive oil, the sentence **en España se come mucho** means *a lot of it is eaten in Spain* (passive: implied subject *olive oil*). But if the conversation is on general eating habits, the same sentence means *people eat a lot in Spain* (impersonal: the verb has no subject):

> **Se habla de ello, pero no lo creo** *People talk about it, but I don't believe it*
>
> **En este país se escribe y se lee poco** *In this country people don't write or read much*

■ With a few verbs, to give the meaning *to get something done*

> **Me voy a hacer un traje** *I'm going to get a suit made* (or *I'm going to make myself a suit*)
>
> **El rey se construyó un palacio de mármol** *The king built (i.e. had himself built) a marble palace*
>
> **Me tuve que operar de apendicitis** *I had to have an operation for appendicitis*
>
> **Me peino en Vidal Sassoon** *I get my hair done at Vidal Sassoon's*

This construction is not used in some parts of Latin America, where **mandar** plus the Infinitive is used to express the idea of ordering something to be done: **mandó construir un palacio** *he had a palace built* (this construction is also possible in Spain).

■ With verbs meaning *eat*, *drink* or other types of consumption, *know*, *see*, *learn* and one or two others, to emphasize the quantity consumed, learned, seen, etc. This device is optional (but usual) and is only possible when a specific quantity is mentioned:

> **Me bebí tres vasos de ron** *I drank three glasses of rum*
>
> **Te has comido una pizza entera** *You've eaten a whole pizza*
>
> **Se leyó el libro entero** *He read the whole book*
>
> **Se lo creyó todo** *He believed every word of it*

Pronominal verbs with inanimate subjects (neither human nor animals)

In this case the verb can only be third-person (since stones, trees, etc. can't speak for themselves). The Pronominal form of the verb shows

■ That the verb has no outside subject (i.e. that the verb is Intransitive). Compare **abrió la puerta** *he/she opened the door* and **se abrió la puerta** *the door opened*.

> **Esta madera se está pudriendo** *This wood is going rotten*
> **El agua se ha enfriado** *The water's got cold*
> **Se le hinchó la mano** *His hand swelled up*

This construction does not apply to all verbs. Several non-pronominal verbs can also refer to more or less spontaneous actions (i.e. actions that have no external subject):

> **La situación ha mejorado** *The situation has improved*
> **El globo reventó** *The balloon burst*
> **La hierba ha crecido** *The grass has grown*
> **Las cantidades han aumentado** *The quantities have increased*

■ To make the passive. This is much more common with inanimate than with human and other animal subjects:

> **Se rehogan la cebolla y el ajo en aceite caliente** *The onion and garlic are sautéed/lightly fried in hot oil*
> **Se compran libros de ocasión** *Second-hand books bought*
> **Esas cosas no debieron decirse** *Those things shouldn't have been said*

Se acepta la propuesta de la oposición *The opposition's proposal is accepted*

Three important points about this construction are:

(a) The verb should agree in number with the subject. Foreign students should respect this rule whatever they may hear or see: sentences like **'se compra libros de ocasión'* are usually considered incorrect.

(b) This construction should not be followed by **por** + the agent of the action. If the person or thing that performed the action must be mentioned, only the Passive with **ser** (p.64) can be used: **el programa fue diseñado por J. González** *the program* (British *programme*) *was designed by J. González* is correct and **'el programa se diseñó por J. González'* is generally considered to be bad Spanish.

(c) The noun in this construction cannot be replaced by a pronoun. In other words one cannot change **se solucionó el problema** *the problem was solved* into **'se lo solucionó'* for *it was solved*, which is **se solucionó**. Use of an object pronoun is only possible if the original sentence referred to a human being and included the preposition **a** (the construction described on p.70). The following examples should make this clear:

> **Se admira mucho *a* Cervantes** *Cervantes is admired a great deal*
> **Se *le* admira mucho** *He is admired a lot*
>
> **Su novela se publicó el año pasado** *His novel was published last year*
> **Se publicó el año pasado** *It was published last year*
>
> **Se *le* puede ver** *He/she can be seen*
> **Se puede ver** (or) **puede verse** *It can be seen*

Unclassifiable pronominal verbs (subject either animate or inanimate)

A number of Spanish pronominal verbs are unclassifiable. The pronominal form merely has an extra nuance of meaning and these verbs must be learned as separate items. This type of verb raises problems that are not appropriate for a grammar of this size, so the following list includes only a brief description of some frequently encountered forms:

Infinitive	non-Pronominal	Pronominal
aparecer	to appear	to materialize (ghosts, visions)
bajar	to go down stairs drop (prices, etc.)	to get out of to get down from (trees, etc.)
caer	to fall/drop	to fall down/over
conocer	to know (a person)	to know only too well
dejar	to leave something	to leave behind accidentally
devolver	to give back, to vomit	parts of Lat. Am. to come back
encontrar	to find	to find by chance
estar	to be (somewhere)	to stay put in a place
ir	to go	to go away, leave
llegar	to arrive	to approach
llevar	to carry, wear	to take away
marchar	to march	to go away
morir	to die	same, but used of loved ones or for lingering deaths
parecer	to seem	to resemble
pasar	to pass (by) to spend time	to go over the mark

Infinitive	*non-Pronominal*	*Pronominal*
regresar	*to come back*	*to return before time (only Lat. Am.)*
salir	*to leave, exit (normally)*	*to walk out,* (fluid, gas) *to leak*
subir	*go up stairs rise (prices, temperature)*	*get in (cars, etc.) climb (trees, etc.)*
volver	*to come back (normally)*	*to turn back, return before time*

In some cases the difference is more or less simply stylistic, the non-pronominal form being rather more formal:

> **Olvidé decírtelo/Me olvidé de decírtelo/Se me olvidó decírtelo** *I forgot to tell you*
> **Espera/Espérate** *Wait!*
> **Calla/Cállate** *Be quiet!*
> **(Me) gasté todo el dinero que traía** *I spent all the money I had*
> **(Se) inventa cada cuento . . .** *He makes up all sorts of stories . . .*

Often the pronominal form suggests an unplanned or accidental action. Compare

> **La lluvia cae del cielo** *Rain falls from the sky* (natural)
> **(Se) cayó de la mesa** *It fell off the table*
> **Me caí en la calle** *I fell over in the street*

Ser, estar and 'there is'/'there are'

Spanish has two words that both translate as *to be*. They can only rarely be used interchangeably

ESTAR

The verb **estar** must be used:

■ To indicate *where* an object or person is (but not where something is *happening*, in which case use **ser**, as explained below):

> **Madrid está en España** *Madrid's in Spain*
> **Dile que no estoy** *Tell him I'm not at home*
> **¿Dónde está la piscina[18]?** *Where's the swimming-pool?*

■ With adjectives and participles to show the state or condition that something or someone is in, not an inherent characteristic. The condition or state is usually temporary—but not always, as the word **muerto** shows:

> **Estoy cansado/deprimido/contento** *I'm tired/depressed/pleased*
> **Está muerto/vivo** *He's dead/alive*
> **La ventana estaba rota** *The window was broken*
> **Las manzanas están verdes** *The apples are unripe* (**las manzanas son verdes** = *apples are green*)

---

[18] **Piscina = la alberca** in much of Latin America.

Estoy con gripe *I've got the flu*
Estoy bien *I'm feeling fine*

Compare **la nieve está negra** *the snow's black* (because of the soot, dirt) and **la nieve es blanca** *snow is white* (its natural state), or **eres muy guapa** *you're very attractive* and **estás muy guapa** *you're **looking** very attractive*.

■ To show that someone's or something's condition has altered (e.g. since you last saw it):

Manuel está calvo *Manuel has gone bald*
Me han dicho que estás casado *They tell me you're married*
¡Qué delgada está! *Hasn't she got thin!*

Use of **ser** implies something more long-standing: **es casado** *he's a married man*, **es delgada** *she's thin/a thin person*.

■ To describe the taste or appearance of something:

Esta sopa está muy buena/rica *This soup tastes very good/appetizing*
Está muy vieja *She's looking very old*

SER

Ser must be used

■ To link two nouns or a pronoun and a noun:

La cebolla es una planta *The onion is a plant*
Mario es profesor *Mario is a teacher*
Yo soy psicólogo *I'm a psychologist*
Esto es un problema *This is a problem*

The pronoun may be implicit in the verb:

Era un hermoso día *It was a lovely day*
Son estudiantes *They're students*
Son las ocho *It's eight o'clock*

The verb **estar** + a Noun or Pronoun means *to be at home, to be there*:

> **Está Mario** *Mario's there*
> **No está** *He's not at home*

Exceptions to this rule are so rare that beginners can ignore them, although the phrase **está un día hermoso** *it's a lovely day* is commonly heard in Spain.

■ To indicate *where* or *when* an event is happening

> **¿Dónde es la fiesta/clase/conferencia?** *Where's the party/class/lecture (being held)?*
> **La Guerra Civil fue en 1936** *The Civil War was in 1936*

But **estar** must be used for location of a thing: **¿Dónde está la habitación?** *Where's the room?*

■ With adjectives and participles, to show that a quality is an intrinsic part of something's nature rather than its condition or state:

> **Soy americano** *I'm American*
> **Eso es diferente** *That's different*
> **Son míos** *They're mine*
> **Son muy grandes** *They're very tall/big*
> **La Tierra es redonda** *The earth is round*

It is true that in such cases **ser** usually refers to a *permanent* quality, compare **soy rubio** *I'm blond* and **estoy irritado** *I'm irritated*. But **muerto** *dead* takes **estar** and the following possibly temporary states take **ser** in standard Spanish:

> **Soy feliz/desgraciado** *I'm happy/unhappy*
> **Soy rico/pobre** *I'm rich/poor* (or **estoy rico/pobre** for a temporary condition)
> **Soy consciente** *I'm aware* (**estoy consciente** in Lat. America)

Note however the phrase **estoy feliz y contento** *I'm happy and contented*. **Estar feliz/desgraciado** is commonly heard in Latin America, but it is usually avoided in writing.

■ In the phrase **ser de** *to be from, to be made from*

> **Soy de Madrid** *I'm from Madrid*
> **Es de oro** *It's made of gold*

CHANGES OF MEANING WITH *SER* AND *ESTAR*

Some adjectives change meaning according to which verb is used:

Adjective	Meaning with **ser**	Meaning with **estar**
aburrido	*boring*	*bored*
bueno	*good*	*tasty*
cansado	*tiresome*	*tired*
consciente	*aware*	*conscious (not knocked out)*
despierto	*sharp-witted*	*awake*
interesado	*self-seeking*	*interested*
listo	*clever/smart*	*ready*
malo	*bad*	*ill*
orgulloso	*proud/haughty*	*proud (of something)*
rico	*rich*	*delicious*
verde	*green/smutty*	*unripe*
vivo	*alert*	*alive*

THERE IS/THERE ARE

The Spanish for *there is/are* is **hay**. This is a special form of the verb **haber**, and the usual forms of this verb are used for the other tenses of **hay**. When used with this meaning, the verb is always third-person and always singular (although use of the plural for *there were/will be*, e.g. **habían/habrán muchos** for **había/habrá muchos** *there were/will be a lot* is extremely common in spoken Latin-American Spanish and also in Castilian as spoken by Catalans. It should be avoided in writing and it is not accepted in Spain). Examples

> **Hay cinco árboles** *There are five trees*
> **Había varias personas** *There were several people*
> **Hubo una tremenda explosión** *There was a tremendous explosion*

■ When **haber** refers back to some noun already mentioned in the sentence it normally requires an object pronoun:

> **Hay un error, o si no *lo* hay, entonces estas cifras son increíbles** *There's a mistake, or if there isn't then these figures are incredible*

■ The basic meaning of **haber** is *exist*. If the meaning is *is there* (i.e. rather than somewhere else) the verb **estar** is used:

> **Está Antonio** *Antonio is there/There's Antonio*
> **Para eso está el diccionario** *That's what the dictionary is there for*

Compare

> **¿Quién hay que sepa ruso?** *Who is there (i.e. who exists) who knows Russian?*

Articles

THE DEFINITE ARTICLE

The four forms of the Spanish Definite Article (the equivalent of *the*) are:

	singular	*plural*
masculine	**el**	**los**
feminine	**la**	**las**

There is also a 'neuter article', **lo**, discussed on pp. 145 ff.

These words stand in front of a noun and agree in number and gender with it: **el hombre** *the man*, **los hombres** *the men*, **la ventana** *the window* (fem.), **las ventanas** *the windows*.

■ When a feminine noun begins with a stressed **a-** sound, the masculine article is used in the singular, but the noun remains feminine and the feminine articles, definite and indefinite, are used in the plural: **el/un águila** *the/an eagle*, but **las águilas** *the eagles*. The following are some common nouns beginning with stressed **a-** or **ha-**:

África	*Africa*
Asia	*Asia*
el agua	*water*
el/un alma	*soul*
el/un ama de casa	*housewife*
el asma	*asthma*
el hambre	*hunger*

el hampa	*criminal underworld*
el/un abra	*mountain pass* (Lat. Am., Spain **el puerto**)
el/un alza	*rise/increase*
el/un ancla	*anchor*
el/un área	*area*
el/un arma	*weapon*
el/un aula	*lecture room/seminar room*
el/un haba	*bean*
el/un habla	*language/speech form*
el/un hacha	*ax/*(British *axe*)
el/un hada	*fairy*
el/un haya	*beech tree*

If any word comes between these nouns and the article, the normal feminine form reappears: **el agua** *the* water, but *la* **misma agua** *the same water*. **La/una** is always used before *adjectives* beginning with stressed a: **la/una amplia área** *the/a wide area*.

Feminine words beginning with an *unstressed* **a-** sound take the normal feminine articles:

> **la/una amnistía** *the/an amnesty*
> **la/una hamaca** *the/a hammock*

La is used before letters of the alphabet beginning with stressed **a-**: **la a, la hache**.

■ **A** *to* and **el** compound to form **al**. **De** *of* and **el** compound to form **del**: **voy al mercado** *I'm going to market*, **vengo del banco** *I've just come from the bank*. This is not done if the article is part of a proper name: **los lectores de** *El País* *the readers of El País*, **vamos a El Paso** *we're going to El Paso*.

USES OF THE DEFINITE ARTICLE

Article usage is subtle, prone to exceptions and may vary slightly between regions, but the general rule is that the

Spanish Definite Article is used as in English except that:

■ It is required before countable nouns that are generalizations:

> **Las ardillas son animales** *Squirrels* (in general) *are animals*
>
> **Me gustan las fresas** *I like strawberries* (i.e. *strawberries in general*)

■ It is used before abstractions or substances in general when they are the subject or object of a verb or when they stand on their own:

> **la astronomía** *astronomy*
> **la democracia** *democracy*
> **el espacio** *space*
> **la gripe** *flu*
> **el oxígeno** *oxygen*
> **El odio destruye todo** *Hatred destroys everything*
> **Admiro la generosidad** *I admire generosity*

Such nouns often appear without the article after prepositions, especially when they are the second noun in the combination noun + **de** + noun and the English translation could be a compound noun (two nouns joined together): **una lección de filosofía** *a philosophy lesson*, **una carta de amor** *a love letter*, **una fábrica de pan** *a bread factory*.

The article is also not used with nouns describing abstractions and substances after **con** *with* and **sin** *without*: **con entusiasmo** *with enthusiasm*, **sin dinero** *without money*, **los españoles nunca comen nada sin pan** *the Spanish never eat anything without bread*.

■ Articles are omitted before quantities and abstractions that refer only to a part, not to the whole (partitive nouns):

> **Trae azúcar** *Bring some sugar*

> **No he puesto sal** *I haven't put any salt in*
> **Repartieron armas** *They distributed weapons*

See the section on Translation Traps for further remarks on the Spanish equivalents of *some* and *any*.

■ The Definite Article replaces Possessive Adjectives (**mi** *my*, **tu** *your*, **su** *his*, etc.) with parts of the body and with personal belongings, especially when these are the object of a verb or whenever an Indirect Object Pronoun identifies the owner:

> **Mario levantó la mano** *Mario raised his hand*
> **Le robaron la cartera** *They stole his/her note-book/wallet*
> **Yo me quité las botas** *I took off my boots*
> **Te torciste el tobillo** *You twisted your ankle*
> **Póngase el sombrero** *Put on your hat*

■ The article should be used before each noun when more than one occurs, whenever the nouns refer to different things or people:

> **el perro y el gato** *the dog and cat*
> **el padre y la madre de Antonio** *Antonio's father and mother*

but

> **el presidente y secretario del comité** *the chairman and secretary of the committee* (same person)

■ It is used before titles like **señor, señora, señorita**, but not when the person is directly addressed and not before foreign titles:

> **Buenos días, señor/señora Rodríguez** *Good morning Mr/Mrs Rodríguez*
> **Le dije buenos días al señor/a la señora Morán/a míster Brown** *I said Good Day to Sr/Sra Morán/to Mister Brown*

■ It is used before the names of a few countries. There is much disagreement on this matter, but students should note the following points:

(a) Always use the article when a country is modified by an adjective or some other word or phrase that does not form part of its official name: **la España contemporánea** *modern Spain*, **el México de los aztecas** *The Mexico of the Aztecs*, but **Gran Bretaña** *Great Britain*, **Corea del Norte** *North Korea*. The United States is either **Estados Unidos** (singular, the usual form) or **Los Estados Unidos** (plural):

> **Estados Unidos denuncia la actitud de Ruritania** or (less commonly) **Los Estados Unidos denuncian . . .** *USA denounces the attitude of Ruritania*

(b) Use the article with **la India** *India*, **el Reino Unido** *the United Kingdom* and **El Salvador**. The article is more often than not used with **el Líbano** *Lebanon* and, in Latin America, with **la Argentina**. It is also frequent in Latin America with **Perú, Ecuador, Paraguay, Uruguay, Brasil**.

■ It is used with names of languages, except after the verb **hablar** and, usually, after **aprender**: **el español es una lengua latina** *Spanish is a Latin language*, **domina el chino** *he's totally fluent in Chinese*, but **hablo/aprendo inglés** *I speak/am learning English*.

■ The article is used with days of the week and seasons (but not after **en**):

> **Viene los lunes** *He comes on Mondays*
> **Las hojas caen durante el otoño** *The leaves fall during Fall/Autumn*
> **El invierno es la peor estación** *Winter is the worst season*

but

> **En invierno nieva mucho** *It snows a lot in Winter*

■ It is used before the names of streets and squares:

> **Vivo en la Plaza de España** *I live in the Plaza de España*
> **un pequeño hotel de la calle de las Monjas** *a little hotel on Nuns' street*

■ It is used before percentages:

> **El cinco por ciento de los mexicanos . . .** *five percent of Mexicans*

■ It is omitted before the second of two nouns joined by **de** when these form a compound noun. Compare:

> **una voz de mujer** *a woman's voice*
> **la voz de la mujer** *the voice of the woman*
>
> **el agua de manantial** *spring water*
> **el agua del manantial** *the water from the spring*

THE INDEFINITE ARTICLE

The forms of the Spanish Definite Article (the equivalent of *a/an*) are:

	singular	plural
masculine	**un**	**unos**
feminine	**una**	**unas**

Un is used before feminine nouns beginning with stressed **a**, e.g. **un arma** *a weapon*, **un área** *an area*. See p.82.

The Indefinite Article is used in much the same way as its English counterpart, except that:

■ It is omitted after **ser**, and after verbs meaning *to become*, before the names of professions and, often, before words denoting sex:

> **Es profesora** *She's a teacher*
> **Quiere hacerse diplomático** *He wants to become a diplomat*
> **No digo eso sólo porque yo sea mujer** *I don't say that just because I'm a woman*

But it is retained if the noun is qualified or modified by some word or phrase:

> **Es un profesor magnífico** *He's a magnificent teacher*
> **Es una mujer inteligente** *She's an intelligent woman*

■ It is omitted after **tener** *to have*, **llevar** *to wear*, **sacar** *to take out* and a few other common verbs, when the direct object is something of which we usually only have one:

> **Tiene mujer/secretaria/paraguas** *He's got a wife/secretary/umbrella*
> **Mi casa tiene jardín y garaje** *My house has a garden and garage*
> **Busca novia** *He's looking for a girlfriend*
> **Lleva corbata** *He's wearing a tie*

but **tengo un dólar** *I've got a dollar*, **tengo una hermana** *I've got a sister* (because in both cases it would be normal to have more than one). But the article reappears if the noun is qualified: **lleva *una* corbata de seda** *he's wearing a silk tie*, **tiene *una* mujer muy atractiva**[19] *he has a very attractive wife*.

■ It is usually omitted after **sin** *without*, **con** *with* and **como** when it means *for/as*:

[19] **Guapo/guapa** is the usual word in Spain for *good-looking*, but it tends to mean *brave/tough* in Latin America, where **buen mozo/buena moza** is often used for *good-looking*. **Atractivo** is used internationally.

un sobre sin estampilla (Spain **sin sello**) *an envelope without a stamp*
un hombre con pasaporte *a man with a passport*
Me lo dio como regalo *He gave it to me as a present*
Ha venido como asesor *He's come as an adviser*

But it is used before **con** when it means *accompanied by*: **ha venido con un amigo** *he's come with a friend*.

■ It is not used before **otro** *another*, or after **qué** *what*, **medio** *half* and **tal** *such a*:

Hay otra película que quiero ver *There's another movie/film I want to see*
¡Qué pena! *What a pity!*
medio kilo *half a kilo*
tal día *such a day*

■ It is used with percentages:

Los precios subieron en un cinco por ciento *Prices rose five percent*

USES OF *UNOS/UNAS*

Spanish is unusual in that the Indefinite Article has a plural form. This is used:

■ To mean *approximately*

Trajeron unos mil kilos *They brought about 1000 kilos*

■ To mean *a/an* before nouns that do not appear in the singular, or to mean *a pair of* before nouns like *scissors*, *shoes*, *pants* that either come in pairs or are symmetrically shaped:

unos zapatos de cuero *a pair of leather shoes*
unas tijeras *a pair of scissors*

> **unos pantalones** *a pair of pants* (Brit. *trousers*)

In the case of nouns that always appear in the plural, e.g. **los celos** *jealousy*, **las vacaciones** *vacation/holidays*, **las ganas** *urge/desire*, and before nouns that would mean a profession if the Indefinite Article were omitted, **unos/unas** must be used whenever **un/una** would be used before a singular noun:

> **unas vacaciones magníficas** *a magnificent vacation/holiday*
> **Yo tenía unas ganas terribles** *I had a terrible urge*
> **Sentía unos celos incontrolables** *She/he felt an uncontrollable jealousy*
> **Sois/son unos payasos** *You're a bunch of clowns* (in the way you act)

Compare

> **Sois/son payasos** *You're clowns* (profession).

■ To mean *a few, a couple of*:

> **Me dejó unos libros** *He left/lent me a few books*
> **Dale unas pesetas** *Give him a couple of pesetas*
> **Unas veces sí, otras no** *Sometimes yes, others no*

Nouns

GENDER OF NOUNS

Spanish nouns are either masculine or feminine and this has major consequences for the shape of any adjectives, articles or pronouns that may be associated with a noun.

The gender of nouns is not related to questions of sex, except when the nouns refer to human beings or to a few well-known animals. There are few absolutely foolproof rules for predicting the gender of the other nouns in the language, so the best rule is to learn every noun with its definite article, which will soon become instinctive. It must be remembered that the grammatical gender of nouns referring to objects and abstractions is basically arbitrary and has nothing to with their meaning. The fact that **el árbol** *tree* is masculine in Spanish is arbitrary: 'tree' is feminine in the closely-related languages Portuguese and French.

The following generalizations can be made:

■ Nouns referring to men or boys are masculine, and nouns referring to women or girls are feminine:

el hombre *man*	**la mujer** *woman*
el modelo *male model*	**la modelo** *female model*
el juez *male judge*	**la juez** *female judge*

This generalization also applies to a few domestic and

well-known wild animals that have special forms to denote
the female of the species:

el caballo *horse*	la yegua *mare*
el león *lion*	la leona *lioness*
el toro *bull*	la vaca *cow*

A longer list of these words appears below at p.97.

There are only a few words that are of invariable gender
and apply to human beings of either sex, e.g.:

el bebé *baby*
el genio *genius*
el personaje *character* (in film, etc.),
la estrella *star* (in films, etc.)
la persona *person*
la víctima *victim*
la visita *visitor* (and *visit*)

■ Apart from those already mentioned and few others like
el lobo/la loba *wolf/she-wolf*, el gato/la gata *tom-cat/she-
cat*, el perro/la perra *dog/bitch*, the names of animals are
of fixed arbitrary gender. The gender of these nouns must
be learned separately from the dictionary:

la ardilla *squirrel*
el avestruz *ostrich*
la culebra *grass snake*
el lagarto *lizard*
la langosta *lobster*
el salmón *salmon*

The invariable words **macho** *male* and **hembra** *female*
can be added if necessary:

el salmón hembra *the female salmon*
las ardillas macho *the male squirrels*

■ Nouns referring to inanimate things (and to plants) are
of fixed gender. As was mentioned before, the gender of
these words cannot be deduced from the meaning of the

word: compare **el cuarto** (masculine) and **la habitación** (feminine) which both mean *room*.

However, the ending of a Spanish nouns that does not refer to a human being often gives a clue to the likely gender of a word:

■ Nouns ending in **-o** are masculine, e.g. **el libro** *book*, **el hombro** *shoulder*. Common exceptions are:

> **la foto** *photo*
> **la libido** *libido*
> **la mano** *hand*
> **la moto** *motor-cycle*
> **la radio** *radio* (in Spain and Argentina, but masculine in northern Latin America)

■ Nouns ending in **-r** are masculine, except **la flor** *flower*, **la coliflor** *cauliflower*, **la labor** *labor*/(Brit. *labour*):

> **el bar** *bar*
> **el calor** *heat*
> **el color** *color/colour*
> **el valor** *value*

■ Nouns ending in a stressed vowel are masculine:

> **(el) Canadá** *Canada*
> **el bisturí** *scalpel*
> **el tisú** *tissue*
> **el sofá** *sofa/couch*

■ Nouns ending in **-aje** are masculine:

> **el viaje** *journey*
> **el equipaje** *baggage*
> **el paisaje** *landscape*

■ Nouns ending in **-ie** are feminine:

> **la intemperie** *bad weather*
> **la serie** *series*

■ Other nouns ending in -e are unpredictable and must be learned separately:

> **el arte** (masculine) *art*
> **las artes** (feminine) *the arts*
> **la fuente** *fountain*
> **el puente** *bridge*
> **la parte** *part*
> **el parte** *bulletin*

■ Nouns ending in -**a** are feminine, with the important exceptions listed at (a) through (c) below:

> **la cama** *bed*
> **la casa** *house*
> **la mariposa** *butterfly*
> **la pera** *pear*

Exceptions:

(a)
> **el alerta** *alert*
> **el cometa** *comet*
> **el día** *day*
> **el insecticida** *insecticide*
> **el mañana** *the morrow/tomorrow* (cf. **la mañana** *morning*)
> **el mapa** *map*
> **el mediodía** *noon*
> **el planeta** *planet*
> **el tranvía** *street-car/tram*
> **el vodka** *vodka*
> **el yoga** *yoga*

(b) Compound nouns consisting of a verb + a noun:

> **el montacargas** *freight elevator/service lift*
> **el guardarropa** *check room/cloakroom*

(c) Words ending in -**ma** that are of Greek origin. These are usually words that have a faintly technical or 'intellectual' character, e.g.

el **aroma** *aroma*
el **clima** *climate*
el **coma** *coma*
el **crucigrama** *crossword puzzle*
el **diagrama** *diagram*
el **dilema** *dilemma*
el **diploma** *diploma*
el **dogma** *dogma*
el **enigma** *enigma*
el **esquema** *scheme*
el **fantasma** *ghost*
el **panorama** *panorama*
el **pijama** *pajamas/pyjamas* (feminine in Latin America)
el **plasma** *plasma*
el **poema** *poem*
el **problema** *problem*
el **programa** *program/programme*
el **síntoma** *symptom*
el **sistema** *system*
el **telegrama** *telegram*
el **tema** *theme/topic/subject*

Words that end in **-ma** and are not of Greek origin are feminine, e.g. **la cama** *bed*, **la forma** *shape*, **la lima** *lime* (the fruit) or *file* (i.e. for wood or fingernails). Two words that are of Greek origin but are nevertheless feminine are **la lágrima** *tear* (i.e. the sort that one weeps) and **la estratagema** *stratagem*.

■ Nouns ending in **-tad**, **-dad** and **-tud** are feminine:

la **ciudad** *city*
la **libertad** *liberty*
la **verdad** *truth*
la **virtud** *virtue*

■ Nouns ending in **-ción** are feminine:

> **la intuición** *intuition*
> **la nación** *nation*
> **la reproducción** *reproduction*

■ Nouns ending in **-is** are feminine:

> **la tesis** *thesis*
> **la crisis** *crisis*
> **la apendicitis** *appendicitis*

Exceptions: **el análisis** *analysis*, **el énfasis** *emphasis*, **el éxtasis** *ecstasy*, **el oasis** *oasis*, **los paréntesis** *brackets*.

■ Feminine words beginning with *stressed* **a-** or **ha-** take the masculine definite article in the singular despite always being feminine in gender: **el agua** *water*, **el alma** *soul*. See p. 82 for discussion.

■ Some words have different meanings according to gender:

el capital *capital (money)*	**la capital** *capital (city)*
el cólera *cholera*	**la cólera** *wrath/anger*
el coma *coma*	**la coma** *comma*
el cometa *comet*	**la cometa** *kite* (the sort you fly)
el corte *cut*	**la corte** *the Court*
el cura *priest*	**la cura** *cure*
el editorial *editorial*	**la editorial** *publishing house*
el frente *front (military)*	**la frente** *forehead*
el guardia *policeman*	**la guardia** *guard*
el mañana *tomorrow/morrow*	**la mañana** *morning*
el margen *margin*	**la margen** *riverbank*
el orden *order* (opposite of *disorder*)	**la orden** *order* (=*command* or *religious order*)
el Papa *Pope*	**la papa** (Lat. Am.) *potato*[20]
el parte *bulletin*	**la parte** *part*

[20] The word used in Spain is **la patata**.

el **pendiente** *earring*	la **pendiente** *slope*
el **pez** *fish*	la **pez** *pitch (i.e. tar)*
el **policía** *policeman*	la **policía** *police force*
el **radio** *radius/radium*	la **radio** *radio* (masc. from Colombia northwards)

FORMS OF NOUNS REFERRING TO FEMALES

The following remarks apply to nouns referring to female human beings and to those few animals for which there is a special word denoting the female.

■ There are special words for the female of some persons and animals:

el **actor**/la **actriz** *actor/actress*
el **alcalde**/la **alcaldesa** *mayor/mayoress*
el **caballo**/la **yegua** *stallion/mare*
el **macho**/el **cabrío** *billy-goat* la **cabra** *she-goat*
el **carnero**/la **oveja** *ram/ewe (sheep)*
el **conde**/la **condesa** *count/countess*
el **duque**/la **duquesa** *duke/duchess*
el **emperador**/la **emperatriz** *emperor/empress*
el **gallo**/la **gallina** *rooster/hen (chicken)*
el **héroe**/la **heroína** *hero/heroine*
el **león**/la **leona** *lion/lioness*
el **marido**/la **mujer** *husband/wife*[21] or *woman*
el **padre**/la **madre** *father/mother*
el **príncipe**/la **princesa** *prince/princess*
el **rey**/la **reina** *king/queen*
el **toro**/la **vaca** *bull/cow*
el **yerno**/la **nuera** *son-in-law/daughter-in-law*

[21] In Latin America **el esposo**/la **esposa** should be used for *husband/wife*, the word **mujer** being reserved for *woman*.

el varón/la hembra *male/female*[22]

With the exception of **la oveja** *sheep/ewe*, **la gallina** *chicken/hen*, **la cabra** *goat/she-goat* and **el toro** *bull*[23], the masculine form of words referring to humans and animals also refers to mixed groups or the species in general:

> **los reyes** *kings/the king and queen/kings* and *queens*
> **los hermanos** *brothers/brothers and sisters*
> **los padres** *fathers/parents*
> **los tíos** *uncles/uncles and aunts*
> **los zorros** *male foxes/foxes*

■ With the exceptions shown, words referring to females are formed from the words referring to males in various ways, according to the ending:

-és > -esa
> **el francés—la francesa** *Frenchman/woman*
> **el inglés—la inglesa** *Englishman/woman*

-o > -a
> **el abogado—la abogada** *lawyer*
> **el americano—la americana** *American*
> **el cerdo** *pig*—**la cerda** *sow*
> **el gitano** *gypsy*—**la gitana** *gypsy woman*
> **el perro** *dog*—**la perra** *bitch*
> **el psicólogo—la psicóloga** *psychologist*

Exceptions: **el/la miembro** *member*, **el/la modelo** *model*, **el/la soldado** *soldier*, **el/la piloto** *pilot*, *racing driver*.

---

[22] **Varón** is a polite word for *male*. **Macho** is used for animals and, pejoratively, for the type of man who tries to dominate women.

[23] **Las vacas** = *cows*. *Cattle* is **el ganado vacuno**. **El ganado** includes cows, horses, sheep, donkeys and pigs, and can be made specific with adjectives like **caballar** (horses), **lanar** (sheep), **menor** (sheep, goats, pigs), etc. These terms are rather technical in style.

-a no change

> **el artista—la artista** *artist*
> **el belga—la belga** *Belgian*

-í no change

> **el iraní—la iraní** *Iranian*
> **el marroquí—la marroquí** *Moroccan*

-e usually no change, but a few change **-e** to **-a** (although the invariable forms are common and are more formal in style) :

> **el estudiante—la estudiante** *student*
> **el amante—la amante** *lover*
> **el principiante—la principianta** *beginner*

-ón > -ona

> **el preguntón—la preguntona** *inquisitive person*
> **el campeón—la campeona** *champion*
> **el león—la leona** *lioness*

Some words denoting professions tend to be invariable in formal language, especially in Spain, but they may form their feminine with **-a** in informal speech, although usage is at present in flux. The formal form is safer and is felt to be more respectful:

masculine	*formal/informal fem.*
el jefe *boss*	**la jefe/la jefa**
el juez *judge*	**la juez/la jueza**
el médico *doctor*	**la médico/la médica**
el primer ministro *prime minister*	**la primer ministro/la primera ministra**
el arquitecto *architect*	**la arquitecto/la arquitecta**
el sargento *sergeant*	**la sargento/la sargenta**

PLURAL OF NOUNS

The plural of Spanish nouns is formed as follows:

■ Nouns ending in an unstressed vowel or in stressed **e** add **-s**:

la casa *house*	las casas *houses*
el libro *book*	los libros *books*
el puente *bridge*	los puentes *bridges*
la tribu *tribe*	las tribus *tribes*
el café *coffee*	los cafés *coffees*
el té *tea*	los tés *teas*

■ Nouns ending in a stressed vowel other than **-e** add **-es**:

el iraní *Iranian*	los iraníes *Iranians*
el marroquí *Moroccan*	los marroquíes *Moroccans*
el tabú *taboo*	los tabúes *taboos*

Exceptions:

el menú *menu*	los menús *menus*
el papá *father*	los papás *fathers*
el sofá *sofa*	los sofás *sofas*
el tisú *paper tissue*	los tisús *tissues*
la mamá *mother*	las mamás *mothers*

There is a growing tendency in informal spoken language to make the plural of all nouns ending in a stressed vowel by simply adding **-s**.

■ Nouns ending in a consonant add **-es**:

el inglés *Englishman*	los ingleses *Englishmen*
la nación *nation*	las naciones *nations*
la red *net/network*	las redes *nets/networks*

As the examples show, an accent written on a vowel disappears after **-es** is added, unless the vowel is **í** or **ú**:

el baúl *trunk (for storage)*   los baúles *trunks*
el país *country*   los países *countries*

Nouns whose singular ends in **-en** require an accent on the second vowel from last in the plural to show that the stress has not shifted:

la imagen *image*   las imágenes *images*
el origen *origin*   los orígenes *origins*
la virgen *virgen*   las vírgenes *virgins*

■ Many recent foreign borrowings add **-s** in the plural even though they end with a consonant:

el bit *bit* (in computing) los bits *bits*
el iceberg *iceberg*   los icebergs *the icebergs*
el show *show*   los shows *shows*

■ The following do not change in the plural:

(a) Nouns whose singular ends in an *unstressed* vowel + **-s**:

la crisis *crisis*   las crisis *crises*
el lunes *Monday*   los lunes *Mondays*
el miércoles *Wednesday*   los miércoles
                              Wednesdays
la tesis *thesis*   las tesis *theses*

(b) Nouns ending in **-x**:

el fax *fax*   los fax *faxes*

(c) A few foreign words which must be learned separately:

el déficit *deficit*   los déficit *deficits*
el láser *laser*   los láser *lasers*

■ In the case of compound nouns consisting of two nouns, only the first noun is pluralized:

el año luz *light year*   los años luz *light
                              years*

el hombre rana *frogman*	**los hombres rana** *frogmen*
el perro guía *guide-dog*	**los perros guía** *guide-dogs*
la ciudad estado *city-state*	**las ciudades estado** *city-states*
la idea clave *key idea*	**las ideas clave** *key ideas*

One important exception is **el país miembro—los países miembros** *member country/member countries*.

■ The following plurals are irregular:

Three nouns show a shift in the position of the accent:

el carácter *character*	**los caracteres** *characters*
el espécimen *specimen*	**los especímenes** *specimens*
el régimen *regimes*	**los regímenes** *regimes*

The plural of the word **lord** *lord* (British title) is **los lores** *lords*.

COLLECTIVE NOUNS

Collective Nouns (see Glossary) are treated as singular, whereas familiar English often treats them as plural.

La minoría votó por el partido nacionalista *The minority voted for the nationalist party*
La mayoría es cristiana *The majority are christian*
El público se está irritando *The audience are/is getting irritated*
El pueblo está descontento *The people are discontented*
La policía es . . . *The police are . . .*

This applies even to collective numerals (see p.196 for more details):

> **Un billón de pesetas fue invertido** *A billion[24] pesetas were invested*
> **La primera treintena** *the first thirty or so*

However, plural agreement is optionally possible when a singular collective noun and a plural non-collective noun are joined by **de**:

> **Una treintena de personas perdieron** (or **perdió**) **la vida**
> **La mayoría de los indígenas son católicos** *The majority of the natives are Catholics*

---

[24] A million million in Spain. The American billion (1000 million) is much used in Latin America.

Personal Pronouns

FORMS OF PERSONAL PRONOUNS

Spanish Personal Pronouns can take different forms depending on Person (1st, 2nd or 3rd), Number (singular or plural) and grammatical function (Subject, Prepositional or Object). In the case of second-person pronouns, there are also different forms depending on the degree of familiarity.

SUBJECT PRONOUNS

yo	*I*
tú	*you* (familiar)
vos	*you* (familiar, Argentina and Central America; see below)
usted	*you* (formal)
él	*he/it*

ella	*she/it*
ello	*it* (neuter gender, explained on p.145)
nosotros	*we* (masculine or masc. and feminine mixed)
nosotras	*we* (feminine only)
vosotros	*you* (familiar, masculine or masc. and feminine mixed. Spain only)
vosotras	*you* (familiar, feminine only. Spain only)
ustedes	*you* (plural. Only formal use in Spain, both formal and familiar in Latin America)
ellos	*they* (masculine or masc. and feminine mixed)
ellas	*they* (feminine only)

Nosotros *we* (object form **nos**) is used to refer to male persons or to males and females mixed. **Nosotras** is used by females when referring to themselves and other females. See below for **vosotros/vosotras**.

OBJECT PRONOUNS

me	*me*
te	*you* (for **tú** or **vos**)
lo	*him/it/you* (**usted**) masculine Direct Object only
la	*her/it/you* (**usted**) feminine Direct Object only
le	*her/it/you* (**usted**) masculine or feminine Indirect Object
nos	*us*
os	*you* informal plural, Spain only
los	*them/you* (**ustedes**) masculine or mixed masc. and fem. Direct Object
las	*them* feminine Direct Object
les	*them/you* (**ustedes**) masculine or feminine Indirect Objects only

| se | 3rd-person reflexive pronoun, singular or plural, discussed on pp.66 ff |

Masculine plural pronouns are always used for groups of people or objects when at least one of them is masculine: **hay dos profesores y treinta profesoras.** *Los* he contado *there are two male teachers and thirty female. I counted them.*

Le and **les** become **se** whenever they precede **lo, la, los** or **las**: see p.114 for details.

Usted and **ustedes** take third-person object pronouns, so **yo la vi ayer** can mean *I saw her/it yesterday* or *I saw you yesterday.* Adding **a usted** or **a ustedes** removes any ambiguity in this case and also makes the form even more formal and polite—**yo las vi a ustedes** *I saw you* (plural)—but it is rarely necessary to do this since context normally makes the meaning clear.

PREPOSITIONAL FORMS OF PERSONAL PRONOUNS

Only the first and second-person singular Personal Pronouns and the so-called 'reflexive' pronoun **se** have special forms, used after most prepositions:

> **de/a/por mí**[25] *of/to/by me*
> **para/contra ti** (no accent!) *for/against you*
> **de sí mismo/de sí misma** *of himself/of herself*

When the preposition is **con** a special form is used:

> **conmigo** *with me*: **ven conmigo** *come with me*
> **contigo** *with you*: **fue contigo** *he/she went with you*
> **consigo** *with himself/herself/yourself/themselves/ yourselves*: **llevan el dinero consigo** *they're carrying the money on them(selves)*

For the rest of the pronouns the ordinary subject forms
    [25] The accent distinguishes it from **mi** *my*.

are used: **contra él/ella/usted** *against him/her/you*, **de nosotros/vosotros/ustedes/ellos/ellas** *of us/you/them*, **con ellos/ustedes** *with them/you*.

The ordinary subject forms **yo** and **tú** are also used after **entre** *between* (**entre tú y yo** *between you and me*), **según** *according to* (**según tú** *according to you*), **excepto**, **menos** and **salvo** *except* (i.e. **excepto tú, menos yo** *except you, except me*), **hasta** when it means *even* (and not as *far as* or *up to*), and **incluso** *even*.

SUBJECT PRONOUNS

These pronouns are required only in special circumstances since Spanish verbs already include their subject pronouns in the ending: **fumo** means *I smoke, I'm smoking*, **fuiste** means *you went*. **Yo fumo** means *I* (and not someone else) *smoke*, **tú fuiste** means *you* (and not someone else) *went*. The pronouns must therefore not be used unnecessarily: '*¿Sabes lo que le ha pasado a Ana? Ella se ha roto el brazo*' *Do you know what's happened to Ana? She's broken her arm* does not make good sense in Spanish because it wrongly stresses the *she*; the **ella** must be deleted. The subject pronouns are used

■ When there is a switch from one pronoun to another, as in

> **Yo estoy aquí todo el día trabajando mientras que tú no haces nada** *I'm here all day working while you do nothing*
> **Te confundiste. Yo soy Juan. Él es Antonio** *You made a mistake. I'm Juan. He's Antonio*

Sometimes the switch is implied rather than explicit **yo sé la respuesta** *I know the answer* (implies *but you don't/he doesn't, etc.*).

■ When the subject pronoun stands in isolation (i.e. without a verb):

—¿**Quién va con Pedro?** —**Yo** *'Who's going with Pedro?' 'Me'*

—¿**Quién fue el primero?** —**Tú y ella** *'Who was first?' 'You and her'*

■ In the case of all pronouns except **yo, tú** and **se**, after prepositions (see above).

■ In the case of **usted** and **ustedes**, from time to time in order to be emphatically polite:

> **No se olvide usted de que tiene que estar aquí mañana a las ocho en punto** *Please don't forget that you must be here tomorrow at eight o'clock sharp*

FORMAL AND INFORMAL MODES OF ADDRESS

■ **Tú** (and the corresponding object and prepositional forms **te** and **ti**) is used to address anyone with whom one is on first-name terms, e.g. relatives, friends, colleagues, children, and also animals. The only exception to the rule about first names might be employees with whom one is not on familiar terms: **Antonia, haga el favor de preparar la cena** *Antonia, please prepare dinner* (speaking to a cook or maid).

Spanish **tú** is used much more widely than French **vous** or German **Sie**: Spaniards under about forty use it even to total strangers of their own age or younger, but it should not be used to older strangers or persons in authority. Latin Americans are generally less ready to use **tú** than Spaniards.

■ **Vos** (object form **te**, possessive adjective **tu**, prepositional form **vos**) is used instead of **tú** in many parts of Latin America, but the only places where this usage is accepted as correct by all social groups are Argentina and most of Central America (but not Mexico). **Vos** tends to be considered 'unrefined' elsewhere in Latin America (if it is used at all), and it is not heard in Spain.

■ **Vosotros** (and the object form **os**) is used only in Spain to address more than one person when one normally addresses them individually as **tú**. Two or more females are addressed as **vosotras**. Latin Americans use **ustedes** (see below).

■ **Usted** (object forms **lo/la/le**) is used everywhere to address strangers, especially older strangers, and persons in authority. It is always used for people with whom one is not on first-name terms. The verb is always in the third-person singular.

  Ustedes (object forms **los/las/les**) is used in Latin America to address two or more people, regardless of one's relationship with them. Latin-Americans use it for small children and even for animals. In Spain it is used to address two persons whom one normally addresses individually as **usted**. The verb is always in the third-person plural.

OBJECT PRONOUNS

The object forms have two basic functions:

(a) To denote the Direct Object (see Glossary) of an action

> **Me criticaron** *They criticized me*
> **Me llamó** *He/she/you called me*
> **Te admiran** *They admire you*
> **No lo sé** *I don't know it*
> **Nos persiguen** *They're persecuting us,*
> **Él os respeta** (Lat. Am. **Él los/las respeta**) *He respects you* (plural)

(b) To denote the Indirect Object (see Glossary) of an action

> **Le dicen** *They say to him/her/you*
> **Usted les mandó una carta** *You sent a letter to them*
> **Dame algo** *Give me something*
> **Dile** *Tell him/her*
> **Nos dice** *He says to us*
> **Os envían** *They send to you* (i.e. *a vosotros*)
> **Les da dinero** *He gives money to them* (or *to you* = *a ustedes*)

It should be noted that the term *Indirect Object* includes not only the meaning *to . . .* but also *from* after verbs meaning removal or taking off/away from, and in some cases it can be translated *for*:

> **Me compró una camisa** *He bought a shirt off me* (or *for me*)
> **Les confiscaron el dinero que llevaban** *They confiscated (i.e. took off them) the money they were carrying*
> **Me robaron cien dólares** *They stole $100 from me*
> **Te escribiré el ensayo** *I'll write the essay for you*

Object Pronouns are also used to show the person affected by something done to his/her body or to some intimate possession:

> **Me sacó una muela** *He took one of my teeth out*
> **Te vas a romper una uña** *You're going to break a finger-nail*
> **Le has manchado la falda** *You've stained her skirt*

The third-person pronouns used for the Indirect Object are unusual in that they differ from the corresponding Third-Person Direct Object Pronouns:

3rd-Person Direct Object Forms

Lo vieron *They saw him/it/you* (**usted**)
La vieron *They saw her/it/you* (**usted**)
Los vieron *They saw them/you* (masculine)
Las vieron *They saw them/you* (feminine)

3rd-Person Indirect Object Forms

Le dijeron *They said **to** him/her/you*
Les dijeron *They said **to** them/you*
Le torcieron el brazo *They twisted his/her/your arm*
Le/les have no separate feminine form.

FURTHER REMARKS ON THE USE OF *LE* AND *LES*

The relationship between **le/les** and **lo/la/los/las** is rather complicated, since **le** and **les** are quite often used as *Direct* Object pronouns as well as for Indirect Objects. This happens:

■ In Central and Northern Spain, and in the standard written language of Spain, when the pronoun refers to a *human male* and is singular:

> **Le vimos** *We saw **him*** (elsewhere **lo vimos**)
> **Lo vimos** *We saw **it***

Le is usual among the 'best' speakers in Spain (academics, schoolteachers, newsreaders, editors of quality publications, most writers), but the Academy in fact prefers **lo vimos** for both *we saw him* and *we saw it*. The **lo** construction is slowly spreading in Spain and is easier for beginners to remember. In Northern Spain one constantly also hears **le/les** used for human female direct objects (i.e. instead of **la**), but this is not approved usage.

Use of **les** for plural human direct objects is also very common in speech in central and northern Spain and is seen in writing in Spain, but it is not approved by the

Academy and other authorities; **los/las** should be used:
los vi ayer *I saw them (masc.) yesterday*, **las vi ayer** *I saw them (fem.) yesterday*.

■ With the following common verbs: (the list is not exhaustive)

> **creer** *to believe* (when its object is human): **yo le creo** *I believe him/her*
>
> **disgustar** *to displease*
>
> **gustar** *to please*: **les gusta** *they like it*
>
> **importar** *to matter to* . . .
>
> **interesar** *to interest*
>
> **llenar** when it means *fulfill* (British *fulfil*) in sentences like **ser ama de casa no le llena** *being a housewife doesn't fulfill her*. Compare **lo/la llena** *he fills it up*.
>
> **pegar** *to beat*: **su marido le pega mucho** *her husband beats her a lot*

■ **Le/les** are also preferred for third-person *human* direct objects in a number of other constructions, and in most parts of the Spanish-speaking world, although this topic is rather advanced for a grammar of this type. The most common cases are:

> (a) Optionally (but usually) after Impersonal **se**:
>
> **Se le** (or **lo**) **reconoció** *He was recognized*

> (b) Optionally when the direct object is **usted(es)** (but **lo/las/los/las** are also correct). Latin-American speakers from some regions may, for example, say
>
> **Perdone, señor, no quería molestarle** *Excuse me, sir, I didn't want to bother you*

even though they would use **lo** in other contexts.

> (c) Often when the subject of the verb is non-human and non-animal. Compare

> *Le* **espera una catástrofe** *A catastrophe awaits her*

and

> *La* **espera su hermana** *Her sister is waiting for her*

Usage fluctuates in some of these cases, especially in Latin America. Colombians especially tend to prefer **lo/la/los/las** where others may use **le**.

ORDER AND POSITION OF OBJECT PRONOUNS

When two or more object pronouns appear in a sentence there are strict rules governing their order and their position in relation to the verb.

The order of object pronouns is:

se	te	me	le lo/la
os	nos	les los/las	

In other words, **se** (discussed on p.66 ff) always comes first, **te/os** always precedes all the rest, **me/nos** always precedes any pronoun beginning with **l**, and **le/les** precedes **lo/la/los/las** (and then becomes **se** as explained after the examples).

This order applies whether the pronouns appear before the verb or as suffixes:

> **Te lo dijo** *He told it to you*
> **Os la entregaron** *They delivered it to you*, Lat. Am. **Se lo entregaron**
> **No te me pongas difícil** *Don't get difficult 'on me'*
> **Me lo enseñó** *He showed it to me*
> **Nos los enviaron** *They sent them to us*
> **Se te dijo** *It was said to you* (see p.73)
> **Se lo comuniqué a usted** *I informed you*
> **Quiero regalártelo** *I want to present it to you/make a present of it to you*

No pueden dárnoslo *They can't give it to us*

Note: Whenever **le** or **les** immediately precede **lo, la, los** or **las, le/les** become **se**. This is the so-called 'rule of two l's': two Spanish object pronouns beginning with **l** can *never* stand side-by-side:

> **Se lo dije** (never *'le lo dije'*) *I told him/her/you/them*
>
> **Se los dieron** (never *'les los dieron'*) *They gave them to him/her/you/them*

The overworked pronoun **se** can therefore (among other things) stand for **a él** *to him*, **a ella** *to her*, **a usted** *to you*, **a ellos** *to them* (masc.), **a ellas** *to them* (fem.) and **a ustedes** *to you* (plural). Usually context makes the meaning clear, but if real ambiguity arises one adds one of the phrases just listed:

> **Se lo dije a ella** *I told **her***
>
> **Se lo quité a ellos** *I took it off/from **them*** (masc.)
>
> **Se lo daré a ustedes** *I'll give it to **you***

These additional phrases should not be used unless emphasis or clarity are absolutely essential.

Familiar Latin-American speech very frequently shows that **se** stands for **les** and not **le** by adding **-s** to the Direct Object pronoun: **se *los* dije** = **se lo dije a ellos/ellas/ustedes** *I told it to them/you*. This is not accepted in written Spanish and is not heard in Spain.

POSITION OF OBJECT PRONOUNS

Object Personal Pronouns are placed:

■ *Before* all finite verb forms (i.e. forms other than the Gerund and Infinitive) *except* the positive Imperative. The pronouns appear in the order given above. No word can come between the pronouns and the verb:

> **Me lo deben** *They/you owe it to me*

Yo no la conozco *I don't know her*

Te lo has olvidado *You've forgotten it* (**olvidarse** = *to forget*)

Siempre la recordaremos *We'll always remember her*

No me lo tires *Don't throw it away for me*

No nos lo digan *Don't tell it to us*

■ *Attached to positive* Imperatives in the order given above:

Dímelo *Tell it to me*

Contestadme (Lat. Am. **Contéstenme**) *Answer me* (plural)

Dénselo a ella *Give* (plural) *it to her* (see p.114 for **se**)

The position of the stress does not change, so a written accent is required when the stress falls more than two syllables from the end of the word formed after the pronouns are added: **organizo** *I organize*, **organízamelo** *organize it for me*.

■ *Attached to* Infinitives and Gerunds in the order given above:

Sería una buena idea vendérnoslo *It would be a good idea to sell it to us*

No creo que sea posible explicárselo *I don't think it's possible to explain it to him* (**selo** for **'lelo'*)

Está pintándomelo *He's painting it for me*

Me llamó pidiéndome dinero *He called me asking for money*

As the examples show, a written accent may be required to show that the stress has not shifted.

However, if the Infinitive or the Gerund is preceded by a Finite Verb (see Glossary), pronouns may be optionally put in front of the latter:

No puede decírmelo/No me lo puede decir *He can't tell it to me*

Queríamos guardártelo/Te lo queríamos guardar *We wanted to keep it for you*

Voy a hacerlo/Lo voy a hacer *I'm going to do it*

Estaba esperándonos/Nos estaba esperando *She/he was waiting for us*

Iba diciéndoselo/Se lo iba diciendo *He was going along saying it to himself/to her/to them, etc.*

The second of these constructions is more usual in everyday language, but it is not possible with all verbs. The best advice for beginners is to use it only with the following verbs:

Verbs followed by Infinitive

acabar de *to have just . . .*
conseguir *to manage to*
deber *must*
empezar a *to begin to*
ir a *to be going to*
parecer *to seem to*
poder *to be able*
preferir *to prefer to*
querer *to want*
saber *to know how to*
soler *to habitually . . .*
tener que *to have to*
tratar de *to try to*
volver a *to . . . again* (**volvió a hacerlo/lo volvió a hacer** *he did it again*)

Verbs followed by Gerund

andar: anda contándoselo a todo el mundo or **se lo anda contando** . . . *he goes around telling everyone*

Quienes/los que piensen así *Those who think/anyone who thinks like that . . .*
No te fíes nunca de quien no dice la verdad *Never trust the person who doesn't tell the truth*

For other uses of **quien/quienes** and also of **quién/quiénes** see the Index.

El de, la de, los de, las de

These mean *the one(s) belonging to*, or *the one(s) from*:

El coche de María es más grande que el de Antonio *Marías's car is bigger than Antonio's*
Las de allí son mejores que las de aquí *The ones* (fem.) *from there are better than the ones from here*

Lo que, lo de

These are neuter equivalents of **el que, el de**. They are ~~re~~quired when they do not refer to a specific noun:

Lo que me irrita *What/the thing that irritates me*
Le sorprendió lo que dijo Ana *What Ana said surprised him*
Lo de Gabriel es increíble *That business of/about Gabriel is incredible*

~~Algui~~en

~~This inv~~ariable word is equivalent to *someone* or, in ques~~tions, any~~*one* (but in negative sentences **nadie** is required;

~~Alg~~uien entró *Someone came in*
~~Vi~~ a alguien en la calle *I saw someone in the street*

---

estar: está haciéndolo or **lo está haciendo** *he's doing it*
seguir: sigue haciéndolo or **lo sigue haciendo** *he's still doing it*

In cases of doubt the suffixed construction is always correct, but it is slightly more formal. The non-suffixed construction should not be used if any word comes between the finite verb and the Infinitive or Gerund: **intentó muchas veces verla** *he often tried to see her*, not *'**la intentó muchas veces ver**'. The suffixed forms should also be used with the Imperative: **vuelve a llamarlos** *call them again*, **ve a verlos** *go and see them.*

REDUNDANT PRONOUNS

Spanish often apparently unnecessarily uses Personal Pronouns when the thing or person is also referred to by a noun in the sentence.

This happens:

■ When the Direct Object noun precedes the verb:

Los libros te *los* mando por correo *I'll send you the books by post* (cf. **te mando los libros por correo**)

■ When the sentence contains a noun that is the Indirect Object:

***Se* lo diré a tu padre** *I'll tell your father* (not *'*lo diré a tu padre*')
Esto *les* parecía bien a sus colegas *This seemed OK to his colleagues*
***Le* robaron mil dólares a Miguel** *They stole 1000 dollars from Miguel*

However, a redundant pronoun is not used when a *Direct* Object comes after the verb. It should be remembered that the presence of the preposition **a** *to* does not necessarily show that the noun is the Indirect Object, since **a** also precedes human *direct* objects in Spanish (see p.157):

> **Vi a Miguel** *I saw Miguel* (not **lo vi a Miguel'*, which, however, is normal in relaxed styles in Argentina and common in spoken Latin-American Spanish elsewhere)
> **La policía seguía a los ladrones** *The police were following the thieves*

EMPHASIS OF PERSONAL PRONOUNS

Subject Pronouns are emphasized simply by using the subject pronoun, since, as is explained on p.107, a Finite Verb in Spanish already contains its subject pronoun:

> **Lo sé** *I know it*
> **Yo lo sé** *I know it (but he doesn't, etc.)*

Object pronouns, direct and indirect, are emphasized by adding **a mí, a ti, a él/ella/usted, a nosotros/as, a vosotros/as** or **a ellos/ellas/ustedes**:

> **A mí nunca me dicen nada** *They never tell **me** anything*
> **A ella sí que la admiro** *I do admire **her*** (emphatic use of **sí**)
> **A ustedes sí los vi** *I did see **you***

TRANSLATING *IT'S ME, IT'S YOU,* ETC.

> **Soy yo** *It's me;* **Eres tú/Es usted** *It's you*
> **Son ellos** *It's them*
> **Son ustedes los que hacen más ruido** *You (plural) are the ones who make most noise*
> **Somos nosotras las que estamos más disgustadas** *It's we women who are most fed up*

| Indefinite Pronouns

This chapter discusses a series of miscellaneous pronouns that unlike the Personal Pronouns do not refer to specific individuals,

El que, la que, los que, las que

These mean *the one(s) that* or *the one(s) who/those that/who.* If the verb is in the subjunctive, the idea of **anyone who** strengthened:

> **El que dice eso es tonto** *The person/man w says that is stupid*
> **El que diga eso . . . Anyone** *who says th*
> **La que dijo eso** *The girl/woman who sa*
> **Los que vinieron ayer** *the ones who* day

El que is not always an indefinite pronoun refer to specific persons or objects:

> **Antonio es el que lleva la bo** *the one wearing the blue b*
> **Esta cerveza es la que m** *beer's the one I like lea*

For other uses of **el que**, see th

Quien/quienes (no a

Quien may replace **el** replace **los que/las q** humans:

Algu

This inv
tions, an
see p. 154

¿**Conoces a alguien que sepa ruso?** *Do you know anyone who knows Russian?*

Algo

This invariable word translates *something* or, in questions, *anything* (but **nada** is required in negative sentences; see p.154):

Me recuerda algo *It reminds me of something*
¿**Tienes algo para mi dolor de cabeza?** *Have you got anything for my headache?*

Alguno

This can be used either as a pronoun or an adjective.

As an adjective it appears before plural nouns with the meaning *some but not others*:

En algunos casos . . . *In some cases*
Algunas mariposas tienen alas muy bonitas *Some butterflies have very pretty wings*

It can also be used as an adjective before singular nouns that do not refer to quantities or substances, in which case it roughly translates *one or other, the odd . . . , one or two . . .* When it comes directly before a singular *masculine* noun it loses its final vowel:

En algún momento de mi vida . . . *At some time or other in my life*
¿**Has encontrado alguna falta?** *Have you found some mistake/any mistakes?*

Alguno is *not* used before non-countable nouns or quantities of objects when the meaning is 'an unspecified amount of':

Necesito pan *I want some bread*
Trajo agua *He brought some water*

> **Tengo que comprar flores** *I've got to buy some flowers*

Used as a pronoun, **alguno** *some of them, the odd . . . , some people, some things*

> **De vez en cuando salía con alguna de sus amigas** *Now and again she went out with the odd girlfriend/with some girlfriend or other*
> **Algunos dicen que . . .** *Some people say that . . .*

For further remarks on the Spanish equivalent of the English 'some' see the chapter on 'Translation Traps'.

Cualquier(a)

This word can also function as an adjective or pronoun. As an adjective it means *any* in the sense of *it doesn't matter which*. When it comes directly before a noun it loses its final -a:

> **en cualquier caso . . .** *in any case . . .*
> **cualquiera que sea la respuesta . . .** *whatever the reply*

It can be put after the noun, in which case it may sound faintly pejorative:

> **Podríamos ir a un cine cualquiera para pasar el rato** *We could go to any cinema to kill time*

As a pronoun it is often followed by **de** and means *any of*:

> **Puedes usar cualquiera de estas dos habitaciones** *You can use any/either of these two rooms*

The plural is **cualesquiera**:

> **cualesquiera que sean sus razones . . .** *whatever his reasons* (also **sean cuáles sean sus razones**)

Uno

This corresponds to the English impersonal pronoun *one*:

> **Si uno tiene que pagar dos veces más, no vale la pena** *If one has to pay twice as much, it isn't worth it*

A female speaker referring to herself would say **una**.

In everyday language **tú** tends to replace **uno** in this kind of sentence:

> **Si tienes que pagar dos veces más, no vale la pena** *If you have to pay twice as much, it isn't worth it*

Uno (or **tú**) must be used to form an impersonal form of a verb that already has **se**:

> **A veces uno tiene que contentarse con lo que tiene** *Sometimes one has to put up with what one has* (never *'se tiene que contentarse'* since a verb cannot have two **se**'s)

Relative Pronouns

These introduce Relative Clauses (see Glossary). There are several possibilities in Spanish, but the most frequent solutions are:

When no preposition precedes:	**que**
When a preposition precedes:	**el que** (people or things)
	quien/quienes (people)
	el cual (see below)
whose	**cuyo**

El que, el cual and **cuyo** agree in number and gender with the noun or pronoun that they refer to:

	Singular	Plural
Masculine	**el que, el cual, cuyo**	**los que, los cuales, cuyos**
Feminine	**la que, la cual, cuya**	**las que, las cuales, cuyas**

Quien has a plural, **quienes,** but no separate feminine form.

- No preposition:

  el perro que mordió a mi hermana *the dog that bit my sister*

  la mujer que vi ayer *the woman that/whom I saw yesterday*

  la carta que recibí de mi nieto *the letter that I got from my grandson*

- With preposition

el bolígrafo[26] **con el que lo escribí** *the ball-point pen that I wrote it with*

los novelistas **a los que/a quienes me refiero** *the novelists I'm referring to*

la mujer **con la que/con quien se casó** *the woman he got married to*

■ Familiar English usually omits a relative pronoun that is the Direct Object of a verb or is accompanied by a Preposition, but Spanish never does this:

el libro *que* leí *the book I read*
el cine *al que* fuimos *the cinema we went to*

■ English constantly puts prepositions at the end of relative clauses. This is *never* possible in Spanish:

la mesa encima de la que había dejado el plato *the table he'd left the plate on* (Spanish must say *the table on which he had left the plate*)

los pronombres de los que estoy hablando *the pronouns I'm talking about*

■ El cual

This is a substitute for **el que,** but it is less used nowadays as it tends to sound rather heavy in familiar styles:

muchachos y muchachas, algunos de los cuales llevaban sombrero *boys and girls, some of whom were wearing hats*

los puntos a los cuales/a los que me he referido *the points that I have referred to*

■ Cuyo

This word means *whose.* It agrees in number and gender with the thing possessed, not with the possessor:

[26] See the preface for a selection of Latin-American words for *ballpoint pen.*

la señora cuyo bolso encontré en el metro[27] *the lady whose bag I found in the subway/underground*

Tolstoy, cuyas novelas figuran entre las más leídas del mundo *Tolstoy, whose novels figure among the most widely read in the world*

---

[27] **El metro = el subte** in Argentina.

| Adjectives

Spanish adjectives (with rare exceptions) agree in number, and a majority also agree in gender, with the noun or pronoun they modify: **un edificio blanco** *a white building* (masc.), **una casa blanca** *a white house* (fem.), **tres edificios blancos/tres casas blancas** *three white buildings/three white houses*, etc.

FORMATION OF PLURAL OF ADJECTIVES

■ Add -s to an unstressed vowel:

> **grande—grandes** *big*
> **roja—rojas** *red* (fem.)

■ Add -es to a consonant or to a stressed vowel:

> **individual—individuales** *individual*
> **iraquí—iraquíes**[28] *Iraqi*

-z is changed to **c** if -es is added:

> **feroz—feroces** *ferocious*
> **feliz—felices** *happy*

FORMATION OF THE FEMININE OF ADJECTIVES:

■ Adjectives ending in -o: the -o changes to -a

---

[28] Familiar speech often simply adds -s to adjectives ending in a stressed vowel, but formal styles require -es.

	Masculine	Feminine	
Singular	**bueno**	**buena**	*good*
Plural	**buenos**	**buenas**	
Singular	**fantástico**	**fantástica**	*fantastic*
Plural	**fantásticos**	**fantásticas**	

■ Adjectives ending in any vowel other than **-o** have no separate feminine:

	Masc.or Fem.	Masc. or Fem.	
	Singular	Plural	
	inherente	**inherentes**	*inherent*
	grande	**grandes**	*big*
	indígena	**indígenas**	*native*
	hindú	**hindúes**	*Hindu*[29]

Exceptions: Adjectives ending in **-ote, -ete**:

	Masculine	Feminine	
Singular	**grandote**	**grandota**	*huge*
Plural	**grandotes**	**grandotas**	

Adjectives ending in consonants have no separate feminine forms:

	Singular	Plural	
	natural	**naturales**	*natural*
	feliz	**felices**	*happy*
	gris	**grises**	*gray/*(Brit. *grey*)

But the following exceptions must be noted:

■ Adjectives ending in **-és**:

	Masculine	Feminine	
Singular	**francés**	**francesa**	*French*
Plural	**franceses**	**francesas**	

[29] Or, in Latin America, (Asian) *Indian*, since **indio** is always taken to mean Amerindian in the Americas.

Exception:

cortés	cortés	*courteous*
corteses	corteses	

■ Adjectives ending in **-n** or **-or**:

	Masculine	*Feminine*	
Singular	chiquitín	chiquitina	*tiny*
Plural	chiquitines	chiquitinas	
Singular	revelador	reveladora	*revealing*
Plural	reveladores	reveladoras	

But comparative adjectives ending in **-or** have no separate feminine form:

	Singular	*Plural*	
	mejor	mejores	*better*
	anterior	anteriores	*former/preceding*
	exterior	exteriores	*outer/exterior*
	inferior	inferiores	*lower/inferior*
	interior	interiores	*inner/interior*
	mayor	mayores	*greater*
	menor	menores	*smaller*
	superior	superiores	*upper/superior*
	peor	peores	*worse*
	posterior	posteriores	*later/subsequent*
	ulterior	ulteriores	*ulterior/further.*

The following two adjectives also have no separate feminine forms:

	Singular	*Plural*	
	marrón	marrones	*brown*
	afín	afines	*related by affinity*

■ **español** and **andaluz**:

	Masculine	*Feminine*	
Singular	español	española	*Spanish*
Plural	españoles	españolas	

Singular	**andaluz**	**andaluza**	*Andalusian*
Plural	**andaluces**	**andaluzas**	

INVARIABLE ADJECTIVES

A small number of adjectives are invariable (at least in literature and careful speech), i.e. they have no separate plural or feminine form, e.g. **las camisas rosa** *pink shirts*, **los rayos ultravioleta** *ultraviolet rays*. The following are the most common:

alerta	*alert*, optional plural **alertas**
ardiendo	*burning*
escarlata	*scarlet*
hembra	*female* (**los ratones hembra** *female mice*)
hirviendo	*boiling*
macho	*male* (**las ratas macho** *male rats*)
malva	*mauve*
modelo	*model* (i.e. *exemplary*)
naranja	*orange*
tabú	*taboo*
violeta	*violet*

Two-word color adjectives of the form *navy blue*, *deep brown*, *signal red* are also invariable:

> **los ojos verde oscuro** *dark green eyes*
> **los zapatos azul marino** *navy blue shoes*
> **las corbatas azul claro** *light blue ties*

In the case of adjectives joined by a hyphen, only the second element agrees:

> **las negociaciones anglo-francesas** *Anglo-French negotiations*

SHORT FORMS OF ADJECTIVES

Grande *big* becomes **gran** immediately before any singular noun: **un gran libro** *a big/great book*, but **dos grandes libros** *two big books*.

The following lose their final –o before a singular *masculine* noun:

bueno *good*	**un buen momento** *a good moment*
malo *bad*	**un mal ejemplo** *a bad example*
tercero *third*	**el tercer día** *the third day*
primero *first*	**el primer año** *the first year*

The adjective/pronouns **alguno** *some* and **ninguno** *none/no* also lose their final vowel before a singular *masculine* noun, and **cualquiera** *any* loses its vowel before any singular noun. They should be sought in the index.

Santo *saint* becomes **san** before the names of male saints not beginning with **Do-** or **To-**: **San José** *St Joseph*, but **Santo Domingo, Santo Toribio**. It is not abbreviated when it means *holy*: **el Santo Padre** *the Holy Father*.

AGREEMENT OF ADJECTIVES

Adjectives agree in number and, when possible, in gender with the noun or pronoun they refer to. Mixed groups of feminine and masculine nouns are treated as masculine:

tres profesores españoles three Spanish teachers (males, or males and females)
tres profesoras españolas three female Spanish teachers

Exceptions to this rule are:

■ Adjectives placed before nouns, which usually agree only with the first noun:

> **su notoria inteligencia y perspicacia** *his well-known intelligence* and *clear-sightedness*

■ Adjectives used as adverbs are always in the masculine singular form:

> **Estamos fatal** *We're feeling awful/We're in a real mess*
> **María habla muy claro** *Maria speaks very clearly*

■ Adjectives that do not refer to any specific noun or pronoun. These are always masculine singular in form:

> **Eso es fantástico** *That's fantastic*
> **Es muy bueno lo que has hecho** *What you've done is really good*

COMPARISON OF ADJECTIVES

■ The Comparative (see Glossary) is formed by using **más** *more* or **menos** *less*. *Than* is **que**:

> **Eres más grande que yo** *You're bigger than me*
> **El terremoto fue más violento que el anterior**
> *The earthquake was more violent than the previous one*
> **Esta silla está menos sucia que la otra** *This seat is less dirty than the other*

There are four special forms which replace **más** + the adjective:

bueno *good*	**mejor** *better*
grande *big*	**mayor** (or **más grande**) *bigger/greater*
malo *bad*	**peor** *worse*
pequeño *small*	**menor** (or **más pequeño**) *smaller*

These must not be used with **más**: **ella es mejor actriz que su hermana** *she's a better actress than her sister.*

Mayor and **menor** usually mean *greater* and *lesser* rather than *bigger* and *smaller*, but **mayor** is also used of physical size: **esta aula es mayor/más grande que la otra** *this lecture room is bigger than the other* (**más grande** is more usual in everyday language).

■ **Más de** or **menos de** must be used before numbers or quantities:

> **Su hijo tiene más de cuarenta años** *His son is more than forty*
>
> **No traigas menos de un kilo** *Don't bring less than a kilo*

The correct number and gender of **del que** (**del/de la/de los/de las que**) must be used if the **que** precedes a verb phrase:

> **Pone más azúcar del que le recomienda el médico** *He puts in more sugar than the doctor recommends him*
>
> **Siempre le da más flores de las que ella se espera** *He always gives her more flowers than she expects*

The form **de lo que** must be used if there is no noun with which **el que** could agree:

> **Es menos tonta de lo que parece** *She's less stupid than she looks*
>
> **más de lo que tú piensas** ... *more than you think* ...

■ *As ... as* is expressed by **tan ... como** (*not* *'*tan que*').

> **Una jirafa es tan alta como un elefante** *A giraffe is as tall as an elephant*
>
> **Este problema no es tan complicado como el anterior** *This problem isn't as complicated as the one before*

■ *The more . . . the more, the less . . . the less*

The standard formula, normal in speech in Spain, is
cuanto más . . . más or **cuanto menos . . . menos**.
Cuanto is often replaced by **mientras** in Latin-American
speech or, in Mexico and some other places, by **entre**:

> **Cuanto más trabajas, más/menos te dan** *The
> more you work, the more/the less they give you*

■ The Superlative (see Glossary) is usually expressed by
using a definite article with the Comparative:

> **Tú eres** *el* **más fuerte** *You're* (masculine) *the
> strongest*
>
> **Eres** *la* **mujer menos sincera que he conocido**
> *You're the least sincere woman I've met/known*

The definite article is omitted:

(1) When a possessive (e.g. **mi, tu, su, nuestro**, etc.)
precedes: **fue nuestro peor momento** *it was our worst
moment*, **es mi mejor amigo** *he's my best friend*. The article is retained if **de** follows: **ésta ha sido la peor de mis
películas** *this was the worst of my films*.

(2) When the adjective does not refer to any specific
noun: **sería menos complicado dejarlo como es** *it
would be less/least complicated to leave it as it is*

(3) After **el que** *the one who*:

> **Ana fue la que más colorada se puso** *Ana
> was the one who blushed most*
>
> **Éste es el que menos estropeado está** *This is
> the one that's least spoilt*

THE SUFFIX -*ÍSIMO*

The suffix -**ísimo** (fem. -**ísima**, plural -**ísimos/ísimas**)
strongly intensifies the meaning of an adjective: **es
grande** *it's big*, **es grandísimo** *it's enormous*.

It is added after removing a final vowel (if there is one):

duro *hard*	**durísimo** *extremely hard*
fácil *easy*	**facilísimo** *extremely easy*

Adjectives whose masculine singular end in **-go, -co** or **-z** require spelling changes:

rico *rich*	**riquísimo** *tremendously rich*[30]
vago *vague/lazy*	**vaguísimo** *very vague/bone idle*
feliz *happy*	**felicísimo** *really happy*

POSITION OF ADJECTIVES

The question of whether a Spanish adjective appears before a noun, as in **un trágico incidente** or after, as in **un incidente trágico** (both translatable as *a tragic incident*) is one of the subtler points of the language. Hard and fast rules are difficult to formulate, but the following guidelines should help to train the ear of beginners.

An adjective *follows* the noun:

■ If it is used for the purposes of contrast. Sometimes the other term in the contrast is missing, but if a contrast is implied, the adjective must follow the noun:

Quiero comprar una camisa *azul I want to buy a blue shirt* (i.e. and not a red/green one, etc. Implied contrast)
Debiste casarte con una mujer *paciente You should have married a patient woman*
El pan *blanco* **cuesta más** *White bread costs more* (i.e. contrasted with others)

---

[30] **Rico** with **estar** means *tastes good*: **el pastel está muy rico** *the cake's delicious*.

■ If it is a scientific, technical or other adjective that is not meant to express any emotional or subjective impression:

la fusión nuclear *nuclear fusion*
un programa gráfico *a graphics program/programme*
la física cuántica *quantum physics*
la vida extraterrestre *extra-terrestrial life*
un líquido caliente *a hot liquid*

■ With very rare exceptions, if it denotes religion, ideology or place of origin:

un niño católico *a Catholic child*
unas actitudes democráticas *democratic attitudes*
un libro francés *a French book*

An adjective *precedes* the noun:

■ If it is an adjective used so often with a specific noun that it virtually forms a set phrase. Swear-words also fall into the this class:

el feroz león africano *the fierce African lion*
la árida meseta castellana *the arid Castilian plain*
los majestuosos Andes *the majestic Andes*
mi adorada esposa *my beloved wife*
este maldito sacacorchos *this damned corkscrew*

■ If it is one of the following common adjectives:

ambos *both*
llamado *so-called*
mero *mere*
mucho *a lot of*
otro *another*
pleno *total, mid-*
poco *little/few*
tanto *so much*

The following adjectives *may* precede the noun, and usually do in emotional, poetic or high-flown styles:

■ Any adjective denoting the speaker's emotional reaction to something:

> **un triste incidente** *a sad incident*
> **un feliz encuentro** *a happy encounter*
> **un sensacional descubrimiento** *a sensational discovery*

■ Adjectives describing shape, color, size, appearance. These especially tend to precede the noun in poetic or emotional styles:

> **la enorme mole del Everest** *the enormous mass of mount Everest*
> **una remota galaxia** *a remote galaxy*
> **la blanca luna** *the white moon*

■ **Grande** and **pequeño** usually precede the noun, although **grande** tends to follow when it is necessary to restrict its meaning to *big/large* rather than *great*:

> **un pequeño problema** *a slight problem*
> **un gran poeta** *a great poet*
> **un gran libro** *a big/great book*
> **un libro grande** *a big book*

Demonstrative Pronouns & Adjectives

These are words that translate *this, these, that, those*. Spanish differs from English in having two words for *that/those*, one resembling the old English *yonder* in that it points to distant things.

	masculine	feminine	
singular	**este**	**esta**	*this, this one*
plural	**estos**	**estas**	*these, these ones*
	(neuter form **esto**: see below)		
singular	**ese**	**esa**	*that, that one*
plural	**esos**	**esas**	*those, those ones*
	(neuter form **eso**: see below)		
singular	**aquel**	**aquella**	*that, that one* (far)
plural	**aquellos**	**aquellas**	*those, those ones* (far)
	(neuter form **aquello**: see p.140)		

When these are used as pronouns, i.e. when they mean *this one*, *those ones*, etc., they may be written with an accent. According to a ruling made by the Royal Spanish Academy in 1959, the accent can be omitted except in those very rare cases where confusion could arise, as in **esta llama** *this flame* and **ésta llama** *this woman is calling*, or **este vale** *this receipt/IOU*, and **éste vale** *this one is okay*. This ruling of the Academy has not met with universal approval and many of the best publishers and most ordinary people always put an accent on the pronouns. In this book the accent is always written on the pronoun forms. The accent must *never* be written on a demonstrative *adjective*: **un libro como ése** or (according to the Academy) **un libro como ese** *a book like that one* (pronoun) is correct, but *'*éste libro*' for **este libro** *this book* (adjective) looks very bad. The neuter forms **esto**, **eso**, and **aquello** are *never* written with an accent.

Difference between *ese* and *aquel*

Aquel and **ese** must be used correctly when a contrast is made between *there* and *further over there*:

> **Ponlo en el estante. No en ése sino en aquél**
> *Put it on the shelf. Not that one but that one over there*

If no such contrast is involved, either **aquel** or **ese** may be used for things that are far from the speaker. **Aquel** is also often used for things that are in the distant past.

> **¿Ven ustedes esas/aquellas montañas?** *Do you see those mountains (over there)?*
> **en aquella/esa época** *at that time* (**aquella** if we are talking of a remote past)

The former . . . the latter

The difference between **ese** and **aquel** is often exploited to mean *the former, the latter*, **aquel** meaning *the former*:

> **Había dos grandes grupos políticos, los Conservadores y los Liberales, aquéllos de tendencias clericales y éstos enconados enemigos de la Iglesia** *There were two large political groups, the Conservatives and the Liberals, the former clerical in tendency and the latter bitter enemies of the Church*

Use of the Neuter Demonstrative Pronouns

These are **esto** *this*, **eso** *that* and **aquello** *that*; **eso** can usually replace **aquello**. These refer to no noun in particular:

> **Eso es horrible** *That's horrible*
> **No quiero hablar de eso/aquello** *I don't want to talk about that* (**aquello** suggests something further in the past)

The following patterns should be noted:

> **Éste es *un* problema** *This one* (male or masculine object) *is a problem*
> **Esto es *un* problema** *This* (i.e. business, matter) *is a problem*
> **Éste es *el* problema** *This is the problem*

| Possessives

There are two sets of possessive adjectives. The Short Forms can function only as adjectives and appear only directly before a noun phrase; these words translate the English *my, your, his, her, its*, etc. The Long Forms function as adjectives or pronouns and translate the English *mine, yours, ours, theirs*, etc. They cannot appear directly before a noun phrase.

THE SHORT FORMS

	Singular	Plural	
	mi	**mis**	*my*
	tu	**tus**	*your* (= **de ti**)
	su	**sus**	*his, her, its*
			your (= **de usted**)
masc.	**nuestro**	**nuestros**	*our*
fem.	**nuestra**	**nuestras**	
masc.	**vuestro**	**vuestros**	*your* (= **de vosotros**)
fem.	**vuestra**	**vuestras**	
	su	**sus**	*their*
			your (= **de ustedes**)

These agree in number and, where possible, in gender, *with the thing possessed*, not with the possessor:

mi hijo *my son*	**mis hijos** *my sons/my children*
tu agenda *your diary*	**tus agendas** *your diaries*
su lápiz *his/her/your/ their pencil*	**sus lápices** *his/her/your/ their pencils*

nuestro coche *our car*	**nuestros coches** *our cars*
nuestra hija *our daughter*	**nuestras hijas** *our daughters*
vuestro amigo *your friend*	**vuestros amigos** *your friends*
vuestra mano *your hand*	**vuestras manos** *your hands*

Vuestro is used only in Spain: **su** replaces it in Latin America.

Su/sus has so many possible meanings that ambiguity occasionally arises. The identity of the possessor can be clarified by adding **de él, de ella, de usted, de ustedes, de ellos** or **de ellas** as required: **su casa de usted y no la de él** *your house, not his*. However, context nearly always makes such clarification unnecessary.

REPLACEMENT OF POSSESSIVE ADJECTIVES BY THE DEFINITE ARTICLE

Spanish Possessive Adjectives differ from their English counterparts in one major respect: they are replaced by the Definite Article when the sentence makes the identity of the possessor clear. This happens when:

■ An Indirect Object pronoun also refers to the possessor, as is normal when an action is done to someone's body or to some intimate possession:

> **Me estrechó la mano** *He/she shook my hand*
> **Le cortaron el pelo** *They cut his hair*
> **Me dejé el dinero en casa** *I've left my money at home*
> **Quítate la blusa** *take off your blouse*
> **Nos aparcó el coche** *He parked our car for us*

■ When the meaning of the sentence makes it obvious

who the possessor is (this replacement is optional, but usual):

> **María levantó la mano** *Maria raised her hand*
> **Mario puso la cartera en el maletín** *Mario put his notebook/wallet in his briefcase*
> **Dame la mano** *Give me your hand*

LONG FORMS

All of these forms agree in number and gender:

	singular	*plural*	
masculine	**mío**	**míos**	*mine*
feminine	**mía**	**mías**	
masculine	**tuyo**	**tuyos**	*yours* (= **de ti**)
feminine	**tuya**	**tuyas**	
masculine	**suyo**	**suyos**	*his/hers/its/*
feminine	**suya**	**suyas**	(*yours* = **de usted** & **de ustedes**)/*theirs*
masculine	**nuestro**	**nuestros**	*ours*
feminine	**nuestra**	**nuestras**	
masculine	**vuestro**	**vuestros**	*yours* (= **de vosotros/de vosotras**)
feminine	**vuestra**	**vuestras**	

Vuestro is replaced by **suyo** in Latin America.

The long forms are used:

■ To translate *a . . . of mine, a . . . of yours*, etc.

> **un amigo mío** *a friend of mine*
> **una tía nuestra** *an aunt of ours*
> **una carta suya** *a letter of his/hers/yours/theirs*

■ To translate *mine, yours*, etc.

Este saco es mío *This jacket is mine* (Spain **esta chaqueta es mía**)
Esta casa es nuestra *This house is ours*

The Definite Article is used (a) when the thing possessed is the Subject or Object of a verb, (b) if the possessive is preceded by a preposition:

De los tres dibujos yo prefiero el tuyo *Of the three drawing I prefer yours*
La mía está abajo *Mine is downstairs* (refers to some feminine object)
Estamos hablando del suyo *We're talking about his/hers/yours/theirs* (refers to some masculine object)

The definite article is not used after the verb **ser** when the thing referred to is owned by the person involved, e.g. **ese reloj es mío** *that watch is mine*. The article is used when the thing referred to does not literally belong to the person involved: **ese asiento debe de ser el tuyo** *that seat must be yours*.

USE OF POSSESSIVES AFTER PREPOSITIONS AND PREPOSITIONAL PHRASES

Colloquial language in Latin-America tends to use long forms of possessives after prepositional phrases, i.e. **delante mío** for **delante de mí** *in front of me*, **detrás nuestro** for **detrás de nosotros/nosotras** *behind us*. This is avoided in standard Spanish and is frowned upon in Spain: the prepositional forms of pronouns should be used (see p.106). However, the possessive construction appears even in the best authors in Argentina.

Neuter Pronouns and Articles

Spanish has a series of words of neuter gender, so called because they do not refer to any specific masculine or feminine noun.

■ **Esto** *this*, **eso** *that*, **aquello** *that* see p.140.

■ **Ello**

Ello is most frequently used after prepositions. It translates *it* when this word does not refer to any specific noun or pronoun. Compare

> **No sé nada de él** *I don't know anything about him/it* (i.e. some male person or some masculine noun)

and

> **No sé nada de ello** *I don't know anything about it* (the situation or problem in general)

■ **Lo**

Lo has various uses. It may be

(a) a third-person masculine Direct Object personal pronoun as in **lo admiro** *I admire him/it:* see p.111.

(b) the Direct Object counterpart of **ello**. This is discussed in the next section.

(c) the neuter article, discussed after the next section.

■ **Lo as a neuter third-person pronoun**

This is the Direct Object form of **ello** and it is used to translate *it* when this does not refer to any noun or pronoun:

> **Su padre había muerto, pero él no lo sabía todavía** *His father had died but he didn't know (it) yet*

Lo is usually required after **ser** and **estar** when these refer back to something already mentioned in the sentence:

> **Dicen que es tonta, pero no lo es** *They say she's stupid, but she isn't*
> **Parece que estoy contento pero no lo estoy** *It looks as if I'm pleased, but I'm not*

For the use of **lo** with **hay** *there is/are*, see p.81.

■ **Lo** used to make abstract nouns from adjectives

Lo + a masculine singular adjective usually corresponds to an English phrase consisting of adjective + *thing*:

> **Lo increíble fue que** *The incredible thing was . . .*
> **lo más importante . . .** *the most important thing*
> **Lo mejor sería no mencionarlo** *The best thing to do would be not to mention it*

■ **Lo** + adverbs or adjectives to translate *how . . .* + adjective or adverb

Lo + an adverb, or **lo** + an adjective that agrees in number and gender, conveniently translates *how* after words implying admiration, blame, surprise, knowledge, etc.

> **Me sorprende lo bien que lo hizo** *I'm surprised at how well he did it*
> **Mira lo blancas que están estas sábanas** *Look how white these sheets are*
> **Ahora me doy cuenta de lo difícil que es** *Now I realize how difficult it is*

The word **cuán** is occasionally used instead in literary styles, but it is very rare in spoken Spanish:

> **Ahora me doy cuenta de cuán difícil es**

■ **Lo más** or **lo menos** + adverb can be used to translate
the idea of *as . . . possible*:

> **Hágalo lo mejor posible** *Do it as well as possible*
> **Lo comió lo más deprisa que pudo** *He ate it as*
> *fast as he could*

| Adverbs

ADVERBS FORMED FROM ADJECTIVES

The usual way of forming an adverb from an adjective is by adding the suffix **-mente** to the singular form of an adjective (to the feminine form if it has one):

igual *equal*	**igualmente** *equally/likewise*
fantástico *fantastic*	**fantásticamente** *fantastically*

If the adjective has an accent, this remains unchanged:

increíble *incredible*	**increíblemente** *incredibly*
esporádico *sporadic*	**esporádicamente** *sporadically*

■ If two adverbs ending in -**mente** are joined by **y/e** *and*, **o/u** *or*, **ni** *nor/and not*, **pero/sino** *but*, the first drops the suffix -**mente**:

> **Se puede justificar económica y (p)sicológicamente** *It can be justified economically and psychologically*
>
> **Contestó irónica pero inteligentemente** *She/he replied ironically but intelligently*

■ Adverbs ending in -**mente** are used sparingly, rarely more than one to a sentence. One adverb ending in -**mente** should not be used to modify another.

> **Se defendieron con un valor increíble** *They defended themselves incredibly bravely* (not *'increíblemente valientemente'*)

■ There are alternative ways of expressing an adverbial idea, and these are preferred if the original sounds clumsy:

inteligentemente—con inteligencia *intelligently*
decididamente—de una manera decidida *decidedly*
increíblemente—de forma increíble *incredibly*
rápidamente—deprisa *quickly*
etc.

OTHER ADVERBS

A large number of Spanish adverbs are independent words not formed from adjectives. These must be learned separately:

abajo *downstairs/down*
arriba *upstairs/up*
(a)dentro *inside*
(a)fuera *outside*
adelante *forward*
atrás *back*
adrede *on purpose*
ahora *now*
apenas *scarcely*
así *thus*
bien *badly*
despacio *slowly*
igual *in the same way*
mal *badly*
mañana *tomorrow*
mucho *much/a lot*
poco *not much*
etc.

Even more numerous are adverbial phrases formed from a preposition + a noun; these must be learned separately. The following are typical:

a contrapelo *unwillingly*

    a gritos *while shouting*
    a mano *by hand*
    a menudo *often*
    a oscuras *in the dark*
    a propósito *on purpose*
    a ratos *occasionally*
    a veces *sometimes*
    con ganas *eagerly*
    de noche/de día *by night/day*
    en balde/en vano *pointlessly/for nothing*
    en cambio *on the other hand*

RECIÉN

The adverb **recién** deserves special mention. It means
just, only in Latin America: **llegó recién** *he's just arrived*
(= **acaba de llegar**), **recién entonces** (colloquial usage)
only then (= **sólo entonces**). In Spain it means *recently,
newly* and appears only in combination with participles :
recién pintado *just painted/recently painted*.

ADJECTIVES AS ADVERBS

Some adjectives may be used as adverbs, in which case
they are invariably masculine singular:

    Trabaja muy duro *He works very hard*
    Hable claro *Speak clearly*
    Estamos fatal *We're feeling dreadful/We're in a
       dreadful mess*

■ Very often normal adjectives can replace adverbs when
the adjective really applies to the subject of the verb and
not to the verb itself. The result is not always easily trans-

lated. The adjective agrees in number and gender with the subject of the verb:

> **Andaban cansados y tristes** *They were walking along (looking) tired and sad*
> **Vivían amargados** *They led bitter lives*
> **Me miró asustada** *She looked at me in alarm*

COMPARATIVE AND SUPERLATIVE OF ADVERBS

The comparative of adverbs is formed by using **más** *more* or **menos** *less*. **Que** is *than*:

> **fácilmente** *easily*   **más fácilmente** more easily
> **a menudo** *often*   **más a menudo** more often

The only irregular forms are

> **bien** *well*—**mejor** *better*
> **mal** *badly*—**peor** *worse*
> **mucho**—*much* **más** *more*
> **poco**—*little* **menos**—*less*

These latter forms do not agree in number when they are adverbs. Compare **son mejores** *they're better* (adjective) and **están mejor** *they're better off/in better condition* (adverb).

■ The superlative of adverbs is usually formed with **el que** or **quien**:

> **Ella es la que lo hará más fácilmente** *She's the one who will do it most/more easily*
> **Antonio es quien mejor canta** *Antonio sings best*
> **Tú eres el que más sabe de todo esto** *You know most about all this*

ADVERBS OF PLACE

The following are particularly frequent:

aquí *here*	**ahí** *(just) there* **allí** *there*
allá *there*	**acá** *here*
(a)dentro *inside*	**(a)fuera** *outside*
abajo *down/downstairs*	**arriba** *up/upstairs*
adelante *forward*	**atrás** *backwards/back*
delante *in front*	**detrás** *behind*

Aquí is the equivalent of *here*. **Ahí** means *just there (close by you)* and **allí** indicates somewhere further away; the distinction should be maintained.

Allá and **acá** are less common in Spain but they are obligatory everywhere when they follow **más**:

> **un poquito más allá/acá** *a bit more that/this way*

Acá replaces **aquí** in many regions of Latin America, especially in Argentina and neighbouring countries.

■ The forms **adentro, afuera** are, in the standard language, generally used only to express motion, and the forms **dentro** and **fuera** are used to indicate static position:

> **Fue adentro** *He went inside* (motion)
> **Estaba dentro/fuera** *He was inside/outside* (static position)

But this distinction is lost in Latin America, where the forms beginning with **a-** are generally used for static position and motion too: **estaba adentro/afuera**

The prepositional phrases are **dentro de** and **fuera de**:

> **dentro/fuera de la casa** *inside/outside the house*

However, the forms **adentro de, afuera de** are commonly heard in Latin America and are accepted in writing in Argentina.

Prepositional phrases are discussed at p.159 ff.

POSITION OF ADVERBS

■ When an adverb or adverbial phrase modifies a verb it generally follows the latter:

> **Canta bien** *He sings well*
> **Hablaba a gritos** *He was talking at the top of his voice*
> **El presidente consiguió también que se modificara la ley** *The President also managed to get the law modified*

■ When an adverb modifies a Modal Verb (see Glossary) plus a participle or Infinitive, the adverb should not be inserted between the modal and the non-finite form:

> **Lo ha hecho siempre/Siempre lo ha hecho** *He's always done it* (never *'**lo ha siempre hecho**')
> **Por fin voy a verla/Voy a verla por fin** *I'm finally going to see her*

■ When an adverb modifies a whole phrase and not just the verb, it usually precedes the whole phrase (as in English):

> **Normalmente viene a las tres** *Normally he comes at three*

Negation

■ The following are the words most commonly used to make negative statements:

apenas	*hardly, scarcely*
nada	*nothing*
nadie	*no one*
ni	*nor, not even*
ninguno	*none*
no	*not*
nunca or **jamás**	*never*

■ Negating a verb

The basic patterns are as follows. Note that if a negative word *follows* a verb, the verb must also be *preceded* by a negative word: this is the so-called double negative construction:

Positive	Negative
Vamos *We're going*	**No vamos** *We aren't going*
Lo han comprado *They've bought it*	**No lo han comprado** *They haven't bought it*
Tengo algo *I have something*	**No tengo nada** *I don't have anything*
Conozco a alguien *I know someone*	**No conozco a nadie** *I don't know anyone*
Ana o María *Ana or Maria*	**ni Ana ni María** *neither Ana nor Maria*
Vino con él o con ella *He came with him or with her*	**No vino ni con él ni con ella** *He didn't come with him or with her* (i.e. with neither of them)

algún día *some day*

ningún día *no day*

Lo/le vi con alguna chica
I saw him with some girl

No lo/le vi con ninguna chica *I didn't see him with any girl*

Siempre llueve *It always rains*

No llueve nunca *It never rains* (or **nunca llueve**)

■ Negatives may be combined:

Apenas conoce a nadie *He hardly knows anyone*

Nunca sale con nadie *He never goes out with anyone*

Nadie compra nada *No one buys anything*

No te he visto nunca en ninguna parte con ninguna de ellas *I've never seen you anywhere with any of those girls/women*

■ Spanish negative words are also used in comparisons, where English uses *anyone, anything, ever*:

Está más guapa que nunca *She's more attractive than ever*

Se acuesta antes que nadie *He goes to bed before anyone else*

Es más impresionante que nada que yo haya visto hasta ahora *It's more impressive than anything I've seen up until now*

■ **Ni**, or **ni siquiera** translate *not . . . even*

Ni (siquiera) pienses en llamarme *Don't even think about calling me*

Ni siquiera se acordó del cumpleaños de su mujer *He didn't even remember his wife's birthday*

■ **Ninguno** may be used as an adjective or a pronoun. Its forms are:

	Singular	Plural
Masculine	**ninguno**	**ningunos**
Feminine	**ninguna**	**ningunas**

But when it comes before a singular masculine noun it loses its final **-o**:

> **Ningún presidente americano se atrevería a decir eso** *No American President would dare to say that*
>
> **Ninguna mujer inteligente defiende el machismo** *No intelligent woman defends machismo*
>
> **¿Libros? No tengo ninguno** *Books? I haven't got a single one*

■ **Nomás** is much used in Latin America (but not in Spain) to mean *just, barely*

> **Los vimos en la entrada nomás** *We saw them right in the entrance* (Spain **en la misma entrada**)
>
> **Te llamaré nomás llegue a casa** *I'll call you as soon as I get home* (Spain **nada más llegue . . .**, **en cuanto llegue . . .**)

■ No words should be inserted between the auxiliary verb **haber** and the Past Participle in Compound tenses:

> **No lo he hecho nunca** *I've never done it* (not *"no lo he nunca hecho'*)

Personal *A*

In Spanish, certain kinds of noun and pronoun must be preceded by **a** when they are the **Direct Object** of a verb. This happens:

■ When the Direct Object represents a *known* human being or animal:

> **Vi a Antonio** *I saw Antonio*
> **Admiro a ese profesor** *I admire that teacher*
> **Llama al camarero**[31] *Call the waiter*
> **Conozco a alguien que sabe chino** *I know someone who knows Chinese*
> **Arrestaron al narcotraficante** *They arrested the drug-pusher*
> **Criticaron al gobierno** *They criticized the government* (collective noun standing for known human beings)
> **Voy a lavar al perro** *I'm going to wash the dog*

Compare **voy a lavar el coche** *I'm going to wash the car*—never *'. . . *al* coche' since the car is non-human. In the case of an unknown human being or animal, **a** is usually omitted; the more impersonal the object the less likely is the use of **a**:

> **Vi (a) un hombre en la calle** *I saw a man in the road*
> **Odio las serpientes** *I hate snakes*

■ In those cases in which word order does not make it clear which is the object and which is the subject of the

---

[31] **Camarero = el mesero** in much of Latin America.

verb. This usually happens in Relative Clauses where the word order is usually Verb-Subject:

> **una medida que afecta al problema** *a measure that affects the problem* (since . . . **que afecta el problema** could mean either . . . *that affects the problem* or . . . *that the problem affects*)

> **Se llamaba al director "Maxi"** *people called the director Maxi* (Impersonal **se**. The *a* avoids confusion with . . . **se llamaba Maxi** *the director's name was Maxi*)

Prepositions

Prepositions—words like *in, of, on, through, to, underneath, without*—stand in front of nouns or pronouns and relate them in various ways to the rest of the sentence: **en España** *in Spain*, **de María** *of Maria*, **encima de la mesa** *on (top) of the table*, etc.

■ Prepositions can also stand in front of verbs: *without looking, by shouting*. In English the verb form used in this case is the *-ing* form, but in Spanish the form used is always the Infinitive: **sin ver** *without seeing*, **(cansado) de hablar** *(tired) of talking*. Prepositions do not appear before a Gerund. A rare exception is **en** + Gerund, as in **en llegando** 'on arriving', but this construction is old-fashioned and is nowadays expressed by **al** + Infinitive, e.g. **al llegar a Madrid** *on arriving in Madrid*.

■ The prepositions **a** 'to' and **de** 'of' combine with the masculine singular Definite Article **el** to form **al** 'to the' and **del** 'of the'. No other combinations of these prepositions are used: compare **a él** 'to *him*' and **de él** 'of *him*'. The combined form is not used when the **el** is part of a proper name: **a El Ferrol** 'to El Ferrol', **de El Cairo** 'from Cairo'.

■ Prepositional phrases consist of more than one word, of which one is always a preposition. They function like prepositions: **a causa de** *because of*, **detrás de** *behind*. The more common of these are included with the simple prepositions in the following list.

ALPHABETICAL LIST OF SPANISH PREPOSITIONS AND THEIR USE

There are minor local variations between Spain and Latin America with respect to prepositional usage. These variations are more numerous in colloquial speech than in written language.

Prepositional usage is often dictated by apparently arbitrary rules and frequently does not correspond between languages: compare English *to dream of someone*, Spanish **soñar *con* alguien** (literally '*to dream with someone*'), or English *to try **to***, Spanish **tratar *de*** (literally '*to try of*').

a[32] *to* (after words denoting motion or giving, sending, showing, beginning, etc.)

> **Vamos a Caracas** *We're going to Caracas*
> **Volaron a Roma** *They flew to Rome*
> **Le dio cien dólares a su hijo** *He gave 100 dollars to his son*
> **Envíe esta carta al Ministerio** *Send this letter to the Ministry*
> **Voy a verla** *I'm going to see her*
> **Empezó a llorar** *He/she began to cry*
> **un viaje a la luna** *a journey to the moon*
> **un homenaje al rey** *a homage to the King*

at, but usually only when it means *towards*:

> **Apuntaba al blanco** *He was aiming at the target*
> **Tiraban piedras a la policía** *They were throwing stones at the police*

---

[32] The preposition *a* is also used in Spanish before human or animal direct objects: **vio a Miguel/a su hermana** *He saw Miguel/his sister*. This is discussed on p.157.

When the English word *at* means *in* or *close to* a place, as in *at the bus-stop*, *at the table*, *at Cambridge*, the Spanish translation is **en** (q.v.), although the following exceptions should be noted:

> **a la salida/entrada** *at the exit/entrance*
> **a la mesa** *at table* (cf. **en la/una *mesa*** *at the/a table*)
> **a mi espalda/derecha/izquierda** *at my back/right/left*
> **a pie de página** *at the foot of the page*

at, before numbers and in several set phrases

> **a las seis** *at six o'clock*
> **a las ocho y media** *at eight-thirty*
> **a doscientos kilómetros por hora** *at 200 km per hour*
> **a treinta kilómetros** *at a distance of thirty km*
> **a los treinta años** *at the age of thirty*
> **al mismo tiempo** *at the same time*
> **al amanecer** *at dawn*

by, *in the manner* of, in set phrases indicating the manner in which something is done

> **a mano, a pie, a caballo** *by hand, by/in pencil, by horse/on horseback*
> **escribir a máquina** *to type*
> **a empujones** *by pushing*
> **arroz a la catalana** *rice cooked Catalan-style*
> **vestido a la inglesa** *dressed in the English style*

in, in set phrases

> **al sol/a la sombra** *in the sun/shade*
> **a lo lejos** *in the distance*

on, in set phrases

> **a la derecha/izquierda** *on the right/left*
> **a la llegada de** *on the arrival of*

 al día siguiente *on the next day*
 al salir de casa *on leaving home*
 estar a dieta *to be on a diet*

onto after verbs of motion

 El gato saltó a la mesa *The cat jumped onto the table*

into after verbs of motion

 Se tiró al agua *He dived into the water*
 Entró corriendo al cuarto *He ran into the room* (Spain . . . **en el cuarto**)

after in set phrases

 Se cansa a los dos minutos *He gets tired after two minutes*
 a los dos días de hacerlo *two days after doing it*

per

 tres veces a la semana *three times per/a week*
 cinco mil dólares al mes *$5,000 per/a month*

of, like, after words meaning *taste, smell, sound like, look like*

 Sabe a ajo *It tastes of garlic*
 Huele a pescado *It smells of fish*
 un olor/sabor a vino *a smell/taste of wine*
 Suena a mentira *It sounds like a lie*
 Se parece a su madre *He looks like his mother*

from, away from, off (after words meaning *steal, take away from, buy, hear*)

 Le compró un coche a su hermano *He bought a car off his brother*
 Les roban dinero a los turistas *They steal money from the tourists*
 Se lo oí decir a Miguel *I heard it from Miguel*

a bordo de *on board of*

a cambio de *in exchange for*

a causa de *because of*

> **a causa del ruido/calor** *because of the noise/heat*

a costa de *at the cost of*

a diferencia de *unlike*

> **a diferencia de algunos de sus amigos** *unlike some of his friends*

a espaldas de *behind the back of*

a excepción de *with the exception of*

a falta de *for lack of/for want of*

a favor de *in favor* (Brit. *favour*) *of*

a fin de *with the aim of*

a finales/a fines de *towards the end of*

> **a finales de junio** *towards the end of June*

a fuerza de *by dint of*

a juicio de *in the opinion of*

a mediados de *towards the middle of*

> **a mediados de julio** *in mid-July*

a modo de *in the manner of*

además de *as well as*

a la hora de *at the moment of*

a lo largo de *throughout/along*

> **a lo largo del río** *along (the length of) the river*
> **a lo largo del siglo** *throughout the century*

a partir de *starting from*

> **a partir de hoy** *from today*
> **a partir de ahora** *from now on*

a pesar de *despite, in spite of*

> **No me lo dio, a pesar de toda su generosidad**
> *He didn't give it to me, despite all his generosity*

a por (Spain only) same as **por** (q.v.) when the latter
means *in search of*

> **Voy a por el médico** *I'm going for the doctor/to
> fetch the doctor*

a principios de *towards the beginning of*

a prueba de . . . *proof*

> **a prueba de bomba** *bomb-proof*

a punto de *on the verge of*

> **Estaba a punto de decirlo** *He was on the verge of
> saying it*

a raíz de (literary) *immediately after/as an immediate result
of*

> **a raíz de la Guerra Civil** *immediately after the
> Civil War*

a riesgo de *at the risk of*

a través de *through/across*

> **a través del llano** *across the plain*

a vista de *in the sight/presence of*

a voluntad de *at the discretion of*

> **El servicio es a voluntad del cliente** *The service
> charge is at the customer's discretion*

acerca de *about* (= *on the subject of*)

> **Me preguntó qué pensaba acerca de todo eso** *He
> asked me what I thought of/about all that*

además de *as well as*

al alcance de *within reach of*

al cabo de *at the end of*

> **al cabo de una semana** *after a week/at the end of a week*

al contrario de *contrary to*

al corriente de *informed about/up to date with*

> **No estoy al corriente de todo lo que ha pasado** *I'm not up to date with everything that's happened*

al estilo de *in the style of*

al frente de *at the head/forefront of*

al lado de *next to*

> **Se sentó al lado de su jefe** *He sat next to his boss*

al nivel de *at the level of*

al tanto de = **al corriente de**

alrededor de *around*

> **un viaje alrededor del mundo** *a journey round the world*
> **alrededor de mil** *around/about 1,000*

ante *in the presence of, faced with*

> **ante este problema** *faced with this problem*
> **ante el juez** *in the presence of/before the judge*

In literary styles it may be an equivalent of **delante de** *in front of* (q.v.).

antes de *before* (time)

> **Tienen que terminarlo antes de las doce** *They've got to finish it before 12 o'clock*

Compare **antes** *que* *rather than*: **cualquier cosa antes que tener que asistir a una de esas reuniones** *anything rather than have to go to one of those meetings.*

bajo *beneath, under*

Debajo de (q.v.) is the usual Spanish translation of *underneath*, although **bajo** is used in literary language to mean our *beneath* with words like **el cielo** *sky*, **el sol** *sun*, **el techo** *roof*: **bajo un cielo azul** *beneath a sky of blue*. **Bajo** is also required with social and political systems, with temperatures and in some set phrases:

> **debajo de la cama** *under the bed*
> **bajo un régimen totalitario** *under a totalitarian regime*
> **bajo cero** *below zero*
> **bajo órdenes** *under orders*
> **Estás bajo aviso** *You've been warned* (lit. 'You're under a warning')
> **bajo la condición de que** . . . *on condition that* . . .

cerca de *near*

> **Vivo cerca del puente** *I live near the bridge*

con *with*. The following special forms should be noted:

> **con + mí = conmigo** *with me*
> **con + ti = contigo** *with you*
> **con + sí = consigo** *with himself/herself/yourself, with themselves/yourselves*
>
> **Vine con mi tía** *I came with my aunt*
> **con amor** *with love, lovingly*
> **Vamos contigo** *We're going with you*
> **Lo abrió con el destornillador** *He opened it with the screwdriver*
> **Es muy cariñoso con ellos** *He's very affectionate with/towards them*

Está enojada (Spain **enfadada**) **con usted** *She's angry with you*

despite (same meaning as **a pesar de**)

Con todos sus esfuerzos, no lo consiguió *Despite all his efforts he didn't achieve it*

Con ser su amigo, no habla bien de él *Despite being his friend, he doesn't speak well of him*

if after an Infinitive (this construction is not particularly common)

Con trabajar un poquito más, aprobará el examen *If he works a little more, he'll pass the examination*

into, against, to, when some idea of a collision or mutual encounter is involved

El autobús chocó con (or **contra**) **un árbol** *The bus ran into a tree*

Me encontré con el jefe *I ran into/unexpectedly met the boss*

Se ve con ella todos los días *He sees/meets her (US meets with her) every day*

Yo me escribo con ella *I write to her regularly/correspond with her*

with . . . in in phrases that mention the contents of some vessel or receptacle

un camión con frutas *a truck/lorry loaded with fruit*

una botella con agua *a bottle with water in it*

con motivo de *on the occasion of*

con motivo del quinto aniversario de . . . *on the occasion of the fifth anniversary of*

con objeto de *with the object/intention of*

con relación a *in respect of/in relation to*

con respecto a *with respect/reference to/in comparison to*

The spelling of the word **el respeto** *respect* (shown to someone) should be noted.

contra *against*

> **Escribió un artículo contra el uso de las drogas**
> *He wrote an article against the use of drugs*
> **Se apoyó contra un árbol** *He leaned against a tree*

Adverbially, the phrase **en contra** is used: **votar en contra** *to vote against*.

de *of* (i.e. *belonging to* or *made of*). English may join nouns to form compound nouns where **de** is normally used in Spanish:

> **el Banco de España** *The Bank of Spain*
> **los zapatos de Antonio** *Antonio's shoes*
> **el ama de casa** *the housewife*
> **un talonario de cheques** *a checkbook* (British cheque-book)
> **la sopa de legumbres** *the vegetable soup*
> **la base de datos** *the database*
> **un chaleco de cuero** *a leather jacket*
> **Murió de paludismo** *He died of/from malaria*

from

> **una carta de mi madre** *a letter from my mother*
> **Es de Almería** *He comes from Almería* (**viene de . . .** means *he's coming from . . .*)
> **Hemos llegado ahora de Madrid** *We've just arrived from Madrid*
> **a partir de ahora** *starting from now*
> **la carretera que va de Madrid a Valencia** *the road that goes from Madrid to Valencia*

See also **desde**, which also means *from*.

off/down from

> **Se bajaron del autobús** *They got off the bus*
> **Bájate de ahí** *Come down from there*

by after verbs meaning *pull, take by, seize*

> **Me tiraba de la oreja** *He/she used to pull me by my ear*
> **Iban cogidos de la mano** *They were walking hand-in-hand*

measuring, costing, old, before quantities, years, etc.

> **una soga de cinco metros** *a rope measuring five meters/metres* (i.e. *five meters long*)
> **el menú de dos mil pesetas** *the 2,000 peseta menu*
> **un niño de tres años** *a three-year old child*
> **Tiene cien metros de largo/profundo** *It's 100 meters/metres long/deep*

about in the sense of *concerning,* after verbs meaning *speak, complain,* etc.

> **Me niego a hablar de eso** *I refuse to talk about that*
> **Se quejó de la mala comida** *He complained about the bad food*
> **Le informaron de lo que pasaba** *They informed him about what was happening*

like, as, in phrases referring to condition or state

> **trabajar de profesor/guía** *to work as a teacher/guide*
> **Vas de marqués por la vida** *You give yourself airs and graces* (literally *you go through life like a marquis*)

Se vistió de payaso *He dressed up as a clown*
estar de broma *to be joking, to be fooling about*

This use can also be translated as *for* or *on* in some phrases:

Se va de viaje *He's going on a journey*
Se fueron de fin de semana *They've gone away for the weekend*

in, after Superlative expressions

El mejor restaurante de España *the best restaurant in Spain*

with to show the cause of some event

Saltaba de alegría *They were jumping with joy*
Enfermó (Latin America **se enfermó**) **de bronquitis** *He fell ill with bronchitis*

if before Infinitives

De ser verdad, provocará un escándalo *If it's true, it'll cause a scandal*

than in the expression **más/menos de** *more/less than*, when a quantity follows (see p.133) and also before clauses (see p.133)

De also appears in many adverbial phrases, e.g.

de broma *as a joke*
de golpe/de repente *suddenly*
de maravilla *fantastically well*
de nuevo *again*
de paso *on the way through*

The use of **de** before **que** is discussed on p.233.

de acuerdo con *in accordance with*

de acuerdo con el Código Penal *in accordance with the Penal Code*
de parte de *on the part of, on behalf of*

>—¿Puedo hablar con Antonio?—Claro. ¿De parte de quién? *'Can I speak to Antonio?' 'Of course. Who's speaking/Who shall I say is speaking?'*

de regreso a *on returning to*

debajo de *underneath*

>**debajo de la mesa** *underneath the table*

Latin Americans often say **abajo de,** but this is not used in Spain.

delante de *in front of*

>**No quiero decirlo delante de ella** *I don't want to say it in front of her*

dentro de *inside*

>**dentro de la casa** *inside the house*

Latin Americans often say **adentro de,** a form not accepted in Spain.

in, i.e. before deadline

>**Llegarán dentro de veinte minutos** *They'll arrive in twenty minutes*

Latin Americans often say **. . . en veinte minutos.**

desde *from* (a place), when some kind of motion is implied or distance is stressed

>**Se veía desde lejos** *It was visible from a distance*
>**Desde aquí hay más de cien kilómetros** *It's more than 100 km from here*
>**Han venido desde Barcelona** *They've come all the way from Barcelona* (cf. **. . . de Barcelona** *. . . from Barcelona*)

There is some overlap in meaning in this case with **de.**

since in time phrases

> **desde entonces** *since then*
> **desde marzo** *since March*
> **Desde niño siempre he creído en Dios** *I've always believed in God since I was a child*

For the phrase **desde hace**, as in **desde hace tres años** *for three years*, see pp.206–7.

después de *after (time)*

detrás de *behind*

durante *during*

> **durante el siglo veinte** *during the twentieth century*

for in expressions of time

> **Durante varios días no hablaste de otra cosa** *You talked of nothing else for several days*
> **durante varias horas** *for several hours*

For other ways of expressing *for n days/minutes*, see p. 205 ff.

en This word combines the meanings of *in, into, on,* and *at*. Spanish-speakers often have difficulty in distinguishing between these English words.

on
> **El plato está en la mesa** *The plate's on the table* (or **encima de**[33])
> **Lo vi en la televisión** *I saw it on television*
> **Flotaba en el agua** *It was floating on/in the water*
> **en la luna** *on the moon*

in
> **Está en el maletero de tu coche** *It's in the trunk/*(British *boot*) *of your car*

---

[33] **Encima de** is the clearest and most usual way of expressing *on top of* a flat surface.

Nací en Caracas *I was born in Caracas*
en el campo *in the countryside*
en 1999/verano/abril/español *in 1999/summer/April/Spanish*
en la mañana/tarde/noche *in the morning/afternoon/by night* (this is Latin-American Spanish: Spain uses **por** with these nouns)

In time phrases of the sort *he'll be here in five minutes*, **dentro de** is more usual than **en** (at least in Spain): **llegará dentro de cinco minutos**.

into   Entró corriendo en la habitación *He ran into the room* (**entrar** is followed by **en** in Spain, usually in Latin America by **a**)
    Introduzca una moneda de cien pesetas en la ranura *Put a 100-peseta coin into the slot*

at   with nouns denoting place, when motion is not implied

    Estudié en Cambridge *I studied at Cambridge*
    en la parada del autobús *at the bus-stop*
    Me senté en una mesa del bar *I sat down at a table in the bar*
    en el semáforo *at the traffic-lights*
    en la puerta *at the door*

En is also used with certain festivals and special days

    en Navidad *at Christmas*
    en los fines de semana *at weekends*

at, by in estimates of quantity, value, price, quality or characteristics

    La casa fue valorada en doscientos mil dólares *The house was valued at 200,000 dollars*
    Me tienen en poca estima *They hold a low opinion of me*

¿En cuánto lo estiman? *How much do they estimate that it's worth?*

Ha bajado en un diez por ciento *It's gone down by ten per cent*

La reconocí en la manera de hablar *I recognized her by her way of speaking*

en busca de *in search of*

en caso de *in case of*

en caso de incendio *in case of fire*

en contra de *in opposition to*

en cuanto a *as for . . . /concerning*

en cuanto a los demás . . . *as far as the rest are concerned . . .*

en forma de *in the shape of*

en lugar de *instead of* (+ noun, pronoun or infinitive)

en medio de *in the middle of*

en medio de la calle *in the middle of the street*

en torno a *around (the subject of)/concerning*

en vez de *instead of* (+ Infinitive)

en vista de *in view of*

en vista de lo ocurrido *in view of what's happened*

encima de *on top of*

El libro está encima de la mesa *The book's on the table*

See also **en**, **sobre**

enfrente de *opposite*

La comisaría está enfrente del museo *The police-station is opposite the museum*

entre *between*

> **entre tú y yo** *between you and me* (note that the prepositional forms of **tú** and **yo**—**ti** and **mí**—are not used when two pronouns follow **entre**)
>
> **entre los dos pinos** *between the two pinetrees*

among, through

> **El sol se veía apenas entre las nubes** *The sun was barely visible among/through the clouds*
>
> **Encontraron la sortija entre la hierba** *They found the ring among/in the grass*
>
> **Recuerdo haberla visto entre la gente que estaba en la fiesta** *I recall seeing her among the people that were at the party*

what with

> **Entre una cosa y otra, se me ha ido el día** *What with one thing and another my day has gone*

The phrases **entre semana** *on weekdays* and **entre sí** *among themselves* or *to himself/herself/themselves* (as in **decía entre sí** *he said to himself*) should be noted.

excepto *except*

Prepositional forms of pronouns are not used with this word.

> **Vinieron todos, excepto Antonio** *They all came, except Antonio*
>
> **Excepto tú y yo** *except you and me*

frente a *opposite*

> **Aparcaron frente a la comisaría** *They parked in front of the police-station*

in contrast with

> **Frente a otros miembros de su partido, atacó la política de la nacionalización** *In contrast with*

> *other members of his party, he attacked the policy of nationalization*

fuera de *outside*

> **fuera de la casa** *outside the house*

Latin Americans often say **afuera de**, a form not accepted in Spain.

hacia *towards*

> **El cometa viaja hacia el sol** *The comet is traveling* (British *travelling*) *towards the Sun*
> **Se volvió hacia ella** *He turned towards her*
> **su actitud hacia sus padres** *his attitude towards his parents*

around (i.e. *approximately*) in time phrases

> **hacia mil novecientos** *around 1900*

hasta *as far as, until*

> **Caminaron hasta la estación** *They walked as far as the station*
> **Las obras continuarán hasta octubre** *The work will continue until October*
> **hasta mañana** *until tomorrow*
> **hasta luego** *good-bye/see you later* (lit. *until then*)

From Colombia northwards **hasta** can also mean *not until . . . not before . . .*:

> **Terminamos hasta ayer** (= **no terminamos hasta ayer**) *We didn't finish until yesterday*

junto a *next to, by*

> **Estuvo esperando junto a la puerta** *He waited by/next to the door*

lejos de *far from*

> **lejos de aquí** *far from here*

mas allá de *beyond*

> **más allá del mar** *beyond/on the other side of the sea*

mediante *by means of*

> **Intentaron solucionar el problema mediante una serie de medidas económicas** *They tried to solve the problem by a series of economic measures*

This word is rather literary, **con** being more usual in everyday language.

no obstante (literary) *notwithstanding* (same as **a pesar de**)

para *for*

This preposition must be carefully distinguished from **por**, which is also sometimes translatable as *for*.

> **Este dinero es para ti** *This money is for you*
> **Necesitamos habitaciones para ocho personas** *We need rooms for eight people*
> **¿Tienen ustedes algo para el dolor de muelas?** *Do you have something for toothache?*
> **¿Para qué lo hiciste?** *What did you do it for?*

to (when it means *in order to*) followed by Infinitive

> **Pon más ajo para darle más sabor** *Put in more garlic to give it more flavor/*(Brit. *flavour*)
> **Se fue de vacaciones para descansar** *He went away on vacation/holiday to rest*
> **Tiene suficiente dinero para vivir** *He's got enough money to live*

by in time phrases

> **Lo necesito para mañana** *I need it by tomorrow*
> **Para entonces ya no servirá** *It'll be no use by then*

for in expressions meaning *to need **for** n days*, etc.

> **Necesito el coche para dos días** *I need the car for two days*

on the point of (with Infinitive. Latin Americans use **por**)

> **Está para/por llover** *It's about to rain*

in . . . view

> **Para ella, él era el más atractivo de todos** *In her view, he was the most attractive of all*
>
> **Para mí que eso suena falso** *In my view, that sounds false*

towards after positive emotions (i.e. love, affection), in combination with **con**

> **el cariño que tenía para con sus hijos** *the affection he had for his children*

por   Various meanings

Although the English translation may sometimes be *for*, its meaning is not the same as **para** and the two words must be carefully distinguished.

As a result of, because of, for (when it means *because of*)

> **Tuvimos que cerrar las ventanas por los mosquitos** *We had to shut the windows because of the mosquitoes*
>
> **Muchas gracias por todo lo que has hecho** *Many thanks for* (i.e. *because of*) *all you have done*
>
> **Lo hice por ti** *I did it because of you/for your sake* (compare **lo hice para ti** *I did/made it for* (i.e. *to give to*) *you*
>
> **Te lo mereces por no decir la verdad** *You deserve it for not telling the truth*
>
> **La admiro por su generosidad** *I admire her for* (i.e. *because of*) *her generosity*

> **Lo hago por dinero** *I do it for money* (i.e. *because of*)
>
> **Llegamos tarde por la nieve** *We arrived late because of the snow*

words meaning *in return for*

> **Te dan doscientas pesetas por libra esterlina** *They give you 200 pesetas to the pound*
>
> **Cambió el coche por otro** *He changed his car for another*

per
> **dos mil kilómetros por hora** *2,000 km an/per hour*
>
> **dos pares de zapatos por persona** *two pairs of shoes per person*

The preposition **a** is used for time: **dos veces al día** *twice per day/a day*

for in the sense of substitution *for*

> **Me tomó por español** *He took me for* (i.e. *confused me with*) *a Spaniard*
>
> **Hazlo por mí** *Do it for* (i.e. *instead of*) *me*

for meaning *in support of*

> **Estamos luchando por la libertad** *We're fighting for freedom*
>
> **No estoy por la pornografía** *I don't support pornography*
>
> **Se esforzó mucho por su hijo** *He made a great effort for his son*

for in the meaning *to the value of*

> **una camisa de seda por cien dólares** *a 100-dollar silk shirt*
>
> **una factura por dos millones de pesos** *a bill for two million pesos*
>
> **Podrás venderlo por un millón** *You'll be able to sell it for a million*

for in the meaning *in search of*. In this case European
Spanish regularly uses **a por**:

> **Tendré que ir (a) por gasolina** *I'll have to go for*
> (i.e. *to get*) *some gas/petrol*
> **Ir por lana y volver trasquilado** *To go for wool*
> *and come back shorn* (proverb used when a plan
> misfires)

by to indicate *by* whom or what something is done

> **Esta novela fue escrita por Juan Goytisolo** *This*
> *novel was written by Juan Goytisolo*
> **La iglesia fue destruida por un terremoto** *The*
> *cathedral was destroyed by an earthquake*

by = *by means of*

> **Los motores diesel funcionan por compresión**
> *Diesel engines work by compression*
> **Funciona por electricidad** *It works on/by electric-*
> *ity*
> **Más por chiripa que por otra cosa** *More by fluke*
> *than by anything else*
> **Consiguió el empleo por enchufe** *He got the job*
> *through connections/by influence*
> **por avión** *by plane* (but **en tren, en coche, en**
> **bicicleta**)
> **por teléfono/fax** *by phone/fax*

however in phrases of the type *however hard you work, how-*
ever tall he is

> **Por muy alto que seas, no lo alcanzarás** *You*
> *won't reach it, however tall you are*
> **Por más deprisa que andemos, no llegaremos a**
> **tiempo** *However fast we walk, we won't get*
> *there in time*

in, around when referring to places or time. In this case it
implies approximate location or time

> **Vivo por aquí** *I live round here*
> **por ahí** *somewhere around there*
> **por enero** *around January*

along, through, via after words indicating motion

> **Andábamos por la calle** *We were walking along the street*
> **Pasaron por San Pedro** *They passed through San Pedro*
> **a Madrid por Segovia** *to Madrid via Segovia*

to before an Infinitive, in the sense of *in order to*.

This overlaps in meaning with the much more frequent **para. Por** is used only when there is a personal or subjective motive, and *para* is usually optionally possible as well:

> **He venido por estar contigo** *I've come to be with you* (i.e. *because I **want** to be with you*)
> **Yo haría cualquier cosa por conseguir ese empleo** *I'd do anything to get that job*

por debajo de *under* (with figures, quantities)

> **muy por debajo de las cifras del año anterior** *well below last year's figures*

salvo = excepto, and like the latter word it does not take prepositional forms of pronouns: **salvo/excepto tú** *except you.*

según *according to*

> **según el parte meteorológico** *according to the weather forecast*
> **según tú** *according to you* (note that the prepositional forms of pronouns—**mí, ti**—are not used after this preposition)

depending on

> **según la cantidad que pongas** *depending on the quantity you put in*

> **según la persona con la que hables** *depending on the person you talk to*)

sin *without*

> **Lo hice sin ayuda** *I did it without help*
> **sin dudar** *without hesitating*
> **sin nada/nadie** *without anything/anyone* (Spanish says *without nothing/no one*)

sobre *on top of*

There is some overlap between this use of **sobre** and **encima de** and **en**. **Sobre** is more specific than **en** in that its spatial meaning is clearly *on top of*, and it is somewhat more literary than **encima de**, which is the usual translation of *on top of*:

> **sobre/encima de/en la mesa** *on (top of) the table*

over with verbs like *fly, pass*

> **El avión voló sobre la ciudad** *The plane flew over the city*
> **Pasó sobre mi cabeza** *It passed over my head*

around (i.e. *roughly*) before times and quantities

> **sobre las tres** *around three o'clock*
> **Tenía sobre cinco metros de largo** *it was about 5 meters/metres long*

over, i.e. *more than, above*, with numbers

> **un aumento sobre el año pasado** *an increase over last year*
> **veinte grados sobre cero** *20 degrees above zero*

about in the meaning *on the subject of*

> **un programa sobre problemas ecológicos** *a program/*(British *programme*) *about ecological problems*
> **hablar sobre . . . .** *to talk on the subject of . . .*

on, over, above in the meaning of *overlooking*

> **una casa sobre el mar** *a house on/overlooking
>   the sea*
> **el castillo que está construido sobre la ciudad**
>   *the castle that is built overlooking the city*

over in the sense of superiority *over*

> **sobre todo** *above all*
> **la superioridad sobre** *superiority over . . .*

tras *after*

This word is literary and is replaced in everyday language
by **detrás de** (space) or **después de** (time).

> **tras (después de) la victoria de los conser-
>   vadores** *after the victory of the conservatives*
> **tras (detrás de) la puerta** *behind the door*
> **año tras año** *year after year* (set phrase)

PREPOSITION FINDER (ENGLISH-SPANISH)

This list gives the Spanish equivalents of the more common English prepositions. The Spanish words should be
checked in the preceding alphabetical list:

about	= *on the subject of* **sobre, de, acerca de**
	= *roughly* **sobre, alrededor de**
	= *all over* **por**
above	**encima de, sobre**
according to	**según, de acuerdo con**
across	**a través de, por**
after	time **después de**
	place **detrás de**

among(st)	**entre**
(a)round	as in *walk round the tree* **alrededor de**
	= *approximately* **sobre, alrededor de**
as far back as	(= *since*) **desde**
at	place (no motion involved) **en**
	place (motion at, towards) **a, contra**
	time **a**
	with numbers **a, en**
before	time **antes de**
	place **delante de** (= *in front of*)
below	place **debajo de**
	numbers **bajo**; = *inferior to* **por debajo de**
beneath	**debajo de, bajo**
beside	**al lado de**
	= *as well as* **además de**
between	**entre**
by	= *done by* **por**
	time **para**
	= *near to* **junto a, al lado de**
	= *by transport* **por, en**
	= *by night* **por**
	= *by doing*, see Gerund,. p.52
by means of	**mediante, por**
during	**durante**
except	**excepto, salvo**
for	= *made/bought/designed/intended for* **para**
	= *as a result of, because of* **por**
	= *on behalf of* **por**
	= *instead of* **por, en lugar de**
	= *in search of* (a) **por**
	time (i.e. *for n days*) **durante, por**; see also p.205.

	= *in exchange for* **a cambio de**
	= *for a quantity, price* **por**
from	**desde, de**
	time **desde, a partir de**
in	time and place **en**
	after superlatives **de**
	= *within* a certain time **dentro de**
in front of	**delante de, ante**
inside	**dentro de, en**
into	**en**
of	**de**
on	**encima de, sobre, en**
	a after verbs of motion
	= *on doing something* **al** + Infinitive
on behalf of	**de parte de**
onto	**a**
out of	place **de**
	motive, reason for **por**
	number **sobre**
outside	**fuera de**
over	= *above* **sobre, encima de**
	= *across* **a través de**
	motive (e.g. *fall out over*) **por**
	number **sobre, encima de**
per	*per day, week* **a**
	per person **por**
since	**desde**
through	= *across* **a través de, entre**
	= *thanks to* **por**
	= *by means of* **mediante, por**

to	place **a** purpose (=*in order to*) **para**; **a** after verbs of motion after **bastante** *enough* **para**
towards	**hacia** = *emotion towards* **hacia, para con**
under	= *underneath* **debajo de** **under** *regime, orders* **bajo** with figures **por debajo de**
underneath	**debajo de**
upon	see *on*
via	**por**
with	**con** emotions *with* (= *arising from*) **de, con**
without	**sin**

| Conjunctions

These are words like *and*, *but*, *so*, used for joining words, phrases or clauses.

■ como

This word has several meanings:

(1) With the subjunctive, *if*: see p.41.

(2) To introduce Relative Clauses after words describing manner:

> **la manera como . . .** *the way that . . .*

(3) To mean *seeing that/as/since*. In this case it must come at the head of the phrase:

> **Como se nos hacía tarde, decidimos dejarlo para el día siguiente** *As/since it was getting late, we decided to leave it for the next day*

In this context **ya que** or **puesto que**, which both mean *seeing that . . .* can also be used.

Cómo (note accent) means *how* and is discussed on p. 202.

■ ni *nor, not even.* See p. 155.

■ o *or*

It is written and pronounced **u** before words beginning with and **o** sound:

> **sociedades u organizaciones** *societies or organizations*
> **mujeres u hombres** *men or women*

■ pero, sino

Spanish has two words for *but*. **Sino** is used in constructions that mean *not A but B*, and especially in the formula

no sólo . . . sino *not only . . . but*:

> **Esto no es vino, sino agua** *This isn't water but wine/This isn't water. It's wine*
> **no sólo en España, sino en Latinoamérica también** *not only in Spain but in Latin America too*

It sometimes means *except*:

> **No se podía hacer otra cosa sino disculparse** *There was nothing else to be done except/but to say sorry*
> **No podía ser sino un mensaje de sus tíos** *It could be nothing else except/but a message from his aunt and uncle*

The form **sino que** must be used when the words introduce a verb phrase:

> **No sólo hablaba alemán, sino que sabía otras cinco lenguas también** *He not only spoke German but he knew five other languages as well*

In other cases *but* is translated **pero**, which differs from **sino** in that it does not suggest incompatibility or replacement, but merely a limiting of meaning.

> **Ana no sabe francés, pero sí sabe escribir a máquina** *Ana doesn't know French, but she can type*
> **Te daré cincuenta dólares, pero no te voy a dar un regalo también** *I'll give you fifty dollars, but I'm not going to give you a present as well*
> **Es inteligente pero perezoso** *He's intelligent but lazy*

■ **porque** *because*

Porque means *because* and it must be distinguished in pronunciation and spelling from **por qué** *why*: Compare **yo comprendo, porque me lo explicaste** *I understand,* *because* *you explained it to me*, and **yo comprendo por qué me lo explicaste** *I understand **why** you explained it to me*.

The phrase **no porque** requires the subjunctive:

> **Lo hizo no porque realmente quisiera hacerlo sino porque se sentía presionado** *He did it not because he really wanted to, but because he felt pressured*

■ **puesto que, ya que** *since* (= *because*)

> **No ha sido posible terminarlo, ya que/puesto que no hay dinero** *It hasn't been possible to finish it, since there's no money*

■ **pues**

This may mean *because* when it is used as a conjunction, but this usage is literary, like the English *for* and it is not heard in spoken Spanish:

> **Se le entendía poco, pues** (i.e. **porque**) **hablaba muy bajo** *One could understand very little of what he said, for he spoke in a very low voice*

In everyday language it is very common in the meaning *in that case*: **si no te gusta, pues vete** *if you don't like, well, in that case go away*.

■ **que**

This word has numerous functions other than as a conjunction, and they must be clearly distinguished.

(1) It may be a Relative Pronoun, as in **la mujer que compró las flores** *the woman **who** bought the flowers*.

(2) It means *than* in comparisons: **eres más alto que yo** *you're taller **than** me*.

(3) **Qué** (note accent) is a separate word and translates *what* in direct and indirect questions: **no sé qué hacer** *I don't know **what** to do*.

The conjunction **que** introduces clauses in the same way as the English *that*:

> **El plomero**[34] **dice que viene esta tarde** *The plumber says he's coming this afternoon/evening*

Unlike its English counterpart, it is not omitted (at least in normal styles): **creo que es verdad** *I think it's true*.

See the chapter on Translation Traps for the phrase **de que**. See p.39 for imperatives phrases like **que venga** *tell him to come/let him come*.

■ **y** *and*

Pronounced as though it were written *i*: **mexicanos y norteamericanos** *Mexicans and Americans*. It is written and pronounced **e** before any word beginning with an **i** sound:

> **la agricultura e industria peruanas** *Peruvian agriculture and industry*
> **Vinieron Mario e Iris** *Mario and Iris came*
> **musulmanes e hindúes** *Muslims and Hindus*

but

> **carbón y hierro** *coal and iron* (because **hierro** begins with a *y* sound)

---

[34] The word for *plumber* in Spain is **el fontanero**.

Numbers, Time, Quantities

CARDINAL NUMBERS

1 un/uno/una
2 dos
3 tres
4 cuatro
5 cinco
6 seis
7 siete
8 ocho
9 nueve
10 diez
11 once
12 doce
13 trece
14 catorce
15 quince
16 dieciséis
17 diecisiete
18 dieciocho
19 diecinueve
20 veinte
21 veintiún/veintiuno/veintiuna
22 veintidós
23 veintitrés
24 veinticuatro
25 veinticinco
26 veintiséis

27 veintisiete
28 veintiocho
29 veintinueve
30 treinta
31 treinta y un/uno/una
32 treinta y dos
33 treinta y tres
34 treinta y cuatro
35 treinta y cinco
36 treinta y seis
37 treinta y siete
38 treinta y ocho
39 treinta y nueve
40 cuarenta
41 cuarenta y un/uno/una
50 cincuenta
60 sesenta
70 setenta
80 ochenta
90 noventa
100 cien/ciento
101 ciento un/uno/una
102 ciento dos
200 doscientos/doscientas
210 doscientos diez/doscientas diez
300 trescientos/trescientas
400 cuatrocientos/cuatrocientas
500 quinientos/quinientas
600 seiscientos/seiscientas
700 setecientos/setecientas
800 ochocientos/ochocientas
900 novecientos/novecientas
1.000 mil
1.050 mil cincuenta
1999 mil novecientos noventa y nueve
2.000 dos mil

66.000 sesenta y seis mil
1.000.000 un millón
1.000.000.000 an American billion: **mil millones**
1.000.000.000.000 a million millions: **un billón**[35]

■ Thousands are separated by periods/full-stops—**10.000** = **diez mil** *10,000*—and decimals are separated by commas: **10,25** = **diez coma veinticinco** = *ten point two five*. But Mexico uses our system—10,000; 10.25, etc.

■ 16 through 29 are written as one word.

■ **Mil** is not pluralized in numbers—**cinco mil** *5000*. It is, however, pluralized when it is used as a noun: **los miles de personas que creen eso** *the thousands of people who believe that*.When used thus **mil** is a masculine noun.

■ **Uno** becomes **un** before a masculine noun, **una** before a feminine noun:

> **Hay treinta y un libros** *There are thirty-one books*
> **Hay treinta y una cartas** *There are thirty-one letters*

but

> **¿Cuántos libros hay? Treinta y uno** *How many books are there? Thirty-one*

■ **Ciento** *one hundred* is used when another number follows—**ciento trece** *113*—but **cien** is used in all other cases: **hay más de cien** *there are more than 100*, **cien hombres** *100 men*.

However, **ciento** is used in percentages: **el quince por ciento** *15%*

[35] In Spain **un billón** is a million million, although for Latin-Americans it is often the same as the US billion (a thousand million). It is a good idea to get this point straight before discussing prices or the national debt!.

■ The hundreds (i.e. 100, 200, 300, 400, 500, 600, 700, 800 and 900) are written as one word and the suffixed form **-cientos** agrees in number with the thing counted:

> **doscient*as* mujeres/mesas** *200 women/tables*
> (fem.)
> **quinient*os* quince hombres/dólares** *515
> men/dollars* (masc.)

The irregular forms **quinientos/as** *500*, **setecientos/as** *700*, and **novecientos/as** *900* should be noted.

■ **Millón** and **billón** are nouns, whereas other numbers are adjectives. They therefore required **de** before the thing counted: **ha costado un millón/billón de dólares** *it cost a million/billion dollars*, but **ha costado un millón tres mil dólares** *it cost one million three thousand dollars*

■ Telephone numbers are said by tens whenever possible, and one begins either by hundreds or by a single digit when there is an odd number of figures:

> **ocho treinta y siete veintidós quince** 837 2215
> or **ochocientos treinta y siete veintidós quince**

Cero is used for *zero*:

> **cero quince cuarenta veintiséis** 015 4026

ORDINAL NUMBERS

Ordinal Numbers higher than ten are rather a mouthful in Spanish and they are usually avoided in all but formal styles. One says **el quince aniversario** rather than **el decimoquinto aniversario** *the 15th anniversary*, or **el capítulo veintiséis** *chapter 26/the 26th chapter*. The higher the number, the rarer the ordinal form. For this reason only ordinal numbers up to 20th and a few other common forms are given here.

The forms ending in **-avo** should strictly speaking be

used only for fractions—**diez quinceavos** *ten fifteenths*.
But they are very commonly used in Latin America to
form the higher ordinal numbers, although this is not usually accepted in Spain.

primer(o)	*first*	
segundo	*second*	
tercer(o)	*third*	
cuarto	*fourth*	
quinto	*fifth*	
sexto	*sixth*	
séptimo/sétimo	*seventh*	
octavo	*eighth*	
noveno	*ninth*	
décimo	*tenth*	
undécimo	*eleventh*	**onceavo**
duodécimo	*twelfth*	**doceavo**
decimotercero	*thirteenth*	**treceavo**
decimocuarto	*fourteenth*	**catorceavo**
decimoquinto	*fifteenth*	**quinceavo**
decimosexto	*sixteenth*	**dieciseisavo**
decimoséptimo	*seventeenth*	**diecisieteavo**
decimoctavo	*eighteenth*	**dieciochavo**
decimonoveno	*nineteenth*	**diecinueveavo**
vigésimo	*twentieth*	**veinteavo**
centésimo	*hundredth*	**centavo**
milésimo	*thousandth*	

■ All these are normal adjectives and agree in number and
gender:

  los treinta primeros hombres *the first thirty men*
  la segunda calle a la derecha *the second street
    on the right*

■ **Primero** and **tercero** lose their final vowel before a
singular masculine noun: **el primer/tercer día** *the*

first/third day, but **la primera/tercera semana** *the first/third week*.

APPROXIMATE NUMBERS

Approximate numbers are formed by adding **-ena** to the cardinal number after removing any final vowel. These numbers exist for 10, 15, the tens 20 through 50 and for 100. They are in common use, although **docena** *dozen* is not used as much as in English:

una decena	*about ten* (note irregular form)
una quincena	*about fifteen*
una veintena	*about twenty, a score*
una treintena	*about thirty*
una centena	*about a hundred* (note irregular form)

Note special form **un millar** *about a thousand*.

Like all collective nouns, these are normally grammatically *singular*: **la primera treintena** *the first thirty or so*, **ha venido una veintena** *about twenty have come*. When **de** + a plural noun follows, either agreement is possible: **una treintena de estudiantes se quedaron/se quedó en el aula** *about thirty students remained in the lecture hall*.

FRACTIONS

The following special words exist:

1/2	**una mitad**
1/3	**un tercio**
2/3	**dos tercios**, etc.

For higher fractions the masculine ordinal number is used, although the feminine form is also found:

1/4 **un cuarto**
1/5 **un quinto**
3/7 **tres séptimos**
7/10 **siete décimos**
tres millonésimos/as *three millionths*

In non-mathematical language the word **parte** is added for values over *half*: **la tercera parte** *a third*, **la quinta parte** *a fifth*.

As was mentioned earlier, decimals are expressed with a comma (although Mexico follows our system):

3,75 = **tres coma setenta y cinco**

■ The main arithmetical signs are:

+ **más**	: **dividido por** or **entre**
– **menos**	× **(multiplicado) por**
² **al cuadrado**	% **por ciento**

Dos más ocho son diez *2 + 8 = 10*
Ocho dividido por dos (or **ocho entre dos**) **son cuatro** *8:2 = 4*
Tres multiplicado por cinco son quince *3 × 5 =15*
Nueve son tres al cuadrado *9=3²*
el treinta por ciento *30%*

TIME

¿Qué hora es? (Lat. Am. often **¿Qué horas son?**) *What's the time?*, **¿Qué hora tiene?** *What time do you have?/What's the time, please?*

Es la una	*it's one o'clock*
Es la una y cinco	*five past/five after one*
Son . . .	*It's . . .*
las dos	*two o'clock*
las once	*eleven o'clock*

las tres y cuarto	*three fifteen*
las cuatro y veinticinco	*four twenty-five*

(also in Lat. Am. **las cuatro con veinticinco minutos**)

las cinco y media	*five thirty*
las seis menos veinte	*twenty before/to six*
las siete menos cuarto	*a quarter before/to seven*
las ocho menos diez	*ten minutes before/to eight*
las nueve en punto	*nine o'clock exactly*
Son menos diez/y diez	*It's ten to/ten past*
Son pasadas las cinco	*It's past five o'clock*
Es medianoche	*It's midnight*
Es mediodía	*It's mid-day*
las siete de la tarde	*seven p.m.*[36]
las tres de la madrugada[37]	*three a.m.*

■ The twenty-four hour clock is much used for timetables and in official documents: **a las quince veinticinco** *at fifteen twenty-five, at three thirty-five p.m.*

■ **Por la mañana, por la tarde** *in the afternoon/evening,* **por la noche** *at night* (Latin Americans may use **en** or **a** for **por**). **Mañana por la mañana** *Tomorrow morning.*

[36] **La tarde** stretches from about 1p.m. to about 8 p.m. and therefore includes both our afternoon and evening.
[37] **La madrugada** is the hours between midnight and 6 a.m. **La mañana** corresponds to our *morning* and can also be used instead of *la madrugada.*

PREPOSITIONS ETC. WITH TIMES OF DAY

a *at*

> **Te veo a las ocho** *I'll see you at eight o'clock*

para *by*

> **Tienes que estar allí para las siete** *You have to be there by seven*

a partir de *from*

> **Las llamadas telefónicas cuestan menos a partir de la una** *Phone calls cost less from/after one o'clock*

al cabo de *after* (i.e. *at the end of*)

> **Al cabo de unos instantes se dio cuenta de que** *After a few moments she realized that . . .*

sobre/a eso de *about*

> **Llegaremos sobre/a eso de las ocho** *We'll arrive around eight*

hasta *until*

> **hasta las cinco** *until five o'clock*

a más tardar *at the latest*

> **Hay que llegar a las tres a más tardar**

DAYS, MONTHS, SEASONS

Days of the week	Months and seasons
lunes *Monday*	**enero** *January*
martes *Tuesday*	**febrero** *February*
miércoles *Wednesday*	**marzo** *March*
jueves *Thursday*	**abril** *April*
viernes *Friday*	**mayo** *May*

Days of the week	Months and seasons
sábado *Saturday*	**junio** *June*
domingo *Sunday*	**julio** *July*
	agosto *August*
hoy *today*	**se(p)tiembre** *September*
ayer *yesterday*	**octubre** *October*
anteayer *the day before yesterday*	**noviembre** *November*
mañana *tomorrow*	**diciembre** *December*
pasado mañana *the day after tomorrow*	**la primavera** *spring*
	el verano *summer*
al día siguiente *the following day*	**el otoño** *autumn/fall*
	el invierno *winter*

Days and months are all masculine and are usually written with a small letter, as are the seasons.

PREPOSITIONS WITH DAYS, MONTHS, SEASONS, ETC.

■ **En** is used for *in* in most cases:

> **en abril** *in April*
> **en el mes de agosto** *in the month of August*
> **en mil novecientos noventa y nueve** *in 1999*
> **en el siglo veinte** *in the twentieth century*
> **en los años ochenta** *in the eighties*

■ With days of the week no preposition is used:

> **Llegaron el martes** *They arrived on Tuesday*
> **Está cerrado los lunes** *It's closed on Mondays*

THE DATE

> **¿A cuántos estamos?** *What's the date?*
> **El once de febrero** *February 11*

No preposition is used and the cardinal numbers are used:

> **Llegué a Managua el quince de enero** *I arrived at Managua on January 15*
> **Llegaremos el primero** (sometimes also **el uno**) **de mayo** *We'll arrive on May 1*

AGE

> **¿Cuántos años tienes?** *How old are you?*
> **¿Qué tiempo tiene?** *How old's the baby?* (if it's possibly less than one)
> **¿Qué edad tiene?** *What's his/her age?*
> **Tengo cuarenta y ocho años** *I'm 48*
> **Mañana cumplo treinta años** *I'm thirty tomorrow*
> **El cumpleaños** *birthday*

MEASUREMENTS

> **¿Cuánto mides?** *How tall are you?*
> **¿Cuánto tiene de largo/longitud?** *How long is it?*
> **¿Cuánto mide?** *How high is it?*
> **¿Cuánto tiene de profundidad?** *How deep is it?*
> **Tiene cien metros de largo/alto/ancho/profundidad** *It's 100 meters/metres long/high/wide/deep*
> **¿Qué número calzas?** *What size shoes do you take?*
> **Mi talla es la cuarenta** *My size is 40* (European system used for dresses, suits)[38]

---

[38] 40 Continental European = 14 British, 12 American. There is much scope for confusion since all three systems are in use in the Spanish-speaking world. Mexico generally uses the American system and Spain the European.

Questions

■ It is often possible in informal styles to turn a simple statement into a question simply by changing the intonation:

> **Tu mamá lo sabe** *Your mother knows*
> **¿Tu mamá lo sabe?** *Does your mother know?* (rising intonation)

■ Alternatively, the order of the verb and its subject can be reversed:

> **¿Lo sabe tu mamá?** *Does your mother know?*
> **¿Conoce Antonio a mi suegro?** *Does Antonio know my father-in-law?*

■ Spanish has a series of words that correspond to our question words:

> **¿cómo?** *how?*
> **¿cuál?/¿cuáles?** *which?*
> **¿cuándo?** *when?*
> **¿dónde?** *where?*
> **¿para qué?** *what for?*
> **¿por qué?** *why?* (contrast with **porque** *because*)
> **¿qué?** *what?/which?*
> **¿quién?/¿quiénes?** *who?*

These question words must be written with an accent and are pronounced as stressed words. This is the case in both Direct and Indirect Questions:

> **¿Cuándo viene?** *When's he coming?* (Direct Question)
> **No sé cuándo viene** *I don't know when he's coming* (Indirect Question)

After these words the verb is put before the subject:

> **¿Cómo van ustedes a Miami?** *How are you going to Miami?*[39]
>
> **¿Por qué dice eso tu jefe?** *Why does your boss say that?*

Who? must be translated by **quiénes** if we are certain that more than one person is involved:

> **¿Quién lo hizo?** *Who did it?*
>
> **¿Quiénes lo hicieron?** *Which persons did it?*

■ Translating *what?*

When the English word is followed by nothing, the Spanish word is **qué**:

> **Tenemos que hacer algo, pero no sabemos qué**
> *We have to do something, but we don't know what*

The English *what + to be* is translated **cuál + ser**, except when *what is?* really means *what is the definition of?* or *how many?*

> **¿Cuál fue la solución que él propuso?** *What was the solution that he suggested?*
>
> **¿Cuál es su profesión?** *What's your profession?*

but

> **¿Qué hora es?** *What's the time?*
>
> **¿Qué es un agujero negro?** *What is (the definition of) a Black Hole?*

When the English *what* precedes a verb other than **ser** it is translated **lo que**, but before an Infinitive by **qué**:

> **No sé lo que quieres** *I don't know what you want*

---

[39] Cubans may use ordinary word order here—**¿Cómo ustedes van . . . ?**, etc.

> **No sé qué decirles** *I don't know what to say to them*

When *what* stands before a noun, it is translated **qué**:

> **Dinero? ¿Qué dinero?** *Money? What money?*
> **No sé en qué canal es** *I don't know what/which channel it's on*

Many Latin-Americans use **cuál** in such sentences, e.g. **¿A cuáles libros te refieres?** for **¿A qué libros te refieres?** *what books are you referring to?*, but this is not done in Spain and is not the case in every Latin-American country.

■ Translating *which?*

When *which* stands alone, it is translated **cuál**, plural **cuáles** (although **quién**, plural **quienes** is more appropriate for human beings):

> **He leído alguno de estos libros, pero no recuerdo cuál** *I've read one or other of these books, but I can't remember which*

Which of? is **cuál de**, plural **cuáles de**. When *which* is an abbreviated form of *which of them* **cuál/cuáles** must also be used:

> **Puedes elegir tres de estos. ¿Cuáles prefieres?** *You can choose three of these. Which (ones of them) do you prefer?*

When *which* can be replaced by *what* it should be translated **qué**. See the previous section for examples.

For *n* Days/Weeks, *Ago*, *Since* and Similar Expressions

■ *for n days, weeks, etc.*

The most frequently used construction in everyday Spanish uses the regular verb **llevar**[40]. Note that Spanish uses the Present or the Imperfect tense where English uses the Perfect or Pluperfect tenses:

> **Llevo seis años estudiando español** *I have been studying Spanish for six years*
>
> **Llevaba seis años estudiando español** *I had been studying Spanish for six years*
>
> **Lleva años aquí** *He/she's been here for years*
>
> **Llevas varios días enfadado** *You've been angry for several days*
>
> **Llevábamos tres horas esperando** *We had been waiting for three hours*

The following constructions with **hacer** are more formal:

> **Estudio español desde hace seis años** *I have been studying Spanish for six years*

or

> **Hace seis años que estudio español**
>
> **Yo estudiaba español desde hacía seis años** *I had been studying Spanish for six years*

[40] Use of **tener**, e.g. **tengo seis años aquí** *I've been here six years*, is common in Latin America, but not in Spain.

or

> **Hacía seis años que yo estudiaba español**

English-speakers are easily misled into thinking that a sentence like ***he estado* tres meses en Nueva York** *I was in New York for three months* means the same as ***llevo* tres meses en Nueva York** *I've been in New York for three months.* The former implies that the speaker has now left the city, whereas the latter clearly indicates that his/her stay is still continuing.

When the period of time is clearly finished, **durante** may be used:

> **La estuvo mirando durante tres minutos** *He gazed at her for three minutes*
>
> **Victoria reinó durante casi cuarenta años** *Victoria reigned for nearly forty years*

In some cases no preposition is used:

> **Estuve tres días en Barcelona** *I was in Barcelona (for) three days*

■ *Ago*

The usual construction uses **hacer**:

> **La vi hace tres días/Hace tres días que la vi** *I saw her three days ago*

■ *Since*

The use of the Present and Imperfect tenses should be noted:

> ***Vivo* aquí desde abril** *I've been living here since April*
>
> **Mi madre *vive* con mi tía desde que murió mi padre** *My mother's been living with my aunt since my father died*
>
> ***Vivíamos* allí desde el año anterior** *We had been living there since the year before*

Spaniards may use the Perfect and Pluperfect tenses in these sentences, but the Present or Imperfect are usually required by Latin-Americans. If the sentence is negated, the Perfect tense is used, or the Preterit in those regions (much of Latin America) where the Perfect is little used:

> **No la he visto/No la vi desde el domingo** *I haven't seen her since Sunday*

■ *The first time that . . .* , etc.

Use of the Spanish Present and Imperfect tenses should be noted in these sentences:

> **Es la primera vez que *olgo* mencionar su nombre** *It is the first time I have heard his name mentioned*
>
> **Era la primera vez que *entraban* en ese edificio** *It was the first time they had entered that building*

Affective Suffixes

'Affective' suffixes are suffixes like **-ito**, **-illo**, **-ón**, **-azo** that add various emotional overtones to a noun, adjective or adverb. In general, foreign learners should avoid using them until they are very fluent in the language, since they can sound silly or even insulting if misused. They are less frequent in some places than in others: Mexicans and Central Americans sprinkle their speech with diminutive suffixes, in Argentina and Spain they are less common (but still much used), and in some places diminutive forms are considered more appropriate in women's speech than men's.

DIMINUTIVE SUFFIXES

The main Diminutive Suffixes are **-ito**, **-ecito** (or **-ico** in some regions), **-illo**, **-ecillo**. Other suffixes like **-uelo**, **-iño**, **-ín** are also encountered, the latter two being regional in use

They are used:

■ To make one's speech especially friendly or affectionate

For this reason they are much used when talking to little children, but they are also often used between strangers in order to make the tone friendly. Compare

> **¿Le pongo un poco de sal?** *Shall I put some salt on it for you?* (neutral tone)
> **¿Le pongo un poquito de sal?** (same thing but more friendly)

> **Eres un comilón** (or **comelón**) *You eat a lot*
> **Eres un comiloncillo** *You sure like your food!* (more friendly)

Ahora se lo traigo *I'll bring it to you now*
Ahorita se lo traigo (same but more friendly).

Ahorita is especially common in Mexico, but Spaniards say **ahora mismo**)

■ To convey the idea of smallness, usually with some feeling of affection:

La casa tiene un jardincito *The house has a little backyard/garden*
¡Mira los pajaritos! *Look at the little birds!*
un cafetín *a little café*

■ Sometimes, especially in the case of **-illo**, to add a sarcastic tone:

¡Qué listillo eres! *Aren't you smart! What a know-all you are!* (sarcastic: **listo** = *clever*)
señorito (roughly) *a spoilt son from a rich family*
miedica *cowardly/'chicken'*

Sometimes diminutive suffixes simply change the original meaning without any emotional overtones:

el palo *a stick*   **el palillo** *a toothpick*
la tesis *thesis*   **la tesina** *dissertation*
la ventana *window*   **la ventanilla** *vehicle window*

AUGMENTATIVE SUFFIXES

The main Augmentative Suffixes are **-ón**, **-azo** and **-ote**. As their name suggests, they indicate increased size or intensity, often (especially in the first two cases) with some overtone of excess or unpleasantness:

mandón *bossy*
aburridón *really boring* (**aburrido** = *boring*)
dramón *a big melodrama* (sarcastic, cf. **el drama** *drama*)

un vinazo *a really strong, heavy wine* (el vino = *wine*)

la palabrota *swearword* (la palabra = *word*)

grandote *enormous* (grande = *big*)

PEJORATIVE SUFFIXES

-ajo, -uco, -ucho, -astro are also sometimes added to nouns and adjectives to add an idea of unpleasantness:

el hotelucho *flophouse/dump of a hotel*

la palabreja *peculiar, horrible word*

la casuca, la casucha *hovel/dingy house* (la casa = *house*)

| Word Order

Word order in questions is mentioned on p.203. Word order with adverbs is mentioned on p.153. Other useful points to remember are:

■ Spanish is unlike English in that it puts a Verb and an Object (if there is one) before the Subject rather than separate them by many intervening words. Spanish does not like to leave verb phrases dangling at the end of the sentence far from their subject. The position of the verbs in italics should be noted in these sentences:

> ***Rompió*** **la ventana el vecino que siempre lleva el sombrero amarillo** *The neighbor/*(Brit. *neighbour) who always wears the yellow hat broke the window*
>
> ***Ganó*** **el partido el equipo que más se había entrenado antes** *The team that had trained most before won the match*
>
> **Me fui porque me *revienta* tener que esperar varias horas en la parada del autobús** *I left because having to wait several hours at the bus-stop gets on my nerves*

The preceding rule is almost always applied in Subordinate and Relative Clauses. The verb is usually not left at the end of the sentence:

> **Esa es la moto que me vendió Alfredo** *That's the motor-bike that Alfredo sold me* (lit. *that sold me Alfredo*)
>
> **Quedará prohibido cuando entre en vigor la nueva ley** *It'll be prohibited when the new law*

> *comes into effect* (lit. *comes into effect the new law*)

■ After adverbs and adverbial phrases, the verb is often put before the subject:

> **Si bien *dice* el refrán que "ojos que no ven, corazón que no llora"** ... *If the proverb is right (literally if well says the proverb that . . .) that 'what the eye doesn't see, the heart doesn't weep about'* ...
>
> **Con la noche *llegan* a su fin las actividades del día** *At nightfall the day's activities come to an end*

■ An English preposition can appear at the end of a sentence, but Spanish prepositions *always* stand before the noun or pronoun that they refer to:

> **La chica a la que di el dinero** *The girl I gave the money* **to** ...
>
> **Las escaleras por las que subieron** *The stairs they went* **up**
>
> **alguien con quien salir** ... *someone to go out* **with** ...

■ No word ever comes between Object Pronouns and their verb:

> **Me lo diste ayer** *You gave it to me yesterday*
>
> **Me has defendido siempre** *You've always defended me*

■ There is a tendency, especially in colloquial speech, to put the most urgent information first. This is required in some contexts, e.g. **¡viene la policía!** *the police are coming!*, but normal word order would also be correct in the following sentences:

> **Dinero tiene, pero no es un millonario** *He's got money, but he's no millionaire* (literally *money he's got . . .*)

> **Invitada está, pero no sé si viene** *She's invited—but I don't know if she'll come* (literally *invited she is . . .*)
>
> **Todos esos detalles ya me los explicaste ayer** *You already explained all those details to me yesterday*

In the last example the Direct Object (**todos estos detalles**) is echoed or resumed by **los**, as explained on p.117.

| Pronunciation

The descriptions given in this section are approximate: it is not possible to give an exact picture in writing of the pronunciation of a foreign language. An attempted representation of the pronunciation is shown between square brackets, e.g. [elpérro] = **el perro** *dog*: the letters in the square brackets should be given their normal Spanish pronunciation, although a few special signs are used, explained below. Where two pronunciations are shown, the Latin-American version is first.

VOWELS

Spanish vowels are neither numerous nor complicated, but none of them is exactly like any English vowel sound. They are all *short* and do not vary in length or quality, whether stressed or not; compare the English pronunciation of *panorama,* which has three different *a* sounds, and the Spanish **panorama**, which has only one kind of *a*.

	Approximate equivalents	
	American English	Southern British
a	*father* (but much shorter)	*father*(shortened), *cut*
	The vowel must be as short as the *a* of *cat*.	
e	*egg*	*egg*
	Not like the *ay* of *day* (which is much too long and ends in a *y* sound), although the first part of this English diphthong is close to Spanish **e**. Spanish **e** is an equivalent of the French *e* in **un café**	

i	*seen* but much shorter and with no trace of a *y* sound at the end	same
o	no exact equivalent? Not like the *o* of *note* (which is too long and ends in a *w* sound) but a very short version of the first part of this sound with rounded lips is good	*hot* (rounded)
u	*good*, but with rounded lips Not like *oo* of *food* (too long, lips not rounded and ends in a *w* sound)	same

Examples: **cama, teme, sin, somos, luz**.

English-speakers, American and British, must learn to pronounce adjacent vowels without a trace of a pause (glottal stop), *y*, *r* or *w* sound between them: **sea o no** *whether it is or not* is [seaonó], not 'sayer-ou-nou', **lo ha hecho** *he's done it* = [loaécho], not 'lo-wa-echou'.

Vowels are not slurred when they are unstressed. **Beca** *(study) grant* is [béka] and nothing like the English word *baker*. The sound of the English *a* in *above* or *e* in *the* does not exist in Spanish.

DIPHTHONGS

American and Southern British

ai, ay	*aisle*
au	*cow*, but with rounded lips
ei, ey	*day*
eu	like *e* in *egg* followed by *w* of *well*
ie, ye	*yes*
ia, ya	*y* of *yes* + Spanish **a**
iu	*y* of *yes* + Spanish **u**
oi, oy	*boy*

ou	*low* but with rounded lips
ua	*w* of *want* (with rounded lips) + Spanish **a**
ue	*went* with rounded lips
uy	Spanish **u** + *y* of *yes*

Examples: **hay** *there is/are*, **causa** *cause*, **ley** *law*, **Europa** *Europe*, **bien** *well*, **ya** *already*, **la viuda** *widow*, **no unió** *he did not join together* (pronounced [nounyó]), **Managua**, **bueno** *good*, **muy** *very*.

Words are run together whenever possible without pauses between them: **nos han dado una fortuna** = [nosandaðounafortúna] *they've given us a fortune*. When one word ends in a vowel and the next one begins with a vowel a diphthong is formed if possible and identical vowels are run together to form a very slightly longer vowel. English speakers must avoid inserting a pause or a *y* or *w*:

> **ha iniciado** [aynisyáðo]/[ayniθyáðo] *has initiated* (**ay** as in English *eye*)
> **la apertura** [lapertúra] *the opening*
> **he indicado** [eyndikáðo] *I have indicated* (**ey** as *ay* in English *day*)
> **he entrado** [entráðo] *I have entered*
> **si han dicho** [syandícho] *if they've said* (**sya** like *cea* in English *oceanic*)
> **no implica** [noymplíka] *it doesn't imply*

TRIPHTHONGS

These arise when one of the above diphthongs is preceded or followed by a *y* sound or a *w* sound:

American and British English

uai, uay	*wise*, but with rounded lips
uei, uey	*ways*, but with rounded lips

iai	*yike*
iei	*Yates*

Examples: **continuáis** *you continue*, **Paraguay**, **continuéis** *you continue* (Subjunctive form), **buey** *ox*, **y aire** [yáy-re] *and air*.

CONSONANTS

p, t, k and **ch** are pronounced as in American and British English except that no puff of breath follows them. A piece of tissue paper hung two inches from the lips should barely move when one says the Spanish words **pipa** *pipe*, **tú** *you*, **kilo** *kilogram*, **chacha** *housemaid* (familiar style, Spain)

t is always pronounced with the tongue against the front teeth and not as in English with the tongue on the ridge of gum behind the front teeth.

c is pronounced as Spanish **k** before **a, o** and **u**: **cama** *bed*, **cosa** *thing*, **el cura** *the priest*.

Before **e** and **i** it is pronounced the same as Spanish **z**, i.e. as *c* in *rice* in Latin America and [θ] (like the *th* of *think*) in Spain: **cinco** [sínko]/[θínko] *five*, **central** [sentrál]/[θentrál] *central*.

b and **v** are pronounced in nearly every position as [ß], a sound that does not exist in English. It is technically known as a voiced bilabial fricative and is made by holding the lips as for *b* and murmuring through them; it should be possible to produce the sound as long as you have breath. The sound of English *v* in *vat* does not exist in Spanish: the pairs of words **tuvo/tubo** [túßo] *he had/tube*, **iba/IVA** [íßa] *he was going/Value Added Tax*, **lavase/la base** [laßáse] *he washed/the base* sound exactly the same in Spanish.

The same two letters are pronounced like the *b* of **big**

only when they come after **n** (even between words) or
when they occur after a pause): **son buenos** [sombwénos]
they're good, **en Bolivia** [embolíßya] *in Bolivia*, **ambos**
[ámbos] *both*. Note that **n** is pronounced **m** before **b** and
v.

d is pronounced [δ] in nearly every position, i.e. like the
English *th* in **this**, **then**: **lado** [láδo] *size*, **los dados**
[losdáδos] *the dice*, **libertad** [lißertáδ] *freedom*. **d** is, however, pronounced like the *d* of *dog* (but with the tongue
against the front teeth) after **n** and **l** and after a pause:
han dicho [andícho] *they've said*, **cuando** [kwándo]
when, **falda** [fálda] *skirt*, **sal de mar** [saldemár] *sea salt*.

f is pronounced as in English.

g is pronounced like Spanish **j** before **e** and **i**: see notes on
j. It is pronounced [γ] in nearly every other position, a
sound that does not exist in English. It is technically
known as a voiced velar fricative and is made by holding
the mouth as for the *g* in *ago* and gently releasing air
through the throat while murmuring; it should be possible
to keep the sound up as long as you have breath: **hago**
[áγo] *I do*, **laguna** [laγúna] *pond*, **Paraguay** [paraγwáy].
   The same letter is pronounced like the English *g* of *go*
only after **n** and at the beginning of a word after a pause:
son grandes [songrándes] *they're big*, **sin ganas** [singá-
nas] *without enthusiasm/appetite*, **tengo** [téngo] *I have*. The
n must be pronounced like the *ng* of *bring* when **g** follows
it.
   The combination **gue** and **gui** are pronounced as the
Spanish **g** of **hago** plus **e** or **i**; the silent **u** merely shows
that the **g** is not pronounced like Spanish **j**: **pague** [páγe]
pay, **la guirnalda** [laγirnálda] *wreath*. In the combinations **güe** and **güi** the **u** is pronounced like *w*, cf. **desagüe**
[desáγwe] *drain*, **nicaragüense** [nikaraγwénse]
Nicaraguan.

h is always silent. Compare the pairs **asta/hasta** *spear/until*, **ha/a** *has/to*, **hecho/echo** *done/I throw out*, which are each pronounced identically. The rule in Spanish is the reverse of English: in Spanish *not* dropping one's aitches tends to sound illiterate.

j is pronounced in Spain and most of Argentina like the *ch* in Scottish *loch* (phonetic sign [χ]). In most of the rest of Latin America it is soft like the *h* in English *hat*. **G** is pronounced like **j** before **e** and **i**: **rojo** [rróχo] *red*, **ajo** [áχo] *garlic*, **jarra** [χárra] *jar*, **general** [χenerál] *general*, **gente** [χénte] *people*, **rígido** [rríχiðo] *rigid*.

l is always pronounced like the *l* in Southern British or Southern Irish *leaf*. It is not pronounced like the *l* in the English *cold*. Americans and Scots tend to use the latter kind of *l* even at the beginning of words like *leaf*, so they must take care over the Spanish sound: **lobo** *wolf*, **sal** *salt*, **natural**, **gol** *goal* (in soccer).

ll varies from region to region. The correct pronunciation in standard Spanish does not correspond to anything in English: it is a palatal **l**, i.e. **l** pronounced with the tongue spread flat against the roof of the mouth. Many English-speakers pronounce it like the *li* in *million*, but this is the Spanish sound **li** in words like **alianza** *alliance*, **exilio** *exile*: the two words **polio** *polio* and **pollo** *chicken* sound quite different. The best solution for English speakers is to pronounce it always like the *y* of *yacht*—as millions of Spanish speakers do. This may sound slovenly to some speakers, but it is much better than the *li* of *million*. In most of the Argentina and Uruguay it is pronounced like the *s* of *pleasure*.

m is pronounced as in English, or sometimes like **n** when it occurs at the end of a word, as in **referéndum**.

n is pronounced as in English before a vowel or **d, t,**

another **n**, or when nothing follows it: **no**, **Londres**
London, **antes** *before*, **innato** *innate*, **son** *they are*.

Before all other consonants it is pronounced with the
mouth in the same position as for the following consonant, i.e.

before **k, j, g** and **c** when pronounced **k**, like *ng* in *song*:
con kilos *with kilos*, **sin gusto** *without taste*, **lengua**
tongue/language, **en Colombia**, **banco** *bank/bench*;

before **m, b, p, v**, like the *m* in *mouse*: **en Madrid**, **han
bajado** *they've got down*, **en París**, **han visto** *they've seen*;

before **ll, y** and **ch**, like **ñ** (see below): **en llamas** *in
flames*, **en Yepes**, **ancho** *wide*, **en Chile**;

before **f** it is pronounced with the tongue and lips in the
position for pronouncing **f**: **son fuertes** *they're strong*, **en
frente** *opposite*.

ñ is difficult for Americans and Britons. It is a palatal *n*,
i.e. an *n* pronounced with the tongue flat against the roof
of the mouth. It is not the same as the *ni* in *onion*, which is
the Spanish **ni** in words like **Sonia**, **milenio** *millennium*.
Students should try their pronunciation of the two words
huraño [uráño] *shy/unsociable* and **uranio** [uranyo] *uranium* on a native Spanish-speaker: if the difference of
meaning is clear, all is well.

q is found only in the combination **que** and **qui**, which
are pronounced [ke] and [ki]. See **k** (first item in list of
consonants) for details: **parque** *park*, **quiso** *he wanted*

r between vowels and at the end of words is rather like the
d in the American English *soda* or the *r* in Scottish English
carry: i.e. a single flap of the tongue against the gum ridge.
It is not like the *r* in American or British *red, rose*. **R** is
never dropped, as it is in southern British English in
words like *cart*, and it is never pronounced with the
tongue curled back, as it is in the USA in words like *far*.

Examples **Carlos, bar, cara** *face*, **mero** *mere*, **decir** *to say*.

At the beginning of a word and after **n**, **l** and **s** it is rolled like Spanish **rr**, e.g. in **Roma, alrededor** *around*, **honra** *honour*, **Israel**.

rr is a rolled **r** (three taps of the tongue). It is important to distinguish between **caro** *dear* and **carro** *car/cart*, **pero** *but* and **perro** *dog*.

s is pronounced like *s* in *hiss*, not as in *rose*.

w is found only in foreign words, where it is pronounced like Spanish **v/b** (see above): **kiwi** [kíßi] *kiwi fruit*, **Kuwait** [kußáyt].

x is the same as in English in Latin America, but in Spain it is often pronounced *s* before a consonant: **explicar** [eksplikár]/[esplikár] *explain*, but **taxi** [táksi].

y is like y in *yacht*. In Argentina it is like the *s* in *pleasure*.

z is always pronounced the same as the Spanish **c** when the latter occurs before **e** and **i**, i.e. like *ss* in *hiss* in Latin America and [θ] (as *th* in *think*) in Spain: **haz** [as]/[aθ] *do*, **las veces** [lasßéses]/[lasßéθes] *the times*.

STRESS (see Glossary)

The position of stress in a Spanish word is often variable and can change the meaning. See the section on Writing Accents (p.222) for details.

Spelling and Punctuation

This chapter presupposes a knowledge of Spanish pronunciation (explained in the previous chapter).

THE ALPHABET

The Spanish alphabet has the following letters:

a **a**	g **ge**	m **eme**	r **erre/ere**	y **i griega**
b **be**	h **hache**	n **ene**	s **ese**	z **zeta**
c **ce**	i **i**	ñ **eñe**	t **te**	
d **de**	j **jota**	o **o**	u **u**	
e **e**	k **ka**	p **pe**	v **uve**	
f **efe**	l **ele**	q **cu**	w **uve doble**	

Letters of the alphabet are all feminine: **la a, una ce**.

Ch and **ll** were counted as separate letters of the alphabet until the Association of Academies of Spanish decided to introduce normal alphabetical order in April 1994. As a result alphabetical order in dictionaries and directories printed before that date will differ from ours, e.g. **chato** came after **cubrir**, **llama** after **luz**.

WRITING ACCENTS

There are three written accents in Spanish: the acute accent, the dieresis and the **tilde**.

The dieresis occurs only in the combinations **güe** and

güe, where it shows that the **u** is not silent as in **nicaragüense** *Nicaraguan*, **el pingüino** *the penguin*.

The **tilde** appears only over **ñ**, and forms an entirely different letter, described on p.220.

■ The acute accent is used for three purposes:

(a) Occasionally to distinguish two words that are spelt the same, e.g. **sólo** *only* and **solo** *alone*.

(b) On question words: **¿cuándo vienes?** *when are you coming?*, **no sabe qué hacer** *he doesn't know what to do*. See p.202 for details.

(c) To show where the stress falls in unpredictably stressed words

This latter function is very important, since the position of stress in a Spanish word is crucial for the meaning: compare **hablo** *I speak* and **habló** *he spoke*.

An accent must be written on the stressed vowel:

(1) Whenever the stress falls more than two full vowels[41] from the end:

> **rápido** *fast*
> **las imágenes** *images*
> **dígamelo** *say it to me*
> **fácilmente** *easily*
> **cámbiate** *change your clothes* (third full vowel from end)

(2) Whenever the word ends in a vowel or **n** or **s** and the stress falls on the final vowel:

> **habló** *he spoke*
> **iraní** *Iranian*
> **cambié** *I changed*

---

[41] By 'full vowel' is meant **a**, **e** and **o** and also **i** when it is pronounced as in **sin** and not like *y* as in **Colombia**, and **u** when it is pronounced as in **uno** and not like *w* as in **continuo**.

> **la nación** *the nation*
> **francés** *French*

Compare the following words which are stressed on the last full vowel but one and therefore do not require an accent: **hablo** *I speak*, **cambio** *I change*, **dicen** *they say*, **la imagen** *the image*, **las naciones** *the nations*, **las series** *the series* (plural).

(3) When the word ends in a consonant other than **n** or **s** and it is *not* stressed on the last vowel:

> **el récord** *the record* (in sport, etc.)
> **el revólver** *the revolver*
> **fácil** *easy*

Compare the following words which are stressed on the last vowel and therefore do not require an accent: **la libertad** *freedom*, **natural** *natural*, **el complot** *conspiracy/plot*.

■ Words of one syllable (i.e. having only one fully pronounced vowel) are not written with an accent:

> **fui** [fwi] *I was*[42]
> **fue** [fwe] *he was*
> **vio** [byo] *he saw*
> **dio** [dyo] *he gave*
> **la fe** *faith*

The only exceptions are accents written to distinguish one word from another: see list below.

Words like **fió** *he entrusted*, **crié** *I bred/raised* have two syllables (i.e. the **i** is pronounced separately).

■ The following words are distinguished by an accent:

> **aun** *even*   **aún** *still/yet*[43]

[42] **fui, fue, vio** and **dio** were written with an accent until 1959.
[43] **Aun** should be pronounced as one syllable [awn] (aw like *ow* in *how*) and **aún** as two [a-ún].

de *of*	**dé** Present Subjunctive of **dar** *to give*
el *the*	**él** *he*
este *this*	**éste** *this one* (see p.138)
ese/aquel *that*	**ése/aquél** *that one* (see p.138)
mas *but* (poetic)	**más** *more*
mi *my*	**mí** *me* (after prepositions)
se pronoun	**sé** *I know*
si *if*	**sí** *yes; himself/herself/ yourself/themselves*, etc.
solo *alone*	**sólo** *only*
te *you*	**té** *tea*
tu *your*	**tú** *you*

DIPHTHONGS AND TRIPHTHONGS: SPELLING AND ACCENT RULES

■ Diphthongs consist of a *y* or *w* sound preceded or followed by a vowel. The pronunciation of the following diphthongs is shown on p.215:

> **au ua ai/ay ia/ya**
> **eu ue ei/ey ie/ye**
> **iu**
> **ou uo oi/oy io/yo**

The sound *y* is always written **y** at the end of words:

> **rey** *king*
> **doy** *I give*

The sound *y* is written either **y** or **hi** at the beginning of words:

> **el yate** *yacht*
> **la hierba** or **la yerba** *grass*

The sound *w* is always written **hu** at the beginning of a word or when it comes between vowels:

> **la huerta** [lawérta] *orchard*
> **ahuecar** [awekár] *to hollow out*

When the combinations of vowel plus **i** or **u** represent two separate vowels and not a diphthong, the **i** or **u** is written with an accent (even if **h** intervenes):

> **dúo** *duo*
> **el búho** *the owl*
> **hacías** *you were doing*
> **prohíben** *they prohibit*
> **se reúnen** *they hold a meeting*

■ Triphthongs consist of one of the above Diphthongs preceded or followed by a *y sound* or a *w* sound:

> **actuáis** [aktwáys] *you act*
> **buey** [bwey] *ox*

Diphthongs and Triphthongs count as one full vowel for the purpose of finding the stress accent:

Regular stress	Irregular
hacia *towards*	ha**cía** *he made*
dio *he gave*	me **fío** *I trust*
aire *air*	**aís**la *he isolates*
sois *you* (**vosotros**) *are*	pro**híbe** *he prohibits*

MISCELLANEOUS SPELLING RULES

The main traps set by the Spanish spelling system are:

■ **b** and **v** are pronounced the same, so words like **vello** *down* (i.e. very fine hair) and **bello** *beautiful* sound the same.

■ The sound **s** (as in English *hiss*) can be spelt three different ways in Latin America:

feroz *ferocious* [ferós]   **as** *ace* [as]   **haz** *do* [as]
hace *does* [áse]   **cinco** *five* [sínko]

The **z** and **c** in the above words are pronounced like *th* of *think* in central and northern Spain.

■ There is no certain way of predicting the spelling of the sound [χ] (like the *ch* in the Scottish *loch*). It is usually written **j** before **a**, **o**, **u** and **g** before **e** and **i**. But there are quite a few words in which the combination **je** occurs, e.g. **el viaje** *journey*, **el equipaje** *baggage*, **el paisaje** *countryside*, **Jesús** *Jesus*, **condujeron** *they drove*, etc.

■ **gue/güe** and **gui/güi**: see p.218.

■ **h** is a silent letter, so there is no difference in sound, for example, between **hecho** *done* and **echo** *I pour out*.

■ **que** and **qui**: the **u** is silent and the **q** is pronounced [k].

■ **r** and **rr**: see p.220

■ A number of alternative spellings exist, the most important of which are:

words beginning with **psic-** (the equivalent of our *psych-*) may be written **sic-**: **psicología** or **sicología** *psychology*, because the **p** is silent;

the words **septiembre** *September* and **séptimo** *seventh* can be spelt without the **p**;

words beginning with **ree-** may be spelt **re-**, e.g. **relegir** or **reelegir** *re-elect*.

In all cases the longer forms are more usual (at least in Spain).

PUNCTUATION

There are variations in punctuation rules depending on country and, to some extent, on publisher. Only the major differences between Spanish and English practice are mentioned.

■ A comma is used to separate decimals (but not in Mexico, which uses the same system as English):

12,75 doce coma setenta y cinco *12.75*

■ A period (British 'full stop') is used to separate thousands

1.000.000 un millón *a million*

Mexico uses our system.

■ In some publications double inverted commas (**las comillas**) are used to enclose quoted words, in others chevrons are used (« »):

Tuvieron problemas por "el fuerte carácter de la suegra" or . . . **«por el fuerte carácter de la suegra»** *They had problems due to 'their mother-in-law's strong character'*

■ Question marks and exclamation marks must be written upside-down at the beginning of questions and exclamations as well as the right way up at the end:

Oye, ¿sabes qué hora es? *Listen, d'you know what time it is?*
Pero, ¡qué tonto! *But what a fool!*

As can be seen, the start of the question or exclamation does not always coincide with the start of the sentence.

A **raya** or double-length dash is used to mark off dialogue in novels and stories:

—Tengo un hijo tuyo —me dijo después—. Allí está.
Y apuntó con el dedo a un muchacho largo con los ojos azorados.
—¡Quítate el sombrero, para que te vea tu padre!

'I've got a son of yours', he said to me afterwards.
'There he is.'
And he pointed to a tall boy with alarmed eyes.
'Take your hat off so your father can see you!'

| Translation Traps

This section covers a number of important miscellaneous points that could not be neatly fitted in elsewhere in the book.

'afternoon'/'evening'
'American'/'Latin-American', 'Spanish-American'
'any'
aun and *aún*
'to become'
de que and *de*
'-ing' forms of English verbs
'to like'
'only'/'alone'
'some'
'Spanish'/'Castilian'
'would'
ya

Afternoon, evening

It is difficult to differentiate these words in Spanish, since **la tarde** runs from about 1 p.m. to after sunset and therefore includes our afternoon and evening. **La noche** begins around 8 or 9 p.m.

American, Latin-American, South American, Spanish-American

In Spain **americano** usually means the same as the English *American*. In Latin America the same word is usually taken to mean *Latin-American* and **norteamericano** is used for our *American*. The adjective **estadounidense** 'pertaining to the USA' is generally found only in newspaper styles.

América Latina or **Latinoamérica** is *Latin America* and is a preferred term since it stresses trans-national identity; the adjective is **latinoamericano**. However, these terms include Brazil, Haiti, Martinique and one or two other places that speak Latin-based languages, and there is no entirely satisfactory word for Spanish-speaking Latin America. **La América de habla española** *Spanish-speaking America* is long-winded, but **Hispanoamérica**, **hispanoamericano** strictly mean *Spanish-America(n)* and some people consider them unfair to the non-European or non-Spanish components of the populations.

América del sur, adjective **sudamericano** or **suramericano** (the latter frowned on by strict grammarians) means *South America* and does not include Central America or the Caribbean.

Any

This word is translated as follows:

(a) Before substances and countable nouns, in negative and interrogative sentences, no Spanish equivalent:

> **No tengo agua/flores** *I haven't got any water/flowers*
> **¿Hay?** *Is there any/Are there any?*
> **¿Hay americanos en tu clase?** *Are there any Americans in your class?*

(b) When it means *it doesn't matter which*: **cualquiera** (see p.122):

> **Puedes elegir cualquiera de ellos** *You can choose any of them*
> **en cualquier sitio y a cualquier hora** *in any place and at any time*

(c) In comparisons: **ninguno** (see p.155):

> **Ella es mejor que ninguno de los hombres**
> *She's better than any of the men*

(d) After **sin** *without*, no Spanish equivalent:

> **Ha venido sin dinero** *He's come without any
> money*

Aun and aún

Aun means *even*, as in **aun en ese caso no lo haría** *even
in that case I wouldn't do it*. **Incluso**[44] means the same
thing, and is nowadays more common.

Aún means the same as **todavía** *yet*: **todavía/aún no
han llegado** *they haven't arrived yet*.

To become

There are several ways of translating this word and words
similar to it in meaning (cf. *to get* angry, *to go* red, *to
turn* nasty):

(a) Use a Pronominal Verb if one exists, e.g. **alegrarse**
to become cheerful, **se cansó** *he/she got/became tired*.

(b) Use **ponerse** for short-lived changes of mood,
appearance: **no te pongas así** *don't get like that*, **esto se
pone difícil** *this is getting difficult*, **se puso colorada** *she
went red*.

(c) Use **volverse** for more permanent changes: **te has
vuelto muy reaccionario** *you've got very reactionary*, **se
volvió loco** *he went mad*.

(d) Use **convertirse en** for total changes of nature, cf.
English *to turn into*: **los alquimistas creían que el
plomo podía convertirse en oro** *alchemists thought lead
could become/turn into gold*.

---

[44] Many Latin Americans say **inclusive** for **incluso**.

(e) Use **hacerse** for conversions to a belief or changes of profession involving qualifications: **se hizo diseñador** *he became a designer*. **Hacerse** is also found in some set phrases with non-human subjects, e.g. **se ha hecho tarde** *it's got late*.

(f) Use **nombrar** for posts, offices, titles: **lo/le han nombrado Ministro de Asuntos Exteriores** *he's become the Minister for Foreign Affairs*.

de que and que

These both translate *that*: **dice que viene** *he says that he's coming*, **la idea de que viene . . .** *the idea that he's coming*.

De que must be used:

(a) After nouns, to show that what follows is a Subordinate Clause and not a Relative Clause. Compare **el argumento que él defiende es absurdo** *the argument that/which he's defending is absurd* (Relative Clause) and **el argumento de que la luna está hecha de queso es absurdo** *the argument that the Moon is made of cheese is absurd* (Subordinator). If the English word *which* could replace *that* in such sentences, **de que** cannot be used.

(b) Before clauses after prepositional phrases, verbs and adjectives that include **de**: Compare

> **antes de la salida del tren** *before the departure of the train*
>
> **antes de que salga el tren** *before the train leaves*
>
> **Estoy seguro de tu amor** *I'm sure of your love*
> **Estoy seguro de que me quieres** *I'm sure that you love me*
>
> **Se queja de que no la dejan dormir** *She complains that they don't let her sleep*

(c) **De que** must *not* be used after verbs meaning *to say, to think, to tell*, etc.

Dice que está enferma *She/he says that she's ill*
(*never* *'*dice de que está enferma*')

'*-ing*' forms of English verbs

This English verb form has many different uses, either as
an adjective, a noun, a participle or, sometimes, as a
gerund. The following are some of the most common
ways of translating the *-ing* form:

(a) When it is a noun it must be translated by the
Infinitive or by a suitable Spanish noun:

Smoking is forbidden **Prohibido fumar**
I like dancing **Me gusta bailar**
hunting and fishing **la caza y la pesca**

In compounds like *driving wheel, fishing rod, diving suit*, the
-ing form is a noun and the translation must be learned
separately: **el volante, la caña de pescar, la escafan-
dra/el traje de buceo.**

(b) When it is an adjective it must be translated by an
adjective:

A boring film **una película aburrida**
An overwhelming majority **una mayoría abru-
madora**
A worrying problem **un problema preocupante**

(c) After a preposition it is translated by the Infinitive:

Do it without complaining **Hazlo sin quejarte**

But when the subject of the *-ing* form is not the same as
the subject of the main verb, the Subjunctive or the
Indicative may be required. See p.29 ff for more details:

I entered without him seeing me **Entré sin que él
me viera**

(d) When the *-ing* form shows when or how an action is done, use the Spanish Gerund:

> *I realized it while walking down the street* **Me di cuenta andando por la calle**
> *He stood looking at me* **Se quedó mirándome**
> *You'll get nothing by shouting like that* **No conseguirás nada gritando así**

(e) For the phrase '*on . . . -ing*' use **al** plus the Infinitive:

> *on entering the room* **al entrar en el cuarto**

(f) To translate 'standing', 'sitting', 'leaning' or other bodily positions, use the Past Participle:

> *I was sitting on the beach* **Yo estaba sentado en la playa**
> *She was leaning against the tree* **Estaba apoyada contra el árbol**
> *He was crouching in the corner* **Estaba agazapado en el rincón**

(g) After many verbs, the *-ing* form must be translated by an Infinitive, often with a preposition:

> *Stop shouting* **Deja de gritar**
> *Start writing* **Empiece a escribir**

See the list of verbs that take the Infinitive on p.44 ff.

To like

Spanish uses the verb **gustar**, which means *to please*, so the English subject must become the object in Spanish:

> **Me gusta el vino** *Wine pleases me = I like wine*
> **No me gusta** *It doesn't please me = I don't like it*
> **¿Te/Le gusta bailar?** *Does dancing please you? = Do you like dancing?*

Le gusta trabajar aquí *Working here pleases/him/her* = *(S)he likes working here*
¿Te gusto? *Do I please you?* = *Do you like me?*
Me gustas *You please me* = *I like you*

Only and alone

Solo (agrees in number and gender: **sola, solos, solas**) is an adjective meaning *alone*: **está sola** *she's on her own*. **Sólo** (with accent) means *only*, and is the same as **solamente**: **sólo sé español** *I only know Spanish*.

Some

This word may be translated in several different ways:
   (a) Before substances and vague quantities of countable nouns: no Spanish equivalent

Pon azúcar *Put in some sugar*
Compra pan/flores *Buy some bread/flowers*
Hay patatas (Lat. Am. **papas**) *There are some potatoes*

(b) Before countable nouns when it means *a small number*: **unos/unas**:

Han venido unos ingleses *Some/a couple of English people have come*

(c) When *some* means *certain*, i.e. *some but not others*: **alguno** (discussed on p.121):

En algunos países está prohibido beber alcohol *In some countries drinking alcohol is forbidden*
Algún día podré comprarlo *I'll be able to buy it some day*

Spanish, Castilian

España is the country, and **español** is the adjective *Spanish*. **El español** is not *the* language of Spain, since Catalan, Basque and Galician also have official status and several other languages are recognized locally. **El castellano** *Castilian* is the official name for the language described in this book, although Castilian-speakers often call it **el español**, which may annoy speakers of the other languages.

What and which

See p.p. 203–4.

Would

This usually forms the Conditional tense in English, in which case it is translated by the Spanish Conditional tense:

> *If we sold more, prices **would** be lower* **Si vendiéramos más, los precios serían más bajos**

But *would* is occasionally used in English narrative to express habitual actions, in which case it must be translated by the Spanish Imperfect tense or by **soler** + Infinitive:

> *Each day he **would** get up (= used to get up) at six and he'd feed the chickens* **Todos los días se levantaba a las seis y daba de comer a las gallinas**
>
> *He **would** (= used to) ring her every night before going to bed* **Solía llamarla todas las noches, antes de acostarse**

Ya

This constantly-used word basically means:

already with a past tense: **ya ha llegado/ha llegado ya** *he's already arrived*;

right now with a present tense or imperative:**ya vienen** *they're coming right now*, **¡dímelo ya!** *tell me right now!*;

for sure/soon with a positive future tense: **no te preocupes: ya llegará** *don't worry, she'll come for sure/she'll be here soon*;

not . . . any more with a negative present or future: **ya no vienen/vendrán** *they're not coming any more*.

Verb Forms

FORMS OF REGULAR VERBS

As the following tables show, one adds the appropriate endings to the stem, which is the form left after removing the -ar, -er or -ir of the Infinitive:

Infinitive	Stem	Examples
hablar	habl-	habl*as* *you speak*
beber	beb-	beb*íamos* *we were drinking*
vivir	viv-	viv*ieron* *they lived*

Each tense has a separate set of endings, which differ for each of the three conjugations, although the endings of certain tenses (e.g. the Future and Conditional) are identical for all verbs, and the differences between the endings of the **-ir** and **-er** conjugations are not numerous.

CONJUGATION OF REGULAR VERB **HABLAR** to speak

Infinitive	**hablar**
Gerund	**hablando**
Past Participle	**hablado**
Imperative	
Tú	**habla**
Vosotros/as	**hablad**
Usted	**hable**
Ustedes	**hablen**

INDICATIVE

Present		*Imperfect*	
hablo	**hablamos**	**hablaba**	**hablábamos**
hablas	**habláis**	**hablabas**	**hablabais**
habla	**hablan**	**hablaba**	**hablaban**

Preterit	
hablé	**hablamos**
hablaste	**hablasteis**
habló	**hablaron**

Present Continuous	*Imperfect Continuous*
estoy hablando	**estaba hablando**
etc.	*etc.*

Preterit Continuous
estuve hablando
etc.

See p.269 for the conjugation of **estar**.

Perfect
he hablado
has hablado
ha hablado

hemos hablado
habéis hablado
han hablado

Pluperfect
había hablado
habías hablado
había hablado

habíamos hablado
habíais hablado
habían hablado

Perfect Continuous
he estado hablando
etc.

Pluperfect Continuous
había estado hablando
etc.

Pretérito anterior
hube hablado
hubiste hablado
hubo hablado

hubimos hablado
hubisteis hablado
hubieron hablado

Future
hablaré   hablaremos
hablarás   hablaréis
hablará   hablarán

Future Perfect
habré hablado
habrás hablado
habrá hablado

habremos hablado
habréis hablado
habrán hablado

Future Continuous
estaré hablando
etc.

Future Perfect Continuous
habré estado hablando
etc.

Conditional
hablaría   hablaríamos
hablarías   hablaríais
hablaría   hablarían

Perfect Conditional
habría hablado
habrías hablado
habría hablado

habríamos hablado
habríais hablado
habrían hablado

The Perfect Conditional may also be formed with the **-ra**
Imperfect Subjunctive of **haber,** *e.g.* **hubiera hablado,** *etc.*

Conditional Continuous
estaría hablando
etc.

Perfect Conditional Continuous
habría estado hablando
or **hubiera estado hablando**
etc.

SUBJUNCTIVE

Present Subjunctive

hable	**hablemos**
hables	**habléis**
hable	**hablen**

Present Subjunctive Continuous
esté hablando
etc.

Imperfect Subjunctives

-ra *form*

hablara	**habláramos**
hablaras	**hablarais**
hablara	**hablaran**

-se *form*

hablase	**hablásemos**
hablases	**hablaseis**
hablase	**hablasen**

Imperfect Subjunctive Continuous
estuviera hablando *or* **estuviese hablando**
etc. *etc.*

Perfect Subjunctive

haya hablado	**hayamos hablado**
hayas hablado	**hayáis hablado**
haya hablado	**hayan hablado**

Perfect Subjunctive Continuous
haya estado hablando
etc.

Pluperfect Subjunctive

hubiera hablado	**hubiéramos hablado**
hubieras hablado	**hubierais hablado**
hubiera hablado	**hubieran hablado**
or **hubiese hablado** *etc.*	

Perfect Subjunctive Continuous
haya estado hablando
etc.

Pluperfect Subjunctive Continuous
hubiera estado hablando
or **hubiese estado hablando**
etc.

Future Subjunctive

hablare	**habláremos**
hablares	**hablareis**
hablare	**hablaren**

CONJUGATION OF REGULAR VERB
BEBER *to drink*

Infinitive	**beber**
Gerund	**bebiendo**
Past Participle	**bebido**
Imperative	
Tú	**bebe**
Vosotros/as	**bebed**
Usted	**beba**
Ustedes	**beban**

INDICATIVE

Present

bebo	**bebemos**
bebes	**bebéis**
bebe	**beben**

Imperfect

bebía	**bebíamos**
bebías	**bebíais**
bebía	**bebían**

Preterit

bebí	**bebimos**
bebiste	**bebisteis**
bebió	**bebieron**

Present Continuous
estoy bebiendo
etc.

Imperfect Continuous
estaba bebiendo
etc.

Preterit Continuous
estuve bebiendo
etc.

Perfect
he bebido   **hemos bebido**
has bebido   **habéis bebido**
ha bebido   **han bebido**

Pluperfect
había bebido   **habíamos bebido**
habías bebido   **habíais bebido**
había bebido   **habían bebido**

Perfect Continuous   *Pluperfect Continuous*
he estado bebiendo   **había estado bebiendo**
etc.   *etc.*

Pretérito anterior
hube bebido   **hubimos bebido**
hubiste bebido   **hubisteis bebido**
hubo bebido   **hubieron bebido**

Future
beberé   **beberemos**
beberás   **beberéis**
beberá   **beberán**

Future Perfect
habré bebido   **habremos bebido**
habrás bebido   **habréis bebido**
habrá bebido   **habrán bebido**

Future Continuous   *Future Perfect Continuous*
estaré bebiendo   **habré estado bebiendo**
etc.   *etc.*

Conditional
bebería   **beberíamos**
beberías   **beberíais**
bebería   **beberían**

Perfect Conditional

habría bebido	habríamos bebido
habrías bebido	habríais bebido
habría bebido	habrían bebido

The Perfect Conditional may also be formed with the **-ra**
Imperfect Subjunctive of **haber**, *e.g.* **hubiera bebido**, *etc.*

Conditional Continuous	*Conditional Perfect Continuous*
estaría bebiendo	habría estado bebiendo
etc.	*or* hubiera estado bebiendo, *etc.*
	etc.

SUBJUNCTIVE

Present Subjunctive		*Present Subjunctive Continuous*
beba	bebamos	esté bebiendo
bebas	bebáis	*etc.*
beba	beban	

Imperfect Subjunctives

-ra *form*		**-se** *form*	
bebiera	bebiéramos	bebiese	bebiésemos
bebieras	bebierais	bebieses	bebieseis
bebiera	bebieran	bebiese	bebiesen

Imperfect Continuous Subjunctive

estuviera bebiendo *or* estuviese bebiendo
etc. *etc.*

Perfect Subjunctive

haya bebido	hayamos bebido
hayas bebido	hayáis bebido
haya bebido	hayan bebido

Pluperfect Subjunctive

hubiera bebido	hubiéramos bebido
hubieras bebido	hubierais bebido
hubiera bebido	hubieran bebido

or hubiese bebido, *etc.*

Perfect Subjunctive Continuous
haya estado bebiendo
etc.

Pluperfect Subjunctive Continuous
hubiera estado bebiendo
or **hubiese estado bebiendo**
etc.

Future Subjunctive

bebiere	bebiéremos
bebieres	bebiereis
bebiere	bebieren

CONJUGATION OF REGULAR VERB **VIVIR**
to live

■ *Only the endings marked with an asterisk differ from those of the* **-er** *conjugation.*

Infinitive	vivir*
Gerund	viviendo
Past Participle	vivido
Imperative	
Tú	vive
Vosotros/as	vivid*
Usted	viva
Ustedes	vivan

INDICATIVE

Present		Imperfect	
vivo	vivimos*	vivía	vivíamos
vives	vivís*	vivías	vivíais
vive	viven	vivía	vivían

Preterit	
viví	vivimos
viviste	vivisteis
vivió	vivieron

Present
estoy viviendo
etc.

Preterit Continuous
estuve viviendo
etc.

Perfect

he vivido	**hemos vivido**
has vivido	**habéis vivido**
ha vivido	**han vivido**

Pluperfect

había vivido	**habíamos vivido**
habías vivido	**habíais vivido**
había vivido	**habían vivido**

Perfect Continuous
he estado viviendo
etc.

Pretérito anterior

hube vivido	**hubimos vivido**
hubiste vivido	**hubisteis vivido**
hubo vivido	**hubieron vivido**

Future

viviré*	**viviremos***
vivirás*	**viviréis***
vivirá*	**vivirán***

Future Perfect

habré vivido	**habremos vivido**
habrás vivido	**habréis vivido**
habrá vivido	**habrán vivido**

Future Continuous
estaré viviendo
etc.

Imperfect Continuous
estaba viviendo
etc.

Pluperfect Continuous
había estado viviendo
etc.

Future Perfect Continuous
habré estado viviendo
etc.

Conditional
viviría*   **viviríamos***
vivirías*   **viviríais***
viviría*   **vivirían***

Conditional Perfect
habría vivido   **habríamos vivido**
habrías vivido   **habríais vivido**
habría vivido   **habrían vivido**

The Perfect Conditional may also be formed with the **-ra**
Imperfect Subjunctive of **haber**, *e.g.* **hubiera vivido**, *etc.*

Conditional Continuous   *Conditional Perfect Continuous*
estaría viviendo   **habría estado viviendo**
etc.   *etc.*

SUBJUNCTIVE

Present Subjunctive   *Present Subjunctive Continuous*
viva   **vivamos**   **esté viviendo**
vivas   **viváis**   *etc.*
viva   **vivan**

Imperfect Subjunctives

-ra *form*   **-se** *form*
viviera   **viviéramos**   **viviese**   **viviésemos**
vivieras   **vivierais**   **vivieses**   **vivieseis**
viviera   **vivieran**   **viviese**   **viviesen**

Imperfect Subjunctive Continuous
estuviera viviendo *or* **estuviese viviendo**
etc.   *etc.*

Perfect Subjunctive
haya vivido   **hayamos vivido**
hayas vivido   **hayáis vivido**
haya vivido   **hayan vivido**

Pluperfect Subjunctive

hubiera vivido	**hubiéramos vivido**
hubieras vivido	**hubierais vivido**
hubiera vivido	**hubieran vivido**
or **hubiese vivido** *etc.*	

Perfect Subjunctive Continuous Pluperfect Subjunctive Continuous

haya estado viviendo *etc.*	**hubiera estado viviendo** *or* **hubiese estado viviendo** *etc.*

Future Subjunctive

viviere	**viviéremos**
vivieres	**viviereis**
viviere	**vivieren**

SPELLING RULES AFFECTING CONJUGATION OF ALL SPANISH VERBS

- Infinitive ends in **-car** $c > qu$ before **e** or **i**. See **sacar** (no.52)
- Infinitive ends in **-gar** $g > gu$ before **e** or **i**. See **pagar** (no. 34)
- Infinitive ends in **-zar** $z > c$ before **e** or **i**. See **rezar** (no. 49)
- Infinitive ends in **-guar**   dieresis needed on **u** before **e**. See **averiguar** (no.7)

■ Infinitive ends in **-cer**: a few verbs are conjugated like **vencer** (no. 61), i.e. $c > z$ before **a** or **o**: these include **ejercer** *to exercise*, **convencer** *to convince*, **mecer** *to rock/sway*. **Escocer** *to sting* and **torcer** *to twist* are conjugated like **cocer** *to cook* (no.12). The rest, which are the vast majority, are conjugated like **parecer** (no. 35) and show a slight irregularity: $c > zc$ before **a**, **o**.

■ Infinitive ends in vowel + **-er** or vowel + **-ir**: a *y* sound is written **y** between vowels. See **poseer** (no. 40) and **construir** (no. 13) for examples.

■ Infinitive ends in **-cir**. Check verb in list.

■ Infinitive ends in **-ger** or **-gir**: **g > j** before **o** or **a**. See **proteger** (no. 43).

■ Infinitive ends in **-ñer, -ñir** or **-llir**: diphthong **ió** in Preterit > **ó**; diphthong **ie** in Preterit and in Imperfect Subjunctive > **e**. See **tañer** (no. 57).

SPANISH VERBS: HINTS AND TIPS FOR LEARNERS

The Spanish verb system is complicated, but there are a number of short cuts that will save learners time and effort.

■ Compound Tense Formation: all verbs

The Compound Tenses (see Glossary) of all verbs are formed with the verb **haber** and the Past Participle, formed as explained on p. 55.

The most frequently used compound tenses are:

Perfect	**he hablado**	*I have spoken, etc.*
Pluperfect	**había hablado**	*I had spoken*
Future	**habré hablado**	*I will have spoken,*
Conditional	**habría** or **hubiera hablado**	*I would have spoken*

The Past Participle is invariable in form in these tenses. The full conjugation of the irregular verb **haber** appears on p.271.

■ Imperfect Indicative: only three verbs are irregular:

ser *to be*: **era eras era éramos erais eran**
ir *to go*: **iba ibas iba íbamos ibais iban**
ver *to see*: **veía veías veía veíamos veíais veían**
(the *e* is unexpected)

In all other cases the endings of the Imperfect are added to the stem left after removing the **-ar**, **-er** or **-ir** of the Infinitive, e.g. **dar** *to give*: **daba, dabas, daba, dábamos, dabais, daban; tener** *to have*: **tenía, tenías, tenía, teníamos, teníais, tenían.**

■ Future and Conditional: with twelve exceptions, all verbs form their Future by adding **-é -ás -á -emos -éis -án** to their Infinitive, and all verbs form their Conditional by adding **-ía -ías -ía -íamos -íais -ían** to their Infinitive (the latter endings are the same as the endings of the Imperfect Indicative of **-er** verbs). The exceptions are the following verbs (and also any compound verbs based on them, e.g. **componer** *to compose*). The Future and Conditional endings are added to the slightly modified form of the Infinitive shown in bold italics:

caber *cabr-* to fit in	querer *querr-* to want
decir *dir-* to say	saber *sabr-* to know
haber *habr-* auxiliary verb	salir *saldr-* to leave
hacer *har-* to do/to make	tener *tendr-* to have
poder *podr-* to be able	valer *valdr-* to be worth
poner *pondr-* to put	venir *vendr-* to come

■ The Present Subjunctive can be formed for nearly all verbs by adding the following endings to the stem left after removing the **-o** of the first-person Present Indicative:

-ar verbs :	-e	-es	-e	-emos	-éis	-en
-er & -ir verbs:	-a	-as	-a	-amos	-áis	-an

Examples:

Infinitive	1st-person singular Present Indicative (stem in Italics)	Present Subjunctive
hablar *to speak*	**habl**o	**hable**, etc.
comer *to eat*	**com**o	**coma**, etc.
vivir *to live*	**viv**o	**viva**, etc.
contar *to tell*	**cuent**o	**cuente**, etc.
perder *to lose*	**pierd**o	**pierda**, etc.
pedir *to ask for*	**pid**o	**pida**, etc.
hacer *to do*	**hag**o	**haga**, etc.
tener *to have*	**teng**o	**tenga**, etc.

The main exceptions are the following verbs, which should be checked in the tables printed below:

> **dar** *to give* (unexpected accent in Subjunctive)
> **estar** *to be* (unexpected accents in Subjunctive)
> **haber**
> **ir** *to go*
> **morir** *to die* and **dormir** *to sleep*
> **saber** *to know*
> **sentir** *to feel* (and all verbs like it)
> **ser** *to be*

In the case of Radical-Changing verbs like **contar**, **mover**, **cerrar**, **perder** only the stressed vowel is altered: c**ue**nte—contemos, p**ie**rda—perdamos, etc.

■ The Imperfect Subjunctive of all verbs is predictable: the endings are added to the stem left after the ending of the third-person singular Preterit is removed (but this stem may require separate learning in the case of Radical-Changing and Irregular verbs):

Infinitive	3rd-person Preterit (stem in italics)	Imperfect Subjunctive
hablar *to speak*	**habló** *he spoke*	**habl**ara, **habl**ase, etc.
sentir *to feel*	**sint**ió *he felt*	**sint**iera, **sint**iese, etc.
estar *to be*	**estuv**o *he was*	**estuv**iera, **estuv**iese, etc.
tener *to have*	**tuv**o *he had/got*	**tuv**iera, **tuv**iese, etc.
decir *to say*	**dij**o *he said*	**dij**era, **dij**ese, etc.

Note the loss of **i** after **j** in words like **dijera/dijese, trajera/trajese, produjera/produjese**.

■ The Imperative

The **vosotros** Imperative (not used in Latin America) is always regularly formed by replacing the **-r** of the Infinitive by **-d**: **hablar—hablad, ir—id, ser—sed**, etc.

The **Usted** and **Ustedes** Imperative are always identical to the 3rd-person Present Subjunctive, singular and plural respectively, e.g. **hacer—haga—hagan**.

The **tú** Imperative is always formed by dropping the **-s** from the 2nd-person singular of the Present Indicative: **cuentas** *you tell*—**¡cuenta!** *tell!*, **pides** *you ask for*—**¡pide!** *ask for!* There are a few important exceptions, shown on p.36.

TABLES OF IRREGULAR VERBS, TYPICAL RADICAL CHANGING VERBS AND EXAMPLES OF VERBS AFFECTED BY SPELLING CHANGES

The Indicative Present and Preterit and the Present Subjunctive are always shown in full, whether they are regular or not. The endings of the Future and Conditional tenses are the same for all verbs. The endings of the

Imperfect Indicative are all regular, with very few exceptions (**ir** and **ser**). The Imperfect Subjunctive endings are always the same as for regular verbs.

1. **Abolir** *to abolish*

This, and a few verbs like it, is a defective verb. Forms in which the ending does not begin with **i** are not used.

Infinitive **abolir**	*Gerund* **aboliendo**
Past Participle **abolido**	*Imperative* **abolid**. *Abole is not found*

INDICATIVE

Present	*Imperfect*	*Preterit*
not found	**abolía**	**abolí**
not found	etc.	**aboliste**
not found		**abolió**
abolimos		**abolimos**
abolís		**abolisteis**
not found		**abolieron**

Future	*Conditional*
aboliré	**aboliría**
etc.	etc.

SUBJUNCTIVE

Present	*Imperfect*
no forms	**aboliera/aboliese**
in use	etc.

2. **Adquirir** *to acquire*

Radical changing verb. Only **inquirir** *to enquire* is conjugated the same way.

Infinitive **adquirir**	*Gerund* **adquiriendo**
Past Participle **adquirido**	*Imperative* **adquiere adquirid**

INDICATIVE

Present	Imperfect	Preterit
adquiero	adquiría	adquirí
adquieres	etc.	adquiriste
adquiere		adquirió
adquirimos		adquirimos
adquirís		adquiristeis
adquieren		adquirieron

Future	Conditional
adquiriré	adquiriría
etc.	etc.

SUBJUNCTIVE

Present	Imperfect
adquiera	adquiriera/adquiriese
adquieras	etc.
adquiera	
adquiramos	
adquiráis	
adquieran	

3. Aislar *to isolate*

The **i** is written with an accent when it is stressed. The accent was introduced in 1959 and does not appear in books printed before then.

Infinitive **aislar** *Gerund* **aislando**
Past Participle **aislado** *Imperative* **aísla aislad**

INDICATIVE

Present	Imperfect	Preterit
aíslo	aislaba	aislé
aíslas	etc.	aislaste
aísla		aisló
aislamos		aislamos
aisláis		aislasteis
aíslan		aislaron

Future	Conditional
aislaré	aislaría
etc.	etc.

SUBJUNCTIVE

Present	Imperfect
aísle	aislara/aislase
aísles	etc.
aísle	
aislemos	
aisléis	
aíslen	

4. Andar *to walk/go about*

Infinitive **andar** *Gerund* **andando**
Past Participle **andado** *Imperative* **anda andad**

Present	Imperfect	Preterit
ando	andaba	anduve
andas	etc.	anduviste
anda		anduvo
andamos		anduvimos
andáis		anduvisteis
andan		anduvieron

Future	Conditional
andaré	andaría
etc.	etc.

SUBJUNCTIVE

Present	Imperfect
ande	anduviera/anduviese
andes	etc.
ande	
andemos	
andéis	
anden	

5. Argüir *to argue (a point)*

The dieresis on the **u** shows that it is pronounced as *w*.

Infinitive **argüir**　　　　*Gerund* **arguyendo**
Past Participle **argüido**　　*Imperative* **arguye argüid**

INDICATIVE

Present	*Imperfect*	*Preterit*
arguyo	argüía	argüí
arguyes	etc.	argüiste
arguye		arguyó
argüimos		argüimos
argüís		argüisteis
arguyen		arguyeron

Future	*Conditional*
argüiré	argüiría
etc.	etc.

SUBJUNCTIVE

Present	*Imperfect*
arguya	arguyera/arguyese
arguyas	etc.
arguya	
arguyamos	
arguyáis	
arguyan	

6. Asir *to grasp/seize*

Infinitive **asir**　　　　*Gerund* **asiendo**
Past Participle **asido**　*Imperative* **ase, asid**

Forms containing g are usually avoided.

INDICATIVE

Present	*Imperfect*	*Preterit*
(asgo)	asía	así
ases	etc.	asiste

Present, continued
ase
asimos
asís
asen

Preterit, continued
asió
asimos
asisteis
asieron

Future
asiré
etc.

Conditional
asiría
etc.

SUBJUNCTIVE

Present
(asga)
(asgas)
(asga)
(asgamos)
(asgáis)
(asgan)

Imperfect
asiera/asiese
etc.

7. **Averiguar** *to ascertain*

The dieresis shows that the **u** is not silent.

Infinitive **averiguar**
Past Participle **averiguado**

Gerund **averiguando**
Imperative **averigua averiguad**

INDICATIVE

Present
averiguo
averiguas
averigua
averiguamos
averiguáis
averiguan

Imperfect
averiguaba
etc.

Preterit
averigüé
averiguaste
averiguó
averiguamos
averiguasteis
averiguaron

Future
averiguaré
etc.

Conditional
averiguaría
etc.

SUBJUNCTIVE

Present	Imperfect
averigüe	averiguara/averiguase
averigües	etc.
averigüe	
averigüemos	
averigüéis	
averigüen	

8. Caber to fit into

Infinitive **caber**	Gerund **cabiendo**
Past Participle **cabido**	Imperative **cabe cabed**

INDICATIVE

Present	Imperfect	Preterit
quepo	cabía	cupe
cabes	etc.	cupiste
cabe		cupo
cabemos		cupimos
cabéis		cupisteis
caben		cupieron

Future	Conditional
cabré	cabría
etc.	etc.

SUBJUNCTIVE

Present	Imperfect
quepa	cupiera/cupiese
quepas	etc.
quepa	
quepamos	
quepáis	
quepan	

9. **Caer** *to fall*

Infinitive **caer**	*Gerund* **cayendo**
Past Participle **caído**	*Imperative* **cae caed**

INDICATIVE

Present	*Imperfect*	*Preterit*
caigo	caía	caí
caes	etc.	caíste
cae		cayó
caemos		caímos
caéis		caísteis
caen		cayeron

Future	*Conditional*
caeré	caeriá
etc.	etc.

SUBJUNCTIVE

Present	*Imperfect*
caiga	cayera/cayese
caigas	etc.
caiga	
caigamos	
caigáis	
caigan	

10. **Cambiar** *to change*

Regular: the **i** is always pronounced like y. However, many verbs ending in **-iar** are conjugated like **liar** (no. 28).

Infinitive **cambiar**	*Gerund* **cambiando**
Past Participle **cambiado**	*Imperative* **cambia cambiad**

INDICATIVE

Present	*Imperfect*	*Preterit*
cambio	cambiaba	cambié
cambias	etc.	cambiaste

Present, continued
cambia
cambiamos
cambiáis
cambian

Preterit, continued
cambió
cambiamos
cambiasteis
cambiaron

Future	*Conditional*
cambiaré	**cambiaría**
etc.	*etc.*

SUBJUNCTIVE

Present	*Imperfect*
cambie	**cambiara/cambiase**
cambies	*etc.*
cambie	
cambiemos	
cambiéis	
cambien	

11. Cerrar *to shut/close*

Radical changing verb.

Infinitive **cerrar**	*Gerund* **cerrando**
Past Participle **cerrado**	*Imperative* **cierra cerrad**

INDICATIVE

Present	*Imperfect*	*Preterit*
cierro	**cerraba**	**cerré**
cierras	*etc.*	**cerraste**
cierra		**cerró**
cerramos		**cerramos**
cerráis		**cerrasteis**
cierran		**cerraron**

Future	*Conditional*
cerraré	**cerraría**
etc.	*etc.*

SUBJUNCTIVE

Present	Imperfect
cierre	cerrara/cerrase
cierres	etc.
cierre	
cerremos	
cerréis	
cierren	

12. Cocer *to boil*

Radical changing verb conjugated like **mover** but with spelling change **c** > **z** before **o** or **a**.

Infinitive **cocer** *Gerund* **cociendo**
Past Participle **cocido** *Imperative* **cuece coced**

INDICATIVE

Present	Imperfect	Preterit
cuezo	cocía	cocí
cueces	etc.	cociste
cuece		coció
cocemos		cocimos
cocéis		cocisteis
cuecen		cocieron

Future	Conditional
coceré	cocería
etc.	etc.

SUBJUNCTIVE

Present	Imperfect
cueza	cociera/cociese
cuezas	etc.
cueza	
cozamos	
cozáis	
cuezan	

13. Construir *to build*

The **y** between vowels should be noted.

Infinitive **construir** *Gerund* **construyendo**
Past Participle **construido** *Imperative* **construye construid**

INDICATIVE

Present	*Imperfect*	*Preterit*
construyo	construía	construí
construyes	etc.	construiste
construye		construyó
construimos		construimos
construís		construisteis
construyen		construyeron

Future	*Conditional*
construiré	construiría
etc.	etc.

SUBJUNCTIVE

Present	*Imperfect*
construya	construyera/construyese
construyas	etc.
construya	
construyamos	
construyáis	
construyan	

14. Contar *to count/tell a story*

Radical changing verb.

Infinitive **contar** *Gerund* **contando**
Past Participle **contado** *Imperative* **cuenta contad**

INDICATIVE

Present	*Imperfect*	*Preterit*
cuento	contaba	conté
cuentas	etc.	contaste

Present, continued
cuenta
contamos
contáis
cuentan

Preterit, continued
contó
contamos
contasteis
contaron

Future
contaré
etc.

Conditional
contaría
etc.

SUBJUNCTIVE

Present
cuente
cuentes
cuente
contemos
contéis
cuenten

Imperfect
contara/contase
etc.

15. **Continuar** *to continue*

The **u** is stressed when possible.

Infinitive **continuar**   *Gerund* **continuando**
Past Participle **continuado** *Imperative* **continúa continuad**

INDICATIVE

Present
continúo
continúas
continúa
continuamos
continuáis
continúan

Imperfect
continuaba
etc.

Preterit
continué
continuaste
continuó
continuamos
continuasteis
continuaron

Future
continuaré
etc.

Conditional
continuaría
etc.

SUBJUNCTIVE

Present	Imperfect
continúe	continuara/continuase
continúes	etc.
continúe	
continuemos	
continuéis	
continúen	

16. Dar *to give*

Infinitive **dar** *Gerund* **dando**
Past Participle **dado** *Imperative* **da dad**

INDICATIVE

Present	Imperfect	Preterit
doy	daba	di
das	dabas	diste
da	daba	dio *(no accent)*
damos	dábamos	dimos
dais	dabais	disteis
dan	daban	dieron
Future	*Conditional*	
daré	daría	
etc.	etc.	

SUBJUNCTIVE

Present	Imperfect
dé	diera/diese
des	etc.
dé	
demos	
deis	
den	

17. Decir *to say*

Infinitive **decir** *Gerund* **diciendo**
Past Participle **dicho** *Imperative* **di decid**

INDICATIVE

Present	Imperfect	Preterit
digo	decía	dije
dices	etc.	dijiste
dice		dijo
decimos		dijimos
decís		dijisteis
dicen		dijeron

Future	Conditional
diré	diría
etc.	etc.

SUBJUNCTIVE

Present	Imperfect
diga	dijera/dijese
digas	etc.
diga	
digamos	
digáis	
digan	

18. **Discernir** to discern

Radical changing verb. This pattern (**e > ie**) is rare in the -**ir** conjugation but common in the -**er** conjugation.

Infinitive **discernir**   Gerund **discerniendo**
Past Participle **discernido**   Imperative **discierne discernid**

INDICATIVE

Present	Imperfect	Preterit
discierno	discernía	discerní
disciernes	etc.	discerniste
discierne		discernió
discernimos		discernimos
discernís		discernisteis
disciernen		discernieron

Future	*Conditional*
discerniré	discerniría
etc.	etc.

SUBJUNCTIVE

Present	*Imperfect*
discierna	discerniera/discerniese
disciernas	etc.
discierna	
discernamos	
discernáis	
disciernan	

19. Dormir *to sleep*

Only **morir** *to die* (past. participle **muerto**) is conjugated similarly.

Infinitive **dormir**	*Gerund* **durmiendo**
Past Participle **dormido**	*Imperative* **duerme dormid**

INDICATIVE

Present	*Imperfect*	*Preterit*
duermo	dormía	dormí
duermes	etc.	dormiste
duerme		durmió
dormimos		dormimos
dormís		dormisteis
duermen		durmieron

Future	*Conditional*
dormiré	dormiría
etc.	etc.

SUBJUNCTIVE

Present	*Imperfect*
duerma	durmiera/durmiese
duermas	etc.
duerma	

Present, continued
durmamos
durmáis
duerman

20. Erguir(se) *to rear up/sit up straight*

Conjugated like **sentir** but with the normal spelling
change **ie** > **ye** at the beginning of words.
The alternative forms are conjugated like **pedir**.

Infinitive **erguir**	*Gerund* **irguiendo**
Past Participle **erguido**	*Imperative* **yergue/irgue erguid**

INDICATIVE

Present	*Imperfect*	*Preterit*
yergo/irgo	**erguía**	**erguí**
yergues/irgues	*etc.*	**erguiste**
yergue/irgue		**irguió**
erguimos		**erguimos**
erguís		**erguisteis**
yerguen/irguen		**irguieron**

Future	*Conditional*
erguiré	**erguiría**
etc.	*etc.*

SUBJUNCTIVE

Present	*Imperfect*
yerga/irga	**irguiera/irguiese**
yergas/irgas	*etc.*
yerga/irga	
yergamos/irgamos	
yergáis/irgáis	
yergan/irgan	

21. Errar *to wander/err*

Conjugated like **cerrar** but with regular spelling change
ie > **ye** at the beginning of words.

Infinitive **errar** *Gerund* **errando**
Past Participle **errado** *Imperative* **yerra errad**

INDICATIVE

Present	*Imperfect*	*Preterit*
yerro	erraba	erré
yerras	etc.	erraste
yerra		erró
erramos		erramos
erráis		errasteis
yerran		erraron

Future	*Conditional*
erraré	erraría

SUBJUNCTIVE

Present	*Imperfect*
yerre	errara/errase
yerres	etc.
yerre	
erremos	
erréis	
yerren	

22. **Estar** *to be*

Infinitive **estar** *Gerund* **estando**
Past Participle **estado** *Imperative* **estate estaos**

INDICATIVE

Present	*Imperfect*	*Preterit*
estoy	estaba	estuve
estás	etc.	estuviste
está		estuvo
estamos		estuvimos
estáis		estuvisteis
están		estuvieron

Future	Conditional
estaré	**estaría**
etc.	etc.

SUBJUNCTIVE

Present	Imperfect
esté	**estuviera/estuviese**
estés	etc.
esté	
estemos	
estéis	
estén	

23. Gruñir *to growl*

The diphthongs **ió** and **ie** become **ó** and **e** after **ñ**.

Infinitive **gruñir**	*Gerund* **gruñendo**
Past Participle **gruñido**	*Imperative* **gruñe gruñid**

INDICATIVE

Present	Imperfect	Preterit
gruño	**gruñía**	**gruñí**
gruñes	etc.	**gruñiste**
gruñe		**gruñó**
gruñimos		**gruñimos**
gruñís		**gruñisteis**
gruñen		**gruñeron**

Future	Conditional
gruñiré	**gruñiría**
etc.	etc.

SUBJUNCTIVE

Present	Imperfect
gruña	**gruñera/gruñese**
gruñas	etc.
gruña	
gruñamos	

Present, continued
gruñáis
gruñan

24. **Haber** (auxiliary verb or *there is/are*)

The 3rd-person present is **hay** when it means *there is/are*.

Infinitive **haber**　　　　　*Gerund* **habiendo**
Past Participle **habido**　　*Imperative not found*

INDICATIVE

Present	*Imperfect*	*Preterit*
he	**había**	**hube**
has	*etc.*	**hubiste**
ha (hay)		**hubo**
hemos		**hubimos**
habéis		**hubisteis**
han		**hubieron**

Future	*Conditional*
habré	**habría**
etc.	*etc.*

SUBJUNCTIVE

Present	*Imperfect*
haya	**hubiera/hubiese**
hayas	*etc.*
haya	
hayamos	
hayáis	
hayan	

25. **Hacer** *to do/to make*

Infinitive **hacer**　　　　　*Gerund* **haciendo**
Past Participle **hecho**　　*Imperative* **haz haced**

INDICATIVE

Present	Imperfect	Preterit
hago	hacía	hice
haces	etc.	hiciste
hace		hizo
hacemos		hicimos
hacéis		hicisteis
hacen		hicieron

Future	Conditional
haré	haría
etc.	etc.

SUBJUNCTIVE

Present	Imperfect
haga	hiciera/hiciese
hagas	etc.
haga	
hagamos	
hagáis	
hagan	

26. Ir *to go*

Infinitive **ir**	Gerund **yendo**
Past Participle **ido**	Imperative **ve id**

The **vosotros** imperative of **irse** is **idos**, not the expected *'íos'.

INDICATIVE

Present	Imperfect	Preterit
voy	iba	fui *(no accent)*
vas	ibas	fuiste
va	iba	fue *(no accent)*
vamos	íbamos	fuimos
vais	ibais	fuisteis
van	iban	fueron

Future	Conditional
iré	**iría**
etc.	*etc.*

SUBJUNCTIVE

Present	Imperfect
vaya	**fuera/fuese**
vayas	*etc.*
vaya	
vayamos	
vayáis	
vayan	

27. **Jugar** *to play (a game)*

The only verb in which stressed **u** becomes **ue**.

Infinitive **jugar**	Gerund **jugando**
Past Participle **jugado**	Imperative **juega jugad**

INDICATIVE

Present	Imperfect	Preterit
juego	**jugaba**	**jugué**
juegas	*etc.*	**jugaste**
juega		**jugó**
jugamos		**jugamos**
jugáis		**jugasteis**
juegan		**jugaron**

Future	Conditional
jugaré	**jugaría**
etc.	*etc.*

SUBJUNCTIVE

Present	Imperfect
juegue	**jugara/jugase**
juegues	*etc.*
juegue	

Present, continued
juguemos
juguéis
jueguen

28. **Liar** *to tie up in a bundle*

The **i** may be stressed. Compare **cambiar**.

Infinitive **liar** *Gerund* **liando**
Past Participle **liado** *Imperative* **lía liad**

INDICATIVE

Present	*Imperfect*	*Preterit*
lío	**liaba**	**lié**
lías	*etc.*	**liaste**
lía		**lió**
liamos		**liamos**
liáis		**liasteis**
lían		**liaron**

Future	*Conditional*
liaré	**liaría**
etc.	*etc.*

SUBJUNCTIVE

Present	*Imperfect*
líe	**liara/liase**
líes	*etc.*
líe	
liemos	
liéis	
líen	

29. **Lucir** *to show off* (transitive)

c > zc before **o** or **a**.

Infinitive **lucir** *Gerund* **luciendo**
Past Participle **lucido** *Imperative* **luce lucid**

INDICATIVE

Present	Imperfect	Preterit
luzco	lucía	lucí
luces	etc.	luciste
luce		lució
lucimos		lucimos
lucís		lucisteis
lucen		lucieron

Future	Conditional
luciré	luciría

SUBJUNCTIVE

Present	Imperfect
luzca	luciera/luciese
luzcas	etc.
luzca	
luzcamos	
luzcáis	
luzcan	

30. Maldecir *to curse*

Conjugated like **decir** except for the Past Participle, Imperative, Future and Conditional.

Infinitive **maldecir** *Gerund* **maldiciendo**
Past Participle **maldecido** *Imperative* **maldice maldecid**

INDICATIVE

Present	Imperfect	Preterit
maldigo	maldecía	maldije
maldices	etc.	maldijiste
maldice		maldijo
maldecimos		maldijimos
maldecís		maldijisteis
maldicen		maldijeron

Future	*Conditional*
maldeciré	**maldeciría**
etc.	*etc.*

SUBJUNCTIVE

Present	*Imperfect*
maldiga	**maldijera/maldijese**
maldigas	*etc.*
maldiga	
maldigamos	
maldigáis	
maldigan	

31. **Mover** *to move*

Radical changing verb.

Infinitive **mover**	*Gerund* **moviendo**
Past Participle **movido**	*Imperative* **mueve, moved**

INDICATIVE

Present	*Imperfect*	*Preterit*
muevo	**movía**	**moví**
mueves	*etc.*	**moviste**
mueve		**movió**
movemos		**movimos**
movéis		**movisteis**
mueven		**movieron**

Future	*Conditional*
moveré	**movería**
etc.	*etc.*

SUBJUNCTIVE

Present	*Imperfect*
mueva	**moviera/moviese**
muevas	*etc.*
mueva	
movamos	

Present, continued
mováis
muevan

32. **Oír** *to hear*

Infinitive **oír**   *Gerund* **oyendo**
Past Participle **oído**   *Imperative* **oye oíd**

INDICATIVE

Present	*Imperfect*	*Preterit*
oigo	**oía**	**oí**
oyes	*etc.*	**oíste**
oye		**oyó**
oímos		**oímos**
oís		**oísteis**
oyen		**oyeron**

Future	*Conditional*
oiré	**oiría**
etc.	*etc.*

SUBJUNCTIVE

Present	*Imperfect*
oiga	**oyera/oyese**
oigas	*etc.*
oiga	
oigamos	
oigáis	
oigan	

33. **Oler** *to smell*

Conjugated like **mover**, but the diphthong **ue** is always
written **hue** at the beginning of a word.

Infinitive **oler**   *Gerund* **oliendo**
Past Participle **olido**   *Imperative* **huele oled**

INDICATIVE

Present	Imperfect	Preterit
huelo	olía	olí
hueles	etc.	oliste
huele		olió
olemos		olimos
oléis		olisteis
huelen		olieron

Future	Conditional
oleré	olería
etc.	etc.

SUBJUNCTIVE

Present	Imperfect
huela	oliera/oliese
huelas	etc.
huela	
olamos	
oláis	
huelan	

34. **Pagar** *to pay*

Regular -**ar** verb, but with spelling changes. The silent *u* keeps the **g** hard (like the **g** in **hago**).

Infinitive **pagar**   *Gerund* **pagando**
Past Participle **pagado**   *Imperative* **paga pagad**

INDICATIVE

Present	Imperfect	Preterit
pago	pagaba	pagué
pagas	etc.	pagaste
paga		pagó
pagamos		pagamos
pagáis		pagasteis
pagan		pagaron

Future	*Conditional*
pagaré	pagaría
etc.	etc.

SUBJUNCTIVE

Present	*Imperfect*
pague	pagara/pagase
pagues	etc.
pague	
paguemos	
paguéis	
paguen	

35. **Parecer** *to seem*

The change **c > zc** before **a** or **o** affects most verbs ending in **-cer** (common exceptions are **vencer, ejercer, torcer, cocer**).

Infinitive **parecer**	*Gerund* **pareciendo**
Past Participle **parecido**	*Imperative* **parece pareced**

INDICATIVE

Present	*Imperfect*	*Preterit*
parezco	parecía	parecí
pareces	etc.	pareciste
parece		pareció
parecemos		parecimos
parecéis		parecisteis
parecen		parecieron

Future	*Conditional*
pareceré	parecería
etc.	etc.

SUBJUNCTIVE

Present	*Imperfect*
parezca	pareciera/pareciese
parezcas	etc.

Present, continued
parezca
parezcamos
parezcáis
parezcan

36. Pedir *to ask for*

Radical changing verb.

Infinitive **pedir**	*Gerund* **pidiendo**
Past Participle **pedido**	*Imperative* **pide pedid**

INDICATIVE

Present	*Imperfect*	*Preterit*
pido	pedía	pedí
pides	etc.	pediste
pide		pidió
pedimos		pedimos
pedís		pedisteis
piden		pidieron

Future	*Conditional*
pediré	pediría
etc.	etc.

SUBJUNCTIVE

Present	*Imperfect*
pida	pidiera/pidiese
pidas	etc.
pida	
pidamos	
pidáis	
pidan	

37. Perder *to lose*

Radical changing verb.

Infinitive **perder**	*Gerund* **perdiendo**
Past Participle **perdido**	*Imperative* **pierde perded**

INDICATIVE

Present	Imperfect	Preterit
pierdo	perdía	perdí
pierdes	etc.	perdiste
pierde		perdió
perdemos		perdimos
perdéis		perdisteis
pierden		perdieron

Future	Conditional
perderé	perdería
etc.	etc.

SUBJUNCTIVE

Present	Imperfect
pierda	perdiera/perdiese
pierdas	etc.
pierda	
perdamos	
perdáis	
pierdan	

38. Poder *to be able*

Infinitive **poder**
Past Participle **podido**

Gerund **pudiendo**
Imperative not found

INDICATIVE

Present	Imperfect	Preterit
puedo	podía	pude
puedes	etc.	pudiste
puede		pudo
podemos		pudimos
podéis		pudisteis
pueden		pudieron

Future	Conditional
podré	podría
etc.	etc.

SUBJUNCTIVE

Present	Imperfect
pueda	pudiera/pudiese
puedas	etc.
pueda	
podamos	
podáis	
puedan	

39. Poner to put

Infinitive **poner**	Gerund **poniendo**
Past Participle **puesto**	Imperative **pon poned**

The **tú** *imperative of compounds takes an accent:* **compón, pospón.**

INDICATIVE

Present	Imperfect	Preterit
pongo	ponía	puse
pones	etc.	pusiste
pone		puso
ponemos		pusimos
ponéis		pusisteis
ponen		pusieron

Future	Conditional
pondré	pondría
etc.	etc.

SUBJUNCTIVE

Present	Imperfect
ponga	pusiera/pusiese
pongas	etc.
ponga	
pongamos	
pongáis	
pongan	

40. **Poseer** *to possess*

Note unstressed **i** > **y** between vowels.

Infinitive **poseer**	*Gerund* **poseyendo**
Past Participle **poseído**	*Imperative* **posee, poseed**

INDICATIVE

Present	*Imperfect*	*Preterit*
poseo	poseía	poseí
posees	etc.	poseíste
posee		poseyó
poseemos		poseímos
poseéis		poseísteis
poseen		poseyeron

Future	*Conditional*
poseeré	poseería
etc.	etc.

SUBJUNCTIVE

Present	*Imperfect*
posea	poseyera/poseyese
poseas	etc.
posea	
poseamos	
poseáis	
posean	

41. **Producir** *to produce*

c > **zc** before **a** and **o**, and irregular Preterit. All verbs whose Infinitive ends in **-ducir** conjugate like this verb.

Infinitive **producir**	*Gerund* **produciendo**
Past Participle **producido**	*Imperative* **produce producid**

INDICATIVE

Present	*Imperfect*	*Preterit*
produzco	producía	produje
produces	etc.	produjiste

Present, continued
produce
producimos
producís
producen

Preterit, continued
produjo
produjimos
produjisteis
produjeron

Future	*Conditional*
produciré	**produciría**
etc.	etc.

SUBJUNCTIVE

Present	*Imperfect*
produzca	**produjera/produjese**
produzcas	etc.
produzca	
produzcamos	
produzcáis	
produzcan	

42. Prohibir *to prohibit*

The **i** of the stem is written with an accent when it is stressed (this spelling rule was introduced in 1959 so the accent does not appear in texts printed before then).

Infinitive **prohibir**   *Gerund* **prohibiendo**
Past Participle **prohibido**   *Imperative* **prohíbe prohibid**

INDICATIVE

Present	*Imperfect*	*Preterit*
prohíbo	**prohibía**	**prohibí**
prohíbes	etc.	**prohibiste**
prohíbe		**prohibió**
prohibimos		**prohibimos**
prohibís		**prohibisteis**
prohíben		**prohibieron**

Future	*Conditional*
prohibiré	**prohibiría**
etc.	etc.

SUBJUNCTIVE

Present	*Imperfect*
prohíba	**prohibiera/prohibiese**
prohíbas	etc.
prohíba	
prohibamos	
prohibáis	
prohíban	

43. **Proteger** *to protect*

Regular verb with spelling changes.

Infinitive **proteger**	*Gerund* **protegiendo**
Past Participle **protegido**	*Imperative* **protege proteged**

INDICATIVE

Present	*Imperfect*	*Preterit*
protejo	**protegía**	**protegí**
proteges	etc.	**protegiste**
protege		**protegió**
protegemos		**protegimos**
protegéis		**protegisteis**
protegen		**protegieron**

Future	*Conditional*
protegeré	**protegería**
etc.	etc.

SUBJUNCTIVE

Present	*Imperfect*
proteja	**protegiera/protegiese**
protejas	etc.
proteja	

Present, continued
protejamos
protejáis
protejan

44. **Querer** *to want/love*

Infinitive **querer**   *Gerund* **queriendo**
Past Participle **querido**   *Imperative* **quiere quered**

INDICATIVE

Present	*Imperfect*	*Preterit*
quiero	**quería**	**quise**
quieres	*etc.*	**quisiste**
quiere		**quiso**
queremos		**quisimos**
queréis		**quisisteis**
quieren		**quisieron**

Future	*Conditional*
querré	**querría**
etc.	*etc.*

SUBJUNCTIVE

Present	*Imperfect*
quiera	**quisiera/quisiese**
quieras	*etc.*
quiera	
queramos	
queráis	
quieran	

45. **Regir** *to govern/direct*

Conjugated like **pedir** but with predictable spelling changes.

Infinitive **regir**   *Gerund* **rigiendo**
Past Participle **regido**   *Imperative* **rige regid**

INDICATIVE

Present	*Imperfect*	*Preterit*
rijo	regía	regí
riges	etc.	registe
rige		rigió
regimos		regimos
regís		registeis
rigen		rigieron

Future	*Conditional*
regiré	regiría
etc.	etc.

SUBJUNCTIVE

Present	*Imperfect*
rija	rigiera/rigiese
rijas	etc.
rija	
rijamos	
rijáis	
rijan	

46. **Reír** *to laugh*

Conjugated like **pedir**.

Infinitive **reír**   *Gerund* **riendo**
Past Participle **reído**   *Imperative* **ríe reíd**

INDICATIVE

Present	*Imperfect*	*Preterit*
río	reía	reí
ríes	etc.	reíste
ríe		rió
reímos		reímos
reís		reísteis
ríen		rieron

Future	Conditional
reiré	reiría
etc.	etc.

SUBJUNCTIVE

Present	Imperfect
ría	riera/riese
rías	etc.
ría	
riamos	
riáis	
rían	

47. Reñir *to scold*

Conjugated like **pedir**, but **ió** becomes **ó** and **ie** becomes **e** after **ñ**.

Infinitive **reñir**   Gerund **riñendo**
Past Participle **reñido**   Imperative **riñe reñid**

INDICATIVE

Present	Imperfect	Preterit
riño	reñía	reñí
riñes	etc.	reñiste
riñe		riñó
reñimos		reñimos
reñís		reñisteis
riñen		riñeron

Future	Conditional
reñiré	reñiría
etc.	etc.

SUBJUNCTIVE

Present	Imperfect
riña	riñera/riñese
riñas	etc.
riña	

Present, continued
riñamos
riñáis
riñan

48. Reunir *to bring together/call a meeting*

The **u** is written with an accent when stressed. The verb
rehusar *to refuse* is similar: **rehúso, rehúsa, rehusamos,**
etc. The accent was introduced in 1959 and is not seen in
books printed before then.

Infinitive **reunir**   *Gerund* **reuniendo**
Past Participle **reunido**   *Imperative* **reúne reunid**

INDICATIVE

Present	*Imperfect*	*Preterit*
reúno	**reunía**	**reuní**
reúnes	*etc.*	**reuniste**
reúne		**reunió**
reunimos		**reunimos**
reunís		**reunisteis**
reúnen		**reunieron**

Future	*Conditional*
reuniré	**reuniría**
etc.	*etc.*

SUBJUNCTIVE

Present	*Imperfect*
reúna	**reuniera/reuniese**
reúnas	*etc.*
reúna	
reunamos	
reunáis	
reúnan	

49. **Rezar** *to pray*

Regular -**ar** verb with spelling changes.

Infinitive **rezar**	Gerund **rezando**
Past Participle **rezado**	Imperative **reza rezad**

INDICATIVE

Present	Imperfect	Preterit
rezo	rezaba	recé
rezas	etc.	rezaste
reza		rezó
rezamos		rezamos
rezáis		rezasteis
rezan		rezaron

Future	Conditional
rezaré	rezaría
etc.	etc.

SUBJUNCTIVE

Present	Imperfect
rece	rezara/rezase
reces	etc.
rece	
recemos	
recéis	
recen	

50. **Roer** *to gnaw*

Infinitive **roer**	Gerund **royendo**
Past Participle **roído**	Imperative **roe roed**

INDICATIVE

Present	Imperfect	Preterit
roo	roía	roí
roes	etc.	roíste
roe		royó

Present, continued	Preterit, continued
roemos	roímos
roéis	roísteis
roen	royeron

The alternative first-person singular present forms **royo** *and* **roigo** *are rarely seen.*

Future	Conditional
roeré	roería
etc.	etc.

SUBJUNCTIVE

Present	Imperfect
roa (roiga, roya)	royera/royese
roas (roigas, royas)	etc.
roa (roiga, roya)	
roamos (roigamos, royamos)	
roáis (roigáis, royáis)	
roan (roigan, royan)	

Bracketed forms are rarely found.

51. **Saber** *to know*

Infinitive **saber**	Gerund **sabiendo**
Past Participle **sabido**	Imperative **sabe sabed**

INDICATIVE

Present	Imperfect	Preterit
sé	sabía	supe
sabes	etc.	supiste
sabe		supo
sabemos		supimos
sabéis		supisteis
saben		supieron

Future	Conditional
sabré	sabría
etc.	etc.

SUBJUNCTIVE

Present	Imperfect
sepa	supiera/supiese
sepas	etc.
sepa	
sepamos	
sepáis	
sepan	

52. Sacar *to take out/extract*

Regular -ar verb with spelling changes.

Infinitive sacar	*Gerund* sacando
Past Participle sacado	*Imperative* saca sacad

INDICATIVE

Present	Imperfect	Preterit
saco	sacaba	saqué
sacas	etc.	sacaste
saca		sacó
sacamos		sacamos
sacáis		sacasteis
sacan		sacaron

Future	Conditional
sacaré	sacaría
etc.	etc.

SUBJUNCTIVE

Present	Imperfect
saque	sacara/sacase
saques	etc.
saque	
saquemos	
saquéis	
saquen	

53. **Salir** *to go out/leave*

Infinitive **salir**   *Gerund* **saliendo**
Past Participle **salido**   *Imperative* **sal salid**

INDICATIVE

Present	*Imperfect*	*Preterit*
salgo	**salía**	**salí**
sales	*etc.*	**saliste**
sale		**salió**
salimos		**salimos**
salís		**salisteis**
salen		**salieron**

Future	*Conditional*
saldré	**saldría**
etc.	*etc.*

SUBJUNCTIVE

Present	*Imperfect*
salga	**saliera/salieses**
salgas	*etc.*
salga	
salgamos	
salgáis	
salgan	

54. **Seguir** *to follow*

Infinitive **seguir**   *Gerund* **siguiendo**
Past Participle **seguido**   *Imperative* **sigue seguid**

INDICATIVE

Present	*Imperfect*	*Preterit*
sigo	**seguía**	**seguí**
sigues	*etc.*	**seguiste**
sigue		**siguió**

Present, continued
seguimos
seguís
siguen

Preterit, continued
seguimos
seguisteis
siguieron

Future
seguiré
etc.

Conditional
seguiría
etc.

SUBJUNCTIVE

Present
siga
sigas
siga
sigamos
sigáis
sigan

Imperfect
siguiera/siguiese
etc.

55. **Sentir** *to feel*

Radical changing verb.

Infinitive **sentir**
Past Participle **sentido**

Gerund **sintiendo**
Imperative **siente sentid**

INDICATIVE

Present
siento
sientes
siente
sentimos
sentís
sienten

Imperfect
sentía
etc.

Preterit
sentí
sentiste
sintió
sentimos
sentisteis
sintieron

Future
sentiré
etc.

Conditional
sentiría
etc.

SUBJUNCTIVE

Present	Imperfect
sienta	sintiera/sintiese
sientas	etc.
sienta	
sintamos	
sintáis	
sientan	

56. Ser *to be*

Infinitive **ser**	*Gerund* **siendo**
Past Participle **sido**	*Imperative* **sé sed**

INDICATIVE

Present	Imperfect	Preterit
soy	era	fui
eres	eras	fuiste
es	era	fue
somos	éramos	fuimos
sois	erais	fuisteis
son	eran	fueron

The accent on the third-person Preterit forms **fuí** *and* **fué** *was abolished in the spelling reforms of 1959.*

Future	Conditional
seré	sería
etc.	etc.

SUBJUNCTIVE

Present	Imperfect
sea	fuera/fuese
seas	fueras/fueses
sea	fuera/fuese
seamos	fuéramos/fuésemos
seáis	fuerais/fueseis
sean	fueran/fuesen

57. **Tañer** *to chime*

ió is simplified to **ó** and **ie** to **e** as usual after **ñ**. This change also affects verbs ending in **-llir** like **bullir** *to seethe*.

Infinitive **tañer**		*Gerund* **tañendo**
Past Participle **tañido**		*Imperative* **tañe tañed**

INDICATIVE

Present	*Imperfect*	*Preterit*
taño	**tañía**	**tañí**
tañes	*etc.*	**tañiste**
tañe		**tañó**
tañemos		**tañimos**
tañéis		**tañisteis**
tañen		**tañeron**

Future	*Conditional*
tañeré	**tañería**
etc.	*etc.*

SUBJUNCTIVE

Present	*Imperfect*
taña	**tañera/tañese**
tañas	*etc.*
taña	
tañamos	
tañáis	
tañan	

58. **Tener** *to have*

Infinitive **tener**		*Gerund* **teniendo**
Past Participle **tenido**		*Imperative* **ten tened**

INDICATIVE

Present	*Imperfect*	*Preterit*
tengo	**tenía**	**tuve**
tienes	*etc.*	**tuviste**

Present continued	Preterit continued
tiene	tuvo
tenemos	tuvimos
tenéis	tuvisteis
tienen	tuvieron

Singular imperative of compounds ends in **-én**: detener *detain/stop* **detén**, retener *retain* **retén**.

Future	Conditional
tendré	tendría
etc.	etc.

SUBJUNCTIVE

Present	Imperfect
tenga	tuviera/tuviese
tengas	etc.
tenga	
tengamos	
tengáis	
tengan	

59. Traer *to bring*

Infinitive **traer**	*Gerund* **trayendo**
Past Participle **traído**	*Imperative* **trae traed**

INDICATIVE

Present	Imperfect	Preterit
traigo	traía	traje
traes	etc.	trajiste
trae		trajo
traemos		trajimos
traéis		trajisteis
traen		trajeron

Future	Conditional
traeré	traería
etc.	etc.

SUBJUNCTIVE

Present	*Imperfect*
traiga	trajera/trajese
traigas	etc.
traiga	
traigamos	
traigáis	
traigan	

60. **Valer** *to be worth*

Infinitive **valer**	*Gerund* **valiendo**
Past Participle **valido**	*Imperative* **vale valed**

INDICATIVE

Present	*Imperfect*	*Preterit*
valgo	valía	valí
vales	etc.	valiste
vale		valió
valemos		valimos
valéis		valisteis
valen		valieron

Future	*Conditional*
valdré	valdría
etc.	etc.

SUBJUNCTIVE

Present	*Imperfect*
valga	valiera/valiese
valgas	etc.
valga	
valgamos	
valgáis	
valgan	

61. **Vencer** *to defeat*

Regular verb with spelling changes.

Infinitive **vencer**	Gerund **venciendo**
Past Participle **vencido**	Imperative **vence venced**

INDICATIVE

Present	Imperfect	Preterit
venzo	vencía	vencí
vences	etc.	venciste
vence		venció
vencemos		vencimos
vencéis		vencisteis
vencen		vencieron

Future	Conditional
venceré	vencería
etc.	etc.

SUBJUNCTIVE

Present	Imperfect
venza	venciera/venciese
venzas	.etc.
venza	
venzamos	
venzáis	
venzan	

62. **Venir** *to come*

Infinitive **venir**	Gerund **viniendo**
Past Participle **venido**	Imperative **ven venid**

INDICATIVE

Present	Imperfect	Preterit
vengo	venía	vine
vienes	etc.	viniste
viene		vino
venimos		vinimos
venís		vinisteis
vienen		vinieron

Future	*Conditional*
vendré	**vendría**
etc.	*etc.*

SUBJUNCTIVE

Present	*Imperfect*
venga	**viniera/viniese**
vengas	*etc.*
venga	
vengamos	
vengáis	
vengan	

63. **Ver** *to see*

Infinitive **ver**	*Gerund* **viendo**
Past Participle **visto**	*Imperative* **ve ved**

INDICATIVE

Present	*Imperfect*	*Preterit*
veo	**veía**	**vi**
ves	*etc.*	**viste**
ve		**vio** *(no accent)*
vemos		**vimos**
veis		**visteis**
ven		**vieron**

Future	*Conditional*
veré	**vería**
etc.	*etc.*

SUBJUNCTIVE

Present	*Imperfect*
vea	**viera/viese**
veas	*etc.*
vea	

Present, continued
veamos
veáis
vean

64. **Yacer** *to lie (as in 'he lay there'. This verb is archaic.)*

Infinitive **yacer**   *Gerund* **yaciendo**
Past Participle **yacido**   *Imperative* **yace/yaz yaced**

INDICATIVE

Present	Imperfect	Preterit
yazco	yacía	yací
yaces	etc.	yaciste
yace		yació
yacemos		yacimos
yacéis		yacisteis
yacen		yacieron

The alternative first-person singular present forms **yago/yazgo** *are rarely seen.*

Future	Conditional
yaceré	yacería

Present	Imperfect
yazca (yazga, yaga)	yaciera/yaciese
yazcas (yazgas, yagas)	etc.
etc.	

65. **Zurcir** *to darn*

Regular verb with spelling changes.

Infinitive **zurcir**   *Gerund* **zurciendo**
Past Participle **zurcido**   *Imperative* **zurce zurcid**

INDICATIVE

Present	Imperfect	Preterit
zurzo	zurcía	zurcí
zurces	etc.	zurciste
zurce		zurció
zurcimos		zurcimos
zurcís		zurcisteis
zurcen		zurcieron

Future	Conditional
zurciré	zurciría
etc.	etc.

SUBJUNCTIVE

Present	Imperfect
zurza	zurciera/zurciese
zurzas	etc.
zurza	
zurzamos	
zurzáis	
zurzan	

LIST OF IRREGULAR AND RADICAL CHANGING VERBS

A few regular verbs that are affected by regular spelling changes are included. Numerous rare or archaic verbs are omitted. The number identifies the model verbs printed on pp.254–302.

Pronominal (i.e. 'reflexive') infinitives are not shown unless the pronominal form is the more usual form.

abastecer to supply   **parecer (35)**
abolir to abolish   **(1)**
aborrecer to detest   **parecer (35)**

abrir *to open*	past participle **abierto**
absolver *to absolve*	**mover (31)** past participle **absuelto**
abstenerse *to abstain*	**tener (58)**
abstraer *to abstract*	**traer (59)**
acentuar *to accentuate*	**continuar (15)**
acertar *to hit the mark*	**cerrar (11)**
acontecer *to occur*	**parecer (35)**
acordar *to agree upon*	**contar (14)**
acostarse *to go to bed*	**contar (14)**
actuar *to act*	**continuar (15)**
adherir *to adhere*	**sentir (55)**
adolecer *to be ill*	**parecer (35)**
adormecer *to put to sleep*	**parecer (35)**
adquirir *to acquire*	**(2)**
advertir *to warn*	**sentir (55)**
aferrarse *to grasp*	**cerrar (11);** may be conjugated regularly
agradecer *to thank*	**parecer (35)**
agredir *to assault*	**abolir (1)**
agriar *to sour*	**cambiar (10)**
aguar *to spoil*	**averiguar (7)**
aislar *to isolate*	**aislar (3)**
alentar *to encourage*	**cerrar (11)**
aliar *to ally*	**liar (28)**
almorzar *to lunch*	**contar (14); z>c** before **e**
amanecer *to dawn*	**parecer (35)**
amnistiar *to amnesty*	**liar (28)**
ampliar *to enlarge*	**liar (28)**
andar *to walk*	**(4)**
anochecer *to grow dark*	**parecer (35)**
ansiar *to yearn for*	**liar (28)**
anteponer *to put in front*	**poner (39)**
aparecer *to appear*	**parecer (35)**
apetecer *to crave*	**parecer (35)**
apostar *to bet*	**contar (14)**

apretar *to squeeze*	**cerrar (11)**
aprobar *to approve,* *pass* (exam.)	**contar (14)**
argüir *to argue*	**(5)**
arraigar *to establish*	**pagar (34)**
arrendar *to lease*	**cerrar (11)**
arrepentirse *to repent*	**sentir (55)**
ascender *to ascend*	**perder (37)**
asentar *to settle*	**cerrar (11)**
asentir *to assent*	**sentir (55)**
asir *to grasp*	**(6)**
atender *to attend*	**perder (37)**
atenerse *to abide by*	**tener (58)**
atenuar *to attenuate*	**continuar (15)**
atraer *to attract*	**traer (59)**
atravesar *to cross*	**cerrar (11)**
atribuir *to attribute*	**construir (13)**
avenir *to reconcile*	**venir (62)**
aventar *to fan*	**cerrar (11)**
avergonzar *to shame*	**contar (14)**, **z>c** before **e**, and diphthong spelt **üe**, e.g. subjunctive **avergüence**
averiar *to spoil*	**liar (28)**
bendecir *to bless*	**maldecir (30)**
biografiar *to write* *biography*	**liar (28)**
caber *to fit in*	**(8)**
caer *to fall*	**(9)**
calentar *to heat*	**(11)**
carecer *to lack*	**parecer (35)**
cegar *to blind*	**cerrar (11)**; **g>gu** before **e**
ceñir *to girdle*	**reñir (47)**
cerrar *to close*	**cerrar (11)**
circunscribir *to* *circumscribe*	past participle **circunscrito**
cocer *to cook*	**(12)**

coger to catch	**proteger (43)**
colar to filter	**contar (14)**
colegir to infer	**regir (45)**
colgar to hang	**contar (14)** g>gu before **e**
comenzar to begin	**cerrar (11)** z>c before **e**
compadecer to pity	**parecer (35)**
comparecer to appear	**parecer (35)**
competir to compete	**pedir (36)**
complacer to please	**parecer (35)**
componer to compose	**poner (39)**
comprobar to check	**contar (14)**
comunicar to communicate	**sacar (52)**
concebir to conceive	**pedir (36)**
conceptuar to deem	**continuar (15)**
concernir to concern	**discernir (18)**; third person only
concertar to harmonize	**cerrar (11)**
conciliar to reconcile	**cambiar (10)**
concluir to terminate	**construir (13)**
concordar to reconcile	**contar (14)**
condescender to condescend	**perder (37)**
conducir to drive	**producir (41)**
conferir to confer	**sentir (55)**
confesar to confess	**cerrar (11)**
confiar to entrust	**liar (28)**
confluir to come together	**construir (13)**
conmover to move (emotionally)	**mover (31)**
conocer to know	**parecer (35)**
conseguir to achieve	**seguir (54)**
consentir to consent	**sentir (55)**
consolar to console	**contar (14)**
consonar to harmonize	**contar (14)**
constituir to constitute	**construir (13)**
constreñir to restrict	**reñir (47)**

construir *to build* — (13)
contar *to count, tell* — (14)
contener *to contain* — **tener (58)**
continuar *to continue* — (15)
contradecir *to contradict* — **decir (17)**
contraer *to contract* — **traer (59)**
contrahacer *to forge* — **hacer (25)**
contravenir *to contravene* — **venir (62)**
contribuir *to contribute* — **construir (13)**
convalecer *to convalesce* — **parecer (35)**
convencer *to convince* — **vencer (61)**
convenir *to agree* — **venir (62)**
convertir *to convert* — **sentir (55)**
corregir *to correct* — **regir (45)**
corroer *to corrode* — **roer (50)**
costar *to cost* — **contar (14)**
crecer *to grow* — **parecer (35)**
creer *to believe* — **poseer (40)**
criar *to rear* — **liar (28)**
cubrir *to cover* — past participle **cubierto**
dar *to give* — (16)
decaer *to decay* — **caer (9)**
decir *to say* — (17)
decrecer *to diminish* — **parecer (35)**
deducir *to deduce* — **producir (41)**
defender *to defend* — **perder (37)**
deferir *to relegate* — **sentir (55)**
demoler *to demolish* — **mover (31)**
demostrar *to demonstrate* — **contar (14)**
denegar *to reject* — **cerrar (11)** g>gu before **e**
denostar *to revile* — **contar (14)**
derretir *to melt* — **pedir (36)**
desacertar *to be wrong* — **cerrar (11)**
desacordar *to put out of tune* — **contar (14)**
desafiar *to challenge* — **liar (28)**

desalentar to dishearten   **cerrar (11)**

desandar to retrace steps   **andar (4)**

desaparecer to disappear   **parecer (35)**

desaprobar to disapprove of   **contar (14)**

desasosegar to unsettle   **cerrar (11) g>gu** before **e**

desatender to disregard   **perder (37)**

descender to descend   **perder (37)**

descolgar to take down   **contar (14) g>gu** before **e**

descollar to stand out   **contar (14)**

descomedirse to be rude   **pedir (36)**

descomponer to break down into parts   **poner (39)**

desconcertar to disconcert   **cerrar (11)**

desconocer not to know   **parecer (35)**

desconsolar to distress   **contar (14)**

descontar to discount   **contar (14)**

desconvenir to disagree   **venir (62)**

describir to describe   past participle **descrito**

descubrir to discover   past participle **descubierto**

desempedrar to take up stones   **cerrar (11)**

desenraizar to uproot   **aislar (3)**

desentenderse to pretend not to know about   **perder (37)**

desenterrar to unearth   **cerrar (11)**

desenvolver to unwrap   **mover (31)**; past participle **desenvuelto**

desfallecer to weaken   **parecer (35)**

deshacer to unmake   **hacer (25)**

desleír to dissolve   **reír (46)**

deslucir to tarnish   **lucir (29)**

desmembrar to dismember   **cerrar (11)**

desmentir to deny   **sentir (55)**

desmerecer *not to deserve* **parecer (35)**

desobedecer *to disobey* **parecer (35)**

desoír *to disregard* **oír (32)**

despedir *to fire* **pedir (36)**

despertar *to awake* **cerrar (11)**

desplegar *to unfold* **cerrar (11); g>gu before e; now often regular**

despoblar *to depopulate* **contar (14)**

desproveer *to deprive of* **poseer (40); past participle desprovisto or desproveído**

desterrar *to exile* **cerrar (11)**

destituir *to dismiss* **construir (13)**

destruir *to destroy* **construir (13)**

desvariar *to rave* **liar 28**

desvergonzarse *to lose all shame* **contar (14); z>c before e; diphthong spelt üe**

desviar *to divert, throw off course* **liar (28)**

desvirtuar *to spoil* **continuar (15)**

detener *to stop, detain* **tener (58)**

detraer *to separate* **traer (59)**

devolver *to give back* **mover (31); past participle devuelto**

diferir *to differ* **sentir (55)**

digerir *to digest* **sentir (55)**

diluir *to dilute* **construir (13)**

discernir *to discern* **(18)**

disentir *to dissent* **sentir (55)**

disminuir *to diminish* **construir (13)**

disolver *to dissolve* **mover (31); past participle disuelto**

disponer *to dispose* **poner (39)**

distender *to distend* **perder (37)**

distraer *to distract* **traer (59)**

distribuir *to distribute* **construir (13)**

divertir *to amuse* **sentir (55)**

doler *to hurt*	**mover (31)**
dormir *to sleep*	**(19)**
efectuar *to effect*	**continuar (15)**
ejercer *to exercise*	**vencer (61)**
elegir *to elect, to choose*	**regir (45)**
embebecer *to fascinate*	**parecer (35)**
embellecer *to embellish*	**parecer (35)**
embestir *to charge (e.g. bull)*	**pedir (36)**
embravecer *to infuriate*	**parecer (35)**
embrutecer *to brutalize*	**parecer (35)**
empedrar *to pave*	**cerrar (11)**
empequeñecer *to dwarf*	**parecer (35)**
empezar *to start*	**cerrar (11); z>c before e**
empobrecer *to impoverish*	**parecer (35)**
enaltecer *to extol*	**parecer (35)**
enardecer *to impassion*	**parecer (35)**
encanecer *to get gray/grey hair*	**parecer (35)**
encarecer *to extol*	**parecer (35)**
encender *to ignite*	**perder (37)**
encerrar *to shut in*	**cerrar (11)**
encomendar *to commend*	**cerrar (11)**
encontrar *to find, meet*	**contar (14)**
encubrir *to cloak, hush up*	past participle **encubierto**
endurecer *to harden*	**parecer (35)**
enflaquecer *to make thin*	**parecer (35)**
enfriar *to chill*	**liar (28)**
enfurecer *to infuriate*	**parecer (35)**
engrandecer *to enlarge*	**parecer (35)**
engreírse *to grow smug*	**reír (46)**
engrosar *to swell (a quantity)*	**contar (14); now usually regular**
enloquecer *to madden*	**parecer (35)**
enmendar *to emend*	**cerrar (11)**
enmudecer *to silence*	**parecer (35)**

ennegrecer *to blacken*	**parecer (35)**
ennoblecer *to ennoble*	**parecer (35)**
enorgullecer *to make proud*	**parecer (35)**
enriquecer *to enrich*	**parecer (35)**
ensombrecer *to darken*	**parecer (35)**
ensordecer *to deafen*	**parecer (35)**
entender *to understand*	**perder (37)**
enternecer *to soften*	**parecer (35)**
enterrar *to bury*	**cerrar (11)**
entreabrir *to half open*	past participle **entreabierto**
entreoír *to hear faintly*	**oír (32)**
entretener *to distract*	**tener (58)**
entrever *to glimpse*	**ver (63)** third-person present singular **entrevé**
entristecer *to sadden*	**parecer (35)**
envanecer *to make vain*	**parecer (35)**
envejecer *to age*	**parecer (35)**
enviar *to send*	**liar (28)**
envilecer *to debase*	**parecer (35)**
envolver *to wrap up*	**mover (31)** past participle **envuelto**
equivaler *to be equal*	**valer (60)**
erguir *to straighten up*	**(20)**
errar *to wander*	**(21)**
escabullirse *to slip away*	**gruñir (23)**
escalofriarse *to shiver*	**liar (28)**
escarmentar *to teach a lesson*	**cerrar (11)**
escarnecer *to scoff*	**parecer (35)**
escocer *to annoy, hurt*	**cocer (12)**
escribir *to write*	past participle **escrito**
esforzarse *to strive*	**contar (14)** z>c before **e**
esparcir *to strew, scatter*	**zurcir (65)**
espiar *to spy on*	**liar (28)**
establecer *to establish*	**parecer (35)**

estar *to be* (22)

estremecer *to shake* parecer (35)

europeizar *to Europeanize* aislar (3)

evacuar *to evacuate* averiguar (7) (no dieresis)

evaluar *to evaluate* continuar (15)

exceptuar *to except* continuar (15)

excluir *to exclude* construir (13)

expedir *to ship* pedir (36)

exponer *to expose* poner (39)

extasiar *to enrapture* liar (28)

extender *to extend* perder (37)

extraer *to extract* traer (59)

extraviar *to mislead* liar (28)

fallecer *to pass away* parecer (35)

favorecer *to favor/favour* parecer (35)

fiar *to entrust, give credit* liar (28)

florecer *to flourish* parecer (35)

fluctuar *to fluctuate* continuar (15)

fluir *to flow* construir (13)

fortalecer *to strengthen* parecer (35)

forzar *to force* contar (14) z>c before e

fotografiar *to photograph* liar (28)

fregar *to scrub* cerrar (11) g>gu before e

freír *to fry* reír (46); past participle **frito**

fruncir *to pucker* zurcir (65)

gemir *to groan* pedir (36)

gloriar(se) *to glory* liar (28)

gobernar *to govern* cerrar (11)

graduar *to grade* continuar (15)

gruñir *to growl* (23)

guarecer *to protect* parecer (35)

guarnecer *to equip* parecer (35)

guiar *to guide* liar (28)

haber auxiliary for forming (24)
  compound tenses, or
  there *is/are*

habituar *to make accustomed to*	**continuar (15)**
hacer *to do, make*	**(25)**
hastiar *to weary*	**liar (28)**
heder *to reek*	**perder (37)**
helar *to freeze*	**cerrar (11)**
henchir *to cram, stuff*	**pedir (36)**
hender *to cleave*	**perder (37)**
hendir = **hender**	**discernir (18)**
herir *to wound*	**sentir (55)**
herrar *to shoe, brand*	**cerrar (11)**
hervir *to boil*	**sentir (55)**
holgar *to take one's ease*	**contar (14)** **g>gu** before **e**
hollar *to trample*	**contar (14)**
huir *to flee*	**construir (13)**
humedecer *to dampen*	**parecer (35)**
impedir *to impede*	**pedir (36)**
imponer *to impose*	**poner (39);** imperative singular **impón**
incensar *to incense*	**cerrar (11)**
incluir *to include*	**construir (13)**
indisponer *to indispose*	**poner (39)**
individuar *to individualize*	**continuar (15)**
inducir *to induce*	**producir (41)**
infatuar *to make big-headed*	**continuar (15)**
inferir *to infer*	**sentir (55)**
influir *to influence*	**construir (13)**
ingerir *to ingest*	**sentir (55)**
inquirir *to investigate*	**adquirir (2)**
insinuar *to hint*	**continuar (15)**
instituir *to institute*	**construir (13)**
instruir *to instruct*	**construir (13)**
interferir *to interfere*	**sentir (55)**
interponer *to interpose*	**poner (39)**
intervenir *to intervene*	**venir (62)**

introducir *to insert*	**producir (41)**
intuir *to intuit*	**construir (13)**
invertir *to invest*	**sentir (55)**
ir *to go*	**(26)**
izar *to raise (flag)*	**rezar (49)**. All verbs ending in **-izar** conjugate like **rezar**.
jugar *to play*	**(27)**
languidecer *to languish*	**parecer (35)**
leer *to read*	**poseer (40)**
liar *to tie up in a bundle*	**(28)**
llegar *to arrive*	**pagar (34)**
llover *to rain*	**mover (31)**; usually only 3rd person
lucir *to sport, show off*	**(29)**
maldecir *to curse*	**(30)**
manifestar *to manifest*	**cerrar (11)**
mantener *to maintain*	**tener (58)**
mecer *to rock (a child)*	**vencer (61)**
medir *to measure*	**pedir (36)**
mentar *to mention by name*	**cerrar (11)**
mentir *to lie*	**sentir (55)**
merecer *to merit*	**parecer (35)**
merendar *to eat an afternoon snack*	**cerrar (11)**
moler *to grind*	**mover (31)**
morder *to bite*	**mover (31)**
morir *to die*	**dormir (19)**; past participle **muerto**
mostrar *to die*	**contar (14)**
mover *to move*	**(31)**
mullir *to fluff up*	**gruñir (23)**
nacer *to be born*	**parecer (35)**
negar *to deny*	**cerrar (11)** g>gu before **e**
nevar *to snow*	**cerrar (11)**; usually 3rd person only

obedecer *to obey*	**parecer (35)**
obtener *to obtain*	**tener (58)**
ofrecer *to offer*	**parecer (35)**
oír *to hear*	**(32)**
oler *to smell*	**(33)**
oponer *to oppose*	**poner (39)**
oscurecer *to darken*	**parecer (35)**
pacer *to graze*	**parecer (35)**
padecer *to suffer*	**parecer (35)**
palidecer *to pale*	**parecer (35)**
parecer *to seem*	**(35)**
pedir *to ask for*	**(36)**
pensar *to think*	**cerrar (11)**
perecer *to perish*	**parecer (35)**
permanecer *to remain*	**parecer (35)**
perpetuar *to perpetuate*	**continuar (15)**
perseguir *to pursue*	**seguir (54)**
pertenecer *to belong*	**parecer (35)**
pervertir *to pervert*	**sentir (55)**
plegar *to fold*	**cerrar (11); g>gu** before **e**
poblar *to people/populate*	**contar (14)**
poder *to be able*	**(38)**
podrir *to rot*	variant of **pudrir**; **-u-** used for all forms save past participle **podrido**
poner *to put*	**(39)**
poseer *to possess*	**(40)**
posponer *to postpone*	**poner (39)**
predecir *to foretell*	**decir (17)**
predisponer *to predispose*	**poner (39)**
preferir *to prefer*	**sentir (55)**
prescribir *to prescribe*	past participle **prescrito**
presuponer *to presuppose*	**poner (39)**
prevalecer *to prevail*	**parecer (35)**
prevaler *to take advantage of*	**valer (60)**

prevenir *to prepare*	**venir (62)**
prever *to foresee*	**ver (63)**; third-pers. present singular **prevé**
probar *to prove*	**contar (14)**
producir *to produce*	**(41)**
proferir *to utter* (usually cries, insults)	**sentir (55)**
prohibir *to prohibit*	**(42)**
promover *to promote*	**mover (31)**
proponer *to propose*	**poner (39)**
proseguir *to continue*	**seguir (54)**
prostituir *to prostitute*	**construir (13)**
proteger *to protect*	**(43)**
proveer *to supply*	**poseer (40)**; past participle **provisto/proveído**
provenir *to arise from*	**venir (62)**
pudrir *to rot*	regular; see **podrir**
puntuar *to punctuate/mark*	**continuar (15)**
quebrar *to snap*	**cerrar (11)**
querer *to want/love*	**(44)**
reaparecer *to reappear*	**parecer (35)**
reblandecer *to soften*	**parecer (35)**
recaer *to relapse*	**caer (9)**
recocer *to warm up (food)*	**cocer (12)**
recomendar *to recommend*	**cerrar (11)**
reconocer *to recognize*	**parecer (35)**
reconvenir *to reprimand*	**venir (62)**
recordar *to remember/remind*	**contar (14)**
recostar(se) *to lean back*	**contar (14)**
redituar *to yield*	**continuar (15)**
reducir *to reduce*	**producir (41)**
reelegir *to re-elect*	**regir (45)**
referir *to refer*	**sentir (55)**
reforzar *to reinforce*	**contar (14)**; z>c before e

refregar *to rub/scrub*	**cerrar (11); g>gu** before **e**
regar *to water*	**cerrar (11); g>gu** before **e**
regir *to govern*	**(45)**
rehacer *to redo*	**hacer (25)**
rehusar *to refuse*	**reunir (48)**
reír *to laugh*	**(46)**
rejuvenecer *to rejuvenate*	**parecer (35)**
remendar *to mend*	**cerrar (11)**
remorder *to grieve* (transitive)	**mover (31)**
remover *to stir up/Lat. Am. to remove*	**mover (31)**
rendir *to yield*	**pedir (36)**
renegar *to deny strongly*	**cerrar (11); g>gu** before **e**
renovar *to renew*	**contar (14)**
reñir *to scold*	**(47)**
repetir *to repeat*	**pedir (36)**
replegar *to fold over*	**cerrar (11); g>gu** before **e**
reponer *to replace*	**poner (39)**
reprobar *to reprove*	**contar (14)**
reproducir *to reproduce*	**producir (41)**
requebrar *to flatter*	**cerrar (11)**
requerir *to require*	**sentir (55)**
resarcir *to compensate for*	**zurcir (65)**
resentirse *to resent*	**sentir (55)**
resfriar *to chill*	**liar (28)**
resollar *to wheeze*	**contar (14)**
resolver *to resolve*	**mover (31); past participle resuelto**
resonar *to echo*	**contar (14)**
resplandecer *to gleam*	**parecer (35)**
restablecer *to re-establish*	**parecer (35)**
restituir *to return*	**construir (13)**
retemblar *to shudder*	**cerrar (11)**
retener *to retain*	**tener (58)**

retorcer *to twist*	**cocer (12); c>z before a, o**
retraer *to draw in*	**traer (59)**
retribuir *to pay*	**construir (13)**
reunir *to bring together*	**(48)**
reventar *to burst*	**cerrar (11)**
reverdecer *to grow green again*	**parecer (35)**
revertir *to revert*	**sentir (55)**
revestir *to put on (clothes)*	**pedir (36)**
revolar *to flutter about*	**contar (14)**
revolcarse *to knock over*	**contar (14) c>qu before e**
revolver *to turn over*	**mover (31); past participle revuelto**
rezar *to pray*	**(49)**
robustecer *to strengthen*	**parecer (35)**
rociar *to sprinkle*	**liar (28)**
rodar *to roll*	**contar (14)**
roer *to gnaw*	**(50)**
rogar *to request*	**contar (14); g>gu before e**
romper *to break*	**past participle roto**
saber *to know*	**(51)**
sacar *to take out*	**(52)**
salir *to come out/leave*	**(53)**
satisfacer *to satisfy*	**hacer (25)**
seducir *to seduce*	**producir (41)**
segar *to reap*	**cerrar (11) g>gu before e**
seguir *to follow*	**(54)**
sembrar *to show*	**cerrar (11)**
sentar *to seat*	**cerrar (11)**
sentir *to feel*	**(55)**
ser *to be*	**(56)**
serrar *to saw*	**cerrar (11)**
servir *to serve*	**pedir (36)**
situar *to situate*	**continuar (15)**
sobre(e)ntender *to infer*	**perder (37)**
sobreponer *to put on top*	**poner (39)**

sobresalir *to jut out*	**salir (53)**
sobrevenir *to happen suddenly*	**venir (62)**
sofreír *to fry lightly*	**reír (46)**; past participle **sofrito**
soldar *to solder*	**contar (14)**
soler *to be used to*	**mover (31)** future, conditional and past and future subjunctives not used
soltar *to release*	**contar (14)**; past participle **suelto**
sonar *to sound*	**contar (14)**
sonreír *to smile*	**reír (46)**
soñar *to dream*	**contar (14)**
sosegar *to calm*	**cerrar (11)** g>gu before **e**
sostener *to support*	**tener (58)**
subarrendar *to sublease*	**cerrar (11)**
subscribir	see **suscribir**
substituir	see **sustituir**
substraer	see **sustraer**
subvenir *to defray costs*	**venir (62)**
subvertir *to subvert*	**sentir (55)**
sugerir *to suggest*	**sentir (55)**
suponer *to suppose*	**poner (39)**
suscribir *to subscribe*	past participle **suscrito**
sustituir *to substitute*	**construir (13)**
sustraer *to remove*	**traer (59)**
tañer *to chime*	**(57)**
temblar *to tremble*	**cerrar (11)**
tender *to tend*	**perder (37)**
tener *to have*	**(58)**
tentar *to tempt*	**cerrar (11)**
teñir *to dye*	**reñir (47)**
torcer *to twist*	**cocer (12)**; c>z before **a**, **o**
tostar *to toast*	**contar (14)**
traducir *to translate*	**producir (41)**
traer *to bring*	**(59)**

tra(n)scender *to transcend* — **perder (37)**

transcribir *to transcribe* — past participle **transcrito**

transferir *to transfer* — **sentir (55)**

transgredir *to transgress* — **abolir (1)**; sometimes regular

transponer *to transpose* — **poner (39)**

trasegar *to switch round* — **cerrar (11)**; g>gu before e

traslucir *to hint at* — **lucir (29)**

trastrocar *to switch round* — **contar (14)**; c>qu before e

trocar *to barter* — **contar (14)**; c>qu before e

tronar *to thunder* — **contar (14)**

tropezar *to stumble* — **cerrar (11)**; z>c before e

tullir *to maim* — **gruñir (23)**

vaciar *to empty* — **liar (28)**

valer *to be worth* — **(60)**

valuar *to value* — **continuar (15)**

variar *to vary* — **liar (28)**

vencer *to win/conquer* — **(61)**

venir *to come* — **(62)**

ver *to see* — **(63)**

verter *to pour out* — **perder (37)**

vestir *to clothe* — **pedir (36)**

volar *to fly* — **contar (14)**

volcar *to upset* — **contar (14)**; c>qu before e

volver *to return* — **mover (31)**; past participle **vuelto**

yacer *to lie* (i.e. *lie down*) — **(64)**

zaherir *to mortify* — **sentir (55)**

zambullir *to plunge* — **gruñir (23)**

zurcir *to darn* **(65)**

Glossary of Grammatical Terms

A few terms not used in this book but often found in Spanish grammars are also included. Terms printed in bold characters are defined elsewhere in the glossary.

Abstract noun A **noun** that refers to something that is not a person or concrete object. The following are abstract nouns: *liberty, impatience, innocence*.

Accent Strictly speaking, the various signs written over certain vowels in Spanish and many other languages, e.g. in the words **café, averigüe**. It is often confusingly used to mean stress; see **Stressed Syllable**.

Active see **Passive**

Adjectival Participles Adjectives formed from some (but by no means all) Spanish verbs by adding **-ante, -ente** or **-iente**, e.g. **preocupante** *worrying*, **hiriente** *wounding*.

Adjective A word that describes a noun, e.g. *a **good** book*, **un *buen* libro**.

Adverb A word that describes a verb, an adjective or another adverb: *he did it **well***, **lo hizo *bien***; *terribly tired*, **terriblemente cansado**; *very quickly*, **muy deprisa**.

Agreement Agreement in Spanish is of three kinds:

   (1) **Number agreement**: the fact that a singular noun or pronoun requires a singular adjective, verb or article, and a plural noun or pronoun a plural adjective, verb or article:

*El **buen** alumno **trabaja** mucho* The good student
works hard

*Los **buenos** alumnos **trabajan** mucho* The good students work hard

(2) **Person agreement**: the fact that a first-person
subject requires a first-person verb and so on:

Person	Singular	Plural
First	**Yo quiero** *I want*	**Nosotros queremos** *We want*
Second	**Tú quieres** *You want*	**Vosotros queréis** *You want*
Third	**Ella quiere** *She wants*	**Ellos quieren** *They want*

(3) **Gender agreement**: the fact that masculine nouns
require masculine adjectives, articles or pronouns,
and feminine nouns require feminine adjectives, articles or pronouns:

Masculine	***un** muchacho **rubio*** *a blond boy*
	este** libro **rojo *this red book*
Feminine	***una** muchacha **rubia*** *a blond girl*
	esta** casa **blanca *this white house*

Anterior Preterit Tense See **Pretérito anterior**

Apposition Two nouns or noun phrases placed side by
side so that the second expands the meaning of the
first: *Don Quixote, **the greatest Spanish novel***. The
words in bold are said to be 'in apposition' to the first
part of the phrase.

Articles Words meaning *the* or *a/an*. See **Definite
Article** and **Indefinite Article**.

Attributive Adjective In Spanish, an adjective that
specifies the type or purpose of a noun: **la industria
hotelera** *the hotel industry*, **problemas sindicales**
trade-union problems. English regularly expresses the
same construction by joining nouns together, e.g. *police
dog, baseball game*.

Auxiliary verb A verb used to form a **Compound Tense** The most common auxiliary verbs in English are *to have* as in *I **have** said*, and *to be* as in *I **am** saying*. The Spanish equivalents are **haber** as in **yo *he* dicho** and **estar** as in **yo *estoy* diciendo**.

Cardinal numbers The ordinary numbers used for counting, e.g. *one, two, three*, etc. See also **Ordinal Numbers**.

Ceceo See **Seseo**.

Clause A group of words that forms part of a sentence and includes a **Finite Verb:** *I'll finish it before she arrives* contains two clauses, *I'll finish it* and *before she arrives*. Often a sentence consists of only one clause, cf. *Jack ate an apple*. Among the types of clause mentioned in this grammar are **Main Clause, Subordinate Clause** and **Relative Clause**, each separately defined below.

Collective Noun A noun that, although it may be singular in form, refers to a group of people or things: *flock, crowd, committee, crew, majority, dozen*, etc.

Comparative Forms of adjectives and adverbs that indicate a *more* or *less* intense quality: *better, worse, more intelligent, less beautiful,* **mejor, peor, más inteligente, menos bello**, etc.

Compound noun A noun formed from two or more nouns joined together: *fire alarm, cat-hair, fish soup, database design textbook*. As the examples show, English can make complex compound nouns, but Spanish has only a few, e.g. **año luz** *light year*, **perro policía** *police-dog*. Generally Spanish creates such nouns either by using **de** *of*—**manual de diseño de bases de datos**—or by using an **Attributive Adjective** (q.v.): **problemas *estudiantiles*** *student problems*.

Compound tenses Tense forms of verbs created in English by using the verb *have* plus a past participle, and in Spanish by using **haber** plus a past participle: *I have done, had finished, I will have left*, **he hecho, había terminado, habré salido**.

Conditional Sentence One that includes a condition and a result, e.g. *if it rains we'll stay at home, if it had rained we would have stayed at home.* Occasionally the *if*-clause is omitted: *it would be have been nice* (i.e. if some condition or other had been met).

Conditional tense The tense of a verb used to express what might or could happen or have happened: *I would be angry, He would have realized*, **me enojaría, se habría dado cuenta**.

Conjugation The general pattern that a verb's forms follow. There are three conjugations in Spanish corresponding to **Infinitives** ending in -**ar**, -**er** and -**ir**. All regular verbs belong to one of these conjugations. Radical changing and irregular verbs follow one of these conjugations in most forms, but some forms are unpredictable.

Conjunction Words or phrases (**Relative Pronouns** excepted) that connect words, phrases and clauses within a sentence. In the following sentence the words in bold are conjunctions: *I bought a shirt **and** a tie, **but when** she saw them, Mary said **that** she didn't like them, **so** I took them back, **although** I liked them myself.*

Consonant Simply defined as all the sounds in a language that are not vowels, i.e. in English and Spanish the sounds corresponding to all the letters of the alphabet except *a, e, i, o, u* and *y* when the latter is pronounced like *i*. See also **Vowel and Semi-vowel**.

Continuous The name given to Spanish verb forms consisting of **estar** plus a gerund, e.g. **estoy fumando** *I'm smoking*. See also **Progressive**.

Definite Article in English *the*, in Spanish **el, la, los, las** when used with the same meaning as the English word.

Demonstrative Adjective A special type of adjective used to point to something: in English *this*, *that* and *those*, in Spanish **este/esta/estos/estas, ese/esa/esos/esas, aquel/aquella/aquellos/aquellas**.

Demonstrative Pronoun A special type of pronoun used to point to something, e.g. *I don't want **this** one, I want **that** one*. In Spanish they usually have the same form as **Demonstrative Adjectives**, but are usually distinguished in writing by an accent. See p.138.

Diphthong In Spanish, a combination of a **Vowel** (q.v.) and a **Semi-vowel** (q.v.), e.g. the **oy** in **soy** or the **ue** in **bueno**.

Direct Object A noun or pronoun that directly experiences the action of a verb: *He hit **me**, Jack saw **Mary**, I wrote **it***. See also **Indirect Object**.

Direct Question see **Indirect Question**.

Feminine see **Gender**

Finite Verb Form A verb form that shows **Tense**, **Person** and **Number**, e.g. *he walked* (Third-person, Past and Singular), **iremos** *we'll go* (First-person, Future and Plural). See also **Non-Finite Verb Form**.

First Person see **Person**

Future Perfect Tense Tense forms that refer to an event that *will have* happened by a certain time: ***I will have died** of hunger by the time you finish cooking dinner*.

Future Tense Strictly speaking, the tense form that refers to the future, usually taken in Spanish to mean forms like **hablaré, iremos**. The term is not very helpful because both Spanish and English have several different ways of expressing the future, cf. *we're going tomorrow*, *we'll go tomorrow, we're going to go tomorrow, we go tomorrow, we're to go tomorrow.*

Gender In Spanish, the fact that nouns and pronouns are either 'masculine' or 'feminine'. Gender is usually obvious if the word refers to a male or a female human being, but all Spanish nouns are either feminine or masculine, even when they refer to sexless objects: **el libro** *book*, **el fusil** *rifle*, **el árbol** *tree* are masculine nouns, **la cama** *bed*, **la cartucha** *cartridge* and **la flor** *flower* are feminine. In the case of such nouns, grammatical gender has obviously got nothing to do with sex. See also **Agreement**.

Generic 'Referring to a whole class or every member of a set of things.' In the sentence *I hate beer/oysters/politics*, the three nouns are said to be generic nouns since they refer to substances, things or abstractions in general. Compare **Partitive**.

Gerund The Spanish verb form created by replacing the ending of the **Infinitive** by -**ando** or -**iendo**, depending on **Conjugation**, e.g. **hablando**, **durmiendo**. The gerund is one of the **Non-Finite Verb Forms** of Spanish and corresponds to some of the uses of the English verb form ending in *-ing*.

Historic Present The **Present Tense** used to make a past event sound dramatic, cf. *There I am resting after all my hard work when she walks in and tells me I'm lazy!*

Imperative See **Mood**.

Imperfect Subjunctive The name traditionally given to the simple (i.e. non-compound) verb forms of the past of the Spanish subjunctive. Examples: **hablara/hablase**, **dijeran/dijesen**. See also **Mood**.

Imperfect Tense A Spanish past tense formed by adding a set of endings (-**aba**, -**abas**, -**aba** or -**ía**, -**ías**, -**ía**, etc.) to the **Stem** of the verb. It usually expresses either habitual actions in the past—**yo fumaba mucho** *I used to smoke a lot*—or events that were in progress at the time but had not yet ended, cf. *I was smoking a lot*.

Impersonal Pronouns Pronouns that refer to unidentifiable persons or things, e.g. *someone, something, anyone,* **alguien, algo, cualquiera,** etc.

Impersonal se One of the many uses of the pronoun **se** as a rough equivalent of the English *one, people*: **se vive mejor en España** *people live better in* Spain, **se come bien en Francia** *people eat well in France*. Compare **Passive se**.

Indefinite Article In English *a/an*, in Spanish **un/una/unos/unas** when used with the same meaning as their English counterparts.

Indicative Mood See **Mood**.

Indirect Object The noun or pronoun that acquires, hears or in some way receives the **Direct Object** (q.v.) of a verb. The word *him* or **le** is the Indirect Object in these sentences and the words in bold italics are the Direct Object: *I sent him **the letter**/*le enviaron **la carta**, *she told him **the truth**/*ella **le** dijo **la verdad**. In Spanish an Indirect Object can also lose as well as receive: **le** robaron **mil pesetas** *they stole 1,000 ptas from him*, **se le** cae el pelo *his hair's falling out* (literally *his hair is falling out* (**caerse**) *from him*).

Indirect Question A question included in a **Subordinate Clause** (q.v.) in a sentence. It is normally introduced by some such expression as *I wonder . . . , Do you know where . . . , I'll ask him when . . .* . Direct question: *When is he coming?*, Indirect Question *I don't know **when he is coming***.

Infinitive The 'dictionary form' of a verb, which always ends in **-r** in Spanish, e.g. **hablar, comer, vivir**. It often corresponds to the English form preceded by *to*— *to speak, to eat , to live*—and sometimes to the form ending in *-ing*, as in **fumar es malo para la salud** *smoking is bad for the health*. It is a **Non-Finite-Verb Form** (q.v.).

Interrogative A feature of words that ask questions, like *why?* (adverb), *when?* (adverb), *who?* (pronoun), *which?* (adjective), Spanish **¿por qué?, ¿cuándo?, ¿quién?, ¿qué?, ¿cuál?**

Intransitive Verb a verb that has no **Direct Object** present or implied: *I go, she came* are intransitive, as are their Spanish equivalents, **voy, vino**: one cannot go *someone* or come *something*. 'Transitive' and 'Intransitive' are often descriptions of the use of a verb rather than of its inherent nature, since many so-called intransitive verbs can take a direct object and then become transitive, cf. *he slept ten hours*, Spanish **durmió diez horas**, or Spanish **lo durmieron** *they put him to sleep*. See also **Transitive verbs**.

Irregular Verb A verb whose forms cannot always be predicted from the usual pattern. English *go-went-gone*, *sleep-slept*, Spanish **soy, eres, es** are typical examples.

Main Clause A **Clause** (q.v.) that could stand alone as a sentence. In *I stood up when she came in*, the words *I stood up* could form a sentence on their own and therefore form the Main Clause; *when she came in* cannot form a sentence without the addition of more words, and is therefore a **Subordinate Clause** (q.v.).

Masculine see **Gender**.

Modal Verbs A verb that indicates the 'mood' of another, e.g. *I may go* (possibility), *you **ought to** do it* (obligation), *she **can't** come* (possibility). The main

Spanish Modal Verbs are **poder, deber, tener que, soler**.

Mood The traditional name given to the three different forms that Spanish and English verbs can take according to the use being made of the verb:

Indicative Mood, used for making statements: *it's raining, you said it*, **yo hablo español**

Subjunctive Mood, almost obsolete in English, but much used in Spanish to show that the verb expresses something hoped, wanted, feared, approved, disapproved, possible or, after **Subordinators** (q.v.) something that has or had not yet happened, e.g. **quiero que** *vayas* I want you to go, **espero que** *venga* I hope that he comes, **antes de que** *saliera* el avión *before the plane left*. The subjunctive occasionally occurs in English, e.g. *if I were you, it is necessary that this be done quickly, if this be true*.

Imperative Mood: The form of a verb used to express a command or order: *tell me the truth*, **dime la verdad**.

Non-Finite Verb Forms Verb forms that cannot express Person, Tense or Number, e.g. *living, to live, lived*—three forms that do not tell us who lived when and how many people were involved. In Spanish the non-finite verb forms are the **Gerund**, the **Infinitive** and the **Past Participle**.

Noun A word that names a person, object or abstraction, e.g. *Peter, woman, table, hope, freedom*. See also **Abstract Noun, Collective Noun**.

Number In grammar, the state of being either singular (i.e. referring to only one person or thing) or plural (referring to more than one).

Object Pronouns in Spanish, pronouns like **me, te, nos, os** that refer either to the **Direct Object** or the **Indirect Object** (q.v.). **Le** and **les** are also object pronouns, although in standard Spanish they usually (but by no means always) refer only to the Indirect Object.

Ordinal Numbers Numerals that indicates the order in which something appears, e.g. *first*/**primero**, *second*/**segundo**, *hundredth*/**centésimo.** Compare **Cardinal Number**.

Partitive 'Referring only to a part of something, not to the whole'. In *Don't forget to buy bread/oysters* the words *bread* and *oysters* are Partitive Nouns: they imply *some* bread, *some* oysters, not all the bread or oysters that exist. Compare **Generic**.

Passive The opposite of **Active**. An active sentence that can be made passive must contain a **Subject**, a **Transitive Verb** and optionally a **Direct Object**: *A car ran him down*/**Lo atropelló un coche**. The equivalent Passive Sentence makes the direct object into the subject: *He was run down by a car*/**Fue atropellado por un coche**. See also **Passive se**.

Passive se One of the uses of the Spanish pronoun **se** to make the equivalent of a **Passive** (q.v.) sentence: **estos libros se publicaron en España** *these books were published in Spain*.

Past Participle The part of the verb used to form **Compound Tenses** and **Passive** sentences. In English it usually ends in -**ed**, in Spanish -**ado** or -**ido**, although there are exceptions in both languages, cf. *broken*/**roto**, *seen*/**visto**. It is a **Non-Finite Verb Form** (q.v.).

Perfect Tense The **Compound Tense** formed in English with the present tense of *to have* plus the **Past Participle**, in Spanish from the present tense of **haber** plus the past participle, e.g. *he has seen*, **ha visto.** It is often called the **pretérito perfecto** in Spanish.

Perfect Tense Continuous (or Continuous Perfect Tense) The tense formed in English with the **Perfect Tense** of *to be* plus the *-ing* form, in Spanish with the perfect tense of **estar** plus the **Gerund**, e.g. *he has been thinking*, **ha estado pensando**.

Perfect of Recency The use of the **Perfect Tense** in Spanish (as opposed to the **Preterit Tense**) to show that an event occurred recently (e.g. since midnight). This is more typical of Spain than Latin America.

Person See **Agreement**

Personal a The term used in Spanish grammar to refer to the preposition **a** when used before **Direct Objects** that refer to human beings, e.g. **vi a Mario** *I saw Mario*. See p.157.

Personal Pronouns Subject pronouns and **Object Pronouns** referring to people or things, e.g. *I*/**yo**, *you*/**tú**/**usted**, *he*/**él**, or *me*/**me**, *him*/**lo**/**le**, *us*/**nos**, etc.

Phrase A meaningful group of words in a sentence that does not contain a **Finite Verb**, e.g. the bold words in *I arrived **at ten o'clock***.

Pluperfect Conditional The tense formed in Spanish by using the **Conditional** form of **haber** + the **Past Participle**: **habrían sido** *they would have been*. The **-ra** form of **haber** may also be used: **hubieran sido** *they would have been*.

Pluperfect Subjunctive The **Subjunctive** version of the Spanish **Pluperfect** (q.v.), formed from the **-ra** or **-se** form of **haber** + the **Past Participle**, e.g. **si me hubieras visto** *if you had seen me*.

Pluperfect Tense The tense formed in English with the past of **had** plus the **Past Participle**, e.g. *I had done*, and in Spanish with the **Imperfect** of **haber** and the **Past Participle**, e.g. **yo había hecho**.

Possessive Adjective An adjective that indicates possession, i.e. *my*/**mi**, *your*/**tu**/**vuestro**/**su**, *his*/**su**, *our*/**nuestro**, etc.

Possessive Pronoun A pronoun that indicates possession. English examples are *mine*, *yours*, *hers*; Spanish examples are **el mío**, **el tuyo**, **el suyo**, etc.

Prefix A letter or letters that usually have no meaning in isolation but are added at the beginning a word to change the meaning, e.g. *pre-* in *pre-school*, *re-* in *represent*.

Preposition A word used before a noun to relate it to the rest of the phrase or sentence, e.g. *on*/**en**, *with*/**con**, *without*/**sin**, *against*/**contra**, etc. In English a preposition can come at the end of a clause or sentence: *the girl he's going out with*. In Spanish a preposition must precede the word it refers to: **la chica con la que sale**.

Prepositional Phrase A phrase used like a **Preposition**, e.g. *on behalf of*/**de parte de**, *in return for*/**a cambio de**.

Present Continuous The name usually given in Spanish grammar to the tense form based on the present of **estar** plus the **Gerund**, e.g. **está cantando** *he is singing*. See also **Progressive**.

Present Participle In Spanish, the name sometimes given to **Adjectival Participles** (q.v.). In English, the name sometimes given to the *-ing* form of verbs, e.g. *walking*, *riding*.

Present Tense The name given to the verb form that indicates events that are happening in the present, e.g. **hablo** *I speak*/*I'm speaking*. The name is misleading since in both languages this tense form can also be used for future, timeless and even past actions. See also **Present Continuous**, **Historic Present**.

Preterit (British spelling 'Preterite') The name given in English to the simple Past Tense in Spanish that denotes a completed action, e.g. **hablé** *I spoke*, **tuve** *I got*, **dijimos** *we said*. In Spanish this tense is often called the **pretérito indefinido**.

Pretérito anterior The Spanish name for the tense form made with the **Preterit** of **haber** and the **Past Participle**, e.g. **hubo hablado** *he had said*. It is nowadays used only in literary styles.

Progressive The name usually given to English verb forms made with *to be* and the *-ing* form of a verb, e.g. *he was singing*, *they are shouting*. The rough Spanish equivalent is the **Continuous**.

Pronominal verb A Spanish verb that has an **Object Pronoun** that is of the same person and number as the subject, e.g. **me afeito** *I'm shaving (myself)*, **te vas** *you're leaving*, **se murieron** *they died*. Traditionally these were called 'reflexive verbs', but the term **Reflexive** correctly refers to just one possible meaning of a Pronominal Verb, not to the *form* of the verb.

Pronoun A word, e.g. *he*, *she*, it, *they*, *I*, **yo**, **tú**, that stands for a noun.

Radical-changing verb In Spanish, verbs that have regular endings but unpredictable vowel changes in certain forms, e.g. **contar** *to tell*, **cuento** *I tell* but **contamos** *we tell*, or **pedir** *to ask for*, **pido** *I ask for*, **pedí** *I asked for*, **pidió** *he asked for*, etc.

Reciprocal One of the meanings that a plural Spanish **Pronominal Verb** can have. The action is done to or for *one another*, e.g. **se quieren** *they love one another*.

Reflexive One of the meanings of a Spanish **Pronominal Verb** which shows that an the action is done by the subject to him or herself, e.g. **me lavo** *I wash myself*.

Regular Verb A verb whose various forms are all predictable from the pattern used by its **Conjugation** (q.v.). Typical Spanish examples are **hablar**, **comer** and **vivir**, which have no irregularities or exceptions.

Relative Clause A clause that modifies or restricts the meaning of a noun or pronoun that occurred earlier in the sentence, e.g. *I was talking to the woman **who lives over the road**, That's the girl **that/whom** I saw yesterday*. In Spanish Relative clauses are always introduced by a **Relative Pronoun** (q.v.), but the pronoun can sometimes be omitted in English, cf. *that's the girl I saw yesterday*.

Relative Pronoun A class of words that introduce a **Relative Clause** (q.v.). English relative pronouns are *who, whom, which, that*; Spanish equivalents are **que, el que, quien, el cual.**

Second Person See **Person**

Semi-Vowel A special kind of vowel that acts like a consonant. There are two Spanish semi-vowels, one pronounced like the *y* of *yes* as in **bien**, the other like the *w* of *wood* as in **bueno**. When a semi-vowel is attached to a **Vowel**, a **Diphthong** is formed.

Seseo In Spanish pronunciation, the use of an **s** sound where Spaniards from Central and Northern Spain use a sound like the *th* of *think*, e.g. in words like **cinco** *five*, **atroz** *atrocious*. Most Andalusians and Canary Islanders and all Latin Americans use **seseo**. Use of the *th* sound is called **ceceo**.

Simple Tense A one-word tense form of a verb, e.g. *he does*, **sabe, toma**. It is the opposite of **Compound Tense** (q.v.).

Stem The part of a verb to which the various endings that indicate Tense, Person and Mood are added. The stem of *kissing* is *kiss*: *kissed, kisses*. The stem of **hablar** is

habl: habl*amos*, habl*aron*, habl*ando* etc. Some irregular verbs have no single identifiable stem, e.g. **ser**—**soy, eres, fui**, etc.

Stressed Syllable The **Syllable** of a word spoken most loudly. Stress is crucial to meaning in both Spanish: and English: compare **hablo** *I speak* with **habló** *he spoke* or the two pronunciations of *invalid* in *the invalid had an invalid ticket*.

Subject The noun or pronoun that performs the action of verb or about which the verb phrase makes a statement: *Mary got up late*, *I am getting tired*, **Miguel conoce a Antonia**.

Subjunctive See **Mood**.

Subordinate Clause A clause in a sentence that depends on a **Main Clause** to make sense. In *Jane got up before the sun rose*, the subordinate clause *before the sun rose* cannot stand alone as a sentence, whereas the main clause *Jane got up* can.

Subordinator A **Conjunction** used to introduce a **Subordinate Clause**, e.g. *I did it **before** you did, Peter phoned **when** she arrived, I paid **although** I wasn't pleased*.

Suffix A letter or letters that (usually) have no meaning in isolation but are added to the end of a word to change the meaning, e.g. *-ness* in *smallness*, *-ito* in **perrito**.

Superlative The form of an adjective or adverb that shows that the quality referred to is the most intense of all: *Molly is the **brightest** student, you're the **best**, **Molly es la más inteligente**, **tú eres el mejor***. See also **Comparative**.

Syllable In Spanish, a portion or element of a word that contains one **Vowel** sound (**Diphthongs** and **Triphthongs** counting as one vowel). **Es** contains one syllable, **era** contains two and **habitación** contains four (**ió** being a diphthong and counting as one vowel).

Tense The form of a verb that indicates *when* the action takes place. *I went*/**yo iba/yo fui/yo he ido** are all past tenses of various kinds, *I'll go/I will go/I'm going to go* are different types of future tense.

Third Person See **Person**.

Transitive Verb A verb that can have a **Direct Object**. The following verbs are transitive: *I hit him*, **La vi** *I saw her*. *I yawned*/**bostecé** is **Intransitive** since we cannot yawn something or someone.

Triphthong The combination of a **Semi-Vowel**, a **Vowel** and another **Semi-Vowel**, e.g. **uéi** in **continuéis** (pronounced 'way').

Verb A word that explains what the **Subject** of a clause or sentence does: *I eat fish*, *You tell tall stories*.

Vowel The sounds of a language that are not classified as consonants and which, in the case of Spanish, can form a **Syllable** (q.v.) on their own or in combination with consonants. Spanish has five vowels: **a, e, i, o, u**. English has the same number of vowel signs, but they are pronounced in more than a dozen different ways.

Index

Prepositional phrases like **en contra, con motivo de**, **debajo de** are listed in alphabetical order on pp.166–183. Only a few important English prepositions are included here. The rest are listed with their Spanish equivalents on pp. 183–6.

For individual Spanish verbs not listed here, see the list on pp. 303–319.